CURRENT TRENDS IN LINGUISTICS

VOLUME 12

CURRENT TRENDS
IN LINGUISTICS

Edited by

THOMAS A. SEBEOK
Research Center for the Language Sciences
Indiana University

VOLUME 12

Linguistics and Adjacent Arts and Sciences

★★★

Associate Editors:
ARTHUR S. ABRAMSON, DELL HYMES, HERBERT RUBENSTEIN
EDWARD STANKIEWICZ

Assistant Editor:
BERNARD SPOLSKY

Assistants to the Editor:
ALEXANDRA DI LUGLIO
LUCIA HADD ZOERCHER

1974

MOUTON

THE HAGUE · PARIS

The research reported herein was performed pursuant to a contract with the U.S. Department of Health, Education, and Welfare, Office of Education, under the authority of Section 602, Title VI, NDEA.

LIBRARY OF CONGRESS CATALOG CARD NUMBER: 64-3663

Printed in The Netherlands by Mouton & Co., Printers, The Hague

PART SEVEN

ANTHROPOLOGY AND SOCIOLOGY

ANTHROPOLOGY AND SOCIOLOGY

AN OVERVIEW

I

The relation of linguistics to anthropology and sociology has an imbalance and a traditional history, both now undergoing significant change. It is no accident, but a reflection of this changing relationship, that two of the contributions to this section are by sociologists, and these contributions deal with topics on which one might have expected an anthropologist to write a decade ago. We are on the threshold of a general social science approach to the study of speech and language. If present trends continue, the distinction between anthropology and sociology in the study of speech and language will be like that between Germanic and Romance linguistics. The distinction will remain, persisting in favored materials, favored methods, influence of seminal figures, and the like. But just as no one can responsibly maintain a general theory that accounts for Germanic findings and not those of Romance, so no one can responsibly maintain a general theory of language as a human institution, on the basis of any one social science alone.

The obvious source of sociological and anthropological interest in language is the series of problems typical of each discipline into which language inescapably enters. For sociologists, as will be seen in the articles by Bernstein and Fishman, problems of social class, of public policy, and of processes involved in social, economic and political change, have given rise to interest. (Where language has entered seriously into study of social interaction, the work has gravitated into an orbit shared with anthropologists and linguists.) For anthropologists, fieldwork in other cultures has long made work with other languages necessary, if only as a means to other ends. A distinguished tradition, through Edward B. Tylor, Horatio Hale, Franz Boas, Alfred L. Kroeber, Leonard Bloomfield, Edward Sapir, Clyde Kluck- hohn, Claude Lévi-Strauss, has long found the study of language essential to understanding of the nature of culture and of man. Each tradition, indeed, can be traced to the Enlightenment, and the common matrix there of all modern social science. If in a passing generation, anthropologists have written chapters about language, sociologists sentences, it is just such a disparity in attention to language that appears to be changing.

These trends are part of a larger trend toward reintegration of the social sciences as traditional differences among them in sphere and subject-matter decrease. On the other hand, that part of the study of language by anthropologists that stems from engagement with other cultures in native North America, Oceania, Africa and elsewhere merges with linguistics proper. That is why, indeed, so much of the linguistic activity of anthropologists is not represented in this section. It is included in other volumes of the series, concerned with the languages of particular areas of the world, and with questions of genetic, areal and typological classifications (see, for example, vol. 10, 1973, and Haas' contribution to vol. 3 of *Current Trends,* 1966). Description and classification of the languages of the world have long depended in part on anthropological traditions of fieldwork and culture history, and just these activities seem likely to continue to make one kind of anthropology and one kind of linguistics the same thing. In this respect anthropology is unique among the social sciences. There have been a few grammars of the language of individual children from psychologists, but no grammars of the language of a community from psychologists, sociologists or political scientists; the prospect of the latter becoming professionally concerned with historical linguistics would depend on the prospect of a quite different kind of historical linguistics, one whose foundations were the empirical study of ongoing change, and whose distinction from the history of language had disappeared.

Where sociology and anthropology claim a distinctive place, then, is where they have distinctive problems and make distinctive contributions to the general field of the study of language.

II

Anthropology has some distinctiveness with regard to its strictly linguistic work, because of its interest in the peoples who speak the languages of the world. Its descriptive and historical work is undertaken as much to learn about actual languages and communities, as to influence technical linguistics. The dominant heritage of anthropology is the humanist one, that 'nothing human is alien', and much of anthropology, as Lévi-Strauss has put it, is a third wave of the humanities, following upon classical and oriental philology, by providing philologies for peoples without philology of their own. The intrinsic value of the materials, and respect for their integrity, for accuracy, and for the communities from which the materials come, must often take precedence over contemplation of technical matters internal to linguistics, or the spinning out of solutions to them. (A colleague recently remarked, 'I've discovered what happened to traditional linguistics; it's alive and well in the meetings of the American Anthropological Association'.) It would indeed be an irremediable loss, if anthropologists were to let go the distinctive materials for which they have taken responsibility, as part of the study, not just of languages, but of ways of life. No doubt such anchoring is maintained sometimes at the expense of theoretical insight into the materials concerned, as well as of the understanding that theoretical contribution can bring, but its value is recognized by many, as when

American Indians seek out linguists in the anthropological tradition to help renew their cultural heritage and self-respect.

III

Where anthropology would be generally considered to have had a distinctive role in recent years would be with regard to the problems of *rate of change* and of *linguistic relativity*. The former is taken up in the volume of this series concerned with diachronic problems (*Current Trends,* vol. 11, 1973), in keeping with what has been said above. Suffice it to say here that the anthropological interest stems from historical problems, for which the lexical evidence with which lexicostatistics and glottochronology work is often all that is available, and for which in any case they provide additional lines of evidence. Criticisms of the mathematics of the subject, once widely accepted, have been shown by Sankoff (1973), and others to be specious; the genuine difficulties are in the limitations on empirical application, not in theoretical foundations. Even here, the mathematicians who have reconstructed the foundation may be most interested in the mathematically interesting problems of family tree subgrouping, to which the linguist can sometimes bring decisive other evidence, and depreciate as particularistic the problems of dating in terms of rates of change, to which linguists can so seldom bring other evidence, and which are crucial to vexed cases of affiliation and to integration of linguistic results with other culture-historical findings.

The difficulty appears to lie in recognizing that problems of dating and rate of change are intrinsic to prehistoric linguistics, quite apart from recent work or the work of any particular scholar. Any historical inference from difference of similarity to difference in closeness makes an assumption about the relationship between similarity and time, i.e., about rate of change. Insofar as degree of similarity is proportional to lapse of time, just so far can an inference to grouping be made. The notion is both indispensable and about as old as modern (post-Renaissance) interest in the grouping of languages; the notion of a sector of 'common words' (basic vocabulary), naturally universal to languages in virtue of their semantic function, and specially probative of relationship, is as old. The crime of lexicostatistics and glottochronology has been to try to make the two notions precise, i.e., to introduce measurement. The nature and limitations of such measurement must remain part of the study of linguistic prehistory, most obviously in cases such as the Malayo-Polynesian (Austronesian) languages where lexical evidence is indispensable to classification, but also in cases where it is the congruence between lexical and grammatical evidence that is in question. In Na-Déné, the North American Indian group of languages that includes Navajo and Apache in the American Southwest, and Eyak, Tlingit and Haida on the North Pacific Coast, and that may ultimately be linked to Chinese and Sino-Tibetan, the grammatical relationship is not in doubt. A leader in current comparative work, Michael Krauss, finds that all lexicostatistic calculations consistently give a pattern of distance in lexical relationship far too great for the apparent degree of grammatical relationship (see Krauss in *Current Trends* 10, 1973). The difficulty, of course, is in knowing how to calibrate degree of grammatical relationship (assuming no further phonological correspondences in lexicon remain to be found). Much of historical and theoretical interest hangs on the possibility of calibration in this case. Again, it has been shown that in some cases of pidginization the resulting glottochronological distance between the pidgin and the dominant source of its basic vocabulary is of a degree of magnitude sharply greater than in cases of normal linguistic change. Here is the possibility of a criterion for the often remarked 'rapid restructuring' characteristics of the formation of a pidgin, a possibility that needs exploration. Whatever the outcome, it will be significant, both to theoretical interpretation of the process of pidginization and to empirical interpretation of cases in which the possibility of past pidginization or creolization has been raised (e.g. Na-Déné). Finally, the interest of questions of differential persistence of basic vocabulary, as between semantic categories, and grammatical classes, or as between cultural traditions, has hardly been taken up, since A. L. Kroeber's discussion (1961, 1963).

Some linguists appear to consider the study of linguistic change justifiable only insofar as it may contribute to 'linguistic theory', the latter term being taken as synonymous with a theory of grammar, not with a theory of language. Others continue to think of linguistic change as of interest in its own right, or for the light it sheds on other aspects of human history. For such linguists, including a number of anthropologists, there can be such a thing as a theory of linguistic change that encompasses more than can be dreamt of in formal grammar. For such scholars the interdependence of the several dimensions of change in human institutions, including the linguistic, will not be expendable. Indeed, the possibility of explaining many particular cases and of a general theory adequate to the facts of linguistic change will depend upon pursuing an integrated approach, combining linguistic and social factors in the study both of ongoing change and of change already accomplished. To the extent that dominant trends in the discipline of linguistics define 'linguistic theory' narrowly, some aspects of the general theory of language will continue to be apportioned among other disciplines, such as anthropology, together with subjects such as pidgin and creole languages (cf. Hymes 1971a), to whose study an integrated approach is indispensable.

IV

The foundations of the problem of linguistic relativity have also been reconstructed, through theoretical critique and analysis, but, as with lexicostatistics and glottochronology, the necessary empirical work on the new foundations has only partially been begun. Both are topics that are sometimes wished away, but remain, because the phenomena do, and because there are those who must deal with them. If in the case of rates of change, and stability of form-meaning connections, the audience is one largely of anthropologists, in the case of linguistic relativity the concern reaches to the condition of our own society, and indeed any society, where attitudes toward differences in ways of speaking, and assumptions as to their relationship to thinking, may shape the futures of children. Difference in way of speaking has often been taken as evidence of inferiority. Social scientists and linguists encountered the issue most often in the past in relation to exotic languages. In modern anthropology and linguistics the prevailing view has been one of appreciation of the particular virtues of linguistic systems different from one's own; such systems have even been found superior in some points of form (e.g. Whorf's comments on Hopi's handling of vibratory phenomena, 1936). Today the issue arises with special force in regard to differences in way of speaking within the same general language, on the part of children of different class and ethnic backgrounds. The issue is likely to remain with us as long as differences in ways of speaking of different social groups remain. Attitudes toward the issue are necessarily colored by awareness of practical consequences, and it is difficult to pursue an analysis of the question without being misunderstood. Facts of difference may be regarded as evidence of particular identity, and valued as such; or regarded as evidence of inferiority, and resented. One and the same person or group may feel impelled to stress distinctiveness in one context, sameness in another.

That languages differ semantically; that these differences are embedded in cultural contexts; that these differences can be difficult to reconcile; such is the common experience of many a translator. For a serious theory of language, especially from a social science standpoint, these phenomena require study and explanation, as essential aspects of the role of language in social life.

The standard anthropological view in the United States in this century has been that languages (and by extension, ways of speaking) are different but equal. The view is rooted in the honorable liberal humanism that is American anthropology's dominant outlook, and shares the virtues and limitations of that outlook. In its classic form the standard view has sometimes seemed to maintain the great significance of linguistic differences in one context, and to deny such differences any significance in another. As evidence of the distinctive world view of an interestingly distinctive culture, differences may be stressed; in social contexts in which stigma or discrimination might occur, such differences may be minimized or explained away, thus allowing one to have one's cake and eat it too. In point of fact, there is merit in a view that distinguishes between semantic configurations as historically derived cultural products, and the cognitive orientations and capacities of present speakers of the language, as will be elaborated below. It remains that the nature of the relation is problematic and requires to be investigated, and little such investigation has been undertaken.

The limited investigations over two summers of the Southwest Project on Comparative Psycholinguistics did establish some relations between linguistic and cognitive differences. Within comparable cultural circumstances, for example, Navajo speakers have been shown to make many more discriminations in terms of shape than Zuni speakers, Navajo being a language with obligatory marking of shape in verbs, and Zuni not (MacLay 1958; see discussion in Hymes 1961). Such findings have been overlooked or even denied by some writers. Just as many anthropologists might refuse to study or analyze differences in genetically inherited abilities, on grounds of giving aid and comfort to the social or theoretical enemy, so many scholars would regard suggestion of significant differences in language, related to thought, as social and theoretical anathema both. Such differences and relationships do exist. At the same time the situation is a mixed one. Some English speakers, for example, make about as many discriminations in terms of shape as Navajo speakers, showing that language is *a* determinant, not *the* determinant of such behavior (Carroll and Casagrande 1958). Such a mixed situation and an unfavorable climate of opinion have not encouraged further investigation, especially when quite superficial differences in linguistic form may be seized upon by persons in our own society to the prejudice of groups of children.

The focus of current linguistic theory on the universal base of language also does not encourage investigation, even though the view that departures from naturalness (universals) involve 'costs' might be taken as a stimulus. Beyond a certain point, the speakers of languages would appear to have been willing or constrained to accept many such 'costs'. A universalizing approach might thus be taken to highlight in a new way the significance of the kinds of difference which concerned Boas, Sapir and Whorf. The pressing task of a universalizing linguistics might be thought to be, not to explain universals and naturalness, which are to be expected, but to explain differences and specific configurations, which are manifold and yet not to be expected. This implication of present theory, however, has yet to be drawn and acted upon.

The patent falsity of the standard anthropological view, that languages are simultaneously different and equal, has not diminished its attractiveness. What is equal, however, is the human *faculté de langage*, the capacity of each normal child to acquire any language and to make use of it in a flexible, adaptive way in the social environment in which it grows up. The very adaptability of language to different environments results in the fact that a given language, as constituted here and now, simply in virtue of its successful adaptation to one setting, is not equally adapted to unlike settings. Adapt*able* is not the same as adapt*ed*. All languages are *potentially* equal, in that one could come to render anything in any language, given sufficient time and trouble, although even then, differences in aptness, in scale and nuance of the means of expression, might remain. The premise of modern linguistics, *tout se tient,* has in part this consequence. Of course not everything quite holds together, or to the same degree, the system being partly open; but mostly it does, and mostly use of language depends on that fact. It is not the case that one can 'say anything in any language', if conditions of acceptability and cost, as are always present in real situations, are admitted. Indeed, it was once the case that syntax could not be carefully discussed in any language on the face of the earth, and it remains a significant fact for many languages today that a language without the terminology of a science cannot be used to give instruction in it. Only certain contemporary languages, in fact, have been developed as languages of all science and technology; it is a serious proposition to suggest that Japanese may be the last language to 'make it' as an independent language of science and technology.

The question of what can be done in a given language, here and now, in relation to the number and status of its speakers, the economic situation, the pressure of surrounding circumstances, is a real and vital question in many countries. Despite the potential equality of all languages, many of those responsible for the development of their countries can not afford the luxury of confusing potentiality with actual equality. We confront a world in which specialization of function among surviving languages will be a paramount reality. One can see this already in regions such as the American Southwest, where the growth of indigenous Indian languages to express new meanings has levelled off, the languages being compartmentalized in function alongside English and Spanish. In some such cases things that once could be done in a language no longer can be, and the language as a means of narrative art and eloquence is moribund or defunct. Speakers of languages themselves make choices of language in terms of what can be done in one or the other, and not only because of their own history as speakers, but in terms of the capacities of the linguistic systems themselves. If linguistic and social theory has not succeeded in relating linguistic means and their meanings in such respects, that is evidence of the need for a theory of language that will be able to do so.

It has sometimes been maintained that the equality of languages consists in each language being equally well adapted to its particular setting. Such a view assumes that each language has only one setting, each setting only one language. Like the notion of linguistic relativity developed by Whorf, this notion interprets differences in structure by assuming a constancy of function. The one assumes that structures have invariantly the function of shaping (or reflecting) outlook, the other that structures have invariantly the function of being adaptive to the whole of a setting. The facts of multilingualism and of diversity of linguistic repertoire point out the inadequacy of the assumption in both cases. With regard to the Sapir-Whorf type of linguistic relativity, notice that ordinary analyses give no basis for recognizing the difference between linguistic structures that are part of the first and only language of a speaker, and structures that are part of a language that is its speaker's second or third; a language that is used only in the home, or one that is used only in the marketplace. The same structures might have one or the other of these functional roles. In short, investigation of the relation between features of language and thought requires prior investigation of verbal repertoire and social function. The study of linguistic relativity, as ordinarily conceived, is dependent upon another kind of linguistic relativity, which might be called sociolinguistic relativity (cf.

Hymes 1966). In general, inferences from linguistic differences to differences of thought make an assumption as to function, and function itself cannot be taken for granted, but is problematic.

The kind of inferences made by Whorf, Lee and others has its place, if taken as inference to a historically derived pattern. Languages do differ in semantic configuration; there is no reason to think the differences to be accidental, and much reason to think the differences to be cumulative products of past choices, past acts of selecting and grouping of features of experience for reporting by speakers of the languages. If a language comes to elaborate aspects, or to change from a verbal system based on aspect to one centered on tense, it is hard to escape the inference that speakers of the language have selectively changed in their reporting of aspectual characteristics of events, and that that is the source of the linguistic change. Such an inference as to pattern, of course, does not speak to the significance of such patterns for present-day speakers of a language, or indeed, to the precise function of such patterns for past speakers. Whether the pattern is to be regarded as a preferred style, as evidence of an inescapable world view, or something else, is a question on which independent evidence must be brought to bear. It is not a question susceptible of answer a priori. In general, the relation of linguistic features to thought and behavior will prove mixed. Absence of any relation or determination in either direction is contraverted by facts such as the occasional influence of grammatical gender, the meaninglessness of a 'four-minute mile' as an ideal target in a metric system, the heuristic value of rhyme, on the one hand, semantic innovation on the other. Perfect relation or determination in either direction is contraverted by known facts as well. Were language the immediately malleable instrument of thought, writers would not wrestle with means of expression, and we should not know of successes. The nature of the relation between language, thought and behavior may itself be something that varies cross-culturally, and even over time in a given culture, and as between individuals. The true subject of an investigation of linguistic relativity may be not only linguistic structures that shape or reflect thought, but also sociolinguistic structures that shape or reflect the degree and way that linguistic structures do so.

In sum, the potential equality and approximate equivalence of linguistic means is one thing, the actual state of affairs another. The subject who can discriminate a vast array of color chips in a laboratory falls back on the convenient common color terms in daily life. That is what the language of daily life is for — to enable one to pick out the book that is some kind of red, not to force one to hit correctly on the fact that the book is vermillion, crimson, scarlet or orient red. Most of us are in that situation most of the time — able perhaps to think through and beyond common terminology, and improvise or revise even if need be, but not able to do that all the time for everything. Like other aspects of human adaptation, the result is one of both benefit and cost. If language is granted a function in human life, that mixture is what one should expect.

The situation of language can be put in relief by a comparison to manual tools. No one seriously doubts that the character of a technology influences what can be done with it; that some technologies are better suited to some purposes, others to others; that some technologies can do things that others cannot. At the same time it is usually clear that technology does not unidirectionally determine other aspects of economic and social life; it is a major condition, but not the only one. A language must be considered a set of verbal tools, or, if one wishes, lingual tools. This is not the only side from which language must be viewed, but it is an essential one. Talk about the significance of language is empty, if one can do nothing with language, if nothing is ever done with language, if language is in no way an instrument of human adaptation and social life. But of course languages are used to name, store, retrieve, report. The very aspect of their structure on which modern linguistics has concentrated is their organization in the service of this 'referential' function. Now, all that is maintained, from a sociolinguistic perspective, is that the character of the tools influences what is done with them; that some sets of verbal tools are better for some things, others for others; that some sets can do things that others can not. The verbal tools do not unidirectionally determine other aspects of mental and social life; they are a major condition, not the only one.

There remains the question of the set of verbal tools pertinent to the given case. As Whorf indicated in his notion of 'fashions of speaking', the usual linguistic description cannot be mechanically pressed into service. Here as elsewhere function governs structure, and the features that are actively, productively used by speakers for a purpose must be identified. More will be said of the implication of this point below.

The points of the preceding analysis perhaps ought to be obvious. My excuse for belaboring the issue is that the relativity of our own attitudes to language and its social role often diverts us from the obvious, and that the issue remains inescapably with us, until further clarified by research on a new, critical basis. A crucial step may be to take the point made by a number of writers, that differences of the sort dramatized by Whorf and others may be found within our own one society and language (e.g., skiers with many terms for snow, vis-a-vis the famous Eskimo case cited by Boas), and make of it a subject of investigation. Given that their terminologies for snow are not identical, investigate the commonalities and differences in the context of snow as between skiers and Eskimos, on the one hand, skiers and non-skiers, on the other. In general, recognize that the pertinent groupings for comparative study of the relation between linguistic means, thought and behavior, are not necessarily given by the names of languages, societies, and cultures, but, like other sociolinguistic phenomena, must be more precisely specified.

V

Lexicostatistics and glottochronology, and linguistic relativity, are associated with the names of two students of Sapir, Morris Swadesh and Whorf, and it is fair to say that the main lines of anthropological concern with language since the last decade of Sapir's life (he died in 1939) have been mediated through what might be called the 'Sapir tradition' (cf. Hymes 1971b). Equally outgrowths of the tradition are the interest in the last twenty years in linguistics as a source of anthropological method and models (a notion Sapir was first to enunciate) and the form of semantic description known as 'componential analysis'. These concerns owe something to Sapir's (and Whorf's) view of language and linguistics as a key to form in culture, so far as their development in the United States is concerned; to the work of Sapir and Swadesh on an etics of semantic description, and to Whorf's particular treatment of grammatical categories and what he called 'cryptotypes' (essentially, semantically characterized grammatical subcategorization and selection, respectively). The attention of Sapir and his students to special languages and forms of speech, and Sapir's own change of outlook in the 1930s toward a person-oriented, social context perspective on speech (cf. Hymes 1970b), has borne fruit in the last ten years in the other main line of current anthropological concern, the patterning of linguistic variation and of the use of language. Here too, linguistics as a source of methods and models has played a part.

Interest in lexicostatistics and glottochronology has remained centered mostly in anthropology and linguistics, and is essentially an aspect of the latter nurtured by the former. As an aspect of semantics, linguistic relativity recurrently attracts attention in psychology, sociology and philosophy, and other fields as well. The interest in linguistic methods and models, also closely tied to 'componential analysis' in the United States, has taken on an independent life, especially in European circles, under the headings of 'structuralism' and 'semiotics'. This latter movement extends far beyond anthropology and sociology into psychoanalysis, contemporary literature and literary criticism, current debate in the Marxist tradition, intellectual history, etc., and may have more influence outside anthropology and sociology than within them. Areas of the greatest importance to anthropology and sociology are the renewed interest in analysis of culturally patterned conduct, such as narrative and ritual, and modes of communication interwoven with language, such as gesture, dress, social space, film, and the like. Some see in structuralism or semiotics a mode of integration of the human sciences as a whole, an integration that would vindicate a vision such as that of Cassirer in his *Philosophy of symbolic forms* (1923), and *Essay on man* (1944), or of Kenneth Burke, in his conception of *Dramatism* (1968). The special significance of such a movement lies in the extent to which it offers a viable method of work, as well as a metaphor or perspective.

These important trends can only be mentioned here. The present overview must be limited to the sphere of the accompanying papers, that is, of work centered on the description and interpretation of specifically linguistic phenomena, as currently treated in the two disciplines of concern. It must be pointed out, however, that the trend toward integration of anthropology and sociology, signalled in this discussion, is but part of the larger trend toward reintegration in which structuralism and semiotics are major forces. The problems of integration faced by anthropology and sociology in the study of language, especially in questions of method and explanation, are something of a microcosm of problems to be faced more generally.

The main contributions of the younger generation of anthropologists and anthropologically-oriented linguists, where not contributions to linguistic description and history as such, have been with respect to the two trends that may be termed *ethnographic semantics* and the *ethnography of speaking* (or, *of communication*). The former, as an aspect of the description of language, may also be considered an aspect of linguistics nurtured by anthropology, being distinctive especially in its concern with domains of cultural importance and problems of the lexicography of a language as a whole. In these respects ethnographic semantics continues an anthropological concern with lexicon that has been subordinated in linguistics proper in the United States. The latter trend, although nurtured by the interest of linguists in functions of speech and culture as communication, has come to appear as an aspect of a general social science approach to language under the rubric of 'sociolinguistics'.

Both trends can be regarded as carrying out along more particular ethnographic lines the concern of the Sapir tradition for the relation of language to culture, voiced most saliently in the notion of linguistic relativity, and as working toward a newly constructed descriptive and methodological base for understanding that relation and that notion. Whereas earlier concern appeared in the form of questions as to the *correlation* between language and culture, as separate entities previously described, the newer ethnographic concerns essentially take the form of description of phenomena of meaning and conduct whose linguistic and cultural aspects are already interrelated in the reality to be described. The principal distinction to be noticed within the current trends is in the tendency of ethnographic semantics to see the integration of language and culture in terms of an integrated code described by its methods, apart from conduct, whereas the ethnography of speaking includes a concern with performances, as events in which structures and meanings emerge through the interaction of codes and settings.

VI

The highpoint of the discussion of linguistic relativity, stimulated by republication of Whorf's writings, coincided with the emergence of the distinctive contribution to Whorf's central concern, meaning, referred to as 'ethnographic semantics'. In the decade from the mid-1950s to the mid-1960s, a limited but penetrating body of work developed in the analysis of folk taxonomies, and the methods therein developed are now a standard, if sometimes controversial, part of the field. There has appeared a textbook collecting a number of major articles under the somewhat over-extended title of *Cognitive anthropology* (Tyler 1969). Anthropologists had often spoken of a language, especially its vocabulary, as an index to culture, but had not made much use of that insight since early in the century. The earlier emphasis, indeed, had tended to be on selective concentration of vocabulary items (such as Eskimo terms for 'snow'), whereas the new emphasis is on structure within domains. The orientation of much of the current work is toward cultural organization of natural domains, such as ethnobotany, ethnozoology, ethnogeography, ethnoastronomy, and the like, and one common term for the subject has been the generalization of such domains as 'ethnoscience': a culture's organization of the universe as disclosed through analysis of its lexical domains. A major line of work has been in kinship, because of the central importance of kinship to life in the societies mostly studied by anthropologists. Here Ward H. Goodenough, Floyd Lounsbury and others have contributed simultaneously to semantic method and cultural analysis, while in the same period, Lévi-Strauss has reshaped ideas on the nature of systems of kin relationship, stimulated by the analogy of linguistics.

Debate continues as to the semantic dimensions that properly define a set of kinship terms, as a matter of general theory, and as an empirical question in particular cases. This issue is of course fundamental throughout ethnoscience and componential analysis, the necessity of validating empirically the dimensions that define a domain having been succinctly demonstrated early on by Conklin (1955) with regard to 'color' terms. The interpretation of Lévi-Strauss' ideas as to elementary structures has given rise to a continuing secondary literature, and the original inspiration of linguistics has been extended by models drawn from a variety of branches of formal analysis in mathematics and logic. Here one may see in capsule form the role of linguistic method for anthropology beyond language; an initial stimulus to formal analysis, supplanted by independent sources of formal analysis, once that approach to a cultural domain is securely launched. In general, the mode of incorporation of componential analysis, and analysis on Lévi-Straussian lines, into semantic and cultural theory remains open, but it is clear that the two lines of work, the one an extension, the other an analogy of structural linguistics, have already transformed the study of kinship.

If ethnographic analysis is an empirical field, currently rejuvenated as part of the general revival of cognitive research since the 1950s, it is also heralded, or stigmatized, depending on viewpoint, as manifestation of fundamental issues in anthropological and sociological theory. The issue has come to be associated with the terms 'emics' and 'etics', devised by Pike (1954, 1967) from 'phonemics' and 'phonetics'. It was Pike's intention simply to generalize linguistic usage, using the two terms to refer to three interdependent aspects of research: a frame of reference in terms of which observations are made and recorded (etic 1); an analysis of structure, validated in terms of the particular system studied (emic); a frame of reference, in terms of which particular emic analyses may be placed (typologically and comparatively), and to whose continuing revision and improvement, as a provisional general theory, particular emic analyses contribute. The two etic moments are of course essentially the same, in that etic 2 may serve as etic 1 to the next investigation; the distinction lies in its role in the unfolding of a particular investigation.

The relationship between 'etic' and 'emic' clearly is dialectical, not one of dichotomy between whose terms a choice is forced; there is feedback between the two as research proceeds in a field of inquiry. The dialectic has sometimes been lost from sight. 'Emic' research, by which has variously been understood 'ethnoscience', 'componential analysis' and other ethnography of linguistic inspiration, has been taken by some to be a form of intellectual imperialism, representing itself as the only method of investigation in anthropology. General issues of 'materialism' vs. 'idealism' in epistemology, of humanistic vs. scientistic attitudes toward man in choice of problems and methods, have been raised. It seems fair to say that linguistics here has been more of a mirror than a model. The intention of 'ethnoscience' and 'componential analysis', and the various ethnographic procedures associated with these names, has been to discover structure that hitherto had eluded anthropologists and linguists, and to insist on the descriptive validity as the central issue of ethnography. Indeed, in Goodenough's writings in the early fifties, the theme of descriptive adequacy, as concerned with a kind of knowledge held by members of a community, was advanced in anthropology before it received due attention in linguistics. In spirit it has carried forward the concern of Boas, Sapir and others that general descriptive concepts be adequate to the realities to which they are applied. It has deepened that Boasian concern with the view that an ethnography, like a grammar, is not merely 'descriptive' in the sense of supplying factual fodder, but itself a theoretical activity, in its procedures and its results.

As to discovery of structure, it is simply the case that previous analyses of kinship terminologies, for example, consisted of lists of terms with definition merely by extension (listing possible kin types), and of a selection of one or another few features considered significant comparatively, as basis for assigning the system to a type. The new work has shown how to provide an analysis of terms by intensional definition, and how to analyze the entire set of terms and features as a system. As to general claims, the new approach has inevitably been a critique of work that did not meet standards of descriptive validity, or, in the particular case of terminological systems, that failed to analyze them as systems; and it has been associated with the particular positions on this or that issue of particular scholars. It has also come to be associated in some cases with use of mathematics and of computers. By a curious irony, indeed, a linguistic approach that was encouraged by Kroeber, Kluckhohn and others, as a source of rigor proper to a humanistic field, an alternative to the 'scientism' imported from other areas by some social scientists, has come to seem a symbol of just such 'scientism' in some quarters. The approach has been criticized on 'humanistic' grounds by some, while being attacked as mentalistic and unscientific by others. Each discipline appears to have its bugaboos, and the bugaboos to have other bugaboos in turn to bite 'em. If some linguists denounce statistical methods as anti-humanistic and as doing violence to the nature of the phenomena (I have in mind some comments on lexicostatistics and on statistical work in stylistics), some anthropologists denounce linguistic methods on the same grounds. (Cf. the reactions of some literary scholars to linguistic analyses of poetry.) There seems no permanent defense, however, against the discovery of new structure.

Because of the intimate association between anthropology and linguistics, anthropological discussions have been concerned with linguistic methods and models, quite generally, apart from their extension through semantic analysis. Lévi-Strauss is of course the most eminent figure, and the vogue of structuralism, sometimes even in spite of the views of its hero-figures, is well known. Suffice it to say here that linguistic methods and models can neither be rejected out of hand, or be made to apply by sleight of hand. As to the latter, attempts at liberal transplantation have usually failed, through being based on surface analogy alone. Where fundamental principles have been understood, there has been some success. The ethnographic work of Goodenough, Conklin, C. O. Frake and others, for example, has seen its task as one of understanding the nature of culture and of cultural description from the same vantage point as that from which modern linguistics understands the nature of language and linguistic description. Rather than seek 'vowel triangles', 'phonemes', or 'deep structures' of culture, it has sought to understand and apply the methodological principles which lead to the discovery of phonemic and other structures — principles of contrastive relevance, distributional class and paradigmatic set, distinctive feature, transformational relation, and to discover their sphere of applicability in other cultural phenomena. The units and patterns resulting from application of the principles have been proper to the cultural domains (on these issues, cf. Hymes 1970b).

In sum, there has been a degree of success in the extension and diffusion of modes of analysis stimulated by linguistics. It will not be possible to write the history of this period of anthropology without recognizing this influence as a major factor. No general prediction as to the limits of language-like methods and models is possible, but three observations can be made. First, a mixed result is to be expected. On the one hand, the role of the human mind in all human activity gives some warrant for anticipating commonality of structure across domains of activity; on the other hand, differences in the modalities employed, and in the purposes to which structures are adapted, and put, give grounds for difference. Second, the test of an application must be that it is possible to invalidate and revise the application in terms of the new field. Linguistics proceeds in just this way, of course, as does any discipline that has a true purchase on its subject matter. Too often anthropological applications have been content with the possibility of an analysis derivative of linguistic method, remaining sterile, because no grounds for developing the analysis independently of linguistics were shown. Yet it may be that Chomsky's transformations of the type before his *Aspects* (1965), for example, fit a particular material better than those of the type after *Aspects*, or that neither do, and a 'generative semantic' model is wanted instead. The diversity of linguistic models makes the choice of model depend on validation in the domain of application, not on the prestige of a particular linguist or school. Finally, whatever the outcome of such applications, the results are of interest to a general field of semiotics, a general science of man. Such a general field must have as one of its concerns the nature of the relations between the various spheres of human activity, the extent and limits of the application of the methods and principles found in each, the degree of generalization possible to these (this discussion draws on Hymes 1970a).

In his penetrating contribution to the present volume Werner surveys the state of ethnographic semantics with close attention to alternative models for the handling of the entire lexicon and the solution of formal problems. His own work has been concentrated among the Navajo, where he and his students have been developing a rich and detailed body of knowledge, at once lexical, semantic and cultural. Werner's work and this review, indeed, exemplify the merging of linguistic and ethnographic analysis in concern for the structure of the knowledge of the members of a community. This is not to say that normal practice in the two fields has merged, and Werner comments on the gap, noting that the anthropologically oriented investigator starts from lexicon, the investigator oriented by contemporary linguistics from grammar. He points out that the effective unification of the two lines of work remains to be accomplished.

This general goal should be kept in mind as the overriding significance of the work discussed by Werner. The discussion is necessarily technical, and close to the technical literature, and not all will agree with the conception of explicit, verbalicable sentences as the criterion of what is psychologically real, or the suggestion that such limits define the limit between verbal and nonverbal, explicit and implicit behavior (2.2 at end). It is indeed important and undeniable that covertness with respect to terms does not imply covertness in the language. Much anthropological attention to semantics has tacitly assumed that semantic coding was a matter of words, neglecting sentences, and often vitiating results. The Voegelins have recently shown, for example, that nodes of a taxonomy of kinship not named by the Hopi are nevertheless directly implicated by certain sentences. Werner's concern with 'occasional' and 'standing' sentences (1.1.2.2) is especially important for all future work. At the same time, there is another distinction, suggested by the term 'standing', which needs to be kept in mind. Werner's distinction has to do with the scope of the information or knowledge contained in sentences ('Here come Mary and her little lamb' vs. 'Mary is the name of a girl', 'A lamb is a young sheep' — as the Voegelin's work indicates, such sentences need not be so expressly definitional in form). Now, as Weinreich once pointed out (*Current Trends* 3, 1966), standing sentences cannot be identified a priori by their form, but must be identified 'emically', empirically in the community in question. Moreover, there is a kind of sentence that might well be called 'standing', even though apparently 'occasional' in appearance, having to do with relations between persons and situations, rather than between terms. If the arrival of a certain girl and her escort is regularly greeted with 'Here come Mary and her little lamb', one has socially a 'standing' sentence, at least for the network of relationships in question. (One should recall here that Kenneth Burke observed many years ago (1941) that recurrent sentences, just as much as words, can be a way of naming situations.) Recently the sociologist Harvey Sacks has shed light on underlying cognitive structures in American society, as to different types of what can be called 'calendar', by attending to and analyzing a sentence recurrent in the calls of elderly divorced or widowed women to the Los Angeles Suicide Prevention Center — 'Nothing ever happens anymore'. It became clear that the sentence referred, not to the public calendar of changing newspaper dates and headlines, but to a private calendar, on which had once occurred birth-days, anniversaries, and the like. Again, 'You can't stop progress' and 'You can't fight city hall' are too recurrent to be called 'occasional', yet not illuminative of the lexical entries for 'progress' and 'city hall' (? 'Progress is something that cannot be stopped', ? 'City hall is something that cannot be fought'); yet from an ethnographic standpoint they may be significant 'standing' sentences indeed. In general the sen-tence that serves as a 'clincher', or that maintains boundaries by offering a choice between acceptance and an argument over group presuppositions, is of vital concern to ethnographic semantics. The study of cultural knowledge can be seen to require integration not only of lexicographic and grammatical study, but also of linguistic and ethnographic, or sociolinguistic, starting points as well.

Given the latter starting point, one may need also to elaborate consideration of the distinction between 'knowing that' and 'knowing how' (2.3, following 29(ii)). Werner is no doubt correct in rejecting the view that competence to produce sen-tences and competence to interpret sentences are identical, if the term 'competence' is to have anything of its normal meaning, ability; competence to understand does outstrip competence to produce. Yet it would be unfortunate if the difference were equated with the difference between 'knowing that' and 'knowing how' without further reflection. Current work in 'ethnomethodology' — a branch of sociological and ethnographic investigation partly inspired by ethnoscience, and concerned with the analysis of conversations and sequences of practical activities, lays great stress upon the active, rather than passive, nature of reception and interpretation. A founder of this line of work, Harold Garfinkel (1967), takes as fundamental that conversations and practical activities make sense to their participants because the participants engage in the 'work' of making them sensible. The processes by which this work is done call upon 'common sense knowledge', and point to universal properties of human rationality. The rationality of everyday life is seen as not a matter of recognition of rational structure alone, but as also an artful accomplish-ment, a making out of reality as rational, that draws on active modes of interpreta-tion whose structures can be discerned. There is more to making sense than making sentences.

It would be unfortunate also if the difference between knowing that and knowing how were equated entirely with the difference between plans and their execution, should that distinction itself be regarded as an absolute dichotomy. The execution of plans often involves feedback to the character of the plan itself. Further, if speakers of a language could never find an instance in the real world of the terms they confidently distinguish, it would be hard not to question their confidence in knowing 'that'. To point out that 'knowing that' does not guarantee 'knowing how' is one thing; the danger of severing the two is another. Here indeed is an important subject — what is taken as criterion of lexical and cultural knowledge in the community itself? One may know that a hole in the ground is a kind of cavity, and an anus a body part, but not be credited with that knowledge, if one consistently fails to make the distinction in practice. One must be concerned not to substitute what a native lexicographer might know for what a native speaker does know, as object of study.

Finally, 'knowing that' involves a great deal of knowledge that sometimes is discussed as 'knowing how'. As Chomsky has stressed, one of the essential goals of linguistic inquiry is to account for the competent speaker's ability to use sentences appropriately (1966). Such an account must consider not only sentences, but also the situations to which they are appropriate, for appropriateness is a relation between the two. Indeed, the relevant features of both terms of the relationship can be regarded as aspects of semantics. Such a semantics is concerned partly with the features of terms and sentences that enter into their appropriate use (properties of social selection and subcategorization), partly with the features of participant roles, scenes, and the like, onto which the features of terms and sentences are mapped to account for appropriateness of deference, insult, and the like. From an ethnographic or sociolinguistic standpoint, then, 'knowing that' entails a conception of 'naming' that is richer than usually entertained in formal semantics. Lexicographic and grammatical semantics must be integrated with analysis of speech acts, and such analysis requires knowledge of social relationships, settings, and the like, inasmuch as one and the same sentence may be intended or taken as a different speech act, according to such features of context. One must be able to account for the fact that naming a person or thing may count as an instance of praising, depreciating, and the like, depending on the name chosen. Knowing that an act of naming is an instance of praising, of course, does not entail that all who know are able to praise, any more than knowing plans for flying a plane suffices to fly it.

The point in question here speaks to a long-standing difficulty with discussions of meaning in linguistics and anthropology. The examples chosen in such discussions bespeak a curious world, in which persons identify internal organs, fly planes, obtain apples, specify kin and otherwise eat, move and inventory their worlds, but never praise, insult, greet, twit or otherwise interact as persons by means of words. Integration of semantic investigation with general analysis of cultural knowledge will not be accomplished without research that recognizes the element of truth in Bronislaw Malinowski's dictum that language is a mode of action, not [only] a countersign of thought.

Malinowski's dictum may be thought to have perished for lack of adequate linguistics; at least that is a theme that runs through commentary on Malinowski's work from Voegelin and Harris (1945) to Berry (1965) and Langendoen (1968). The dictum lives again, transfigured, in the work known as 'ethnomethodology', from which vantage point Cicourel writes in his contribution to this volume. Some of the work of the sociologists associated with this label concentrates upon formal properties of conversation, and can be taken as of interest for its empirical and analytical results, apart from the orientation of its authors (e.g. Schegloff 1968). Cicourel is at pains to stress the underlying orientation, and to show that the work is not to be understood as an addition or extension of familiar work, but as a radical critique.

The work which Cicourel treats is ethnographic, in a sense, and semantic, in another, but it is ethnography practiced in our own society, not in an exotic one, and it is a semantics that pushes beyond words and sentences to a concern with elementary modes of reasoning. Whereas Malinowski has been recurrently criticized for his stress on 'context of situation', on the grounds that context is external to meaning and inherently incapable of accounting for it, Cicourel joins a stress on situated interaction with a stress on 'mentalistic' bases of meaning that finds linguistic 'mentalism' itself superficial. Whorf had maintained (1956 [1936]:74) that

The very essence of linguistics is the quest for meaning, and, as the science refines its procedure, it inevitably becomes, as a matter of this quest, more psychological and cultural, while retaining that almost mathematical precision of statement which it gets from the highly systematic nature of the linguistic realm of fact.

Cicourel agrees that the quest for meaning leads linguistics further into psychological and cultural considerations, but calls fundamentally into question the basis of the almost mathematical precision of linguistics. That precision, he maintains, depends upon the social norms of the community of linguists, upon the assumption by the linguist of a role like that of a judge, rather than from an accurate reflection of the nature of the linguistic realm of 'fact'.

From the standpoint of contemporary linguistics, Cicourel may be said to take seriously the notions of 'competence' and 'performance' as concerns of linguistic theory. Such notions imply human abilities. Unless the use of the term is to be considered rhetorical hyperbole, 'competence' implies concern with the creative aspect of language use in a thorough-going way. The ethnomethodological standpoint agrees wholeheartedly with linguistics in seeing everyday use of language as creative, but it sees creativity as dependent on abilities wider and deeper than those involved in sentences as such. The empirical concluding section of Cicourel's paper discusses work with communication among the deaf that is designed to make just this point, in a striking, limiting case. The preceding sections deal with work on the organization of memory, and work in artificial intelligence, in order to make the point in terms of the capacities and abilities of human beings quite generally.

Again, Cicourel may be said to take seriously the principle that 'text does *not* signal all its own structure', agreeing with contemporary linguistics, but pointing beyond contemporary practice. Linguists have commonly considered dimensions of meaning beyond their practice as a matter of infinite particulars which no one could reasonably be expected to incorporate in a science. Cicourel does lay great stress on particulars, and in a way that might indeed suggest that not much more could be done than to muse upon the perversity of reality. Open-ended particularity is not the whole story, however, and practitioners of ethnomethodology search for recurrent forms of 'glossing', of practical reasoning; they seek universal properties of human reason, on the one hand, and implicit cognitive structures shared by members of a community, on the other, not just what might be called a 'bill of particulars' against the research of others. The instance of implicit types of 'calendar' has already been cited from the work of Harvey Sacks, who has suggested generic principles of practical reasoning as well. Such work impinges on linguistic work in an empirical, as well as critical, way. Sacks has given reason to think, for example, that the interpretation of some 'performative' utterances is based, not on underlying linguistic structures, but on underlying principles of interpretation of experience that are quite general, and that obtain in the interpretation of pictures as well as of sentences. Meaningfulness, semantic interpretation, in short, are endemic in human orientation to the world, and accurate generalizations cannot be captured by analyses that make an environing tunnel of some one mode of handling experience.

For the linguist and anthropologist interested in verbal art, narrative is an especially interesting sphere of application of such an approach. Boas long ago (1888) noted that traditional narratives among the Central Eskimo presuppose a community already acquainted with their content and meaning; the actual narration would be succinct to the point of opacity. The same may be found in other groups, such as the Wasco-Wishram Chinook of central Oregon and Washington. In the words of Mrs. Ida White (Michael Silverstein, personal communication) 'White people make stories long, Indians make stories short'. The interesting point is that Indians also make stories longer when telling them to whites, i.e. when a knowledgeable audience cannot be assumed. In general the more authentic a narration (or manifestation of other cultural knowledge), the more that it is likely to presuppose, the more elliptical (from an observer's standpoint) it is likely to be. In the case of phenomena such as Chinookan myth narratives, the tradition is multiform, but not infinitely diverse. Meanings valid across situations and persons can be established. Myths have their uses as ingredients of emergent, opportunistic meanings as well, providing a store of quotations and references that can be used to jibe and joke. (As Washington Irving observed long ago in *The crayon miscellany* (1835), the dour Indian is an image in part produced by the constraints of interaction under circumstances of unshared understanding and uncertainty (cf. Basso 1970).)

In short, the spheres of meaning that lie beyond ordinary linguistic practice have both particularity and conventionality. Cicourel stresses the emergent particularities of situations, perhaps because a flood of particularity does not embarrass his aims. It justifies both critique of linguistic practice and a setting of the goal of inquiry as the universal processes of reasoning which incessantly make use of particulars. It is important to point out the sphere of stable understandings and meanings lying between linguistic rules and experiential flux, or, perhaps more to the point, between linguistic rules and processes of practical reasoning.

Ethnomethodology is a salient example of the convergence of anthropology and sociology in their concern with speech and language. Twenty years ago it might have been inconceivable that a report on current trends would bracket treatments of meaning by an anthropological linguist and a sociologist renowned for his work on methodology.

Cicourel, although dealing with situated interaction, focusses upon information in general, upon functions of language such as naming, describing, reporting (cf. his discussion of Lakoff's treatment of co-referentiality), not upon properties of interaction often studied by sociologists, such as structures of role relationship, status and the like. He notes the dependence of meaning upon modalities beyond the linguistic, notably the visual, but not the dependence of meaning upon other dimensions of the verbal itself — the social meanings encoded in stylistic features and choices, including choice of a language, or of language itself, as means. This use of the social situation to attack the generically human and mentalistic, makes for the convergence just noted. Cicourel's general perspective, however, is consistent with concern with these other aspects of meaning, and indeed, precise investigation of situated meanings requires explicit attention to all aspects of conventional verbal meaning. Some of Cicourel's own research, such as that on bilingual code-switching in conjunction with John Gumperz, has shown as much.

In general, if ethnomethodology has a face toward ethnographic semantics, it has also a face toward the ethnography of speaking. The work of Schegloff (1968), already mentioned, is a significant example. The difference between the two aspects of ethnomethodology may be said to depend on whether attention is focussed upon the properties of practical reasoning as such, or upon the forms it takes in a given case, given ways of 'glossing', as it were. From ways of glossing to ways of speaking is not a difficult step — the two intersect —, and the ethnomethodological critique of syntactic semantics as a linguist's construction is akin to the critique of the notions of 'language' and 'meaning', as constructions, that inform the ethnography of speaking. To this I now turn.

VII

For most linguistic work today the object of analysis is either a language or LAN-

GUAGE. The world of relevant data comes under one or the other heading. Meaning is equivalent to referential meaning, as has been mentioned. The heart of the ethnography of speaking, and of a sociolinguistic perspective, is to see the data of linguistics as organized in terms of ways of speaking — speech codes, styles, genres, routines and the like, and to see the data of linguistics as encompassing conventional stylistic as well as referential means, social as well as referential meaning. That entails stylistic means at each usual level of organization — phonological, lexical, syntactic, but also stylistic means that cut across and integrate these levels. To a considerable extent, the ethnography of speaking, and sociolinguistics generally, are concerned with the pursuit of *social* meaning. Social meaning may be analyzed apart from referential meaning, as when choice of a code or style or manner of pronunciation has a meaning. Ultimately, the study of meaning must integrate social and referential meaning, as interdependent aspects of discourse. At the present time, a great deal of sociolinguistic research is concentrated upon the identification and analysis of ways of speaking, and their social meanings, and upon their distribution, or patterns of use. In part this concentration reflects matters of practical concern, especially where way of speaking is equated with the ordinary notion of language ('who speaks what language to whom . . .'). In part this concentration, especially where the number and kind of ways of speaking in a community is taken as problematic, reflects a sense of the great gap to be filled in our knowledge of the actual structure of language as an instrument of social life.

Linguists have tended to stop at the grammar's edge, and if social scientists have analyzed many kinds of structure in social life, they have tended to ignore the organization of linguistic means. They have analyzed social relationships and actions without attending to ways of speaking as specific conditions for implementing and defining them. Much of the structure and precise meaning of social life has been left unstudied between the two in consequence. Both linguists and social scientists have taken the notion and functions of language for granted, failing to recognize that the functions of language, a language, any way of speaking, are problematic in a given case, and that indeed, functions and social meanings define the relevant units, or organizations, of linguistic means.

A major exception has been Basil Bernstein. He has almost single-handedly made language a respectable, serious topic within British sociology, and has influenced the study of language in other countries and disciplines as well. A sense of a single common language appears to have masked fundamental questions for most sociologists. Their theoretical orientations have led them to discuss the role of language, a priori and in general, but not to investigate language's role, in ways that would demonstrate empirical connections between linguistic means and social life. Bernstein's originality and impact consist in having seen that major theories of social order, such as those of Marx and Durkheim, are incomplete, perhaps ultimately unintelligible, if the role of linguistic means in maintenance and change of social order is not made explicit; and in having done something about it. (Social order should be taken to include symbolic order of the sort often distinguished as cultural.)

In his contribution here Bernstein gives the first account of the theoretical origins of his work, origins which have hitherto lain implicit behind empirical reports and analytical discussions. The significance of the work to education and other applications of social science is obvious. It must be noted that there has been a fair amount of misunderstanding of Bernstein's intentions, especially when the context of social class in England in which his concepts were formulated is ignored, and when the concepts are applied mechanically to class and ethnic differences in the United States. While Bernstein does consider an elaborated code superior in as much as it allows for its own reconstruction — thereby being able to serve an emancipatory role, he does not regard an elaborated code as without its own possibilities of misuse and damage to children, nor does he regard a restricted code as simply impoverished and inadequate. The basic point is that the two types of speech codes derive from two types of orientation, two matrices of social control and interaction. The social issues arising from their relationship have to do with the conflict into which they are brought in school and other situations. There are values and adequacies realizable in a restricted code that have a significance of their own. (Recall the discussion of linguistic relativity earlier in this overview.) Indeed, Bernstein's analysis of the relationship between the two ideal types of code allows for empirical investigation of their relative occurrence across classes, family types, and other parameters. The main thrust of his practical recommendations is that an elaborated code variant be made effectively available to all children, for their own defense and advantage, not that restricted codes be suppressed or stigmatized. Indeed, in his view the failure of children to acquire such a code variant in schools that profess to provide it is an indictment of the schools, not the children.

The great significance of Bernstein's view for the study of language is that it brings out the role of social factors in giving organization and meaning to linguistic features; it shows that such organization both exists and does not play merely a limiting role, but is indispensable to the accomplishment and finding of meaning. For social science generally, the great significance is to show that functions of language can not be speculated about or postulated in the abstract. It is not enough to theorize about the social role of language in symbolic interaction or the maintenance of social order; one must investigate the role. Nor can the unit of study be simply the 'language' or 'dialect' of the traditional usage. The varieties in which linguistic resources are organized must be empirically determined in the given case. Bernstein shows that 'English', for example, is simply not the relevant unit. It serves to designate a historically derived set of contents, but its relation to productive ways of speaking is problematic. The same holds true for any 'language'.

It follows, as Bernstein has indicated, that consideration of linguistic relativity must be based in sociolinguistic descriptions of relevant units. It is not enough to know that a feature is present in the general language, or even that it is grammatically obligatory in some respect; one must also know something of mode and frequency of use. Distinctive patterns of cognitive orientation are not regarded as automatic consequences of structure, but as emerging out of interaction between linguistic resources and social relationships, as the former are selected in terms of the latter.

The problems posed by Bernstein require much further work, before a general theory can be confidently proposed. The types of code and social relationship that he has defined need to be investigated in other settings. Their social and linguistic dimensions no doubt will be elaborated and refined. A major task of sociolinguistic research, indeed, is to do just this: to provide empirical studies, and comparative analyses, leading to a general typology and theory of the relation between modes of social control and the organization of linguistic resources for use.

A variety of work that contributes to such a goal is reviewed by Pride in his contribution to this volume. Writing from a standpoint within linguistics, Pride is first concerned to argue to linguists what is obvious to social scientists, namely the significance of context. Pride argues directly for transcendence of convenient dichotomies, and for an integrated approach to linguistic description, integration here meaning the incorporation of social meaning and use. His discussion of language and social stratification properly focusses on the path-breaking work of Labov. Pride's concern here is not with Labov's demonstration of the social motivation of sound change, and mechanisms of linguistic change generally — a demonstration that appears likely to rank in retrospect with the demonstration of the regularity of sound change a century before — but with the variables analyzed by Labov as constituting New York City a speech community. Pride's general point is not to dispute Labov's findings, but to argue for the dependence of significance on the functions chosen for investigation, such that other social dimensions might disclose other regularities in New York City speech.

In his discussion of social goals of language use Pride calls attention to significant work on code-switching, and on the varieties and levels of language involved, but also looks beyond it to an underlying theoretical problem. It is cause for rejoicing to have anything like a satisfactory description of such phenomena, but Pride notes that the terms that designate varieties and levels, and that are employed to designate the dimensions on which they contrast, are often ad hoc, and suspiciously dichotomous. We know very little as to what is meant by 'high' vs. 'low', or 'prestigeful' vs. 'non-prestigeful' in a way that would make valid comparison across situations and studies possible. The same point informs Pride's discussion of perception of social and linguistic variation. The possibility and necessity of sociolinguistic description has been shown by a number of admirable studies, but, Pride suggests, the general methodological and theoretical bases for such description have only begun to be built. The richness of the phenomena to be considered requires modesty as to present accomplishment. There is great need both for well described cases, and for theory of a middle range to link them. The preponderance of dichot-

omies among concepts may be a sign that theory is yet at an early stage, analogous
to an early stage in language typology, before Joseph H. Greenberg had shown how
to use gross categories as measurable dimensions, and (as had Roman Jakobson)
how to see specific traits as implying universal relations, such that a language could
be characterized by a profile of co-present features, not forced into one of a few
pigeon-holes (see Greenberg's contribution to *Current Trends* 3, 1966). The situation may be seen as analogous also to an earlier stage in description of kinship or
phonological systems, when ethnographers might expect to encounter social relationships or phone types not provided for in manuals, and to contribute to the adequacy
of an etic framework, by news of additional elements proper to its scope.

The need is apparent enough — there are few well described cases, and no
systematic typology, no general analysis as to underlying features and configurations, for even such well known varieties of language and its uses as languages of
concealment and forms of speech play — such phenomena as medieval German
Rotwelsh, contemporary American Pig Latin and 'op' talk, the eight varieties of
Chinese secret language described by Chao (1931), the twelve types of Hanunóo
speech modification reported by Conklin (1955), the complementary processes of
novel forms for common meanings, novel meanings for common forms, as between
Zuni sacred and slang usage (Newman 1955), as well as argots based simply on
special vocabulary or vocabulary substitution, as Irish traveller cant (Harper and
Hudson 1971). The same holds true for other forms of 'special language', variously
labelled 'abnormal types of speech', 'men's and women's language', 'honorific languages', and the like. There are well known cases but little in the way of comparative and theoretical understanding. There is great need simply for more well described cases and for the sort of comparison and analysis that Tylor, Louis Henry
Morgan and others began to perform successfully for other social phenomena a
century ago, and to whose indispensable role Kroeber has called attention in our
own time. We hardly know the range of possibilities in such genres of speech, let
alone what recurrent types might be usefully distinguished and named, and what
explorations would be adequate.

Explanation will require more than building on existing work, however; it will
require reconsideration of the basis of description and comparison. Here in fact is
one implication of Pride's call for an integrated approach. Distinguishable genres
of speech use have been usually treated as marginal phenomena. They have been
noted mostly when they intruded themselves upon the normal course of description,
by their frequency (so that understanding of conversation required understanding
of them), their cultural salience (e.g. religious use), or their complication of grammar. If suffixes have alternates, accountable neither by linguistic environment or
free variation, and tied obviously to sex role of speaker, then sex role of speaker is
entered into the statement of contexts of complementary distribution at that point;
given the interest, one has material for a note on men's and women's speech, even
more so if all phonological forms have alternates on such a basis (as in Yana).

Most cases described by linguists are of this third sort. Notice two things about them. The existence of differences in speech is discovered as a byproduct of another purpose. The differences are described, in effect, when their description is necessary to preserve the integrity of a description built upon the referential function of language. The alternates appear as such, as in complementary distribution, precisely in relation to that function; two alternates may both signify, e.g. first person singular possessive (as when in Wishram-Wasco Chinook, *n-* is used as the obligatory first person singular possessive prefix of kin terms only with the stems for 'father' and 'mother' (*wi-n-amš*, *wa-n-aqš*), while elsewhere a phonologically conditioned *k-~č-* occurs). From the standpoint of social function, as stylistic elements, the forms are not alternates, but contrast in meaning. (In the case in question, the relation of the terms for 'father' and 'mother' to other terms is not one of allomorphy but social distinction, morphologically marked.) If repetition and contrast are fundamental principles of linguistic analysis, then it is fair to say that linguistics has proceeded almost entirely in terms of one kind of repetition and contrast, that serving referential function, grammatically conceived, and has almost ignored repetition and contrast from the standpoint of stylistic or social meaning. (Reference of course is social, but the term 'social' has presently a marked meaning (contrasting with 'referential') as well as the unmarked meaning (subsuming 'referential' vs. 'social').) From one standpoint, two utterances of 'On the fourth floor' in a New York city department store are repetitions. From another standpoint, the two contrast, as less formal : more formal, in terms of a difference in overt linguistic form clearly marked and motivated (manifesting what Labov terms a linguistic variable).

Bloomfield once said that linguistics ignores the difference between 'I'm hungry', said by a beggar and by a child wishing to avoid going to bed, treating only what is the same. E. Colin Cherry has defined pragmatics as having the converse concern, to treat what is different. From an integrated perspective such as that advocated by Pride, a perspective that is properly linguistic, since it is concerned with the description of repetition and contrast in linguistic form — an adequate approach will describe both what is the same and what is different, insofar as both aspects of the meaning of the whole are expressed by means having conventional, interpretable status in the competencies of the community in question.

Such an approach requires that 'meaning' be conceived more broadly than 'naming' and 'reporting (neutrally)', and that procedures for investigating linguistic form in a community have a social as well as a referential base. Not only word-lists and a knowledge of grammatical categories, but also a knowledge of social roles and relationships, must provide some of the context of inquiry. Only then will the basis for a comparative analysis and adequate explanation of speech differences due to social role, concealment, play, and the like, be possible. In the past we have perhaps tended to think that explanation of these matters was as simple as saying that communities in which role, or concealment, or the like, was intrusive in morphology or phonological form must simply be interested in sex role, status concealment, or the like. An unintentional implication of such explanation would be that other communities lacked such interest, even did not mark sex role, status, concealment, or the like at all. Given the universal importance of sex role and status, the universal occurrence of occasions and motives for verbal concealment and play, it is probable that such concerns have verbal expression in every human community. If only cases intrusive in grammar are described, such universal functions of language must appear as curiosities. If description begins with a recognition of such functions, and seeks their verbal expression, then the grammatically intrusive cases can be put into a general context, and the reasons why such functions find different forms of verbal expression becomes susceptible of explanation.

The implication of Pride's call for an integrated approach, then, is a new basis for description of what is there. The linguistic resources of communities are not to be thought of simply as languages and dialects; their organization is not to be considered a matter of grammars and dictionaries alone. A community is to be described in terms of verbal repertoire, into which different languages and dialects may enter, not only as alternates, but sometimes as aspects of a single style or fashion of speaking. The necessary general concept will be that of the *variety*, or *way of speaking*. The methodological basis for identifying varieties, or ways of speaking, will add to the rules of phonology and grammar the notions of rules of co-occurrence and rules of alternation, as developed recently by Susan Ervin-Tripp (1972). Rules of co-occurrence specify what features go together to define a style, variety, or, in general, a recognized way of speaking. Rules of alternation specify the contexts of choice between ways of speaking, that is, they deal with the set of ways of speaking as if the verbal repertoire constituted a paradigm. The specification requires discovering the dimensions on which the ways of speaking contrast, the meanings associated with each, and the privileges of occurrence of each. These two concepts can be seen as culminating a general logic of linguistics in the twentieth century, toward development of analytic concepts both concrete, in the sense of constituting a description of each language, and universal, in the sense of entering into a general theory of language. The work of Boas, Sapir, Kroeber and others with American Indian grammatical structures, the notions of phoneme and morpheme, and current work in syntax and semantics may be seen as successive stages in such a development.

Social meanings and functions, to be sure, come into attention increasingly today because they intrude in the practice of linguistics, as they attempt to deal with speech acts, with disagreements in the intuitions of native speakers as to acceptability, with appropriateness, etc. But from a longer perspective, the recognition of social meaning as a basis for description, of sociolinguistics as an approach to integrated description, is a culmination of a natural development intrinsic to the gradual extension of the organizing principles of linguistic methodology from sound through syntax to meaning.

The most general conception of the field of linguistics, then, and certainly of the field of sociolinguistics, as approached from the standpoint of linguistics (Hymes 1972), can be expressed as: *the means of speech in human communities, and their meanings to those who use them.*

VIII

The concern just stated must clearly involve contributions from social scientists as well as from linguists. If one branch of linguistic description should become partly sociological or ethnographic in character, some branches of the social sciences must become partly linguistic in character. Otherwise the functions, meanings, causes and occasions of means of speech can not be adequately identified and explained. In his remarkably comprehensive review, Fishman approaches the subject from a properly social science standpoint. Whereas for Pride some argument with linguists as to context and social organization is found necessary, for Fishman the point can be taken for granted. The central problem is to describe and explain the characteristics of context and organization, as these presently exist and change over time.

As starting point for sociolinguistic description, Fishman adopts the principle of contrast in way of speaking, 'switching' as it is commonly called, from one variety to another (such switching is in effect a sociolinguistic commutation test), and a definition of speech community in terms of the sharing both of at least one variety and of norms for its appropriate use (1.3; 3.3; cf. Hymes 1967). He provides a comprehensive, yet precise definition of the sociology of language:

the study of the characteristics of language varieties, the characteristics of their functions, and the characteristics of their speakers, as these three constantly interact, change, and change one another, both within and between speech communities (1.3 at end).

(this definition can be taken as including and articulating the formulation given just above).

The importance of the sociology of language perspective is brought out especially in Fishman's treatment of the characteristics of speech communities, role relationships, domains of use, and bilingualism, regarding dominance configurations, and actual capacities for competence in bilingual situations. Such considerations are essential to bridge the gap noted by Bernstein between the abstract ideal competence dealt with in grammatical theory and the real competence of persons in the ensemble of their social relations. Most of the world, indeed, is multilingual, or at least multivarietal. Again, Fishman's discussion of a typology of contact situations, and of questionable generalizations, points up present lacks in understanding of linguistic change, if linguistic change is conceived as change both in and of language.

It may be worth noting in this connection that the discussion of bilingualism, as in sections 6.2 and 7.4, is more general than the term 'bilingualism' might itself be taken to imply. The considerations advanced apply to all cases of a plurality of varieties, or styles, not merely to cases of different languages, two at a time. Indeed, it might be desirable to introduce a new term, rather than to subsume such phenomena under 'bilingualism'. One such term would be 'multivarietalism' (together with 'multivarietal' for 'bilingual'), taking as basis the concept of variety which Fishman uses in his definition of the sociology of language. (An alternative in keeping with the Greek-derived set of terms suggested in Hymes (1968) would be to add *-typic* as a base form (to *-chronic, -topic, -(a)gelic, -telic, -critic)*; the prefix would be *poly-* (alongside *a-, di-, dia-, pan-, syn-)*; and the full form, *polytypic*.)

Fishman is an outstanding figure in the development of the new interest in language among sociologists in the United States, through his own research and advocacy, and through organizing and encouraging the work of others. Much of his own attention has gone to large-scale processes of language development, maintenance and shift, societal bilingualism, and language policy and applied sociology of language, to which he gives careful attention here within a broad frame of reference, sensitive to the meanings of the phenomena to their participants, as well as to patterns and processes as such.

Fishman's preference for the general term, 'sociology of language', reflects a concern that the larger scale phenomena, and problems of social structure and process essential to explanation, not be lost from sight, or considered marginal, as the association of 'sociolinguistics' with the interests of linguistically-oriented scholars might suggest. Too often linguists have been either naive as to the social dimensions of their work, or have leapt into amateur sociology without stopping to gain a basis for sociological insight from their own sphere of competence. On the other hand, when confronted with an analysis by multiple regression (as in 5.3 of the present paper), a linguist may not but wonder about the rest of the variance, beyond the 36.2 percent accounted for. Is it free variation, in a technical sense? Or accounted for in terms of some linguistic factors? Or accounted for in terms of social factors that might be detected in participant observation? What indeed is the occurrence of the variable in natural conversation, as distinct from experimental situations? What social meaning does it there appear to have? Could the variability in the occurrence of the plural suffix be incorporated formally into linguistic rules of the sort that Labov has devised for the copula in English?

The greatest strength of an approach from the linguistic and ethnographic side is likely to be in extension of what is known to be structured in speech. The greatest strength of an approach from the sociological and ethnological side is likely to be in comparative and evolutionary perspective, and in explanation of the occurrence, maintenance or loss of such socially-implicated structures. The one is likely to be most important to progress in understanding what is there to be explained, from phonological variation to entire varieties and genres. The other is likely to be most important to progress in understanding the conditions that give rise to different patterns of variables, varieties and genres. Both are essential to the future of socio-linguistic research. In the course of this future the distinction between anthropology and sociology will increasingly disappear, as both merge in the world wide study of contemporary mankind.

DELL HYMES

REFERENCES

BASSO, K. 1970. To give up on words: Silence in the Western Apache culture. SJA 26.213–30.

BERRY, J. 1965. Introduction to: Coral gardens and their magic, by Bronislaw Malinowski, Part II. Bloomington, Indiana University Press.

BOAS, F. 1888. The central Eskimo. B[A]E–AR 6.

BURKE, K. 1941. The philosophy of literary form. Baton Rouge, Louisiana State University Press.

——. 1968. Dramatism. International Encyclopedia of the Social Sciences, ed. by David Sills, 7.445–52. New York, Macmillan.

CARROLL, J. B., and J. CASAGRANDE. 1958. The function of language classifications in behavior. Readings in social psychology, ed. by E. Maccoby, T. H. Newcomb, and E. L. Hartley, pp. 18–31. 3rd ed. New York, Holt.

CASSIRER, E. 1923. Philosophie der symbolischen Formen: Die Sprache. Berlin, Bruno Cassirer. (English translation, New Haven, Yale University Press, 1953.)

——. 1944. An essay on man. An introduction to a philosophy of human culture. New Haven, Yale University Press.

CHAO, Y. R. 1931. Eight varieties of secret language based on the principle of fanch-ieh. Academia sinica, National Research Institute of History and Philology, Bulletin 2.312–54. Peiping. [Text in Chinese.]

CHOMSKY, N. 1965. Aspects of the theory of syntax. Cambridge, Mass., M.I.T. Press.

——. 1966. Cartesian linguistics. New York, Harper and Row.

CONKLIN, H. C. 1955. Hanunóo color categories. SJA 11.339–44.

——. 1956. Tagalog speech disguise. Lg 32.136–39.

ERVIN-TRIPP, S. 1972. Rules of co-occurrence and alternation. Directions in sociolinguistics: The ethnography of communication, ed. by J. J. Gumperz and D. Hymes. New York, Holt, Rinehart, Winston.

GARFINKEL, H. 1967. Studies in ethnomethodology. New York, Prentice-Hall.

GREENBERG, JOSEPH H. 1966. Language universals. CTL 3.61–112.

HAAS, MARY R. 1966. Historical linguistics and the genetic relationship of languages. CTL 3.113–159.

HARPER, J., and C. HUDSON. 1971. Irish traveller cant. JEL 5.78–86.

HYMES, D. 1961. Linguistic aspects of cross-cultural personality study. Studying personality cross-culturally, ed. by B. Kaplan, pp. 313–59. New York, Harper and Row.

——. 1966. Two types of linguistic relativity. Sociolinguistics, ed. by W. Bright, pp. 114–57. The Hague, Mouton.

——. 1967. Models of interaction of language and social setting. JSocI 23/2.8–28.

——. 1968. Linguistics: The field. International Encyclopedia of the Social Sciences, ed. by D. Sills, 9.351–71. New York, Macmillan.

——. 1970a. Linguistic models in archaeology; Discussion. Archéologie et calculateurs. Problèmes semiologiques et mathématiques, 81–118; 118–20. (Colloques Internationaux du Centre National de la Recherche Scientifique). Paris, C.N.R.S. (colloquium organized by J. C. Gardin).

——. 1970b. Linguistic method of ethnography. Method and theory in linguistics, ed. by P. L. Garvin, pp. 249–325. The Hague, Mouton.

——. 1971a. Introduction to Part III. Pidginization and creolization of languages, ed. by D. Hymes. Cambridge, Cambridge University Press.

——. 1971b. Morris Swadesh and the first 'Yale School'. Origin and diversification of languages, by M. Swadesh, ed. by J. F. Sherzer. Chicago, Aldine.

——. 1972. Introduction. Language in society 1/1 : 1ff. Cambridge, Cambridge University Press.

IRVING, W. 1835. The Crayon miscellany. Philadelphia, Carey, Lea and Blanchard.

KRAUSS, M. 1973. Na-Déné. CTL 10.903–78.

KROEBER, A. L. 1961. Semantic contribution of lexicostatistics. IJAL 27.1–8.

——. 1963. Yokuts dialect survey. Anthropological Records 11/3. Berkeley and Los Angeles, University of California Press.

LANGENDOEN, T. S. 1968. The London school of linguistics. Cambridge, Mass., M.I.T. Press.

MacLAY, H. 1958. An experimental study of language and non-linguistic behavior. SJA 14.220–29.

NEWMAN, S. S. 1955. Vocabulary levels: Zuni sacred and slang usage. SJA 11.345–54.

PIKE, K. L. 1954–1960. Language in relation to a unified theory of the structure of human behavior, I–III. Glendale, California, Summer Institute of Linguistics. (2nd ed., The Hague, Mouton, 1967.)

SANKOFF, D. 1973. Glottochronology. CTL 11.93–112.

SCHEGLOFF, E. A. 1968. Sequencing in conversational openings. AmA 70.1075–95.

TYLER, S. A., ed. 1969. Cognitive anthropology. New York, Holt, Rinehart and Winston.

VOEGELIN, C. F., and Z. S. HARRIS. 1945. Linguistics in ethnology. SJA 1.455–65.

WEINREICH, URIEL. 1966. Explorations in semantic theory. CTL 3.395–478.

WHORF, BENJAMIN LEE. 1936. The punctual and segmentative aspects of verbs in Hopi. Lg 12.127–31. *Also in* Language, thought and reality: Selected writings of Benjamin Lee Whorf, ed. by John B. Carroll, pp. 51–56. Cambridge, Mass., M.I.T. Press (1956).

——. 1956 [1936]. A linguistic consideration of thinking in primitive communities. Language, thought and reality: Selected writings of Benjamin Lee Whorf, ed. by John B. Carroll, pp. 65–86. Cambridge, Mass., M.I.T. Press. *Also in* Language in culture and society, ed. by Dell Hymes, pp. 129–41. New York, Harper & Row (1964).

SOME NEW DEVELOPMENTS IN ETHNOSEMANTICS AND THE THEORY AND PRACTICE OF LEXICAL/SEMANTIC FIELDS[1]

OSWALD WERNER

WITH WILLIAM HAGEDORN, GEORGE ROTH, EMILE SCHEPERS, AND LUIS URIARTE

0. INTRODUCTION

The major aspects of this introduction focus on several disclaimers. These are intended as warnings to the reader's expectations. The following account makes no pretenses of a well-balanced presentation of ethnosemantics or ethnoscience (also known as ethnoepistemology or ethnognosiology[2]) in general. It is a highly selective and therefore subjective compilation of what we consider to be the major advances in the field within the last few years. If we have slighted someone, or if we did not give a particular source its full due we accept responsibility. Any omission is due to ignorance rather than malice. On several authors we had divided opinions. In evaluating their contributions, in several cases, when at first they did not seem to meet our content criteria, we changed our opinions in the course of our study and discussions. We usually opted for inclusion and cannot recall a single case where we 'excluded' an article or an author who was previously selected for discussion.

Our biases are clear and explicit. They are stated in Werner and Fenton (1970) and slightly modified in Werner (1969). For the moment we side with Conklin (e.g. 1962). That is, our bias is lexicographic or lexicological — a belief that better 'dic-

[1] This work was supported by a grant from the National Institute of Mental Health MH-10940-04. This support is gratefully acknowledged. I am grateful for the comments of Carl F. Voegelin, Paul Friedrich and the encouragement of Brent Berlin.
[2] There is some confusion about the most appropriate terminology to be used as the name of the endeavor outlined in these pages. Ethnoscience is perhaps best known and is appropriate insofar as we are dealing with folk science, that is from folk-anatomy to folk-zoology. Since it is largely lexicography or the description of lexical/semantic fields, ethnosemantics is appropriate. However, since the field is broader than either of the above terms suggest, that is, deals with the total range of cultural knowledge, ethnoepistemology seems more adequate, but since English does not make the distinction between *Erkentnisslehre* (Epistemology) and *Kentnisslehre* (Gnosiology), and the latter seems more appropriate because it deals with the study of knowledge rather than the acquisition of knowledge, ethnognosiology seems to be the most adequate term. Unfortunately gnosiology is no neutral and has heavy associations with gnosticism. Thus we are stuck with a terminological problem

tionaries' will result in better ethnographies. Following Casagrande and Colby (among others) we accept translation as the key problem of ethnography (see Casagrande 1954:335; Colby 1966:13), but we depart sharply from Colby's view that ethnosemantics should restrict itself to culturally important domains, and not concern itself with general semantic theories (Colby 1966:16). We do not consider the two goals exclusive. Advances in the lexicographic description of culturally relevant domains is futile without concern for their fit into the picture of a general description of the *entire* vocabulary.

We put the word 'dictionaries' in quotes above to indicate our agreement with Williams that our attention should be focused on networks rather than linearly alphabetized dictionaries and that this interest will require new technologies (models and devices) of description (Williams 1966:20). We too consider the problem of the representation of lexical/semantic fields, and thus of cultural knowledge, an urgent task of ethnosemantics. It is for this reason that we have devoted the entire second half of this paper to field representations that are sometimes explicit but more often merely implied in the literature.

The compound term 'lexical/semantic fields' is necessary because we are not clear about where the lexicon ends and semantics begins, or even if the assumption of such a postulated boundary, stratum, or whatever, is fruitful. In part this grows out of our uncertainty about the status of semantic 'components' or 'features'; especially the relation of these to the vocabulary of English in general and to the vocabularies of the studied source languages in particular. We would like to draw the reader's attention on this point especially to the enlightened critique of componential analysis by John Lyons (1968:470–80). More will be said about the problem of components later in this work.

Although a disproportionately large segment of ethnosemantic research effort was and is directed toward the examination of kinship terminological lexical/semantic fields, we will refer to them only sparingly. Our view is restricted to insights that have bearing on the representation and understanding of the structure of the ENTIRE lexicon.

We will take into account few of the advances in semantic theory within the framework of transformational generative grammar. This is due to the fact that we are attempting to review anthropological advances, and not because we think that 'their' advances are of no relevance.

The view represented by the generative semantics school seems to converge with our views. To accomplish a meaningful integration of ethnosemantics and transformational generative semantics will require a major undertaking and may be premature at this point. It will suffice to point out the complementarity of the two fields: The approach in transformational generative grammar is from the grammar to the lexicon. It shows sophistication in grammatical elaboration but maintains relatively simple views regarding the lexicon. Anthropologists have pursued the problem by starting with the lexicon and/or lexical fields. Their concern shows some sophistication in dealing with the lexicon, but works with relatively simple views with regard to grammar. The latter attempts can hardly be called at present anything but rudimentary. We would like to see more effort spent in this direction. Nevertheless some convergences with the 'generative semantics school' of transformational grammar (Lakoff, McCawley, Ross and others, see McCawley in bibliography) may be, we hope, more substantive than mere expressions of the *Zeitgeist*.

Finally, we must point out that our selective approach to ethnosemantics is counterbalanced by excellent general reviews, especially the work of Hymes (1964), Sturtevant (1964), Colby (1966), and the unpublished topical bibliographies collected by Conklin (1967) in ethnoscience and Albert (1968) in the general field of semiotics.

In this context we cannot fail to mention the major critics, especially Burling (1964), Lyons (1968), Berreman (1966), and Harris (1964 but esp. 1968). The first two are inside critics, who have made substantive contributions to semantics and who will be discussed in Section 2. The other two have at times made valid points, especially in debunking excessive claims.

Some of the early enthusiasm seems to have settled now. The claims need to be followed up by hard work.

Returning to the two 'outside' critics, both operate with a limiting philosophy of science: Berreman's critique is based on secondhand translated information of the navigational techniques on Truk; Harris's on Ernest Mach's view of theory as a convenient summary of data (see e.g. Toulmin's (1953:150 ff.) critique of Mach and possibly also of 'etic nomothetic historical materialism').

The 'etic-emic' distinction has in recent years come to mean different things to different people. It has consequently suffered so much from what Weinreich called 'desemanticisation' that we do not consider it a useful conceptual distinction. If 'etic' is used to mean, from 'tokens', 'universal units' of a phonetic theory, 'arbitrary units' imposed on reality, to 'nomothetic historical materialism', and 'emic' is used to mean from 'type', 'non-arbitrary, psychologically real, language specific, phonological units' to 'idiographic synchronic (a- or anti-historical) mentalism', the usefulness of this dichotomy is hopelessly obscured. Furthermore, it is unclear why language should be blessed with at least four 'emic-etic' 'strata' (Lamb 1965:45) (phonemic, morphemic, lexemic and sememic) while all other behavior makes do with just one (the behavioreme). One could also argue that all science is 'emic' because scientists study 'laws of nature' which deal with types rather than tokens, or that all languages are 'etic' since *every* language system is imposed on 'reality'. If 'etic' units deal with observationally adequate units and 'emic' units with descriptively adequate units, then the two sets of units are not independent. Both are derivatives of the theory we are using, that is, that which constitutes relevant observations is theory dependent. Considering that in anthropology we have at least two levels of theories: theories of specific cultures (also called ethnographies) and theories of culture, we must consider the possibility of 'etic' units of a culture, 'emic' units of a culture, 'etic' units of culture (in general) and 'emic' units of culture (in general). That makes the words 'etic' and 'emic' part of the vocabulary of the theory of theories and impressively abstract.

Reserving 'etic' for an initial typology (Leach's butterfly collecting stage of a science, 1961:2–5) and 'emic' for a set of theoretical structural units, may give us at times a USEFUL METAPHOR OF SPEAKING. This is not unlike the 19th century language typology (with the additions of Sapir) which at times is a useful shorthand for talking about languages as being isolating, agglutinative, inflectional or polysynthetic.

1. NEW DEVELOPMENTS

1.1 *Lexical/Semantic Fields*

1.1.1 *Folk definitions*

Weinreich in 1962 lamented the fact that folk definitions could, except for their general unavailability, become an important source for the empirical foundation of lexicography (Weinreich 1962:42). Wallace also (1965:233) proposed the use of folk definitions, but primarily for validation. About 18 months after the appearance of Weinreich's article, Casagrande and Hale circulated the early version of an article which appeared later in the Festschrift in honor of Harry Hoijer (Casagrande and Hale 1967:6). This article makes three major contributions to ethnosemantics:

(A) The extensive use of folk definitions (ibid.:165),

(B) The analysis of folk definitions into atomic definitions (the attribute 'atomic' is ours), and

(C) The demonstration that atomic definitions fall into types known from word association studies and from which it follows that atomic definitions are binary semantic relations (ibid.:168).

Although Weinreich anticipated that folk definitions would reveal cultural norms and that one would expect folk definitions to be closely tied to the 'psychological reality' of the culture, Casagrande and Hale have strikingly established that the 13 plus atomic definitional types which they find in Papago are very likely language universals. In any case, they are equally applicable to definitions found in English monolingual dictionaries, as in Navajo folk definitions, or Navajo definitions constructed by native Navajo research assistants. Considering the fact that we compare Papago folk definition with English monolingual commercial dictionary definitions, the latter distinction may not be very important.

1.1.2 *Binary lexical/semantic relations*

The indeterminancy of the exact number of different binary semantic relations rests on at least six independent pieces of evidence:

1.1.2.1 *First consideration: STAGE OF.* Both Conklin and Frake have extensively investigated folk-botanies. Not surprisingly they consider the relation

1a '____ is a stage of ____.' or (A) STAGE (B), important. For example in English:
1b sapling n. 1. A young tree (*Webster's Collegiate* 1953:750) and
1c 'A sapling is a stage of a tree'.

This relation is not contained in Casagrande and Hale's set.

1.1.2.2 *Second consideration: SPATIAL.* Casagrande and Hale's spatial relation, defined as:

2a '____ is oriented spatially with respect to ____.'

is not unique and in English contains at least the following (non-exhaustive) set:

2b '____ is a part of ____.'
  '____ is above ____.'
  '____ is below ____.'
  '____ is next to ____.'
  '____ connects ____ and ____.'
  '____ is between ____ and ____.'

Before continuing a clarification is in order. Sentences like **1** and **2**, including sentences containing other relations, need to be STANDING SENTENCES (analogous to 'standing orders' in Medicine or Army) and are usually or predominantly generic, that is, they should always be true or generally true (perhaps 'sometimes', if 'sometimes' designates a subset of the cases of 'always' but always to be found in that subset; i.e. there is at least one x so that ...). In other words, we would like to contrast occasional sentences, e.g.

3a 'Here comes Mary and her little lamb.'

from standing sentences, e.g.

3b 'Mary is the name of a girl.'
  'A girl is a young female.'
  'A lamb is a young sheep.'
  'A sheep is an animal.'
  'Sheep are domesticated.'

and so on.

Such standing sentences contain the knowledge or information necessary for the understanding of occasional sentences.

1.1.2.3 *Third consideration: ANTONYMY.* In his recent book Lyons demonstrated that antonymy is complex. Hale (1971) showed that the principle of antonymy can be generalized and probably is found in all languages. Possibly the relation of antonymy and grading (Casagrande and Hale 1967) may turn out to be equivalent or closely related.

According to Lyons, antonymy consists of at least three distinct semantic relations:

4   *Complementarity* (Lyons 1968:460): e.g.

4a   single : married, male : female

4b   '____is married' implies '____ is not single'. and
      '____ is single' implies '____ is not married'.

That is, a set U of and all possible values of dichotomous variables x1 and x2 are related as follows:

4c $x_1 \cup x_2 = U$ and
     $x_1 \subset U$ implies $x_2 = \bar{x}_1$ (x_2 is the complement of x_1), and $x_1 = \bar{x}_2$.

One of the problems ethnographers face with the relation of complementarity (especially where it has to be translated into or from another language) is that for most speakers of English the sentence

4d   '____ is the complement of ____.'

is not meaningful. However, it may be meaningful and easily verbalizable in a few other languages (although we are unaware of such languages).

Leach's notion that the intersticies between generally acceptable vocabulary are often filled by taboo words (Leach 1964:35) is applicable here. If

4e   'Male is the complement of female.'

then words like 'homosexual', 'hermaphrodite', 'lesbian' considered as interstitial are certainly today more taboo-ish than male and female, and have been more so historically.

Lyons feels that the simple dichotomy of male : female does not account for the biological or behavioral classification satisfactorily. The weakening of the taboo, appears to signal changes in our (world) view of sexuality toward greater acceptance of variation. Further evidence with regard to homosexuality especially, is to be found in the fact that while some segments of English-speaking peoples consider homosexuality with neutrality, most of us accept it as an 'abnormality', and a number of the American public would consider it a 'perversion', and practitioners of homosexuality as 'perverts'. Especially colloquial designations of homosexuality are still more strongly tabooed and/or offending than those for the sex-act (e.g. *cock-sucker*).

5 *Antonymy* (proper) or 'oppositeness' par excellence (Lyons 1968:63) which is regularly gradable: e.g.

5a big : little, large : small, etc.

Comparison may be inherent as Lyons asserts but interestingly it also involves ordering:

5b 'There is nothing smaller than smallest.'
'Smallest is smaller than smaller.'
'Smaller is smaller than small.'
'Small is smaller than big.'
'Big is smaller than bigger.'
'Bigger is smaller than biggest.'
'There is nothing bigger than biggest.'
'Biggest is bigger than bigger.'
'Bigger is bigger than big.'
'Big is bigger than small.'
'Small is bigger than smaller.'
'Smaller is bigger than smallest.'

The relations 'bigger' and 'smaller' are complementary; they are irreflexive, asymmetrical and transitive and represent a complete order. All antonyms are complete orders and represent with a neutral zero point (where 'X is small or large' is undecidable) a seven point ordinal scale. The neutral zero point is implied, because it is not the case that:

5c '"_____ is small" implies "_____ is not big"' (see **7e**)

The norms for the scale are considered implicit, although we find this less likely than considering the norm perhaps discourse dependent. It may very well be quite explicit within a particular universe of discourse (for details we refer the reader again to Lyons' excellent discussion 1968:463–467).

6 *Converseness* (Lyons 1968:467), e.g.
6a buy : sell, husband : wife, father : son

is equivalent to reciprocals or reciprocal components as used in componential analyses especially by Romney and D'Andrade (1964) and Goodenough (1967). Similar to

6b '_____ is bigger than _____' implies '_____ is smaller than _____'
    1   2   2   1

6c '_____ buys _____ from _____' implies '_____ sells _____ to _____.'
  1   2   3   3   2   1

But whereas the relation of antonymy in **6b** is gradable, the relation in **6c** is not.

Complementarity, antonymy and converseness are not unrelated, as Lyons points out. The interrelationship is complex as the following examples imply:

(With a slight change in notation: quotes replaced by parentheses and slot markers by variables X,Y,Z: implication by IMPL (= IF____THEN____) and 'it is not the case' by NOT.)

7a ((X is married to Y) IMPL (Y is married to X)
7b ((X is single) IMPL NOT (X is married))

7c ((X is male) IMPL NOT (X is female))
7d ((X is a husband) IMPL NOT (X is a wife) (?)
7e (NOT((X is small) IMPL NOT (X is big))),

because

7f ((X is small) IMPL (X is smaller than norm))

only where norm corresponds to the neutral (zero) point on the scale in general or with reference to a particular discourse.

7g ((X was sold) IMPL (X was bought)), but
7h ((X was brought) IMPL (X was taken))), because in
7i (X brought Y to Z), the speaker assumes in fact, or fictiously a position at Z:
7j 'McNulty brought whiskey to the tribe.' (Z = the tribe)
7k (X took Y to Z); with the speaker at non-Z
7l 'McNulty took whiskey to the tribe' (speaker at non-tribe).

Because of their multiple senses, 'bring' and 'take' are still more complex

7m ((X brought Y to Z) IMPL (Z took Y from X) OR NOT (Z /did/ take Y from X))), i.e. Z refused.

'Bring' and 'give' are related in this sense also. That is,

8a ((X brought Y to Z) IMPL (X carried Y to Z) AND (X gave Y to Z))
8b ((X took Y to Z) IMPL ((X carried Y to Z) AND (Z took Y from X) OR NOT (Z /did/ take Y from X))).

Furthermore, the relation of implication appears to have at least two senses: one of synonymy as in **7b**.

9a ((X is single) MEANS THE SAME AS NOT (X is married)) and one of logical necessity; as in **7g**:
9b ((X was sold) REQUIRES (X was bought); and
9c NOT ((X was sold) MEANS THE SAME AS (X was bought))

The two verbs 'buy' and 'sell' are strongly directional. English has a directionally neutral verb in 'trade', the only one available, for example in Navajo:

10a hastiin lh8i7i7' shich'8i' nayiisnii'.[3]
　　　 horse toward me he traded it (he sold it)
10b hastiin lh8i7i7' shaa nayiisnii'.
　　　 man horse from me he traded it (he bought it)

---

[3] The Navajo orthography used in this paper is essentially that of Young and Morgan 1943 made computer-compatible. The modifications are in detail: Nasalization is marked by '8' PRECEDING the vowel segment; tone is marked by '7' FOLLOWING the vowel segment. For example, '*adą́ą́dą́ą́*' 'yesterday' becomes *ad8a7a7d8a7a7*'. Syllabic *n* becomes *n9* (or plain *n*); high tone *n* becomes *n6*. (The

It appears in this context that almost every lexical item behaves idiosyncratically. It was this fear that made structural linguists abandon the lexicon (e.g. Gleason's laments, 1962:86). However it appears to be plausible that while individual lexical items may behave idiosyncratically in their relations to the rest of the lexicon, the nature of the relations appears regular and limited to a relatively small number of basic relations. We will take up the relations or the organization of the lexical fields in the next section in some detail.

Casagrande and Hale (1967) introduced 14 types of semantic relationships which we prefer to call atomic definitions. In this they go beyond a transformationalist tenet (a notion which predates transformational generative grammarians), that complex sentences (definitions) consist of simple 'kernelized' sentences.

We take putatively the even stronger stand, implied by Casagrande and Hale, as well as Frake (1964) and Williams (1966), that atomic semantic relations are always binary with a very simple 'grammatical' structure: (C should be construed as meaning lexicon, or lexical/semantic structure)

11a $C \rightarrow (A) \ REL(i) \ (B)$
11b $A \rightarrow a$
11c $A \rightarrow C$
11d $A \rightarrow b$
11e $B \rightarrow C$

Where REL(i) is a set of i atomic lexical/semantic relations.

We generally restrict ourselves to REL(j) a subset of REL(i) that are verbalizable, i.e. that are also lexical relations. We assume that the remaining REL(i) can be inferred. For example we inferred REL(i) = COMPLEMENT OF in **4d** and in a sense 'lexicalized' it although it may not exist in the explicit English folk system. The A and B are nonterminal symbols which may be simple or complex; if complex, they are nested binary semantic relations of indefinite depth and of the same structure as C; if simple, they are terminal and may be attributes, but their status for the moment is unclear (see below).

Lexical entries following Chomsky (1965:84) are of the form ((C), (P)) where (C) is a 'semantic representation' and (P) marks the recognition of this bundle (C) as a lexical/semantic entity and represents a phonetic label for it and attached to it.

If (A) and (B) are the (C(i)) of some particular lexical items (P(i)), then (C(i)) now written as C(i) may be more complex than **11** implies:

---

tail of the '9' is pointing down: low tone; the tail of the '6' is pointing up: high tone.) Consonants are identical with Young and Morgan (1943.iii–vi) with the following changes: ł (barred el) becomes lh, tł and tł' becomes tl and tl' respectively. x is used in place of h in cases where ambiguity or misreading may result. For example, *alhtso* 'all completed' and *alhtsxo* (instead of the misleading *alhtsho* 'truly all completed' indicating the heavy aspiration of the affricate *ts*. In an attempt to be concise, the initial glottal stop before vowels (as in the examples above) is automatically assumed and not written.

12 $C(i) - \bigcup\limits_{j=1}^{n} \dfrac{((C(i))\ \text{REL}(j)(B))}{((A)\ \text{REL}(j)(C(i)))}$

That is, the lexical/semantic representation ($C(i)$) of a lexical entry (($C(i)$), ($P(i)$)) is the lexical/semantic NETWORK in which the ($C(i)$) is embedded (note that Dixon 1971 recommends a mixed strategy of features AND relations).

For the Casagrande and Hale lexical/semantic relation of type 8 (class inclusion or taxonomy, TAXN), limiting conditions (on the structure of these taxonomic tree structures) are easily supplied (as we shall demonstrate in the next section). Little or nothing is known about constraints on the structure of the other relations.

Formula **12** implies that the lexical/semantic representation of a lexical entry is the union of all predicates ($C(i)$ REL(j) $B(i)$ simple and complex) of ($C(i)$) AND all subjects (A REL(i) $C(i)$) to which ($C(i)$) may be predicate. But since (A) and (B) are complex the network could go on indefinitely and circularly. How to limit the (A) and (B) for any relation except taxonomies and perhaps part-to-whole is not known. This limitation could be interpreted as the limitation of $C(i)$ to some 'immediate vicinity' of $C(i)$. Note that because of the transitivity of the relation of taxonomy (TAXN) every node of a taxonomy is in the 'immediate vicinity' of every other node.

The binarization of lexical/semantic relations seems easy to accomplish for languages like English which are largely 'isolating'. It seems much more difficult for languages that are largely 'polysynthetic', e.g. American Indian languages like Navajo; although Casagrande and Hale seem to have had little difficulty with Papago.

1.1.2.4 *Fourth consideration: Frake (1964).* Binarization of semantic relations is proposed by Williams (1966), but the ideas of Frake (1964:136–42) are particularly provocative and disturbing. Frake proposes the following six (lexical) semantic relations (questions eliciting the relations) in Subanun:

13a ?k   ?w   ?u   ?i   ?p   ?s
species, genus, use, ingredient, part, source.

Frake arranges his relations in the form of paired queries that elicit the relation depending on the direction of questioning. Thus for example Frake's (ibid.:136) relation ?k/?w corresponds to our TAXN and $\overline{\text{TAXN}}$ (with bar = inverse).

13b Frake's (ibid.:142): (*buŋa*) ?k/?w (*gayu*)
Ours: (*buŋa*) TAXN (*gayu*), and (*gayu*) $\overline{\text{TAXN}}$ (*buŋa*)
(*gayu*: translation label 'tree')
(*buŋa*: translation label in this context 'areca palm')

Similar to the above example, all six relations listed in **13a** combine as follows:

13c ?k/?w   species/genus
?k/?u   species/use

ʔi/ʔu   ingredient/use
ʔp/ʔs   part/source
ʔu/ʔs   use/source

The occurrence of the same query for one direction in combination with more than one query in the other is disturbing. For example, 'use' occurs with 'species', 'ingredient' and 'source', etc. This fact appears to indicate that the basic linkage is, as Frake claims, the query, and not as we claim the explicit sentences, which may, or may not have inverses.

We propose the following solution to Frake's problem: First, we follow the convention that if we have a relation of the form:

14   (A)TAXN(B) we diagram it: $\circ \leftarrow$ TAXN $\longrightarrow \circ$
                                     (A)   (B)

i.e., for any left to right sentence we draw a right to left arrow; from dominating to subordinating term. It appears that in all languages the less general term is always mentioned first, i.e. is the subject, and the general term, the predicate, is second (Koutsoudas, personal communication).

We can then write Frake's sentences (ibid.:135, Fig. 1a and b) in the following way: (members of list Sk abbreviated as (Sk)).

15a (Sk) is used for (spice)   (Sk) USE FOR (Spice)
15b (spice) is used for (yeast)   (spice) USE FOR (yeast)

(We assume yeast refers to spiced, storable yeast cakes; ibid.: 135)

15c (yeast) is used for (beer)   (yeast) USE FOR (beer)
15d (beer) is used for (drinks)   (beer) USE FOR (drinks)

It is difficult to evaluate the Subanun part without a Subanun speaker. Let us raise some objections, possibly unfairly, assuming that the above example is strictly in English. Unless 'spices' is a complex category or a blend of plants, **15a** should be

15a' (Sk) USE AS (spice);

similarly 'drinks' is ambiguous in English. 'drink-1' is synonymous with 'beverage'; 'drink-2' is 'that which is drunk'; and 'drink-3' is synonymous with 'the act of drinking'. This changes **15d** to

15d'   (beer) USE FOR (drink-s-2)
15d'' (beer) USE FOR (drink-3), or (drinking)
15d''' (beer) USE AS (drink-1)

These represent at least two different relations IN ENGLISH (we are also not doing Frake full justice by pluralizing only **15d'**). Whereas, as we shall see, USE FOR is related to 'ingredient of', in this context, and possibly others in other contexts (e.g.

'A knife is *used for* cutting'); USE AS is akin to 'used in the same way as the dominating class' e.g. 'Beer is used the same way any beverage is used, namely, to drink'. That is,

15e ((((beer) TAXN (drink-1)) AND/OR ((drink) USE FOR (drinking))) IMPL ((beer) USE FOR ((drinking)) AND/OR ((beer) USE AS (drink-1)) AND/OR ((drink-1) USE AS (beer))))

Using the other half of Frake's Fig. 1. (leaving out 'Beer is a kind of drink' already contained in **15e**).

15f	(yeast) is an ingredient of (beer)	(yeast) INGR. OF (beer)
15g	(spice) is an ingredient of (yeast)	(spice) INGR. OF (yeast)
15h	(SK) is an ingredient of (yeast)	(SK) INGR. OF (spice)
15i	(Sk) is a kind of (spice)	(Sk) TAXN (spice)

We can now rediagram Frake's Figure 1 as Diagram **16**, opposite.

The inevitable result of the reinvestigation of anyone's proposed semantic structure is the discovery of more specialized relations. In our case we have expanded Frake's USE, to three relations: USEFOR, USAME, and USTEAD. USEFOR may be further ambiguous. We have established that the direction of USEFOR is *the same as and* parallel to INGR. OF, which is irreflexive, asymmetrical and transitive and therefore related to PARTOF, and more complexly (see section 2.), to TAXN. Frake's interlinkages now assume the form (we introduce the convention '/' 'opposed direction', '//' 'parallel direction', and 'Ø' 'non directional'):

17a Interlinkages:

Frake's	Our's
?k/?w	TAXN/TAXN
?k/?u	TAXN/TAXN and ØUSAME
?i/?u	INGR. OF//USEFOR
?p/?s	PARTOF/PARTOF

(although this may be more complex)

?u/?s	USEFOR//PARTOF

(this too, may be more complex)

Our critique of Frake should not be construed as a slight of his contribution. He was, to the best of our knowledge, the first to show in print that semantic relations beyond, and far more complex than taxonomies, can be represented graphically, and that lexical fields are complex networks of such relations. He, Williams, and Casagrande and Hale take credit for the binarization of these atomic relations.

We have not committed ourselves to any particular elicitation technique and we

16   ((drink-1) = (beverage)) OR (drink-s-2)

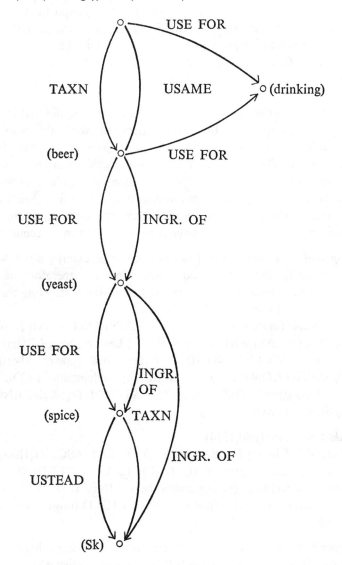

(Note the abbreviations: TAXN = is a kind of; USE FOR = is used for; USTEAD = is used instead of; USAME = is used the same as; INGR. OF = is an ingredient of; SK = a list of spices.)

feel that such commitment is, although heuristically important, of little theoretical interest as long as our lexical structures are formal and fully explicit. However, assuming that we have been eliciting folk-definitions, we have analyzed these complex definitional sentences into simple constituent sentences and these further into binary semantic relations. Our oversimplified recursive semantic grammar **11** applies to intra-sentence structure.

1.1.2.5 *Fifth Consideration: Sanday's* (1968) recent work implies that inter-sentence structure may also be important. In her experiment she asked subjects to list kinship terms in any order (the fact that she performed two separate listing experiments need not concern us here). The 'random' order or listing was not at all random but followed what she terms 'decision rules'. These decision rules are amazingly analogous to 'components'. She demonstrates that human beings may find their way through the semantic space of kinship in a number of different structured ways. Her flow charts of decision (or search) procedures are given here in string form for economy of space.

18   *The reciprocal structure* (Sanday 1968:573); complementarity is (COMPL) represented here in the form of a linear string. Since her operators may be called localized decision rules, we will abandon that distinction. Note that SEX is a kind of COMPL (notation slightly changed).
((Father) SEX (mother)) LINEAL DESCENDING COMPL ((son) SEX (daughter)) COLLATERAL ASCENDING ((brother) SEX (sister)) RETURN TO LINEAL ASCENDING ((grandfather) SEX (grandmother)) LINEAL DESCENDING COMPL ((grandson) SEX (granddaughter)) COLLATERAL ASCENDING ((uncle) SEX (aunt)) COLLATERAL DESCENDING COMPL ((niece) SEX (nephew)) ...

19a   *The ladder structure* (ibid.:514).
((brother) SEX (sister)) LINEAL (father)) LINEAL ASCENDING, PARENT ((grandfather) SEX (grandmother)) LINEAL ASCENDING, PARENT ((greatgrandfather) SEX (greatgrandmother)) LINEAL DESCENDING ((son) SEX (daughter)) LINEAL DESCENDING, CHILD ((grandson) SEX (granddaughter)) ...

Rules: 1. generate lineal ascendants and descendants in a cluster using the lineal path; 2. Generate collaterals /and affinals -added/ in ... separate cluster/s/.

20a   *The cluster structure* (ibid.:514–15 given here by rules only).

Rules: 1. generate close (to ego) lineals and collaterals by family cluster; 2. generate remaining ascending generation lineals and collaterals similarly; 3. generate affinals and more distant consanguineals in modified clusters.

21a   *The tree structure*. 'This structure corresponds to the tree structure of the genealogist and is highly particularizing in that maternal and paternal lines are carefully separated as are affinals (including spouses and parent's siblings) and consanguineals' (ibid.:518).

A folk-definition or a text of explanation can be construed as a 'random' listing task. Not only the relations *in* the sentences but the succession of items *between* sentences may have significant semantic implications. The situation is more complex than in the case of 'random' listings of terms. The collocations of terms in the deep structure may differ markedly from their collocation in the surface structure. Perhaps one way of getting around this problem would be the elicitation of associational lists, or associational chains instead of simple associational pairs.

However, Sanday's work already seems to point to the integration of Lounsbury's transformational (skewing and merging) rules (Lounsbury 1964a, b, 1965 including Lamb's 1965 simplified symbolism) into lexical/semantic field descriptions. These look to us like Sanday's decision rules. They define paths from the so-called 'etic' vocabulary that every language has, namely the basic kin types and/or 'relative products' of these types, to classes of further outlying kinsmen and may form structures analogous to Sanday's cluster structure. Similarly, Burling's (1965) assertion that Burmese prefer 'relative product' to 'class product' definitions seems to indicate culturally conditioned 'styles of decision' affecting retrieval of information from a person's cognitive (lexical/semantic) structure. These may be analogous to Hymes' (1961) cognitive styles, to Robert's (1959, 1962, 1963) arrays of cultural models which he calls 'templates', or to Wallace's (1961) 'mazeways', etc.

Lexical domains, in which parallel paths like the so-called 'etic' vocabulary of basic kin types plus 'relative products' exist alongside the actual, so called 'emic' kinship terms 'proper', are probably rare, although paraphrase may be interpreted in exactly this way: after all, the 'relative product' constructions are paraphrases of the terms for the kinship terminology 'proper'.

This seems to imply that Lounsbury's 'transformations' and other than 'class product' definitions or paraphrases may play an important part in a paraphrase theory of the general vocabulary. That this is so, however, remains to be demonstrated.

Sanday's work implies further that the organization of the semantic or cognitive space for cultural knowledge (general cultural knowledge) may differ from the organization of space of personal experience. The first organization was reflected in her 'random' listing tasks of kin terms. The personal organization was reflected in her second listing task, of each subject's individual kinsman.

Unfortunately Casagrande and Hale did not publish the full text of any of their 800 Papago folk definitions. Neither are Werner's (1965) Navajo folk definitions adequate since they are not spontaneously elicited definitions but were CONSTRUCTED from a large number of informant responses.

The application of Sanday's concern for serial order as another manifestation of lexical/semantic field structure and the ways in which this structure is applied by humans to 'information retrieval' will have to await further implementation.

In Sanday's system 'components' are decision rules which seem to be closely connected with the collocation of terms in retrieval and hence probably also in human information storage. According to this notion 'components' are relations between 'naming units' (Mathiot 1963).

Sanday's flow charts are probably closely related, in ways not clear to us, to Bock's (1968) rules for generating English kinship terms.

1.1.2.6 *Sixth consideration: Bendix* (1966) arrived at a similar point of view by a different method and following different aims. Without mentioning it explicitly Bendix was influenced by Weinreich's (1962) quest for the reduction of the metalanguage of definitions, that is, Weinreich postulated that it may be possible to find a zero level set of the vocabulary of natural languages. Every member on this list may be defined 'somehow' ostensively. Terms of level 1. could then be defined exclusively by the vocabulary of the zero level; level 2. by terms of level 1. and zero, ... the nth level by terms of any level equal to or smaller than n-1. Monolingual dictionaries and componential definitions according to Weinreich face the problem that the object language and the metalanguage of the definitions are about equally rich. This, of course raises the question of the relationship between components and lexical items, as Lyons has shown (1968:479). We will expand this point in the next section (see also Dixon 1971).

Bendix's approach is important and we present his tabular summary. Note that he has succeeded in reducing the complexity of the metalanguage and that his 'components' are sentence representations (Bendix 1966:76, for further refinement of his work see Bendix 1971).

22

	h+	h—	BR	As	Cc	Ac	ch
A gets B	+						
A finds B	+		+				+
C gives A B	+				+		
C gets A B	(+)		+		+		
C lends A B	+		+	+			
A borrows B from C	+		+	+			+
A takes B from C	+		+				+
A gets rid of B		+					+
A loses B		+	+				+
A keeps B	+		+				

Explanation of symbols:
h+ = A has B after time T (T = time referent of verb)
h— = A not-has B after T
BR = B an-R ... before T (i.e. B is in a relation [to a D or to A or to C] before time T, including A or C has B before time T).

As = B not-is A's
Cc = C causes (...)
Ac = A causes (...)
ch = chance causes (...)

Bendix also notes that although the relation

23a (A)HAS(B)

looks simple it contains at least three interpretations (compare the complexity of the relation USE, see **16**).

23b (A)HAS(B) may be interpreted: (1) accidental
(2) inherent
(3) characteristic of A

The first case is of limited interest since we have excluded occasional sentences. Accidental possession of (B) by (A) could not be part of a standing and/or generic sentence. Inherent and characteristic of (A) 'have' seems to be quite similar. The latter 'characteristic of (A)' is the basis of 'metonymic' taxonomies which Price (1967) postulates as being more important in Huichol than 'attribute' taxonomies. The distinction between these two types of taxonomies confuses the taxonomic relation with the method of naming (labeling) taxa. Scientific taxonomies which are surely 'true' taxonomies contain numerous examples of metonymic naming:

24 chordates; animate beings that have a notochord;
vertebrates: animate beings that have a spinal column;
mammals: animate beings that have mammary glands;
marsupials: animate beings that have a marsupium (pouch);
placentals: animate beings that gestate their young inside their body in a placenta and give live birth; etc.

Metonymically labeled taxons are strange to speakers of English because this method of naming is uncommon. In other languages it may be more common.

Whereas we cannot think of a good English non-scientific example, in Navajo *bizhe7e7' ho7lo7ni7* '(has foam) beer' comes to mind; in German *Tiergarten* '(animal garden), zoo' faces the problem of an alternate interpretation analogous to English *icehouse*: 'the house has ice', 'a house for ice'. ('*Ein Haus für Tiere*', '*Ein Haus das Tiere hat*'.) Only the Navajo example contains the unalienable possession as in 'vertebrates have vertebrae', but not '**... for vertebrae*'.

Bendix demonstrated within the limits of his thesis that semantic analysis can proceed without a clearly delimited domain of lexical items. The set does not need to belong to any clearly defined domain. However, in general we prefer to follow Werner's (1965) suggestion that in working with the general vocabulary it is relatively easy to acquire an initial set of terms. The problem is to extend these terms to the full extent of a cultural domain. Few terminologies are as clearly delimited as kinship terms and even here the analysis of the extensions to domains outside of kinship proper has generally been avoided. It appears that domain boundaries are not sharp and the nature of the 'fuzzyness' is an interesting theoretical question. Meanwhile lexical/semantic fields can be investigated without full awareness of every conceivable ramification.

1.1.3 *Priority of organization*

Contributions at present will be more significant if they explore the nature of the ORGANIZATION or structure of general lexical/semantic fields rather than attempt substantive contributions or exhaustive description of selected domains. We should caution, however, that the two approaches are not totally independent. For example, Metzger and Williams (1966) have shown conclusively that exhaustiveness in a domain is achievable. That the domain of firewood was trivial is a misguided criticism. Metzger and Williams aptly demonstrated the importance of firewood to the Tzeltal, with their comparison to the Tzotzil and the Mestizo Spanish classification. More importantly, their work confirms that cultural classifications, i.e. cultural knowledge, reaches down to the last splinter of firewood. The importance of this insight to the problem of ethnographic translation hardly requires amplification.

1.1.4 *Domain boundary and grammatical analysis*

Problems of domain boundaries are closely connected with grammatical analysis — a field generally neglected by practitioners of ethnosemantics. There is a growing evidence in the literature that grammatical classifications often intersect explicit taxonomies. Mathiot (1962) has shown (her results were supported by Casagrande and Hale 1967, but note also Pilcher's 1967 explicit and cogent critique of Mathiot 1962), that the bird terminology in Papago falls into two grammatical categories (individual and aggregate) depending on the bird's ability to fly. Mathiot's (1962) notion that in Papago terminal taxonomic nodes tend to belong to the class of individual nouns, but non-terminal taxa tend to be aggregate, needs to be checked for analogies in other languages. Haas has shown (1967) in her rejoinder to the Brights (1965) that the grammatical classification can often provide the answers to 'covert' taxa. Although the Brights were unable to elicit a term for animal in Yurok the membership of the animal terms in the animate class of nouns disambiguates the domain boundary. Friedrich's (1968) extensions of a front/back metaphor in Tarascan across a large number of domains opens new areas of investigation. Werner and Begishe's (fieldnotes) part-to-whole classification of human bones and the skewed intersection of this classification with the Navajo object classes: elongated rigid (about 100 terms), compact (round) object class (four terms: skull, Atlas bone, hip bone and knee cap), Basso's (1968) investigation of Apache classificatory verb stems and Tyler's (1965) inclusion of pronominals with the kin-terms of Koya all point to a need for greater attention to grammatical classification and its general role in folk classifications and lexical/semantic fields.

1.2 Developments Outside of Lexical/Semantic Fields Proper

1.2.1 Field techniques

All field techniques require some kind of evaluation. Durbin (1966) has developed an interesting typology for the evaluation of linguistic as well as other kinds of behavior:

Behavior may be:

A. not possible (impossible to do by humans);

B. possible, which may be further:

B.1 not permissible or tabooed sometimes to the extent that existence of this kind of behavior is inconceivable. Also not occurring or not known.

B.2 permissible, which may be further:

B.2.a not acceptable or deviant. It is permissible to the extent that deviant behavior is recognized and labeled. This takes into account culturally patterned forms of deviance.

B.2.b acceptable.

The problem of acceptability is complex as Maclay and Sleator (1960) have emphasized, but the problem decreases in proportion to the complexity of the lexical/semantic fields which we construct. That is, the more complex our structure becomes, the more we view acceptability in some total context, the less elusive it becomes. Putting it another way, the more complex our theoretical structures are the more vulnerable they become and mistakes (lack of fit) will tend to show up more glaringly. Therefore a test of acceptability of an entire lexical/semantic system is preferable to the testing of isolated utterances. If we could construct a lexical/semantic field with some decision rules similar to Sanday's (1968) we could compare the output to similar tasks performed by human beings. If there is a close match between the two outputs, the lexical/semantic system could be called 'psychologically valid'. It would be this match of the two outputs '... which should decide the question of "correctness" (if, indeed, this question is decidable)' (Lyons 1968:477).

One of the most important methods of investigation in linguistics is comparison of form and meaning (Garvin 1964). There are various ways to get at this variation:

(1) THE FRAME ANALYSIS METHOD: Given two terms, queries about one, the other, or both, and answers to the queries, what kind of relationship can we postulate to hold between the two terms? If we vary the queries and responses how does this affect the linkage of the two terms?

All other techniques rest on more clear-cut informant decisions; although generally working 'down' is considerably easier than working 'up'; general and most specific terms are easier to elicit than intermediate terms (Fowler and Leland 1967; Perchonock and Werner 1969).

(2) SLIP SORTING TECHNIQUE: Literate informants are asked to sort slips into piles of items 'that belong together' (Perchonock and Werner 1969). This method may be extended to the triad test (which one of three is most unlike the remaining two)

applied by Romney and D'Andrade (1964) and Berlin, Breedlove and Raven (1968) and others.

(3) TREE DRAWING METHOD: Informants are asked (after a brief orientation) to draw classificatory trees. Unfortunately many of the resulting connecting line linkages are not easily verbalizable. Since the relations are not explicitly stated, 'mixing' of 'decision rules' obscures the true semantic relations represented. However, the method provides a first list and informant hunches that can be followed up by other techniques (Werner and Fenton 1970).

(4) FOLK DEFINITIONS: The informants are asked to define terms. The definitions can be analyzed into simple sentences and these into simple binary relations following Casagrande and Hale. Sanday's work indicates the order of presentation within the definition and inter-sentence order may contain important additional clues. Concordances of folk definitions are unusually helpful in finding all occurrences of the same term (Werner 1967), i.e. in different folk definitions.

(5) TEXTS AND MYTHS: These can be analyzed similar to the folk definitions. The intra-sentence linkages may be more tenuous.

Myth and traditional texts are often incomprehensible to non-members of the language/culture community. In situations like this, ancillary eliciting as first proposed by Voegelin and Voegelin (1957) extends the usefulness of these texts for ethnoscience. Each sentence is queried and becomes the source of another textlet. The textlets may serve for further ancillary eliciting or can be analysed into Casagrande and Hale (1967) atomic definitions following Werner (1967).

(6) VERBAL PLANS: It is relatively easy to ask a person what he has done on a particular day. Isolating the verbphrases, one can then ask more questions about these, and so on. The technique is described by Werner (1966b; see also 4.4).

(7) PARAPHRASE TECHNIQUES. Mathiot (1967) mentions two types: 'active' paraphrase which is paraphrase attempted by the investigator and 'passive' paraphrase where the informant is asked to rephrase. Informant translation is always problematic because the informant's fluency in domain dependent discourse and in the investigators' language cannot be easily ascertained (see Werner and Campbell 1970 and Voegelin and Voegelin 1960). Bendix (1966:18–19) describes what he calls 'the open-ended interpretation test' as follows: To get at the contrast 'give' and 'lend', the informant is asked to interpret the sentence: 'He didn't give it to me, he lent it to me'; for example, 'It is not the case that ((he had it) and then (he caused that (I have it now))), but ((he had it) and then (he caused that (I have it now) but (It is not mine))).

Obviously the informant must be quite sophisticated, though the task can be simplified by using simpler sentences (see Bendix's refinements in 1971).

(8) TEST BY SYLLOGISTIC ARGUMENT: Bendix (1966:20–23) describes it as follows:

(a) He's only given it to me

(c) And so it isn't really mine

(b) He's only lent it to me

'... the informant is asked to select that sentence from among the first two (a, b) which makes more sense followed by the third (c)' (ibid.: 21). The informant may also be asked which set of two sentences is easier (harder) to interpret or which makes more (or less) sense:

> (d) 'Since he's only given it to me, it isn't really mine.'
> (e) 'Since he's only lent it to me, it isn't really mine.'

(9) RANKING TEST WITH 'BUT': (Bendix 1966:23) Similar to the sentences (d) and (e) but where one of the second clauses negates the assertion of the first:

> (g) 'He's lost his watch, but he knows where it is.'
> (h) 'He's lost his watch, but he doesn't know where it is.'

This method can be extended in chains

> (i) 'He's lost his watch, but did so intentionally.'
> (j) 'He's lost his watch, but didn't do so intentionally.'

As Bendix points out there are dangers unless the sentences are carefully formulated and the informant is allowed enough freedom to explain that he chose (i) as an example of deceptive behavior. All these tests test for the presence or absence of 'components' or predicates. For example (i) and (j) test for 'intention IS NOT AN ASPECT OF losing something'. Where IS ASPECT OF seems to be the PART OF relation of abstract terms (Werner with Begishe 1969). For further details we refer the reader to Bendix's monograph (1966) and his article (1971).

(10) SANDAY'S SEQUENTIAL DECISION TEST: Although Sanday (1968) never intended to have her method used for eliciting there is no reason why it could not be used that way. It could be applied to: lists of randomly elicited vocabulary following the presentation of a stimulus starter word; checks on the inter-sentence order in folk-definitions, or texts, e.g. myths. The interpretation may not be easy, but may alert the investigator to further questioning by any one of the other techniques.

(11) CONCORDANCES: Particularly if texts and open-ended interviews and folk definitions are used for eliciting it is easy to accumulate large bodies of data in relatively short periods of time. Much of the information contained in such text is often of marginal relevance to specific subdomains under investigation. A concordance will bring together all the occurrences of a lexical item in relevant contexts. It is an invaluable aid in compiling the sentences in which terms occur and it may also be very useful in checking on inter-sentence collocations. A detailed description of the use of concordance can be found in Werner (1967). If on-line facilities are available and large bodies of text are in computer storage, search programs for individual lexical items with specifiable amounts of context may be more useful (see Werner 1966a:37).

1.2.2 *Validation and cross cultural comparison and other developments*

Most validation has been attempted with kinship terminologies, which will be mentioned only briefly. Sanday's (1968) contribution has been discussed before because it has wider implications. Romney and D'Andrade (1964) have used factor analysis on informant judgments about their Yankee kinship space. The ambiguity or indeterminancy of the component of 'collateral distance' is also supported by a paper by Steinberg (1967). Wallace (1965:244–45) noted that only culture specific dimensions produced a psychologically valid analysis, raising again the question of the status of components. Outside of kinship, Berlin et al. (1968) will be taken up in the next section. D'Andrade (1965), again using statistical methods, demonstrated that measurement of character trait descriptions by adjectives may have instead measured their semantic distance. Another paper by D'Andrade et al. (1966) deals with Mexican Spanish and American English medical terminology and could be perhaps best considered a short-cut method contrasted with the longwinded deterministic methods, but whereas the application of a lexicon seems relatively clear, the factor analyses are less so. An integration of statistical techniques, however, with the deterministic techniques emphasized in this paper is an urgent but special undertaking beyond the scope of this paper.

In comparative studies of kinship, Lounsbury's total approach (papers from 1956 to 1965) is predicated on cross cultural comparison of various PUBLISHED kinship terminologies: 'I do not imagine a satisfactory sociological explanation can be given from the study of a single society. This is not because the explanation is not to be found there, but because we may not yet know precisely what to look for' (Lounsbury 1965:181). Buchler's typology of Crow systems by scale analysis is interesting and in part rests on Lounsbury's work (Buchler 1964, in spite of Scheffler's 1967 sharp critique). Outside of kinship a notable typology and a search for universal components is Buchler and Freeze's (1966) dealing with pronominal systems. Metzger and Williams's (1966) comparison of firewood in three contiguous ethnic groups was mentioned before.

Lounsbury also advocates structural analysis for better studies of change (Lounsbury 1964b). A lead which is followed by Basso (1967) in his study of the nature of semantic change in Apache extension of body parts to part of the automobile (see also Haile 1942 for Navajo). An interesting comparative and evolutionary paper is Berlin and Kay's (1967), implying that the evolution of color categories became lexically coded in the languages of the world in a fixed temporal order.

Historical reconstruction in kinship is the aim of most of Friedrich's work (1962, 1964) and the work of Frisch and Schutz (1967).

Hymes (e.g. 1962), Sarles (1966) and Moehrman (1968) and others are trying to expand ethnoscience, if not ethnosemantics, to phenomena of human interactions.

2. SOME EXPLICIT AND FORMALIZED NOTIONS CONCERNING LEXICAL/SEMANTIC FIELDS

Readers interested in the general history of ideas on lexical/semantic fields are referred to Suzanne Oehman's article (1953) in English. In German Oehman's dissertation (1951) and Gipper (1963) (a generally fascinating book) are possibly the best sources. The German field theorists come from a philological tradition and make no attempts at formalization. The translation of their insights into formal field properties will require time.

The structure of lexical/semantic fields mirrors the structure of cultural knowledge. The task of ethnosemantics is the explication of cultural knowledge. (The notational conventions — an extension of notation in logic — are discussed in Appendix A, Section 4.1. It is essential to the understanding of the rest of the paper.)

2.1 *The Linear or Thesaurus Model*

The possibility of this kind of description of the entire vocabulary of a language is mentioned in passing by Weinreich:

First, 'The grouping of synonyms along a continuum yields a thesaurus like Roget's. No doubt significant aspects of the vocabulary structure can be studied on the basis of the thesaurus alone ...' (Weinreich 1962:30).

Second, 'For example, the list of words in a thesaurus can be interpreted as a series of one dimensional projections (mappings) of the multidimensional semantic structure of the vocabulary. The dimensions of the vocabulary might be studied in terms of intersections of synonymy lines (= cross-references between the paragraphs of the thesaurus)' (ibid.).

The first part of Weinreich's statement is no doubt true. Werner and Campbell (1970) used the thesaurus in addition to the dictionary to obtain a larger number of paraphrases for an English sentence. Werner's structural description of 'thought' in English (1969) is based on *Webster's New Collegiate Dictionary* (1953) and iteration through the dictionary by looking up every word in every definition, and so on. A quick check of *Roget's International Thesaurus*, 3rd ed. (1962) contains a large number of entries in the index alone. These are listed in 4.2, Appendix B.

The list of mostly classificatory sentences obtained by analyzing the articles in the dictionary are in 4.3, Appendix C.

The reader can check for himself the amount of overlap between the information inferred from the *Collegiate Dictionary* and the index of the *Thesaurus* (Compare Appendix A and Appendix B). Checking the *Thesaurus* paragraphs would reveal an even greater divergence between the two lists. Weinreich's conclusion is sound: although we do not know the quality or the precise nature of the structural information provided by the *Thesaurus*, the fact is that it does help by bringing additional lexical items and relations into focus.

There are two more points to be made:

First, that the existence of dictionaries and thesauri in a language simplifies the task of the structural investigation of lexical/semantic fields considerably. Perhaps this aid of dictionaries and thesauri is qualitatively less than adequate, but it makes up for this lack, by quantitative near exhaustiveness. In linguistic anthropology one starts almost always with nothing. Even where dictionaries are available few of those dealing with 'exotic' languages can match the 200 or more years of the accumulated American and European lexicographic tradition.

Second, that the size of the lexicon of any language is a major obstacle to the study of lexical/semantic fields. Although we went only to the *index* of the thesaurus and only to a *collegiate* dictionary (see Appendix B), the sheer bulk of lexical items and their relations is overwhelming. Such bulk is in no way restricted to European languages or the languages of so called high cultures (e.g. see Nielsen and Nessheim's Lapp dictionary (1962) or Werner and Begishe's (1969) work on Navajo thought (*nitsaʔhaʔ-kees*).

In order to assess Weinreich's second claim we will look at a more concrete and perhaps less ramified lexical item, the English word 'bachelor'.

25

p. 692 BACHELOR degree — 915.6 — 915. TITLE

     degree,
     academic degree;
     bachelor,
     baccalaureate,
     baccalaureus /L./;
     master,
     masterate;
     doctor,
     doctorate.

       knight — 916.6 — 916. NOBILITY
     knight,
     cavalier,
     chevalier,
     caballero /Sp./,
     Ritter /Ger./,
     "a very parfit gentil knight" /Chaucer/;
     Knight-errant,
     knight-adventurer;
     companion;
     bachelor,
     knight bachelor;
     baronet,

knight baronet;
banneret,
knight banneret;
Bayard,
Gawain,
Lancelot,
Sidney,
Sir Galahad,
Don Quixote.

celibate — 932.3 — 932. CELIBACY
bachelor,
bach /slang/,
single man,
lone wolf /coll./.
Other *relevant* entries under 932. CELIBACY (no cross reference)
932.1
celibacy,
singleness,
single blessedness;
bachelorhood,
bachelorship;
spinsterhood,
maidenhood,
maidenhead,
virginity;
monasticism,
monachism;
misogamy,
misogyny.

932.7 (adj.)
unmarried,
unwedded,
unwed,
single,
sole /law/,
spouseless,
wifeless,
husbandless;
bachelorly,
bachelorlike;

spinsterly,
spinsterish,
spinsterlike;
old-maidish,
old-maidenish,
maiden,
maidenly;
virgin,
virginal.

We have excluded most of the paragraphs under 932., CELIBACY, because its content is irrelevant. We have also excluded all further entries in the index. The latter are, exhaustively: bachelor girl 932.4; bachelorhood 932.1 (included) ; bachelor like 932.7. (included); bachelor's wife 931.9; the latter cited with 'Coeleb's wife' and next to (separated by semicolon) 'commonlaw wife' and 'concubine'.

Quite obviously Weinreich's proposal does not work with an *ordinary* Thesaurus. Bachelor is not cross referenced to 'human', or 'physical object' (concrete). 'Male' is implied only by the third entry under 932.3. Unless one knows English well, the synonymous expressions 'wifeless man', 'unmarried man', are not connected. The usually voluntary character of 'celibate' is not contrasted. Neither of the preceding paragraphs (915., TITLE, or 916., NOBILITY) is of much help. The only surprise is perhaps the relatively close collocation of 915.6. 'degree' and 916. NOBILITY.

We assume that Weinreich had a different kind of a thesaurus in mind. The illustration opposite is an attempt to use the resources of the existing thesauri to implement Weinreich's view.

Example 26 displays the entire lexicon of English as a linear 'projection of the multidimensional structure of the vocabulary'. We have provided our own system of cross referencing between the 'paragraphs' that seem to us plausibly connectable. The nature or interpretation of the 'synonymy lines' is questionable. For example, we wanted to express the fact that 'bachelor' designates a male human being. The only way we could do this was by connecting 'bachelor' to 'mankind' and to 'masculinity'. Although the relation of 'bachelor' to 'man(human)' and 'male human' is taxonomic, this fact is concealed by connections to 'mankind' and 'masculinity'. The model is not particularly helpful. The entries and connections are arbitrary and the linearization of the multidimensionality of the vocabulary seems to obscure rather than to clarify the relations in the lexical/semantic fields.

Thesauri and dictionaries contain important clues to the relationships that may hold between lexical items, but most of these clues are covert rather than explicit. The articles in dictionaries from which the sentences in App. C were more or less directly derived are more explicit than the thesauri. The 'synonymic continuum' from CLASS ONE: ABSTRACT RELATIONS, to 1040 Religious Institutions, is of little or no help

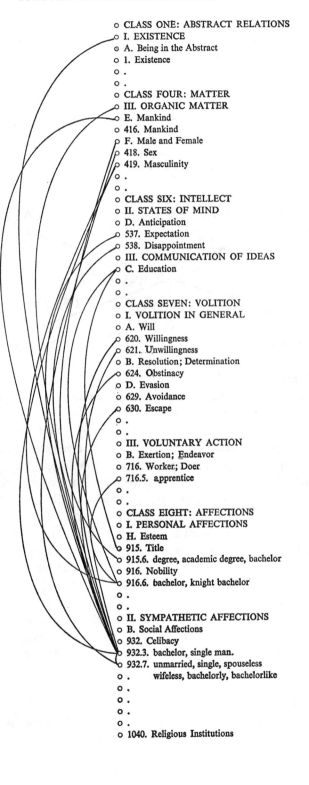

o CLASS ONE: ABSTRACT RELATIONS
o I. EXISTENCE
o A. Being in the Abstract
o 1. Existence
o .
o .
o CLASS FOUR: MATTER
o III. ORGANIC MATTER
o E. Mankind
o 416. Mankind
o F. Male and Female
o 418. Sex
o 419. Masculinity
o .
o .
o CLASS SIX: INTELLECT
o II. STATES OF MIND
o D. Anticipation
o 537. Expectation
o 538. Disappointment
o III. COMMUNICATION OF IDEAS
o C. Education
o .
o .
o CLASS SEVEN: VOLITION
o I. VOLITION IN GENERAL
o A. Will
o 620. Willingness
o 621.. Unwillingness
o B. Resolution; Determination
o 624. Obstinacy
o D. Evasion
o 629. Avoidance
o 630. Escape
o .
o .
o III. VOLUNTARY ACTION
o B. Exertion; Endeavor
o 716. Worker; Doer
o 716.5. apprentice
o .
o .
o CLASS EIGHT: AFFECTIONS
o I. PERSONAL AFFECTIONS
o H. Esteem
o 915. Title
o 915.6. degree, academic degree, bachelor
o 916. Nobility
o 916.6. bachelor, knight bachelor
o .
o .
o II. SYMPATHETIC AFFECTIONS
o B. Social Affections
o 932. Celibacy
o 932.3. bachelor, single man.
o 932.7. unmarried, single, spouseless
o .   wifeless, bachelorly, bachelorlike
o .
o .
o .
o .
o 1040. Religious Institutions

in the description of lexical/semantic fields. Note for example, that none or few of the rich multiplicity of semantic features of 'bachelor' observed by Bolinger (1965) appear.

2.2 *The Field or Single Page Model*

This model is discussed at some length by Bierman (1964:240ff.). Imagine a dictionary with one page, albeit a very large page. All English words appear on this one page. And it is arranged something like this:

27

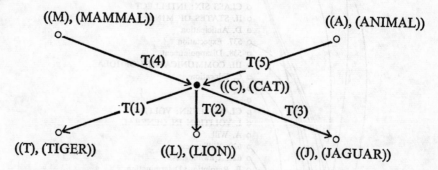

... 'A star of meaning!' ... 'My dictionary is really a word map. Points represent words and when there is a line between points we know that two words can be combined into a sentence. Thus, when I want to know the combinatory meaning of a word I look on the dictionary and follow the various lines to other words. There are as many lines as combinatory possibilities.' ... 'You've given us a spatial analogue for the idea of combinatorial meaning' (Bierman 1964:240).

We are adapting Bierman's model to our view by first proposing that the node '•', which is to be defined, is labeled in the usual canonical dictionary entry fashion as ((C), (P)). It is immediately apparent that folk-taxonomies diagrammed as labeled directed tree graphs represent Bierman's model in general, and the 'star of meaning' in particular, if we extend Bierman's notions. In his view the center of the 'star of meaning' is the term to be defined. Implicitly, at least, he seems to imply that only sentences qualify for representation as arrows for which ((C), (P)) is subject. We have to extend this notion to include explicitly not only those sentences where ((C), (P)) is the subject (the first member of the sentence), but to those where ((C,(P)) is the predicate as well. Note in this context that according to our convention the direction of the arrow is reversed (at least in taxonomies): the specific term in taxonomic sentences is the subject and the general term is the predicate and our arrows run from the genus to the species.

Counting incoming and outgoing edges equally is congruent with our view that concepts such as 'noun' and 'verb' are conventional language–specific categories, expressing only notions such as 'used predominantly as subject', or 'used predominantly as predicate'. Werner and Fenton (1970) define what they call an *extended Aristotelian definition* in a taxonomy as the path from the most general known node to the term to be defined, *plus* the subtree dominated by the term to be defined.

The subtree could be interpreted as definition by enumeration, but that is misleading. (We have not mentioned referents at all, except when we specifically talked about *examples* of particular ((C),(P)), that is, (x) ex ((C),(P)) or 'there is an x so that ex ((C),(P)) is *an example* of ((C),(P))'. In this context of definitions we are not talking about relations of a lexical item to the 'real' world, but to relations *among* lexical items.

A theory of reference is quite outside our view; a theory of lexical/semantic fields is primarily a theory of Bierman's combinatorial meaning or connotation and a theory of paraphrase. There are philosophers who claim that a theory of reference is impossible in principle (e.g. Polanyi 1958:87). We recognize that in any case it might be very difficult.

Similar to ostensive 'definitions', a 'definition' by enumeration of members of the class fails because it is not automatically clear — for example, for an observer from another culture — what criteria were selected and included in (C) from all the possible criteria that differentiate the criterial bundle of attributes (C) and link it to the 'noise' (P).

Because of the transitivity of the relation of taxonomy (or set inclusion) every extended Aristotelian definition is freely convertible into 'the star of meaning'.

28a   28b

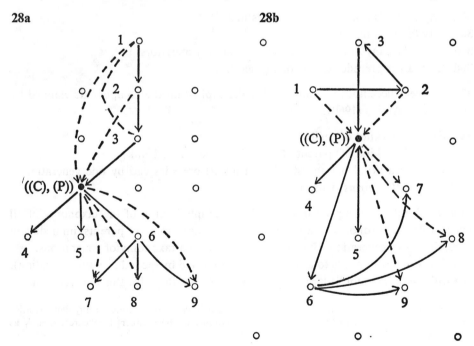

Note: For the 'star of meaning' of ((C),(P)) in **16b** the lines 12, 23, 67, 68, 69 are superfluous, they are drawn in to show more clearly the correspondence with **16a**. (12 and 23 are part of the 'stars' of nodes 1, 2, and 3, similarly 67, 68, 69 are part of the stars of nodes 6, 7, 8 and 9.)

The 'star' of ((C),(P)) is relevant only insofar as we are interested in the meaning of ((C),(P)). The moment we focus on the problem of lexical/semantic fields we are interested in all possible connections between all the nodes represented in the field, or on the single page.

What is the connection between semantic features, components, or markers and the star of meaning? Components can be overt or covert. Overt components are directly accessible through the 'star of meaning' if we restrict ourselves to relations for which actual sentences can be elicited. Thus we will not talk about covert taxonomies (we return to this in 2.5) and define the relation of taxonomy, such that (a), it must be overt, explicitly verbalizable in a natural language (e.g. English) and (b) the linking relation must be of the form

30   '____ is a kind of ____.' (in English), or
       '____ ____ a7t'e7.' (for example, in Navajo).

By this heuristic we separate the relatively simply task of discovering overt taxonomies from the more difficult task of finding the covert 'components'.

If we apply this heuristic principle to 'father' in the Yankee kinship system, we find that it takes us a long way toward the solution of the componential analysis (this may, or may not be true generally):

30a 'My father is a man' ('My father is male.')
30b 'My father is my parent.'
30c 'My father, my father's father, etc., … are my ancestors.'[4]
30d 'My father precedes me by one generation.

The four sentences above contain and make explicit all the components claimed by Wallace and Atkins (1960):

31 'Father is a (kind of) male.'
         is a (kind of) parent.' (ascending generation, 1 link)
         is a (kind of) ancestor.' (is a lineal) precedes ego by one generation.
         (confirms, 1 link)

Thus the Yankee kinship term 'father' is at the intersection of the taxonomy of all males, with the taxonomy of all ancestors, the subtaxonomy of parents, immediately preceding ego's generation, that is, intersecting with a taxonomy of generations.

This taxonomy happens to be ordered (first followed by second … with generation). We will use the symbol 'is larger than' and 'is smaller than' for this new relation.

---

[4] Not all informants agree with this statement. Some Americans do not consider any living relative an ancestor; others seem to feel only nameless (unknown to the speaker) forebearers qualify as ancestors.

There appears to be very little difference between components as attributes in the 'star of meaning', or pairs of items linked by semantic relations. The 'stars of meaning' of all superior dominating nodes in taxonomies are contained in all subordinate nodes. When we mark a lexical item like father as (+male) we tend to forget that it is rooted in the standing sentence of English cultural knowledge (for explanation of (F') see Appendix A, 4.1):

32a 'A father is a man.' (in the sense of male)

   or

   $(\text{father}) = ((\text{man}) \cup (\text{F'}))\text{TAXN}(\text{man})$

or, if we read (x) (...) 'there is an x such that ...', and { } stands for 'or'

32 $(\text{father}) = \begin{cases}(x)\,(((\text{man}) \cup (x)\text{TAXN}\,(\text{man})) \\ (y)\,((\text{parent}) \cup (y))\text{TAXN}\,(\text{parent})) \\ (z)\,((\text{ancestor}) \cup (z))\text{TAXN}\,(\text{ancestor}))\end{cases}$

Covert categories may be of two kinds. For example in 'slap' it is easy to elicit a sentence

33 'A slap is a kind of hit with an open hand.'

More difficult are such terms as 'collateral' in English. Sentences such as

34 A _____ is a distant relative.
      kinship term

do not elicit unique answers. If the published componential analyses of the Yankee system are compared, they differ from each other only by the fact that collateral distance was defined by every investigator somewhat differently. The multiplicity of solutions is therefore an important characteristic of the Yankee system. There may be subcultural variation (see Sanday's suggestive work, 1968), or the variation may be idiosyncratic. In each case we would have to establish subtypes, by subculture or by each person. The multiplicity of combinatorial possibilities which Burling (1964) has demonstrated, has nothing to do with the nonuniqueness of the solutions. The non-uniqueness of Yankee solutions is part of the empirical constraints which would, in a more rigid culture (at least as far as definition of the collateral distance of relatives is concerned) drastically reduce the number of solutions to one or at most a few. We should keep in mind therefore that variants may have important implications for actual kinship behavior.

Analyses of Yankee kinship would have probably been less controversial if the technical term(s) 'collateral' ('colineal', 'ablineal') had not been introduced. We know at the present time no better way of keeping semantic analyses 'psychologically' real than to restrict (as a first step), eliciting to sentences that are easily verbalizable in the informants' language. If the limits of verbalizable relations are reached, then and then only is it time to begin looking for more covert attributes. We do not yet understand the nature of the boundary between verbal and non-verbal (implicit) behavior. Sticking to the verbalizable for the investigation of lexical/semantic fields will pay off in the long run by a better understanding of the limits of language, and thus the boundary of explicit culture and that which is known only tacitly.

Bierman's model, which all who have worked in ethnosemantics have used for years (at least implicitly), is a good first heuristic model. Whether it has any deep theoretical significance depends on how successfully it can be integrated with the insights into the workings of language gained since the Transformational Revolution.

2.3 *The Inverse of Bierman's Model*

For certain applications, for example, the empirical analysis of verbal plans (which are comparable to verbal directions for performance, similar to directions for mixing photographic developers, which are printed on the container) an inverse of Bierman's model has demonstrated its usefulness (see Werner 1966b).

Inversion refers to the replacement of edges by nodes and nodes by edges in Bierman's model (2.2). We will demonstrate inversion on a simple taxonomy rather than by working out general rules. We feel the illustration is more transparent. Since this model is largely exploratory, we will try to draw some tentative conclusions and reserve a general statement of the inversion for another publication. In part, our reluctance to develop general rules is due to the fact that we are unable to account fully for the 'wellformedness' of the inversion and have to supplement it with empirical evidence. Recall the simple 'star of meaning' **27** (a sample taxonomy) representation of (cat) on Bierman's first model.

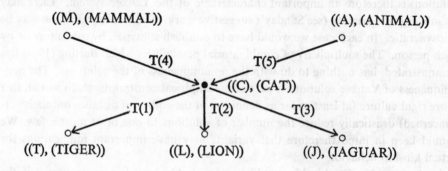

We construct the 'incidence matrix' of graph **27** by using the labels of the edges T(1) to T(5) (representing the relation of TAXN) for the columns and the nodes (suppressing the phonological part in square brackets) for the rows. We use the values of +1 for 'outgoing' and −1 for 'incoming' edges.

35a

	T(1)	T(2)	T(3)	T(4)	T(5)
(C)	+1	+1	+1	−1	−1
(T)	−1	0	0	0	0
(L)	0	−1	0	0	0
(J)	0	0	−1	0	0
(M)	0	0	0	+1	0
(A)	0	0	0	0	+1

We invert matrix **35a** simply by inverting rows and columns

35b

	(C)	(T)	(L)	(J)	(M)	(A)
T(1)	+1	−1	0	0	0	0
T(2)	+1	0	−1	0	0	0
T(3)	+1	0	0	−1	0	0
T(4)	−1	0	0	0	+1	0
T(5)	−1	0	0	0	0	+1
T	+1	−1	−1	−1	+1	+1

We obtain the sum of the columns and label it T and justify it as follows: T represents the relation of taxonomy TAXN. Since all these relations are identical, we will represent TAXN by a single node T. The sum of the columns of matrix **35b** shows that six edges connect to node T: Three are 'incoming' and three are 'outgoing'. The inversion fails to interpret *where* three of these edges 'come from' or where three of them 'go to'. We provide these nodes, at first without interpretation (the 'black' nodes):

35c

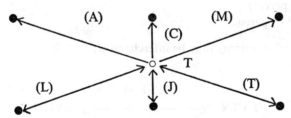

The interpretation of the 'black' nodes follows from Exs. **5**, Appendix A

35d

$$(L') \quad T \quad (A)$$
$$\circ \longrightarrow \circ \longrightarrow \circ$$

If (L)TAXN(A) represents 'A lion is a kind of animal'; then formulas **5a-c** in Appendix A interpret the 'black' nodes.

35e (lion) = (animal) ∪ (L') ⊃ (animal)

35f (L) = ((A)ATTR(L')) TAX (A)

We redraw graph **35d** as follows

35g

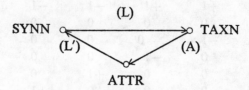

The link between (A) and (L′) is (A)ATTR(L′), that is, (L′) is an attribute added by set theoretical union to (A); (A)ATTR(L′) = (L) is the relation of synonymy; and (L)TAXN(A) is self explanatory.

Generalization (F) (see Appendix A) may now be read off immediately: If (L′) tends toward the empty set the relation of TAXN will approach SYNN, i.e. the relation of synonymy is the limiting case of the relation of taxonomy (see also Lyons 1968:455-56).

Whereas the attribute (L′) has no phonological association, the generality of the 'triangle' can be seen if we chose a verbalizable attribute.

36a

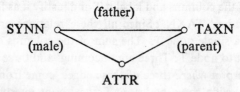

(father) = ((parent) ATTR (male))
'Father is a male parent.'
(father) TAXN (parent)
'Father is a kind of parent.'

But synonymy and taxonomy may be interchanged:

36b

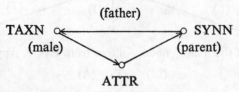

(father) TAXN (male)
'Father is a kind of male.'
(father) = ((male) ATTR (parent))
'Father is a parental male.'

The last sentence sounds unusual but is by no means impossible. Note again the closeness of the relation of taxonomy and synonymy in 'A male parent is a kind of a parent' and 'A parental male is a kind of a male.'

The situation is still more complex. The symmetry of 'father' is unusual. It reflects the fact that 'father' is a member of both the taxonomy of 'male' and the taxonomy of 'parent.' This does not seem to be true of complex naming units:

37a   **37b**

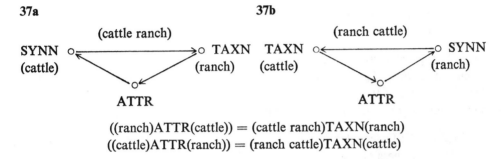

$$((ranch)ATTR(cattle)) = (cattle\ ranch)TAXN(ranch)$$
$$((cattle)ATTR(ranch)) = (ranch\ cattle)TAXN(cattle)$$

It is not the case that 'A cattle ranch is a kind of cattle', nor that 'Ranch cattle is a kind of ranch'. The asymmetry may be more conspicuous when one of the combinatorial possibilities is not recognized as a general term or naming unit of the language. In the above example 'ranch cattle' is slightly more unusual than 'cattle ranch'. 'Bread basket' is common, but 'basket bread' is quite unusual, although it is not difficult to think up appropriate contexts (Katz and Fodor's game 1963:489n). The situation seems intermediate for adjectival constructions:

38a

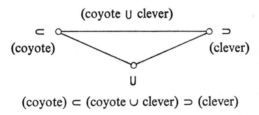

$$(coyote) \subset (coyote \cup clever) \supset (clever)$$

38a is noncommittal and nondirectional (coyote ∪ clever) should be interpreted as noncommittal with respect to the choice of the topic. After a speaker makes a decision about his topic the relation ∪ and ATTR are no longer exactly the same. If the choice of topic is made with regard to 'coyote' we get:

38b   ((coyote)ATTR(clever))TAXN(coyote); conversely

38c   ((clever)ATTR(coyote))TAXN(clever-ness)

There is a neutral way of talking in the declarative mode in **b**

38d   'The coyote is clever.'

but there is no doubt that the topic is a (kind of) coyote. Nominalized **c** yields:

38e 'The *coyote* that is clever ...'
　　　'Clever *coyote* ...'

Correspondingly **c** may be nominalized

38f 'The *cleverness* of the coyote ...'
　　　'The coyote's *cleverness* ...'

but **f,** the topic clever(ness), does not possess a simple declarative form with predicate (comment) coyote. That is, whereas (coyote)ATTR(clever) is representable as **d,** the declarative form of the attribution, (*clever*) ATTR(coyote) is representable only in a more complex construction in which it is topicalized:

38g ((*clever*)ATTR(coyote))ATTR(proverbial)
　　　'The cleverness of the coyote is proverbial.'

This is, however, not generally true of all possible attributes of clever:

39　(clever)ATTR(admire)
　　　'Clever(ness) is admir(able).'

We have glossed over a number of difficulties, especially with regard to grammatical formants such as '-ness', 'of', 'from' and others. The inclusion of these does not seem impossible in principle, especially since every edge that we have marked 'simple' may be part of deeper complex 'triangles' itself. A more systematic investigation is called for; our presentation is at best suggestive.

　　It is apparent that the relation of attribution ATTR and set theoretical union are not strictly analogous. After their union the members of two sets lose their identity and are irretrievable. This in fact does take place in what we may term 'taxonomic attribution'.

40a　(lion) = ((animal) $\cup$ (L'))

Above the right side is an unordered set with the identities of (animal) and (L') merged. This is probably due to the fact that there is no word or naming unit in the language *((L'),(L')). (Subsets of (L') are, of course, named, e.g. 'Lions are yellow'.) In cases of attribution where both sides of the semantic relation have a phonological manifestation the relation ATTR contrasts with $\cup$ by being asymmetrical:

41a　(A)ATTR(B) $\neq$ (B)ATTR(A)

Loosely speaking the relation ATTR 'remembers' the order of the elements and in nominalizations this 'remembering' means the retention of the first argument of ATTR as the head of the resulting phrase. It is conceivable that attributive relations are coded in our heads by the relation of union,

41b　(A) $\cup$ (B) = (B) $\cup$ (A)

but as two distinct sets to be operated on. The relation is converted to ATTR *after* a speaker decides what he wants for his topic. We have, however, no formal means of representing the co-occurrence restriction if (A)ATTR(B) does occur, but (B)ATTR(A) does not. On the other hand, we know of no good cases where (B) ATTR (A) is not justifiable in some, often bizarre, contexts. Admitting that language should be able to account for bizarre occurrences and that, therefore, (B) ATTR (A) ought to be legitimate, the asymmetry remains and needs to be noted and studied in detail especially with reference to the growing literature on nominalization in transformational grammar.

The inverse of Bierman's model has the advantage that it establishes the unity of Werner's (1966b) 'Plans' and the rest of semantics. However, we feel that Werner's separation of what he calls pragmatics from semantics was too sharp. First, his pragmatics is not about 'knowing how' rather than 'knowing that' (following Ryle's distinction (1946)) as he has claimed. In the terminology of lexical fields, 'pragmatics' is that part of the lexical field where the semantic relation 'is followed by' (FLBY) predominates. For example;

42   (someone returns on and with the horse)
SYNN
((someone starts after the horse)
FLBY
(someone finds the horse)
FLBY
(someone returns home on and with the horse))

(part of Werner's Fig. 4, 1966b:56–57, only the English part of the Navajo example; slight corrections added; for the Navajo graph and detail see Appendix D).

'Knowing how' is knowing how to act. 'Knowing that' is knowing a fact. Although the distinction may at times be not very sharp it seems to be quite distinct in 'pragmatics'. The plan **42** and in Appendix D is not 'know how' to find one's horse, if one is a Navajo (given the full details of Werner's plan), but 'knowing that to know how'. In other words, it is a plan for action but does not ensure the 'knower' that he can actually find his horse. Another example for clarification: Navajo informants know *habid* 'stomach' and *hate7li7* 'spleen'. They know *that* both are *haghi' bilh haz'a7anii* 'internal organs' and a lot more. However, given the chance and willingness on the part of the informant, it is irrelevant as to whether or not they could find the spleen in a cadaver. The two domains of knowledge are relatively independent: one is the ability to manipulate lexical relations and/or symbols (including propositions); the other the ability to manipulate the world. The relative independence of the two types of knowledge is also supported by the fact that most of us can understand more of any language than we can produce. Our competence to interpret sentences ('to know that') outstrips our competence to know how to construct certain sentences and/or use certain lexical units ('to know how').

Werner's 'pragmatics' is the competence to verbalize plans for action and should be considered as one of the (perhaps major) prerequisites for knowing how to execute them. However, as Miller, Galanter and Pribram (1960) point out, no amount of verbal direction (or verbal plans) is sufficient to know how to, for example, fly a plane.

In the inverse of Bierman's model, Werner's 'pragmatic ambiguity' or 'pragmatic paraphrase' (Werner 1966b:54) is a special case of paraphrase in general. The most detailed paraphrase Werner (1966b:65n) and Begishe were able to elicit for **42** in Navajo is the longest path through the diagram in Appendix D. Note that every possible path through the diagram is a permissible paraphrase. This can be seen by reading off the English translation labels in the proper sequence. The Navajo reference is to the so–called fourth person (or 3a.), 'specifically human actor' (Werner 1966a).

All nodes should be labeled FLBY (followed by), especially since other activities, especially 'standing' activities or 'standing plans' may include the topmost labeled edge 'one returns on and with the horse'. The dotted lines in Appendix D connect synonymous (or near synonymous) terms.

We will use an 'atomic' plan to demonstrate the similarity between 'pragmatic paraphrase' and paraphrase in general. An atomic plan is a plan for which further 'pragmatic' structure is elicitable only with great difficulty. These plans therefore, correspond closely to dictionary definitions of the verb. However, this difficulty should not be construed as an absolute difficulty. Kinesiologists have shown that terms like 'walk' *can* be described; so have army manuals which describe how to do an 'about face'. Such descriptions tend to be very lengthy. We have seen a description of 'walking' several pages long (Gardner, Gray and O'Rahilly 1963:318–320). Apparently in natural languages verbs are shorthand labels for very complex descriptions of actions and/or motions, or even 'posture' (see Hewes 1966).

We will use as our example the 'atomic plan' for 'splitting wood'. In light of the preceding paragraph the label 'plan' may be misleading. We will not go into further detailed description of the minute muscular and object movements that cause the splitting of the wood. We will explore the dictionary definition of 'splitting'. A detailed description of the plan 'splitting wood' (with reference to Eastern or Central Europe, based on Werner's experience) is given in Werner's paper (ibid. 47–48). The *Collegiate dictionary* (1953:817) gives the relevant definition in edited form:

43a ((split), (SPLIT)) SYNN ((to divide with the layers), (SPLIT))

The following relevant evidence (our judgment) is from *Webster's Collegiate dictionary* (1953) (marked WCD: page number) and a few intuitions of our own (marked (00):

43b 'Divide' is to cause to be separate. (WCD:243)
43c 'Divide' is to cause to become divided. (00)
43d 'Cause' is effecting of result. (WCD:132)
43e 'Cause' is causing of result. (00)

43f 'Cut' is to divide into parts with an edged instrument. (WCD:205)

43g 'Cut' is to cause division into parts by means of an edged instrument. (00) (in this case, an ax)

43h 'With' means by way of. (WCD:984)

43i 'With' means in the direction of. (00)

43j 'With' means parallel with (to). (00) (in this case)

43k 'With' means in the relation parallel to. (00)

43l 'Sever' is to divide by cutting. (WCD: 775)

43m 'To split' is to sever. (00) (in this case).

43n 'The cause' is a human causation. (00) (in this case)

We are now prepared to diagram 'splitting (wood)' in the form of a system of triangles each with nodes labeled TAXN & SYNN and ATTR.

43o

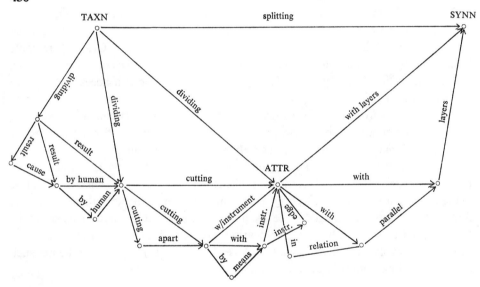

43p (splitting) TAXN (dividing) ATTR ____ (((((cause) ATTR (resulting)) ATTR ((by) ATTR (human))) ATTR ((cutting) ATTR (((by) ATTR (means)) ATTR ((instrument) ATTR (edged))))) ATTR ____ ((((with) ATTR (relation)) ATTR (parallel)) ATTR (layers)))

Paraphrased (more or less accurately) in ordinary English:

43q 'Splitting is dividing, which is with the layers.'

43r '... dividing, which is cutting with an instrument parallel with the layers.'

43s '... dividing, which is cutting apart with an edged instrument parallel with the layers.'

43t dividing, which is cutting apart, which is the result of human cause by means of an edged instrument in parallel relation (with) to the layers.

The above are only a few of the possible paths through the graph **43o**. In spite of the imperfection of our model we are prepared to define paraphrase:

44   Any two paths between two points in the lexical field (represented as the inverse of Bierman's model) represent paraphrases of each other.

Generalizing further we can state that texts may be viewed as paraphrases of their titles. A title like 'The Sapir-Whorf Hypothesis', or a query about the title 'Discuss the Sapir-Whorf Hypothesis', requires (for example, in an examination) abstracts (i.e. shorter texts than original texts) of the readings and lecture notes strung together in an integrated paraphrase. The original input was linear, the coding non-linear as a network and the retrieval (the paraphrase or answer), a linear output. Thus Bierman's inverse model is a first approximation of a paraphrase retrieval device. Considering that potentially it paraphrases questions and that paraphrase is one of the few tests of knowledge (i.e. of understanding a question) the model is a putative and simple minded representation of cultural knowledge.

Obviously it would be wrong to over-value this model. Tremendous amounts of work need to be done. Problems abound, for example, as one passes through the graphs, the nodes keep changing labels. What does that mean? Or, is there some basic order that corresponds to some deep or lexical/semantic structure? Or, finally, can the bracketing (e.g. **43p**) be made unambiguous, and if so is it necessary? We do not know the answers.

Whatever the problems, it remains a fact that, similar to Bierman's model, the inverse of Bierman's model is also an important heuristic device for the eliciting of semantic information, in one's own, as well as in another culture.

Note for example that graph **43o** makes some of the different senses (different from the ones in **43o**) of 'splitting' relatively explicit: We can ask where changes could be made in the graph without affecting the use of the label 'splitting'. Inspecting it we find that the causation need not be by human agent; that the action need not be 'cutting', but could be a 'ripping' or 'tearing' apart; and finally, that an instrument need not be involved. 'Division with the layers' (WCD:817) turns out to be not such a bad general paraphrase ('definition') after all.

2.4   *The 'Componential' Lexical/Semantic Field*

Anthropologists have found two structures useful in the analysis of ethnosemantic data. Both of these are formally defined by Werner and Fenton (1970). We will repeat very briefly:

45a   If U is the universe of the labeled nodes of a taxonomy then the relation TAXN is a relation in U and TAXN applies to every pair of U if and only if TAXN is irreflexive ((A) TAXN (A) is not a member of TAXN), asymmetric (If (A) TAX (B) then (B) TAXN (A) is not part of (TAXN), and transitive (If (A) TAXN (B) and (B) TAXN (C) then (A) TAXN (C)). Taxonomies have usually a unique 'origin' or 'beginner' (If (A) TAXN (B) and if there is no (B) TAXN (X), then (B) is an 'origin' or a 'beginner');

However a condition of a unique 'origin' or 'beginner' is not necessary.

If there is no unique 'origin' or 'beginner' the number of 'origins' or 'beginners' is usually small.

Taxonomies may also intersect, if (A) TAXN (B) and (A) TAXN (C) and (D) TAXN (B), it is possible to also have (D) TAXN (C). This will be elaborated further.

45b An important heuristic corollary of taxonomies is that the relation of TAXN between two nodes (A) and (B), (A) TAXN (B) will be recognized only if there exists a sentence in the language under investigation which corresponds to English '(A) is a (kind of) (B)' where (A) and (B) are phonological representations associated with semantic representations (A) and (B) respectively, i.e. ((A), (A)) and ((B), (B)) are the relevant lexical entries.

Far more important for us will be the definition of a paradigm. We modify it slightly

46a If U is the universe of the 'components' of a paradigm then the relation PDGM is synonymous with the relation $\cup$ called union, in U and is constructed in the following manner: The set U is partitioned into n subsets called dimensions D(i) so that the intersection of all D(i) is null ($\bigcup_{i=1}^{n} D(i) = \emptyset$), and the union of all D(i) is the set U ($\bigcup_{i=1}^{n} D(i) = U$). A paradigm is then the subset C(i) of U containing exactly one element from each dimension D(i).

To construct a paradigm we define a 'star' operation, '*' as follows:

46b D(0) * D(1) * D(2) *...* D(i) *...* D(n) = {{d(0), d(1), d(2), ..., d(i), ..., d(n)} so that one and only one d(i) is taken from every D(i)}

46c The relation PDGM in U is irreflexive, symmetrical and intransitive, therefore not a hierarchy. *It cannot be represented by a unique labeled tree.*

46d Generally the relation PDGM cannot be represented as a sentence of a natural language. Occasionally it may correspond to attribution, but attribution is symmetrical only in unusual circumstances (see examples **36** to **38**).

46e We will call a paradigm asymmetrical if we can specify (1) conditions under which one or more of the dimensions D(i) neutralize to the null set (D(i) $\Rightarrow \emptyset$).

(2) conditions under which one or more dimensions D(i) neutralize partially so that the new set D(i)' is a subset of the old dimension D(i), i.e., (D(i)' $\subset$ D(i)).

Werner and Fenton (1970) propose three possible solutions to the interrelationship between taxonomies and paradigms:

(1) Taxonomies and paradigms alternate. That is, a paradigm is the structuring of

a single level of a taxonomy. Trivially, every taxonomy consists of a one dimensional paradigm. The single dimension is formed by the individual bundle of attributes which distinguish every node on a particular level from every other node.

(2) Taxonomies and paradigms do not alternate necessarily through the entire system. It may be more economical at times to include several levels of a taxonomy in parts of the paradigm. There may or may not be natural boundaries between such structured levels of a taxonomy. Werner and Fenton consider this the most conservative solution.

(3) We intend to apply their third solution to the entire lexicon of a language. This solution asserts the 'relative independence' of the paradigmatic definitions $C(i)$ (see **41a**) and lexical field relations which are superimposed on the multidimensional semantic grid.

Werner and Fenton (1970) note but fail to develop fully that 'The lexical field of taxonomy may be particularly important because its semantic representation is closely linked to the paradigm by the condition of set theoretical inclusion... The taxonomic field is therefore the automatic by-product of the correct componential paradigmatic solution.'

The apparent contradiction of 'relative independence' and 'closely linked' is due to the failure of the star operation to be easily applicable to taxonomies. This we shall remedy with the introduction of a new operation called 'circle star' or '⊛'.

We consider the entire vocabulary of a language to be a multidimensional space. Although the 'components' within a 'componential definition' $C(i)$ are not ordered, the dimensions are strictly ordered according to their generality. We define the 'circle star' operation as follows: Given the dimensions $D(o), D(1), D(2), ..., D(i), ...,$ $D(n)$ we form F the lexical/semantic field.

47 $F \rightarrow D(o) \circledast D(1) \circledast D(2) \circledast ... \circledast D(i) \circledast ... \circledast D(n) =$
   $D(o)$,
   $D(o) * D(1)$,
   $D(o) * D(1) * D(2)$,
   . . . .
   $D(o) * D(1) * D(2) * ... * D(i)$,
   . . . .
   $D(o) * D(1) * D(2) * ... * D(i) * ... * D(n)$

The 'star' operation is applied anew each time a new dimension is added until all dimensions are exhausted. The 'circle star' operation corresponds to the 'star' operation applied repeatedly in the above manner.

Since all sets of $D(o)$ are contained in the paradigmatic definitions in $C(i)$ of the set $D(o) * D(1)$, all members of set $D(o)$ represent superordinate taxa to $D(o) * D(1)$, and so on. If the taxonomy of the entire language has one unique 'origin' or 'beginner', then $D(o)$ has but one value; the most general set of attributes or the most general attribute available in the language. More likely, perhaps every language operates with a *set* of very general taxa. In that case D(o) will be appropriately multi-valued; one value for each major taxonomy.

We will use as a partial and limited illustration of the 'circle star' operation the taxonomy and asymmetrical paradigm published by Berlin, Breedlove and Raven (1968).

The dimensions are as follows (there is an obvious misprint in Table 4 (p. 295) which disagrees with Fig. 3 (p. 294); we will assume their (A) to be the marker of the attribute (vine (x)) 'the uniting feature of the total set' (ibid.: 294) and dimension B accordingly as stem *and* leaf texture, etc.):

48a D(o) a certain vine called /'ak'/ = {(vine (x))}
   D(1) stem and leaf texture   = {b(1) hairy; b(2) spiney}
   D(2) flower color   = {c(1) white; c(2) yellow}
   D(3) fruit shape   = {d(1) disk-like; d(2) elongated}
   D(4) leaf color   = {e(1) relatively light; e(2) relatively dark}
   D(5) fruit size   = {f(1) large; f(2) small}
   D(6) color of meat of fruit   = {g(1) yellow; g(2) white}

48b The 'circle star' operation:
   F → D(o) ⊛ D(1) ⊛ D(2) ⊛ D(3) ⊛ D(4) ⊛ D(5) ⊛ D(6)
   1.   D(o)
   2.   D(o) * D(1)
   3.   D(o) * D(1) * D(2)
   4.   D(o) * D(1) * D(2) * D(3)
   5.   D(o) * D(1) * D(2) * D(3) * D(4)
   6.   D(o) * D(1) * D(2) * D(3) * D(4) * D(5)
   7.   D(o) * D(1) * D(2) * D(3) * D(4) * D(5) * D(6)

Obviously D(o) represents ((vine(X)), /'ak'/) (we have substituted slashes to symbolize the phonemic transcription of Berlin et al. (1968)).

This structure with 177 combinatorial possibilities is obviously too rich for the mere five plant names dominated by /'ak'/ given in Table 4 (p. 295): (transcription slightly modified; the English and Latin botanical terms are merely translation labels).

48c (((vine (x)), /'ak'/)   *vines*
   (((vine (x)), b(1), c(1), d(1), e(1)), /bohch/)   *large gourd*
   (((vine (x)), b(1), c(1), d(2), e(1)), /tsu/)   *bottle gourd*
   (((vine (x)), b(2), c(2), d(2), e(1), f(2), g(2)), /mayil/)   *cucurbita ficico*
   (((vine (x)), b(2), c(2), d(1), e(2), f(1), g(2)), /ch'um/)   *cucurbita moschata*
   (((vine (x)), b(2), c(2), d(1), e(2), f(2), g(1)), /ts'ol/)   *cucurbita pepo*

In order to reduce the structure we reduce the number of dimensions by combining them and noting their restricted co-occurrence in **48c**.

Flower color and leaf texture do not vary independently. We therefore set up a single dimension: (The effect of these rules is restated in English under each reduction rule).

49a $D(1) * D(2) \Rightarrow D(12) = ((b(1), c(1)), (b(2), c(2)))$

That is, hairy stem and leaf do not co-occur with yellow flowers, nor spiney stem and leaf with white flowers.

Further simplification is obtained if we collapse in the same manner dimensions three with four and five with six:

49b $D(3) * D(4) \Rightarrow D(34) = ((d(1), e(1)), (d(1), e(2)), (d(2), e(1)))$

That is, elongated fruit shape and relatively dark leaf color do not co-occur.

49c $D(5) * D(6) \Rightarrow D(56) = ((f(1), g(2)), (f(2), g(1)), (f(2), g(2)))$

That is, large fruit and yellow meat do not co-occur.

This simplifies the 'circle star' operation considerably.

50a $F \rightarrow D(o) \circledast D(12) \circledast D(34) \circledast D(56)$
     1. $D(o)$
     2. $D(o) * D(12)$
     3. $D(o) * D(12) * D(34)$
     4. $D(o) * D(12) * D(34) * D(56)$

Leaf and stem texture and flower color are insufficient attributes for the characterization of any plants in Tzeltal. They are not specific enough for naming. Therefore we have to eliminate line 2 by a neutralization rule

50b   If $D(34) * D(56) \Rightarrow \emptyset$ (i.e. are not present), then set $D(o) * D(12) \Rightarrow \emptyset$ (i.e. is also absent)

That is, if further attributes are lacking, leaf and stem texture and flower color alone are insufficient for naming. Neutralization rule **50b** is of the same type as Werner and Fenton's (1970) 'total neutralization' of a dimension or of several dimensions. In order to further reduce the structure of **50a** we need 'partial neutralization' rules.

50c   If $D(12) \Rightarrow (b(1), c(1))$, then
         $D(34) \Rightarrow ((d(1), e(1)), (d(2), e(1)))$ and
         $D(56) \Rightarrow \emptyset$

That is, if leaf texture is hairy and flower color is white, then only relatively light leaf color occurs, and fruit size and color of the meat of the fruit are irrelevant.

50d   If $D(12) \Rightarrow (b(2), c(2))$, then
         $D(34) \Rightarrow ((d(1), e(2)), (d(2), e(1)))$ and
         $D(56) \Rightarrow \emptyset$

That is, if leaf and stem texture are spiney and the flower color is yellow the fruit shape and leaf color are either disk–like and relatively dark or elongated and relatively light respectively, and fruit size and the color of the meat of the fruit is relevant.

Note that the asymmetry expressed by the neutralization rules are *empirical facts* of the Tzeltal flora provided the discriminational judgments of the Tzeltal people are set to work. That is, the 'components' and their combination express the Tzeltal's knowledge of botany rather than of their language. It is clear from Berlin et al. (1968) that the values of their dimensions are based on informant responses. Unfortunately no Tzeltal sentences are presented. We suspect that the neutralization rules correspond to Tzeltal cultural knowledge and are very likely on a level of awareness which is easily accessible through language.

The application of the 'circle star' operation of **50a** and the neutralization rules **50b** to **50d** give the correct solution; the single level taxonomy:

50e

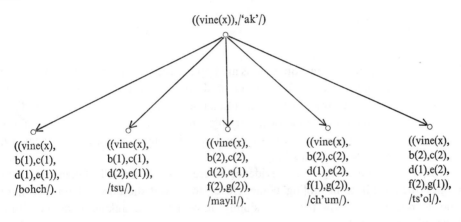

We provide the following schema, **50f**, in order to give a graphic illustration of the clustering of the five terms. The term /'ak'/ is the dominating node for all of these terms. As Berlin et al. have found in their 'triad test' /bohch/ and /tsu/ are related. While the latter is closest to /mayil/, /ts'o/ is also near to /mayil/, similarly /ch'um/ is close to /ts'o/. If we were looking for covert unlabeled taxa on the basis of shared features /tsu/ and /mayil/ appear about equally as close as /tsu/ and /bohch/. The informant's responses and 'additional evidence' point to the clustering of /bohch/ with /tsu/ and /ch'um/ with /ts'ol/, the latter two with /mayil/ exactly as presented by Berlin et al. (1968:296).

We accept the clustering as a 'psychological fact'; the Tzeltal seem clearly aware of it. The clustering is also the result of the asymmetry of the paradigm which structures the single level taxonomy of /'ak'/.

50f

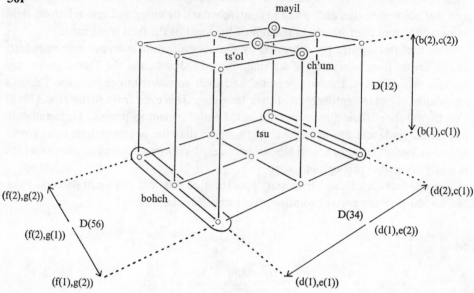

If the 'circle star' and/or 'star' operations are applied with the appropriate empirically justified neutralization rules, there is no need to proliferate 'zero lexemes'. This should obviously not distract from the fact that the maximally asymmetrical paradigm is a taxonomy and an asymmetrical paradigm may convert to a taxonomy if the clustering of terms reaches consciousness and there is a need to create a new category, for example, for ease of expression.

It would be interesting to see evidence where this has actually taken place. In English the kinship term 'sibling' comes closest to it. But should we claim that those who do not use or know the term 'sibling' have a covert, unlabeled taxon within their cultural competence?

We will now try to demonstrate that the 'circle star' operation in conjunction with a convention of 'indexing' substantially simplifies the presentation of the Berlin et al. (1968) data and other data as well. The definition of dimensions is the same as before in **48a**, however we will start immediately with the 'collapsed' dimensions of **50a**. The componential definitions remain the same as in **48c**.

In order to make this relatively abstract representation heuristically most useful we will develop its representation first for the taxonomy **50e** without paradigmatic structuring. This corresponds closely to the *first stage* of our method in lexicographic fieldwork (e.g. Werner and Begishe 1969b), when a large number of taxonomic relations is elicited. This procedure follows our heuristic corollary **45b** requiring explicit sentences of classification in the language in question. This is what Werner and Begishe (1969b and c) have done for the Navajo vocabulary of *hats'i7i7s* 'body' and *nitsa7ha7kees* 'thought'.

The *next step* in the field procedures is to work out the contrasts on each level of taxonomy by eliciting additional non–taxonomic sentences. Such sentences may and sometimes do identify some components as belonging to intersecting taxonomies. (see our example of 'father' in **36**). Accordingly we will introduce the expansion of taxonomic levels to paradigms as a second step.

We now write the 'circle star' operation of the first stage of eliciting as follows:

51a $F \rightarrow D(o) \circledast D(123456)$ with

$D(123456) = (k(1), k(2), k(3), k(4), k(5))$

1. $D(o)$
2. $D(o) * D(123456)$

Where $D(123456)$ stands for the contraction of the five dimensions and $k(1)$ to $k(5)$ correspond to the attribute clusters of the five lexical items /bohch, tsu, mayil, ts'ol/ and /ch'um/.

We can now commence the second step of investigating the paradigmatic structure of our single level taxonomy:

51b $\begin{Bmatrix} k(1) \\ k(2) \end{Bmatrix} \rightarrow D(o) * D(12) * 1D(34)$

Where the prefix '1' is a convention which indicates that $D(34)$ is to combine *only* with the first element of $D(12)$, and $1D(34)$, as in this case, may assume a value or values different from $D(34)$, but $1D(34) \subseteq D(34)$.

51c $1D(34) \Rightarrow ((d(1), e(1)), (d(2), e(1)))$

That is, if the leaf and stem are hairy and the flower white, then the leaves *cannot* be relatively dark and the fruit *cannot* be disk-like (i.e. NOT(d(1), e(2) the third member of $D(34)$).

51d $\begin{Bmatrix} k(3) \\ k(4) \\ k(5) \end{Bmatrix} \rightarrow D(o) * D(12) * 2D(34) * \begin{Bmatrix} 1D(56) \\ 2D(56) \end{Bmatrix}$

$2D(34) \Rightarrow ((d(1), e(2)), (d(2), e(1)))$

$1D(56) \Rightarrow ((f(1), g(2)), (f(2), g(1)))$

$2D(56) \Rightarrow (f(2), g(2))$

That is, if the leaf and stem are spiney and the flowers yellow, then, (1) the leaf color is relatively dark and the fruit is disk-like, large with white meat or disk-like, small with yellow meat; or, (2) The leaf color is relatively light and the fruit is elongated, small with white meat. We have thus made the structure of $D(123456)$ explicit and can rewrite **51a**:

52a $F \rightarrow D(o) \circledast D(12) * \begin{Bmatrix} 1D(34) \\ 2D(34) * \begin{Bmatrix} 1D(56) \\ 2D(56) \end{Bmatrix} \end{Bmatrix}$

Note that no additional rules are required. The format of **52a** takes care of all 'neutralizations'.

Thus we apply the 'circle star' operator only up to the point to which it is productive. Had we applied it beyond D(12) in **52a** it would have resulted in two additional lines which represent no *lexical* reality. That is, if we had used the 'circle star' operation throughout **52a**, it would have given us three *additional* lexically unlabeled *taxonomic* nodes, i.e. the unlabeled, covert nodes postulated by Berlin et al. (1968). Whether one uses such covert, unlabeled taxons or not seems to us a matter of taste. We prefer to avoid unlabeled nodes although their avoidance does make our formulae, like **36a** *more complex* since we have to use two operators: 'circle star' and 'star'. If we allow for covert nodes the 'circle star' operation could have been used exclusively.

A compromise solution is possible. If the structures on one level of a taxonomy are *well worked out* then we will permit covert taxonomic labels, but only if the condition of taxonomy is met: (A) ⊃ (B), for (A) the subordinate taxon, and (B) the dominating taxon.

We can graph **52a** in the following fashion for somewhat greater clarity (the dotted lines connect covert nodes):

52b

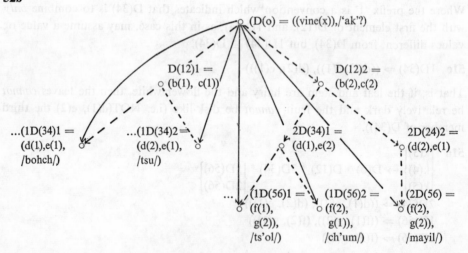

Note that /mayil/ is overspecified. If that is disregarded we are left with the three covert, unlabeled nodes of Berlin et al. (1968). Thus by ignoring the redundancy of (f(2), g(2)) the proximity of /mayil/ to /tsu/ becomes apparent as it did in our previous illustration **50f**. It is an interesting question as to why the Tzeltal informants do not recognize this similarity. We hypothesize that in graphs like **52b** sharing of a bundle of attributes (components) by two terms on the same branch of the tree graph (sister nodes) is perceived as greater similarity than between two terms with the same number of shared components which are on different branches.

In graph **52b** the dotted lines represent Tzeltal covert, implicit taxonomy of /'ak'/; the solid lines the overt, explicit taxonomy **50e**. Because the relation of taxonomy — overt as well as covert — is transitive, the overt explicit taxonomy *is* fully *contained* in the covert implicit taxonomy. This is as it should be: (as we remarked before) explicit knowledge must be contained in a wider implicit knowledge. The intuitively correct outcome is reassuring.

In the first solution we used one 'circle star' rule **50a**, one neutralization rule **50b**, and two partial neutralization rules **50c** and **50d**. The second solution required in the end only one rule with all the 'neutralizations' 'built in' (**52a**). We will now attempt to make our second solution general.

First we define the semantic representations at an arbitrary node in a taxonomy.

53a $d(i,j,k,m)$ with the following meaning:

  i = the i-th level of the taxonomy
  j = the j-th node on the i-th level (from left to right)
  k = the in degree of the (i, j)-th node
  m = the out degree of the (i, j)-th node

53b i = $\emptyset$ for nodes on the initial level
  i = i for nodes on the i-th level
  j = 1 leftmost node on a level
  j = j rightmost node on a level
  k = $\emptyset$ in degree zero, 'origins' or 'beginners'
  k = 1 regular taxonomy
  k > intersection of taxonomies
  m = the out degree of the (i, j)-th node or the number of nodes dominated by the (i,j)-th node.
  m = $\emptyset$ terminal nodes of a taxonomy

The rules of combination for an arbitrary node $d(i, j, k, m)$ of a taxonomy are (assuming k on the $(i+1)$-st level is equal 1).

53c $F \rightarrow \ldots \circledast d(i,j,k,m,) \circledast d(i+1, j+1, 1, n) \circledast \ldots$

  . . . .

  $d(i+1, j+m, 1, p)$

The d on the $(i+1)$-st level are a dimension $D((i+1), ((j+1)$ to $(j+m), m)$. It has m members $d((i+1), \ldots)$ and all members have the indegree of 1.

The next step in the analysis is to determine whether the dimensions $D((i+1), \ldots)$ are further structured. The number of combinatorial possibilities without empirical constraints is so great that it is difficult to give a general account of all possible paradigmatic solutions (see Burling 1964, and Nerlove and Romney 1967).

The notation of **47c** applied to **46a** yields

54 $F \rightarrow D(\emptyset), 1, \emptyset, 2) ~^\circledast D(1, 1–2, 1, 2–2) * \begin{Bmatrix} D(2, 1–2, 1, \emptyset) \\ D(2, 1–2, 1, 2) \end{Bmatrix}$
$* \begin{Bmatrix} D(3, 1–2, 1, \emptyset) \\ D(3, 1, 1, \emptyset) \end{Bmatrix}$

Where 1–2 in the j column means there are two values for the dimension, and 2–2 in the m column that each of the two values has an outdegree of 2. Following our previous discussion, the 'star' operation after D(1, ...) may be replaced by the 'circle star' operation if covert, implicit nodes are permitted.

There are numerous problems. We are uncertain whether our general statement (or our particular example) is capable of producing intersecting taxonomies. More importantly, rule **52a** or **54** are rules for the formation for 'set-strings' of components (or binary semantic relations) which are unordered. Some of these 'set-strings' are well formed and part of our solution; others are not. Possibly they could be generated more economically with some kind of formal 'set grammar' or some set generation rules. In fact, our rules **52a** and **54** are set generating rules; the neutralization rules, whether separately stated as in the first solution, or 'built in' as in the second solution, are environmental constraints.

Perhaps the major problem of the 'componential model' is that although it automatically generates all componential sets with overt, explicit associated phonological representations of lexical items or naming units (if we wish we can also generate componential sets that are unlabeled), and all taxonomic relations are an automatic by-product of the generation, other lexical relations cannot be represented at present at all; for example, the relation of general attribution. This relation is representable only within a taxonomy. We have no device to show attributive relations *between* taxonomies, as in our previous examples of 'cattle ranch' and 'ranch cattle'. This hopefully does not mean that such 'devices' cannot be found in principle.

On the other hand, the model provides us with a powerful strategy of investigation, at least of fields that are taxonomically structured. Explicit, verbalizable taxonomies are, therefore, our first goal, followed by subsequent investigations of each level for paradigms, symmetrical or asymmetrical and covert taxons or taxonomies. We have no rules for the proper componential or implicit solution. However, we have one important check, namely, that the appropriate taxonomic relations *must* be an automatic by-product of our componential solutions.

3. CONCLUSION

Of the four models proposed in these pages the first was of the least utility. The other three, regardless of their theoretical motivation, or the absence thereof, suggest potentially fruitful avenues of investigation; they are heuristic devices. But ultimately they go beyond that. We have presented three viable models for the representation of the entire vocabulary of a language.

Bierman's one page dictionary model seems to be in part included in the componential solution. We have found a congruence between binary semantic relations (as actual sentences, parts of sentences, or implicitly) and components, features or semantic markers. So far the one page model is most useful for eliciting taxonomies. The componential model implies that this is the proper procedure, and that all other relations are deeper and are better approached *after* the taxonomic relations have been worked out.

Bierman's inverse model allowed us to see the close relationship between taxonomy and synonymy and the interdependence of taxonomy, synonymy and attribution. It allowed us to view attribution as a much broader and encompassing relation than heretofore. It also helped us to see how more complex relations involving complex plans fit into the ethnosemantic framework.

Although we are keenly interested in theory, the payoff of these pages has been primarily in heuristics. We sincerely hope that others will become interested in our four (minus one) models and will through them (or in spite of them) contribute to researches into the formal nature of lexical/semantic fields and thus into the nature of the structure of cultural knowledge.

4. APPENDICES

4.1 *Appendix A: Some Notational Conventions and Generalizations*

Following Reichenbach (1947:80) it has become customary to symbolize the following sentences as $f(x)$:

1a 'A lion is an animal.'   as $A(L)$
     (L)   (A)
1b 'Lions are dangerous.'   as $D(L)$
     (L)   (D)
1c 'The head is part of a lion.'   as $PL(H)$
     (H)   (PL)
1d 'Lions eat zebras.'   as $EZ(L)$
     (L)   (EZ)

The last two sentences could be considered two–place or two–argument functions and could be written:

1e $P(H, L)$ and
1f $E(L, Z)$.

We reject this notation in favor of a relational notation.

Sentence **1a** expresses the relation of taxonomy. We symbolized this in section 1. as follows:

2a $(L)TAXN(A)$

We can symbolize the relation in **1b** similarly, but the relation is not taxonomic but attributive:

2b   (L)ATTR(D)

The functional notation of Reichenbach fails to distinguish the fact that in f(x) the relation between x and f is not always the same. 'In symbolic logic, this syntactical relation is created by the parentheses' (Reichenbach 1947:81-2). The syntactic relation of the parentheses is semantically ambiguous. Since our problem is semantic we prefer to make the relation created by the parentheses explicit and unambiguous. By following the relational convention we do not negate the fact that different semantic relations may be realized in the same way syntactically.

Examples **1c** and **d** are more complex. The predicates are nested (Weinreich 1963:130 ff.) rather than linked.

Stated explicitly, Reichenbach's function 'alpha' (Reichenbach 1947:229) is not, as he claims, a dispensable constant (Weinreich 1963:158n). This 'metarelation alpha', contrary to Reichenbach and in agreement with Weinreich, has the empirical content of 'semantic relation' (ibid.). In Reichenbach's notation f(x) is represented in the 'ALPHA' notation

3   ALPHA(f, x), which corresponds after application to **3** to **2a** TAXN(A, L); or **3** to **2b** ATTR(L, D).

Although there are advantages to be gained by using the 'Polish' system of notation (namely **2b**) we prefer for the sake of clarity to retain the notational convention of **2a**.

We consider lexical items to be of the form ((C), (P)). Since we are dealing with semantic relations except in the citation of actual sentences we will suppress (P), the phonological representation.

We know that semantic components are unordered or a set; generally

4a $C(n) = \{a, b, c, ..., i, ... n\}$, specifically
4b $C(animal) = \{animal\}$
4c $C(lion) = \{lion\}$

(We will use parentheses for the ease of typing and typesetting.)

Where animal and lion are the 'components' of 'animal' and 'lion' respectively. What is meant by

4d   (lion) TAXN (animal)?

Considering that C(tiger) = (tiger) we also get

4e   (tiger) TAXN (animal)

That is, both (tiger) and (lion) must contain all features of (animal) since both tigers and lions are animals. Both must contain something *in addition to* (animal) that distinguishes them from (animal), as well as from each other: Some bundle of features (L') in the case of 'lion', and some bundle of features (T') in the case of 'tiger'. However, since both (animal) and (lion) are unordered sets the 'in addition to' must be set-theoretical union:

5a (lion) = (animal) $\cup$ (L') and

5b (lion) TAXN (animal) = (animal) $\cup$ (L') TAX (animal) =

5c (animal) $\cup$ (L') $\supset$ (animal)

We conclude (without committing ourselves with regard to the nature of semantic components, assuming only that the bundles of components associated with lexical items are unordered) that the relation of TAXN (taxonomy = '____ is a (kind of) ___') corresponds to set-theoretical inclusion; that is, all the components of 'animal' are contained among the components of 'lion'.

This appears counter-intuitive: the class of lions *is contained* in the class of animals. But in the preceding sentence we are not talking about the components or features; more precisely, attributes of lions, but about *actual* lions or *examples* of lions ex((lion), (LION)). If we introduce the convention that (x)ex((C),(P)) = 'there is an x such that ex is an example of ((C), (P))', then

6 All (x)ex((lion), (LION)) $\subset$ All (x)ex((animal), (ANIMAL))

'The extension of a term is the class of entities to which the term is applicable or refers; the intension of a term is the set of attributes which characterize any entity to which the term is correctly applied. Extension [our **6**] and intension [our **5c**] vary inversely in relation to one another: The greater the extension of a term, the less the intension; and conversely' (Lyons 1968:454). In other words, the more general a term the fewer attributes it has. From this follow some important generalizations:

(A) This allows us to deal with transitive sentences like **1d**:

7a 'Lions eat Zebras'   EZ(L)

7b 'Zebras are eaten by lions'   EL(Z)

   (Z)   (EL)

Nominalized with 'eating' as the head construction:

7c 'The eating of zebras by lions ...'

7d 'The eating by lions of zebras ...' but

7e 'Zebra eating by lions ...'

Because

7f (The eating of zebras by lions)TAXN(eating) and

7g (Zebra eating by lions)TAXN(eating), it follows, because of

7h ((A) $\cup$ (attributes)) $\supset$ (A) and

7i (Zebra eating)TAXN(eating), (writing modifier always to the right of the modified term), that

7j   (((eat)ATTR(zebra))ATTR(lion))TAXN(eat), or
7k   (((eat) ∪ (zebra)) ∪ (lion)) ⊃ (eat)

The structure of the non-nominalized transitive sentence is thus:

7l   (lion ∪ ((eat) ∪ (zebra))

Should (eat) turn out to be more complex, as the generative semanticists claim, this can be easily accommodated since we did not commit ourselves with regard to the complexity of the bundle of attributes of (eat) that is, the internal structure of (eat). Causatives, volitionals, tenses, modes, etc. 'within' (eat) are easily accommodated as additional modifiers of some basic, deeper level.

The relation of ATTR (attribution, or union ∪, can accommodate the three different possible nominalizations of **7a** and its semantic structure **7l**:

8a   'Zebra eating lions ...'
8b   (*lion*)ATTR((eat)ATTR(zebra)) ...
8c   'Zebras eaten by lions ...'
8d   ((*zebra*)ATTR(eat))ATTR(lion) ...
8e   'Zebra eating by lions ...'
8f   ((*eat*)ATTR(zebra))ATTR(lion) ...

Note that
8g   'Zebra eating ...'

corresponds to ((*eat*)ATTR(zebra)) and

8h   'Eaten zebras ...'

corresponds to (*zebra*)ATTR(eat) ....

Although our notation is unambiguous we have supplied the italics in the incomplete sentences to mark the head of the phrase and the subject of the main sentence.

Our notational convention has the advantage that it treats nouns and verbs alike as contentives. (This is congruent with the possibility of nominalization of the verbs for use as subject and the possible use of nouns as verbs and attributes.) Additional complexity can be introduced as it becomes known, for example:

9a   'The heart is part of the body.'
9b   (heart)TAXN((part)ATTR(body))

which explains the taxonomic conversion of the part-to-whole relation

9c   'The heart is a kind of body part.'
9d   'Zebra eating is for lions.' ('... is for of lions.')
9e   ((eat)ATTR(zebra))ATTR((for)ATTR(lion))

Plurality is probably also an attribute which, for these examples, we have suppressed. Our notational convention completely binarizes all semantic relations and all well formed semantic relations obey the simple 'grammar' of **11a** in section 1. In a similar fashion most of Casagrande and Hale's semantic relations may be reduced to two: the relation of attribution ATTR or union and the relation of taxonomy TAXN or inclusion. We are at a loss concerning the interpretation of set-theoretical intersection.

(B) 'Things, entities or concepts' are convenient bundles of attributes. 'Convenience' refers to 'entitativity' (some perception of the attributes as belonging together) and naming. For example the attributes (L') in **5a** are not a 'convenient' bundle of attributes, only (animal) or 'animalness' and (animal, L') = (animal) U (L'), or 'lionness' are 'convenient' bundles of attributes. The bundle (L') is used nowhere else in the entire vocabulary.

Concepts are proliferated by attribution, our relation ATTR in **2b** corresponds to set-theoretical union of attributes. The relation of taxonomy and attribution are closely related:

10a $((A)ATTR(B))TAXN(A)$

is equivalent to

10b $((A) \cup (B)) \supset (A)$

Semantics is a calculus of attributes.

(C) General concepts are learned before specific concepts. The smaller the vocabulary of a person the more general must be its application. We learn discrimination of attributes as we learn more. The less we know, the fewer attributes we distinguish. The anecdote of children applying 'mama' to all humans, then to all females, and finally to their mother is a case in point (Kuhn 1962). We should not be deceived by the sound of 'mama' and its adult associations.

(D) The principle of the economy of attributes. In order for language to be an effective tool of communication it must be less rich than the world. We are constantly forced to suppress attributes in favor of others that are more criterial for our classes of objects and hence our lives. An overly rich language would be as useless as a 1:1 scale map (Polanyi 1958:81).

(E) Attributes are predicates. Bundles of attributes are also potential predicates. The noun-verb distinction appears to be a convention, stating approximately, 'This bundle of attributes in this language is preferably used as a subject or object' ..., '... and this preferably as a predicate'.

(F) If following **5c** we have (animal) $\cup$ (L') $\supset$ (animal) and we replace $\supset$ by $\supseteq$; i.e. (animal) is contained or equal to (the same as) the attributes (animal) in union with the attributes (L') that characterize a lion, then synonymy is the limiting case. That is:

$$\text{If } (B) \supseteq (A)$$
$$\text{And } (A) \supseteq (B)$$
$$\text{Then } (A) = (B)$$

and $((A), (A))$ and $((B), (B))$ are synonyms. Synonymy is the limiting case of the relation of taxonomy. Two taxa on different levels of a taxonomy and directly (distance 1) connected to that node are partial synonyms. If $(C) \supset (A)$, then A and C are partial synonyms (see also Lyons 1968:455–56).

(G) Our formalism makes the relation of taxonomy completely explicit.

10c If $(C) \supset (A)$ then $(C)\text{TAXN}(A)$ or $((C), (C))\text{TAXN}((A), (A))$.

The relation of class inclusion automatically takes care of multiple intersecting taxonomies which Werner and Fenton (1970) have called 'Supertaxonomies'. That is

10d If $(C) \supset \begin{Bmatrix} (A1) \\ (A2) \\ \vdots \\ (An) \end{Bmatrix}$, then $(C)\text{TAX} \begin{Bmatrix} (A1) \\ (A2) \\ \vdots \\ (An) \end{Bmatrix}$

We can illustrate the full impact of this fact as follows:

10e

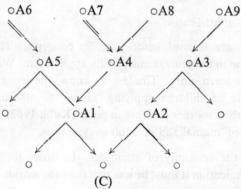

(C)

$(C) \supset (A1)$, $(C) \supset (A2)$ where $(C) = (A1) \cup (A2) \cup (C1)$ and $(A1) \nparallel (A2)$ and $(A1) \cap (A2) = \emptyset$. Note, however, that, for example: $(A1) \supset (A5) \supset (A6)$; $(A2) \supset (A3) \supset (A9)$.

(H) Many attributes such as (L') for lions and (T') for tigers are not verbalized because of the principle of the economy of semantic features. Taxonomies bring lexical items together into systems and by linking them taxonomically $(A) \cup (K) \supset (A)$. We are thus avoiding the need for the verbalization of the highly unique class attribute (K). In other words taxonomies allow us to reduce the number of verbalized attributes. The 'occasional sentences' of a language constantly create new combinations of attributes, usually in the form of complex sentences. If a complex sentence occurs too frequently we tend to invent a new term and reduce complexity.

4.2 *Appendix B: The Entries of 'Think' and 'Thought' (in* Roget's International Thesaurus, 3rd ed., 1962)

Words not contained in the retrievals from about 50 articles of the *Webster's Collegiate Dictionary* (1953) are underscored.

think
nouns idea 478.1
  opinion 500.4
verbs cogitate 477.7
  ~ about 477.10
  reason 481.15
  suppose 498.9
  opine 500.9
  care 531.6
  expect 537.4
  intend 651.4
NOT THINK
  not consider 479.2
  neglect 532.6
NOT TO BE THOUGHT
  OF
  impossible 509.6
  rejected 636.3
  refused 774.7
  prohibited 776.7
  hopeless 887.14
  objectionable
    967.25
THINK BACK 535.11
THINK BEST 635.14
THINK BETTER OF
  reconsider 477.14
  repent 871.7
THINK FIT
  will 619.2
  be willing 620.3
  prefer 635.14
THINK HARD
  think 477.8
  remember 535.21
THINK HIGHLY OF
  value 670.12
  respect 962.4
THINK IT OVER
  477.13
THINK LITTLE OF
  underestimate 497.2
  disregard 529.3
  not hesitate 622.10
  unimportant 671.11
THINK NOTHING OF
  underestimate 497.2
  not hesitate 622.10
  unimportant 671.11
  take it easy 730.10
  disdain 964.3
THINK OF
  think 477.15
  judge 493.8
  remember 535.11
  intend 651.7

be considerate
  936.11
THINK OUT 166.14
THINK OUT LOUD
  discuss 481.16
  speculate 498.8
  soliloquize 596.3
THINK OVER 477.12
THINK THE WORLD OF
  929.18
THINK THROUGH
  477.10
THINK TWICE
  be uncertain 513.10
  be cautious 893.5
THINK UP 166.14
thinkable
  possible 508.6
  imaginable 533.26
thinker
  wise man 467.1
  reasoner 481.12
thinking
nouns thought 477.1
  opinion 500.4
adjs. mental 465.6
  thoughtful 477.20
thinking machine
  348.16
thought
  small amount 35.4
  tinge 44.7
  thinking 477.1
  idea 478.1
  reasoning 481
  opinion 500.4
  heed 528.1
  expectation 537.1
  considerateness
    936.3
ENGAGED IN THOUGHT
  477.21
GIVE THOUGHT TO
  477.10
NOT GIVE A THOUGHT
  TO 532.6
NOT GIVE IT ANOTHER
  THOUGHT 945.5
thought-challenging
  528.19
thoughted 478.12
thought-free 479.4
thought-freeness 479.1

thoughtful
  judicious 466.19
  contemplative
    477.20
  careful 531.10
  serious 869.3
  considerate 936.17
thoughtfulness
  judiciousness 466.7
  pensiveness 477.3
  care 531.1
  seriousness 869.1
  considerateness
    936.3
thought-giving 528.19
thought-inspiring
  528.19
thoughtless
  foolish 469.8.9
  thought-free 479.4
  giddy 530.16
  careless 552.11
  impulsive 628.10
  improvident 719.15
  inconsiderate
    937.16
thoughtlessness
  foolishness 469.1
  injudiciousness
    469.2
  thought-freeness
    479.1
  inattention 529.1
  giddiness 530.5
  carelessness 532.2
  impulsiveness 628.3
  improvidence 719.2
  inconsiderateness
    937.3
thought-provoking
  interesting 528.19
  suggestive 544.6
thoughts 477.4
PUT OUT OF ONE'S
  THOUGHTS 529.4
UPPERMOST IN ONE'S
  THOUGHTS 535.23
thought transference
  1032.9

4.3   *Appendix C: List of Sentences on 'Thought'* (*from* Webster's Collegiate Dictionary, 1953).

(1)   Entity is a thing or being for thought.

Thought is an act of thinking.

Thought is an act of thought.

Thought is a kind of entity of mind.

Thought is a kind of act of an entity of mind.

Thought is a kind of act of mind.

Thought is the process of thinking.

Thought is the product of thinking.

Thought is that which is in one's mind.

Thought is a kind of process of mind.

Thought is a kind of product of mind.

Thought is a kind of content of mind.

What is in one's mind is included in one's mind.

What is included in one's mind is the content of one's mind.

A product is anything produced, as by generation, growth, labor of thought.

Thought is a kind of process.

Thought is a kind of product of the process of mind.

Thought is a kind of product of thought.

Thought is the capacity to think.

Thought is the capacity of thought.

An act of mind is a kind of an act.

$$\left.\begin{array}{l} \text{Act of mind (thought)} \\ \text{Process of mind (thought)} \\ \text{Product of thought (mind)} \\ \text{Content of mind (thought)} \\ \text{Capacity of thought (mind)} \end{array}\right\} \text{is a kind of entity of mind.}$$

$$\left.\begin{array}{l} \text{Thought} \\ \text{Thinking} \\ \text{Adduction} \\ \text{(Deduction)} \\ \text{Comprehension} \\ \text{Conception} \\ \text{Conclusion} \\ \text{Perception} \\ \text{Realization} \\ \text{Understanding} \end{array}\right\} \text{is a kind of act of thought.}$$

$$\left.\begin{array}{l}\text{Thought}\\ \text{Thinking}\\ \text{Cogitation}\\ \text{Cogitating}\\ \text{Imagining}\\ \text{Meditation}\\ \text{Meditating}\\ \text{Reasoning}\\ \text{Reflection}\\ \text{Reflecting}\end{array}\right\}$$ is a kind of process of thought.

$$\left.\begin{array}{l}\text{Thought}\\ \text{Thinking}\\ \text{Adduction}\\ \text{Deduction}\\ \text{Comprehension}\\ \text{Conclusion}\\ \text{Fancy}\\ \text{Idea}\\ \text{Judgment}\\ \text{Notion}\\ \text{Opinion}\\ \text{Perception}\\ \text{Reason}\\ \text{Understanding}\\ \text{Principle}\\ \text{System (of thought)}\\ \text{View (point)}\\ \text{Conception}\\ \text{Realization}\end{array}\right\}$$ is a kind of result of thought.

$$\left.\begin{array}{l}\text{Adduction}\\ \text{Deduction}\\ \text{Comprehension}\\ \text{Conception}\\ \text{Judgment}\\ \text{Perception}\\ \text{Reason}\\ \text{Understanding}\end{array}\right\}$$ is a kind of $$\left.\begin{array}{l}\text{capacity}\\ \text{power}\\ \text{faculty}\\ \text{ability}\end{array}\right\}$$ of thought.

Thought is a $$\left.\begin{array}{l}\text{distinct entity}\\ \text{real thing}\\ \text{existent being}\\ \text{mental object (mind?)}\end{array}\right\}$$

Reason is the power of comprehension.

Reason is the power of inference.

Reason is a kind of power.

Thought is reasoning power.

Capacity of thought is capacity of reason.

The capacity of reason is an aspect of the capacity of thought.

Reason is the $\begin{Bmatrix} \text{capacity} \\ \text{power} \\ \text{faculty} \end{Bmatrix}$ of reasoning.

Comprehension is an aspect of reason.

Inference is an aspect of reason.

Reason is an aspect of $\begin{Bmatrix} \text{intellect.} \\ \text{sanity.} \\ \text{sense.} \end{Bmatrix}$

$\begin{Bmatrix} \text{Reason} \\ \text{Intellect} \\ \text{Sense} \\ \text{Sanity} \end{Bmatrix}$ is good.

Lack of $\begin{Bmatrix} \text{reason} \\ \text{intellect} \\ \text{sense} \\ \text{sanity} \end{Bmatrix}$ is bad.

$\begin{Bmatrix} \text{Comprehension} \\ \text{Inference} \end{Bmatrix}$ is an aspect of reason.

Intellect is an aspect of reason.

$\begin{Bmatrix} \text{Comprehension} \\ \text{Inference} \end{Bmatrix}$ is an aspect of intellect.

$\begin{Bmatrix} \text{Adduction} \\ \text{Deduction} \end{Bmatrix}$ is a kind of inference.

$\begin{Bmatrix} \text{Conception} \\ \text{Judgment} \end{Bmatrix}$ is an aspect of intellect.

Judgment is an aspect of sense.

Perception is an aspect of sense.

Imagination is an aspect of intellect.

The capacity of reasoning is an aspect of the capacity of thought.

$\begin{Bmatrix} \text{Act of mind (thought)} \\ \text{Process of mind (thought)} \end{Bmatrix}$ is an aspect of the capacity of thought.

$\begin{Bmatrix} \text{Product of thought} \\ \text{Content of thought} \end{Bmatrix}$ is an aspect of the capacity of thought (mind).

Thought is reasoning power.

Capacity of thought is an aspect of the capacity of reason.

Thought is an aspect of reason.

Reason is a capacity which can be evaluated.

Good judgment is part of good sense.

Good judgment is part of good intellect.

The $\begin{bmatrix} \text{content} \\ \text{product} \end{bmatrix}$ of his reasoning was $\begin{bmatrix} \text{wicked.} \\ \text{righteous.} \end{bmatrix}$

4.4 *Appendix D: lh8i7i7' ni7dzi7lo7o7s* 'one returns with the horse' (dotted lines connect homophones on different levels)

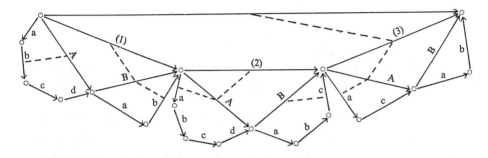

(1) *lh8i7i7' bike7e7' dashdiigha7a7h* 'one starts after the horse'

   A. *hasht'e' a7zhdiil'8iih* 'one prepares to go'

      (a) *ha'e7etsoh biih jigha7a7h* 'one puts on coat'

      (b) *hach'ah a7jiilh'8iih* 'one puts on hat'

      (c) *aza7a7t'i'i7 dashdiijih* 'one takes bridle'

      (d) *beeldle7i7 dashdiilhtsos* 'one takes blanket'

   B. *lh8i7i7' bike7e7' dashdiigha7a7h* 'one starts after the horse'

      (a) *ch'i7ji7gha7a7h* 'one goes out'

      (b) *lh8i7i7' (bike7tsi7i7n be'jitl'o7o7hy8e7edo7o7 jidilhkah)* 'one starts tracking the horse (from where it was hobbled)'

(2) *lh8i7i7' bik'i7 ji7gha7a7h* 'one finds the horse'

   A. *lh8i7i7' baaji7gha7a7h* 'one catches the horse'

      (a) *lh8i7i7' bik'i7ji7gha7a7h* 'one finds the horse'

      (b) *lh8i7i7' baazhdilnih* 'one gets hold of the horse'

      (c) *lh8i7i7' biza'jilht'ih* 'one puts bridle on'

      (d) *lh8i7i7' bike7tsi7i7n k'e'ji'a'* 'one unties the hobble'

   B. *lh8i7i7' holh nikina7ldlosh* 'one starts back on the horse'

      (a) *lh8i7i7' bika7a7' dah'ajiltsos* 'one puts (blanket) on the horse'

      (b) *lh8i7i7' bika7a7' dashnidaah* 'one gets on the horse'

      (c) *lh8i7i7' holh dahni7diildlosh* 'one starts back (home on the horse)'

(3) *lh8i7i7' holh na7ldlosh* 'one returns home with and on the horse'

   A. *lh8i7i7' ni7ji7dlo7o7s* 'one brings back (home) the horse'

(a) *lh8i7i7' holh na7ldlozh* 'one returns with and on the horse'
(b) *lh8i7i7' bik'i ahdajigha7a7h* 'one gets off the horse'
B. *lh8i7i7' dahjiitl'o7o7h* 'one ties horse (to a post, tree, etc.)'
(a) *lh8i7i7' beeldle7i7 bik'i nidzilhtsos* 'one takes off blanket'
(b) *lh8i7i7' dahjiitl'o7o7h* 'one ties the horse'

REFERENCES

ALBERT, ETHEL M. 1968. Semiotics and semantics, a partial interdisciplinary bibliography to 1967 (Draft). [Mimeo.]

BASSO, K.H. 1967. Semantic aspects of linguistic acculturation. AmA 69.471–77.

——. 1968. The Western Apache classificatory verb system: A formal analysis. SJA 24.252–66.

BENDIX, E.H. 1966. Componential analysis of general vocabulary: The semantic structure of a set of verbs in English, Hindi and Japanese. IJAL 32, Part II.

——. 1971. The data of semantic description. *In* Steinberg and Jakobovits 1971, pp. 393–409.

BERLIN, B., D.E. BREEDLOVE, and P.H. RAVEN. 1968. Covert categories and folk taxonomies. AmA 70.290–99.

BERLIN, B., and P. KAY. 1967. Basic color terms: Their universality and evolution. Berkeley and Los Angeles, University of California Press.

BERREMAN, G.D. 1966. Anemic and emetic analyses in social anthropology. AmA 68.346–54.

BIERMAN, A.K. 1964. Logic: A dialogue. San Francisco, Holden-Day, Inc.

BOCK, P.K. 1968. Some generative rules for American kinship terminology. AnL 10/6.1–6.

BOLINGER, D. 1965. The atomization of meaning. Lg 41.555–73.

BRIGHT, JANE O., and W. BRIGHT. 1965. Semantic structures in northwestern California and the Sapir-Whorf hypothesis. AmA 67, Part 2.249–58.

BUCHLER, I.R. 1964. Measuring the development of kinship terminologies, Scalogram and transformational accounts of Crow-type systems. AmA 66.765–88.

BUCHLER, I.R., and R. FREEZE. 1966. The distinctive features of pronominal systems. AnL 8/8.78–105.

BURLING, R. 1964. Cognition and componential analysis: God's truth or hocus-pocus? AmA 66.20–28.

——. 1965. Burmese kinship terminology. AmA 67, Part 2.

CASAGRANDE, J. 1954. The ends of translation. IJAL 20.335–40.

CASAGRANDE, J.B., and K.L. HALE. 1964. (Early version of Casagrande and Hale 1967.) [mimeo]

——. 1967. Semantic relations in Papago folk-definitions. *In* Hymes and Bittle 1967, pp. 165–96.

CHOMSKY, N. 1965. Aspects of a theory of syntax. Cambridge, Mass., M.I.T. Press.

COLBY, B.N. 1966. Ethnographic semantics: A preliminary survey. CAnth 7/1.3–32.

CONKLIN, H.C. 1962. Folk taxonomy. *In* Householder and Saporta 1962, pp. 119–41.

——. 1967. Ethnoscience, references. [Mimeo.]

D'ANDRADE, R.G. 1965. Trait psychology and componential analysis. AmA 67, Part 2. 215–28.

D'ANDRADE, R.G., N. QUINN, S.B. NERLOVE, and A.K. ROMNEY. 1966. Categories of disease in American English and Mexican-Spanish [mimeo].

DIXON, R.M.W. 1971. A method of semantic description, illustrated for Dyirbal verbs. *In* Steinberg and Jakobovits 1971, pp. 436–71.

DURBIN, M. 1966. The goals of ethnoscience. AnL 8/8.22–41.

FODOR, J.A., and J.J. KATZ. 1964. The structure of language: Readings in the philosophy of language. Englewood Cliffs, N.J., Prentice Hall.

FOWLER, CATHERINE S., and JOY LELAND. 1967. Some Northern Paiute native categories. Ethnology 6.381–404.

FRAKE, C.O. 1964. Notes on queries in ethnography. AmA 66, Part 2. 132–45.

FRIEDRICH, P. 1962. An evolutionary sketch of Russian kinship. Proceedings of the 1962 Annual Spring Meeting of the American Ethnological Society. Seattle, University of Washington Press.

——. 1964. Semantic structure and social structure: An instance from Russian. *In* Goodenough 1964, pp. 141–66.

——. 1968. Paper read at the 67th Annual Meeting of the American Anthropological Association, November 1968, Seattle, Washington.

FRISCH, J.A., and N.W. SCHUTZ. 1967. Componential analysis and semantic reconstruction: The proto-central Yuman kinship system. Ethnology 6.272–93.

GARDNER, E., D.J. GRAY, and R. O'RAHILLY. 1963. Anatomy. Philadelphia, W.B. Saunders Co.

GARVIN, P.L., 1964. On linguistic method. The Hague, Mouton.

GARVIN, P.L., and B. SPOLSKY, eds. 1966. Computation in linguistics: A case book. Bloomington, Indiana University Press.

GIPPER, H. 1963. Bausteine zur Sprachinhaltsforschung. Düsseldorf, Paedagogischer Verlag Schwann.

GLADWIN, T., and W.C. STURTEVANT, eds. 1962. Anthropology and human behavior. Washington, D.C., The Anthropological Society of Washington.

GLEASON, H.A. 1962. The relation of lexicon and grammar. *In* Householder and Saporta 1962, pp. 85–102.

GOODENOUGH, W.H., ed. 1964. Explorations in cultural anthropology. New York, McGraw Hill.

——. 1964. Introduction. Explorations in cultural anthropology, ed. by W.H. Goodenough, pp. 1–24. New York, McGraw Hill.

——. 1965. Yankee kinship terminology: A problem in componential analysis. AmA 67, Part 2. 259–87.

——. 1967. Componential analysis. Science 156.1203–09.

GREENBERG, J.H. 1963. Universals of language. Cambridge, Mass., M.I.T. Press.

HAAS, MARY R. 1967. Language and taxonomy in northwestern California. AmA 69.358–62.

HAILE, FR. BERARD. 1941–48. Learning Navaho, 4 vols. St. Michaels, Arizona.

HALE, K. 1971. A note on Walbiri tradition of antonymy. *In* Steinberg and Jakobovits 1971, pp. 472–84.

HAMMEL, E.A., ed. 1965. Formal/semantic analysis. AmA 67, Part 2. 2–7.

HARRIS, M. 1964. The nature of cultural things. New York, Random House.

——. 1968. The rise of anthropological theory. New York, Thomas Y. Crowell.

HEWES, G.W. 1966. The domain of posture. AnL 8/8.106–12.

HOUSEHOLDER, F.W., and S. SAPORTA, eds. 1962. Problems in lexicography. IJAL 28/4.

HYMES, D.H. 1961. On typology of cognitive styles in language (with example from Chinook). AnL 3/1.22–54.

——. 1962. The ethnography of speaking. *In* Gladwin and Sturtevant 1962, pp. 13–53.

——. 1964. Directions in (ethno-) linguistic theory. AmA 66, Part 2. 6–56.

HYMES, D.H., and W.E. BITTLE, eds. 1967. Studies in Southwestern ethnolinguistics. The Hague, Mouton.

KATZ, J.J., and J.A. FODOR. 1963. The structure of a semantic theory. Lg 39.170–210. (Reprinted in Fodor and Katz 1964, pp. 479–518)

KUHN, T. 1962. The structure of scientific revolutions. Chicago, University of Chicago Press.

LAMB, S.M. 1965. Kinship terminology and linguistic structure. AmA 67, Part 2. 37–64.

LEACH, E.L. 1961. Rethinking anthropology. *In* Rethinking Anthropology, by E.L. Leach, pp. 1–27. London School of Economics Monographs on Social Anthropology 22.

——. 1964. Anthropological aspects of language: Animal categories and verbal abuse. *In* Lenneberg 1964, pp. 23–64.

LENNEBERG, E.H., ed. 1964. New directions in the study of language. Cambridge, Mass., M.I.T. Press.

LOUNSBURY, F.G. 1956. A semantic analysis of Pawnee kinship usage. Lg 32/1.158–94.

——. 1964a. A formal account of the Crow-Omaha type kinship terminology. *In* Goodenough 1964, pp. 351–93.

——. 1964b. The structural analysis of kinship semantics. PICL 9. 1073–93.

——. 1965. Another view of Trobriand kinship categories. AmA 67, Part 2. 142–85.

LYONS, J. 1968. Introduction to theoretical linguistics. Cambridge, Cambridge University Press. [esp. pp. 463–67.]

MCCAWLEY, J.D. 1968a. Concerning the base component of a transformational grammar. FL 4.243–69.

——. 1968b. Review of CTL 3, 1966. Lg 44.556–93.

MACLAY, H., and MARY D. SLEATOR. 1960. Response to language: Judgments of grammaticalness. IJAL 26.275–82.

MATHIOT, MADELEINE. 1962. Noun classes and folk taxonomy in Papago. AmA 64.340–50.

——. 1963. A procedure for investigating language and culture relations. M.S.

——. 1967. The place of the dictionary in linguistic description. Lg 43.703–24.

METZGER, D., and G. WILLIAMS. 1966. Some procedures and results in the study of native categories, Tzeltal 'firewood'. AmA 68.389–407.

MILLER, G.A., E. GALANTER, and K.H. PRIBRAM. 1960. Plans and the structure of behavior. New York, Henry Holt.

MOEHRMAN, M. 1968. Analysis of Lue conversation: Providing accounts, finding breaches and taking sides. Working Paper 12, Language-Behavior Research Laboratory, University of California, Berkeley.

NAROLL, R., and R. COHEN, eds. 1970. Handbook of anthropology. New York, History Press.

NERLOVE, SARA, and A.K. ROMNEY. 1967. Sibling terminology and cross-sex behavior. AmA 69.179–87.

NIELSEN, K., and A. NESSHEIM. 1962. Lappisk ordbok—Lapp dictionary. Oslo, Universitetsforlaget. [especially Vol. 4, Systematic Part]

OEHMAN, SUZANNE. 1951. Wortinhalt und Weltbild. Stockholm.

——. 1953. Theories of the linguistic field. Word 9.123–34.

PERCHONOCK, NORMA, and O. WERNER. 1969. Ethnoscience methodology and categories of Navajo foods. Ethnology 8.229–42.

PIKE, K. 1954–60. Language in relation to a unified theory of the structure of human behavior. Glendale, Calif., Summer Institute of Linguistics.

PILCHER, W.W. 1967. Some comments on the folk taxonomy of the Papago. AmA 69.204–08.

POLANYI, M. 1958. Personal knowledge. Harper Torchbook.

PRICE, P.D. 1967. Two types of taxonomy: A Huichol ethnobotanical example. AnL 9/7.1–12.

REICHENBACH, H. 1947. Elements of symbolic logic. New York, Macmillan.

ROBERTS, J.M., M.J. ARTH, and R.R. BUSK. 1959. Games in culture. AmA 61.597–605.

ROBERTS, J.M., and B. SUTTON-SMITH. 1962. Child training and game involvement. Ethnology 1.166–85.

ROBERTS, J.M., B. SUTTON-SMITH, and A. KENDON. 1963. Strategy in games and folk tales. Journal of Social Psychology 63.185–99.

Roget's International Thesaurus. 1962. 3rd ed. New York, Thomas Y. Crowell.

ROMNEY, A. K., and R. G. D'ANDRADE. 1964. Cognitive aspects of English kin terms. *In* Romney and D'Andrade 1964, pp. 146–70.

——, eds. 1964. Transcultural studies in cognition. AmA 66, Part 2.

RYLE, G. 1946. Knowing how and knowing that. Proceedings of the Aristotelian Society 46. London, Harrison and Sons Ltd.

SANDAY, PEGGY R. 1968. The 'psychological reality' of American English kinship terms: An information processing approach. AmA 70.508–23,

SARLES, H. B. 1966. The dynamic study of interaction as ethnoscientific strategy. AnL 8/8.66–70.

SCHEFFLER, H. W. 1967. On scaling kinship terminologies. SWJ 23.159–75.

STEINBERG, D. D. 1967. The word sort: An instrument for semantic analysis. Psychon. Sci. 12.

STEINBERG, D. D., and L. JAKOBOVITS, eds. 1971. Semantics; an interdisciplinary reader in philosophy, linguistics and psychology. London, Cambridge University Press.

STURTEVANT, W. C. 1964. Studies in ethnoscience. AmA 66, Part 2.99–131.

TYLER, S. A. 1965. Koya language morphology and patterns of kinship behavior. AmA 67.1428–40.

——. 1966. Context and variation in Koya kinship terminology. AmA 68.693–707.

——, ed. 1969. Cognitive anthropology. New York, Holt, Rinehart and Winston.

VOEGELIN, C. F., and FLORENCE M. VOEGELIN. 1957. Hopi domains: A lexical approach to the problem of selection. Suppl. to IJAL 23/2 = IJAL Memoir 14.

——. 1960. Selection and Hopi ethics, linguistics and translation. AnL 2.48–77.

WALLACE, A. F. C. 1961. Culture and personality. New York, Random House.

——. 1965. The problem of the psychological validity of componential analyses. AmA 67, Part 2.229–48.

WALLACE, A. F. C., and J. ATKINS. 1960. The meaning of kinship terms. AmA 62.58–80.

Webster's New Collegiate Dictionary. 1953. G. C. Meriam Co.

WEINREICH, U. 1962. Lexicographic definition in descriptive semantics. *In* Householder and Saporta 1962, pp. 25–44.

——. 1963. On the semantic structure of language. *In* Greenberg 1963, pp. 114–71.

WERNER, O. 1965. Semantics of Navajo medical terms: I. IJAL 31.1–17.

——. 1966a. Computers and anthropological linguistics. *In* Garvin and Spolsky 1966, pp. 1–41.

——. 1966b. Pragmatics and ethnoscience. AnL 8/8.42–65.

——. 1967. Systematized lexicography or 'ethnoscience', the use of computer made concordances. BS 10/5.5–8.

——. 1969. The basic assumptions of ethnoscience. Semiotica 1. 329-38.

WERNER, O., and K. Y. BEGISHE. 1968a. The anatomical atlas of the Navajo. Fifth and Sixth revised versions. MS.

——. 1968b. Styles of learning: The evidence from Navajo. MS.

WERNER, O., and D.T. CAMPBELL. 1970. Translating, working through interpreters and the problem of decentering. *In* Naroll and Cohen 1970.

WERNER, O., and JOANN FENTON. 1970. Method and theory in ethnoscience. *In* Naroll and Cohen 1970.

WILLIAMS, G. E. 1966. Linguistic reflection of cultural systems. AnL 8/8.13–21.

YOUNG, R. W., and W. MORGAN. 1943. The Navaho language. Education Division, Office of Indian Affairs, Phoenix, Arizona. Reprinted 1967, Deseret Book Company, Salt Lake City, Utah.

SOCIAL CLASS, LANGUAGE AND SOCIALISATION

BASIL B. BERNSTEIN[1]

INTRODUCTION

It may be helpful to make explicit the theoretical origins of the thesis I have been developing over the past decade. Although, initially, the thesis appeared to be concerned with the problem of educability, this problem was imbedded in and was stimulated by the wider question of the relationships between symbolic orders and social structure. The basic theoretical question, which dictated the approach to the initially narrow but important empirical problem, was concerned with the fundamental structure and changes in the structure of cultural transmission. Indeed, any detailed examination of what superficially may seem to be a string of somewhat repetitive papers, I think would show three things:

1. The gradual emergence of the dominance of the major theoretical problem from the local, empirical problem of the social antecedents of the educability of different groups of children.

2. Attempts to develop both the generality of the thesis and to develop increasing specificity at the contextual level.

3. Entailed in (2) were attempts to clarify both the logical and empirical status of the basic organising concept, code. Unfortunately, until recently these attempts were more readily seen in the *planning* and *analysis* of the empirical research than available as formal statements.

Looking back with hindsight, I think I would have created less misunderstanding if I had written about sociolinguistic codes rather than linguistic codes. Through using only the latter concept it gave the impression that I was reifying syntax and at the cost of semantics. Or at worse, suggesting that there was a one to one relation between meaning and a given syntax. Also, by defining the codes in a context free fashion, I robbed myself of properly understanding, at a theoretical

[1] This work was supported by grants from the Department of Education and Science, the Ford Foundation and the Nuffield Foundation, to whom grateful acknowledgement is made. I would also like to take the opportunity of acknowledging my debt to Professor Courtney Cazden, Dr. Mary Douglas, Professor John Gumperz, Professor Dell Hymes, and in particular to Professor Michael Halliday. I am also grateful for the constant constructive criticism I have received from members of the Sociological Research Unit, University of London Institute of Education.

level, their significance. *I should point out that nearly all the empirical planning was directed to trying to find out the code realisations in different contexts.*

The concept of sociolinguistic code points to the social structuring of meanings *and* to their diverse but *related* contextual linguistic realisations. A careful reading of the papers always shows the emphasis given to the form of the social relationship, that is, the structuring of relevant meanings. Indeed, role is defined as a complex coding activity controlling the creation and organisation of specific meanings and the conditions for their transmission and reception. The general sociolinguistic thesis attempts to explore how symbolic systems are both realisations and regulators of the structure of social relationships. The particular symbolic system is that of speech, *not* language.

It is pertinent, at this point, to make explicit earlier work in the social sciences which formed the implicit starting point of the thesis. It will then be seen, I hope, that the thesis is an integration of different streams of thought. The major starting points are Durkheim and Marx, and a small number of other thinkers have been drawn into the basic matrix. I shall very briefly, and so selectively, outline this matrix and some of the problems to which it gave rise.

Durkheim's work is a truly magnificent insight into the relationships between symbolic orders, social relationships and the structuring of experience. In a sense, if Marx turned Hegel on his head, then Durkheim attempted to turn Kant on his head. For in *Primitive classification* and in *The elementary forms of the religious life*, Durkheim attempted to derive the basic categories of thought from the structuring of the social relation. It is beside the point as to his success. He raised the whole question of the relation between the classifications and frames of the symbolic order *and* the structuring of experience. In his study of different forms of social integration he pointed to the implicit, condensed, symbolic structure of mechanical solidarity and the more explicit and differentiated symbolic structures of organic solidarity. Cassirer, the early cultural anthropologists, and in particular Sapir (I was not aware of von Humboldt until much later) sensitised me to the cultural properties of speech. Whorf, particularly where he refers to the fashions of speaking, frames of consistency, alerted me to the selective effect of the culture (acting through its patterning of social relationships) upon the *patterning* of grammar *together* with the pattern's semantic and thus cognitive significance. Whorf more than anyone, I think, opened up, at least for me, the question of the deep structure of linguistically regulated communication.

In all the above work I found two difficulties. If we grant the fundamental linkage of symbolic systems, social structure and the shaping of experience, it is still unclear *how* such shaping takes place. The *processes* underlying the social structuring of experience are not explicit. The second difficulty is in dealing with the question of change of symbolic systems. George Herbert Mead is of central importance in the solution of the first difficulty, the HOW. Mead outlined in general terms the relationships between role, reflexiveness and speech, and in so doing provided the basis of the solution to the HOW. It is still the case that the Meadian solution does not allow us to deal with the problem of change. For the concept, which enables role to be related to a higher order concept, 'the generalised other' is, itself, not subject to systematic enquiry. Even if 'the generalised other' is placed within a Durkheimian framework, we are still left with the problem of change. Indeed, in Mead change is introduced only at the cost of the re-emergence of a traditional Western dichotomy in the concepts of the 'I' and the 'me'. The 'I' is both the indeterminate response to the 'me' and yet at the same time shapes it. The Meadian 'I' points to the voluntarism in the affairs of men, the fundamental creativity of man, made possible by speech; a little before Chomsky.

Thus Meadian thought helps to solve the puzzle of the HOW but it does not help with the question of change in the structuring of experience; although both Mead implicitly and Durkheim explicitly pointed to the conditions which bring about pathological structuring of experience.

One major theory of the development of and change in symbolic structures is, of course, that of Marx. Although Marx is less concerned with the internal structure and the process of transmission of symbolic systems he does give us a key to their institutionalisation and change. The key is given in terms of the social significance of society's productive system and the power relationships to which the productive system gives rise. Further, access to, control over, orientation of and *change* in critical symbolic systems, according to the theory, is governed by these power relationships as these are embodied in the class structure. It is not only capital, in the strict economic sense, which is subject to appropriation, manipulation and exploitation, but also *cultural* capital in the form of the symbolic systems through which man can extend and change the boundaries of his experience.

I am not putting forward a matrix of thought necessary for the study of the basic structure and change in the structure of cultural transmission, *only* the specific matrix which underlies my own approach. Essentially and briefly I have used Durkheim and Marx at the macro level and Mead at the micro level, to realise a sociolinguistic thesis which could meet with a range of work in anthropology, linguistics, sociology and psychology.

OTHER VIEWS OF THE RELATION OF LINGUISTIC
AND CULTURAL SYSTEMS

I want also to make clear two views I am not concerned with. Chomsky in *Aspects of the theory of syntax* neatly severs the study of the rule system of language from the study of the social rules which determine their contextual use. He does this by making a distinction between competence and performance. Competence refers to the child's tacit understanding of the rule system, performance relates to the essentially social use to which the rule system is put. Competence refers to man abstracted from contextual constraints. Performance refers to man in the grip of the contextual constraints which determine his speech acts. Competence refers to the Ideal, performance refers to the Fall. In this sense Chomsky's notion of competence is Platonic. Competence has its source in the very biology of man. There is no difference between men in terms of their access to the linguistic rule system. Here Chomsky, like many other linguists before him, announces the communality of man, all men have equal access to the creative act which is language. On the other hand, performance is under the control of the social — performances are culturally specific acts, they refer to the choices which are made in specific speech encounters. Thus from one point of view, Chomsky indicates the tragedy of man, the potentiality of competence and the degeneration of performance (this view explicitly derives from Hymes 1966).

Clearly, much is to be gained in rigour and explanatory power through the severing of the relationship between the formal properties of the grammar and the meanings which are realised in its use. But if we are to study speech, *la parole*, we are inevitably involved in a study of a rather different rule system, we are involved in a study of rules, formal and informal, which regulate the options we take up in various contexts in which we find ourselves. This second rule system is the cultural system.

This raises immediately the question of the causal relationship between the linguistic rule system and the cultural system. Clearly, specific linguistic rule systems are part of the cultural system, but it has been argued that the linguistic rule system in various ways shapes the cultural system. This very briefly is the view of those who hold a narrow form of the linguistic relativity hypothesis. I do not intend to get involved in that particular quagmire. Instead, I shall take the view that the code which the linguist invents to explain the formal properties of the grammar is capable of generating any number of speech codes, and there is no reason for believing that any one language code is better than another in this respect. On this argument, language is a set of rules to which all speech codes must comply, but which speech codes are realised is a function of the culture acting through social relationship in specific contexts. Different speech forms or codes symbolize the form of the social relationship, regulate the nature of the speech encounters, and create for the speakers different orders of relevance and relation. The experience of the speakers is then transformed by what is made significant or relevant by the speech form.

This is a sociological argument because the speech form is taken as a consequence of the form of the social relation or put more generally, is a quality of a social structure. Let me qualify this immediately. Because the speech form is initially a function of a given social arrangement, it does not mean that the speech form does not in turn modify or even change that social structure which initially evolved the speech form. This formulation, indeed, invites the question: under what conditions does a given speech form free itself sufficiently from its embodiment in the social structure so that the system of meanings it realises points to alternative realities, alternative arrangements in the affairs of men? Here we become concerned immediately with the antecedents and consequences of the boundary maintaining principles of a culture or sub-culture. I am here suggesting a relationship between forms of boundary maintenance at the cultural level and forms of speech.

LANGUAGE, SOCIALISATION AND CLASS

I am required to consider the relationship between language and socialisation. It should be clear that I am not concerned with language, but with speech, and concerned more specifically with the contextual constraints upon speech. Now what about socialisation? I shall take the term to refer to the process whereby a child acquires a specific cultural identity, *and* to his responses to such an identity. Socialisation refers to the process whereby the biological is transformed into a specific cultural being. It follows from this that the process of socialisation is a complex process of control, whereby a particular moral, cognitive and affective awareness is evoked in the child and given a specific form and content. Socialisation sensitizes the child to various orderings of society as these are made substantive in the various roles he is expected to play. In a sense then socialisation is a process for making people safe. The process acts selectively on the possibilities of man by creating through time a sense of the inevitability of a given social arrangement, and through limiting the areas of permitted change. The basic agencies of socialisation in contemporary societies are the family, the peer group, school and work. It is through these agencies, and in particular through their relationship to each other, that the various orderings of society are made manifest.

Now it is quite clear that given this view of socialisation it is necessary to limit the discussion. I shall limit our discussion to socialisation within the family, but it should be obvious that the focussing and filtering of the child's experience within the family in a large measure is a microcosm of the macroscopic orderings of society. Our question now becomes: what are the sociological factors which affect linguistic performances within the family critical to the process of socialisation?

Without a shadow of doubt the most formative influence upon the procedures of socialisation, from a sociological viewpoint, is social class. The class structure influences work and educational roles and brings families into a special relationship with each other and deeply penetrates the structure of life experiences within the family. The class system has deeply marked the distribution of knowledge within society. It has given differential access to the sense that the world is permeable. It has sealed off communities from each other and has ranked these communities on a scale of individuous worth. We have three components, knowledge, possibility, invidious insulation. It would be a little naive to believe that differences in knowledge, differences in the sense of the possible, combined with invidious insulation, rooted in differential *material* well-being would not affect the forms of control and innovation in the socialising procedures of different social classes. I shall go on to argue that the deep structure of communication itself is affected, but not in any final or irrevocable way.

As an approach to my argument, let me glance at the social distribution of knowledge. We can see that the class system has affected the distribution of knowledge. Historically and now, only a tiny percentage of the population has been socialised into knowledge at the level of the meta-languages of control and innovation, whereas the mass of the population has been socialised into knowledge at the level of context-tied operations.

A tiny percentage of the population has been given access to the principles of intellectual change whereas the rest have been denied such access. This suggests that we might be able to distinguish between two orders of meaning. One we could call universalistic, the other particularistic. Universalistic meanings are those in which principles and operations are made linguistically explicit whereas particularistic orders of meaning are meanings in which principles and operations are relatively linguistically implicit. If orders of meaning are universalistic, then the meanings are less tied to a given context. The meta-languages of public forms of thought as these apply to objects and persons realise meanings of a universalistic type. Where meanings have this characteristic then individuals may have access to the grounds of their experience and can change the grounds. Where orders of meaning are particularistic, where principles are linguistically implicit, then such meanings are less context independent and *more* context bound; that is, tied to a local relationship and to a local social structure. Where the meaning system is particularistic, much of the meaning is imbedded in the context and may be restricted to those who share a similar contextual history. Where meanings are universalistic, they are in principle available to all because the principles and operations have been made explicit and so public.

I shall argue that forms of socialisation orient the child towards speech codes which control access to relatively context-tied or relatively context-independent meanings. Thus I shall argue that elaborated codes orient their users towards universalistic meanings, whereas restricted codes orient, sensitize, their users to particularistic meanings: that the linguistic realisation of the two orders are different, and so are the social relationships which realise them. Elaborated codes are less tied to a given or local structure and thus contain the potentiality of change in principles. In the case of elaborated codes the speech is freed from its evoking social structure and takes on an autonomy. A university is a place organised around talk. Restricted codes are more tied to a local social structure and have a reduced potential for change in principles. Where codes are elaborated, the socialised has more access to the grounds of his own socialisation, and so can enter into a reflexive relationship to the social order he has taken over. Where codes are restricted, the socialised has less access to the grounds of his socialisation, and thus reflexiveness may be limited in range. *One of the effects of the class system is to limit access to elaborated codes.*

I shall go on to suggest that restricted codes have their basis in condensed symbols whereas elaborated codes have their basis in articulated symbols. That restricted codes draw upon metaphor whereas elaborated codes draw upon rationality. That these codes constrain the contextual use of language in critical socialising contexts and in this way regulate the orders of relevance and relation which the socialised takes over. From this point of view, change in habitual speech codes involves changes in the means by which object and person relationships are realised.

ELABORATED AND RESTRICTED SPEECH VARIANTS

I want first to start with the notions of elaborated and restricted speech variants. A variant can be considered as the contextual constraints upon grammatical-lexical choices.

Sapir, Malinowski, Firth, Vygotsky, Luria have all pointed out from different points of view that the closer the identifications of speakers, the greater the range of shared interests, the more probable that the speech will take a specific form. The range of syntactic alternatives is likely to be reduced and the lexis to be drawn from a narrow range. Thus, the form of these social relations is acting selectively on the meanings to be verbally realised. In these relationships the intent of the other person can be taken for granted as the speech is played out against a back-drop of common assumptions, common history, common interests. As a result, there is less need to raise meanings to the level of explicitness or elaboration. There is a reduced need to make explicit through syntactic choices the logical structure of the communication. Further, if the speaker wishes to individualise his communication, he is likely to do this by varying the expressive associates of the speech. Under these conditions, the speech is likely to have a strong metaphoric element. In these situations the speaker may be more concerned with how something is said, when it is said; silence takes on a variety of meanings. Often in these encounters the speech cannot be understood apart from the context, and the context cannot be read by those who do not share the history of the relationship. Thus the form of the social relationship acts selectively on the meanings to be verbalised, which in turn affect the syntactic and lexical choices. The unspoken assumptions underlying the relationship are not available to those who are outside the relationship. For these are limited, and restricted to the speakers. The symbolic form of the communication is condensed yet the specific cultural history of the relationship is alive in its form. We can say that the roles of the speakers are communalised roles. Thus, we can make a relationship between restricted social relationships based upon communalised roles and the verbal realisation of their meaning. In the language of the earlier part of this paper, restricted social relationships based upon communalised role evoke particularistic, that is, context-tied meanings, realised through a restricted speech variant.

Imagine a husband and wife have just come out of the cinema, and are talking about the film: 'What do you think?' 'It had a lot to say'. 'Yes, I thought so too — let's go to the Millers, there may be something going there'. They arrive at the Millers, who ask about the film. An hour is spent in the complex, moral, political, aesthetic subtleties of the film and its place in the contemporary scene. Here we have an elaborated variant, the meanings now have to be made public to others who have not seen the film. The speech shows careful editing, at both the grammatical and lexical levels, it is no longer context tied. The meanings are explicit, elaborated and individualised. Whilst expressive channels are clearly relevant, the burden of meaning inheres predominantly in the verbal channel. The experience of the listeners cannot be taken for granted. Thus each member of the group is on his own as he offers his interpretation. Elaborated variants of this kind involve the speakers in particular role relationship, and *if you cannot manage the role, you can't produce the appropriate speech.* For as the speaker proceeds to individualise his meanings, he is differentiated from others like a figure from its ground.

The roles receive less support from each other. There is a measure of isolation. *Difference* lies at the basis of the social relationship, and is made verbally active, whereas in the other context it is *consensus*. The insides of the speaker have become psychologically active through the verbal aspect of the communication. Various defensive strategies may be used to decrease potential vulnerability of self and to increase the vulnerability of others. The verbal aspect of the communication becomes a vehicle for the transmission of individuated symbols. The 'I' stands over the 'We'. Meanings which are discreet to the speaker must be offered so that they are intelligible to the listener. Communalised roles have given way to individualised roles, condensed symbols to articulated symbols. Elaborated speech variants of this type realise universalistic meanings in the sense that they are less context-tied. Thus individualised roles are realised through elaborated speech variants which involve complex editing at the grammatical and lexical levels and which point to universalistic meanings.

Let me give another example. Consider the two following stories which Peter Hawkins, Assistant Research Officer in the Sociological Research Unit, University of London Institute of Education, constructed as a result of his analysis of the speech of middle-class and working-class five-year-old children. The children were given a series of four pictures which told a story and they were invited to tell the story. The first picture showed some boys playing football, in the second the ball goes through the window of a house, the third shows a woman looking out of the window and a man making an ominous gesture, and in the fourth the children are moving away.

Here are the two stories:

(1) Three boys are playing football and one boy kicks the ball   and it goes through the window   the ball breaks the window   and the boys are looking at it   and a man comes out and shouts at them   because they've broken the window   so they run away   and then that lady looks out of her window   and she tells the boys off.

(2) They're playing football   and he kicks it and it goes through there   it breaks the window and they're looking at it   and he comes out   and shouts at them   because they've broken it   so they run away   and then she looks out   and she tells them off.

With the first story the reader does not have to have the four pictures which were used as the basis for the story, whereas in the case of the second story the reader would require the initial pictures in order to make sense of the story. The first story is free of the context which generated it, whereas the second story is much more closely tied to its context. As a result the meanings of the second story are implicit, whereas the meanings of the first story are explicit. It is not that the working-class children do not have in their passive vocabulary the vocabulary used by the middle-class children. Nor is it the case that the children differ in their tacit understanding of the linguistic rule system. Rather, what we have here are differences in the use of language arising out of a specific context. One child makes explicit the meanings which he is realising through language for the person he is tellling the story to, whereas the second child does not to the same extent. The first child takes very little for granted, whereas the second child takes a great deal for granted. Thus for the first child the task was seen as a context in which his meanings were required to be made explicit, whereas the task for the second child was not seen as a task which required such explication of meaning. It would not be difficult to imagine a context where the first child would produce speech rather like the second. What we are dealing with here are differences between the children in the way they realise in language use apparently the same context. We could say that the speech of the first child generated universalistic meanings in the sense that the meanings are freed from the context and so understandable by all. Whereas the speech of the second child generated particularistic meanings, in the sense that the meanings are closely tied to the context and would be only fully understood by others if they had access to the context which originally generated the speech.

It is again important to stress that the second child has access to a more differentiated noun phrase, but there is a restriction on its *use*. Geoffrey Turner, Linguist in the Sociological Research Unit, shows that working-class, five-year-old children in the same contexts examined by Hawkins, use fewer linguistic expressions of uncertainty when compared with the middle-class children. This does not mean that working-class children do *not* have access to such expressions, but that the eliciting speech context did not provoke them. Telling a story from pictures, talking about scenes on cards, *formally framed* contexts may not encourage working-class children to consider the possibilities of alternate meanings and so there is a reduction in the linguistic expressions of uncertainty. Again, working-class children have access to a wide range of syntactic choices which involve the use of logical operators, 'because', 'but', 'either', 'or', 'only'. The constraints exist on the conditions for their *use*. Formally framed contexts used for eliciting context independent universalistic meanings may evoke in the working-class child, relative to the middle-class child, restricted speech variants, because the working-class child has difficulty in managing the role relationships which such contexts require. This problem is further complicated when such contexts carry meanings very much removed from the child's cultural experience. In the same way we can show that there are constraints upon the middle-class child's use of language. Turner found that when middle-class children were asked to role play in the picture story series, a higher percentage of these children, when compared with working-class children, initially refused. When the middle-class children were asked 'What is the man saying?', or linguistically equivalent questions, a relatively higher percentage said 'I don't know'. When this question was followed by the hypothetical question 'What do you think the man might be saying?' they offered their interpretations. The working-class children role played without difficulty. It seems then that middle-class children at five need to have a very precise instruction to *hypothesise in that particular context*. This may be because they are more concerned here with getting their answers right or correct. When the children were invited to tell a story about some doll-like figures (a little boy, a little girl, a sailor and a dog), the working-class children's stories were freer, longer, more imaginative than the stories of the middle-class children. The latter children's stories were tighter, constrained within a strong narrative frame. It was as if these children were dominated by what they took to be the *form* of a narrative and the content was secondary. This is an example of the concern of the middle-class child with the structure of the contextual frame.

It may be worthwhile to amplify this further. A number of studies have shown that when working-class black children are asked to associate to a series of words, their responses show considerable diversity, both from the meaning and form-class of the stimulus word. In the analysis offered in the text this may be because the children for the following reasons are less constrained. The form-class of the stimulus word may have reduced associative significance and so would less constrain the selection of potential words *or* phrases. With such a weakening of the grammatical frame a greater range of alternatives are possible candidates for selection. Further, the closely controlled middle-class linguistic socialisation of the young child may point the child towards both the grammatical significance of the stimulus word and towards a tight logical ordering of semantic space. Middle-class children may well have access to deep interpretive rules which regulate their linguistic responses in certain formalised contexts. The consequences may limit their imagination through the tightness of the frame which these interpretive rules create. It may even be that with *five*-year-old children, the middle-class child will innovate *more* with the arrangements of objects (i.e. bricks) than in his linguistic usage. His linguistic usage is under close supervision by adults. He has more *autonomy* in his play.

To return to our previous discussion, we can say briefly that as we move from communalised to individualised roles, so speech takes on an increasingly reflexive function. The unique selves of others become palpable through speech and enter into our own self, the grounds of our experience are made verbally explicit; the security of the condensed symbol is gone. It has been replaced by rationality. There is a change in the basis of our vulnerability.

FOUR CONTEXTS

So far, then, I have discussed certain types of speech variants and the role relationships which occasion them. I am now going to raise the generality of the discussion and focus upon the title of the paper. The socialisation of the young in the family proceeds within a critical set of inter-related contexts. Analytically, we may distinguish four contexts.

1. The regulative context — these are authority relationships where the child is made aware of the rules of the moral order and their various backings.

2. The instructional context, where the child learns about the objective nature of objects and persons, and acquires skills of various kinds.

3. The imaginative or innovating contexts, where the child is encouraged to experiment and re-create his world on his own terms, and in his own way.

4. The interpersonal context, where the child is made aware of affective states — his own, and others.

I am suggesting that the critical orderings of a culture or subculture are made substantive — are made palpable — through the forms of its linguistic realisations of these four contexts — initially in the family and kin.

Now if the linguistic realisation of these four contexts involves the predominant use of restricted speech variants, I shall postulate that the deep structure of the communication is a restricted code having its basis in communalised roles, realising context bound meanings, i.e., particularistic meaning orders. Clearly the specific grammatical and lexical choices will vary from one context to another.

If the linguistic realisation of these four contexts involve the predominant usage of elaborated speech variants, I shall postulate that the deep structure of the communication is an elaborated code having its basis in individualised roles realising context free, universalistic, meanings.

In order to prevent misunderstanding some expansion of this point is necessary. It is likely that where the code is restricted, the speech in the regulative context may well be limited to command and simple rule announcing statements. The latter statements are not context dependent in the sense previously given for they announce general rules. We need to supplement the context independent (universalistic) and context dependent (particularistic) criteria with criteria which refer to the extent to which the speech in the regulative context varies in terms of its *contextual specificity*. If the speech is context-specific then the socialiser cuts his meanings to the *specific* attributes/intentions of the socialised, the specific characteristics of the problem, the specific requirements of the context. Thus the general rule may be transmitted with degrees of *contextual specificity*. When this occurs the rule is individualised (fitted to the local circumstances) in the process of its transmission. Thus with code elaboration we should expect:

1. Some developed grounds for the rule.
2. Some qualification of it in the light of the particular issue.
3. Considerable *specificity* in terms of the socialised, the context and the issue.

This does *not* mean that there would be an *absence* of command statements. It is also likely that with code elaboration the socialised would be *given* opportunities (role options) to question.

Bernstein and Cook (1965) Cook (1970) have developed a semantic coding grid which sets out with considerable delicacy a general category system which has been applied to a limited regulative context. G. Turner, linguist to the Sociological Research Unit, is attempting a linguistic realisation of the same grid.

We can express the two sets of criteria diagrammatically. A limited application is given by Henderson (1970):

Realisation of the Regulative Context

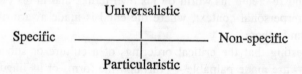

It may be necessary to utilise the two sets of criteria for *all* four socialising contexts. Bernstein (1967, published 1972) suggested that code realisation would vary with context.

If we look at the linguistic realisation of the regulative context in greater detail we may be able to clear up another source of possible misunderstanding. In this context it is very likely that syntactic markers of the logical distribution of meaning will be extensively used.

'If you do that, then . . . .'
'Either you . . . or . . . .'
'You can do that but if . . . .'
'You do that and you'll pay for it'

Thus it is very likely that young children may well in the *regulative* context have access to a range of syntactic markers which express the logical/hypothetical irrespective of code restriction or elaboration. However, where the code is restricted it is expected that there will be reduced specificity in the sense outlined earlier. Further, the speech in the control situation is likely to be well-organised in the sense that the sentences come as wholes. The child responds to the total *frame*. However, I would suggest that the informal *instructional* contexts within the family may well be limited in range and frequency. Thus the child, of course, would have access to and so have *available*, the hypotheticals, conditionals, disjunctives etc. but these might be rarely used in *instructional* contexts. In the same way, as we have suggested earlier, all children have access to linguistic expressions of uncertainty but they may differ in the context in which they receive and realise such expressions.

I must emphasise that because the code is restricted it does not mean that speakers at no time will not use elaborated speech variants. Only that the use of such variants will be infrequent in the socialisation of the child in his family.

Now, all children have access to restricted codes and their various systems of condensed meaning, because the roles the code pre-supposes are universal. But there may well be selective access to elaborated codes because there is selective access to the role system which evokes its use. Society is likely to evaluate differently the experiences realised through these two codes. I cannot here go into details, but the different focussing of experience through a restricted code creates a major problem of educability only where the school produces discontinuity between its symbolic orders and those of the child. Our schools are not made for these children; why should the children respond? To ask the child to switch to an elaborated code which presupposes different role relationships and systems of meaning without a sensitive understanding of the required contexts may create for the child a bewildering and potentially damaging experience.

FAMILY TYPES AND COMMUNICATION STRUCTURES

So far, then, I have sketched out a relationship between speech codes and socialisation through the organisation of roles through which the culture is made psychologically active in persons. I have indicated that access to the roles and thus to the codes is broadly related to social class. However, it is clearly the case that social class groups today are by no means homogeneous groups. Further, the division between elaborated and restricted codes is too simple. Finally, I have not indicated in any detail how these codes are evoked by families, and how the family types may shape their focus.

What I shall do now is to introduce a distinction between family types and their communication structures. These family types can be found empirically within each social class, although any one type may be rather more modal at any given historical period.

I shall distinguish between families according to the strength of their boundary maintaining procedures. Let me first give some idea of what I mean by boundary maintaining procedures. I shall first look at boundary maintenance as it is revealed in the symbolic ordering of space. Consider the lavatory. In one house, the room is pristine, bare and sharp, containing only the necessities for which the room is dedicated. In another there is a picture on the wall, in the third there are books, in the fourth all surfaces are covered with curious postcards. We have a continuum from a room celebrating the purity of categories to one celebrating the mixture of categories, from strong to weak boundary maintenance. Consider the kitchen. In one kitchen, shoes may not be placed on the table, nor the child's chamber pot — all objects and utensils have an assigned place. In another kitchen the boundaries separating the different classes of objects are weak. The symbolic ordering of space can give us indications of the relative strength of boundary maintaining procedures. Let us now look at the relationship between family members. Where boundary procedures are strong, the differentiation of members and the authority structure is based upon clear-cut, unambiguous definitions of the status of the member of the family. The boundaries between the statuses are strong and the social identities of the members very much a function of their age, sex and age-relation status. As a shorthand, we can characterise the family as *positional*.

On the other hand, where boundary procedures are weak or flexible, the differentiation between members and the authority relationships are less on the basis of position, because here the status boundaries are blurred. Where boundary procedures are weak, the differentiation between members is based more upon *differences between persons*. In such families the relationships become more egocentric and the unique attributes of family members more and more are made substantive in the communication structure. We will call these *person-centred* families. Such families do not reduce but increase the substantive expression of ambiguity and ambivalence. In person-centred families, the role system would be continuously evoking, accommodating and assimilating the different interests, attributes of its members. In such families, unlike positional families, the members would be making their roles, rather than stepping into them. In a person-centred family, the child's developing self is differentiated by continuous adjustment to the verbally realised and elaborated intentions, qualifications and motives of others. The boundary between self and other is blurred. In positional families, the child takes over and responds to the formal pattern of obligation and privilege. It should be possible to see, without going into details, that the communication structure within these two types of family are somewhat differently focussed. We might then expect that the reflexiveness induced by positional families is sensitized to the general attributes of persons, whereas the reflexiveness produced by person-centred families is more sensitive towards the particular aspects of persons. Think of the difference between Dartington Hall or Gordonstoun Public Schools in England, or the difference between West Point and a progressive school in the USA. Thus, in person-centred families, the insides of the members are made public through the communication structure, and thus more of the person has been invaded and subject to control. Speech in such families is a major media of control. In positional families of course, speech is relevant but it symbolizes the boundaries given by the formal structure of the relationships. So far as the child is concerned, in positional families he attains a strong sense of social identity at the cost of autonomy; in person-centred families, the child attains a strong sense of autonomy but his social identity may be weak. Such ambiguity in the sense of identity, the lack of boundary, may move such children towards a radically closed value system.

If we now place these family types in the framework of the previous discussion, we can see that although the code may be elaborated, it may be differently focussed according to the family type. Thus, we can have an elaborate code focussing upon persons or an elaborated code in a positional family may focus more upon objects. We can expect the same with a restricted code. Normally, with code restriction we should expect a positional family, however, if it showed signs of person-centred, then we might expect the children to be in a situation of potential code switch.

Where the code is elaborated, and focussed by a person-centred family, then these children may well develop acute identity problems, concerned with authenticity, of limiting responsibility — they may come to see language as phony, a system of counterfeit masking the absence of belief. They may move towards the restricted codes of the various peer group sub-cultures, or seek the condensed symbols of affective experience, or both.

One of the difficulties of this approach is to avoid implicit value judgements about the relative worth of speech systems and the cultures which they symbolize. Let it be said immediately that a restricted code gives access to a vast potential of meanings, of delicacy, subtlety and diversity of cultural forms, to a unique aesthetic whose basis in condensed symbols may influence the form of the imagining. Yet, in complex industrialized societies, its differently focussed experience may be dis-valued, and humiliated within schools or seen, at best, to be irrelevant to the educational endeavour. For the schools are predicated upon elaborated code and its system of social relationships. Although an elaborated code does not entail any specific value system, the value system of the middle class penetrates the texture of the very learning context itself.

Elaborated codes give access to alternative realities yet they carry the potential of alienation, of feeling from thought, of self from other, of private belief *from role obligation.*

SOURCES OF CHANGE

Finally I should like to consider briefly the source of change of linguistic codes. The first major source of change I suggest is to be located in the division of labour. As the division of labour changes from simple to complex, then this changes the social and knowledge characteristics of occupational roles. In this process there is an extension of access, through education, to elaborated codes, but access is controlled by the class system. The focussing of the codes I have suggested is brought about by the boundary maintaining procedures within the family. However, we can generalise and say that the focussing of the codes is related to the boundary maintaining procedures as these affect the major socialising agencies, family, age group, education and work. We need, therefore, to consider together with the question of the degree and type of complexity of the division of labour the value orientations of society which it is hypothesised affect the boundary maintaining procedures. It is the case that we can have societies with a similar complexity in their division of labour but who differ in their boundary maintaining procedures.

I suggest then that it is important to make a distinction between societies in terms of their boundary maintaining procedures if we are to deal with this question of the focussing of codes. One possible way of examining the relative strength of boundary maintenance, at a somewhat high level of abstraction, is to consider the strength of the *constraints* upon the choice of values which legitimize authority/power relationships. Thus in societies where there is weak constraint upon such legitimising values, that is, where there are a variety of formally permitted legitimising values, we might expect a marked shift towards person type control. Whereas in societies with strong constraints upon legitimising values, where there is a severe *restriction* upon the choice, we might expect a marked shift towards positional control.

I shall illustrate these relationships with reference to the family:

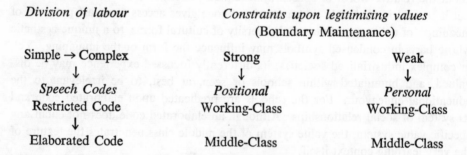

Division of labour	*Constraints upon legitimising values* (Boundary Maintenance)	
	Strong	Weak
Simple → Complex	↓	↓
↓	Positional	Personal
Speech Codes	Working-Class	Working-Class
Restricted Code		
↓		
Elaborated Code	Middle-Class	Middle-Class

Thus the division of labour influences the availability of elaborated codes; the class system affects their distribution; the focussing of codes can be related to the boundary maintaining procedures, i.e. the value system. I must point out that this is only a coarse interpretive framework.

CONCLUSION

I have tried to show how the class system acts upon the deep structure of communication in the process of socialisation. I refined the crudity of this analysis by showing how speech codes may be differently focussed through family types. Finally, it is conceivable that there are general aspects of the analysis which might provide a starting point for the consideration of symbolic orders other than languages (see Douglas 1970). I must point out that there is more to socialisation than the forms of its linguistic realisation.

BIBLIOGRAPHY

BERNSTEIN, B. 1970a. Education cannot compensate for society. New Society No. 387, February, 1970.

——. 1972. Family role systems, socialisation and communication. Directions in sociolinguistics, ed. by D. Hymes and J. J. Gumperz. New York, Holt, Rinehart and Winston. Also appeared as Manuscript, Sociological Research Unit, University of London Institute of Education (1967).

BERNSTEIN, B., and J. COOK. 1965. Coding grid for maternal control. Available from Department of Sociology, University of London Institute of Education.

BERNSTEIN, B., and D. HENDERSON. 1969. Social class differences in the relevance of language to socialisation. Sociology 3/1.

BRIGHT, W., ed. 1966. Sociolinguistics. The Hague, Mouton.

CARROLL, J. B., ed. 1956. Language, thought and reality: Selected writings of Benjamin Lee Whorf. New York, John Wiley & Sons, Inc.

CAZDEN, C. B. 1969. Sub-cultural differences in child language: An interdisciplinary review. Merrill-Palmer Quarterly 12.

CHOMSKY, N. 1965. Aspects of the theory of syntax. Cambridge, M.I.T. Press.

COOK, J. 1970. An enquiry into patterns of communication and control between mothers and their children in different social classes. Ph.D. Thesis, awaiting submission to the University of London (1970).

COULTHARD, M. 1969. A discussion of restricted and elaborated codes. Educational Review 22/1.

DOUGLAS, M. 1970. Natural symbols. London, Barrie & Rockliff, The Cresset Press/New York, Pantheon.

FISHMAN, J. A. 1960. A systematisation of the Whorfian hypothesis. BS 5.

HALLIDAY, M. A. K. 1969. Relevant models of language. Educational Review 22/1.

HAWKINS, P. R. 1969. Social class, the nominal group and reference. L & S 12/2.125-35.

HENDERSON, D. 1970. Contextual specificity, discretion and cognitive socialisation: With special reference to language. Sociology 4/3.

HOIJER, H., ed. 1954. Language in culture. American Anthropological Association Memoir No. 79 — also published by the University of Chicago Press.

HYMES, D. 1966. On communicative competence. Research Planning Conference on Language Development among Disadvantaged Children. Ferkauf Graduate School, Yeshiva University. *Also in* Hymes and Gumperz, 1972.

——. 1967. Models of the interaction of language and social setting. Journal of Social Issues 23.

HYMES, D., and J. J. GUMPERZ, eds. 1972. Directions in sociolinguistics. New York, Holt, Rinehart and Winston.

LABOV, W. 1965. Stages in the acquisition of standard English. Social dialects and language learning, ed. by W. Shuy. Champaign, Illinois, National Council of Teachers of English.

——. 1966. The social stratification of English in New York City. Washington, D.C., Center for Applied Linguistics.

MANDELBAUM, D., ed. 1949. Selected writings of Edward Sapir. University of California Press.

PARSONS, T., and E. A. SHILS, eds. 1951. Toward a general theory of action. Cambridge, Mass.; Harvard University Press. Also Harper Torchbooks TB1083N. [Chapter 1, especially]

SCHATZMAN, L., and A. L. STRAUSS. 1955. Social class and modes of communication. American Journal of Sociology 60.328–38.

TURNER, G., and R. E. PICKVANCE. 1970. Social class differences in the expression of uncertainty in five-year-old children. L & S 13.

WILLIAMS, F., and R. C. NAREMORE. 1969. On the functional analysis of social class differences in modes of speech. Speech Monographs 36/2.

ETHNOMETHODOLOGY

AARON V. CICOUREL *

The term ethnomethodology was coined by Harold Garfinkel (1967) to index the study of everyday practical reasoning as constitutive of all human activities. A basic consideration in the study of practical reasoning is members' use of everyday talk or accounts to describe the factual status of their experiences and activities. This abstract opening statement is not intended as a crisp explanation of the term 'ethnomethodology', but a delaying action so that a more elaborate discussion will evolve gradually in later sections.

In this chapter I restrict myself to selected aspects of generative-transformational linguistics to address more general issues in the problem of meaning. The term 'linguistics', however, is to be used in a generic way despite my more narrow reference to some features of generative-transformational grammar. I will trade on a presumed knowledge by the reader of current issues in generative-transformational linguistics in my development of ethnomethodology and its perspective on language and meaning.

A further restriction should be noted. I have not addressed various issues in conversational analysis that constitute an important part of sociolinguistics (Sacks 1966, dittoed materials 1967, 1970; Schegloff 1968; Turner 1970). The analysis of conversations can include (a) how conversations can be started and terminated by different speaker-hearer strategies, (b) the relationship between the speaker's social status and his rights to talk under specific interactional circumstances, (c) how certain markers signal that additional information is expected or that a hearer is available for further talk about a particular topic, (d) how topics are introduced or avoided or changed or prolonged within and over different conversations, (e) how different chunks of a conversation can be seen as tied together to communicate particular kinds of information not evident from the sequential character of the dialogue, (f) how speaker-hearers use particular lexical items or phrases to convey context-restricted or context-free impressions, and (g) how we structure our speech to accomplish activities like making excuses, distrusting and mocking others, and the like. My reasons for excluding the above issues in this chapter is that the

* This paper draws upon research sponsored by the Ford Foundation for the study of communicative competence in children and classroom performance. I am grateful to Hugh Mehan, Sybillyn Jennings, and Thomas Petersen for their extensive and very helpful remarks.

research cited relies almost exclusively on transcripts of (presumably obtrusively obtained) naturally occurring conversations that deliberately ignore or defer consideration of non-oral features of interaction. Even when intonational or acoustical information is presupposed in the analysis, the use of such information is usually tacit and not central to the description of the conversation. I am primarily concerned with the articulation of oral and non-oral features in a general theory of everyday communication, particularly as non-oral features are forced on us in the study of deaf communication.

The ethnomethodologist is interested in the modern linguist's use of speech or talk to construct a grammar that will describe the structure of language. But this interest in the linguist's activities assumes that every attempt to describe the structure of language relies on practical reasoning as a tacit and unexamined resource for finding in talk (but primarily idealized talk) an innovative but rule-governed structure (competence) that is said to transcend actual displays (performance). The ethnomethodologist's central concern is the study of members' necessary reliance on practical or mundane reasoning to communicate with others, and the fact that members count on this tacit use of practical reasoning for more abstract activities like constructing mathematical proofs or developing re-write rules in linguistics.

Ethnomethodologists and linguists employ somewhat different conceptions of meaning but both rely on the production of speech or accounts as a point of departure. For the linguist the meaning of speech becomes fairly restricted; it is tied to the establishment of relationships and reference in speech through the use of formal types of reasoning that seeks to produce determinate outcomes. For the ethnomethodologist talk and action are produced and understood as indexical (Bar-Hillel 1954; Garfinkel 1967; Cicourel 1968a) displays of the everyday world. The linguist relies heavily on a conception of meaning based on syntax, while the ethnomethodologist addresses the interpretive abilities presupposed by the necessary interplay between competence and situated performance. This chapter relies on elements of linguistic theory to present an ethnomethodological view of the problem of meaning. A partial outline is contained in the following overview.

I. Linguistic and ethnomethodological approaches to the problem of meaning differ markedly. The former has stressed formal properties of language that would be relevant for the development of logical relationships and rules to describe the association between sound patterns and the objects and events or experiences to which they refer, while the latter approach has been concerned with the process whereby rules said to cover interactional settings are constructed as well as with the assessment of claimed measurement of the actual implementation of rules in specific circumstances. Ethnomethodology emphasizes the interpretive work required to recognize that an abstract rule exists that could fit a particular occasion, while linguists minimize the relevance of interactional context-sensitive features when stressing the importance of syntactic rules for semantic analysis. Recent work on generative semantics (Lakoff 1968; McCawley 1968a, 1968b; Ross, forthcoming) has been moving toward the inclusion of the consideration of context and presuppositions as developed in philosophical studies of language and anthropological linguistics, and these works have been helpful in formulating the present chapter.

The ethnomethodologist views meaning as situated, self-organizing and reflexive interaction between the organization of memory, practical reasoning, and talk. Linguistic rules are seen as normative constructions divorced from the cognitive reflection and ethnographic settings in which speech is produced and understood. Universal grammatical structures inferred from proscribed and prescribed forms of talk can be described as general rules or policies or practices, under which situated innovative language displays of familiar forms are subsumed. Syntactic and phonological rules provide linguists with carefully constructed normative ideals that can be studied and described independently of actual use in social settings. The researcher's context-free description or account, however, presumes and tacitly relies on an intuitive use of ethnographic particulars and interpretive procedures that are never made explicit, though occasionally touched upon in an abstract way.

The term generative semantics, therefore, is not, for the ethnomethodologist, a syntax-based theory of meaning and reference. The acquisition and use of general rules of syntax and phonology presuppose a tacit reliance on cognitive activities embedded in the organization of memory within an interactional setting. Settings or some kind of imagery must be recalled, invented, or imagined to make utterances, stripped of their situated occurrence, appear plausible. There is a continual reflexive monitoring by the speaker-hearer to provide self-organizing information processing during activities like reading a text or discussing a setting different from the one being experienced. The conception of generative semantics proposed here assumes that the speaker-hearer selectively consults and intuitively presupposes features or particulars in a setting to invoke the tacit or explicit phonological, syntactic, lexical, social, or legal rules to order and justify his speech.

II. The use of memory and interpretive procedures (Cicourel 1968a; 1973) for recoding or chunking activities illustrates how practical reasoning requires indexical procedures for expressing reflexive thoughts that interact with visual and auditory particulars in a setting. In contrast, the notion of a rule of grammar, like any normative practice or policy, is invoked to construct a correspondence theory that minimizes the role of intuitive reasoning in linking a rule or practice with particular occasions of speech usage. Those particulars remembered or selectively witnessed (intended) are tied to standardized conceptions of meaning so that categorization by rule can simulate a sense of adequacy for intended meanings and reference. Linguistic analyses and studies of artificial intelligence achieve their elegance by examining utterances that are divested of the non-syntactic particulars presupposed in their production. These utterances, while not as 'purified' as those constructed by logicians, are conveniently produced by the linguist by drawing on his native abilities with the language, or by making use of elicitation procedures that guarantee the selectivity necessary for fitting utterances to idealized syntactic or phonological rules. The student of artificial intelligence and the linguist achieve elegant description by relying on idealized utterances and their practical reasoning and intuitive knowledge of language to legislate non-syntactic ambiguity and contradictions out of their constructed realities.

III. A recent study of children in quasi-experimental and natural classroom settings is discussed in the final section to clarify issues in the problem of meaning by revealing how situated reconstructions of past experiences, and unfolding auditory and visual cues, are central for the child's production of oral expressions that adults evaluate as phonologically, syntactically, and semantically 'correct'. The child's understanding of presumed 'clear' stimulus sentences by an experimenter or teacher does not always coincide with the adult's conception of a correct correspondence between a stimulus and a response.

Additional work on manual sign language provides an even broader theoretical and empirical basis for suggesting that the problem of meaning in a general theory of communication cannot be conceived as part of an oral language tradition that is syntactically organized. Many versions of sign language emerge depending on the frequency of interaction between participants as dyads or in larger groups. The self-organizing nature of sign activity among deaf strangers underscores the situated basis of meaning because there are no standard rules of orthography and grammar that force members to express themselves via idealized or rule-modified constructions that have been divested of non-syntactic particulars. Only when signs are set up in correspondence with oral language grammatical structures and a standardized lexicon does sign language give any appearance of having formal context-free properties.

I

Recent linguistic work (Lakoff 1968) suggests that one version of the generative semantics proposed by syntactically-oriented generative-transformational linguists will be forced to adopt more of a situated interactional approach to meaning if notions like counterpart theory, and the idea of sentences containing contradictory references to different possible worlds are pursued. One consequence of adopting an interactional perspective wherein syntactic rules play a minor role in problems of meaning and doing reference is that current reliance on sentence boundaries and a static lexicon of the 'look-up' sort will have to be altered radically. The notion of 'sentence' is being re-examined in response to recent work on performative theory and embedding in phrase structure rules. Unless the syntactic basis for meaning is altered we must view the linguist as a judge: he would be a specialist for interpreting a highly formal system of rules, practices, or policies so that these rules could be invoked to justify the claim that a particular instance of speech can be said to fall under a rule or practice or policy (Rawls 1955; Cicourel 1967, 1968b). The analogy between judges and linguists is central to my argument because in each case the features or particulars that serve as empirical displays (e.g., the details of a police report, the intent of an action that leads to bodily harm, the sentences offered as candidates for grammaticality, lexical items assigned meaning by reference to a dictionary and classificatory bundles of features) are always idealized accounts whose 'legality' is decided by the judge or linguist by consulting a rule structure he has imposed on the ambiguity and looseness of everyday language. The judge and linguist assign normative sense to sentences or their structure and thus detach utterances from their common sense and situated meaning, transforming them into context-free claims about social reality. The linguist, of course, would claim that many of his judgments (e.g. number agreement) render context irrelevant.

When lawyers are taught about legal activities by the use of textbook materials that include the 'facts' of a case, a large number of contingencies or particulars are eliminated so that a coherent story appears that reduces possible ambiguities in the description of an unfolding scene over clock-time. The language of the lawyer's argument is a carefully edited grammatical text whose structure is managed, just as a linguist's candidate sentences are edited or the informant's utterances are constrained through the linguist's elicitation procedures. The utterances used by linguists for constructing rules that account for linguistic descriptions are generally posed as context-free. The self-contained or bounded nature of these utterances eliminates the ambiguities that members must incorporate into their production of speech when carrying out everyday conversations. In actual exchanges editing is constrained by a concern for chaining sequences, but can also trade on visual and auditory information.

If we view a speaker-hearer's utterances as accounts that are situated, edited versions of information that is being processed, then fragments of utterances, pauses, ellipsis, auditory and visual information not verbalized can no longer be ignored but must be incorporated into the linguist's theories. The differentials in meaning emerge within the contingencies of an interaction setting where the ethnographic context, the biographies of the participants, and subtleties of voice intonation, gestures, and body posturing all contribute to the information that is continually being processed while utterances are being produced. To include such contingencies would obviously go beyond the goals of most linguists. The linguist is dealing with an 'idealized speaker-hearer' who often turns out to be himself or his wife turned informant, someone who is tacitly reflective at least about sentences he dreams up or is asked to assess. This reflective activity divorces the formal sense of the utterance from the contingencies mentioned above, while simultaneously producing a tacit (but suppressed) ethnographic context that could yield the utterance. But even this tacit context is often irrelevant for the linguist interested in showing what sentences must look like if rules that seem to hold for one class of sentences must also cover another sentence whose structure seems a bit odd. The linguist makes explicit use of his own or an esoteric informant's native intuition or 'feel' for the language without addressing the cognitive aspects of his production of language.

We can illustrate some of the problems mentioned above by discussing Lakoff's paper on the problem of reference. He proposes two readings of the following sentence (Lakoff's numbering):

(2) 'I dreamed that I was playing the piano.'

The first reading is called the 'participant reading' and Lakoff describes this as a feeling that he is sitting at a piano, seeing the keyboard, with his fingers hitting the keys. He adds an 'etc.' to his description to imply further particulars are possible. In the second reading (called the 'observer reading'), he sees himself (or someone like himself) sitting at the piano, playing it, as if he were sitting in a movie watching himself perform. What is of interest in Lakoff's distinction between participant and observer readings of a sentence is that all readings imply perspectival views of possible speaker-hearers, and the kinds of ethnographic conditions that might render these readings (or others) plausible. The ethnographic particulars are integral to the interpretations offered. A consequence of including specific ethnographic conditions is that sentences can be seen as meaningful and also satisfying syntactic rules, yet a dictionary look-up of each lexical item can only locate the sentence for a reader by tacitly trading on a native's intuitive reasoning and conception of ethnographic particulars. In situated everyday conversation, however, we also have many sentences that are either grammatically improper or are not understandable by reference to a dictionary. My concern is to show that as soon as the linguist entertains alternative possible readings he tacitly invokes situated circumstances that render problematic the context-free readings possible by reference to syntactic rules and a dictionary. Each reader can supply many features or particulars that are privileged to the perspectival view or account of the observer to justify a specific reading of an utterance.

Lakoff then presents two additional sentences that are said to represent participant and observer readings of the same action:

(3) 'I enjoyed robbing the bank.'
(4) 'I enjoyed my robbing the bank.'

Sentence (3) is said to be a participant reading that refers to an enjoyment of a bank robbing experience, while (4) is said to be an observer reading where there is a reflexive observing or possible contemplation of an event. To call the act reflexive suggests that the speaker-hearer's thoughts provide a self-organizing basis for the intended reference. His thoughts may be only partially indexed by the utterance produced, making it difficult for an observer to determine the intended referent. Lakoff is interested in showing that sentences like (5), (6), (7), (8),

(9), and (10) cannot be handled by the theory of referential indices (If two NPs have the same referential indices, they have the same 'intended reference'.), for sentences like (9) and (10) would have the same underlying or deep structure, yet include two different semantic references.

> (5) 'As a participant, I enjoyed robbing the bank.'
> (6)* 'As an outside observer, I enjoyed robbing the bank.'
> (7)* 'As a participant, I enjoyed my robbing the bank.'
> (8) 'As an outside observer, I enjoyed my robbing the bank.'
> (9) 'I imagined robbing the bank.' (participant)
> (10) 'I imagined myself robbing the bank.' (observer)

The point being stressed by Lakoff is that syntactic distinctions cannot handle the problem of the 'same' intended reference within the same sentence or different sentences where both participant and observer readings refer to different kinds of discourse or possible worlds. The subjects of (9) and (10) have the same reference in the same world, while the subjects of the verbs *imagine* and *rob* have the same physical reference but the worlds (participant and observer) are different. Lakoff's distinction can be extended by noting that imagining presupposes not only my participating but also observing myself as a participant. Thus Lakoff (referring to another sentence) distinguishes between the actual world in which one can do dreaming activity, and the world of the dream itself. A person's identity must be referenced differently when different realities are entertained and the person assumes two identities because the actual world (read: the world within my reach or grasp) is conceived as two possible worlds (read: the world within my reach and the world within my dreams: cf. Schutz 1964). Lakoff presents another sentence to show how two types of people (read: with ideological differences) in one possible world are reduced to a single individual in another possible world (read: the ideological world reconstructed by the speaker-hearer).

> (15) 'You think that Nixon and Humphrey are different people and that *they* will campaign against each other and one of *them* will lose, but I think that Nixon and Humphrey are the same person and that *he* will win.'

Lakoff has touched upon the construction of multiple realities by members (be they informants or researchers) described more extensively by Alfred Schutz (1962), by recognizing that generative transformational grammar cannot handle the complicated problems of reference posed by different possible worlds. The same syntactic markers confuse different possible worlds in the surface or deep structure constructions, but it is clear that the speaker-hearer (informant and researcher) must supply meanings that must be attributed on the basis of what seems 'obvious' or what 'anyone knows' to be the intentions of the speaker-hearer.

When Lakoff argues that within the first half of the same sentence (15) Nixon and Humphrey have different referential indices, and therefore cannot have the same index in the second half of the sentence, he wants to show that syntactic grounds for doing reference are inadequate. The possible semantic solution suggested by Lakoff would require a logic through which different possible worlds can be represented, such that a single entity in one world can be represented as two different entities in another world. By insisting on a normative system of rules to gloss what members in everyday life resolve routinely despite syntactic limitations, the linguist or logician seeks to organize our speech acts such that linguistics or logic becomes a policy science. Natural ways developed by members for coping with inherent gaps and inconsistencies in lay theories of language use would be ignored, while more elegant rule systems would be constructed that could logically hope to resolve the ambiguities of doing reference as outlined in the work by Lakoff. Much of language can be viewed as normatively learned in that existing forms of speech become progressively reified and standardized by historical accidents and power relationships within a community or country. The result of normative language legislation is that some forms are rewarded or honored more as marks of social achievement or intellectual status, and other forms of speech are justified by reference to scientifically-based psychological theories of learning and testing.

Linguists insist that the acquisition and use of natural language is miraculous because it is characterized by the ability to understand and produce an indefinite number of expressions that are new to one's experience. Chomsky (no date) notes the creative nature of language and the independence of its appropriate use from any clear-cut stimulus configurations in some conditioned sense. He suggests these very characteristics may preclude detailed knowledge about the human use of language as an instrument for expressing thought and feeling. He goes on to discuss several other important issues that I want to link to Lakoff's paper and to the problem of meaning as situated phenomena that require the interaction of the speaker-hearer's (a) standardized or typified use of information to provide for memory generalization and the resolution of ambiguity; and (b) continual reflexiveness of thought, talk, and situation.

Doubts about the phonetic representation are expressed by Chomsky in the same argument by raising the question of the legitimacy of this abstraction process. He raises the issue of whether our understanding of the use of language must go beyond grammatical structure when we use formal rules for interpreting surface structure as phonetic form. Anyone who has done field research with children and adults in his own and foreign communities will recognize the difficulties of locating phonetic representations for many sounds. We utilize phonetic categories as normative rules that we force on materials. By incorporating scientific knowledge into our everyday use of language as well as our teaching children how they are to represent themselves through sound patterns, the linguist ignores the interaction between what is learned normatively and what is claimed as linguistic universals or an acquisition device.

Linguists do not study the abstraction process itself when they devise notions like deep and surface structures, phonetic and semantic representations. Yet these abstractions are employed as descriptions of language competence and use. Notions like deep and surface structure cannot alone recover the abstraction 'everyday language' because the pragmatics of everyday language use is always embedded reflexively in the setting of its production. Some of these situated and reflexive features are illustrated by Lakoff's distinction between participant and observer readings of a sentence and the idea of different possible worlds that cannot be referenced by the theory of referential indices. Deep structure is an arbitrary (but heuristically useful) notion constructed by the linguist to deal with the fact that surface structure is indexical; it always implies more information than is displayed. Proposing transformational rules to link deep and surface structures does not alter the arbitrariness of deep structure which the linguist constructs by selectively consulting the particulars of a setting and his own reflections about how a given utterance may have been produced.

Despite his expressed cautions about the abstraction process, Chomsky shifts from a treatment of the formal rules of grammar as describing the structure of language to a reification of the grammar as characterizing part of the speaker-hearer's knowledge of a language. The linguist's heuristically useful constructs for depicting an ideal speaker-hearer have become rules that a person who has learned a language has mastered. The linguist's heuristically developed rules constitute the person's knowledge of the language.

The claims about what constitutes a person's knowledge of a language are presented by Chomsky in the context of showing how certain sentences appear to have deep and surface structures that are similar if not identical, while other sentences differ in their deep and surface representation. He goes on to alter previous formulations by noting how surface structure can be important in determining the semantic interpretation of a sentence. This observation requires a discussion of how different meanings are presupposed in the surface structure of a sentence in the sense outlined by Lakoff when he talks of different possible worlds, and the readings possible by a participant as opposed to an observer, or both readings in the same sentence. Chomsky has further modified earlier versions of his theory by noting how different intonational contours can alter the surface meaning of a sentence. Differences of intonation can lead to complicated conceptions of the presuppositions involved. Speaker-hearers make use of presuppositions on every occasion of speech. The serious question discussed in more detail later in the chapter is how the presuppositions are to be located by reference to a rather rigid system of rules claimed for the speaker-hearer. Or, how are we to locate presuppositions by reference to intonational contours that influence the way information is processed and then presumably indexed by sound patterns? Much of contemporary linguistics operates within a theory of grammar characterized by three components – the phonological, syntactic, and semantic – along with an elusive lexicon. By introducing the idea of presupposition, and treating intonation seriously, the linguist, whatever his view of the interrelations among these components, will find it hard to avoid bringing in additional types of information that have been glossed with the label 'pragmatics'.

The picture that emerges from Chomsky's paper is that deep structure endows an utterance with predication and modifications that enter into the problem of determining meaning, while the surface structure in part handles matters of focus and presupposition, pronominal reference, and topic, among others. Recalling Lakoff's remarks that possible worlds can contain contradictions, the fascinating changes taking place within generative semantics lead one to ask if linguists can hold on to the formal syntactic distinctions (like sentence boundaries) as both observers' rules for explaining speaker-hearers' utterances, and as claims that the formal notions are also part of universal grammar and the speaker-hearer's mental structures?

The idea of a deep structure with transformational rules that provide for a surface structure is an important heuristic device because it calls attention to the indexicality of everyday language; however, it also raises serious questions about the term 'natural' in referring to language use. The naturalness of language becomes problematic because it is not clear how linguists' formulations, teachers' curricula, educational psychologists' and psycholinguists' assessment tests, and educated adults' models, interact in a speech community. The linguist's use of elicitation procedures to discover evidence for linguistic universals presupposes an ideal language structure. Speech acts may be called 'natural' by an observer when he senses that members appear to be oblivious to 'correct' or ungrammatical usage. We have, however, little knowledge about uneducated everyday language use (even in non-literate societies) despite many field studies. In addition, we ignore the extent to which our studies of competence and use are continually infused with formal normative elements that derive from monitoring one's own output or having it monitored for one by others. What seems to be natural about everyday speech is that groups have always developed various kinds of normative rules or conventions for such purposes as determining kinship relationships, performing public ceremonies, and interpersonal address.

The linguistic expert uses his own capabilities as a native speaker-hearer or those of an informant to formulate the grammatical utterances of a language. The idealized sentences produced are the work of an expert, even when the sentences are elicited from an informant prompted about what he is expected to say. Using his own native competence (or that of an informant) the linguist provides us with conceptions of what is possible or believable about an utterance up for grammatical or semantic review. He will note that we cannot ignore the universal character of disjunctions as underlying yes-no questions, or that imperatives have second person subjects, and the like. But these conceptions or presuppositions (like participant and observer readings or intonation stress) must be in agreement with the normatively constructed logical schema adopted for representing syntactic relationships.

Lakoff's distinctions are important because he attempts to push the syntactic framework to its limits to show that it cannot cover reference work that endows the speaker-hearer with the ability to live with apparent contradictions and multiple realities that defy traditional two-valued logic. Logical frameworks are subdomains of everyday language that have been cleansed of difficulties that would confound the correspondence theory necessary for idealized outcomes. Therefore, grammatical or logical utterances retain their rule-governed structure because they have been cleansed and divorced from their occasions of use, and other particulars about the biographies of the participants, the features of the setting tacitly taken into account, the reflexive thinking and use of talk, and so on. For the linguist the book he is now reading is proof that language behavior can be understood independently of the occasions that produced it. The speaker-hearer (linguist, logician) can consult his own speech for evidence that his enterprise is a success because his mastery of the formal normative framework becomes a referential schema or system of general rules to justify claims that utterances he produces or those of a native informant can be described by reference to these rules. The linguist constructs a self-validating circle that tacitly utilizes unexplicated common knowledge as a basic resource for recognizing topics, constructing appropriate presuppositions, and eliminating possible alternatives not suggested by the logical possibilities of idealized normative rules.

Linguists prefer to live with different kinds of conveniently constructed glosses, while the ethnomethodologist prefers to treat the glossing itself as an activity that becomes the phenomenon of interest while recognizing that no one can escape some level of glossing in order to claim knowledge about something. But this claim to knowledge, this use of some level of glossing for communication, is also a claim for a privileged position. Different levels of glossing produce different self-validating circles and hence different claims about what is known. We can perhaps achieve glimpses of our glossing activity by making it clear that every attempt to simulate or avoid the glossing activity is itself a glossing operation. This means showing the absurdity of efforts to be uncompromisingly literal in our descriptions of observed events or activities in which we participate.

II

In this section I rely on selected topics in recent work on visual and linguistic memory organization and studies of artificial intelligence to provide a more general framework for examining the semantic issues addressed in section I. Ethnomethodology and semantic issues in linguistics both presuppose that cognition and thought are central for understanding linguistic competence, but employ different models of the speaker-hearer. Linguists imply that the same mechanisms govern both the production and comprehension of speech. The ethnomethodologist seeks to locate the comprehension of speech in an emergent interactional setting that makes speech production both a topic and a resource for the participant. This section explores the treatment of everyday language as an abstract topic for creating strong rule systems to justify claims about grammaticality and meaning by linguists and cognitively oriented students of artificial intelligence and their failure within these enterprises to study how everyday language and meaning are and remain *tacit* resources for applying and interpreting these systems. The constructed rule system guarantees that a correspondence theory of measurement will be constitutive of utterances that are candidates for grammaticality or computer procedures that are intended to establish artificial constructions of meaning and reference.

A central issue in studies of artificial intelligence is how to deal with the short- and long-term storage of information. Linguists have not given the problem of memory much attention because recall and recognition are not problematic issues in discussions of deep and surface structure and the transformational rules that link them. The linguist claims a certain kind of immunity from contamination by memory problems largely by ignoring performance issues and focusing on a corpus of materials that is divorced from interactional settings. The linguists, however, share with the students of artificial intelligence an interest in syntactic, semantic, and lexical problems, and the use of edited sentences generated primarily by a native speaker-hearer who is either the researcher himself, or an informant who acts like a research assistant. Recent work in artificial intelligence has posed inter-action between a machine programmed to generate English sentences, and a native-speaking subject or informant-researcher (Greenberger 1962; Reitman 1965; Minsky 1968; and Simon 1969). Ethnomethodologists (Garfinkel 1967) have used a kind of 'talking-out-loud' procedure similar to those used by students of artificial intelligence (De Groot 1965; Quillian 1968; Simon and Barenfeld 1969) for generating material designed to make visible how language and meaning are embedded in and created by a cognitive information processing system. Quillian (1968), Colby *et al.* (1969) and Simon and Barenfeld (1969) study information processing by having the speaker-hearer engage in some task like thinking out loud about chess moves, stating and justifying beliefs, or having a coder-subject encode sentences of English text into the format of a previously created memory model. The authors of these studies view the protocols as displays of information processing. Yet the task alters the routine ways humans confront such problems by asking for explicit statements of activities seldom discussed while actually being experienced.

The ethnomethodologist collects talking-out-loud protocols and employs them to reveal the taken-for-granted features of daily activities after making everyday routines appear strange to subjects. Garfinkel (1967) demonstrated this idea by having subjects ask questions of a 'counselor' about their problems. The coun-selor's 'answers', however, were randomized 'yes' and 'no' responses. Subjects were able to reorient their thinking to absorb apparent contradictions and ambiguities. Another procedure is to have persons give accounts of some recent activity and then show each subject an audio or video tape of the activity while asking for another account of the activity. The ethnomethodologist sees these constructed accounts as indefinite elaborations of ostensibly the 'same' scene, where various accounts produce different outputs. Specifying that someone did the task 'correctly' or made a 'proper' chess move, or reasoned 'correctly' is not a goal of ethnomethodological analysis. Instead there is a deep concern with treating the temporally constituted production and comprehension processes as the phenomena of interest. This means that the grammatical structure of speech acts is merely one part of indexical activity or the production process and no more 'natural' than raising or lowering the voice, stepping closer to or farther from someone during a conversation, or relying on facial expressions and body movements to communicate the intent of one's thinking.

The use of grammatical rules to order speech provides an elegant and powerful tool for organizing and standardizing the production of verbal acts that index cognition and thought. Rules of grammar and programs of artificial intelligence are designed to eliminate ambiguities and contradictions and to produce outcomes that are internally consistent. The production of rule-governed utterances or programs are normative constructions that are subject to specifiable constraints if they are to code and recode or chunk information according to specifiable search procedures or algorithms (Miller 1956; Norman 1969). Our human experiences continually outstrip our ability to express them in speech acts. We must assume that a number of tacit properties are operative or plausible when we code, recode, and then use information to communicate with others. The organization of memory and the intuitive procedures we use to interpret an interactional setting are strained by the indexical structure of language. Our ability to assign meaning to utterances is contingent on an understanding of various possible sources of information in a complex setting. Syntactic rules do not appear to be central but clearly useful for achieving normative agreement.

The organization of memory can only be meaningful vis-à-vis the settings in which speech and non-oral communication occur. The setting is not merely a passive vehicle for witnessing universals of language; the setting is constitutive of how properties of cognition as displays of practical reasoning render a scene sensible or socially meaningful. Speech, like one's social and personal identity, requires continuous performances if rules or attributes said to transcend the setting (like presumed personality traits said to be somehow embedded in the actor) are to be recognized as operative. If we seldom speak to others in public settings our performances suffer, and we avoid such occasions. If we do not write often then even a simple letter becomes difficult, while a governmental form proves torturous. Persons who become deaf after adolescence quickly lose their ability to speak like natives because the reflexive feedback of a temporally constituted scene that includes intonation, body movements, gestures, visual and auditory details, is altered as a source of information. The organization of cognition that served us on previous occasions is reconstituted in each new setting while we normatively reconstruct our speech, our social identity, and culture itself. The discovery of constancies reflects the normative organization of everyday experience by an inescapable reliance on memory and practical reasoning.

Speech as used in everyday conversation provides the native with his own measurement system because members ritualize certain forms of speech. The more obvious examples of normative features of speech are to be found in ceremonies and rituals that we call religious or developmental as in rites of passage, or legal as in marriage or judicial activities. Thus, everyday talk is indexically constitutive of its own explication on each occasion of use. As a measurement system of cognitive activity speech indexes some particulars, but we must feel, perceive, recover, invent, or imagine many more particulars to assign sense to a setting. Some set of phrase structure rules and transformational rules does not produce language; we must ask how the particulars of language production as a situated accomplishment of each occasion can be linked reflexively by speaker-hearers to some normative system of grammatical, legal, or other rules. We examine our talk in order to find, among other things, its normative character.

Chunking or recoding is a way of describing formal indexical activity. Miller's (1956) work on the span of immediate memory is important for showing that regardless of the information content (which limits absolute judgment) of different items, our immediate memory seems to be limited by the number of items. Miller distinguishes between *bits* of information that seem to be constant for absolute judgment, and *chunks* of information that seem to be constant for immediate memory span. Miller reports that by regrouping two or more digits into code items that remained at seven or less, subjects could extend the number of digits that could be retained in immediate memory. This efficient regrouping or recoding of old items into new items is called *chunking* by Miller. We expand the number of items we can remember by building larger and larger chunks so that each chunk contains more information than previously. The span of immediate memory appears to be independent of the number of bits that can be grouped into a chunk.

The term 'short-term memory', however, seems to refer to a type of psychological experiment rather than to describe the recoding process as it operates in humans (Norman 1969). We are not very clear about how members carry out chunking because most of the recoding experiments have been done with fairly simple stimuli. Miller notes that we engage in recoding operations continuously on objects, facts, images, arguments, events told as stories, and that these operations are more complicated than the presumed unidimensional stimuli used in psychological experiments. We continuously recode our experiences into verbal reports that we remember, and then use the verbal recall as a way of recovering the events recoded, or to give accounts to others about our experiences. Miller suggests that particular speaker-hearers develop idiosyncratic ways of recoding that become embedded in their life history.

All language use seems to reflect some kind of underlying competence and also represents at least two kinds of compromise the speaker-hearer must negotiate: (a) the language employed is part of an indexical process whose most primitive formal output can be loosely characterized as chunked or recoded information; and (b) the products of chunking are normative displays that are culture-specific and also constrained by differential abilities, educational training, use, or occupation. The negotiation means that within the indexicality of language actual use can always vary in different contexts or occasions; variations emerge because participants locate and elaborate particulars differently by relying on speech, visual and auditory information, biographical information, and a reflexive elaboration of their own memory or general cognitive procedures.

Language chunking or recoding is constitutive of our efforts to express our experiences. The role of rules for generating admissible sound patterns expressed logically as bundles of features and strings of words that are normatively segmented into logically constructed units called sentences is only one (though often useful) element among various chunks of particulars that convey meaning and do reference in everyday exchanges. To say that something is rule-governed presupposes that members will agree that certain behaviors or activities are being followed correctly or incorrectly. This means that indexical expressions (Bar-Hillel 1954; Garfinkel 1967; Cicourel 1968a; Garfinkel and Sacks 1969) or any given instance verbalized (or produced non-orally) as a chunk of particulars must be subsumed under general rules such that the speaker-hearer will presume that others would agree with his reasoning and recognize the instance or event or object as falling under a class, policy, practice, or general rule (Rawls 1956; Hart 1961; Cicourel 1967, 1968b).

Linguists have advanced a convincing argument for biologically based (Chomsky 1965) universals of language. I do not wish to quarrel with the biological foundations of language (Lenneberg 1968) here, but do wish to question the idea of 'linguistic universals'. The linguistic argument states that every human group studied has a spoken language with a lexicon and a grammar, where the lexicon seems to be organized into normatively consistent bits and chunks. Each language provides for pronominal displays, contains notions of time, space, and number, as well as notions like true and false, and can be described as having phonological and syntactic levels of structure. It seems clear that biological competence is presupposed in these activities. But we can also call the 'universals' normative constructions imposed initially by certain 'experts' in a tribe or linguists in a society or nation-state. The idea is that forms of communication other than oral language can convey these activities. This view argues that 'linguistic universals' are cultural products of normative chunking or recoding activities. A linguist would want to argue that the *same* linguistic norms keep turning up in different languages. He would claim that this consistency cannot be dismissed as the product of the researchers' methods for discovering language regularities.

I want to treat each linguistic universal as a particular kind of gloss imposed by the ingenious constructions of the researcher (and lay scribes and grammarians). Each glossing practice (Garfinkel and Sacks 1969) represents the researcher's native ability to begin with any level of indexicality designated as 'correct' speech or any language display in conformity with some general rule or practice. The researcher then seeks to reduce the chunk or gloss to constituent or basic elements. I do not think that work in acoustical phonetics alters this assertion because the native intuition of a speaker-hearer is essential for recognizing meaningful patterns in physical displays of human speech. Normative grammatical constructions we learn as natives help us find noun phrases and verb phrases in all languages, or we can train members to use an alphabet in such a way that the sounds of any language will fall under the general rules involving vowels and consonants. Similarly, we can use a case system to find that all languages can be forced into this kind of construction providing we are willing to employ the handy notion of ellipsis or presuppositions about tacit knowledge. The use of speech or talk is a tacit presupposition of common sense or mundane reasoning for speaker-hearers. Hence we rely on an intuitive use of talk as a constitutive self-organizing feature of practical reasoning to examine reflexively talk as a resource for claiming that we have discovered universals in every normatively organized society.

Linguistic rules are one of the formal ways humans have normatively discovered to construct chunking or recoding procedures for handling verbal information that indexes a variety of experiences embedded in an interactional scene. The construction of meaning and reference can be facilitated by such rules for generating and processing information in everyday interaction, even when the information is produced and stored independently of oral language. But meaning and reference can be generated and communicated by modes other than oral language.

A consequence of treating linguistic universals as normative constructions is that solutions to the problems of meaning and reference can be facilitated because the idea of universals forces a wide variety of complex experiences and information processing procedures into a social framework for displaying ostensive forms of agreement, consensus, or understanding. But the ability to produce grammatical and ungrammatical strings of sound patterns that can be coded into a standard orthography tells very little about the difficult problem of how the child is able to index information and assign meanings in specific contexts. The central issues in the biological argument are that a child must be able to acquire the language in question despite the fact that his parents do not know how to teach it to him in some systematic way that would include schedules of reward and punishment. The child must possess the ability to learn to produce a wide variety of utterances that others will be able to comprehend, and to understand an unlimited number of diverse utterances he has never heard before. Humans' species-specific cog-

nitive properties that permit the production and understanding of unlimited utterances preclude a conditioning argument for the acquisition of language, but the
normative construction of rules means that mistakes are recognizable and, therefore, conditioning successes *are* possible.

Our ability to create subdomains of everyday language by eliminating or de-
leting particulars that create ambiguity or contradictions (e.g. logical or mathematical systems) also gives rise to conceptions of language production based on
the notion of rule-governed linguistic universals. But how we understand what we
can produce seems to extend beyond the way the linguist conceives of the grammar
of phrase structure and transformational rules (Quillian 1968). We find we can
attribute children's capabilities to imitate sentences given by adults (in the home,
in the classroom, in a psycholinguistic experiment) to the idea of a short-term store
or primary memory that requires rehearsal if it is to be transferred to a long-term
store or secondary memory (Norman 1969). The ways in which we decide that
the child understands what he can produce or what adults produce is not very
clear. Much of what is attributed to linguistic competence is based on the child's
ability to generate or produce utterances. Neither the biological foundations of
language nor the biological basis of cognition need be questioned to understand
that the production of utterances seems to be dependent on the cognitive ability
to learn and use normative linguistic rules. Rehearsal is essential for discussions
of primary and secondary memory regardless of whether or not one believes in a
unitary theory or prefers to distinguish short-term and long-term storage mechanisms. The idea of rehearsal must include reflexive exchanges with others where
the individual's own thoughts become the object of rehearsal and elaboration or
situated indexical activity.

The problem becomes more complicated when we recognize the role of visual
perception in remembering and planning (Miller, Galanter, and Pribram 1960).
An interactional setting complicates the use and understanding of language because
of visual and auditory information and reflexive thoughts by speaker-hearers. The
idea of one kind of memory for pictorial material and another for linguistic material
(Haber 1968; 1969; 1970) suggests that pictorial and linguistic material are inter-
actionally productive features of understanding in all settings. Subjects seem to
remember pictures better than a name associated with a picture. We can extend
this point to say that we can understand more than we can formulate according
to normatively (grammatically) correct rules and appropriate lexical designations
for objects and events. Haber's experiments suggest that subjects retain information about fine details of pictures even though these details may not be routinely
available to the subject for reporting to the experimenter. After viewing a detailed
picture subjects are given a word-association task initially linked with a blank
projection screen and then are asked nondirective questions about the picture. The
subjects' first ten spoken words are used to elicit additional associations that appear
to facilitate his later recall of details absent from the earlier report. Haber con-

cludes that the pictures were not stored by the subjects in the form of words, but that the pictures and their details had to be attached to words during a period of intense associative activity. Thus because pictures are not stored in or coded initially into words their particulars cannot be recalled in detail through words unless the memory of the subject is aided by an activity like the free-association exercise. Haber notes that we could probably improve recall considerably if we could increase the attachment of words to visual images. This suggests that the recoding or indexical activities of pictorial and linguistic memory can be linked, resulting in an improved ability to remember pictures or feelings not associated with words. Having demonstrated that the iconic image is visual, Haber and his associates conclude that the visual image is accurately conveyed to the short-term memory and locate the source of errors in later processing stages of memory.

An interesting problem raised by the work of Haber and his associates inheres in the language subjects use to describe the visual images. Apparently the experimenter has no difficulty deciding that subjects had accurately reported and recalled the initial stimulus presented, and that the image was conveyed by the subject's visual processing system to his memory system. Subjects achieve perfect recall at the instant after they are shown an array of letters tachistoscopically. The subject must extract information from visual stimuli and then attach linguistic terms or glosses to this visual coding process.

Haber implies we have the ability to retain all the 'relevant' information of an iconic sort for a matter of milliseconds effecting a transfer to short-term store. Haber notes that words are remembered as ideas. The subject's linguistic reports therefore become further indexical expressions of reported perceptual memory. The researcher and subject employ normatively organized linguistic indexical expressions of recorded perceptual information to convince each other that agreement has been attained.

How do we represent iconic information linguistically? How do we recover the indexical particulars that escape perception due to the subject's limited capacity to retain all of the items or details in a display? The problem is not merely one of information loss, but of information transformation and distortion that only the subject can partially monitor. How do we account for the description of the normative recoding process itself so as not to fall into the trap of believing that our procedures elicit all 'relevant' particulars because what is available to the subject is thought to be controlled experimentally? The limitation of memory capacity is only describable within the constraints of the experimenter's limitations as a native speaker-hearer.

This problem will be discussed vis-à-vis the deaf (and could also include the blind) in the last section of the chapter in order to underscore the normative organization of manual signs when one is deaf (or verbal displays when one is blind) and cannot speak, or can speak but without auditory feedback. Even with children who can hear, speak, and see, psycholinguistic research makes limited use of visual and auditory information processing ideas and 'substantive' findings for understanding that the child is using more than linguistic rules and responding to considerably more than a presumed controlled auditory stimulus sentence. The setting itself provides a self-organizing collection of particulars that the child selectively invokes and reorganizes to process the experimenter's linguistic stimulus.

Recent work on artificial intelligence studies reveals how much more complicated the linguistic model must become to describe understanding in an actual setting. Researches by De Groot (1965; 1966), Simon (1969), and Simon and Barenfeld (1969) articulate information processing theories using computer simulation with formal human problem solving by examining the substantive problem of chess move choices. Simon and Barenfeld go beyond problem-solving heuristic search procedures by demonstrating that subjects impose considerable structure on the problem situation in the course of the first few seconds of exposure. Not linguistic but perceptual information processing is central to the Simon and Barenfeld research. Simon and Barenfeld monitor subjects' eye movements during the initial few seconds after the problems have been presented to them by the experimenter. This is combined with an attempt to test the subjects' abilities to extract and retain information from the complex visual displays of a chess board within a few seconds of exposure. Simon and Barenfeld stress that the game player seems preoccupied with extracting information about position so as to generate possible moves and understand their consequences rather than with trying to find actual solutions. Thus a combination of eye fixation and peripheral vision provides reflexive information about the subject's relative attention to specific and more distant squares. The experimenter must discover the possible squares perceived and those from which information was extracted by the retention test. According to the authors there is consistency in the research results of Russian, Dutch, and American subjects' abilities to extract information while moving from one to another square of the chess board. The maximum rate is estimated at about four fixations per second.

The Simon and Barenfeld work presumes that relations among the squares, between squares and pieces, and among pieces are extracted from the board by eye movements and some level of expertise carried in short- and long-term perceptual storage. The authors discuss the chess perception program called PERCEIVER, in which the machine simulates the initial sequences of eye movements of human subjects, and the program posits relations among pieces on the board as well as processes that will generate these perceptions in some particular sequence. Thus the machine program can specify what should and will be done under some sort of optimal human conditions, but the machine operates under an all-or-none principle in extracting information, while the human player relies on momentary and past indexical experience to decide what is 'important'. Past reflexive experience is central for humans. A grand master or master chess player is capable of reproducing a chess position without error after a few seconds of exposure. A random board reduces a grand master to the level of a weaker player.

The Simon and Barenfeld paper is central to our earlier discussion because the chess player's ability to place pieces correctly is linked to the role of short- and long-term memory. The chess player must chunk or recode (Miller 1956) information if his expertise is to be maintained. The ability to transfer information from short-term to long-term store has been estimated to be a matter of five seconds. Therefore short-term store is probably operative in order to make maximum use of information that is limited by fixation time. What constitutes a 'chunk' of information is not clear. Simon and Barenfeld say that it means 'any configuration that is familiar to the subject'.

I will summarize my use of Miller, Haber, and Simon and Barenfeld to indicate how these works help to clarify related issues about meaning and reference. The role of perceptual processes and their primary and secondary memory do not necessarily involve ever speaking to another participant in a chess game. Encounters in everyday life may only require a few seconds devoted to extracting information from a setting to generate action but without any necessary recourse to speaking. The experimenter creates an artificial problem by having the subjects produce talking-out-loud protocols to monitor perceptual processes, information extraction, and storage in primary memory. This forced linguistic information processing may involve a different memory mechanism and a transformation or distortion of the presumed 'basic' data.

There are many activities accomplished each day that do not have to be described verbally. Our experiences of the everyday world are not always mapped into verbal constructions, yet we may assume that speaker-hearers proficient in the normative use of language probably incorporate normative rules of language use into their thinking and thus are able to describe experiences as if the verbal categories were constitutive of the experiences. But if we follow Haber's work (and the research he builds on and cites), then visual information processing must also include a linguistic operation involving an inherent tacit recoding if information is to be reportable to others including experimenters. In playing chess, it may never be necessary to report the nature of one's move, and we would therefore expect players to be incapable of describing all of the information they may have situationally recognized as relevant and which they may have extracted from the board by a sequence of visual fixations. The reflexive elaboration of information continually extracted while attending the board with the help of short- and long-term memory means that these experiences retain a sense of vagueness because the player must rely on verbal expressions of perceptual activities. Forcing a player to transform his chess thinking experiences into verbal reports means producing glosses experimenters call basic data.

Studying visual memory by requiring the subject to demonstrate recognition of previously exposed photographic slides or their mirror images by pressing a button avoids total reliance on verbal reports of pictorial memory. Similarly, when subjects are asked to draw in the details (Haber 1970) of a previously shown photograph, we obtain some idea of aspects of pictorial memory that can be retrieved but not easily obtained through verbal reports. Such a measure cannot be used with children, however, for their ability to draw is not developed, and the researcher must employ everyday language as if it were neutral to the description of pictorial memory that he seeks.

When children (ages 5-6) are given sentences to imitate they sometimes repeat the sentences perfectly, but when they are asked to act out what the sentences intend they cannot (by adult conceptions) always carry out the 'correct' activity. We also find that sentences that seem to be acted out 'properly' are not imitated 'properly' (Jennings 1969). Finally, some sentences that are imitated and/or acted out properly (again by adult conceptions of what is 'proper') may not be understood according to adult conceptions when the child is asked to explain what is supposed to happen. When the imitation involves objects and activities that may be strange to the child or which are innovative, the researcher cannot be certain what imagery the sentences arouse. The production of imitated sentences may be 'mechanical' (Cicourel 1973) because perceptual information (including cues the child attributes to the experimenter) at the child's disposal may be more significant in the carrying out of a verbal stimulus than the child's understanding of the grammatical rules that are supposedly being tested. The child's eye movements and fixations are seldom a concern of the developmental psycholinguist (though of central interest to his colleagues in perceptual development), nor does the psycholinguist concern himself with how verbal categories get attached to perceptual and auditory experiences. The particular occasion presupposes cognitive abilities that are invariant to, but must also incorporate, the complexity of the setting.

Researchers may find that they must continually consult the child's response to learn something about the possible world their stimulus questions may have produced. The child's interpretation of what he is expected to do remains somewhat foreign to the researcher's conception of language acquisition. An adult's world is presupposed to provide the frames for transforming the unknown world of the child into a presumed measurable enterprise. The researcher's questions provide the frames for establishing correct and incorrect responses that can stand independently of the possible worlds the child constructs.

If a sentence generates imagery that is seldom verbalized, then the elegant syntactic rules in the linguist's conception of language structure will not help unless the recipient of the sentence is practiced in the ways of attaching verbal categories to such experiences in normatively acceptable constructions. But skilled speaker-hearers recognize the indexicality of their constructions. When subjects are requested to provide more and more detailed accounts, we create frustrating and often insurmountable difficulties. Yet every account seems to be amenable to indefinite elaboration.

We force experimental subjects to chunk their (selective) experiences in order to capture how they process information. But we also make the linguist's mistake in such experiments by treating the verbal reports as if they were basic data rather than expressions whose understanding requires going beyond linguistic information. This glossing process is not understood to be the heart of meaning and reference and thus is not examined.

Notice that Lakoff's sentences like (2) and (9) involve activities which presuppose experiences imagined or recalled and a visual ethnographic context integral to any discussion of meaning and reference. The details of imagery derived from visual stimulation that are relived when one goes to bed hours after the original experience have, Hebb (1968) notes, a convincing realism except in one respect — the fine detail is missing. When the linguist asks us to consider various sentences that can be generated by our facility with rules he is not concerned with the way in which the sentences may stimulate our short- and long-term memory or strain it reflexively as we attempt to create and process information derived from complex settings.

An objective statement or expression, therefore, can be viewed as one which has been idealized in regard to its inherent indexicality. Contextual particulars are ignored, while logically consistent assumptions are constructed and made explicit. Objective and indexical expressions are both constructions in that they include only elements that presume the recipient is a 'well-socialized' speaker-hearer who will interpret the utterances in specific and predictable ways. Logical, mathematical, or scientific constructions, despite monitoring to eliminate contradiction, are like everyday expressions because they presume that the reader or speaker-hearer has been socialized to the utterances produced and can be counted on to assign them specific rule-governed meanings.

Simon's (1969) statement that man is a simple behaving system who generates complex behavior largely because of the complexity of his environment, implies that because behavior is adapted to goals stimulated by the environment and man's thinking about his environment, behavior is an artificial construction. Simon remarks that there is an inner environment (biologically limiting) that places constraints on the kinds of information processing of which the organism is capable. My treatment of indexicality and reflexivity in this paper are also at issue in Simon's conclusion (1969: 51–52) that the relationship between language and thinking can be stated as an 'overstrong' Whorfian hypothesis: 'Only the expressible is thinkable.' Simon then says that if this can be accepted: 'Only the thinkable is expressible.' This can be interpreted as saying that despite the biological basis of language, its actual expression is artificial in a normative rule-governed sense. However, if only the expressible is thinkable, then our normative constructions (ideal syntactically organized utterances, logical and mathematical subdomains) reflexively fold back on our thinking to make thinking compatible with our attempts to communicate intersubjectively. Language generates its own system of measurement, and every expression of language would contain only those particulars that reflect the thoughts that led to the expressions. Innovative ways of thinking would always appear in innovative expressions.

The generative transformational linguistic view states that the syntactic component is the fundamental link between the phonological and semantic components. Remarks by Quillian (1968) and others cited above state that our memory includes what can be said in language, what is sensed in perception, and properties and relationships of thinking more general than syntactic rules could reflect. The attribution of meaning may not be expressible in all instances of communication. The speaker-hearer must recognize that multiple meanings can exist for different expressions or their sub-parts. The information that is created and processed is embedded in and constitutive of the context of interaction. A sentence that is formally syntactically or semantically anomalous need not be anomalous for the speaker-hearer. And as Quillian notes, even if we honor the transformational linguists' model for the production of utterances, we will need a more complex model to study the understanding of sentences.

Simon must ask how the expressible and thinkable can be so interrelated if our understanding of the expressible is only partially dependent on the production of the expressible. What is expressed in an account suffers from the same difficulties as the language itself because no language can ever mark or provide for those particulars necessary for its production *and* comprehension. Hence even as we speak of these difficulties we count on the reader supplying particulars that the language does not and cannot carry in some 'obvious' or clearcut way. Much of language production can be mechanical in the sense that it is rule-governed because of the normative constraints imposed on the speaker, but our understanding of interactional scenes or texts is not entirely reliant on what is expressible, for what is thinkable can only be expressed indexically if at all.

III

I have tried to discuss ethnomethodological ideas within the framework of cognition or information processing and information generation. But beyond the scope of this framework the ethnomethodologist proposes that invariant properties of cognition and thought are plausible only within a world taken for granted and known through a self-preserving practical reasoning or a 'mundaneity principle' (Pollner 1970). Operating within the mundaneity principle, the speaker-hearer seeks to create and sustain coherence by organizing information into practical chunks and normatively acceptable categories. The theories of linguists and students of artificial intelligence examined operate within the mundaneity principle but are correspondence schemes carved out of practical reasoning and selective displays of everyday language. They rely on an unexamined nativeness that provides for a world that is self-organizing and pre-constituted. This nativeness cannot be discovered and examined if it is treated as an obvious phenomenon within a correspondence theory of reality; the latter does not recognize this nativeness as constitutive of knowledge processes, a precondition of our inquiries, and an endless, tacit resource for everything we do.

The ethnomethodologist also employs glosses while operating within the mundaneity principle at different levels, and these glosses remain a member's account of practices said to make up the properties of mundane reasoning. Because these glosses recommend that a sense of 'stepping back' is possible to obtain a perhaps absurd and hence 'objective' view of the world, the ethnomethodologist is also vulnerable to the charge of having adopted a privileged position. In recognizing that we can generate only different glosses of our experiences, the ethnomethodologist tries to underscore the pitfalls of viewing indexical expressions as if they could be repaired and thus transformed into context-free objective statements. Our inquiries therefore cannot ignore the mundaneity principle when dealing with substantive outcomes or claims about the structure of syntactic rules, the nature of information processing, the organization of perceptual and linguistic memory, or the elegance of linguistic productions. What is of interest is how language, memory, and our senses can be seen to preserve the mundaneity principle and provide the ways by which members create what Simon calls the sciences of the artificial. The sciences of the artificial (standardized or grammatically correct versions of language, logical or mathematical systems, and scientific theories about the universe) generate a dialectic between science and practical reasoning (Schutz 1964; Garfinkel 1967; Pollner 1970) that proposes science as a superior way of discovering truth. The sciences of the artificial presuppose mundane reasoning, and this practical reasoning is a constant resource for constructing a meaningful and viable science. The everyday world is an indispensable tacit resource for the creator of the sciences of the artificial, but is seldom a topic of inquiry (Zimmerman and Pollner 1970).

I, with several of my graduate students, have conducted a series of studies into the acquisition and use of oral language and manual sign language at home and communicative competence in the school. Central questions in our work are how the world comes to be formulated and reformulated by and for the child in terms of an adult's conception of clock-time; and how the very existence of this world depends on adult formulations of the child's reasoning and language acquisition. There are two kinds of glosses here: (a) those used by parents, teachers, and clinicians for describing normal development, and (b) those employed by researchers for demonstrating that child development and language acquisition are descriptive sciences.

In the research we seek a kind of 'indefinite triangulation' procedure that would reveal the irreparable but practical nature of accounts used by subjects and researchers. I use the expression 'indefinite triangulation' to suggest that every procedure that seems to 'lock in' evidence, thus to claim a level of adequacy, can itself be subjected to the same sort of analysis that will in turn produce yet another indefinite arrangement of new particulars or a rearrangement of previously established particulars in 'authoritative', 'final', 'formal' accounts. The indefinite triangulation notion attempts to make visible the practicality and inherent reflexivity of everyday accounts. The elaboration of circumstances and particulars of an occasion can be subjected to an indefinite re-elaboration of the 'same' or 'new' circumstances and particulars.

The triangulation procedure varies with the research problem. When gathering information on language acquisition in the home setting we left a tape recorder for about one hour during lunch. A transcription of the tape was done by a typist who had been instructed to render a verbatim record. Then the transcript, the first version of this scene, was read by the mother while she listened to the tape; her comments produced another version of the interaction. The typist was next asked to listen again to the tape and to describe what she thought was 'going on' correcting her original transcript as she deemed necessary. In this elaboration and correction a different version of the scene was always produced. My phonetic transcription of the tapes created still another version. With a number of different versions of an interaction scene, the problem is deciding which version captures the child's language, the child's referencing ability, the parent's constructions, and so on.

The reader could now say that we should have simply combined the different versions to produce the 'best' one possible, but the point is that different versions could have been produced indefinitely by simply hiring different typists and providing the mother with different transcripts. The mother could not always remember the context in which the interaction occurred, especially if we waited several days before playing the tape for her. The mother's equivocation about the meaning of the child's utterances or her own statements, because of her inability to recall the ethnographic particulars available at the time of the interaction, points to the situated nature of meaning.

In another study with Kenneth Jennings and Sybillyn Jennings we employed a procedure in which sentences having direct and indirect object constructions (in active and passive voice) were acted out and imitated by pairs of pre-school and kindergarten children (ages 3-6). There was a table of toys beside the children that they identified before the test began. The sentences typically require one child to give an object to, or receive an object from, the other child. Child A, upon recognizing that he is the agent, must convert the information from the sentence into a search procedure that requires him to scan the table and pick out an appropriate object and then give it to child B.

We used video tapes to show from a different view the problem indexicality raises for language acquisition studies. Multiple versions of the scene become apparent when the researcher finds that although a forced coding of the child's responses can be made at the time of presenting the stimulus sentences, subsequent viewings of the tape reveal that the original coding was often ambiguous and could be changed (Jennings 1969). By coding the child's responses as if they were motivated only by the stimulus sentence, psycholinguists might typically infer that the child does or does not have an internalized rule for comprehending active and passive and direct and indirect object constructions. But repeated tests of different children and repeated viewings of the tapes revealed that various schemes of interpretation and analysis could emerge and be supported. The conclusion of this discussion is that repeated viewings of the tapes provide the researcher with different versions of the phenomenon because different particulars are noticed each time even though some particulars may be remembered over several occasions. Each hearing of the oral part suggests new inferences because closer attention is paid to intonational features. Concentrating on any particular aspect of the scene such as watching the child's eyes provides a basis for additional conjectures.

Children generate their own interpretations of the setting and search the setting for additional information. If child A starts to move first, child B may not move because he may assume that child A 'knows better' what to do. If child A moves with the first NP, then child B may not even pay attention to the rest of the stimulus sentence. This suggests that the stimulus sentence may not be retained long enough for the child to process the oral stimulus and link it to the perceptual information he needs to carry out the task. The child may be responding to the noun he hears first, regardless of the noun's assignment in a deep structure. He may receive only a selective version or some fragment of the sentence due to a form of interference generated by himself, his partner, or the experimenter.

Still other problems emerged when it was found that some sentences could be imitated accurately but not acted out 'appropriately' while other sentences could not always be imitated accurately but could be acted out 'correctly'. Psycholinguists do not always treat such problems as part of a more general information processing task where the interplay between perceptual and linguistic memory and routine interference from the experiment can reduce the number of chunks the child has to process. It seems clear that the issue is not simply one of testing the child's internalization of grammatical rules. Rather it points out once again that syntax is only one among several factors that the child must attend in deciding the meaning of an utterance in an interactional setting.

When the child is asked to explain his actions or the intended actions of a stimulus sentence he may be forced to generate linguistic constructions or information that is not in one-to-one correspondence with his perceptual memory or the immediate perceptual display as it is selectively organized by him. We investigated the 'naturalness' of the stimulus sentence by asking four children (7; 9; 10; 12 years) to act out some 'bizarre' sentences. A few weeks later we sought explanations from the children in an interview. The stimulus sentence seemed to provide the child with an occasion to explore reflexively various possibilities that could possess what for him seemed to constitute reasonable accounts to justify his interpretation of the stimulus sentence. This sometimes meant that a bizarre sentence was rejected by the child because the surface subject of the sentence which was taken to be the agent lacked features deemed appropriate to the action, for example, 'A lamppost can't give a table a book'. In other cases the child carried out the instruction reporting that he was, say, the fire hydrant. The syntactic structure of the stimulus sentence obviously provides valuable information to the child, but this information may not be central to his performance because of the influence of the interactional particulars experienced reflexively in the setting or imagined as relevant.

When I assisted Marshall Shumsky with his dissertation we worked out another variation of the indefinite triangulation procedure to generate different accounts of the 'same' scene. Several conditions of differential participation in one session of Shumsky's on-going encounter group were arranged. Some experienced participants who came only infrequently were specifically asked to be at the video session. A member with limited experience in the group was to come when the session was well underway. One of the older members, the member who came late, and the participant who had joined most recently were interrogated about their experiences in the day's session. We were interested in obtaining each participant's reconstruction of the group experience and comparing the vocabulary the older and newer group members used to express their opinions and feelings.

Shumsky placed one of the older members on the 'hot seat' of intensive group focus soon after the session began. As soon as attention was diverted from him, he was removed from the session and asked to provide an account of what had occurred in the group to that point. After this account was audio-taped, he was shown portions of the video tape which depicted his 'hot seat' experience, and he was again asked to address particulars identified by the interviewer.

The group member with limited experience arrived an hour and a half after the group started. She was allowed to participate for about 10 minutes, then she was removed from the group and was interrogated in the way described above. Of particular interest here was the way she described the part of the session she did not experience directly but saw on video tape. Finally, the participant with the least experience in the group was interviewed. One month later the same group members were interviewed independently of each other. They were asked to provide reconstructions, and then they were shown the same video segments they had seen before.

The participants' conceptions of the group experience, the motives they attributed to others, were all varied and often contradictory. With each interview individual utterances or fragments were used as different particulars to provide different meanings of 'what happened'. The expressions utilized could not be examined to recover the particulars used during each interview. Some knowledge about the recoding process and the role of memory and general information processing activity can be gained by observing how subjects reconstruct their expressions of what happened. When participants were repeatedly shown a video-tape of the session they provided new interpretations because on different viewings they noticed someone's intonational shifts, his facial expressions, his use of particular lexical items, changes in body position, the movement of the eyes, and the like.

Participants in group interaction (as in the perceptual experiments described by Haber) receive more information than they are aware of or can possibly verbalize. It is not clear how selective particulars (ignored, stored, or available only by prodding or by verbal associations) are utilized to construct accounts, nor how perceptual, somesthetic, kinesthetic, and auditory information become selectively processed by a reflexive self. The speaker-hearer must process information so as always to be 'seeing' the meaning or intentions of his own actions, as well as the actions of others, in a retrospective and prospective way that is situated and is contingent on an open horizon of unfolding possibilities (Schutz 1964; Garfinkel 1967; Cicourel 1968a).

The meaning of any lexical item or string of items can be described by reference to syntactic rules and constraints. The meaning of any received or produced utterance for the speaker-hearer is embedded in a larger context that is activated and deepened by the complexity of the setting, and the reflexive availability of short-term and long-term store that are themselves influenced by normative linguistic and non-linguistic social practices.

Memory can be seen as socially organized information that members learn to store as idealized normal forms or typifications of their experiences. These normal forms are socially distributed among any population and available as a stock of knowledge for assigning and reassigning meanings, but must interface with situated social interaction (Schutz 1964).

Ease and facility of expression in a given context are contingent upon the ability to transcend one's own talk, and the talk of others, while making use of information generating and information processing procedures. These procedures include syntactic and phonological rules and dictionary information as normal form expressions embedded in a complex environmental context. Thus many of the utterances of the encounter group do not provide grammatically relevant information for understanding what seems to be going on. The grammatical structures available provide information for the linguist, but are not clear resources for participants or observers. The verbal accounts given of what happened are contingent displays whose indexicality cannot be repaired by coding devices for making data more 'precise' or improving methods of research by additional experimental controls.

In research being done with Robert MacKay, Hugh Mehan, and David Roth, studying communicative competence and language use in the classroom, we have been using another variation of the indefinite triangulation procedure. Two first grade classes in two elementary schools with different mixtures of Anglo, Chicano, and Black students have been observed for eight months. Various standard psycholinguistic, reading, and intelligence tests, and specially designed variations on them have been used to assess children's understanding of general classroom instructions and materials presented in lesson form and on tests. A major task of the research is the examination of the assumptions which test constructors must make about the child's world to develop measures of intelligence and general knowledge.

Triangulation was used as a research strategy by obtaining the teacher's account of her plans and expectations for a lesson she was to present. Then, both the lesson presented to the class and the teacher's subsequent assessment of the impact of the lesson in interaction with some of the children were video-taped. We also observed the lesson and asked several children about their conception of what the lesson was about. A brief, general overview of the lesson was gathered from the teacher. After a few days the teacher was interviewed about the lesson once again. She was first asked to reconstruct the lesson, its purpose and goals, then she was shown a video tape of the lesson and asked to describe aspects of the lesson and the children's reactions toward it.

As in the encounter group study and the study of language acquisition in the home, different accounts of the 'same' scene were obtained. The different accounts reveal the difficulty of trying to repair each glossed level of information to claim 'adequate' objectivity because these glosses too can be infinitely changed and expanded. Each account draws upon both stated and unstated particulars and is contingent on the social constraints of the actual lesson. One's selective storage, or changing memory of the setting, or a selective or changing audio- or video-taped recovery of the setting, provides an important basis for indefinite accounts of the 'same' scene.

When we contrast the teacher's accounts with the children's accounts it is sometimes difficult to recognize that everyone presumably witnessed the 'same' event. The children seem to receive and organize the lesson in terms of their own orientations at the time of the event. Interferences are routine and may be self-generated, initiated by other students, or by the teacher in response to a particular student. Where each child sits, who sits next to him, and the teacher's ability to follow his gaze contribute both to the parts of the lesson the child picks up and to the teacher's conception of what the child has assimilated.

The classroom research is too extensive to describe adequately here. The work, however, underscores the problems mentioned earlier about the child's ability to utilize perceptual experiences, or his memory of these experiences, in contexts where verbal expressions are necessary for the teacher to assess the child's ability and achievement. It becomes impossible to separate competence from performance because the linguist's and psycholinguist's models are not realistically based on the ways in which children seem to develop and display cognitive abilities that transcend language use itself. The child may be forced to process information couched in grammatically correct sentences produced by the teacher as a way of satisfying educational goals, but this does not constitute a test of how the child receives, organizes, and generates information nor is it a test of what he understands about the setting or task. The teacher's utterances and intentions in combination with the use of perceptual materials for conveying a lesson may appear to be ambiguous and/or contradictory for the child. The child's ability to produce utterances recognized by the psycholinguist and teacher as grammatically adequate may not index his ability to understand the syntactic or lexical complexities of his productions, or how he processes the complexities the teacher or researcher produces.

Our bilingual Chicano subjects present a more complicated situation because these children appear to have learned two grammars and two phonological systems that are not integrated. For some tasks the children may understand similar instructions in both Spanish and English, yet not be able to produce utterances that convey what they seem to know. The children seem capable of switching from one language to the other to indicate their intentions, but they are not always capable of translating from one language into the other. Depending on the initial structure of an utterance, adults seem capable of starting in Spanish, while inserting English items within the Spanish grammatical frame, and vice versa. Our subjects were unable to engage consistently in this form of systematic switching, yet a few of them seemed to be moving in this direction. The bilingual child who relies on pointing and gesturing appears to be attempting to transcend his apparent inability to make his knowledge, thinking, and intentions comprehensible by normative verbal reports.

In describing the last research project, being done in collaboration with Robert Boese, I must trade somewhat more on the reader's imagination because the material derives from a study of manual sign language used by deaf adults and hearing children born to deaf adults. The two children we studied (called Freddy and Andy) were video-taped in the home when they were one to two and two to three years of age.

To orient the reader to the study of manual sign language, we distinguish, for example, between native sign language as a first language, whose initial normative structure seems to be a product of the interactional scenes of only those persons who communicate with each other frequently in a household setting, relying on primary and secondary memory in order to recreate signs that can be recognizable as the 'same' across different occasions (Cicourel 1973; Cicourel and Boese, in press; Cicourel and Boese 1969 and 1970; Boese 1971) and signing learned as a second language. As soon as deaf persons move out of a family setting into a deaf community or into contact with speaker-hearers, the picture can change considerably if the hearing society or culture has developed a standardized orthographic system, a normative grammar, and a lexicon. Deaf persons who have been taught to speak and read lips as a second language may also create normative signs by establishing a correspondence between a native sign and a lexical item in the oral language. Hearing persons who have learned to sign as a second language have been instrumental in creating this correspondence.

Because many speaker-hearers have learned to use manual signs and have helped to standardize many native signs so that they are in correspondence with oral lexical items, we must distinguish between (a) native signers who have had no contact with oral language in its standardized normative form, (b) native signers exposed to oral language who have standardized normative signs in their repertoire in correspondence with an oral lexicon, and (c) second language signers who have first learned an oral language as speaker-hearers and then acquired a knowledge of standardized normative and perhaps some native signs that they incorporate into their conception of language as an oral-written system of communication. Second language signers, therefore, do not *think* in terms of an (as yet unknown) competence to generate and understand signs in situated contexts. As speaker-hearers, we may never know how to understand this competence that deaf persons rely on tacitly. We might imagine deaf linguists, relying on a standardized idiographic normative sign language developed by deaf scholars, someday attempting to describe this competence just as oralists attempt to describe the competence-performance of a speaker-hearer.

Speaker-hearers concerned with teaching the deaf how to speak, read lips, and read and write oral language often cite the fact that manual sign language has few if any of the characteristics of oral language. They cite particularly the absence of inflections and order constraints, considered necessary for oral language, but ignore the absence of many of these normative constructions in other oral languages. The detailed standardization found in oral languages is lacking in sign language and clearly limits the power of sign language. A normative system that is generalized as rules is a powerful way of generating abstract meanings and doing complicated reference. Some sort of standardized ideographic system is not precluded for sign language, though the ones that have been attempted thus far have always used oral language as the point of departure. Despite the powerful generative system of rules said to describe oral language, the translation of signs into oral reports compounds the indexicality problem. Contextual features are central in sign language, but we are poorly informed about communication that depends extensively on seldom-studied perceptual, kinesthetic, and somesthetic information. Because signs are not ordered in ways associated with normative uses of oral language, serious questions may be raised about syntactically based linguistic universals (Schlesinger, no date).

To argue that the uneducated deaf are dependent on kinesthetic, somesthetic, and perceptual information articulated with non-linguistic primary and secondary memory, means that standardized oral syntax plays a minimal role in communication within this group. The educated deaf person making use of manual signs that have been set in correspondence with an oral lexicon does not utilize an intuitive understanding of oral syntax for signing, but will convert information obtained from the oral system into his sign system (Cicourel and Boese, in press). Finger spelling and lip movements will be seen as signs even though they have a direct correspondence with oral letters of the alphabet and words (sound patterns). The argument is similar to saying that an adult who learns a second language as a non-native will always tend to translate the second language into his own as a means of understanding this second language. The native signer's dependence on his perceptual, somesthetic, and kinesthetic memory to generate and understand manual signs underscores the deep involvement of all communication in the unfolding context of interaction despite the existence of abstract powerful normative systems of oral language syntax. This means oral language syntax is of limited value to deaf persons using manual signs who cannot experience oral language as speaker-hearers do. The feedback necessary for monitoring output and understanding inputs based on intonational differences is lacking.

Before closing this section and the chapter, I want to present a limited amount of data from our study of two hearing children. Freddy and Andy were born to deaf parents whose primary language during the course of our research was sign. There are many problems inherent in understanding manual sign language because oral language glosses must be used to further index signs whose meanings are themselves embedded in different experiences and memory and in a complex interactional setting. Our attempts to reconstruct and attribute meaning to the video tapes were hampered by an unexpected realization that it was very difficult to recapture the contextual cues used at the time of the initial recording. The fact that so much of the meaning was tied to the setting itself made it imperative that we reconstruct some of the unstated conditions of the context for even a poor beginning.

Some serious consequences and rewards emerged from our somewhat embarrassed realization that the video tapes were very difficult to understand six to eight months after participating in the interaction we recorded. Our involvement in the setting at the time of the filming seemed 'routine', and our understanding of what appeared to be 'happening' seemed rather 'obvious'. But the observation that understanding the video tape was quite difficult underscores the central argument of this chapter; the researchers, as participants, are heavily dependent on tacit contextual particulars for producing an account of the setting. The video tape does not capture the way participants' situated experiences produce emergent meanings as a reflexive accomplishment. Our memories were not adequate for recovering the sense of social structure experienced at the time of recording, and our glosses of what happened required considerable intensive viewing in order to reconstruct a plausible account. This translation problem might lead the reader to conclude that if there had been a simultaneous translation by a sign/oral language 'bilingual' interpreter the matter could have been resolved. But a simultaneous verbal gloss (translation) at the time of the original signing interaction, even by a bilingual who is a native signer, does not guarantee as much accuracy as might be expected. It is like the problem of attaching verbal expressions to perceptual experiences and memory; the information lost and transformed by the recoding process is difficult to recover, much less identify.

Several layers of glossing occur, each with its own indexicality or chunking operations which mask particulars integral to each layer. The rendition of an oral gloss of the manual signs is a recoding problem that poses many difficulties because thinking in sign language as a native can not readily be transformed into an oral gloss. The interpretation of thinking-out-loud protocols is difficult enough; adding the manual sign activity only compounds our problem.

One way of trying to repair the reflexivity and indexicality problems posed by the translation from one medium to another, would be to analyze the normative signs used by the deaf mother or father with the child. One could observe how the child modifies these normative signs while creating his own signs. But such repair work presupposes some understanding of how sign language is generated independently of imposing oral syntax as a schema of analysis. The translation of parent-child interaction by a bilingual interpreter at the time of actual interaction merely transforms the problem of how signs can be viewed as a generative semantics *qua* sign language, into a traditional problem in developmental, oral language psycholinguistics. The translation and simultaneous transformation of the problem into an oral psycholinguistic one permits the researcher to find 'pivot structures', noun phrases and verb phrases, uses of the active voice, direct object constructions, and the like, but these glosses are created by the translator for the benefit of an oral or speaking-hearing audience interested in demonstrating that linguistic universals as constructed (normatively) for oral language, 'must exist' for the deaf as well.

The perplexing difficulties of the problem can be illustrated by the following materials from our study of manual sign language acquisition. The material on the left hand side of the page was translated by a native signer (Robert Boese) whose parents were both deaf though he is a speaker-hearer, while the right side was translated by a second-language signer (Marian Boese). Robert Boese learned to speak and understand verbal sound patterns when he began attending public school around seven or eight years of age. This phenomenon of hearing children of deaf parents learning to speak without difficulty is reported by Lenneberg (1968, 1969). The signing was done by Freddy at two years of age.

Tape III Translation — Video Segment 240-253 — April 1, 1970

Native Signer	Second Language Signer
First Viewing: 253 – 'Come.'	Nothing recorded.
Second Viewing: Nothing recorded.	Second Viewing: 243 – 'car, car, car' 250 – 'bird, outside'
Third Viewing: 243 – 'Oh, I hear a truck, I hear something out there, there now is a truck moving out	243 – 'car, car' 249 – 'stopped, stopped'

there, there is a car, truck.'
246 – 'Oh, now there is a car out
there, a truck, and it is moving.'
250 – 'A bird, there is a bird out
there, flying very fast, high bird.'
253 – 'Come'.

Fourth Viewing: 243 – 'Oh, I hear   Nothing recorded.
out there, a sound, a truck, I hear
something outside, car out there,
moving.'

246 – 'Car out there, car outside, car
moving; car outside, like a dump-
truck; there is a truck out there (247)
and it is a kind of (248) dump-truck;
I hear it, you hear it, it is a dump-
truck, it makes (249) a big noise, and
it is dumping things out there; a
truck out there, it is dumping something, it makes a fast stop; there is
a truck there, and it is dumping
things, it dumps the things out, and
then it stops.'

250 – 'Oh, bird, bird out there, bird.'

Fifth Viewing: 243 – 'Car, truck, ac-   Nothing recorded.
celerator, beep-beep; I hear, down
the hill, (244) there is a car out there;
there is a truck moving back and
forth there; I hear a car out there,
beep, it is moving, there is a car out
there, a truck, moving.'

245 – 'Steering wheel.'
246 – 'There is a car out there, a
truck; there is a car out there, (247)
dumps the things down, and hear
the stop and opens up, and (248)
stops.'

250 – 'Bird is flying in the air, bird
is flying very hard; (251) it is a bird,
bird out there, come, come [moves

toward window]; it is a (252) bird,
there is a bird flying out there, there,
out there, (253) oh, I hear a sound,
hear the truck, come on, come over
here.'

Sixth Viewing: Not attempted.   250 – 'Bird, bird, bird'

There is an obvious discrepancy in these free translations between the first and second language signers' attribution of particulars to a video scene of about thirty seconds duration. The native signer took many liberties in his translation and inserted articles freely as well as verb inflections and adverbs. It was difficult to synchronize the two readings because of technical problems such as the tape stretching and the difficulty of accurately noting the reading of the counter each time. But there were other kinds of inferences, for example, a facial expression would be recorded as an *oh*; meanings would be attributed to the signers and included in the translation on the basis of body movements integral to the native translator's use of tacit knowledge in signing. The interpretation of a sign or series of signs is always embedded in the total context wherein the observer or participant makes reflexive use of memory. While studying the present burst of signing it was not clear initially what Freddy was trying to express until we accidentally turned up the volume (thought to be irrelevant at the time) of the video recorder and discovered what sounded like a big truck.

The reader might claim (from even a quick glance at the translations) that there is consistency in interpretation even though there are many variations in the ways the translations are expressed each time. We could transform the materials of the free verbal gloss into sentences that are normatively ideal for a linguistic analysis and thus 'clean up' the transcript to produce bounded sentences that seem to 'make sense'. But such tidy sentences would merely satisfy our preconceptions of the 'correct' utterances we should be able to find if we are to lend support to the linguistic universals' thesis as formulated by speaking-hearing linguists for oral language.

There are two substantive points the reader should attend: (1) The native translator reports 'I hear out there, a sound, a truck . . .' and 'it makes a big noise'. The translation suggests the child is relying on his hearing, but this interpretation did not occur until after we accidentally heard the noise of the truck apparently passing by outside. If we had relied only on the signs, the elaboration reported would have taken a different form. (2) Difficulties in translation may be attributable to the vagueness of the child's signing ability as occurs in oral 'baby talk'.

We have also found that translations of adult signing do not alter this problem, particularly when native signs are used extensively.

We encountered two other problems: (a) the translator's use of short- and long-term memory of the original setting and video tape to create consistency in his analysis across successive interpretations of roughly the 'same' video scene; and (b) the extent to which the elaboration of particulars was produced to satisfy the translator's desire to communicate with a speaking-hearing audience. We are convinced that an independent native signer would have considerable difficulty coming up with even a free gloss of minimal coherency unless he was told many ethnographic particulars about the setting and the kinds of signs taught to (and modified by) the child, as well as the signs invented by the child almost daily. The verbal gloss attributed to the above burst of signing contains all the features necessary for claiming grammaticality in oral language (word order, NPs, VPs, agreement between subject and predicate, etc.), but these features cannot be found as 'natural' structures of sign language unless negotiated and imposed by establishing an arbitrary correspondence between oral syntax, on oral lexicon, and manual signs. Such an imposition tells us nothing about how native signers generate meanings and do reference with a system of signs embedded in each contextual setting, rather it suggests how a bilingual native signer can provide a translation intelligible to speaker-hearers.

It might be easier to understand the difficulties of repairing the indexicality of translating signs into oral glosses that would satisfy syntactic rules or a standardized lexicon, if we examine attempts to provide verbal glosses for a presumed literal description of the signing itself.

Tape III — Verbal Gloss of Literal Description — Segment 240–253

Native Signer

240 – 'Freddy sitting position, legs apart, arms down, hands (241) close together, twisting and turning his fingers, index (242) and thumb together.'

243 – 'Freddy turns his head, his head was down, and now he turns his head to his right and upwards and looks at mother. Then he looks straight ahead, moving head to upright position, his head pointed in front of him with eyes facing straight ahead of him.'

243 – [Repeating of numbers indicates rewinding the tape.] 'He moves his hand, with his index finger, other fingers kind of closed, points with arm half stretched out in front of himself, his index finger, as well as

Second Language Signer

242 – 'Freddy looks up and looks towards Bob and Mother and he looks towards his Father, looks back towards Bob.'

242 – [Rewinds tape] 'He looks up, he looks towards his father.' (I just realized that I have to stop the machine faster than that because by the time I have said 'he looks up' and 'by the time he looks over to his mother,' he has already said a whole string of thoughts and that is almost up to 243.)

242 – (missed it that time.)

242 – 'Freddy looks over to Bob and his mother, to his father, back again and there are, I would say, five separable signs to 243.'

his other fingers, but mainly his index finger, points toward his ear, moves head towards me, slightly to the left, head shifting to the right, right hand with palm open, 45 degree angle, and jerking hand motion up and down, vibrating it, kind of like the accelerator motion, and then points again, with his index finger, and then partially closes his hand, his right hand, all motion with right hand, giving an up and down motion, as if holding on to a steering wheel, with movement going slightly up and down, with arm in front of him, moving it up and down.'

243 – 'With his index finger, he points back and forth, back and forth, with his right hand, touches his mother, having turned his head from down to up and right, then points to me with his right hand, having moved a bit to the left, and both hands, with both of them he does hands clenched, a griplike hold, attempts to draw, as if holding imaginary steering wheel, grasping each other.'

242 – (I feel hampered by the equipment and feel really frustrated by the equipment . . . It stops it and then jiggles all the tape and I want to stop it faster and I find the lever very hard to work.)

242 – 'He looks up, and the first sign or movement, let's not say signs anymore, the first movement he does is something like he has hands both in front of him at the point of looking up from them. I still haven't decided where he looks first.'

243 – 'He is looking up, looks at his mother and down, back to his mother and in looking towards his mother, at 242½; so he looks to his mother, his dad, then his mother, and then looking back to his mother he signs at the same time this time. Then his first motion is: he takes his hands, his right hand away from the object that he has just above his lap, as he is sitting on the couch. The left hand and the object, in the same position, and takes the right hand, lifts the right hand up, and does something with it towards his chest, his upper chest, that is all between 242½ and 243.'

242 – 'Towards chest, away from chest, up towards mother, with that same right hand.'

242 – 'He looks up, looks back, . . . I do not know how to describe that, that burst of motion.'

I have arbitrarily cut off the amount of detail that can be presented. A more elaborated account can be found in Cicourel and Boese (1969, 1970) and Boese

(1971). Yet I hope the illustration is sufficient to give the reader a sense of the problem. It is quite difficult to match a segment of the free oral gloss with the segment of verbal gloss of the literal description. Each translator encountered rapid bursts which were resistant to description as physical movements. Trying to describe them verbally often seemed ridiculous unless many liberties could be taken. Note that the native signer provides a kind of detail different from the second language signer. He addresses details of body movement, notes the coordination of movements of different parts of the body, and is particularly aware of the movement of the child's hands and fingers. Researchers reading this chapter would probably want to claim that translators should be trained (as linguistic informants are trained) to use a similar vocabulary so as to produce similar accounts thus 'cleaning up' the description.

This would guarantee that the translation would follow the logical structure of normative oral syntax. Interrogating the native signer in sign would not alter the translation problem of providing the reader with normative oral syntax.

The reader will notice also that the native signer adds interpretations that provide specific cultural content to his descriptions, for example, referring to a movement of the hands as 'kind of like the accelerator motion' or 'holding on to a steering wheel'. The iconic nature of the steering wheel idea seems clear. We assume that both describer and reader are socialized to similar kinds of tacit knowledge about their environment that is available to their imagery and activated by actual or recalled movements glossed by the use of specific lexical items. But saying that 'his index finger, points toward his ear' presumes that the reader can imagine the relevance of the configuration in the particular context to signify the child's movements indicate he is 'hearing' something. Recall that we were unable to claim to 'know' and lock-in this interpretation of the movements described until we accidentally turned up the volume of the video recorder, which occurred after we had stopped analyzing this segment of tape and had gone on to another segment.

A central problem in making the translations was the desire to 'make sense' of what was 'happening' even though each viewing of the tape made the translators feel somewhat anomic and uncertain about the 'real' meaning of what was being displayed on the tape. The apparent uniformity of the two versions of the 'same' video tape display is only possible by selectively choosing particulars that can be justified by reference to oral syntactic general rules that enable the translators to decide to close off further guessing, speculation, uncertainty, bewilderment, and the like. Were we to avoid the use of a descriptive vocabulary or the labels with which we achieve social 'thingness' in our everyday use of oral language, but were to rely instead on a physical description, it would be difficult to link the physical descriptions to the kind of glossing that selectively settles on a particular use of lexical items to achieve socially meaningful descriptions. For example, the description, 'with his index finger, he points back and forth, back and forth, with his right hand, touches his mother, having turned his head from down to up and right . . .'

does not readily convey very much information. Yet notice how many perceptual particulars are being attended that cannot be made visible to the reader, but which the viewer recoded as 'touches his mother' and 'turned his head'. Can we presume that the translator is motivated by having settled on a particular substantive characterization that seems appropriate to the setting or by a general rule he guesses might be relevant? Do we assume instead that the translator is merely doing his best to detach himself from a meaning of the scene he wants to intend substantively and is rendering a literal physical description? In that case we would have to negotiate a correspondence between a presumed 'neutral' descriptive vocabulary employed, and a socially 'acceptable' or 'plausible' interpretation of 'what happened' in socially meaningful terms. Several meta-languages, each with an unexplored indexicality, provide a dubious correspondence. We thus would bypass the native signer's language, for we would not know how this section of tape would be described by one native signer to another.

In our work on sign language (Cicourel and Boese 1969 and 1970; Boese 1971), we indicate how it is possible to 'clean up' the messy versions produced by repeated translations to construct an account that appears to be free of ambiguity-producing particulars or contradictions. Yet each cleaned-up translation, each attribution of meaning can be subjected to an indefinite elaboration that views sign language as a context-sensitive, self-organizing medium of communication generating meanings accomplishing reference independently of those processes we find in oral language.

A reader trained in linguistics might want to suggest that something like a distinctive feature system is needed. The physical movements of the hands and body could be described by a small number of distinctive features that chunk into more complex labels like 'open', 'closed', 'away', 'towards', 'circular', and the like. Training translators to perform like coders produces the same kind of agreement that linguists (or sociologists using questionnaires) generate when they force their hearing of sounds into a finite number of complex symbols represented by the IPA and the various invented symbols any field researcher finds necessary to develop because of *his* hearing of the sounds. Distinctive features are convenient, elegant, and practical devices for producing a sense of linguistic structure. These interpretations provide a constructed sense of unity and correspondence. I am not saying that we should abandon such constructions for some as-yet-unannounced 'new' and 'objective' procedure. I have none to offer. I am saying that the inherent indexicality and reflexiveness of our constructions of social (linguistic, psychological, political, economic) reality are phenomena worthy of study in their own right. The ethnomethodologist finds the construction of different glosses of central interest, and he views research procedures as members' practices for preserving the mundaneity or meaningfulness of the world (Pollner 1970). But an examination of these practices reveals the irremedial indexicality of all communication by showing how the indefinite elaboration is resolved to achieve practical outcomes.

Paraphrasing Simon (1969), we can say that the thesis that humans possess a bio-logically determined competence for language leads to the notion of an inner environment placing limits on how humans process information. Language itself is the most artificial and 'the most human of all human constructions' (Simon 1969: 51-52). But it does not follow, as Simon would assert, that only the expressible is thinkable, and that if this is true, only the thinkable is expressible. The thinkable is expressible only through indexical expressions. Our reflexive use of the par-ticulars of the setting (the intonation of language use, the social and physical eco-logy, the biography of the speakers, the social significance of the occasion, etc.) and our kinesthetic, somesthetic, perceptual, and linguistic memory, to mention some of the apparently central ingredients, all contribute to the irreparable in-dexicality of communication. We can refer to these constraints and information processing features, but we find it difficult to describe in detail our ability to make tacit use of them. Everyday language is fascinating because subdomains of its rather awesome flexible structure permit us to construct other artificial languages like logical and mathematical systems or computer programs that can be set up in correspondence with objects, events, and operations. We can produce elegant ma-chines or linguistic algorithms that enable us to make certain classes of predictions and produce complex activities that humans cannot do or that require very special training and abilities. But our ability to construct machines or develop complex logical systems always presupposes a necessary reliance on the presuppositions of practical or mundane reasoning with its constraints of indexicality and reflexivity that are inherent in the development and in all uses of the sciences of the ar-tificial.

When we try to deal with manual sign languages as used by deaf persons (or the use of oral language by persons who cannot see), the limitations of our speech about signs should be quite apparent. How we go about constructing translations that seek to link speaking-hearing interpretations of the everyday world with deaf manual signers' conceptions of their everyday world, provides us with challenging problems of the processing of information and the creation of expressions re-presenting different levels of glossing. If language is artificial, then oral language conceptions of linguistic universals are equally artificial vis-a-vis other possible non-oral languages. If we hope to construct a theory of meaning that enables us to understand how we assign sense to our everyday worlds and establish reference, then we cannot assume that oral language syntax is the basic ingredient of a theory of meaning. The interactional context, as reflexively experienced over an exchange, or as imagined or invented when the scene is displaced or is known through a text, remains the heart of a general theory of meaning.

REFERENCES

BAR-HILLEL, YEHOSHUA. 1954. Indexical expressions. Mind 58.359–79.

BOESE, ROBERT J. 1971. Native sign language and the problem of meaning. Unpublished Ph.D. dissertation. University of California, Santa Barbara.

CHOMSKY, NOAM. 1965. Aspects of the theory of syntax. Cambridge, M.I.T. Press.

——. No date. Form and meaning in natural language. Amsterdam, North Holland Publishing Co.

CICOUREL, AARON V. 1967. Kinship, marriage, and divorce in comparative family law. Law and Society Review.

——. 1968a. The acquisition of social structure: Towards a developmental sociology of language and meaning. Understanding everyday life, ed. by Jack Douglas, 1970. (Reprinted from Rassagna di Sociologia.)

——. 1968b. The social organization of juvenile justice. New York, Wiley.

——. 1973. Generative semantics and the structure of social interaction. Cognitive sociology. London, Penguin.

CICOUREL, AARON V., and R. BOESE. 1969 and 1970. The acquisition of manual sign language and generative semantics. Duplicated. Paper presented at the American Sociological meetings, September, 1969, and International Conference on the Education of the Deaf, Stockholm, August, 1970.

COLBY, KENNETH M., L. TESLER, and H. ENEA. 1969. Experiments with a search algorithm on the data base of a human belief structure. Palo Alto, Stanford Artificial Intelligence Project.

DE GROOT, ADRIAAN D. 1965. Thought and choice in chess. The Hague, Mouton.

——. 1966. Perception and memory versus thought: Some old ideas and recent findings. Problem solving, ed. by B. Kleinmuntz, pp. 19–50. New York, Wiley.

GARFINKEL, HAROLD. 1967. Studies in ethnomethodology. Englewood Cliffs, N. J., Prentice-Hall.

GARFINKEL, HAROLD, and H. SACKS. 1969. On formal structures of practical activities. Theoretical sociology: Perspectives and developments, ed. by J. C. McKinney and E. Tiryakian. New York, Appleton-Century-Crofts.

GREENBERGER, MARTIN, ed. 1962. Computers and the world of the future. Cambridge, M.I.T. Press.

HABER, RALPH N., ed. 1968. Contemporary theory and research in visual perception. New York, Holt, Rinehart and Winston.

——, ed. 1969. Information-processing approaches to visual perception. New York, Holt, Rinehart and Winston.

——. 1970. How we remember what we see. SA 222/5.104–12.

HART, H. L. A. 1961. The concept of law. Oxford, Oxford Press.

HEBB, D. O. 1968. Concerning imagery. PsychRev 75.466–77.

JENNINGS, SYBILLYN. 1969. Report of continuing research on linguistic comprehension. Duplicated.

LAKOFF, GEORGE. 1968. Counterparts, or the problem of reference in transformational grammar. Summer meeting, Linguistic Society of America.

LENNEBERG, ERIC. 1968. The biological foundations of language. New York, Wiley.

——. 1969. On explaining language. Science 164.635–43.

McCAWLEY, JAMES D. 1968a. Concerning the base component of a transformational grammar. FL 4.234–69.

——. 1968b. The role of semantics in a grammar. Universals in linguistic theory, ed. by Emmon Bach and Robert T. Harms, pp. 125–69. New York, Holt, Rinehart and Winston.

MILLER, GEORGE A. 1956. The magical number seven, plus or minus two: Some limits on our capacity for processing information. PsychRev 63.81–96.

MILLER, GEORGE A., E. GALANTER, and K. PRIBRAM. 1960. Plans and the structure of behavior. New York, Holt, Rinehart and Winston.

MINSKY, MARVIN, ed. 1968. Semantic information processing. Cambridge, M.I.T. Press.

NORMAN, DONALD A. 1969. Memory and attention. New York, Wiley.

POLLNER, MELVIN. 1970. On the foundations of mundane reasoning. Unpublished Ph.D. dissertation. University of California, Santa Barbara.

QUILLIAN, M. ROSS. 1968. Semantic memory. Semantic information processing, ed. by M. Minsky, pp. 227–70. Cambridge, M.I.T. Press.

RAWLS, JOHN. 1955. Two concepts of rules. PhilRev 54.3–32.

REITMAN, W. R. 1965. Cognition and thought. New York, Wiley.

ROSS, JOHN ROBERT. Forthcoming. On declarative sentences. Readings in transformational grammar, ed. by R. Jacobs and P. Rosenbaum.

SACKS, HARVEY. 1966. The search for help: No one to turn to. Unpublished Ph. D. dissertation. University of California, Berkeley.

——. 1967 and 1970. Dittoed lectures. University of California, Irvine.

SCHEGLOFF, EMANUEL A. 1968. Sequencing in conversational openings. AmA 70.1075–95.

SCHLESINGER, I. M. No date. The grammar of sign language: Some implications for the theory of language. Duplicated.

SCHUTZ, ALFRED. 1962. Collected papers I: The problem of social reality. The Hague, Nijhoff.

——. 1964. Collected papers II: Studies in social theory. The Hague, Nijhoff.

SIMON, HERBERT. 1969. The sciences of the artificial. Cambridge, M.I.T. Press.

SIMON, HERBERT, and M. BARENFELD. 1969. Information-processing analysis of perceptual processes in problem solving. PsychRev 76.473–83.

TURNER, ROY. 1970. Words, utterances, and activities. Understanding everyday life, ed. by Jack Douglas.

ZIMMERMAN, DON H., and MELVIN POLLNER. 1970. The everyday world as a phenomenon. People and information, ed. by H. Pepinsky.

SOCIOLINGUISTICS

J. B. PRIDE

FORM AND FUNCTION

What sociolinguistics is is best defined in terms of what it does. Whether it amounts to a subdiscipline (Grimshaw 1966), a byproduct of developments in the two supposedly parent disciplines of linguistics and sociology (Fishman 1968a), an area of research that links linguistics with anthropology and sociology (Hymes 1971), or whatever, perhaps does not matter so very much in the long run. What it does is simply to investigate all those varieties and uses of language that may be termed broadly social. The development of linguistics has on the whole been such as to tend to obscure the plain fact that this aspect of language is as important as any other, and more important than most: hence, it can be argued, the need for a special label for what linguistics itself might have become but did not.[1]

---

[1] Jakobson (1963: 277) poses the rhetorical question: 'Do we today not conceive language as a whole in and for itself and simultaneously as a constituent part of culture and society?' — well, it depends who 'we' are. Firth (1935: 27) maintained that 'sociological linguistics is the great field for future research'. This may well be so, emphasis still resting however on the word future. The ebb and flow of the disciplinary allegiances of sociolinguistics can be roughly traced through the following references, all of which say much the same thing as Firth was saying, only the audiences differing: Boas (1911), Sapir (1929: 'It is peculiarly important that linguists, who are often accused, and accused justly, of failure to look beyond the pretty patterns of their subject matter, should become aware of what their science may mean for the interpretation of human conduct in general. Whether they like it or not, they must become increasingly concerned with the many anthropological, sociological, and psychological problems which invade the field of linguistics'), Malinowski (1937), Carroll (1953 : 113, fn. 6), Weinreich (1953 : 4, 5), Pike (1954–1960, Part I : 1–7, 21, etc.), Putnam and O'Hern (1955), Pickford (1956 : 211, 212, 220–223), Lévi-Strauss (1958 : 41), Weinreich (1958: '. . . we at last see untranslateability of languages and bi-culturalism of speakers taken seriously and subjected to empirical study. It is probably safe to say that as the machinery of social science is brought to bear on problems of attitude and motivation in contact situations, it will become possible to deal with psychological and social factors in the regulation of interference which so far have eluded investigation': 792, 793), Ferguson (1959: 'Descriptive linguists in their understandable zeal to describe the internal structure of the language they are studying often fail to provide even the most elementary data about the sociocultural setting in which the language functions': 437), Ferguson and Gumperz (1960: 2, 10, 11), Diebold (1961 : 496, 497), Gumperz (1961), Hymes (1961a : 337; 1961b : 66), Ferguson (1962 : 3), Sebeok (1963 : 58), Hymes (1964a, b, c; compare 1964b : 31 ff. with Katz and Fodor 1963), Klein (1965 : 210), Mitchell (1965 : 19), Hall (1965: '. . . there is the ever-present danger that . . . ultra-structured grammar will lose touch with linguistic reality, which is that of individual humans speaking to and responding to the speech of other individual humans in the

A simple and by no means original analogy may serve quite well to explain the primary motivations of sociolinguistics. Suppose language were like a game, say of football. Football has its rules, and its players move about the field in more or less characteristic ways, but no-one forgets that the object of the game is to score and to prevent goals. Language is like that, only it has more complicated rules and many goals. Hence its moves, rule-governed and goal-directed, are correspondingly more complex. Moreover, rules and goals are closely interrelated. The rules of grammar for example match the goal of grammaticality, the two together providing for one type of rule-governed creativity. No doubt different, or partly different, rules match those manifold objectives of language that go under such everyday headings as appropriateness, effectiveness, and so on; correspondingly, sociolinguistic performance must be interpreted quite differently from performance as measured against grammaticality.[2]

The goals of verbal behaviour constitute a very large part of its meaning,[3] hence what one is saying is that sociolinguistics studies the social meaning of language in relation to sociolinguistic rules, the two together governing performance — or, as one might say, the language user's moves, observable and unobservable. The recipient for his part is normally as alive to the social as to any other dimensions of meaning, even if in so doing he attends only to such structurally peripheral features as voice quality, hesitations, and so forth. The setting (or context, context of situation, etc.) in which verbal behaviour takes place is also part of its meaning, and to the extent that the connection here too is rule-governed so we may regard the setting as meaningful, rather than as some kind of jumble of stage props.

The history of linguistics itself has been characterised at times by a persistent and false separation of form, meaning, and context, at times by the playing down or outright exclusion of one or the other. The early structuralist's excessive regard for the forms of language, identified and defined without recourse to meaning, is still reflected in more recent linguistic theory, even where some attention is given to the fact of situationally-related formal variety. One notes for example the neo-Firthian's stipulation of a logical dependence of an 'inter-level' called context on form rather than on situational meaning (Halliday 1961; Ellis 1966). Halliday argues against the attempt to link language form to unobservables, on the grounds that the latter 'are only observable as (exponents of) the forms they are set up to explain' (: 245, fn. 13). Hence the need for an inter-level between form and situation the subcategories of which (called 'registers') are formally, and only formally, defined. But if distinctions at the 'inter-level' of context were logically wholly

---

context of their social relationships': 345), Bright (1966: Introduction), Fishman (1966 : 424, fn. 2), Grimshaw (1966: 'Most sociologists have only the vaguest idea of the activity carried on in the growing academic subdiscipline labelled sociolinguistics': 319).

[2] Hymes (1972) discusses some of the ambiguities inherent in Chomsky's use of the term performance.

[3] Pike's discussion (1954–1960) of the 'feature mode' of an emic unit stresses meaning as purpose; see also the last sentence of fn. 9 below.

dependent on form, not at all on situation, then what is it that guides the linguist's own discriminations of formal differences among texts, and by what criteria could such differences ever be regarded as below the threshold of significance for the purpose of distinguishing contextual registers? It is at the situational level, unobservable as well as observable, that form derives much of its meaning.

The transformational linguist is of course concerned to exclude the notion of context entirely from the rightful territory of linguistics.[4] Indeed expulsion would be a better word if one turns to their treatment of Malinowski and Firth. Langendoen (1964) for example refers to the exercise which requires provision of a feasible context of situation for given utterances as an argument against the assertion that contexts of situation are needed to yield their semantic interpretation. In his more recent book on *The London school of linguistics*, he argues briefly for 'general rules which amalgamate the meaning of nouns and adjectives to yield the meaning of noun phrases ...' (Langendoen 1968: 64), and refers to Katz and Fodor (1963) for exemplification. Three answers to this viewpoint are: first, at least some part of the semantic meaning of any utterance (or word, etc.) will have derived historically from and will always be susceptible to, contexts of use; second, the potential ranges of semantic meanings of most utterances (or words, etc.) are very large indeed, and forbid reference to 'the' meaning independently of the context or contexts which may activate and affect part(s) of 'it' (Whiteley 1966:150, 151); and third, Langendoen is alluding to a view of context which places great emphasis on observable aspects of environment (including linguistic environment) and social action — a degree of emphasis which sociolinguists on the whole no longer subscribe to. Langendoen stresses the infinite diversity of context, but this objection, justifiable in itself,[5] could apply equally well of course to the study of linguistic form — whether or not, but particularly if, form turns out to be some kind of function of context in any case.

Rather similarly, Lyons (1968) has argued the need for situationally neutral or 'restricted' contexts in which to carry out semantic analysis. Lyons regards the question 'how much meaning' as logically prior to 'what meaning'. Given a particular situational context, predictability or expectancy is the basic measure of how much meaning a word, phrase, etc. has. A phrase like *How do you do?* might well, in this sense, have 'no meaning' on occasion: '... it is certainly in accord with general, everyday usage to say that the meaningfulness of utterances, and parts of utterances, varies in inverse proportion to their degree of expectancy in context' (:415). But this is surely not the case. On the one hand it is not at all difficult to think of everyday occasions in which meaningfulness increases with predictability,

---

[4] A perspective which has been most pungently expressed by Katz and Fodor (1963 : 489).

[5] Malinowski saw linguistics as preferably 'an empirical study, carried out on living human beings within the context of their practical activities' (1937 : 63). But contextual discriminations do indeed have to be reduced, by both analyst and language user alike: see Sections III and IV below.

while conversely originality does not in itself necessarily carry with it greater increments of meaningfulness. To argue otherwise is to accept the implications of an information theory view of language; this in turn (as Lyons points out: 98, 419, and elsewhere) necessitates as complete a neutralisation of situational variation as possible. However, if one takes such a theoretical stand, then little is gained by illustrating it with reference to 'general everyday usage'.

Lyons's stipulation that situation has to be, as it were, neutralised before one can make progress with the analysis of meaning leads him to contrast phatic communion (which has as its main purpose the establishment and maintenance of a feeling of social solidarity and well-being) with that part of the use of utterances 'which is to be distinguished as their meaning (if they have meaning in terms of our definition)'. It may be as well to point out however that phatic communion is only one aspect of what one might refer to as sociolinguistic communion. If phatic communion, then why not power communion, or prestige communion, or transactional communion, etc.? Lyons seems to wish to isolate the sociolinguistic factor of solidarity as specially unworthy of semantic treatment (so too does Weinreich, 1963, who compares it with the 'doorbell', true semantic meaning with the 'elevator'), ignoring many other equally or more important sociolinguistic factors.

The ideally neutralised context (called 'restricted'), is, it is explained, one which has not 'developed', in the sense that 'participants in a conversation do not draw upon their previous knowledge of one another or the information communicated in earlier utterances, but ... share the more general beliefs, conventions and presuppositions governing the particular universe of discourse in the society to which they belong' (: 419). But it is precisely what is shared by participants in such contexts that constitutes much of the subject matter of sociolinguistics. Synonymy, for example, which Lyons regards as a basic 'sense-relation' between words, depends on contextually-dependent interchangeability: if two words can be freely interchanged in a given context then they are synonymous. But in what terms does one characterise the given context in the first place? Which of the 'general beliefs, conventions and presuppositions governing the particular universe of discourse' to which the given participants subscribe apply the more directly to choice of language on the occasion in question? Unless this problem is tackled, the notion of synonymy will remain either quite vague or dependent on information relating to relatively trivial contextual features. Synonymy may depend crucially for example upon whether participants are or are not old friends of equal status (specifying what is meant by status), and upon many other aspects of the subject matter of sociolinguistics. Lyons's position in this respect is very close to that of the componential analyst who adopts a de-contextualised approach to semantic field analysis. But in Whiteley's words, the componential analyst's significata and connotata 'belong to a conceptual model which is constantly under review from the social context' (1966: 149); or, as Hymes puts it: '... speech situations provide some of the frames necessary to recognize contrast' (Hymes 1964b:38).

The exclusion of contextual factors (whether observable or non-observable) from linguistic analysis is indeed still all too common practice, and, we are saying, amounts to the exclusion of several important aspects of meaning. In this respect little has changed since the time of de Saussure, since although few would now deny that 'phonetic and semantic criteria of identity are needed if we are to know what we are talking about' (Haugen 1951:218), not many wish to go very much further than to acknowledge features of language as meaningful, period, in some rather vague and unspecified sense. Haas (1966) for example, in an extremely lucid — if biassed — assessment of the goals of linguistic theory, points out that 'relations in the proposed analysis obtain almost invariably within determinate significant units, ultimately within meaningful units' (:121). Contrastive elements, it is explained, appear in a network of syntagmatic, paradigmatic, and functional relations to units of higher level — the last being 'usually passed over in silence', and 'significant, not arbitrary' (:125). But the author is still careful to set very narrow limits on the proper interest of autonomous linguistics in what constitutes meaningfulness. Thus Firth is credited not only with ejecting the 'sporadically intrusive semantic entities' which are said to have made Bloomfield's position difficult, but also with ensuring that 'situational context' stays 'safely outside the utterance' (:118).

Sociolinguistics sets no such limits. Among other things it admits the study of contrastiveness among variant features in what Haas calls 'functions' (i.e. significant units left incomplete by the removal of a variable: *the boys — home* would be called a 'sentence function', 125) in terms of contrastiveness among the social significance of those functions (compare, as a trivial example, *the boys went home, the boys pushed off home,* etc.). It also studies the determinant power of 'constants', or 'markers', which are not necessarily contrastive: phonological features for example which serve to characterise utterances as, say, commands or as upper-middle-class, etc.

The difficulty of dissociating the notions of form, meaning, and context from each other has not inhibited proposals for (or, largely outside 'pure' linguistics, attempts at) statistical correlation. Lyons (1966) for example, writes, of the category 'noun': 'if we have a language-neutral and workable notion of "thing" . . . the question whether there is any correlation between the class of elements which denote things in a given language and one or other of the distributionally valid syntactic classes of elements in that language is open to empirical investigation' (:214). The former type of class, in Lyons's view, may be a fundamental substantive linguistic universal resting upon the distinction between 'things' and 'properties' in the perceptual world, alongside 'such general notions as "inherent" v. "contingent", "change of state", "number", "sex", "animacy", "position", "motion", "direction", etc. . . . "deictic", or "orientational", features of the spatio-temporal situations of utterances' (:233). . . . 'There must be some point at which the categories of logic, epistemology and syntax are in correspondence with one another' (:234). The usefulness of the suggestion seems to turn on whether distributional classes can or can not be defined in *purely* distributional terms. Lyons takes it for granted that they can be (1966:210, 1968:147), or at least that since neither meaning nor distribution is 'completely determined' by the other the two notions are at least 'theoretically distinct' (1968:73). But if they cannot be so defined, then correlation with 'general notions' will necessarily remain suspect. The closer any such correlation, indeed the more likely it is that the same criteria have been involved on both sides (Carroll 1960, provides a good example of what is liable to turn up when unusually arbitrary sets of would-be correlates are chosen). Needless to say the difficulty applies no less where meaning is socially rather than logically defined, and simply reflects once again the error in trying to dissociate language from use. Referring to the problem of 'linguistic relativity', Lyons points out that 'neither extreme nominalism nor extreme realism is an acceptable approach' (1966:234) — but neither here nor in any other analytical pursuit can one properly reconcile the two by techniques of correlation.[6]

Terminological dichotomies abound in linguistics: in particular doubt for the sociolinguist are the related distinctions between *langue* and *parole*, competence and performance, and language and the use of language. The last of these is a metalinguistic accident lying all too handy for those who feel the need to wedge apart concepts which should be accepted as ultimately inseparable. Miller (1965) for example writes: '. . . the psycholinguist's task is to propose and test performance models for language use but he must rely on the linguist to give him a precise specification of what it is a language user is trying to use' (:17). Similarly in sociolinguistics there has been the drive to match choice of language (and languages) with sociological findings, each independently arrived at. One can do this, of course, in certain cases, but the choices of real interest may as often as not be scarcely identifiable at all without reference in the first place to social use.

Insofar as language can be so separated from the use of language then the two are indeed statistically correlateable. The drift of sociolinguistic evidence, however, suggests rather not only some limitation of interest in but also the ultimate impossibility of explanation by correlation; and this is so because, as we shall go on to illustrate, one cannot ignore the central role of latent meaning in all aspects of social (as of any other) verbal behaviour.

2. LANGUAGE AND SOCIAL STRATIFICATION

The resistance of some of the more meaningful social groups to objective identification and measurement is well reflected in both sociological and sociolinguistic research. There have been some attempts (beside programmatic statements) to make use of linguistic evidence for the clarification of groups and dimensions of

---

[6] Compare again Halliday (1961 : 245, fn. 13): 'The linguistic statement of context attempts to relate language form to (abstractions from) other (i.e. extra-textual) observables.'

interpersonal relationship — such evidence being supposed to be relatively concrete and measurable as well as immune from conscious suppression. Pickford (1956), for example, sees language as 'one of the clues' to the analysis of social class, Brown and Ford (1961) seek to match forms of address in American English with what they regard as semantic dimensions of social structure 'that may possibly be universal' (234), and so forth. The main difficulty here, namely that linguistic markers of sociological categories may be so much functions of those categories as to be very awkward to isolate, is brought out most effectively by Labov's work on social dialects.

Working from an earlier sociological survey of the Lower East Side of New York City, Labov (1964, 1966a, b) explored certain linguistic characteristics of ten socio-economic subgroups or classes, defined in terms of the three combined indicators of occupation, education, and family income. The realisations of five phonological variables, the values of which 'may cover a wide range of phonemic and phonetic units', are correlated both with class and with 'speaking styles', the latter on a five-point scale of formality which ranges from casual speech to the reading of minimal pairs, the context of elicitation in each case being the interview. The variables in question, chosen for their frequency, immunity from conscious suppression (but not from conscious distortion), and quantifiability, are (r), (eh), (oh), (the), and (dh) — using Labov's own form of notation. Values are shown to extend over wide and unbroken articulatory continua, and to be correlated with both class and style, such that both 'sharp stratification' into two major class groups (as in the case of (th)) and 'fine stratification' (as in the case of (r)) can be observed; in addition to this, a 'crossover pattern' appears in certain cases (such as (r) and (eh)) such that the next-to-highest class pronunciation displays a marked degree of 'hypercorrection' in more formal styles. Labov argues that this last phenomenon points to processes of linguistic change in being. Behind the evidence for hypercorrection he finds more general indications of evaluative norms which, while performance norms may be relatively unstable or show only social or only stylistic variation, are markedly unanimous, hence 'define New York City as a single speech community'. Bound up in turn with patterns of subjective evaluation are patterns of social mobility, such that for example hypercorrection in the use of (r), (r) values for 'mobility type', and responses to subjective evaluation tests alike, tell the same story, namely that 'linguistic behavior reflects participation in a set of norms' rather than sets of habits which are produced by close contact and past experience. Social groups in this respect are primarily reference groups.

Social mobility had been the main theme of Labov's earlier enquiry (1963) into a most noticeable centralisation of the diphthongs /ay/ and /aw/ by some of the inhabitants of Martha's Vineyard, Massachusetts. As he puts it, the overall significance of this sound change was its association with a positive orientation towards the island. 'I think we use a totally different type of English language' is how one Martha's Vineyard informant put it. And this of course is a sentiment which asserts itself in many parts of the world in many different ways, and with many differing aspects.[7] Social change and linguistic change are seen here as mutually responsive.

Labov's investigations are undoubtedly of considerable interest in demonstrating the operation of social values in one area of linguistic behaviour, and the consequent difficulty of establishing clear boundaries between linguistic variants. They also indicate that the relative variability of observable linguistic social group markers might be best interpreted in terms of processes of sound change. Labov draws inferences based on both direct observation of performance and on indications of subjective evaluations of usage on the part of language users. Evidence for change from performance is provided for example by lower class pronunciations of (oh) which would seem to exclude them from the normal pattern of social-with-stylistic variation (1966a:228, ch. 9), by the hypercorrect behaviour in more formal styles of the lower middle class for (r) (eh) (oh), and more generally by taking account of linguistic correlates of social mobility in relation particularly to age. The last type of inference depends upon assumptions such as that increasing age will tend to bring increasing contact with higher status groups, that stigmatisation of a linguistic feature will lead to its less frequent use in the speech of the young than in the speech of the old, that newly introduced prestige features will tend to be used more by the relatively insecure middle-aged than by either the young or the old, and above all that prestige in this particular setting always attaches to the highest ranking socio-economic group — and is most envied by the next in line. A separate account of relationships between social mobility, social aspiration, and linguistic change in this same context is provided by Labov (1966b). Statistical evidence is provided for a closer linguistic correspondence between 'lower middle class upward mobility type' and 'upper middle class' sections of the community than between the former and 'lower middle class stable mobility type', particularly in non-casual relationships and settings — both in terms of performance and the subjective endorsement of norms. Moreover, evaluative norms (particularly for the 18–39 age group) are very much more uniform than performance.[8]

The orientation of Labov's work towards interpersonal relationships seen only or mainly in terms of degrees of formality and towards a certain type of social class is not uncharacteristic of much of the work that has been done so far on social dialects, at any rate in the United States. The Detroit Dialect Study (Shuy *et al.* 1967) for example, which aims to describe certain linguistic features of the various English-speaking subcultures of Detroit, contrasts the speech of the 'so-called dis-

---

[7] The Filipino critic for example who writes 'Upon this new, or rather newest, English, Filipino writers will erect the literary language' (Passin 1963) is no less intent on asserting a social reference group by the use of linguistic hypercorrection.

[8] McCormack (1969) notes: 'Labov's data seem to call into question the theory that it is "social class" rather than an assemblage of individual status strivings which gets expressed by prestigious markers in New York City speech' (: 467). This is precisely the point — made very clearly by Labov himself.

advantaged with that of the more socio-economically successful' in respect of forms considered (by the fieldworkers themselves) to be socially stigmatised as well as relatively easily quantifiable. These include such features as multiple negation, pronominal apposition, and nasalisation of vowels. Data was obtained from interviews in three styles — conversational, short answers, and reading. The use of multiple negation, for example, is shown to reflect at least four socio-economic groupings (but in differing degrees for children and adults, men and women, negroes and whites: thus younger children have clearly not yet arrived at the fine social discriminations of their elders and betters in this respect, negroes are more sensitive to this feature but less sensitive to pronominal apposition than whites, and so forth). It is argued that the more conscious a grammatical index of social stratification the finer it will stratify, and that multiple negation is consequently a prime problem for the Detroit teacher. In its educational aspect this study is aimed at promoting bi-dialectalism (between 'standard' and 'home' styles of speech) appropriate to the occasion, topic, etc., and some awareness (among teachers in the first instance) of the use by the community of several social dialects, distinguished from each other not so much by the presence or absence of certain linguistic features as by differing frequencies of use. As in the case of Labov's work, emphasis falls upon quantifiable markers of socio-economic class stratification, associated feelings of correctness and prestige, and discrete points on a formality scale.

One would not wish to dispute the local validity of the underlying assumptions here — empirical evidences for which are certainly not lacking; the questions posed in Labov's subjective evaluation forms (1966a:410ff.) are no doubt well attuned to the realities of New York culture (thus, would such and such a snatch of speech be 'acceptable' for a television personality, an executive secretary, etc., or would it not be 'good' enough?), and Labov makes it quite clear in any case that other types of subjective reaction are possible, unrelated perhaps to class hierarchies and associated attitudes. But the point has still to be made that reference to dimensions of interpersonal relationship besides that of formality, and to groups besides those of socio-economic class, might point to the functioning of quite different linguistic variables; and of course vice-versa.

3. SOCIAL GOALS OF LANGUAGE USE

Labov shows then how linguistic markers of sociological categories may be so much functions of those categories as to be very difficult to isolate, by measuring degrees of phonological variation on continuous scales against sociological (including evaluative) variables which are kept very much more discrete. In working generally from the latter towards the former the analysis is made finally linguistic rather than sociological. But linguistic variation is still very precisely circumscribed. This is characteristic: one can find few examples of work which attempt to analyse lin-

guistic variation really open-endedly; so that although the expression free variation
has been used often enough to designate the interests of sociolinguistics, linguistic
variation is characteristically allowed very much less free rein in analysis than social
or otherwise contextual variation. This is not necessarily a bad thing, since sociolinguistics is centred upon the study of formal systems as functions of social
factors. Yet much attention has still to be given to the task of clarifying what such
factors may be, how much part of the knowledge of language users. In this Section
we shall take a brief look at a very few of the more insightful approaches to the
analysis of the social goals of language use.

Of basic importance are those investigations into social constraints upon code-
switching where the languages and dialects concerned are distinct enough from each
other to enable the analyst to be reasonably certain of what is being switched with
what. Rubin's studies in Paraguay (1962, 1968) for example are of this sort, and
display an instructive methodological shift from an earlier relatively simple hypothesis (that choice of Spanish or Guarani on the part of bilinguals can be fundamentally referred to the two axes of power and solidarity) to a subsequent espousal
of a more complex set of factors organised in a more interesting manner. Working
from questionnaires given to bilinguals in a rural area and in a town area, Rubin
arranges certain factors in an apparent order of importance: from rural/urban
locality, formality, intimacy, seriousness, to a number of others such as first language learned, school pressures, predicted language proficiency, sex, and so on
(1968:100–112). Formality is regarded as a matter of behaviour that is 'expected'
or 'permitted', in relation to social identities as functions of relative status (Goodenough 1961, 1965; also Pride 1970a, b, on Goodenough 1965), in relation to
occasions ('if the dance floor is brick, then the dance is more formal than if the
floor is packed earth', 106), and in relation to topics. Intimacy is in effect another
term for solidarity, and arises particularly from shared values and frequent contacts.
These various factors, suggested as appropriate to a culture which has not developed a sharply defined class system, are assumed to have the character of ordered
series of decisions or a 'system of ordered priorities' (:112). Three questions seem
worth asking here: first, what evidence is there that factors derived from a questionnaire will necessarily reflect ordered psychological decisions? [9] second, what
evidence is there that respondents were sufficiently aware of their own usage to be
able to provide accurate replies? and third, to what extent were the derived variables (inevitably) implicit in the questions themselves, which is to say in the investigator's mind while compiling them?

---

[9] Insofar as they do, it will still be the case that factorisation will tend to disguise the particular
rank orders of particular components. Thus, Denison (1968 : 583) refers to a 'hierarchy of situational factors' which correlate with language selection in Sauris; yet particular topics for example may on particular occasions (or indeed on most or even all occasions) dominate all other
factors; other topics may be quite neutral with respect to language selection, unless co-occurring
with certain other factors, and so on. Pike (1954–1960 : 68, 69) states very relevantly that 'purpose'
will determine choice of order in his 'etic classificatory criteria' for utterance types.

Rubin's later work then to some extent displaces the two general factors of power and solidarity in favour of a more complex 'decision path'. Tanner (1967) works with these same two axes but differentiates each into more particular components which, with respect to choice of low Javanese and high Javanese in certain settings, may clash — hence invite the use of 'everyday Indonesian'. Choice of code is seen also in relation to a number of other factors, each of which has its apparent counterpart elsewhere in sociolinguistic literature, including: public or private setting (cf. Stewart 1962); academic discussion, or joking and gossip (cf. Rubin: seriousness of discourse); and business transactions (cf. Gumperz 1966: transactional versus personal occasions). It may be an interesting question whether the factors of power (or 'vertical social distance') — differentiated into, for example, academic, class, and age distance, on the one hand, and of solidarity (or 'horizontal social distance') — differentiated into friendship and ethnic group distance, etc., on the other, are not very much more fundamental notions than, say, socio-economic class and formality. Whatever the labels one uses, will there always or often tend to be two such overriding axes where choice of language is concerned?

There is some evidence on this score, most obviously with respect to the very frequent availability of two languages (dialects, varieties or variants) rather than three or more on any given occasion. When say choice exists between *tu* and *vous,* or between Spanish and Guarani, or between high and low Javanese, or between standard and dialectal English, one must correspondingly expect some sort of two-termed choice at the social level. Generally speaking, local informants will tend to readily fall in with (or suggest) either-this-or-that explanation for choice of either-this-or-that language (dialect, etc.). Sociolinguistic investigation which proceeds from a given set of language data towards social constraints upon language choice will normally tend either to refine upon such explanations (showing for example that 'power' has many facets which may not all act in quite the same way: Tanner 1967; that code mixing may be unconscious even though explainable in terms of conscious attitudes: Blom and Gumperz 1972 etc.); or, alternatively, will favour a larger number of dimensions (Friedrich 1966), these perhaps being seen as hierarchically ordered in one respect or another (Rubin 1968; Denison 1968).

Examples of each type are not lacking. Fishman (1968b: 974, 975) sees Spanish-English code-switching among Puerto Ricans in New York as answering to 'two complementary sets of domains' or 'institutional arenas in which cultural identifications are enacted'. Cultural identifications in turn are seen in terms of the 'high' and the 'low' culture, the one emphasising distance and power relationships, formality and ritual (one notices the association of power with formality), the other ethnicity, spontaneity, comradeship, intimacy, etc. English and Spanish are called respectively the high and the low language, Spanish in New York contrasting nicely in this respect with Spanish in Paraguay: where Guarani is the 'sweeter' language in the one setting (Rubin 1968 : 107), it is Spanish which has that 'certain little thing to it' that parents under pressure to do a favour are presumed to respond to in the other.

Ferguson (1959) had earlier used the terms high and low to designate those fairly clearly distinguishable language varieties which stand in a relationship of diglossia, which is to say in markedly complementary positions in respect of various types of prestige, domains of use, order of learning, modes of borrowing, structural features, etc. — the four defining languages being Arabic, Modern Greek, Swiss German (with Standard German), and Haitian Creole (with French). Diglossia presents an extreme case of linguistic-with-social dichotomy. Grammatical differences in each of Ferguson's four defining cases are clearly marked, lexical and phonological differences less so. Householder (1962) shows, with respect to Greek diglossia, how unpredictable (at any rate to the outsider) the various uses and evaluations may be. Nearly all art, literary, and theatrical criticism is in D(himotiki); yet art history, biography, and scientific writing might well be in K(atharevusa). Principal news stories in the papers are likely to be in K, as are social as well as business letters. And 'of course the most loyal supporters of K are the poor people who don't know it and can't use it'(129). Topics generally are important, and the language of books will correspondingly tend to govern the language of spoken discussion about their subject matters (:130). Householder points out that the grammatical dichotomy is very much less conscious in people's minds than the finer lexical distinctions.[10]

The most fundamental social factors in diglossia are attitudinal ones, and are liable to be culturally very relative. It is not enough for example to understand that H is believed in some given community to be 'somehow more beautiful, more logical, better able to express important thoughts, and the like' (Ferguson 1959: 431). Nader (1962) argues convincingly for more refined interpretations of prestige feelings in particular cases; her examples are with special reference to the various attitudes one might encounter towards dialects of Arabic in the Lebanon, and to their situations of use. Fischer (1958), Hymes (1961b) and several others have called for more precise handling of this notion in relation to language, but such has not yet been forthcoming, whether in respect of diglossic or any other types of situation. 'High' and 'low', as they stand, are in danger of being mere labels for whatever it may be that invites the use of this language rather than that.

Avoidance of this danger is one of the motivations for Fishman's emphasis on the categories of domain and role-relationship (1966:341), to a lesser extent on topic and locale, and generally on data that can be empirically observed and (it is hoped) predicted. 'Value clusters are much grosser and looser abstractions than speech varieties' (1968b:974); and analysis should progress 'from descriptive adequacy alone to predictive power with respect to the what and the how of variety use' (1968b:981). Although Fishman's approach is prevailingly towards the con-

---

[10] While such evidence must be no more than merely suggestive for non-diglossic contexts, one is still prompted by it to question the breadth of application of markers of social status (those favoured for example by Labov and Shuy) which, though they may be relatively immune in mid-speech from conscious suppression, are nevertheless among those most consciously thought about.

crete, away from the abstract, some attention is given in his Report on Puerto Rican code-switching in New York to the concept of 'network types', such as 'predominantly open and closed relationships' — the former specified as those which allow relatively greater freedom of choice as between high and low language. Network types are not regarded as standing in a branching relationship with role-relations. Thus 'shared experience of great danger, great intimacy, etc.' may bear no predictable relationship with such role-relations as may apply at the time. Social relations, in comparison, are 'specifiable in terms of much more precise and naturalistically real role-relationships' (1968b: 977), and the analyst is urged to shun a 'basic reliance on purported inter-personal meanings' (: 1034). A rather different view is put forward in the same Report by Hoffman (1968: 63) to the effect that it is the unpredictable choice that holds the greatest interest. Hoffman does not unfortunately offer many examples of what might motivate unexpected choices (reprimanding a child versus discussing educational goals and aspirations with him, expression of anger versus warning of impending anger, argument versus discussion, group therapy situations versus situations which do not threaten personal dignity, kidding and joking, and so on), but notes: 'Respondents were not able to explain why they switched, but remembered that it was always done without conscious effort' (: 66). It is consciousness of language choice that is seen by Fishman, however, as the significant pointer to reality: 'Domain ... is an abstraction that ... corresponds closely to the way many bilinguals think of their language-choice regularities' (Fishman 1968b: 1042). In this connection the transcripts of discussions with a group of Puerto Rican high school students are instructive, since one notices in the students' remarks more or less equal consideration of domain etc., on the one hand, and status relations, cultural values, and rather pragmatic purposes such as asking for a favour, etc., on the other. It is very evident that besides domain analysis two further levels of analysis are relevant here: first, that which looks for underlying explanations for such observable regularities; and second, that which looks at instances of code-switching which are not marked by observable changes in the environment at all (these being a frequent subject of debate in the Puerto Rican transcripts).

The last type of verbal behaviour is evidenced by Blom and Gumperz (1972), in their discussion of the use of Ranamål (a rural dialect in northern Norway) and Bokmål (the standard variety of Norwegian used in that part of the country) as symbols of local and national Norwegian social values respectively. Status distinctions, local and non-local descent, and use of and loyalty to dialect or standard speech tend to go hand in hand in this setting, code-switching being both narrowly constrained by observable features of the situation (locale, participants, etc.) and itself serving (as 'metaphorical switching') to define or alter a situation which otherwise would lack overt marking. The code chosen will always tend to carry its distinct set of social values, code mixing accordingly conveying corresponding mixtures of these same social values. In lesser depth of detail, Stewart (1962) seeks to explain Haitian Creole and French diglossia in terms of the contrasts public/ private and formalised/unformalised, along with otherwise unobservable changes in 'mood of discourse' which may reflect feelings of solidarity, sympathy, casualness, intimacy, etc. (:157, 158).

Denison (1971) is also concerned with this same general phenomenon. He suggests that in Sauris ('a German linguistic island' in N.E. Italy of some 800 inhabitants), while there seems to be a high degree of correlation between language and setting (Friulian in bars, German in the home, Italian at church and in school), there nevertheless 'turns out to be a more accurately predictive correlation with some other factor or factors present'. They include generation, formality, 'conjugal dispute', rural or non-rural topics, above all feelings of social identity with the village, region, or nation ('When a villager speaks Italian he sees himself as part of the Italian nation', for example), feelings which Denison symbolises as low, mid, and high respectively. An interesting point is that the increasing use of Italian by parents to children does not seem to be bringing with it any conflict between the function of the home as an extension of school (Italian as H) and the dimension of intimacy (German as L now only among adults). In this small community therefore Italian may be in process of taking on a broader range of functions than hitherto, and in part independently of school pressures and 'high' prestige — in effect developing into the local standard language (on functional heterogeneity as a property of standard language see Havránek 1932 and Haugen 1966). Code-switching tactics in Sauris may be expected to change accordingly; for example the rural population may in time no longer wish or need or be able to 'defend itself' against the patronising use of Friulian by neighbouring middle-class citizens by replying in Italian — as Denison reports they frequently have to do at present. Code-switching of this sort, which deploys the symbolic resources of available codes, can indeed create situations.

The recognition of high, mid, and low languages in Sauris is roughly paralleled in the discussion of *krama, madya,* and *ngoko* speech levels in Javanese provided by Geertz (1960:248–260). These are obligatory (Geertz calls them 'involuntary' and 'unintentional'), and symbolise relative status and familiarity. In addition, special honorific words can raise the high and low levels of speech in such a way as to provide for three dialects each dispersed into three (lowest dialect) or five (highest and middle) levels. 'The higher the level of language spoken to an individual . . . the thicker the wall of etiquette protecting his emotional life' (:255). The need for respect and the need for familiarity on the same occasion are especially well handled by honorific usage in the highest dialect (cf. Tanner 1967, who sees a role for Indonesian in resolving such difficulties), while the 'average middle rank urbanite' can draw on levels of language appropriate to his wide range of social contacts. Other factors mentioned appear to relate more or less directly to status and familiarity (setting, subject matter, third persons, etc.), but Geertz nevertheless considers that a 'complete listing of the determinants of level selection would

... involve a thorough analysis of the whole framework of Javanese culture' (: 258).

Not the least interesting aspect of the Javanese linguistic scene to explore would be that of borrowing from Indonesian into Javanese. Geertz quotes: 'Someone then noted that even when one goes to a political meeting in the village and they use Javanese, many of the words are Indonesian words which, although the people in the audience perhaps cannot use them or at least cannot make them into whole Indonesian sentences, they nevertheless understand quite well' (:260). In this general connection, Whiteley (1967) has made a useful study of borrowing from English into the Swahili spoken in Dar-es-Salaam which lends further structure to the 'general agreement that Swahili is associated with the informal, relaxed, leisured, and popular aspects of life, while English is reserved for the formal, serious, official, and cultured situations' (: 126). Patterns and degrees of assimilation at a phonological and morphological level are sought, and — along with distinctions between established and probationary loans, and loans which conform to the existing patterns of Swahili and those which are more innovatory — related to the speech (and attitudes: 130) of monolingual and bilingual speakers, subject or discourse, and social contexts. The author raises a suggestive type of question: what might the role of the individual as innovator be in these respects in a multilingual urban context 'where linguistic loyalties are liable to sudden and profound change'? Who sets the fashion? [11]

Certainly borrowing and language learning (or bilingualism) are related, in incidence and motivation if less directly in structural description. The linguistic impact of one language upon another, whether this takes the form of integration or interference (Haugen 1956:40; also Diebold 1961:497, 498), may well be accompanied by a degree of bilingualism in the community, the initial and important yet often neglected stages of which Diebold calls 'incipient bilingualism'. In the Mexican context incipient bilingualism is one result of greater social contact with and participation in national life, the Huave otherwise being 'almost a second-rate citizen' (:501). Spanish in the Huave-speaking area of Mexico is thus instrumental for upward social mobility. Several studies by Lambert (1967, for example) take up the question of language learning motivation as a theoretical issue, his postulation of 'instrumental' alongside 'integrative' motivations being very clearly connected in various ways with such language-related notions as power and solidarity, status and familiarity, etc. Lambert, Gardner, Olton and Tunstall (1961) investigated the effects of each type of motivation on the work of high school pupils studying French in three American localities (Louisiana, Maine, Connecticut), and their relationships to measures of intelligence and aptitude, it being hypothesised that integrative

---

[11] Whiteley considers that the mere use of loans in any language does not amount to a special style of discourse; this one feels is debateable, not only for instance in the light of Javanese-Indonesian borrowing but also as illustrated by the development of English for some time after the Norman conquest. Additional features (intonational, syntactical, etc.) will of course always tend to characterise the discourse in question, but may not always be so criterial.

motivations are the more important in the long run. Motivations of this sort are inferred from the results of questionnaires and are described in terms such as: 'a subject's dissatisfaction or discouragement with his place in society', 'prejudiced orientations towards foreign peoples', attitudes towards (the same) voices speaking French and English on tape, social inquisitiveness, number of French friends, parents' attitudes, and so on. The statistical results, which are relative to the particular locality, are not however altogether convincing, either in respect of general factors or in respect of individual components (Pride 1970a); moreover they do not show whether or not there were higher correlations between integrative motivation and achievement for the very high achievers; more generally they do not allow for variation in such respects as the teachers' skills and language proficiencies, or (above all) for the various selections and presentations of material; these for example might be such as not only to involve ('integrate') the learner in some aspects of the other culture, but also, conversely, to involve the teacher (hence the language he selects and the way he presents it) in some part of the learner's own culture. Within every neat dichotomy there may lurk many a necessary qualification, and perhaps nowhere is this more true and less suspected than in the study of aims and objectives in language use.

4. PERCEPTION OF SOCIAL AND LINGUISTIC VARIATION

The approaches to sociolinguistic description referred to in the last Section start out by and large by postulating a small number of fairly simple (usually dichotomous) contextual contrasts and go on in varying degree to elaborate the detail of their various component parts. It is with such elaboration that the prospects of cross-cultural equivalence seem to recede. And the fact that each individual component factor may operate in its own particular way (both independently and in its manner of occurrence with others) seems to lessen the validity or extensibility of such uniform labels as power and solidarity even for any given setting. One can only say that both Friedrich (1966) and Haugen (commenting in the same volume) were right in a sense, the one wishing to preserve the distinctions between each of the ten contextual factors which he saw as constraining the use of Russian personal pronouns in nineteenth century Russian literature, the other seeing the twin pronominal choice necessarily matching twin social constraints (see also Hymes 1971).

These two difficulties may furthermore be compounded by seemingly incompatible underlying assumptions on the part of different investigators. How is one for example to interpret the senses of such terms as 'personal' and 'individual' in the studies of code-switching carried out by Gumperz (1966) and Bernstein (1972)? Gumperz contrasts the bearing of personal and transactional relationships on choice of code in a Norwegian setting. Bernstein draws a threefold contrast between imperative, positional, and personal modes of social control, in respect of social dialects in Britain. But whereas Gumperz sees the peer-group, the group of friends, the family circle, etc. as allowing scope to 'all the facets of an individual's personality' (not least linguistic scope), Bernstein regards the effects of such closed groups to be such as to favour the use of language which is altogether more predictable and less individualising than the more elaborated language which is instead 'oriented to persons'. Personal language in Gumperz's sense in rural Norway will tend to be dialectal rather than standard, whereas personal language in Bernstein's sense in Britain will tend to be standard rather than dialectal. The absence of fit here is obviously more than cross-cultural (Norwegian-British) in origin.

Further than this, there is the question of degree. Stewart (1962) suggests that the contrast public/private plays an important role in determining language use. But how public is public? Whiteley (1968) writes of the rural Kenya context: 'To say, for example, that an Area Council is held in Swahili may merely mean that the Government Officer addressing the meeting cannot speak the local language: it says nothing about the impact of Swahili ... on the community, who both during and after the meeting discuss the issues heatedly in the local language'. And how private is private? '... when we who are known as outsiders stepped up to a group of locals engaged in conversation, our arrival marked an alteration in the casual posture of the group ... looks changed and predictably our inquiries were answered in the standard' (Blom and Gumperz 1972); but at some stage 'we' may come to be accepted as insiders. ... Public/private, non-casual/casual, out-group/in-group, etc. are all more than simple dichotomies in this respect (on the problematical nature of the last-mentioned in the Japanese and Korean contexts, see Martin 1964:411). Each of Labov's contextual situations and five non-phonological cues for the identification of casual speech (1964:167, 168; 1966a:101ff.) is necessarily only a very rough guide; laughter for example may be nervous or affected, perhaps accompanied — by certain people — by quite formal and controlled language.

The question of just how many discriminations are or can be perceived and handled by the language user on any one contextual or linguistic dimension may well be of fundamental relevance to the analysis of stylistic variation in language. One should neither assume unbroken continuities of expression (on any linguistic level) matching continuities of situation, nor this-or-that alternatives on either side, but rather something in between.[12] On the linguistic side, seemingly endless diversity in certain respects may not be what the receiver is attending to: he may be more concerned with those features which present themselves to him as distinctly finite series of alternatives, sociolinguistic phonemes so to speak. It seems certain, for example, that each of a limited number of tone groups in English (at least partly

---

[12] See Miller (1956), Goodenough (1965 : 17, 18), and Pride (1970a, b). A good example (referred to in the last Section) of descriptive work which makes more than implicit assumptions of this sort is provided by Geertz (1960), who shows elsewhere (1961 : 20 ff.) in a similar fashion how the Javanese linguistic etiquette system interlocks with that of kin term ranking.

independent of grammatical and lexical structure[13]) contributes its specific social meanings. The perception of such groups involves not only the perception of physical cues but also the perception of situational meanings. Each type of perception will depend to some extent on the other. Judgements of social class, for example, may in part be a function of the ability to judge linguistic niceties: perception of the more discrete transition points on the phonological variable scales which Labov describes will, if nothing more, at any rate colour the language user's perception of class boundaries. And vice-versa. In this sense linguistic and non-linguistic, language and situation, language and the use of language, even language and society, are all false dichotomies.

REFERENCES

BERNSTEIN, B. 1972. A sociolinguistic approach to socialisation; with some reference to educability. Directions in sociolinguistics, ed. by D. H. Hymes and J. J. Gumperz, pp. 465–98. New York, Holt, Rinehart and Winston.

BLOM, J.-P., and J. J. GUMPERZ. 1972. Some social determinants of verbal behavior. Directions in sociolinguistics, ed. by D. H. Hymes and J. J. Gumperz, pp. 407–34. New York, Holt, Rinehart and Winston.

BOAS, F. 1911. Introduction. Handbook of American Indian languages, ed. by F. Boas, pp. 59–73. Washington, D.C., Smithsonian Institution.

BRIGHT, W., ed. 1966. Sociolinguistics. The Hague, Mouton.

BROWN, R. W., and M. FORD. 1961. Address in American English. JAbSoc-Psych 62.375–85. (Reprinted in Hymes 1964c: 234–44.)

CARROLL, J. B. 1953. The study of language. Cambridge, Mass., Harvard University Press.

——. 1960. Vectors of prose style. Style in language, ed. by T. A. Sebeok, pp. 283–92. New York, Wiley.

DENISON, N. 1968. Sauris, a trilingual community in diatypic perspective. Man 3.578–92.

——. 1971. Some observations on language variety and plurilingualism. Social anthropology and language, ed. by E. Ardener, pp. 157–85. London, Tavistock.

DIEBOLD, A. R., JR. 1961. Incipient bilingualism. Lg 37.97–112. (Reprinted in Hymes 1964c : 495–506.)

ELLIS, J. O. 1966. On contextual meaning. In memory of J. R. Firth, ed. by C. E. Bazell, J. C. Catford, M. A. K. Halliday, and R. H. Robins, pp. 79–95. London, Longmans.

[13] Only partly. As Mitchell (1969) points out: 'The dissatisfaction one feels with present intonational analyses may well be due in no small measure to the analyst's belief in the independence of intonation from the remainder of the formal textual complex.' He goes on: '... but this apart, the inconvenient fact for the analyst is that speech, like other forms of behaviour, is on-going in the circumstances of use' (: 164).

FERGUSON, C. A. 1959. Diglossia. Word 15.325–40. (Reprinted in Hymes 1964c : 429–37.)

——. 1962. Background to second language problems. Study of the role of second languages in Asia, Africa, and Latin America, ed. by F. A. Rice, pp. 1–7. Washington, D.C., Center for Applied Linguistics.

FERGUSON, C. A., and J. J. GUMPERZ. 1960. Linguistic diversity in South Asia: studies in regional, social, and functional variation. (RCAFL-P 13 (= IJAL 26/3, Part 3.))

FIRTH, J. R. 1935. The techniques of semantics. Papers in linguistics 1934–1951, pp. 7–35. London, Oxford University Press. (Also in TPhS 1935.36–72.)

FISCHER, J. L. 1958. Social influences in the choice of a linguistic variant. Word 14.47–56. (Reprinted in Hymes 1964c:483–88.)

FISHMAN, J. A. 1966. Language maintenance and language shift as a field of inquiry. Language loyalty in the United States, pp. 424–58. The Hague, Mouton.

——. 1968a. Review of J. O. Hertzler, A sociology of language. Lg 43.586–604.

——. 1968b. Bilingualism in the barrio. Final report, contract no. OEC-1-7-062817-0297. U.S. Department of Health, Education and Welfare. Also Language Science Series, Indiana University Press, 1971.

FODOR, J. A., and J. J. KATZ, eds. 1963. The structure of language. New York, Prentice-Hall.

FRIEDRICH, P. 1966. The structural implications of Russian pronominal usage. Sociolinguistics, ed. by W. Bright, pp. 214–59. The Hague, Mouton.

GEERTZ, C. 1960. The religion of Java. Glencoe, Ill., Free Press.

——. 1961. The Javanese family. Glencoe, Ill., Free Press.

GOODENOUGH, W. H. 1961. Education and identity. Anthropology and education, ed. by F. C. Gruber, pp. 84–103. Philadelphia, University of Pennsylvania Press.

——. 1965. Rethinking status and role. The relevance of models for social anthropology, ed. by M. Banton, pp. 1–24. London, Tavistock.

GRIMSHAW, A. D. 1966. Directions for research in sociolinguistics: Suggestions of a non-linguist sociologist. Explorations in sociolinguistics, ed. by S. Lieberson = Sociological Inquiry 36. (Also RCAFL-P 44; and Part II of IJAL 33.)

GUMPERZ, J. J. 1961. Speech variation and the study of Indian civilisation. AmA 63.976–88. (Reprinted in Hymes 1964c:416–23.)

——. 1966. On the ethnology of linguistic change. Sociolinguistics, ed. by W. Bright, pp. 27–48. The Hague, Mouton.

HAAS, W. 1966. Linguistic relevance. In memory of J. R. Firth, ed. by C. E. Bazell, J. C. Catford, M. A. K. Halliday, and R. H. Robins, pp. 116–47. London, Longmans.

HALL, R. A. 1965. Fact and fiction in grammatical analysis. FL 1.337–45.

HALLIDAY, M. A. K. 1961. Categories of the theory of grammar. Word 17.241–92.

HAUGEN, E. 1951. Directions in modern linguistics. Lg 27.211–22.

——. 1956. Bilingualism in the Americas: A bibliography and research guide. University, Alabama, University of Alabama Press.

——. 1966. Language, dialect, nation. AmA 68.922–35.

HAVRÁNEK, B. 1932. The functional differentiation of the standard language. Reprinted in: A Prague School reader on aesthetics, literary structure, and style, ed. P. L. Garvin (1964), pp. 3–16. Washington, D.C., Georgetown University Press.

HOFFMAN, G. 1968. Final Report, contract no. OEC–1–7–062817–0297. U.S. Department of Health, Education and Welfare.

HOUSEHOLDER, F. W. 1962. Greek diglossia. MSLL 15.109–29.

HYMES, D. H. 1961a. Linguistic aspects of cross-cultural personality study. Studying personality cross-culturally, ed. by B. Kaplan, pp. 313–61. New York, Harper and Row.

——. 1961b. Functions of speech: An evolutionary approach. Anthropology and education, ed. by F. C. Gruber, pp. 55–84. Philadelphia, University of Pennsylvania Press.

——. 1964a. Introduction: Towards ethnographies of communication. The ethnography of communication, ed. by J. J. Gumperz and D. H. Hymes, pp. 1–34. AmA, Special Publication. = Ama 66/6, Part 2.

——. 1964b. Directions in (ethno)-linguistic theory. Transcultural studies of cognition, ed. by A. K. Romney and R. G. D'Andrade, pp. 6–56. AmA, Special Publication. = AmA 66/3, Part 2.

——, ed. 1964c. Language in culture and society: A reader in linguistics and anthropology. New York, Harper and Row.

——. 1971. Sociolinguistics and the ethnography of speaking. Social anthropology and linguistics, ed. by E. Ardener, pp. 47–95. London, Tavistock (= ASA Monographs 10).

——. 1972. On communicative competence. Sociolinguistics, ed. by J. B. Pride and J. Holmes, pp. 269–94. Harmondsworth, Penguin.

JAKOBSON, R. 1963. Implications of language universals for linguistics. Universals of language, ed. by J. H. Greenberg, pp. 208–19. Cambridge, M.I.T. Press.

KATZ, J. J., and J. A. FODOR. 1963. The structure of a semantic theory. Lg 39.170–210. (Reprinted in The structure of language, ed. by J. A. Fodor and J. J. Katz, q.v.)

KLEIN, J. 1965. Samples from English culture. London, Routledge and Kegan Paul.

LABOV, W. 1963. The social motivation of a sound change. Word 19.273–309.

——. 1964. Phonological correlates of social stratification. The ethnography of communication, ed. by J. J. Gumperz and D. H. Hymes, pp. 164–76. AmA, Special Publication. = AmA 66/6, Part 2.

——. 1966a. The social stratification of English in New York City. Washington, D.C., Center for Applied Linguistics.

——. 1966b. The effect of social mobility on linguistic behaviour. Explorations in sociolinguistics, ed. by S. Lieberson = Sociological Inquiry 36. (Also RCAFL-P 44; and Part II of IJAL 33.)

LAMBERT, W. E. 1967. A social psychology of bilingualism. Problems of bilingualism, ed. by J. Macnamara, pp. 91–109. (Journal of Social Issues 23.)

LAMBERT, W. E., R. C. GARDNER, R. OLTON, and K. TUNSTALL. 1961. A study of the roles of attitudes and motivation in second-language learning. McGill University. (Mimeo)

LANGENDOEN, D. T. 1964. Review of Studies in linguistic analysis, special volume of the Philological Society. Oxford.

——. 1968. The London school of linguistics: A study of the linguistic theories of B. Malinowski and J. R. Firth. Research Monograph no. 46. Cambridge, Mass., M.I.T. Press.

LÉVI-STRAUSS, C. 1958. Anthropologie structurale. Paris, Plon. (Chapter 2 translated by D. H. Hymes in Hymes 1964c:40–51.)

LYONS, J. 1966. Towards a notional theory of the parts of speech. JL 2.209–236.

——. 1968. Introduction to theoretical linguistics. London, Cambridge University Press.

MALINOWSKI, B. 1937. Review of M. M. Lewis, Infant speech: A study of the beginnings of language. Nature 140. (Reprinted in Hymes 1964c:63–65.)

MARTIN, S. E. 1964. Speech levels in Japan and Korea. Language in culture and society, ed. by D. H. Hymes, pp. 407–12. New York, Harper & Row.

McCORMACK, W. C. 1969. Review of Explorations in sociolinguistics, ed. by S Lieberson. Lg. 45.463–69.

MILLER, G. A. 1956. The magical number seven, plus or minus two: Some limits on our capacity for processing information. PsychRev 63.81–97.

——. 1965. Some preliminaries to psycholinguistics. American Psychologist 20.15–20.

MITCHELL, T. F. 1965. On the nature of linguistics and its place in university studies. Leeds University Press.

——. 1969. Review of D. Abercrombie, Elements of general phonetics. JL 5.153–64.

NADER, L. 1962. A note on attitudes and the use of language. AnL 4/6.24–29. (Reprinted in Readings in the sociology of language, ed. by J. A. Fishman, pp. 276–81. The Hague, Mouton, 1968.)

PASSIN, H. 1963. Writer and journalist in the transitional society. Communications and political development, ed. by L. W. Pye, pp. 83–123. Princeton, N.J., Princeton University Press.

PICKFORD, G. R. 1956. American linguistic geography: A sociological appraisal. Word 12.211–33.

PIKE, K. L. 1954–1960. Language in relation to a unified theory of human behavior. Glendale, California, Summer Institute of Linguistics. (Also The Hague, Mouton, 1967.)

PRIDE, J. B. 1970a. The social meaning of language. Oxford University Press.

——. 1970b. Customs and cases of verbal behaviour. Social anthropology and language, ed. by E. Ardener, pp. 95–121. London, Tavistock.

PUTNAM, G. N., and E. M. O'HERN. 1955. The status significance of an isolated urban dialect. Language Dissertations, no. 53.

RUBIN, J. 1962. Bilingualism in Paraguay. AmA 4.52–58.

——. 1968. National bilingualism in Paraguay. The Hague, Mouton.

SAPIR, E. 1929. The status of linguistics as a science. Lg 5.207–214. Also in Selected writings of Edward Sapir, ed. by D. G. Mandelbaum, pp. 160–66. Berkeley and Los Angeles, 1949.)

SEBEOK, T. A. 1963. The informational model of language. Natural language and the computer, ed. by P. Garvin, pp. 47–64. New York, McGraw Hill.

SHUY, R. W., W. A. WOLFRAM, and W. K. RILEY. 1967. Linguistic correlates of social stratification in Detroit speech. Final report, Cooperative Research Project 6–1347, U.S. Office of Education.

——. 1968. Field techniques in an urban language study. Urban Language Series 3. Washington, D.C., Center for Applied Linguistics.

STEWART, W. A. 1962. The functional distribution of Creole and French in Haiti. MSLL 15.149–59.

TANNER, N. 1967. Speech and society among the Indonesian elite: A case study of a multilingual society. AnL 9/3.15ff.

WEINREICH, U. 1953. Languages in contact. The Hague, Mouton.

——. 1958. Research frontiers in bilingualism studies. PICL 8.786–97.

——. 1963. On the semantic structure of language. Universals of language, ed. by J. Greenberg, pp. 114–71. Cambridge, Mass., M.I.T. Press.

WHITELEY, W. H. 1966. Social anthropology, meaning and linguistics. Man 1.139–57.

——. 1967. Loanwords in linguistic description: A case study from Tanzania, East Africa. Approaches in linguistic methodology, ed. by I. Rauch and C. T. Scott, pp. 125–43. Madison, University of Wisconsin Press.

——. 1968. Preliminary report on the Kenya Survey. Bulletin of the Survey of Language Use and Language Teaching in Eastern Africa 2/1.9–10.

THE SOCIOLOGY OF LANGUAGE:
AN INTERDISCIPLINARY SOCIAL SCIENCE
APPROACH TO LANGUAGE IN SOCIETY

JOSHUA A. FISHMAN

1. INTRODUCTION

Man is constantly using language — spoken language, written language, printed language — and man is constantly linked to others via shared norms of behavior. The sociology of language examines the interaction between these two aspects of human behavior: use of language and the social organization of behavior. Briefly put, the sociology of language focuses upon the entire gamut of topics related to the social organization of language behavior, including not only language usage per se but also language attitudes, overt behaviors toward language and toward language users.

1.1 *Sociolinguistic Headlines*

The latter concern of the sociology of language — overt behavior toward language and toward language users — is a concern shared by political and educational leaders in many parts of the world and is an aspect of sociolinguistics that frequently makes headlines in the newspapers. Many French-Canadian university students oppose the continuation of public education in English in the Province of Quebec. Many Flemings in Belgium protest vociferously against anything less than full equality — at the very least — for Dutch in the Brussels area. Some Welsh nationalists daub out English signs along the highways in Wales and many Irish revivalists seek stronger governmental support for the restoration of Irish than that made available during a half a century of Irish independence. Jews throughout the world protest the Soviet government's extermination of Yiddish writers and the forced closing of Yiddish schools, theaters and publications.

Swahili, Pilipino, Indonesian, Malay and the various provincial languages of India are all being consciously expanded in vocabulary and standardized in spelling and grammar so that they can increasingly function as the exclusive language of government and of higher culture and technology. The successful revival and modernization of Hebrew has encouraged other smaller communities — the Catalans, the Provençals, the Frisians, the Bretons — to strive to save *their* ethnic mother tongues (or their traditional cultural tongues) from oblivion. New and revised writing systems are being accepted — and at times, rejected — in many parts of the world by communities that hitherto had little interest in literacy in general or in literacy in their mother tongues in particular.

Such examples of consciously organized behavior toward language and toward users of particular languages can be listed almost endlessly. The list becomes truly endless if we include examples from earlier periods of history, such as the displacement of Latin as the language of religion, culture and government in Western Christendom and the successive cultivation of once lowly vernaculars — first in Western Europe, and then, subsequently, in Central, Southern and Eastern Europe, and, finally, in Africa and Asia as well. Instead of being viewed (as was formerly the case) as merely fit for folksy talk and for common folk, the vernaculars have come to be viewed, used and developed as *independent* languages, as languages suitable for *all* higher purposes, and as languages of state-*building* and state-*deserving* nationalities. All of these examples, too, feed into the modern sociology of language, providing it with historical breadth and depth in addition to its ongoing interest in current language throughout the world.

1.2 *Subdivisions of the Sociology of Language*

However, the subject matter of the sociology of language reaches far beyond interest in case studies and very far beyond cataloging and classifying the instances of language conflict and language planning reported in chronicles, old and new. The ultimate quest of the sociology of language is pursued diligently and in many universities throughout the United States and other parts of the world, and is very far from dealing directly with headlines or news reports. One part of this quest is concerned with describing the generally accepted social organization of language usage within a speech community (or, to be more exact, within speech- and writing-communities). This part of the sociology of language — *descriptive sociology of language* — seeks to answer the question 'who speaks (or writes) what language (or what language variety) to whom and when and to what end?' *Descriptive sociology of language* tries to disclose the norms of language usage — that is to say, generally accepted social patterns of language use and of behavior and attitude toward language — for particular social networks and communities, both large and small. Another part of the sociology of language — *dynamic sociology of language* — seeks to answer the question 'what accounts for different rates of change in the social organization of language use and behavior toward language?' *Dynamic sociology of language* tries to explain why and how the social organization of language use and behavior toward language can be selectively different in the *same* social networks or communities on two different occasions. Dynamic sociology of language also seeks to explain why and how once similar social networks or communities can arrive at quite different social organizations of language use and behavior toward language.

These two subdivisions taken together, i.e. descriptive sociology of language *plus* dynamic sociology of language, constitute the sociology of language, a *whole* which is *greater than the mere sum of its parts.*

1.3   *Language* is *Content; the Medium* is *(at Least Partly) the Message*

Newspaper headlines with all of their stridency may serve to remind us of a truism that is too frequently overlooked by too many Americans, namely, that language is not merely a *means* of interpersonal communication and influence. It is not merely a *carrier* of content, whether latent, or manifest. Language itself *is* content, a referent for loyalties and animosities, an indicator of social statuses and personal relationships, a marker of situations and topics as well as of the societal goals and the large-scale value-laden arenas of interaction that typify every speech community.

Any speech community of even moderate complexity reveals several varieties of language, all of which are functionally differentiated from each other. In some cases the varieties may represent different occupational or interest specializations ('shop talk', 'hippy talk', etc.) and, therefore, contain vocabulary, pronunciation and phraseology which are not generally used or even known throughout the broader speech community. As a result, the speakers of specialized varieties may not always employ them. Not only must they switch to other varieties of language when they interact in less specialized (or differently specialized) networks within the broader speech community of which they are a part, but most of them do not even use their specialized varieties all of the time with one another. On some occasions, interlocutors who *can* speak a particular specialized variety to one another nevertheless do not do so, but, instead switch to a different variety of language which is either in wider use or which is indicative of quite a different set of interests and relationships than is associated with their specialized variety. This type of switching represents the raw data of descriptive sociology of language, the discipline that seeks to determine (among other things) who speaks what variety of what language to whom, when and concerning what.

The varieties of language that exist within a speech community need not all represent occupational or interest specializations. Some varieties may represent social class (economic, educational, ethnic) distinctions within co-territorial populations. 'Brooklynese' and 'Cockney' English within New York and London, respectively, do not connote foreignness or even a particular section of the city as much as lower class status in terms of income, education or ethnicity. Nevertheless, many individuals who have left lower class status behind can and do switch back and forth between Brooklynese and more regionally standard New York English when speaking to each other, depending on their feelings toward each other, the topic under discussion, where they happen to be when they are conversing and several other factors, all of which can exhibit variation and, as a result, can be signalled by switching from one variety of English to another.

A speech community that has available to it several varieties of language may be said to possess a *verbal repertoire*. Such repertoires may not only consist of different specialized varieties and different social class varieties but may also reveal different regional varieties (Boston English, Southern English, Midwestern English and other widely, and roughly, designated dialects of American English are regional varieties), if the speech community is sufficiently large such that enclaves come to arise within it on a geographic basis alone. Furthermore, multilingual speech communities may employ, for the purpose of *intragroup* communication, all of the above types or varieties of language within each of the codes that the community recognizes as 'distinct' languages (e.g. within Yiddish *and* Hebrew, among most pre-World War II Eastern European Jews; within English *and* Hindi, among many upper-class individuals in India today, etc.).

Regardless of the nature of the language varieties involved in the verbal repertoire of a speech community (occupational, social class, regional, etc.) and regardless of the interaction between them (for initially regional dialects may come to represent social varieties as well, and vice versa) descriptive sociology of language seeks to disclose their linguistic and functional characteristics and to determine how much of the entire speech community's verbal repertoire is available to various smaller interaction networks within that community since the entire verbal repertoire of a speech community may be more extensive than the verbal repertoire controlled by subgroups within that community. Dynamic sociology of language on the other hand seeks to determine how changes in the fortunes and interactions of networks of speakers alter the ranges (complexity) of their verbal repertoires.

All in all, the sociology of language seeks to discover not only the societal rules or norms that explain and constrain language behavior and *the behavior toward language* in speech communities but it also seeks to determine the symbolic value of language varieties for their speakers. That language varieties come to have symbolic or symptomatic value, in and of themselves, is an inevitable consequence of their functional differentiation. If certain varieties are indicative of certain interests, of certain backgrounds, or of certain origins, then they come to represent the ties and aspirations, the limitations and the opportunities with which these interests, backgrounds and origins, in turn, are associated. Language varieties rise and fall in symbolic value as the status of their most characteristic or marked functions rises and falls. Varieties come to represent intimacy and equality if they are most typically learned and employed in interactions that stress such bonds between interlocutors. Other varieties come to represent educated status or national identification as a result of the attainments associated with their use and their users and as a result of their realization in situations and relationships that pertain to formal learning or to particular ideologies. However, these functions are capable of change (and of being consciously changed), just as the linguistic features of the varieties themselves may change (and may be consciously changed), and just as the demographic distribution of users of a variety within a particular speech community may change.

The step-by-step elevation of most modern European vernaculars to their current positions as languages of culture and technology is only one example of how dramatically the operative and symbolic functions of languages can change. Similar changes are ongoing today:

Since the preservation of adequate control over the labour force loomed so large in the minds of the early planters, various devices have evolved, of which the maintenance of caste-like distance was perhaps the one most significantly affecting race relations. One thinks immediately of the frequently cited admonition in the *Rabaul Times* of August 8, 1926, by a veteran Territorian, "Never talk to the boys in any circumstances. Apart from your house-boy and boss-boy, never allow any native to approach you in the field or on the bungalow veranda." This free advice to the uninitiated planters was, no doubt, intended to preserve "White prestige", but it was also conceived as a protective device to "keep labour in its place". So also the Melanesian Pidgin, which had come into being as a medium of interchange in trade, subsequently acquired, on the plantations, the character of a language of command by which the ruling caste "talked down" to its subordinates and "put them in their place". A wide range of plantation etiquette symbolizing proper deference by workers toward their masters and expressed in expected form of address and servile conduct gave further protection to the system and any signs of insubordination or "cheekiness" on the part of the workers might be vigorously punished and rationalised by the planter as a "threat to the system." (Lind 1969 : 36).

Yet today, barely half a century since Melanesian Pidgin began to expand, it has been renamed Neo-Melanesian and is being groomed by many New Guineans to become their country's national language, and, as such to be used in government, education, mass media, religion and high culture more generally (Wurm and Laycock 1961/62).

The sociology of language is the study of the characteristics of language varieties, the characteristics of their functions, and the characteristics of their speakers as these three constantly interact, change, and change one another, both within and between speech communities.

2. SOME REASONS WHY THE SOCIOLOGY OF LANGUAGE HAS ONLY RECENTLY BEGUN TO DEVELOP

Given the obvious importance of the sociology of language, given its apparent interest for all who are interested in either or both of its parent disciplines (as well as for all who wish better to understand events and processes all over the world), and, finally, given the substantial applied promise of the sociology of language for governmental use, it is quite natural to ask: why is the sociology of language only coming into its own? Actually, the sociology of language, as a field of interest within linguistics and the social sciences, is not as new as its recent prominence may suggest. The 19th and early 20th century witnessed many studies and publications that belonged to this field (many are cited in Hertzler 1965). Nevertheless, it is quite true that the disciplinary priorities and biases of both fields were such

JOSHUA A. FISHMAN

Type of Behavior	Linguistics	Social Sciences
Invariant	Classical Interest	No Interest
Moderately Variable	Recent Growing Interest	Classical Interest
Highly Variable	Possible Future Interest	Recent Growing Interest

Fig. 1. The Changing Interests and Emphases of Linguistics and the Social Sciences with Respect to Variation in Behavior (after Labov).

that those earlier attempts were prematurely set aside and only recently has momentum been attained in this field to enable it to attract and train specialists devoted to it per se (Ferguson 1965; Fishman 1967b).

2.1 Invariant Behavior

Linguistics has classically been interested in completely regular or fully predictable behavior. The p in 'pun' is always aspirated by native speakers of English. The p in 'spin' is always unaspirated by these speakers. This is the kind of entirely determined relationship that linguistics has classically sought and found — to such an extent that a highly respected linguist wrote a few decades ago: 'if it exists to some degree, it's not linguistics' (Joos 1950). The implication of this view is quite clear: linguistics is not interested in 'sometimes things'. The phonemes it describes are either completely determinable occurrences or non-occurrences. Wherever some other lesser state of determinacy was noted, e.g. in usage, this was defined as 'exolinguistic', as 'free variations' that was outside of the realm or the heartland of linguistics proper.

The social sciences on the other hand, were (and remain) singularly uninterested in apparently invariant behavior. Any such behavior could only prompt the observation 'so what?' from the social sciences since their preserve was and is societally patterned variation in behavior and the locations of those factors that parsimoniously explain and predict such variation. If one were to observe to a social scientist that the same individuals who always wore clothing when they were strolling on Fifth Avenue never wore any when they were bathing or showering, his reaction to this brand of societal invariance would be 'so what?'

Given the above basic difference in orientations between its two parent disciplines, it is not even necessary to add that linguistics was classically too code-oriented to be concerned with societal patterns in language usage, or that sociology, e.g., was classically too stratificationally oriented to be concerned with contextual speaking (or writing) differences within strata. Fortunately, both fields have recently moved beyond their classical interests (see Figure 1) and, as a result, fostered the kinds of joint interests on which the sociology of language now depends.

2.2 *Moderately Variable Behavior*

Linguistics has, in recent years, plunged further and further into 'sometimes things' in the realm of language behavior. Some of the same speakers who say 'ain't' on certain occasions do *not* use it on others, and some of the same cotton-pickers who have such a colorful and unique vocabulary, phonology and grammar on occasions also share other varieties with their many non-cotton-picking friends and associates. This is the kind of societally patterned variation in behavior that social scientists not only recognize and understand, but it is the kind they are particularly well prepared to help linguists study and explain. When such behavior is reported the social scientist is oriented toward locating the smallest number of societal factors that can account for or predict the usage variation that has been reported.

2.3 *Highly Variable Behavior*

Finally (and even more recently), even more complex societally patterned variation in behavior has come to be of interest to the social scientist. This behavior is so complexly patterned or determined that a goodly number of explanatory variables must be utilized and combined, with various quantitative weights and controls, in order that their total impact as well as their separate contributions can be gauged. This kind of highly variable and complexly patterned societal behavior obviously exists (and plentifully so) with respect to language too. However, linguists generally lack the skills of study design, data collection and data analysis that are required in order to undertake to clarify such multiply determined language behavior. At this level, more than at any other, the corpus of language per se is insufficient to explain a major proportion of the variation in language behavior that obtains. Nor are a few demographic (age, sex, education), nor a few contextual (formality-informality in role relationships), nor a few situational factors sufficient for this purpose. Rather, predictors of all of these kinds are needed and, to the extent that this is so, their joint or combined use will result in far greater explanatory or predictive power than would any two or three of them alone. The social sciences themselves have only rather recently become accustomed to working with large numbers of complexly interrelated and differentially weighted variables. This is obviously a level of analysis which will become available to the sociology of language only if there is genuine cooperation between linguists and social scientists.

The sociology of language is thus a by-product of a very necessary and very recent awareness on the part of linguists and the social sciences that they do indeed need each other in order to explore their joint interests in a productive and provocative manner. This cooperative attitude has yielded important results in the few years that it has been actively pursued (Grimshaw 1969; Hymes 1967a) and we may expect even more from it in the future when a greater number of individuals who are themselves specialists in *both fields simultaneously* (or in the joint field per se) will have been trained.

2.4 *Variability and Predictability*

While it is, of course, true that the more variable behavior is, the more the factors that need to be located in order to account for it in any substantial way, the less predictable the behavior is until the proper factors have been located and combined or weighted in the most appropriate ways. Ultimately, however, if the quest for rigorous data collection and data analysis is successful, as high a level of predictability or explanability may be attained with respect to complexly determined and highly variable behaviors as with the far less and the somewhat less complexly determined and variable ones. Thus, the methodological differences that have existed between linguistics and sociology have been primarily differences in the extent to which a very few well chosen parameters could account substantially for the behaviors that the respective disciplines choose to highlight. Ultimately, all disciplines of human behavior — including linguistics and sociology — strive to locate and to interrelate the most parsimonious set of explanatory-predictive variables in order to maximally account for the variability to which their attention is directed.

With respect to societally patterned language behavior, there is doubtlessly variability that can be well-nigh perfectly accounted for by a very few well selected intra-code positional factors. Social scientists should recognize such behavior for it not only leads them to recognition of linguistics per se but to the clearer realization that the entire world of socially patterned variability in language behavior still remains to be explored — and to be explored by linguists and social scientists together — after the variability explainable on the basis of intra-code factors alone has been accounted for. However, at that level of inquiry it is *not* possible to simply put linguistics aside and, turning to more exciting and difficult tasks, simply to 'do social science'. Studies of more complexly determined and more highly variable socially patterned language behaviors still require rigorous descriptions and analyses of language usage per se and for such analyses the social sciences will always be dependent on linguistics.

3. SOME BASIC SOCIOLINGUISTIC CONCEPTS

The sociology of language deals with quite a range of topics: small group interaction and large group membership, language use and language attitudes, language-and-behavior norms as well as changes in these norms. We expect to deal with all of these topics, at least briefly, in this presentation, and, necessarily, to introduce the technical terms and concepts which specialized fields of discourse inevitably require.

However, before moving into any of these more specialized substantive topics there are a number of basic sociolinguistic concepts that are of such general intertopic utility that we had best pause to consider them here, rather than to permit them to remain as primitives any longer.

3.1 Language-Dialect-Variety

The term *variety* is frequently utilized in the sociology of language as a non-judgmental designation. The very fact that an objective, unemotional, technical term is *needed* in order to refer to 'a kind of language' is, in itself, an indication that the expression 'a language' is often a judgmental one, a term that is *indicative* of emotion and opinion, as well as a term that *elicits* emotion and opinion. This is an important fact about languages and one to which we will return repeatedly. As a result, we will use the term 'variety' in order not to become trapped in the very phenomena that we seek to investigate, namely, when and by whom is a certain variety considered to be a language and when and by whom is it considered something else.

Those varieties that initially and basically represent divergent geographic origins are known as *dialects* (Ferguson and Gumperz 1960; Halliday, MacIntosh and Strevens 1964b). It is in this purely objective sense of the word that it is used in such terms as *dialectology* and *dialect geography* within linguistics, and it is in this sense that the sociology of language employs it as well. However, dialects may easily come to represent (to stand for, to connote, to symbolize) other factors than geographic ones. If immigrants from region A come to be a large portion of the poor, the disliked and the illiterate in region B, then their speech variety (dialect A) will come to stand for much more than geographic origin alone in the minds of the inhabitants of region B. Dialect A will come to stand for lower social status (educationally, occupationally) than will dialect B. In this way what was once *regional variety* (in the sense that at a particular time its speakers were viewed as merely concentrated in a particular area) may come to be viewed (and to function) much more importantly as a *social variety* or *sociolect* (Blanc 1964) once social differentiation comes to the fore. Furthermore, if the speakers of variety A are given hardly any access into the interaction networks of region B, if they marry primarily only each other, engage primarily in their original regional customs and continue to value only each other's company, they may, in time, come to consider themselves a different society, with goals, beliefs and traditions of their own. As a result, variety A may no longer be viewed as a social variety but, rather, as an *ethnic* or *religious* variety and, indeed, it may come to be cultivated as such to the point of being viewed as a separate *language* (Kloss 1967; Fishman 1968c). However, within the community of A speakers there may come to be some who have learned B as well. They may utilize A with each other for purposes of intimacy and in-group solidarity but they may also use

B with each other for occupational and deferential purposes. Thus, for them, A and B will be contrasted and complementary *functional varieties,* with B also being (or including) a *specialized* (occupational or other experiential) *variety* and, therefore, in some ways different than variety B as used by others (M. Weinreich 1953).

The above theoretical sketch has more than general didactic value. It represents the route that many varieties — regional and social — have travelled in the past and the route on which still others are embarked at this very time (Haugen 1966c; Deutsch 1966). Nevertheless, it is the *general* point that is of particular value to us at this juncture. Varieties may be viewed as regional at one time and social at another. Varieties may be reacted to as regional within the speech community of their users and as social (or ethnic) by outsiders. Varieties may have additional functional uses for some of their users that they do not have for others who possess fewer contrasted varieties in their verbal repertoires. Thus, the term variety — unlike the term dialect — indicates no particular linguistic status (other than difference) vis-a-vis other varieties. A dialect must be a regional *sub*-unit in relation to a language, particularly in its vernacular or spoken realization. 'Language' is a superordinate designation; 'dialect' is a subordinate designation. Both terms require that the entire taxonomy to which they pertain be known before they themselves can be accepted. The sociology of language is interested in them only insofar as members of speech communities contend over which is which, and why. As the result of such contention varieties hitherto considered to be dialects may throw off their subordination and be 'promoted' by their speakers to official and independent status, whereas formerly independent languages may be subordinated. The term variety, on the other hand, merely designates a member of a verbal repertoire. Its use implies only that there are other varieties as well. These can be specified by outsiders on the basis of the phonological, lexical and grammatical differences that they (the varieties) manifest. Their functional allocations, however, as language or as dialects, are derivable only from societal observation of their uses and users rather than from any characteristics of the codes themselves.

Varieties change over time but varieties are also *changed*, either by drift or by design. Varieties that have been used in palaces and universities may later come to be used only by the rural and unlettered. In this process their lexicons may well become impoverished (hundreds or thousands of the terms once needed dropping into disuse). At the same time lexicons, grammars as well as phonologies may become much influenced by other temporarily more prestigeful and possibily genetically unrelated varieties. Conversely, varieties that had never been used outside of the most humble speech networks may be elevated in function, increased in lexicon and purified or enriched in whatever direction their circumstantially improved speakers may desire (Kloss 1952; Fishman 1968c). All varieties of all languages are equally expandable and changeable; all are equally contractable and interpenetrable under the influence of foreign models. Their virtues are in the eyes (or ears) of their beholders. Their functions depend on the norms of the speech communities that employ them. These norms, in turn, change as speech communities change in self-concept, in their relations with surrounding communities and in their objective circumstances. Finally, such changes usually lead to changes in the varieties themselves. Speech communities and their varieties are not only interrelated systems; they are completely interdependent systems as well. It is this interdependence that the sociology of language examines.

3.2 Major Types of Attitudes and Behaviors Toward Language

One of the best known societal behaviors toward language is *standardization,* i.e., 'the codification and acceptance, within a community of users, of a formal set of norms defining "correct" usage' (Stewart 1968). Codification is, typically, the concern of such language 'gatekeepers' as scribes, storytellers, grammarians, teachers and writers, i.e. of certain groups that arise in most diversified societies and whose use of language is professional and conscious. Given codification as a goal, this desired 'good' is formulated and presented to all or part of the speech community via such means as grammars, dictionaries, spellers, style manuals, and exemplary texts, whether written or oral. Finally, the acceptance of the formally codified (i.e. the standardized) variety of a language is advanced via such agencies and authorities as the government, the educational system, the mass media, the religious institutions and the cultural 'establishment'. The standard variety then becomes associated with such institutions, the types of interactions that most commonly occur within them, and the values or goals they represent (Haugen 1966a).

Note that not all languages have standard varieties. Note also, that where a standard variety does exist it does not necessarily displace the non-standard varieties from the linguistic repertoire of the speech community for functions that are distinct from but complementary to those of the standard variety. Note, additionally, that there may be several competing standard varieties in the same speech community. Note, finally, that hitherto non-standard varieties may themselves undergo standardization whereas hitherto standardized varieties may undergo de-standardization as their speakers no longer view them as worthy of codification and cultivation. Standardization is not a property of any language per se, but a characteristic societal treatment of language given sufficient societal diversity and need for symbolic elaboration.

Another common societal view of language is that which is concerned with its *autonomy,* i.e. with the uniqueness and independence of the linguistic system or, at least, of some variety within that system. *Autonomy* is often of little concern to speech communities whose languages differ markedly from each other. These may be said to be autonomous by dint of sheer *abstand* or linguistic distance between them (Kloss 1952, 1967). On the other hand, where languages seem to be quite similar to each other — phonologically, lexically and grammatically — it may be of great concern to establish their autonomy from each other, or at least that of the weaker from the stronger. Were such autonomy not to be established it might occur to some that one was 'no more than' a dialect (a regional variety) of the other, a subservience which may become part of a rationale for political subservience as well.

A major vehicle of fostering autonomy views concerning a language is its standardization. The availability of dictionaries and grammars is taken as a sure sign that a particular variety is 'really a language'. However, the availability of dictionaries and grammars not only *represents* autonomy, but also cultivates and increases it by introducing new vocabulary and stressing those phonological and grammatical alternatives that are most different from those of any given autonomy-threatening contrast language. 'Heroes are made, not born.' The same is true of the autonomy of genetically (historically) related languages. Their autonomy has to be worked on. It is not autonomy by *abstand*, but, rather, by *ausbau* (by effort, and, often, by fiat or decree), and pertains particularly to their standard (and most particularly to their written standard) varieties.

It is a characteristic of the newly rich to supply their own ancestors. In a similar vein those speech communities, the autonomy of whose standard variety is based most completely on *ausbau*-activity, are also most likely to be concerned with its *historicity*, that is with its 'respectable' ancestry in times long past. As a result, many speech communities create and cultivate myths and genealogies concerning the origin and development of their standard varieties in order to de-emphasize the numerous components of more recent vintage that they contain (Ferguson 1959b). As a result of the widespread preference for historicity, currently utilized (and recently liberated or standardized) varieties are found to be derived from ancient prototypes that had largely been forgotten, or are found to be the language of the gods, or to have been created by the same miraculous and mysterious forces and processes that created the speech community itself, etc. Thus, a variety achieves historicity by coming to be associated with some great ideological or national movement or tradition (Fishman 1965c). Usually, historicity provides the ex post facto rationale for functional changes that have transpired with respect to the verbal repertoire of a speech community.

Finally, a speech community's behavior toward any one or another of the varieties in its linguistic repertoire is likely to be determined, at least in part, by the degree to which these varieties have visible *vitality*, i.e. interaction networks that actually employ them natively for one or more vital functions. The more numerous and the more important the native speakers of a particular variety are the greater its vitality and the greater its potential for standardization, autonomy and historicity. Conversely, the fewer the number and the lower the status of the native speakers of a variety, the more it may be reacted to as if it were somehow a defective or contaminated instrument, unworthy of serious efforts or functions, and lacking in proper parentage or uniqueness. As usual, such biased views are likely to be self-fulfilling in that when the numbers and the resources of the users of a given variety dwindle they are less likely to be able to protect its standardization, autonomy or historicity from the inroads of other speech communities and their verbal repertoires and language-enforcing resources.

ATTRIBUTES *				VARIETY-TYPE	SYMBOL
1	2	3	4		
+	+	+	+	Standard	S
—	+	+	+	Vernacular	V
—	—	+	+	Dialect	D
—	—	—	+	Creole	K
—	—	—	—	Pidgin	P
+	+	+	—	Classical	C
+	+	—	—	Artificial	A

Fig. 2. Evaluations of different types of language varieties (Stewart 1968).
* 1 = standardization, 2 = autonomy, 3 = historicity, 4 = vitality.

Given these four widespread patterns of societal belief and behavior toward language, it is possible to define seven different kinds of varieties, depending upon their absence or presence at any given time (Figure 2). Note, however, that any speech community may include in its repertoire a number of such varieties which are differentiable on the basis of the four widespread belief-and-behavior systems just discussed. Furthermore, occupational, social class and other experiential sub-varieties are likely to exist within most of the varieties listed in Figure 2. Indeed, the members of any given community may not agree as to whether standardization, autonomy, historicity and/or vitality are absent or present in connection with one or more of the varieties in their repertoire. After all, these dimensions are highly evaluational, rather than objective characteristics of language varieties per se, and as such, variation in evaluations may be expected both synchronically (at any particular time) as well as diachronically (across time).

In some speech communities deference due an interlocutor with whom one stands in a particular role-relationship may be indicated by switching from one social class variety or from one dialect to another. In other speech communities this very same function may be realized by switching from a dialect to the standard variety (which latter variety, alone, may possess formal verb-forms and pronouns of respect). In yet another speech community a switch from one language to another (or from a dialect of one language to the standard variety of another) may be the accepted and recognized realization pattern for deferential interaction. While the precise nature of the switch will depend on the repertoire available to the speech community, switching as such and the differentia and concepts by means of which it may be noted and explained are of constant interest to sociolinguistic method and theory.

3.3 *Speech Community*

Speech community (a term probably translated from the German *Sprachgemein-schaft*), like variety, is a neutral term. Unlike other societal designations it does not imply any particular size nor any particular basis of communality. A speech community is one all of whose members share at least a single speech variety and the norms for its appropriate use. A speech community may be as small as a single closed interaction network, all of whose members regard each other in but a single capacity. Neither of these limitations, however, is typical for speech communities throughout the world and neither is typical for those that have been studied by sociologists of language.

Isolated bands and nomadic clans not only represent small speech communities but speech communities that also exhaust their members' entire network-range while providing little specialization of roles or statuses. Such speech communities usually possess very limited verbal repertoires in terms of different varieties, primarily because one individual's life experiences and responsibilities are pretty much like another's. Nevertheless, such similarity is likely to be more apparent than real. Even small and total societies are likely to differentiate between men and women, between minors and adults, between children and parents, between leaders and followers. Indeed, such societies are likely to have more contact with the 'outside world' than is commonly imagined, whether for purposes of trade or exogamy (Owens 1965). Thus, even small total societies reveal functionally differentiated linguistic repertoires (and, not infrequently, intra-group bilingualism as well) based upon behaviorally differentiated interaction networks.

Such small and total (or nearly total) societies differ, of course, from equally small or even smaller family networks, friendship networks, interest networks, or occupational networks within such larger speech communities as tribes, cities or countries. In the latter cases the interaction networks are not as redundant as in the former (i.e. one more frequently interacts with *different* people in one's various roles as son, friend, work colleague, party member, etc.). However, varieties are needed not only by diverse small networks but also by large networks of individuals who rarely, if ever, interact but who have certain interests, views and allegiances in common. Thus, not only are network redundancy and network size attributes that characterize and differentiate speech communities but so is the extent to which their existence is experiential rather than merely referential.

One of the characteristics of large and diversified speech communities is that some of the varieties within their verbal repertoires are primarily experientially acquired and reinforced by dint of actual verbal interaction within particular networks, while others are primarily referentially acquired and reinforced by dint of symbolic integration within reference-networks which may rarely or never exist in any physical sense. The 'nation' or the 'region' are likely to constitute a speech community of this latter type and the standard ('national') language or the regional language is likely to represent its corresponding linguistic variety.

Many American cities present ample evidence of both of these bases — verbal interaction and symbolic integration — for the functioning of speech communities. Every day hundreds of thousands of residents of Connecticut, up-State (northern) New York and various parts of Pennsylvania and New Jersey come to New York City to work and shop. In terms of waking hours of actual face-to-face verbal interaction these speakers of dialects that differ from New York City English may talk more, and more frequently, to New Yorkers than they do to inhabitants of their places of residence and to speakers of their local dialects. How then can we explain the fact that not only do most of them differentially utilize the markers of their local dialects (and not only during the evenings, weekends and holidays when they are at home rather than at work) but the simultaneous fact that many of them can and do also employ a more regionally neutral variety, which is their approximation to 'Standard American', as distinct from New York City English on the one hand and Lower Connecticut Village English on the other? Obviously, the 'Standard American' of these commuters to New York City cannot be based on much verbal interaction with a separate network known as 'the American people'. Nor can it be based upon any other interaction network, however referred to, whose speakers use 'Standard American' and it alone. There is no other alternative but to conclude that the speech community of 'Standard American' represents a reference group for the denizens of Connecticut villages while 'Standard American' itself is a variety that has the functions of 'symbolic integration with the nation' in their linguistic repertoire.

Thus, some speech communities and their linguistic repertoires are preserved primarily by communication gaps that separate them from other communities and their repertoires. Other speech communities and their repertoires are preserved primarily by the force of symbolic (attitudinal) integration even in the absence of face-to-face interaction. Many speech communities contain networks of both types. Many networks contain both kinds of members. Societal norms that define communicative appropriateness can apply with equal force and regularity regardless of whether direct interaction or symbolic integration underlies their implementation.

As mentioned earlier, the standard variety of a language is likely to be that variety that stands for the nation as a whole and for its most exalted institutions of government, education and High Culture in general. It is this variety which comes to be associated with the mission, glory, history and uniqueness of an entire 'people' and, indeed, it is this variety which helps unite individuals who do not otherwise constitute an interaction network into a symbolic speech community or 'people'. Thus it is that standard varieties and larger-than-face-to-face speech communities are historically and functionally interdependent. While interaction networks of speakers of standard varieties doubtlessly do exist (literati, scholars, social and educational elites, etc.), these are likely to arrive at somewhat specialized usages, on the one hand, as well as to require a non-standard variety, on the other hand, if they are to engage in more intimate and informal kinds of interactions as well. Thus, the standard language per se, without further differentiation or accompaniment, is most fitted for communication across large but referential (or non-interacting) networks, such as those involving the mass media, governmental pronouncements, legal codes and textbooks. The standard variety is the 'safest' for those communications in which a speaker cannot know his diversified and numerous listeners (Joos 1959). However, the more the communication is expected to live on, independently of both speaker and listener (or sender and receiver), over an appreciable period of time, the more it will be viewed as archaic (or classical) rather than merely 'standard'.

A basic definitional property of speech communities is that they are *not* defined as communities of those who 'speak the same language' (nothwithstanding Bloomfield 1933), but, rather, as communities set off by density of communication or/and by symbolic integration with respect to communicative competence *regardless of the number of languages or varieties employed* (Gumperz 1964a). The complexity of speech communities thus defined varies with the extent of variation in the experiential and attitudinal networks which they subsume. Speech communities can be so selected as to include greater or lesser diversity on each of these grounds. In general the verbal repertoire of a speech community is a reflection of its role repertoire (in terms of both implemented and ideologized roles). This reflection pertains not only to repertoire *range* but also to repertoire *access* and *fluidity*.

Speech communities with a larger role repertoire reveal a larger verbal repertoire as well (Gumperz 1962). Communities most of whose members are restricted in daily experiences and in life aspirations, will also tend to show little linguistic range in terms of differentiable varieties. This tends to be the case not only in the small, total communities that were mentioned earlier but also, some suspect, in large, democratic, industrialized communities of the most modern sort. Actually, both kinds of speech communities show more repertoire range (in terms of verbal repertoire and in terms of role repertoire) than is obvious on superficial inspection. Nevertheless, they both tend to have narrower (and less diversified) ranges than are encountered in the stratified speech communities that exist in intermediate societies of the traditional, non-Western World. Whereas the modern, relatively open speech community tends to reveal several varieties of the same language, the more traditional speech community will typically reveal varieties of several languages (see Figure 3).

These two types of speech communities are also quite likely to differ in the extent to which their members have *access* to the roles and to the varieties available in the respective repertoires of their communities. In the more traditional speech communities' access to certain roles is severely restricted and is attained, in those cases in which access to new roles *is* available, on the basis of *ascription*. Those whose ancestry is inappropriate cannot attain certain new roles, regardless of their personal achievement. Similarly, access to an expanded verbal repertoire is also severely

Societal Domain	Speech Community 1	Speech Community 2	Speech Community 3	Speech Community 4
Home	a_1	c_1	c_1	d_1
School and Culture	a_2	b_3/c_2	b_2/c_2	a_2
Work	a_3	c_3	d_2	d_2
Government	a_2	b_1	a_2	a_2
Church	e_1	b_2	b_2	e_1
	(Moscow, 1960)	(Mea Shearim, 1966)	(Ostropol, 1905)	(Ostropol, 1905)
	[Russians]	[Jews]	[Jews]	[Ukrainians]

Fig. 3. Speech Communities and Verbal Repertoires (based upon concepts of Gumperz, 1964a and elsewhere).
Some communities have more obviously diversified repertoires than others (e.g., SC1 utilizes 3 varieties of one language and one of another, whereas SC3 utilizes varieties of four different languages). Varieties that are related to one societal domain in one SC (e.g., b_2 in SC2) may be associated with more or different societal domains in another SC (e.g., b_2 in SC3). All speakers of varieties of a particular language do not necessarily constitute a single speech community.

restricted, most varieties not learned in childhood being available only to those who can afford to devote many years of patient and painstaking formal study to their acquisition. Both of these conditions are not nearly so likely to exist in modern, personal-achievement-oriented societies, although their lack of completely equal and open access is evident to all students of the disadvantaged (including Negro non-standard speech) in the midst of America's plenty.

In more traditional societies in which status is based on ascription there is also likely to be more role *compartmentalization*. Thus, not only are certain individuals barred from enacting certain roles but, in general, the rights and duties that constitute particular roles are more distinct and the transition from one role to the next, for members of those classes who may enter into them, are ritually governed, as are the roles themselves. Such societies also tend to reveal marked verbal compartmentalization as well (McCormack 1968). When an individual speaks language or variety A he takes great care not to switch into B and not to slip into traces of B, whether phonologically, lexically or grammatically. Each variety is kept separate and uncontaminated from the other just as is each role. How different such compartmentalization is from the fluidity of modern democratic speech communities in which there is such frequent change from one role to the other and from one variety to another that individuals are frequently father and pal or teacher and colleague simultaneously or in rapid succession! The result of such frequent and easy role shifts is often that the roles themselves become more similar and less distinctive or clearcut. The same occurs in the verbal repertoire as speakers change from one variety (or language) to another with greater frequency and fluidity. The varieties too tend to become more similar as the roles in which they are appropriate become more and more alike. This is particularly likely to occur, as we will see below, among lower class speakers whose mastery of the more formal roles and varieties available to their speech communities is likely to be marginal at best.

Thus, just as varieties are characterizable by a small number of attributes and their combinations, so is this true of the attributes that characterize speech communities at the most general level. The interactional basis of speech communities, their symbolic-integrative basis, their size, repertoire range, repertoire access and repertoire compartmentalization are all concepts that we will need to refer to again and again in the pages that follow.

4. INTERACTIONAL SOCIOLOGY OF LANGUAGE: MICRO– AND MACRO–

Boss	Carmen, do you have a minute?
Secretary	Yes, Mr. Gonzalez.
Boss	I have a letter to dictate to you.
Secretary	Fine. Let me get my pen and pad. I'll be right back.
Boss	Okay.
Secretary	Okay.
Boss	Okay, this is addressed to Mr. William Bolger.
Secretary	That's B-o-r-g-e-r?
Boss	B-o-l
Secretary	Oh, oh, I see.
Boss	Okay. His address is in the files.
Secretary	Okay.
Boss	Okay. Dear Bill, Many thanks for telling me about your work with the Science Research Project. The information you gave me ought to prove most helpful.
Secretary	That was "The information you gave me ought to prove most helpful".
Boss	Correct.
Secretary	Okay.
Boss	Okay, ah. I very much appreciate the time you gave me. Never mind, strike that out. Ah, enclosed are two of the forms that you let me borrow. I'll be sending back the data sheets very soon. Thanks again. I hope that your hospital stay will be as pleasant as possible and that your back will be soon in top shape. Will soon be in top shape. It was nice seeing you again. Sincerely, Louis Gonzalez.
Secretary	Do you have the enciosures for the letter Mr. Gonzalez?
Boss	Oh yes, here they are.
Secretary	Okay.
Boss	Ah, this man William Bolger got his organization to contribute a

	lot of money to the Puerto Rican parade. He's very much for it.
	¿Tú fuiste a la parada?
	(Did you go to the parade?)
Secretary	Sí, yo fuí.
	(Yes, I went.)
Boss	¿Si?
	(Yes?)
Secretary	Uh huh.
Boss	¿Y cómo te estuvo?
	(and how did you like it?)
Secretary	Ay, lo mas bonita.
	(Oh, very pretty.)
Boss	Sí, porque yo fuí y yo nuca había participado en la parada y
	(Yes, because I went and I had never participated in the parade and
	este año me dió curiosidad por ir a ver como era y estuvo eso
	this year I became curious to go and see how it was and that was
	fenómeno. Fuí con mi señora y con mis nenes y a ellos también
	a phenomenon. I went with my wife and my children and they also
	le gustó mucho. Eh, y tuve un día bien agradable. Ahora lo que
	liked it very much. And I had a very pleasant day. Now
	me molesta a mí es que las personas cuando viene una cosa así,
	what bothers me is that people when something like this comes along,
	la parada Puertorriqueña o la fiesta de San Juan, corren de la
	the Puerto Rican parade, or the festival of San Juan, they run from
	casa a participar porque es una actividad festiva, alegre, y sin
	the house to participate because it is a festive activity, happy, and
	embargo, cuando tenen que ir a la iglesia, o la misa para pedirle ...
	then, when they have to go to church or to mass, to mass, to ask ...)
Secretary	(Laughter)
Boss	A Diós entonce no van
	(God then they don't go.)
Secretary	Sí, entonces no van.
	(Yes, then they don't go.)
Boss	Pero, así es la vida, caramba. Do you think that you could get this
	letter out today?
	(But that's life, you know.)
Secretary	Oh yes, I'll have it this afternoon for you.
Boss	Okay, food, fine then.
Secretary	Okay.
Boss	Okay.

If we carefully consider the above conversation it becomes evident that it reveals considerable internal variation. Speaker A does not always speak in the same way nor does his interlocutor, Speaker B. Were it possible for us to listen to the original tapes of this conversation, several kinds of variation within each of them would become evident to us: variations in speed of speaking, variations in the extent to which Spanish phonology creeps into English discourse, and, vice versa, variations in the extent to which English phonology creeps into the Spanish discourse, etc. However, even from the conventionally (orthographically) rendered transcription available to us on the previous pages one kind of variation remains exceedingly clear: that from Spanish to English or from English to Spanish for each speaker. It is precisely because bilingual code switching is often more noticeable than other kinds of sociolinguistic variation that bilingualism is so commonly examined in socio-linguistic theory and research. However, the concepts and findings that derive from such examinations must be provocative and illuminating for the sociology of language more generally. And, indeed, that *is* the case, for the societal patterning of bilingual interaction is merely an instance (hopefully a more obvious and, therefore, pedagogically useful instance) of the vastly more general phenomenon of societal patterning of variation in verbal interaction.

How shall we describe or measure the phenomenon of interest to us: societal patterning of variation in verbal interaction? Usefully accurate description or measurement is certainly the basic problem of every scientific field of endeavor. Most of mankind has constantly been immersed in a veritable ocean of cross-currents of talk. Nevertheless, as with most other aspects of everyday social behavior, it is only in very recent days that man has begun to recognize the latent order and regularity in the manifest chaos of verbal interaction that surrounds him.

4.1 How Should Talk be Described Contextually?

How should 'talk' be described contextually in order to best reveal or discover its social systematization (assuming that its 'basic' linguistic description is already available)? Let us begin with some passages of actual 'talk', making sure to preserve its verbatim form (preferably by utilizing sensitive audio and visual recording equipment) rather than merely summarizing the content of such talk. The smallest socio-linguistic unit that will be of interest to us is a *speech act*: a joke, an interjection, an opening remark (Schegloff 1968) a question, in general — a segment of talk that is also societally recognizable and reoccurring. Speech acts are normally parts of somewhat larger *speech events,* such as conversations, introductions, lectures, prayers, arguments, etc. (Hymes 1967), which, of course, must also be societally recognizable and reoccurring.

If we note that a switch has occurred from variety *a* to variety *b* — perhaps from a kind of Spanish to a kind of English, or from more formal English to less formal English, or from regionally neutral, informal Spanish to Jíbarro (rural) informal

Spanish — the first question that presents itself is whether one variety tends to be used (or used more often) in certain kinds of speech acts or events whereas the other tends to be used (or used more often) in others. Thus, were we aware of the speech acts recognized by bilingual Puerto Rican youngsters in New York, we might venture to explain a switch such as the following:

First girl	Yes, and don't tell me that the United States is the only one that has been able to in Puerto Rico . . . .
Boy	Okay so you have a couple of people like Moscoso and Luís Ferrer.
First girl	¡Un momento!
Boy	¡Bueno!
First girl	¡Un momento!
Boy	Have you got people capable of starting something like . . . like General Motors

as being related to the act of interruption or disagreement in the midst of a somewhat specialized argument. There may be a problem, however, when testing this interpretation, in determining the speech acts and speech events that are to be recognized within a speech community.

Certainly, it is not appropriate to simply apply the system of acts and events that has been determined for one speech community in the study of another, without determining first its appropriateness in the second community. Similarly, it is not sufficient for the investigator, no matter how much experience he has had with the verbal behavior of a particular speech community, merely to devise as detailed a listing of speech acts and events as he can. Such a list runs the decided risk of being *etic* rather than *emic*, i.e. of making far too many, as well as behaviorally inconsequential, differentiations, just as was often the case with phon*etic* vs. phone*mic* analysis in linguistics proper. An *emic* set of speech acts and events must be one that is validated as meaningful via final recourse to the native members of a speech community rather than via appeal to the investigator's ingenuity or intuition alone.

An *emic* set of speech acts and speech events is best approximated, perhaps along a never-ending asymptote, by playing back recorded samples of 'talk' to native speakers and by encouraging them to react to and comment upon the reasons for the use of variety *a* 'here' as contrasted with the use of variety *b* 'there'. The more the sensitive investigator observes the speech community that he seeks to sociolinguistically describe the more hunches he will have concerning functionally different speech acts and speech events. However, even the best hunches require verification *from within the speech community*. Such verification may take various shapes. The views of both naive and skilled informants may be cited and tabulated as they comment upon recorded instances of variation in 'talk' and as they reply to the investigator's patient probes and queries as to 'Why didn't he say "Just a minute!" instead of "¡Momento!"'? Would it have meant something different if he *had* said that instead? When is it appropriate to say "¡Momento!" and when is it appropriate to say "Just a minute!" (assuming the persons involved know both languages equally well)?', etc. Once the investigator has *demonstrated* (not merely assumed or argued) the validity of his sets of functionally different speech acts and events he may then proceed to utilize them in the collection and analysis of samples of talk which are *independent* of those already utilized for validational purposes. Such, at least, is the rationale of research procedure at this micro-level of sociolinguistic analysis, although the field itself is still too young and too linguistically oriented to have produced many instances of such cross-validation of its *social* units selected for purposes of *socio*linguistic analysis.

4.2 *Micro-level Analysis in the Sociology of Language*

Sociolinguistic description may merely begin — rather than end — with the specification and the utilization of speech acts and events, depending on the purpose of a particular research enterprise. The more linguistically oriented a particular study may be, the more likely it is to remain content with micro-level analysis, since the micro-level in the sociology of language is already a much higher (i.e. a more contextual and complicated) level of analysis than that traditionally employed within linguistics proper. However, the more societally oriented a particular sociolinguistic study may be, the more concerned with investigating social processes and societal organization, per se, the more likely it is to seek successively more macro-level analyses. Micro-level sociology of language (sometimes referred to as ethnomethodological) constitutes one of the levels within sociolinguistic inquiry (Garfinkel 1967; Garfinkel and Sachs in press). The various levels do not differ in the degree to which they are correct or accurate. They differ in purpose and, therefore, in method. We can trace only a few of the successive levels in this section, primarily in order to demonstrate their similarities and their differences.

One of the awarenesses to which an investigator may come after pondering a mountain of sociolinguistic data at the level of speech acts and events is that variation in 'talk' is more common and differently proportioned or distributed between certain interlocutors than it is between others (Schegloff 1968). Thus, whereas either the boy or the girl in Conversation 2 may initiate the switch from one language to another, it may seem from Conversation 1 that the boss is the initiator of switching far more frequently than is the secretary. Therefore, while a great deal of switching is functionally *metaphorical*, i.e. it indicates a contrast in emphasis (from humor to seriousness, from agreement to disagreement, from the inessential or secondary to the essential or primary, in any interchange already underway in a particular language variety), interlocutors may vary in the extent to which they may appropriately initiate or engage in such switching, depending on their *role-relationship* to each other. Note, however, that it is necessary for a certain appropriateness to exist between a variety and certain characteristics of the societal setting before it is possible to utilize another variety for metaphorical or contrastive purposes.

4.3 *Role-relationships*

Any two interlocutors within a given speech community (or, more narrowly, within a given speech network within a speech community) must recognize the role-relationship that exists between them at any particular time. Such recognition is part of the communality of norms and behaviors upon which the existence of speech communities depend. Father-son, husband-wife, teacher-pupil, clergyman-layman, employer-employee, friend-friend: these are but some examples of the role-relationships that may exist in various (but not in all) speech communities (Goodenough 1965). Role-relationships are implicitly recognized and accepted sets of mutual rights and obligations between members of the same socio-cultural system. One of the ways in which members reveal such common membership to each other, as well as their recognition of the rights and obligations that they owe toward each other, is via appropriate variation (which, of course, may include appropriate non-variation) of the way(s) they talk to each other. Perhaps children should generally be seen and not heard, but when they *are* heard, most societies insist that they talk differently to their parents than they do to their friends (Fischer 1968). One of the frequent comments about American travelers abroad is that they know (*at most*) only one variety of the language of the country they are visiting. As a result, they speak in the same way to a child, a professor, a bootblack and a shopkeeper, thus revealing not only their foreignness, but also their ignorance (of the appropriate ways of signalling local role-relationships).

It is probably not necessary, at this point, to dwell upon the kinds of variation in talk that may be required (or prohibited) by certain role-relationships. In addition, and this too should require no extensive discussion at this point, whether the variation required is from one language to another or from one geographic, social or occupational variety to another, the functionally differential role-relationships must be *emically* validated rather than merely *etically* enumerated. There are certainly sociolinguistic allo-roles in most speech communities. However, two other characterizations of role-relationships do merit mention at this point, particularly because they have proved to be useful in sociolinguistic description and analysis.

Role-relationships vary in the extent to which their mutual rights and obligations must or must not be *continually stressed*. The king-subject role-relationship may retain more invariant stress than the shopkeeper-customer relationship. If shopkeepers and their customers may also interact with each other as friends, as relatives, as members of the same political party, etc., whereas kings and their subjects (in the same speech community) may not experience a similar degree of role change, access and/or fluidity *vis-a-vis each other,* then we would expect to encounter more variation in the 'talk' of two individuals who encounter each other as shopkeeper and customer than we would expect between two individuals who encounter each other as king and subject. In addition, a shopkeeper and his customer may be able to set aside their roles entirely and interact entirely on the basis of their individual and momentary needs and inclinations. This may not be permissible for the king and his subjects. Thus, we would say that a shopkeeper and his customer may engage in both *personal* and *transactional* interactions (Gumperz 1964b), whereas the king and his subjects engage only in transactional interactions. Transactional interactions are those which stress the mutual rights and obligations of their participants. Personal interactions are more informal, more fluid, more varied.

In part, speech acts and events are differentially distributed throughout various role-relationships because personal and transactional interactions are differentially permitted in various role-relationships. The sociology of language is necessarily of interest to those investigators who are concerned with determining the functionally different role-relationships that exist within a given community. Micro-level sociology of language, at least, is concerned with the validation of such relationships, via demonstration of differential role access, role range and role fluidity, as well as via the demonstration of differential proportions of personal and transactional interaction, through the data of 'talk'. Role relationships may be used as data-organizing units both with respect to variation in talk as well as with respect to other variations in interpersonal behavior. That is the reason why role relations are so frequently examined in the sociology of language.

4.4 *The Situation: Congruent and Incongruent*

It has probably occurred to the reader that if the shopkeeper and his customer are not to interact only as such but, rather, also as friends, lovers, relatives, or party-members, that more than their roles are likely to change. After all, neither the *time* nor the *place* of the storekeeper-customer role-relationship is really ideal for any of the other relationships mentioned. Lovers require a time and a place of their own, and the same is true — or, at least, is typical — for other role-relationships as well. These three ingredients (the *implementation* of the rights and duties of a particular role-relationship, in the *place* (locale) most appropriate or most typical for that relationship, and at the *time* societally defined as appropriate for that relationship), taken together, constitute a construct that has proven itself to be of great value in the sociology of language: the *social situation* (Bock 1964; see Figure 4).

SITUATION: 'CLASS'	*Time*: Class Meeting
Space: Classroom	*Roles*: + Teacher + Pupil ± Student-Teacher

Fig. 4. The Social Situation (Bock 1964).

+ indicates obligatory occurrence.
± indicates optional occurrence.

The simplest type of social situation for micro-level sociology of language to describe and analyze is the congruent situation in which all three ingredients 'go together' in the culturally accepted way. This is not to say that the investigator may assume that there is only one place and one time appropriate for the realization of a particular role-relationship. Quite the contrary. As with the wakes studied by Bock on a Micmac Indian Reserve, there may be various times and various places for the appropriate realization of particular role-relationships (see Figure 5). Nevertheless, the total number of permissible combinations is likely to be small and, small or not, there is likely to be little ambiguity among members of the society or culture under study as to what the situation in question is and what its requirements are with respect to their participation in it. As a result, if there are language usage norms with respect to situations these are likely to be most clearly and uniformly realized in avowedly congruent situations.

However, lovers quarrel. Although they meet in the proper time and place they do not invariably behave toward each other as lovers should. Similarly, if a secretary and her boss are required to meet in the office at 3:00 A. M. in order to complete an emergency report, it may well be difficult for them to maintain the usual secretary-boss relationship. Finally, if priest and parishioner meet at the Yonkers Raceway during the time normally set aside for confessions this must have some impact on the normal priest-parishioner role-relationship. However, in all such instances of initial incongruency (wrong behavior, wrong time, or wrong place) the resulting interaction — whether sociolinguistic or otherwise — is normally far from random or chaotic. One party to the interaction or another, if not both, reinterpret(s) the seeming incongruency so as to yield a congruent situation, at least phenomenologically, for that particular encounter, where one does not exist socioculturally.

Because of incongruent behavior toward each other lovers may reinterpret each other as employer and employee and the date situation is reinterpreted as a dispassionate work situation. Because of the incongruent time, secretary and boss may view the work situation as more akin to a date than is their usual custom. Because of the incongruent place priest and parishioner may pretend not to recognize each other, or to treat each other as 'old pals'. In short, after a bit of 'fumbling around' in which various and varying tentative redefinitions may be tried out, a new congruent situation is interpreted as existing and *its* behavioral and sociolinguistic requirements are implemented (Blom and Gumperz 1972; Fishman 1968b). Thus, whereas bilingual Puerto Rican parents and their children in New York are most likely to talk to each other in Spanish at home when conversing about family matters, they will probably speak in English to each other in the Public School building (Fishman, Cooper and Ma 1968). As far as they are concerned, these are two different situations, perhaps calling for two different role-relationships and requiring the utilization of two different languages or varieties.

Situational contrasts need not be as discontinuous as most of our examples have thus far implied. Furthermore, within a basically Spanish-speaking situation one

M-14		T-1	T-2	T-3	T-4	T-5
S-1: Bier	s-1.1: nucleus	R-1	R-1	R-1	R-1	R-1
Area	s-1.2: margin	±r-2			±r-2	
S-2: Front Area			R-3	R-4		r-2.1
S-3: Audience Area			R-2	R-2	±R-2 ±R-4	r-2.2 R-4
S-4: Marginal	s-4.1: kitchen				r-2.1	
Area	s-4.2: outside	r-2.2			±r-2.2 ±R-4	

Fig. 5. Situation-Matrix # 14: Indian Wake (Bock 1964).

14.SC–A: Place of Wake — External distribution into 9.S–A.1: House site (usually that occupied by deceased)
  S–1: Bier Area
  s–1.1: nucleus — contains coffin
  s–1.2: margin — area immediately surrounding coffin
  S–2: Front Area — focal region of performances during T–2, –3, and –5.
  S–3: Audience Area — seating area for R–2: Mourner
  S–4: Marginal Area — residual space, including
  s–4.1: kitchen area
  s–4.2: outside of house

14.TC–A: Time of Wake — External distribution (see discussion above).
          TC–A = //T–1/T–2//:T–3/T–4://± T–5//:T–3/T–4://
  T–1: Gathering Time — participants arrive at SC–A: Place of Wake
  T–2: Prayer Time — saying of the Rosary by R–3: Prayer Leader
  T–3: Singing Time — several hymns sung with brief pauses in between
  T–4: Intermission — longer pause in singing
  T–5: Meal Time — optional serving of meal (about midnight)

14.RC–A: Participant Roles — External distribution noted for each:
  R–1: Corpse — from 3.RC–A: Band Member
  R–2: Mourner
  r–2.1: Host — member of 9.RC–A: Household Group (of deceased)
  r–2.2: Other — residual category
  R–3: Prayer Leader
  r–3.1: Priest — from 3.R–B.1.1: Priest
  r–3.2: Other — from 14.R–4
  R–4: Singer — usually from 11.R–A.4: Choir Member

or another member of a bilingual speech community may still switch to English (or, in Paraguay, to Guarani) in the midst of a speech event for purely metaphorical (i.e. for emphatic or contrastive) purposes. Such *metaphorical switching* would not be possible, however, if there were no general norm assigning the particular situation, as one of a class of such situations, to one language rather than to the other. However, in contrast to the frequently unilateral and fluid back-and-forth nature of metaphorical switching (perhaps to indicate a personal interlude in a basically transactional interaction) there stands the frequently more reciprocal and unidirectional nature of *situational* switching.

More generally put, *situational switching is governed by common allocation,* i.e. by widespread normative views and regulations that commonly allocate a particular variety to a particular cluster of topics, places, persons and purposes. *Metaphorical switching, on the other hand, is governed by uncommon or contrastive allocation.* It is operative as a departure from the common allocations that are normally operative. Without well established normative views and regulations relative to the functional allocation of varieties within the repertoire of a speech community neither situational nor metaphorical switching could effectively obtain. A switch to Cockney where Received Pronounciation (and grammar) is called for may elicit a brief raising of eyebrows or a pause in the conversation — until it is clear from the speaker's demeanor and from the fact that he has reverted to *RP* that no change in situation was intended. However, such metaphorical switching can be risky. Someone might feel that Cockney for the situation at hand is in poor taste. Metaphorical switching is a luxury that can be afforded only by those that comfortably share not only the same *set* of situational norms but also *the same view as to their inviolability.* Since most of us are members of several speech networks, each with somewhat different sociolinguistic norms, the chances that situational shifting and metaphorical switching will be misunderstood and conflicting — particularly where the norms pertaining to variety selection have few or insufficiently powerful guardians — are obviously great.

4.5 *The Transition to Macro-Level Sociology of Language*

The situational analysis of language and behavior represents the boundary area between micro-level and macro-level sociology of language. The very fact that a baseball conversation 'belongs' to one speech variety and an electrical engineering lecture 'belongs' to another speech variety is a major key to an even more generalized description of sociolinguistic variation. The very fact that humor during a formal lecture is realized through a metaphorical switch to another variety must be indicative of an underlying sociolinguistic regularity, perhaps of the view that lecture-like or formal situations are generally associated with one language or variety whereas levity or intimacy is tied to another (Joos 1959). The large-scale aggregative regularities that obtain between varieties and societally recognized functions are examined via the construct termed *domain* (Fishman 1965d, Fishman in press).

Sociolinguistic domains are societal constructs derived from painstaking analysis and summarization of patently congruent situations (see Fishman, Cooper, and Ma 1968 for many examples of the extraction of *emic* domains via factor analysis as well as for examples of the validation of initially etic domains). The macro-sociologist or social psychologist may well inquire: What is the significance of the fact that school situations and 'schoolish' situations (the latter being initially incongruent situations reinterpreted in the direction of their most salient component) are related to variety *a*? Frequently, it is helpful to recognize a number of behaviorally separate domains (behaviorally separate in that they are derived from discontinuous social situations) all of which are commonly associated with a particular variety or language. Thus, in many bilingual speech communities such domains as school, church, professional work-sphere and government have been verified and found to be congruent with a language or variety that we will refer to as *H* (although for purely labelling purposes we may refer to it as *a* or *X* or *1*). Similarly, such domains as family, neighborhood and lower work-sphere have been validated and found to be congruent with a language or variety that we will refer to as *L* (or *b*, or *Y* or *2*). All in all, the fact that a complex speech community contains various superposed varieties — in some cases, various languages, and, in others, various varieties of the same language — is now well documented. The existence of complementary varieties for intra-group purposes is known as *diglossia* (Ferguson 1959a) and the communities in which diglossia is encountered are referred to as *diglossic*. Domains are particularly useful constructs for the macro-level (i.e. community-wide) functional description of societally patterned variation in 'talk' within large and complex diglossic speech communities, about which more will be said in section 7, below.

Some members of diglossic speech communities can verbalize the relationship between certain broad categories of behavior and certain broad categories of 'talk'. More educated and verbally more fluent members of speech communities can tell an investigator about such relationships at great length and in great detail. Less educated and verbally limited members can only grope to express a regularity which they vaguely realize to exist. However, the fact that the formulation of a regular association between language (variety) and large scale situational behaviors may be difficult to come by is no more indicative of a dubious relationship than is the fact that grammatical regularities can rarely be explicitly formulated by native speakers is to be considered as calling the abstracted rules themselves into question.

As with all constructs (including situations, role-relationships and speech events), domains originate in the integrative intuition of the investigator. If the investigator notes that student-teacher interactions in classrooms, school corridors, school auditoriums and in school laboratories of elementary schools, high schools, colleges and universities are all realized via *H* as long as these interactions are focused upon educational technicality and specialization, he may begin to suspect that these hypothetically congruent situations all belong to a single (educational) *domain*. If he further finds that hypothetically incongruent situations involving an educational and a non-educational ingredient are, by and large, predictably resolved in terms of H rather than L if the third ingredient is an educational time, place or role-relationship, he may feel further justified in positing an educational domain. Finally, if informants tell him that the predicted language or variety would be appropriate in all of the examples he can think of that derive from his notion of the educational domain, whereas they proclaim that it would not be appropriate for examples that he draws from a contrasted domain, then the construct is as usefully validated as is that of situation or event — with one major difference.

Whereas particular speech acts (and speech excerpts of an even briefer nature) can be apportioned to the speech and social situations in which they transpire, the same cannot be done with respect to such acts or excerpts in relationship to societal domains. Domains are extrapolated from the *data* of 'talk', rather than being an actual component of the *process* of talk. However, domains are as real as the very social institutions of a speech community, and indeed they show a marked paralleling with such major social institutions (Barker 1947). There is an undeniable difference between the social institution, 'the family', and any particular family, but there is no doubt that the societal norms concerning the former must be derived from data on many instances of the latter. Once such societal norms are formulated they can be utilized to test predictions concerning the distributions of societally patterned variations in talk across all instances of one domain vs. all instances of another.

Thus, domains and social situations reveal the links that exist between micro-level and macro-level sociology of language. The members of diglossic speech communities can come to have certain views concerning their varieties or languages because these varieties are associated (in behavior and in attitude) with particular domains. The H variety (or language) is considered to reflect certain values and relationships within the speech community, whereas the L variety is considered to reflect others. Certain individuals and groups may come to advocate the expansion of the functions of L into additional domains. Others may advocate the displacement of L entirely and the use of H solely. Neither of these revisionist views could be held or advocated without recognition of the reality of domains of language-and-behavior in the existing norms of communicative appropriateness. The high culture values with which certain varieties are associated and the intimacy and folksiness values with which others are congruent are both derivable from domain-appropriate norms governing characteristic verbal interaction.

4.6 *On the Reality of Sociolinguistic Compositing*

So little (if, indeed, any) microsociolinguistic data has been subjected to rigorous quantitative analysis or obtained via experimentally controlled variation that it is fitting that we pause to examine a study that has attempted to do so even if it deals only with sociolinguistic normative views and claims. The study in question (Fishman and Greenfield 1970) is concerned with the relative importance of persons, places and topics in the perception of congruent and incongruent situations and with the impact of perceived congruency or incongruency on claimed language use in different domains. Since domains are a higher order generalization from *congruent situations* (i.e. from situations in which individuals interact in appropriate role-relationships with eath other, in the appropriate locales for these role-relationships, and discuss topics appropriate to their role-relationships) it was first necessary to test intuitive and rather clinical estimates of the widespread congruences that were felt to obtain. After more than a year of participant observation and other data-gathering experiences it seemed to Greenfield (1968) that five domains could be generalized from the innumerable situations that he had encountered. He tentatively labeled these 'family', 'friendship', 'religion', 'education' and 'employment' and proceeded to determine whether a typical *situation* could be presented for each domain as a means of collecting self-report data on language choice. As indicated below each domain was represented by a congruent person (interlocutor), place and topic in the self-report instrument that Greenfield constructed for high school students.

Domain	Interlocutor	Place	Topic
Family	Parent	Home	How to be a good son or daughter
Friendship	Friend	Beach	How to play a certain game
Religion	Priest	Church	How to be a good Christian
Education	Teacher	School	How to solve an algebra problem
Employment	Employer	Workplace	How to do your job more efficiently

Greenfield's hypothesis was that within the Puerto Rican speech community, among individuals who knew Spanish and English equally well, Spanish was primarily associated with family and with friendship (the two, family and friendship constituting the intimacy value cluster), while English was primarily associated with religion, work and education (the three constituting the status-stressing value cluster). In order to test this hypothesis he first presented two seemingly congruent situational components and requested his subjects (a) to select a third component in order to complete the situation, as well as (b) to indicate their likelihood of using Spanish or English if they were involved in such a situation and if they and their Puerto Rican interlocutors knew Spanish and English equally well. Section I of Table 1 shows that Greenfield's predictions were uniformly confirmed among those subjects who selected congruent third components. Spanish was decreasingly reported for family, friendship, religion, employment and education, regardless of whether the third component selected was a person, place or topic.

TABLE I

*Spanish and English Usage Self-ratings in Various Situations
for Components Selected*

1. *Congruent Situations:* Two 'congruent' components presented; S selects third congruent component and language appropriate to situation. 1 = all Spanish, 5 = all English.

Congruent Persons Selected

	Parent	Friend	Total	Priest	Teacher	Employer	Total
Mean	2.77	3.60	3.27	4.69	4.92	4.79	4.81
S.D.	1.48	1.20	1.12	.61	.27	.41	.34
N	13	15	15	13	13	14	15

Congruent Places Selected

	Home	Beach	Total	Church	School	Work Place	Total
Mean	2.33	3.50	2.60	3.80	4.79	4.27	4.27
S.D.	1.07	1.26	1.10	1.51	.58	1.34	.94
N	15	6	15	15	14	15	15

Congruent Topics Selected

	Family	Friendship	Total	Religious	Education	Employment	Total
Mean	1.69	3.30	2.64	3.80	4.78	4.44	4.38
S.D.	.92	1.20	.95	1.47	1.53	1.12	.73
N	16	18	18	15	18	18	18

2. *Incongruent Situations:* Two 'incongruent' components presented; S selects third component and language appropriate to situation. 1 = all Spanish, 5 = all English.

Persons Selected

	Parent	Friend	Total	Priest	Teacher	Employer	Total
Mean	2.90	3.92	3.60	4.68	4.77	4.44	4.70
S.D.	1.20	.64	.70	.59	.48	.68	.52
N	16	16	16	14	15	9	15

Places Selected

	Home	Beach	Total	Church	School	Work Place	Total
Mean	2.63	3.86	2.77	3.71	4.39	4.42	4.10
S.D.	.77	.94	.70	1.32	1.90	.96	.82
N	15	5	15	15	15	15	15

Topics Selected

	Family	Friendship	Total	Religious	Education	Employment	Total
Mean	2.83	3.81	3.26	3.07	3.66	3.81	3.49
S.D.	1.04	1.13	1.02	1.00	1.20	.85	.76
N	18	16	18	18	17	18	18

However, as Blom and Gumperz (1972), Fishman (1968b) and others have indicated, seemingly incongruent situations frequently occur and are rendered understandable and acceptable (just as are the seemingly ungrammatical sentences that we hear in most spontaneous speech). Interlocutors reinterpret incongruencies in order to salvage some semblance of the congruency in terms of which they understand and function within their social order. Were this not the case then no seemingly congruent domains could arise and be maintained out of the incongruencies of daily life. In order to test this assumption Greenfield proceeded to present his subjects with two incongruent components (e.g. with a person from one hypothetical domain and with a place from another hypothetical domain) and asked them to select a third component in order to complete the situation as well as to indicate their likelihood of using Spanish or English in a situation so constituted. Greenfield found that the third component was overwhelmingly selected from either one or the other of any two domains from which he had selected the first two components. Furthermore, in their attempts to render a seemingly incongruous situation somewhat more congruent his subject's language preferences left the relationship between domains and language choice substantially unaltered (directionally), regardless of whether persons, places or topics were involved. Nevertheless, all domains became somewhat less different from each other than they had been in the fully congruent situations. Apparently, both individual indecisiveness as well as sociolinguistic norms governing domain regularity must be combined and compromised when incongruencies appear. Language choice is much more clearcut and polarized in 'usual' situations governed neatly by sociolinguistic norms of communicative appropriateness than they are in 'unusual' situations which must be resolved by individual interpretation.

Yet, another (and, for this presentation, final) indication of the construct validity of domains as analytic parameters for the study of large-scale sociolinguistic patterns is yielded by Edelman's data (1968). Here we note that when the word naming responses of bilingual Puerto-Rican children in Jersey City were analyzed in accord with the domains derived from Greenfield's and Fishman's data reported above, significant and instructive findings were obtained. The most Spanish domain for all children was 'family' (Table II A). The most English domain for all children was 'education'. The analysis of variance (Table II B) indicates that not only did the children's responses differ significantly by age (older children giving more responses in both languages than did younger children), by language (English yielding more responses than does Spanish), and by domain (church yielding fewer responses than does any other domain), but that these three variables *interact significantly* as well. This means that one language is much more associated with certain domains than is the other and that this is differentially so by age. This is exactly the kind of finding for which domain analysis is particularly suited. Its utility for inter-society comparisons and for gauging language shift would seem to be quite promising, but its major value should be in describing and demonstrating the dependence of communicative appropriateness on the compositing appropriateness of members of speech communities, whether monolingual or bilingual.

One thing appears to be clear from the theoretical and empirical work cited: there are classes of events recognized by each speech network or community such that several seemingly different situations are classed as being of the same kind. No speech network has a linguistic repertoire that is as differentiated as the complete list of apparently different role relations, topics and locales in which its members are involved. Just *where the boundaries come* that do differentiate between the *class of situations* generally requiring one variety and another class of situations generally requiring another variety must be empirically determined by the investigator, and constitutes one of the major tasks of descriptive sociology of language. Such classes of situations are referred to as *domains*. The various domains and the appropriate usage in each domain must be discovered from the data of numerous discrete situations and the shifting or non-shifting which they reveal. This is a central task of descriptive sociology of language, and it can only be accomplished by painstaking research — utilizing *all* of the available social science methods: participant observation, interviews, surveys and experiments too. The compositing concerns of some researchers in the sociology of language are thus far from being research strategies alone. Ultimately they also seek to reveal the behavioral parsimony of members of speech communities all of whom inevitably come to rely on a relatively functional sociolinguistic typology to guide them through the infinite encounters of daily interaction.

TABLE II A

Mean number of words named by young schoolchildren
(Edelman 1968) (N = 34)

Age	Language	Domain				
		Family	Education	Religion	Friendship	Total
6–8	English	6.2	8.2	6.6	8.3	7.3
	Spanish	7.6	6.2	5.8	6.4	6.5
	Total	6.9	7.2	6.2	7.4	6.9
9–11	English	11.7	12.8	8.7	10.9	11.0
	Spanish	10.5	9.4	7.2	9.7	9.2
	Total	11.1	11.1	7.9	10.3	10.1
Total	English	9.0	10.5	7.7	9.6	9.2
	Spanish	9.0	7.8	6.5	8.0	7.8
	Total	9.0	9.1	7.1	9.0	8.5

TABLE II B

Analysis of variance of young schoolchildren's word-naming scores

Source	Sum of Squares	df	Mean Square	F_{95}	F_{95}	F_{99}
Between Subjects	1844.12	33				
C (age)	689.30	1	689.30	19.67*	4.17	7.56
D (sex)	15.54	1	15.54	.44	4.17	7.56
CD	87.87	1	87.87	2.51	4.17	7.56
error (b)	1051.41	30		35.05		
Within Subjects	1795.88	238				
A (language)	123.13	1	123.13	9.73*	4.17	7.56
B (domain)	192.54	3	64.18	8.51*	2.71	4.00
AB	65.12	3	21.71	11.67*	2.71	4.00
AC	16.50	1	16.50	1.30	4.17	7.56
AD	42.08	1	42.08	3.32	4.17	7.56
BC	61.54	3	20.51	2.72	2.71	4.00
BD	2.89	3	.96	.13	2.71	4.00
ABC	23.99	3	8.00	4.30*	2.71	4.00
ABD	6.70	3	2.23	1.20	2.71	4.00
ACD	14.62	1	14.62	1.15	4.17	7.56
BCD	13.53	3	4.51	.60	2.71	4.00
ABCD	7.98	3	2.66	1.43	2.71	4.00
error (w)	1225.26	210				
error$_1$ (w)	379.88	30	12.66			
error$_2$ (w)	678.31	30	7.54			
error$_3$ (w)	167.07	90	1.86			
Total	3640.00	271				

* Significant at or above the .01 level.

4.7 *Sociology of Language: Multilevel and Multimethod*

The list of constructs utilized in the sociolinguistic description and analysis of samples of 'talk' is far from exhausted. We have not mentioned several of the social units long advocated by Hymes (1962), such as participant vs. audience roles, the purposes and the outcomes of speech events, the tone or manner of communication, the channel of communication employed (oral, written, telegraphic), nor all of the various parameters and components for the analysis of talk data that he has more

(S)   SETTING or SCENE: time and place; also, psychological setting and cultural definition as a *type* of scene

(P)   PARTICIPANTS or PERSONNEL: e.g., addressor-addressee-audience

(E)   ENDS: ends in view (goals, purposes) and ends as outcomes

(A)   ART CHARACTERISTICS: the form *and* the content of what is said

(K)   KEY: the tone, manner or spirit in which an act is done

(I)   INSTRUMENTALITIES: channel (the choice of oral, written, telegraphic or other medium) and code (Spanish, English, etc.) or subcode (dialect, sociolect)

(N)   NORMS OF INTERACTION and of INTERPRETATION: specific behaviors and properties that may accompany acts of speech, as well as shared rules for understanding what occurs in speech acts

(G)   GENRES: categories or types of speech acts and speech events: e.g., conversation, curse, prayer, lecture, etc.

Fig. 6A. Components of speech events: a heuristic schema (Hymes 1967b).

recently advanced (Hymes 1967b; see Figure 6A); we have not discussed such social psychological parameters as the saliency of individual vs. collective needs (Herman 1961), nor the several functions of speech so revealingly discussed by Ervin-Tripp. Suffice it to say that there are several levels and approaches to sociolinguistic description and a host of linguistic, sociopsychological and societal constructs within each (see Figure 6B). One's choice from among them depends on the particular problem at hand (Ervin-Tripp 1964). This is necessarily so. The sociology of language is of interest to students of small societies as well as to students of national and international integration. It must help clarify the change from one face-to-face situation to another. It must also help clarify the different language-related beliefs and behaviors of entire social sectors and classes. In some cases the variation between closely related varieties must be highlighted. In other cases the variation between obviously unrelated languages is of concern.

It would be foolhardy to claim that one and the same method of data collection and data analysis be utilized for such a variety of problems and purposes. It is one of the hallmarks of scientific social inquiry that methods are selected as a *result* of problem specifications rather than independently of them. The sociology of language is neither methodologically nor theoretically uniform. Nevertheless, it is gratifying to note that for those who seek such ties the links between micro- and macro-constructs and methods exist (as do a number of constructs and methods that have wide applicability through the entire range of the sociology of language). Just as there is no societally unencumbered verbal interaction so are there no large-scale relationships between language and society that do not depend on individual

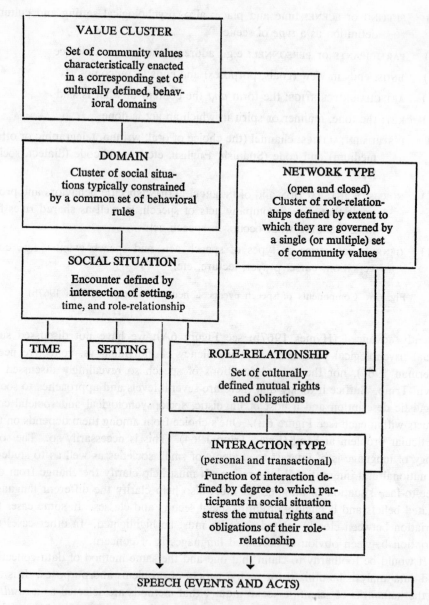

Fig. 6B. Relationships among some constructs employed in sociolinguistic analysis.

From: Robert L. Cooper, "How can we measure the roles which a bilingual's languages play in his everyday behavior?", in L. G. Kelly, ed., *The description and measurement of bilingualism.* Toronto, Toronto University Press, 1969, p. 202.

interaction for their realization. Although there is no mechanical part-whole relationship between them, micro-level and macro-level sociology of language are both conceptually and methodologically complementary.

5. SOCIETAL DIFFERENTIATION AND REPERTOIRE RANGE

Speech communities — particularly those at the citywide, regional or national levels — obviously vary in the degrees and kinds of language diversity that they reveal. What do such differences imply with respect to the social differentiation and organization of the communities and networks to which they apply? If we examine the varieties of Javanese required by linguistic etiquette in the communities described by Geertz (1960), the varieties of Baghdadi Arabic described by Blanc (1964), the varieties of Hindi or Kannada described by Gumperz (1958) or McCormack (1960), and the varieties of Indonesian described by Tanner (1967), it is clear that these compose different kinds of repertoires than do the varieties of Norwegian described by Haugen (1961) or the varieties of American English described by Labov (1963, 1964, 1965) or by Levine and Crockett (1966). In addition, the types of speech communities in which these varieties are encountered also differ strikingly, as do the larger national or regional units in which the communities are imbedded. To put it very briefly, the speech communities in the first cluster seem to be much more stratified socially and to employ much more diversified repertoires linguistically than do those in the second. The documented co-occurrence of linguistic heterogeneity and societal heterogeneity — when both are examined in intra-group perspective — is a major contribution of the sociology of language to the study of social organization and social change.

5.1 *The Significance of Pervasive Linguistic Discontinuity*

Prior to the development of the sociology of language per se, area-dialectology had already clearly indicated that discontinuous populations (i.e. populations that lived at some distance from each other or that were impeded in their communication with each other by physical or political barriers) frequently revealed substantial phonological and morphological differences between their language systems (see e.g. Herzog 1965 and Kandori 1968 for examples of such work today). Where such differences did not obtain despite the absence of communicational frequency and socio-cultural unity, recency of settlement from a single source or other similar unifying factors (conquest, religious conversion, etc.) were assumed and encountered. Indeed, if we view the entire world as a single geographic area we tend to find similar (i.e. genetically related) languages clustered contiguously or closely to each other ('language families' are normally clustered geographically, except for the confounding fact of colonization and distant migration). Some parts of the world, of course, are famous for their concentration of highly diversified languages found in close proximity to each other. However, these same areas are also noted for their mountains, jungles, deserts and rivers, i.e. for barriers that have limited travel, commerce and common endeavor.

More difficult to explain are those variations in language and behavior that are *co-territorial*. In such instances sheer physical distance cannot be invoked as either a casual or a maintenance variable for the variations encountered. In such cases cultural and social factors alone must be examined and they alone must be meaningfully related to the *degree* and *kind* of language differences noted. In reviewing co-territorial linguistic diversity throughout history it becomes clear that it can be maintained in an extremely stable manner. Throughout the world — but particularly throughout the ancient and traditional world — populations have lived side by side for centuries without learning each other's language(s) and without significantly modifying or giving up their distinctly discontinuous repertoires. Except for the relatively few middlemen that connect them (merchants, translators, etc.) such populations represent distinct speech communities although they may be citizens of the same country, of the same city, and, indeed, of the same neighborhood. However, the maintenance of such well-nigh complete linguistic and socio-cultural cleavage — equal in degree and kind to that encountered between territorially discontinuous populations — is usually indicative of population relocation some time in the past that has subsequently been buttressed and maintained by socio-cultural (including ethnic and religious) differences. The *former* differences are responsible for the origin of the differences noted by Blanc (1964) between the Moslem Arabic, Christian Arabic and Jewish Arabic of Baghdad. The *latter* differences are responsible for the *maintenance* of these cleavages in as sharp a manner, or nearly so, as initially established.

While it may often be relatively difficult to overcome the cleavage between separate but co-territorial speech communities it is not impossible to do so. The forced conversion of various Jewish and Christian communities during certain periods of Islamic rule, the urban-industrial assimilation of hitherto rural or small town immigrants and their children in the United States (Nahirny and Fishman 1965; Fishman 1965a, 1965e, 1966c), the very similar assimilation of tribal populations moving to Wolof-speaking Dakar (Tabouret-Keller 1968), the Hellenization and Romanization of many 'barbarian' elites in ancient Rome and Alexandria, the convergence between illiterate speakers of Marathi and Kannada in India (Gumperz 1967) — these are all examples of the fusing into one of populations that originally functioned as largely separate though co-territorial speech communities. Conversely, the mutual alienation of populations that originally considered themselves to be united can create far-going linguistic differences between them where none, or few, existed previously. In general, the more far-going the linguistic differences between any two co-territorial populations (i.e. the more the differences are basically gram-

matical-syntactic and morphological — rather than primarily phonological or lexical), the more their linguistic repertoires are compartmentalized from each other
so as to reveal little if any interference, and the more they reveal functionally
different verbal repertoires in terms of the sociolinguistic parameters reviewed in
section 4, above — then the greater the interactional and socio-cultural gap between
the speech communities involved.

Geertz's data (see Figures 7A, B and C) might well be examined in the light of the
above generalization concerning the social significance of marked grammatical discontinuity between the repertoires of co-territorial speech communities. In Geertz's
case we are dealing with co-territorial speech networks that differ greatly in
verbal repertoires but that cannot be considered to be either of separate
geographic origin or of separate cultural or religious self-definition. Here we find
three different social classes or strata within Java each differing in repertoire range
and each lacking entirely one or more speech varieties available to at least one of
the others. While the intra-network variation shown by Geertz is probably less than

7A. Dialect of Non-Prijaji, Urbanized, Somewhat Educated Persons

Level	are	you	going	to eat	rice	and	cas-sava	now	Complete sentence
3a	me-napa	pandje-nengan	badé	ḍahar	sekul	kali-jan	kaspé	same-nika	*Menapa pandjenengan baḍé ḍahar sekul kalijan kaspé samenika?*
3		sam-péjan		neḍa					*Menapa sampéjan baḍé neḍa sekul kalijan kaspé samenika?*
2	napa	sam-péjan	ad-jeng	neḍa		lan		saniki	*Napa sampéjan adjeng neḍa sekul lan kaspé saniki?*
1a	apa		arep		sega			saiki	*Apa sampéjan arep neḍa sega lan kaspé saiki?*
1	apa	kowé	arep	man-gan	sega			saiki	*Apa kowé arep mangan sega lan kaspé saiki?*

7B. Dialect of Peasants and Uneducated Townspeople

Level	are	you	going	to eat	rice	and	cas-sava	now	Complete sentence
2	napa	sam-péjan	ad-jeng	neḍa	sekul	lan	kaspé	saniki	*Napa sampéjan adjeng neḍa sekul lan kaspé saniki?*
1a	apa		arep		sega			saiki	*Apa sampéjan arep neḍa sega lan kaspé saiki?*
1	apa	kowé	arep	man-gan	sega			saiki	*Apa kowé arep mangan sega lan kaspé saiki?*

7C. *Dialect of the Prijajis*

Level	are	you	going	to eat	rice	and	cas-sava	now	Complete sentence
3a	me-napa	pandje-nengan	badé	ḍahar	sekul	kali-jan	kaspé	same-nika	Menapa pandjenengan baḍé ḍahar sekul kalijan kaspé samenika?
3		sam-péjan		neḍa					Menapa sampéjan baḍé neḍa sekul kalijan kaspé samenika?
1b	apa	pandje-nengan	arep	ḍahar	sega	lan	kaspé	saiki	Apa pandjenengan arep ḍahar sega lan kaspé saiki?
1a		sam-péjan		neḍa					Apa sampéjan arep neḍa sega lan kaspé saiki?
1		kowé		man-gan					Apa kowé arep mangan sega lan kaspé saiki?

Fig. 7. Social class differences in Javanese linguistic repertoires (Geertz 1960).

that which actually exists (thus, we may assume that metaphorical switching also occurs in Java and, if it does, level 2 (for example) may be employed on occasions which are normatively viewed and regulated as being more appropriate for level 1b or 1a), let us consider this to be merely an artifact of the data model that Geertz employs and ask ourselves (a) what *kind(s) of variations* does it reveal and (b) what kind(s) of repertoire differences does it reveal.

Geertz's data clearly indicate that social class differences exist (or existed at the time his fieldwork was done) in Javanese verbal behavior. In addition, however, the data also indicate that contextual-situational variation also exists in Javanese verbal behavior. The very fact that both of these types of variation regularly co-occur is an indication that although stratificational differences involved are rigid and deep, nevertheless the strata constitute a single integrated speech community with shared normative expectations and regulations vis-a-vis intra-strata and inter-strata communication.

The fact that networks in each stratum lack at least one variety available to networks drawn from the other strata is a sign of fargoing discontinuity also in their respective behavioral repertoires. Networks from certain strata are not expected to engage in certain role-relationships and as a result, lack entirely certain morpho-syntactic co-occurrences available to networks from other strata. Thus, in these latter respects, the variation that occurs is *stratificational only* and not contextual at all. This stratificational discontinuity in morpho-syntactic co-occurrences is shown graphically in Figure 8 for the forms *apa, napa* and *menapa*. The strata that do possess these forms use them for identical contexts of interaction and with apparently equal frequency of realization. However, there is in each case also a

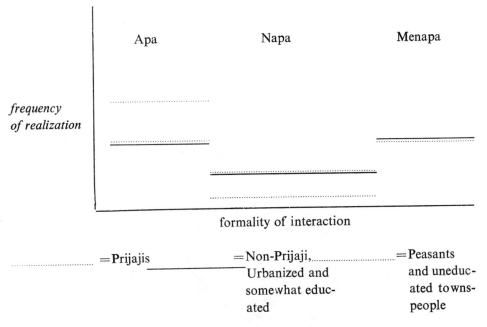

Fig. 8. Verbal and behavioral discontinuity.

stratum that lacks these forms. The graphic representation of social and verbal discontinuity should be kept in mind for comparison with other graphs presented further below (e.g. Figures 9a and 9b).

5.2 *More Marginal but Systematic Linguistic Differences between Social Strata*

However, most co-territorial populations that differ in verbal repertoire cannot be considered fully separate speech communities, even if the differences between them can be considered as basically geographic in origin. There are very many areas today, primarily urban in nature, where sub-populations that differ in social class, religion or ethnic affiliation nevertheless view themselves as sharing many common norms and standards and where these sub-populations interact sufficiently (or are sufficiently exposed to common educational institutions and media) to be termed a single speech community. It is hardly surprising, therefore, that the linguistic differences between such socio-cultural sub-populations (or networks) within the same speech community are more linguistically marginal (i.e. lexical and, to a lesser degree, morpho-phonological) rather than syntactic and all-embracing. It is clear that the social class variation that exists in New York City English is of this kind rather than of the kind that develops between clearly separate, non-interacting and

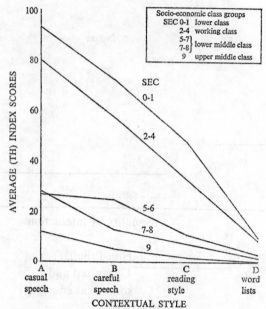

Figure 9a. *Class stratification diagram for (th)*
(Labov, 1964)

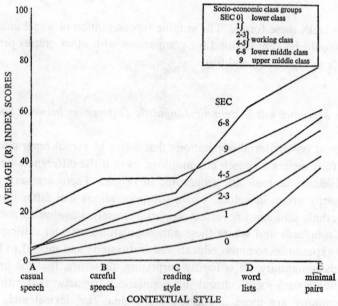

Fig. 9b. *Class stratification diagram for (r)*
(Labov, 1964)

Fig. 9a. Class stratification diagram for (th) (Labov 1964).
Fig. 9b. Class stratification diagram for (r) (Labov 1964).

mutually alienated speech communities. One of the surest indications of this is the fact that (if we delete features attributable to Southern Negro, Puerto Rican and other recent geographically derived differences) few of the characteristic phonological features of lower class speech in New York are entirely absent from the speech of other classes in New York City, just as few of the characteristic phonological features of its upper-class speech are entirely lacking from the lower class speech of that city. What does differentiate between the social classes in New York is the degree to which certain phonological *variables* are realized in *certain ways* on *particular occasions*, rather than their complete absence from the repertoire of any particular class.

Labov's studies of the phonological correlates of social stratification (1964, 1965, 1966a, 1966b, 1966c, 1968) illustrate this point. In one of his studies (1964) Labov gathered four different samples of speech (each by a different method calculated to elicit material approximating a different kind of speech situation) from four different social classes of informants. Studying such variables as *th* (as in *thing, through*), *eh* (the height of the vowel in *bad, ask, half, dance*), *r* (the presence or absence of final and preconsonantal /r/) and *oh* (the height of the vowel in *off, chocolate, all, coffee*), Labov found that *all* social classes yielded some values of each variable in nearly every speech situation (see Figure 9). However, the differences between the social classes remained clear enough. Lower class speakers were less likely to pronounce the fricative form of the [Θ] when saying 'thing' or 'through' than were working class speakers; working class speakers less likely to pronounce it than lower middle class speakers; lower middle class speakers, less likely to yield it than upper middle class speakers. Speakers of all classes were more likely to pronounce the standard fricative form (rather than the sub-standard affricate [t Θ] or lenis stop [t] in reading wordlists than they were when reading passages; more likely to pronounce it when reading passages, than when being interviewed (= careful speech); more likely to pronounce it when being interviewed than then recounting 'a situation where you thought you were in serious danger of being killed' (= casual speech).

This may be considered a hallmark of social class differences in speech where the classes as a whole share *continuous* experiences, goals and expectations, i.e. neither their role repertoires nor role access have been fully compartmentalized. As long as individuals in each class can differ in repertoire, depending on their personal opportunities and experiences with respect to interaction with various speech networks, there can be no complete discontinuity in repertoires, no complete freezing of social class position, and no overriding alienation into separate religious, ethnic or other relatively fixed and immutable speech communities.

Of course, not all variables yield such dramatic and clearcut social class differences as those found in connection with *th* in New York. With respect to *r, eh,* and *oh* Labov's data reveals much more *similarity* between the several social classes, although the differences between contexts and between classes remain quite clear. Labov's data also reveal a recurring *reversal with* respect to the lower middle class's performance on word and passage reading lists. This reversal, dubbed *hypercorrection*, shows the lower middle class to be more 'correct' (more careful, more inclined to use the standard or cultured pronunciation) than is the upper middle class at its most correct or careful. Such a reversal may well indicate a variable that has become a stereotype rather than merely a marker of class position. As such it tends to be used (or overused) by those who are insecure about their social position, i.e. by those who are striving to create a more advantageous social position for themselves in a speech community in which upward social mobility seems to be possible. This explanation is not dissimilar from that which Labov utilized to explain observed differences in centralization of /ai/ and /au/ on Martha's Vineyard, Massachusetts (1963). Such centralization was most common among minority group members of the island community (of Portuguese and Indian extraction) who sought to *stress their positive orientation to Martha's Vineyard*, rather than among the old Yankees whose feelings toward the Vinyeard were more low-keyed and required no linguistic underscoring. Whether consciously employed or not the 'Pygmalion effect' in language is a striking indicator of reference group behavior and of social aspirations more generally (Ross 1956).

Similar results to Labov's (in the sense that the proportional realizations of particular variables were found to differ regularly and smoothly both between *social classes* and between *contexts*) have been reported by Lindenfeld (1969). Examining syntactic variation in French, Lindenfeld found that nominalization, relativization and sentence length (but not subordination) showed both types of variation, although upper middle class speakers were much more likely to reveal contextual variation than were lower class speakers (Figure 10). This may be taken as a sign that the socio-economically more favored subjects had more of a real repertoire range behaviorally so that the difference between formal and informal interactions was very real for them. For lower class speakers, on the other hand, this difference may be quite hypothetical in that it tends to have much less functional reality associated with it.

The demographic differentials observed in usage are as related to the societal allocation of codes as are the more directly contextual or functional differentials. The fact that an extensive cluster of phonological, lexical and grammatical realizations is more widely or characteristically employed by one particular social class than by another is commonly related to the fact that the social class in question is also more likely or characteristically engaged in particular pursuits or involved in particular situations. Demographic and contextual variations are particularly likely to be redundant in relatively closed societies in which role access is restricted and in which roles tend to be ascribed and compartmentalized. However, the awareness of verbal and behavioral repertoires — a central awareness indeed in the sociology of language — should not keep us from realizing that even in relatively open societies there is often appreciable redundancy between demographic and contextual differentials in usage. Both Labov's and Lindenfeld's data referred to previously reveal

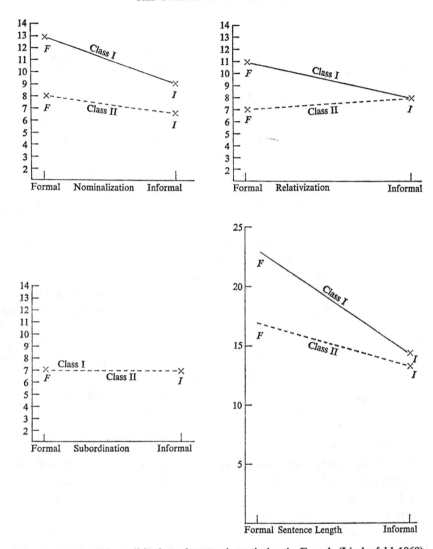

Fig. 10. The social conditioning of syntactic variation in French (Lindenfeld 1969).

this redundancy when they show that for most levels of formality one social class is much more likely to yield a particular variant than are the others, even though repertoire continuity exists. This redundancy strengthens the normative sense of members of speech communities and, indeed, enables them to guide their own speech behavior more appropriately, as well as to comment upon it validly to one another and to outside investigators and to do so over and above the metaphorical variation that undoubtedly obtains round about them.

5.3 *The Implications of Either Contextual-Situational or Demographic Variation*

The foregoing comparisons of social class differences and contextual-situational differences in language usage suffer in at least two ways. Neither Geertz nor Labov nor Lindenfeld have been able to indicate which of these two sources of language variation is the stronger for their data. In order to answer this question a more quantitative approach is needed to the study of social class or other demographic-group variation in usage. In addition, neither Geertz nor Labov nor Lindenfeld have asked the question 'what could it mean — insofar as the overall societal organization of language behavior — if only *one or another* of these two sources of usage variation obtained?' In order to answer these two questions let us take another look at data obtained in the study of *Bilingualism in the barrio* (Fishman, Cooper, Ma, et al. 1968).

The data we will review was obtained as part of an interdisciplinary project on the measurement and description of widespread and relatively stable bilingualism in a Puerto Rican neighborhood in the Greater New York City area. The neighborhood studied by a team of linguists, psychologists, and sociologists included 431 Puerto Ricans (or individuals of Puerto Rican parentage) living in ninety households. All these individuals were covered in a language census that obtained the demographic data utilized for the purposes of this report at the same time that it obtained detailed self-reports on bilingual usage and ability (Fishman 1969d). The linguistic data utilized for this report was obtained in the course of two to four hour interviews and testing sessions with a random-stratified sample of those Puerto Ricans living in the study neighborhood who were over the age of 12.

5.31 *Speech contexts*

The interviews and testing sessions were designed to elicit speech data in five different contexts that form a continuum from most formal or careful to most informal or casual as follows:

Context D: Word Reading. Subjects were asked to read two different lists of separate words, one in English and one in Spanish. The speech data obtained in this fashion was considered to be representative of the most careful pronunciation available to the subjects.

Context C: Paragraph Reading. Subjects were asked to read four different paragraphs, two in English and two in Spanish. The speech data obtained in this fashion was considered to be representative of (somewhat less) careful pronunciation.

Context WN: Word Naming. Subjects were asked to 'name as many words as come to mind that have to do with (domain locales)'. This task was performed separately in English and in Spanish for each of the following domain-locales: home, neighborhood, school, work, church. The speech data obtained in this fashion was considered to be representative of intermediate pronunciation (neither markedly careful nor casual).

Context B: Careful Conversation. Subjects were asked factual questions concerning five taped 'playlets' to which they had just listened. Ideally, half of the questions were asked (and answered) in Spanish and half were asked and answered in English. The speech data obtained in this fashion was considered to be representative of somewhat (but not completely) casual pronunciation.

Context A: Casual Conversation. Subjects were asked their personal opinions and preferences with respect to the problems that figured in the 'playlets' to which they had just listened. The speech data obtained in this fashion was considered to be representative of the most informal pronunciation that could be elicited by an interviewer.

Only the last three contexts (WN, B, A) will be examined in the discussion that follows in view of the restricted corpuses obtained in the two reading contexts in the study population.

5.32 *Linguistic variables*

The taped speech samples obtained for the above mentioned five contexts were independently scored by two linguists on seven Spanish and ten English variables. The reliability of scoring varied only slightly and irregularly from context to context and from one language to the other, the reliability coefficients obtained ranged from 0.73 to 0.94 with a median of 0.90. A full report on the contextual variation encountered for each variable as well as on the factorial relationship between all variables is available elsewhere (Ma and Herasimchuk 1968). The present discussion deals only with selected values on one Spanish and one English variable in order to illustrate a method of analysis hitherto not utilized in sociolinguistic research. The particular linguistic values selected for presentation in this study are further explained in the Results section below.

5.33 *Demographic variables*

Four demographic factors (sex, age, education, and birthplace) are included in the analyses presented in this report. Social class, a variable frequently utilized in other sociolinguistic research on phonological variables, was not utilized in the present research due to the severe restriction in range that our overwhelmingly lower-class Puerto Rican subjects revealed in this connection. An extensive analysis of the demographic variation encountered in our study neighborhood is available elsewhere (Fishman 1968c). The reliability coefficients for the various items of obtained demographic information are all 0.90 or higher.

Sex has consistently proved to be a non-significant demographic variable in accounting for phonological variation in Puerto Rican Spanish. It was included in the present study merely in order to provide a comparison with prior studies.

Age was categorized in two separate ways. As a three-category variable the categories employed were <25, 25–34, >34. As a two-category variable the categories utilized were <25 and >25. By categorizing age in two different ways we will be able to tell whether one categorization is more related to linguistic variation than the other and, at the same time, sum both age categorizations into one age variable.

Education was categorized in three different ways. As a four-category variable the categories were <7 years, all in Puerto Rico; 7 or more years, all in Puerto Rico; partially in Puerto Rico and partially in continental U.S.A.; all in continental U.S.A. As a two-category variable education was categorized in two different ways: first, all in Puerto Rico vs. all or part in continental U.S.A. and, second, all U.S.A. vs. all or part in Puerto Rico. Once again our analytic technique enabled us to sum these three different ways of categorizing education as well as to tell whether there is any difference between them in explaining linguistic variation.

Birthplace was categorized in two different ways. As a four-category variable the categories used were highland Puerto Rico, coastal Puerto Rico other than San Juan and suburbs, San Juan and suburbs, and continental U.S.A. As a two-category variable the categories utilized were highland Puerto Rico vs. all other birthplaces. As in the other two instances of multiple categorization of demographic variables, we will be able both to compare the effectiveness of these two categorizations of birthplace in explaining linguistic variation and to sum them into one birthplace variable.

5.34 *Statistical analysis*

The statistical technique utilized in this report is that of analysis of variance via multiple regression analysis. Analysis of variance is a technique designed to answer questions concerning the separate significance as well as the interactional significance of several simultaneous effects. In the context of the present study, analyses of variance can tell us whether context, age, education, or birthplace are separately significant in explaining variation in the production of a particular linguistic variant or whether the interaction between any two of them, e.g. between context and birthplace, has explanatory significance. Multiple regression analysis is a technique designed to answer questions concerning the value of utilizing additional explanatory parameters beyond those already utilized at any given stage in the explanatory process (Bottenberg and Ward 1963; Cohen 1965, 1968a, 1968b). In the context of the present study multiple regression analysis can tell us whether or not certain explanatory parameters (e.g. context plus age) are already so powerful in explaining variation in the production of a particular linguistic variant that it is not necessary or productive to add other explanatory parameters even if the latter, too, are significantly related per se to the variation in question.

5.35 *Hypotheses*

Spanish variables. Our general hypothesis regarding linguistic variation in Puerto Rican Spanish (PRS) in the speech community under study is that it will consist of contextual variation primarily and demographic variation only secondarily. Except for regionally related differences between speakers of highland origin and speakers of coastal origin we consider our subjects as constituting a single speech community. Our subjects have all learned the norms of Spanish communicative competence pretty much in the same way and at the same developmental period of their lives. These norms incorporate contextual variation. Too few of our subjects have had too little exposure to formal, educated Spanish to constitute an educated network of the speech community. Such a network might develop speech norms of its own that could significantly (i.e. raise or lower) the contextual variation norms that exist for the speech community as a whole.

Our general hypothesis is that beyond a highland-coastal difference in a few variables no significant demographic factors will be encountered in explaining any linguistic variation that may exist in Puerto Rican Spanish above and beyond contextual variation. This hypothesis will be tested here against one illustrative Spanish variant where a variant is described as one of the realizations that a variable can assume.

English variables. With respect to linguistic variation in Puerto Rican English in the speech community under study our general hypothesis is that it will consist of demographic variation primarily and contextual variation secondarily (if at all). We do not view our subjects as constituting a unitary English speech community with its own contextual norms of communicative competence in that language. In general, the English-speaking horizons and experiences of most of our subjects are still too limited for contextual varieties of English to have developed (or to have been adopted) and to have been stabilized. On the other hand, there are within the speech community those whose English has been significantly modified by substantial influences stemming from outside the community, such as those that derive from American education in particular and increased time in the continental United States in general. We would expect their English to differ from those with other demographic characteristics who have not had these experiences. We expect these differences between demographic groups to be pervasive in their use of English rather than contextualized along a casualness-carefulness dimension for intra-group purposes. This hypothesis will be tested here against one illustrative English variant.

5.36 *Results*

Spanish variant SpC-0. SpC-0 refers to the dropping of the plural marker *s* when the following word begins with a consonant. An example of this realization is (*los*) *muchacho comen* as opposed to the standard realization (*los*) *muchachos comen* (SpC1) or the common PRS variation (*los*) *muchachoh comen* (CpC-2). This variable (SpC) had a very high number of occurrences, and the realization in question showed considerable contextual variation, accounting for just 17 percent of the cases of CpC in the most formal context but 62 percent in the least formal context (Ma and Herasimchuk 1968). *s* in this morphophonemic environment

was realized quite differently from *s* in other environments. For instance, *s* before
a consonant within a word showed zero realization only 11 percent of the time in
the least formal context. Similarly, *s* marking a plural article preceding a word
beginning with a consonant was realized as zero only 23 percent of the time in the
least formal context. In these environments S-2 or [h] was the preferred realization
81 percent and 70 percent of all times respectively in style A. Thus SpC is definitely a favorable environment for zero realization of *s*, with the further advantage,
for our present purposes, that there was substantial variation in the realization of
SpC-0 across contexts. Under these circumstances, then, we decided to ask whether
other parameters of a directly demographic nature might also be significantly related
to differential production of SpC-0.

If we examine the first column in Table III (labeled r), we will note that only
context, in each of its aspects, correlates significantly with differential use of SpC-0.
The second aspect of context (that which differentiates between word naming and
B + A) correlates with SpC-0 as well (0.423) as do both aspects taken together
(column 3, R = 0.424).

The fact that only the two aspects of context correlate significantly with SpC-0
is corroborated in column 8, where only the two aspects of context yield significant
F ratios. Thus we can safely conclude that in the speech community under study
demographic differences are not significantly related to differential use of SpC-0,
whereas contextual differences are so related. However, if we are to stop our prediction of SpC-0 with context alone, we will have accounted for only 18 percent of
the casual variance (see column 6). If we add sex of speaker to the prediction of
SpC-0, we can account for 24.4 percent of the casual variance. This increase is due
to the fact that there is a slight tendency (column 1: $r = -0.240$) for males to use
SpC-0 more frequently than females.

If we continue to add successive demographic variables, our multiple prediction
of SpC-0 continues to rise (see column 5) and finally reaches the appreciable figure
of 0.602. A multiple correlation of this magnitude accounts for 36.2 percent of the
casual variance in SpC-0, a substantial increase beyond that accounted for by context alone.

Although none of the demographic variables is significantly related to differential
use of SpC-0, sex of speaker approaches such significance. This, however, is due to
the fact that in the speech community under study more women than men are of
highland origin in Puerto Rico. The context by birthplace interaction, therefore,
also approaches significance, which indicates that some birthplace groups show
more contextual variation than do others.

Table IV reveals the mean number of occurrences of SpC-0 in the three different
contexts for our sample as a whole and for two different birthplace subsamples.
This table confirms that the effective contextual difference comes between WN and
the two conversational styles. Table II also confirms the greater contextual sensi-

TABLE III

Analysis of Variance via Multiple Regression Analysis of Puerto Rican Spanish SpC–0 (n = 34)

Source	(1) r	(2) r^2	(3) R	(4) R^2	(5) Cum R^2	(6) Cum R^2	(7) $\triangle R^2$	(8) F_{r^2}	(9) F_{R^2}	(10) $F\triangle R^2$
1. Context: WN vs. B vs. A	0.380*	0.144						5.4*		
2. Context: WN vs. all other	−0.423*	0.180	0.424	0.180	0.424	0.180		7.0*	3.0	
3. Sex	−0.240	0.058	0.240	0.058	0.494	0.244	0.064	2.0	2.0	2.5
4. Age: <25 vs. 25–34 vs. >34	−0.055	0.003						<1		
5. Age: <25 vs. all other	−0.021	0.000	0.156	0.024	0.509	0.259	0.015	<1	<1	<1
6. Educ: <7 yrs. PR vs. 7+ yrs. PR vs. PR and US vs. US only	−0.116	0.013						<1		
7. Educ: all PR vs. other	0.111	0.012						<1		
8. Educ: all USA vs. other	−0.022	0.001	0.193	0.037	0.535	0.286	0.037	<1	<1	<1
9. Birthplace: Highland vs. Coastal vs. San Juan vs. USA	0.063	0.004						<1		
10. Birthplace: Highland vs. all other	−0.163	0.027	0.216	0.047	0.585	0.342	0.056	<1	<1	<1
11. Context × Birthplace	0.239	0.057	0.239		0.602	0.362	0.020	2.0	2.0	<1

* Significant at 0.05 level.

TABLE IV

Contextual Differences in Mean Number of Occurrences of SpC-0, for Total Sample and For Birthplace Groups

Birthplace groups	Contexts			Total
	WN	B	A	
Highland	27.13	57.27	66.58	49.17
Other	30.38	53.29	57.05	56.09
Total	29.13	54.17	59.87	54.39

TABLE V

Analysis of Variance via Multiple Regression Analysis of Puerto Rican English EH–2 (n = 26)

Source	(1) r	(2) r^2	(3) R	(4) R^2	(5) Cum R^2	(6) Cum R^2	(7) $\triangle R^2$	(8) F_{r^2}	(9) F_{R^2}	(10) $F_{\triangle R^2}$
1. Context: WN vs. B vs. A	0.174	0.030						<1		
2. Context WN vs. all other	−0.112	0.013	0.189	0.036	0.189	0.036		<1		
3. Sex	−0.136	0.018	0.136		0.241	0.058	0.022	<1	<1	<1
4. Age: <25 vs. 25–34 vs. >34	−0.524	0.275						9.1†		
5. Age: <25 vs. all other	0.555	0.308	0.556	0.309	0.582	0.338	0.280	10.7†	5.17*	4.2*
6. Educ: <7 yrs. PR vs. 7+ yrs. PR vs. PR and US vs. US only	−0.717	0.514						25.2†		
7. Educ: all PR vs. other	−0.722	0.521						26.1†		
8. Educ: all USA vs. other	0.589	0.347	0.753	0.567	0.785	0.616	0.278	12.8†	9.45†	4.1*
9. Birthplace: Highland vs. Coastal vs. San Juan vs. USA	0.446	0.199						6.0*		
10. Birthplace: Highland vs. all other	−0.309	0.095	0.491	0.241	0.810	0.656	0.040	2.5	3.67	<1
11. Context × Birthplace	0.428	0.183	0.428	0.183	0.815	0.664	0.008	5.4*	5.4*	<1

* Significant at 0.05 level.　　　　† Significant at 0.001 level.

tivity of highland born subjects for whom we find greater average contextual differences than those found for other subjects.

English variant EH-2. EH-2 represents the Standard American English sound [æ], as in *cat, bad, ham*. Two other variants of this EH variable were recognized: EH-1, as in New York City [kɛət, bɛəd, hɛəm], and EH-3, as in accented English 'cah'nt', 'bahd', 'hahm'. EH-2 serves fairly effectively to differentiate accented from native English speakers, as the sound is not available in Spanish phonology. Mastery of this phone seems to imply mastery of a number of other typically English sounds not available in Spanish.

Use of the three variants of EH changed but slightly and irregularly with context (Ma and Herasimchuk 1968), which supports the hypothesis of more or less fixed usage of one sound by any given speaker. EH-2 showed an overall higher incidence of occurrence and, for this reason, was chosen over EH-1 for testing. It is also less ambiguously American; EH-1 can be approximated by the Spanish [ɛ] of [e], so a score of EH-1 does not clearly isolate the the sound as English but rather marks some form or other of dialect realization. For reasons both of numerical frequency and of phonological exclusiveness, then, EH-2 is a very good variant for the statistical testing of relationships between differential use of sounds and the characteristics of their users.

Table V reveals quite a different picture from that shown in Table III. The values in column 1 indicate that neither of the two aspects of context are significantly related to differential use of EH-2. Indeed even when both aspects of context are taken together, it is still the least important multiple predictor of EH-2 except for sex of speaker (column 3). If we utilize context alone, we are able to account for only 3.6 percent of the causal variance pertaining to differential use of EH-2 (column 6). If we add sex of speaker to context, our prediction rises only to 5.8 percent. However, as soon as we consider such demographic variables as age, education, and birthplace the picture changes radically.

Of the three major demographic variables related to differential use of EH-2, the most important is clearly education (column 1). If we combine all three aspects of education, we obtain a multiple correlation of 0.753 (column 3), which itself accounts for 56.7 percent of the causal variance (column 4).

Those of our subjects who were partly or entirely educated in the United States are more likely to utilize EH-2 than those entirely educated in Puerto Rico (note minus correlations in column 1). This relationship between differential use of EH-2 and education is further clarified in Table VI which reveals it to be consistent for each speech context.

TABLE VI

Contextual Differences in Mean Number of Occurrences of EH-2 for total Sample and for Educational Groups

Educational groups	Contexts			Total
	WN	*B*	*A*	
Educated entirely in Puerto Rico	15.75	16.43	19.40	16.46
Educated partially or entirely in USA	60.71	64.43	65.17	63.35
Total	35.79	38.57	51.71	40.20

If education is now combined with the variables that precede it in Table V (context, sex of speaker, and age), then the resulting cumulative multiple correlation with EH-2 rises to 0.785 (column 5), and we have accounted for 61.6 percent of the causal variance in differential use of EH-2 (column 6).

Although neither age nor birthplace are as strongly related to EH-2 as is education, their independent correlations with EH-2 are clearly significant (columns 1 and 8). When all three of them are added to context and sex of speaker, we arrive at a cumulative correlation of 0.810 (column 5), which indicates that we have accounted for 65.6 percent of the causal variance in differential use of EH-2 (column 6).

Although context itself is not significantly related to differential use of EH-2, the interaction between context and birthplace is significantly related to such use. This implies that certain birthplace groups show more contextual variation than do others. Whereas our sample as a whole increasingly uses EH-2 as it proceeds from *WN* (35.79) to *B* (38.57) to *A* (51.71), this variation occurs primarily between *B* and *A* for our highland-born subjects and between *WN* and *B* for other subjects, with the latter using EH-2 more frequently in all contexts.

Incremental prediction of EH-2. Not only are age and education significant variables in accounting for differential use of EH-2 but they are also incrementally significant in this respect. Column 10 of Table V reveals that it pays to add age as a predictor of differential use of EH-2 when one has previously used only context and sex of speaker in this connection. Another way of saying this is that 0.338 (column 6), the cumulative prediction of EH-2 based on three variables (context, sex of speaker, and age), is significantly better than the cumulative prediction based on only the first two (0.058). Similarly, Table V indicates that it pays to add education as well to our prediction of differential use of EH-2, even after context, sex of speaker, and age have been used cumulatively in this connection. The cumulative prediction of EH-2 based upon these four variables (0.616) is significantly greater than that based on the first three (0.338).

The same cannot be said, however, with respect to birthplace or the interaction between birthplace and context. Although it is true that their cumulative addition to the prediction of differential use of EH-2 (after context, sex of speaker, age, and education have been cumulatively utilized for this purpose) does increase the multiple prediction of EH-2 from 0.616 to 0.656 to 0.664, these increases, though welcome, are not statistically significant. Thus, if birthplace were an expensive or difficult measure to obtain, we would be justified in deciding to forego it because it does not produce a significant increment in our efforts to account for differential use of EH-2.

There have recently been several other studies of the importance of demographic factors in accounting for the variability of usage (see e.g. Ellis 1967; Huffine 1966; Jernudd 1969; McCormack 1968). The study just reported gains considerably from the fact that it sought to compare demographic with contextual variation, and to do so in quantitative terms, as well as to do so separately for each of the languages used in a functioning community (rather than by a random sample of speakers).

5.37 *Conclusions*

The foregoing analysis of SpC-0 shows that its variable realization was primarily attributable to contextual-situational variation along a continuum of formality-informality. Whereas demographic factors (not social class in this case since our subjects were so uniformally of the lower class) added to the overall prediction of this variable — as did the interaction between demographic factors and speech context — it is clear that these are of lesser importance than the speech-community-wide norms relating SpC-0 to informality rather than to formality. Scores of other Spanish phonological variables behave in this same way in the Puerto Rican neighborhood under study. As a result we may consider it a single, relatively homogeneous speech network as far as Spanish phonology is concerned, i.e. one in which experiential differences have not resulted in the formation of significantly different groups within the population with substantially unique speech norms of their own. Our Puerto Rican subjects are behaving more like Labov's Lower East Siders than like Geertz's Javanese in this respect.

Just the opposite seems to be true vis-a-vis variability in the realization of English phonology. In connection with EH-2 — and scores of other English variables — no neighborhood-wide contextual-situational variation has as yet developed. Those individuals who have spent larger proportions of their lives in the USA and who have obtained more formal education in the USA have a different English phonology than do their more recently arrived and less American-educated neighbors. Instead of a single set of speech community norms with respect to English phonology there are several different demographic subgroups (social classes if you like) each with their own substantially different English phonologies used consistently in all contexts (by and large). Our Puerto Rican subjects are behaving more like Geertz's Javanese than like Labov's Lower East Siders in this respect. Without common contextual norms vis-a-vis English phonology they are fragmented into more and less advantaged discontinuous strata insofar as English phonology is concerned.

More generally stated in conclusion, the existence of societally shared contextual variation is a sure indication of the existence of a speech community or speech network. Societally shared contextual variation is indicative of social interaction governed by common normative regulations. On the other hand, demographic variation alone is not necessarily indicative of the existence of a speech community or speech network. Indeed, demographic variation in usage is, in and of itself, ambiguous in this very respect. On the one hand, it may be merely indicative of separate experiential groups (e.g. separate castes, social classes, regional origin groups, etc.) that are required to interact in marginal or limited ways. On the other hand, demographic variation may be indicative of relatively pervasive, inflexible and compartmentalized role-relationships within a speech community, such that members of network X always utilize variety x, members of network Y always utilize variety y, etc. Sorenson (1967) has described multilingual speech communities of this kind in the Northwest Amazon region.

The co-occurrences of contextual and demographic variations must not, therefore, be considered a necessary feature of speech communities. It reflects a degree of interaction, a degree of complexity of stratification, and a degree of shared open-network access and repertoire fluidity that are by no means encountered everywhere.

5.4 *Non-proletarians of all Regions, Unite!*

In a relatively open and fluid society there will be few characteristics of lower class speech that are not also present (albeit to a lesser extent) in the speech of the working and lower middle classes. Whether we look to phonological features such as those examined by Labov or to morphological units such as those reported by Fischer (1958) (Fischer studied the variation between *-in'* and *-ing* for the present participle ending, i.e. *runnin'* vs. *running* — and found that the former realization was more common when children were talking to each other than when they were talking to him, more common among boys than among girls and more common among 'typical boys' than among 'model boys'), we find not a clearcut cleavage between the social classes but a difference in rate of realization of particular variants of particular variables for particular contexts. Even the widely publicized distinction between the 'restricted code' of lower class speakers and the 'elaborated code' of middle class speakers (Bernstein 1964, 1966) is of this type, since Bernstein includes the cocktail party and the religious service among the social situations in which restricted codes are realized. Thus, even in the somewhat more stratified British setting the middle class is found to share some of the features of what is considered to be 'typically' lower class speech. Obviously then, 'typicality', if it has any meaning at all in relatively open societies, must refer largely to repertoire *range* rather than primarily to unique features of the repertoire.

This is the most suitable point at which to observe that between Bernstein's view that lower class speech is typically more restricted and Labov's view that lower class speech is typically more informal there is an implied contradiction, if 'restricted' is defined as *more* predictable and informal as *less* predictable. Actually, the contradiction is more apparent than real. In terms of speech repertoire range both investigators would agree that the range of the lower class is typically narrower than that of the middle and upper middle classes. This is what Bernstein is reacting to when he considers lower class speech more restricted and, therefore, more predictable. On the other hand both investigators would certainly agree that the phonological, lexical or grammatical markers of lower class speech more commonly resemble those of informal usage within the larger speech community. However, as far as redundancy of speech is concerned, one must distinguish between predictability *between* varieties and predictability *within* any of them. Lower class usage may well be more predictable or redundant when *between*-variety variation is considered, as Bernstein claims, and yet be more eliptical and incomplete than middle or upper middle class usage when *within*-variety variation is considered. When Joos and others point to the greater redundancy (ritualization, predictability) of frozen and other more formal styles, they are reacting to within-variety rather than between-variety variation. Thus, rather than being in conflict, Bernstein and Labov, taken together, sensitize us additionally to two different but equally important types of variation in the speech behavior of socially variegated speech communities.

Those speech networks with the widest range of experiences, interactions and interests are also those that have the greatest linguistic repertoire range. In many speech communities these networks are likely to be in one or another of the middle classes since some networks within these classes are most likely to maintain direct contact with the lower and working classes below them (in employer-employee, teacher-pupil and other role-relationships), as well as with the upper class above them (in educational, recreational and cultural interactions). However, whereas the repertoire ranges of the upper and lower classes are likely to be equally discontinuous (even if not equally restricted) there is likely to be a very major distinction between them if the larger speech community (the region, the country) is considered. Lower classes tend to be regionally and occupationally separated from each other to a far greater extent than do upper and middle classes (Gumperz 1958). Thus, there may well be several different lower class varieties in a country (depending on regional and on occupational or other specializations), while at the same time upper- and upper-middle class speech may attain greater uniformity and greater regional neutrality. The more advantaged classes travel more frequently, engage in joint enterprises more frequently, control the agencies of language uniformation (schools, media, language planning agencies and government per se). They more quickly arrive at a common standard, at least for formal occasions, than do the lower classes who remain fragmented and parochial. Differences such as these are illustrated in Nancy Tanner's case study of an Indonesian elite group (1967, see Figure 11). Whereas the lower classes speak only their local ethnic language, the middle and upper classes also speak several varieties of Indonesian (including a regionally neutral variety that is least influenced by local characteristics) and the elites speak English and Dutch as well. One can predict that as these elites lose their local ties and affiliations and assume Pan-Indonesian roles, establishing speech communities of their own in Djakarta and in a few other large cities, their need for local languages and for locally influenced and informal Indonesian will lessen and their stylistic variation will proceed, as it has with elites in England, France, Germany, Russia and elsewhere in the world, via contrasts with foreign tongues.

Another way of arriving at the conclusions indicated above concerning the greater discontinuity between the lower class varieties than between upper or middle class varieties in most relatively open societies is to consider the differences referred to

in Figure 12. Here we note that when all other factors are held constant, co-territorial groups of diverse regional origin may frequently be expected to differ most
profoundly linguistically. The lower classes are exactly those whose regional origins
are most diversified in most cities the world over. Indeed, the lower classes are
likely to be more heterogeneous than the upper classes in exactly those factors —
whether they be diversity of origin or diversity of experience — that are associated
with more than peripheral lexical differences between co-territorial populations.
They are far more likely to be regionally, socially, culturally, occupationally and
religiously diverse than are the upper classes whose self-uniformizing tendencies and
capacities have already been mentioned. Indeed, it is only in connection with sex
and age variability that the lower classes are often more homogeneous than the
upper but these generally tend to be associated only with the more marginal linguistic differences.

As a result of the differential experiences and opportunities vis-a-vis uniformation
to which they are exposed, social class differences in relatively open societies have
commonly arrived at the following state of affairs: (a) the middle and upper middle
classes have larger repertoires in language and in social behavior than do the lower
classes; (b) the lower classes tend to remain more diverse — regionally, ethnically,

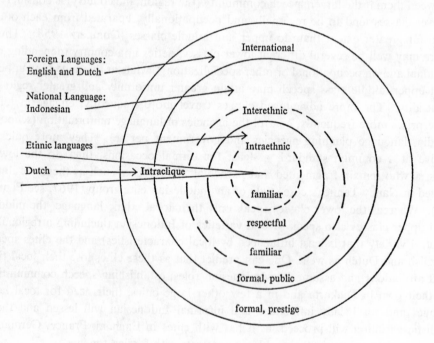

Fig. 11. Functional specialization of codes in Indonesia and among the Case Study Group
(Tanner 1967).

NETWORKS DRAWN FROM DIVERSE**	Lexical Differences	Phonological Differences	Grammatical Differences
EXTRA-REGIONAL			
Origin Groups	++	++	++
RACIAL Groups	++	++	++
Ethnic Groups	++	+	+
OCCUPATIONAL Groups	++	+	+
Religious Groups	+	+	+
AGE Groups	++	—	—
SEX Groups	++	—	—

Fig. 12. Extent of Linguistic Differences and Extent of Socio-Cultural Differences Within Various Kinds of Speech Networks (as judged by Stanford students native to the Lower Peninsula)*.

* Legend: ++ = Substantial differences are judged to exist between categories (e.g., between different age groups) on the diversity parameter in question. + = Moderate differences are judged to exist between categories in the diversity parameter in question. — = Negligible or no differences are judged to exist between categories on the diversity parameter in question.
** Categories are compared on the assumption that all other bases of group-functioning are held constant when networks are selected at the level of any given diversity parameter. Thus, when considering networks drawn from diverse occupational groups, judges were asked to assume that racial, ethnic, religious and other diversity parameters were held constant.

religiously, racially, etc. — than the upper classes and, therefore, there are preserved more and more discontinuous varieties of lower class speech than of upper class speech. These two tendencies are not in conflict with each other, except as social conflict itself may exist and, therefore, come to disturb whatever societal and usage patterns have been stabilized. They are both due to societal differentials in normal social class role ranges and in exposure to the uniformizing institutions of the larger polity.

5.5 Diversification vs. Massification

One further consideration deserves at least brief attention in our review of societal differentiation and language variation; namely, the common view that there is a trend toward overall uniformation, in language and in other social behavior, as industrialization progresses (Bell 1961; Boulding 1963; Hertzler 1965; Hodges 1964). It is undeniable that life in urbanized and industrial countries is in some ways more uniform than is the case in countries where local and regional particularisms remain relatively untouched. Nevertheless, it seems to be erroneous to think of preindustrial rural heterogeneity and industrial urban homogeneity as either accurate or mutually exclusive designations. Both stages of development seem to foster as well as to inhibit certain kinds of uniformation and differentiation in language as well as in other aspects of behavior.

Certainly, the preindustrial rural society is not as internally heterogeneous as is the urban society with its variety of classes, religions, ethnic groups, and interest groups. Thus, the supposedly uniformizing effect of urbanization and industrialization must pertain to inter-regional or inter-urban comparisons rather than to intra-urban or intra-local ones. Nevertheless, the best available evidence indicates that no trend toward inter-regional homogeneity in religion, politics or other generalized behaviors is apparent in the United States (Glenn 1966, 1967), nor are such trends apparent in other countries, such as England, France, Holland or Belgium that have been industrialized or urbanized for the greatest length of time. There the differences in values, tastes, social and political orientations between manual and non-manual workers seems to be as great or greater than they are today in the United States (Hamilton 1965; Bonjean 1966; Schnore 1966; Broom and Glenn 1966, etc.).

At the language level both uniformation and differentiation are found to go on simultaneously, indicative of the fact that the traditional and the modern are frequently *combined* into new constellations rather than *displaced* one by the other. Uniformation pressures seem to be strongest in conjunction with only certain varieties within a speech community's verbal repertoire as well as in conjunction with only some of the interaction networks of that community. The language variety associated with school, government and industry tends to be adopted differentially, the degree of its adoption varying with the degree of interaction in these domains. Not only need such adoption not be displacive (particularly when populations remain in their former places of residence) but — even though the adoption may be quite uniform and official for an entire country — it may remain an entirely passive rather than active component in the repertoire of many interaction networks. Thus, even though television and radio listening are most frequent and prolonged among the lower classes their overt repertoires seem to be little influenced by such viewing or listening.

Finally, it should be recognized that urbanization may also foster certain kinds of differentiation. Whereas the number of different ethnic groups (and, therefore, the number of mutually exclusive language groups) may decline, new social differentiation and new occupational and interest groups normally follow in the wake of industrialization. These latter commonly develop sociolects and specialized usages of their own, thus expanding the repertoires of many speakers. Even the rise of languages of wider communication frequently results in differentiation rather than in uniformation. The spread of English as a second language in the past 50 years has resulted in there being more varieties of English today (including Indian English, East African English, Franglais, Spanglish and others) rather than less. It is, of course, true that certain languages, now as in the past, are in danger of dying out. Nevertheless, others frequently regarded as 'mere varieties' rather than as full-fledged languages, are constantly being 'born' in terms of differentiating themselves within the linguistic repertoires of certain interaction networks, and, at times, of entire speech communities. Modernization is a complex phenomenon. While it depresses the status and decreases the number of speakers of certain varieties (e.g. in recent years: Frisian, Romansch, Landsmal, Yiddish) it raises the status and increases the speakers of others (Macedonian, Neo-Melanesian, Indonesian, Swahili, etc.).

Our own American environment is an atypical example. It reveals the uniformation that results from the rapid urbanization and industrialization of *dislocated* populations. We must not confuse the American experience with that of the rest of the world (Greenberg 1965). In addition, we must come to recognize that American uniformation, whether in speech or in diet, is at times a surface phenomenon. It is an added variety to the repertoires that are still there and that are still substantial if we will but scratch a little deeper (Fishman 1967a).

6. SOCIETAL BILINGUALISM: STABLE AND TRANSITIONAL

Societal bilingualism has been referred to so many times in the previous pages that it is time that we pause to consider it in its own right rather than as a means of illustrating more general sociolinguistic phenomena. The psychological literature on bilingualism is so much more extensive than its sociological counterpart that workers in the former field have often failed to establish contact with those in the latter. It is the purpose of this section to relate these two research traditions to each other by tracing the interaction between their two major constructs: bilingualism (on the part of psychologists and psycholinguists) and diglossia (on the part of sociologists and sociolinguists).

6.1 *Diglossia*

In the few years that have elapsed since Ferguson (1959a) first advanced it, the term diglossia has not only become widely accepted by sociolinguists and sociologists of language, but it has been further extended and refined. Initially it was used in connection with a *society* that recognized two (or more) languages or varieties for intrasocietal communication. The use within a single society of several separate codes (and their stable maintenance rather than the displacement of one by the other over time) was found to be dependent on each code's serving functions distinct from those considered appropriate for the other code. Whereas one set of behaviors, attitudes and values supported, and was expressed in, one language, another set of behaviors, attitudes and values supported and was expressed in the other. Both sets of behaviors, attitudes and values were fully accepted as culturally legitimate and complementary (i.e. non-conflictual) and indeed, little if any conflict between them was possible in view of the functional separation between them. This separation was most often along the lines of a H(igh) language, on the one hand, utilized in conjunction with religion, education and other aspects of High Culture, and a L(ow) language, on the other hand, utilized in conjunction with everyday pursuits of hearth, home and lower work sphere. Ferguson spoke of H as 'superposed' because it is normally learned later and in a more formal setting than L and is, thereby, superposed upon it.

To this original edifice others have added several significant considerations. Gumperz (1961, 1962, 1964a, 1964b, 1966) is primarily responsible for our greater awareness that diglossia exists not only in multilingual societies which officially recognize several 'languages', and not only in societies that utilize vernacular and classical varieties but, also, in societies which employ separate dialects, registers, or *functionally differentiated language varieties of whatever kind*. He has also done the lion's share of the work in providing the conceptual apparatus by means of which investigators of multilingual speech communities seek to discern the societal patterns that govern the use of one variety rather than another, particularly at the level of small group interaction. Fishman (1964, 1965a, 1965c, 1965d, 1965e, 1966a, 1968c), on the other hand, has attempted to trace the maintenance of diglossia as well as its disruption at the national or societal level. In addition he has attempted to relate diglossia to psychologically pertinent considerations such as compound and coordinate bilingualism (1965b). Finally, Kaye (1970) has indicated that diglossia is often a far more flexible, changeable and even ill-defined status, particularly in its linguistic aspects, than has often been presumed. The present section represents an extension and integration of these several previous attempts.

For purposes of simplicity it seems best to represent the possible relationships between bilingualism and diglossia by means of a four-fold table such as shown in Figure 13.

DIGLOSSIA

+   —

BILINGUALISM

+	1. Both diglossia and bilingualism	2. Bilingualism without diglossia
—	3. Diglossia without bilingualism	4. Neither diglossia nor bilingualism

Fig. 13. The Relationships between Bilingualism and Diglossia.

(Joan Rubin 1968)

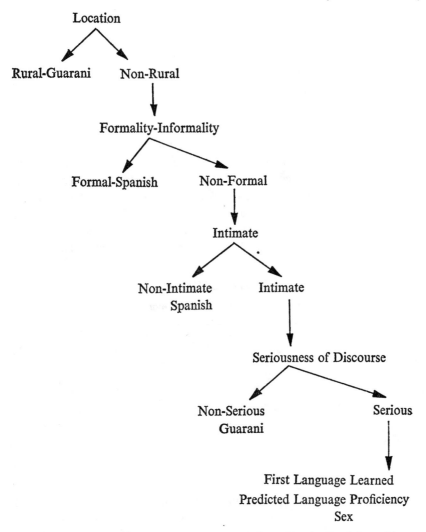

Fig. 14. National Bilingualism in Paraguay. Ordered dimensions in the claims of language in a diglossic society.

6.2   *Speech Communities Characterized by both Diglossia and Bilingualism*

The first quadrant of Figure 13 refers to those speech communities in which both diglossia and bilingualism are widespread. At times such communities comprise an entire nation, but of course this requires extremely widespread (if not all-pervasive) bilingualism and, as a result, there are really few nations that are fully bilingual and diglossic. An approximation to such a nation is Paraguay, where more than half of

JOSHUA A. FISHMAN

the population speaks both Spanish and Guarani (Rubin 1962, 1968). A substantial proportion of the formerly monolingual rural population has added Spanish to its linguistic repertoire in connection with matters of education, religion, government, and High Culture (although in the rural areas social distance or status stressing more generally may still be expressed in Guarani). On the other hand, the vast majority of city dwellers (being relatively new from the country) maintain Guarani for matters of intimacy and primary group solidarity, even in the midst of their more newly acquired Spanish urbanity (see Figure 14). Note that Guarani is not an 'official' language (i.e. recognized and utilized for purposes of government, formal education, the courts, etc.) in Paraguay, although it was finally recognized as a 'national language' at the 1967 constitutional convention. It is not uncommon for the H variety alone to be recognized as 'official' in diglossic settings without this fact threatening in the acceptance or the stability of the L variety within the speech community. However, the existence of a particular 'official' or 'main' language should not divert the investigator from recognizing the fact of widespread and stable multilingualism at the levels of societal and interpersonal functioning (see Table VII).

TABLE VII

Linguistic Unity and Diversity, by World Region

Region	No. of Countries by Percent of Population Speaking Main Language									Total
	90–100	80–89	70–79	60–69	50–59	40–49	30–39	20–29	10–19	10–100%
Europe	17	4	2	2	2	–	–	–	–	27
East and South Asia	5	3	4	3	1	4	–	1	–	21
Oceania a	2	–	–	–	–	–	–	–	–	2
Middle East and Northern Africa	8	6	2	3	1	2	–	–	–	22
Tropical and Southern Africa	3	–	–	2	5	8	7	5	3	33
The Americas	15	6	–	–	2	2	1	–	–	26
World Total	50	19	8	10	11	16	8	6	3	131

Source: Table 1 (Rustow, D. 1967).
a Not including New Guinea, for which no breakdown by individual languages was available.

Below the level of nationwide functioning there are many more examples of stable diglossia co-occurring with widespread bilingualism. The Swiss-German cantons may be mentioned since their entire population of school age and older alternates between High German (H) and Swiss German (L), each with its own firmly established and highly valued functions (Ferguson 1959a; U. Weinreich 1951, 1953a). Hughes (1970) has demonstrated how English (H) and French (L) diglossia-and-bilingualism are peripheral and external in many Montreal agencies and businesses in which clients (or customers) and management (or owners) must interact although coming from different origins. On the other hand, in plants (where no customers/ clients are present) the communication between workers and management reveals bilingualism-and-diglossia of a hierarchical and internal nature. Traditional (pre- World War I) Eastern European Jewish males communicated with each other in Hebrew (H) and Yiddish (L). In more recent days many of their descendants have continued to do so in various countries of resettlement, even while adding to their repertoire a Western language (notably English) in certain domains of *intra-group* communication as well as for broader *intergroup* contacts (Fishman 1965a, 1965e; U. Weinreich 1953b; M. Weinreich 1953). This development differs significantly from the traditional Eastern European Jewish pattern in which males whose occu- pational activities brought them into regular contact with various strata of the non- Jewish coterritorial population utilized one or more coterritorial languages (which involved H and L varieties of their own, such as Russian, German or Polish on the one hand, and Ukrainian, Byelorussian or 'Baltic' varieties, on the other), but did so primarily for *intergroup* purposes. A similar example is that of upper and upper middle class males throughout the Arabic world who use classical (Koranic) Arabic for traditional Islamic studies, vernacular (Egyptian, Syrian, Lebanese, Iraqui, etc.) Arabic for informal conversation, and, not infrequently, also a Western language (French or English, most usually) for purposes of *intragroup* scientific or techno- logical communication (Blanc 1964; Ferguson 1959a; Nader 1962).

All of the foregoing examples have in common the existence of a fairly large and complex speech community such that its members have available to them both a range of *compartmentalized* roles as well as ready *access* to these roles. If the *role repertoires* of these speech communities were of lesser range, then their *linguistic repertoires* would also be(come) more restricted in range, with the result that one or more separate languages or varieties would be(come) superfluous. In addition, were the roles not compartmentalized, i.e. were they not *kept separate* by dint of association with quite separate (though complementary) values, domains of activity and everyday situations, one language (or variety) would displace the other as role and value distinctions merged and became blurred. Finally, were widespread access not available to the range of compartmentalized roles (and compartmentalized lan- guages or varieties) then the bilingual population would be a small, privileged caste or class (as it is or was throughout most of traditional India or China) rather than a broadly based population segment.

These observations must lead us to the conclusion that many modern speech communities that are normally thought of as monolingual are, rather, marked by both diglossia and bilingualism, if their several registers are viewed as separate varieties of languages in the same sense as the examples listed above. Wherever speech communities exist whose speakers engage in a considerable range of roles (and this is coming to be the case for all but the extremely upper and lower levels of complex societies), wherever the access to several roles is encouraged or facilitated by powerful social institutions and processes, and finally, wherever the roles are clearly differentiated (in terms of when, where and with whom they are felt to be appropriate), both diglossia and bilingualism may be said to exist. The benefit of this approach to the topic at hand is that it provides a single theoretical framework for viewing bilingual speech communities and speech communities whose linguistic diversity is realized through varieties not (yet) recognized as constituting separate 'languages'. Thus, rather than becoming fewer in modern times, the number of speech communities characterized by diglossia and the widespread command of diversified linguistic repertoires has increased greatly as a consequence of modernization and growing social complexity (Fishman 1966b). In such communities each generation begins anew on a monolingual or restricted repertoire base of hearth and home and must be rendered bilingual or provided with a fuller repertoire by the formal institutions of education, religion, government or work sphere. In diglossic-bilingual speech communities children do *not* attain their full repertoires at home or in their neighborhood playgroups. Indeed, those who most commonly remain at home or in the home neighborhood (the pre-school young and the post-work old) are most likely to be functionally monolingual, as Lieberson's tables on French-English bilingualism in Montreal amply reveal (see Table VIII). Once established, and in the absence of rapid and extensive social change, bilingualism under circumstances of diglossia becomes an ingredient in the situational and metaphorical switching patterns available for the purposes of intra-communal communicative appropriateness. Many conversations and utterances demonstrably 'mean something else', depending on the language in which they are expressed (Table IX) even when all other factors are kept constant (Kimple et al. 1969).

6.3 *Diglossia without Bilingualism*

Departing from the co-occurrence of bilingualism and diglossia we come first to polities in which diglossia obtains whereas bilingualism is generally absent (quadrant 3). Here we find two or more speech communities united politically, religiously and/or economically into a single functioning unit notwithstanding the socio-cultural cleavages that separate them. At the level of this larger (but not always voluntary) unity, two or more languages or varieties must be recognized as obtaining. However one (or both) of the speech communities involved is (are) marked by relatively impermiable group boundaries such that for 'outsiders' (and this may well mean those not born into the speech community, i.e. an emphasis on ascribed rather than on achieved status) role access and linguistic access are severely restricted. At the same time linguistic repertoires in one or both groups are limited due to role specialization.

Examples of such situations are not hard to find (see, e.g. the many instances listed by Kloss 1966a). Pre-World War I European elites often stood in this relation-

Table VIII

Percentage Bilingual, by Age and Sex, Montreal Area, 1931–61 (Lieberson 1965)

	Males					Females				
	Montreal-Verdun		Montreal-Outremont-Verdun			Montreal-Verdun		Montreal-Outremont-Verdun		
Age	1931 (1)	1941 (2)	1941 (3)	1951 (4)	1961 (5)	1931 (6)	1941 (7)	1941 (8)	1951 (9)	1961 (10)
0- 4	4.1	5.7	5.7	3.3	2.5	4.0	5.6	5.7	3.4	2.5
5- 9	18.2	11.3	11.5	9.7	9.9	18.0	11.5	11.8	9.7	9.6
10-14	43.4	22.2	22.6	20.5	22.4	41.4	21.9	22.3	20.1	21.9
15-19	62.4	51.4	51.7	50.6	49.6	54.7	43.1	43.5	44.5	46.7
20-24	67.2	67.1	67.2	64.9	59.4	53.3	51.5	51.7	48.2	44.4
25-34	61.9	68.8	68.8	63.8	59.7	49.0	47.8	48.1	47.8	41.1
35-44	62.2	63.6	63.7	68.1	65.3	44.5	40.9	41.2	45.2	45.5
45-54	59.3	60.3	60.3	62.7	63.6	41.6	35.6	36.0	37.4	42.6
55-64	57.4	53.7	53.8	57.3	57.2	37.1	31.2	31.6	30.8	34.5
65-69	56.4	49.4	49.6	49.7	52.0	34.3	28.0	28.5	26.5	28.5
70+	51.2	42.9	43.3	42.2	44.0	31.2	24.4	24.7	23.5	24.5

Socio-economic class groups
SEC 0-1 lower class
2-4 working class
5-7} lower middle class
7-8} upper middle class
9 upper middle class

Socio-economic class groups
SEC 0} lower class
1}
2-3} working class
4-5}
6-8 lower middle class
9 upper middle class

TABLE IX

The Interpretation of Language Switching
(English-Spanish) given both Bilingualism and Diglossia (Kimple et al., 1969)

A

Analysis of variance for items requiring subjective judgment: conversation 1
(Boy calls girl for date)

Item no.	Source	df	MS	F
10 (Length of family's residence in N.Y.C.)	Treatments	3	4.13	3.50*
	Within	45	1.75	
11 (Length of boy's residence in N.Y.C.)	Treatments	3	11.70	6.69**
	Within	45	1.18	
12 (Kind of job held by girl's father)	Treatments	3	2.46	3.97*
	Within	45	.62	
13	Treatments	3	.17	.23
	Within	45	.73	
14	Treatments	3	.18	.51
	Within	45	.35	
15	Treatments	3	.32	.76
	Within	45	.42	
16 (Naturalness of conversation between boy + girl)	Treatments	3	2.32	7.03**
	Within	45	.33	
17 (Naturalness of conversation between mother + girl)	Treatments	3	2.19	3.91*
	Within	45	.56	
18	Treatments	3	.67	1.45
	Within	45	.46	

* $p < .05$
** $p < .01$

B

Analysis of variance for items requiring subjective judgment: conversation 2
(Invitation to stay for dinner)

Item no.	Source	df	MS	F
9	Treatments	3	.37	.73
	Within	45	.51	
10	Treatments	3	3.33	1.29
	Within	45	2.58	
11	Treatments	3	1.42	1.89
	Within	45	.75	
12	Treatments	3	.06	.65
	Within	45	.93	
13 (Naturalness of conversation between mother + guest)	Treatments	3	2.97	5.82**
	Within	45	.51	
14 (Naturalness of conversation between boy + guest)	Treatments	3	3.96	8.25**
	Within	45	.48	

** $p < .01$

ship with their countrymen, the elites speaking French or some other fashionable H tongue for their *intra-group* purposes (at various times and in various places: Danish, Salish, Provençal, Russian, etc.) and the masses speaking another, not necessarily linguistically related, language for their intra-group purposes. Since the majority of elites and the majority of the masses never interacted with one another they *did not form a single speech community* (i.e. their linguistic repertoires were discontinuous) and their inter-communications were via translators or interpreters (a certain sign of *intra-group* monolingualism). Since the majority of the elites and the majority of the masses led lives characterized by extremely narrow role repertoires their linguistic repertoires too were too narrow to permit widespread societal bilingualism to develop. Nevertheless, the body politic in all of its economic and national manifestations tied these two groups together into a 'unity' that revealed an upper and a lower class, each with a language appropriate to its own restricted concerns. Some have suggested that the modicum of direct interaction that does occur between servants and masters who differ in mother tongue contributes to bringing into being the marginal languages (pidgins) for which settings are known (Grimshaw 1972).

Thus, the existence of national diglossia does *not* imply widespread bilingualism amongst rural or recently urbanized African groups (as distinguished from somewhat more Westernized populations in those settings); nor amongst most lower caste

Hindus, as distinguished from their more fortunate compatriots the Brahmins, nor amongst most lower class French-Canadians, as distinguished from their upper and upper-middle class city cousins, etc. In general, this pattern is characteristic of polities that are economically underdeveloped and unmobilized, combining groups that are locked into opposite extremes of the social spectrum and, therefore, groups that operate within extremely restricted and discontinuous linguistic repertoires (Friederich 1962; Fishman 1969a; Pool 1969). Obviously such polities are bound to experience language problems as their social patterns alter as a result of industrialization, widespread literacy and education, democratization, and modernization more generally. Since few polities that exhibit diglossia without bilingualism developed out of prior socio-cultural consensus or unity, rapid educational, political or economic development experienced by their disadvantaged groups or classes is very likely to lead to demands for secessionism or for equality for their submerged language(s). The linguistic states of Eastern Europe and India, and the language problems of Wales and Belgium stem from origins such as these. This is the pattern of development that may yet convulse many African and Asian nations if their de-ethnicized and Westernized elites continue to fail to foster widespread and stable bilingual speech communities that incorporate the masses and that recognize both the official language(s) of wider communication and the local languages of hearth and home (Figure 15).

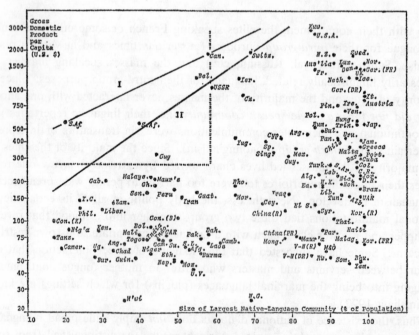

Fig. 15. Gross Domestic Product per Capita (U.S.$) and Size of Largest Native Language Community (% of Population), c. 1962 (Pool 1969).

6.4   *Bilingualism without Diglossia*

We turn next to those situations in which bilingualism obtains whereas diglossia is generally absent (quadrant 2). Here we see more clearly than before that bilingualism is essentially a characterization of *individual* linguistic versatility whereas *diglossia is a characterization of the social allocation of functions* to different languages or varieties. Under what circumstances do bilinguals function without the benefit of a well understood and widely accepted social consensus as to *which* language is to be used between which interlocutors, for communication concerning *what* topics or for *what* purposes? Under what circumstances do the varieties or languages involved lack well defined or protected separate functions? Briefly put, these are circumstances of rapid social change, of great social unrest, of widespread abandonment of prior norms before the consolidation of new ones. Children typically become bilingual at a very early age, when they are still largely confined to home and neighborhood, since their elders (both adult and school age) carry into the domains of intimacy a language learned outside its confines. Formal institutions tend to render individuals increasingly monolingual in a language other than that of hearth and home. Ultimately, the language of school and government replaces the language of home and neighborhood, precisely because it comes to provide status in the latter domains as well as in the former, due to the extensive social change to which home and neighborhood have been exposed (see section 7, below).

Many studies of bilingualism and intelligence or of bilingualism and school achievement have been conducted within the context of bilingualism without diglossia (for a review see Macnamara 1966), often without sufficient understanding on the part of the investigators that this was but one of several possible contexts for the study of bilingualism (Corpas 1969; Metraux 1965). As a result many of the purported 'disadvantages' of bilingualism have been falsely generalized to the phenomenon at large rather than related to the absence or presence of social patterns that reach substantially beyond bilingualism (Fishman 1965b, 1966a).

The history of industrialization in the Western world (as well as in those parts of Africa and Asia which have experienced industrialization under Western 'auspices') is such that the means (capital, plant, organization) of production have often been controlled by one speech community while the productive manpower was drawn from another (Deutsch 1966). Initially, both speech communities may have maintained their separate diglossia-with-bilingualism patterns or, alternatively, that of an overarching diglossia without bilingualism. In either case, the needs as well as the consequences of rapid and massive industrialization and urbanization were frequently such that members of the speech community providing productive manpower rapidly abandoned their traditional socio-cultural patterns and learned (or were taught) the language associated with the means of production much earlier than their absorption into the socio-cultural patterns and privileges to which that language pertained. In response to this imbalance some react(ed) by further stressing the advantages of the newly gained language of education and industry while others react(ed) by seeking to replace the latter by an elaborated version of their own largely pre-industrial, pre-urban, pre-mobilization tongue (Fishman 1968c).

Under circumstances such as these no well established, socially recognized and protected functional differentiation of languages obtains in many speech communities of the lower and lower middle classes. Dislocated immigrants and their children (for whom a separate 'political solution' is seldom possible) are particularly inclined to use their mother tongue and other tongue for intra-group communication in *seemingly* random fashion (Fishman, Cooper and Ma 1968; Nahirny and Fishman 1965; Herman 1961). Since the formerly separate roles of the home domain, the school domain and the work domain are all disturbed by the massive dislocation of values and norms that result from simultaneous immigration and industrialization, the language of work (and of the school) comes to be used at home. As role compartmentalization and value complementarity decrease under the impact of foreign models and massive change, the linguistic repertoire also becomes less compartmentalized. Languages and varieties formerly kept apart come to influence each other phonetically, lexically, semantically and even grammatically much more than before. Instead of two (or more) carefully separated languages each under the eye of caretaker groups of teachers, preachers and writers, several intervening varieties may obtain differing in degree of interpenetration. Under these circumstances the languages of immigrants may come to be ridiculed as 'debased' and 'broken' while at the same time their standard varieties are given no language maintenance support.

Thus, bilingualism without diglossia tends to be transitional both in terms of the linguistic repertoires of speech communities as well as in terms of the speech varieties involved per se. Without separate though complementary norms and values to establish and maintain functional separation of the speech varieties, that language or variety which is fortunate enough to be associated with the predominant drift of social forces tends to displace the other(s). Furthermore, pidginization (the crystallization of new fusion languages or varieties) is likely to set in when members of the 'work force' are so dislocated as not to be able to maintain or develop significantly compartmentalized, limited access roles (in which they might be able to safeguard a stable mother tongue variety), on the one hand, and when social change stops short of permitting them to interact sufficiently with those members of the 'power class' who might serve as standard other-tongue models, on the other hand.

6.5 *Neither Diglossia nor Bilingualism*

Only very small, isolated and undifferentiated speech communities may be said to reveal neither diglossia nor bilingualism (Gumperz 1962; Fishman 1965c). Given little role differentiation or compartmentalization and frequent face-to-face interaction between all members of the speech community, no fully differentiated registers

or varieties may establish themselves. Given self-sufficiency, no regular or significant contacts with other speech communities may be maintained. Nevertheless,
such groups — be they bands or clans — are easier to hypothesize than to find
(Owens 1965; Sorensen 1967). All speech communities seem to have certain ceremonies or pursuits to which access is limited, if only on an age basis. Thus, all
linguistic repertoires contain certain terms that are unknown to certain members of
the speech community, and certain terms that are used differently by different subsets of speakers. In addition, metaphorical switching for purposes of emphasis, humor,
satire, or criticism must be available in some form even in relatively undifferentiated
communities. Finally, such factors as exogamy, warfare, expansion of population,
economic growth and contact with others all lead to internal diversification and,
consequently, to repertoire diversification. Such diversification is the beginning
of bilingualism. Its societal normification is the hallmark of diglossia. Quadrant
four tends to be self-liquidating.

Many efforts are now underway to bring to pass a rapprochement between psychological, linguistic and sociological work on bilingualism (Fishman and Terry
1969). The student of bilingualism, most particularly the student of bilingualism
in the context of social issues and social change, should benefit from an awareness
of the various possible relationships between individual bilingualism and societal
diglossia illustrated in this section. One of the fruits of such awareness will be that
problems of transition and dislocation will not be mistaken for the entire gamut of
societal bilingualism.

7. LANGUAGE MAINTENANCE AND LANGUAGE SHIFT

Modern history reveals at least five major instances of language shift, i.e. where
huge populations adopted a new language or variety into their repertoires, whether
or not at the same time they also gave up a language or variety that they had previously used. The instances referred to are (a) the vernacularization of European
governmental, technical, educational, cultural activity, (b) the Anglification/Hispa-
nization of the populations of North/South America respectively (Table X), (c) the
adoption of English and French as languages of elitist wider communication
throughout much of the world, but particularly so in Africa and Asia, (d) the
Russification of Soviet-controlled populations, and most recently (e) the growing
displacement of imported languages of wider communication and the parallel vernacularization of governmental, technical, educational and cultural efforts in many
parts of Africa and Asia. Having previously noted (section 5) that divergence and
differentiation of the verbal repertoire are reflections of societal distance and segmentation, we must now point out that the socio-cultural changes that carry with
them changes in verbal repertoires are themselves differentially associated with the
various speech communities and speech networks of any polity. As a result, not
only are the verbal repertoires of communities and networks that experience the

TABLE X

1940–1960 Totals for 23 Non-English Mother Tongues in the USA
(Fishman 1966c)

Language	1940 Total	1960 Total	Total Change	
			n	%
Norwegian	658,220	321,774	—336,446	—51.1
Swedish	830,900	415,597	—415,303	—50.0
Danish	226,740	147,619	—79,121	—65.1
Dutch/Flemish	289,580	321,613	+32,033	+11.1
French	1,412,060	1,043,220	—368,840	—26.1
German	4,949,780	3,145,772	—1,804,008	—36.4
Polish	2,416,320	2,184,936	—231,384	—9.6
Czech	520,440	217,771	—302,669	—58.2
Slovak	484,360	260,000	—224,360	—46.3
Hungarian	453,000	404,114	—48,886	—10.8
Serbo-Croatian	153,080	184,094	+31,014	+20.3
Slovenian	178,640	67,108	—111,532	—62.4
Russian	585,080	460,834	—124,246	—21.2
Ukrainian	83,600	252,974	+169,374	+202.6
Lithuanian	272,680	206,043	—66,637	—24.4
Finnish	230,420	110,168	—120,252	—52.2
Rumanian	65,520	58,019	—7,501	—11.4
Yiddish	1,751,100	964,605	—786,495	—44.9
Greek	273,520	292,031	+18,511	+6.8
Italian	3,766,820	3,673,141	—93,679	—2.5
Spanish	1,861,400	3,335,961	+1,474,561	+79.2
Portuguese	215,660	181,109	—34,551	—16.0
Arabic	107,420	103,908	—3,512	—3.3
Total	21,786,540	18,352,351	—3,434,189	—15.8

In 1940 the numerically strongest mother tongues in the United States were German, Italian, Polish, Spanish, Yiddish, and French, in that order. Each of these languages was claimed by approximately a million and a half or more individuals. In 1960 these same languages remained the 'big six' although their order had changed to Italian, Spanish, German, Polish, French, and Yiddish. Among them, only Spanish registered gains (and substantial gains at that) in this 20-year interval. The losses among the 'big six' varied from a low of 2.5% for Italian to a high of 44.9% for Yiddish. The only other languages to gain in overall number of claimants during this period (disregarding the generational distribution of gains) were Ukrainian, Serbo-Croatian, 'Dutch'/Flemish, and Greek. The greatest gain of all was that of Ukrainian (202.6%!). Most mother tongues, including five of the 'big six', suffered substantial losses during this period, the sharpest being that of Danish (65.1%). All in all, the 23 non-English mother tongues for which a 1940-1960 comparison is possible lost approximately one-sixth of their claimants during this interval. Yet the total number of claimants of non-English mother tongues in the United States is still quite substantial, encompassing nearly 11% of the total 1960 population (and an appreciably higher proportion of the white population).[6]

[6]   The 1940 and 1960 totals shown in Table X must not be taken as the totals for *all* non-English mother tongue claimants in those years. Figures for Armenian were reported in 1940 but not in 1960. Figures for Chinese and Japanese were reported in 1960 but not in 1940. Total figures for 'All other' languages were reported in both years. None of these inconsistent or non-specific listings are included in Table X. Adding in these figures, as well as the necessary generational estimates based upon them, the two totals would become 1940: 22,036,240; 1960: 19,381,786.

greatest socio-cultural change the most likely to be altered, but the repertoires of those who gain most in economic, political or other socio-cultural status are the most likely to be adopted or copied by others who see opportunities for desirable changes in their own status by so doing.

The study of language maintenance and language shift focuses upon cell 2 of Figure 13 above and is basically concerned with the relationship between degree of change (or degree of stability) in language usage patterns, on the one hand, and ongoing psychological, cultural or social processes, on the other hand, in populations that utilize more than one speech variety for intra-group or for inter-group purposes. That languages (or language varieties) *sometimes* displace each other, among *some* speakers, particularly in *certain* interpersonal or system-wide interactions, has long aroused curiosity and comment. However, it is only in quite recent years that this topic has been recognized as a field of systematic inquiry among professional students of language behavior. It is suggested here that the three major topical subdivisions of this field are: (a) habitual language use at more than one point in time or space; (b) antecedent, concurrent or consequent psychological, social and cultural processes and their relationship to stability or change in habitual language use; and (c) behavior toward language, including directed maintenance or shift efforts. It is the purpose of this section to discuss each of these three topical subdivisions briefly, to indicate their current stage of development, and to offer suggestions for their further development.

7.1 *Habitual Language Use at More Than One Point in Time*

The basic datum of the study of language maintenance and language shift is that some demonstrable change has occurred in the pattern of habitual language use. The consequences that are of *primary* concern to the student of language maintenance and language shift are *not* interference phenomena per se but, rather, degrees of maintenance or displacement in conjunction with several sources and domains of variance in language behavior. Thus, the very first requirement of inquiry in this field is a conceptualization of variance in language behavior whereby language maintenance and language displacement can be accurately and appropriately ascertained. In the course of their labors linguists, psychologists, anthropologists and other specialists have developed a large number of quantitative and qualitative characterizations of variance in language behavior. By choosing from among them and adding to them judiciously, it may be possible to arrive at provocative insights into more sociolinguistic concerns as well. Whether those aspects of variance in language behavior that have, in the past, been conceived of as *qualitative* can be rendered ultimately commensurable with those that have more frequently been considered *quantitative* is a topic to which we will return, after first considering the two aspects separately.

7.11 *Degree of bilingualism*

For the student of language maintenance and language shift the *quantification* of habitual language use is related to the much older question of ascertaining *degree of bilingualism*. This question, in turn, has been tackled by a great number of investigators from different disciplines, each being concerned with a somewhat different nuance. Linguists have been most concerned with the analysis of bilingualism from the point of view of *switching or interference*. The measures that they have proposed from their disciplinary point of departure distinguish between phonetic, lexical and grammatical proficiency and intactness (Mackay 1962). At the other extreme stand educators who are concerned with bilingualism in terms of *total performance contrasts* in very complex contexts such as the school or even the society (Manuel 1963). Psychologists have usually studied degrees of bilingualism in terms of speed, automaticity, or habit strength (Macnamara 1966). Sociologists have relied upon relative frequencies of use in *different settings* (Hayden and Fishman 1964; Hofman 1966a, 1966b; Nahirny and Fishman 1965). Thus, since a great number of different kinds of bilingualism scores or quotients are already available, the sociolinguistically oriented student of language maintenance and language shift must decide which, if any, are appropriate to his own concerns. Since the study of this topic cannot be reduced to or equated with the concerns of any particular discipline it seems highly likely that a *combination or organization of approaches* to the measurement and description of bilingualism will uniquely characterize the study of language maintenance and language shift.

7.12 *The need for a combination of interrelated measures*

It would seem that the linguist's interest in itemizing examples of interference and switching introduces an outside criterion into the study of language maintenance and language shift which may not at all correspond to that utilized by speech communities or speech networks under study. The linguist's distinction between what is English and what is French and the distinction made by English-French bilinguals may differ so widely that the linguist's *conclusions* about the drift or shift, based upon interference and switch data, may be seriously in error.

However, even where a linguist is obviously interested only in a carefully delimited question about the relative frequency of a particular instance or class of interferences or shifts, it is clear that it may be far easier to answer this question in some cases than in others (e.g. it may be easier to answer in connection with encoding than in connection with inner speech; it may be easier to answer in connection with writing than in connection with speaking; it may be easier to answer in connection with formal and technical communication than in connection with intimate communication, for the 'density', stability and clarity of interference and switching varies for the same individual from occasion to occasion and from situation to situation. Although interference and switching are lawful behaviors, there are advanced cases of language shift in which even linguists will be hard pressed to determine the answer to 'which language is being used?', particularly if a single supra-level answer is required.

Similarly, concern with relative proficiency, relative ease and automaticity, and relative frequency of language use in a contact setting are also not necessarily indicative of overall language maintenance or shift. Conclusions based on such measures may be particularly far off the mark in bilingualism-plus-diglossia settings in which most speakers use both languages equally well (correctly), effortlessly and frequently but differ *primarily* in connection with the topics, persons, and places (or, more generally, the *situations* and situation types or domains) in which these languages are used. Thus, in conclusion, the contribution that the student of language maintenance and language shift can make to the measurement of bilingualism, is precisely his awareness (a) that *various* measures are needed if the social realities of multilingual settings are to be reflected and (b) that the measures *can be organized* in terms of relatively *general variance considerations*. Of the many approaches to variance in language use that have been suggested the following is both simple enough for easy presentation as well as sufficiently involved to imply that even greater complexity exists not too far below the surface.

7.13 *Media variance: written, read and spoken language*

Degree of maintenance and shift may be quite different in these very different media. Where literacy has been attained prior to interaction with an 'other tongue', reading and writing in the mother tongue may resist shift longer than speaking. Where literacy is attained subsequent to (or as a result of) such interaction the reverse may hold true (Fishman 1965e). More generally, the linguist's disinclination to be concerned with the written language is a luxury that cannot be afforded in the study of language maintenance and language shift, where the contrasts involved are so frequently between languages that vary greatly in the extent to which they have literacy or other 'higher' functions for the speech networks under study.

7.14 *Overtness variance*

Degree of maintenance and shift may be quite different in connection with *inner speech* (in which ego is both source and target), *comprehension* (decoding, in which ego is target), and *production* (encoding, in which ego is the source). Where language shift is unconscious or resisted, inner speech may be most resistant to interference, switching and disuse of the mother tongue. Where language shift is conscious and desired, this may less frequently be the case (Fishman 1965f).

7.141 *Location of bilingualism: The domains of language behavior.* The *qualitative* aspects of bilingualism are most easily illustrated in connection with the *location* of language maintenance and language shift in terms of *domains* of language behavior. What is of concern to us here is the most parsimonious and fruitful designation of the societally or institutionally clusterable occasions in which one language (variant, dialect, style, etc.) is habitually employed and normatively expected rather than (or in addition to) another.

7.142 *The domains of language behavior and the compound-coordinate distinction.* If the concept of *domains of language behavior* proves to be as fruitful and as manageable a one as seems to be likely on the basis of recent empirical evidence it may also yield beneficial results in connection with other areas of research on bilingualism, e.g. in connection with the distinction between *coordinate* and *compound* bilingualism (Ervin and Osgood 1954 : 140). The latter distinction arose out of an awareness (mentioned by several investigators over the years) that there are 'at least two major types of bilingual functioning', one (the compound type) being 'characteristic of bilingualism acquired by a child who grows up in a home where two languages are spoken more or less interchangeably by the same people and in the same situations' and the other (the coordinate) being 'typical of the "true" bilingual, who has learned to speak one language with his parents, for example, and the other language in school and at work. The total situations, both external and emotional, and the total behaviors occurring when one language is being used will differ from those occurring with the other.' From our previous discussion of domains of language behavior it is clear that these two types of bilingual functioning (more accurately put, two extremes of a continuum of psycho-neurological organization) have been distinguished on the bases of some awareness, however rudimentary, that *bilinguals vary with respect to the number and overlap of domains in which they habitually employ each of their languages.* However, this is true not only initially, in the acquisition of bilingualism (with which the compound-coordinate distinction is primarily concerned) but also subsequently, *throughout* life. Initially coordinate bilinguals may become exposed to widespread bilingualism in which both languages are used rather freely over a larger set of overlapping domains. Similarly, compound bilinguals may become exposed to a more restrictive or dichotomized environment in which each language is assigned to very specific and non-overlapping domains.

Going one step further it appears that the domain concept may facilitate a number of worthwhile contributions to the understanding of the compound-coordinate distinction in conjunction with language maintenance and language shift per se. Thus, domain analysis may help organize and clarify the previously unstructured awareness that language maintenance and language shift proceed quite unevenly across the several sources and domains of variance in habitual language use. Certain domains may well appear to be more maintenance-prone than others (e.g. the family domain in comparison to the occupational domain) across all multilingual settings characterized by urbanization and economic development, regardless of whether immigrant-host or co-indigenous populations are involved. Under the impact of these same socio-cultural processes other domains (e.g. religion) may be found to be strongly maintenance oriented during the early stages of interaction and strongly shift oriented once an authoritative decision is reached that their organizational base can be better secured via shift. Certain interactions between domains and other sources of variance may remain protective of contextually 'dis-

advantaged' languages (e.g. family domain: internal speech, husband-wife role relations), even when language shift has advanced so far that a given domain as such
has been engulfed. On the other hand, if a strict domain separation becomes institutionalized such that each language is associated with a number of important but
distinct domains, bilingualism may well become both universal and stabilized even
though an entire population consists of bilinguals interacting with other bilinguals.
Finally, in conjunction with language maintenance and language shift among American immigrant groups, the interaction between domain analysis and the compound-
coordinate distinction may prove to be particularly edifying.

As suggested by Figure 16, most late 19th and early 20th century immigrants to

BILINGUAL FUNCTIONING TYPE	DOMAIN OVERLAP TYPE	
	Overlapping Domains	Non-Overlapping Domains
Compound ('Interdependent' or fused)	2. Second Stage: More im-migrants know more English and therefore can speak to each other either in mother tongue or in English (still mediated by the mother tongue) in several domains of behavior. Increased interference.	1. Initial Stage: The immi-grant learns English via his mother tongue. English is used only in those few do-mains (work sphere, govern-mental sphere) in which mother tongue cannot be used. Minimal interference. Only a few immigrants know a little English.
Coordinate ('Independent')	3. Third Stage: The lan-guages function indepedently of each other. The number of bilinguals is at its maxi-mum. Domain overlap is at its maximum. The second generation during childhood. Stabilized interference.	4. Fourth Stage: English has displaced the mother tongue from all but the most private or restricted domains. Interference de-clines. In most cases both languages function indepen-dently; in others the mother tongue is mediated by Eng-lish (reverse direction of Stage 1, but same type).

Fig. 16. Type of bilingual functioning and domain overlap during successive stages of immigrant acculturation.

America from Eastern and Southern Europe began as compound bilinguals, with English assigned to quite specific and restricted domains. With the passage of time (involving increased interaction with English-speaking Americans, social mobility, and acculturation with respect to other-than-language behaviors as well) their bilingualism became characterized, first, by far greater domain overlap (and by far greater interference) and then by progressively greater coordinate functioning. Finally, language displacement advanced so far that the mother tongue remained only in a few restricted and non-overlapping domains. Indeed, in some cases, compound bilingualism once more became the rule, except that the ethnic mother tongue came to be utilized via English (rather than vice-versa, as was the case in early immigrant days). Thus the domain concept may help place the compound-coordinate distinction in socio-cultural perspective, in much the same way as it may well serve the entire area of language maintenance and language shift.

7.143 *The dominance configuration.* Section 7.142, above, clearly indicates the need for basic tools of a complex and sophisticated sort. Precise measurement of *degree of maintenance or displacement* will be possible only when more diversified measures of degree of bilingualism (including attention to media and overtness variance) are at hand. Precise measurement of *domains of maintenance or displacement* will be possible only after concerted attention is given to the construction of instruments that are based upon a careful consideration of the various domains of language behavior (and the role-relations, topics and locales — these being the three components of situational variation) mentioned in a scattered international literature. The availability of such instruments will also facilitate work in several related fields of study, such as the success of intensive second-language learning programs, accurate current language facility censuses, applied 'language reinforcement' efforts, etc. Given such instruments, the inter-correlations between the several components of variance in degree of bilingualism will become amenable to study, as will the variation of such inter-correlations with age or with varying degrees of language ability, opportunity and motivation. The relationship between maintenance or displacement in the various domains of language will also become subject to scrutiny. Speculation concerning the relationship between shifts in degree and direction of bilingualism and shifts in the domains of bilingualism will finally become subject to investigation. Finally, out of all the foregoing, it will become possible to speak much more meaningfully about the *dominance configurations* of bilinguals and of changes in these configurations in language maintenance —- language shift contexts.

7.144 *Some preliminary suggestions.* Figures 17 and 18 are primarily intended to serve as possible presentation formats for dominance configurations based upon several *domains* and *sources of variance* in language behavior mentioned earlier in this discussion. The types of language use data favored by linguists, psychologists and educators have been set aside temporarily in favor of grosser 'frequency use' data. However, of primary interest at this time are the suggested parameters rather

Sources of Variance

Media	Overtness	Family role-rels. 1 2 3	Neighb. role-rels. 1 2	Work role-rels. 1 2 3	Jew Rel/Cult role-rels. 1 2
Speaking	Production Comprehension Inner				
Reading	Production Comprehension				
Writing	Production Comprehension				

Fig. 17. Intragroup Yiddish-English maintenance and shift in the United States: 1940–1970 summary comparisons for immigrant generation 'Secularists' Arriving Prior to World War I ('Dummy Table' for Dominance Configuration).

than the rough data presented. An inspection of these figures reveals several general characteristics of the dominance configuration: (a) the dominance configuration summarizes multilingual language use data for a particular population studied at two points in time and space; (b) a complete cross-tabulation of all theoretically possible sources and domains of variance in language behavior does not actually obtain. In some instances, logical difficulties arise. In others, occurrences are logically possible but either necessarily rare or rare for the particular populations under study; (c) each cell in the dominance configuration summarizes detailed process data pertaining to the particular role-relations (parent-child, teacher-pupil, etc.) pertinent to it and the situations, network types (open and closed) and/or transaction types (interactional and personal) encountered; (d) some of the domains utilized do not correspond to those listed in section 7.2 below, nor are all of the domains previously listed utilized here. This should sensitize us further to the probability that no invariant set of domains can prove to be maximally revealing, notwithstanding the efforts expended in pursuit of such a set (Dohrenwend and Smith 1962; Jones and Lambert 1959; Mackey 1962; Schermerhorn 1964); (e) an exhaustive analysis of the data of dominance configurations may well require sophisticated pattern analysis or other mathematical techniques which do not necessarily assume equal weight and simple additivity for each entry in each cell; (f) a much more refined presentation of language maintenance or language shift becomes possible than that which is provided by means of mother tongue census statistics (Kloss 1929; Nelson 1947). Word naming scores, self-ratings of frequency of usage,

Media	Overtness	Domains	Role-Relations	Summary Ratings 1950	1970
Speaking	Production	Family	Husband-Wife	Y	Y
			Parent-Child	Y	E
			Grandparent-Grandchild	–	E
			Other: same generation	Y	Y
			Other: younger generation	E	E
		Neighbor-hood	Friends	Y	E
			Acquaintances	Y	E
		Work	Employer-Employer	E	E
			Employer-Employee	E	E
			Employee-Employee	E	E
		Jewish Rel./Cult	Supporter-Writer, Teacher, etc.	Y	Y
			Supporter-Supporter	Y	Y

Fig. 18. Part of 'dummy table' in greater detail.

observed occurrences of various phonological, lexical, or grammatical realizations, all of these and many other types of scores or indices can be utilized for dominance configuration analysis of speech communities or networks. The need to *summarize* and *group* language usage data necessarily leads to some loss of refinement when proceeding from specific instances of actual speech in face-to-face interaction to grouped or categorized data. However, such summarization or simplification is an inevitable aspect of the scientific process of discovering meaning in continuous multivariate data by attending to differential relationships, central tendencies, relative variabilities and other similar characterizations. Moreover, the ultimate 'summary' nature of the dominance configuration and the further possibilities of collapsing domains according to higher order psychological or sociological similarities (e.g. 'public' vs. 'private' language use) obviates the proliferation of atomized findings.

All in all, the dominance configuration represents a great and difficult challenge to students of bilingualism and of language maintenance or language shift. It is possible that once this challenge is recognized, serious problems of configurational analysis will also arise, as they have in other substantive areas requiring attention to *patterns* of quantitative or qualitative measures. However, it is unnecessary to prejudge this matter. It does seem fitting to conclude that the dominance configuration — if it is to have maximal analytic value — might best be limited to those aspects of *degree of bilingualism* and of *location of bilingualism* which further inquiry may reveal to be of greatest relative *importance* and *independence*. Focused attention on the study of spoken production (as initially suggested by Table XI) has amply demonstrated the rich yield that a self-imposed limitation of this kind can produce in appropriately selected speech communities (Fishman, Cooper, Ma et al. 1968).

TABLE XI

Claimed Frequency of Mother Tongue Use in Conversations by Oldest and Youngest Children of Four Ethnic Backgrounds (Fishman 1966c)

In Conversation with:	GERMAN Almost Always N	%	Frequently N	%	Almost Never N	%	JEWISH Almost Always N	%	Frequently N	%	Almost Never N	%
Grandparents	6	26.1	6	26.1	11	47.8	6	20.0	9	30.0	15	50.0
Father	7	18.4	10	26.4	21	55.2	5	15.0	23	34.3	34	50.7
Mother	5	16.1	4	12.9	22	71.0	5	9.8	19	37.4	27	52.9
Brothers and Sisters	2	8.7	2	8.7	19	82.6	5	–	7	18.9	30	81.1
Friends	3	10.0	7	23.3	20	66.7	–	–	10	22.7	34	77.3
Husband and Wife	2	11.1	1	5.6	15	83.3	–	–	1	4.5	21	95.5
Own Child	1	5.6	3	16.7	14	77.8	–	–	1	5.3	18	94.7

In Conversation with:	POLISH Almost Always N	%	Frequently N	%	Almost Never N	%	UKRAINIAN Almost Always N	%	Frequently N	%	Almost Never N	%
Grandparents	15	57.6	5	19.2	6	23.2	26	96.3	–	–	1	3.7
Father	22	38.3	17	26.7	21	35.0	42	84.0	6	12.0	2	4.0
Mother	16	29.1	14	25.4	25	45.5	41	89.1	5	10.9	–	–
Brothers and Sisters	7	19.4	5	13.8	24	66.7	20	50.0	18	45.0	2	5.0
Friends	4	9.8	9	21.9	28	68.3	15	27.3	20	36.4	20	36.4
Husband and Wife	3	15.0	–	–	17	85.0	4	36.4	3	27.3	4	36.4
Own Child	3	20.0	–	–	12	80.0	4	50.0	3	37.5	1	12.5

* Data reported by parents. The German and Polish parents studied were primarily second generation individuals. The Jewish and Ukrainian parents studied were primarily first generation individuals. All parents were ethnic, cultural or organizational 'leaders'.

7.2 *Psychological, Social and Cultural Processes Related to Stability or Change in Habitual Language Use*

The second major topical subdivision of the study of language maintenance and language shift deals with the psychological, social and cultural processes associated with habitual language use. Under certain conditions of interaction the relative incidence and configuration of bilingualism stabilizes and remains fairly constant over time within various bilingual-diglossic speech communities. However, under other circumstances one variety or another may continue to gain speakers to the end that bilingualism initially increases and then decreases as the variety in question becomes the predominant language of the old and the mother tongue of the young. The second subdivision of the study of language maintenance and language shift seeks to determine the processes that distinguish between such obviously different conditions of interaction as well as processes whereby the one condition is transformed into the other. The processes pertaining to this topical subdivision may be conceived of either as antecedent, concurrent (contextual), or consequent variables, depending on the design of particular studies. Their major common characteristic is that they are primarily *outside* of language per se.

7.21 *The paucity of cross-cultural and diachronic regularities*

Just as an understanding of social-behavior-through-language must depend upon a general theory of society, so the understanding of language maintenance or language shift must depend on a theory of socio-cultural contact and socio-cultural change. Furthermore, it would seem that since we are concerned with the possibility of stability or change in language behavior on the one hand, we must be equally concerned with all of the forces contributing to stability or to change in societal behavior more generally, on the other. Thus the selection of psychological, social and cultural variables for the study of language maintenance and language shift may well be guided not only by impressions of what seem to be the most relevant processes in a particular contact situation but also by more general theories of personal, social, and cultural change. This is not to imply that all forces leading to *change* in other-than-language behaviors *necessarily* also lead to language *shift*. Indeed, whether or not this is the case (or, put more precisely, a determination of the circumstances under which language and non-language behaviors change concurrently, consecutively or independently) constitutes one of the major intellectual challenges currently facing this field of inquiry. If this challenge is to be met, it will be necessary for the study of language maintenance and language shift to be conducted within the context of studies of intergroup contacts that attend to important other-than-language processes as well: urbanization (ruralization), industrialization (or its abandonment), nationalism (or de-ethnization), nativism (or cosmopolitanization), religious revitalization (or secularization), etc.

Our current state of generalizeable knowledge in the area of language maintenance and language shift is insufficient for the positing of relationships of cross-cultural or diachronic validity. Indeed, many of the most popularly cited factors purportedly influencing maintenance and shift have actually been found to 'cut both ways' in different contexts or to have no general significance when viewed in broader perspective. Thus, Kloss illustrates that no uniform consequences for language maintenance or language shift are derivable from (a) absence or presence of higher education in the mother tongue, (b) larger or smaller numbers of speakers, (c) greater or lesser between-group similarity, and (d) positive or hostile attitudes of the majority toward the minority (Kloss 1966b: 9–13). The presence of so many ambivalent factors is a clear indication that complex interactions between partially contributory factors (rather than a single overpowering factor) must frequently be involved and that a typology of *contact situations* (as well as a theory of socio-cultural change) may be required before greater regularity among such factors can be recognized.

Although debunking represents a rather primitive level of scientific development it may be a necessary stage on the path to greater maturity. Although we *cannot* currently formulate universally applicable regularities in our area of inquiry we *can* indicate that several attempts along these lines fall somewhat short of their mark:

7.211   *A few questionable generalizations.*

7.2111   *Language maintenance is a function of intactness of group membership or group loyalty, particularly of such ideologized expressions of group loyalty as nationalism.* Among the evidence pointing to the need for refining or justifying this view is that which reveals that the Guayqueries of Venezuela preserved their groupness by preserving their property relations while giving up their language and religion (Hohenthal and McCorkle 1955), that lower caste groups in India pursue Sanskritization (emulation) rather than solidarity as a means of *group* mobility, that 'the Raetoromans, like the Italian Swiss, cultivate the fullest possible loyalty to their language without aspiring to such nationalistic goals as political independence' (Weinreich 1953a: 100), that the 'Yiddishist' movement in Eastern Europe before and after World War I similarly concentrated on a language program rather than on political organization (Weinreich 1953a: 100), that second and third generation Americans frequently maintain 'cultural (refinement) bilingualism' after ethnic group loyalty disappears at any functional level and, vice versa, that vestiges of behavioral ethnicity often remain generations after language facility has been lost (Fishman and Nahirny 1966); that many Auslandsdeutsche maintained their self identification as Germans in the midst of Polish or Ukrainian majorities, long after completely giving up their German mother tongue (Kuhn 1930, 1934); that language loyalty is low in many newly developing and highly nationalistic African states (Brosnahan 1963a-b; Spencer 1963), etc. Thus, it would seem, on the one hand, that language maintenance has continued under various and highly different forms of group membership, some of which have involved significant changes in traditional social relationships and in pre-established role-relations. On the other hand, it appears that group loyalty can be similarly (if not more) ubiquitous, continuing both with and without language maintenance. The American readiness to use language as an index of acculturation may, in itself, be quite culture bound (Samora and Deane 1956). Hymes's observation that 'some languages do not enjoy the status of a symbol crucial to group identity' (Hymes 1962:30) and Weinreich's observation that 'the connection (between language maintenance and group maintenance) is thus at least flexible and cannot be taken entirely for granted' (Weinreich 1953a:100) really represent important intellectual challenges for the study of language maintenance and language shift. We very much need a more refined understanding of the circumstances under which behaviors toward language and behaviors toward the group are related to each other in particular ways. We can recognize today that the pre-World War II views of many German students of language maintenance and language shift (as to whether language and language consciousness created — or are derived from — race, peoplehood and consciousness of kind) were too simplified and too colored by then current political considerations. However, the fact remains that the relationship between language-saliency and group-saliency is almost as speculative today as it was at that time, although it seems clear that a language undergoing massive displacement may be retained most fully by increasingly atypical and self-consciously mobilized populations as displacement progresses. Nevertheless, it is also clear that ideologies normally mobilize only a relatively younger, more active and, perhaps, more alienated or dislocated segment of any large population. Language maintenance may depend *most* on nationalist ideologies in populations whose lives have otherwise been *greatly dislocated* and it may also depend *least* on such ideologies in those populations that have best preserved their total social context against the winds of change (Fishman 1971).

The nationalism of several African and Asian countries seems to be much more characterized by *nationism* than by the nationalistic elaboration of ethnicity per se. It is much more concerned with the instrumental political and economic conditions of *nationhood* than with the socio-cultural content of *peoplehood*. The political and administrative limits of new nations are now usually defined in advance of their formation rather than in the process of their formation. The new nations are less frequently formed as the result of the 'painful but glorious' unification of hitherto particularistics who have grouped to define the language, the history, the customs, and the missions that unite them and set them apart from others. They are formed along supra-ethnic lines that normally follow colonial demarcations which depended on the fortunes of conquest and the skills of treaty-making. Political and economic self-determination are much more prominent considerations in the new nations than is cultural self-determination of the European pre- and post-World War I variety. Political leadership is much more evident than cultural leadership. The Western experience has typically been that industrialization preceded urbanization and (particularly in Eastern Europe) that nationalism preceded nationism and that the first set of phenomena preceded the second. In the new nations, the reverse sequences seem to be more common, and these may be among the major socio-cultural determinants de-emphasizing language issues in connection with local or regional languages, on the one hand, and which favor continued use of supra-regional and colonial languages on the other. Indeed, it may be that language concerns are most noticeable today where we find socio-cultural distinctions remaining (even after the attainment of considerably more politico-operational integration than has currently been attained in most new nations), particularly when hitherto backward, exploited or disadvantaged groups begin to experience great and rapid economic and cultural development in their own areas of primary population concentration (as, e.g., the French-Canadians, Flemings, Jura-regionists, etc.). The displacement of Western languages of wider communication in Africa and Asia is coming — particularly in connection with mass education and governmental operations and services — and it is coming on socio-cultural integrative grounds, but it is still just coming, rather than having arrived together with independence.

7.2112 *Urban dwellers are more inclined to shift; rural dwellers (more conservative and more isolated) are less inclined to shift.* This is one of the most reasonable and best documented generalizations in the study of language maintenance and language shift. Nevertheless, it runs counter to the first mentioned generalization, above, in that *consciousness* of ethnicity and the *espousal* of nationalism have been primarily urban phenomena. Language revival movements, language loyalty movements, and organized language maintenance efforts have commonly originated and had their greatest impact in the cities. Intelligentsia and middle class elements, both of which are almost exclusively urban, have frequently been the prime movers of language maintenance in those societies which possess both rural and urban populations. Indeed, urban groups have been 'prime movers', organizers or mobilizers more generally, that is in connection with other than language matters as well as in connection with language behavior and behavior toward language. Thus, whereas small rural groups may have been more successful in establishing relatively selfcontained traditional interaction patterns and social structures, urban groups, exposed to interaction in more fragmented and specialized networks, may reveal more conscious, organized and novel attempts to preserve or revive or change their traditional language. The urban environment does facilitate change. However, the *direction of such change* has not always favored language shift at the expense of language maintenance. *When* it has favored the one and *when* the other (and when urban-inspired language shift has actually signified a return to a languishing ancestral language) represents a further challenge to this field of study.

Discussions of rurality-urbanness in relation to language maintenance have often unwittingly combined two related but importantly separate factors: separation and concentration. Thus, rurality is often not so much significant for language maintenance because of a higher relative concentration of own-mother-tongue population as because rural populations can isolate themselves consciously — or are more isolated even without particularly wanting to be — from differently speaking popu-

TABLE XII

Mother Tongue of Second Generation Foreign White Stock for Urban and Rural Population in U.S. and Selected States (1940) (Haugen 1953).

		Norway	Sweden	Denmark	Neth.	Germany	Austria	Poland	Finland	Italy
U.S. Urban	Stock	312,980	538,500	164,480	143,100	2,570,740	596,360	1,608,600	85,000	2,612,740
	Language	127,160	222,860	44,600	48,020	1,397,260		1,176,580	54,480	1,832,000
	Retention	40.7	41.4	27.1	33.6	42.6*		73.3	64.0	70.2
U.S. Rural Non-farm	Stock	134,660	148,360	64,380	48,120	651,360	125,680	186,000	35,140	283,100
	Language	72,080	63,100	19,120	18,320	412,380		151,420	24,420	193,300
	Retention	53.5	42.4	29.7	38.2	50.5		81.4	69.8	68.3
U.S. Rural	Stock	214,960	169,460	76,780	70,100	776,740	59,300	117,780	46,940	75,360
	Language	145,000	88,080	31,740	36,900	626,060		100,820	39,560	55,380
	Retention	67.5	52.5	41.3	52.6	70.7		85.6	84.3	73.6
Wis. Urban	Stock	30,600	14,680	12,820	8,520	214,080	17,040	60,980	2,460	18,260
	Language	14,900	6,260	5,100	3,480	145,120		53,600	1,460	13,800
	Retention	48.6	42.7	39.7	40.9	61.3		83.2	59.3	75.7
Wis. Rural Non-farm	Stock	17,980	6,920	4,860	2,840	63,640	4,200	7,740	1,480	2,440
	Language	11,500	3,020	1,620	1,700	46,220		7,200	1,180	1,820
	Retention	64.0	43.7	33.4	59.9	64.5		93.5	79.8	74.6
Wis. Rural	Stock	33,820	12,360	6,800	6,140	103,100	6,400	18,080	3,780	1,380
	Language	24,660	6,540	2,960	3,840	81,880		17,660	2,980	960
	Retention	72.9	52.9	43.5	62.6	70.7		97.8	79.8	69.6
Minn. Urban	Stock	73,720	87,880	13,380	2,920	91,340	10,880	19,180	12,540	8,760
	Language	37,320	44,000	4,380	760	58,840		13,840	9,240	5,460
	Retention	50.7	50.2	32.7	26.0	55.7		72.3	73.6	62.4
Minn. Rural Non-farm	Stock	33,980	24,260	5,320	2,340	42,820	1,920	2,540	5,680	1,720
	Language	22,640	13,260	2,120	960	32,380		2,420	4,300	1,240
	Retention	66.8	54.6	39.2	41.0	70.7		95.3	75.8	72.2
Minn. Rural	Stock	69,240	49,820	10,860	7,760	90,500	3,560	6,920	15,880	380
	Language	52,660	32,020	4,580	4,440	69,560		7,400	14,300	200
	Retention	76.2	64.4	42.2	57.2	72.4		?	90.2	—
N.Y. Urban	Stock	27,700	44,380	12,160	12,380	433,180	207,960	365,220	7,500	952,440
	Language	9,620	17,260	2,000	2,440	210,780		196,580	3,500	664,760
	Retention	34.8	38.9	16.4	19.7	32.1		53.8	46.7	69.8
N.Y. Rural Non-farm	Stock	3,280	7,980	2,660	4,000	62,320	10,280	27,420	1,240	52,140
	Language	660	2,560	500	1,200	25,180		21,440	520	33,340
	Retention	20.1	32.1	18.8	30.0	33.4		78.3	41.9	63.8
N.Y. Rural	Stock	680	2,560	900	3,430	22,620	3,880	14,920	880	8,240
	Language	160	1,180	200	1,680	12,100		13,260	640	5,720
	Retention	—	46.2	—	49.0	42.5		88.9	—	69.6

* Figures for Switzerland have everywhere been added to the German stock.

lations. Data from several countries illustrate this aspect of rurality. In the United States in 1940 the 'second generation foreign white stock' (that is native born individuals of foreign born parents) was regularly more retentive of its ethnic mother tongues — regardless of whether this stock was derived from less retentive old-immigrant (Scandinavian and German) or from more retentive new-immigrant (Southern and Eastern European) groups — if living in rural than if living in urban areas (Haugen 1953: Table XII). Seemingly, at that time, it was more possible to hand on more traditional ways of life, including the traditional mother tongue, in rural areas, particularly in those that were populated largely by others of the same language background. Such separation no longer made much difference in the United States in 1960 (Fishman 1966c).

Similarly, non-rurality in India (as well as a more advanced level of education which accompanies non-rurality) is positively related to claiming English as a subsidiary language in contemporary India (Table XIII), but it is negatively related to the claiming of Hindi as a subsidiary language (Table XIV). Seemingly, the acquisition of English depends on institutions, higher schools, government bureaus, organizations and media (newspaper, motion pictures) not readily available in the rural areas. However, the acquisition of Hindi (in non-Hindi mother tongue areas) depends more on lower schools, on radio broadcasts and on federal governmental agricultural demonstration and assistance programs and these *are* available in rural areas. Thus, rurality in India means well nigh full separation from English acquisition opportunities and, therefore, a relative intensification of Hindi acquisition opportunities. Language shift is occurring in both settings, but in different directions as a result of the differential separations that rurality represents for English and for Hindi (Das Gupta and Fishman 1971). Of course, separation need not depend on rurality and can occur — although less readily — in urban areas as well. Lieberson and Curry (1971) have shown that 'separating occupations' can serve language maintenance quite as well as does the separation factor in rurality (Table XV).

The impact of population concentration, i.e. the proportion that speakers of language X are of the total co-territorial population of a particular administrative unit, is quite another matter from rurality per se. Of course, rurality *is* related to population concentration in general but as we have used it here, concentration is a proportional matter rather than merely an absolute one. Once again, there is much evidence that population concentration is important in language maintenance, but this is true in urban rather than in rural settings. Thus, Lieberson and Curry (1971) have shown that in cities in which the proportion of non-English-speaking immigrants was higher in 1900, the proportion of second generation Americans unable to speak English was also higher (Table XVI). Sixty years later, those non-English mother tongues that were numerically in the strongest position in the United States were exactly those that constituted the highest relative proportions of the total populations of the states in which their claimants were concentrated (Table XVII). Seemingly, a relatively large community of speakers is necessary, in many immigrant settings at least,

TABLE XIII

The Best Predictors of District Variation in English Claiming (N = 129 districts)
(Das Gupta and Fishman, 1971)

Cumulative Predictor	r	CumR	CumR²	△R²	F△R²
% Male Pri + Jr.	−.146	.678	.459	.007	1.6
% Male Matric +	.176*	.497	.247	.134	22.3***
Rural Pop/Total Pop	.054	.649	.421	.174	37.8***
% Immigrants	.038	.659	.434	.013	2.8
% Female Matric	.057	.670	.448	.014	3.1
Crude Literacy	−.067	.672	.452	.004	< 1
% Female Pri +Jr.	−.336**	.336	.113	—	—
Agricult/% Rural	−.122	.679	.461	.002	< 1
Workers in Retail	.039	.679	.462	.001	< 1
Persons/Sq. mile	.056	.680	.463	.001	< 1
Workers in Manuf.	−.005	.681	.463	.000	0.0
Scheduled caste	.021	.681	.464	.001	< 1

   *   significant at .05 level
   **   significant at .01 level
  ***   significant at .001 level

TABLE XIV

Ten Best Predictors of District Variation in Hindi Claiming (N = 75 districts)
(Das Gupta and Fishman, 1971)

Cumulative Predictor	r	CumR	CumR²	△R²	F△R²
% Male Pri + Jr.	.425**	.425	.181	—	—
Crude Literacy	−.167	.619	.384	.203	23.6***
% Female Matric +	−.019	.635	.403	.019	2.2
% Male Matric +	−.163	.680	.462	.059	7.7**
Agricult/% Rural	.303**	.719	.518	.056	8.0**
% Immigrants	−.086	.736	.542	.024	3.6
% Female Pri + Jr.	.055	.744	.553	.011	1.6
Rural Pop/Total Pop	.030	.746	.556	.003	< 1
Persons/Sq. Mile	−.120	.747	.558	.002	< 1
Scheduled caste	.046	.748	.559	.001	< 1
Workers in Manuf.	−.051	.752	.565	.006	< 1
Workers in Retail	−.142	.753	.566	.001	< 1

   * = significant at .05 level
   ** = significant at .01 level
  *** = significant at .001 level

TABLE XV

Foreign Born White Males Unable to Speak English, By Occupation, 1890
(Lieberson and Curry 1971)

Occupation	Per Cent Unable to Speak English
All	23
Agricultural Laborers	28
Miners (coal)	55
Stock Raisers, Herders	52
Professional Service	8
Dentists	4
Lawyers	2
Bartenders	6
Launderers	30
Auctioneers	4
Clerks and Copyists	6
Salesmen	5
Artificial Flower Makers	30
Brick and Tile Makers	46
Harness and Saddle Makers	10
Iron and Steel Workers	33
Printers, Lithographers	8
Tailors	29
Tobacco and Cigar Factory Operatives	44

Persons born in England, Ireland, Scotland, and Canada (English) are excluded since it is assumed that virtually all could speak English prior to migration.

in order for language maintenance to be most useful as well as most likely in the increasingly urban context with which it is faced. Under circumstances of high relative concentration, non-English schools, publications, broadcasting, organization activity, and, above all, non-English family patterns can more readily be maintained in interactional American urban environments. Thus, not only is an inter-group diglossia fostered in urban centers with a high relative concentration on non-English speakers, but in addition, intra-group diglossia, in terms of the separate societal allocation of functions, becomes more of a possibility. Soviet developments during the past few decades also seem to reveal similar processes with respect to

JOSHUA A. FISHMAN

TABLE XVI

Proportion Unable to Speak English in Cities,
Second Generation Cross-Tabulated by Foreign Born, 1900
(Lieberson and Curry 1971)

Cities Classified by Proportion of Foreign Born Unable to Speak English	Mean Proportion Unable to Speak English Among	
	Foreign Born	Second Generation
.10+	.1957	.0065
.05 to .09	.0682	.0005
.05 or less	.0267	.0003

Data based on 20% sample of cities with 25,000 or more population. 'Foreign born' refers to Foreign Born Whites; 'Second Generation' refers to Native Whites of Foreign Parentage.

the co-existence of Russian and the languages of at least the major Soviet minorities (Table XVIII).

7.2113 *The more prestigeful language displaces the less prestigeful language.* Our earlier discussions of *sources of variance* and *domains of language behavior* may have prepared us for the realization that language prestige is not a unit trait or tag that can be associated with a given language under all circumstances. Indeed, our earlier discussions were necessary precisely *because* the prestige of languages can vary noticeably from one context to another for the same interlocutors, as well as from one speech network to another within the same speech community. It is for this very reason that Weinreich recommends that 'as a technical terms . . . "prestige" had better be restricted to a language's value in social advance' (Weinreich 1953a : 79). However, even this limitation does not make the concept 'prestige' any more useful for research purposes since social advance itself is relative to various reference groups. Advance in family and neighborhood standing, say, requires a different language than advance in occupational or governmental standing. The fact that an overall hierarchy of reference groups may exist does not mean that the top-most reference group will be dominant in each face-to-face situation.

It may be precisely because 'prestige' obscures so many different considerations and has been used with so many different connotations that the relationship between prestige data and language maintenance or language shift data has been more uneven than might otherwise be expected. Thus, whereas Hall claims that 'it is hard to think of any modern instance in which an entire speech community is under pressure to learn a sub-standard variety of a second language' (Hall 1952:19), it is really not very hard to do so. A Low German dialect displaced Lithuanian in East

TABLE XVII

External Concentration (in Selected States), Internal Concentration and Urbanness (in the United States) of Foreign Born Claimants of 23 Non-English Mother Tongues
(Fishman 1966c)

Composite Ranking of overall strength: 1960	Foreign Born Claimants in selected States*: 1960	Total Population in selected States*: 1960	'External' Concentration	Rank	% Urban	Rank	'Internal' Concentration: No. of States
1 Spanish	467,147	25,296,881	.01846	2	.848	12	2
2 German	694,824	53,900,032	.01196	3	.837	13	4
3 Italian	692,155	34,168,452	.02026	1	.932	5	3
4 French	173,775	40,183,320	.00432	6	.836	14	4
5 Polish							
6 Dutch/	340,347	46,006,022	.00739	5	.905	8	4
Flemish	72,823	46,389,484	.00157	15	.787	20	4
7 Hungarian	110,170	32,555,483	.00338	8	.900	9	3
8 Yiddish	295,308	16,782,304	.00760	4	.982	1	1
9 Ukrainian	58,678	34,168,452	.00172	14	.910	7	3
10 Russian	157,917	43,818,874	.00360	7	.927	6	3
11 Greek	89,429	47,729,244	.00185	13	.944	2	4
12 Norwegian	76,492	38,766,586	.00197	11	.765	21	4
13 Swedish	109,102	45,994,530	.00237	10	.806	17	4
14 Slovak	85,925	43,874,849	.00196	12	.831	16	4
15 Slovenian	16,692	31,106,921	.00054	21	.825	18	3
16 Serbo-							
Croatian	47,577	46,824,125	.00102	17	.880	11	4
17 Lithuanian	60,203	43,331,406	.00139	16	.899	10	4
18 Portuguese	56,257	20,865,782	.00270	9	.834	15	2
19 Czech	45,376	52,287,063	.00087	18	.803	19	4
20 Arabic	26,630	55,177,677	.00048	22	.937	4	5
21 Danish	37,415	45,338,203	.00083	19	.764	22	4
22 Rumanian	12,946	33,246,795	.00039	23	.739	3	3
23 Finnish	32,242	48,838,144	.00066	20	.669	23	5
				U.S.A.	.699		

* 'Selected states' = least number of states required in order to include 50% of claimants.

Prussia before World War I, although many Lithuanians there were highly conversant with Standard German (Gerullis 1932). Unstandardized Schwyzertutsch is replacing Romansh, although several generations of Raetoromans have known Standard German as well (Weinreich 1951: 284–286). Standard German completely displaced Danish in a trilingual area of Schleswig, but it was itself then increasingly displaced by the local Low German dialect (Selk 1937). Obviously, Schwyzertutsch maintains itself quite successfully in competition with Standard German, Landsmaal achieved considerable success (into the 1930s, at the very least) in competition with Dano-Norwegian; Yiddish won speakers and adherents among

TABLE XVIII

*Proportions of Russians in populations of Union Republics in 1926 and 1959,
and percentage of migrant and non-migrant populations using Russian as native
language* (Lewis 1971)

Republic	% of Russians in population			% using Russian 1959	
	1926	1959		non-migrant	migrant
		Total	Urban		
Russia	78	83.0	87.2	–	–
Ukraine	9	16.9	29.9	12.0	23.0
Belorussia	8	8.2	19.4	15.0	28.0
Uzbekistan	6	13.5	33.4	0.3	12.6
Kazakhistan	20	42.7	57.6	1.2	4.3
Azerbaidjhan	10	13.6	24.9	1.2	9.3
Armenia	2	3.2	4.5	8.0	15.0
Georgia	4	10.1	18.8	0.4	8.0
Lithuania	–	8.5	17.0	0.1	3.5
Moldavia	9	10.2	30.8	3.0	15.0
Latvia	–	26.6	34.5	1.4	25.0
Tadzhikstan	5	13.3	35.3	0.5	18.0
Turkmenia	8	17.5	35.4	0.6	6.7
Estonia	–	20.1	30.8	0.5	25.0
Kirgisia	12	30.1	51.8	0.3	16.0

Sources:
a) Figures for 1926 and 1959 are drawn from the respective Census returns.
b) Volova, N. G., "Voprosy Dvuyazychaya na Severnom Kaukaza", *Sovetskaya Etnografiya*,
   1967, No. 1, 27–40.

Russified, Polonized and Germanized Jewish elites in Eastern Europe before and
after World War I; Castillian-speaking workers settling in more industrialized Cata-
lonia tend to shift to Catalan, etc. Indeed the entire process whereby a few classical
languages were displaced by 'lowly' vernaculars and whereby some of the latter, in
turn, were later displaced by still other and even 'less prestigeful' vernaculars
(Deutsch 1942; the latter varieties are still referred to as 'dialects' in many popular
(as well as in all too many socio-linguistically insensitive though scholarly) publications, e.g. Yiddish, Ukrainian, Byelo-Russian, Flemish, Afrikaans, Macedonian,
to mention only European derivatives) indicates that the prestige notion is easily
discredited unless serious qualifications and contextual redefinitions are attempted.
This too may be an appropriate task for the study of language maintenance and
language shift.

Quite clearly it is not some mystically invariant prestige of a language or variety that need concern us, but, rather the highly variant fates and fortunes of its speakers. The triumphs of English, Spanish (and Portuguese) in the New World is a triumph of physical might, of economic control and of ideological power. None of these are language factors per se, but languages that happen to be associated with such powerful forces and developments that can open up advantages to their speakers far beyond those available to non-speakers of these languages. Under circumstances in which desired socio-cultural change follows from verbal repertoire change, schools and media and organizations and programs have no difficulty facilitating shift (as e.g. in Israel, see Figure 19). Without such circumstances — and they are usually differentially available to various population segments — neither better pedagogic approaches nor more intense exhortation can have major impact on language shift.

7.22 *Toward more general theory and a more inclusive comparative approach*

7.221 When bilingual speech networks are in touch with each other on the one hand, as well as with monolingual speech networks on the other, they are *differentially* involved in the crucial socio-cultural processes that influence or regulate their interaction. These processes serve to increase or decrease interaction between populations or sub-populations in question, to either detach them from or to confirm them in their accustomed sources of authority, to either lead them to influence others or to be particularly receptive to influence from others, to either emphasize or minimize their own groupness and its various manifestations, to either rise or fall in relative power or control over their own and each other's welfare, to either view with positiveness or negativeness the drift of the interaction between them and to react toward this drift on the basis of such views. We must look to these engulfing socio-cultural processes and, particularly, to indices of individual and group involvement in them, in our efforts to explain the direction or rate of language maintenance and language shift.

7.222 However, after having appropriately selected and specified one or more variables from among the endless subtleties that make up the 'process' of socio-cultural change, it may still be found that their cross-cultural and diachronic study reveals inconsistent results. The 'same' process (e.g. 'urbanization', as measured by constant indices such as those selected and cross-culturally applied by Reissman 1964) may result in language shift *away* from hitherto traditional languages in some cases, in language shift *back* to traditional languages in other cases, while revealing significantly unaltered maintenance of the status quo in still others. Under such circumstances a typology of contact situations might serve to control or regularize a number of group or contextual characteristics, in the manner of moderator variables, and, by so doing, reveal greater order in the data.

We all have an intuitive impression that the 'American immigrant case' is different from the 'Brazilian immigrant case' (Willems 1943); that the 'Spanish conquest case' (Bright 1960; Dozier 1951) is different from the 'Anglo-American

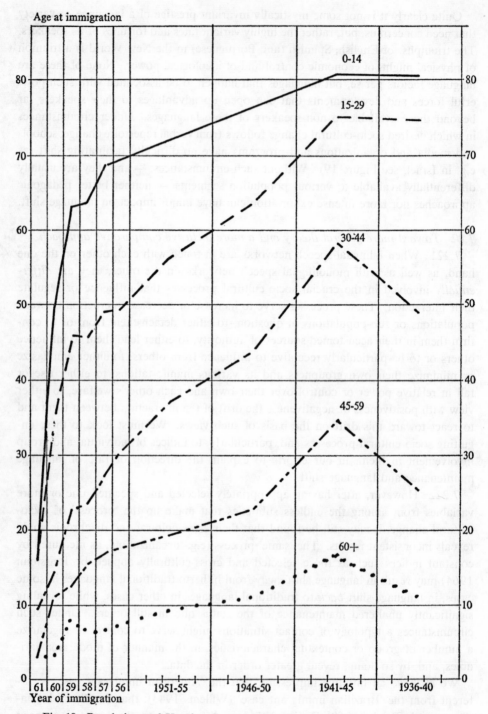

Fig. 19. Population and Housing Census, 1961; Government of Israel, Jerusalem.

conquest case' (Cook 1943; Gulick 1958); that the 'immigrant case', in general, is different from the 'conquest case' in general; that the 'Yiddish speaking immigrant to America case' (Fishman 1965f) is different from 'German speaking immigrant to America case' (Kloss 1966b), etc. The question remains how best to systematize these intuitive impressions, i.e. what variables or attributes to utilize in order that contact situations might be classified in accord with the differences between them that we sense to exist. In the terms of R. A. Schermerhorn's recently formulated typology (1964) the 'American immigrant case' immediately prior to World War I would be characterized as revealing (i) sharply unequal power configurations between non-English speaking immigrants and English-speaking 'old-Americans'; (ii) incorporation (rather than extrusion or colonization) as the *type of control* exercized by American core society over the immigrants; (iii) marked plurality and recent immigration (rather than duality, intermediate plurality without recent immigration, or any other of a continuum of patterns) as the *plurality pattern*; (iv) intermediate stratification and substantial mobility within the *stratification pattern*; (v) widespread mutual legitimization of acculturation and de-ethnization as the *interpretation of contact* in philosophical or group image terms; and (vi) growing industrialization, mass culture and social participation as *major social forces*.

Given the above typological framework, it has proved possible to summarize the current status of language maintenance and language shift among pre-World War I immigrants in terms of a very few *pre-contact factors, host factors,* and *product factors.* Unfortunately, Schermerhorn's typology for intergroup contacts is so recent that it has not yet been widely *tested* on either practical or theoretical grounds, whether in conjunction with language maintenance-language shift or in conjunction with other topics in the area of intergroup relations. While it may be expected that any typology based upon six parameters, each with several subdivisions, is likely to be somewhat unwieldy and require simplification, it is clear that Schermerhorn's system has at least heuristic value for the sociology of language from Verdoodt's efforts to put it to use in such fashion (1971).

At the opposite extreme of complexity from Schermerhorn's typology is one which is derivable from an intensive review of the extensive literature an Auslandsdeutschtum (Kuhn 1934). One of the major differentiations among the German settlers seems to have been the *original legitimization and concentration of their settlements.* A three-way break is recognizable here: *Stammsiedlungen* (settlements founded as a result of official invitation and assistance from non-German governments), *Tochtersiedlungen* (settlements founded by those who left the earlier Stammsiedlungen and who settled elsewhere as *groups*, but without governmental invitation or assistance), and *Einsiedlungen* (the in-migration of German individuals or of small occupationally homogeneous groups into non-German communities). Another related distinction is that between the relative 'cultural development' of the settlers and their hosts. During the decade before the Second World War the two most frequently recognized co-occurrences were (a) *Einsiedlungen* of 'culturally

Table **XIX**

The Non-English and the Ethnic Group Press, 1910–1960 (Fishman 1966c)

A   Proportions of Types of Publication, 1930 and 1960
Number

Ethnic Groups	1930 Mother Tongue		1930 Mixed		1930 English		1930 Total	1960 Mother Tongue		1960 Mixed		1960 English		1960 Total
	n	%	n	%	n	%	n	n	%	n	%	n	%	n
French	28	80	6	17	1	3	35	13	76	3	18	1	6	17
Spanish	61	81	9	12	5	7	75	31	65	13	27	4	8	48
German	146	59	22	9	78	32	246	41	37	9	8	60	55	110
Jewish	20	21	13	14	62	65	95	15	14	4	4	85	82	104
Hungarian	35	90	4	10	0	0	39	32	94	1	3	1	3	34
Ukrainian	6	86	1	14	0	0	7	14	74	3	16	2	10	19
Italian	85	68	38	30	2	2	125	21	16	20	43	5	11	46
Polish	84	95	2	2	2	2	88	37	86	2	5	4	9	43
Greek	15	71	4	19	2	10	21	9	47	5	26	5	26	19
Czech	44	98	1	2	0	0	45	19	83	4	17	0	0	23
Other Slavic	53	79	14	21	0	0	67	46	68	19	28	3	4	68
Scandinavian	62	63	17	17	19	19	98	20	43	5	11	21	46	46
Other Germanic	13	56	5	22	5	22	23	1	8	2	15	10	77	13
Other Romance	15	94	1	6	0	0	16	7	88	1	12	0	0	8
Near Eastern	8	89	0	0	1	11	9	10	63	1	6	5	31	16
Far Eastern	18	67	6	22	3	11	27	12	57	8	38	1	5	21
All Others	44	86	6	12	1	2	51	49	78	7	11	7	11	63
Total	737	69	149	14	181	17	1067	377	54	107	15	214	31	698

B   Proportions of Types of Publication, 1930 and 1960
Circulation

Ethnic Groups	1930 Mother Tongue		1930 Mixed		1930 English		1930 Total	1960 Mother Tongue		1960 Mixed		1960 English		1960 Total
	n	%	n	%	n	%	n	n	%	n	%	n	%	n
French	151[a]	94	10	6	—	—	161	118[a]	96	5	4	—	—	123
Spanish	298	98	3	1	3	1	304	268	81	54	16	7	2	329
German	1354	67	65	3	598	30	2017	281	10	146	5	2274	84	2701
Jewish	775	72	34	3	264	25	1073	179	9	63	3	1826	88	2068
Hungarian	238	96	9	4	0	0	247	198	95	4	2	6	3	208
Ukrainian	51	100	—	—	0	0	51	47	62	27	36	2	2	76
Italian	613	83	114	15	16	2	743	270	56	164	34	47	10	481
Polish	999	96	23	2	15	1	1037	690	96	9	1	18	2	717
Greek	74	77	12	12	10	10	96	65	62	15	14	24	23	104
Czech	513	100	—	—	0	—	513	274	94	17	6	0	0	291
Other Slavic	730	74	167	17	93	9	990	216	45	243	51	17	4	476
Scandinavian	580	85	82	12	21	3	683	120	26	40	9	303	65	463
Other Germanic	22	58	16	42	—	—	38	4	2	15	6	216	92	235
Other Romance	130	100	—	—	0	0	130	25	86	4	4	0	0	29
Near Eastern	38	100	0	0	—	—	38	37	69	6	11	11	20	54
Far Eastern	346	87	52	13	—	—	398	67	57	45	38	6	5	118
All Others	296	98	7	2	—	—	303	253	85	26	9	20	7	299
Total	7216	82	591	7	1023	12	8830	3118	35	889	10	4784	54	8791

[a] Last three digits have been dropped in all circulation figures.

more mature' Germans living in the midst of a 'culturally less developed' population, as opposed to (b) *Stamm- und Tochtersiedlungen* of 'culturally younger' Germans surrounded by a 'more mature, nation-oriented' population. Thus, although
only two diagonal cells of a theoretically complete two-by-two typology are extensively discussed it is possible to find examples of the remaining cells as well. Even
when limited to the two co-occurrences mentioned above very interesting and consistent differences appear both in rate and in stages of language shift and acculturation. The implications of this rough typology and of the regularities that it has
suggested deserve consideration in connection with quite different intergroup contact
settings.

7.223 Although the study of language maintenance or language shift *need* not
be completely limited to the comparison of separate cases it is nevertheless un-
deniably true that the comparative method is quite central to inquiry within this
topic area. Certainly the comparative mothed is indispensable in our pursuit of
cross-cultural and diachronic regularities. Assuming that a relatively uniform set of
appropriate socio-cultural process-measures could be selected and applied and,
assuming that a recognizably superior typology of contact situations were available,
it would then become possible to study:

(i) The same language group in two separate interaction contexts that are judged
to be highly similar (with respect to primary socio-cultural process(es) and contact
type), e.g. two separate German *Stammsiedlungen* in rural Poland.

(ii) The same language group in two separate interaction contexts judged to be
quite dissimilar (with respect to major socio-cultural process(es) and contact type,
e.g. one German-Swiss community in contact with Swiss Raetoromans and another
German-Swiss community in Cincinnati, Ohio.

(iii) Different language groups in two separate interaction contexts judged to be
highly similar (with respect to major socio-cultural process(es) and contact type),
e.g. a Polish-speaking and a Slovak-speaking community, both of rural origin, in
Cincinnati, Ohio.

(iv) Different language groups in two separate interaction contexts judged to be
quite dissimilar (with respect to major socio-cultural process(es) and contact type),
e.g. a German *Stammsiedlung* in rural Poland and a Slovak community in Cincinnati, Ohio.

Thus, by judiciously contrasting groups, socio-cultural processes and types of
contact situations (*not* necessarily taken two at a time, if higher level interaction
designs prove to be feasible) it should become possible to more meaningfully apportion the variance in language maintenance or language shift outcomes. Furthermore, the greater our insight with respect to socio-cultural processes and the more
appropriate our typology of intergroup contact situations, the more possible it becomes to meaningfully assemble and analyze language maintenance and language
shift files. Such files would permit both cross-cultural and diachronic analysis, of
primary as well as of secondary data, based upon comparable data, collected and

organized in accord with uniform sets of socio-cultural processes and contact categories. This state of affairs is still far off but it is the goal toward which we might attempt to move within this second topical subdivision of the study of language maintenance and language shift, once more basic methodological and conceptual questions reach a somewhat more advanced level of clarification.

7.3 *Behavior Toward Language*

The third (and final) major topical subdivision of the study of language maintenance and language shift is concerned with behavior toward language (rather than with language behavior or behavior through language, particularly, with more focused and conscious behaviors on behalf of either maintenance or shift per se. Strictly speaking, this subdivision may be properly considered a subtopic under 7.2, above. However, it is of such central significance to this entire field of inquiry that it may appropriately receive separate recognition. Three major categories of behaviors toward language are discernible within this topical subdivision:

7.31 *Attitudinal-affective behaviors*

We know all too little about language oriented attitudes and emotions (running the gamut from language loyalty — of which language nationalism is only one expression — to language antipathy — of which conscious language abandonment is only one expression) as distinguished from attitudes and emotions toward the 'typical' speakers of particular language variants. The features of language that are considered attractive or unattractive, proper or improper, distinctive or commonplace, have largely remained unstudied. However, in multilingual settings, particularly in those in which a variety of 'social types' are associated with each language that is in fairly widespread use, languages per se (rather than merely the customs, values and cultural contributions of their model speakers) are reacted to as 'beautiful' or 'ugly', 'musical' or 'harsh', 'rich' or 'poor', etc. Generally speaking, these are language stereotypes (Fishman 1956). However, the absence or presence of a 'kernel of truth' (or of verifiability itself) is entirely unrelated to the mobilizing power of such views.

The manifold possible relationships between language attitudes and language use also remain largely unstudied at the present time. Although Lambert reports a positive relationship between success in school-based second language learning and favorable attitudes toward the second language and its speakers (Lambert et al. 1963), this finding need not be paralleled in all natural multilingual contact settings. Thus, Ruth Johnston reports a very low correlation between subjective and objective (external) assimilation in the language area (1963b). Many older Polish immigrants in Australia identified strongly with English, although they hardly spoke or understood it several years after their resettlement. On the other hand, many young immigrants spoke English faultlessly and yet identified strongly with Polish, although they spoke it very poorly (1963a). Similarly, in summarizing his findings concerning current language maintenance among pre-Word War I arrivals in the United States coming from rural Eastern and Southern European backgrounds, Fishman reported a long-term distinction between attitudes and use, namely, an increased esteem for non-English mother tongues concomitant with the increased relegation of these languages to fewer and narrower domains of language use (Fishman 1965e). In the latter case, the particular non-English mother tongues in question were now found to be viewed positively and nostalgically by older first and second generation in-dividuals who had formerly characterized these tongues as ugly, corrupted and grammarless in pre-World War II days. Younger second and third generation in-dividuals were found to view these mother tongues (almost always via translations) with less emotion but with even more positive valence. Instead of a 'third genera-tion return' (Hansen 1940) there seemed to be an 'attitudinal halo-ization' within large segments of all generations, albeit unaccompanied by increased usage. This development (a negative relationship over time between *use rates* and *attitudinal positiveness)* was not predictable from most earlier studies of language maintenance or language shift in immigrant or non-immigrant settings. We are far from knowing whether its explanation in American contextual terms (i.e. in terms of the greater acceptability of marginal rather than either primordial or ideologized ethnicity) would also apply to other settings in which similar circumstances might obtain. Recent methodological clarification of the language-attitude area (Fishman and Agheyisi 1970) should now make it possible for workers to move ahead in this area along a broad front of little explored topics and approaches.

7.32 *Overt behavioral implementation of attitudes, feelings and beliefs*

Both language reinforcement ('language movements') and language planning may be subsumed under this heading. Language reinforcement may proceed along voluntary as well as along official routes and encompasses organizational protection, statutory protection, agitation and creative production. As for language planning, it has not always been recognized that much (if not most) of its activity (codifica-tion, regularization, simplification, purification, elaboration, and the implementation and evaluation of all of the foregoing) occurs in the context of language mainte-nance or language shift (Fishman 1966c: Ch. 21).

The possible relationships between language reinforcement (or language plan-ning), on the one hand, and the waxing or waning of actual language use (or of other socio-cultural processes) are largely unknown at this time. Data from the American immigrant case imply that a number of unexpected relationships may obtain in that novel reinforcements may be introduced as actual language use di-minishes. Thus, as even some of the more 'exotic' mother tongues (i.e. mother tongues not usually considered to be among the major carriers of European civiliza-tion and, therefore, hitherto usually associated only with foreign ethnicity in the minds of 'average Americans' (Hayden and Fishman 1964)) have ceased to be primarily associated with immigrant disadvantages or with full-blown religio-ethnic distinctiveness among their own sometime-and-erstwhile-speakers, they have been increasingly introduced as languages of study at the university, college and public high school levels (Haugen 1953; Kloss 1966b). At the same time, massive displacement seems to have had greater inhibitory impact on language planning efforts in the American immigrant case than it had on language reinforcement efforts. The latter are essentially conservative and seem to require less in the way of highly specialized leadership. The former are frequently innovative and dependent upon expert personnel working in concert with compliance producing or persuasive authority. To what extent this differential impact also holds true in other types of language shift settings is currently unknown but worthy of study.

Advocates of languages that are undergoing displacement are often much more exposed to (and identified with) the values and methods of their linguistic competitors than were their less exposed (and less threatened) predecessors. As a result, they are more likely to adopt organized protective and publicity measures from more 'advantaged' co-territorial (other-tongue) models to serve language maintenance purposes (Fishman 1969a). The introduction of a few ethnically infused languages into the curricula of American high schools, colleges and universities represents just such a recent innovation on behalf of mother tongue maintenance — and an even more de-ethnicized one (Nahirny and Fishman 1965) than was the innovative establishment of ethnic group newspapers, schools, cultural organizations and camps prior to World War I. In contrast, the normal processes of controlled *language change* and the more aroused processes of conscious *language planning* may require more than 'last ditch' ingenuity. However, to what extent reinforcement and planning are differently balanced given varying degrees of displacement or augmentation is currently unknown but worthy of study. In addition to its importance in its own right, the overall study of the relationship between language attitudes and language behaviors (Fishman 1969c) will also gain greatly from attention to topics such as this.

7.33 *Cognitive aspects of language response*

Constantly flitting between the above two categories and overlapping partially with the one, with the other, or with both are such matters as: *consciousness* of mother tongue (or 'other tongue') as an entity separate from folkways more generally; *knowledge* of synchronic variants, language history and literature; and *perceptions of language as a component of 'groupness'*. We have little systematic information concerning the circumstances under which language consciousness, language knowledge and language-related groupness-perceptions do or do not enter into reference group behavior in contact situations. As a result, it is difficult to say at this time whether or when language maintenance and language shift are ideologically mediated as distinguished from their more obvious situational and instrumental determinants discussed thus far. We recognize very gross long-term contrasts in this connection, namely, that there were periods and regions when language 'was in no way regarded as a political or cultural factor, still less as an object of political or cultural struggle' (Kohn 1945:6); that there were other periods and regions marked by a sharp increase in such regard, so that language became a principle 'in the name of which people ... (rallied) themselves and their fellow speakers consciously and explicitly to resist changes in either the functions of their language (as a result of language shift) or in the structure or vocabulary (as a consequence of interference)' (Weinreich 1953:99), and that there currently seems to be less of this than previously, particularly if we compare African with European nationbuilding. However, gross differentiations such as these are patently insufficient to enable us to clarify the conditions under which language becomes a prominent component in *perceptions* of 'own-groupness' and 'other-groupness'. This topic (language-related groupness-perception) is, of course, closely related to one previously mentioned, namely, the role of language in group membership and in group functioning (see section 7.2111, above). In the American immigrant case we have seen a growing dissociation between self-perceived ethnic identification and language maintenance. Far from being viewed as necessary components of groupness (whether in the sense of resultants or contributors) non-English mother tongues appear to be viewed increasingly in terms of non-ethnic *cultural* and non-ethnic *practical* considerations. At the same time, some form of ethnic self-identification is frequently still reported by many of those who no longer claim any facility at all in their ethnic mother tongues, implying that in several American immigrant-derived groups some kind of ethnicity usually appears to be a much more stable phenomenon than language maintenance. Indeed, some groups are able to maintain newspapers, schools and organization long after they have lost their non-ethnic mother tongues (Table XIXA and Table XIXB). Most immigrants became bilingual much before they embarked on de-ethnization or seriously contemplated the possibility of bi-culturism. However, there were obviously exceptions to this process, both in the United States and in other contact settings. We certainly do not seem to be in a position to indicate the underlying regularities in this subtle area of inquiry at the present time, except to point out that the segments of the population among which language consciousness, language interest, and language-related groupness-perceptions are likely to be in evidence are normally quite small and elitist in nature (Tables XXa and XXb).

We know very little about the interaction *among* the three components of behavior toward language or about the interaction *between* any of these components and the larger psychological, social and cultural processes discussed earlier. Rather than being a 'natural', omnipresent condition, either in monolingual or in multilingual settings, heightened and integrated behaviors toward language may be related to somewhat rare and advanced symbolic and ideological extensions of primordial ethnicity. Such extensions may well require a particular level of socio-cultural development and a particular group of custodians for their preservation and further

JOSHUA A. FISHMAN

TABLE XX

Attitudes and beliefs with respect to Spanish among Ordinary Puerto Ricans (OPR) and Intellectuals, Leaders and Artists (ILA) in the Greater New York Metropolitan Area (Fishman 1969e)

A. Is it necessary to know Spanish to be Puerto Rican?

Response	OPR (n = 32)	ILA (n = 20)
No	20 (62%)	2 (10%)
Yes	12 (38%)	18 (90%)

B. Are there many 'Nuyorquinos' who do not speak or understand Spanish?

Response	OPR (n = 29)	ILA (n = 20)
Yes (many do not understand)	2 (7%)	1 (5%)
Most understand little and speak poorly	3 (10%)	4 (20%)
Most understand well but speak poorly	3 (10%)	14 (70%)
Most speak and understand without real difficulty	21 (73%)	1 (5%)

elaboration. They almost certainly require a relatively advanced level of elitist concentration on intra-elitist concerns, often in advance of elitist concerns for communication within the masses. Nevertheless, none of these desiderata need have invariable consequences for behavior toward language. Even where heightened and integrated behaviors toward language are culturally present they will not be equally operative in all situations or among all population subgroups. Furthermore, even where they are culturally present they need not be uniformly related to other symbolically elaborated forms of behavior. Thus, this area remains the most unsystematized topical subdivision of the study of language maintenance and language shift. Perhaps it can be clarified in the future as a result of concomitant clarification and constant interrelation in connection with the two other major subdivisions within this field of inquiry.

7.34 *Interference and switching*

Within the topical subdivision of behavior toward language we once again meet the topic of interference and switching, first introduced in section 7.1, above. The absence or presence of interference and switching can have cognitive, affective and overt implementational implications for language maintenance and language shift. Certainly, both interference and switching are related to the domains and variance sources of bilingualism, on the one hand, and to socio-cultural processes and type of interaction, on the other hand. Moreover, within this topical subdivision it is appropriate to stress that where attitudes and awareness concerning purism obtain, interference is sometimes viewed as *an imperfection* — not in the speaker or in his productions but *in the language itself*. At the opposite pole, there are multilingual contact situations in which conscious, purposive interference obtains. In these instances speakers attempt to incorporate into their language usage as many elements or features as possible from another language including (in very advanced cases) interference in stress patterns, intonation, and *Denkformen*. In either case (i.e. when interference occurs although it is considered undesirable, or when interference occurs and is considered desirable) interference is not always considered to be all of one piece. Certain occurrences are considered to be more acceptable, excusable, permissible, necessary than others. In either case it can become a factor in hastening language shift, particularly since bilinguals tend to interpret interference in each of the languages known to them quite differently. Finally, at a point when language shift is appreciably advanced, certain sounds and forms of the language undergoing displacement may become so difficult for the average speaker (while errors in connection with them may become so stigmatized among purists) that this in itself may accelerate further shift. All in all, recognition of interference, attitudes toward interference, and the behavioral consequences of interference represent interesting and important topics within the field of language maintenance and language shift.

7.4 *A Glance Back and a Glance Ahead*

Various language maintenance and language shift phenomena have long been of interest to scholars and to laymen. Several sub-topics within this area have undisputed relevance to the daily concerns and joys of millions. Others, of more theoretical interest, are closely related to topics of recognized concern to linguists, anthropologists, sociologists, psychologists, political scientists, educators, etc. Culture contact and language contact will always be with us, and out of these contacts will come modifications in habitual behavior as well as attempts to restrain or channel such modifications. Whether (or when) language habits change more or less quickly than others, whether or when language loyalties are more or less powerful than others, indeed, whether (or when) men can live in a supraethnic tomorrow without strong links (linguistic or non-linguistic) to their ethnic yesterday and today — these are questions to which there are currently no definitive answers. However, interest in social-psychological aspects of language behavior is currently growing (whether under that name or under the name of sociolinguistics, anthropological linguistics, ethnolinguistics, the ethnography of speaking, the ethnography of communication, the sociology of language, or some other designation). In most instances, there is some recognition of *behavior toward language* as a crucial topic within the field of social behavior through language. This growing interest will undoubtedly contribute answers to many of the currently unanswerable questions within the field of language maintenance and language shift.

Three major subdivisions of the study of language maintenance and language shift have been suggested. The first deals with the precise establishment of habitual language use in a contact situation. This requires instruments just beginning to become available for the measurement of *degree of bilingualism* and of *location of bilingualism* along sociologically relevant dimensions. Degree of bilingualism, hitherto recognizable in terms of automaticity, proficiency, and code-intactness at the phonetic, lexical and grammatical levels, must also be investigated with respect to media variance and overtness variance. *Location of bilingualism* requires investigation with respect to functional diversification in appropriately designated domains of language, each domain being abstracted from patterned role-relations, topics, locales and/or other lower order phenomena. The complex relationships between the several components of degree of bilingualism and location of bilingualism may be represented by a *dominance configuration* which, in turn, may or may not be reducible to a single index of direction of bilingualism. The drift of language maintenance or language shift may be established by diachronic measures pertaining to some or all of the above factors.

The second major topical subdivision of the study of language maintenance and language shift deals with psychological, social and cultural processes that are associated with ascertained changes in habitual language use. No conceptual systematization of these processes is currently available although several preliminary typologies of 'contact situations' exist and require further refinement in cross-cultural perspective. The greatest encouragement in this topical subdivision comes from the accelerating interdisciplinary work on socio-cultural and politico-operational change (including work on development and modernization). To the extent that the study of language maintenance and language shift will become increasingly linked to ongoing theoretical and empirical refinements in the study of psycho-socio-cultural stability and change more generally, the more rapidly will mutually rewarding progress occur.

The third (and final) major subdivision of the study of language maintenance and language shift pertains to behavior toward language, including (but not limited to) more focused and conscious behaviors on behalf of maintenance or shift. Three major sub-topics within this topic are recognizable: Attitudinal-affective behaviors (loyalty, antipathy, etc.), overt behavioral implementation (control or regulation of habitual language use via reinforcement, planning, prohibition, etc.), and (overlapping partially with each of the two foregoing sub-topics) cognitive behaviors (language consciousness, language knowledge, language-related group-perceptions, etc.).

Two socio-linguistic patterns, that of the urban American immigrant and that of the urban French-Canadian nationalist, have been repeated many times in the past century. The increasing use of Russian alone by Soviet minorities — particularly the smaller ones — whether they be immigrants to large urban centers in other regions or outnumbered by Russians and various other immigrants into their own regions, has followed the same path as the increasing use of English alone by immigrants to the United States, the increasing use of Spanish alone by indigenous Indian populations moving to urban centers throughout Latin America, or the increasing use of Wolof alone by the diverse Senegalese populations that began to move to Dakar more than a generation ago. Similarly, the increasing use of the mother tongue in the domains of education, industry and government (which had previously 'belonged', so to speak, to English), that has increasingly typified French-Canada, is not at all unlike the growing displacement of English or another Western language of wider communication in Puerto Rico, Tanzania, Kenya, India, Pakistan, Malaysia and the Philippines. The one group of cases illustrates the general inability of dislocated populations to maintain domain separation and, therefore, a sufficiently distinctive functional allocation of codes in their verbal repertoires, such as to render their mother tongues necessary for membership and status even within the home, neighborhood and other intra-group domains. The other group of cases illustrates the generally far greater ability of sedentary populations to withstand the onslaught of foreign-inspired political, educational, social and economic domination. If domain separation is maintained, at least between the L domains of home and neighborhood and the H domains of government, education and religion, a subsequent mobilization of the indigenous population around a new, nationalist proto-elite may yet lead to the introduction (or re-introduction) of the vernacular into those domains from which it has been barred or displaced.

In the urban American immigrant case — as in all instances in which severely dislocated populations have been presented with tangible opportunities to share in new role-relationships and in vastly improved power- and status-networks — a new language initially entered the verbal repertoire of the speech community for marginal metaphorical purposes only. Situational *and* metaphorical switching *both* were possible only with respect to several varieties of the ethnic mother tongue or its H + L matrix. However, with the passage of time *intra-group* power, status and even membership per se, all come to be granted on the basis of mastery of the new language. As a result, the ethnic mother tongue became increasingly relegated to metaphorical purposes (humor, contrast, tenderness) and, therefore, to oblivion as a third generation arose that had itself directly experienced none of the situations upon which the metaphorical functions of the ethnic mother tongue rested in the usage of 'old timers' and the second generation.

In the case of less dislocated populations — where the absence of widespread social mobility or of physical extirpation from established roles and networks helped preserve the distinction between intra-group and extra-group domains — the new language normally gained metaphorical recognition *only* insofar as the majority of intra-group networks and role relations were concerned. As a result, it served primarily as an intergroup H for the few well-placed individuals with inter-group roles. Little wonder then that among the rank and file of such less dislocated populations — including the Alsatians discussed by Tabouret-Keller (1968) and by Verdoodt (1971) and the Swabians discussed by Fishman and Luders (1972) — H varieties do not displace L varieties and indeed, are themselves easily displaced by yet newer H varieties resulting from the temporary intrusions of new political authorities.

The above sketch is still more suggested then demonstrated. It depends more on theoretical parsimony than on empirical data. The exhaustive study of language maintenance and language shift ultimately requires not merely theory but also theory tested and revised in the light of hard data. Since the basic instruments and theory required for the establishment of degree and direction of language maintenance or language shift are now beginning to be available (certainly this is true relative to the situation five years ago) it would now seem to be most crucial to devote increasing amounts of theoretical and empirical attention to comparative (cross-network, cross-speech community, cross-polity and cross-cultural) study of the psycho-socio-cultural antecedents and concomitants of language maintenance and language shift. The next few years will doubtlessly see the greatest progress precisely along these lines, i.e. along lines for which the social anthropologist, social psychologist and sociologist — rather than the linguist — must take primary responsibility.

8. SOCIO-CULTURAL ORGANIZATION: LANGUAGE CONSTRAINT AND LANGUAGE REFLECTIONS

One of the major lines of social and behavioral science interest in language during the past century has been that which has claimed that the radically differing structures of the languages of the world constrain the cognitive functioning of their speakers in different ways. It is only in relatively recent years — and partially as a result of the contributions of psycholinguists and sociolinguists — that this view (which we shall refer to as the linguistic relativity view) has come to be replaced by others: (a) that languages primarily reflect rather than create socio-cultural regularities in values and orientations and (b) that languages throughout the world share a far larger number of structural universals than has heretofore been recognized. While we cannot here examine the work related to language universals (Greenberg 1966; Osgood 1960), since it is both highly technical and hardly sociolinguistic in nature, we *can* pause to consider the linguistic relativity view itself as well as the linguistic reflection view which is increasingly coming to replace it in the interests and in the convictions of social scientists. It is quite clear why so much interest has been aroused by the question of language as restraint and language as reflection of socio-cultural organizations. Both of these views are unidirectional. One posits that language structure and language usage are fundamental and 'given' and that all behavior is influenced thereby. The other claims that social organization and behavior are prior and language merely reflects these. A position on one side or another of this argument must be taken by those who are interested in changing or influencing the 'real world' of behavior.

8.1 *Grammatical Structure Constrains Cognition*

The strongest claim of the adherents of linguistic relativity — whether by Whorf (1940, 1941), Hoijer (1951, 1954), Trager (1959), Kluckhohn (1961), or by others — is that cognitive organization is directly constrained by linguistic structure. Some languages recognize far more tenses than do others. Some languages recognize gender of nouns (and, therefore, also require markers of gender in the verb and adjective systems) whereas others do not. Some languages build into the verb system recognition of certainty or uncertainty of past, present, or future action. Other languages build into the verb system a recognition of the size, shape and color of nouns referred to. There are languages that signify affirmation and negation by different sets of pronouns just as there are languages that utilize different sets of pronouns in order to indicate tense and absence or presence of emphasis. Some languages utilize tone and vowel length in their phonological systems whereas English and most other modern European languages utilize neither. There are languages that utilize only twelve phonemes while others require more than fifty. A list of such striking structural differences between languages could go on and on — without in any way denying that each language is a perfectly adequate instrument (probably the *most* adequate instrument) for expressing the needs and interests of its speakers. That the societies using these very different languages differ one from the other in many ways is obvious to all. Is it not possible, therefore, that those socio-cultural differences — including ways of reasoning, perceiving, learning, distinguishing, remembering, etc. — are directly relatable to the structured differences between the languages themselves? The Whorfian hypothesis claims that this is indeed the case (Fishman 1960).

Intriguing though this claim may be, it is necessary to admit that many years of intensive research have not succeeded in demonstrating it to be tenable. Although many have tried to do so no one has successfully predicted and demonstrated a cognitive difference between two populations on the basis of the grammatical or other structural differences between their languages alone. Speakers of tone languages and of vowel length languages and of many-voweled languages do *not* seem to hear better than do speakers of languages that lack all of these features. Speakers of languages that code for color, shape and size in the very verb form itself do not tend to categorize or classify a random set of items much differently than do speakers of languages whose verbs merely encode tense, person and number (Carroll and Casagrande 1958). Whorf's claims (namely, that '. . . the background linguistic system (in other words, the grammar) of each language is not merely a reproducing instrument for voicing ideas, but rather is itself the shaper of ideas, the program and guide for the individual's mental activity, for his analysis of impressions, for his synthesis of his mental stock in trade. Formulation of ideas is not an independent process, strictly rational in the old sense, but it is part of a particular grammar and differs, from slightly to greatly, between grammars' (1940) seem to be overstated and no one-to-one correspondence between grammatical structure and either cognitive or socio-cultural structure measured independently of language has ever been obtained. Several of the basic principles of sociolinguistic theory may help explain why this is so, although the psychological maxim that most men think about what they are talking about (i.e. that language structure is *always being struggled with via cognitive processes*) should also be kept in mind.

In contrast with the older anthropological-linguistic approach of Whorf, Sapir, Kluckhohn, Korzybski and others who pursued this problem during the first half of the twentieth century, sociolinguistics is less likely to think of *entire languages or entire societies* as categorizable or typable in an overall way. The very concepts of linguistic repertoire, role repertoire, repertoire range and repertoire compartmentalization argue against any such neat classification once functional realities are brought into consideration. Any reasonably complex speech community contains various speech networks that vary with respect to the nature and ranges of their speech repertoires. Structural features that may be present in the speech of certain interaction networks may be lacking (or marginally represented) in the speech of others. Structural features that may be present in certain varieties within the verbal repertoire of a particular interaction network may be absent (or marginally represented) in other varieties within that very same repertoire. Mother-tongue speakers of language X may be other-tongue speakers of language Y. These two languages may co-exist in a stable diglossic pattern throughout the speech community and yet be as structurally different as any two languages chosen at random.

Certainly, all that has been said above about the difficulty in setting up 'whole-language' typologies is equally true when we turn to the question of 'whole-society' typologies. Role repertoires vary from one interaction network to the next and roles themselves vary from one situation to the next within the same role-repertoire. Distinctions that are appropriately made in one setting are inappropriate in another and behaviors that occur within certain interaction networks do not occur in still others within the same culture. The existence of structured biculturism is as real as the existence of structured bilingualism and both of these phenomena tend to counteract any neat and simple linguistic relativity of the kind that Whorf had in mind.

Nevertheless, there are at least two large areas in which a limited degree of linguistic relativity *may* be said to obtain: (a) the structuring of verbal interaction and (b) the structuring of lexical components. The first area of concern points to the fact that the role of language (when to speak, to whom to speak, the importance of speaking per se relative to inactive silence or relative to other appropriate action) varies greatly from society to society (Hymes 1966). However, this type of relativity has nothing to do with the *structure* of language per se in which Whorf was so interested. The second area of concern deals with lexical taxonomies and with their consequences in cognition and behavior. However, these border on being linguistic *reflections* of socio-cultural structure rather than being clearly and solely linguistic *constraints* that inevitably and interminably must bring about the particular behaviors to which they are supposedly related. It is to a consideration of these lexical taxonomies that we now turn.

8.2 *Lexical Structure Constrains Cognition*

For many years it was believed that the only tightly structured levels of language were the grammatical (morphological and syntactic), on the one hand, and the phonological, on the other. These two levels certainly received the brunt of linguistic attention and constituted the levels of analysis of which linguists were most proud in their interactions with other social and behavioral scientists. By contrast, the lexical level was considered to be unstructured and exposed to infinite expansion (as words were added to any languages) and infinite interference (as words were borrowed from other languages). A small but hardy group of lexicographers (dictionary makers) and etymologists (students of word origins) continued to be enamoured of words per se but the majority of linguists acted as though the lexicon was the black sheep, rather than a bona fide member in good standing, of the linguistic family. The discovery of structured parsimony in parts of the lexicon has done much to revive linguistic interest in the lexical level of analysis. The discovery as such is one in which psychologists, anthropologists and sociologists were every bit as active as were linguists themselves (if not more so). This may also explain why the interrelationship between lexical organization *and* behavioral organization has been so prominent in conjunction with the investigation of lexical structure.

The psychological contributions to this area of analysis take us back to one level of the Whorfian hypothesis (see Level 2 in Figure 20). Psychologists had long before demonstrated that the availability of verbal labels was an asset in learning, perception and memory tasks (see, e.g. Carmichael et al. 1932; Lehmann 1889; Maier 1930). A new generation of psychologists has recently set out to determine whether this could be demonstrated both interlinguistically (i.e. by comparing different languages) as well as intralinguistically (i.e. within a given language) on a structured set of behaviors that correspond *to a structured portion of lexicon.*

	Data of (Cognitive) Behavior	
Data of Language Characteristics	Non-linguistic data	Language data ('cultural themes')
Lexical or 'semantic' characteristics	Level 1	Level 2
Grammatical characteristics	Level 3	Level 4

Fig. 20. Schematic Systematization of the Whorfian Hypothesis (Fishman 1960)

Level 1 of the Whorfian ('linguistic relativity') hypothesis predicts that speakers of languages that make certain lexical distinctions are enabled thereby to talk about certain matters (for example, different kinds of snow among speakers of Eskimo and different kinds of horses among speakers of Arabic) that cannot as easily be discussed by speakers of languages that do not make these lexical distinctions. Similarly, Level 3 of the Whorfian hypothesis predicts that speakers of languages that possess particular grammatical features (absence of tense in the verb system, as in Hopi, or whether adjectives normally precede or follow the noun, as in English vs. French) predispose these speakers to certain cultural styles or emphases (timelessness; inductiveness vs. deductiveness). These two levels of the Whorfian hypothesis have often been criticized for their anecdotal nature as well as for their circularity in that they utilized verbal evidence for both their independent (causal) and dependent (consequential) variables. Level 2 of the Whorfian hypothesis predicts that the availability of certain lexical items or distinctions enables the speakers of these languages to remember, perceive, or learn certain non-linguistic tasks more rapidly or completely than can the speakers of languages that lack these particular lexical items or distinctions. This level of the Whorfian hypothesis has been demonstrated several times—most recently and forcefully in connection with the differing color terminologies of English and Zuni—but it is difficult to argue that the absence of lexical items or distinctions in a particular language is more a *cause* of behavioral differences than a *reflection* of the differing socio-cultural concerns or norms of its speakers. As soon as speakers of Zuni become interested in orange (color) they devise a term for it. Language relativity should be more stable and less manipulable than that! Level 4 of the Whorfian hypothesis is the most demanding of all. It predicts that grammatical characteristics of languages facilitate or render more difficult various non-linguistic behaviors on the part of their speakers. This level has yet to be successfully demonstrated via experimental studies of cognitive behavior.

They chose the color spectrum to work with because it is a real continuum that tends to be environmentally present in all cultures. Nevertheless, the investigators hypothesized that language labels for the color spectrum are culturally idiosyncratic. These labels not only chop up the color continuum into purely conventional segments in every language community, but they probably do so differently in different language communities. By a series of ingenious experiments, Brown and Lenneberg (1954), Lenneberg (1953, 1957), Lantz and Stefflre (1964) and others have demonstrated that this was indeed true. They have demonstrated that those colors for which a language has readily available labels are more unhesitatingly named than are colors for which no such handy labels are available. They have shown that the colors for which a language has readily available labels (i.e. highly codable colors) are more readily recognized or remembered when they must be selected from among many colors after a delay subsequent to their initial presentation. They have demonstrated that somewhat different segments of the color spectrum are highly codable in different language communities. Finally, they have shown that the learning of nonsense-syllable associations for colors is predictably easier for highly codable colors than for less codable colors that require a phrase — often an individually formulated phrase — in order to be named.

All in all, this series of experiments has forcefully shown that the availability of a structured set of terms has both intralinguistic as well as interlinguistic consequences. However, in addition, it has underscored the equally important fact that every speech community has exactly such terms for those phenomena that are of concern to it. Certainly, artists, painters, and fashion-buyers have a structured color terminology that goes far beyond that available to ordinary speakers of English. The relative absence or presence of particular color terms in the lexicon of a given speech network is thus not a reflection of the state of that network's *code per se* as much as it is a reflection of the color interests, sensitivities and conventions of that network at a particular time in its history.

A color terminology is merely one kind of *folk-taxonomy*, i.e. it is an example of the many emic semantic grids that are contained in the lexicons of all speech communities. Other such examples are the kinship terminologies of speech communities, their disease or illness terminologies, their plant terminologies, their terms of address, etc. (Basso 1967; Conklin 1962; Frake 1961, 1962; Pospisil 1965; Friederich 1966; Metzger and Williams 1966; Price 1967; Wittermans 1967, etc.). In each of these instances the particular lexicons involved constitute 'un systeme on tout se tient'. Each such system is considered by its users to be both literally exhaustive and objectively correct. Nevertheless, each system is socially particularistic, i.e. for all of its self-evident objectivity ('what other kind of kinship system could there *possibly* be?' — we can imagine the average member of each of the scores of such systems asking himself), it is a reflection of locally accepted conventions rather than a necessary reflection either of nature or of language per se. This last is particularly well demonstrated in the work of Friederich (on Russian kinship terms), Wittermans (on Javanese terms of address), and Basso (on Western Apache anatomical terms and their extension to auto parts; see Figure 21).

The Russian revolution brought with it such fargoing social change that the kinship terms in use in Czarist days had to be changed to some degree. In contrast with the refined stratificational distinctions that existed in Czarist days — distinctions that recognized gradations of power, wealth and proximity within the universe of kin, not unlike those that were recognized in the larger universe of social and economic relationships — Soviet society stressed far fewer and broader distinctions.

As a result, various kinship terms were abandoned entirely, others were merged and other were expanded. A very similar development transpired in Javanese with respect to its highly stratified system of terms of address. The impact of post-war independence, industrialization, urbanization and the resulting modification or abandonment of traditional role-relationships led to the discontinuation of certain terms of address and the broadening of others, particularly of those that implied relatively egalitarian status between interlocutors. Howell's review of changes in the pronouns of address in Japan (1967) also makes the same point, as did his earlier study of status markers in Korean (1965). Not only does he indicate how individuals change the pronouns that they use in referring to themselves and to each other, as their attitudes and roles vis-a-vis each other change, but he implies that widespread and cumulative changes of this kind have occurred in Japan since the war, to the end that certain pronouns have been practically replaced by others. Certainly the best known study of this kind is Brown and Gilman's review of wide-spread Western European social change with respect to the use of informal (T) vs. formal (V) pronouns and verb forms for the third person singular (1960). Feudalism, renaissance, reformation, the French Revolution, 19th century liberalism and 20th century democratization each had recognizable and cumulative impact. As a result, both T and V forms were retained in interclass communication (except in the case of English) but their differential use came to indicate differences primarily in *solidarity* or differences in *solidarity and in power* rather than differences in *power alone* as had been the case in the early middle ages (see Figure 22).

Note that the complexities of the pre-revolutionary kinship taxonomies in Russia did not keep Russians from thinking about or from engaging in revolution. Note also that the revolution did not entirely scrap the pre-existing kinship taxonomy. Similarly, the Apache anatomical taxonomy did not preclude (but rather assisted) taxonomic organization of automobile parts. Thus, while we are clearly indicating the untenability of any strong linguistic *relativity* position when we show that semantic taxonomies are subject to change, expansion and contraction as the socio-cultural realities of their users change, we are also demonstrating that their linguistic *reflection* of social reality is also likely to be both slow and partial. Nevertheless, as between the two, the taxonomic *reflection* of socio-cultural reality is more likely to have widespread heuristic utility at any given time, however much the existence of such taxonomies is likely to be *constraining* in the momentary cognitive behavior of individual members or socio-cultural systems.

The emic distinctions which underlie these taxonomies are differentially constraining for various interaction networks within any speech community. Some networks (e.g. the networks of quantitative scientists) can repeatedly rise above the cognitive constraints of the taxonomies current in their speech communities. These networks are likely to be the ones that are most actively engaged in social change and in taxonomic change as well. Other networks are unable to break out of the socio-cultural taxonomies that surround them. In such cases, as, e.g. in connection

ndɛ bi tsi ("man's body").									ni ("face")		ɛbiyɪ' ("entrails")					
łikɔ ("fat")	dɔ ("chin and jaw")	wos ("shoulder")	gən ("hand and arm")	kai ("thigh and buttock")	zε' ("mouth")	kε' ("foot")	ʔən ("back")	inda ("eye")	čį ("nose")	ta ("forehead")	tsəs ("vein")	zɪk ("liver")	pɪt ("stomach")	čɪ ("intestine")	ji ("heart")	jisolɛ ("lung")

a. TAXONOMIC STRUCTURE OF ANATOMICAL SET

Note: Black bars indicate position of additional (unextended) anatomical terms.

nałbil bɪ tsi ("automobile's body")									ni[a]		ɛbiyɪ' ("machinery under hood")					
łikɔ ("grease")	dɔ ("front bumper")	wos ("front fender")	gən ("front wheel")	kai ("rear fender")	zε' ("gas pipe opening")	kε' ("rear wheel")	ʔən ("bed of truck")	inda ("headlight")	čį ("hood")	ta ("front of cab," "top")	tsəs ("electrical wiring")	zɪk ("battery")	pɪt ("gas tank")	čɪ ("radiator hose")	ji ("distributor")	jisolɛ ("radiator")

b. TAXONOMIC STRUCTURE OF EXTENDED SET

[a] 'Area extending from top of windshield to bumper'

Fig. 21. Lexical structure and social change: Western Apache examples
(Keith H. Basso, "Semantic aspects of linguistic acculturation", *American Anthropologist*, 69 (1967), 471-477).

with Kantrowitz's race relations taxonomy among White and Negro prison inmates (1967; see Figure 23), or Price's botanical taxonomies among the Huichols (1967), these taxonomies may be taken not only as useful *reflections* of the cognitive world of the speech community from which they are derived but also as forceful *constraints* on the cognitive behavior of most, if not all, of the individual members of these networks.

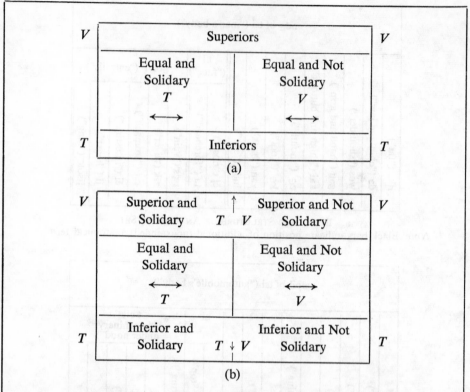

Fig. 22. The two-dimensional semantic (a) in equilibrium and (b) under tension (Brown) and Gilman 1960).

Solidarity comes into the European pronouns as a means of differentiating address among power equals. It introduces a second dimension into the semantic system on the level of power equivalents. So long as solidarity was confined to this level, the two-dimensional system was in equilibrium (see a), and it seems to have remained here for a considerable time in all our languages. It is from the long reign of the two-dimensional semantic that T derives its common definition as the pronoun of either condescension or intimacy and V its definition as the pronoun of reverence or formality. These definitions are still current but usage has, in fact, gone somewhat beyond them.

The dimension of solidarity is potentially applicable to all persons addressed. Power superiors may be solidary (parents, elder siblings) or not solidary (officials whom one seldom sees). Power inferiors, similarly, may be as solidary as the old family retainer and as remote as the waiter in a strange restaurant. Extension of the solidarity dimension along the dotted lines of Figure (b) creates six categories of persons defined by their relations to a speaker. Rules of address are in conflict for persons in the upper left and lower right categories. For the upper left, power indicates V and solidarity T. For the lower right, power indicates T and solidarity V.

Well into the nineteenth century the power semantic prevailed and waiters, common soldiers, and employees were called T while parents, masters, and elder brothers were called V. However, all our evidence consistently indicates that in the past century the solidarity semantic has gained supremacy. The abstract result is a simple one-dimensional system with the reciprocal T for the solidary and the reciprocal V for the nonsolidary.

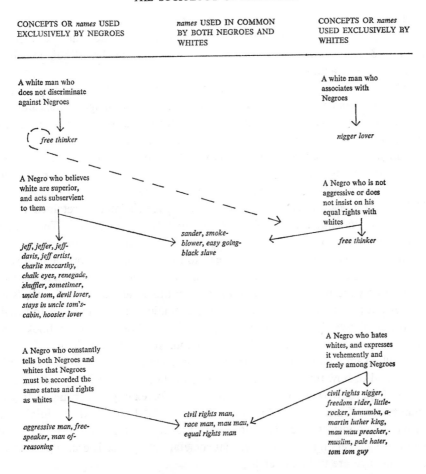

Fig. 23. Selected examples of vocabulary used by White and Negro Prison Inmates (N. Kantro-witz, American Dialect Society, Chicago, 1967).

8.3 Lexical Structure Reflects Social Organization

There are, however, more pervasive (and, therefore, seemingly less systematic) ways in which lexicons in particular and languages as a whole are reflective of the speech communities that employ them. In a very real sense a language variety is an inventory of the concerns and interests of those who employ it at any given time. If any portion of this inventory reveals features not present in other portions this may be indicative of particular stresses or influences in certain interaction networks within the speech community as a whole or in certain role-relationships within the community's total role-repertoire. Thus, Epstein's study of linguistic innovation on the Copperbelt of Northern Rhodesia (1959) revealed that the English and other Western influences on the local languages were largely limited to matters dealing with urban, industrial and generally non-traditional pursuits and relationships. Similarly, M. Weinreich's meticulous inquiry into the non-Germanic elements in Yiddish (1953) sheds much light on the dynamics of German-Jewish relations in the 11th century Rhineland.

Like all other immigrants to differently-speaking milieus, Jews, learning a variety of medieval German in the 11th century, brought to this language-learning task sociolinguistic norms which incorporated their prior verbal repertoire. In this case the repertoire consisted of a vernacular (Loez, a variety of Romance) and a set of sacred languages (Hebrew-Aramaic). However, the pre-existing sociolinguistic norms did not impinge upon the newly acquired Germanic code in either a random fashion or on an equal-sampling basis. Quite the contrary. Both the Romance and the Hebraic-Aramaic elements in Yiddish were overwhelmingly retained to deal with a specific domain: traditional religious pursuits and concerns. The Christo-logical overtones of many common German words, for example *lesen* (to read) and *segnen* (to bless), were strong enough to lead to the retention of more neutral words of Romance origin (*levenen* and *bentshn*) in their stead. Similarly, Hebrew and Aramaic terms were retained not only for all traditional and sanctified objects and ceremonies but also in doublets with certain Germanic elements in order to provide contrastive emphases: *bukh* (book) vs. *seyfer* (religious book, scholarly book); *lerer* (teacher) vs. *melamed* or *rebi* (teacher of religious subjects), etc. Thus, Yiddish is a wonderful example of how *all* languages in contact borrow from each other selectively and of how this very selectivity is indication of the primary interests and emphases of the borrowers and the donors alike (for examples pertaining to early Christianity see Knott 1956; Mohrman 1947, 1957). Indeed, M. Weinreich has conclusively demonstrated (1953, 1967, etc.) that a language not only reflects the society of its speakers but, conversely, that societal data per se is crucial if language usage and change are to be understood.

Findling's work too (1969) is interpretable in this fashion, demonstrating as it does that Spanish and English among Puerto Rican youngsters and adults in the Greater New York Metropolitan area reflect different psycho-social needs and con-flicts. In word-association tasks Findling found his subjects mentioning humans more frequently in English than in Spanish and more frequently in the work and education domains than in the home and neighborhood (Tables XXIA and XXIB). According to various previous studies in the area of personality theory, the pre-valence of human terms in such unstructured tasks is indicative of 'need affiliation', that is, the need to be accepted into positive relationships with others. Findling therefore maintains that the language of Puerto Ricans in New York reveals this need to be stronger (because less gratified) in English interactions and in Anglo-controlled domains than in Spanish interactions and Puerto Rican controlled do-mains. Knowing, or suspecting, as we do from other sources, that Puerto Ricans in New York are struggling for acceptance in an Anglo-dominated world, Findling's interpretations seem reasonable and intriguing indeed.

Table XXI A

Analysis of Variance of Human Ratio (Need Affiliation) Scores
(Findling 1969)

Source of Variance	Sum of Squares	df	Mean Square	F	F_{95}	F_{99}
Between subjects	19,573.09	31				
Occupation (C)	110.73	1	110.73	.17	4.17	7.56
Error (b)	19,463.08	30	648.77			
Within subjects	65,904.10	288				
Language (A)	701.69	1	701.69	3.78*	4.17	7.56
Domain (B)	12,043.27	4	3,010.82	12.10**	2.44	3.47
AB	239.49	4	59.87	.48	2.44	3.47
AC	181.84	1	181.84	.98	4.17	7.56
BC	1,855.50	4	463.87	1.86	2.44	3.47
ABC	446.16	4	111.54	.89	2.44	3.47
Error (w)	50,436.15	270				
Error₁ (w)	5,571.17	30	185.71			
Error₂ (w)	29,851.83	120	248.77			
Error₃ (w)	15,013.15	120	125.11			
Total	18,477.19	319				

* $p > .07$
** $p > .01$

Table XXI B

Mean Need Affiliation Ratio Scores by Language and Domain (Findling 1969)

Language	Domain					
	Work	Education	Religion	Neighborhood	Home	Total
English	33	24	20	17	14	22
Spanish	28	23	17	13	14	19
Total	30	23	18	15	14	20

8.4   *Language Behavior and Societal Behavior: A Circular Process of Mutual Creations*

The difference between the language constraint view and the language reflection view is related to the difference between being interested in language as *langue* and language as *parole*. It is also related to the difference between being interested in inter-cultural variation and being interested in intra-societal variation. Obviously, the sociology of language is more fully at home with the latter level of analysis, in both cases, than with the former. However, the latter level too can be overstated, particularly if it is claimed that not only is language behavior a *complete* index to social behavior, but, also, that it is nothing more than an index of such behavior. While indices are merely passive, language behavior is an active force as well as a reflective one. Language behavior feeds back upon the social reality it reflects and helps to reinforce it (or to change it) in accord with the values and goals of particular interlocutors.

When Weinreich relates that Yiddish (then Judeo-German) came to be the vernacular of Rhineland Jewry because Jews and non-Jews on the eastern shore of the Rhine shared open networks and because higher status in these Jewish-Gentile networks also came to provide Jews with higher status in their own closed networks, he is saying much more than that language usage reflects social interaction. Of course, Judeo-German was a reflection of the fact that Jews and Gentiles participated in common open networks. However, Judeo-German also helped implement and reinforce these networks, and, thus, became a co-participant in creating or preserving the social reality that it reflected. Similarly, when Weinreich tells us that Judeo-German became increasingly more indigeneously normed (and therefore increasingly more Yiddish and less Judeo-German) he is referring to much more than a linguistic reflection of the primacy of its closed networks for this Jewish community. He is also telling us that the uniquely Jewish aspects of Yiddish (in phonology, lexicon and grammar) also helped foster the primacy of Jewish closed networks for its speakers. As a result, Yiddish not only reflected (as it does today) the cohesiveness and separateness of its speakers, but it helped to preserve and to augment these characteristics as well.

Thus, both unidirectional views are outgrowths of an artificial search for independent variables and original causes. The original cause of any societal behavior may well be of some interest but it is historical interest rather than a dynamic one with respect to life as it continues round about us. If we can put aside the issue of 'what first caused what' we are left with the fascinating process of ongoing and intertwined conversation and interaction. In these processes language and societal behavior are equal partners rather than one or the other of them being 'boss' and 'giving orders' to the other.

9. APPLIED SOCIOLOGY OF LANGUAGE

One of he wisest maxims that Kurt Lewin bequeathed to social psychology is that which claims that 'nothing is as practical as a good theory'. In addition, social science theory is undoubtedly enriched by attempting to cope with the real problems of the workaday world. Thus, if social science theory is *really* any good (really powerful, really correct), it should have relevance for practitioners whose work brings them into contact with larger or smaller groups of human beings. Applied sociology of language attempts both to enrich the sociology of language and to assist in the solution of societal language problems. The applied sociology of language is of particular interest whenever: (a) language varieties must be 'developed' in order to function in the vastly new settings, role-relationships or purpose in which certain important networks of their speakers come to be involved, or (b) whenever important networks of a speech community must be taught varieties (or varieties in particular media or uses) that they do not know well (or at all) so that these networks may function in the vastly new settings, role-relationships or purposes that might then become open (or more open) to them. In many instances (a) and (b) co-occur, that is, language varieties must be both developed and taught in order that important networks within a speech community may be fruitfully involved in the new settings, role-relationships and purposes that have become available to them. This is but another way of saying that planned language change and planned social change are highly interrelated activities and that the sociology of language is pertinent to their interaction.

Comments on the uses of sociology of language must keep in mind for separate categories of actual and potential users, namely, linguists and sociologists on the one hand, and the users of linguistics as well as the users of sociology on the other hand. The sociology of language, as a hybrid or bridge-building specialization, is useful not *only* as it pertains to the front line of contact between science and society but *also* as it enables those in theoretical heartlands to understand their basic fields afresh and in refreshing ways. Application and applicability are themselves an endless array of concentric circles that surround all immediate problems in an ever-widening and interlocking flow. It is never wise to rigidly declare some knowledge 'useful' and other 'useless', for neither knowledge nor usefulness (nor even the very problems to which both are referred) hold still long enough for such judgments to be more than myopic indicators of how near or far we stand with respect to a particular and often fleeting goal. All knowledge is useful, and if at any point in time we nevertheless grope toward a consideration of the 'uses of X', it is merely because for some particular purposes at some particular time some knowledge may seem *more useful* than others.

This section proceeds by reviewing a few recognized topics within applied linguistics in order to illustrate and document a point of view with respect to the usefulness of the sociology of language. Its point of departure is Charles A. Ferguson's well known attempt to divide applied linguistics into its five most common American branches: the creation and revision of writing systems, literacy efforts, translation work, language teaching efforts, and language policy efforts (Ferguson and Morgan 1959; for a German and a Soviet view see Kandler 1955 and Andreev and Zinder 1959). Although it will be impossible to give equally detailed attention to all five of these branches of applied linguistics here, it would seem that essentially similar questions must be addressed to each of them, namely, what has been accomplished *without* formal sociolinguistic awareness and sophistication?; what has the sociology of language *contributed* to more recent applied linguistic efforts in these topical areas?; finally, what more *could* the sociology of language contribute to these (and even to other) applied linguistic concerns if its practitioners were to really take *both* parts of this hybrid field with *equal seriousness* and with the deep technical and theoretical proficiency that they *both* require.

9.1 *Creation of Writing Systems*

The sophistication of phonological theory, both that of the early part of this century as well as that of very recent years, and the recent linguistic interest in theories of writing systems and in the relations between such systems and spoken language are, and have long been, powerful linguistic contributions to the worldwide efforts to create writing systems for pre-literate peoples. However, the very sophistication of the linguist's professional skills in code description and code creation merely intensified the separation trauma when it became obvious that it was necessary to go outside the code and to confront the real world if writing systems were not only to be devised (this being the only apparent concern of Pike 1947 or Ray 1963) but also *employed*. The first steps in this direction were moderate indeed. These consisted of Vachek's (1945/49 and 1948) and Bolinger's (1946) protests (among others) that the writing system must be viewed separately from the spoken code, i.e. that it could not properly be viewed as merely the phonetic transcription of the spoken code, and that it was basically a 'visual system' (being not unlike the language interaction of the deaf in this respect) with regularities all its own.

The reverberations of these early protests are still with us. As Berry has pointed out (1958), new alphabets have clearly become less purely phonemic and more inclined to the 'use of reason and expedience' (rather than to rely on phonemicization alone) in their pursuit of acceptance. Indeed, the latter concern, that of acceptance, has tended to replace the former, that of 'reduction to writing', and, as a result, arguments pertaining to intra-(written) code phenomena have tended to recede evermore into the background. While 'phonetic ambiguity' is still considered a 'bad' thing and while it is generally agreed that 'words pronounced differently should be kept graphically apart' (Bradley 1913–14) it is considered to be an even 'worse thing' if alphabets of exquisite perfection remain unused or unaccepted. More and more work on the creation of writing systems has shown awareness of the fact that such nonacceptance is only to a relatively minor degree governed by intra-code ambiguities, inconsistencies or irrelevancies (all of these being rampant characteristics of the most widely used writing systems today and throughout history). Time and again in recent years the greater importance of extra-code phenomena has been hinted at (Gelb 1952; Bowers 1968), pointed to (Sjoberg 1964, 1966; Walker 1969) and, finally, even listed and catalogued (Nida 1954; Smalley 1964).

9.2 Desired Similarity and Dissimilarity

Perhaps because their attention is basically directed toward intra-code factors, linguists and applied linguists were quickest to notice those extra-code factors in the adoption or rejection of writing systems which indicated societal preferences or antipathies for writing conventions associated with some other language or languages. Thus, among the 'practical limitations to a phonemic orthography' Nida (1954) discussed the fact that both the Otomi and the Quechua 'suffer from cultural insecurity' and want their writing systems not only to 'look like Spanish' but to operate with the same graphematic alternances as does Spanish, *whether these are needed or not* in terms of their own phonemic system. In a related but crucially different vein Hans Wolff recommended (1954) that Nigerian orthographies be created not only in terms of tried and true technically linguistic criteria (such as 'accuracy, economy and consistency') but that 'similarity to the orthographies of related languages' also be used as a guide. Of course, Wolff was merely following in the footsteps of the Westermann Script of the late '20s, which, in its fuller, more generally applicable form, became the All-Africa Script of the International African Institute (Anon. 1920; see also Tucker 1971). However, he was also following in the tradition that placed the linguist or other outside expert in the position of judging not only *which languages* were sufficiently related in order to deserve a common writing system, but that placed them in the position of deciding whether such similarity in writing systems was or was not a 'good thing' and whether it was or was not desired by the speech communities involved.

However, once having stepped outside of the charmingly closed circle of intra-code considerations, Pandora's box had been opened never again to be shut. In very recent days, to mention only such examples, Serdyuchenko has assured us that the Cyrillic alphabet is used as the model in 'the creation of new written languages in the USSR' only because of the widespread and still growing interest in subsequently more easily learning Russian, just as Sjoberg (1966) mentions Tlingit insistence that their orthography 'follow the rather chaotic orthographic patterns of English wherever possible in order to conform to the demands of the broader society' (p. 217), and the Institut Français d'Afrique Noire concludes that speakers of African vernaculars in Francophone countries want their orthographies to look as French as possible (Smalley 1964). Walker (1969), like Serdyuchenko before him (1962), is

quite willing to champion such modeling at the explicit expense of maximal phonemic efficiency. Recently the Bamako Meeting on the Use of the Mother Tongue
for Literacy (February 28 – March 5, 1966, UNESCO sponsored) went a step
further. It not only recommended that new writing systems be similar to those of
unrelated but important languages for the learners (Bowers 1968), but it also warned
of 'possible repercussions of a technical and economic nature' following upon the
adoption of Non-European diacritics and special letters in the standard transcrip-
tions of West African languages (Ferru 1966). Such letters and diacritics, it is
pointed out, increase the cost of printing and typing, as well as the cost of manufacturing printing and typing equipment, and do so at the time when the per capita
cost of printed or typed material is already likely to be troublesomely high in view
of the limited number of consumers available for them in newly literate societies.
On these same grounds the Institut d'Afrique Noire insisted as far back as 1959
that 'when symbols have to be made up they should be typable on a standard
French typewriter' (Smalley 1964).

The obverse case has been less fully documented, namely, that in which newly
literate communities have desired a more *distinctive* writing system, one that they
could call *their own* or one that would more effectively differentiate their language
from others with respect to which they sought not similarity but rather *dissimilarity*.
Dickens' (1953) discussion of the Ashante rejection of the Akuapem-based writing
system for standard Twi (in the late 30s and early 40s) is one such case. Another
is Ferguson's brief reference to the fact that St. Stefan of Perm (14th century) purposely created a separate alphabet for the Komi (giving 'some of the letters an
appearance suggestive of the Tamga signs in use among the Komi as property
markers and decorations' (1967 : 259) 'so that the Komi could regard the writing
system as distinctively theirs and not an alphabet used for another language'. There
must be many examples of this kind, e.g. St. Mesrop's creation of the Armenian
alphabet in the fifth century, utilizing in part characters like those of far-distant
brother-Menophysite Christians in Ethiopia with whom contact had probably been
made (according to Olderogge) as a result of the presence of both Armenian and
Ethiopian churches in Jerusalem. Another such example is Sequoyah's syllabary
which was 'not associated with aliens but developed within the Cherokee language
community itself' (Walker 1969 : 149; also see White 1962). Finally, to the above
cases there must be added the few preliminary studies of indigenous African and
Asian scripts of relatively small communities that weathered competitive pressures
precisely because of their real or assumed local origins (e.g. Dalby 1967, 1968; Hair
1963; Stern 1968; G. Stewart 1967). Perhaps the relative reluctance to document
such cases is not unrelated to the more general reluctance of those who practice
applied linguistics upon others to recognize the frequent desires of non-literate
peoples to be themselves (albeit 'in a modern way'), rather than merely to be imita-
tive copies of *ourselves* (whether we be Chinese, Russian, Arab, French, British,
American, Spanish, or Portuguese).

9.3 'A Little More Complicated Than That'

If economics answers all questions with 'supply and demand', psychology with 'stimulus and response' and education with 'it all depends', then the first contribution of the sociology of language to applied linguistics is doubtlessly to stress the fact that the relations and interpenetrations between language and society are 'a little more complicated than that', whatever *that* may be. Indeed, although it is half a century since Radin (1924) first implied that the adoption (actually, the borrowing) of an alphabet by an aboriginal people was a fascinatingly complex and internally differentiated chain of social processes, we have not to this very day seriously followed up this seeming complexity, let alone tried to reduce it to some underlying set of basic dimensions. Our technical expertise and theoretical sophistication lead us more readily to agree with Burns' (1953) early conclusion, based on sad experience with the failure of 'linguistics without sociology' in Haiti, that the choice of an orthography has widespread social and political implications. They also lead us to continually admire Garvin's accounts (1954, also see 1959) of his attempts to achieve consumer consensus and participation in the creation of a standard orthography for Ponape, and to share his disappointment that even this was not enough to assure the use of that orthography. Beyond such agreement and admiration, however, we can only suggest that the process of gaining acceptance for technically sound writing systems is even 'a little more complicated than that'. In spelling out this complexity, applied sociology of language uniquely stresses that it is crucial to systematically look *outside* of the linguistic system itself if one is to locate the reasons for the differential acceptance or rejection of programs of linguistic change. Modern sociology of language can contribute most by linking this particular topic of applied linguistics with the body of theory and practice that has grown up in connection with the acceptance of other systematic innovations, the planning of social change more generally, and the amelioration of the inevitable dislocations that follow upon the introduction of innumerable innovations and changes of which new writing systems are merely symptomatic.

The creation of writing systems is itself necessarily an outgrowth of culture contact, if not of political and economic domination from outside. Thus, the creation of a writing system is singularly unlikely to be viewed dispassionately and its propagation and acceptance by indigenous networks are necessarily viewed as having implications for group loyalty and group identity. Latinization, Arabization, Cyrillization or Sinoization are not merely fargoing indications of desired (and frequently of subsidized or directed) social change and cognitive-emotional reorganization, but they have immediate consequences for the relevance of traditional elitist skills and implications for the distribution of new skills and statuses related to literacy and to the philosophy or ideology which is the carrier of literacy.

The creation of writing systems is significant only insofar as it leads to the acceptance and implementation of writing systems. The latter are broadly revolutionary rather than narrowly technical acts. They succeed or fail far less on the basis of the adequacy of their intra-code phonological systems or on the basis of their fidelity to model systems, than on the basis of the success of the larger revolutions with which they are associated; revolutions in the production and consumption of economic goods (leading to new rural-urban population distributions, new jobs, new training programs, new avocations, new pastimes, and new purposive social groups) and revolutions in the distributions of power and influence. All of these both lead to and depend upon an increasing number of new texts and new written records. Thus, when sociolinguistic attention is finally directed to the creation of writing systems it will be focused upon the organization, functioning and disorganization of an increasingly literate society. This is potentially a very useful addition to the linguist's disciplinary focus because even more than writing changes speech (via 'spelling pronunciations') literacy changes speakers and societies. It is this perspective on the creation of writing systems — as always, a perspective which is outside of the linguistic system alone — that is part of the programmatic promise of the sociology of writing systems.

How will such attention improve or alter the creation of writing systems? Precisely by relating the problem of creation to the problem of acceptance, of impact, of possible dislocation, of possible manipulation, of possible exploitation, of possible redistribution of power and, in general, of the dependency of the very best writing system on revolutionary processes at their most pragmatic as well as at their most symbolic.

9.4 *Orthographic Reform*

To some extent such liberation and immersion are more advanced with respect to the study and planning of orthographic *reforms*, perhaps because the truly vast amount of technical linguistic effort invested in these reforms has yielded such meager results. Even though orthographic reform may be so sweeping as to involve the complete replacement of one writing system by another (and, in that sense, it may be viewed as a subcategory of the topic just reviewed), it deals with already literate networks and as a result, more clearly reveals the social ramifications and reverberations of seemingly technical linguistic adjustments.

If the introduction of a newly created writing system easily threatens to change established lines of relative advantage and disadvantage, practical and symbolic, the revision of traditional orthographies most often obviously *attempts* to do so. Orthographic change represents departure from an established written tradition and, as such, it *must* cope with the gatekeepers of that written tradition, the poets, priests, principals and professors, and the institutions and symbols that they create and serve, or be destined to oblivion. Indeed, the greater and grander the tradition of literacy, literature and liturgy in an orthographic community, the less likely that even minor systematic orthographic change will be freely accepted and the less likely that any orthographic change will be considered minor.

In this connection we have a larger number of rather detailed and, to some extent, *sociolinguistically oriented* descriptions, than is the case for the creation of writing systems, but, as yet we have no sociological analyses or hypotheses per se. The socio-culturally contextualized descriptions of orthographic reforms in the USSR (Kolarz 1967; Ornstein 1959; Quelquejay and Bennigsen 1961; Serdyuchenko 1965, Weinreich 1953b; Winner 1952), Turkey (Rossi 1927, 1929, 1935, 1942, 1953; Heyd 1954; Özmen 1967; Gallagher 1967 and 1969), Norway (Haugen 1966a, which contains an exhaustive bibliography of other studies) and Vietnam (Haudricourt 1943; Nguyen dinh Hoa 1960; Thompson 1965) again point to the literally revolutionary nature of the societal processes that have often accompanied system-wide orthographic change. On the other hand, the available descriptions of far less successful attempts to bring about orthographic change under less dramatic circumstances, e.g. in Japan (DeFrancis 1947; Holton 1947; Meyenberg 1934; Scharshmidt 1924; Toshio 1967), Haiti (Valdman 1968; Burns 1953) and Israel (Rabin 1969), or to bring about the orthographic unification of closely related languages in the absence of accompanying societal unification, e.g. in India (Anon. 1963; Jones 1942; Ray 1960), Africa (Dickens 1953; Ward 1945) and Indonesia-Malaysia (Alisjahbana 1969 and in press), all indicate the difficulties encountered and the failures experienced thus far.

However, there is no justification for interpreting the above cited investigations as implying 'revolutionary success and non-revolutionary failure' as the proper summation of experience with orthographic reform. In earlier centuries a great deal of orthographic reform seems to have been accomplished both quietly and successfully without the involvement of mobilized populations or, indeed, of any other population segments than 'the authorities' whose business it was to make wise decisions for the community. The initial orthographic distinctions between Serbian and Croatian, or between Ruthenian (Ukrainian) and Polish, were decided upon by representatives of God and/or Caesar who sought to cultivate differences between speech communities that were otherwise 'in danger' of religious, political and linguistic unification. Indeed, the Ausbau languages (in Kloss's sense, 1952) are all instances of the success of applied linguistics and should be carefully studied as such. The restoration of written Czech (and Slovak) in Latin script was engineered by Count Sedlnitzsky, the administrative director of the Austro-Hungarian police and one of the most influential officials under the Emperor Francis (early 19th century), by subsidizing the publication of the Orthodox prayer book in Latin letters as 'an important device to fight the political danger of the Pro-Russian Pan-Slav movement' (Fischel 1919:57). The Roumanian shift from Cyrillic to Latin script in 1863 was accomplished by a painless edict which sought to further that nation's self-defined Latinizing and Christianizing role in the heathen 'Slavo-Moslem' Balkans (Kolarz 1964). In more recent days Irish orthography has been changed without arousing unusual interest or opposition (Macnamara 1969), as was the type font (from an 'Irish looking' font to an ordinary roman font). Indeed, the relative ease with which these changes were made may be a reflection of the lack of widespread Irish interest or concern for the Language Revival.

Not only *has* there been much successful orthographic reform without revolutionary change (particularly where mass mobilization along language-related lines was absent for one reason or another) but there has also been a good bit of unsuccessful orthographic reform even when these have been accompanied by revolutionary social changes. Thus, the Soviet 'rationalization' of Yiddish orthography (Szajkowski 1966) initially aimed at both the *phonetization* of words of Hebrew-Aramaic origin, as well as at the *discontinuation* of the social final letters of the traditional Hebrew alphabet. However, twenty-five years after the October revolution, the names of the grandfathers of Modern Yiddish literature were neither spelled

מענדעלע מויבער ספֿאָרים, ייצכאָק לייבוש פֿערעצ און שאָלעם אלייכעם

(as they *had* been throughout the 20s and 30s), nor were they spelled

מענדעלע מוכד ספֿדים, יעהק לייבוש פֿדן אזו שלום עליכם

(as they *had* been before the Revolution and continued to be everywhere outside of the Soviet Union), but, rather, in an attempt to reach a compromise that would maximize the propaganda value of the few permitted Yiddish publications primarily distributed to and published for readers outside of the USSR:

מענדעלע טויכעד ספֿאָדים ייעכאָק לייבוש מעדעץ און שאָלעם אלייכעם

However, even in its heyday the Soviet revolution in Yiddish orthography could not overcome the visual traditions of the orthographic community. The initial silent aleph at the beginning of words that would otherwise begin with the vowels י and ו was *never* dropped, regardless of its phonemic uselessness, perhaps because the initial silent aleph in such cases was considered to be too strong a visual convention to be tampered with (Hebrew writing itself — i.e. the visual precursor to written Yiddish — never beginning words with vocalic י or ו).

A far more widely renowned revolutionary attempt at orthographic reform which has failed (certainly thus far) is the once promised phonetization of (Northern Mandarin) Chinese. While the basic sources available to us in English (DeFrancis 1950 and 1968; Mills 1956 and Hsia 1956) all agree that the Latinized New Writing was abandoned sometime late in the fifties, the reason for this abandonment can still only be surmised.

By 1956 it had become necessary to defend the 'Han (Chinese) language phonetization draft plan' as being concerned with an alphabet (Latin) which was truly progressive and international rather than necessarily related to any anti-proletarian class (Chinese Written Language Reform Committee 1956; Wu Yu-Chang 1956). By 1959 Chou En-lai had officially demoted phonetization from its original goal of immediate 'liberation and development of the whole Chinese language from the shackless of the monosyllabic Chinese characters' (Ni Hai-shu 1949, cited by De-Francis 1968) to third place and the indefinite future, after both simplification of the traditional characters and adoption of a spoken standard for 'Common Speech' had been attained (Chou En-lai 1965). While work on the first two tasks is constantly going on in a very direct fashion (see, e.g. Anon. 1963 and Wu Yu-Chang 1965) work on the latter is primarily nominal (that is, phonetization is kept alive as a distant goal but is not substantively advanced) and indirect (i.e. phonetization is utilized for subsidiary purposes, such as annotating novel or complex Chinese characters in technical texts, furthering instruction in the Common Speech among speakers of other regional languages, or creating 'initial alphabetic scripts' for illiterate non-Chinese speaking minorities). Indeed, while phonetization has recently been reported to be superior for such special purposes as telegraphic communication (Wu Yu-Chang 1964) and minority group initial literacy (Li Hui 1960) the traditional characters have again been proclaimed as superior in connection with general education for the bulk of the population among whom these characters are viewed as symbolic of education and the standard pronunciation (Serruys 1962)! The goal of phonetization is, seemingly, still a long way off and may or may not be reached any more rapidly than the withering away of the state (see several references to this effect in Kwan-wai Chiu 1970).

From the foregoing examples it is clear that if we but dichotomize both 'success' (acceptance) and 'revolutionary social change' we have examples of all four possible types of co-occurrences: successful orthographic revision with and without revolutionary social change and revolutionary social change with and without successful follow-through of planned orthographic revision. The discussions of revolutionary social change thus far encountered in studies of either the creation of writing systems or the revision of orthographies is still far too crude to be considered as more than rough labeling. As sociolinguistic description it is regrettably out of touch with the sizable modernization literature in economics, political science, sociology and anthropology. It lacks both the concepts and the technical data collection methods and data analysis skills needed to inquire into the intensity, extensity or continuity of the change forces and processes or the counter-change forces and processes that underly the gross labels so frequently encountered.

It is also unfortunate that there are *so few* localized case studies of *variation in sub-group reactions* to new writing systems or to revised orthographies and, conversely, proportionally *so many* commentaries, studies, evaluations, and recommendations that deal with entire countries, continents, and even the world at large. The result is an imbalance with respect to the usual mutual stimulation between micro-analysis and its emphases on process and function concerns, on the one hand, and macro-analysis and its emphases on structure, quantification, compositing and weighing of parameters on the other hand. Either type of study, when pursued too long without correction from the other, becomes myopic and, therefore dangerous for theory as well as (or even more so) for application. However, whereas both macro- and micro-studies are equally necessary for the growth of general socio-linguistic theory, the future of *applied* sociology of language is particularly tied to *within-context* studies (within nation X, within region Y, within district Z) and, therefore, to ever more detailed studies of differential acceptance processes, rather than to studies of large-scale between-context variation (the latter not having an immediate applied significance for any particular within-context problem).

9.5 *Language Planning*

Perhaps the area of applied linguistics which most clearly illustrates the full complexity of societal phenomena which the sociology of language may someday enable us to understand is that which is concerned with language planning. Just as sociolinguistic inquiry into the creation of writing systems and into the revision of orthographies permits us to first recognize and to then refine our appreciation of the magnitudes of social change and social planning (if not social dislocation) with which such activities are commonly associated, so the systematic sociolinguistic study of language *planning* as a whole (incorporating the creation of writing systems and the revision of orthographies, but going beyond them to conscious governmental efforts to manipulate both the structure and the functional allocation of codes within a polity) enables us to appreciate the societal complexity impinging on the determination, implementation and evaluation of language *policy* as a whole. The study of language planning is the study of organized efforts to find solutions to societal language problems (Jernudd and Das Gupta 1969). As such, it is necessarily most dependent — of all the fields of applied language concerns — on the sociology of language and on the social sciences as a whole in order to move from theory to informed practice (Figure 24).

Of the language planning studies recently completed or currently underway a few have dealt with the cost-benefit analysis of alternative or hypothetically alternative decisions between which governmental or other bodies must choose (Jernudd 1969; Thorburn 1969). Others have discussed the pressure functions focused upon decision making/decision implementing bodies in the language field (whether the latter be legislative-executive within government or political-religious-literary-academic outside of government) from a variety of special interest groups running the gamut from professional associations of educators, to manufacturers of typewriters and publishers of textbooks, to spokesmen for literary, journalistic and ideological groupings, etc. (Das Gupta 1969). There are now several theoretical models (happily commensurable) of the interaction of sentimental and instrumental integrative and disintegrative forces in the language planning process (Kelman 1969; Fishman 1969f). There are recent critiques and integrations of the literature on the evaluation of planned change in education, industry, agriculture and other areas of conscious societal planning, in an effort to suggest evaluative methods that might be most fruitfully adopted for the evaluation of success or failure in language planning (Macnamara 1966; Rubin 1969). A four-country study has recently gotten underway (involving linguists, anthropologists, political scientists, sociologists, psychologists and educationists) in order to obtain roughly comparable data concerning

Les grandes enquêtes de l'Office du Vocabulaire français de Paris

Depuis quelques années, l'opinion publique est alertée sur les dangers que court la langue française, et divers organismes, tant officiels que privés, ont été créés pour assurer la défense d'un idiome parlé par la communauté sans cesse grandissante des francophones: 90 millions aujourd'hui, ils seront 200 millions avant l'an 2000. Mais comment obtenir que la langue française, ciment de cette francophonie dont on parle tant, ne s'altère pas, ne dégénère pas, ne devienne pas un jargon à la syntaxe désordonnée et au vocabulaire truffé de néologismes mal assimilés?

Les règles du bon langage, on peut connaître. Les atteintes au bon langage, tout le monde les connaît également, ou peut les connaître à la lecture de maints ouvrages ou articles de presse. Ce que l'on connaît mal, c'est le moyen d'obtenir que les règles soient mieux respectées et l'invasion des néologismes contenue. L'opinion sait que l'usage est à corriger selon les principes d'une norme raisonnable. Mais elle ignore comment la norme, une fois établie, peut descendre jusqu'à l'usage, c'est-à-dire comment l'usage peut être *orienté,* simon *dirige* par la norme de manière efficace.

Précisément, la troisième Biennale de la langue française a inscrit à l'ordre du jour de ses prochains travaux une formule significative d'enquête: *De la norme à l'usage.* L'Office du Vocabulaire français, qui, on le sait, est à l'origine des Biennales, entend participer à cette recherche et fournir aux orateurs de la Biennale qui désireront s'informer sur l'opinion du grand public éclairé, une riche documentation. Celle-ci sera puisée à la meilleure source qui soit: le groupe que constituent les membres consultants de l'Office du Vocabulaire français.

C'est pourquoi nous vous demandons de bien vouloir répondre au questionnaire que voici:

1. Pensez-vous, d'une manière trés générale, qu'il soit possible d'agir sur les habitudes de langage d'une grande communauté humaine?

   N.B. – A cette première question, les membres de l'Office du Vocabulaire français répondront, de toute évidence, par un « oui». Mais toute personne qui répondra « non » devra développer ses raisons, qui pourront être constructives.

2. Pensez-vous que l'Enseignement soit le seul dispensateur de la norme et que nulle action sur l'usage ne soit concevable hors de l'école?

3. Croyez-vous que les adultes puissent recevoir un enseignement prolongué de la langue française, de la même manière qu'ils reçoivent, par les publications spécialisées, par les revues de vulgarisation scientifique ou technique, un enseignement prolongé en histoire, en physique, en histoire naturelle, en géographie... et même en astronautique?

Nous vous serions reconnaissants de bien vouloir répondre à ces questions, en portant en tête de votre lettre vos nom et prénom, profession, adresse.
Vous voudrez bien ajouter, également en tête de votre réponse, selon votre choix:
J'accepte que mon nom figure dans un compte rendu de synthèse (signature);
Je désire garder l'anonymat (id.).
Les réponses devront être adressées au secrétariat de

l'Office du Vocabulaire français, 17, rue de Montparnasse, Paris-VIe, France

Fig. 24. (*Le Travailleur,* June 7, 1969).

the processes of language planning per se in each of the above contexts (decision making, pressure functions, national integration, implementation and evaluation). Obviously, the study of language planning is rapidly moving away from intra-code efficiency considerations alone (the latter being the primary emphasis of Tauli 1968) and moving steadily into ever-richer contextual concerns. Hopefully, as language planning and social planning agencies become more aware of the possible contributions of applied sociology of language they may become more inclined to involve sociolinguists and other language specialists in *guiding* the decision making *process* itself rather than merely in *implementing* decisions *already reached*. Several signs already point in this direction. Thus, the several nations of East Africa are interested in the current 'Survey of Language Use and Language Teaching' (Prator 1967) in order to adopt or revise language operations in schools, mass media, public services, etc., on the basis of more precise information as to the age, number, location and interactions of the speakers of various local languages. Similarly, the Philippine government has long followed a policy of evaluating language policy in the area of education via research projects dealing with such matters as the advisability of initiating education in the local mother tongues and introducing the national language (Filipino) only in some optimal subsequent year (Ramos et al. 1967). The Irish government has sponsored 'motivation research' and opinion polls in order to determine how its citizens view the Irish language and how they react to the government's efforts to 'restore' it to wider functions (Anon. 1968). One of the most widely cited guides to governmental language policies and their educational implications is an applied sociolinguistic report issued by Unesco and dealing with "The use of the vernacular in education" (Anon. 1953). Once a policy is adopted it is then necessary to implement it. Such implementation not only takes the obvious route of requiring and/or encouraging the functional re-allocation of varieties but also their phonological, lexical and grammatical realization along prescribed lines. Language agencies, institutes, academies or boards are commonly authorized to develop or plan the variety selected by policymakers. Such agencies are increasingly likely to seek feedback concerning the effectiveness or the acceptability of the 'products' (orthographies, dictionaries, grammars, spellers, textbooks, translation series, subsidized literary works, etc.) that they have produced. Sociologists of language have already produced many studies which language agencies are likely to find extremely useful in terms of their implications for the work that such agencies conduct.

The difficulties encountered and the lessons learned in planned lexical expansion to cope with the terminology of modern technology, education, government and daily life are recounted by Alisjahbana (1962, 1965, 1971), Bacon (1966), Morag (1959), Passin (1963) and Tietze (1962) in their accounts of language planning in Indonesia, Central Asia, Japan, Israel and Turkey, respectively. The problems of planned language standardization have been illuminated by Ferguson (1968), Garvin (1959), Guxman (1960), Ray (1963), U. Weinreich (1953b), Havranek (1964), Valdman (1968) and Twaddell (1959) in sufficiently general terms to be of interest in any speech community where this process needs to be set in motion.

Even the very process of government involvement in language issues has begun to be documented. In this connection one must mention the reports of the Irish government on its efforts to restore the Irish language (Anon. 1965); Goodman's review of Soviet efforts to provide — as well as deny — indigenous *standard* languages to the peoples under their control (Goodman 1960); Haugen's many insightful reports of the Norwegian government's attempts to cope with language conflict by both protecting and limiting the linguistic divergence of its citizenry (Haugen 1961, 1966a, 1966b); Heyd's account of language reform in modern Turkey (Heyd 1954); Lunt's account of the studied efforts in Titoist Yugoslavia to separate Macedonian from Serbian and from Bulgarian (Lunt 1959) and Mayner's comments on the attempts to fuse Serbian and Croatian in that country (Mayner 1967); the contrasts between different parts of Africa noted by Mazrui (1967), Armstrong (1968), Polomé (1968) and Whiteley (1968); Mill's report of how Communist China advanced and retreated in connection with the writing reform it so desperately needs (Mills 1956); Wurm's descriptions of the very beginnings of language policy in reference to Pidgin English ('Neo-Melanesian') in New Guinea (Wurm and Laycock 1961–62), and several others (e.g. Brosnahan 1963a; LePage 1964; Fishman 1968c) of more general or conceptual relevance.

One of the most necessary areas of applied sociology of language is that which deals with educational problems, related to language policy formulation or evaluation. In this connection there have been studies of the organization and operation of bilingual schools (Gaarder 1967); of the academic consequences of compulsory education via the weaker language for most learners (Macnamara 1966, 1967); of different approaches to teaching a hitherto untaught mother tongue (Davis 1967); of varying South American and West Indian approaches of teaching both local and 'wider' languages (Burns 1968; LePage 1968; Rubin 1968); of difficulties in teaching English (as the compulsory school language for non-English speakers) encountered by teachers who are themselves non-native speakers of English (Lanham 1965); and, more specifically, of the role problem of teaching standard English to speakers of very discrepant, non-standard varieties of that language (Stewart 1964, 1965). A more generalized interest in applied sociology of language is that shown by the recent Canadian Royal Commission on Bilingualism and Biculturism (Royal Commission 1965, 1967, 1968). It authorized studies not only on bilingual schooling but also on bilingualism in broadcasting, in industrial operations, in military operations and in the operation of various other societal enterprises.

Nothwithstanding the obvious recent strengthening of applied sociology of language, several nations throughout the world are currently engaged in language planning without anything like the information available to them in other areas of planning. Sociolinguistic research on language planning must aim, first, to locate, then to apportion, the variation in behavior-toward-language which is to be observed in language planning contexts. It must seek detailed knowledge of how orthographic decisions (or script decisions, or, national language decisions, or nomenclature decisions, etc.) are arrived at, how they are differentially reacted to or followed up by agencies inside and outside government, how they are differentially accepted or resisted by various population segments, how they are differentially evaluated and how subsequent policies and plans are differentially modified as a result of feedback from prior policy and planning. The sociology of language is just now beginning to describe the variation that constantly obtains in all of these connections. After this has been done sufficiently well and in sufficiently many contexts it should begin to successfully account for this variation and, at that point, be able to offer suggestions that are useful from the point of view of those seeking to influence, implement or evaluate language planning in the future.

9.6 *Some Straws in the Wind*

However, even in the absence of the amount of detail and sophistication that is needed before practical information becomes available, 'sociolinguistically motivated' changes in applied linguistics are clearly on the increase. Not only are such topics as the creation of writing systems, the reform of orthographies and language planning more generally, marked (as we have seen) by a constantly increasing awareness of societal interpenetration and of the need for truly professional competence (which is more than simply being either critical or admiring) if one is to understand, let alone influence, the societal forces at work, but such awareness is growing in most other fields of applied linguistics as well.

The planning, implementation and evaluation of literary campaigns increasingly ceased being merely applied linguistics plus education pedagogy plus ethnography as the period of immediate post World War II exuberance was left behind (Smith 1956). What is currently being developed in this field goes beyond advice on how to establish proper local contacts and obtain official cooperation (Young 1944; Russell 1948), important though such advice undoubtedly is. It goes beyond care to adapt programs to local needs (Jeffries 1958), to utilize a variety of methods on a variety of fronts (Ivanova and Voskresensky 1959), or to evaluate outcomes broadly enough to include health, economic and other pertinent indices (UNESCO 1951). Current efforts to advance literacy are increasingly based upon efforts to more fully understand the meaning and impact of literacy via small pilot studies which seek to recognize and weigh alternatives (Correa and Tinbergen 1962; Lewis 1971; McClusker 1963) and clarify the societal dimensions of literacy enterprises in different contexts (Goody 1968; Hayes 1965; Nida 1967; Schofield 1968; Wurm 1966).

A similar systematic intrusion of societal considerations has become noticeable in the field of *translation*. It is here, in particular, that sociolinguistic differentiation of language into varieties and of speech communities into situations is beginning to be felt, perhaps more so than in any other field of applied linguistics. One cannot read Catford's *Linguistic theory of translation* (1965) without being delighted by the fact that it is far broader than 'immaculate linguistics' alone, and one cannot read Wonderly's *Bible translations for popular use* (1968) without wishing that its sensitivity to social varieties and social occasions were part of the professional orientation of translation for far more worldly purposes as well. Certainly the deep concern with recognizing the significance of functional variation in language variety use, the sensitivity shown with respect to the *situational analysis* of repertoires of social and linguistic behavior — viewing Bible reading and listening as kinds of situations that may require particular kinds of language — and the repeated attention given to the contextual-functional differences between written and spoken language (and the multiple varieties of each) must sooner or later feed back into religious work on the creation of writing systems and on literacy more generally. This is, indeed, the beginning of technical sociolinguistic utility for an applied field. Having once embarked along the path of recognizing that all of the factors influencing communicative appropriateness in a particular speech community also influence the acceptability and the impact of translations in that community, the probability of mutual enrichment between application and theory for both fields of endeavor (translation and sociology of language) is indeed very great.

The same may yet be the case for the huge field of language teaching, where the contacts with the sociology of language are still far more tenuous, if only because the contacts between an elephant and a sparrow must always be rather incomplete. Nevertheless, although the problems and prospects of language teaching could easily swallow up or trample underfoot not only all of the sociology of language but also all of sociology, psychology and linguistics per se, first linguistics and, more recently, the sociology of language *have* had some impact on the beast. A valuable introduction to sociology of language has been presented to language teachers generally by Halliday, McIntosh and Strevens (1964a). In this introduction teachers are urged to recognize the different uses (and, therefore, the different varieties) of language that coexist within speech communities rather than, as has usually been the case thus far, to persist in the erroneous and deadening fiction that there is always *only one* (and always the *same* one) correct variety.

More recently we have witnessed a deluge of 'sociolinguistically oriented' interest in the language of disadvantaged speakers of non-standard English with Bernstein's work (e.g. 1964) being best known in England and Labov's (1965) or McDavid's (1958) in the U.S.A. Most of the products of this interest seek to contrastively highlight the basic structure of the speech of such communities so that teachers may be able to more successfully recognize and overcome the difficulties that learners will encounter when confronted with the phonological and grammatical structures of standard (school) English (e.g. Labov 1966b; Labov et al. 1968; Wulfram 1969; Baratz and Shuy 1969). Nevertheless much (if not all) of what is currently offered to teachers in this connection is merely 'sociolinguistically oriented' (in that it recognizes that minority group members often utilize varieties of English unfamiliar to others) rather than sociology of language proper (Fishman 1969b; Fishman and Lueders 1972). 'Sociolinguistically oriented' advice is now also being directed toward teachers of bilinguals (Andersson 1969; Boyd 1968; Gaarder 1965). Such teachers are admonished that learners should be encouraged to maintain or acquire repertoires (incorporating several varieties) in each of their languages — rather than to displace all non-standard varieties in favor of one artificial standard version of each. Teachers of bilinguals are being urged to enable their students to select from each repertoire in accord with the norms for communicative appropriateness of the particular networks with which they (the pupils) seek mutually accepting interaction (Fishman and Lovas 1970; Mackey 1970). Nevertheless, the teachers of bilinguals (particularly in countries of mass immigration) have just begun to be shown how to influence the bilingual settings in which they and their students live and in which one or another of their languages may be roundly ignored, if not attacked, as soon as school is over (Andersson and Boyer 1970; John and Horner 1970).

Of course, the distance is still considerable between 'sociolinguistically oriented' advice or sensitivity training for teachers and any more complete interrelationship between teaching methodology and sociology of language. Thus the education of bilinguals is still viewed primarily within the context of disadvantaged and dislocated minorities (whose lot in life will be far easier if only they learn English, French, Russian, etc.) rather than within the broader context of worldwide experience with bilingual education — whether in conjunction with elitist bilingualism, traditional bilingualism, or, more generally, widespread and stable (i.e. non-dislocated) bilingualism. As a result, the education of speakers of non-standard English is being pondered without awareness, for example of the fact that most students entering German, French, Italian, and other schools during the past century have also been speakers of non-standard varieties of their respective languages. A true meeting of education and the sociology of language will enable *both* to discover why proportionally so many dialect speakers *do* and *did* seem to become readers and speakers of the standard language (and even of classical languages) in other parts of the world whereas so few seem to accomplish this in the U.S.A. today (Fishman and Lueders 1972). As with many other social science fields, a severe test of the power of the sociology of language will be its ability to be useful in the world of affairs. The education of non-literates, of bilinguals and of non-standard speakers are all fields about which the sociology of language must have more to say if it is really a discipline worth listening to at all.

BIBLIOGRAPHY

ALISJAHBANA, S. TAKDIR. 1962. The modernization of the Indonesian language in practice. Indonesian language and literature: Two essays, by S. T. Alisjahbana, pp. 1–22. New Haven, Conn., Yale University Southeast Asia Studies.

——. 1965. New national languages: A problem modern linguistics has failed to solve. Lingua 15.515–30.

——. 1969. Some planning processes in the development of the Indonesian/ Malay language. Consultative Meeting on Language Planning Processes. Honolulu, EWC-IAP. *Also in* Rubin and Jernudd 1971.

——. ed. 1971. The modernization of the language of Asia. Kuala Lumpur, University of Malaysia Press.

ANDERSSON, THEODORE. 1969. Bilingual schooling: Oasis or mirage? Hispania 52.69–74.

ANDERSSON, THEODORE, and MILDRED BOYER, eds. 1970. Bilingual schooling in the United States. 2 vols. Washington, D.C., USGPO.

ANDREEV, N. D., and L. R. ZINDER. 1959. Osnovnye problemy prikladnoj lingvistiki. VJa 1959/4.1–9.

ANON. 1930. Practical orthography of African languages. International Institute of African languages and cultures, Memorandum 1. Rev. ed. Oxford, Oxford University Press.

——. 1953. The use of vernacular languages in education. Paris, UNESCO.

——. 1963. A common script for Indian languages. Delhi, Ministry of Scientific Research and Cultural Affairs.

——. 1965. The restoration of the Irish language. Dublin, The Stationery Office. [Also note Progress Report for the period ended 31 March, 1966 and Progress Report for the period ended 31 March, 1968. Dublin, The Stationery Office, 1966 and 1968.]

——. 1968. A motivational research study for the greater use of the Irish language. 2 vols. Croton-on-Hudson, N.Y., Ernest Dichter International Institute for Motivational Research.

ARMSTRONG, ROBERT. 1968. Language policies and language practices in West Africa. *In* Fishman, Ferguson, and Das Gupta 1968, pp. 227–36.

BACON, ELIZABETH E. 1966. Russian influence on Central Asian languages. Central Asians under Russian rule, by E. E. Bacon, pp. 184–201. Ithaca, N.Y., Cornell University Press.

BARATZ, JOAN, and ROGER W. SHUY. 1969. Teaching black children to read. Washington, D.C., Center for Applied Linguistics.

BARKER, GEORGE C. 1947. Social functions of language in a Mexican-American community. Acta Americana 5.185–202.

BASSO, KEITH H. 1967. Semantic aspects of linguistic acculturation. AmA 69.-471–77.

BELL, DANIEL. 1961. The end of ideology. New York, Collier.

BERNSTEIN, BASIL. 1964. Elaborated and restricted codes: Their social origins and some consequences. AmA 66/6, Part 2.55–69.

——. 1966. Elaborated, and restricted codes: An outline. Sociological Inquiry 36.254–61.

BERRY, JACK. 1958. The making of alphabets. PICL 8.752–64. *Also in* Fishman 1968a, pp. 737–53.

BLANC, CHAIM. 1964. Communal dialects in Baghdad. Cambridge, Mass., Harvard University Press.

BLOM, JAN–PETER, and JOHN J. GUMPERZ. 1972. Some social determinants of verbal behavior. *In* Gumperz and Hymes 1972, pp. 407–34.

BLOOMFIELD, LEONARD. 1933. Language. New York, Holt.

BOCK, PHILIP K. 1964. Social structure and language structure. SJA 20.393–403. *Also in* Fishman 1968a, pp. 212–222.

BOLINGER, D. L. 1946. Visual morphemes. Lg 22.333–40.

BONJEAN, CHARLES M. 1966. Mass, class and the industrial community: A comparative analysis of managers, businessmen and workers. AJSoc 72.149–62.

BOTTENBERG, R. A., and K. H. WARD, JR. 1963. Applied multiple linear regression. Lackland, Texas, Lackland Air Force Base PRL-TDR-63-6.

BOULDING, KENNETH. 1963. The death of the city: A frightened look at post-civilization. The historian and the city, ed. by Oscar Handlin and John Burchard, p. 145ff. Cambridge, Mass., MIT Press and Harvard University Press.

BOWERS, JOHN. 1968. Language problems and literacy. *In* Fishman, Ferguson and Das Gupta 1968, pp. 381–401.

BOYD, DOROTHY L. 1968. Bilingualism as an educational objective. The Educational Forum 32.309–13.

BRADLEY, HENRY. 1913–14. On the relation between spoken and written language. Proceedings of the British Academy 6.212–32.

BRIGHT, WILLIAM. 1960. Animals of acculturation in the California Indian languages. UCPL 4/4.215–46.

BROOM, LEONARD, and NORVAL D. GLENN. 1966. Negro-White differences in reported attitudes and behavior. Sociology and Social Research 50.187–200.

BROSNAHAN, L. F. 1963a. Some historical cases of language imposition. Language in Africa, ed. by Robert Spencer, pp. 7–24. Cambridge, Cambridge University Press.

——. 1963b. Some aspects of the linguistic situation in tropical Africa. Lingua 12.54–65.

BROWN, ROGER W., and ALBERT GILMAN. 1960. The pronouns of power and solidarity. Style in language, ed. by Thomas A. Sebeok, pp. 253–76. Cambridge, Mass. and New York, Technology Press of MIT and Wiley. *Also in* Fishman 1968a, pp. 252–75.

BROWN, ROGER W., and ERIC H. LENNEBERG. 1954. A study in language and cognition. JAbSocPsych 49.454–62.

BURNS, DONALD. 1953. Social and political implications in the choice of an orthography. FAE 5/2.80–85.

——. 1968. Bilingual education in the Andes of Peru. *In* Fishman, Ferguson and Das Gupta 1968, pp. 403–14.

CARMICHAEL, L., H. P. HOGAN, and A. A. WALTER. 1932. An experimental study of the effect of language on the perception of visually perceived form. JExPsych 15.73–86.

CARROLL, JOHN B., and J. B. CASAGRANDE. 1958. The function of language classifications in behavior. Readings in social psychology, ed. by E. Maccoby, T. Newcomb, and E. Hartley, pp. 18–31. New York, Holt.

CATFORD, J. C. 1965. A linguistic theory of translation. London, Oxford University Press.

CHINESE WRITTEN LANGUAGE REFORM COMMITTEE. 1956. Several points concerning the Han language phoneticization plan (draft) explained. Current Background 1956/380, March 15.4–13.

CHOMSKY, NOAM. 1957. Syntactic structures. The Hague, Mouton.

——. 1965. Aspects of the theory of syntax. Cambridge, Mass., MIT Press.

CHOU EN-LAI. 1965. Current tasks of reforming the written language. *In* Reform of the written language, pp. 7–29. Peking, Chinese Foreign Language Press.

COHEN, JACK. 1965. Some statistical issues in psychological research. Handbook of clinical psychology, ed. by B. B. Wolmand, pp. 95–121. New York, McGraw-Hill.

——. 1968a. Prognostic factors in functional psychosis: A study in multivariate methodology. Invited address at the New York Academy of Sciences, March 18, 1968. Mimeographed.

——. 1968b. Multiple regression as a general data-analytic system. PsychB 70.425–43.

CONKLIN, HAROLD C. 1962. Lexicographic treatment of folk taxonomies. Problems in lexicography, ed. by Fred W. Householder and Sol Saporta, pp. 119–41. RCAFL-P 21.

COOK, S. F. 1943. The conflict between the California Indian and white civilization. Ibero-Americana 21.1–194, 22.1–55, 23.1–115, 24.1–29.

CORPAS, JORGE PINEROS. 1969. Inconvenientes de la enseñanza bilingüe a la luz de la fisiologia cerebral. Noticias Culturales 1969/99.1–4. Bogatá.

CORREA, HECTOR, and JAN TINBERGEN. 1962. Quantitative adaptation of education to accelerated growth. Kyklos 15.776–85.

DALBY, DAVID. 1967. A survey of the indigenous scripts of Liberia and Sierra Leone: Vai, Mende, Loma, Kpelle and Bassa. AfrLS 8.1–51.

——. 1968. The indigenous scripts of West Africa and Surinam: Their inspiration and design. AfrLS 9.156–97.

DAS GUPTA, JYOTIRINDRA. 1969. Religious loyalty, language conflict and political mobilization. Consultative Meeting on Language Planning Processes. Honolulu, EWC-IAC. *Also in* Rubin and Jernudd, 1971.

DAS GUPTA, JYOTIRINDRA, and JOSHUA A. FISHMAN. 1971. Interstate migration and subsidiary language-claiming; an analysis of selected Indian census data. International Migration Review 5.227–49.

DAVIS, FREDERICK B. 1967. Philippine language-teaching experiments. Philippine Center for Language Study 5. Quezon City, Alemar-Phoenix.

DEFRANCIS, JOHN. 1947. Japanese language reform: Politics and phonetics. Far Eastern Survey 16/19.217–20.

———. 1950. Nationalism and language reform in China. Princeton, N.J., Princeton University Press.

———. 1968. Language and script reform (in China). CTL 2.130–50. *Also in* Fishman 1971, pp. 450–75.

DE SAUSSURE, FERDINAND. 1959. Course in general linguistics (translated from the French by Wade Baskin). New York, Philosophical Library. Original publication 1916: Cours de linguistique générale. Paris, Payot.

DEUTSCH, KARL W. 1942. The trend of European nationalism — the language aspect. American Political Science Review 36.533–41.

———. 1966. Nationalism and social communication. 2nd ed. Cambridge, Mass., MIT Press.

DICKENS, K. J. 1953. Unification: The Akan dialects of the Gold Coast. *In* Anon. 1953, pp. 115–23.

DOHRENWEND, BRUCE P., and ROBERT J. SMITH. 1962. Toward a theory of acculturation. SJA 18.30–39.

DOZIER, EDWARD P. 1951. Resistance to acculturation and assimilation in an Indian pueblo. AmA 53.56–66.

EDELMAN, MARTIN, ROBERT L. COOPER, and JOSHUA A. FISHMAN. 1968. The contextualization of school children's bilingualism. Irish Journal of Education 2.106–111.

ELLIS, DEAN S. 1967. Speech and social status in America. Social Forces 45.-431–37.

EPSTEIN, A. L. 1959. Linguistic innovation and culture on the Copperbelt, Northern Rhodesia. SJA 15.235–53. *Also in* Fishman 1968a, pp. 320–39.

ERVIN, SUSAN M., and CHARLES E. OSGOOD. 1954. Second language learning and bilingualism. JAbSocPsych 49/Supplement. 139–46.

ERVIN-TRIPP, SUSAN. 1964. An analysis of the interaction of language, topic and listener. AmA 66, Part 2.86–102. *Also in* Fishman 1968a, pp. 192–211.

———. 1969. Sociolinguistics. Advances in experimental social psychology, ed. by L. Berkowitz, 4.91–165. New York, Academic Press. *Also in* Fishman 1971.

FERGUSON, CHARLES A. 1959a. Diglossia. Word 15.325–40.

———. 1959b. Myths about Arabic. MSLL 12.75–82. *Also in* Fishman 1968, pp. 375–81.

——. 1965. Directions in sociolinguistics; Report on an interdisciplinary seminar. SSRC Items 19/1.1–4.

——. 1967. St. Stefan of Perm and applied linguistics. To honor Roman Jakobson 1.643–53. The Hague, Mouton. *Also in* Fishman, Ferguson and Das Gupta 1968, pp. 253–66.

——. 1968. Language development. *In* Fishman, Ferguson and Das Gupta, 1968, pp. 27–35.

FERGUSON, CHARLES A., and JOHN J. GUMPERZ, eds. 1960. Linguistic diversity in South Asia: Studies in regional, social and functional variation. IJAL 4/1.

FERGUSON, CHARLES A., and RALEIGH MORGAN, JR. 1959. Selected readings in applied linguistics. Linguistic Reporter 1959, Supplement 2, 4 pp.

FERRU, JEAN LOUIS. 1966. Possible repercussions of a technical and economic nature of the adoption of particular letters for the standard transcription of West African languages. Mamako /Mali /Meeting on the standardization of African alphabets, Feb. 28–March 5, 1966. UNESCO/CLT Baling.

FINDLING, JOAN. 1969. Bilingual need affiliation and future orientation in extra group and intragroup domains. MLJ 53.227–31. *Also in* Fishman 1971.

FISCHEL, A. 1919. Der Panslawismus bis zum Weltkrieg. Stuttgart/Berlin, Cotta.

FISCHER, JOHN L. 1958. Social influences in the choice of a linguistic variant. Word 14.47–56.

FISHMAN, JOSHUA A. 1956. The process and function of social stereotyping. JSocPsych 43.27–64.

——. 1960 A systematization of the Whorfian hypothesis. BS 8.323–39.

——. 1964. Language maintenance and language shift as a field of inquiry. Linguistics 9.32–70.

——. 1965a. Yiddish in America. RCAFL-P 36.

——. 1965b. Bilingualism intelligence and language learning. MLJ 49.227–37.

——. 1965c. Varieties of ethnicity and language consciousness. MSLL 18.69–79.

——. 1965d. Who speaks what language to whom and when? Linguistique 1965/2.67–88.

——. 1965e. Language maintenance and language shift: The American immigrant case within a general theoretical perspective. Sociologus 16.19–38.

——. 1965f. Language maintenance and language shift in certain urban immigrant environments: The case of Yiddish in the United States. Europa Ethnica 22.146–58.

——. 1966a. Bilingual sequences at the societal level. On Teaching English to Speakers of Other Languages 2.139–44.

——. 1966b. Some contrasts between linguistically homogeneous and linguistically heterogeneous politics. Sociological Inquiry 36.146–58. Revised and expanded in Fishman, Ferguson and Das Gupta 1968, pp. 53–68.

——. 1966c. Language loyalty in the United States. The Hague, Mouton.

———. 1966d. Planned reinforcement of language maintenance in the United States: Suggestions for the conservation of a neglected national resource. *In* Fishman 1966c, Chapter 21.

———. 1967a. The breadth and depth of English in the United States. University Quarterly 1967 (March).133–40.

———. 1967b. A sociology of language (review). Lg 43.586–604.

———, ed. 1968a. Readings in the sociology of language. The Hague, Mouton.

———. 1968b. Sociolinguistic perspective in the study of bilingualism. Linguistics 39.21–50.

———. 1968c. Sociolinguistics and the language problems of developing nations. International Social Science Journal 20.211–25.

———. 1969a. National language and languages of wider communication in the developing nations. AnL 11.111–35.

———. 1969b. Literacy and the language barrier. Science 165.1108–09.

———. 1969c. Bilingual attitudes and behaviors. Language Sciences 5.5–11. *Also in* Fishman, Cooper and Ma 1968 and Language Science Series, Bloomington Ind., 1971.

———. 1969d. A sociolinguistic census of a bilingual neighborhood. AJSoc 75.323 –39. *Also in* Fishman, Cooper and Ma 1971.

———. 1969e. Puerto Rican intellectuals in New York: Some intragroup and intergroup contrasts. Canadian Journal of Behavioral Science 1.215–26.

———. 1969f. The impact of nationalism on language planning: Some comparisons between early twentieth century Europe and subsequent developments in South and South-East Asia. Consultative meeting on language planning processes. Honolulu, EWC-IAP. *Also in* Rubin and Jernudd 1971.

———. 1971. The links between micro- and macro-sociolinguistics in the study of who speaks what language to whom and when. *In* Gumperz and Hymes 1972, pp. 435–53. *Also in* Fishman, Cooper and Ma 1971.

———, ed. 1971. Advances in the sociology of language. The Hague, Mouton.

FISHMAN, JOSHUA A., and REBECCA AGHEYISI. 1970. Language attitude studies. AnL 12.137–57.

FISHMAN, JOSHUA A., ROBERT C. COOPER, and ROXANA MA, et al. 1968. Bilingualism in the barrio. Final report to the Department of Health, Education and Welfare under Contract OEC–1–7–062817–0297. New York, Yeshiva University. *Also* Language Science Series, Bloomington, Ind., 1971.

FISHMAN, JOSHUA A., CHARLES A. FERGUSON, and J. DAS GUPTA, eds. 1968. Language problems of developing nations. New York, John Wiley.

FISHMAN, JOSHUA A., and LAWRENCE GREENFIELD. 1970. Situational measures of normative language views in relation to person, place and topic among Puerto Rican bilinguals. *In* Fishman, Cooper and Ma 1971; *also* Anthropos 65.602–18.

FISHMAN, JOSHUA A., and ELEANOR HERASIMCHUK. 1969. The multiple prediction of phonological variables in a bilingual speech community. AmA 71.648–57. *Also in* Fishman, Cooper and Ma 1971.

FISHMAN, JOSHUA A., and JOHN C. LOVAS. 1970. Bilingual education in socio-linguistic perspective. TESOL Quarterly.

FISHMAN, JOSHUA A., and ERIKA LUEDERS. 1972. What has the sociology of language to say to the teacher? (on teaching the standard variety to speakers of dialectal or sociological varieties). The functions of language, ed. by Courtney Cazden, Vera John and Dell H. Hymes, pp. 67–83. New York, Teachers College Press.

FISHMAN, JOSHUA A., and VLADIMIR C. NAHIRNY. 1966. The ethnic group school in the United States. *In* Fishman 1966c, Chapter 6. *Also* Sociology of Education 37.306–17 (1964).

FISHMAN, JOSHUA A., and CHARLES TERRY. 1969. The validity of census data on bilingualism in a Puerto Rican neighborhood. American Sociological Review 34.636–50.

FRAKE, CHARLES O. 1961. The diagnosis of disease among the Subanun of Mindanao. AmA 63.113–32.

——. 1962. The ethnographic study of cognitive systems. Anthropology and behavior, ed. by Thomas Gladwin and William C. Sturtevant, pp. 77–85. Washington, D.C., Anthropological Society of Washington. *Also in* Fishman 1968a, pp. 434–46.

FRIEDERICH, PAUL. 1962. Language and politics in India. Daedalus, Summer 1962, pp. 543–59.

——. 1966. The linguistic reflex of social change: From Tsarist to Soviet Russian kinship. Sociological Inquiry 36.159–85.

GAARDER, A. BRUCE. 1965. Teaching the bilingual child: Research, development and policy. MLJ 49.165–75.

——. 1967. Organization of the bilingual school. Journal of Social Issues 23.-110–20.

GALLAGHER, CHARLES F. 1967. Language rationalization and scientific progress. Paper prepared for Conference on Science and Social Change, California Institute of Technology, October 18–20, 1967.

——. 1969. Language reform and social modernization in Turkey. Consultative Meeting on Language Planning Processes. Honolulu, EWC-IAP. *Also in* Rubin and Jernudd 1971.

GARFINKEL, HAROLD. 1967. Studies in ethnomethodology. New York, Prentice Hall.

GARFINKEL, HAROLD, and H. SACKS, eds. In press. Contributions in ethnomethodology. Bloomington, Ind., Indiana University Press.

GARVIN, PAUL L. 1954. Literacy as problem in language and culture. MSLL 7.117–29.

——. 1959. The standard language problem: Concepts and methods. AnL 1/2.28–31.

GEERTZ, CLIFFORD. 1960. Linguistic etiquette. Religion of Java, by C. Geertz. Glencoe, Ill., Free Press. *Also in* Fishman 1968a, pp. 282–95.

GELB, I. J. 1952. A study of writing. Chicago, University of Chicago Press.

GERULLIS, GEORG. 1932. Muttersprache und Zweisprachigkeit in einem preussischlitauischen Dorf. Studi Baltici 2.59–67.

GLENN, NORVAL D. 1966. The trend in differences in attitudes and behavior by educational level. Sociology of Education 39.255–75.

——. 1967. Differentiation and massification: Some trend data from national surveys. Social Forces 46.172–79.

GLENN, NORVAL D., and J. L. SIMMONS. 1967. Are regional cultural differences diminishing? Public Opinion Quarterly 31.167–93.

GOODENOUGH, WARD H. 1965. Rethinking 'status' and 'role': Toward a general model of the cultural organization of social relationships. The relevance of models for social anthropology, ed. by M. Banton, pp. 1–24. New York, Praeger.

GOODMAN, ELLIOT R. 1960. World state and world language. The Soviet design for a world state, by E. R. Goodman, pp. 264–84. New York, Columbia University press. *Also in* Fishman 1968a, pp. 717–36.

GOODY, JACK. 1968. Literacy in traditional societies. London, Cambridge University Press.

GREENBERG, JOSEPH H. 1965. Urbanism, migration and language. Urbanization and migration in West Africa, ed. by Hilda Kuper, pp. 50–59. Los Angeles and Berkeley, University of California Press.

——. 1966. Universals of language. 2nd ed. Cambridge, Mass., The MIT Press.

GREENFIELD, LAWRENCE. 1968. Situational measures of language use in relation to person, place and topic among Puerto Rican bilinguals. *In* Fishman, Cooper and Ma 1968.

GRIMSHAW, ALLEN D. 1969. Sociolinguistics and the sociologist. The American Sociologist 4/312.21.

——. 1972. Some social sources and some social functions of pidgin and creole languages. Handbook of communication, ed. by W. Schramm et al. New York, Rand McNally.

GULICK, JOHN. 1958. Language and passive resistance among the eastern Cherokees. Ethnohistory 5.60–81.

GUMPERZ, JOHN J. 1958. Dialect differences and social stratification in a north Indian village. AmA 60.668–82.

——. 1961. Speech variation and the study of Indian civilization. AmA 63.976–88.

——. 1962. Types of linguistic communities. AnL 4/1.288–40. *Also in* Fishman 1968a, pp. 460–76.

——. 1964a. Linguistic and social interaction in two communities. AmA 66/2.37–53.

——. 1964b. Hindi-Punjabi code-switching in Delhi. PICL 9.1115–24.

——. 1966. On the ethnology of linguistic change. Sociolinguistics, ed. by William Bright, pp. 27–38. The Hague, Mouton.

——. 1967. The linguistic markers of bilingualism. Journal of Social Issues 23/2.48–57.

GUMPERZ, JOHN J., and DELL H. HYMES, eds. 1972. The ethnography of communication: Directions in sociolinguistics. New York, Holt, Rinehart and Winston.

GUXMAN, M. M. 1960. Some general regularities in the formation and development of national languages. Voprosy formirovanija Nacial'nyx jazykov, ed. by M. M. Guxman, pp. 295–307. Moscow. *Also in* Fishman 1968a, pp. 766–79.

HAIR, P. E. H. 1963. Notes on the discovery of the Vai script, with a bibliography. Sierra Leone Language Review 2.36–49.

HALL, ROBERT A., JR. 1952. Bilingualism and applied linguistics. ZPhon 6.13–30.

HALLIDAY, M. A. K., ANGUS MACINTOSH, and PETER STREVENS. 1964a. The linguistic sciences and language teaching. London, Longmans.

——. 1964b. The users and uses of language. *In* Halliday, MacIntosh and Strevens 1964a. *Also in* Fishman 1968a, pp. 139–69.

HAMILTON, RICHARD F. 1965. Affluence and the worker: The West German case. American Journal of Sociology 71.144–52.

HANSEN, MARCUS L. 1940. The immigrant in American history, ed. by Arthur M. Schlesinger. Cambridge, Mass., Harvard University Press.

HAUDRICOURT, A. G. 1943. De l'origine des particularités de l'alphabet Vietnamien. Dan Vietnam 1943/3.66–68.

HAUGEN, EINAR. 1953. The Norwegian language in America; a study in bilingual behavior. 2 vols. Philadelphia, University of Pennsylvania Press. 2nd ed., Bloomington, Ind., Indiana University Press.

——. 1961. Language planning in modern Norway. Scandinavian Studies 33.68–81. *Also in* Fishman 1968a, pp. 673–87.

——. 1966a. Language planning and language conflict; the case of modern Norwegian. Cambridge, Mass., Harvard University Press.

——. 1966b. Linguistics and language planning. Sociolinguistics, ed. by William Bright, pp. 50–66. The Hague, Mouton.

——. 1966c. Dialect, language, nation. AmA 68.922–35.

HAVRANEK, BOHUSLAV. 1964. The functional differentiation of the standard language. A Prague School reader on esthetics, literary structure and styles, ed. by Paul L. Garvin, pp. 1–18. Washington, D.C., Georgetown University Press.

HAYDEN, ROBERT G., and JOSHUA A. FISHMAN. 1964. The impact of exposure to ethnic mother tongues on foreign language teachers in American high schools and colleges. MLJ 48.262–74. *Also in* Fishman 1966c, ch. 13.

HAYES, ALFRED S. 1965. Recommendations of the work conference on literacy. Washington, D.C., Center for Applied Linguistics.

HERMAN, SIMON N. 1961. Explorations in the social psychology of language choice. Human Relations 14.149–64. *Also in* Fishman 1968a, pp. 492–511.

HERTZLER, JOYCE O. 1965. The sociology of language. New York, Random House.

HERZOG, MARVIN I. 1965. The Yiddish language in northern Poland: Its geography and history. RCAFL-P 37.

HEYD, URIEL. 1954. Language reform in modern Turkey. Jerusalem, Israel Oriental Society.

HODGES, HAROLD M. 1964. Social stratification: Class in America. Cambridge, Schenkman.

HOFMAN, JOHN E. 1966a. Mother tongue retentiveness in ethnic parishes. *In* Fishman 1966c, Chapter 9.

——. 1966b. The language transition in some Lutheran denominations. *In* Fishman 1966c, Chapter 10. *Also in* Fishman 1968a, pp. 620–38.

HOHENTHAL, W. D., and T. McCORKLE. 1955. The problem of aboriginal persistence. SJA 11.288–300.

HOIJER, H. 1951. Cultural implications of the Navaho linguistic categories. Lg 27.111–20.

——. 1954. The Sapir-Whorf Hypothesis. Language in culture, ed. by H. Hoijer, pp. 92–104. American Anthropological Association Memoir 79. Chicago, University of Chicago Press.

HOLTON, DANIEL C. 1947. Idiographs and ideas. Far Eastern Survey 16/19.-220–23.

HOWELL, RICHARD W. 1965. Linguistic status markers in Korean. Kroeber Anthropological Society Papers 55.91–97.

——. 1967. Terms of address as indices of social change. Paper read at the American Sociological Association Meeting, San Francisco, Sept. 1967.

HUFFINE, CAROL L. 1966. Inter-socio-economic clan language differences: A research report. Sociology and Social Research 50/3.351–55.

HUGHES, EVERETT C. 1970. The linguistic division of labor in industrial and urban societies. MSLL 23.103–20. *Also in* Fishman 1971.

HSIA, TAO-TAI. 1956. China's language reforms. New Haven, Conn., Yale University Press.

HYMES, DELL H. 1962. The ethnography of speaking. Anthropology and human behavior, ed. by T. Gladwin and W. C. Sturtevant, pp. 13–53. Washington, D.C., Anthropological Society of Washington. *Also in* Fishman 1968a, pp. 99–138.

——. 1966. Two types of linguistic relativity. Sociolinguistics, ed. by William Bright, pp. 114–57. The Hague, Mouton.

——. 1967a. Why linguistics needs the sociologist. Social Research 34/7.632–47.

——. 1967b. Models of interaction of language and social setting. Journal of Social Issues 23/2.2–28.

IVANOVA, A. M., and V. D. VOSKRESENSKY. 1959. Abolition of adult illiteracy in USSR, 1917–1940. Fundamental and Adult Education 77/3.131–86.

JEFFRIES, W. F. 1958. The literacy campaign in Northern Nigeria. Fundamental and Adult Education 10/1.2–6.

JERNUDD, BJORN H. 1969. Notes on economic analysis and language planning. Consultative Meeting on Language Planning Processes. Honolulu, EWC-IAP. *Also in* Rubin and Jernudd 1971.

JERNUDD, BJORN H., and JYOTIRINDRA DAS GUPTA. 1969. Towards a theory of language planning. Consultative Meeting on Language Planning Processes. Honolulu, EWC-IAP. *Also in* Rubin and Jernudd, 1971.

JERNUDD, BJORN H., and TOMMY WILLINGSSON. 1968. A sociolectical study of the Stockholm region. Svenska Landsmal och Svenskt Folkliv 289.140–47.

JOHN, VERA, and VIVIAN HORNER. 1970. Early childhood bilingual education. New York, Modern Language Association.

JOHNSTON, RUTH. 1963a. Factors in the assimilation of selected groups of Polish Post-War immigrants in western Australia. Unpublished Ph.D. Dissertation, University of Western Australia, Perth. *Subsequently*: Immigrant assimilation; a study of Polish people in western Australia. Perth, Paterson Brokensha. 1965.

——. 1963b. A new approach to the meaning of assimilation. Human Relations 16.295–98.

JONES, D. 1942. Problems of a national script for India. Hartford, Conn., Hartford Seminary Foundation.

JONES, FRANK E., and WALLACE E. LAMBERT. 1959. Attitudes towards immigrants in a Canadian community. Public Opinion Quarterly 23.538–46.

JOOS, MARTIN. 1950. Description of language design. JAcS 22.701–08. *Also in* Readings in linguistics, ed. by M. Joos, pp. 349–56. Washington, D.C., American Council of Learned Societies. 1958.

——. 1959. The isolation of styles. MSLL 12.107–13. *Also in* Fishman 1968a, pp. 185–91.

KANDLER, C. 1955. Zum Aufbau der angewandten Sprachwissenschaft. Sprachforum 1.3–9.

KANDORI, TAKEHIKO. 1968. Study of dialects in Japan. Orbis 17.47–56.

KANTROWITZ, NATHAN. 1967. The vocabulary of race relations in a prison. Paper presented at the American Dialect Society Meeting, Chicago, Dec. 1967.

KAYE, ALAN S. 1970. Modern Standard Arabic and the colloquials. Lingua 24.374–91.

KELMAN, HERBERT C. 1969. Language as an aid and barrier to involvement in the national system. Consultative Meeting on Language Planning Processes. Honolulu, EWC-IAP. *Also in* Rubin and Jernudd, 1971 *and* Fishman 1971.

KIMPLE, JAMES JR., ROBERT L. COOPER, and JOSHUA A. FISHMAN. 1969. Language switching in the interpretation of conversations. Lingua 23.127–34.

KLOSS, HEINZ. 1929. Sprachtabellen als Grundlage für Sprachstatistik, Sprachen-karten und für eine allgemeine Soziologie der Sprachgemeinschaften. Viertel-jahrsschrift für Politik and Geschichte 1/7.103–17.

——. 1952. Die Entwicklung Neuer Germanischer Kultursprachen. Munich, Pohl.

——. 1966a. Types of multilingual communities: A discussion of ten variables. Sociological Inquiry 36.135–45.

——. 1966b. German-American language maintenance efforts. *In* Fishman 1966c, chapter 15.

——. 1967. 'Abstand' languages and 'Ausbau' languages. AnL 9/7.29–41.

KLUCKHOHN, CLYDE. 1961. Notes on some anthropological aspects of communication. AmA 63.895–910.

KNOTT, BETTY I. 1956. The Christian 'special language' in the inscriptions. Vigiliae Christianae 10.65–79.

KOHN, HANS. 1965. The idea of nationalism: A study of its origin and background. New York, Macmillan.

KOLARZ, WALTER. 1946. Myths and realities in Eastern Europe. London, Lindsay Drummon.

——. 1967. Russia and her colonies. Hamden, Conn., Archon Books. (Originally published in 1952.)

——. 1969. The peoples of the Soviet Far East. Hamden, Conn., Archon Books. (Originally: 1954.)

KUHN, WALTER. 1930. Die jungen deutschen Sprachinseln in Galizien: Ein Bei-trag zur Methode der Sprachinselforschung. Munster, Aschendorffsche Ver-lagsbuchhandlung.

——. 1934. Deutsche Sprachinselforschung. Plauen, Gunther Wolff.

KWAN-WAI CHIU, ROSALINE. 1970. Language contact and language planning in China (1900–1967); A selected bibliography. Quebec, Les Presses de l'Uni-versité Laval.

LABOV, WILLIAM. 1963. The social motivation of a sound change. Word 19.-273–309.

——. 1964. Phonological correlates of social stratification. AmA 66/2.164–76.

——. 1965. On the mechanism of linguistic change. MSLL 18.91–114.

——. 1966a. The effect of social mobility on linguistic behavior. Sociological Inquiry 36.186–203.

——. 1966b. Hypercorrection by the lower middle class as a factor in linguistic change. Sociolinguistics, ed. by William Bright, pp. 84–101. The Hague.

——. 1966c. The social stratification of English in New York City. Washington, D.C., Center for Applied Linguistics.

——. 1966d. Stages in the acquisition of Standard English. Social dialects and language learning, ed. by Roger W. Shuy, Champaign, Ill., NCTE.

——. 1968. The reflection of social processes in linguistic structures. *In* Fishman 1968a, pp. 240–51.

LABOV, WILLIAM, PAUL COHEN, CLARENCE ROBINS, and JOHN LEWIS. 1968. A study of the non-standard English of Negro and Puerto Rican speakers in New York City. 2 vols. Final Report, Cooperative Research Project no. 3288. New York, Columbia University.

LAMBERT, WALLACE E., R. C. GARDNER, H. C. BARICK, and K. TUNSTALL. 1963. Attitudinal and cognitive aspects of intense study of a second language. JAbSocPsych 66.358–68.

LANHAM, L. W. 1965. Teaching English to Africans: A crisis in education. Optima Dec. 15 (1965), pp. 197–204.

LANTZ, DELEE, and VOLNEY STEFFLRE. 1964. Language and cognition revisited. JAbSocPsych 49.454–62.

LEHMANN, A. 1889. Über Wiedererkennen. Philos. Stud. 5.96–156.

LENNEBERG, ERIC H. 1953. Cognition in ethnolinguistics. Lg 29.463–71.

——. 1957. A probabilistic approach to language learning. BS 2.1–12.

LePAGE, ROBERT. 1964. The national language question. London, Oxford University Press.

——. 1968. Problems to be faced in the use of English as the medium of education in four West Indian territories. *In* Fishman, Ferguson and Das Gupta 1968, pp. 431–41.

LEVINE, LEWIS L., and H. J. CROCKETT. 1966. Speech variation in a Piedmont community: Postvocalic *r*. Sociological Inguiry 36.204–26.

LEWIS, E. GLYNN. 1971. Migration and language in the USSR. International Migration Review 5.147–79. *Also in* Fishman 1971.

LEWIS, W. ARTHUR. 1961. Education and economic development. Social and Economic Studies 10/2.113–27.

LI HUI. 1960. The phonetic alphabet — short cut to literacy. Peking Review 13/28 (July 12, 1960).

LIEBERSON, STANLEY. 1965. Bilingualism in Montreal: A demographic analysis. AJSoc 71.10–25. *Also in* Fishman 1971.

LIEBERSON, STANLEY, and TIMOTHY J. CURRY. 1971. Language shift in the United States: Some demographic clues. The International Migration Review 5.125–37.

LIND, ANDREW W. 1969. Race relations in New Guinea. Current Affairs Bulletin 44/3.34–48. Sydney, Australia.

LINDENFELD, JACQUELINE. 1969. The social conditioning of syntactic variation in French. AmA 71.890–98. *Also in* Fishman 1971.

LUNT, HORACE G. 1959. The creation of Standard Macedonian: Some facts and attitudes. AnL 1/5.19–26.

MA, ROXANNA, and ELEANOR HERASIMCHUK. 1968. The linguistic dimensions of a bilingual neighborhood. *In* Fishman, Cooper and Ma 1968. *Also in* Fishman 1971.

McCLUSKER, HENRY F., JR. 1963. An approach for educational planning in the developing countries. Menlo Park, Calif., Stanford Research Institute.

McCORMACK, WILLIAM C. 1960. Social dialects in Dhawar Kannada. Linguistic diversity in South Asia, ed. by C. A. Ferguson and J. J. Gumperz. IJAL 4/1.79–91.

——. 1968. Occupation and residence in relation to Dharwar dialects. Social structure and social change in India, ed. by M. Singer and B. S. Cohn, pp. 475–86. VFPA.

McDAVID, RAVEN I., JR. 1958. The dialects of American English. *Chapter in* The structure of American English, ed. by W. Nelson Francis. New York, Ronald.

MACKEY, WILLIAM F. 1962. The description of bilingualism. CJL 7.51–85.

——. 1970. A typology of bilingual education. The Foreign Language Annals 3.596–608. *Also in* Fishman 1971.

MACNAMARA, JOHN. 1966. Bilingualism in primary education. Edinburgh, Edinburgh University Press.

——. 1967. The effects of instruction in a weaker language. Journal of Social Issues 23.121–35.

——. 1969. Successes and failures in the movement for the restoration of Irish. Consultative Meeting on Language Planning Processes. Honolulu, EWC-IAP. *Also in* Rubin and Jernudd 1971.

MAIER, NORMAN R. F. 1930. Reasoning in humans I: On direction. Journal of Comparative Psychology 10.115–43.

MANUEL, HERSCHEL T. 1963. The preparation and evaluation of interlanguage testing materials. Austin, University of Texas. Mimeographed report, Cooperative Research Project no. 681.

MAYNER, THOMAS F. 1967. Language and nationalism in Yugoslavia. Canadian Slavic Studies 1.333–47.

MAZRUI, ALI A. 1967. The national language question in East Africa. East Africa Journal 1967/3.12–19.

METRAUX, RUTH W. 1965. A study of bilingualism among children of U.S.-French parents. FR 38.650–55.

METZGER, DUANE, and GERALD E. WILLIAMS. 1966. Some procedures and results in the study of native categories: Tzeltal 'firewood'. AmA 68.389–407.

MEYENBERG, ERWIN. 1934. Der heutige Stand der Romazi-Bewegung in Japan. F&F 10/23–24.

MILLS, H. C. 1956. Language reform in China. Far Eastern Quarterly 15.517–40.

MOHRMAN, CHRISTINE. 1947. Le latin commun et la latin des Chrétiens. Vigiliae Christiannae 1.1–12.

——. 1957. Linguistic problems in the early Christian church. Vigiliae Christiannae 11.11–36.

MORAG, SHELOMO. 1959. Planned and unplanned development in modern Hebrew. Lingua 87.247–63.

NADER, LAURA. 1962. A note on attitudes and the use of language. AnL 4/6.24–29. Also in Fishman 1968a, pp. 276–81.

NAHIRNY, VLADIMIR C., and JOSHUA A. FISHMAN. 1965. American immigrant groups: Ethnic identification and the problem of generations. Sociological Review 13.311–26.

NELSON, LOWRY. 1947. Speaking of tongues. AJSoc 54.202–10.

NGUYEN DINH HOA. 1960. The Vietnamese language. Saigon, Department of National Education, Vietnam Culture Series 2.

NIDA, EUGENE A. 1954. Practical limitations to a phonemic orthography. BT 5.35–39, 58–62.

——. 1967. Sociological dimensions of literacy and literature. World literacy manual, ed. by Floyd Shacklock et al., Chap. 11. New York, Committee on Literacy and Christian Literature.

ORNSTEIN, JACOB. 1959. Soviet language policy: Theory and practice. SEEJ 17.1–24.

OSGOOD, CHARLES E. 1960. The cross-cultural generality of visual-verbal-synesthetic tendencies. BS 5.146–49.

OWENS, ROGER C. 1965. The patrilocal band: A linguistically and culturally hybrid social unit. AmA 67.675–90.

ÖZMEN, YÜCEL. 1967. A sociolinguistic analysis of language reform in Turkey 1932–1967, with special reference to the activities of the Turk Dil Kurumu. Master's Thesis, Georgetown University, Washington, D.C. Unpublished.

PASSIN, HERBERT. 1963. Writer and journalist in the transitional society. Communication and political development, ed. by Lucian W. Pye, pp. 82–123. Princeton, N.J., Princeton University Press. Also in Fishman, Ferguson and Das Gupta 1968, pp. 442–58.

PIKE, KENNETH L. 1947. Phonemics: A technique for reducing languages to writing. Ann Arbor, University of Michigan Press.

POLOMÉ, EDGAR. 1968. The choice of official languages in the Democratic Republic of the Congo. In Fishman, Ferguson and Das Gupta 1968, pp. 295–312.

POOL, JONATHAN. 1969. National development and language diversity. La Monda

Lingvo-Problemo 1.129–92. *Also in* Fishman 1971.

POSPISIL, LEOPOLD. 1965. A formal semantic analysis of substantive law: Kapauka Papuan laws of land tenure. AmA 67, Part 2.186–214.

PRATOR, CLIFFORD H. 1967. The survey of language use and language teaching in East Africa. Linguistic Reporter 9/8.

PRICE, P. DAVID. 1967. Two types of taxonomy: A Huichol ethnobotanical example. AnL 9/7.1–28.

QUELQUEJAY, C., and A. BENNIGSEN. 1961. The evolution of the Muslim nationalities of the USSR and their linguistic problems. London, Central Asian Research Center.

RABIN, CHAIM. 1969. Spelling reform: Israel, 1968. Consultative Meeting on Language Planning Processes. Honolulu, EWC-IAP. *Also in* Rubin and Jernudd 1971.

RADIN, PAUL. 1924. The adoption of an alphabet by an aboriginal people. Cambridge University Reporter (Proceedings of the Cambridge Philological Society), Nov. 25, 1924, pp. 27–34.

RAMOS, MAXIMO, JOSE V. AGUILAR, and BONIFACIO P. SIBAYAN. 1967. The determination and implementation of language policy. Philippine Center for Language Study, Monograph 2. Quezon City, Alemar-Phoenix.

RAY, PUNYA SLOKA. 1963. Language standardization (esp. Ch. 9, "Comparative description and evaluation of writing systems", pp. 106–20). The Hague, Mouton.

READ, ALLEN WALKER. 1964. The splitting and coalescing of widespread languages. PICL 9.1129–34.

REISSMAN, LEONARD. 1964. The urban process: Cities in industrial societies. New York, Free Press.

ROSS, ALLAN S. C. 1956. U and non-U; an essay in sociological linguistics. Nobless oblige, ed. by N. Mitford, pp. 11–38. London, Hamish Hamilton.

ROSSI, ETTORE. 1927. La questione dell' alfabeto per le lingue turche. Oriente Moderno 7.295–310.

——. 1929. Il nuovo alfabeto latino introdotto in Turchia. Oriente Moderno 9.32–48.

——. 1935. La riforma linguistica in Turchia. Oriente Moderno 15.45–57.

——. 1942. Un decennio di riforma linguistica in Turchia. Oriente Moderno 22.466–77.

——. 1953. Venticinque anni di rivoluzione dell' alfabeto e venti di riforma linguistica in Turchia. Oriente Moderno 33.378–84.

ROYAL COMMISSION ON BILINGUALISM AND BICULTURALISM. 1965. A preliminary report. Ottawa, Queen's Printer.

——. 1967. Book I: General introduction, the official languages. Ottawa, Queen's Printer.

——. 1968. Book II: Education. Ottawa, Queen's Printer.

RUBIN, JOAN. 1962. Bilingualism in Paraguay. AnL 4/1.52–58.

——. 1968. Language and education in Paraguay. *In* Fishman, Ferguson, and Das Gupta 1968, pp. 477–88.

——. 1969. Education and language planning. Consultative Meeting on Language Planning Processes. Honolulu, EWC-IAP. 1971; *also in* Fishman 1971.

RUBIN, J. and B. JERNUDD, eds. 1971. Can language be planned? Honolulu, East-West Center Press.

RUSSELL, J. K. 1948. Starting a literacy campaign. Books for Africa 18/2.17–20.

RUSTOW, DANKWART A. 1967. A world of nations: Problems of political modernization. Washington, Brookings Institution. *Also*, adapted as "Language, modernization and nationhood — an attempt at typology", *in* Fishman, Ferguson, and Das Gupta 1968, pp. 87–106.

SAMORA, JULIAN, and WM. N. DEANE. 1956. A language usage as a possible index of acculturation. Sociology and Social Research 40.307–11.

SCHARSCHMIDT, CLEMENS. 1924. Schriftreform in Japan: Ein Kulturproblem. Mitteilungen des Seminars für Orientalische Sprachen 26/27, no. 1, 183–86.

SCHEGLOFF, EMANUEL A. 1968. Sequencing in conversational openings. AmA 70.1075–95. *Also in* Fishman 1971.

SCHERMERHORN, RICHARD A. 1964. Toward a general theory of minority groups. Phylon 25.238–46.

SCHNORE, LEO. 1966. The rural-urban variable: An urbanite's perspective. Rural Sociology 21.137.

SCHOFIELD, R. S. 1968. The measurement of literacy in pre-industrial England. Literacy in traditional societies, ed. by Jack Goody. London, Cambridge Univ. Press.

SELK, PAUL. 1937. Die sprachlichen Verhältnisse im deutsch-dänischen Sprachgebiet südlich der Grenze. Flensburg, Verlag Heimat und Erbe. (Ergänzungsband, 1940.)

SERDYUCHENKO, G. P. 1962. The eradication of illiteracy and the creation of new written languages in the U.S.S.R. International Journal of Adult and Youth Education 14/1.23–29.

——. 1965. Elimination of illiteracy among the people who had no alphabets. Moscow, U.S.S.R., Commission for UNESCO, Ministry of Education, RSFSR, 16 p.

SERRUYS, PAUL L. M. 1962. Survey of the Chinese language reform and the anti-illiteracy movement in Communist China. Studies in Communist Chinese Terminology 8. Berkeley, Center for Chinese Studies. University of Californa.

SHUY, ROGER W., ed. 1966. Social dialects and language learning. Champaign, Ill., NCTE.

SJOBERG, ANDRÉE F. 1964. Writing, speech and society: Some changing interrelationships. PICL 9.892–97.

———. 1966. Socio-cultural and linguistic factors in the development of writing systems for preliterate peoples. Sociolinguistics, ed. by Wm. Bright, pp. 260–76, The Hague, Mouton.

SMALLEY, WILLIAM A. 1964. Orthography studies: Articles on new written systems. London, United Bible Societies. Help for Translators, vol. 6.

SMITH, ALFRED G. 1956. Literacy promotion in an underdeveloped area. Madison, University of Wisconsin. Unpublished Ph.D. thesis.

SORENSEN, ARTHUR P., JR. 1967. Multilingualism in the Northwest Amazon. AmA 69.670–84.

SPENCER, JOHN, ed. 1963. Language in Africa. Cambridge, Cambridge University Press.

STERN, THEODORE. 1968. Three Pwo Karan scripts: A study of alphabet formation. AnL 10/1.1–39.

STEWART, GAIL. 1967. Present-day usage of the Vai script in Liberia. AfrLR 7.71–74.

STEWART, WILLIAM A. 1964. Non-standard speech and the teaching of English. Washington, D.C., Center for Applied Linguistics.

———. 1965. Sociolinguistic factors affecting English teaching. Social dialects and language learning, ed. by Roger W. Shuy, pp. 10–18. Champaign, Ill., NCTE.

———. 1968. A sociolinguistic typology for describing national multilingualism. In Fishman 1968a.

SZAJKOWSKI, ZOSA. 1966. Catalogue of the exhibition on the history of Yiddish orthography from the spelling rules of the early sixteenth century to the standardized orthography of 1936. New York, Yivo Institute for Jewish Research.

TABOURET-KELLER, ANDRÉE. 1968. Sociological factors of language maintenance and language shift: A methodological approach based on European and African examples. In Fishman, Ferguson and Das Gupta 1968, pp. 107–18.

TANNER, NANCY. 1967. Speech and society among the Indonesian elite: A case study of a multilingual community. AnL 9/3.15–40.

TAULI, VALTER. 1968. Introduction to a theory of language planning. Acta Universitatis Upsaliensis, Studia Philologiae Scandinavicae Upsaliensia.

THOMPSON, LAURENCE C. 1965. A Vietnamese grammar. Seattle, University of Washington Press.

THORBURN, THOMAS. 1969. Cost-benefit analysis in language planning. Consultative Meeting on Language Planning Processes. Honolulu, EWC-IAP. Also in Rubin and Jernudd 1971 and Fishman 1971.

TIETZE, ANDREAS. 1962. Problems of Turkish lexicography. IJAL 28.263–72.

TOSHIO, YAMADA. 1967. The writing system: Historical research and modern development. CTL 2.693–731.

TRAGER, GEORGE L. 1959. The systematization of the Whorf hypothesis. AnL 1/1.25–31.

TUCKER, A. N. 1971. Orthographic systems and conventions in sub-Saharan Africa. CTL 7. 618–53.

TWADDELL, W. I. 1959. Standard German. AnL 1/3.1–7.

UNESCO. 1951. The Haiti Pilot Project. Paris, Unesco.

VACHEK, JOSEPH. 1945–1949. Some remarks on writing and phonetic transcription. AL (Copenhagen) 5.86–93.

——. 1948. Written language and printed language. Recueil linguistique de Bratislava 1.67–75. *Also in* A Prague School reader in linguistics, ed. by J. Vachek, pp. 4530–60. Bloomington, Indiana University Press. 1964.

VALDMAN, ALBERT. 1968. Language standardization in a diglossia situation: Haiti. *In* Fishman, Ferguson and Das Gupta 1968, pp. 313–26.

VERDOODT, ALBERT. 1971. The differential impact of immigrant French speakers on indigenous German speakers: A case study in the light of two theories. International Migration Review 5.138–46. *Also in* Fishman 1971.

WALKER, WILLARD. 1969. Notes on native writing systems and the design of native literacy programs. AnL 11/5.148–66.

WARD, IDA C. 1945. Report of an investigation of some Gold Coast language problems. London, Crown Agents for the Colonies.

WEINREICH, MAX. 1953. Yidishkayt and Yiddish: On the impact of religion on language in Ashkenazic Jewry. *In* Morecai M. Kaplan Jubilee Volume, New York, Jewish Theological Seminary of America. *Also in* Fishman 1968a, pp. 382–413.

——. 1967. The reality of Jewishness versus the ghetto myth: The sociolinguistic roots of Yiddish. To honor Roman Jakobson, pp. 2199–2211. The Hague, Mouton.

WEINREICH, URIEL. 1951. Research problems on bilingualism, with special reference to Switzerland. Unpublished Ph.D. dissertation, Columbia University.

——. 1953a. Languages in contact. New York, Linguistic Circle of New York.

——. 1953b. The Russification of Soviet minority languages. Problems of Communism 2/6.46–57.

——. 1962. Multilingual dialectology and the new Yiddish Atlas. AnL 4/1.6–22.

WHITE, JOHN K. 1962. On the revival of printing in the Cherokee language. CAnthr 3.511–14.

WHITELEY, W. H. 1968. Ideal and reality in national language policy: A case study from Tanzania. *In* Fishman, Ferguson and Das Gupta 1968, pp. 327–44.

WHORF, BENJAMIN L. 1940. Science and linguistics. Technology Review 44.229–31, 247–48.

——. 1941. The relation of habitual thought to behavior and to language. Language, culture and personality, ed. by Leslie Spier, pp. 75–93. Menasha, Wisc., Sapir Memorial Publication Fund.

WILLEMS, EMILIO. 1943. Linguistic changes in German-Brazilian communities. Acta Americana 1.448–63.

WINNER, T. G. 1952. Problems of alphabetic reform among the Turkic peoples of Soviet Central Asia. Slavonic and East European Review 1952.132–47.

WITTERMANS, ELIZABETH P. 1967. Indonesian terms of address in a situation of rapid social change. Social Forces 46.48–52.

WOLFF, HANS. 1959. Nigerian orthography. Zaria, Gaskiya Corp.

WOLFRAM, WALTER A. 1969. A sociolinguistic description of Detroit Negro speech. Washington, D.C., Center for Applied Linguistics.

WONDERLY, WILLIAM L. 1968. Bible translations for popular use. London, United Bible Societies.

WU YU-CHANG. 1956. Concerning the draft Han Language Phonetization Plan. Current Background 1956/380 (March 15).4–20.

——. 1964. Widening the use of the phonetic script. China Reconstructs 13/6.29–31.

——. 1965. Report of the current tasks of reforming the written language and the draft scheme for a Chinese phonetic alphabet. In Reform of the Chinese written language. Peking, Foreign Language Press.

WURM, S. A. 1966. Language and literacy. New Guinea on the threshold, ed. by E. K. Fisk, pp. 135–48. Canberra, Australian National University.

WURM, S. A., and D. C. LAYCOCK. 1961–1962. The question of language and dialect in New Guinea. Oceania 32.128–43.

YOUNG, R. R. 1944. An adult literacy campaign in Sierra Leone. Oversea Education 15/3.97–100.

PART EIGHT

LINGUISTICS AND EDUCATION

LINGUISTICS AND ECONOMICS

FERRUCCIO ROSSI-LANDI

> In der Anatomie des Menschen
> ist ein Schlüssel zur Anatomie des Affen.
> KARL MARX
>
> El lenguaje es obra del hombre,
> y el hombre no ha de ser esclavo del lenguaje.
> JOSÉ MARTÍ

1. INTRODUCTION

> Thought, rising from the concrete to the abstract, does not get
> farther away *from* the truth, but gets closer to it ... Man's con-
> sciousness not only reflects the objective world, but it creates it
> as well.
> V. I. LENIN

1.1 *Foreword*

The title of this essay indicates a juxtaposition of two different disciplines, economics and linguistics. Such juxtaposition does in fact take place here, but in ways
and within limits which must be set forth in the beginning to avoid misunderstandings. In what follows neither economics nor linguistics is simply assumed as it
appears today in the texts of the specialists. Rather we are interested primarily
in the objects to which the two disciplines give attention: that is, to human language as the principal object of linguistic science and to economic exchange as
the principal object of the science of economics. Such "objects" are taken up in
the inquiry to the degree in which they lend themselves to being considered in a
unitary way. It is my intention to begin a semiotic elaboration of the two social
processes which we can identify provisionally as "the production and circulation
of goods (in the form of commodities)" and as "the production and circulation
of sentences (in the form of verbal messages)". These are two fundamental
modes of human social development. Although they usually appear in disjoined
fields, here we formulate the hypothesis that they are "the same thing" at least in
the sense in which the two principal branches of one tree may be considered "the
same thing". The essay is dedicated to some aspects of this relative "sameness".

I will maintain that when goods circulate in the form of commodities they "are" messages; and that when sentences circulate in the form of verbal messages they "are" commodities. These two assertions will be justified by means of a conceptual framework derived from a general theory of man and of society. It is the theory of the *anthropogenic character of work* originating in Hegel and Marx. According to this theory, man is the result of his own work, and it is through such work that he has progressively severed himself from the other animals. One of the most important aspects of this theory is that everything that has value (and therefore, as we shall see, everything that has *meaning*) is always a product of human work; value is something that man has introduced and continues to introduce into the world (theory of labor-value[1]). All social sign systems also have meaning and value as products of human work. The background of this research is therefore that of a radical materialism, not mechanicistic but dialectical and historical. An alternative to the conscious use of these general ideas and the connected world-view is not the supposed emancipation from general ideas and from acting within a world-view, although many specialists are often subject to such an illusion. The real alternative, always to be found, is, instead, that of the conscious or unconscious use of *other* general ideas, and of a *different* world-view.

The ideas presented in this essay then, have not been elaborated inside two or more specialistic disciplines, rather they have been drawn in a deductive or applicative way from a nucleus of ideas whose founding power we acknowledge. In the application of such ideas to sign systems generally, and in particular to the sign systems of language and of economy, some unaccustomed aspects of these systems have come to our attention. As a consequence of the procedure followed, the bibliographical apparatus, especially for the part regarding linguistics, has an extrinsic character: it is aimed more at the verification, or at least at the clarification, of what is said than at its foundation; it serves rather to comfort the reader of

---

[1] In the fourth edition of Book one of *Kapital*, 1890, Friedrich Engels added to footnote 16 of Chapter I the following remark: «Die englische Sprache hat den Vorzug, zwei verschiedne Worte für diese zwei verschiednen Aspekte der Arbeit zu haben. Die Arbeit, die Gebrauchswerte schafft und qualitativ bestimmt ist, heißt *work*, im Gegensatz zu *labour*; die Arbeit, die Wert schafft und nur quantitativ gemessen wird, heißt *labour*, im Gegensatz zu *work*. Siehe Note zur englischen Übersetzung, p. 14». In the Dent translation of *Kapital*, which we shall use for our quotes, Engels' addition is omitted; and *Arbeit* is generally rendered by *labour*. Engels' addition is reported instead in both the Italian and the French translations, as it was in the English translation by Samuel Moore and E. Aveling, London 1887, Tome I, p. 14, note 1. In short, according to Engels the English language has the advantage of distinguishing between a more specific and a more generic productive activity — that is, between *work* and *labor*. I made the decision to use 'work' rather than 'labor' as a fundamental term because in this essay attention is mainly given to *specific* work, productive of *use*-values, while *generic* work, productive of "values" (cf. footnote 12) is considered as a derivation from the former. An additional point is that 'work' can be used together with 'worked' and 'works', while the same derivations from 'labor' would bear different meanings. In stereotyped expressions like 'theory of labor-value', the term 'labor' was however retained. Because of such terminological decisions, the English wordings may sound a little awkward whenever 'labor' might have been preferable to 'work' from the point of view of common usage.

Current trends in linguistics than to justify the author. There are cases in which it may even seem to have a post-eventum character. We have been trying to see what sense the developments of the theory of labor-value assume within the disciplines to which they would traditionally belong. This operation, even if technically immature, has given two types of results. On the one hand, we have come across indications which coincide with various notions commonly accepted by linguists and semioticians; on the other hand, various other equally common notions have been contradicted. We outline here, in a preliminary form and merely as an example, some of the points the reader will meet in the course of the exposition.

Let us begin with the points where the results coincide. In the study of exchange within the realm of social production from the point of view of communication, it is possible to distinguish various kinds of material bodies which are carriers of signs; with the thinning of their materiality, these bodies become more and more irrelevant to the sign they carry: this seems to offer an anthropological explanation for the Saussurian doctrine of the *arbitraire du signe*. — One of the types of value belonging to signs is identified with the *position* of the signs within total sign production; that is, a sign has the value (among others) which belongs to it as a result of the portion of work carried out to produce it. It is worth repeating that this identification came about through an exclusively deductive procedure beginning from the theory of labor-value. In the author's view, the most important point was that this fit together with other deductions drawn from the same theory. The fact that such masters of the field as Saussure, Hjelmslev, and Wittgenstein had reached much the same conclusion by a different path was taken into account only later on, as a confirmation, when the above congruence had already emerged independent of their authoritative research. — In a not dissimilar way, the application of the equation of value of commodity exchange to linguistic exchange has pointed to an interesting direction for the study of the sentence. The opposition between use-value and exchange-value, internal to every single linguistic sign that comes to be part of a sentence, "unfolds", so to speak, within the sentence itself. The sentence holds together precisely because this "unfolding" takes place — it is of such "unfolding" that it consists. Here verification has shown that in spite of their very different terminology, Tesnière and Greimas in France had reached positions not dissimilar by a different path (to make ourselves immediately understandable, let us recall Tesnière's well-known remark regarding the sentence as a "theatrical action", taken up by Greimas in *Sémantique structurale*). — Strictly connected to the two cases mentioned is the technique of pushing aside the semantic dimension for the purposes of syntactic inquiry. More than a similarity of results, we find here that the approach drawn from the founding notion of labor-value may be of help in understanding the *reasons* why linguists are both doing a right thing and going astray when they leave aside the semantic dimension. — Other cases regard the problem of the acquisition of language in its relation to the non-parallelism between use of the language and intelligence brought to light by Eric Lenneberg and others. According to the theory of labor-value applied to language, we learn to speak so easily *precisely because* we don't have to contribute our intelligence; and we don't have to contribute our intelligence because the products of linguistic work which has already been done are offered to us to be used.

On the other hand, however, the indications obtained deductively do not seem reconcilable with some of the principles of contemporary linguistic and semiotic research. For example, it does not appear that any privileged position belongs to language and to *verbal* communication within the realm of social communication. *All* non-verbal sign systems, with paraverbal or postverbal systems as an obvious exception, enjoy their own independence from verbal sign systems; indeed, *beneath* verbal sign-systems there exists a "language of things" tied to material production. — In spite of the enormous complexity of their relations, the qualification as social applies to animal aggregates only in an extended sense of the word, because in them there is lacking the work which is at the foundation of human societies. — Entrusting meaning and context to the semantic dimension alone, considering extraneous to them the syntactic and pragmatic dimensions, does not make sense from the point of view of labor-value. According to this point of view, meaning and context are present instead in all three dimensions, and should be described by using the terminology of each of them. — Moreover, the Saussurian *parole* turns out to be an individualistic myth which should give way to the recognition of the *collective character of speech.* — Finally, plurality of articulation is to be found not only in the genetic code and in language, but also in other social sign systems. — Whether these and other similar indications which have been obtained by applying the theory of the anthropogenic character of work, and in particular of labor-value, to language, are correct or not; and whether they must be substituted for the ideas they seem to exclude, and in what measure, or made to agree with them — is for the reader to decide.

It is suggested that the reader consider the whole of the present research within the dialectic of contradiction and agreement — even if, given the intricacy of the problems and the multiform vastness of the literature, often this dialectic will emerge only in passing, in spite of the length of the essay. The reader will find, then, a certain number of new and (at least provisionally) unacceptable assertions. At the same time he may find that numerous assertions are a restatement of the obvious or are taken for granted, and will object perhaps that some of these things have already been said very clearly. I answer him with Roman Jakobson's remark that «only the things which have been said very clearly often fall into complete oblivion» (1953, French transl. 1963 : 40); and add that of the various assertions, the new as well as the obvious, those which will seem unacceptable and those which will seem to have been accepted for too long, at least come from a unitary basis and involve each other reciprocally. This brings up several questions. In the first place it is clear that errors to be found in these pages will have to be localized *aut* in the process of deduction from, or application of, the theory of labor-value, *aut* in the theory itself. At this level, either the theory has been applied wrongly here, or it is false. In the second place, however, the application of the theory of labor-value to language has *also* given results which coincide with various commonly accepted notions, and this would remain unexplained. Where does the separation take place? — All this sends us back to that unity of approach in which the author finds an excuse for the imprecisions and the provisional character of his exposition. To an endeavor which is voluntarily pioneeristic and interdisciplinary, one will perhaps concede a certain number of extenuating circumstances.

In this first section we recall and briefly comment on some notions of semiotics. Readers acquainted with semiotic literature may skip over them and begin with Section Two. My aim is to secure a minimum terminological and conceptual framework, fairly widely accepted and common enough, necessary and sufficient to the ends of the discussion. At the same time, though always within the realm of habitual notions, I shall be trying to bring the reader little by little towards the theory I have decided to adopt and apply.

1.2 *Sign Systems*

Everything that is understood by 'human communication' — in the widest sense of effective transfer of information and meaning — is sign exchange (cf. 2.4.1 and 2.4.2). With this we do not at all want to exclude the fact that communication is itself a wholly material process. Clearly, in order for there to be communication there must be a transfer of matter-or-energy from one place to another, in space and time, even if this transfer is reduced to the movement of sound waves, in the case of acoustic communication and of light waves (or photons), in the case of visual communication. When we consider the exiguousness of the material transfer as compared to the behavior that may follow upon it, the notion arises of communication as a servomechanism. Signs too are *also* material objects external to our bodies. But they are not *just* or *only* that. For the transfer of an object or even only of a movement from one place to another to assume sign value and become a *message*, it is necessary that various conditions be realized concomitantly; one of these conditions is that a *code* be operating. We will clarify little by little some of these conditions.[2] Let us say for the moment that a code is an organized and strati-

---

[2] *Only some*, and limited to the purposes of the present enquiry. Since this is a comparative study of some basic features of human production, and not an introduction to semiotics as such, a number of issues usually considered fundamental for semiotics by contemporary scholars (including the present writer) remain outside our scope. Such are, for example, the questions concerning different kinds of signs (signals, symbols, icons, and the like) and different kinds of meanings (signification, denotation, connotation, and the like), as well as the dimensions of semiosis, and the relations between metalanguage and object-language. See also footnote 4

fied totality made up of the sign products of "completed" work, that is, of work which has been done previously to the moment in which sign work is resumed; and a message is a product of new sign work which uses as materials some of the elements of the code. Messages and codes exist together in reality. Any given message is what it is only because there is a code; any given code is what it is only because messages can be obtained from it. Between a code and "its" messages there is a constant dialectical relationship. It is only when we consider a code in its structural abstraction that we can provisionally leave its messages aside; and it is only when we receive messages in a "natural" (unconscious, or completely spontaneous) way, that we ignore or simply do not refer to the codes from which they are obtained. The fact that the first of these two cases is limited to the scientific enquiries of some linguists and other semioticians, while the second is what normally happens, confers to the opposition an interesting lack of symmetry.

The totality of communication is subdivided in sectors, each of which consists of (i) at least one code as a structured totality, (ii) the rules which regulate the use of the signs, that is, the modalities of the codification, decodification, and interpretation of the messages, (iii) the group of conditions which permit such operations, that is, the presence of (at least) one transmitter, one receiver, a channel (contact) and a context.[3] Here we need in the first place an expression designating any sector

---

ad finem. Generic reference can be made to the writings of Peirce, Vailati, Saussure, Morris; and, more recently, Prieto, Greimas, Šaumjan, Jakobson, and Sebeok.

Under certain conditions, a low-level imput signal is transformed by a control-system into a higher-level movement. The control-system of communication is based on code and context, while on the other hand some code and some context must be operating for any servomechanism to exist. Thus in order to speak even of a servomechanism we must have already introduced the basic notions of semiotics. It is however apparent that to approach all sorts of communication in terms of the servomechanism involved helps to clarify some basic features of communication itself. For servomechanism in general, see H. Lauer, R. N. Lesnick, and L. E. Matson, 1960. Current notions of cybernetics could be discussed from the vantage point of communication as a servomechanism. Our main interest, however, doesn't lie in individual speech processes (such as those proposed in Liberman's motor theory of speech, for example), but rather in the "natural" or "spontaneous" emergence, within social reproduction, of the collective servomechanism of communication as an articulation internal to the moment of exchange. See for this 2.4.1-2.

[3]   This is, of course, a highly condensed way of presenting the situation. Let us refer to footnote 2 above, and to the text as well, for the limits of our exposition. Alternative and more complete descriptions of the conditions permitting codification, decodification, and interpretation of messages, whether verbal or non-verbal, can be found in Peirce II, 227° fll.; VIII, 342°-379°; and *passim;* Morris 1938 (Ital. transl. with commentary, 1954); Jakobson 1961; Rossi-Landi 1961, ch.s VII and VIII; Sebeok 1965, 1969; Eco 1968 : 15-70; Britton 1970; and in many others. It should be added at this point that if we turned to the *nature* of codes and messages, the proper place for their study would be at the boundaries between semiotics and other disciplines and would lead us to examine — to put it in philosophical jargon – the very *possibility* of codes and messages, *i.e.* their *foundation.* At the same time, such a study would help in the definition of semiotics as a discipline by assuming 'code' and 'message' as its fundamental terms. Whether or not these two notions can be traced back to 'mediated-taking-account-of', as proposed by Charles Morris in 1938, cannot be examined here. But it must be said that whenever such fundamental terms are traced back to something else we find ourselves outside the field of semiotics proper, perhaps dealing with a meta-semiotics. The procedure of explaining the terms

of communication in a neutral way, with reference, that is, not to its differential characteristics, but only to the fact that it is a sector of communication and consequently must be made up of the elements listed above. We will use *sign system*, which has several advantages. First, it introduces from the beginning the notion of the sign as the dialectical sum of *signans* and *signatum*, and thus renders central the notion of meaning, excluding the possibility that we might be referring to mere systems of *signantia*. In the second place it excludes the possibility that we might be thinking of communication as the mere arithmetical sum of messages as distinct from their codes. Sign systems are dialectical sums of codes and messages actually used by transmitters and receivers in favorable conditions. This is why they also include the rules for their own use (for qualifications see 2.3.3 and 5.2.3). Thus we refuse as ambiguous and incomplete the idea that codes are used *in order to* communicate. We will see more clearly in what follows (5.2.1.1) the importance of this refusal. Believing that codes are used in order to communicate means admitting that *first* codes existed (at least an *ur*-code) and *afterwards* communication began (cf. Eco 1968: 251–370). There is in such a belief an anthropomorphical projection of the fact that each of us finds his own language and the other codes of the community to which he belongs ready-made at the moment of his birth for him to learn and use. In this way justice is not done to other and more fundamental aspects of communication: like the contemporaneous genesis of any signal and of its use; or the modifications which, in this field as in others, use always brings to the object used; or the unconscious character of a large part of communication. On the other hand, the notion of sign system also excludes belief in a communication from which codes are absent — usually an anti-scientific temptation induced by the difficulties encountered in deciphering this or that code; what is more, it excludes the belief in a communication which *precedes* the formation of codes (cf. among many others Cherry 1966², 7: «There is no communication without a system of signs»). As to the question whether in principle *there can be* forms of communication from which precedently stratified codes are absent, judgment is suspended here, although we do not conceal a negative attitude towards such an idea. The

---

fundamental for semiotics by means of other terms was partially followed — more philosophically than semiotically, and thereby with aims and terminology very different from those of semioticians — by Husserl in the three volumes of *Ideen,* Merleau-Ponty (especially 1945, but also 1960 and 1942), Lévi-Strauss (1958, 1962, 1964), Sartre (1960), and others who enquired into the origin and formation of codes as symbolic selections of experience and as a set of relations of the human body to all the rest of the world. Solìmini (1968 : 103-127) has summarized some of these enquiries.

The main obstacle to any enquiry of a meta-semiotic (or para-semiotic, or quasi-semiotic) kind is that it is very difficult to single out, or even to imagine, a situation in which no sign is present. Even if we say that there is no social relation, whether among men or among non-human animals, without signs, and trace back social aggregation to pre-social levels of life, we then also find that life itself is based on messages and codes. In my opinion, the only way to overcome this difficulty consists in approaching totalities of increasing complexity: sign systems are parts of such totalities, and develop with them. This is, indeed, the line of the present enquiry.

very identity between codes and messages found in animal communication (with the partial single exception, perhaps, of birds) does not refute but confirms the simultaneous presence of messages and codes (cf. Sebeok 1970: 125).

Our insistence on a unitary reference to the totality composed of codes and messages, including all the conditions which make possible their existence and their use, moreover, considers as unessential the question as to the status of this or that sector of communication — whether it has already been broken down by semiotic inquiry into the parts of which it is composed, that is, traced back to a code and to its use as construction, transmission, reception, and interpretation of messages; or whether it is still a virgin territory, or has been explored only in some of its aspects separated from others.

Let us instead divide all sign systems into *natural* and *social*. For example the genetic code (Sebeok 1963; Borek 1965; Sullivan 1968; Masters 1970) and the other codes found in nature by human interpretation (the code of sea and sailing, "written in things" but put into operation by sailors: Rossi-Landi 1968d: 296–303), belong to the field of natural sign systems. Here there is the problem of the measure of man's intervention in giving rise to signs which he finds, so to say, out there. In what way can we delimit the realm of signs within the realm of nature? It can be maintained that it is not proper to talk of mere nature through the thickness of codes, lexicons, and ideologies as in fact we do talk about it, and that as a matter of fact we should be doing the opposite operation of limiting the realm of nature within the realm of signs (Marx and Engels, *Die deutsche Ideologie:* 42–45; Engl. transl.: 57–61; Korsch 1938: ch. IV; Schmidt 1962: ch. II). One intricate and important aspect of the question is whether sign systems underlying the relations of animals in their aggregates should also be considered as only natural. Do animal aggregates constitute societies in the proper sense? Since what follows concerns only human sign systems, we will not be tackling these questions; for a treatment of them readers can see specialized literature (listed writings by Sebeok; Bronowski 1967; *Animal communication*, 1968, and *Approaches to animal communication*, 1969). In the following, only properly human sign systems belonging to the "second evolution" are considered social in the full sense. A "second evolution" superimposed itself upon merely natural evolution with the advent of the dialectic between use and exchange as a result of the division of labor. If, ideally, we were to fix the phenomenon of homination as the unitary initial phenomenon, then human social sign systems would be by definition subsequent to it; but we would be more nearly correct in saying that social sign systems *are* both homination and all that followed from it, that is, they are human prehistory and history considered from the point of view of general semiotics.

Let us proceed by distinguishing all *social sign systems* into two large classes: *verbal* and *non-verbal*. Since the two classes both belong to the social, it will not be necessary to add the adjective 'social' on each occurrence: 'verbal' is not opposed to 'natural' but — within the social — to 'non-verbal'. The adjectives 'human' and 'social' and the syntagm 'sign: verbal or non-verbal' all indicate the same zone of reality, shedding light on diverse aspects or levels of it.

Verbal sign systems are those that have languages and their various specifications and elaborations as codes. These codes are founded on distinctions made by man in sound material, the so-called articulate sounds. These are objects produced by man with his own body, but which are arranged, nevertheless, in supra-individual structures, and become immediately institutionalized. We are dealing with languages here only in the historical or universal sense, the most common sense of the word (English, Italian, Cheremis, Hopi); we are not just considering them separately (for example, English, insofar as it is distinct from Hopi, or Italian from Cheremis), but rather as particular cases of speech, that is, of the human capacity to use consistent codes of articulate sounds for normal expressive and communicative ends. Such ends are to be considered common to all the members of the community in which a given language is spoken, and, at a fundamental level, to all men, regardless of the particular language they speak. Furthermore, our enquiry is limited to the practico-communicative use of a language, leaving aside things like the poetic elaborations to which a language may be submitted or the formation of technical "languages", within and beyond a language, for special aims — whether these be internal to the community in which the language is spoken (like ceremonial language), or, instead, common to various communities (for example many ideological languages), or even actually or potentially panhuman (for example mathematical language).

The terms *language* and *linguistic* suffer from an irremediable polysemia — especially in English due to the cryptotypic character of the opposition between language in general and languages, an opposition which is instead phenotypically present in the neo-Latin languages. There's no one-to-one correspondence between English as an object-language and the semiotic metalanguage that studies this sector of the language (see footnote 4 hereafter). This is why, in our classification, we have preferred to call languages and their various specifications and elaborations, 'verbal sign systems'. As we go on, however, we will use 'language' and its derivatives whenever we are not particularly concerned with the opposition between verbal and non-verbal sign systems or with the presence of verbal sign systems that are not identical to languages as they are commonly understood. It remains to be mentioned that the notion of *verbal* sign systems does not take into account the distinction between *spoken* and *written* because it is logically anterior to it. In general, every verbal sign system can be written or spoken, and if it is spoken only, it can be transcribed. This is not a subdivision of all verbal sign systems into two subclasses; it is an internal subdivision for each separate verbal sign system. At any rate the distinction between spoken and written is not directly relevant. We have made these remarks only because they are handy for clarification of the subsequent use of 'verbal'.

All the other social sign systems are *non-verbal*. By this we mean that they do not use codes founded on articulated sounds but rather codes founded on other types of objects. Such objects, which we will also call "bodies", already exist "in nature"; or they have been produced by man for other purposes; or they are produced with the purpose of being used as signs; or they are used as signs in the very act in which they are produced. Throughout the discussion we will be running into some of the inexhaustible complications implicit in these apparently rather obvious distinctions. It is a virtue of modern semiotic science to have brought numerous non-verbal sign systems to light and to have begun to make comparisons between them and to classify them. If here we risk a considerably simplified classification, it is only in view of what we have to say — with the forewarning, moreover, that verbal sign systems (as we will specify as each case arises) can also present characteristics belonging to this or that class of non-verbal sign systems, from which they remain distinct, however, because they *are* verbal. We can distinguish, then, sign systems which are (i) *kinesic* and *postural*: movements made, communication by gestures, facial and other expressions, physical attitudes and positions assumed; (ii) *proxemic*: regarding man's use of space, and the meaning of spatial relations as elaborated specifically in every culture and human group; (iii) *tactile, olfactory, gustative*; as well as *visual* and *auditory*, to the extent in which we exclude other non-verbal sign systems also founded on sight and hearing; (iv) *objectual:* founded on objects which man manipulates, produces, and uses (here also "verbal objects", that is, articulate sounds, are excluded): we have clothes, cosmetics, ornaments, utensils and machines, constructions of every sort (this is the field of so-called "material production"); music and the figurative arts enter into this class although they are not exhausted within it; (v) *institutional:* all kinds of social organizations, especially kinship systems, rites, ceremonies, mores, manners, juridical systems, religions, the economic market as the circulation and exchange of goods in the form of commodities, and so on (language too is institutional). One sees that — generally and with some complications or exceptions — the first three classes of sign systems refer to the human body, the human organism; while the last two refer to something external to the human organism. In fact the distinction between *organic* and *instrumental* sign systems is a current one (Jakobson 1970a: 3–16): in the former case man *behaves*; in the latter man behaves *with* or *by means of* — that is, he uses or applies — *something*.

One essential characteristic of all social sign systems — whether verbal or non-verbal, organic or instrumental, conscious or unconscious, more or less openly institutional — is that they do not exist *in nature*, and are instead *products of human work* (for our uses of *work* and *labor* see footnote 1 above and Section Two below, especially 2.3 and footnote 6). This is the characteristic to which we will most often return. We must bear in mind that not only are messages the products of human work but so are the modalities of codification and decodification, the rules for the use of codes, and the codes themselves, the addresser and the addressee, the channels, the context. Any social sign system whatsoever must be seen in its entirety as the product of human work. This is one good reason for saying that 'social' is equivalent to 'human'.

Naturally the character of being a product appears more or less clearly according to the social sign systems examined. It is usually accepted by everybody for objectual non-verbal sign systems; it is fairly well recognized for institutional sign systems (for some of these last, however, the very fact of their being sign systems has still not been fully accepted). For the other non-verbal sign systems listed, that is, for all those united under the heading 'organic sign systems', the character of being a product of human work is usually much less recognized, when it is not simply denied. Finally, widely varied positions appear when the question arises of attributing to language the character of being a proper product. In my opinion these uncertainties and divergences depend upon a confused or overly limited notion of work, beginning with the fact that the *programs* to which every piece of meaningful behavior unconsciously refers have not yet been, or are just beginning to be, studied (1.4). It is clear that if by 'work' we only mean, *e.g.* the behavior of the artisan who modifies and puts together various objects (for example boards, glue, and nails) by means of utensils, and who offers a new object as a product (for example, a table), then the character of being a product of work would belong only to objectual sign systems, and perhaps not even to all of them. But the notion of work must be enlarged in an anthropogenic sense, and distinguished from that of mere activity. We will clarify this enlargement and this distinction in 1.4, when we discuss the communicative programs which underlie organic sign behaviors themselves; in 2.2, when we examine the possibility of generalizing the notion of artefact (for this spelling see 2.1); and throughout the whole of the discussion. As we have said, however, our principal aim is not to show that all sign systems are products of work, but rather to examine the relations between the sign systems of material production and economic exchange on the one hand, and the sign system of linguistic production and exchange on the other. Thus we will remain prevalently on the ground of social sign systems of the objectual and institutional type.

In theory, relations between sign systems obtain in the following cases:

a. Between social sign systems and natural sign systems, that is:
   a.a. between verbal sign systems and natural sign systems;
   a.b. between non-verbal sign systems and natural sign systems.

b. Within the realm of natural sign systems, that is, among various types of natural sign systems.

c. Within the realm of social sign systems, that is:
   c.a. between verbal sign systems and non-verbal sign systems;
   c.b. within the realm of verbal sign systems, that is, among various verbal sign systems;
   c.c. within the realm of non-verbal sign systems, that is, among various non-verbal sign systems.

All of these relations may be studied. In this essay we privilege a group of reciprocal relations to be located in *c.a.* (see the last part of footnote 4 below).

1.3   *The Autonomy of Non-Verbal Sign Systems*

Non-meaningful behavior does not exist. It is with the whole of his social organization that man communicates. No man can operate without consciously or unconsciously using some sign systems. These are propositions that recall those with which the social character of any human action is usually asserted. They raise the problem of the relation between a general semiotics and a general theory of society (cf. for ex. Carpenter 1969: 43–45; Kristeva 1969: 27–59 *passim*; Lotman 1967). It seems to me that there are two opposite solutions. One might on the one hand maintain that sign systems exist *within* social reality. But one has by this assertion divorced sign systems from social reality already, thus losing sight of the operations of social practice as what they are — essentially, sign operations none of which can take place alone because they all belong to one or more sign systems. Semiotics would seem accordingly to be a superimposed and auxiliary discipline. On the other hand, one might maintain that sign systems are *themselves* social reality. But this could lead us to believing that there is nothing more to social reality than sign systems. Social reality, instead, is based on need, work, and exploitation, that is, on factors which brutally beset the very body of man in its psycho-physical materiality and not just the sign systems practised by him (cf. for his notion of the human body Di Siena and Rossi-Landi, 1970). One possible line of mediating between the two solutions could begin with the remark that without social sign systems the contents of reality *would not be lived as social*. There's a big difference between shooting wolves on the moorlands, and shooting men on the street. Even considering as primary the fact that the organisms of the wolves and of the men are lacerated equally by the lead, the sign systems which the wolves put into operation while living this experience, though certainly not inexistent, are incomparably less complex and less pregnant with consequences than are those which the men put into operation. The human body lacerated by lead is a biological fact; but the various and complex interpretations that one can and must give for this fact are social, beginning with the victim's own interpretation. It is not through biological measures that one can stop men from shooting; and even if one succeeded, the *adoption* of such measures certainly would not itself be a biological fact; it would be a highly social fact. We can glimpse how the knowledge of sign systems is necessary not only for knowing social reality but also for operating upon it. This is particularly true in situations of a high level of reactionary sign elaboration, like the present mass societies dominated by money, consumption, and exploitation.

All this concerns all the social sign systems in principle, the verbal as well as non-verbal. But full recognition of the importance of non-verbal sign systems is still hindered by a number of factors. Of these factors, perhaps the most insidious, because it is put into operation even by those who do study non-verbal sign systems, lies in the excessive pre-eminence attributed to language. Language is substituted for non-verbal sign systems, or unduly projected upon them. Let us consider the following steps: (i) One recognizes the existence of political, economic, juridical, and other *languages* (Ital. *linguaggi*).[4] This restricted use of 'language' describes a set of systematic ways of employing certain linguistic techniques and of developing them according to special aims, and this to an analogous (though not identical) degree within the various historical languages (Ital. *lingue*). This is obvious. (ii) It is also obvious that there are particular sectors of the historical languages dominated by those systematic ways of using certain linguistic techniques. That is, the technical specifications of language (*linguaggio*) are to be found within the various languages (*lingue*). But all this is not sufficient for bringing to light non-verbal sign systems *as such*. We must add that: (iii) politics, the economy, jurisprudence, as well as fashions, cuisine, games, and so forth, are *themselves* social sign systems, subjectable to enquiry just as much as verbal sign systems are. The central point is that: (iv) we are dealing with non-verbal sign systems which not only are distinct from verbal sign systems, but also not reducible to them.

Naturally, every time we approach a non-verbal sign system *ex novo*, we must

---

[4] Clearly different usages of 'language' are involved here, with the additional complication that they differ not only within any given language but also from language to language. All the different usages of 'language', 'speech', 'idiom', and 'tongue' make up a field which is in no way identical, though it is obviously similar, to the field made up by all the different usages of 'linguaggio', 'lingua', 'favella', 'parola', and 'idioma' in Italian. In 1.2 we spoke of the irremediable polysemia of the terms 'language' and 'linguistic', especially in English. In the following, as already stated, we shall be using 'language' in a rather conservative manner, with reference to verbal (oral or written) codes and messages *i.e.* to a sector of *human* sign behavior. For non-verbal human sign behavior and for animal sign behavior we shall instead speak of sign systems, and we shall specify what system is being described as the various cases arise. 'Language' will be used as the Italian *linguaggio* (French *langage*), while the Italian *lingua* (French *langue*) will be rendered by '*a* language', or '*the* language'. Restricted uses of 'language' are explained in the text.

The *Oxford English Dictionary* and the *Random House Dictionary of the English Language* list some 14 senses of 'language'. One has the impression *both* that the various sciences of language correspond, at least to some extent, to the various senses listed, *and* that such a correspondence is not complete and could be, so to say, improved to the advantage of scientific enquiry. It is refreshing to hear Shakespeare stating that «Ther's a language in her eye, her cheake, her lip», and Mozley remarking that «all action is ... besides being action, language».

This is perhaps also the place to spend a few more words on the complexity of the relations obtaining in the field of sign systems. We may list the relations among verbal sign systems, among non-verbal sign systems, and among verbal *vs.* non-verbal sign systems. The complexity would of course further increase if we were to consider the additional relations emerging when *post-verbal* sign systems (which form when verbal languages already exist, or grow upon them) and *para-verbal* sign systems (which form alongside verbal languages, or refer to them) are also taken into account. For these and other complications, which are left aside here, the reader is referred to the enquiries contained in other Sections of the present volume and in other volumes of the *Current trends* (especially Volume 3, on *Theoretical foundations*), as well as to their bibliographies.

discuss accurately the extent to which it is in fact distinct and independent from language, and not reducible to it. One much debated question is whether in order to justify the existence and operation of a given non-verbal sign system, it is necessary for a *previous verbal agreement* to have taken place among the users of the system. Often the discussion shifts to the origin of sign systems in general. When the burden of making non-verbal sign systems possible is attributed to language, then the problem ends by being that of the autonomous origin of language. If a previous verbal agreement was necessary for the institution of a given non-verbal sign system, itself born precisely as a consequence of that agreement, in fact, the agreement must have taken place between men to whom that very non-verbal sign system was lacking. In some cases, such as the institution of the Morse code, this is completely obvious and does not merit discussion. But in other cases, especially those of the use of utensils and of the most simple institutions, one would be forced to introduce the notion of a humanity that reproduced itself by means of speech alone, if one wanted to maintain the idea of a previous verbal agreement. The speakers would have been men only halfway, half men and half apes, people who talked but didn't work, and who did not possess any institution other than language — which is absurd. Moreover, the idea of a previous agreement takes us back to the *contractualistic prejudice*, that is to the notion of already-formed individuals, who start discussing in order to draw up that very contract to which instead the power to form them is attributed (Rossi-Landi 1967a: 99–109). This vicious circle is an ideological projection in the field of signs of a social situation which has contingently permitted the formation and the free self-expression of individuals of a particular type, that is, sufficiently privileged to feel themselves detached from their own formation, which allows the overgrowth of consciousness in its self-regulating certainty. The old American university joke 'don't put Descartes before the horse' contains an involuntary criticism of this operation precisely while referring to its principal modern doctrinal source.

In the prospect of a more correct evaluation of non-verbal sign systems, let us begin by totally refusing the position of those who make non-verbal depend upon verbal sign systems, and who see the ruling structure in language. We maintain in this essay, sometimes in an open way and sometimes implicitly, (i) that all social sign systems developed parallel to the progressive interpretation of natural sign systems, and moreover (ii) that all social sign systems, regardless of the distinction between verbal and non-verbal, have been from the beginning — to the extent in which they developed together in every given community — in conditions of reciprocal structural independence and at the same time of reciprocal influence. This does not mean that there was no hierarchy imposed by real needs on sign systems; but it does mean that all basic social sign systems are "primary modelling systems" — according to the terminology of Lotman, who considers primary only the system of language, and secondary instead all non-verbal sign systems (Ital. transl. 1969: 311). If all social sign systems have primary modelling power, the extrapolation made by splitting off any one of them from all the others assumes a risky abstract character. When we study any social sign system we automatically find that we have to study various others (cf. some steps in this direction in Key 1970). The ideal situation towards which to move, indeed, would be that of a unitary examination of all sign systems presenting any sort of reciprocal dependence. The very idea of a social sign system isolated from others is not a correct one. Since man lives in nature and is (also) nature himself, not even the notion of studying social sign systems while isolating them from natural sign systems, can be correct. That all these descriptive distinctions must never be mistaken for ontological distinctions, is something over which there reigns a certain agreement; much more in words than in fact, however, given the profound difficulties that a criticism founded on consistent general principles succeeds so often in identifying beneath the sharply-outlined and compact surface of so much specialistic research.

To use one of Wittgenstein's well-known images, all sign systems are, then, at least to some extent, original "games", not reducible the one to the others. This does not mean, though, that there are not reciprocal influences among them. Ideologies, for example, depend upon the division of labor and of power. But these relations do not work equally in both directions. The English language is able to describe the natural sign system of the sea and the non-verbal sign system of fashion, while the natural sign system of the sea and the non-verbal sign system of fashion are not able to describe the English language. On the other hand, the capacity to interpret English or any other language cannot at all be substituted for the capacity to interpret the sign system of the sea or of fashion. The linguist is neither a sailor nor a tailor. Saussure, Slocum, and Christian Dior were masters of different arts.

The priority usually assigned to verbal sign systems is normally explained in various ways. We recall briefly three reasons suitable for beginning a realistic explanation of this attribution. A first reason is that the languages were the first social sign systems upon which attention was focused with conscious effort. It was about language itself that a sign-curiosity developed. Only in a second moment did this curiosity and the instruments elaborated for its satisfaction begin to extend themselves outside of language, moving over to other systems — whether or not these had been studied from other standpoints —— and considering them as sign systems within which codes and messages could be distinguished. The sign nature of non-verbal systems began to emerge all around a zone of awareness which had originally been limited to verbal sign systems. (The awareness of the programmed character of every form of communication, see 1.4, also grew little by little in this way but still more slowly, and culminated unilaterally in the construction of computers.)

The second reason has to do with the very nature of verbal sign systems as compared to non-verbal ones; as such it offers a sort of meta-explanation of the preceding reason. The articulated sounds upon which the codes of languages are founded are institutionalized objects produced by the human body. They are at the same time internal and external to the organism. This means that language, in one of its aspects, is kin to non-verbal sign systems of the objectual type; that in another aspect, it is kin to non-verbal sign systems of the institutional type; and that in still another aspect it is kin to the various types of sign systems which can be united under the heading of organic. These family relations confer to language proper a coverage which non-verbal sign systems usually do not possess. Each of us learns to produce by himself, with his organism, the articulated sounds of language without having to resort to anything external; still the sounds are objects existing in the external world; lastly they constitute an institutionalized, supra-individual, system. Clearly in spite of its complexity language presents itself as a more inviting and apparently nearer, almost handier, object of study. A colossal inversion.

The third is, I believe, the most important reason. It is an ideological reason: a projection of the way in which power has been handed down in more or less all of the historical societies, at least until a few decades ago. Language has always been the depository of power *par excellence*. The dominating classes, castes, and groups have always used language for their aims. The opposition between head and hand (Farrington 1947: ch. I) has been from the beginning an opposition between verbal and non-verbal sign systems respectively. It seems to have been more intense particularly during the periods when class distinctions were clearest; we are thinking, within European history, of language research done by Athenian citizens, who deputized material production to the great human machine of slavery; of medieval language research, prerogative of a privileged class of literate monks; or of sixteenth and seventeenth century linguistics, contemporary to the formation of the bourgeoisie; or the imposing foundation of linguistics in the nineteenth century, subservient to the take-off of bourgeois power.

One will notice that these reasons explain the fact that a priority has been and still is attributed to language; but they don't justify it. Moreover, they do not regard the priority as such. The reasons for which language has been and still is considered predominant over the other sign systems are not reasons in favor of its actual predominance.

There are, however, arguments that directly touch the question of priority or predominance. We continually see how other social sign systems, the non-verbal ones, contribute in a necessary way to the formation of the very stuff of all our lives. There are no alternatives to this situation. Consequently one doesn't see why non-verbal sign systems should be considered, as a group, less important than language. It is even difficult to understand what may be meant by a 'priority of language' in the absolute. Since in the absolute — that is, on its own account, without the other sign systems — language does not in fact exist, what in the world is meant when its priority is asserted? It seems a little like asserting the priority of digestion upon breathing, or of rivers upon seas, or worse, of downhill roads upon uphill roads. Since language and all other sign systems of a community are in reciprocal relations in reality, we don't understand in what possible way one can attribute to any one of these sign systems a *real* priority.

But even if we did want to assert the *priority* or *predominance of* language over the other sign systems and we had good reasons for such an assertion, it wouldn't follow in the least that all the other sign systems would be *dependent upon* language. There are, if anything, good reasons for saying the contrary: not for all non-verbal sign systems, of course, but for many of them. Certainly it can be said that language depends upon sign systems that we find already present in the other animals, and this because of the biological continuity between them and man. Since they came before language, language must have been conditioned by them. Moreover, language continues to be fed and sustained by all the non-verbal sign systems to which it refers. It would be senseless to ask that the butter be passed to us at the table, if we did not know how to recognize it with our eyes and move it with our hands. If we took away from language sailing, fashion, eating meals together, and little by little all the other human activities that express themselves in as many non-verbal sign systems, the only thing left would be the soul talking to itself. Language, on its own, simply does not exist in reality. On its own, it exists only as an object of study isolated by means of deliberate specialistic abstractions.

Some relations between speaking a language and the rest of meaningful behavior were once caught very accurately by Bertold Brecht in California when he wrote in 1946: «I don't have the least hope of ever being able to learn everyday American . . . . It is not just that I lack the words, not just the knowledge of the syntax. Rather, I lack a very precise behavior [*Habitus*] which I simply don't see any possibility of learning . . . I should learn to become a "nice fellow"» (1968: 298-299). Unable to assimilate the very different culture in which he found himself immersed, Brecht did not succeed in assimilating the language. But what does it mean to refuse a culture as distinguished from its language? What is left of a culture when we have taken its language away? Evidently, all the rest of the culture consists in nothing other than non-verbal sign systems. Not succeeding in mastering the non-verbal sign systems of a culture for him new and different, Brecht also refused its concomitant verbal sign system.

We will try to present by means of a brief analysis the way in which a non-verbal sign system is not only distinct but also (in one of the meanings of the term) independent from language. Let us consider the objective non-verbal sign system composed of the physical objects of daily household use: like socks, shoes, shorts, trousers, belt; or like matches, cigarettes, ashtrays, pipes, pipecleaners, swabs, tobacco-pouches; or like soap, towel, comb, brush, toothpaste, toothbrush, etc. Let's take the case of silverware and start off paradigmatically with the knife. Here it is necessary to anticipate some of what we will be saying in Section Three about the homology between linguistic products and material products. A table knife is an artefact, a manufactured object, that is, a social object provided with specific properties that make it useful. It is not just an *instrument* occasionally potentiating the human body, but rather is an object produced according to a model for precise aims: it is autonomous and finished in itself, an object that can be used and re-used in any moment and in diverse circumstances by any member of the community, with some minor exceptions (very small children, paralytics, and so on). Moreover, we find knives in any human community. A knife, then, is both species-specific and species-consistent. In a word, a knife is a veritable *utensil*. As such it has the level of complexity and the utility not just of a mere word or of a syntagm, as complex as this may be, but of a proper *sentence* or *judgment*. The utensil in fact consists in parts which are preproduced and put together according to certain rules, like the sentence. It is as if, in the language of things, the knife, every time we **asked** it, **replied**: **I am used for cutting**.

A knife is used for cutting. But what? It is easy to reply that it is used for cutting bread, fruit, meat, and so on; it is *not* used for cutting steel, stone, glass (it is not relevant to our argument whether or not in some technical language the utensils with which one cuts very hard objects are also called knives); *it can be used* for cutting paper, leather, and wood, but this is not its usual use (so much so that there are other types of knives, and moreover, other utensils, for cutting paper, leather, wood); it cannot be used for cutting air or water because these, not being solid, are not in the proper sense cuttable objects. Now, in what has been called the **language of things** (in our terminology a set of non-verbal sign systems) everything that can be done with a knife is equivalent to everything with which a knife can be put into a real relation, and thus constitutes the **discourses** (groups of interconnected sentences) of which the knife can be a part. The syntactic relations of the sentence **'knife'**, suitable for generating finished and meaningful discourse, depend upon its semantic value, upon what it tells us. In fact, **proper discourses** of the type **'the knife cuts the steel'** do not exist, even if this is a meaningful discourse. Absurd, or rather metaphorical, is instead a **discourse** like **'the knife cuts the water and the air'**. Transcribing: the discourse **'the knife cuts the steel'** is equivalent to 'that which is used for cutting is employed according to its proper use upon a thing which cannot be cut because it is too hard'; and the **discourse 'the knife cuts the water'** is equivalent to 'that which is used for cutting is employed according to its proper use upon a thing which is not a cuttable object because it is liquid'.

The essential point in the preceding discussion is that all the words, syntagms, sentences, and discourses printed in bold face should not be construed as they are presented on this page, that is, as verbal words, syntagms, sentences, and discourses in which we are *talking about* the knife and its relationships; they should instead be interpreted, so to say by making a jump outside of language, at *the level of things*, as homologous indications of relationships regarding the knife insofar as we use it as such (and not as an object of discourse). The description of the discourses in bold face as proper, improper, absurd, metaphorical, and so on, is not, then, a meta-linguistic description, that is, a discourse about a discourse, but it is a meta-sign or meta-communicative description in which we refer to an object belonging to a non-verbal sign system by means of discourses in the proper sense, that is, belonging to the language as a verbal sign system. **'The knife cuts the air'** is a **metaphorical discourse** beyond or beneath any verbal description. That is, the piece of behavior which consists in cutting the air with a knife is itself metaphorical: it is such at the level of things.

One gathers this clearly in terms of possible daily experiences. If we see our table-companion cut his bread with his knife, it seems normal to us. If we see him try to cut steel we understand what he wants to do: it "makes sense" even though we think that it is impossible. If he starts cutting the air or water instead, his behavior seems absurd or metaphorical to us. All this takes place in a way distinct and independent from the verbal sign systems to which we resort when we want to *talk about* these pieces of behavior, report them or make comments about them with words.

We can make analogous considerations as to the semantic relationships to which a knife is subject within the little system to which it belongs together with the spoon, the fork, and the other silverware. This system is a **semantic** or **semiotic field,** or simply a **sign field** (cf. footnote 66), at the level of things. It is, in its turn, only a part of the vaster system of table ware: the little knife-fork-spoon, etc. system is in relation to the system bowl-plate-saucer-glass, etc.; these two little systems are in relation to the system of food and drink; and so on, working in a field which it would be well worthwhile to interpret and describe minutely (as Lévi-Strauss 1964, 1966, 1968 has begun doing; cf. also Barthes 1967 for the terminology of fashion). It is on the basis of all these semantic relations that we must judge the **models of discourses** (**correct, incorrect,** or **absurd** as they may be) **at the level of things,** like **'to cut the meat with the knife', 'to skewer the potato with the knife', 'to cut the meat with the spoon', 'to drink the broth with the fork',** and so on.

The considerations we have just made are in principle applicable, *mutatis mutandis,* to any non-verbal sign system. A fundamental heuristic instrument is the principle that man communicates not only with his verbal behavior but also with all of his non-verbal behavior. Human behavior is included entirely within verbal and non-verbal social sign systems and natural sign systems: whatever we may say or do is programmed by the sign systems of which we make use, or believe we *make* use.

The notion of the language of things opens the path for a consideration of what is probably the most profound sign dimension imaginable as far as man is concerned. Marx in fact talked about a *Sprache des wirklichen Lebens* referring to the *material behavior* of men in a work relationship. It is a question of *objective meanings, anterior to the formation of consciousness,* which men communicate to one another unconsciously during the course of their productive operation (Trân duc Thao 1966: 14). It will be precisely through a consideration of this "language of things" which is present in the exchange of commodities without men's being aware

of it, that in Section Four we will reach the notion of economics as a central
sector of semiotics. First we must fortify ourselves with numerous other considerations.

1.4 *The Programs of Communication*

There is certainly a confirmation of the views of two great American scholars,
Franz Boas and George Herbert Mead, in the modern Soviet conception of culture
as information (Lotman 1967) and of its transmission as conservation of sign systems suitable for controlling the behavior of individuals (*Simpozium* 1962). Boas
in fact had seen very well that communication is the constitutive and central process of every culture (Boas 1911; cf. Emeneau 1966, Jakobson 1966); and Mead
maintained that everything we call *mind* is a system for communication, making it
advisable to explain the mind in terms of signs rather than trying to explain the
signs by means of some sort of ontological notion of the mind (1934; cf. Morris
1932: 322–325; 1970: 33–36, 126–128). As a matter of fact, a history of such doctrines should go back to the structural historicism, or genetic structuralism, inaugurated by classical German thought, beginning with Kant: especially that of
Hegel and the Hegelian left, that is, of the materialistic overturning of the dialectic
culminating in Marx. Indeed, it would not have been possible to "put man into
sign systems" if there hadn't been a previous success in making man depend upon
Reason, then upon the Idea, and finally upon the Modes of Production: that is,
upon supra-personal entities, endowed with a movement and self-preserving structure of their own, which act and express themselves through human individuals. So
that we could begin to see the semiotic position of man correctly, it was necessary
to abandon pre-Kantian ontological dualism and to then proceed in a direction
both social and materialistic. In 1914 Lenin, commenting on Hegel's "syllogism of
action", wrote that «human practice, repeating itself billions of times, fixes itself
in the consciousness of man by means of logical figures. These figures have the
solidity of a prejudice and an axiomatic character just (and only) because of this
repetition that happens billions of times» (*Works*, It. ed.: XXXVIII, 201). In 1927
the essay by Edward Sapir appeared on «The unconscious patterning of behavior
in society».

Considering the human individual as a part of a wider organization also means
recognizing (i) that experience takes place in an environment already shaped by
man, so that *every single individual*, when he is born and develops, in a certain
sense finds *everything ready-made*; and (ii) that the very behavior of the individual
is anchored to something that precedes and guides it, that is, *it is programmed*.
Now, we know that every piece of human behavior *is* communication (Watzlawick, Beavin, and Jackson, 1967), that communication supports every human behavior. But communication exists only insofar as messages are transmitted, and

these in their turn require the use of codes. The notion of communication sends us back to the notion of sign systems. Summing up these elements we come across the thesis, or if you prefer, the working hypothesis, according to which sign systems include programs of behavior, and communication itself is always programmed.

This had been glimpsed by Whorf (1956; as is well known, his writings go back to the thirties), who maintained that our very perception of the physical world is programmed by the language we speak. His was a case of exasperated glottocentrism in which it is not difficult to recognize an idealistic deviation (Rossi-Landi 1968b). Still, it is an important pointer because it can be extended from verbal sign systems, to which Whorf's research was substantially limited, to non-verbal sign systems, that is, to the totality of culture (Hall 1959, 1966), with particular attention to so-called material production.

As a matter of fact, many of the things that used to be said about verbal sign systems alone must now be said about non-verbal sign systems; and the very fact of concentrating our attention upon the latter leads us to say much that is new for both. For example, Boas used to counterpose the unconscious character of linguistic (verbal) activity to the externally conscious activity of cultural institutions. We know today that there are forms of communication still more profound and less noticed than the verbal ones. We continually send and receive non-verbal messages without even suspecting it. In comparison with such messages as these, the very verbal messages which appeared barely conscious to Boas are usually much closer to the threshold of consciousness or are more easily brought to it. Even if we don't know *what happens* when we speak, at least we know *that* we are speaking. As scanty as may be the intentionality we usually put into common speech, as fluid and as natural as the daily use of linguistic instruments and materials may appear to us (see 2.3.3, 5.2, and 6.5), the fact remains that the situation of linguistic exchange is immediately distinguishable from a situation in which such exchange does not take place. We can't even say this, though, for many other types of messages — but not only because we have just started studying them. The fundamental reason is that the use of social sign systems invests different levels of consciousness, from full consciousness to the most profound unconsciousness. It could not be otherwise, since the entire human psyche *is* this use. New semiotic research is in fact revealing vast series of mechanisms supporting the non-verbal strata of communication, that is, non-verbal sign systems, the existence of which formerly no one even suspected. These sign systems can require the use of language, or accompany it, or even precede it (as in the ease of the "language of things": cf. the end of the previous section).

As a general comment on the tardy discovery of non-verbal sign systems, we can say that they remained submerged in confused and unexplored zones of a "nature" and a "society" which were not felt as dialectically related and therefore not prone to be investigated beyond well-determined limits. With a naturalistic or positivistic residue, it was maintained that natural factors were something independent from

socialization; or else, with a spiritualistic residue, it was maintained that socialization was a set of creativistic processes, that is, that there was a gap between
them and nature. Now, since social sign systems by definition are human products,
it certainly wasn't possible to find them in nature as detached from the social; and
on the other hand, since they operate as machines conditioning our behavior, it
wasn't even possible to find them within processes of a creativistic type. The anti-
nomy is overcome and the natural begins to rejoin the social only when we realize
that man is himself a product of his own work, and therefore also that the field
of social conditioning to which the individual is submitted is immensely larger than
we used to think. This is, in my opinion, the main path for introducing the notion
of *communication as the execution of programs* by means of (which also means:
within) social sign systems, whether verbal or non-verbal.

Saying that every piece of behavior is meaningful is, then, the equivalent of
saying that every piece of behavior is a program in realization, the execution of
an already established program (*Simpozium* 1962; Scheflen 1968, with bibliography). In every interaction, that is, in every social process during which two or
more persons or groups influence each other reciprocally by means of various types
of messages (Watzlawick, Beavin, and Jackson, 1967: 50; Gerbner 1967: 43 and
passim) a program supporting the interaction itself can be individuated. The program prescribes both the individual or group roles and the relationships which are
being instituted among its various executors. Diverse types of signals (kinesic, proxemic, and so on) are used during the transaction prescribed by the program; these
serve to regulate and integrate the various pieces of behavior in a totality. One
essential characteristic of such signals is that they are transmitted, received, and
interpreted for the most part unconsciously. The verbal portion of the transaction,
if any, not only transmits verbal meanings, but also, indirectly, meanings which do
not reach the level of verbal expression even if they are presupposed by it. These
are meanings contained in relations between the code and the context, or in non-
verbal sign systems which remain permanently unconscious even when they are
a prerequisite to verbal communication (Rossi-Landi 1961: ch.s vii and viii).

Every piece of behavior exists within a given culture in the form of sequences
or aggregates of fixed and conventional units (Watzlawick, Beavin, and Jackson,
1967 : 118 fll.). It is precisely because of this that it is meaningful. The members
of that culture have learned to act in such a way as to forge their own behavior
in the form of these sequences, thus making them recognizable and predictable.
To the units themselves various names have been given: for example, Pike calls
them behavioremes (1967: ch. V and *passim*), Scheflen, "structural or behavioral
units". These denominations, however, do not take sign systems into proper account. It would be better to call the units "non-verbal sentences". The most interesting points are the following: (i) the execution of behavioral units, or non-
verbal sentences, is what is meant by 'meaningful behavior'; and (ii) the execution
itself must come about *according to a program*. The executor follows instructions

which are implicit in what he is executing for the very good reason that they have been *codified in it.* Which means that the sign system to which the meaningful behavior belongs has been previously produced: it is a result of past human work. When he realizes a program by behaving in a certain way, the executor *transmits messages* interpretable in terms of a *code common* to all the members of the community. The previous human work which put the code into operation was, therefore, a social, communitary work: one *becomes* a member of the community insofar as, even without knowing it, one accepts its products and learns to use them. «Only by becoming part of the network of the sign systems functioning in a given community does man acquire those characteristics which differentiate his behavior from that of the animals» (*Simpozium* 1962, Ital. transl.: 36). *Communication is the execution of programs.* Learning to execute the programs, one learns to communicate and become part of the process of "social reproduction" (2.4). It is from birth that a child produces, exchanges, and consumes signs, non-verbal first and then little by little also verbal ones. As soon as he opens his eyes (according to some, perhaps even earlier), he is ensnared by extremely complex codes. His "spontaneity" certainly does not consist in acting without schemata, but rather in the way in which he reacts to prescribed schemata and in the particular ways in which he learns them and adapts himself to them. The process of homination stands over us and accompanies us in everything we do, much more than we are used to believing. The animalesque regression often found in prisoners of war or famished survivors of shipwrecks, or in various forms of organized sadism, confirms the relative subtlety and precariousness of the social sign systems which allow us to exist as men-animals with the added dimension of sociality.

New research on meaningful non-verbal behavior leads us to trace programs not only in objective and institutional sign systems, where everybody would expect to find them, but also in organic ones. Running through the classification of non-verbal sign systems again we find actions founded on the movements of the body, as Birdwhistell first showed in 1952; or the structure of a simple meal consumed at home (Pike 1967: 122–8); or a psychoanalytic session, any party or reunion, dating, the way in which a mother treats her baby (Scheflen 1964, 1965, 1966); or proxemic behavior (Hall 1959, 1966); or the economic market (Rossi-Landi 1966a, 1968b and c; in this essay, Section Four); and so on. Man becomes part of programs which then determine his behavior in *an automatic, i.e., unconscious way* for the rest of his life (Ivanov 1965, Ital. transl.: 45). Current research is piling up evidence for all this. There is, however, an armchair argument that all the above interactions are programmed, indeed, that they must be so in principle. It is a *reductio ad absurdum* (Ryle 1945) which begins when one asks oneself what would happen if they weren't programmed. If non-programmed interactions did exist, the relative behavior would be incomprehensible and unpredictable and it would be impossible to set up any human relations. But human behavior is, to a large extent, comprehensible and predictable, and human relations do exist. It follows that interactions *are* programmed, that is, that they belong to sign systems into which every individual enters at birth. Both verbal and non-verbal communication depend properly upon a common behavioral morphology induced in us by the fact that we belong in common to the same sign systems. The meaning of such systems is shared by those who transmit and receive messages, whether or not they are conscious of doing so. This is a point which seems to put down, or diminish in importance, the usual opposition between voluntary and involuntary signs, as well as the more complex distinctions between signs which are emitted voluntarily or involuntarily on the one hand, and, on the other, signs received and interpreted — voluntarily or involuntarily — without the transmitter's knowing it.

It is interesting to compare these ideas with what Wittgenstein and then Ryle were saying in the thirties and forties about human behavior. Ryle's insistence on non-verbal behavior capable of exhibiting intelligence because it is (i) learned and (ii) executed according to rules (1949: ch. II and *passim*) bears an especially close resemblance to more rigorous notions which have been reached by considering all meaningful behavior as programmed, that is, by studying its codification and decodification. But, in a word, both Wittgenstein and Ryle were talking about *public* as opposed to private behavior; they certainly weren't talking about *social* behavior.

It is also interesting to notice how we are moving farther and farther away from the pseudo-profound problems of incommunicability, typical of a bourgeois society in decay and without hope. It becomes increasingly difficult to understand how many scholars, although they believe by a sort of act of faith in communicability, continue to think about it as an insoluble general philosophical problem. It is thus for the left-overs of the existentialistic school; but also for many scholars who are not reducible to it, and — alas — even for numerous linguists, probably of idealistic or at any rate over-humanistic descent. We understand each other because, without knowing it, we do everything according to programs; we become members of a community as we become actors in numerous sign systems. Such systems, certainly, would not exist without us, the individuals who act in the communicative processes. But the contrary is also true: we would not exist as individuals without the sign systems of which we are the executors. As individuals we "do the work" (later we will say more precisely: "we expend labor-power of a sign type"); but so that our expenditure of labor-power may *give rise to products, that is, make sense*, there must be materials upon which to exercise it, instruments for applying it, and modalities for its expenditure. All this is furnished, indeed, imposed upon us by the social sign systems.

What we have said does not imply that in executing a program man must necessarily feel that he is a slave of fixed rules. Freedom is a human invention (Di Siena 1969; Rossi-Landi 1969c) and is therefore itself founded upon communication, that is upon programs: if programs did not exist, we would never even find ourselves in one of those conditions which we do call "free". The more so, we could never introduce new freedom into history. Liberation is in fact an enlargement of human planning, and planning is the *conscious* use of programs. Moreover, the programs themselves can prefigure measures of freedom in the form of choices or legitimate variations. The game of chess, on the one hand, and the code of a language, on the other, to mention a comparison which merits its longevity, both offer good examples of programs with a *certain amount* of freedom. We are less conscious of the code of a language than we are of that of chess both because the former is much more complex and because language is necessary while chess is not. Moreover, although it is a human product, language was certainly not invented in the same sense that chess and all other games must have been. Still less conscious because still less conditional are those non-verbal codes which we practice by the antique heredity of an evolution which is not only social but also biological.

One important aspect of the relations between verbal and non-verbal sign systems is the following. A non-verbal communicative program can be executed with or without verbal accompaniment. The fact that in the second case we say that it takes place "in silence" shows how the notion of silence has been traditionally reserved to the absence of verbal signs alone. It seems evident that we should also talk about non-verbal silence, and distinguish between them all the possible silences according to the specific sign system of which each of them denounces the absence.

When verbal accompaniment is present, at least two programs are developing contemporaneously, one non-verbal and one verbal. In some cases the executor of the programs is talking about something completely different. Sometimes it may even seem that the conversation has been introduced by mere habit, without its having anything to do with the non-verbal program it accompanies. In other cases a program can be accompanied by a commentary regarding it: for example one can teach manually the use of a machine and at the same time talk about it, describing the operations which are taking place, or recalling those done previously, or anticipating orally operations which will take place later on. In still other cases, finally, the discourse which accompanies a non-verbal execution distorts, falsifies, rationalizes, hides, mystifies, conceals the other program, or diverts the attention of the participants or spectators. On top of all this, the verbal accompaniment of a non-verbal program may even reach the point of representing the entire program in men's consciousness. The relationship between verbal canals and the totality of the communications which are taking place at various levels remains unknown to them. The verbal comment on the non-verbal programs is then transmitted by tradition «without anyone's knowing how it has been derived from the action as a totality, or what its relation to it may be» (Scheflen 1968: 51). In other words, we act without knowing how and why; and this "how" and this "why" are all the more difficult to discover because the action is accompanied by a verbal comment which traditionally represents it *and thus also hides it*. As Ivanov says:

The models of the world introduced into a man at a fairly early age (by teaching) often act (as a model of the world and as a program of behavior) in an automatic manner independently from their degree of correspondence to the conscious models of the world which the individual constructs in a subsequent phase. Becoming conscious of these semiotic models and programs which act unconsciously is therefore the indispensible condition for the conscious control of the behavior of the individual and of the collectivity [1965, from the Ital. transl.: 53].

An excellent example of all this lies in one of the objects central to our enquiry, economic exchange interpreted semiotically. Economic exchange is sustained by laws which have been put into operation over and over again for thousands of years; nevertheless, it was demystified and made conscious only by the Marxian analysis of commodities (1868). Since an exchange of some sort is the immediate result of the division of labor (cf. 2.4.3), we go back to the primordial stages of homination. We must assume that already at that time non-verbal group behavioral programs were beginning to be unconsciously forged, learned, and handed down. The verbal discourse that usually accompanies these programs has the peculiar character of not regarding them or even of contributing to their concealment. This is the case of the merchant who vaunts the quality of his merchandise only in order to sell it, even when he himself is not convinced of its worth or is perhaps quite conscious of its defects; it is moreover the case of the buyer who disburses money for that merchandise — thus putting into operation the non-verbal behavioral program of the economic exchange — insofar as he executes at the same time a verbal behavioral program induced in him by advertising or by other verbal elaborations of values wide-spread in the community to which he belongs; and it is, finally, also the case of numerous economic theories which, not succeeding in bringing to light the real dialectic of market, enroll themselves objectively in the service of very definite interests.

Bringing the programs of non-verbal communication to consciousness, and recognizing the structures and modalities of the use of non-verbal sign systems, can therefore work a powerful demystification. The dialectic between non-verbal and verbal programs is of exceptional importance for the study of *linguistic alienation*, of which one essential dimension consists precisely in the handing down of discourses which lack a real object or are detached from it, and in this case, indeed, are apt to conceal or estrange it. We can see also how scholars who limit their study to linguistic exchange alone, ignoring all the rest, are forced to substitute that enormous rest with something else. As Lenin says, «expelling the laws of science means, in fact, secretly introducing the laws of religion» (*Works*, It. ed.: XX, 190). And then we find that such scholars resort «to merely subjective approaches and to cultural myths» (Scheflen 1968: 51), from which they extract the data they use as a starting point. The data instead should regard communication as a whole, that is, all the programs in question. For some developments of these ideas see 4.3 and 7.4.

Let's sum up. Whatever he does, every man always executes programs *because* he cannot avoid using verbal and non-verbal sign systems which were established before he came into existence. Or rather, since these systems exist and he is a part of them, man is always in the position of executing programs (which are similar to those of a totally automated machine: cf. 3.2.3). If this is valid even in the field of organic non-verbal sign systems, so much the more so must it hold for objectual and institutional ones. Whether the execution of the programs is conscious or unconscious is something completely irrelevant to the existence of programs. Even if, naturally, an unconscious program is different from a conscious program, the main fact here is that there is always a program. Still, the measure of our consciousness of the entire situation — between the two extreme limits of the full practical and theoretical possession of the operations which are made, on the one hand, and on the other hand, of the totally unconscious, apparently only biological character of the action — has an enormous importance for human life. This is the meeting ground between semiotic enquiry and praxis.

2. WORK AND PRODUCTION

> Die Arbeit is *gehemmte Begierde.*
> G. W. F. HEGEL

2.1   *About Artefacts and Work*

An *artefact* in the most general sense, from *artĕ* and *factum*, is any product of human work, that is, something that did not exist in nature and that has required man's intervention for its existence. Since dictionaries admit of both the spellings *artifact* and *artefact*, let us use the latter, although it is less common, because it brings out the Latin roots. The notion of artefact is connected to the problem of the relation-distinction between *man* and *nature* and shares its profundity. Man and nature are measurelessly polysemous terms which pass from one to the other the difficulties of their own relations. The artefact is part of this relation as a product of work: so much so that we can say that nature is everything that is *not* artefact; and that man as well, insofar as he is not artefact, is nature (*remains* such), while insofar as he is the product of his own work, he is no longer nature, and is, indeed, himself the most important artefact.

The notion of artefact, in its position between the notion of man and that of nature, sends us back, therefore, necessarily, to the mediating notion of *work* (cf. footnote 1). Work is what transforms nature in artefact. In every single working process, the materials from which one starts are assumed as something natural insofar as they are *given* to us; the product, that *for which* we must work, will be non-natural. From the general point of view of work, we could say that everything from which we start is "natural" (and ends up by being felt as "nature"); while everything at which we arrive is artefact.

This is true for man, too. The essential point is the following: if we don't want to admit that something *human* exists for man without the intervention of man himself, we must hold to the principle that every artefact, however understood, is the result of work which man has done and can do again. Generalizing, between any product or human result as absent, and the same product or result as present, there is a difference that can be explained (for which reasons can be given) only in terms of the work carried out by men to obtain it. The most general category of these products is man himself, the historical result of his own work.

An essential methodological aspect of the notion of artefact is to be found in the use which is made of it in palethnology and archeology. Here it is said that an artefact is a prehistoric object produced by man *in so far as it is distinct from* a similar object formed naturally (cf. Gerow 1964: 37; Rouse 1953: 57–76; Bidney 1953; Oakley 1959; and the entry "Artefact" (or "Artifact") in the listed dictionaries). Since palethnologists and archeologists deal with the dawn of humanity and therefore with very simple objects, what counts for them is a mere *difference from* something similar. Thus for example the fact that a pebble bears some human trace, that is, that it has been modified by man for some end, is enough to rank it as an artefact. It does not matter if in nature there are many almost identical or even indistinguishable pebbles; what matters is that *that* pebble has been modified.

2.2   *Material Production and Linguistic Production*

What we have just said also suits another kind of object — the sounds emitted by human organisms. As we know, such sounds are the stuff of the codes of verbal sign systems. For simplicity's sake, in what follows we will call them, directly, linguistic sounds. The fact, then, that any sound bears the imprint of man is enough to make us regard it as produced in some way instead of simply emitted, and we can therefore recognize in it the character of artefact. Naturally we have no trace of the sounds produced before the era of the phonograph, and we cannot even imagine their system abstractly before the era of writing. This circumstance has certainly retarded the consideration of linguistic sounds as artefacts: perhaps, so that this characterization of them could appear in all its clarity, the development of the techniques of the registration and interpretation of unwritten languages was necessary.[5]

---

[5] Reference can be made to Bloomfield 1924, Bloch and Trager 1942, Pike 1947, Nida 1946, Gudschinsky 1967, Samarin 1967 (with extensive bibliography). New technical means of enquiry allow of a more comprehensive approach. Our own behavior doesn't appear to us in its real dialectical texture of "nature" and "history" but rather in a texture of "nature" and "history" which corresponds to the present state of the various techniques by which we approach it. One general consequence of this is that "nature" and "history" themselves – whatever we have come to understand by these immensely complicated notions — present themselves as unrelated, or as scarcely related, since the dialectic linking them together in the very essence of man remains

The fact that ceramic artefacts last through the millennia while ones made of wood disintegrate, certainly does not hinder us from considering the wooden ones artefacts as well: in the same way we do not doubt that prehistoric man possessed a brain although we find only its bone casing. Sound objects exist in nature as, for instance, geological objects do; and both kinds can be worked upon — with increasingly complex procedures into which numerous products of previous elaborations enter as materials — until they reach the heights respectively of a tragedy and of a temple. All sound objects constituting a language are the fruit of human work, that is, artefacts. Words, sentences, and discourses certainly do not exist in nature without the intervention of man; not even the individual variants of a phoneme exist in nature with the characteristics that make them suitable for the scope for which they were made. Often the emission of a single sound is enough to give immediate evidence of the possible presence of man. A very brief spoken chain, even one belonging to a completely unknown language, usually overcomes every obstacle, that is, takes away all doubt: a man is there (if it happens to have been a parrot that emitted just those sounds, a man has taught them to him). This means that the operations with which linguistic objects are produced are so specific and precise that we recognize them immediately in their products. It's even clearer in the case of writing, which, augmenting the corporality of linguistic objects in the direction of permanence, permits us to see a language according to designs which can be arranged, composed, and discomposed spatially, like other physical designs.

For the moment we won't raise the question of the meaning of this or that sound fragment belonging to a language; in the same way, we won't be asking ourselves about the meaning of this or that fragment of, for example, geological material which has gone into various non-verbal sign systems of the objectual type. What interests us is the difference between a natural sound or stone, and a sound or stone to which, *überhaupt*, the title of artefact belongs. The difference lies in the fact that the latter are products of human work. This is their most general value or meaning; it is precisely this that makes them available for the assumption of more and more determinate meanings at successive stages.

We sustain then the Vichian and Marxian thesis that the notion of artefact is in principle applicable to language (besides Vico and Marx, cf. Berlin 1960 and 1965 for an interpretation of Vico). Sign systems, both verbal and non-verbal, are systems of artefacts. Non-verbal production exists; so does verbal production.

In 2.4 we will come back to the material nature of any artefact, but also to the

---

at least partially hidden in the darkness. If this situation is not taken account of, then the fact that the sciences of nature are technically more advanced than the sciences of history would appear to grant the erroneous conclusion that man is more a natural than an historical being. — For further sources and/or comments on the notions of artefact as applied to language — or, more specifically, as obtaining in verbal as well as in non-verbal sign systems —, cf. the "paleontology" of language put forward by André Leroi-Gourhan (especially 1964 : 161-166) and Gordon Childe's analysis of the overall use made by man of *precedent* products (for inst. in 1936, new edition 1961; ch. I).

fact that *no* artefact is *only* material. The description and explanation of any arte-fact can never limit itself to its structure as described in merely physical terms. It is immediately clear that there is a difference between the naked branch of a tree that the wind has broken off, and that lies on the ground without anybody's paying any attention to it, and the same branch used as a walking-cane (only metaphoric-ally, with an anthropomorphic projection, could we say that "the wind has worked on the branch"). It is essential to understand that the difference does not regard the physical body of the branch, and that in spite of this it is not a difference to be located outside of the realm of material things (2.3.1). In order to shed light on just what it is that makes an artefact an artefact, we must explain that it has been produced in order to be used, that it can be employed in a number of ways, and so on: in short, it is a result-of-work and is therefore something not just natural but social as well. We have the two propositions (i) all artefacts are material, and (ii) all artefacts belong to social sign systems: they must be assumed together.

From the semiotic point of view, the principal *systematic* difference between non-verbal and verbal artefacts is to be sought elsewhere, that is, in the aims for which they are produced. While verbal artefacts are produced just and only for use as signs, and any other use of them is occasional or subsidiary, non-verbal artefacts are not used as signs *only*, and indeed, the majority of them are produced for other aims. The use-values are distributed differently. Even in the cases in which non-verbal objects are produced expressly for use as signs, like, for example, signal flags, they conserve beyond their sign use a "residue" which semiotic en-quiry must take into account (2.4.2, 4.1). One can blow one's nose on signal flags; on phonemes, one cannot, and not even generated sentences are big enough.

We now want to examine the principal notions we have introduced somewhat more systematically.

2.3 *Work*

The first notion to be analyzed is also the most important and the most difficult — the notion of work. It is scarcely believable how very little has been written about it. As Tilgher (1928) and later Foucault (1966: 262 fll.) observed, it is a recent notion, connected to a renovation of culture and of society. Believe it or not, the entries "work" and "labor" do not appear in the *Encyclopedia of philos-ophy*; and only the entry "labor" is to be found in the *Encyclopedia of the social sciences*, but only within phrases and exclusively for some of its descriptive socio-logical aspects. Almost nothing seems to have been done of recent for an organic classification of the various types of work man is able to do, of the internal structure of work considered in its operative generality, of the levels reached successively by various cycles of production. The general idea of work was formed by Smith and Ricardo, dealt with forcefully by Hegel especially in his youth, placed at the foundation of his whole theoretical edifice by Marx. Now it is as if this general idea had been deliberately cancelled or broken into small pieces.[6] In this long section, we have to resort almost exclusively to Hegel, to the treatment of alienated

[6] Unsurprisingly, little or no help can be found in the texts of economists posterior to the "classical school", *i.e.* generally, of the marginalists. Let us indicate a few passages where the reader can easily satisfy himself that this is the case: Marshall, II, III, and *passim*; Fraser, XI, 9 and XIII, 1°-4°; Böhm-Bawerk, I, 1°, with the long footnote at the end of the chapter where a welter of problems which would require a much wider discussion is surprisingly compressed; von Mises, I, V and *passim*; Samuelson, 1970 *passim* under *labor* and *work*. — Something better can be extracted from anthropologists and archeologists: see, for example, Gehlen 1962[7], «Introduction»: 5° and 6°, where "operating" (in the sense of *Handlung*) is distinguished from language and from impulses (in the sense of *Antriebe*); the well-known volumes by Gordon Childe; or Mead 1968. — In the field of sociology let us take up as an example Talcott Parsons' "theory of action" as we find it in 1937 (1949[2]), or perhaps more clearly in the essays «Values, motives, and systems of action», written together with Edward A. Shils and appearing in *Toward a general theory of action*, 1951 (1965), and «The dimensions of action-space», written together with Robert F. Bales and appearing in *Working papers in the theory of action*, 1953. Of Parsons, Shils, and Bales' approaches to "action" it can be said that they concern actions which are already seen as social, or actions which assume as their object something which is already social itself. It is only in function of a pre-introduced social dimension that their theory is articulated into operations internal to human action in general, or typical of various kinds of human action. — A much more comprehensive approach was developed in the fifties by Silvio Ceccato (cf. now his 1966 collection of essays), who was operating under a triple influence: that of Marx (undeclared), of Dingler and Bridgman as founders of operational schools, and of Gentile as a theorist of Action idealistically conceived. Ceccato's study of work was basically a splitting of Gentile's Pure Act of the immaterial Spirit into separate procedures — but even so, work *was* studied in some of its many differences. — Max Weber, now 1964 and 1972 (Part First on the fundamental sociological concepts), and Kotarbińsky, 1948, 1971 should also be considered here. Some other books variously dealing with work and its structures are Tilgher (1943[3]), Welty (1946), ad Chenu (1955). For Freud, see footnote 10 below

Let us now take a look into the analytical indexes of the two big American encyclopedias. In the *Encyclopedia of philosophy*, under *Labor* there is just one reference to the "Labor theory of value" which is dealt with in one and a half lines in the second column of page 172 in Volume V, the entry being Marx. There are also three references under *Work*. These concern the history of the concept of energy (II, 511); William Reich's distinction between "compulsive-unpleasurable" work and "natural joyful" work (VII, 109); and John Ruskin's positive point that the separation of the work from man produces only an alienated being (which is right, of course, but utterly useless within Ruskin's own doctrine of labor as the "exertion of perfect life") (VII, 234). Thus there is nothing like labor or work for North-American philosophers, at least insofar as they are faithfully represented by their *Encyclopedia*.

One passes to the other *Encyclopedia* with great hopes. Certainly, one thinks, it must be a question of academic divisions. It must be that in the United States philosophers have decided to hand over the general treatment of work and labor to the social sciences. The entry WORK, however, doesn't exist. The main reference in the general Index is to the *sociology of work*, which is a section of an entry dedicated to INDUSTRIAL RELATIONS, and here we learn «that the activity of man in industrial society no longer has much in common with that of the earlier *homo faber*, since it is no longer bound to be either rural or industrial» (VII, 231). Since this statement is representative of one particular manner of looking at one tenth of mankind at the most, the authoress is very cloistered indeed. But of course, we are also given words of caution against *general* definitions of work (*ib.*) — lest we may find that we have something in common with people from underdeveloped countries, or of different color, or of a lower social class. Another reference is to *work tasks,* this being a paragraph in Section X, "Acquisition of skill", belonging to the entry LEARNING. The word 'labor', as hinted in the text, appears only within

work in the *Manuskripte* of 1844 and in the *Grundrisse*, to *Kapital* (especially the fifth chapter of the First Book, which remains the fundamental text on the topic), and to some pages of Engels.[7]

2.3.1 *Work and activity*

In the first place, we must distinguish between *work* and mere *activity*. According to Aristotle, activity bears its own ends within it, while the ends of work are detached from it (*Et.nic.* I, 1 1094a; VI, 4, 1140a; *Magna Moralia*, II, 12, 1211b). As Hegel, the Adam Smith scholar, noticed, the activity that satisfies need in an immediate way is pre-human. In order for man to develop, it is necessary that the immediacy be broken: that between need and satisfaction work be inserted. It is

---

phrases: *Labor economics*, subdivided into "Labor force", "Labor relations", and "Labor unions". I am not in the least saying that these topics shouldn't be dealt with, or that the gigantic entry which comprehends them is defective within its limits (VIII, 469-546). I just want to point out that the notion of labor or work is never faced on its own ground. This is also true of the only entry where some words are spent about labor in general (with the stress on value, however, and not on labor): "Value, labor theory of" (XVI, 279-283), a section of the entry VALUE, which contains an historical sketch of the theory as maintained by Smith, Ricardo, and Marx. The point of view is professionally economic, which doesn't prevent the short paragraph summarizing Chapter I of *Kapital* (281-282) from being ludicrous. No mention of Hegel or of dialectics is made, and the idea that exchange may be of general importance for the study of man doesn't even begin to dawn. We are here in the darkest night of unimaginative separatistic academic delusion.

In the previous edition of this very *Encyclopedia* (1932), however, an entry LABOR did exist (VIII, 615-620). It was written by Emil Lederer, a distinguished Heidelberg professor, who, having fled from Germany when Hitler rose to power, also taught at Columbia for some years. Although it was not intended to say anything from an anthropological, or philosophical, or psychological, or operational point of view, Lederer's entry did trace a short history of the notion of labor and did insist upon its central importance: «The various attitudes toward labor are of course very closely dependent upon the social and economic status of the laboring masses in any particular society, while at the same time they help to create that status. The conception of the value of labor constitutes a determinate ideology ...» (617). Actually, the entry began with the words «The valuation placed upon labor is a significant element in the ideology dominating any period, for it reflects the social structure as well as the scale of social values»; and it ended with a reference to «the conception of an organization of the entire economy in the interest of society as a whole», which had «greatly enhanced the significance of labor in modern society». All this has been suppressed in the «entirely new, entirely expressive of the times» 1968 edition, «a historical document of its time», as the honorary editor Alvin Johnson so rightly affirms in his Foreword (I, xiii). Or, how to turn into a paper tiger.

[7] Marx's main *loci* are in the *Ökonomisch-philosophische Manuskripte* of 1844, Third Manuscript, cf. pp. 584 fll. of the *Frühe Schriften* 1962 edition, pp. 128 fll. of Milligan's translation; *Kritik der Hegelschen Dialektik und Philosophie überhaupt*, cf. p. 645 of the *Frühe Schriften* and p. 177 of Milligan's transl.; *Grundrisse der Kritik der politischen Ökonomie* of 1857-58, Dietz Verlag, pp. 264-270, 504 fll., and *passim*: see in McLellan's anthology pp. 87-93, 504 fll., and *passim*. In *Kapital*, besides Chapter 5 of Book First, there are in the three Books, as well as in the *Theorien über den Mehrwert*, a high number of passages which can only be found through integral reading or by means of an analytical index (like the 200 page Index appended to the Italian translation). For Engels see especially Chapter 10 of *Dialektik der Natur*, entitled «Anteil der Arbeit an der Menschwerdung des Affen» (rather poorly rendered by «The part played by Labor in the transition from ape to man» in Dutt's translation), and also *Antidühring*, ch. VI. For additional information on Marx's *Grundrisse*, cf. footnote 18; for Hegel, footnote 8.

only with work that something universal arises in man. Work is «appetite [or desire] *held in check*»; in it consciousness «goes out of itself in the element of the lasting»; and, therefore, work *forms* the object.[8] Activity is expenditure without a product; work aims at something. One works, that is, for some end. And still, not even this lasa clause is strictly necessitating. With regard to what interests us most here, a modification brought to an object, one can admit that man also works without being at all conscious that he is doing it for some end. The end can be supra-individual because imposed by a social program which remains unconscious. In this sense work is differentiated from activity because it is the execution of programs which are indifferently conscious or unconscious. Still, in order to distinguish work from activity from the point of view of the object, it must be possible to find in the history of this object at least the dialectic between a "before" and an "after": that is, once two temporal moments have been distinguished, in the second the object presents some characteristics not to be found in the first. Applying this criterion fully we can arrive at the limit-case of two objects which seem identical in all their observable properties, but of which one is a product and the other is only-natural, because we know that only the first has *passed through* at least one modification by the intervention of man; and this even if it is a modification that

---

[8] *Phenomenologie des Geistes*, p. 149 in Hoffmeister's edition; for a different English wording, cf. Baillie's transl., p. 238. It should be noticed that consciousness of labor emerges in the bondsman *within* the dialectic of Lordship and Bondage — here lies the main root of the conception according to which class-struggle, as an explicatory principle, is prior to anything else. That since the beginning of his activity Hegel was fully aware of the central importance of work in homination is clearly shown by his lessons on "Realphilosophie" delivered at Jena in 1803-4 and in 1805-6, now in *Jenenser Realphilosophie*, ed. by J. Hoffmeister, which were in their turn anticipated by the so-called Frankfurt Systematic Fragment of 1800 (now in *Hegels theologische Jugendschriften*, ed. by H. Nohl: 345-351), and by the *System der Sittlichkeit* of 1802 (now in *Sämtliche Werke*, VII: *Schriften zur Politik und Rechtsphilosophie*, ed. by G. Lasson, 1932²: 415-499). Hegel carefully studied Stuart's *Inquiry* (cf. Rosenkranz: 107), but the copy which he annotated on the margins was never found. The relationship of Hegel to Adam Smith was pointed out especially by Lukács in *Der junge Hegel*, 1948: II, iv-v and III, v-vii.

The more matter-of-fact approach used by Marx is also clearly shown if we compare Hegel's often cryptic remarks with such a simply-worded statement as the following: «Primarily, labour is a process going on between man and nature, a process in which man, through his own activity, initiates, regulates, and controls the material reactions between himself and nature. He confronts nature as one of her own forces, setting in motion arms and legs, head and hands, in order to appropriate nature's productions in a form suitable to his own wants. By thus acting on the external world and changing it, he at the same time changes his own nature. He develops the potentialities that slumber within him, and subjects these inner forces to his own control» (Paul's translation, I, p. 169). [«Die Arbeit ist zunächst ein Prozess zwischen Mensch und Natur, ein Prozess, worin der Mensch seinen Stoffwechsel mit der Natur durch seine eigne Tat vermittelt, regelt und kontrolliert. Er tritt dem Naturstoff selbst als eine Naturmacht gegenüber. Die seiner Leiblichkeit angehörigen Naturkräfte, Arme und Beine, Kopf und Hand, setzt er in Bewegung, um sich den Naturstoff in einer für sein eignes Leben brauchbaren Form anzueignen. Indem er durch diese Bewegung auf die Natur ausser ihm wirkt und sie verändert, verändert er zugleich seine eigne Natur. Er entwickelt die in ihr schlummernden Potenzen und unterwirft das Spiel ihrer Kräfte seiner eignen Botmässigkeit» (*Kapital*, Dietz Verlag XXIII: 192)].

does not regard the structure of its body but only its position relative to other objects. These are cases difficult to imagine as soon as one has left the most rudimentary level; but talking about them is of help in concentrating attention on man's work already at that level. Let us take the case of two identical pebbles, one of which has been found far away from its proper geological site, in a place and in a position announcing the intervention of man. The artefact is germinated. The extreme simplicity of the situation permits us to grasp the intervention of man in the nascent state. One will kindly note that the case of two or more identical tokens of the same model remains outside the discourse. Here we are dealing, at a more basic level, with two objects whatsoever, in order to decide if one has had a model of some sort and the other none. In the more rudimentary cases, like that of the pebble which was simply transported far from its proper site, having a model may have amounted to a vaguely planning intention. Obviously, if five pebbles bear the same imprint of work, as primitive as it may be, and ten others don't, the first five are tokens of some model, the other ten are not.

But how can we distinguish, then, between artefacts and the merely natural "products" of a human presence, like the footprints left by a man on the sand, or his feces? Aren't these perhaps also "signs" of man because they result from modifications made by him on materials which precede his intervention, in the first case by walking, and in the second by defecating (I mean, unintentionally)?[9] Certainly they are signs for an interpreter who arrives afterwards; but they are not themselves products. For the footprints to be also the products of human work, for example, they must be left there *on purpose*. This very specification indicates that usually they are not. We may respond to this last difficulty beginning from the recognition that the use of 'products' for things like the footprints and the feces *is not a proper use*. It is here that a distinction must be drawn between the work which gives us products in the proper sense, and mere activity, which at the most leaves traces *capable* of becoming products if work is superimposed upon it. The modification brought by work is usually willed, planned, intentional. But one can will, plan, and have intentions also in an unconscious way, by passive application of models received. This only moves the question backwards; it certainly does not take it outside the realm of the social. The *human* unconscious is certainly not something anterior to homination; it is by definition subsequent to it, and is therefore itself a product. Freud with deep insight called the production of dreams by the unconscious, *work*.[10] Even the worker who unconsciously applies models he

[9] This is not a joke, if we consider that even detecation and urination (i) may be directed to leave signs, as the male wolf does to mark off the family boundaries (Mowat 1963), and (ii) must be, to some extent, performed according to programs, as both parents and pet-lovers know only too well.

[10] *Dream-work* [*Traumarbeit*] is the title of Chapter VI of *The interpretation of dreams* ("Standard Edition": IV, 277-338 and V, 339-508; *Gesammelte Werke*, II-III: 283-515), as well as of Lecture XI of the *Introductory lectures on psycho-analysis* (*Gesammelte Werke*, XI: 173-186, "Standard Edition", XV: 170-183). The manifest dream-content is the product of dream-work upon latent dream-thoughts, or unconscious thinking. The latent dream-

has received, who executes programs of which he ignores the very existence, must *have learned how* to make every given modification that he does in fact make. In front of this basic point, it becomes a secondary question whether the worker makes those modifications heedingly or unheedingly, and whether or not he is aware of having been subjected to a process of learning.

That work is distinguished from mere activity because it leads to products, means then that work is situated necessarily in a social dimension. *Work is human social activity.* Physiological activity and any other activity not based on learning of some sort, is not. But even this formulation could also be understood the other way around, with the result of making us put the cart before the horse. We must not start off from a notion, however rudimentary, of the social, and *then* add the notion of work to it. We must *start off from work*: it is work that creates the social dimension from the beginning. Some anthropoids began to differentiate themselves from the others *because*, and *following upon the fact that*, they began to carry out a new type of activity by "holding their appetite in check" — they started to work.

2.3.2 *Elements of the working process*

Once work has been distinguished from mere activity, one can proceed to describe its internal articulations. They have been analyzed once and for all by Marx in chapter V of the First Book of *Kapital*, to which we refer the reader again. A normal complete working situation is formed insofar as the following "moments" (elements, factors) come together:

 (i)   the materials on which one works;
 (ii) the instruments (or utensils) with which one works;
 (iii) the worker;
 (iv) the working operations;
 (v)   the end for which one works;
 (vi) the product of the work.

Thus, for example, a carpenter uses a plane on rough wood with the aim of obtaining as a product a smooth plank.

---

thoughts are the material which the dream-work transforms into the manifest dream. Why should you want to confuse the material with the activity which forms it? (*G.W.*: XI, 229; Standard Edition: XV, 223; cf. also, in the S.E.: 113-125, 128-9, and *passim;* and the exceedingly important essay, «The antithetical meaning of primal words», XI, 155-161; «Über den Gegensinn der Urwerte», *G.W.*: VIII, 214-221). As is well-known, however, Freud was always suspicious of political doctrines founded on work, and dedicated very little attention to the real processes of work as they take place out there in the world. It is as if this eminent representative of *Mittel*-European bourgeoisie and of the decaying Hapsburgic Empire had put all the work worthy of examination within the individual, and most of it so deep there that the individual himself could not quite grasp it — one of the most grandiose and elaborate ways one can imagine of avoiding the problems of work. The only labor which Hegel knows and recognizes is *abstractly mental* labor — says Marx in his *Critique of Hegelian philosophy*: cf. p. 646 in the *Frühe Schriften* edition and p. 177 in Milligan's translation. The idealistic side to a nevertheless basically materialistic approach like Freud's was in this way clearly grasped by Marx in advance.

The scheme of the six listed moments constitutes a simple model for the study of the internal relations among the moments themselves. Moreover, the various working situations can be measured on this model. This is not the place for a systematic study of the scheme; a few remarks can, however, indicate the direction such a study would take. The materials can be mere objects gathered in nature; or they can themselves be the results of previous work ("raw material", "semi-manufactured items", and the like). The instruments can also be parts of the body of the worker (we work also "with our own hands"); that is, the worker can use himself as an instrument. Then there are *instruments* which are simply used to prolong the body of the worker, and instruments which are in turn the products of a precise work cycle, that is, *utensils* (we take up this distinction again in 3.2.1 and 3.2.2). The end is a conscious or unconscious, desired or endured, "mental" anticipation of the product, and hence determines the finalistic character of work, its taking place according to a program. From this point of view, as Marx says, work is a *zweckmässige Tätigkeit*, an activity conforming to a scope. The operations of work can flow without apparent interruptions (6.5), or they can arrange themselves in successive cycles, that is, stratify in the discrete form of products taken up again successively. The work expended is the factor that keeps all the factors together, mediating between them.

Every working situation constitutes a totality outside of which the elements which make it up lose their character of parts, that is, "degrade" dialectically. This does not deny that each of them can be put back into the same or other working situations, that is, reassume the character of part of a totality. Basically, this means three things. First, the function of being material, worker, end, instrument (or utensil), and product, depends on the position assumed within the working situation. Second, changing the position changes the function as well. The rough wood on which the carpenter works is, in its turn, the product of different and previous work; and so on. Third, the worker himself can function as material, or as instrument, or as end, or as the product of various pieces of work. This constitutes a necessary enlargement of the vision of work beyond the restricted limits of usual "material" work. A sick man can be transformed into a healthy man; a recruit into a veteran; a Daddy's boy into a red guard. A teacher is used by the system as an instrument to inculcate an ideology in the students; a policeman, to keep a dominating class in power; an advertising agent, to make us buy certain products. An entire army is at once material, instrument, worker, end, and product, within the realm of a vast political operation, in which, in their turn, finalistically determined intranational and international class interests are expressed. Already in this rapid fanning of cases we may glimpse the various "positions" that men can assume in diverse situations which are, if only in a wide sense, working situations (one doesn't see why on earth they shouldn't be viewed as pieces of work, since all the "moments" present in the simpler model can be clearly traced in them).

The basic situation remains that of the use of the worker's labor-power on the part of capital. Capital's complex *program* makes the workers act as its own instruments, and the workers themselves must therefore also be products and materials (cf. 1.4 on the historical genesis of the notion of supra-personal programming). It was in fact the study of this situation, that allowed Marx to enucleate the general characteristics of work. His treatment of the working process begins with the words *Der Gebrauch der Arbeitskraft ist die Arbeit selbst*, «the use of labor-power is work itself». The mature and complex situation of industrial capitalism permitted Marx, following the indications of Hegel, to identify the working situation in general and to re-affirm the anthropogenic character of work. This is one of the senses in which in the anatomy of man there is a key for the anatomy of the ape.

As a result of work, every artefact is the attained end of a working process in which — in a more or less explicit and articulable way — materials, instruments, worker, and working operations, have come together. Every artefact is a product. It therefore constitutes a *new totality*, which, once it is put into operation, functions necessarily in a new way with regard to the various ways in which its isolated parts used to function. If (going in the opposite direction) we have a compound artefact, and break it down into the parts which went together to constitute it, we find that each of them, in its isolation preceding the synthesis of work, functions in a different way from the way in which the artefact functions as a totality. The handle of a bucket or of a pot doesn't function as the bucket or the pot does; nor does a phoneme function as a word functions. We find again this renovation and complication of the functioning at successive levels, in such a way that sequences can be constructed. For example, a piece of crude iron does not function as a bucket or pot handle, and these handles do not function as a bucket or as a pot, nor do these utensils, in turn, function as a *sāqiya* (pot wheel of the Nile), or as the chain of buckets described by Vitruvius. In a not dissimilar way, [ī] does not function as [luv], nor [luv] as [love], nor [love] as [love you], nor [love you] as [I love you], nor [I love you] as [I love you and want to marry you as soon as I come back from my trip, provided grandmother doesn't opposite it]. Moreover, no grouping of the separated parts which does not give that very artefact as a result, can function as the artefact does. A series of pots arranged in an orderly way on the sand next to a well does not pull the water up however hard one may turn the wheel; and the words in our example must have just that order, so that, using them, I can transmit the appropriate message to my sweetheart. If I dispose them in another order, however accurately, for instance by a CVC criterion, there is no crying them aloud or singing them to the *Greensleeves* tune which can make them mean what I want them to. We must remember, however, that neither the pots and their pieces, nor the sentences and their pieces, lose *all* value through misarrangements. We still partially recognize them for what they are. But if, at a certain level of complication, we want a determinate working synthesis, it must be just that; no other disposition of its pieces will do. This shows both the specific importance of work and the "dignity" of products as coagulated human work. The artefact as a new totality can be used for a certain number of ends which are interconnected because of the artefact's specific structure, and it has that structure because it is the product of a well determined working cycle and not of others.

The use of artefacts is further work that we do with them, using them as materials or as instruments. The most common case is that in which the use — that is, the new work — begins with a totality, already starts off from it. The totality is used as it is. Only for very particular aims is the totality broken down into the parts which make it up, and such parts examined independently from each other. We will see later the importance of these facts for the study of language as work.

The most common articles in the field of material production are the *utensils* of daily life; in the field of linguistic production, *sentences*. We are dealing, in fact, with products belonging to more or less the same level of complexity.

In what precedes, many readers have perhaps glimpsed further dimensions of work. We must take a look at them now.

2.3.3 *Work at different levels*

Prima facie, to produce an object is not to use it (except when we try it out to see whether it works). To use an object is not to produce it; it is, at most, to consider how it is made and try to repair it when it functions badly (cf. 6.5). Given any artefact whatsoever, we can distinguish between the work that is anterior and the work that is subsequent to it. The former is usually called productive work, the latter, use. We will insist in this section, and then again in 2.4.1, on the unity of these moments. Meanwhile, let us begin to single out some of their differential aspects.

The difficulty of productive work usually becomes greater in relation to its complexity. Producing a chair is more difficult than producing a smooth plank; producing a television set is more difficult than producing a chair; producing a car with an automatic shift is more difficult than producing a small sailboat with a simple sloop rigging. Instead, using a television set is almost as easy as using a chair; using a car, more so with an automatic shift, is much easier than using mainsail and jib in the various points of sailing; using a relatively simple instrument like a violin is immensely more difficult than using a rather complicated apparatus like the radiotelephone.

By these little examples, I certainly do not intend to start a classification which ranks from easy to difficult; ease and difficulty are always relative to numerous factors. But I wanted to give a quick idea of the asymmetries to be found between work and use. The basic factor for explaining these asymmetries, their secret, so to say, lies in the past work accumulated within every artifact. In a certain sense, using a car means not only utilizing the work which went immediately into forming it, but also all the planning that preceded its production, and moreover, also everything that preceded the car in the field of means of transportation. In principle, this "everything" extends indefinitely both backwards and on every side. You and

I can use our cars today because before there were cars there were carriages, because the processing of iron has reached a very high level, because electric power has been discovered, because a network of roads exists, because service stations function, and so on. Every time we use something, we are not dabbling our toes in a mud puddle, but taking a few armstrokes on the surface of a deep sea. The statement that "a man abandoned nude in the desert can't use a car, nor can he play the organ — but wouldn't be able to do so even if he wore his dinner-jacket with cane, top-hat, and monocle", grotesquely reminds us of how we each depend completely upon everything produced by our contemporaries and by our ancestors right back to the primordial tribes.

We may be able to clarify the relations between productive work and use by means of the distinction between models/programs and tokens/executions. Production regards both the models and the programs, both the tokens and the executions. When we produce a token we do it according to a model; when we behave in a certain way, we do it according to a program; the model and, respectively, the program, are thus confirmed, reproduced in the token and the execution. Reproduction does not regard, instead, the tokens and executions — except in the case of the reproduction of a unique prototype representing its own model, or in the case of a unique execution having its own program within it (it is the case of a one-member class). One can, instead, produce a model that precedes its own token, or a program that precedes the execution. Finally, in the case of a model that remains without tokens and of a never-executed program, we have the case of a no-member class.

If, from the level of productive work, anterior to the artefact, we move to the level of use, subsequent to the artefact, we find that the use also takes place according to models or programs. Actually, even production according to a model must take place according to a program. In this case, one would say, the model is a part of the program of production. Anyway, whether all models — both of production and of use — come under the general notion of program, or not, is a question we do not need to decide here. Let us content ourselves with calling those belonging to production, *models*, and those belonging to use, *programs*. There are obvious differences between the model according to which an artefact is constructed, for example, an electric drill, or a movie camera, and the instructions, that is, the program for their use, which accompany every token electric drill or movie camera. The program of use is connected to the model of production; but at the same time it is generally not reducible to it, on the contrary, it differs from it radically. This appears also in the types of performance required anteriorly and subsequently to the artefact: a good driver can be ignorant about motors; and nobody expects a surgeon to be an expert in the art of tempering steel and manufacturing scalpels from it. Let us say then, that we cannot use an artefact without at the same time following a program of use, with the aim of realizing it. In this sense, the work done with an artefact is "only" an execution. But the execution sends us back necessarily to the production of that very artefact; moreover, since to use means to destroy or to consume, the request arises for the production of other tokens (cf. 2.4.1 below). The execution of the program for use contains a multiple appeal to the model of the production.

When we use a token of an artefact in a new piece of work, the use shows clearly that it is part of productive work at a level higher than that of the production of the artefact itself. But productive work and use are always interwoven to the point of seeming inextricable. Let us consider a very simple, indeed, an artificially simplified, example: that of the production and of the use of a common hammer, assuming that the parts of the hammer have already been produced, and limiting the discussion to one of these parts, the handle. Even in such an elementary and limited case we already have to distinguish between:

(i) the use of a handle to make a hammer, that is, the work on the handle, *vs.* the use of a handle as a part of a hammer which has already been made, *vs.* the use of the handle by itself (that is for some aim that doesn't have anything to do with the hammer, though it remains a handle which is actually or potentially part of a hammer);

(ii) the work with which the handle is produced *vs.* the work with which the hammer is produced;

(iii) the work with which a hammer is produced *vs.* the use of the hammer as a finished artefact constituting an autonomous totality.

Reflecting on this situation, we must conclude that we are dealing with a typical dialectical situation of unity-distinction. Use *is* work; at the same time, use is distinguished from work. Use is work, because in all the listed cases of use programmed operations take place. Suppose we wanted to distinguish between a use of the hammer which is not directly productive, for example its domestic use for driving nails into the wall, and a use for further productive aims which require the hammer, for example its use in a carpenter's workshop. We should specify that the one who is driving the nails is not an electrician hanging a light fixture, nor a decorator arranging pictures, nor any worker or artisan. After having said this, we should add that the nail driver does not practice any of these arts himself. At this rate, we would end up by having to specify that he does not set himself any aim at all, and that he is driving nails for pleasure alone. But this won't do either, and for two reasons. First of all, if the nail driver did not set himself any aim, he would not even set himself that of driving nails. In the second place, even if he drove nails at random and for mere pleasure, he has to follow rules all the same — he still must have learned to drive nails. For example, it is the nail that has to be placed against the wall, and point-first; the hammer must be held by the handle; and so on. In conclusion, even our occasional nail driver is still doing work: if he does it badly, he bends the nails, damages the wall, and bangs his fingers.

The only method for distinguishing use from work in which the present writer succeeds in having any faith consists in saying that, given a certain artefact, use is subsequent to it while work is anterior to it. The artefact is here only a milestone for making the distinction. *Use is work subsequent to the artefact* — it is such every time the discussion is expressly limited to the state of things immediately before and immediately after the artefact.

From this we can obtain the following. In the course of the millennia (and, where basic artefacts are concerned, in the course of hundreds of thousands of years), humanity has produced (i) models for production, (ii) tokens of these models, (iii) programs for the use of the tokens, (iv) executions of these programs. Work is irradiated, distributed, and deposited on all this in unequal ways; at the same time it is what holds everything together. We have work in the most commonly accepted sense in the production of tokens. It is usually admitted that the production of their relative models is also work. That also the production of programs for use, and especially their execution, is also work, may sound irksome to some ears — especially in fields traditionally reserved for the "free activity of the spirit" or even only for "the individual". The fact is that the program, coming after the artefact, is reconnected to the model of production only across the artefact itself, so to say by piercing it through. The artefact opposes to this the thick skin of its own totality which does not want to let itself disintegrate. It is there, ready for use, *as if* it had not been produced by work. It *may seem* that the use of an artefact, the execution of a program, are not work, because the artefact bears in itself the work that has produced it, is itself work in a crystallized form. Work has made of it something remote from mere naturality, thus conferring upon it what can be called a *new* naturality. Using an artefact means taking this new naturality as a starting point and then heedlessly drawing upon the past work crystallized in it. About this work we may know nothing at all, but it helps and sustains us. Using an artefact means enjoying the interest on a patrimony, an interest granted to us through enculturation. Looking again synthetically at the situation in the direction of the flow of work, which is the direction of the process of homination: The flux of work is coagulated in the artefact and then goes ahead mediated by its own product, with a leap or after a pause, like the flux of a river when it encounters a lock-gate, or perhaps like a nervous impulse when it crosses a synapse.

The individual learns to use many programs, or to obey them. The programs are arranged in various types of sign systems, whose complete description would be equal to the complete description of culture. Only in a few cases does the individual learn the programs for use in a direct and explicit way, in the form of instructions given and received. In the great majority of cases he learns them only implicitly, while he is learning to execute them. Every individual learns just a very small part of the models of production (we used to say, just those "of his trade"). We must therefore keep the *social work* of the production of models, of tokens according to models, and of the programs for the use of the tokens, quite distinct from the *individual work* of the use of tokens as occurs in the execution of programs. This distinction does not at all touch the fact that the individual use of tokens is itself work, and social work.

Let us run through our little example of the hammer again, but backwards this time, and inserting the dialectic between models and tokens and between programs and execution. What happens with regard to work at different levels when I use a hammer? Which are the levels of work referred to directly or indirectly? First of all, I am working, since use is work. I am working subsequent to the artefact, because there it is, already produced. I am executing a program for its use, otherwise I wouldn't even know which end was up on the token of a hammer that I have in my hand. And as for the program, then, I must have learned it somehow or other. It depends upon the properties of the artefact, which have been united and organized in the artefact by the productive work that has realized in it a token of a very precise model. The program for the use is therefore connected to the model of production. But it is an indirect connection because it is mediated by the artefact as a totality complete in itself, as a stable result of previous work. It is only, so to say, by penetrating into the totality of the artefact, and then coming out again on the other side, that one makes the connection between the program for use and the model of production: here we find the river lock-gate or synapse quality which is typical of the artefact. Meanwhile, in using the hammer I am in a certain sense using its parts; but I am not using them separately. The handle and the head of the hammer remain what they are; and the same is true for any parts at a lower level to which we might eventually reduce these two pieces constitutive of the hammer. However, when I expend the work that consists in using these pieces together, I am presupposing, though I am ignoring, or simply don't deal with, the fact that these pieces have been first produced, and then put together, to form the object I am using.

This description of the way work is articulated in the use of a simple artefact, is certainly not exhaustive. The complexity to be found in this articulation even in the case of such a very elementary use, however, should suffice to give a glimpse of the way in which work, product, and use are stratified dialectically.

To learn to get along in a world that work has completely transformed and stratified into countless layers of products, amounts to becoming a *homo sapiens*. We don't certainly mean to deny the ecological and biological complexities of the other animals' behavior when we say that man is distant from them to the exact extent in which the other animals have not learned to get along in a world *of their own* that *their* work has completely transformed and stratified into countless layers of products. What is then the ideology that may lie in the assimilation of man to the other animals from the viewpoint of semiotics? It may well be the ideology of an advanced industrial society which represents its products as natural, taking the attention away from the work which has made them into products. The restitution of man to himself, instead, can come about only by bringing all the dimensions of work to full and operative consciousness.

As we know (cf. 1.4) all learning takes place in so far as behavioral programs which are always meaningful are proposed to us or imposed upon us. Every piece of meaningful behavior is work, though often unconscious work, since it produces something that did not exist in nature before, and could never come into existence if not as a result of that behavior. If we consider now a list of successive pieces of work like the one indicated in 2.3.2, we find a very interesting fact. As work gets more complicated and we pass from one level to the next one, the possibility of choice diminishes for the interpreter. This means that information increases. The phenomenon is to be found in both fields of material production and linguistic production. When all we encounter is the bare moneme [luv], we are left free to interpret it in the most generic way; we have an enormous possibility of choice and therefore receive very limited information. Much more precise is the information we receive from the complex sentence 'I love you and want to marry you as soon as I get back from my trip, provided grandmother doesn't oppose it'. In a similar way, if we find a handle, any handle, we have little information and vast interpretative possibilities. If, instead, we find the chain of buckets described by Vitruvius, our possibilities of interpretation are limited to the chain of buckets described by Vitruvius; if we have a transistor, or a wizzen topgallant, our possibilities are limited to the uses of those highly specified products. This point concerns the information which can be drawn from material objects as messages belonging to various non-verbal sign systems, and not directly their uses; it is, however, obvious that such information is mainly information *about* their uses.

The layers of work, product, and use constitute an immensely complex vertical mass from which increasingly precise messages can be drawn. The more our position is subsequent to successive series of artefacts, the fewer are our interpretative possibilities with regard to each of them. Primordial man still had before him all the choices possible for an animal with his biological set-up; but he didn't have the objects to choose, nor was he aware of his position, so he certainly was not freer than we are. Freedom is a late and complex human product, founded on the liberation from need and on the intensification of consciousness. As Davydov puts it (1962, It. transl. 1966: 42), «the most general features of "freedom" as such (in its difference from "non-freedom") coincide with the most general features of work, of human production». This is the meaning of the great difficulty and profundity of every revolutionary reconstruction of history. Such a reconstruction finds itself in front of a barrier composed of all the established sign systems, beginning with those that protect and transmit exploitation; to overcome them, the most basic human relations must be put into question again. It is necessary, so to say, to run through homination again, but knowing that we are doing so. The most profound sense of the "Great proletarian cultural revolution" (but the deep-seated meanings of *wuchan jieji wenhua da geming* should be carefully discussed) promoted by Mao Tse-tung is perhaps just this: that it has faced sign systems squarely with the intention of changing them instead of limiting itself to the political seizure of power and the redistribution of wealth. This is equivalent to saying that in China a serious attempt is being made at socially producing a radically new kind of man.

The articulation of work regards not only and most obviously all non-verbal as well as verbal sign systems and hence everything we mean by 'language'; it constitutes, indeed, in my opinion, the unique basis for an explanation of the way in which language functions as a constitutive sector of the social, that is of language not just reduced to a little formal system, but met with in all its reality. Here it is not a question of choosing between different interpretations of language but between different conceptions of man. Basic ideas are under discussion; in no case can we shirk the responsibility of declaring our own, or take refuge in the illusion that they may not shine through the texture of our specialistic technicalities as well. *If* man is the product of his own work, *then* work is the unique dimension for the explanation of that essential part of man — language. The only equally fundamental alternative consists in saying that man is *not* the product of his own work; one has then to find another explanation.

All the rest of this essay is dedicated to showing *some aspects* of the articulation of work in the field of language. This is perhaps the place for an anticipatory sketch. The speaker is a linguistic worker: in him is to be found the spring of linguistic operations, of the expenditure of linguistic labor-power. Such expenditure invests already existing products, united in the system of the language. As an extremely complex, human, social product, language offers to every linguistic worker an immediately accessible patrimony (as we shall say, a "constant capital") of linguistic materials, instruments, and "money" (5.2.1.1 and 5.2.1.2). Using the artefacts of language, the linguistic worker is in a position subsequent, not anterior, to them. He carries out programs for the use of linguistic artefacts which are shown to him ready-made by those who teach him to speak (and thus back through the generations). The sense in which each speaker himself "reproduces" tokens according to models of production is a very attenuated sense; rather, he is perhaps similar to one who picks up a hammer in his hand instead of leaving it in the closet. He does not so much reproduce them as he *repeats* them, *takes them up again*. This is the job of a machine, indeed, a computer, of still unequalled complexity, his organism (Rossi-Landi 1968c: 188–190). It was in this sense, perhaps, that Wittgenstein said that «everyday language is a part of the human organism and is no less complicated than it» (*Tractatus:* 4.002). This is also the site of possible confusion between the biological nature and the social nature of language. As a product of work, human language is *entirely social*; no contradiction arises when we add that, naturally, we are talking about hominoidea, that is, about extremely complex organisms. Not only does the second evolution not exclude the first; it presupposes it. The dialectic of work, product, and use as it applies in the field of language, and indeed of all social sign systems, accounts for current exaggerations of every linguistic worker's individual contribution, which according to some would be downright creativistic. It also helps to explain the opposition, which we may encounter, to the operation of placing work at the foundation of language.

Not only is the production model unconscious, but so is the repetition of tokens. Tokens are used (usually in the very act in which they are repeated) according to programs which are unconscious in their turn. To become aware of the programs for the use of linguistic artefacts we have to study the operation of things which are already produced. The single linguistic worker rarely goes back from the programs for use to the production models, crossing backwards over the artefacts, though this is not impossible. It usually happens only in research, in the invention of new words which do satisfy a new social need, and in the case of so-called poetic "creation" (modifications brought to programs, or even to a few production models).

The speaker repeats or takes up again tokens of linguistic artefacts, and uses them in new work which consists in the execution of social programs. No objection is made to the idea that in such execution we may also find small individual variations of the type found in the handling of the various utensils. In so doing, the speaker produces sentences and messages. Messages are sentences, or fragments or combinations of them, effectively transmitted. Every message has its own end within it, the end of being received and interpreted, and possibly acted upon. In front of the multitude of messages, however, it is reasonable to extrapolate some common end, and distinguish it from the messages as products. This is how we come to the generalization that the primary ends of the speaker are to express himself and to communicate.

The essential aspect of all this is that, exactly as it happens in the field of material production, the speaker uses the products of previous work even without being conscious of it, and usually considers these products natural (spontaneously *physiocratic conception* of language). At the most he arrives at considering the language as capital and speech as a sort of commerce (*mercantilistic conception* of language: cf. Ryle 1961: 223–229). When we apply the more mature theory of labor-value to language, we see in the articulations of work the appropriate design for beginning to explain some tangles of difficulties which up to now have remained mysterious, like the facility of language learning, reciprocal understanding among speakers, the "generation" of sentences, the relations between *langue* and *parole*, the spontaneous flow of speech, and many others. We will say what we can about them later on. First we must examine a further aspect of work, and try to situate linguistic (or more generally, sign) work within the realm of a global conception of social reproduction.

2.3.4 *Differentiated work and undifferentiated work*

Everything we have said so far about work regards the specific work with which we produce different objects or execute different programs. Let us take the case, new and original for us, of the production of a hammer and of its use. The work with which a hammer is produced is different from the work with which a pair of socks is produced. The hammer and the socks belong to two different zones of the enormous objectual sign system which comprehends all "objects of common use" (as they are significantly called). The difference between the two pieces of work is to be found in the first place in the two different series of operations into which they can be divided. But this doesn't suffice. If we take the two entire working situations into consideration, we see that all the moments or elements that make them up are different. Not even the worker is an exception, because even if it is always Titius who produces a hammer today and a pair of socks tomorrow, the operations he carries out are different and therefore, in a strict sense, we are dealing with two different moments of Titius or even with two different Titiuses.

It is always possible to reduce two different kinds of work, either wholly or in part, to the same elementary operations. The worker, both when he produces socks and when he produces hammers, must carry out certain simple movements like pulling, pushing, pressing, applying, turning, cutting, and so on — apart from whether or not all such movements may be in turn reducible to *bringing together* and *separating*, as Pietro Verri (1771; 1964: 135) says with great ingenuity. The point is valid for the other elements of the working process as well; the wood and the iron destined to become a hammer, and the wool destined to become a pair of socks, both consist of molecules; the same for the hammer and the finished pair of socks. But the fact remains that each of the elements of the two working processes is different from the corresponding element in the other; so much the more so are the two working processes different when each is seen as a whole. Producing a hammer means doing work which is different from the work which is done to produce a pair of socks.

Work is, then, *differentiated*. It is *concrete, specific* work with which we modify something by impressing in matter qualities suitable for satisfying «human wants of some sort or another», as Marx says (*Kapital* I,1.: 49; Engl trans.: 35). And he adds: «The nature of such wants, whether, for instance, they spring from the stomach or from fancy, makes no difference. Neither are we here concerned to know how the object satisfies these wants, whether directly as means of subsistence [untranslated clause: *d.h. als Gegenstand des Genusses*, that is, as an object of enjoyment], or indirectly as means of production» (*ibidem*). The capacity of any object whatsoever to satisfy a human want or need, «being limited [bedingt] by the physical properties of the commodity, it has no existence apart from them» (*ib.* 50, Engl. 36). An object with such qualities is called a *useful object*, or a *good*, or a *value*. Since such value is realized in *use*, or rather, in *consumption*, we had better specify that it is a *use-value*. There are numberless different artefacts, numberless different use-values, suitable for satisfying numberless different needs. At this point it should be clear that each of them is the result of a different set of working operations. There are as many different working processes for obtaining artefacts as there are different kinds of artefacts. Work is differentiated into as many cases.

Each type of work is defined by its scope and therefore possesses an inherent qualitative differentiation. This is the social division of labor into working processes, the one independent from the other (the case of the parcellization of work for a single scope, for example in assembly lines, doesn't concern us here). The work called specific or concrete or differentiated is work that produces use-values.

We have encountered up to this point three different dimensions of work. The first is that of the working process generalized and broken down into its minimal constitutive elements (2.3.2). The second is that of the different levels of work, anterior and subsequent to the artefact, as productive work that realizes models, and as use (directly productive or not) that executes programs (2.3.3). The third is that of the differences existing among all the possible working processes productive of different use-values, as indicated briefly just above. There is another way to look at work, a fourth dimension of work, which is directly opposed to the third and indirectly also to the first two. Work can be seen also as an *undifferentiated totality* — leaving aside its productive differentiations, its constitutive moments, and its levels. The undifferentiated totality of work can then be subdivided in another way which is radically different from all previous subdivisions. This is one of the most difficult conceptual knots of all of political economy and of every general theory of work. For an exhaustive study of it I cannot but refer to those who have dealt with it more thoroughly.[11] I will try to explain very briefly in what follows, and limited to the applicative ends of the present research, (i) what the "undifferentiated totality" of work consists in; (ii) what the new subdivision of such undifferentiated totality is; (iii) what values correspond to the new subdivisions of the undifferentiated totality of work, and how they differ from use-values.

(i) The undifferentiated totality of work is all the socially useful work expended

---

[11]   Apart from the texts of Smith and Ricardo and the translations of Marx available, good contemporary expositions in English are to be found in Dobb (1937, rev. ed. 1940, repr. 1960: chs. I, III, and *passim*; cf. also, for historical information, 1946, rev. ed. 1963; 1948, sixth ed. 1966; and 1967a and b), and Sweezy (1942, especially Part One). A few examples of a more general treatment are Boudin (1907, repr. 1967), who deals with the labor theory of value with reference to Böhm-Bawerk's historically important criticism (ch. V); Hilferding's 1904 answer to Böhm-Bawerk (Engl. trans. 1966); Lindsay (1925, repr. 1947), who indulges in a partial exposition of the theory before piling up several pages of undevastating criticism (ch. III); Schumpeter (1950 : 23-25), whose criticism, as Rosdolsky rightly observes (1971 : 6), is put forward *as if* Marx were only a positive scientist, and not also, basically, a dialectic thinker; and Korsch (1938, repr. 1963), who says relatively little about the relation between work and value but has the remarkable merit of placing what he does say within the right general framework (Part Two: 83-164). — Some essays which appeared in *Science & society* may also be recalled: Primbs (1965, where a number of American books on dialectical materialism are inspected among which additional analyses of the conceptual knot of undifferentiated labor can be found); Hodges (1965), followed by a discussion in XXX, 2°; Goldway (1967) and in general the whole issue of *Science & society* where it appears; Sherman (1970); and Duffield (1970). — The literature, of course, is immense; but the examples of analysis starting with work as such — with what can and must be said about work itself — are, as we know (cf. note 6) very rare. What usually happens is that after a few remarks about two "kinds of work" an author goes on to inspect their possible relations with two kinds of value — the problem of how work can be approached and articulated on its own merits isn't usually felt.

in a given community. If we consider all the artefacts of a given community not according to their differences but rather only for their common quality of being all products of work, it is clear that in correspondence to them there is all the work which has, in fact, produced them. At the level of a philological joke, perhaps with a touch of Heideggerian semi-profundity: all the *ars* corresponds to all the *facta*. If the *facta* are assumed only according to the viewpoint of their being *facta*, then the *ars* as well is assumed only according to the viewpoint of its being *ars*. Nothing is said about the differences between the various *facta* and the various *artes* — between the various artefacts and the various working processes which have presided differentially over their production.

(ii) The notion of undifferentiated work may be reached by abstracting from the specific determinations of productive activity. Undifferentiated work is mere *expenditure of human labor-power*. The differences among the various working processes do not count any more. We have moved from a qualitative to a quantitative consideration. The whole quantity of the artefacts produced corresponds to the whole quantity of the work expended. But the artefacts are a plurality and are exchanged the ones with the others. Thus the question arises of the quantity of undifferentiated work that, within the community of which we are speaking, belongs to every artefact. Work is at this point measured only according to its quantity — both the work actually expended in the present and that expended in the past and deposited in the variety of artefacts on which the life of the community rests.

(iii) A new and different kind of value of the artefacts corresponds to the new way of subdividing undifferentiated work. Every artefact possesses not only a use-value, a capacity to satisfy needs, which comes to it from the differentiated work with which it is produced; it also possesses a value *tout court* [12] which comes to it from the *quota* or *ratio* of undifferentiated work expended for its production. We can identify this value as the *position* which the artefact assumes in the system of all the arte-

---

[12]   This terminology might give rise to misunderstanding owing to the presence of the same term, 'value', in different expressions. It has however taken such a deep root in the relevant literature that it isn't possible to change it any longer without raising even bigger misunderstandings. The following little table, which also comprehends some graphic devices, may be of use to avoid confusion:

— *use-value* [Germ. *Gebrauchswert*, Ital. *valore d'uso*]: utility, capacity to satisfy a human need; it comes from differentiated work (or simply *work*, according to Engels' remark on English usage: cf. footnote 1);

— *value tout court*, *i.e.* value without adjectives; sometimes hereafter put in quotation marks ("value"), or specified as value-as-position. This kind of value comes from a *ratio* of undifferentiated work (or, of *labor*, according to Engels' distinction). The phenomenal form of "value", that is, the form in which it usually appears to us and is grasped by us in reality, is *exchange-value* [Germ. *Tauschwert*, Ital. *valore di scambio*].

The following is the main opposition: the opposition between use-value and "value" (as position). But since in the reality of the market (as well as, as we shall see, in the reality of other social institutions) what we directly encounter is exchange-value, the *most frequent* opposition is that between use-value and exchange-value. See 4.2, 5.1 and 6.1-4 hereafter.

facts, and which is acknowledged to it within the community. This value-as-position does not satisfy needs; it does not have anything to do with the particular qualities of the body of the artefact. It is only an abstract property on the basis of which artefacts are measured with each other, that is, fundamentally, they are *exchanged*. It is value-as-position that makes artefacts into commodities. It emerges and is specified as *exchange-value* when two or more (types of) artefacts enter in a particular sort of relationship, the relationship which sustains commodity exchange already at the level of *barter*, the developments of which constitute a *market*. Notice: the value does not *derive* from the exchange; it is the exchange that comes about according to value-as-position.

In 4.2 we shall have to deal with this dialectic in the field of exogamic exchange; and in Section Five, with reference to language, we will return to the opposition between use-value and value-as-position, and the expression of the latter in the form of exchange-value. We will furnish at that point also a few simple schemata of the ethographic type, as well as some examples. Let us add here a few remarks with an aim at glimpsing, meanwhile, the importance of the dialectic of the various types of value for the comprehension of signs. In every sign system, whether verbal or non-verbal, every sign is an artefact (autonomous, or borne by another artefact: 2.4.2). As such, every sign possesses both a use-value and a value-as-position which is expressed as exchange-value owing to the plurality of signs and their entering into relations within the system. Moreover, every sign system in its entirety possesses not only use-values but also the values which come to it from its relations with all other sign systems. In the minimum case of a single sign, as in that of an entire sign system, the network of the value-as-position relations, expressed in exchange-values, derive in the last analysis from the subdivision of undifferentiated work, that is, from the quantity of mere expenditure of labor power that belongs to each of them. The quantity of the various *artes*, various only as to quantity, determines the position of the various *facta*, various only as to quantity.

A passage from the Marxian analysis of the commodity will conclude this section in the most appropriate way:

As use-values, commodities are, above all, of different qualities, but as exchange-values they are merely different quantities, and consequently do not contain an atom of use-value.

If then we leave out of consideration the use-value of commodities, they have only one common property left, that of being products of labour. But even the product of labour itself has undergone a change in our hands. If we make abstraction from its use-value, we make abstraction at the same time from the material elements and shapes that make the product a use-value; we see in it no longer a table, a house, yarn, or any other useful thing. Its existence as a material thing is put out of sight. Neither can it any longer be regarded as the product of the labour of the joiner, the mason, the spinner, or of any other definite kind of productive labour. Along with the useful qualities of the products themselves, we put out of sight both the useful character of the various kinds of labour embodied in them, and the concrete forms of that labour; there is nothing left but what is common to them all; all are reduced to one and the same sort of labour, human labour in the abstract.

Let us now consider the residue of each of these products; it consists of the same unsubstantial reality [actually, *gespenstige Gegenständlichkeit, i.e.* 'a ghostly objectivity'] in each, a mere congelation of homogeneous [actually, *unterschiedsloser, i.e.* 'without differences left in it'] human labour, of labour-power expended without regard to the mode of its expenditure. All that these things now tell us is, that human labour-power has been expended in their production, that human labour is embodied in them. When looked at as crystals of this social substance, common to them all, they are – values. [*Das Kapital*, I, 1°; 52; Engl. transl.: 37-38]

2.4 *Schema of Social Reproduction*

In this section we try to identify the place of communication in the process by which every society is formed, proceeds, and persists in time, reproducing itself. At the basis of this process lies the fact that man, a social animal of a particular type, works and by working produces himself. This means that he institutes relations with nature and with himself as a kind. The relations of man with nature are, from the very beginning, relations between men. We will call this whole situation *social reproduction*.[13]

2.4.1 *Production, exchange, and consumption*

We can distinguish three fundamental moments in social reproduction: production, exchange, and consumption. As Marx showed once and for all, these three moments are so closely interconnected that only by deliberate abstraction can one

---

[13] Italian *riproduzione sociale*. It was felt by some English-speaking readers of this passage that 'social reproduction' wouldn't do in English because of its biological associations. Let us examine, however, some of the proposed alternatives. 'Social propagation' is not satisfactory because it gives the idea of something which increases in size or extension or power; this is not necessarily the case, for a society may also reproduce itself while diminishing in size and/or extension and/or power. Nor would 'cultural evolution' do, because what is conveyed by the Italian *riproduzione sociale* is merely the fact that a society goes on, not the fact that it evolves. 'Economic anthropology' wouldn't do either, for what we have in mind is *not* economic life as a subsystem of society but, rather, the *whole system of society* in the process of being handed down from generation to generation by keeping on producing and using the basic things which are necessary to human life. Reference to ethnology would make things worse, not better. Perhaps the best thing to do is just to say that 'social reproduction' is an expression defined by its use in sub-sections 2.4.1 and 2.4.2 and in this note, and leave it at that. It is noteworthy, however, that a difficulty is found in translating into English a basic term which is almost immediately clear and unambiguous in another S.A.E. language. As a point of linguistic relativity, it seems that the Italian reader slides back to the noun from the adjective, and *modifies* the noun; while to the English reader the noun is a citadel that the adjective can only *qualify*. The obligatory position of the English adjective before the noun may be connected with the phenomenon.

talk about them separately.[14] The goods men need, "use-values", must in fact be produced and consumed, consumed and produced; with the social division of labor the exchange of produced goods is inserted as the abstractly intermediate moment between the abstractly initial and terminal moments of production and consumption. As we have just seen, exchange takes place according to values which are different from the use-values, although they presuppose them. In the restricted sense of economics proper, we can begin to speak of exchange only from the moment in which there is production for the market. But in a vaster sense the process is at the root of homination. In various ways, to be inspected, the dialectic between use and exchange is inherent in the dialectic between production and consumption and has been so since primordial times. Any human activity is connected to it (2.4.3). As we will try to show below (in 2.4.2; then in 5.2 and in 6.1, 6.2, and 6.3), it is already contained in any form of communication.

The whole process of social reproduction is a material process. With this we want to assert both that needs and the conditions of material life determine all the rest, and that there are no ontological dimensions distinct from that of matter. The two assertions are much more strictly interconnected than might seem at first glance. It is indeed only when one denies that the needs and conditions of material life determine all the rest, that one fancies ontological dimensions, distinct from the material one, to which that very "rest" would belong. We maintain instead that *any* phenomenon is in principle always liable to be explained in terms of material modifications. Such modifications can be external or internal to man: by which we mean to say, unmetaphorically, that they can take place either outside or inside the human organism (or both). While much is already known about material

---

[14] One should also distinguish between mere *transfer* and *distribution, i.e.* the organization of all transfers according to social rules with the aim of reaching all the members of the social group. In this case we then have *exchange in a proper, or better in a restricted, sense* when what has been distributed is redistributed according to individual need. But it is also correct to speak of exchange at the level of transfer, provided transfer is not limited to the externally material level of an object moving from one spot to another — as we are presently going to see. On the interconnection of production, exchange, and consumption see Marx's «Einleitung of 1857», in *Grundrisse*: 10-21 (McLellan's translation: 22-33). «Circulation — says Marx — is but a certain aspect of exchange, or it may be defined as exchange considered as a whole. Since *exchange* is an intermediary factor between production and its dependant, distribution, on the one hand, and consumption on the other, and the latter appears only as a constituent of production, exchange is manifestly also a constituent part of production ... The result we arrive at is not that production, distribution, exchange and consumption are identical, but that they are all members of one entity, different aspects of one unit. Production predominates not only over production itself in the opposite sense of that term [actually, *in der gegensätzlichen Bestimmung der Produktion*, that is, «in its own antithetic determination»: meaning that the total process of production predominates over production *as distinguished from* exchange *and* consumption], but over the other elements as well. With production the process constantly starts over again. That exchange and consumption cannot be the predominating elements is self-evident. The same is true of distribution in the narrow sense of distribution of products; as for distribution in the sense of distribution of the agents of production, it is itself but a factor of production ... A mutual interaction takes place between the various elements. Such is the case with every organic body [*Ganzen*]» [McLellan's translation: 32-33].

modifications external to man, as far as the modifications internal to his organism are concerned, we must make a distinction. There is already a fairly stable body of knowledge about some of them, for example, the physiological processes that man has in common with other animals; but very little is known about others. The modifications internal to man about which we know the least are those which take place in his central nervous system, and which preside over the activities most specific to him (not shared, or shared only in part, by the other animals) — the so-called mental, or spiritual, activities. The ancient notion of a non-material dimension proper to man sends its roots down into this lack of knowledge (though that is, of course, only part of the story), and not by chance. It is an illusion still fed by philosophy and pre-scientific thought in general, and it is laden with the insoluble (because irremediably metaphorical) problems of the ontological dualism of mind and body.

Bearing in mind the fundamental materiality of every human activity, and of the whole process of social reproduction with it, let us take a closer look at the various moments of the process, with particular attention to its intermediate moment — exchange.

The production of goods as use-values is in the first place external material production, what anthropologists and economists usually deal with. It gives rise to physical objects detached from the organism of man, objects which man fashions in nature and can manipulate in various ways. *Bodies* are produced this way, *not signs*. We must specify with care what kind of negation this is.

Non-human animals also produce their signs; signs were certainly produced by primates chronologically (and not only evolutionally) anterior to the advent of man. We must assume that when some of the primates started to work, thus beginning to become men, they produced as many or more signs than the other animals. When work emerged, it must have been from the beginning accompanied by, or better, inextricably connected to, *signs of a new* type suitable for favoring working operations. We are speaking here of both verbal signs (or pre-verbal, *e.g.* in the form of cries), and non-verbal signs — down to the level of the "language of things" we had a look at in 1.4 (we shall come back to it in 3.3 and 4.2). But the point here is to distinguish the production *of signs* from the production *of bodies* suitable for satisfying corporal needs like hunger or the need for shelter. The disarticulated thigh of an animal that has been killed with a club, and a roof put together with branches, are themselves *also* signs: so they are for the members of the tribe and indeed for all human animals able to interpret them, and so will they be for the ethnologist. Meanwhile, however, *they are* non-sign bodies.

In an analogous way, the consumption of goods as use-values is in the first place a consumption of external material objects. Since it is human consumption, it is difficult for signs to be absent from it; but in its specificity as material consumption, *it does not* itself *consume signs*. It consumes bodies. Even the bodies consumed, when the act of consumption does not destroy them, may assume sign value later on; they may indeed function as signs even when they are consumed. But so far we are talking about the consumption of bodies, not about the consumption of signs.

Thus I can produce beets by cultivating my garden and consume them by eating them myself. I am a man, hence I continually use various types of signs. My products can be interpreted by other men. But what I produce and consume are the bodies of the beets. Or you can fashion a branch to produce a walking-stick and then consume it little by little leaning on it when you walk. The walking-stick as such is not a sign even if it can be, or become, one; using a walking-stick does not mean using signs. The fact that the beets, when I eat them, immediately become internal to my organism and cease to exist as beets, while the walking-stick remains external to yours in spite of your using it, regards the modality of the consumption, not the external character of the objects consumed. One could naturally discuss at length the various types of objects which are produced and consumed, the various ways of using and consuming them, and the way in which various types of signs enter into play in all this. We have already said something about it, and we shall say something else later on. Here what interests us is that we haven't yet met with the *direct* production and *direct* consumption of signs.

In order to encounter human signs throughout the whole course from production to consumption, we must introduce the dimension of exchange at least in the embryonic sense of some sort of distribution or some sort of transfer, at least at the level of cooperation in work. This is *almost* a tautology. But it is worth while repeating that the first completely human signs can only have been formed with the social division of labor and in a way inextricably connected to material production. Considering the nature of the objects exchanged, we have to distinguish between an exchange which is material and external, made possible by the production of a surplus and placed between production and consumption as described so far; and exchange specifically of signs. If I give you my beets, or you give me your walking-stick, a transfer takes place of objects detached from our organisms. The same happens if we exchange the two objects, that is, if I give you the beets *in order to get* the walking-stick, and you give me the walking-stick *in order to get* the beets. The latter is the elementary economic situation known as barter, with which the dialectic of exchange begins. Now it is clear that not even a mere transfer can avoid resorting to signs of some sort. However, in the situation of barter, and generally of exchange, we come across something that is qualitatively new. Exchange not only cannot *limit itself* to external material objects; it is not even enough to say that during an exchange there is *also* the use of signs. There is something more, and it is precisely that real and proper *messages* are now produced, transmitted, and received (consumed). External material exchange is at the same time an exchange of messages, a resorting to codes. For two material objects to get *exchanged*, it is necessary that the two men who exchange them use sign systems.[15] The exchange is therefore, in first approximation, double: bodies are exchanged and, at the same time, messages are exchanged. As we shall see better here below, it is not a question of having two classes, one beside the other; rather, two processes are developing which are overlapping and contemporaneous, even if with some notable asymmetries. By now the dialectic between use and exchange is operating in all of its complexity.

According to our assumption, even the exchange of messages must be resolvable in material processes. Nevertheless one rightly feels that here we are dealing with a materiality different from that which is usually attributed to the physical objects of the external world that we have called bodies. Messages, certainly, (i) are themselves *also* material objects external to our organism, at least as transfer of energy (1.2). But they are not *only* this. They are immersed in networks of relations which we do not find only in the physically considered external world, or better, the description of which is not exhausted by the description of objects in the external world and their relations. We must look for those sign objects that messages are, according to two other dimensions as well: (ii) within us, and (iii) in networks of relations which are not natural because we have constructed them. According to the first dimension the exchange of messages is external material exchange, like the exchange of any other object. According to the second dimension, it is *internal* because it involves material modifications within our organism. This means that, along with exchange, the human organism became adapted for accepting such modifications: work has changed the human organism. According to the third dimension, the exchange of messages belongs to a reality different from natural reality. This different reality is society, defined as the organized whole of all products of human work, and of all relations between individuals. Society is the aspect assumed by matter at the human level. Work has transformed matter into society.

When we want to give a description of man that is adequate in principle, the social dimension is what must be resorted to. In order to move towards such a description, it is not enough, in the first instance, to describe how the human body as a piece of nature behaves; it is also necessary, in the second instance, to describe what happens within man, the modifications of his organism. After having passed thus from the outside to the inside, penetrating man in order to look for material modifications internal to him, it is nevertheless necessary, in the third instance, to make the opposite operation, that is, to return to the outside from the inside. What we encounter in this "exit", which is a dialectical return, is no longer mere nature; it is society, something *newly external* to the individual. Society in this sense is general like nature (and can or indeed usually does manifest itself once more as nature). There is nothing mysterious or metaphysical in the above "passages": every child learns to go through them in the first years, even though of course he

---

[15] For the crucial distinction between signs and messages, cf. 1.2 above and 3.2.1-2, 4.3, 5.1, and 6.1-3 below.

doesn't put to himself the problem of giving more or less adequate descriptions of them.

As we know, man finds himself immersed in sign systems from birth onwards, beginning with the non-verbal sign system of the objects of common use produced by the culture to which he belongs, and with the verbal sign system *par excellence*, his mother tongue. Every *in-fans* is also an *in-ficiens* who becomes a child and then develops into an adult because he learns to manipulate such systems at least in part — but it must be an initial and substantial part. They precede him in time, contain him in space, and impose precise behavioral programs upon him. Collaboration and reciprocal understanding are made possible by all this (1.4).

Scholars who willingly make the first passage, from the outside to the inside, will maintain at this point that the relations the brain has with other brains — communitary relations between the individuals to whom those brains belong — must deposit investigable traces within any given brain. As soon as the techniques for this research are developed sufficiently, we should be able to find, for example, traces in the brain of a Cheremis folksinger different from the traces we find in the brain of a Hopi ceramist (leaving the task of investigating Cheremis ceramists to the editor of *Word ways, The journal of recreational linguistics*). This line of thought is legitimate but premature. At the present state of knowledge, in spite of very recent progress in the chemical study of memory, we are far from having at our disposal such minutely differential traces. But the main point is that even when we did find them, *they would be mute for us* if we did not already know music, ceramics, and the Cheremis and Hopi languages, as something that extends far beyond the brains of the Cheremis folksinger and the Hopi ceramist. Music, ceramics, the Cheremis and Hopi languages, and all non-verbal and verbal sign systems are social institutions. The materials and the instruments of the programs that make human relations possible are contained in them. Not only are sign systems not something we can begin understanding only after having better understood the brain; they are themselves the foundation for the study of the brain. Nobody learns a language in treatises of differential neurology, but rather in grammars, linguistic texts, and by consulting native speakers. Speakers let their brains function and in so doing they activate and make available sign systems they have learned as children. Being in a position subsequent to the sign artefacts to be studied, speakers use them and make them employable by those who hadn't known them before — a little as a warehouseman who brings the objects we ask for to the counter and shows us how they work. The whole process of learning a sign system never makes any reference to things like electric potential or chemical reactions.

Thinkers have always tried theoretically to penetrate into the black box of the brain. Whether it is a question of the Stoics' τλεκόν (Mates 1953: 11-26); or of Bradley's *idea as meaning*, that is, of a part of the content of the idea constructed and used artificially by men as something general (1922², repr. 1958: for example 5–6, 38 note 8); or of Peirce's interpretant, the transcribability of a sign by other signs (I, §§ 553–555; II, §§ 92–94), taken up by Morris as disposition to respond (1946: 17 fll.); or of Saussure's *signifié* as a state of consciousness or psychic event that accompanies the *signifiant* (1967–1968, ed. Engler: 146–51, 257–8); or of the "mental work" of semantization studied by Ceccato (1964: 183-6, 1966: 256 fll.); and so on — we find everywhere, in spite of the differences of viewpoint and terminology, the appeal to something man produces and uses within himself. Semiotic literature, however, is also showing in an increasingly precise manner how sign exchange is immediately *external* to the individual *again* because it requires or indeed presupposes the existence of supra-individual sign systems.

2.4.2 *Exchange of bodies and exchange of signs*

We have talked so far about exchange in general only as the abstractly intermediate moment between production and consumption. Let us now see how it is articulated internally with the aim of beginning to bring out its sign aspect. Our hypothesis is that, at a higher dialectical level, exchange comprehends in itself the very tripartition between production, exchange, and consumption. This triad internal to exchange does not regard, however, the material objects already produced and destined for consumption, but rather the signs that must enter into play so that between production and consumption exchange may be inserted. We have sign production, sign exchange in a restricted and specific sense (exchange of messages), and sign consumption. *Sign* production, exchange, and consumption are part of exchange generally understood as the element mediating between external material production and consumption. Between external material production and consumption, the process of exchange is inserted as something unitary and dual at the same time: external material objects that are not signs are exchanged, and messages are exchanged as well — that is, communication takes place. It is *as if* two processes were taking place contemporaneously. One is that of the material transfer of a physical body from one pair of hands to another pair of hands. The other is that of all the sign work that must take place so that the transfer may have *a complete sense of exchange* for the two men to whom the two pairs of hands belong. It is *within* the sign aspect of exchange that we find production, exchange, and consumption again. The *differentia specifica* of the sign and of the message, "what makes a sign a sign and a message a message", is to be located and investigated in this reappearance of the triad of social reproduction within the moment of exchange.

Asymmetries between the two aspects of the process of exchange emerge as soon as we consider the different ways in which each is necessary to the other. For the exchange of external material objects (exchange, not mere transfer) to be present, there must also be an exchange of messages. Material exchange is *also* a form of communication; indeed, it is mainly such a form, because if there were no exchange of messages in it, it would be a mere transfer. It is in a different sense, and to a different extent, that the non-sign aspect of exchange is necessary to the sign aspect. For the existence of an exchange of messages it is not essential that an exchange of non-sign objects, that is, external material bodies produced for other aims and suitable for satisfying other needs, also take place. It is enough that the bodies produced for the purpose of bearing signs be transmitted *in their relative physical indifference.*

It almost seems as if, once he had learned the gist of the game in the division of labor and in the immediate distribution of goods, man had begun to practice it on its own. The holding of surplus in the form of a reserve and its being then distributed among members of the community did certainly have an influence here. But still more influential is the fact that primitive communities, even when they leave free access to subsistence goods, institute *non-mercantile exchange* in other social zones. We shall return to this point both in 2.4.3 and then again in 4.1–2. What happened was that in this way the sign aspect of exchange detached itself, so to say, from the non-sign aspect, and assumed various measures of autonomy. We can communicate even without exchanging non-sign material objects (naturally we must still use sign-bearing bodies, or at least resort to the modifications of energy that transmit them). As sign-exchange became more complicated, social structure became more complicated too.

Communication is sign exchange: production of signs and messages, exchange of messages, consumption of messages and of signs (cf. 6.1). With a more concise formula, to be used below also in a graphically thriftier way, it is "sign-[production-exchange-consumption]". This entire process can in turn be subdivided according to various criteria. It can be wholly or partially conscious or unconscious, voluntary or involuntary, occasional or systematic, and so on. For our aims, the principal subdivision is that between verbal and non-verbal which we sketched in 1.2. We have verbal and non-verbal sign production-exchange-consumption. But things are not all this simple; indeed, as everybody knows, they are very complex. There is here another aspect of that complexity to be examined. We have just had a look at various types of non-verbal sign systems. Let us now consider the opposition between verbal and non-verbal according to various *working conditions* of the bodies used. This will permit us to study it more closely and to propose a unitary criterion for further subdivisions. Let us concentrate on two main approaches.

FIRST APPROACH. — *Non-verbal* sign production-exchange-consumption can be carried out with bodies already existing "in nature" or with bodies already produced for other aims: as, respectively, women who circulate as messages in exogamic systems and goods exchanged on the economic market.[16] In these cases

---

[16] This distinction, which I deem sufficient for our present aims, would certainly need further clarification if we were to face professional objections of a philosophical kind. The phrase 'bodies already existing in nature' cannot be construed as meaning "bodies independent of the historical process" — unless it is taken to mean *"purely* natural bodies". The point is that as soon as there is something historical, nature, so-to-say, is no longer alone. No intermediate interpretation is therefore available. But this is obviously not what is meant by our distinction:

exchange takes place fully according to both of its aspects: the material aspect and the sign aspect are manifest, so to say, at the same level, or with the same force. Or, non-verbal sign production-exchange-consumption can take place *with* bodies purposely produced as sign bearers, like street signs or signal banners. In this case material production remains; but sign exchange and consumption are detached from it because the object of the exchange is not the body of, say, the street sign as such but rather the sign borne by it (its sign value). Intermediate cases are those of objects produced for the purpose of functioning as non-verbal signs and delivered to the interpreter: a bouquet of flowers sent as a message of love or devotion and then kept by the receiver also for the use that is made of its non-sign body (flowers have a nice smell, signs do not). Another intermediate case could be that of an object that serves exclusively as a sign, *and* is either ignored or thrown away as soon as it is used. These are cases of *ostension* (as studied by

_____

women "already existing" and later on assumed into a sign system and made to circulate as messages, also belong to historically determined social groups. They certainly don't exist in a "purely natural way", for this would mean that they existed outside of or before history; all human persons, instead, *are* social, *i.e.* historical products. — Actually, what underlies the distinction between bodies already existing in nature and bodies already produced for other aims is, first, a classification of various types of production, and second, a clarification of the way in which "what exists already" is to be understood in function of new working processes which are in our case sign processes (see 2.3.3).

Let us take the opportunity of this prudential footnote for a few more methodological remarks:

(i) According to one current usage of the term 'material', that of anthropologists in the phrase 'material culture', the quality of being material would belong to both non-sign products and non-verbal sign products, while it would not belong to verbal products (one possible root of this illusion has been hinted at above in the text). Here 'material' is construed as 'externally material', and this hands down (through implicit negation) the blunder that verbal signs aren't material, and useless difficulties are raised as to the nature of non-verbal signs (are they at the same time material and non-material?). What is playing here is a tension among various uses or levels of the whole terminology referring to matter: a terminology well worth examining with a due amount of care. Suffice it here to repeat that, first, all *internal* material processes are one case of material processes in general and keep on developing in the presence, and not in the absence, of other material processes; and second, the internal material processes of communication are to be understood against the background of an already present social dimension — when social messages circulate, the "second reality" external to man is existing as much as the "first reality" of nature is.

(ii) Differences between the production of signs and the use made of signs while producing something else should be investigated. The ways in which signs enter into the constitution of various kinds of products, or otherwise accompany the products in their social route, can be described in detail. Cf. on this 4.3.

(iii) The very opposition between internal and external with reference to the human organism turns out to be over-simplified and static when we submit it to dialectical probing. As hinted at, what is working here is a complex dialectic which takes us from the inside to the outside, and then again to the inside and again to the outside: it is only within such a dialectic that the terms 'inside' and 'outside' acquire their full meaning. Cf. on this Husserl's *Ideen* and Trân duc Thao 1951 (Ital. transl. 1970a) and 1973 (forthcoming).

Throwing some light also on the problems now raised does certainly belong to the range of this investigation; a systematic treatment of them, however, falls outside of our present scope.

I. Osolsobě; cf. Jakobson 1970a: 9); but it is not our job to enter into their study, interesting though they may be.

Verbal production-exchange-consumption, instead, takes place *only* with bodies produced for that purpose: articulated sounds, for which, in principle, no use is usually recognized other than that of functioning as verbal signs. Although articulated sounds are (also) bodies, the pre-eminence of the sign aspect of the exchange has gone still further. It is by now irrelevant which body bears the sign. The body, some body, is necessary, and it must be always the same one; but what counts is by now only the sign. This is the fount of the Saussurian *arbitraire du signe.* In the case of writing, the verbal sign reacquires a greater corporality, both because it is more permanent in its graphic shape than it is as a sound, and because it needs a substratum. This can be relatively labile, like paper, but also very lasting, like stone or bronze. With the advent of writing, then, as already in an embryonic way with the seal, a sort of pendular movement takes place, backwards towards the corporality of non-verbal sign-systems. There would be much still to investigate on this point by applying the theory of labor-value. But, as we said at the beginning, this too is a topic that remains programmatically outside of the range of the present essay.

All signs, non-verbal as well as verbal, can be interiorized. That is, the individual can entertain them "in thought" or use them unconsciously, without physically operating upon any object external to him. Interiorization leaves a residue, that of the bodies that have been used as signs but do not for this reason cease being bodies. Strictly, this also happens when the interiorization regards verbal signs; and we can understand how, in this case, the illusion that they have been interiorized *without residue* can arise. Since the bodies of verbal signs are produced and reproduced on purpose, and are of use only in the brief moment of their repetition, there is a sense in which, if I don't use them, I make or let them disappear. And since the physical nature of these bodies is irrelevant to their functioning as signs (only the fact that they are different from each other in a systematic way has value), even when the bodies disappear the signs seem to survive without them, they seem to outlive their own bodies. Unfortunately, however, they don't end up in a heaven for signs at all. Only a cancelling of the external bodies has taken place, and the internal material processes are left at work by themselves. That the disappearance of the bodies of signs is illusory, can be seen immediately. Even in the case of non-verbal signs, their bodies — in spite of the fact that I have left them there in the external world — are malignant enough to keep on functioning as signs for other people. In the field of verbal signs, the fact that I do not pronounce words, that is, that I do not personally reproduce bodies consisting in articulated sounds, certainly does not keep others from doing so. In both cases, the sign systems from which I thought I had somehow subtracted myself survive my every decision or illusion to the contrary. I had limited myself to *not executing* a given program, or not executing it in public.

What happens then, when we cut ourselves off from the external bodies of signs and only internal material processes are at work? A *new* passage from outside to inside has taken place. Society has been interiorized. This passage from outside to inside must not be confused with the previous passage in the same direction, which consisted of an interiorization of nature. It is distant from it by two degrees. Just this is the confusion resorted to by those who believe they can explain social things with biological facts, for example, sign systems with innate brain structures. The interiorization of sign systems is a late and so to say contingent process which does not touch the supra-personal and objective social substance of sign systems. Still, we may find in this interiorization, especially of verbal sign systems, an interesting track for moving towards an acceptable definition of consciousness and thought, or more generally, of the mental: the mind is *what is left* when the immediate practical relation to the external world has been annulled, and processes are taking place which only regard the matter constitutive of the human nervous system and the energies that move in it, considering, however, such processes not just as the support of sign systems, but rather as their interiorized product.

SECOND APPROACH. — Instead of beginning with the distinction between non-verbal and verbal, we begin with the distinction between bodies which already exist "in nature" or are produced for other aims (women destined to become exogamic messages, goods destined to become commodities) on the one hand, and bodies produced for the purpose of bearing signs. If what is used are already existing bodies, or those produced for other aims, sign production-exchange-consumption can only be non-verbal. If bodies produced on purpose are used, sign production-exchange-consumption can be either non-verbal or verbal. When the articulated sounds of verbal production-exchange-consumption are used in conversation and in writing, bodies external to man's organism are also at work; when instead those sounds and their relations have been introjected, as in visual reading or in thought, a cancellation or annullment of the external bodies, as we have described it above, has taken place; and only internal material processes are at work. The advantage of this second approach, if seen as complementary to the first, lies in the fact that it underlines the originally external character of all objects produced, exchanged and consumed, signs included.

We believe it will be useful to summarize by means of two tables the main distinctions advanced so far on the matter of social reproduction and of sign and non-sign exchange (facing).

2.4.3 *Non-mercantile exchange*

Our discussion of exchange and of its anthropogenic power (second only to that of work) would not be complete even within the narrow limits we have set for ourselves, if we neglected a group of problems which have emerged here and there between the lines, but which we have so far left aside. If by 'exchange' we meant only mercantile exchange in a strict sense, that is, the exchange of commodities,

TABLE I

SCHEMA OF SOCIAL REPRODUCTION

Social reproduction always comprehends, in a constitutive way, three indissolubly correlated moments:

1. External material **production** which, although *it uses signs*, produces not signs but bodies.

2. EXCHANGE, which is always, at the same time and constitutively,

   - external material EXCHANGE, that is, the process of exchanging not signs but bodies;

   - sign EXCHANGE, that is, communication, including as such within it:
     - sign **production**,
     - sign EXCHANGE in the strict sense, and
     - sign c o n s u m p t i o n.

3. External material c o n s u m p t i o n, which, even when *it uses signs*, consumes not signs but bodies.

TABLE II

FURTHER SUBDIVISIONS OF EXCHANGE,

regarding equally sign **production**, sign EXCHANGE, and sign c o n s u m p t i o n:

a. *Beginning from a distinction between non-verbal and verbal:*

   a.a. Non-verbal communication: non-verbal production-exchange-consumption: can take place

   a.a.a. with bodies already existing "in nature", or with bodies produced for other aims;

   a.a.b. with bodies produced for the purpose of bearing signs;

   a.b. Verbal communication: verbal production-exchange-consumption, only with bodies produced for the purpose of bearing signs.

b. *Beginning from different working conditions of the bodies:*

   b.a. Comunication as a sign production-exchange-consumption done with bodies already existing in nature, or with bodies produced for other aims: non-verbal only.

   b.b. Communication as production-exchange-consumption of bodies produced for the purpose of bearing signs: it can be

   b.b.a. non-verbal,
   b.b.b. verbal.

then a large part of what we have been building up should be exposed to radical criticism. We would be facing indeed a number of difficulties, which can be summarized as follows. One cannot assume the existence of mercantile exchange — in the sense of a proper market where independent private producers appear, each with his own commodities to exchange — in primitive societies; and the more so, the more one goes back towards primordial times. Marx and Engels are the first to be explicit on this point. Not all products are commodities, not even when they are consumed by persons other than the producer.[17] Now if the distinction between undifferentiated and differentiated work were applicable only to full-winged commodities, outside of the field of commodities it would not be permissible to attribute a "value" (value-as-position) to any other product. It wouldn't then be possible to maintain that non-verbal and verbal sign systems are interpretable by means of the dialectic between use-value and exchange-value, according to the two kinds of work that determine them. One of our fundamental hypotheses would then begin tottering. Everything that is not a commodity would have use-value only. The theory of labor-value would be inapplicable outside the field of the production and exchange of commodities proper, or its application would be only metaphorical.

We have already hinted in passing at the solution of these difficulties: non-mercantile exchange exists in social zones which are severed from that of the market, and precede it. Marx himself in the *Grundrisse*[18] asserts that «man is isolated

---

[17] In *Kapital* Marx makes it clear that his concern is purely with what happens «in a society of commodity producers». The division of labor, he says, «is essential to the production of commodities; although it is not true, conversely, that there is no social division of labour in the absence of commodity production. In the primitive communities of India there is social division of labour, but the products of this community production do not become commodities. To take an example that lies nearer to our hand, in every factory there is a systematic division of labour, but this division of labour is not brought into being by an exchange of individual products among the workers in the factory. The only products which confront one another as commodities are those produced by reciprocally independent enterprises» (Dietz Verlag: XXXIII, 56-57; English transl.: 11). In a passage reintroduced by Engels into the fourth edition of Book First of *Kapital* after Marx's death, we read again that «The medieval peasant produced cense-corn for the seigneur and tithe-corn for the priest; but the fact that they were produced for others did not make commodities of cense-corn and tithe-corn. To become a commodity, a product must pass by way of *exchange* into the hands of the other person for whom it is a use-value.» And in a footnote Engels comments: «It has often and wrongfully been supposed that Marx regarded as commodities all products that were consumed by other persons than the producers» (*ib.*: 55 and 9-10 respectively).

[18] The *Grundrisse der Kritik der politischen Ökonomie (Rohentwurf)* [*Fundamental traits of the critique of political economy (rough draft)*] were written in 1857-1858 and comprehend the real text of the famous «Einleitung of 1857», usually published in a somewhat altered version as an Appendix to *Zur Kritik der politischen Ökonomie* (1859). They first appeared in Moscow in 1939 but were practically unknown in the Western world until Dietz Verlag of Berlin reprinted them in 1953. Among the first to speak of the *Grundrisse* in English were Hobsbawm (1964) and especially Nicolaus (1968), who must be credited with the first global exposition of the work. An important event for readers limited to the English language is *Marx's Grundrisse*, a short anthology prepared by David McLellan (1971), although the translation may appear flabby to readers of the German text (or even of the Italian translation). The most analytical use made

[actually: *vereinzelt sich*] only through the historical process» and that «exchange is one main instrument of this isolation [*Vereinzelung*]» (395, 396; Engl. transl.: 96, retouched). Evidently here Marx is not talking about mercantile exchange, because the private producers who come to the market with their goods to exchange are already individuals, perfectly isolated from one another. These are indeed necessary conditions for a market to exist at all. Already in Marx, then, there exist two distinct concepts of exchange: mercantile exchange in the proper sense, limited to the rise of bourgeois and capitalistic society, that is of a society in which goods are produced *for the market*, which is a narrow sense; and a more general concept, which refers to any process in which some sort of exchange takes place between men. Mercantile exchange is only one among many types of exchange, even though it is the one through which the general structure of every possible exchange was discovered.

Contemporary anthropological research gives us empirical data on which to articulate a general doctrine of exchange. Let us recall a few points. The nineteenth century idea that primitives dedicated all their forces to mere subsistence has by now toppled. Already Malinowski had shown how the property rights of primitive societies formed composite systems (1922, chapter III on the "Kula"; 1929: 22-27). We must distinguish between various types of goods, subdivided in heterogeneous categories which vary from case to case. It is only in a mercantile

---

of the *Grundrisse* for the purpose of clarifying theoretical issues is so far, to my knowledge, Rosdolsky's (1955, 1967; Ital. transl. 1971). Of the whole *Grundrisse* there are a bad French translation by Dangeville (1967-1968), duly chopped up by Howard (1969), and a painstaking Italian translation by Grillo (1968-1970). For additional information, see Nicolaus and McLellan.

The publication of the *Grundrisse*, or better their diffusion, has definitively rejoined the "early" or "philosophical" Marx of the *Manuscripts of 1844*, who used to be the object of existential interpretation like Fromm's (1963), or worse of shallow pseudo-religious interpretation like Tucker's (1961), to the "mature" and "scientific" Marx of *Kapital*, who, taken in isolation from his previous production, was made the victim of structuralistic interpretations like Althusser's (1965, 1966), the more misleading the more sophisticated and clever. As Lukács (1923); French transl. published against Lukács' will and to his utter dissatisfaction, 1960; Ital. transl. with a new 50 page introduction by the author, 1967; Engl. transl. 1971) and Korsch (1923, 1938) had foreseen alhough they could'nt have known the *Grundrisse*, several basic characteristics of Marx's thought have now been finally demonstrated by Marx himself. Among them are the gapless *continuity* (which doesn't imply repetitiveness) of his investigations from beginning to end, the inseparability of his economic analyses and doctrines from the general framework of his vision and from the great tradition of German thought, and his constant use of the Hegelian dialectical method. Of a particular interest for our present concern is what is said in the *Grundrisse* about the so-called "Asiatic mode of production" and, in general, precapitalist economic formations, on the one hand (cf. the text above); and, on the other, what is said about capital when it becomes itself a means of production (we shall be coming back to this in 7.3 and 7.4, *passim*). Once the scope and central position of the *Grundrisse* are duly taken into account, *Kapital*, in spite of its magnitude, appears to contain "only" the most profound analysis ever made of one mode of production historically determined and doomed to disappear; while Marx's whole approach, of which *Kapital* exhibits "only" a part, allows of a global interpretation of human history as the reality we first have to cope with whenever we begin to think or to act.

economy that a generalized exchange of all types of goods arises (the consequences of which bring about, with capitalism, a universal merchandization: cf. note 50). In pre-capitalistic economies, instead, and the more so in primitive ones, various systems of exchange are to be found. What is more, these are non-communicating systems (Godelier 1969: 101–110). While the mercantile system is open, these are "closed" systems. Only one of these closed systems regards subsistence goods; and since these goods, in general, are available to all, the very system within which the market will later be formed is originally subtracted from the dimension of exchange. As Godelier writes:

> Competition within the group begins .... more often than not beyond the sphere of production and of the appropriation of subsistence goods, and it does not cause the loss of physical existence but that of the social *status* of the individuals. By excluding the problems of access to the means of production (land) and to subsistence goods from the competition between its members, the primitive community guarantees their survival and assures its own physical continuity; while by authorizing competition for the rare goods that give access to women and to authority, it assures its existence as a *society* [Godelier 1969: 103].

To repeat, primitive societies do not limit themselves to producing goods destined for subsistence. The fact that such goods are common property, or anyhow freely available, eliminates the market in the modern sense. Primitive economies do produce surplus, but this is destined to the support of *social structures other than the market*, which function by means of numerous *forms of non-mercantile exchange*. The productive forces remain what they are, sufficient for the subsistence of all the members of the community. Surplus work is directed towards the production of special goods, which are exchanged in a non-mercantile way.

Now, goods which are not destined to be exchanged on the market are also products of human work. What work produces them? It will naturally be a specific working cycle for each of them as a use-value, that is, differentiated work (at the vanishing point, the "natural" utility of goods must at least have been identified). But, on the other hand, non-mercantile goods are exchanged also; it follows that the dialectic between use and exchange enters into play for them too. Besides being endowed with a use-value, non-mercantile goods must also possess an exchange-value as the phenomenal form of their value *tout court* (value-as-position within the system to which they belong). For non-mercantile goods as well, then, we must refer not only to the notion of differentiated work, of the specific work expended to produce each of them, but also to that of undifferentiated work, of the portion of such work pertaining to each of them within the system to which they belong, and, more generally, within the wider system which is made up of all the artefacts produced by the community.

All this permits some important clarifications. In the first place, the continuity between the sign systems already used by pre-human animals and those used by men is not wrongfully broken. It would have been, had we been forced to locate the formation of sign systems too far ahead in social evolution, at a level which was no longer primitive or indeed even no longer primordial. And this would have been inevitable had we been able to talk about exchange only beginning with the formation of an economy which in some way was mercantile. But since pre-human animals can have very complicated sign systems, one doesn't see why human animals shouldn't have had at least equally complicated sign systems from the start. The point is that there is no need to antedate mercantile exchange, even in an early or immature form, in order to justify the fact that they had them. The continuity between pre-human animals and human animals is preserved insofar as men continue to be animals and inherit as such the non-verbal sign systems of their biological predecessors. At the same time, the continuity is partially broken, but only and precisely with the advent of work and with the institution of various orders of exchange that are not originally mercantile. Work and exchange preside over the formation of consciousness and of language.

The second clarification is offered to us by the fact that what we have just said is immediately transcribable into semiotic terminology. Having started from this terminology in the previous section, we moved away from it here with the intent of tracing it back to more basic terms, that is, of looking for a more adequate foundation. We can now face the rest of our discussion with a unified terminology. The passage from pre-human animals to human animals — we can now say — comes about with the increasing complication of basic sign systems: both non-verbal ones which are enriched by the sign value of all non-verbal artefacts produced by work, and verbal ones which are being formed as products of a fundamental branch of work, indispensable from the beginning.

Finally, a third clarification regards the generalization of an anthropogenic character — usually attributed *either* to work alone *or* to language alone[19] — to work *together with* language in the first instance; and, in the second, to work with all the sign systems that derive from it. This is the same as insisting upon the inextricably unitary character of work and of all its products in all sign systems. At the same time, two branches of production emerge as essential for the understanding of man: material production of common use objects (everyday utensils and tools), linguistic production of verbal messages. We are now ready to concentrate our attention upon them.

---

[19] 'Usually' here means that an historical inquiry would show how the attention of scholars fell *either* to the side of work, in the sense of material production, *or* to the side of language, in the sense of verbal communication. For concentration on language, suffice it to recall Sapir's classical opening of the entry LANGUAGE in the *Encyclopedia of the social sciences,* 1933, IX : 155 (now in Sapir 1963 : 7), where we read: «Of all aspects of culture, it is a fair guess that language was the first to receive a highly developed form and that its essential perfection is a prerequisite to the development of culture as a whole». For concentration on material work and production, see Lukács' otherwise magnificent Hegelian analysis of the founding power of work (1948, 1967[3]: II, iv and v; III, v, vi, and vii). For some words of criticism of either unilateral approach, cf. 1.3 above and Section Three hereafter.

3. THE HOMOLOGY BETWEEN LINGUISTIC PRODUCTION AND MATERIAL PRODUCTION

The one divides into two.
MAO TSE-TUNG

Between material artefacts like wooden planks, shoes, or automobiles, and linguistic artefacts like words, sentences, or discourses, a constitutive homology can be traced. It can be baptized with the brief expression *homology of production*. If we use 'production' in its general sense, the homology is internal to it, and thus present *between* the two types or branches of production here distinguished as fundamental.[20]

Man has never produced linguistic artefacts without producing material artefacts at the same time. It is only by abstraction that we place the former under examination without the latter. Wherever we look, we find artefacts belonging to the two classes existing together. That the material resist the wear of time longer than the linguistic artefacts do and can thus remain alone as witnesses to societies which have disappeared, does not concern the human essence of work expressed in them, nor the fact that they have been produced, but only some of the modalities man has utilized for the manipulation of these materials (cf. 2.2). A civilization which is "only material" or "only linguistic" does not exist in reality. Moreover, the production of utensils and sentences and of their developments, if considered in a unitary way, enjoys a privileged definitory power when compared to any other factor.[21] No definition or characterization of man is as radical as that which places in the *definiens* his capacity to produce material (*faber*) and linguistic (*loquens*) artefacts. But indeed, that material artefacts may be produced without the concomitant production of linguistic artefacts, and vice versa, is not even *thinkable*. Man would not have been able to work on any object without communicating with other workers, at least with rudimentary languages at the beginning bordering on gestures. Conversely, verbal communication presupposes a world of real objects to which language refers, and thus the advent of the capacity to distinguish and manipulate such objects. To put it in phenomenological jargon, such a capacity

[20] In what follows we shall proceed to make some systematic comparisons, which we label "homological", first, between production-exchange-consumption of signs and production-exchange-consumption of bodies other than signs (without forgetting that exchange is in both cases also exchange of signs); and second, between verbal and non-verbal production-exchange-consumption. Let us telescope these two orders of comparisons into one comparison of a more simple and direct kind, the comparison between *verbal* or (in the proper sense) *linguistic* production-exchange-consumption, and externally material (or, as it is usually called, simply *material*) production-exchange-consumption. And since it is not possible to consider production without necessarily bringing in the exchange and the consumption of the produced objects, because exchange and consumption are themselves moments and factors of production, let's use as an additional simplification *linguistic production* vs. *material production,* as we did in 2.2.
[21] Cf. note 19. — The prohibition of incest as a basic or indeed founding social rule belongs to exogamy, *i.e.* to a form of non-mercantile exchange which presupposes both material and linguistic production.

is rooted in the *constitution of things*.[22] Let us conclude that the homology of production is at the same time a logico-structural and a historico-genetical homology. Those particular animals that come together in communitary groups and, with the passage from unity to plurality, little by little become men, operate in a basically similar way when they organize all their sign systems, as different as these systems may seem at first glance. It would be strange if the opposite were true, since sign systems express the relations of social organization as it grew from the beginning. As Thao says «the cry of the animal becomes human language by *articulating itself* on the structure of productive work» (1970a: 222). There would be no division of labor without the existence of some form of communication; communication, however, would not arise without the division of labor.[23]

The similarities between the two orders of artefacts, the material and the linguistic, are presented in this chapter as pre-eminent over their differences (which, certainly, nobody wants to deny) for the good reason that the latter are accepted as obvious by everyone. When, at the level of reflection, we run into the similarities for the first time, they come to us as a surprise and can even arouse adversion or suspicion. For this very reason, insistence on the similarities has a methodological function and a demystificatory power. It is only after the similarities are clearly assessed that the correct differences between the two orders of artefacts — correct, as it were, from both points of view — should be expected to display themselves in a way that will allow us to proceed to put them in their proper arrangement. We usually talk instead about the differences without having at all taken

---

[22] Although language is by no means limited to *describing* the world (as is shown in great detail, among others, by Wittgenstein 1953), it would be impossible to imagine a system of words *i.e.* of linguistic objects operating independently of a system of non-linguistic objects; and since the latter are produced by men in various senses, which go from the pregnant sense of bringing into physical reality something which didn't exist before production to the attenuated sense of intervening upon nature by means of distinctions (cf. footnotes 16 and 26) — it follows that what man does to and with non-linguistic objects is essential to language, though in a problematic and reciprocal way (some comments on this in Rossi-Landi 1968b : 34-39). To put it in a nutshell, there is some sort of unbreakable continuity underlying whatever waves and leaps may appear at the surface of the processes which go from words to objects and from objects to words. Nobody, as far as I know, has ever gone as deep into these things as Hegel in the *Wissenschaft der Logik* and Husserl in the three books of *Ideen* and in the *Analysen zur passiven Synthesis*; but the task of reformulating their investigations in historico-materialistic terms has only begun. Cf. the pioneering works of Thomson, Schaff, and Thao.

[23] For communication itself *is, inter alia,* a division of labor; and it would be arduous to imagine that in a situation where the main daily problem was survival through cooperation, our earliest ancestors possessed the leisure and talent to build up systems of signs for systems of signs' sake. Bloomfields statement that «the division of labor, and, with it, the whole working of human society, is due to language» (1964, 1933[1]: 2.2., p. 24) is ambiguous not because of what it does say but because of what it does not say, *i.e.* because it doesn't expressly make clear that "language in its turn, and with it the whole working of human society, is due to the division of labor". It is remarkable how these things were felt by various authors. For instance, at the beginning of the Eleventh Century Ratnakīrti was stating that «whatever is unproductive is no object of knowledge» («ajanakasyāprameyātvat» in *Kṣaṇabhaṅyasiddhiḥ Vyatirekātnikā*, 81.09).

account of the similarities: thus, from the beginning, the discussion leans in only one direction. Or still worse, we talk about what would *emerge* as different if and only if we kept both orders of production always under our eyes and examined them in a comparative fashion from beginning to end — and this is exactly what does not happen at all. As a result of our failure to compare the two orders, whatever we say about linguistic production is doomed to regard only a part split off from a totality which itself remains in the shadows. This being the situation, it seems advisable for a semiotician who has run across the homology of production, to concern himself expressly with the similarities between the two orders, at the risk of giving the impression that he underrates their (obvious) differences.

Linguistic production and material production develop according to parallel modalities and levels of complexity for which unitary explanations may be given. There is no reason why the internal articulations of work as we have described them shouldn't be valid for both. When we reconstruct the phases of production in a parallel way we find that for every linguistic level (distinctive features, phonemes, monemes,[24] words, phrases, sentences, and higher units of discourse) there is a corresponding level of non-verbal linguistic work, that is, a corresponding phase in the elaboration of non-sound material — this from the standpoint of language. But we can also take the opposite standpoint, and recognize in language the moments and levels of the various processes of "material", non-verbal, production. In this way we begin to carry out the program mentioned in 1.2, 1.4, and 2.3.3.

3.1   *Analogy, Isomorphism, and Homology*

Before we start to examine the homology of production a little more closely, we had better say something about the differences between analogy, isomorphism, and homology.[25] Since these notions are akin to each other at least apparently, they

---

[24] For the reasons stated in note 32, we are going to use *moneme* in the European sense, as made clear by Martinet, rather than the North-American *morpheme*. A *moneme* in Martinet's sense can be either a *lexeme* (also called a *semanteme*) as a unit of sense, or a *morpheme* as a modifier of sense. Thus, according to this terminology, *unacceptable* divides into the lexeme *accept* and the two morphemes *un* and *able*.

[25] To select just a few items out of a pretty large literature, cf. Melandri's extensive study of analogy (1968), Max Black on models and metaphors (1962, repr. 1966), *L'analogie* (1969), Paul on figurative language (1970), and Schlanger on the metaphors of the organism (1971). Our use of the terms 'homologous' and 'homology' has something akin to the use of these terms in biology, where they refer to a fundamental similarity due to community of descent, to a correspondence in structure and in origin (biological homomorphism is instead correspondence in form or external appearance but not in type of structure and in origin). The question may therefore be legitimately raised whether the homology we are going to describe is the object of discovery or of invention. In other words, does the homology between material and linguistic production exist in reality, or is it only an intellectual tool? In my view the dilemma is spurious, and the correct answer is that the homology is a successful intellectual tool for the study of reality *because* homology really exists. This answer is grounded on the materialistic

are also prone to easy confusion. It strikes the eye that differences and similarities
— the basic corner-stones of thought[26] — enter into all three cases: and indeed,
nothing less than the dialectic between similarity and difference is what has a
different arrangement in the three different cases.

If we say that two processes, two conditions, two parts of the same or of two
distinct totalities, etc. — let us say briefly, in the most general term, "two things"
— are *homologous*, we are saying both that they are different and that between
them there is *a similarity according to some criterion*. If they were identical according to all criteria, we couldn't even distinguish the one from the other (conversely, to mention an illustrious Leibnizian problem: "indiscernables are identical"[27]). But, on the other hand, if there weren't some sort of similarity between
the two "things", each would wander about on its own, and there wouldn't be any
reason for considering them together, for making them the object of a unitary discourse. Notice in passing that in what we have said the two "things" have been
taken up as already constituted. We will continue, for simplicity's sake, to take
them up in this way, that is, we shall not be going back to before "the thing". In
a discussion expressly dedicated to the dialectic between similarity and difference,
or to that of the constitution of the thing, it would be necessary to specify that
differences and similarities enter into play in the constitution of the thing itself.[28]

What are the similarities and differences that are in action when we talk about

---

theory of knowledge used by Marx, Lenin, Lukács and Mao Tse-tung. According to this
theory, we find, *i.e.* "discover" in the essence of things what we have built, *i.e.* "invented" at
the theoretical level in order to go through the surface of things, when we succeed in this
operation. A dialectic of reality *vs.* appearance, essence *vs.* manifestations, and initial totalities
vs. structured wholes is involved, and it develops through the so-called "concrete-abstract-
concrete circle", or "praxis-theory-praxis circle". Cf. my essay on Mao Tse-tung's contribution
to dialectics (1971 : 519-540).

[26] «The intellect has the dual necessity of perceiving the identical and the different, the
constant and the variable, the one and the multiple ... The principle of identity and the principle of diversity are equally necessary to understand the universe» (Cattaneo, *Logica*, 1855-
1856, ch. II, now in 1960, III : 227-228). Dingler put the *sheer relation of difference* — with
equality and similarity as its special cases — at the foundation of his epistemological construction. The point is that underneath the level of differentiation only unnameable "presence"
exists (1942, 1949). Perhaps this is part of what Lao-tse meant when he began his treatise with
the words «The Tao of which one can speak (or, that can be named) is no longer the eternal
Tao». Hegel however comes to his doctrine of "Something and an Other" only after dealing
with Being, Nothing, and Becoming, and with the Determinate Being as such. On Dingler cf.
Kramps 1955, Kramps (ed.) 1956, Sandborn 1952, and the entry DINGLER in the *Encyclopedia
of philosophy*. And see footnote 28 hereafter.

[27] Cf. Ayer 1953 (now in 1954a: ch. 2); Parkinson 1965; and, for a review of recent Leibnizian
literature, Costa 1971.

[28] Taking up again the digression contained in note 26, it may be observed that the very
notion of a thing involves at least one difference internal to that thing. If there are no internal
differences, there is no thing. In other words, an entity without internal differences is a non-
thing, *i.e.* it is not something one can describe. According to Mao Tse-tung, however, the difference must be a contradiction, and there is no thing unless there is at least one contradiction
internal to it. Contradiction is the origin of movement — the very stuff of the universe (1937,
now in *Selected works*, I, 1967 : 315-319).

homology instead of talking about analogy or isomorphism? The first point to clarify is that, given two different artefacts, for example a type of sentence and a type of utensil, belonging with all their diversity to linguistic production and to material production respectively, the similarities which they will present to homological enquiry are not similarities to be traced empirically, by an *a posteriori* application of some criterion to heterogeneous and genetically disconnected situations. It is completely clear not only to the reader but also to the present writer, that there are differences between sentences and utensils. To neglect such differences would be simply silly. We have already hinted at them jokingly by observing that, for example, we can't blow our noses on sentences as we can on signal flags. A first difference between analogy and homology is just this: that tracing an *analogy* means operating subsequent to the artefact, assuming two artefacts as already produced, and operating on them *a posteriori* with the intention of finding objective similarities.

In the case of *homology*, instead, the two different artefacts are taken into consideration all along the range of the work regarding them. Thus the fact emerges that in the developments leading to them there is a common anthropogenic root both in the philogenetic and in the ontogenetic sense. We predicate the homology of at least two different manifestations of the same structure-in-becoming; this is possible insofar as the two manifestations present correspondences whose root lies in something essential common to both of them. What counts for seeing them as homologous is certainly not some immediate external similarity between two artefacts, found subsequently to them, but rather something that they have in common at a stage previous to the stage where they come to assume their full-winged status, *i.e.* some factor belonging to the process by which they have been produced. When we study homology as the manifestation of the same essence in different fields, we have to be careful not to be led astray by the differences of the fields, for this could make us lose sight of the homological factor. But on the other hand, we must also take into account the differences of the fields and thus also the differences of the manifestations. One may feel tempted to say that a relation between materials and forms enters here into play and that in the homology we are confronted with the results of the application of the same form to different *materials*. But this would be inadequate or indeed wrong, because what we are dealing with here are dynamic, and not static relations. What we have here is not just a model which is being repeated in different tokens; but, as we said, a structure-in-becoming. The whole dialectic is set into motion. Man develops himself by working; indeed, even before he develops *as man*, "he" *becomes a* man for the first time by virtue of the fact that "he" starts to work. In this process of becoming he expresses himself *in*, *with*, and *on* different materials which condition the techniques of expression and in this sense give rise to different products. But the work *is* unitary. This can be grasped at an elementary level — even today with so much history behind us, and a multitude of sign systems of every sort available to us — in the cases in which there is a choice possible between two different codes for expressing or "delivering" the same thing. The poet expresses his love in a lyric, the painter in a picture, the shoemaker makes a marvellous pair of shoes for his girl, the sportsman takes her skiing with him. The same things, or very similar things, can be said with words, with gestures, with objects, with various types of silence, and by behaving in various ways.

Analogy is similarity, direct similarity between objects of any sort, isolated and kept immobile; the similarity is here traced *a posteriori*, from a position subsequent to the artefact, according to some criterion put to work contingently. An analogy provisionally reunites what is divided, or at least what is not united in a necessary way, superimposing upon any two objects whatsoever a third element extraneous to them; and it is just this third element that serves to bring the similarity to the fore. The homology shows that what appeared, or usually appears, to be divided is actually genetically united. With two brief formulae: analogy is the superimposition of the one upon the two; homology is the recognition of the original unity, that is, the genetic bringing-back of the two to the one. Using the analogical method means starting from two to arrive at one: the assumption is that the processes under consideration are separate at the origin. Using the homological method means, instead, starting from one to arrive at two, that is, recognizing that the real and original process has consisted in the division of one into two. The "struggle between the two lines" in China exemplifies the opposition we are talking about. The victory of Mao Tse-tung's line over that of Liu Shao-chi is presented as a victory of the homological method over the analogical method, of dialectics over empiricism.

An extreme case of the analogy is *isomorphism*. The Latin sentence *i vitelli dei romani sono belli* and the Italian sentence *i vitelli dei romani sono belli* are isomorphic to the point of showing up as identical. Except that the Latin sentence means *go, oh Vitellius, at the sound of war of the Roman god*, while the Italian sentence means *the calves of the Romans are beautiful*. The following are, instead, homologous: the Latin sentence, *i vitelli dei romani sono belli*, the Italian sentence, *vai o Vitellio al suono di guerra del dio romano*, and the English sentence, *go, oh Vitellius, at the sound of war of the Roman god*. In these little games, the essence that is expressed differently is the same message in different languages. Quite different slices of reality are taken into consideration when we substitute one of the above messages for another under the auspices of an isomorphic factor extraneous to them. The linguistic operations for producing the different messages examined continue to be very different. An illustrious example of isomorphism is the belief that the structures of language correspond to those of the world understood ontologically, as such subtracted from human production by definition, and then, so to say, "regained" by the procedure of a *post-eventum* comparison of the two orders of products. Thus isomorphism is a dialectical halt that from the beginning stands in the way of starting any sort of homological research. We could even say that it is its dialectical overturning, or at least its caricature.

The search for correspondences between the structure of a language and the structure of a society is, then, also analogical instead of homological. It is the case, for example, of Sommerfelt (1938), who carries out an enquiry on the relations between the structure of the language and the structure of the society in an Australian tribe, the Aranta. We can get an idea of his approach just by looking at his subtitle: «Caractères sociaux d'une langue de type archaïque». Sommerfelt follows the analogical procedure of contraposing *the* language *to the* society. This is an error from which, once it is committed in the very foundation of one's own research, one can never get free (cf. Rossi-Landi 1968c, 135-8; 1969b, 84-6). A homological approach, instead, consists in a study of the social *from the inside*, in the attempt to see how the human essence variously manifests itself within the reality of society. Naturally, what one actually ends up by studying is a certain number of *objects* isolated by abstraction; but it is of basic importance that the approach be the one indicated. We can, accordingly, view the language as one fundamental social factor in a position of comparison with other fundamental social factors. This is a job which is radically different from any and every comparison *of* the language *to* the society. Simple as the difference is, in my opinion it indicates whether an approach is healthy or wrong-headed. Because if I compare *the* language *to the* society I have already pulled *the* language *out of the* society — and then I will be faced with the impossible task of putting back together that which already exists together in reality but which I myself have separated by thought. Since (i) I have produced that separation myself and have superimposed it on reality, and (ii) I am now producing additional thought as a development of a separaiton I have made, it follows that (iii) whatever I now do I can't but confirm the separation, even if — at a stage which is now too far removed from the initial steps — I am instead aiming at bringing separated items back together. This is also the limit which B. L. Whorf never crossed in his research, stimulating as it nevertheless is (Rossi-Landi 1968b).

When we take instead the point of view of work, of what man does, and we study results obtained in different fields by means of the same or substantially similar working operations, then, between these different results we can find structures of similarity which bring us back, precisely, to work. The *deduction* of the homology is permitted by a properly understood genetic method, that is, by a genetic method which includes the structural study of synchronic and symmetrical phases of the processes under examination. The homological element breaks through specializations: it obliges us to take different things into account contemporaneously; it disturbs the independent play of separate sub-totalities; it refers to a vaster totality whose laws are not those of its parts. In other words, the homological method is an anti-separatistic method, as such unpleasant for specialists.[29]

---

[29] These statements refer to the big issue of a "unitary or global science of man" *vs.* the segregationism of the particular sciences, and of the "science of what should be done" *vs.* the science of what has been done. There are here some of the many issues which surround our

The homology may sound surprising. In order to accept it one must admit into the realm of founding thoughts the total, indivisible unity of man and his every production. Those who do not wholly admit this unity find themselves faced with an asymmetrical conjunction of heterogeneous elements and have to shoulder the weight of their explanation. This amounts to an impossible research for extra-human causes of the human. The process of the autogeneration of man is excluded, or at least the root of it is excluded; and just this exclusion, in the form of a bad negation, seems to confirm the non-unity. It is the antique superstition, or illusion, or perversion, of the ontological dualism of mind and body, in which, ultimately, the subdivision of society into at least one ruling and one subaltern class is expressed. As is well known, this subdivision presents itself again at the ideological level in the most unexpected ways, within the most modern theories, often hidden under the veil of new terminology which can be very difficult to disentangle and demystify. In such a way, the "interiority" of which Trân duc Thao speaks, «where the horror of bourgeois thought for the hard materiality of productive work is hidden» (1970a: 223), is handed down.

But we mustn't accept the homology indiscriminately either. It should be taken in the first place as a methodological instrument valid within its limits. It is the task of empirical research, inspired by the principle of homology, to establish what those limits are in the various cases. When we say that sign systems are systems of artefacts, for example, we certainly do not intend to deny the existence of languages as relatively neutral sets of instruments and materials (and, as we shall see in 5.2.1.2, of linguistic "money"). As such, languages are objects to study *also* by themselves, in their relatively objective structures and as to how they work. In much the same way material machines exist with their structures and the way they work, and all of us in our everyday lives use material artefacts, even very complex machines, and money. The common use of a language corresponds to the common use of all the objects that surround us in the society in which we live and into which we were born. It is not this or that individual factory or industrial enterprise that is going to be compared to linguistic production in the following pages (it would be a very dull idea), but the entire non-linguistic production of a community considered in its initial and founding phase. We know, moreover, that one can use artefacts also for ends which are not directly working ends, and that it is not impossible to distinguish sheer use from productive work (2.3.3). Thus it happens that, for example, words are used for the pleasure of their sounds, without really satisfying any need other than that perhaps recognizable in the pleasure itself; in the same way, we can toy about with various objects and draw from their

---

central issue of the homology of material and linguistic production, issues which cannot be dealt with within this monograph but must at least be mentioned to avoid that what is said in these pages may resemble the emerging portion of an iceberg unaware of its own nature. My own views on the science of man are sketched in 1958a, 1967b, 1967c, and 1969b (now also in 1972: 253-339).

use a pleasure of some sort, which doesn't have anything to do with production as such. Even these pleasures, games, and toyings-about belong to verbal and non-verbal sign systems. Lévi-Strauss dwelt on some of their aspects when he dealt with *bricolage* (1962: 26–47). But not even pleasures, games, and toyings-about can be subtracted from the condition of being programmed in the codes of the society in which they take place. And, anyway, they presuppose the existence of the whole system of social products — both of the things one toys about with, and of man as a toyer-about. The *bricoleur* is himself a historico-social product. The basis can only reside in production. If produced objects didn't exist, there wouldn't be anything to use either productively or unproductively, and indeed, even the users wouldn't exist. If this is valid for material objects, it is necessarily valid for language also. We shall return to this point in 7.2, with particular attention to the opposition between play and work.

In conclusion, it would be well to remember that here we are always talking at the level of models and not at that of tokens: we are talking about things like shoes or hammers in general (about the fact that shoes and hammers do exist), or this or that sentence in general (about the fact that this or that sentence does exist), and not about *the* shoes I am wearing at the moment or about my uttering, *hic et nunc*, *a* sentence. Similarly we are always talking about programs, not single executions. These and other methodological remarks, for the foundation of which a unitary theoretical schema has been provided in Section Two, will from now on be considered obvious and taken for granted. Both in the case of linguistic production, *i.e.* of verbal sign systems, and in the case of "material" production, *i.e.* of non-verbal sign systems of the objectual type, they refer to the premises of the processes to be examined. We will try not to repeat ourselves any more about these premises. It is the processes to be examined, not the premises as such, that lend themselves to global and unitary considerations leading to the detection of the homology of production. Let us therefore proceed to inspect how such a homology is articulated.

3.2 *Homological Steps of Production*

The homology of production can be traced by contraposing successive levels of production, in which material and linguistic production correspond. The levels follow one another only in a unidirectional way, going from what is more simple because less work has gone into it to what is more complex because more work has gone into it. Differences which are also qualitative spring from the quantity and the progressive complication of the working processes; once reached, every totality is worth more than the mere sum of its parts (2.3.3). By splitting a product of a given level into its constitutive parts we descend to a lower level, and this amounts to destroying it.

The homological schema of production, like any other schema, is artificial. The description of the cycles of operations which must be carried out successively in order to arrive at producing a complete and functioning automobile is artificial if it is compared either to the automobile itself as a concrete object ready for use, or to the functioning of that object. The operations by means of which the various pieces are put together in an assembly line are not in the least the operations carried out by the totality reached, that is, by the same pieces as soon as they are able to be taken as a whole (2.3.2). Even more artificial is the schema of a natural process like breathing. The physiological description of breathing isolates one process from what is occurring in the organism, it generalizes to all organisms some minimal common conditions, and it unites data of very different provenience in its own explanations (for example: the mechanical description of the filling up and emptying of the lungs and the chemical description of the transformation of hemoglobin into oxyhemoglobin).

Artificial both for material and for linguistic production, the homological schema may seem less acceptable for the latter since schematizing what man has done and is doing with objects external to him comes more naturally than schematizing processes which take place within his organism, whatever man is or is not doing with external objects at the moment. Two considerations come to our aid here. The first is that linguistic production is a material process also; the second is that in order to understand any other internal material process, like breathing, we can advance and indeed can't avoid advancing explanatory schemata.

While the schema is shaped in a unidirectional way, there is only a partial unidirectional character immanent in production as such. As a matter of fact production does move in all directions — the more so, the more mature it is. In the reality of both material and linguistic production, moreover, the level which is usually taken as a starting point is not that of the greatest simplicity in the schema but, if anything (as we hinted at the end of 2.3.2), that of completed sentences or utensils (which *in the schema* appear at a middle-low level). Production can go both from the simpler to the more complex, and from the more complex to the simpler, so to say turning back on itself and retro-acting on its own previous phases. This turning-back and retro-action can be seen clearly on the yardstick of a unidirectional schema; in unconscious or only partially conscious practice, it can and usually does happen that we don't pay any heed to it. Products belonging to higher levels are also used to produce products belonging to lower levels. Simple pieces of sheet steel are today cut out by means of complex machinery. It is by means of long, fussy, specialistic arguments that we delimit the meanings of single words or discuss the nature of phonemes and morphemes. It is part of the circular and dialectical structure of productive processes and their relations that complex machinery and long pieces of reasoning are already themselves composed precisely of objects like the ones they serve to produce.

In spite of all this the schema, artificial as it is, regards real production as we may suppose that it developed phylogenetically and as it repeats itself by jumps and with abbreviations in the realm of ontogenesis. We shall come back to this in 3.3, when we see how the linguistic doctrine of double articulation applies to the homological schema not only in the field of linguistic production but also in that of material production and must indeed be extended in both; and then in 6.5, when we deal with the spontaneous flow of speech in its relations to past linguistic work.

All artefacts, whether material or linguistic, derive from precedent objects by virtue of some working synthesis. Given an artefact as a starting point, it will always be possible to trace it back to pieces which are more simple than the artefact itself. In these terms, and taking into account that the anteriority of materials over products (that is, respective simplicity and complexity) is ranked according to a schema, the question arises again as to the *type of work* which will be called upon to justify the passages. What sort of work is it whereby "pieces" are combined in the ways required for obtaining a product under examination? With reference to the group of ideas brought forward in the previous Section, we can specify that the notion of work to bear in mind here is that of the differentiated and specific work which gives rise to use-values. But we must add the following qualifications: (i) such work is assumed in its operative generality; (ii) the community — either of material workers or of speakers —, not the individual, is posited as the worker; (iii) we are therefore going to deal in an abstract way with *the work which has socially produced models and programs*.

3.2.1. *Before utensils and sentences*

In this sub-section we deal with products that precede the utensil and the sentence respectively, that is, products that we find within the utensil and the sentence as their parts when we dismantle them to see how they are made.

First level: Pre-significant items. — Where and how does work begin? In 2.3.4 we remarked how any external material work can be broken down into simple operations. These must be operations that a human organism can perform alone and even in the nude upon objects that constitute his immediate environment. The most simple real operations one can imagine are operations like pulling, pushing, adding, taking away, turning, tracing, pressing; and like superimposing, overturning, heaping, flattening, sharpening, breaking, splitting, scraping, curving, spreading, reuniting, inserting, piercing. Whoever gives some thought to this list will soon realize that — apart from synonyms — it is not easy to add other equally simple operations which are neither immediately reducible to one of those already listed nor a combination of two or more of them. Notice that they must be operations carried out directly by the organism, not only without utensils but also without instruments and, indeed, without any intermediary. We also remarked about how all these elements of work can perhaps be reduced to the two basic operations identified by Verri, bringing together and separating, in which finding similarities, and respectively differences, seem to be reflected. It happens, then, that at a certain stage man (like other animals before him) is able to make some distinctions and some modifications *between* and *in* the physical materials existing in nature, the former being results of perceptive operations and the latter of manipulative operations. All results belonging to this level, *i.e.* the most elementary modifications brought by man to his own natural external environment, will be called hereafter *matteremes*.

If we look for equally elementary elements in the field of linguistic production, we find that the first modifications made on sound material by the speaker are precisely the ones the linguists call *phonemes* as the minimal distinctive units traceable in a spoken chain.[30] Matteremes and phonemes can in turn be broken down. Phonemes can be broken down phonetically into acustico-articulatory "coefficients" or pertinent "features"; matteremes into movements of the human members and displacements of the objects upon which they act (we could talk here about visual-motor coefficients and pertinent features in non-sound material). What interest us are minimal working units producing minimal distinctive units. *Both* in the flow of vocal emission *and* in the flow of corporal movements, we single out some identifiable units which function as pigeon-holes able to accommodate individual variants.

The initial results of work lend themselves to various considerations. First of all, we cannot go below them and continue talking about work. A material object, whether a sound object or not, which bears not even one of the modifications able to make it a mattereme or a phoneme, is part and parcel of the field of "mere nature", it belongs to the world of the "unmanipulated" (compare on this subject Dingler's notion of *Unberührte*, 1942; 1955: 20–33, partially drawn from Husserl's *epoché* and certainly related to *Lebenswelt*). Here a very complicated tangle of problems arises, but we must limit ourselves to mentioning only two of their aspects. The reference to mere nature as unmanipulated can be understood either in the sense of what Hjelmslev calls substance (of the *signatum* as of the *signans*), or as the postulation of an undifferentiated level anterior to any human intervention. The notion of a substance not formed by man lets us glimpse the totality of

---

[30]   At the risk of seeming to espouse one linguistic school instead of another, or more broadly and worse, linguistics *vs.* other social sciences — something that would be against the spirit of a homological investigation —, some terminological decisions had to be taken at this point in order to avoid useless periphrases. The problem is that some situations, on whose existence and structure sufficient agreement might otherwise be reached, are described in very different ways, and with terminologies which cannot be unified, not only by various schools of linguists but also by psychiatrists, anthropologists, archeologists, semioticians, philosophers, and other ists, ans, and ers. On the terminological frolics of even only the linguists, to the astonishment of the non-linguist, cf. Marouzeau 1963 (1951¹), Matoré 1953, Vachek 1966, Pei 1966. The crowding waves of terminology clearly appear in Ivić 1965. As anticipated in footnote 24, we are going to use some terms in Martinet's sense because they allow the doctrine of double articulation to be taken up, discussed, and enlarged — which is the final aim of this section — without having to change terminology as we go on. The main writings where Martinet expounded his views on double articulation are listed in the Bibliographical References.

materials virgin in nature; it belongs to disciplines which are not specifically semiotic, like physics, chemistry, and biology. By this I only want to say that the chemical composition of a matchere or the acoustical structure of a phoneme remain outside the semiotic discourse, or belong only to its fringes (cf. 1.2 at the beginning).

If we postulate instead a level of the undifferentiated, we find that the passage to the differentiated can be caught in three ways: in the realm of genetic psychology (animal as well as human), or as the first moment in a doctrine of the formation of consciousness (Hegel, Husserl), or as the basic step for a theory of the scientific grasp of reality (the *Ergreifung des Wirklichen*, according to a posthumous formulation by Dingler 1955). The study of any substance, whether in Hjelmslev's sense or not, naturally requires that the substance receive forms, and therefore that the level of *originary* differentiations has been abandoned much earlier (cf. Fischer-Jørgensen's approach to the patterning of elementary units). This also amounts to saying that not even the substance of the *signatum* — in spite of its pre-sign indifference — can be studied without systems of signs coming into play. Thus the difference emerges between the study of things upon which work has been done and things upon which work has not been done, taking for granted that the study itself requires complex products of (sign and non-sign) work. It is submitted that the *status* of the genetic code may perhaps be re-considered from this angle. Anything that is studied by humanity is studied at the level attained by humanity.

In the second place, the number of mattheremes and phonemes is limited. It is surprising to notice how these first building stones of every successive material and linguistic working process appear in both fields with approximately the same number or quantity. Man is able to articulate, recognize, and use within natural sound material some few tens of phonemes because his articulatory and acoustic apparatuses are what they are; in the same way, he is able to articulate, recognize, and use only some few tens of mattheremes as basic modifications operated on the non-sound material furnished by nature to him. His hands, his senses, and his brain are what they are (even if they can be modified precisely as a consequence of his work). The number of mattheremes as well as of phonemes is also limited in view of the kinds of working processes that will have to be done upon them.

In the third place, mattheremes and phonemes have no other signification[31] than that of being destined to serve as elements in further units which are only slightly more complex than they are. These further units are the first human products to be endowed with a stable and independent signification. Since we have linguistics

---

[31] That mattheremes and phonemes *have* an instrumental signification, or that they have *only* that, are perhaps debatable issues. It may be that in special circumstances, for instance, mattheremes and phonemes also convey a signification of their own. But since phonemes are elements in linguistic production as mattheremes are elements in material production, let us content ourselves with the notion that they are lumps or bundles of distinctive features (as Bloomfield would put it) in the two fields.

while we don't have any corresponding discipline devoted to the study of material production in all its details (there are, of course, bits and pieces of such study in the realms of philosophy, psychology, and education, and also, but in a scattered way, in the practice of technologies), the elaboration of simple elements into elements which are step by step more complex is perhaps going to have a more familiar look in the field of linguistic production than in that of material production. And still we are always dealing with one and the same thing. It is the one that divides into two. We can discern here one of the senses in which work is appetite held in check, desire under control. In order to carry out a piece of work, man needs a utensil; in order to build the utensil, he must pass through various stages previous to it, beginning with the stage at which he has to effect in nature modifications which lack an independent signification, and which will assume their proper function only when they are further combined with one another.

At this level we can also catch the first irreducible differences between man and the other animals; or at least we can grasp the initial emergence of things which will prove later on to be irreducible differences. Matteremes and phonemes have the simplicity and the availability of mere intermediaries, or at most, of quite elementary instruments. They are therefore remote from utensils proper. Non-human animals too use intermediaries and quite elementary instruments. They move a branch to bring a piece of fruit nearer, *i.e.* they obtain the fruit through the mediation "moved-branch", which makes an intermediary of the branch; they use a stone to crack nuts, that is, they work on the nuts with the elementary instrument of the stone (which, one will notice, recedes into the un-worked-upon as soon as it ceases being used: it has simply been assumed as an elementary instrument). To the same order of considerations belongs the fact that non-human animals also communicate, often in complex ways. These have only begun in the last few years to be subjected to systematic enquiries which probably have many surprises in store for us. There don't seem to exist any animals other than man, however, that produce modifications lacking a stable signification of their own *for the purpose* of combining them later on by means of a working synthesis, in this way producing artefacts endowed with a signification that begins to become specific and stable (in different terminology, this is the situation indicated by Jakobson as the production of "tools to build tools", 1967: 103; see also Tétry 1948). Leaving aside minor exceptions about which very little is known, and while we are waiting for empirical discoveries which will demonstrate the contrary, it turns out that a proper *activity of combining by successive levels* is after all typical of man alone. This activity is, as we know, work.

As soon as we leave the first level and move towards the second, we cross the zone in which Martinet's "second articulation" takes place: the articulation of monemes in phonemes and, as we shall see, of objectemes in matteremes.

Second level: Irreducibly significant items. — At this level we encounter stable, characterizing, and completed modifications made on materials by means of combinations of matteremes or of phonemes. At this point separate, independent new items have been created in the matter of the world. Each of these items already has some sort of a signification, it is already a "significant unit" different from all the others. It can not be broken down without destroying its signification; nor can this signification be traced back to significant elements that precede it at a more elementary level. However, we are not dealing here (if not in a minority of cases) with such completed significations as those we shall begin to encounter only at the next level, the third. The set of these pieces or significant units forms the first articulation of utensils and sentences, as will become clearer for both of the fields of production just as soon as we have all the levels up to that of sentences and utensils laid out in front of us.

Let's examine our old friend the hammer again. It is composed of a head and a handle. According to artisan terminology, the head is in turn composed of a face, a peen, and an eye. The peen is the tapered striking end of the head opposite the face; sometimes it is divided into a claw and serves as a lever for extracting nails. The eye is the hole into which the handle is introduced; it can be circular, oval, or square. The face is the flat part used for hitting: it is that part of the whole head, and thus of the whole hammer, that enters into direct contact with the nail or any other object one is working upon. Let's call these three significant aspects of the head of the hammer *objectemes*.

Objectemes are at one and the same time parts and functions. They *are* parts — or, this is the aspect of them that emerges — every time it is easy to distinguish the objectemes from each other within the higher level unit to which they belong. Whenever this discrete aspect does not emerge we consider them as functions instead. Is there anything like a hierarchy among the parts making up the head of a hammer? There seems to be one in this sense: since the hammer is mainly used for hammering and you hammer specifically with the face, this is the principal significant unit, while the others concur to make its workings more precise, or equip it with additional signification in various ways. Let us call the part or aspect or function that bears the principal signification a *lexobjecteme* and the others *morphobjectemes*. The face of the head of the hammer is a lexobjecteme; the peen and the eye are morphobjectemes.

In the field of linguistic production the significant units described above are pieces of a complexity inferior to or, at the most, equal to that of the word.[32] As announced we are going to use Martinet's term *monemes* for such pieces or significant units in linguistic production. We can also further transpose the hierarchy of material objects to the linguistic field, and specify that monemes subdivide into *lexemes* (also called *semantemes*) when they constitute the significant nucleus, and *morphemes* when they serve to modify the nucleus. Thus 'love' and 's' are both monemes; but the former is a lexeme, the latter a morpheme (as a completed word,

---

[32] For the problem of what should be called a "linguistic unit", cf. Ebeling 1960; for words in particular, Krámský 1969.

'loves' belongs to the third level of this schema). It belongs to the nature of object-emes and monemes that they can be taken apart, for each of them is the result of combinations made with results of previous operations. The working process leading to any given moneme or objecteme is always the same. Thus the moneme 'love' can be analyzed into phonemes, as the objecteme face (of the hammer) into matter-emes. As categories or pigeon-holes, phonemes and matteremes cannot undergo any change; or better, a change brought to phonemes and matteremes would affect to some extent the whole of whatever sign system is built upon them. Their combination gives rise to a high number of monemes, and of objectemes respectively, usually several thousand or tens of thousands for every historical language and for every objectual, non-verbal sign system of a given community.

The signification of all the products described up to this point lies in the first place in this, that they are all *products of work*. This includes the way in which they are produced, the functions which they have to be able to carry out and their lending themselves to different uses for different ends, the relations into which they enter with other products of work, and so on. Just these, and not others, are the factors that constitute their signification in the general sense. Let us think for a moment instead about the consequences we would have to face if we wanted to attribute to products a signification *that accompanied them*, that is, if we wanted to think of them only as *signantia* and started searching for their respective *signata*. With things put in these terms, signification ought to join the products of work in a realm different from that of matter. This would mean resorting to a dualistic conception of human activity, and therefore, in the last analysis, bringing into play some non-human factor of what is human. It is certainly legitimate to ask oneself what is the signification (what they are used for) of the monemes constituting the word 'loves', *i.e.* 'love' and 's'; in the same way it is legitimate to ask ourselves what is the signification (what they are used for) of the parts constituting the head of the hammer, *i.e.* the peen, the eye, and the face. But we would never dream of relegating the signification of these "material" pieces to a different realm; in the same way it is advisable not to try to do it with "linguistic" pieces.

An argument upon which we cannot dwell here, but which would complete this sketch of a homological schema, concerns the place of the noises[33] and the cries that men produce. It seems to me that the noise and the cry correspond somehow to the intermediary and to the elementary instrument. The production of a noise in the field of signs is like the use of an intermediary in the field of material objects. A cry is like an elementary instrument, used and then left there. Noise and cry on the one hand, intermediary and elementary instrument on the other, do in

---

[33] We speak here of noises actually produced by men and which are either intended to mean something or can be construed as meaning something by an onlooker independent of the intention of the producer. No reference to 'noise' as used in information theory is involved at this stage. It follows that when the channel of the noise-message is disturbed, we shall have to say that there is a noise diminishing the quantity of information carried by another noise. Total noise deprived of internal differences would have as much information as total silence.

fact present the character of being used, but without there having been previous work done upon them. A discussion of them would therefore enter almost fully into the first two levels distinguished above: in the first level because very little or no work has been exercised upon them, in the second because of the use that can be made of them anyhow (while a phoneme or a mattereme does not have any distinct use *per se*).

Third level: "Completed" pieces. — If we go on towards more complex units, in the field of material production we find, *in the first instance*, the pieces constituting a utensil, those whose parts we have so far described as objectemes. With restrictions which we will specify later, let us call these "completed" pieces; and since we lack a specialistic term we will keep on using this expression even when it seems unsatisfactory.

Often, perhaps in the majority of cases, these pieces are more or less easily separable from each other: for example the head and the handle of a hammer, the vamp and the sole of a shoe, the lens and the frame of a pair of glasses. A hammer is a complete utensil (more about this later on); the head and the handle are the "completed pieces" which make it up; the face, the peen, and the eye are the objectemes of which the head consists. The difference between an objecteme and a "completed piece" is clear in cases like these. A stable modification made by man in non-sound matter, endowed with a generic signification and able to be used in various ways, for example a wooden plank of a given form, is an objecteme. A semi-finished product which already lends itself, and is limited, to a particular use or working process, for example a wooden plank that has been reinforced, varnished, and accurately smoothed, and under which legs can be attached to obtain a table, is a "completed piece". Here various objectemes have been joined to each other in such a way as to form units which in turn are immediately able to give rise to finished utensils. In fact, putting two or more "completed pieces" together usually suffices to give us a utensil in its turn complete and ready for use. By this we do not at all mean to exclude that there may be utensils made up of a single "completed piece" (for example, a walking stick made from a single piece of wood, without other additions). However, we must distinguish carefully between utensils made up of a single "completed piece" and the isolated use of a "completed piece", perhaps as a substitute for a utensil which we lack. Nor should we ignore the existence of groups of "completed pieces" which may even be fairly complex but which are not yet organized in such a way as to constitute a utensil proper.

In this first instance, we said above — for a little thought shows us that things are not that simple. For expository purposes we have used some examples rather than others, and in so doing the situation has undergone a process of simplification. The combination of matteremes in objectemes, of objectemes in "completed pieces", and of "completed pieces" in utensils is obvious in the case of the hammer as in all artefacts which are at the same time equally simple and equally easy to take apart. It is not at all obvious for other, less simple utensils, or for utensils which are equally simple but not equally easy to take apart. A tree cultivated in the garden, regularly fertilized, pruned, and protected from the cold, is an artefact too. Certainly, there is a sense in which we can say that a tree in flower is the sum of its own natural growth, plus the fertilizer, the plastic that protected it during the winter, and the pruning operations. But the sense in which we are dealing with component parts which have been pre-produced and then put together is different from that of the hammer. A big oil jar appears to us as a single piece. If we wanted to distinguish "completed pieces", objectemes, and matteremes in it, we certainly wouldn't succeed with the same comfortably discontinuous progression that we find in other cases, and perhaps we would not even succeed in doing it convincingly. Its matteremes have been resolved step by step into objectemes, which have been resolved in turn into "completed pieces", which, without a break in continuity, constitute the finished artefact, the utensil, jar. A plastic toy of a complex shape but stamped out by a single operation does not possess matteremes and objectemes independent from those belonging in an ideal way to the project according to which the matrix used in the stamping machine has been realized. Sailor's knots, from the simplest to the most incredibly complex, are artefacts realized by operating on a single "completed piece"; we can use a longer or shorter stretch of rope, the only limits to this being that there must be enough rope for tying and using the various knots; the objectemes of the rope are a large number of intertwined fibers.

Examples could be multiplied. Those offered here are already sufficient for raising a number of points which limit or alter the notion of "completed pieces", and in part also the notion of objectemes, as well as the relations between the two. There are artefacts produced by letting natural forces develop, or by assisting them. There are others in which no separation or difference can be found between matteremes and objectemes — artefacts, that is, in which the production of matteremes slowly assumes the status of a production of objectemes without a break in continuity. There are still other artefacts in which continuity is to be found in the process by which objectemes become "pieces" of the finished utensil (pieces which are therefore no longer "completed" *by themselves*). Others in which it is difficult or even impossible to distinguish between the level of objectemes and that of "completed pieces". There are also artefacts in which the objectemes that go together to form "completed pieces", or some of these objectemes, can be traced only as *functions* present in the "completed pieces", this being clear sometimes only from the vantage point of the finished utensil. And there are even artefacts where the level of the utensil seems to be reached directly by mere accumulation of matteremes.

All this shows how the level of "completed pieces" — as products at an intermediate stage between objectemes and utensils — may even be a sheer abstraction by which we are trying provisionally to fix some stage of the very complicated processes of material production. At this point it is useful to distinguish various families of objectual sign systems. Some utensils belong to families that we may call analytic, where every "completed piece", so to say by "isolating" itself, tends to remain always the same, as such always distinguishable from all the others; the difference between "completed pieces" and objectemes here tends to disappear. Then there are families where "completed pieces" which are homologous to each other are produced by means of different objectemes. These objectemes carry out the same function (even without having anything else in common) only because of the way in which they are fixed in constant objectual nuclei, that is, in lexob-jectemes. And there are families where, instead, the objectemes are the ones that remain always equal to themselves, so that they reappear with the same function in the formulation of different "completed pieces" by being so to say pasted on to each other in different ways. The different "completed pieces" can here be reduced to constituent objectemes of a clearly inferior level (this is the family to which the hammer belongs). One of the conclusions to be drawn when we consider the multiplicity of the families of objectual artefacts, is that they harbor remarkable differences in the relations between objectemes and "completed pieces". We can imagine that, given an objectual sign system, the *ratio* between the number of the objectemes and the number of "completed pieces" may be calculated, and that the result may offer an index of the analyticity of the utensils belonging to that family. The closer such *ratio* is to 1, the less one will be able to distinguish between ob-jectemes and "finished pieces", and the more the utensil will be composed directly of objectemes.

These and other similar particularities of the various arts and trades have certainly been well-recognized throughout the millennia by their respective master artisans, even though they set them out and commented on them almost exclusively in their own language, practising and refining the non-verbal codes of their arts, and verbally talking about them only for the purpose of handing the art down to others. The masters of the verbal arts, shut up as they were in a class isolation which convinced them of the superiority of intellectual over manual labor, certain-ly did not pay attention to the way in which the master artisans of the non-verbal arts were aware on their own of what they were doing all the time. Recently things have changed, however. Part of the immense complexity and variety of produc-tion seems to have made an impression on the masters of verbal arts also. We face difficulties very similar to the non-verbal difficulties described in the last few pages, in the linguistic field as well, just as soon as we begin to deal with "com-pleted pieces" of a level higher than that of monemes, like so-called "words" and other "linguistic units" (syntagms, locutions, dictions, phrases). Thus, for in-stance, one recognized master of the verbal arts explains how the difference between a completed word and a moneme, for example between the English word *unacceptable* and the three monemes *un*, *accept*, and *able* (which in his termi-nology are "morphemes"), may seem at first glance just as acceptable as instead it turns out to be unacceptable as soon as we try to establish general rules capable of explaining the exceptions and of being extended beyond the limits of any individual historical language (Lyons 1968: Chapter Five). This is not the place to take up current discussions about the nature of words and other units in which it may seem convenient to subdivide the spoken chain. The variety of human languages, we must admit, is almost as great as the variety of objectual sign systems — even if we mustn't forget that in the latter very different bodily residues come into play, because their *signantia* are made of multiple substances instead of being limited (perhaps in a slightly monotonous way) to sound (or at the most graphic) substance.

Not directly relevant for the immediate ends of our classification by successive levels — which in turn only has the purpose of setting forth the homology of production — are the different ways in which, in the various languages, distinctions can be drawn within the *continuum* that goes from a word-moneme constituted by a single phoneme up to an extended and complex syntagm. Before going ahead to the level of sentences and utensils, we have only to recall one more thing, *i.e.* that it is within the last two levels distinguished, the second and the third, that the "first articulation" takes place. This is the articulation of utensils and sentences in "completed pieces" and/or objectemes, and, respectively, in words and/or monemes. In a general theory of material production it is necessary to renounce the naïve view that utensils are always and only the combinations of prefabricated pieces — almost as if there were a sort of universal lexicon of such pieces, so that to obtain utensils it would be enough to apply constant rules to equally constant classes of pieces. Contemporary linguistic theory has arrived at a similar renunciation and is now a long way from maintaining that there are rules operating directly upon word-classes and that sentences are generated by applying such rules to all the lovely ready-made words listed in the dictionary. The fact remains that the utensil and the sentence occupy a recognizedly central position in their respective productions and that they are, after all, reducible to simpler elements.

3.2.2 *Utensils and sentences*

Fourth level: Utensils and sentences. — This is, in an order of rising complexity, the first level at which we encounter fully finished though still very simple artefacts lending themselves to *uses* or *working processes* which are complete in their turn. Let's call artefacts at this level *utensils,* generalizing the term somewhat, and, respectively, *sentences.* Sentences are verbal utensils, so that it may be said that all utensils divide into material (or, non-verbal) and linguistic (or, verbal) utensils, and that the latter are also called sentences[34]. For clarity's sake, however, we

---

[34] Alternatively, we may confine ourselves to speaking only in terms of sentences, and specify that there are *verbal sentences* and *non-verbal sentences*; and that the latter, which are also called utensils, belong to a number of non-verbal sign-systems of the objectual kind (cf. 1.3

shall mainly use 'utensils' for *material utensils*, and 'sentences' for *linguistic utensils*; and in using 'utensils' for both we shall always add the clause 'whether material or linguistic', or 'whether non-verbal or verbal'.

Examples of various types of simple material utensils are hammers, sickles, flags, stilettos, bottles, shoes, handkerchiefs, pots, spoons, pipes, tobacco pouches, cages, stools, chairs; and so are lawns and the trees and bushes in the garden insofar as they comply with the double character of being products of work and objects for use (even if one doesn't usually call them utensils). Simple pieces of more complex machines, like gears or tire inner tubes are also simple utensils, although they are usually employed only within more complex totalities. Examples of simple sentences are: 'the water is hot', 'the daisy is a flower', 'the apple is tasty', 'the sun will shine', 'it's raining', 'Amelia laughed', 'the children were play-ing', 'children like toys', 'Eve ate the apple', 'Adam ate the apple too', 'the snake smiled', 'hurray for Europe!', 'down with Europe-centrism!', 'he came here', 'come here!', 'are you coming here?', 'aren't you coming here?', 'why don't you come here?', 'why didn't you come here yesterday?', 'she didn't want to come', 'they will not be able to get there', and so on. These are sentences in the traditional sense. Let us say in traditional jargon that they are all composed of subject, verb, and predicate, or of subject and intransitive verb, in some cases with slight syn-tactical complications which are not supposed to involve any necessary reference to *other* sentences.

Simple utensils, whether verbal or non-verbal, present the differential character with regard to previous products, of possessing *in se* the *form* of the use or of the working process to which they lend themselves. Shoes are used for wearing, hammers for hammering, pipes for smoking, lawns for restful walking, and so on. Instead, the "completed pieces" and/or the objectemes of which they are made up, although they lend themselves to various uses, do not possess this form. With the finished utensil, as simple as it may be, the material productive process has arrived at its first halt; a working cycle has reached a conclusion, though a provisional one. The same can be said for verbal utensils, *i.e.* for simple sentences: as complex and as diverse as their genesis may be in the various languages, sentences possess, differently from words and/or monemes, the form of the use to which they lend

---

ad finem). While for the use of 'sentence' we may refer to current linguistic discussion — after all, in the early thirties there were 160 definitions of 'sentence' available in the literature, as Ivić reports (1956 : 203 note 1) —, the use of 'utensil' requires a few comments. As explained in the text, we use it here in the largest and perhaps in an extended sense, to mean any artefact of the objectual kind belonging to the level where some sort of *completeness has at least dawned*. In this usage utensils comprehend not only tools or implements which can be used in further work, like hammers, or to make something simply available, like corkscrews; not only pieces which are not used by themselves but go into something more complex as distinguish-able and necessary elements, like carbureters or loudspeakers; but also all useful objects destined for consumption, *i.e.* for the production of consumers (cf. 2.4 and footnote 14), like a loaf of bread or the wine contained in a bottle (immediate consumption), or like a pair of shoes or a bottle containing wine or any other liquid (protracted, or instrumental consumption).

themselves — whether it is a question of using them just as they are as messages, or instead of combining them with other simple sentences to obtain complex sentences and then discourses. If I say 'laughed' I don't yet know who was laughing *or not laughing*, while if I say 'Amelia laughed' I know that a person of the female sex did *not* do any of the many things that are excluded by the indication of the thing she was doing, that is, laughing.

Common to all the pieces of the first three levels (putting it in a unitary way: previous to the utensil, and respectively to the sentence) is the fact that they are not usually used alone; they are not ends in themselves. They are *instrumental pieces* whose ends lie outside of them, serving precisely and only for this, the production of pieces of a higher level, beginning with the level which we have here distinguished as the fourth, *i.e.* with utensils and sentences. Nobody ever set himself the task of producing sixty-six hammer handles without any regard to their respective heads, without at least supposing that somebody else was going to produce the heads; nobody ever went about plowing thirty-three acres of land in the certitude that he would never be able to sow it, or in the ignorance of the existence of seeds. Nobody repeats a given moneme, well-identified as such, ninety-nine times without ever going on to combine it with others. When things like this do happen we talk about pathology, or we have to construct very complicated explanatory contexts. We *usually* don't have any use for an isolated word or piece of a utensil. It does not at all follow from this that we don't know what their signification or function is. But the idea of the utensil must be operating for anybody to be able to go back to the first level and then come down again through the second and third, following the flux of work, to the fourth, where the realization of the idea itself takes place. In the same way, we can isolate and discuss words and monemes only if we possess the idea of the sentence. In a different sense, however, the utensil and the sentence do presuppose their own parts. We will come back to some aspects of this situation in 3.3.

The fact is that the notion of what is presupposed must not be made absolute. To begin with, the notion of a generative idea must not be made absolute, as is typical in old and new idealism, since even the idea which it seems indispensable to possess cannot itself have avoided being formed little by little in the course of social evolution. As far back as we try to go, we will still have to stop at the period in which the type of activity called work appeared on the planet, in so far as the appetite of certain primates was held in check and between their needs and the respective satisfaction of the needs something universal was inserted. It is in fact tautological that there are no *human* ideas previous to homination. Isn't it a little ridiculous to imagine that one fine morning, even if we may concede that he had slept on a fortuitous bed of fronds, a single anthropoid merrily woke up *with* the idea of a sentence or a utensil all formed in his brain. (A geometrical idea, as Husserl says in Appendix III of the *Krisis*, would make the performance particularly stirring; but also the idea of nothing more than a pot would do.) And that that very anthropoid went about realizing his idea by *facing an intact nature for the first time*.

But on the other hand, not even the notion of the elements of the lowest level should be made absolute. For, unless we indulge in a sort of childish evolution-istic mechanicism, it would be almost insane to suppose that first man produced matteremes and phonemes without doing anything else, and only afterwards dedi-cated himself to the production of objectemes and monemes, passing over to the production of "finished pieces" and words at a still successive stage. And then again that, perhaps after having rested for some tens of thousands of years, he made the further step of starting to combine the previous products (which meanwhile had lain there waiting for him) into utensils and sentences.

The central character of the utensil and of the sentence in the process of pro-duction, and thus also in the process of social reproduction as a whole, lies pre-cisely in this duality or reciprocity: they presuppose the pieces that go together in forming them, and are in turn presupposed by them. Of utensils and sentences, and of these alone, we can say that they are the finished items of the lowest level, in which the reciprocity of presupposition is fully present. That is: it is fully pre-sent, as we will mention, also in items of a higher level. Moreover it is also pre-sent, but not *fully* present, in the relation between monemes and words and be-tween phonemes and monemes, and respectively between objectemes and "com-pleted pieces", and between matteremes and objectemes.

All this amounts to saying two complementary things: the first, that sentences and utensils have been developed together with their own component pieces; the second, that the quality of being utensils and sentences is not an absolute quality but rather a relative quality. There are available sentences and utensils that are always such, but also utensils and sentences that *become* such in given circum-stances but stop being such when those circumstances dissolve. Thus sailor's knots are utensils with respect to the rope that functions as a "completed piece"; but the rope is a utensil with regard to the strands of which it is composed. 'It's a lovely day for fishing trout' is a sentence; but so are, if taken by themselves in given circumstances, 'it's a lovely day', 'a day for fishing', 'fishing trout', and even 'trout!'.

These considerations bring us to the next level of our schema.

Fifth level: Aggregates of utensils. — In addition to simple utensils there are also compound utensils. The notion of compound utensils is in turn a compound notion. Space and time, to which the real responsibility must be attributed for the accidental death of the passer-by hit by the Hegelian roofing-tile, manifest their dominion even here. Compound utensils may be implements with a multiple use, which always remain what they are themselves but are built in such a way as to be applicable in different working processes; or they may rest on the joint use of two different utensils which must be applied, either contemporaneously or one after the other, in the same working process, or in two working processes one of which is subordinate to the other or both of which concur to one purpose. Some examples are: a sofa bed, a complete suit made up of trousers, jacket, and vest, simple gardening tools seen as a whole, a group of weights for a scale, a wallet for documents, notes, and coins. In the field of linguistic production we have sentences combined or interconnected in various ways, like those in the following discourse: 'Rome is the capital of Italy, it has almost three million inhabitants, it is situated about half-way between Florence and Naples, it possesses many beautiful monuments, the traffic is terrible there, it is the seat of both the Papacy and the largest official Communist Party in the West'.

One soon realizes that the distinction between simple utensils and sentences and compound ones is much more arduous than it may seem at first glance, or than it may appear from the examination of a single group of examples. If the disjunction of the levels is to be measured on the yardstick offered by such substantial differences as those between matteremes and objectemes (respectively between phonemes and monemes), or the differences between objectemes (or "completed pieces") and utensils (respectively, between monemes — or words — and sentences), we might perhaps decide to renounce distinguishing the fifth level from the fourth. There is not an equally important leap here between simple and complex. What is simple and what is complex with regard to utensils and sentences depends upon too many criteria. Probably only the application of distributional criteria to a single "text" of objectemes or monemes, or even better, to the totality of an objectual or verbal sign system, would permit us at the present stage of research to provisionally stratify categories of utensils and sentences according to a larger or smaller degree of complexity; provisionally, since distributional procedures can be nothing other than rationalistic-formal approximations imposed on material which has been collected only empirically — one way for keeping side-by-side the two disjoined members of a process which in reality is unitary and dialectical.

Still, once two or more utensils, or two or more sentences which are distinct from each other (without repeating the reservations about the various ways in which they are composed) have been joined in some way for an end which cannot be accomplished by a single utensil or a single sentence, a situation arises which we do not have the liberty to ignore. What we are concerned with here is this, that the two or more utensils or sentences *have entered into a relation with each other*. Dealing with work in the last section we saw how at a certain point the working process coagulates in an artefact which then remains there like a river-lock or synapse, conditioning every other working process by its own presence. Utensils and sentences, as we mentioned then, and as we have been trying to show in the preceding pages, are the most typical examples of artefacts endowed with this character. In 6.4 we shall come back to the sentence and try to examine it in terms of the "unfolding" of the values internal to the words (or monemes) composing it. Well then, when two or more utensils or sentences enter into relationship, the dialectic internal to a single utensil or sentence *begins* to become a dialectic external to each of them. This amounts to saying that a new totality *begins* to form, dialectically posterior to that of the utensil or sentence. The dawning of this new totality had to be pointed out somehow to the reader, and this is the sense of the distinction made between the fourth level and the fifth. As soon as a dialectic *external* to the utensil or sentence has *fully* emerged, we have reached a further level, the sixth: we are, in fact, at the threshold of a fascinating stage, that of mechanism.

3.2.3 *After utensils and sentences*

Once we have reached and recognized the utensil — either material or linguistic — as the central unit of all production, everything that follows it in order of complexity is a combination of utensils. The property of being useful for something, as we know, does certainly not belong to utensils alone: it belongs to all artefacts (with the partial and perhaps niggling reservations made in 2.1 and 2.3.1) and is the most general matrix for possessing a signification (3.2.1). The utensil is "only" an artefact at an intermediate level between the first elementary modifications which man brings to nature and his highest constructions. At the same time, the utensil is the definitive sign of the irreversible separation of man from all other animals, not only because it is a finished product of work and requires the dialectic of exchange, but also because, more specifically, it has been obtained through a double selection of instrumental artefacts of a lower level, and therefore presupposes the use of communitary codes (we shall come back to this last point at the end of the section). As Hegel says: «The plough is nobler than the immediate pleasures which are procured through it and which are the aims. The tool preserves itself, while the immediate pleasures vanish away and are forgotten».[35]

Sixth level: Mechanism. — The first new totality built by man after the utensil is the mechanism. We shall describe a material (non-verbal) mechanism as a *machine*, and a linguistic (verbal) mechanism as a *syllogism* (see below in the text, and note 38). Machines are utensils combined and organized for an end, endowed with the capability of working in a uniform way, even prescinding from how and where they are used and from who uses them. When it has assumed the rank of a mechanism, the artefact is called upon to carry out a working process which is already present or anticipated in its structure. The relation between working process and structure has become so close that the working process is at this point more or less obligatory; other working processes are excluded because they are impossible, or have an effect incompatible with the one expected, or are absurd. All this can be caught in the first place almost intuitively — although the

---

[35] «Der Pflug ist ehrenvoller, als unmittelbar die Genüsse sind, welche durch ihn bereitet werden und die Zwecke sind. Das Werkzeug erhält sich, während die unmittelbaren Genüsse vergehen und vergessen werden» (*Wissenschaft der Logik*, Drittes Buch, Zweiter Abschnitt, Die Objektivität, 3. Kapitel (Teleologie), Lasson's Herausgebung, II : 398). For an alternative English wording see Johnston and Struthers' translation, Volume Two: 388.

"intuition" to which we have recourse here is nothing other than the only partially conscious stratification of the common experiences we have as individuals belonging to non-primitive communities. Consider, in the field of material production, the way in which looms "work", and bicycles, record players, lathes, electric saws, typewriters. What we aim at describing here is the system of the differences between such artefacts and the more simple artefacts we have so far discussed as belonging to lower levels. Not that the advent of the mechanism has excluded the worker; it continues to require him. But while at previous levels the worker had to carry out the whole working process himself, here it suffices that he put the machine he has decided to use in motion. Naturally, he has to have learned this too; but the machine functions "on its own", in one way and not in another, according to an operational cycle fixed beforehand. While external material operations done by anyone who uses a simple utensil still have an internal material guide, the working operations of a machine no longer need a guide of this sort for the good reason that they *are* themselves external material operations carried out according to a plan (cf. 2.4.1, and Section Two generally). The functioning of a machine appears as something pseudo-natural which has been generated by society. The machine bears its own programs and imposes them. Man, not satisfied with programming himself as an individual, has come to the point of programming the behavior of pieces of matter external to him. The modifications which a material machine has to be able to bring about in the world if it functions well, are constant and impersonal modifications: the loom always weaves, impersonally. The worker has gone outside of himself, he has inscribed himself in nature, he has ordered her to guide his own working steps.

Between the level of the utensil and that of the mechanism, then, we have a real substantial difference, a qualitative leap due to the formation of a new totality. Just as the totality "utensil" is not reducible to the pieces of which it is composed, neither is the totality "machine". We can of course think of the vanishing point where a utensil is used as a machine; and there can be cases of utensils that so to say shade off into machines as well as cases of machines used as utensils. For example, the literature is uncertain whether to call a plow a utensil or a machine; and the expression 'machine-tool' is in current usage. The complexity of production compels us — as the case arises — not to forget these prudential remarks. Still the new totality of mechanism imposes itself. Using a screwdriver merely as a weight for a scale is not only using it in an improper way, but also wasting it. What need is there to use a specific utensil like a screwdriver for its weight alone, one can ask oneself. But the waste and the regression are immeasurably more serious if the weight is a high precision, water-proof, self-winding watch.

In what, then, does a machine that is no longer a utensil consist? What "additions" must the structure of the utensil receive for a new totality of a higher level to be born? Does a minimal level of mechanism exist beneath which we cannot talk about machines and revert instead to utensils? I want to hazard an answer, or better a proposal, as abstract as it may sound. So that an artefact may proceed to the rank of a machine, there must be at the start (at least) two pieces which condition each other reciprocally. Each of these two pieces must have a recognizable sense and a precise function. In brief, there must be (at least) two utensils. Now, if the two utensils confined themselves to contrasting with one another, one of the two might take the upper hand, or there might not even be any decisive action between the two. Nothing new would be formed. The two utensils must instead (i) find themselves in *opposition*, and (ii) this opposition must be overcome dialectically, that is, it must give rise to a synthesis. The kernel of mechanism lies precisely in this, that an artefact in the position of synthesis carries out the role of at least two utensils in opposition to each other. The two elements must become three, and binarism give way to dialectic. Let's take it up again. Two utensils act upon each other; this reciprocal action, whether or not it is physically represented by a third artefact of a higher level, is the dialectical sum of the work that the two utensils can carry out separately (or of essential parts of this work). The two elements have become three. When this happens, the mechanism dawns.

Thus, for example, the archer draws the string of a bow and thereby bends the wood, storing up energy which will later be discharged all at once into the arrow. In the first phase the string acts upon the wood, in the second, the wood upon the arrow through the string. The string so to say belongs to the bow when it is drawn, and belongs to the arrow when it is released. The string is the mediating element. Although they are processed in such a way as to work together, wood, string, and arrow can be useful for something and be considered utensils each on its own account; but the machine "bow-and-arrows" (one of the most primitive machines) consists of the sum of the *two actions* of drawing and releasing, and cannot be reduced to one of them alone. Notice that the two actions are similar but certainly not identical; indeed, the machine "bow-and-arrows" benefits precisely from the way they differ. They are moreover separated in time; finally, the man who has accumulated energy by drawing the bow can release it at his discretion, triggering the machine without otherwise intervening in the process. A similar mechanism is to be found in the oar and the rowlock: one rows by applying a force to the arm of a lever, which, resting on a fulcrum, transmits the force to the resistance of the water and thus moves the boat. The oar and the rowlock are utensils, the whole made up of the two together is a machine.

Let us consider now the wheel-and-axle and its differences from a mere roller. The roller is among the most primitive of utensils, at the confines of the mere instrument, even when it is produced on purpose. If one uses the trunk of a tree which has been struck down by lightning as a roller, the level of the utensil is not even reached and what one is using is only an instrument which then is abandoned there, left to itself like a cry which serves only once for attracting attention. The roller comprehends in itself the functions of both wheel and axle, but in a still unseparated manner. In the wheel-and-axle instead the two functions have been externalized for they have been embodied in two materially independent artefacts. An internal dialectic has become external. Man has discovered and extracted it and is by now able to reproduce it and make it work at his orders. At this stage, *post eventum*, he can also look backwards and say that that dialectic was present already in the roller, though in an undistinguished and indeed "undistinguishable" manner. The wheel-and-axle is manufactured according to a plan and carries out its function insofar as the wheel rotates on the axle, which in turn forms one piece with a cart. In this way the cart is easier to push. Because of its exploiting in this way rotary motion, the wheel-and-axle deserves to be considered a primitive machine.

Another example, perhaps a heterodox one, could be that of a pot filled with water and put over a fire of wood which has been arranged under it and lighted on purpose. Much human knowledge already goes into this simple procedure. Used in this way for boiling something, the pot is not just a mere container. It acts on the fire because it arrests the flame and receives it according to its shape and structure; the fire, naturally, acts on it by heating it. The water can be heated by the fire by virtue of the pot; and the pot can avoid getting burned by virtue of the water to which it transmits the heat received from the fire. The pot is the mediating element. Hot water is the result of the operation within this machine, much as the hurled arrow within the machine bow-and-arrows. An arrow, then, is expected to hit some target as hot water is expected to boil raw food: with these achievements the machine has been successfully applied. There is, then, a reciprocal action between the water-filled pot and the fire which is synthetically overcome by the operation of boiling. It is remarkable that the whole operation is described in terms of what happens primarily to the water (the importance of boiling when compared to roasting is well-known: in some Amerindian languages, 'to boil' is synonymous with 'to banquet'). One boils something by putting a water-filled pot and a proper fire in the above relation and letting this elementary machine do its job.

Other primitive machines, just a little more complicated than utensils, are traps, bow drills (both derived from the bow or kin to it), bellows and blow pipes, bolas (which already require a complex play of forces). Generally, all so-called "simple machines" of elementary physics and their derivatives are primitive.[36] This is not the place for dwelling technically on the nature of these machines, the formal description of which belongs to abstract scientific discourse, *i.e.* to a recent development of human thought. Reference to the section on statics in any text of mechanics

---

[36] For a description of mans earliest technological endeavors, cf. Volume I of *A history of technology*, 1965 impression with corrections (1954[1]), especially Parts I, II, and III. Papers by Oakley, Childe, Harrison, Sommerfelt, Leach, Leakey, Forde, Forbes, and Bradford, as listed in the References, will easily be connected by topic to various moments of the treatment given in the text. Cf. also Hooke in Part VII of Volume I, and references to earlier developments in Volume II (for instance Jope). Other histories of science and/or technology where im-

will suffice. It is advisable to recall, however, that every simple machine is a device in which a resistant force is counter-balanced by a motive force. The machine is the result of *the play of* these *two forces* — whether this happens through the exploitation of the equilibrium of the bodies around an axis of simple rotation (lever, winch, and pulley); or the motive force counter-balances only a small component of the resistant force, releasing the residual component on a fixed tie (inclined plane, wedge, and screw); or, finally, the forces are transformed into pressure by making them act upon pistons with conveniently different areas, according to Pascal's principle of the equivalence of pressure in all the particles of a liquid in a state of rest (hydraulic press).[37]

In the field of linguistic production, the difference between the level of mechanism and previous levels can be struck in the bullseye as soon as one considers the *syllogism*.[38] The syllogism starts from two sentences (from the enunciation of

---

portant observations on the dawning of mechanism can be found are Derry and Williams (1960), Kranzberg and Pursell (eds., 1967), Lilley (1966), Bernal (1965). Cf. Forbes 1958, Oakley 1959 and 1961 (in *Social life of early man*: 176-193), and the works of Gordon Childe. See also the *Dictionnaire archéologique des techniques*, 1963-1964; and other essays in *Social life of early man*, 1961.

What should be *called* a utensil or instrument or tool, and what should be called a machine, is to some extent open to discussion. For instance Störig (1965 : 26) uses 'instruments' [*Werkzeug*] for the hammer, 'machine' for the plough and the cart. The difference rests on the amount of thinking which goes into the machine as compared with the instrument: «even simple machines like the lever, the pump, or, for instance, the ballistas used in forgone wars presuppose a theoretical foundation» (26). The genealogy of earliest machines is also open to disagreement, and one comes across many statement like the following by Larssen (1969² : 15): the bow «may be regarded as the *first device* for storing up energy, to be released at will» (italics mine). Whether there are or not simpler and earlier examples, will depend on how one conceives of man's will, and on what is meant by 'releasing'.

In Hegel's *Jenaer Realphilosophie* of 1805-1806 mechanism is viewed as a modification of man's work (Hoffmeister's edition: 197fll. and 213 fll.), and the machine is defined as relationship of the abstract forms of space and time, *i.e.* as abstract external activity (215). Hegel was always deeply interested in the mechanical process; his most thorough treatment is, of course, in the *Wissenschaft der Logik*: cf., in Lasson's edition, II: 359-406 (English transl. Vol. II: 350-394). And see footnote 38 hereafter.

[37] As noted by Störig (1965 : 27), Bernal (Volume I: 117 fll.), Forti (Volume I: 27-32), and practically all students of technology who don't confine themselves to externally material artefacts, there are also "non-material" instruments and machines, beginning with the zero and the value acquired by figures according to their position. These, however, belong to the other division of our dual enquiry, *i.e.* to linguistic production (actually, to sign production in general). More on this below in the text.

[38] We are all so accustomed to the term syllogism in its contemporary technical sense, that it isn't entirely useless to recall that it came from σύν and λόγος, that the Greek term has a host of different meanings circling around the notion of "collecting" or "putting together", and that a huge number of related terms also derive from the union of σύν with some form of a verb of action, especially λέγω (the συλλογεύς, for example, was the man who called in confiscated property). In studying the dawning of syllogism as homologous to the dawning of mechanism, we have to keep in mind the pre-scientific linguistic family from which it arose and to which linguistically it still belongs. Otherwise we would fall into an anti-genetic fallacy.

The Hegel of Jena had already anticipated the idea that the work of man with the instrument is essentially a syllogism (cf. Lukács 1948, new edition 1967: 433, and *passim*). In the *Wissenschaft der Logik* the syllogism and the mechanism have a parallel treatment: the former

two propositions), which are put to work together. The conclusion is the dialectical sum of the two premises. The content of the conclusion was present in the premises, but it emerges from them on the condition of their entering into reciprocal action. We cannot have less than three pieces if we want to talk about a syllogism. The elementary form of the syllogism, indeed of the various possible syllogisms, is homologous to the elementary form of the various possible mechanisms in the field of material production. One has to distinguish here in both fields between the study of pure and elementary forms and the study of whatever is actually produced in reality. As they are non-existent or extremely rare in material production, pure and elementary forms are also rare in the field of linguistic production. This amounts to saying that we are not expected to find and discuss the mechanism only in the formalized study of mechanics or logic, but rather all along the variety of everything that assumes some sort of mechanical power in either field.[39]

For a verbal mechanism to begin emerging, a more or less correct and complete argument, or just any grouping of sentences organized for some end, capable of communicating something in an at least relatively unambiguous way to any interpreter, is sufficient. One important requirement is that a double disconnection take place: the group of sentences must function *regardless of* (i) their immediate, actual use by whoever has emitted them, whether or not he is responsible for having organized them in that way; and (ii) the context they belonged to originally or in which they happen to be placed later on. This means that a given message, usually a non-rudimentary one, is already inserted in the structure of the linguistic

---

is the final stage of "Subjectivity", the latter is the initial stage of "Objectivity" (cf. footnote 36). For Hegel, as is well known, things had mainly to go from the inside to the outside; or, they had to be prepared within the subject's mind before they could be used in the external natural world. We needn't in the least accept his idealistic bias in order to be able fully to appreciate the depth and rigor of his treatment of both mechanism and syllogism, beginning with his vision into their homological structure.

[39] Although we must admit of some parochial, academic, insular, cultural, ideological, social, and political limitations of theirs, Oxford-Cambridge philosophers, especially in the Fifties, did certainly have the merit of dealing carefully with *informal linguistic mechanisms* as found in the sort of language they called natural, common, and everyday. Once the key for the understanding of this jargon is given — *i.e.*, once one realizes that 'natural' meant "social", 'common' meant "the dons'", and 'everyday' meant "used for the purposes of philosophical analysis" — it can be said that Oxford-Cambridge philosophers dealt informally with *subtle linguistic mechanisms* to be found in the peculiar English language they were speaking within the walls of their clubs. In so doing they duly attacked the myth that everything can be formalized: they did it so thoroughly, that sometimes it almost looked like they were endorsing the opposite myth that nothing can be formalized. They certainly adored language in such a would-be monogamous way, that they were blinded by their own passion, up to the point of ignoring that language was already married to the professional linguist, and that on top of that (possibly because of the linguist's *laissez-faire* tolerance) was having more or less public relations with other lovers of less distinguished descent as well, such as, *horresco referens*, the psychologist, the sociologist, and even the anthropologist (whether cultural or not). Meanwhile the semiotician was duly holding his desire in check.

mechanism in such a way that it cannot avoid being received as such by whomsoever does receive it, independently of the circumstances. Or, to put it negatively: we are by now a long way from the contingent and indiscriminate use of a simple sentence for the aims of immediate expressive and communicative contact. The needs that are satisfied by using linguistic mechanisms are sophisticated needs which can only be thought of as forming in a well organized (though "primitive") culture. Sound material has received a type of elaboration which constitutes a new level with regard to all previous levels.

The first linguistic mechanisms, probably, developed along with the emergence, if not of writing itself, at least of consolidated techniques for the oral handing-down of knowledge. One can assume that their development was parallel to the production of the first material machines. If men had not learned to make a group of utensils function by itself, impersonally, it is unlikely that they could have learned to report anything in an equally impersonal way, regardless of the immediate performance of individual linguistic workers *i.e.* speakers. As we said, any connection among sentences apt to form a whole is sufficient for a linguistic mechanism to emerge. We can see this when examining any narrative passage in which a number of sentences of the factual kind (statements) are linked together in such a way that each of them is specified by the simultaneous presence of all the others and a global effect is obtained. Any grouping of sentences organized in this way functions by itself precisely because it becomes a communicative mechanism which stands alone. A small chain of interconnected sentences, *prima facie*, can seem much more simple than a formal syllogism. The opposite is true. If I say 'It's raining', 'water gets you wet', 'I want to go for a walk', 'I don't want to get wet', and 'I go back in the house', I am using several disconnected sentences. But if I say 'I wanted to go for a walk, but as soon as I went out, I came back in again because it was raining', I communicate in an unambiguous way a remarkable quantity of information which presupposes an already rather crowded network of formal relations between the various sentences. The simple group of sentences 'I wanted to go for a walk, but as soon as I went out, I came back in again because it was raining' already functions as a complete, impersonal, communicative mechanism. This doesn't have anything to do with the fact that it is you or I or somebody else who is making that utterance.

As often in these cases, the field of infantile language learning offers good examples. Whether we are dealing with material or linguistic mechanisms, it takes many months for a child to learn to make function properly a mechanism which the environment does make available to him. Meanwhile he already knows how to express himself by using phonemes, monemes, words, syntagms, and finished sentences; in the same way he already knows how to get about with matteremes, objectemes, "completed pieces" of utensils and their aggregates, and finished utensils. The machine and the syllogism, by objectifying the world, mark the advent of rationality.

Going ahead in the direction of increasing complexity, our schema offers four more levels. We can deal with these more rapidly because we have already met all but one of the dialectical leaps which are most important for us. These are the leaps between intact nature and matteremes; between matteremes and object-emes; between objectemes and utensils; between utensils and machines; and thus for linguistic production. We shall examine one more leap, leading to automated machines and program-bearing codes, presently. Apart from such a leap, at the higher levels which remain to be seen we find material and linguistic artefacts a thorough examination of which would take us far beyond the limits of the present research. Moreover, the complexity of the artefacts renders the distinction between levels more and more uncertain.

Seventh level: Complex and self-sufficient mechanisms.   —   Here we find machines able to carry out multiple working processes. Their difference from simple machines is usually only quantitative, but as such it can be enormous. The whole historical development of technology from the origins up until a few decades ago enters into it. As examples we give automobiles, automatic looms, printing machines, office calculators. In the field of linguistic production we find all arte-facts usually described as lectures, speeches, essays, books. Hundreds or thousands of sentences and syllogisms, and respectively of utensils and mechanisms, are or-ganized here with an eye to sets of ends which can vary remarkably from case to case with regard to their different applications. The human performer, however, is still there. For the program to be carried out, the erogation of human labor is still required from beginning to end, though relieved by the presence of mechan-isms. In other words, there is still, at this level, a difference — which will instead disappear at level nine — between the program and its various executions. A professor can teach the same things, or extremely similar things, an indefinite number of times, repeating the same course. In much the same way, the artisan operator of an automatic loom can always weave according to the same program, producing the same type of material. Not for this is the loom operator reduced to that type of material, or the lecture operator to that course. They both have alternative programs in their pockets. Many different types of material can be woven, and of lectures delivered, by using the same complex mechanism. But further comment on the artefacts belonging to this level is unnecessary for our aims.

Eighth level: Total mechanism or automation. — We can consider this level as a development of the level of simple mechanism, from which it is distinguished by a new qualitative leap. It is listed here after the level of complex mechanism because it presupposes its *quantitative* presence, its historical accumulation. One does not immediately get to automation by starting from a simple machine. Between the abacus and the computer there is not only a qualitative leap but also a differ-ence of quantity. We could also say that the quantitative accumulation of techno-logical development has its outlet in a qualitative leap which can be seen as a recovery and development of the qualitative level of departure. In terms of our schema: level eight is a dialectical return to level six, that is, a recovery of level six at higher level, and this is made possible by the developments described as belonging to level seven.

Here we find *self-regulating* automatic machines, capable of substituting man entirely in complex and protracted working processes which previously were not conceivable as detached from continuous human intervention. Such machines are not made up only of a plurality of complex and self-sufficient mechanisms, like those encountered at the previous level; they also include all the programming necessary for passing from one mechanism to another according to a plan, for example: (i) subjecting a product to successive and independent working processes; (ii) putting semi-finished products aside to take them up again later together with other semi-finished products; (iii) taking account of the fact that each artefact, as soon as it is produced at any given stage of the total program, immediately possesses a reality of its own; (iv) respecting the qualitative leaps whenever they occur; and so on. The elements of the working process (2.3.2) and the diverse levels of work (2.3.3) are here all part of the machine. It is precisely because of this that at the level of total mechanism the machine is able to substitute man in an entire cycle of production, thus inserting itself in the very process of social reproduction. Think of the *possibility* of a program beginning with geological prospecting and the excavation of minerals and arriving at the stage where airplanes ready for use are manufactured (including automatic pilots and, with further refinements, automatic political hi-jackings).

Now let us ask the usual question: what do we find in the field of linguistic production that corresponds to a completely automated machine? The interesting answer is that we could even not find anything: it may be that we have already found everything there was to find. In fact, just as soon as we set foot on the ground of material automation, we find ourselves already on the ground of linguistic production as well. At the level of automation, material and linguistic production are reunited, as it were, and exhibit their homology up to the point of beginning to resolve it in identity. This happens for *one sector* of linguistic production in correspondence to *one sector* of material production. In other words, there is a sector where the two overlap — the special technical or formal language which is realized in the matter of the machine as an integral part of it. It is the zone of the relations between hard-ware and soft-ware. The typical case is of course the computer.

Still we can hit on an independent linguistic production at this level as well. It is a question of self-sufficient codes functioning in social reality in such a way as to condition and absorb more or less completely the individuals who use them. If by deliberate abstraction we want to remain on the ground of language alone, we shall be dealing with sub-codes or lexicons fed by an historical language: for example, ritual and ceremonial "languages", or literary production (but see level nine). These are portions of historical languages which become specialized for some separate aims forming relatively limited *post-linguistic sign systems* investigated by *semiology* as a sector of *linguistics* (which is, in turn, a sector *of semiotics*[40]).

But as soon as we give up the abstraction of an independent language and widen our discussion to all verbal and non-verbal social sign systems having to do with the problem under examination (as, in principle, one should always do: giving the upper hand to the object of inquiry instead of to the inquiry about the object), we find again the same communicative programs we were talking about in 1.4 and elsewhere in Section One. We shall then have to face not only ritual and ceremonial "languages" as something parasitic on a historical language, such as the ritual or ceremonial terminology belonging to the Navajo language, studied by anglophones, or that belonging to the English language, unstudied by the Navajophones; but also *non-verbal sign systems* of rites and ceremonies, pregnant with their non-sign residues and carrying all their typical power to absorb and condition the individual — a power often only very partially experienced [*erlebt*] by individuals at the level of consciousness.

Thus we have arrived, after a long tour, at the point where it is possible to specify the following. Programs of communication, and sign systems in general, are self-regulating machines of a complexity which is *at least equal* to that of a perfectly automated material machine. When the enormous development of mechanical and electronic technology permitted man to realize this kind of machines in matter, they were necessarily founded on sign systems proper. This is the sense in which reference to a totally automated machine automatically involves reference to a sign system with *at least* one program contained in it. The same point is more accurately made by saying that totally automated machines, in principle, have been able to develop only because verbal and non-verbal sign systems of an even greater

---

[40] If we say that semiotics is the general science of signs, linguistics is the science of all verbal sign systems, and semiology deals with post-linguistic (post-verbal) sign systems, this seems to be the correct terminology. On the European Continent, however, there has been a tendency to use 'semiology' instead of 'semiotics', sometimes reserving the latter term to the objects studied, *i.e.* to the sign systems themselves (which could rather be called semiosic systems, from *semiosis*). The Saussurian descent of these by now highly confusing usages is obvious. They often express the tendency of the literary critic who deals professionally with post-linguistic signs, to reduce all semiotic enquiry to the boundaries of his own tradition and interests, in this way putting a part in the place of the whole it belongs to (cf. Rossi-Landi 1967a: 90-93).
More generally, the literary man as distinguished from the scientific man finds it delightful to think that there are systems of signs proper only as a result of the cultural use of language, when man is at least partially aware of what he is doing as an individual. Now since linguistics is the science of language, it is easy to jump to the conclusion that linguistics is the queen of all sciences. But in this way, paradoxically, linguistics loses its pilot role instead of affirming it. For there is no boat with a helmsman on board unless there are waters all around on which the boat floats and which must be crossed at the helmsman's guidance.

complexity existed already. Machines have been built from the beginning by imitation of such systems. Before mechanical and electronic technology made it possible consciously to manufacture these complex machines in external matter, they *existed socially* — even if mainly at an unconscious level — in the form of verbal and non-verbal sign systems. As we know, verbal and non-verbal sign systems require material processes internal to the individual; at the same time, since they are social, they constitute the form which matter has reached as the result of the stratification of human work for tens of millenia (cf. 1.4, 2.4.1, 2.4.3, and level ten below; also, the treatment of "linguistic capital" in Section Five; and, for some remarks of a slightly more speculative kind, Rossi-Landi 1968c: 188–191).

We insist on the fact that machines have been built from the start by imitating already existing human sign systems also in order to reassert their character as products and servants of man, while at the same time vindicating a structural continuity between producer and products.

Ninth level: Non-repeatable production. — We can relegate to this level, in both fields of production, artefacts which are usually considered *original*. While using the term 'original', however, we are not entering into questions of value (whether artistic or of any other kind). The term is used only descriptively, the assumption being that there must be a recognizable kernel of objective originality at a stage less complicated than the stage at which any question of value is usually raised. One doesn't even begin talking about the original value of a shovel or of the sentence 'it is raining'. Original production in the descriptive sense is in the first place a single person's or individual group's production, projected and realized only once for ends and through modalities which are unique and, at the extreme, unrepeatable. The program is set out in the act of its realization; or, the model is one with the single token produced. In the field of material production this is the case of "unique prototypes". Instead of unique prototypes we may also have a very limited number of tokens, but then each token is cared for and modified individually, bears variants which are all original, and can itself be proposed as a prototype. This type of production is exemplified by a very special automobile or yacht made-to-order; an ocean liner or a non-conventional dam; or, at a higher level, enterprises like the transfer of the temple of Abū-Sìmbel following upon the creation of Lake Nasser. Altogether, every artefact which is the final result of purposely projected and realized working cycles and possesses a unique character can be described as belonging to this level.

In the field of language, this is the place of literary and scientific production viewed as the construction of special languages; while the production of non-verbal arts, as well as that part of scientific production which cannot be reduced to scientific languages, exemplify non-repeatability and originality within the respective non-verbal sign systems. It is worthwhile to add that the printing of the works of a poet leads us completely outside of the level under examination. The production of books is a production of tokens according to a material program and does not have anything to do with the production *of the text*.[41] The poet realizes his model in the very act in which he realizes the unique token of the model. The typographer takes only the non-sign body of the text as the model to be reproduced, while the text as such remains the unrepeatable model of itself. If things weren't like this, misprints would be welcome, or at least they would not arouse protest. With the necessary variations, much the same would hold good for the production of any original artefact as distinguished from the various ways in which it can be reproduced. That, on the other hand, any "original" literary text is the expression of a social group even without the author's knowing it, so that the author is in the position of acting as an individual channel for a collective work (Goldmann 1959, 1964, 1970a, 1970b), confirms the social character of original production itself.

We can attempt to say that we find here a dialectic between levels, not dissimilar from that found for automation. The products of level nine are a further development of those of level seven, but they are made possible by the quantitative accumulation of products of level eight. Even without entering into questions of aesthetic or other assessment, there is something more to an original book than to a book which has only been compiled. It is in comparison with a current, average assembly line car that a special model Ferrari is something new; and if Nicholson, Stephens, or Harlé accepted to project and build a yacht for the America's Cup, it wouldn't cease being a yacht because of such a special and highly competent planning. But the original book, the special model Ferrari, and the yacht for the America's Cup, because of their self-contained character and perfection, also presuppose the developments of total mechanism. This, at first glance, seems clearer in the field of material than in that of linguistic production; but it becomes clear here too as soon as we recall how total mechanism was operating in the form of sub-codes or lexicons even before it was able fully to manifest itself in the form of artefacts which are deliberately planned and manufactured in the external material world. This is the sense in which we say that every poet has his own self-contained and self-sufficient language; or that the Pyramids, the taming of the Yellow River, or mass anti-polio vaccination, are unique phenomena. In other words, original production arises in both fields as a sign subsystem which conveys in its way a vision of the world, partial as this may be, offering to interpretation all the richness of the layers accumulated in it.

Tenth level: Global production. — We will only say a few words about our tenth and last level, although it is the one upon which one might enlarge the most. It is a widely varied level, or perhaps it is not just one level at all, but many; for our purposes, however, we don't need to examine them one by one. Let us locate

---

[41] It is the particular merit of the French school of Marx-inspired semioticians (actually, semiologists) to have studied this highly complicated layer of sign production. Cf. Macherey 1966, Kristeva 1969, and the journals *La nouvelle critique*, *Tel Quel*, and *Communications*. Cf. also Goldmann's writings quoted below in the text.

here all artefacts that result in one way or another from the work of any historic-ally real "productive unit". So we'd better have a look at this last notion. A pro-ductive unit can be a man, a more or less wide and/or permanent social group, a whole culture; the widest productive unit one can think of is mankind as the total-ity *hominum sapientium*. In other words, the overall production of a single indi-vidual, of various social groups, of various cultures, of mankind as a whole can be examined.

Social sign systems, whether verbal or non-verbal, belong by right to each of the last three levels we have distinguished. As we saw, they already appear at the level of complete mechanism; their originality and unrepeatability shows that it is convenient to consider them at level nine too; finally, their global character makes them an appropriate object of study for anybody who wants to see things from the point of view of productive units. A culture as a whole is a system of sign systems, a sort of enormous historical "language" transmitting messages to whom it may concern. That a whole sign system may be viewed from the outside is apparent, if only we concentrate in the appropriate manner on even very simple cases. A glance at a written page, without really reading and retaining anything of it, suf-fices for us to decree what language it is written in (provided we are at least a little acquainted with it, of course); and there are artefacts one single token of which suf-fices for the identification of a material culture. By considering, moreover, how a simple artefact abandoned in a deserted place does inform us of the fact that man has worked near there, we can glimpse the methodological possibility of examining from the outside even the total production of humanity. A single artefact appears to be sufficient for distinguishing man not only from the other animals but also from everything non-human which has ever existed on the planet.

We mustn't forget that all these are comments made about provisionally dis-tinguished levels in an artificial schema, the aim of which is to exhibit progressive homological complications of production in two expressly privileged fields. The *level of complication* at which *complete* sign systems begin to appear shouldn't be confused with the items that every sign system must include. A sign system does not *consist* only of automated mechanisms, but also of artefacts of previous levels. Verbal and objectual sign systems are already present in reality as soon as senten-ces and utensils begin to develop. As for organic sign systems, it would seem that they begin to form at even lower levels. It remains to be seen, however, whether or not they possess at least the two articulations that lead to sentences and to utensils and are therefore typical of the initial phases of verbal and objectual sign systems. But a structural comparison between the production of utensils and sen-tences and the production of "organic artefacts" lies entirely outside the scope of the present enquiry.

What is, in conclusion, the relation between (i) a verbal sign system and a non-verbal sign system of an objectual type, and (ii), the homological schema of lin-guistic and material production? We shall try to say that the schema is a sounding-

ARTIFICIAL SCHEME OF PROGRESSIVE COMPLEXITY	MATERIAL PRODUCTION	LINGUISTIC PRODUCTION
Zero level: intact, unworked-upon nature	material non-sound substance	material sound substance
First level: pre-significant items	matteremes	phonemes
	intermediary-noise	
Second level: irreducibly significant items	objectemes (lexobjectemes or morphobjectemes)	monemes (lexemes or morphemes)
	instrument-cry	
Third level: "completed pieces"	"finished pieces" of utensils; syntagms, expressions, parts of speech, phrases in the "language of things"	words; syntagms, expressions, parts of speech, phrases
Fourth level: utensils and sentences	simple utensils, *i.e.* material sentences	simple sentences, *i.e.* linguistic utensils
Fifth level: aggregates of utensils	compound utensils	compound sentences
Sixth level: mechanism	machines of a simple type, *i.e.* material syllogisms	syllogisms, organized groupings of interconnected sentences: *i.e.*, linguistic mechanisms
Seventh level: complex and self-sufficient mechanisms	self-sufficient mechanisms	lectures, speeches, essays, books
Eighth level: total mechanism or automation	automated machines	sub-codes and lexicons (post-linguistic)
	objectual and verbal program-bearing codes	
Ninth level: non-repeatable production	special constructions, unique prototypes	"original" literary and scientific production
	objectual and verbal program-bearing codes	
Tenth level: global production	all objectual sign systems of a "productive unit"	all verbal sign systems of a "productive unit"

rod inserted vertically into any sign system and describing its stratification, with no claim at describing also its width and coverage. Some clarifications in this regard are to be found in Section 3.3.

Meanwhile, a table as on the preceding page allowing a comprehensive glance at our ten levels may be of help for grasping some of their interconnections.

3.3 *Plurality of articulations*

Let's examine one essential character of the homological schema of production again. Some passages between levels require proper qualitative leaps, others do not; or at least, some of the qualitative leaps are decidedly more important than others. The most important qualitative leaps are: from intact nature to matteremes and phonemes (the schema begins with matteremes and phonemes as *first results* of work); from matteremes and phonemes to objectemes and monemes; from objectemes and monemes to utensils and sentences; from utensils and sentences to mechanisms and syllogisms; from mechanisms and syllogisms to automated machines, that is, to non-verbal and verbal program-bearing codes. Extrapolating these five levels means further simplifying an already simplified schema, paring it to the bone. This further simplification is useful for a new order of reflections which were already implicit in the exposition of the schema, and which we want to delineate more clearly now. As we shall presently see, even the schema "pared to the bone" appears to be a relatively complex one if we compare it to current tenets on the same basic issues.

For each of the levels in which a qualitative leap is realized, the artefacts, whose production is made possible by that leap and whose structure is characterized by it, so to say *pour out of the productive process* and *stay there waiting*. Let us try to see what are the real processes hinted at by these metaphors. Artefacts are all bound together, whatever level they belong to, by the general process of production. There is among them all a continuous dialectical play by virtue of which the modifications brought by work to artefacts of any one of the levels end up sooner or later by reverberating at all the levels. But artefacts, as we know, are new totalities superior to the sums of their parts; work is coagulated in them, furnishing them with a skin that opposes a more or less long-lasting resistance to the entry of new influences from the outside (2.3.2 and 2.3.3). Artefacts tend to remain what they are even when they are used in new productive processes. The more so, of course, they don't lose their properties if they are *not* used. Indeed this is necessary, otherwise any worker wanting to start a new piece of work at a given level wouldn't find anything ready to start working with and would always have to begin from scratch. The absurdity of this will be taken up again at the end of the section. Meanwhile, let us find an expression describing the condition of artefacts that have poured out of the productive process and of their forming groups by levels. *Faute de mieux* we choose *parking lots of artefacts*.[42] New workers learn to use "parked" artefacts in new working processes, or else they simply consume them to satisfy a need. Generally, we use arte-facts leaving aside the fact that they *are* artefacts, *i.e.* products. The consumer goes to the parking lot, gets his car, and goes on about his business. A dialectical terminology avoids in its way the anti-climax introduced by talking about parking lots and cars: the artefacts are assumed "in their new immediacy", "in themselves and by themselves".[43]

That artefacts pour out of the productive process, arrange themselves in parking lots, and are used in themselves and by themselves, is particularly evident when we are dealing with artefacts destined for immediate consumption (even if it should never be forgotten that *consumption is production anyhow*: 2.4.1). One does not "work" any more on food which is ready to be eaten, if not in the possible but not essential sense, which is also an attenuated one, that usually men eat according to ceremonial or ritual programs. The parking lot of all food ready to be eaten is available to the market. The parking lot of all "units" ready to be used is available to the linguistic market.[44] Less evident is the fact that there are parking lots of artefacts not destined for immediate consumption. If we take another look at the

[42] Let us insist that this expression is not entirely satisfactory and should be used more to *label the situation described* than for the associations it bears. Alternative expressions could be 'working store', 'provisional dump', and the like. One of the difficulties of the expression 'parking lot of artefacts' is examined below (footnote 44). Another is that a parking lot in the usual sense is a place for numerable, physically existent objects; while some of the objects we want to describe as "poured out of the productive process" and "waiting for us" are brought into existence only when, and insofar as, they are used to build something else.

[43] Cf. 2.3.3. — While this is certainly not the place for a treatment, however cursory, of dialectics, let us recall the importance of the synthetic moment of a dialectic triad. We may call it after Hegel's fashion (*Enzyklopädie*: §§ 18 and 81) the "in itself and by itself" moment, and add that it is taken up "in its new immediacy", as Marx, Lenin, and Mao Tse-tung do; or we may content ourselves with saying that it is the final stage of a process of growth which comprehends in itself the various elements gone into the process; and add that the object is then taken up in its final stage as it is, without going back to the process of its growth any longer. In either case the dialectical leap signalled by the presence-and-the-new-use of an artefact is cleary indicated.

[44] Here the problem may arise of the nature or ontological *status* of linguistic parking lots as distinguished from material parking lots, and with it the question of finding their proper place or *locus*. It is a complex question which can also be a futile or dangerous one. Linguistic objects are a part of verbal sign systems. Now once one has admitted that verbal sign systems "are in" the nervous system of individuals ("internal material" dimension and the question of differential traces: 2.4.1-2) and that they constitute, moreover, groups of univocal sound stimuli commonly emitted and received in speech-acts, as well as groups of the corresponding graphical stimuli listed in dictionaries and grammars and used in everything that is printed (5.1, 5.2.3), 6.5), one has said all that it is possible to say about their ontological *status* and about their locus at *this level of generality*. One must be very careful if he wants to avoid useless elucubrations. Linguistic objects are artefacts, as such they share the problems which arise for any artefact. The fundamental distinctions between models and tokens and between programs and executions (2.2, 2.3.3, 3.1 *ad finem*) cut across the opposition between material artefacts and linguistic artefacts, and vanify any worries one may have about the "non-materiality" (and therefore about the possibility of placing them) of linguistic artefacts alone.

A deeper look into the ontological nature and the localization of *all* artefacts can take

homological schema of production, concentrating on the five levels at which a qualitative leap occurs, we find that we have to list the following *parking lots of artefacts*:

parking lot of matteremes and (respectively) of phonemes;

parking lot of objectemes and monemes;

parking lot of utensils and sentences;

parking lot of mechanisms and syllogisms;

parking lot of automated machines and of non-verbal and verbal program-bearing codes.

We are dealing with parking lots which are very different from each other in nature, structure, and use. Many considerations of a descriptive type could be made about them. For example, the lower the level, the more intersubjective is the parking lot in principle. A polished stone is less culture-bound than a mortar and pestle, and a simple mortar and pestle is less culture-bound than a carpenter's tools. Japanese and Italian phonemes are similar even if the two languages are very different. The most vast and multiform parking lots can be found at the fourth and the sixth levels of the schema: a curve developing along the axis of the abscissa and indicating the extent of the parking lots, would have its highest ordinates at these levels. The wealth and variety of forms, in fact, are greater for utensils and mechanisms and for sentences and syllogisms than they are for matteremes and phonemes at one end of the schema and for codes and programs (considered in their formal abstraction) at the other.

But these and other similar descriptive features, on which it would be easy to harp at length and minutely, are not central to our argument. What interests us here above all is that we have five levels of parking lots of artefacts, each of which is *composed of* artefacts of the previous level *plus* the work done to compose them, and will serve (together with new work to be done) to compose artefacts of the subsequent level. As we know, the process often takes place through quantitative accumulations realized at intermediate levels, *i.e.* at levels that are not marked by qualitative leaps themselves, or not by equally decisive ones. Thus objectemes

---

various paths. Let's recall two of them: the path of research into the way the nervous system works together with the construction of the relative cybernetic models, and the path of the dialectical and social study of the relations between products and producers, with special attention given above all to the fact that the former reflect the latter in an imperious though mystified manner. The second path was opened by Marx in one of his most profound and overwhelming analyses, the fourteen pages dedicated to «The mystery of the fetishistic character of commodities» (actually, «Der Fetischcharakter der Ware und sein Geheimnis») (*Das Kapital*, Erster Band, 1. Kap., 4; Paul's translation I: 43-58). The commodities Marx talks about, *and likewise any other sign object*, indifferently non-verbal or verbal, certainly do not have sign value by themselves, independent of man. On the other hand, the system of commodities *and likewise any other sign system* certainly cannot be reduced to facts of the human consciousness, rather it rises up in front of man as a formidable reality. Overcoming the opposition between these two orders of problems, mediating the one by the other, is a job that is waiting for both general Marxist theory and general semiotic theory (cf. the conclusion to Section One).

and monemes are composed of matteremes and phonemes; utensils and sentences are composed of objectemes and monemes; mechanisms and syllogisms are composed of utensils and sentences; automated machines and non-verbal or verbal program-bearing codes are composed of mechanisms and syllogisms (and in them the two branches of production approach one another again up to the point of appearing reunited: the homology finds a ground upon which it may be resolved in identity).

At this point we must ask ourselves if the expression 'composed of' has the same sense at the various levels; or, in Oxonian jargon, we may ask what its "logic" is. But we'd better transform this way of putting it into a question about the real processes under examination, as distinguished from a question about the ways in which we describe such processes. The main question, then, is the following. Is the dialectic presiding over qualitative leaps always the same at the various levels, or is it at least a similar dialectic? Or, rather, is it a dialectic that changes substantially with the changing of levels? For example, when we pass from the level of sentences to that of syllogisms, are the operations presiding over this passage substantially similar or dissimilar to the operations by which we passed from the level of monemes to that of sentences? Is the work which brings together sentences in such a way as to build a syllogism the same sort of work which is applied to the task of bringing together monemes in such a way as to build a sentence? The answer to such questions — apart from anything that might be said at the level of linguistic usages, whether popular or donnish — is that *it must necessarily be a similar dialectic as far as the substantial part of the whole process is concerned.* And the substantial part is nothing else than the *articulation of work.* We know that all the objectemes and monemes we use are produced with a few tens of matteremes and phonemes. Moreover we know that it is with a few thousand objectemes and monemes that utensils and sentences we use are produced. *Hic Rhodus, hic salta.* Does a process of the same kind obtain when we produce mechanisms and syllogisms by means of utensils and sentences, and then automated machines and program-bearing codes by means of mechanisms and syllogisms? Is there in these two cases as well a parking lot of artefacts upon which production can draw — a parking lot, we mean, which can be held under practical, operational control because of its being numerically *limited* (even though it may be a very high number)? Obviously yes, as we have seen during the exposition of the schema (3.2.3, and *passim*). Thus the problem is resolved already. But it is worth our while to look at its facets a little longer.

The conventional reply to the last two questions we asked sounds more or less like this (try it and see). The two questions don't make sense for language because there is an "infinite number" of sentences which are produced by the "free creative activity of individual speakers". So there is no parking lot of sentences, leaving alone syllogisms. As far as material production is concerned, the problem is not even raised. Thus *the progression of production is interrupted* on the linguistic

side at the level of sentences, without even taking further developments into account. On the side of material production, the progression is *not even introduced*.
In this way various pieces of knowledge are left to wander about on their own,
without any attempt to bring them together; indeed, obstacles are erected against
their unification. Suffice it to think of the programs governing every form of verbal
and non-verbal communication. These programs are artefacts of the highest level
and as such they presuppose the progressive and organic play of all previous levels.
How in the world could we ever arrive at a theoretical foundation for the simultaneous presence of (i), the common use of language understood as the free production of sentences, and (ii), the programs governing every form of verbal communication from a level of elaboration higher than the level at which the very production of sentences takes place?

These are basic difficulties. In order to overcome them, or at least to face them
on their proper theoretical ground, it is necessary to make great sacrifices, leaving
the security of the sown field and hazarding into virgin territory. Let's say this,
then. *Even in the case of utensils and sentences, and then of mechanisms and
syllogisms, we can only be dealing with dominable parking lots which are numerically limited and subject to precise organizational choices.* Otherwise, it would be
simply impossible to proceed to a higher level and produce more complex artefacts, for the techniques which are used in this as in any production could never
have been invented and much less transmitted to new workers. Techniques exist
only for what is selected and determined. You don't build anything with the indeterminate, or worse, with the infinite.

Let's take up again the important case of sentences as materials for the construction of syllogisms. We shall maintain in 7.1 that, as big as their number may
be, it is certainly not an "infinite" number. Indeed, sentences are all reducible in
principle into tribes, families, and sub-families, the structures of which are transmitted from generation to generation as an essential part of linguistic know-how.
Syllogisms can be constructed by man because he has succeeded in isolating some
typical cases of sentence-making, choosing them from all possible sentences and
conferring an organization upon them. This is the most important point, lending
itself to generalization as regards the constructive relations between artefacts of all
the levels. As we saw in dealing with the level of mechanism (3.2.3), a syllogism
occurs when at least two sentences are put in opposition and this opposition is
overcome dialectically (binarism thus giving way to dialectic); and moreover, when
one prescinds from both the immediately existential use of the sentences and the
context they happen to belong to. In this way a permanent and autonomous formal relation, the syllogism, is instituted among sentences. Well then, we do not
see any difference in principle between these operations of selection, freezing, and
organization of reciprocal relations and the operations that govern the formation
of linguistic artefacts of either a lower or a higher level.

We shall have the opportunity of returning to all this later on. Meanwhile, let's draw a first general conclusion from what we have been developing. Production is articulated in *four* main successive phases, those conjoining the *five* listed parking lots of artefacts. Production — material as well as linguistic — rests on a *quadruple articulation*. In order to grasp this articulation it is necessary to move continually back and forth along the schema. Articulation in fact is the relation of any given artefact to a number of artefacts that precede it; as such it is a passage from unity to plurality. This passage is possible, however, and makes sense, only insofar as there is a previous possession of that unity. Thus we shall say that every objecteme and moneme *is articulated in* a certain number of matteremes and respectively of phonemes. This means that *in order to build* a given objecteme or moneme, some matteremes and phonemes *are required* which have been selected and isolated from all other possible matteremes and phonemes and organized in a certain way. Work is necessary too, of course; and indeed, its notion has been introduced already in terms of 'building' in general, and, specifically, in terms of 'selection', 'isolation', and 'organization'. Another aspect of articulation is that when we have an objecteme or a moneme, we have at the same time certain matteremes or phonemes. And since *these* matteremes and *these* phonemes do not and cannot exist without *the other* matteremes and phonemes that are produced by the community, the notion of the parking lots of matteremes and phonemes turns out to have been already introduced as well. Considerations of the same sort are valid for all the other articulations, up to the highest level. We shall also say, therefore, that automated machines and program-bearing codes are articulated in mechanisms and syllogisms. That is, certain sets of mechanisms or syllogisms which have been selected and isolated from all possible others and organized in a particular way are necessary for the construction of any given automated machine or program-bearing code. Thus when we have an automated machine or program-bearing code we already have those mechanisms and syllogisms and therefore we already have their relative parking lots.

   Maintaining the existence of a quadruple articulation, and maintaining it both for the field of linguistic production and for that of material production, means moving away radically from the common doctrine according to which only a double articulation exists, and only with regard to language (of which it is held to constitute a differential characteristic, perhaps the most important one). Let's look at the two points separately.

It is still a current conception that language is a system of words and expressions *by means of which* the speakers of a given linguistic community "express feelings and thoughts", "analyze experience", and "communicate with each other". This amounts to saying that language is an instrument which we use for further ends. In the course of the next Sections we shall come back repeatedly to this conception of language, attacking it from various points of view (cf. especially 5.2.1–3; 6.5; 7.1, 7.3.1, and 7.4). Notice, for the moment, that if this is what language is, then the place for locating the other three parking lots we distinguished is outside of language. An alternative would consist in extending the notion of language to include all five parking lots. In this case the notion of language would be stretched until it became identical with the notion of "verbal sign system" (1.2). A verbal sign system, in fact, includes all five parking lots by definition, for it consists of codes and messages and thus of the program for realizing the messages, which also means that all lower-level parking lots are already involved in its construction and, of course, continue to be used.

Neither of the alternatives — restricting language to the first two parking lots or extending it to all five — seems sufficient to us. The problem is, instead, how to tie language to work in the proper ways. The precariousness of the Saussurian notion of individual *parole* begins to emerge here. It is a very partial conception of linguistic work, able only to put a two-parking-lot language in motion, but certainly not capable of justifying higher-level parking lots. If *parole* is individual work, whatever factor there is which binds the innumerable individual *paroles* in communion, thus making communication possible, remains totally unexplained. One doesn't understand how on earth the parking lots of sentences that all speakers learn to produce univocally, and then also more complex parking lots, were ever produced. Really, one doesn't even understand how the first two parking lots have ever been produced. There have been well known attempts to overcome these difficulties by enriching the two parking lots attributed to language [*langue*] with operative and generative rules and by introducing intermediate ideas for the purpose of linking individual *parole* to language [*langue*] as a collective patrimony. One of these "linking ideas" is the contradictory invention of a "speech pact" to which already-speaking-individuals adhere (cf. 1.3). The Saussurian opposition between a two-parking-lot collective *langue* and an individual *parole* has thus been substantially accepted. Remedies to its deficiencies have been proposed in the form of various corrections or integrations made for the purpose of sewing up again precisely that which had been irremediably lacerated from the beginning.

In order to put all the five parking lots of linguistic artefacts in motion, the overall power of linguistic work is required. According to the present writer, the first notion to introduce is that of a *collective parole* or *speech* (Rossi-Landi 1961, especially chapters V and VI; 1968c: 186–7 and *passim*; cf. also 2.3.3, and further developments in Sections Five and Seven). Making some sort of "terminological decision" and leaving it at that is of course of little importance. The basic task consists in *not interrupting* the continuity of articulations in favor of something abstract. And this instead is exactly what happens when language is postulated as a two-layer system of phonemes and monemes and all the rest of linguistic production is left vague; or else one "passes the buck" to other disciplines with the self-congratulatory excuse that it doesn't enter into the field of linguistics; or again, one loads it all onto that mean slice of linguistic work which is individual *parole*. Whether in the course of a reconstruction of the continuity of linguistic production the notion of language turns out to be extended, or whether its restricted notion is arranged within a vaster organism, may also be, from the point of view of basic theoretical decisions, a secondary question. What is important is to turn to the primacy of work.

The reconstruction of the totality of the articulations is intended to be a move towards a more faithful and pregnant representation of reality. A child immediately learns together with words the use of the most common sentences, just as he immediately learns the use of the simple utensils currently employed in the community to which he belongs. Moreover, a child does not just learn the use of sentences and utensils, but that of mechanisms and syllogisms as well, with a remarkable homology in this learning process of his. Thus he learns, for example, to recognize the generic sense of a little discourse, that is made to him with the purpose of inducing him to behave in a certain way, homologically to the way in which he learns the generic use of an everyday mechanism, let us say a watch. He will be able to use the watch and the little discourse in a superficial but practically adequate way much before he begins to look at all into the way they function, and much before he even glimpses anything of the principles guiding the construction and functioning of such complex mechanisms. Simple sentences present themselves to whoever is learning to speak together with their combinations — 'it's raining', 'I'm going outside', and 'I'll get wet' present themselves together with 'if I go outside when it's raining, then I'll get wet'. In a homological manner, complex machines present themselves together with the simple machines and with the utensils that make them up. Finally, the child immediately learns to execute, or at least to comply with, verbal and non-verbal programs so much so that one can assume (as we saw in 1.4) that he is entangled in them from birth. It is necessary to take account of all this in a unitary way and not by bits and pieces. We must acquire the capacity to face both philogenetic and onto-genetic homination in their totality.

There is a question which has been hiding between the lines so far, and which may seem futilely numerological, or at the most intellectually elegant; we want, instead, to attribute much importance to it. While adding *three* parking lots to the two which are usually recognized in language, we have only added *two* articulations. We have brought the parking lots of linguistic artefacts from two to five, but the articulations from two to four. Let us take a look into the reasons for this apparent asymmetry.

According to the doctrine of linguistic double articulation, sentences produced by speakers are traced back to parking lots of monemes in which they are articulated, but they aren't seen as forming a parking lot themselves. The speaker, according to the doctrine, produces sentences "freely" and in "infinite" number. Rules do exist which he has to follow somehow; but they are either immanent in the production of sentences — or they are biological features of the human organism, and with this the progression of production is interrupted in the most radical way. Consequently, parking lots of a level higher than that of monemes (or at the most of words) wouldn't exist. But our highest parking lot is instead that of program-bearing codes. Therefore we have to ask ourselves whether or not, above codes and programs, there may be working processes that have to program-bearing codes the same type of relation that sentences are supposed to have to the parking lot of monemes. If they did exist, they would be working processes not belonging to any parking lot but still traceable to the parking lot immediately previous to them, that of program-bearing codes. Then there would be a sixth articulation (to tell the truth, this would be the first articulation, all the others descending by one unit along the numerical scale), consisting in the articulability of verbal behavior (freely produced in infinite number) in what we could call "programmatic units", in the same way that sentences can be articulated in "meaningful units" (monemes). *Prima facie*, such an hypothesis would seem to fit into what we were saying in 1.4 about the programs of communication and their being reducible to sequences or aggregates of fixed and conventional units (Pike, Scheflen, etc.).

The temptation to admit this sixth (first) articulation is remarkable, also because it may appear as necessary for the justification of the free human use of the codes and programs themselves, beginning with the work consisting in their production. We'd better renounce this temptation, however. Accepting the existence of behavior of a level higher than that of the parking lot of the highest level, does not so much mean affirming the freedom of that behavior as deferring to another parking lot the property of belonging to the highest possible level. In other words, we only make this property slide, leaving the rest as it is. Let us explain. Communication *is* the execution of programs. Behavioral units in which the behavior of those who execute programs is to be articulated, are by definition units of a *lower* level. By opening the door to a further level of linguistic production, we would then find an impossible choice in front of us. On the one hand, we could not avoid formulating the pseudo-problem of a further level, still higher than the level just produced; that is, we would run the risk of an infinite regression. On the other hand, it could happen that, in order to get around the regression, we might not know how to refute a conception of man — of his most intimate and motivating portion — as an entity winging its way above its own parking lots of artefacts (to which, however, with a further contradiction, we would still have to resort for an explanation of what man himself was). But this would mean that we hadn't understood anything at all about communication as the execution of programs and that we were regressing to a romantic vision of human activity.

Let us therefore refuse these philosophical complications *toto corde* and state that the freedom of human behavior cannot reside in something that wings its way above all the parking lots of artefacts, but rather in conscious and original ways of using units of any level — up to the point of modifying from within the verbal and non-verbal sign systems to which we cannot avoid belonging. The very work that has produced codes, programs, and whole sign systems, if it is work, cannot have been exempt from programs. Original planning itself is either new use of sign systems, or doesn't make sense (cf. 1.4). If we want to find the fount of all human programming, we must look for it in needs and in the work done for their satisfaction, certainly not in something human precedent to work. Consequently, it seems more correct (and healthier) methodologically, to include all human behavior within the apparatus of the five parking lots here distinguished and the four articulations which join them internally.

All human communication takes place by using the parking lots of artefacts and the articulations *that can be distinguished*. Beyond the parking lots of artefacts and the articulations that can be distinguished, communication does not obtain. This is a definition, or if you prefer, a characterization, of communication, made in terms of elements that must be working together for it to exist at all. It should be clear that we are not in the least defending *a certain number* of parking lots and articulations. Empirical research and the work of theoretical systematization can always bring us to modify our descriptive data and their arrangement. For example, in the examination of a given language or objectual sign system, we might find it convenient to single out the level of words and "completed pieces", recognizing in it a qualitative leap as important as the leaps occurring at the levels we have selected in this Section, our present aim being the construction of a schema as general as possible. When this is the case, the parking lots will become six, and the articulations five. The same thing can happen with aggregates of sentences and of utensils. And so on. Questions of this sort should always remain open. What we have to defend, instead, from a general theoretical point of view is the notion of the *system of all parking lots*. This system should be viewed as an autonomous and irreducible bloc of interdependent levels. We are moving away from the conventional doctrine of the articulations also in this: that we don't defer to anything external, on the contrary, we contend that everything that happens within a given field is in principle capable of being explained with the conceptual instruments that define the field itself.

Let's go on to the second point. Not only is the articulation quadruple instead of double. It exists, and is quadruple, also in the field of material production. In this field as well there is a full realization of that thrift which linguists rightly insist on when they observe how a few thousand monemes suffice to produce an enormous number of sentences, and a few tens of phonemes suffice for the production of all the monemes of a language. If a utensil entirely new in all of its constituent parts, that is, different from every other artefact, were necessary for every material working process; and still worse, if entirely new modifications, different from all the others, were necessary for the construction of the parts of every distinct utensil, then there would never have been anything like technological development on the planet. This would simply mean that man would never have learned to dominate nature. Instead we know that a utensil is composed of objectemes which are in turn composed of matteremes, and that objectemes and matteremes have the homological level of monemes and phonemes.

The structural similarity of the parking lots of the same level permits us to find and recognize more or less the same artefacts in all equally developed cultures. This happens insofar as the artefacts are assimilated to each other by means of an operation which we could baptize "material translation". One finds, for example, that a given group of objectemes, taken as a whole, corresponds to another group of objectemes with a completely different origin. One can say then, that two different utensils belonging to two different cultures are equivalent: one of the two utensils has been "translated" into the other, so that it can be employed in the place of the other. Even the observation that the form of the *signans*, since it is articulated into phonemes void of *signata,* withdraws from the value of its corresponding *signatum* and in this way acquires a greater stability (Martinet 1960, 1966[6]: 22), is an observation that is equally valid in the field of material production. Matteremes, in fact, as modification of the first level, are not significant by themselves. A matttereme is a modification that anyone can bring to formless material even independently of the use that he may make of it, if and when he combines it with other such non-significant elements, in this way forming a significant unit, *i.e.* an objecteme, which may in turn become the part of some utensil. A mattereme, moreover, is a stable modification. A piece of wood which has been cut, and a polished stone, remain cut and polished independently of the use that may be made of them — indeed, independently of their being later used or not used at all.

To conclude this long section we want to insist again on the presence of the articulations in the field of material production through the negation of the negation that they exist. We want to make a little intellectual experiment founded on a *reductio ad absurdum.* What would happen if every time we started a given working process we found ourselves in the condition of having to procure a completely new utensil, appropriate just and only for that? Let's suppose, for example, that somebody wanted to start hammering on a planet void of hammers (*adgnosco veteris vestigia flammae!, Aen.* IV, 23). Naturally, the hypothesis itself is odd: not because it is absurd to imagine planets without hammers, but because it is contradictory to bring to the limelight an actor without a part, a specific operator without a specific utensil, assuming that on a planet void of hammers one would want to hammer, just hammer, nothing else but hammer. We can reduce the oddness, though not eliminate it, by supposing that it makes sense to want to use a type of hammer that while being a hammer is different in all of its aspects from all existing hammers. Our argument, anyhow, begins with the vision of a future hammerer who finds himself forced to start all over again from scratch.

What will he have to do when the desire to hammer descends upon him? He will have to begin to examine the thousands and thousands of objectemes available, choose the ones most suitable for his aims, transform the objectemes he has selected in completed pieces and finally combine these pieces with each other in an original way. Specifically for the hammer: our future hammerer will have to select some metallic or at least solid and resistant bodies from the sea of objectemes, bodies neither too big nor too tiny for making up part of a manageable object, of a cylindrical or polyhedric shape, presenting a flat surface suitable for violent contact with hittable objects, that is, suitable for functioning as the face of the head. Then, in the bodies he has found, if there aren't any already, he will have to make some holes into which he can introduce the handle which meanwhile he will have had to produce by means of an equally complicated research. The enterprise seems desperate: our future hammerer might declare that he felt himself to be reduced to the condition of a Robinson Crusoe.

He would be wrong. His apparently desperate enterprise, in fact, already presupposes the existence of a parking lot of previously produced objectemes. Contrary to first appearances, starting to "search for" a hammer on a planet already populated with objectemes means finding oneself already in a relatively privileged position. *All* you have to do is to draw on the appropriate objectual parking lot, choose the suitable objectemes and combine them. A big waste of work, but posterior to previous products already bearing distinct significations.

If he didn't have any objectemes either, then the future hammerer really would be in difficult waters. In that case he would have to produce objectemes from the start, resorting to their constituent elements, matteremes. Fortunately, somebody may say, there are only a few tens of matteremes. But the fact is that these few tens of constituent elements lacking autonomous signification permit, in their various combinations, the production of billions and billions of objectemes. The hammerer, therefore, will have to choose the right combinations for producing the objectemes he needs. He will have to know how to use rigorous selective and organizational criteria from the very beginning.

Even so, however, the hammerer still wouldn't have reached the worst conditions imaginable. After all, we were still assuming that from the start he had at his disposal at least one parking lot of matteremes well-distinguished from each other and fully possessed one by one. We have conceded to him that he may be able to realize matteremes — the matteremes he can realize, given his biological equipment and given the objective structure of the planet. And if, instead, the future hammerer didn't even possess the art of producing matteremes? If he didn't even know yet what the most rudimentary modifications are which he will be able to bring to matter, and if he couldn't succeed even in following, directing, and remembering the movements of his own limbs and the resulting changes in the external world (which, we grant, he is able to feel as external)?

At this point we can call a halt to the hammerer's tribulations. We don't have any need to put ourselves in his shoes and follow his regression to the state of a new-born *homo sapiens*, then of pre-semiotic ape, and so on down to the state of a protozoon. Let us rejoice about it: matteremes already exist. Indeed, so do objectemes. And even utensils exist, and mechanisms made of utensils too, as well as automated machines made of mechanisms and partially overlapping program-bearing codes. Quadruple articulation of material production already exists. Quadruple thrift has already been taken advantage of. It is on a planet which has already been completely transformed by human work that we have opened our eyes; it is through an atmosphere already teeming with highly articulated sounds that we have uttered our first whimpers. Let us therefore feel consoled. Humanity, even if it has developed in an unsatisfactory and dangerous way, has at least already developed. The fatigue of starting everything over again from scratch does not lie ahead of us. If anything, we shall have consciously to undo what has already been done, and to rebuild it at the service of a better human condition. Let the reader not lend an ear to certain linguists, then, when they malignantly try to make him believe that only a double articulation exists, and only in the field with which they themselves are concerned.[45]

---

[45] It would be well to recall, at least in a note, the homological approximations of two authors who are as original as they are relatively neglected, George Thomson and Trân duc Thao. George Thomson advanced the hypothesis that *human* rhythm (as such distinguishable from the *solely* physiological rhythm which man has in common with the other animals) had its origin in the use of utensils. Taking up an idea of Bücher's, later also developed by Paget for the physiological part, he maintained the originary homology between the articulation of the hands and of the vocal organs as the premise for the elaboration made by consciousness of such reflected actions into socially accepted communicative systems (Thomson 1961 [1955]: 445-454; Bücher 1919; Paget 1930).

Trân duc Thao (who was at one time minister of Instruction under Ho Chi Minh), beginning from a Marxist interpretation or integration of Husserl, whose unpublished manuscripts he studied at Louvain, reconstructed some of the main aspects of animal behavior in terms of the development of "sensorial certainty". They are the passage from the "ghostly object" to the "real object" or "thing", and then the series in which appear the forms of the *intermediary*, the *instrument* (individual and temporary), the *utensil* (collective and permanent) and *language* (considering the last two as forms at the same level). Thao makes the sign equivalent to the instrument understood as the development of a merely intermediary object. We then have «the use of the *utensil*, when ... the mediating object is no longer simply utilized in the present situation, but is also a product which is consumed ... thus assuming for consciousness the sense of an instrument which is of itself efficacious» (1951: 213). The important point for us, noticed by Thao, is that the development of the instrument into utensil requires a common activity, that is, collective habits, techniques acquired by a group; and that therefore «the immediate acts of collaboration and of tradition diversify by articulating themselves according to these techniques and they rise in this way to the form of language ... In the exercise of language the subject has the consciousness of realizing a common value and a transmission of power» (216). Going ahead in this analysis, Thao arrives at the assertion that, «with the use of verbal schemata, real behavior already begins *de facto* to rise up to the level of utensil», which indicates that «the constitution of the vocal sign presents itself as a first form of the process of making» (221; but see all of pages 217-230, and the essays to be collected in 1973 as well). These ideas, in one so deeply acquainted with Marx and Husserl, which came to my

4. FROM LANGUAGE TO ECONOMY

> If commodities could speak,
> they would say ...
> KARL MARX

4.1 *The Corporal Residue of Non-verbal Messages*

An important part of semiotic research still consists in "going" from the verbal to the non-verbal, that is, in the application of the mentality, the methods, and the instruments developed in the study of verbal sign systems, especially of languages, to this or that non-verbal sign system. One well-known and much-discussed example is given by Lévi-Strauss, who applies notions of structural linguistics in the field of anthropology, studying the rules of matrimony and kinship systems «as a kind of language, that is, a group of operations destined to assure a certain type of communication between individuals and groups». According to Lévi-Strauss, the fact that "the message" is constituted of the *women of the group* who *circulate* between clans, stirpes, or families (and not, as in language itself, of the *words of the group* circulating between individuals), does not in any way alter the identity of the phenomenon considered in the two cases. Lévi-Strauss generalizes his own comparative approach affirming that «in every society, communication takes place on at least three levels»: of woman, of goods and services, and of messages as such. With regard to the other two forms, economic exchanges would have an intermediate position: this because goods and services, unlike women, are not persons, while, unlike phonemes, but in this like women, they are values. Still, «just as soon as the economic system reaches a certain degree of complexity» symbols and signs are necessary for the exchange of goods and services (Lévi-Strauss 1949 and 1967²; 1958: 69, 326, 327 and *passim*).

This last statement is remarkable for the variety of interpretations which can be made of it. Here we take three distinct propositions from it, beginning with the

---

knowledge several years after I had presented the homology of production in *Language as labor and trade*, have been of great comfort to me and have encouraged me to develop the homology further in this section.

Many specifications could be added to what has been said above in the text. We are dealing, in fact, with arduous problems more often hinted at than faced squarely. It can seem easy to talk about them only when one subtracts a portion of them from the material dimension and from the dialectical flux: because then the portion of them which has been subtracted, taking vigor from traditional, unanalyzed values (these are always class values), absorbs and hides within itself all the unresolved difficulties. As Mao Tse-tung says, «idealism and metaphysics are the easiest things in the world, because people can talk as much nonsense as they like ... Materialism and dialectics, on the other hand, need effort» (1955, now in Chapter XXII of any edition of *Quotations from Chairman Mao Tse-tung*). Some typical ways to "forget about difficulties" — and favorite subjects for big discources — are (i) a "mind" which is seen as being able to do by itself the work that must instead laboriously be sought for and described in material terms on the one hand and in social terms on the other; (ii) sign universals of *the biological sort*, as such withdrawn from historical development or even made precedent to homination; (iii) sign systems and processes isolated from all the rest and examined only as self-sufficient machines.

proposition, certainly a just one, that (i) the economic market does not take place without *the use of* a language. This amounts to saying that a market from which all languages are absent has never been seen. For this point we refer the reader to the discussion in Section Three of the homology between linguistic production and material production. However, it would be an error to proceed from the proposition affirming the *simultaneous presence* of the two productions to either of the following two propositions: (ii) the market would not be a non-verbal sign system if a (verbal) language were not a *constitutive part* of it; (iii) the economic market has non-sign residues within the field of its being *a market*.

Keeping, as we must, (ii) well-distinguished from (i), we can free ourselves from it immediately by repeating the statement that non-verbal sign systems enjoy the *status* of existing to the same extent that verbal sign systems do. In other words, the language as a verbal sign system must be distinguished from any non-verbal sign system. Proposition (iii), instead, indicates a rather intricate situation which we must examine more closely. Here there is a tangle of problems regarding the double use of non-verbal codes, that is, regarding the *bodies* of non-verbal signs as the bearers of properties which are not just or only sign properties.

The women of whom Lévi-Strauss speaks, even if they are *communicated* from family to family and therefore function as messages, are also flesh-and-blood persons. Although it is fundamental and necessary under any other aspect, this character of theirs is extra-verbal, indeed, extra-sign, and thus does not concern semiotic inquiry as such. Semiotics as applied to kinship systems does not study mates as mates, but rather mates as messages: that is, *prima facie*, not their use-values, but instead their exchange-values. But this is only the first layer of the situation.

On the other hand, the corporality of verbal messages lies in the very sign vehicles which constitute their codes: indispensable, but relevant only insofar as they are the vehicles of something other than themselves. This seems to hold true even when verbal sign vehicles are studied on their own account, in their objective structure, for particular ends like those of phonetic inquiry or formal logic, or those of poetic language and the doctrines dedicated to it. And anyway, as we have said from the beginning, in this piece of research we are dealing only with the practico-communicative use of a language. One can moreover recognize a corporality in verbal messages by the fact that they are produced and emitted by human bodies, of which they constitute modifications (or by machines produced by human bodies: in which case one talks about modifications intervening in *extensions of the bodies themselves*). But such corporality does not exist by itself outside the sign system to which those messages belong. In other words, the use-value of verbal messages does not exist outside of their existence as messages, as it does in the case of mates. Such value must then be sought *within* their function as messages, as we will try to show. From this it follows, however, that also in the case of mates a use-value must be found *also* within their function *as messages*, independently of the use-value they already have *as mates* (and that can therefore determine, so to speak from the outside, the type of exchange which takes place).

Let's take the case of roast chickens. In the non-verbal sign systems of etiquette and cuisine, in their turn connected to those of the market and of production, chicken is still partially a highly-prized food in Italy, while it is a popular or even "cheap" food in the United States (and also has a low price). But the corporality of roast chickens, their use-value, is in turn completely independent of the value that they assume in the above non-verbal sign systems.

The *way* in which we use sound material to construct words, and words to confection verbal messages, regards their *bodies* much more and much less than the way in which we use the bodies of other objects (which nevertheless do assume sign value in non-verbal sign systems) when we leave aside the fact that such bodies can function *also* as signs: much more, because the only use of the bodies of words lies in their function as signs; much less, because we can't do anything else with them. The meaning that any non-verbal object comes to assume in a sign system is connected to the use that is made of it as an object: if chicken weren't edible it could never assume the sign value of refined or of "cheap" food in the "language" of etiquette or of cuisine. The same thing happens to commodities: the assumption of an (exchange-)value by any product, that is, its transformation into a commodity, requires, as is well-known, that it have a use-value, even if it doesn't depend upon it in a direct way. It is a question of various non-verbal sign systems, that is, of non-verbal objects that assume this or that type of sign value, thus coming together to form a system of their own. Still the fact remains that raising a chicken or eating it are not by themselves sign operations, or not primarily. A chicken does not develop in nature, nor is it produced and consumed, as a sign; but rather, precisely, as a chicken.

Every time that we apply conceptual instruments originating in linguistics to objects different from those constituting a language in the usual sense, we come upon what I have elsewhere called the *corporal residue of non-verbal messages* (R.-L. 1968c, ch. II). The danger to avoid at this point is that of becoming bogged down in this corporality in the sense of assimilating the production and consumption of those objects *as messages* to their production and consumption *as objects*. In order to avoid this danger it is, in the first place, necessary to make a distinction between the production and consumption of *the body* and the production and consumption of *the sign*. We have already given a fairly systematic discussion of this point in 2.4.1 and 2.4.2; but it is worth-while insisting in a more analytic and exemplificatory way on some of the aspects of the distinction (to say it in a brief way) between "body" and "sign". For this purpose we find particularly fruitful (i) a closer analysis of how the dialectic of exchange takes place already in the field of the non-mercantile exchange of mates (cf. 2.4.3); and (ii) an examination of commodities as messages, of the sign character of the economy and thus of the

semiotic character of economic science. We shall find that the fundamental processes of *exchanging* and *communicating*, which are usually studied separately as
if each of them belonged to a separate field of reality, are instead present together
in various fields and can be dealt with in a unitary manner.

4.2   *Dialectic of Exogamic Exchange*

In the exchange of mates the dialectical crossing of use-values and exchange-
values, which was first brought to light by Marx in the analysis of the commodity,
is fully realized. Such a crossing is always present whenever exchange occurs
(whether mercantile *or non-mercantile*, 2.4.3); moreover, we are going to place
it at the basis of a study of the formation of sentences (cf. Section Six). Let us,
then, take advantage of the fact that the crossing of use- and exchange-values is
easier to understand in the case of exogamy, and explain it in some detail. What
follows is by no means an empirical generalization from fieldwork in anthropology
or related disciplines. It is, by application of one main procedure in the dialectical
method, a *model* constructed by determined abstraction, *i.e.* an *abstract* instrument
for enquiring into the structure of exchange (cf. footnote 25).

We shall assume *as a paradigm* the case of a human male adult who is at the
same time potent, heterosexual, and non-incestuous. Let's call him M_1 and examine his social behavior with regard to two categories of women, those who
are related to him by blood, and all the others. Let's call these two categories,
simply, "blood relations" and "other women": by which we understand that
coming under one category or another is a property that belongs to every given
woman in relation to a given man. Insofar as he is non-incestuous, M_1 gives up
the use of his own mother, sisters, and daughters (as well as grandmothers, aunts,
nieces, and other more or less close kin) for sexual purposes. Insofar as he is
heterosexual, he uses sexually — or is willing to use, or has used in the past —
at least one woman belonging to another category.[46] Let's look now at another
human adult male, also potent, heterosexual, and non-incestuous, and moreover
not bound to M_1 by any kinship relation. Let's call him M_2 and repeat the same
line of reasoning for him. We will find, naturally, that the women who are "blood
relations" of M_1, the ones M_1 gives up, belong to the category "other women" for
M_2; while the women who are "blood relations" of M_2, the ones M_2 gives up, belong
to the category "other women" for M_1. The two categories of women, "blood relations" and "other women", have crossed each other. M_1 gives up his own blood rela-

---

[46] It should be clear that in this context the use of 'using' is just a usage to be found in the
relevant literature *describing* exogamy and other basic social processes. As such it is a neutral,
pre- or post-sexual usage, and no lack of respect either to the users or to the used is involved.
If the issue were the exchange of men, we would have to describe the ways in which women "use"
men in an equally asceptic manner.

tions and has free access to all the other women, including the blood relations of M_2; and thus, symmetrically, for M_2. If we add M_3, M_4, and so on, until we have listed all the men who in a given social group are potent, heterosexual, and non-incestuous, we have the same situation for all: each one gives up his own blood relations and has free access to all the other women, that is, to the blood relations of all the other men.

The situation is worth-while examining more intimately, in terms of values. What each man of the group gives up when he gives up his own blood relations is their use-value. Now the use-value of women for men originally lies in the properties, possessed by the female body, of satisfying the male sexual need and of generating children. These properties, however, cannot be isolated from the ability, acquired by women through enculturation, to carry out services useful to all the members of the group. From the beginning, in fact, everything has become social: even the "values of the female body" appear as social variables, so much so that they differ from culture to culture. And it isn't enough to generate children, it is also necessary to submit them in their turn to the specific processes of socialization required by the group. As adult members of the community and objects of exogamic exchange, women themselves are complex social products; the use-values they bear come from the specific work with which the community "produces" them.[47] By giving up his own use of his own blood relations, every man of the group makes them available to all the other men of the group as use-values. The blood relations of M_1 are offered to M_2, M_3, and so on, to whom access is given to their use-values. With this giving-up, and this offer, M_1 acquires the right of access to those who are "other women" for him, that is, to the blood relations of M_2, M_3, and so on (cf. Godelier 1969: 97–8).

Thus a non-mercantile exchange has been instituted. In order to bring forth the dialectic more clearly we will reduce the analysis to the most elementary case: let's isolate one female blood relation of M_1, and call her W_1, and one female blood relation of M_2 and call her W_2. The situation is then the following: M_1 gives up the use-value of W_1 in order to be able to enjoy the use-value of W_2,

[47] Cf. note 16. — What is involved here again is the notion of the social production of human beings in general. As far as exogamy is concerned, we are dealing with the social production of *women liable to be exchanged* for the purpose of mating. While it is clear that mateable women are "produced" in an attenuated sense if compared with the production of, say, hunting instruments, the fact remains that if all human beings are social products so are mateable women. Some aspects of the issue, to be carefully distinguished are the following: (i) the production of the body of human persons is, of course, basically natural; up to a certain point, there is little difference here among various families of mammals; (ii) even by non-human animals, however, there is at least *some* social production of individuals (cf. Ford and Beach, 1951, repr. 1965); (iii) the social production of human individuals varies enormously in time and space, and is inextricably connected with class struggle (cf. for example Poole's 1971 remarks on the origins of the "bourgeois production of women" and on literary myths which try to justify at the ideological level the view of women as part of the material patrimony, etc.).

while M_2 gives up the use-value of W_2 in order to be able to enjoy the use-value of W_1. W_1 has acquired a "value" that allows her to be exchanged with W_2, who has in turn acquired a "value" that allows her to be exchanged with W_1.[48]

It is then by crossing the different values, that M_1 and M_2 present themselves in the arena of non-mercantile exchange with W_1 and W_2, and exchange them. We'd better say a few more words on this interweaving of values. By permitting W_1 to assume an exchange-value, M_1 suppresses her use-value for him. M_2 does the same with W_2. The whole operation emerges only because W_1 and W_2 are contraposed and exchanged. If W_2, or to be precise, the use-value of W_2, didn't exist, desired by M_1, he would not set aside the use-value of W_1; and thus for M_2 who desires the use-value of W_1 and in order to obtain it sets aside the use-value of W_2. If, in the arena of (non-mercantile) exchange, we use the simple formula of equality, '$W_1 = W_2$', in the moment in which we affirm the equality of the two W under the aspect of their exchangeability, we can also specify that it is the use-value of W_2 that "cancels" (*auslöscht*, as Marx says) the use-value of W_1, expressing its "value".[49] If we turn the formula around, that is, we say '$W_2 = W_1$', the use-value of W_1 will cancel that of W_2, with what follows. The first formula, in fact, expresses the point of view of M_1 as the one who has brought W_1 into the arena of (non-mercantile) exchange; the second expresses the point of view of M_2 as the one who has brought W_2. M_1's end lies in W_2 as M_2's end lies in W_1; and it is just because of this that the process starts to move which, by crossing the values, leads to exchange.

With this brief analysis, which we should remember in the course of this Section and then in Section Six, we believe we have shown two things. The first is that exchange proceeds directly from work, of which it constitutes a dialectical complication. If work is "desire held in check", so also is exchange from the time in which it begins to develop as barter. M_1 *gives up* W_1 *in order to acquire* W_2 *through* an exchange. The desire is, at this point, held in check in an institutionalized way. The division of labor has assumed the social figure of a production for others, where the producer prescinds from the use-value of his own products. With the formation of a production for the market, a degeneration of the holding-in-check will take place. The second thing is that the dialectic discovered by Marx in the analysis of the elementary form of value of the commodity also holds good for the exchange of mates, and therefore, we can imagine, for other cases of non-mercantile exchange too. Actually, if we define exchange in terms of a crossing

[48] Cf. 2.3.4 at (iii) and footnote 12. — Let us recall that, according to this terminology, (i) 'value' is opposed to 'use-value', while 'exchange-value' can be used instead of 'value' when reference is made to the actual process of exchange; and (ii) exchange-value is then the phenomenal form of value. For further details, cf. 6.2-4.
[49] 'Setting aside', 'suppressing', 'giving up', and the like, are quasi-synonyms describing various moments of the unitary behavior of M_1 with regards to W_1. 'Cancelling', instead, is a specific description of the action exercised by a use-value on another use-value through the dialectical crossing of exchange.

of different values, it follows that some type of crossing must obtain for any exchange to exist, whether mercantile or not.

4.3   *Commodities as Messages*

Prima facie, a commodity presents itself as the *simple* object of an act of barter,
or of selling and purchasing. But one comes very soon to see that the simplicity
of commodities is only apparent. Or better, a commodity as a physical object
may be as simple as you want; but it cannot exist in isolation, and it acquires its
signification only in a special context. Even the most elementary cases of barter,
below the level of exchange proper, presuppose a pretty complicated network of
social relationships. The fact is that all commodities belong to non-verbal sign
systems, and function as messages within highly programmed non-verbal communicative situations.

A commodity appears on the market as the bearer of several layers of signification; interpretation must distinguish between these different layers and trace
them back to the sign-systems they belong to. A commodity doesn't go to the
market by itself; it needs somebody who sells it; and it isn't sold until somebody
buys it, that is, accepts it in exchange for money, or for other commodities in the
case of barter. A product doesn't transform itself into a commodity like a caterpillar
into a butterfly; it undergoes such a transformation because there are men who
put it into significant relations, that is, make it a member of a non-verbal sign
system. But when a commodity is used to satisfy a need, this means that its character of being a commodity is so to say dropped off, forgotten. In short, a commodity *is a commodity* rather than being a product or a useful article because,
and insofar as, it operates as a message of a certain kind. It is remarkable that
Marx's analysis of commodities is crowded with references to their status as messages, which so to say creep up from thought towards verbal expression in such
clauses as «if commodities could speak, they would say ...»; «the coat means
more when brought into a value relation with the linen than it means apart from
such a relation»; «the linen ... conveys its thoughts in the only language it knows
— the language of commodities» (*Das Kapital*, I: 97 and 66; English translation:
58, 21, and 22); and many others.

The shop-keeper who displays his goods in the shop-window is accepting and
applying semiotic rules which allow him to tell any potential buyer his intention
to sell goods as commodities. The important fact here is that such semiotic rules
are being used quite independently of whether any given commodity is or is not
accompanied by a price-tag, or by a label conveying additional verbal information
about the commodity itself. A commodity *may also* be the bearer of *verbal* signs
(for instance, a word may be printed on a scarf), and there are verbal commodities; but in no way is it necessary for a commodity to have anything to do with

verbal signs, and whether it does or not has nothing to do with its being a commodity. Since being a commodity means, among other things, functioning as a *non-verbal* sign, we find here a clear example of reciprocal independence between verbal and non-verbal sign systems (cf. 1.3).

There are of course products which *signify as products*, *i.e.*, which are products insofar as they are interpreted by men according to some code other than the code of commodities. They may be non-veɪbal, like traffic-signs, or verbal, like books. The sign-function here is also to be found in the use-value of articles — within their capacity to satisfy human needs. The property, however, of being a commodity belongs to another order of signification. If the case at hand is that of a commodity which also signifies as a mere product, as traffic-signs and books do, *i.e.* which signifies something before becoming a commodity and independently of this additional condition it may attain, we have then to deal with two kinds of signification, the one superimposed on the other.

In other words, the sign function may be present in two ways: (i) within the use-value of the commodity; this sign function has nothing to do with the fact that the object is a commodity, because it is a sign function which exists already at the product level; (ii) within the commodity as such, that is in its *exchange-value* (see footnote 48). It is the latter kind of signification, exchange-value, that turns any object whatsoever into a commodity. If this kind of signification didn't exist, the object could only be described as a product or as a useful article; it would belong to the realm of production and respectively to the realm of mere usefulness; it wouldn't have reached the level of commodities.

In addition to all this we have to consider that products or useful articles are themselves the carriers of non-verbal significations. The signification of a product is the value of the specific human labor crystallized in it, of all the operations which have gone into its production (2.3.2). The signification of a useful article is its capacity to satisfy a human need. These significations belong to social sign systems of the non-verbal kind and are also linked to biological systems of signification. By taking all the cases examined into account and presenting them, as it were, from bottom to top, the following classification of five levels as regards the sign-functioning of commodities can be attempted:

I. For man even a non-produced good, like the water of a spring or the edible fruit of a wild tree, bears signification: this lies in its capacity to satisfy a human need, to be used for some end.

II. The greater part of goods, however, are produced. Even the water of a spring, or the fruit of a wild tree, is partially a product of human work if man has deliberately gone there in order to reach it. Products bear with them the signification of being goods; and, *in addition*, they also bear the signification of the operations which have been necessary for producing them according to a plan. Notice that the type of work under consideration here is specific work: the specific procedures required for the production of that product as distinct from all others, together with the end or group of ends for which the product can be used (cf. 2.3.1, 2.3.2).

III. Almost all products are commodities. Today indeed one speaks of the universal transformation of everything into commodities, and of commodities into independent entities and fetishes.[50] Commodities are messages that bear a third kind of signification, superimposed on the first two, and coming synthetically into being only at this level. The kernel of this third signification is the "value" deriving, as we know (2.3.4), from the *ratio* of human work which belongs to each commodity within the global production of a community or group of communities. The consequences of the formation of this third significant layer are enormous for human life. It is here that, to begin with, we find "the fetish-character of the commodity" first brought to full light by Marx in a classic section of *Kapital*.

So that a commodity may be a commodity, it is then necessary that the message which it constitutes draw upon all three of the layers of signification which we have set forth. We consider as a particular, indeed an exceptional, case, that in which a mere good — as distinguished from a true product — becomes a commodity. In this case our second level is left out. For example, one could even exchange — or, sell and buy — a stone which has been picked up on an uninhabited mountainside, transmitting it as a commodity; in this case we would say

---

[50] The Italian *mercificazione* and *feticizzazione* (as the French *marchandization* and *fétichization*) express the process by which anything can be and usually is automatically transformed into, or assumes the status of, a commodity and respectively a fetish, this transformation being a general feature of contemporary neo-capitalistic societies. Of course much of the original pregnancy gets lost in a periphrastic translation. Here and elsewhere, the English language shows a sort of resistance to the transmission of general ideas of a dialectic character — a fact well known to translators of Hegelian or Marxian texts, and on which there is general agreement among Continental scholars.

The following is a convincing passage by a scholar who went through the terrible job of rewriting in English a book he had previously produced in German: «As to terminology, the reader will find some unusual terms, or usual terms applied with a somewhat modified meaning. This was unavoidable in a book that had to deal with Hegelian and Marxian terms which can by no means be translated into conventional English. We have not availed ourselves of all the liberties which were declared necessary in an article contributed by Engels to the November 1885 issue of *The Commonwealth*. We have refrained from linguistic innovations as far as possible and even from coining new English terms corresponding to the many new-coined German terms used by Hegel, Marx, and present-day Marxists. However, we have followed the advice of Engels to risk a heresy rather than to render the difficult German words and phrases by more or less indefinite terms which do not grate upon our ears but obscure the meaning of Marx» (Korsch 1938[1], 1963: 13).

As one can now read even in the *Times literary supplement* («Coming to terms with class», 1971, No. 3,615, p. 2), «Lukács dissects skillfully and profoundly the process of "reification" in capitalist society, whereby what are essentially human relations are transformed into entities apparently possessing an independent existence of their own (commodities, exchange-value, laws of the market). This process not only stands in the way of any true understanding of reality, except at its most superficial empirical level, but protects and perpetuates exploitation, since both exploiters and exploited see themselves as subject to the rigid compulsion of external realities though these are in fact merely the relations which bourgeois society has itself created».

that the stone is a good without being a product because it doesn't consist of previously existing materials put together by work, *i.e.*, it is not manufactured. Naturally one could maintain that even the stone is a product in the sense that it has been fixed by attention and picked up by human hands instead of being left in its indistinct naturality. The immense value of a stone collected on the moon clearly shows how work gives its value to an object even in cases where it doesn't modify its internal structure. The risk involved in a discussion like this is that of starting a perfectly useless academic argument on the relations between idealism and empiricism in the theory of knowledge. Or else it is a question here also of distinguishing — as in the case of the women-messages of Lévi-Strauss — between the various senses of such terms as 'producing', 'product', and the like. It seems to me that the case of the stone picked up on the (terrestrial) mountainside and then sold is not only very rare but also artificial. And anyhow, the distinction between idealism and empiricism cannot be drawn by an arm-chair study of the theory of knowledge as it has been developed through the centuries by feudal and bourgeois philosophers, but rather by investigating how things actually developed in the reality of historical development. In this reality we see that a virgin nature from which non-produced goods might be drawn has ceased to exist from remote millennia, and that the notion of such virgin nature is in its turn a well-defined historico-ideological product (Marx and Engels, *Die deutsche Ideologie*; Lukács 1923, English transl. 1971; Korsch 1923; 1934-36, English transl. 1963; Di Siena 1969; Rossi-Landi, 1969b and 1969c). Let's drop, then, the particular case of the direct passage from the level of the good to that of the commodity, and consider normal and paradigmatic the case in which the three distinct levels pile up one upon the other in the order in which we have set them forth.

There are two more levels, which for the sake of simplicity we list as fourth and fifth, but which we could consider as variations or complications of the second and the third. These two variations or additional layers occur frequently, but they are not at all necessary for the existence of a complete three-level commodity-formation.

IV. A product, independently of its being a commodity, can signify as a product: it can be, that is, a *sign product*, a product only insofar as men interpret it by means of a given code. We gave two obvious examples already: a book is a sign product of the verbal subspecies, a street-sign is a sign product of the non-verbal subspecies. As we know, this sign character of theirs does not regard the commodity-formation. Even in a perfectly socialist society, from which the typical commodity-formation of the capitalist mode of production is absent, books and street-signs will continue to be produced. The sign character we are talking about regards the product *as a product*, before the alternative between making of it a commodity and simply using it even arises. This fourth level, then, is really a variation of the second. In the case of a sign product, the commodity-message will bear anyway *also* this signification. And here is, finally, the last level:

V. The body of the commodity can be the bearer of further signs regarding the commodity itself or other things. For example, the commodity can have a tag indicating its price or its use or the fact that it belongs to a certain sector of production. A typical case of a commodity-message bearing all five significations, that is, which signifies contemporaneously at all five of the levels distinguished, is that of a book displayed in the shop-window of a bookstore with a price tag attached and a paper band describing the book itself or the series to which it belongs.

We have used the term 'signification' at all five levels. Certainly it would be helpful to distinguish even in their names the various ways of signifying to which we have referred. The signification of a good for human life as the satisfier of a need is certainly not the same thing, nor does it perform the same function, as the verbal signification of the pages of a book. The issue is not only terminological; indeed, it is connected with a tangle of problems. 'Meaning', 'sense', 'significance', 'signification', 'denotation', 'connotation', and the like, are terms unequally used in the various languages, and their "families" oppose remarkable difficulties to being transported from one language into another. One could even feel tempted to say that there is one such family in each individual language, and conclude that meaning is not an exportable article — that the "commodities of meaning" are to be consumed only on the domestic market (cf. Rossi-Landi 1955 and 1961). Fortunately there have been numerous attempts at putting in order all the members of one national family, or a number of families on the international market; and unfortunately, a host of new terms have been introduced, to be learned in special contexts. This is the situation as it appears to anybody who sticks his neck out of his own special orchard. In front of it the most important thing for fruitful spade-work in a new field of semiotics seems to be not to unduly extend this or that terminological model beyond the field in which it has been elaborated and in which it has a specific job to do. Once we have admitted that talking about signification at all five of the listed levels sounds generic, we must also understand that in this unitary use a just demand for generality is expressed. What ties all the levels together is the presence of some sort of signification. If we want to begin from the trunk, we have to examine what sign system is at work at each of the levels described. The first thing to realize is that at least one different sign system is operating at each level.

Keeping all five of the levels of the sign function of the produced-good-which-has-become-a-commodity well in mind, means avoiding underrating the play of the factors that concur dialectically in its coming into existence, and thus also avoiding overly simple solutions.[51] We call this play *dialectical* because here we are not

---

[51] Let us consider as an example some statements by Lefebvre (1966, ch. VIII), which at first glance seem to be kin to the content of this section: «Toute marchandise est un signe, mais n'est pas qu'un *simple* signe ... Le monde de la marchandise ... constitue un système de signes, un langage, un champ sémiotique. Il nous parle, avec quelle éloquence persuasive et contraignante ... [these last three dots are Lefebvre's] ... L'objet se perçoit d'abord dans son rapport au besoin. Sans ce rapport, il ne nous dit rien; mais aussitôt, sous nos yeux, en tant

dealing with the mere arithmetical sum of various factors, but rather with their having concurred in the formation of something that serves us for something else in its new immediacy, through a qualitative leap, as is typically the case of the

que marchandise, l'objet se change en signe. Il unit en lui le signifiant (l'objet susceptible d'être échangé) et le signifié (la satisfaction possible, virtuelle, pas seulement différée mais dépendante de l'achat)» (p. 342). This is a very confused way of referring to the complex situation which has been analyzed above. Lefebvre passes through the distinctions we have noted without seeing them at all. He makes something of a mess when talking of the signification of commodities. He collects in a single *signifié* of the commodity as such, the significations that come to the commodity-message from the level of products and from the level of mere goods; and instead, he puts the whole signification of the commodity as such in a notion he has of the *signifiant* of the commodity. In this way everything that has genetically gone into a commodity is flattened into the idea of a *signifié* of the commodity considered as a mere sign; and the message character of the commodity as such is flattened into the idea of a *signifiant* of that very sign. In short, Lefebvre reduces the five levels distinguished above to a mere Saussurian opposition of *signifiant* and *signifié* within a presumptive commodity-sign. Thus Lefebvre, though his research doubtlessly has a Marxian flavor and though he does present himself as a Marxist, falls completely under the ferocious criticism of Karl Marx, who had already denounced with due energy the danger of considering commodities as mere signs (see below in the text, and footnote 52).

One can therefore consider completely erroneous Lefebvre's identification of the *signifiant* of a commodity-sign with the commodity-object susceptible of being exchanged on the market, as well as the identification of its *signifié* with the potential satisfaction to be had from the body of the commodity. To put it better, rather than simply erroneous, it appears in the first place to be arbitrary; and in the second place to be seriously out of phase with regard to reality. It is arbitrary because one could turn it over, or move it around in various ways, and then discuss uselessly and endlessly about the various operations made. In fact, even if one were to accept the hypothesis that Lefebvre was right in maintaining that the commodity is a mere sign, one could turn what he says upside down and maintain that what functions as *signifiant* is the presence of the material body; this would seem to be kin to what is usually said about the materiality of the verbal *signifiants* themselves as opposed to the (let us say in the first instance) "non-material" character of the *signifiés*. The *signifiés* would then be concepts *à la* Saussure; interpretable, on the other hand, as *uses* of the respective *signifiants*, as ways of employing them. Let us go ahead and say that the uses *are not material* in the sense in which the objects used are material (what is important is to avoid making the idealistic leap that brings one to consider them as *immaterial*). The same is true for a hammer too, or a pair of shoes: the uses of such objects are not in their turn material objects. Accepting the hypothesis, then, that it is the material body of the commodity that functions as the *signifiant*, where would the *signifié* of the commodity be? This is what one can vainly begin to hunt for. Where would it be? In the exchange–value of the commodity as such, for example? This distribution of the rôles of *signifiant* and *signifié* would be just as gratuitous as the one made by Lefebvre.

The most serious error, however, remains that of mistaken phasing: the over-simplified view of the formation of a commodity-sign at a level which is already much too high, that is, a level much more complex than the one at which the signs of the non-verbal sign system of economics *begin* to function.

Parsons' approach to money as a specialized language, to the circulation of money as the communication of messages having meanings according to a code, etc. (1967: 357-360; 1968: 465), the importance of which was stressed by Jakobson (1967: 84; 1970b: 427-428), should also be discussed. It seems to me that a treatment of money as a language (better: as a sign system) should be founded on the underlying layers of production and exchange of commodities, rather than isolated from them — and this is true for *any* treatment of money, deliberately semiotic or not.

product which becomes a commodity prescinding from the specific working process from which it derives as a product. It appears then, among other things, that the nature of the commodity as a message belonging to the sign system of mercantile exchange cannot be fully grasped unless one keeps in mind the whole dialectic of work and production, resorting to it in order to delve out whatever internal relations are buried in the "mystery of commodities".

4.4   Economics as a Sector of Semiotics

Every economic discussion is founded on the triad of production-exchange-consumption, that is, on the entire process of social reproduction (2.4). The way in which the economic discourse refers to each of the three terms is, however, radically different. The demystification of economics shows that it does not regard production and consumption as such (even though, given the continuous circle between production and consumption, they are, *in fact*, present as second level objects of the discourse). It is with other instruments that the initial and terminal moments of the triad of social reproduction are usually faced. From the viewpoint of production, the description of how a particular good is produced belongs to various branches of technology; the description of its characteristics or properties, that constitute its particular use-value, to merceology; and the description of the value of the goods produced, taking the general situation into account, to sociology and history. Economics proposes itself as the study of the intermediate moment of social reproduction — of something that happens *between* production and consumption, that is, of exchange. It is hardly necessary to add that when we talk about exchange we are also talking about its developments: the transformation of the product into commodity, the development of the market as a system of commodities, money as the universal equivalent of commodities, the formation and use of capital, and so on.

Obviously economics cannot avoid making constant *reference* also to production and consumption: still it is not part of its job to consider them from the inside, but rather from the outside, insofar as they constitute the two social zones in the midst of which exchange and its developments are inserted. The paradigm-case of a possible piece of behavior of an elementary sort will clarify the issue. If I produce something and consume it right away or let somebody else consume it, *i.e.*, if not even the embryo of exchange or barter is present, the "economic" moment is simply absent. Only the production of a good, of a use-value, has occurred; the production has not had time to *assume* an exchange-value, that is, to *become* a commodity. So that an economic moment in the proper sense can take place, it is necessary that a mediation constituted by exchange be inserted between production and consumption. An additional sign system must begin operating. Indeed, as we have seen in 2.4.3, if the exchange is to be mercantile in the proper sense two independent producers must present themselves on the market. While the mediation of exchange is taking place, the product is so to say suspended; and during this *suspension*, extraneous both to production as such and to consumption as such, it assumes values of another type, radically different from those for which it had been produced originally as an object of consumption, capable of satisfying a need. Making production contiguous to consumption would amount to eliminating the very object of economic science as it is usually understood. If this happened in an integral way, economics as the study of the market and of the individual use of resources would be entirely substituted by social planning of production in function of human needs. And since such a study cannot even start without facing the distinction between "natural" and "artificial" needs, as well as other categories of human needs, a general theory of man would be almost immediately involved. As we know, this is not an alternative between the sheer presence and the absence of any such theory, but rather between the conscious use of an adequate theory and the passive acceptance of whatever theory happens to be handed down in a certain society at a given moment. In other words, a general theory of man is dialectically prior to social planning; but no social planning can avoid conveying an attempt at bringing about a determinate conception of man (cf. Rossi-Landi 1968c, ch. 6).

In semiotic terms — with references to the classifications set forward in the previous Sections, to the hypothesis of the homology of production discussed in Section Three, and to what we just said in 4.3 about commodities as messages — the following characterization can be attempted. Economics proper is the study of the non-verbal sign system which makes it possible for particular types of messages, usually called "commodities", to circulate. More briefly, and with a formula: *economics is the study of commodity-messages*. External to the commodity-messages lie the production and the consumption of the bodies of the commodities — sign or non-sign bodies as they may be with regard to their *status as products*.

Notice that we say "commodity-messages", not "commodity-signs". A message is made up of signs that are already complete for they consist of the synthetic union of at least one *signans* and one *signatum*. A message gets to be built and to function as it does as a feature of real social life. We are thus two stages distant from the *danger*, denounced by Marx with just force, of *considering commodities only as signantia* (instead of as the union of *signantia* and *signata*).[52] Such

---

[52]   Marx: *Kapital*, I: 2, 105-106; English transl.: 66-67. Cf. the brief discussion of Lefebvre in the preceding footnote. It is hardly necessary to remind the reader that Marx was writing in an epoch in which linguistic science was much more rudimentary than it is today, and the very concepts of semiotics and of information theory hadn't yet begun to develop. A certain amount of interpretation and "translation" is therefore necessary whenever we construe his texts in contemporary semiotic terms. But this happens with all great thinkers; or indeed, there is no alternative to the interpretation of past messages according to present interests, for there is no alternative to a progressive variation of the code of the receiver as compared to the code of the transmitter. While it is the historian's task to learn as much as possible to think in terms of the transmitter's code, it is the task of the theoretician, as well as of the man of action, to make as much sense as possible of earlier messages within the contemporary code.

partial considerations would be cases of reductionism, that is, they would amount to using a part for the whole. The danger is avoided by considering commodities, instead, as proper messages composed of various complete signs. Messages function in society, not within some abstract system; they circulate in the real world, and it isn't enough to dissect them according to some partial interest in their formal appearance. With commodity-messages information is transmitted about human work, about the way in which the society is organized, about exploitation. If we come to know of just one commodity which exists in a given community, *i.e.*, if we have received from that community just one commodity-message, what we have *ipso jure* come to know is that in that community there is a production for the market — with all that is involved in it. The distinction between signs and messages, here as elsewhere, is decisive. A message is an organized group of full-winged signs that is electively used. It is something codified: the use of a code has already taken place for a message to exist at all. A sign can be just repeated, but a message is usually manufactured. There is new human work in it. The fact that a commodity is a complex message and not a mere sign can be seen by investigating the type of codification that makes the form of commodities possible at a level higher than the level of products. Therefore the various levels are all taken into account, if only in an indirect way, whenever a commodity-message is described.

The economist, however, can leave out of consideration what happens *within* the processes of the production and consumption of goods, and consider the use-values of the bodies of commodities only insofar as they are the bearers of particular exchange-values. Why is he able to do this? Because, as a student of messages, he deals with the way in which, *after* material production, a product (whether a sign-product or not) becomes a commodity (that is, a message belonging to a certain sign-system); and then, *before* material consumption, it becomes a product again. He studies the way in which the product is codified into a commodity, and the commodity de-codified into a product. (Let's recall that it *can* be a question of a mere *good*, in the sense that it isn't *necessary* for the thing to have been produced in the proper sense of the word.) The economist thus studies not only the way in which the message is exchanged but also (*as a message*) produced and consumed. It is *within exchange* in the wide sense, as distinguished from production and consumption in the wide sense, that he finds *those* processes of production and consumption that interest him as a semiotician (cf. 2.4.2). Economics offers an excellent model for the study of non-verbal sign systems because one finds very clearly here the formation of a message on the substratum of a material object, which then, when this character of being a message ceases, usually conserves a corporal residue.

One part of the greatness of Marx as a thinker of general ideas — of the fact that in writings of his apparently dedicated to the economic problem alone one continues to find incomparable stimuli for many different studies — can be presented in just this way. After having eliminated from economic consideration production as a group of technological processes and consumption as a group of physiological processes, he described for the first time *both* the exchange of commodities *and* the production and consumption of the commodities themselves as commodities. He described, that is, the *entire process* of the functioning of commodities as messages within a non-verbal sign system programmed by every society which has arrived at the stage of production for the market. An economic science, in fact, that does not study the commodity as a message, limits itself to the acceptance of commodities as simply given or "natural"; and an economic science that, though it does see a message in the commodity, considers only its exchange while ignoring its production and consumption, can never make a proper use of the theory of labor-value nor ever come to face the deep-seated problems of exploitation. The Marxian demystification of bourgeois economy, because of its studying commodities as messages and of its considering the entire trajectory of these messages, offers the first complete dialectical model of a socially real communicative process, and the first conscious grasp of a non-verbal sign programming (cf. 7.5) which was accepted and repeated unconsciously by billions of people. Semiotics as the general science of sign systems has its most important root in *Kapital*. The systematic exploration of non-verbal socially real communicative processes, and thus also of the codes that, hidden beneath them, support them, begins with the Marxian demystification of the bourgeois economy and particularly with the analysis of the commodity. It was Marx who first brought to light the reciprocal relations between men on the one hand and those omnipresent products of theirs, non-verbal messages, on the other hand, as well as the relations between these messages themselves. Precisely the fact of leaving aside the production and consumption of the bodies which bear these messages makes Marxian economics a typically semiotic science; but precisely the fact of considering the entire communicative process of commodity-messages makes it a completely human science, a complete science of the social.

The reasons are by now clear why the economists referred to here can only be those of the so-called Classical School, Smith, Ricardo, and Marx, with the addition of some of their contemporaries, and some of their current continuators or commentators.[53] The thinkers of the Classical School face the economic

---

[53] Among others writing in English, we recall again Baran, Dobb, and Sweezy (cf. footnote 11 and the References). Pierro Sraffa — the English-writing Italian Marxist editor of Ricardo's works, a fellow of Trinity College of Cambridge, and, according to Wittgenstein, the main influence on his passing over from the static world of the *Tractatus* to the mobile (even if not historical) world of the *Untersuchungen* — would require a discussion apart. His *Production of commodities by means of commodities* is the first big scientific step in bringing economic *thought*, as distinguished from economic statistics or sociologistic analyses, back where it belongs, *i.e.* to the categories of the Classical School, after the long marginalistic parenthesis expressing the bourgeois reaction to the development of Marxism as a demystifying and revolutionary science. — Cf. Wittgenstein 1953, Foreword: x; Sraffa 1960; Napoleoni 1963: 194-201; Vitello 1963: 124; Pietranera 1961, 1966²; Pesenti 1970; Rossi-Landi 1966a, b (now in 1968c, ch.s 2 and 3: especially 95-97 and 105-112).

problem squarely, trying to resolve it within a theory of society, which, with Marx-after-Hegel, also has the bearing of a general theory of man and history. They deal with the economic problem in all of its extent, as an organic part of human *reality* — for human reality is basically the totality of social sign systems.

Naturally, all of this gets lost if the situation of simple economic exchange, or indeed of mere barter, is interpreted as a sheer material passage, as such filmable in all of its aspects — the physical transfer of two objects from the hands of one person to the hands of another, and vice-versa. According to a point of view of this sort (see for example Samuelson, 1949, 1970[8]), it is through the observation of a large number of material transfers of objects between two persons that the economist collects his basic protocol statements; he can then quantify them, and by going ahead in this manner he will finally derive the *laws of economics*. When one asks such economists if it isn't possible to investigate *within* exchange, recon-structing the sign processes without which exchange would not take place and beginning, for example, from the fundamental distinction between the use-values and exchange-values of the exchanged objects, the answer that one usually gets is that such questions regard "the psychology of the subjects" and cannot lend them-selves to the quantification necessary for the construction of "an intersubjective science in the modern sense". In this way what is set aside as mystificatory and ideological is precisely the analysis of the value of the commodity — which is the irreplaceable foundation not only of every demystificatory investigation and of every doctrine of ideologies, but also of every over-all semiotic approach to social reality. In the place of investigations aiming at unburying deep social processes which go on unnoticed and affect our whole lives, one then puts an "objective reality" made up of "facts" which are supposed to be fully describable by means of "perceptive judgments": a veritable tombstone, smooth and flawless, which nobody should ever dare to lift.

5. FROM ECONOMY TO LANGUAGE

> Utilitas expressit nomina rerum.
> LUCRETIUS

5.1 *Messages as Commodities*

The messages which we exchange when speaking a given language make up the linguistic community to which we belong, that is, the society as a whole in its speech-aspect. Here 'linguistic' is used as a derivative of the Latin *lingua* (*a* lan-guage): to contrast "a language" with its corresponding "linguistic community" is partly equivalent to contrasting the code with the totality of messages expressed in it. The concepts "a language as a code" and "linguistic community as totality of messages" indicate two reciprocally necessary elements within the sphere of an existing totality. The one necessarily implies the other; but to say only this would be incomplete, and furthermore inexact, for a language can outlive its own linguistic community of origin when it is studied within and by another linguistic community — just as the products of non-linguistic work survive, and an abandoned factory is adapted and used for new production processes.

A linguistic community appears as a sort of *immense market, in which words, syntagms and sentences, used as verbal messages, circulate in the same way as commodities do*. We can ask ourselves what are the regularities which determine the circulation of these messages, starting from the *values* according to which they are *exchanged and consumed*.

A market is a system of equivalences and at the same time of differences. In order that the situation of mercantile exchange may be realized, it is in fact necessary to have commodities embodying, first and foremost, use-values. Without use-values there would be no exchange-values. We have therefore, immediately, a system of differences: the differences between the individual use-values and their respective exchange-values. Furthermore the use-values are themselves based on differences: they refer to needs and to ways of satisfying them; they are the result of production processes and bear properties to which the description "different" can be very fittingly applied. When use-values constitute a system, this is consequently a system of differences; but for the same reason it is also a system of equivalences; and the other aspect of this system, that of exchange-values, is a system of equivalences, and for the same reason also one of differences. A market comes into being precisely in the dialectical inter-play of all these factors. We maintain that the same is true in a linguistic community.

However, the products of non-verbal work do not cover the entire field of objects capable of satisfying non-verbal needs, while *all* verbal signs are by definition produced by man himself (cf. 2.4.1-2). Using some terms in a static rather than dialectical manner: "unproduced" objects exist "in nature"; their existence "precedes" that of "man" or is "independent" of him, such as air and water, which satisfy precisely his most fundamental needs. But only so-called "natural" signs can be regarded as equivalents to so-called "natural" products: neither of them are produced in the proper sense of the word, that is by specificially human work. Without the activity of an organism to "interpret" them, not even the most rudimental signs would be signs; without their identification, seizure and consumption by an organism, not even objects like air or water would serve to satisfy needs. All this not only does not contradict the characterization of *verbal* signs as products, but on the contrary gives a useful indication precisely for the demarcation of mere activity from work (2.3.1).

Messages too, like all the products of human work, have, first and foremost, a use-value or utility insofar as they satisfy needs. The needs satisfied by messages are those of expression and communication, with all the varying stratifications which historically have piled up and become entangled around them. Without verbal signs, these needs are not given full satisfaction *on the human level*. Once the conception of language as work has been accepted, the first hypothesis for research which presents itself is this: that not only the products of non-verbal work but also words and syntagms are used, and messages are transmitted and received, not only according to their use-value, but also and principally according to their exchange-value. As a first approximation: in the case of words and syntagms considered in the abstract, their exchange-value is to be sought in the reciprocal relationships into which they enter within the language of which they are a part, within the code when it is considered independently from the further linguistic work through which they are converted into messages. In the case of messages, their exchange-value is to be sought in their being transmitted and received within the sphere of a linguistic community, that is, in their circulating on a linguistic market of which they themselves are the constituent parts.

The terminology of values, as we encounter it in the texts of the classical economists and notably in Marx, has been put aside by marginalist economics, but survives in an attenuated form precisely in the works of linguists, for whom it is often normal to regard the *value* of a word or expression, and even of a message, as equivalent to their *meaning*. Common speech assists us too on this point with many idiomatic and proverbial expressions. It is difficult to consider these facts as purely accidental analogies; and it is remarkable that they have been paid such little attention. Saussure himself has many things to say about it, even if he does not appear to possess a theory of linguistic work, the most viable foundation for any theory of linguistic value.[54]

With things put in these terms, the basic proposition to be examined is the following: *the field of linguistic value corresponds entirely to the field of meaning*. To put it in a slightly more determined manner: 'having a value' has the same value as 'having a meaning', 'being worth something' is equivalent to 'meaning something'. However, one must avoid right from the start overestimating this correspondence or equivalence. The pie of all that which is (or has) linguistic value is divided into slices which do not correspond to the traditional slices into which people used to divide or still do divide the pie of meaning. Linguistic value, furthermore, is here introduced at a certain level in the elaboration of a general structure, which is that of work and production considered homologically

---

[54] Saussure's insistence on linguistic values is so well known that it is certainly not for us to re-expound it here. We are going to make some use of it in 6.3. Cf., however, ch. V of his *Cours* (1915, 1955[5]; English transl. 1966), his "notes" published by Robert Godel in the *Cahiers* (1954, 1957), Godel 1957, and especially Engler's critical edition (1967-1968) and De Mauro's abundant commentary on the Italian translation (1967). The whole notion of linguistic work developed in the present research (and first stated in 1961: ch.s IV and VI; cf. also 1967a: 99-109; 1968c: 185-192), contains a criticism of the Saussurian *parole* which we see as only one secondary case of linguistic work. One could say that Saussure did start a comparison between linguistics and economics and was fully aware of it (*Cours*: 114-117; English transl.: 79-81), but that his whole *Weltanschauung* and his intellectual tools, in spite of his towering stature, remained "marginalistic" — an expression of bourgeois individualism with all that goes with it.

in the linguistic and "material" fields. We are proceeding here from work to value, and consider value as a general property of that which has been produced by work. This is contrary to what happens in many theories of meaning, where meaning is placed as the foundation of a whole structure which then seems to have been fabricated so as to explain meaning itself; not to speak of those cases in which it is precisely meaning which is neglected, that is to say the machine of the language is considered with no regard to the values which it produces. It would be misleading, at least at this stage, to attempt comparisons between this or that type of meaning and this or that type of linguistic value.

Let us say rather that the types of linguistic value which we shall be able to distinguish will constitute a new subdivision carried out within the field tradition-ally indicated by the generic use of the word 'meaning' (as of *significato*, or *Bedeutung)*. We reaffirm that the theory of linguistic value as a product of linguistic work is an attempt to explain meaning by tracing it back to something else. In this way even the possible suspicion that linguistic values should not be called "use-" and "exchange-values" is dismissed as being terminological. To para-phrase Wittgenstein's celebrated remark, that «the meaning of a word is its use in the language» (1953: 43⁰), the path followed in this investigation consists in stating not only that the meaning of a word is its *value* or rather its *values* in the language, but also and principally that these values are to be traced back to the human work which makes them into what they are. This tracing back of value to work presents right away the following advantages: (i) the notion of linguistic use is included in that of linguistic work which, as a part of the notion of work in general, already possesses an articulated structure of its own; (ii) the important distinction between use and meaning is not lost (*even* Wittgenstein had reservations as to the reducibility of the latter to the former: 1953, I, 138⁰ and II, xi, 215); (iii) one does not run the risk of seeing in meaning only what is done with a pro-duct which has already been produced, that is, the risk of reducing use to con-sumption; (iv) nor does one run the opposite risk of seeing in meaning only its production.

Every message appears on the linguistic market as a *unit* of use-value and ex-change-value. It must in fact have a use-value, that is, it must be able to satisfy some communicative need, in order to be able to assume an exchange-value; but on the other hand it must present itself as an exchange-value so that it can be possible for people to reach its use-value and enjoy it. It is through a complex dialectic between the two types of value that, when I tell you something, you understand it. The elegant but peripheral question arises of whether, for such a dialectic to obtain, it is sufficient to have a use-value which, existing in the ab-sence of an objectively retraceable communicative situation, is *only* expressive. The question will be ignored hereafter because even an "only expressive" use-value must nonetheless belong to a code, which in its turn refers to previous com-municative situations.

When we examine a message from the angle of the two types of value, use- and exchange-value, which are enclosed within it, we find that in this field too the notion of linguistic work must in its turn be broken up in correspondence with the values which it is called upon to justify: to determine exchange-value one must use a different notion of work from that which serves to determine use-value (2.3.4).

Use-values satisfy varieties of needs (wants). So linguistic work bringing about use-values capable of satisfying different needs must also be work which varies and differentiates itself with the variation of its products: concrete and specific work, giving equally concrete and specific products which can be easily distinguished from each other. It is, in the field of verbal as of non-verbal sign systems, the same type of work which in the field of material production produces the bodies of goods in their quality of useful things, that is of use-values: objects and situations with specified properties capable of satisfying human needs. Any type of message (verbal or non-verbal, intentional or only detected from the outside) is primarily a thing whose qualities enable it to satisfy expressive and communicative needs. Verbal messages, those which make use of the constant capital constituted by the language, satisfy expressive and communicative needs such as expressing, denoting, connoting, showing, distinguishing, informing, reporting, qualifying, commanding, begging, reasoning, and so on, and also the complex need of connecting up various pieces of linguistic material at various levels of elaboration. In the literature of contemporary linguistic analysis, the study of the workings of language in general and of the different languages from the point of view of the satisfaction given to various expressive and communicative needs has only just begun to be felt as a requirement for the science. The labor hitherto accomplished by linguists and philosophers, huge as it is, is mostly limited to this or that aspect of the workings of the linguistic machine or — at the opposite extreme — to various aspects of existential situations in which individual speech acts occur.

The determination of exchange-values is closer to what linguists habitually do and does not present, as a research undertaken descriptively and *a posteriori*, the difficulties which appear to impede the determination of use-values. But the abstract and general *notion* of exchange-value and of the type of linguistic work which justifies it is more difficult to grasp.

The new-born *homo sapiens* finds himself immediately and insurmountably surrounded by (i) all the useful things that the society to which he belongs has already produced and continues to produce as tokens, *according to determined models*, (ii) the programs for their use, and (iii) the executions of such programs (2.3.3). This is just as true for the products of linguistic work as it is for the products of material work — for verbal sign systems as for non-verbal sign systems. Within the field of non-verbal sign systems, both the sign quality and the materiality of the sign-carrying bodies operate on the baby. He will find words and syntagms already opposed to each other in the system of the

language which was constituted before his birth and which he is learning
as his mother-tongue; subsequently he will discover that words and syntagms are also globally opposed, as parts operating within that particular system,
to all the words and all the syntagms of every other system of the same kind, that
is, of every other language. For both types of work the models were originally
developed as forms of social planning for the satisfaction of needs. The infant
learns to use the products and therefore sets in motion the programs to which
socially he adheres; in so doing he consumes tokens and also exercises, indirectly,
an action in favor of the models which have presided over production. But he is
certainly not aware of the specific work which is the basis of production according to models, and even less does he learn the construction of new models.
It will be only very partially, and much later, that he is possibly going to learn
how to deal with new models; and then only if he learns thoroughly, and with
originality, given professions. As we have seen (1.4), the very programs which
govern the forms of execution are indeed largely unconscious. The tokens produced in conformity with the models are for the most part used only in their new
immediacy, as materials and instruments. As such, the objects progressively produced come to belong to systems which are institutionalized according to programs
not necessarily connected with a planning aimed at the satisfaction of needs, and indeed quite often detached from it. The dialectic between models, tokens, programs
and executions interposes here an insurmountable thickness or barrier (2.3.3).
Both in the world of commodities and in that of verbal messages, it is the social
programming of the use of already produced items, and not the operative rules
for the satisfaction of needs, which determines exchange and circulation and which
decides what the exchange-value of the objects produced will be. As far as their
exchange-value is concerned, commodities and verbal messages appear detached
from the operations which do, in fact, produce them.

What all verbal messages have in common when their use-value is left aside is
precisely the quality of being simply messages, that is, the mere *results* of linguistic
work.[55] When we observe the linguistic market we notice that everyone speaks;
everyone is capable of using words and syntagms and of producing verbal messages. This is independent of the particular relationship which each word-as-pro-
duct and each message-as-product must nonetheless have with the specific linguistic work which has determined its use-value. Given the existence of a language spoken by a certain human group and of its linguistic market, we have here

---

[55] Wittgenstein seems to be pointing to this when he speaks of words *in general* as compared
with tools *in general* (1953: I, 11°, 12°, and 13°), or when he states that «the clothing of our
language makes everything alike» (*ib.*: II, xi, p. 224). This was anticipated in the *Tractatus,* for
instance, 4.02: «we understand the sense of a propositional sign without its having been explained to us»; 4.002: «the proposition *shows* [zeigt] its sense»; 4.121: on the logical form
"mirrored" in propositions; and *passim.*

a phenomenon which we could call "inevitability of meaning",[56] *i.e.*, the grasping of meaning as something natural (it is the social pseudo-naturalness of which we have already spoken). A hearer cannot help *beginning* to interpret in a given way an expression uttered by a speaker of his own linguistic community, whatever further interpretation he may then give to that same expression according to differing context and to his own personal inclinations.[57] If I say or write 'water', the reader will not take it to mean "earth" or "fire", and if I say 'if . . . then . . .', he will not take it to mean "neither . . . nor . . ." or "equal by definition to . . .". None of us, as a speaker, has it within his personal power to get out of this.

All the same, the inevitability of meaning, the fact that we cannot shirk the initial signification of each message which, as it were, impinges on us, does not

---

[56] «. . . when there is sense there must be perfect order. — So there must be perfect order even in the vaguest sentence» (1953: I, 98°); «. . . the sentence must . . . have *a* definite sense. An indefinite sense — that would really not be sense *at all*» (*ib.*: I, 99°): these are just two of the many passages where Wittgenstein is saying, or almost saying, that no speaker can *escape* the "apprehension" of sense. Cf. also *Pragmatics of human communication* (1967: 2.2, on "The impossibility of not communicating", pp. 48-49): «Behavior has no opposite . . . There is no such thing as nonbehavior or . . . one cannot *not* behave. Now, if it is accepted that all behavior in an interactional situation has message value, *i.e.*, is communicative, it follows that no matter how one may try, one cannot *not* communicate». It will be noticed that while Wittgenstein is stating something about the nature or structure of the message, and the authors of *Pragmatics of human communication* are stating something about (or from the point of view of) the sender of the message, our main point in the text concerns the receiver. Given the communicative situation, the three approaches converge, and the general formula may be attempted that "one cannot help communicating — by means of a message endowed with a definite sense — to a receiver who cannot help interpreting the message according to that sense". But this is only true of an *initial portion* (in the interpretation) of the message: cf. below in the text and footnote 57.

[57] In my book of 1961, ch.s VII and VIII, I tried to deal with this problem in terms of a distinction between "initial meanings" and "additional meanings", opposing this distinction to other distinctions such as — with regards to meanings — direct *vs.* indirect, immediate *vs.* mediated, explicit *vs.* implicit, literal *vs.* metaphorical, present *vs.* latent, and so on. Once the initial meaning has been grasped — which, as said before, is "inevitable" —, additional meanings are either spontaneously or purposively extricated from various layers of context. The initial meaning, whatever it may be, can trigger further interpretation (though it doesn't trigger it necessarily). The main point is that no descriptive or systematic definition of 'initial meaning' holds water. The only possible definition is rather a methodological one: the initial meaning is any meaning one starts with *de facto* in any given case (or class of cases) of interpretation. Whereupon the difficulty arises that in many cases (or groups of cases) the meaning one does start with belongs to a more complex, and not to a simpler, level than the additional meanings delved out by further interpretation. In other words, there is no possibility of simply pairing 'initial' to either immediate, or explicit, or literal, or present meaning — though there are of course measures of overlapping. Some messages are received and interpreted, for instance, for their metaphorical import, while their literal (underlying?) sense may *or may not* be discussed at a later stage. The first answer to some other messages is such that one has to construe it as an unconscious response to a latent aspect of the message, etc. Two complementary orders of enquiry open up at this point, and present themselves as unavoidable: the enquiry into the relations between meaning and context (cf. Slama-Cazacu, 1961), and the enquiry into universes of discourse (a notion first introduced by Augustus De Morgan in 1846 and clearly related to the current notions of semantic, or semiotic, field: cf. Rossi-Landi 1958a, 1958b, and 1961 ch. II; also 6.3 and footnote 66 hereafter).

involve in the least that the reader or I are in control of the linguistic working processes with which those words and those syntagms are produced and those verbal messages are made up and transmitted. When we begin to discuss these processes in a systematic manner, we in fact realize how immensely complicated they are and we run into the most serious disagreement on their effective nature and importance and consequently also on the nature of their results. On the level of common linguistic exchange, we all know how to use, with fluency, those same terms over which argument amongst scientists and philosophers has been raging for thousands of years: terms like 'number', 'cause', 'duty', 'part', 'movement', and very many others. We all produce correct sentences, but only over the last few years has scientific investigation given rise to hypotheses of working models which attempt to explain how this happens.[58] Here the possible deception hidden in the idiom of linguistic use reappears, the empirico-mercantilistic reductionism that sees language in action as the mere use of words and syntagms which have already been produced while ignoring their production. In an important sense, knowing how to use a word is not at all the same as knowing how it functions — in *this sense*, consumption is not production. The ability to understand the exchange-value of words, syntagms and verbal messages is mere expenditure of linguistic labor-power: that is, we are always dealing with linguistic work, but considered in its abstractness, as generic and undifferentiated productive activity. It is in relation to this type of linguistic work that linguistic exchange-values are determined as distinct from linguistic use-values. An insight on this can be gained if we consider how certain people, who "speak badly", "do not know the language very well", "cannot express themselves convincingly", and so forth, are sometimes capable of understanding thoroughly this or that sector of specific linguistic work producing linguistic use-values. We all know of stuttering poets, logicians who make a mess of every period, language analysts who seem to suffer from aphasia: these are cases which recall those of the inept businessman or the bankrupt banker who turn out to be excellent artesans in only one of the innumerable fields in which the capacity to produce something is exercised.

Studying commodities as messages and economic science as a sector of semiotics, we proceeded to "leave aside" the corporal non-sign residue of economic objects. With this we certainly did not wish to deny that a product, indeed a mere good, also may have a signification even before it is transformed into a commodity: in a

---

[58] Whether they belong to Chomsky's generative grammar, or to Ceccato's study of "mental operations" (cf. 2.4.1 *ad finem*), or to other attempts at describing what goes on in language, the danger of all such models is that they may refer only to the activity of the linguist who "reconstructs" the activity of the common speaker within his specialized jargon. Alternatively the models may pay for the "glory" of approximating a "realistic description" of what the speaker is actually doing with the "shame" of becoming mentalistic (cf., on Chomsky, Ponzio 1971b; on "mental operations", 6.5 below). Wrong or provisional models, however, are better than no models at all insofar as they contribute to overcoming that pseudo-natural approach to language which considers it as the "free", relatively unconditioned activity of speakers. Cf. 7.1 and 7.2 below.

product, as we said, there is all the signification that it receives from the work which is crystallized in it, in a mere good there is the signification of the use-value for the satisfaction of a need. As Hegel says, language (to be here understood as a general sign capacity) penetrates everything men make their own. The leaving aside of the corporal residue of non-verbal messages, moreover, brought us on to the fundamental affirmation that *merchandization is a form of semioticization* (cf. 4.3 and footnote 50), in fact that it is the constitution of a special non-verbal sign system in which men effectively and systematically exchange messages of a certain type (whether they are aware of it or not, and even though they are usually victims of it).

The leaving aside of the corporal residue of commodities is an essential condition for being able to consider them as messages. This means that when we proceed in this section to the complementary operation of applying in the field of the verbal, considerations on non-verbal signs drawn from the sign system of commodities, we find that the leaving-aside has *already been done*: it must have been done previous to the new application. To pick out those structures which are communicative of meaning in the economic market means to progressively disregard some of its other aspects, connected with the body of the objects of which those structures are also formed; instead, to apply those structures elsewhere means to have already disregarded the corporal aspects, to have done so *before* the new application. One can perhaps discuss whether this is always and completely necessary in cases where the application is made with respect to another type of non-verbal sign system, for example in the case where we pass from the non-verbal sign system of commodities to the non-verbal sign system of kinship relations. Disregarding the corporal aspect, on the other hand, is completely necessary in the case of a verbal sign system, of a language, because the non-sign aspects of a language exist *only* insofar as the sign aspects exist. One could say that in verbal language the operation of disregarding was carried out, in a "naturally" social way, since the very birth of language (cf. 2.4.2).

In other words, we can set up a comparison between the verbal sign system of a language and the non-verbal sign system of commodities or "economic language", insofar as we have recognized a sign nature in the latter; and this recognition has been possible to the extent that, following Marx's teaching, we have, as it were, *looked through the corporal density* of the economic market, beyond its non-sign aspects. It is then possible to state not only that capital is a non-verbal sign system, *i.e.* a kind of "language" (*langue*), but also that a language is a kind of capital. We arrive at the two orders of statements by starting from the same premises and developing them in a parallel manner. The comparison is made not between two heterogeneous activities, but between two sign systems; and when we find that the non-verbal sign system of commodities presents certain features, we can argue that the same features, or fairly similar features, must also be possessed by the verbal sign system of the language. The two systems both belong in fact to the same fundamental situation of social reproduction in the intermediate moment of exchange (cf. 2.4 and footnote 13).

We repeat that this should not surprise us. Man has succeeded in producing and using verbal messages in the sphere of the same real process — historical evolution — within which he has also produced and used non-linguistic objects and has organized them into non-verbal sign systems.

5.2 Linguistic Capital

Let us now try to introduce into the study of language some of the conceptual instruments developed in the study of the work and production which are usually called "material", *i.e.* (from the semiotic point of view), non-verbal. As already announced in 1.3 and hinted at again a moment ago, this is complementary to the now fairly wide-spread operation of applying conceptual instruments originally formed in the study of verbal language, to non-verbal sign systems. Just as we speak of determinate negations and abstractions, so we can speak of determinate extensions: the extension being attempted here is determined — through reaction and complementarity — above all by the existence of a science of verbal sign systems which has even taken on, rightly or wrongly, the functions of a pathfinder-science.

5.2.1 Constant linguistic capital

Capital is distinguished, according to Marx, into a (relatively) *constant* or *fixed* portion and a *variable* portion. The constant part is made up of materials, instruments,[59] and money; the variable part is the workers. The two parts are in relationship of continuous reciprocal action. They are both necessary to social reproduction, that is, to production, exchange, and consumption.

We maintain that a language is homologous to what is understood by the constant part of a capital (or accumulated wealth, or patrimony[60]). In order to demonstrate this we must be able to trace in the language, linguistic materials, linguistic instruments, and linguistic money as constituent and indispensable parts of the language itself.

[59] Or *utensils*: the difference being, as we know (1.3, 3.2.1), the difference between an object which occasionally potentiates the human body and an object produced according to a model for precise aims, surviving its production and available for further use in the future. Now, since not all instruments are utensils while all utensils are instruments at a higher level (in the sense that they are instruments plus something else), it is convenient to speak here broadly of all linguistic instruments rather than only of linguistic utensils. The formation of sentences as verbal utensils (3.2.2) will be examined again in Section Six.

[60] I use these synonyms to avoid the over-interpretation which would make linguistic capital homologous with what is usually understood by 'capital' in an advanced capitalistic society like ours. Accumulated money and patrimonies of various description obviously existed even before the formation of capitalism in the modern historical sense, as exchange existed even before the formation of mercantile exchange (cf. 2.4.3); and references to language as a sort of wealth are frequent in the literature (cf. 5.2.1.2), as they are in common speech.

5.2.1.1 *Linguistic instruments and materials* — It is a widespread view that a language is a system of verbal *signantia* and of rules for their use, and that by applying these rules the *signantia* function as complete signs, *i.e.* as the dialectical sums of *signantia* and *signata*; and, furthermore, that a language is a system of rules for the combination of these signs at successive levels of elaboration. This is the system that we use to communicate, that is, to construct, transmit, receive and interpret verbal messages. The study of the dynamic relationships among the various elements of the language, of what happens inside the system when it is used, is the main task of traditional linguistics. In our terminology, it belongs to the treatment of that part of the working process which is more specifically linguistic because it refers to the language as a code and to the various stages of linguistic elaboration. But this is not our present concern. We shall concentrate instead on the customary approach to a language in its entirety as an instrument. The discussion thus begins to shift from the working process to the mode of production. An examination of the former is only the first step for an examination of the latter.

Let us examine some features of the instrumental view of the language. If the language is an instrument, we find ourselves working *with* it, *by means of* it, *on* something else. This amounts to saying that the language turns out to be inserted in a broader totality — the totality of the communicative process by means of which verbal messages are produced, where it constitutes a part alongside other parts. But what then, according to the view under examination, will be the nature of these other parts? What will their relationship to the part represented by the language be?

If all that we understand by instrument or utensil (or aggregate of instruments and utensils) belongs to the language, then the other parts of the whole communicative process must perforce be linguistic workers on the one hand, and materials and products on the other. Of linguistic workers we shall say more further on. Let us deal here with materials and products. What is the *status* of materials? If, after identifying the instruments alone as linguistic, we wished to consider the materials too as linguistic, we should find ourselves extending the very conception of the language as an instrument backwards to include items previously described as materials — that is, we should be taking up the matter at some other point as a consequence of having displaced the *locus* where the distinction between instruments and materials is drawn. According to this view, therefore, materials are not allowed to be linguistic; and the construction of messages by means of the language lies in working on non-linguistic materials by means of linguistic instruments. As for the nature of messages, it would be partly linguistic and partly non-linguistic. It would be linguistic because messages are products of linguistic work done with definitionally linguistic instruments, and it is therefore impossible for them not to receive the imprint of these instruments and of the operations performed with them. It would, however, also be non-linguistic because — and to the degree that —

materials assumed to be non-linguistic enter into the messages. In other words, something of the non-linguistic nature of the materials must after all continue to exist, surviving the operations which they undergo — rather in the way that the wooden nature of the material used by the carpenter remains part of his product even if the carpenter's operations and instruments are not themselves made of wood. Things of this sort, particularly the non-linguistic nature of the materials, are contained in the current definitions of a language as an instrument for organizing and communicating "feelings", "thoughts", and "experiences". "Feelings", "thoughts", and "experiences", indeed, show up as "non- or pre-linguistic materials" which many linguists, concentrating in an exclusive or excessive manner on the language as a complete system in itself, willingly abandon to other fields of study — to psychologists, sociologists, philosophers, and all the other unfortunate "non-linguists". In a similar manner, a purely instrumental conception of economic science abandons to the "non-economists" the very dialectic between use and exchange (cf. 4.4).

The view under examination is vulnerable to serious criticism. What on earth is «experience as such, prior to all attempts to transmit it to others», i.e. experience as (linguistically) described, for example, by Martinet (1962: 21, with what follows)? Faced with the difficulties raised by this "simple" question, one is almost tempted to say that a "functional" view of language consists precisely in leaving them brilliantly aside, artificially simplifying the problems for the benefit of specialists. The feelings or thoughts or experiences which are completely extraneous to language — entirely pre-linguistic, and on which the instruments of a language are supposed to act — are items very difficult if not impossible to identify. Do they not form and become distinguishable only insofar as we learn to speak, that is, insofar as we are, as it were, taken into service within the verbal sign system of our mother tongue? And does not all this so-called "non-linguistic material" itself vary, at least to some degree, also in relation to our mother tongue, or even in relation to the language which we happen to be speaking at a given moment? According to the instrumental view of language, the feedback of the different languages on the varying of experience remains inexplicable; it becomes impossible to tackle the problems of the constitutive action of language-in-general on the formation of consciousness and experience; and the reciprocal influences of verbal and non-verbal sign systems are simply ignored.[61]

The instruments of a language are not instruments in the absolute. We mean

---

[61] The semiotic enterprise is then always apt to reduce itself to the mere contemplation of self-contained sign systems. On the contrary, the continuity between those sectors of human experience vaguely described by such umbrella-terms as 'language', 'communication', 'thought', 'social life', and the like, should always be stressed — and it is better to over- than to understress it. The notion of thought as something non-linguistic, for instance, is even more untenable than the notion of thought as something merely linguistic; and so are the notions of culture, or of society, or of *human* activity in general. To distinguish language from all the rest as a mere instrument is absurd.

both that they are themselves the products of previous linguistic work *and* that they are liable to turn into materials again. There are no limits to the ways in which any language can be worked upon. If a language consisted only of instruments that always remained instruments, this elaboration would not be possible. Indeed, if instruments were not in their turn products liable to become materials again, we would be forced to the awkward conclusion that the language's whole armory had been furnished to us once and for all. Always equal to itself, unable to evolve, this serene equipment would serve to encapsulate and transmit non-linguistic and thereby muddy feelings, thoughts and experiences. If you want to enjoy the revival of a most ancient dualistic doctrine opposing earth and heaven, here you have it. According to such doctrine, all the variations in the messages produced would depend solely upon the proneness of the terrestrial, non-linguistic materials, which are worked upon by the language, to undergo change, to be affected by contingent factors; or, at the most, they would depend on small personal variations in the use of the supra-personal, unchangeable, heavenly instruments of the language. The linguist is turned into a theologian.

In order to overcome these difficulties, it is necessary to admit that a language consists not only of instruments but also of materials, and that both are the products of previous linguistic work. In using a language we work with linguistic instruments on materials which are (at least partially) linguistic. In any given moment, the linguistic instruments and materials that we use appear as the products of previous linguistic work. Someone could object that at least the original materials and instruments, in the beginning of human evolution, could not themselves have been linguistic. The big problem which should be dealt with here is the problem of the origin of "the linguistic": both in the sense of the origin of language in general, and in the sense of the way in which non-linguistic elements are absorbed into the linguistic function every time speech is used. But the problem of where linguistic instruments and materials originally come from is only an interesting pseudo-problem. One can certainly reply that they come from messages, *i.e.* from the products of previous linguistic work, which leave behind them an instrumental residue. But with what are these messages constructed, if not already with linguistic materials and instruments? A vicious circle seems to form, which might lead one to wonder whether in the beginning there was *the* code or *the* message. The logic of this question is not unlike that of the famous question about the chicken and the egg. Both these pseudo-problems are resolved when we consider the antinomies that seem to constitute them, as totalities which descend from previous totalities. Probably the verbal code-and-messages totality, typical of linguistic work, can be traced back to a previous and less complex non-verbal code-and-messages totality, typical of a communicative form of work which is still to be found both in men and animals. (*En passant*: there are interesting similarities between the concepts of sign and cell, word and seed or reproductive cell, message and organism.) Here too, moreover, non-verbal work comes to our aid with homologies:

the hand is already an instrument with which instruments are produced; and the first instrument with which work was done was produced by work. Approaching the language in more than merely instrumental terms is a decisive step towards the basic principle that *the linguistic and the non-linguistic necessarily stand together*: they can be distinguished and opposed to each other only within one totality which includes them both. To put it in a graphic formula which lends itself to changes in tones of voice: you cannot have something *non*-linguistic which is non-*linguistic* before and unless you have the linguistic too. An important consequence of this principle is that it helps explain the way in which we carry along with us the whole linguistic experience of the species. Each child, when he begins to speak, is already using immensely complicated instruments *and materials*. The same is true for the use of material products, *i.e.* for the acquisition of non-verbal sign systems. The point will be taken up again in 6.5.

Let us say then that a language consists not only of instruments but also of materials. This fact begins to reveal the homology of the language with the part of material capital called constant or fixed. But we know that constant capital is also made up of money. We must therefore ask ourselves if a dimension corresponding to money can be found in languages — if "linguistic money" also exists.

5.2.1.2. *Linguistic "money"*. — The idea of money applied to language has an unaccustomed sound; its formulation is not easy. And yet, this is the aspect which has most strongly caught the attention of various scholars and men of letters. Horace spoke of the "coinage of words"; Francis Bacon of the "money of intellectual things"; Hegel, Marx, and Lenin of logic as the money of thought. Bacon indeed went so far as to write that «words are the tokens current and accepted for conceits, as moneys are for values» (*The advancement of learning*, Book VI, I). Lévi-Strauss reminds us that while we (Europeans and Americans) are always talking and thus abusing the language, «the greater part of those cultures which we call primitive use language parsimoniously — one does not talk on any occasion and about anything. Verbal manifestations are often limited to prescribed circumstances, outside of which words are saved» (1958: 78; text somewhat different in the English transl., 1963). The philosopher of law Bruno Leoni attempted to make a parallel not only between language and money in general but also between production, exchange, and falsification of coins and of words (1962: 541-567). The many pages in which Saussure compares the value of signs to economic value are well known.

I shall mention three possible explanations of the fact that linguistic money has attracted attention more than the other features of linguistic capital. The first is that we make use of our language in a "natural" manner. This is, as we know, a pseudo-naturality, but one which creates a zone very difficult to pass beyond; it is hard to recognize a form of work in its various articulations, or even only the use of previous products, in a fundamental daily activity common to everyone such as is the speaking of one's mother tongue. Only over the last decades have we begun to be aware of the programs which we realize when communicating. The second explanation is that the primitive conception of money as true wealth, or even worse, as the source of wealth, may have contributed to emphasizing precisely and solely that aspect of language which is its wealth. No theory tracing value back to work was yet available, and the vision of social reality was distorted by the presence of exploitation to the point of being completely overturned. These two factors made it acceptable to see wealth in a language and also to place such wealth over and above other aspects of the language, or even to make the latter depend on linguistic wealth. To see constant linguistic capital only in the shape of money was in effect an ideological reflection of the life-situation of someone who lives off his income without ever concerning himself with the instruments and materials of work. Work itself, the prerogative of the servile classes, in this way turned out to be doubly remote.

A third explanation of the reduction of constant linguistic capital to mere money lies in the fact that any language shows in a macroscopic way its own character of being a means of universal exchange. He who speaks can address anyone, he can say anything — similarly a person who has money in his pocket can go into any shop and buy any commodity, since it is with money that all other commodities are bought and sold. The very limitations to these freedoms, reference to which was made already (5.1) and will be made again further on (7.3.1.1), accentuate rather than diminish the significance of the homology. Furthermore, the patrimony of the language is present universally and necessarily within every given linguistic community. Not only can everyone make use of it, but it is also true that no-one can entirely escape from it. It is on the yardstick of a language that we measure all messages that are exchanged: they have a value insofar as such a measurement is possible and gives a result which is at least partially positive (cf. Rossi-Landi 1961: chapters V and VI). Without going so far as to consider linguistic money as a real and proper "excluded commodity", one can perhaps say that it is the general equivalent of all possible communications in the sense that it controls them all, placing a limitation on each. Secondarily, it is reasonable to admit that some linguistic values take on the functions of privileged commodities, those which can be immediately exchanged for all other commodities, or a majority of them. Much the same thing happens on the market with precious stones. I am referring for example to terms called precisely terms of value, or to the existential use of the verb *to be*; and here one may see what George Thomson was saying about the relationship between the formation of a monetary economy and the formation of the Parmenidean One and later of the notion of substance (1949-1955, II: ch. XIV).

It is possible to distinguish further elements of homology between the exchange of so-called material goods and the exchange of sign goods in communication by studying, in the field of language, the progression: barter — simple exchange — mercantile production — capitalist production — neocapitalist production. Barter would correspond to the communicative exchange of one or more meanings in an immediate manner. On the other hand we would have a schema similar to that of exchange through money, that is, a Commodity-Money-Commodity transaction, when the linguistic exchange is broken in two by the permanence of words and syntagms in the language, *i.e.* by the fact that a part of the linguistic capital is now passed down from generation to generation as something essential and indispensable. The language lies in the memory rather like money in a coffer. Linguistic money would be found to subsist precisely in this permanence of the wealth of the language outside actual communicative transactions.

The shift from occasional linguistic barter to subsequent and more complicated levels of exchange can be made clearer by introducing the notion of *linguistic need*. In correspondence to *occasional barter* — the satisfaction of one's own needs through a private exchange between two producers — we would have a linguistic barter performed for the satisfaction of immediate expressive or communicative needs. The fact that already in such cases words are employed is not dissimilar from the fact that in barter the various types of goods must already have been produced and are susceptible of being considered objects of exchange, and it does not constitute for this reason a difficulty in the homological survey of this phase of the development. Corresponding to *simple mercantile production*, where money has been introduced and production is directed towards *consumption*, we would have the institutionalization of linguistic materials, that is, the social possibility of keeping them apart or of "conserving" them separately from their live meaning, independent of the use that can be made of them — a procedure which can be accomplished through writing or even through memorization and handing down of ritual or technological formulae which no longer represent in an immediate manner the specific linguistic work that produced them. Here then communication as immediate and direct linguistic exchange is interrupted by "words and syntagms kept in storage"; in social terms what happens is that linguistic circulation is interrupted by whoever "possesses" these words and syntagms. It is difficult, at this level, for real linguistic crises to appear. What we will finally have is *"capitalistic" linguistic production*: a linguistic capitalism corresponding to capitalistic production aimed at *profit*, with its crises and depressions. In a system of linguistic production for profit, profit would be limited to those who possess the sources and the means of comunication, *i.e.* the control of codes and channels; while the common linguistic worker, or common speaker, would continue to produce for consumption (cf. 7.3-4).

Another way of saying the same thing is the following. Linguistic money is that aspect of the language which permits and indeed promotes communication with anyone whomsoever in addition to and beyond the needs which emerge in the division of labor. This allows the development of an indeterminate number of ever more complicated, and to a large extent artificial, linguistic needs (Rossi-Landi 1968b: 54–5).

So far, we have discerned in the language the aspects of instruments, materials, and money. We can therefore describe a language as fixed or constant capital. What will be the nature of the variable linguistic capital, which, added to the constant capital, determines total linguistic capital and sets it in motion?

5.2.2 *Linguistic capital, variable*

Fixed or constant capital is inanimate if variable capital is not added to it. In the case of language (as in general of social sign systems), the variable capital must be sought in the speakers and identified as the value of the *linguistic labor-power* expended by them. Men who speak and understand a given language, who are able to express themselves and communicate in it, expend this capacity of theirs whether they are in the position of transmitter (speaker or writer) or in that of receiver (listener or reader). We are speaking here of the normal quantity of success in communicating which presides over every exchange; and since we are dealing with a considerable quantity, by dialectical law this turns into quality each time that an infant *has learnt* to speak; without a qualitative leap of this kind, no social-linguistic community could ever have been formed. Linguistic labor-power can thus be defined as the mere capacity, generically understood, to use a language, to speak in it; it qualifies one as belonging to a verbal sign system.

The attribute 'constant' when applied to capital doesn't certainly imply an ontological fixity or even only a naturalistic one; rather, it indicates a difference in comparison with variable capital. Constancy and variation are both relative and one can grasp them very well by considering the permanence of a language from generation to generation. The historical tempo of individual linguistic workers is quicker than that of the language — the variable part of linguistic capital *becomes* more rapidly than its constant part.

If we take away variable capital we are left with only materials, instruments, and money, which without work are dead things. Before being dead, a language must have been alive; it is precisely the notion of a dead language that *we arrive at* when variable capital is taken away. On the other hand, *the addition* of variable capital to constant capital appears clearly when we consider the case of a linguist who succeeds in interpreting a dead language: he is like one who enters an abandoned factory and little by little starts up the machinery, whose workings he has learned to understand; and puts to use once more the materials which were left there waiting. To take away all constant capital, concentrating one's attention solely on variable capital, would mean instead limiting the discussion to man's body understood in its psycho-physical materiality — full of potentiality, but at the same time wholly unexpressed.[62]

---

[62]   As we know, man is more than a biologically organized piece of matter because he belongs to sign systems, *i.e.* to a higher level of organized matter. What lurks in the operation of concentrating on variable capital and forgetting about constant capital — to put it more traditionally, on speakers rather than on codes, or worse on *parole* rather than on *langue* — is the danger of subsequently making the further substitutive step of searching into man's biological body for a basis of social codes. Linguistic innatism of the biological kind is thus born — a

For the capital of language [langage] to continue to operate, it is necessary that not only its constant portion, that is, *the* language [langue] but also its variable portion, that is, the linguistic workers, survive. But how does one *produce linguistic workers*? The answer, which is only apparently obvious, is that they are produced *by* language [langage], that is, by their being a portion of linguistic production, a controllable and exploitable element of it. If we carry out the operations that, in economics, make us sort out wages from other prices, and if we consider the working class as a commodity, then we are struck by this fact, that we are dealing with a *talking commodity*. The language must continue to function; for this to happen, those who speak it must continue to exist; the transmission of language from generation to generation is also a transmission of linguistic exploitation and alienation. The most important point regarding variable linguistic capital is just this — the way in which it is handed down.

The relationship between constant linguistic capital and variable linguistic capital, that is the *organic structure* of linguistic capital, also lends itself to interesting considerations. We can suppose that a truly primitive language (much more primitive than those of societies we commonly call primitive) constituted a constant capital of little value, which as such allowed a certain freedom to the speaker. The very conversational parsimony of the primitives, described by Lévi-Strauss and other anthropologists, is an indication of a certain amount of closeness to the specific linguistic elaborations with which we obtain use-values — to the relative independence and integrity of the craftsman. As constant capital grows, any interruption or defect or modification in the working of the machines endangers an ever greater value. Not for nothing purists are conservatives and the avant-garde revolutionaries. The more complex and regulated the structure of constant capital, the more the speaker is atomized, reduced to the condition of an individual who works without freedom inside an immense machine. At this point, as Marx says in the *Grundrisse*, the worker's activity «is limited to mediating the work of the machine»; it is an activity which is «determined and regulated in every direction by the machinery's motion» ... «The accumulation of knowledge and talent, of the general productive forces of the social brain, is thus, with regard to work, absorbed into capital and manifests itself therefore as a property of capital, and more precisely of *capital fixe* [French in the German text], to the extent to which this enters into the productive process as a real means of production» (trans. from the German text; pp. 584, 586; Italian transl., II: 390, 392). It would seem that the extreme stage one can reach is that of coming once more to believe that a language is something only natural: a force which cannot be opposed, a necessary condition. At this point linguistic exchange-values put themselves forward again as linguistic use-values, they appear as if they were themselves linguistic use-values. The worker's

---

very important case of "biologism" as a basic error in thinking and as an ideological projection of the fear of change. Cf. 2.4.2 above, and 5.2.3 below.

resignation is complete since it is no longer even felt as resignation. The transition from capitalism to neo-capitalism, linguistic as well as non-linguistic, is accomplished.[63]

5.2.3 *Total linguistic capital and its operation*

The operation of total linguistic capital, *i.e.* of a language as constant linguistic capital together with its speakers as variable linguistic capital, is communication: production, circulation and accumulation of messages within a linguistic community, on a communicative market. The process must be viewed as something unitary and circular: there is no speaker without a listener, no listener without a speaker, nor speaker and listener without messages which go from one to the other, nor comprehensible messages without a code in common, nor a code in common without previous linguistic-communicative work. *The whole situation takes shape little by little in its entirety.* It is only much later, at a much higher level of dialectical elaboration — the spiral having already turned innumerable times upon itself —, that each individual begins first to distinguish himself within the process of communication, and then to assign himself a particular position as a speaker, that is, as an expender of linguistic labor-power. Linguistic labor-power supports and animates the whole edifice. To perform this function, it was unknowingly forged over hundreds of thousands of years by supra-personal and therefore objective structures; and these structures were in their turn produced by linguistic work which accumulated from the first beginnings of mankind. The question of the origins, which presents itself again at this stage of the argument, is once more a question of going back from one totality to a previous, less complicated totality. *Linguistic* labor power descends from communicative labor-power which is already present in pre-human animals; but an immense qualitative leap has occurred through the division of labor and the institution of exchange (cf. Sections Two and Three, *passim*).

If communication is the operation of *total* linguistic capital, it is not possible to characterize it as a function of only a portion of that capital. When people say that communication takes place *by means of the language*, that is, with only the constant capital, and then add that the language *is made use of* by the speakers, they seem to be repeating a banality which merely describes the surface of things; but in reality, on closer examination, we find that they slide into considering the language and the speakers as separate entities, each one produced independently of

---

[63] This process has been described along more or less Marxian lines by Lukács 1923 (Engl. transl. 1971); Benjamin 1955: 148fll.; Horkheimer 1947; Adorno 1963, 1964, and 1966; Horkheimer and Adorno 1942-1944; Marcuse 1964. For a general interpretation see Scalia 1966 and especially Perlini 1968a and b, 1969. Banfi 1965 and 1966 are careful examinations of the "return" of exchange-values as "new" use-values. The *Grundrisse* are now the main text for the whole discussion (see footnote 18). See also Section Seven hereafter, especially the last three subsections (7.3-5).

the other. The old, impossible problem of joining together again what has been arbitrarily divided will then rear its malignant head. What gets lost is the simultaneity of the formation, and the reciprocal influence, of the two parts of the same totality. The situation is even more distorted if we suppose that only a part of the language is made use of — only the materials, or only the instruments, or only the "money". We have seen the difficulties that one runs into by developing the reductive hypothesis that the speakers are able to communicate by means of linguistic instruments alone (5.2.1.1), or the supposition that this can take place by means of linguistic money alone (5.2.1.2). The third reductive hypothesis would be that speaking consists in using linguistic materials alone. In this case both the instrumental part of the language and everything in it which has the character of a monetary generalization of linguistic values would be pushed back *into* the speakers; their activity would take on a pseudo-creative character liable to impede any developments in depth of the research; the social dimension of language would then become impossible to understand. It is worthwhile noticing that this third reduction can be either spiritualistic or biologistic. Spiritualism and biologism are pseudo-explanatory devices which substitute for a properly social approach two complementary errors: whether it is the soul alone or the body alone to be made the mysterious carrier of social activity, is, in the last analysis, almost irrelevant.

If at this point someone were to ask whether the rules for the use of constant capital, including programs as their systematic developments, belong to constant capital itself, or, rather, to the workers, he would be posing not only a just and important question, but also a relatively original one in the field of theoretical Marxism. To arrive at a correct answer, let us first consider two partial replies. If rules and programs belonged only to constant capital, workers as the variable part of capital would find themselves learning rules and programs as something objective, detached from themselves; the active intervention of individual workers, or of groups of workers, on rules and programs would then be impossible — unless one takes into consideration the case of a change operated by them with regard to constant capital. Such a change is certainly foreseeable; it is, however, difficult to understand how it could be performed by workers who find their *own* operations located entirely outside themselves, extraneous to their bodies. To say the least, the idea creeps up of second-order rules and programs governing the use of objective rules and programs. The second partial reply is that rules and programs belong exclusively to the workers. In this case, however, it would remain to be seen how it is that you have on the one hand the instruments, materials, and money, and on the other hand workers who are the bearers of rules and programs and are capable of applying them to objects extraneous to the workers themselves. The appropriate reply is to be found, once again, in a synthesis of the two partial replies. Rules and programs constitute the meeting place, the ground for exchange and reciprocal influence, between constant capital and variable capital. If we consider that it is work which mediates all the factors of the working process, then this is the only way to interpret rules and programs. Articulated into programs, broken up into working operations governed by systems of rules, variable capital and constant capital interact in specific ways — so that workers modify objects and are modified by them.

There is of course no prohibition against considering a language separately, "on its own", as is often said, as a relatively immobile structure. Much in the same way, there is no prohibition against studying any form of production *in the abstract*: as presumed reciprocal action of materials, instruments, and money, leaving out men; or only as the relationship of instruments and materials, leaving out all the rest. For a variety of purposes, these types of separatistic make-believe are indispensable. But he who believes that in such cases work, without which the objects studied remain inanimate, has been eliminated, is forgetting that he is introducing it himself as a scholar.

And yet, what often happens is precisely that the language and the speakers are presented to us as separate entities which confront each other in the act of speech. What is then lacking is nothing less than the most important dimension — work. Ancient anti-dialectical and anti-materialistic resistances are certainly operating here. They were originally built up as ideological defenses of class privilege. The doctrine of Sense Data, for example, was an ideological projection of the wish that the substance of reality could not be changed. The doctrine of the so-called Moments of the Spirit was an ideological projection of the wish that all experience should allow itself to be dominated by something higher, pre-arranged and immutable. In both cases it was a question of imposing a fixed capital, not to be touched because already in the hands of the ruling class, while ignoring the variable capital or rather admitting it only *a posteriori*. This ideological use of fixed capital undergoes interesting metamorphoses. Today, for example, we often find it transferred into the Structures of the Language. What must instead be proposed as primary and foremost is a totality comprehensive of both the language and its speakers as its intrinsic and constitutive parts. It must be shown how total linguistic capital is itself the social reality which proceeds with its own motion, a motion which includes both the language and its speakers — its constant as well as its variable portion.

Messages, as the products of the operation of total linguistic capital, can exhaust themselves in the act of reception, that is, upon linguistic consumption or fruition. Or else they can retro-act on the constant capital of the linguistic community, bringing about modifications in the units and in the aggregates of which the language is made up, and in the rules for the use and the combination of both. Another path that messages can follow is that of their piling up and organizing themselves in the form of higher level capital, remaining available for further and more complex linguistic elaborations to be undertaken with that language within that community. Here I am referring to the ceremonial, ritual, folkloristic patrimony, both oral and written, as well as to poetic and literary activities; and I believe that here we could bring out elements homologous with financial capital.

Inside the limits within which translating is possible, the patrimonies thus formed in the various languages exert reciprocal influences. This is therefore the place to add that beyond the national linguistic markets corresponding to the various languages, the plurality of the languages and the exchanges that take place among them determine various international linguistic markets and tend to build up one planetary linguistic market. The ways in which we receive and absorb messages translated from other languages present in fact remarkable similarities with the ways in which we absorb commodities imported from other markets. They are still messages and commodities, even if "we" have not produced them; and, in both cases, there is the same interplay between similarity (recognizability, usability) and difference (originality, strangeness, or amusement).

6. DIALECTIC OF LINGUISTIC VALUES

> After a fashion, it is with the human being as with the commodity. Since the human being does not come into the world bringing a mirror with him, nor yet as a Fichtean philosopher able to say "I am myself", he first recognises himself as reflected in other men. The man Peter grasps his relation to himself as a human being through becoming aware of his relation to the man Paul as a being of like kind with himself. Thereupon Paul, with flesh and bone, with all his Pauline corporeality, becomes for Peter the phenomenal form of the human kind.
>
> KARL MARX

The mere opposition between use-value and exchange-value is insufficient, not only with respect to the complexity of language, but also for the purposes of an elementary approach to a theory of linguistic labor-value. Enlarging the discussion semiotically, the same is true for any social sign system interpreted by means of a theory of sign labor-value. We must now say something about two necessary qualifications.

The first qualification regards the fact that the opposition almost indiscriminately applied up to the present stage to "words, syntagms, and messages", must be examined separately for each of these. The second qualification regards the fact that — as hinted at in 2.3.4 under (iii) — there are not two values, but three. The two points are closely interwoven; in what follows we shall first examine each of them separately, and then together within a wider approach.

6.1 *Use-Value and Exchange-Value, from Word to Message*

The dialectic found in the opposition between use-value and (exchange-)value is present at various levels of linguistic work and of its products. These levels come usually together and they are circularly interconnected; but it is convenient to distinguish between them for the purpose of analysis. At the *level of every single word* (or *moneme*, or *linguistic sign*[64]), we find a *first opposition* between a *signatum* and a *signans*: the linguistic work of *semantization* produces the word as the unity of the two. By putting the dialectic between use and exchange to work at this level, one can see an embryonic form of use-value in the *signatum* and of (exchange-)value in the *signans* (the two, let us recall, always exist together). A need, insofar as it is satisfied by the work of semantization, is a *signatum* exchanged by means of a *signans*. This does justice to the conventional character of the *signantia* by which, in different linguistic communities, the same or very similar *signata* are transmitted.

When we look at a word as already formed, it presents a *new opposition* of use-value and (exchange-)value superimposed upon the previous opposition. Since as a matter of fact isolated words do not exist (a point not to be confused with the *isolated use* of a word), we find ourselves already at the *level of words in the plural*, as they appear one next to the other within the system of a language. The use-value of a word in a language is its use; a *signatum* as something external to the word does not exist. But since when we use a word we use it precisely in its capacity as that very unity of *signans* and *signatum*, the use we can make of it depends in turn upon the properties it possesses. The word as a unity of *signans* and *signatum* is a product of linguistic work; its use is further linguistic work. The (exchange-)value the word has in the language proceeds from its entering into relationships with other words. This is what I had in the back of my mind when I kept on adding the term 'syntagms' to the term 'words', for with a syntagm the stage of separate linguistic units gives way to the stage of initial association between two or more words.

There is a *third opposition* between use-value and exchange-value at the *level of communication*. A message can be transmitted and received because it embodies in its turn the dual character of being a use-value and an (exchange-)value. It is manufactured as use-value but transmitted as (exchange-)value; it is received as (exchange-)value but interpreted as use-value. Signs become a message and the message becomes signs again. The homology with what happens in economic communication is startling here: we will come back to it in 6.3 and 6.4.

The main dialectic leaps are then *two*, taking place *in between* the following *three* levels: (i) When a single word is used, it is already a unity of pieces put together synthetically; it already has the value that comes to it as the product of this work of synthesis. This is its use-value as a complete word. (ii) When two or more

---

[64] For *monemes* and *words* cf. notes 24 and 32, and the theory of linguistic production from phonemes to sentences in 3.2.1. *Linguistic* sign is a notoriously more comprehensive term, to be preferred to monemes, words, and other such terms; in the following, however, it will be sufficient to resort to the common usage of the word *word* as the basic linguistic unit.

words are united in any expression whatsoever, each of them is connected to the others within the expression according to its value and to the (exchange-)value it has in the language: words act upon one another with their values, and these actions form the unity of the expression. (iii) A message in turn is the bearer of a duality of use-value and (exchange-)value when it is transmitted and received.

6.2   Use-Value, "Value" as Position, and Exchange-Value

As we know one has to distinguish between the *use-value* and (simply) the *value* of every word and every message individually considered, and find their *exchange-value* in the establishment of relationships among them. The fundamental texts for the study of the dialectic of the three values are — naturally in addition to *Kapital* (beginning with the first chapter of Book I) and to the *Grundrisse* — «The form of value», 1867, and the «Randglossen zu A. Wagners *Lehrbuch der politischen Ökonomie*», 1881-82. In the «Randglossen» Marx begins not from value, but from the commodity: this is the «*concrete social figure* of the product of work». Analyzing the commodity «in the *form in which it appears* [in der *Form, worin sie erscheint*]», we find *in first place* the opposition between use-value and exchange-value; but then, «a further analysis of the latter ... shows that exchange-value is only a "phenomenal *form*" [Erscheinungs*form*], an independent mode of presentation of the value contained in the commodity» (Dietz Verlag, XIX, 369).[65] This amounts to discovering that, in reality, the commodity *is* use-value and "value"; and this discovery is made possible by the fact that the commodity *manifests itself* as use-value and exchange-value, that is, it possesses an independent phenomenal form which represents its "value". A commodity acquires its own phenomenal form — by which its "value" is expressed — in the relationship between different commodities (one of the texts where this transition is formulated with greatest clarity is «The form of value»). It is not that a commodity, even in isolation, doesn't possess a "value" corresponding to the portion of undifferentiated work pertaining to it; the point is that such "value" cannot emerge until a commodity enters into relationship with at least another commodity, whereupon its "value" becomes manifest as exchange-value. Or, a commodity acquires a full-winged *status* as a commodity only by entering the situation of exchange. In this sense «commodities themselves are not things» (Marx: *Theorien über den Mehrwert*, Dietz XXVI, 3°: 268). The wrong operation, for which Marx rebukes Wagner, consists in beginning with value and then subdividing it into use-value and exchange-value; as if an entity, value, existed on its own, and we could grasp it as such. It

---

[65]   Cf. note 12, and 2.3.4 on differentiated and undifferentiated work. The dialectic of reality and appearance, of essence and phenomenon or manifestation is present in Marx's statement. We hinted at it in passing in footnote 25 as an object of study for the materialistic theory of knowledge, strictly interwoven with other dialectical processes.

is clear that this would be an idealistic hypothesis sending us back to a realm of values detached from reality. The correct operation, instead, consists of finding the opposition between use-value and "value" *within the commodity*: and of then recognizing that exchange-value is a phenomenal form of the latter. We have talked commodities; but we know the same basic dialectic obtains and must obtain in other forms of exchange as well (2.4.3, 4.2, and *passim*).

6.3   *The Dialectic of the Three Values at Diverse Levels*

By bringing into a single approach the two qualifications made, let us look at how they work at the level of words (in the plural). The "value" of *a word*, as distinct from its use-value, can be understood *as its position within a language*, just as the "value" of a commodity is its position within the market. This does not mean, however, that either language or market may be conceived of as something previous to words and commodities. As we know, a commodity in the first place is not just an external object, a body to be described according to its physical or chemical properties; it is an object potentially related to man because of its being endowed with properties suitable for the satisfaction of a need. This is the use-value of a commodity; or, the commodity is, to begin with, a use-value (4.2). As such it can be compared to a word. A word, as the unity of *signans* and *signatum*, is the bearer of the property of being usable for communication; this is where its use-value resides. The position of the word in the language, its "value", is brought to light by the exchange-value that the word assumes upon entering into an active relationship with other words.

When dealing with *redouter* [dread], *craindre* [fear], and *avoir peur* [be afraid], Saussure expressly asks himself what the "value" of each of these words may be, and concludes that they «have value only through their opposition: if *redouter* did not exist, all its content would go to its competitors, etc.» (1915, 1964: 160; Engl. transl.: 116; Godel 1957: 90). It is clear that he is not investigating here what each of these words may *mean*, what its *signification* may be, that is, what specific linguistic work may have constituted those three relationships of *signans-signatum* (*signifiant-signifié*). If the problem that Saussure is setting himself were the latter, he couldn't deny the words under examination a value independent from their opposition and previous to it. Saussure is asking instead what the value may be of those words in the *sign field*[66] *to which they belong*; and he finds it represented by

[66] We prefer *sign field* to the more used *semantic field* in order not to exclude from the start meaning-as-value from the syntactic and pragmatic dimensions of semiotics. If we wanted instead to relegate meaning-as-value to the semantic dimension alone, we would then have to introduce a semantics-of-syntax and a semantics-of-pragmatics. It would follow that also a semantics-of-semiotics would have to be introduced. The issue certainly is not merely terminological; indeed, it raises a group of basic difficulties that every theory of signs should consider its duty to face and should be able to solve. These difficulties cannot be dealt with in the

their reciprocal opposition, that is, by their exchange-value: «the value of just any term is accordingly determined by its environment [par se qui l'entoure]»; «un signe dépend d'un système de signes ... Toutes les grandeurs dépendent les unes des autres» (1915, 1964: 160; Engl. transl.: 116; and 1908–9: 20). Actually, he goes even further, and states that the content of a word «is really fixed only by the concurrence of everything that exists outside it. Being part of a system, it is endowed not only with a signification but also and especially with a value, *and this is something quite different*» (1915, 1964: 160; Engl. transl.: 115; for all these quotes, cf. Engler's edition: 256 fll.; my own italics).

The "value" of words depends upon how linguistic work of the "generic" or "undifferentiated" kind (2.3.4) is subdivided in the sign field to which the words belong. When we make this quantitative consideration, we are referring to work in general as mere expenditure of human linguistic labor-power, constitutive of the substance of value — the "measurer" of exchange-value. This is why all of its content would go to its competitors if *redouter* did not exist: because the *same quantity* of undifferentiated linguistic work, continuing to be expended, would be distributed into two rather than three pieces. It is, however, precisely on the subject of underlying work that continues to be expended that Saussure remained silent. His conception of work is still a conception of personal or private performances in spite of his appeal to the social sanction that such performances (are expected to) receive and to the obvious fact that a language *is* a social product (cf. especially 1908-9). The "official" Saussure, in the passage quoted, also seems to be saying that a sign field subdivided into three signs is operating; but if these three signs weren't *signantia-signata*, each of the pairs being joined in that specific way by the specific linguistic work of the community, *the problem would not even arise*.

The "value" of words, like that of commodities, is measured according to the average linguistic work socially necessary for their production (*Das Kapital*, I, 5°: 204; English transl. by Paul, vol. I: 183). This point comes forward as soon as we consider how the *total* value of a language can be traced back to nothing else than the total social work of the community speaking that language. The totality of the linguistic work of a community brings into being the totality of the value of *all* the words that constitute that language. When normally developed languages are concerned, it is not usually possible to keep in mind at any given moment, or even in the course of a single piece of research, the position of every word (its "value") with regard to all the other words of that language. This position is therefore to be determined by studying the limited *sign field* of the word

---

present essay, but reference can be made to the fact that as early as 1938 Charles Morris was clearly stating that meaning is present in all the dimensions of semiosis, and *certainly not only in the semantic dimension* (1938: VI, 1°). How it happened that the presence of meaning was confined to the semantic dimension, so that the phrases 'taking account of, or giving up, meaning' and 'taking account of, or giving up, the semantic dimension (or, semantics *tout court*)' came to be felt as homonymous, is an interesting subject for historical enquiry.

under examination (Greimas 1966: 174 and *passim*). The word one has decided
to examine will therefore exercise the function of a provisional nucleus around
which the sign field is arranged (cf. Ducháček 1968: 26).

Every sign field belongs in turn to broader sign fields (cf. already Trier 1931,
Leisi 1961[2], Ullmann 1962 and 1957[2]); and so on until we arrive at the sign totality
of the language. A path complementary to that of finding sign fields arranged
around a "word of departure" (the word one starts with) consists in subdividing
the language (aprioristically with regard to the piece of research that is being started)
into categories organized according to some criterion, in order then to accommodate
within them various groups of words. That one must, in part, resort to such subdivisions is shown by the very process of singling out partial sign fields. Our linguistic "knowing-how" is always present in us every time we begin any enquiry; it
is to something we know already that we have to resort, as soon as we begin
wondering about any problem.

Let us imagine a rudimentary ethogram according to which a community of
animals has only one signal, for example, a breeding signal. All the sign activity
of the animal group would go into the emission and reception of that single message. Now, this activity can already be viewed in two ways: according to its quality
— that is, according to the physiological, behavioral, ecological, or other processes
that make it what it is, and in which it consists; or it can be viewed according to
its quantity. This double approach is different from what is usually understood
as an ethogram since not only does it not expunge semantics (or, at least, what is
usually understood by semantics: cf. footnote 66), but it introduces it instead at the
level of departure. If the signals become two, for example, one for the breeding
situation and one for danger, the approach becomes more complicated, but does
not change. We would have now, in fact, two distinct qualities pertaining to the
activities carried out for each of the two signals, that is, two different processes or
groups of processes; and, moreover, we would have the quantity of the global
activity, divisible into the two quantities of activity that separately belong to the
two types of signals. Let us go on to imagine that, for example, two out of every
three signals regard sex, and one, danger. Given *all* the sign activity carried out,
one would thus find that two thirds of this total activity go into the production of
signals for breeding and one third goes into the production of signals for danger.
The signals can be used separately: we shall then say that the quantity of activity
expended for one of the two types is equal to the total quantity *minus* the quantity
expended for the other type of signal. It is clear that as soon as these quantitative
considerations come into play, the qualitative differences between the two processes
are set aside: we are not talking about them now, even though their existence is a
premise in the new argument. This is a first, rudimentary situation in which we, the
investigators, can discern an embryo of the opposition between use-value and
"value" in each of the two types of signals. That is, again: each of the two types
of signals bears within it both a use-value, which comes to it from the processes

by which it is produced, and a "value", which comes to it from its position in the system to which it belongs.

A slightly more complicated paradigm is offered us by the ethogramic hypothesis of an "animal tribe" in which the whole "language" consists of only three groups of signals centered around the notions of requesting, accepting, and refusing. If I now designate these three groups with the English words 'come on!', 'yes!', and 'no!', it is clear that I am using a rather forced prolexis in which the English language is used as a metalanguage with regard to that primordial object-"language". In the case described, all the linguistic work of the tribe is distributed among those three groups of signals, and determines their "value" according to the quantity of such distribution. The three groups of signals constitute three sign fields outside of which that "language" does not exist; they therefore assume a reciprocal exchange-value which depends upon that quantity. This is indicated by the possible combinations of signals which belong to different groups: a signal from the 'come on!' group may be answered with a signal from the 'yes!' group, thus excluding the 'no!' group, or vice-versa. A signal from the 'yes!' group may be answered with another from the same group or with one from the 'no!' group; but it becomes useless to answer with one from the 'come on!' group. And so on. The most important factor is that the group of signals which has been provisionally excluded continues to exist in the very act in which it is being negated: it is in fact precisely this oppositional permanence of the excluded group that determines the "value" of the group whose signal we are using instead. Here too what we find is a form of what is often called binarism — just a case of dialectic.

The examination of the relationships between the groups of signals is certainly not something that can regard the signals themselves as isolated from their real function. If a word did not have a specific use-value, it would not have its possible exchange-values either. If 'dog' could not be used to distinguish dogs from wolves, and, in another direction, from cats, it would not be possible to put 'wolves' and 'dogs' together as 'canines' as distinct from 'felines', or 'dogs' and 'cats' as 'domestic animals' as distinct from 'wild animals'; and if 'white', 'black', and 'brown' did not distinguish certain colors, it would not be possible to say that 'this dog is brown' while 'that one is white and black'. The conjunctions, oppositions, and implications of words bring to light their "value" — the position that each of them has in the language; and this sends us back again to the existence of their use-value. Our saying, however, that 'dog' is used to distinguish (among other things) dogs from wolves and cats, does not mean that we are making a reference to the complex procedures of distinction and cataloging by which that linguistic use-value, in the form of that unity of *signans* and *signatum*, has been developed in the praxis of a community which has *become* a community of speakers precisely by carrying out that work. When we use a word according to its exchange-value with other words, we always presuppose its use-value; but this doesn't mean that we go through those communitary procedures again. In other words, original meanings are always necessarily presupposed; they make up the indispensable dimension which underlies any enquiry into sign systems; but, at the same time, they are something that is temporarily set aside. We will come back to this point soon.

For the "value" of a word to get expressed *as* exchange-value, *speech* — the actual use of the language for expressive and communicative ends — must come into play. Now, speech always refers to the already-spoken and, indeed, includes it: it takes place *on*, *with*, and *in* the language understood as an institution, as the constant portion of capital, consisting of linguistic materials, instruments, and money, that we examined in Section Five. Whenever we speak, the constant capital of the language is there, ready to let itself be used according to all the combinations possible with it. But constant capital, as the already spoken, in turn, always pre-supposed past speech. Exchange-value must therefore be sought already in the verbal sign system of the language as including the programs which pre-delimit all possible exchanges, that is, all possible messages. It is not for nothing that ex-change-value is the form of money in embryo (4.1.1). Here too, the parallel with commodities and the market in the ordinary sense comes to our aid: the equation of value 'x commodity $A = y$ commodity B' does not regard any real act of barter; it is a formula that expresses the dialectical nucleus, the minimum and original structure for any possible act of barter to take place. In the same way, the equation of linguistic value 'A is B' — where 'A' and 'B' are two words and 'is' is a third word indicating an operation regarding the other two (or else it is such an operation as indicated by a suffix and/or the relationship between the other words, as in 'Charles laughs') — does not regard an actually communicated message, it isn't an act of speech; it is only a formula expressing the dialectical nucleus, the minimum and original structure of every possible message of that kind.

Here too, then, as for the commodity, exchange-value is the *phenomenal form of value*, which is realized in speech (speech including, as stated, the already-spoken) as the external form of the social relationship between the speakers of at least two words. This relationship is equivalent to that between at least two speakers: just as «to become a commodity the product must be transferred to the other person, to whom it serves as a use value, through exchange» (*Das Kapital*, I: 55; Engl. transl.: 41). «Exchange-value does not exist in the singular» («Randglossen . . .»: 358). It is through speech that the opposition, internal to every word, between use-value and "value" is expressed or made manifest. The sentence is the possible message: this possibility is founded on the dialectical crossing of the values borne by the words in the language.

Remembering that the language is a result of a common production, let us con-sider the following passage from Marx:

When consumed in common, the means of production give up a smaller part of their value to each single product; partly because the total value they part with is spread over a greater quantity of products, and partly because their value, though absolutely greater, is, having regard to their sphere of action in the process, relatively less than the value of isolated means of production. Owing to this, the value of a part of the constant capital falls, and in proportion to the magnitude of the fall, the total value of the commodity also falls [*Das Kapital*, I, 10°: 334; Engl. transl.: 324-325].

In Italian everyone commonly says 'dammi dell'acqua' [give me some water] or 'l'acqua è limpida' [the water is clear]. Such a common consumption of these means of linguistic production distributes their value over a large number of messages. The value of these means of linguistic production is greater in the absolute, but it becomes relatively less if we consider their sphere of action. Just the opposite happens when one says something unusual like 'acqua tinta e neve' [painted water and snow], 'non scuse / d'aprir lo core all'acque della pace' [don't refuse to open your heart to the waters of peace], or 'una montagna ... lieta / d'acqua e di fronde' [a mountain ... serene with water and foliage] (respectively: *Inferno* IV, 10; *Purgatory* XV, 131; *Inferno* XIV, 98): the value insofar as it comes from isolated means of production goes entirely onto that product, in that message. This could be the beginning of an enquiry in which modern theories on the consumption of sign objects (artistic objects, particularly) are traced back to, interpreted by means of, and ultimately founded on, an articulated theory of the sign work that produces them.

6.4 *Dialectic of Values in the Definition*

It will be well to give for what we have said up until now in this chapter some other examples which, in their culturally intuitive immediacy, may be more useful than abstract discussion. They are examples that belong to what we have called the level of words in the plural, that is, of expression and sentence making; more particularly, they regard the definition and the judgment, which, being typical of language, constitute the very nucleus of syntactic structuring (cf. Jakobson 1970: 16). We want to apply to such cases the most simple and fundamental equation, '*x* commodity $A = y$ commodity *B*'. Let us consider the definition, which is also a value judgment:

'*God is omnipotent*'.

Here the quantity (x,y) is reduced to one for both of the terms: there is only one God, and he is omnipotent. (It would be easy to quantify: for example, by asserting that gods, or a certain type and number of gods, are omnipotent; or else by graduating the power of the various beings.) Let us follow literally the beginning of the Marxian analysis of the commodity. The value-as-position of a word can only be expressed relatively to at least another word. Within the equation which is instituted between them, the first word plays an active part, the second word a passive one. Thus, 'God' expresses its own "value" in, and by the merit of, 'omnipotent'; 'omnipotent', indeed, serves to express the "value" of

'God'. This comes about by means of the use-value of 'omnipotent', which, in its form of equivalent to 'God', operates a sort of cancellation of the use-value of 'God', mirroring and expressing only its "value". It is relative to the use-value of 'omnipotent', that 'God' expresses its own "value" and therefore assumes an exchange-value. The result of this intricate network of operations, only hinted at here, is that 'God' can be put into the linguistic circulation as the bearer of such value. In terms of work, the amount of average, undifferentiated, human linguistic work (in a given society) with which 'God' is "measured" (the importance of 'God' in that society) is brought to light by setting 'God' in relation to the use-value of 'omnipotent'. The opposition internal to the linguistic "commodity" is represented by an external opposition, it unfolds in it. The sentence as a unity has been created and can be used as a message.

Generalizing, we can say that this corresponds to one of the ways in which words are reintroduced into the use of the language by means of definition; at the same time, it gives us the following definition of one type of definition: two words or groups of words are set in an equation which establishes such a relation between them, that in force of this relation the second group as use-value reveals the exchange-value of the first, at the same time "cancelling" its use-value. The sign of the relationship is represented by the copula 'is' or by 'has' or by some other verb or linguistic sign indicating the active part of the first term of the equation.[67]

Through the *total or unfolded form of value* (what Marx expresses with the multiple equation 'z commodity $A = u$ commodity B, or $= v$ commodity C ... etc.') we move on to the *general form of value*, in which a certain number of commodities express their own values by means of a single excluded commodity. The excluded commodity, upon which as use-value the exchange-value of all the other commodities as objectified quantity of work are measured, corresponds linguistically to the known term in a definitory series. A good example can be found in the following Crocean definitions of Art:

> '*Art is intuition,* or
> *feeling locked in an image,* or
> *individual theoretical moment of the Spirit*'.

This means that art is measured as the unknown term upon the others as known terms, and, turning it the other way around, that it can be the only known term of the series. In this way Benedetto Croce introduced the exchange-value 'art *as* intuition, or *as* feeling locked in an image, or *as* individual theoretical moment of the Spirit' into the linguistic "market". After which, his followers were able to write, 'art, which *as we know*, is intuition, etc.' Just as they could have written 'ten pounds of tea, which *as we know*, are worth twenty yards of cloth, etc.'.

---

[67] For the possibility of interpreting the sign '=' in linguistic terms, as referred to common language, cf. Vailati's fundamental essay «La grammatica dell'algebra», 1911: 871-889 (repr. 1966 : 131-157). For the not necessarily mercantile character of sign exchange, cf. 2.4.3; for another example of the dialectic of use-value and exchange-value, 4.2.

We can now see a little more clearly what is beneath the cancellation of meaning, that is — as one usually says (footnote 66) — of the semantic dimension. As is well known, this cancellation is considered necessary by many linguists and semioticians for the systematic development of their research.[68] Already at the level of the simple sentence, the dialectic between use and exchange, between use-value or utility and "value" as position, demands that the use-value of the grammatical subject be provisionally set aside ("cancelled" as Marx would say) so that it may be put into linguistic circulation. In this way, as we have just said, the opposition between use-value and "value", internal to the subject, can become an opposition external to it which unfolds in the sentence; indeed, the *sentence* in its elementary form *is this unfolding*, this transfer of the opposition from inside to outside the grammatical subject. In order for this to come about, it is necessary that the subject enter in contact with other words, these too necessarily endowed with both use-value and "value", in such a way that a crossing may take place among the various values. From this crossing, which each of us unconsciously learns to bring about when he learns to speak, a new quality emerges. A leap, or dialectical strengthening, takes place: the sentence is *something more* than the sum of its parts. What happens, therefore, when we concentrate our attention on that "something more", is that we leave aside what the parts of the new totality were *before* they became such parts.

I believe that many linguists and semioticians have felt just this: that *if one wanted to talk about the structure of the sentence, one shouldn't talk any longer about* the use-value of the various words, that is about their original meaning (signification). They felt that it was necessary, instead, to concentrate attention on the relations of words insofar as they had already concurred in the making up of a sentence — with a formula which I believe an unhappy one, one had to "abandon semantics in favor of syntax". Still, since they did not use the theory of labor-value, and thus were not able to distinguish (while at the same time keeping present) the two kinds of value, of use and position, as the fruits of two different kinds of work, they believed that the setting aside of the use-value of words was equivalent to cancelling it completely. That, moreover, with the contact between (at least) two words, as between (at least) two commodities, a third type of value, exchange-value, should emerge as the phenomenal form of "value", was an ulterior difficulty that couldn't certainly be faced alone, outside of the complex theoretical schema that serves to explain it. The procedure was discontinuous instead of being dialectical. As we said, what enters into the equation as the first term becomes exchange-value because and insofar as it is invested by the cancelling power of the

[68] A few references for the discussion are Bloch and Trager 1942; Jakobson, Fant, and Halle 1951 (1961); Ullmann 1951 (1957²); Harris 1951 (1963); Hocket 1954; Martinet 1960 (1966⁶); Burger 1961; Ullmann 1962; Harris 1962 (1965); Rossi-Landi 1966a (1968c); De Mauro 1967. It may be of interest to notice that the different *status* of the sign-carrying body in non-verbal *vs.* verbal sign systems makes it a little cumbersome to deal with sheer *signantia* when the bodies aren't just articulated sounds . . .

second term of the equation itself: for this reason only "it is no longer" a use-value. Both the new and provisional exchange-value of the first term and the exchange-value of the equation seen as a whole, were instead taken into account by linguists only as they appeared *at the end* of the dialectical process, while the process remained ignored — or better, let us repeat, its underlying presence was indeed felt, but the tendency was to dismiss it as being an obstacle to clear and distinct work.

6.5   *The Flow of Speech and Past Linguistic Work*

In spite of its complexity, linguistic work is usually carried out by speakers and listeners without any heed to the techniques put into operation. The use of language *manifests* itself as natural; seemingly man talks as a bird flies or a fish swims. This apparent naturality is instead a *social pseudo-naturality*, that is, a level of sociality so high and complex that it seems natural. An offshore yacht gives us the impression of proceeding in a totally natural way only when everything is perfectly ship-shape: this is obtained when a highly elaborated, complex, and costly machine, which is at any rate very remote from mere nature, is exploited to the full by a thoroughly trained, that is, highly socialized, crew.

The reasons why the speaker and listener do not think at all about the machine of language are as profound and tangled as language itself, and it is not possible to separate them from each other in reality. Still, because of the problems they raise, we attempt to list some of them. (i) Language learning takes place through ten or fifteen years of novitiate, during which time a large portion of our resources are committed to the task. (ii) In a preponderant measure the object of learning has been a constant linguistic capital, that is, an already constituted patrimony of linguistic materials, instruments, and money, together with the rules for using them (5.2). (iii) All this has come about alongside of and jointly with the learning of the non-verbal sign systems without which the verbal sign systems would not make sense, indeed, would not exist (1.3). (iv) Finally, almost everything has taken place according to programs that have been imposed upon us without our knowledge (1.4). We expend verbal and non-verbal sign labor-power putting an immensely complicated social machine in motion, a little as if we were punching the right buttons of a computer by chance. Clearly this is a very difficult situation to unravel. In the rest of this section, on the basis of what we have previously said, we will touch on some points of it. In order to use linguistic materials, instruments, and money, that is, to produce with them sentences to be transmitted as messages, we must have rules and programs. As pointed out before (5.2.3), these rules and programs are the *locus* of the dialectical conjunction between the constant portion and the variable portion of total capital. Learning the rules and applying the programs does not at all mean *running historically through the production* of sign systems *again*. The speaker produces sentences and messages; this does not mean that he produces the relative codes; it doesn't even mean that he invents the programs (2.3.3). To the contrary: if sign systems *and* programs didn't exist, the speaker wouldn't produce anything, indeed, he wouldn't even be a speaker. Avoiding the empirico-mercantilistic prejudice of those who study language while ignoring linguistic work (5.2) does not necessarily mean falling into the opposite error of believing that everything is produced *ex-novo* by every speaker. The production of sign systems consists in social processes carried out through tens or hundreds of thousands of years. Certainly the ontogenesis cannot but consist in a sort of "entrance" of the individual into a number of sign systems; thus we may even say that the child, in a sense, recapitulates their production, although in a highly abbreviated and partial manner. But it would be excessive to think that the child lives this production over mechanically step by step from the beginning (Solìmini 1968: 108–114), and it would be absurd to think that every individual runs through it from the beginning every time he uses a code to produce a message. The same happens in any material working cycle: no one, when he learns to use those instruments on those materials for given ends, reconstructs, on his own, the history of the working cycle to which they belong. Ideas of this sort can only come from wild exaggeration of the powers of individual consciousness, subtracted from, indeed, made prior to, the historical and social processes which have instead produced it. No one would say that the miner reconstructs the history of the extraction of minerals in his own consciousness. But the same is true for the speaker.

The theory of labor-value applied to language is a social theory which permits the mediation between research limiting itself to the study of already produced linguistic artefacts, and research attributing to individual linguistic operators a sort of possession of production itself. A conspicuous example of the former were the philosophers of Wittgensteinian descent who analyzed common language (the variegated school of Ryle, Wisdom, and Austin); conspicuous examples of the latter can still be found in various forms of mentalism, especially in those who study the so-called "mental operations", "constitutive of language". We have already made some remarks about the former, let us dedicate a few words to the latter. Studying individual mental operations supporting speech amounts to trying to find the social dimension by exploring the individual. The assumption here — certainly an idealistic residue — is that the individual, by the fact of having learned to use a language, that is, to produce sentences and messages, has also learned linguistic production. Since he doesn't know it, though, and can't talk about it, he must have also *forgotten* it, somehow. Production therefore should be present within the individual in some latent form. The idea then is to search for it there. According to this approach, it should be possible to *bring back* every individual to the awareness of what he is doing when he speaks. What isn't clarified here is that such awareness can only exist as the result of a very specific process. But a process of the kind is especially that of research, when a particular piece of language is lifted out of the spontaneous flow of speech and made into an object of study (I don't mean to exclude other cases in which a similar isolation of the linguistic object may take place: cf. Rossi-Landi 1968c: 20-21, 161-164). When awareness is instead assumed as something present but hidden within what every speaker does, it is gratuitously attributed to the speaker as a point of arrival in a univocal, predetermined, and potentially necessary psychic process — the process of becoming aware. At this stage awareness is dealt with as an item in the furnishing of consciousness, and this seems to be nothing other than one more *Ersatz* of the soul.

It'll be healthy to compare rapidly the two positions sketched above to similar positions that could be maintained in the field of non-verbal sign systems as well. Let's take the case, belonging to our main argument, of manipulative and transformative work and products, that is of the various objectual sign systems. With its appeal to the nursery as the school of language, the Oxonian position as applied to objectual sign systems would contain two tenets, of which the first is entirely acceptable and the second must be entirely rejected. The first tenet would be that in the nursery everyone begins to learn to use a huge number of objects of common use produced by the culture to which he belongs — combs and brushes, silver and glasses, keys and drawers, pencils and erasers, and so on. The second tenet would be that the production of all the above objects has nothing to do with their use. There they are, ready-made for use, and there are plenty of them. Why should we bother with the social processes by which they are produced? But in this way the second tenet, and the whole theory with it, looks like a bird trampling on the soil of everyday practice while we expected it to take off and perform some handsome piece of flying before us. *We know* that artefacts are ready-made, good gracious! but we also have an interest in learning more about them. It's over-gentlemanly to assume the artefacts as naturally given to us. The appeal to what is ordinary, everyday, and common, if you leave it at that, is like studying a market as given instead of as produced. Precisely by presenting itself as social while it stops at a level of pseudo-naturality, the theory under examination impedes our going back to the social work from which that very pseudo-naturality derives.

In the study of mental operations one would suppose instead that in learning to *use* brushes, keys, and pencils, one has also secretly learned the procedures by which they are produced.

In the normal use of a fully possessed mother tongue, for the aims and within the limits of daily communication, what happens is that, *with their entry into new linguistic working processes* as *objects of work* and *means of production*, the words and their combinations *lose their character of products and now function only as objective factors of living work* (cf. *Das Kapital*, I: 197; awkward Engl. transl.: I, 182). In this extraordinary remark of Marx's there is enclosed, in my opinion, a substantial indication for a new approach to some of the central problems of contemporary semiotics and linguistics, like the strictly interconnected problems of language learning, deep structures, and linguistic universals. Deep structures can be seen as stratifications of previous linguistic work, generalized results of past speech (Lévi-Strauss would call them "sedimented history"). The idealistic and individualistic LAD ("Language Acquisition Device"), who looks so pale, must give way in front of a history-fed and therefore rubicund LASSIE ("Language As Sign Stratification In Evolution") (Rossi-Landi, «LAD and LASSIE», forthcoming). From the time when we begin to learn to speak, we succeed in putting into motion remote results because the "right buttons" for doing it immediately with success are put in front of us: the buttons are the stimuli of products which are still actual, but which for the speaker have lost their product character. The speaker treats the words as means with which to speak, as objects that he elaborates in speaking, as parts of a wealth he feels to be his own. Certainly, one cannot speak without materials and instruments with which to speak; therefore when one begins to speak, the presence of these products *is* presupposed. But in this process of speech it is indifferent that the words are *products of past work*, «as it is indifferent, in the act of nutrition, that the bread is the *product* of the past work of the farmer, the miller, the baker, etc.» (*Das Kapital*, I: 197; awkward Engl. transl.: I, 182). When in the process of speech the words as means of linguistic production make themselves felt in «their character of products of past work, this happens by means of their defects» (*ibidem*). A word, a syntagm, a sentence which does not function communicatively as we wish, which for example (as one may say) "doesn't get the idea across", sends us back to the specific communicative program in which it serves as an instrument, or to the productive work from which it derives. In the first case, we are usually dealing with the performance of a single speaker, in the second with the work of society that has constructed and put together those pieces of language. We must resist the temptation of assimilating the second case to the first. The knife that doesn't cut and the thread that breaks continually (these are Marx's examples) bring another worker to the mind of the one who is using them in a new working process — a given knife-maker and a given spinner respectively. This is equivalent to the case in which a piece of language is badly used in a given text I am examining. If I were the one who had produced that knife before using it for cutting something, the "other worker", the one I would get mad at, would be myself in a previous moment; and it is easy to imagine the linguistic counterpart. But saying that a word, a syntagm, a sentence, doesn't get the idea across *in general*, saying that one is employing linguistic products which are insufficient to whomsoever may be using them and however they may be used, corresponds to saying that a given *type* of knife does not serve for that given work; then one has to use sentences or knives of different existing types, or *in extremis* invent a new type. In this second group of cases the defect in the product of past work sends us back not just to a single worker, but to society; and we may even be dealing not just with a defect, but with an insufficiency with regard to new aims.

In order to *recognize* that any linguistic element doesn't do the job, I must have learned how to use it. But in no case *must I* (and in the great majority of cases it is irrelevant that I *might*) have learned to produce the objects which I am using either badly or well, and of which I am now recognizing either the merits or the defects.

7. LANGUAGE AS A SECTOR OF SOCIETY

οὐ μόνον δεῖ τἀληϑὲς εἰπεῖν ἀλλὰ καὶ αἴτιον τοῦ φεύδους.

ARISTOTLE

There develops a multiplicity of social relations that are spontaneous in their growth and are quite outside the control of the actors.

KARL MARX

This final section is mainly dedicated to some of the problems belonging to the exploitation of sign systems and to the linguistic alienation which is connected with it. The topic has already been hinted at in a more or less occasional way when dealing with economics as a sector of semiotics in Section Four and in the course of the treatment of linguistic capital in Section Five (especially *ad finem*). Actually, it has been implicit since the beginning of this research. If (i) between material and linguistic production there obtains a homology founded on the ways in which human work is expended, and (ii) exploitation does take place in the field of material production, it follows that (iii) also linguistic production must be the object of some sort of exploitation. As alienation exists in various other fields, it must also exist in the field of language. Indeed, a very simple and preliminary way of presenting it would consist in stating that language, as a *sector of* society, must share the basic features of the totality it belongs to. Society *is* alienated; and so is language.

Before concentrating on our main topic, however, it is opportune to dedicate some attention to two additional features of linguistic production: its finite character, and the relation between work and play in language. This will help to clear the air of some possibly lingering doubts about the homology of production, and will thereby put us in a better position for beginning the examination of our subject from its root — linguistic private property.

7.1 *The Finite Character of Linguistic Production*

An objection may be raised against the homology between material production and linguistic production. In material production the number of products is finite; whereas it is typical of linguistic production that, given a particular language, an indeterminate (some *love* to say infinite) number of words and sentences can be produced with it. Whereas each material product can be used only a finite number of times, there is supposedly no limit to the usability of words and sentences. To this objection another has been added as a corollary. Because of the two-fold indeterminateness or infinitude of language, nobody ever tries to take over linguistic capital: there is an abundance of words and sentences for all who want them. From this it would follow that in the sphere of language we find neither exploitation, nor private property, nor alienation in the sense given in these pages.

Let us concentrate in this section on the idea of indeterminateness or infinitude. It is an idea which it is better to sack on the spot. Things are actually completely different from the way in which they are usually presented by the lovers of infinitude. A given language, in the course of its historical existence, is the sum of all the linguistic signs which have progressively made it up. These clearly run into very high figures; as do the sentences produced with the code of the language. But we do not see here any substantial differences with what takes place in the field of material production (apart from the obvious phenomenal differences). All of the techniques which sustain material production in the human community in which a given language is spoken enable an also very high number *of utensils* to be produced with the materials available; and each of these sentences and utensils can be used very many times. But once the wealth of both forms of production has been recognized, it must not be forgotten that they have their historical limits; you can recognize at a glance, for example, if a sentence is Latin or English; and a Bermuda, that is, Marconi-rigged, sloop with bulb keel is certainly from the twentieth century. Both the number of objects produced and the number of times they are used is in either case finite, not infinite. Certainly no-one can be interested in establishing how many times pots of pasta were put on the fire to boil during the Kingdom of Napels; or how many times the English may have said 'tis . . .' or 'it's raining' or other variant ways of saying the same thing, from the time of the Magna Charta down to that of Queen Victoria. But since the number of citizens of those kingdoms was in both cases finite, as were the meteorological and culinary occasions, there is no reason to suppose that the use made of pots or of utterances on the rain was particularly excessive, or maniacal. Those linguists who insist so much on the usability of the language really make one think that they must have a very slight acquaintance with manual work: otherwise they should perforce be struck by the fact that the systems of material products are actually just as usable, and with just as much individual liberty (or lack of it).

There is therefore reason to ask oneself where the notion of infinitude applied to language comes from. It necessarily sends us back to something which lies outside the natural, biological, and historical delimitations which make up the everyday texture of human life. Now what can stand raised up above such delimitations? Even in the cases where the old idealistic terminology has been abandoned, the first thing that comes to mind is some sort of *category of the Spirit*. Man would have by definition a capacity which is supra-historical and precisely for this reason infinite; this capacity would find expression in the infinitude of linguistic use.

This hoary philosophical notion, which we still find living in the crannies of contemporary linguistics, is to be repudiated at the root. In any case, to start with, we should remark that this should be a question not only of the Spirit's producing words and sentences, but also of the spirit's producing objectemes and utensils made up of objectemes. This far the young Hegel had already applied himself. In a number of countries in old Europe, disdain for material production, typical of a bourgeoisie feudally placed over a rural mass immobilized in underconsumption, had instead taken a big step backwards, had sanctioned a further delimitation: the spirit invoked was only that of linguistic production (which was moreover mystified as a creative activity). But the fact is that we are now living in a neo-capitalistic *régime*: the structures of production press in on us from all sides, permeating more and more every aspect of our lives. It is no longer possible to ignore them. And now lo and behold — what a novel idea! — the "free, spontaneous, infinite activity of the Spirit", withdrawn from material production and reduced to linguistic production already, is neo-capitalistically transferred from the Producer to the Products and thus turns out to be perceivable within the *structures of the language*. The language, product and instrument, would contain itself the dimensions of infinitude. It is like saying that the liberty conceded by the capitalist exercising his dominion would manifest itself in the infinite possibilities of elaborating the production line, the factory — objectified capitalist production.

If we think of the language as capital we can catch a glimpse of just how deep the implications of such a transfer are. In fact the toiling masses are emerging; the countries subject to imperialist domination are claiming their independence. All this provokes a typical ruling-class reaction also with regard to the language: it is presented as everybody's common property. "You are free, dear linguistic workers and dear under-developed peoples. So what are you looking for? Haven't you already got the structures of the language, with which you can produce all the sentences you like?" The structural conception of the language, plus the insertion of a sort of infinitude into its structure, plus the re-affirmed separation between linguistic workers and the language (between the variable and constant portions of capital), jointly play the mystificatory role of concealing the appropriation of linguistic goods on the part of the ruling class. But of this later on.

There are meanwhile at least two other essential points to be clarified. The first is that the homological study of the two orders of production, the material and the linguistic, must be carried out adhering progressively to the *same level of elaboration* for both. For example, if you wanted to indicate a divergence in the order of magnitude of sentences on the one hand, and of, shall we say, automobiles on the other, then you would be quite right to say that the homology does not stand up. An automobile, like other artefacts more complex than the mere mechanism, belongs to a level of complexity where, on the linguistic side, we would have to name such things as speeches, essays, lessons, or books (cf. 3.2.3).

It thus happens that the argument of the indeterminateness or infinitude of linguistic production can take on an appearance of validity whenever on the other side, as an example of material production, a product of a different level is given. We spoke for example of a utensil such as a pot for boiling water and of a sentence such as 'it's raining'. Billions of pots may have been produced by a certain community in the course of its historical life-time, and "innumerable" uses may have been made of them. Automobile production, on the other hand, presents itself as much more "finite" (even if we complain of its relative enormity); and the same is true of the production of speeches, essays, lessons, and books (even if we complain of their quantitative excess). As we know, the level of pots is that of simple utensils, usable because they are complete in themselves; and as such it corresponds to that of sentences. Below sentences and *simple* utensils, there are *parts* of sentences and *parts* of utensils: these parts, as a rule, are not used in isolation. It is clear that if a sentence, or even worse, a word, is placed on the same level as that of an automobile, the constructive significance of the homological scheme turns out to be completely distorted and it then becomes plausible to speak differentially of the availability and versatility of the language compared to the limited nature of material capital.

The second point concerns the differences between *models* and *tokens* and between *programs* and *executions* (cf. 2.3.3, especially *ad finem*, for the articulation of this double opposition in the field of language). We must ask ourselves what the *status* and dialectic are — of models and tokens, and of programs and executions — in *both* orders of production; and not only in one of the two. Models certainly do not exist only in linguistic production, nor tokens solely in material production, or vice-versa. The same is true of programs and executions. Of which use do so many linguists preach the numerical limitedness or unlimitedness? Of the use of models, tokens, or programs? And do they make any distinction between models and programs?[69] Whatever the number of executions of programs continuously

---

[69] They certainly don't, whenever the whole dialectic of models and tokens, and of programs and executions, is *not* taken into account. One could have a look here at such notions as that of archeological types (Gordon Childe's writings from 1936 to 1956 are exemplary in this respect; cf. also Sabbatini 1967-1970 for an extension to history), or at the current treatment of patterns and functions in anthropological research. — Part of what is involved can be brought out by considering the process of teaching the use of any elementary utensil. If I teach a child the use of a pot which I put into his hands, I am transmitting to him a token (the "material" pot); in another, probably overstretched sense of the phrase, I am also handing down to him at least one execution (*the* execution or *the* executions which I perform together with him and for his sake during the teaching process). Moreover, I am transmitting to him a program as something distinguished from the above execution or executions, for the child is expected to be able to use the pot even without my assistance, executing the program on his own. Indeed, teaching may be defined as "transmission of programs". In an attenuated sense, lastly, I am also handing down to the child a model, the model of that kind of pot, even if I am not expressly teaching him how to manufacture pots: because knowing the use of the pot and having learnt how to get about on this planet, at a certain point he may go back by himself from the pot to the operations which produce it. To sum up, models and tokens, programs and executions are all handed down from generation to generation; but they are handed down in different manners, at different levels, and with different implications. The bearing of all this on the transmission and acquisition of language should be obvious.

carried out by speakers, and numerous though the tokens reproduced by them may be (we have seen that it is *in any case* a finite number), the question is this: what and how many are the models and programs which the speakers in fact follow — apart from innovatory exceptions (which obviously exist in material production too)? There is a widespread impression that linguistic production is easier or comes more naturally than material production; this arises not only from systematically forgetting past work, *i.e.* the work which has gone into it (see 6.5), but also from an unsystematic approach in the use of the oppositions between models and tokens and between programs and executions — I mean an unsystematic approach on the part of those who get the above impression. If we wish to be objective with regard to both orders of production, then the minimum of which we must be assured is that when we speak of models or programs for one side we must also do the same for the other; and the same must be done for tokens and executions.[70] However it is only recently that the distinction has been made not only between models and tokens but also between programs and executions, thus also distinguishing the two oppositions the one from the other.

The question of linguistic models and programs is naturally also that of the language as a conservative institution. To study the models and programs which speakers in fact follow means taking a decisive step towards the study of linguistic alienation. The speaker can even illude himself that he is free because he produces all the tokens that he likes to produce and he executes as he pleases all the programs that he has learnt. But the programs remain for the most part what they are. It is not the speaker who invented them: he is limited to producing them with precisely his reproductive and executive activity. This illusion of freedom, which is then an illusion of naturalness, is on the whole the more deeply rooted the less able the speaker is to express himself in *other* languages, different from his mother tongue: never having thoroughly assimilated other models and programs prevents him from feeling the determinant weight of his own. You can arrive at the ridiculous and pathetic absurdity of a linguist who believes that certain reproductive and executive activities are "free" and "natural" only because he personally is not capable of doing them according to models and programs different from those in which, being born in a particular linguistic community, he in fact does them. At this point the notoriously vast and difficult problems of so-called "linguistic relativity" are reopened; these problems are closely connected

---

[70] Charles Sanders Peirce, of course, examined some of these problems with his usual insight; Saussure deals repeatedly with some others of them; and a good treatment of the opposition between models and tokens is to be found in Price 1953. — This is perhaps the right place to recall that within the apparently unitary opposition between material and linguistic production two complementary and overlapping distinctions are telescoped — between verbal sign production and non-verbal sign production, and between sign production *tout court* and the production of items other than signs (cf. notes 12 and 20 and Section Three in general). The dialectic of models *vs.* tokens and programs *vs.* executions would also apply to a non-telescoped treatment of production.

to those of ideology. Beyond linguistic relativity we find ourselves faced with linguistic exploitation and alienation, which we shall be discussing presently (7.3 and 7.4).

7.2 *Work and Play in Language*

Even when the homology between material production and linguistic production has been accepted, at least as a suitable hypothesis for research, it remains to be seen whether the correspondences which can be traced between the two types of production are valid for the *whole* of linguistic activity.[71] It can be maintained that the production of goods is obviously instrumental: whether they are immediately consumed, or kept in storage, or used for the production of further goods, all material goods are supposed to be of *some* use. Now there are ways of using language which are also clearly instrumental. Prayers and orders, for instance, are aimed at getting something. But can we consider *every* use of language to be instrumental? Would it not be better to distinguish between obviously instrumental uses of language ("practico-communicative", as they are sometimes called; or, to delimit the field even further, "intentionally pragmatic") and other uses, for example "cognitive" or "expressive"? Will it not then be more fitting to withdraw language from the homology with material production in all the cases where the aims of linguistic production are not instrumental or where no aim can be detected in it? There are cases, for example, where it would seem that language is more easily assimilated to play, in Schiller's sense of the word, than to work. The conceptual framework of the working process with its articulations into materials, instruments, etc., and that of capital with its opposition between constant portion and variable portion, and so forth, would then in fact be acceptable in the field of language only for some of its uses, while for others they should be abandoned.

We hold this objection to be fundamentally erroneous on account of its insufficient vision of reality. However, in contrast to certain others, it does raise important questions; and it is well worth discussing. We could of course stop at the simplest reply: the interpretation put forward in these pages is not intended to be exhaustive. Our homological study of linguistic and material *production* takes its starting point from a voluntary and expressly stated delimitation of the field. As we have said, the theoretical schema proposed *can be seen* as an application of certain categories of economic science in its classical (Ricardian-Marxian) phase to the structure of a language and to its *practico-communicative* use. Given these delimitations, it could be argued that *nothing is said about what can be done with a language once it has been produced.* Even the *production of messages* comes into the notion of practico-communicative use of the language; so that, given the

---

[71] Since the thesis to be examined is that not all language is work and production, we say on purpose here linguistic *activity* rather than linguistic work.

same delimitations, we do not here take up a position even on what happens to the messages once they have been put into circulation.

It is obvious that one can also use linguistic products for purposes which are not declaredly those of work, simply by consuming them. But it does not follow at all from this that other uses of language, different from the ones here examined, can be assimilated to activities basically different from productive activity, for example, to play, again in Schiller's sense of the word. To clarify this point, let us distinguish two successive levels of overall interpretation.

FIRST LEVEL. If it is true that production is to be distinguished from the other things that can be done with the objects produced, it is equally true that their foundation lies in production. *If there were no objects produced, there would be nothing that could be used in an indifferently productive or non-productive way.* As Marx says, «in order to be able to plunder, there must be something to plunder, *i.e.* there must be production» («Einleitung» of 1857: 19; McLellan's transl.: 31); in the same way there must be something already produced, with which to play. He who intends to counterpose non-productive uses to productive ones is describing two branches which have already diversified themselves from a common trunk; but he is certainly not going back to the trunk itself. In other words, non-productive uses are a species of the genus production, they are not a different genus. This was discussed already in 2.3.3 and will appear more clearly at our second level of interpretation.

SECOND LEVEL. A fundamental investigation by Marx concerns the "identity" between consumption and production («Einleitung» of 1857: 10–21; McLellan's transl.: 22–33). It is not possible to reassume Marx's analysis here. Let it suffice to recall that we are not dealing with a mere identification of an idealistic sort, something which was explicitly denounced and refuted by Marx; but rather with an articulated study of the complex internal relations which obtain between production and consumption *within the totality to which both belong.* This text of Marx's is one of the best examples which can be given on the use of totalities and on the way of identifying their structures. The position of a thing in the system of categorial propositions is *ipso jure* an explanation of its genesis. The principal conclusion of Marx's research is that you cannot even speak of consumption without at the same time finding yourself speaking about production, and vice-versa: where you find one you will find the other, and neither acquires its full meaning in isolation. In particular, «consumption provides the ideal object of production, as its image, its wants, its impulse and its purpose ... Consumption thus appears as a factor of production» («Einleitung» of 1857: 9, 15; McLellan's transl.: 25, 27).

There is no reason why, also in the case of language, we shouldn't raise the question of whether uses which are non-productive in the narrow sense — uses describable as consumption — are or are not productive in the wider and deeper sense of the intimate relationships between production and consumption. In my opinion the reply to this question is whole-heartedly affirmative. Even if we leave aside the fact that expression and knowledge *pre-suppose a language* which has already been produced (first level), and even if we admit that, *in a narrow sense*, using a language is not the same as producing it, something more basic remains: the dialectical relationships which obtain between production and the use of the objects produced, *i.e.* between production and consumption, impose that expression and knowledge be subsumed under the more general category of production. Not for nothing are new expressions (for example poetic) and new factual propositions (for example psychological) continually flowing back into the reservoir of the language and eventually modifying it, in this way affecting future speakers; not for nothing are various languages born, do they develop, and die; not for nothing is the presence of a language a distinguishing mark of human society just as the presence of material artefacts is; and not for nothing does the edifice of social reproduction, to which also the expressive and cognitive uses of language belong, have its foundation in the modes of production and in class struggle.

Certainly the language (*langue*) was originally formed to be used also for expression. There was therefore in the beginning a need to express oneself and to communicate. But one cannot postulate an expressive use *of the language* before the language was formed, nor can one identify a need as being linguistic when the language did not yet exist. While making these distinctions, we are already using highly evolved linguistic materials and utensils. The distinctions of which we speak present themselves at a very high level of super-structural elaboration. But the matter does not end here. It is not correct to call linguistic an expressive need which is previous to the formation of the language. Otherwise even the way my dog looks at me would be linguistic (from *lingua*): after all, I am sure he is trying to communicate with me in his own way.

We repeat that a need requiring for its satisfaction instrumental mediations develops together with the instruments capable of taking us through such mediations. At least on the philogenetic level, one cannot postulate a need which remains unsatisfied without postulating, as a long-term result, the end of the need itself. This can take place either as a renunciation of the need, *i.e.* through adaptation to the situation in which it is not satisfied; or as the disappearance, as a result of non-adaptation, of the individuals who feel the need in question; or indeed, in an extreme case, as the end of the species. The discussion here seems to pass naturally from the biological to the historico-social field: it would appear permissible to state that in a society which does not satisfy certain needs, those individuals who are not able to "renounce them" are destined to disappear. This kind of social survival of the fittest is a real phenomenon. But it cannot be generalized to the point of social Darwinism. Against every form of social Darwinism it must be proclaimed that, in a society which is incapable of satisfying certain needs, unsatisfied individuals or groups can act in a revolutionary way. This is precisely the alternative which biologism would like to cancel out: biologism, that is, the conception that in the anatomy of the ape there is a key to the anatomy of man —

exactly the contrary of the Marxian statement used as a motto to this whole investigation.

One of the greatest dangers of present-day consumer society is that the situation in which we find ourselves appears to have become colored with social Darwinism in a spontaneous and incontrovertible way. The neo-capitalist system represents itself as nature, clothed with the naturalness of a biological process (see references given in footnote 63). In a sort of ghostly pseudo-naturalness more and more artificially-induced needs serving to perpetuate the system are being satisfied: with the result that we find ourselves being turned upside-down, and are prone to believe that the *other* needs, previously (and correctly) considered of basic importance, may now be doomed to disappear. We are therefore further away than ever from expression and knowledge as something independent from production. In the claim for the independence of expression and knowledge from production there is a precise ideological bourgeois heritage, which consists in denying the founding power of work and its universality. The purpose is to subtract something from work; *there must be something which has not been produced* and which, *therefore*, cannot be modified with new working processes. To withdraw expression and knowledge from the circle of production and consumption amounts to viewing them as at least partly raised above the historical flux; to claim for them some kind of independence from historico-social circumstances leads to nothing other than to making them ultimately into something reserved for the ruling class. In front of producers, or rather *above* them, there would be people who limit themselves to using the products — for other and nobler ends.

Nonetheless there does remain the fact that with words and with discourse we can also play, amuse ourselves, without thinking in the least of their production. Play is a fundamental *animal* activity: it is that also for men insofar as they are animals. But once the division of labor has taken place and private property has been set up, play can't avoid becoming a part of consumption. This is the case for men. If play serves to reproduce the consumer, it also serves to nourish production. The matter will perhaps become clearer when we consider that we "play" not only with linguistic objects but also with material objects. We drive around in automobiles to admire the countryside and in this way consume the automobile and reproduce ourselves as consumers of automobiles. When we play we execute programs, and even when we invent something we certainly do not do so from scratch. Outside the production-consumption dialectic, play is an indeterminate abstraction.

All this is not intended to deny that in play — sometimes baptized rather pompously "ludic dimension" — there is a survival of the spontaneous contact of man with nature and with other men. We have to admit that in the classless society of the future the "ludic dimension" may get the upper hand over an essential part of what is now called work. In a certain sense this may appear as a return to something lost; but, in a more important sense, it will be a new acquisition. In both senses one can perhaps say that contemporary Chinese are closer to the "ludic dimension" than we Europeans or Americans.

No-one can allow himself to ignore the relations which exist between play, pleasure, and art; or the impulse to play as a vehicle of social liberation, as Marcuse says, precisely when commenting on Schiller (1962 [1955]: 169–179). On the disalienating character of a *free* activity one can even reach a certain agreement, which is probably destined to cease as soon as one starts discussing what an activity properly called free should be and the political means for obtaining it. In view of the fact, however, that human nature in general, considered in the abstract, either does not exist or is reduced to the biological, and that this reduction itself presents big problems, it is (to say the least) dangerous, theoretically and ideologically dangerous, to speak of play and of "ludic dimension" outside precise historical determinations. We must therefore ask ourselves how such determinations are obtained. The answer is that first and foremost they concern production and consumption, *that is*, class division, *that is*, exploitation. Each time we pose a fundamental problem, we come back to the political dimension; and each time that is the new point of departure from which the discussion must begin.

The way in which bourgeois thinkers have recognized as fundamental a "ludic dimension" in man has above all the significance of an ideology — of a *social design* concerning the future (Rossi-Landi 1967c, 1968a). However, this social design has not expressed its real nature, and has instead taken on the naturalistic, *i.e.* pseudo-universal, appearance of a description of something which supposedly already exists. Schiller himself, far from describing a constant of human nature, was, without being aware of it, expressing a class desire. He was giving voice, in a mystified form, to a particular utopian design concerning a future society. As Lukács remarks in his *Contributions to the history of aesthetics* (Section I of the essay on Schiller, now in 1969: 17-47), Schiller's unconscious design reflected the particular political situation of the German bourgeoisie to which the poet belonged. Naturally even a utopian design can have a liberating value of its kind, or at least can propose an attitude of conflict. In the weighing up of this liberating value or attitude of conflict, the practical value of all attitudes is acknowledged. It is then legitimate to ask each one if he prefers to play about with theoretical visions of a utopian kind or if he wants to *work for* a future society founded on play. In view of the fact that a society founded upon play presupposes liberation from need, then working seriously for such a society means aiming at liberating man from need. The political consequences are immediate. There are choices to be made, and to be made at once. No one can consciously avoid them.

The appeal to play in language can be presented as an argument against the characterization of language itself as work and trade. It is however interesting to notice that this very appeal contains an oblique reference to linguistic alienation. If language is alienated and if play is a vehicle of liberation, what we find ourselves in front of is the hypothesis of a *disalienating ludic form of language*. In other words the desire that language *be* also play cannot be dissociated from the desire that it *become disalienated*; and this means that it *is* alienated. But in order that such a desire may go beyond the folk-singer level at which it is usually expressed, and assume the character of a real and proper design, *i.e.* of a politically significant project, we must begin to describe language in such a way as to make the project have a sense. What we come back to is precisely the characterization of language as work and trade, which — as it is here maintained — is indispensable for a frontal study of linguistic alienation.

7.3   *The Exploitation of Sign Systems*

7.3.1   *Linguistic private property*

Do we have private ownership of sign systems? More in particular, can we say that there is anything like private property in the field of language and verbal communication which are our present concern? Everyone speaks a language, everyone uses it; the words are available to all and therefore all possess in common the goods of the language, whereas only a few possess economic goods (cf. Jakobson on this, 1963a: 33). So it would appear that the answer is negative. If, however, we look at the field of material production, we find that everyone consumes some goods, everyone buys or uses certain commodities, all can handle money; and yet we talk about private property — and how!

The major misunderstanding as regards linguistic private property is that the supra-individual, public, social character of the language is considered sufficient to exclude the possibility of the language itself being subject to private ownership. The two notions, that of the language and that of private property, are juxtaposed abstractly upon each other in such a way as to make them screech. But this is only the external appearance of things, favored by the logico-formal rather than dialectical mentality with which the theme is usually treated.

Going beyond appearances, the essential points seem to be two. First of all, the above operations of production and consumption — both economic and linguistic operations — are not performed "freely" except in very particular and delimited senses; secondly it is not possible to talk about "private" without at the same time talking about "public". Let us look at the two points in this order.

7.3.1.1   *The conditioning of speech.* — The use of the language is free only in appearance, or rather only at a superficial level. There isn't much difference here from the freedom of a person who goes about with some money in his pocket and "decides" to buy one object instead of another: this freedom too is only apparent and superficial. In any such case it is our task to assess just how great is the freedom of the citizen who — bombarded as he is from infancy, daily and without let-up, by both official and concealed propaganda, by both open and hidden persuasion — receives from the system a salary calculated to the last farthing for

social reproduction, including of course the reproduction of exploitation. Our citizen finds himself being able to quench his thirst with one type of drink rather than another; at the most, he can decide whether to buy, on pay-day, this or that make of refrigerator or motor-bicycle. In a homologous manner, it is a question of assessing inside just what limits of freedom and individual independence the typically social operation of speaking is performed. It should be clear that verbal communication takes place only among historically determined individuals or groups and can only be performed in a given language, *i.e.* within and by means of a determined structure. This structure itself is always, to some extent, both an ideological product and an ideological instrument *already*. Lastly, the audience is always determined as well (Perelman and Olbrechts-Tyteca, 1958, have rightly denounced the philosophical vagaries contained in the notion of a "universal audience"). It is impossible to imagine what a verbal intercourse held outside *all* historico-social situations would be like; and yet, this is precisely what one should imagine in order to postulate a basic freedom of *parole*. Even if (according to the hypothesis rejected in 5.2.1.1) the language were only an aggregate of neutral instruments for the communication of non-linguistic materials, the conditioning would exercise itself on these materials as well as on the speakers; but if we do consider the language as an aggregate or better a system not only of instruments but also of materials, themselves already linguistic, and of linguistic money too, we come to see that the conditioning of speech must be traced within each one of the parts that make up total linguistic capital. We speak, and there is verbal intercourse, only insofar as linguistic capital operates in its entirety. Even the uttering of the simplest of verbal messages already requires the whole huge machine of language to have functioned in the past and to be functioning at the moment. In a perfectly homologous manner, even the use of a simple object, of an *objecteme* which is only a part of a utensil, requires the past and contemporary existence of material production. To suppose the contrary would mean describing the historical present in the conceptual terms of the remotest past, that of the earliest forming of something human, unduly reducing the complex to the simple with a strange mechanicistic contortion.

In what sense, then, is it possible to say that words are "available to all"? I believe there to be two answers, which are in any case already implicit in what has been said on linguistic capital and on the finite character of verbal production. On the one hand, the *parole* as an individual production is not of itself immediately and rigidly constrained by the code of the language: in the same way, even though there is the non-verbal system of utensils for daily use, there is a margin of freedom, or choice, or style, or individual whim in the use of this or that utensil or group of utensils. On the other hand, each time we begin to speak, all of the language is already present: there it is, contained in our speakers' memories, in the books which describe it, in the objects and institutions which represent its meanings. Here too there is no substantial difference from material products, which theoretically exist on the planet even *for* those who cannot use them, or not immediately, or not like other people. Shops are full of commodities even when we cannot buy them; some nations live on waste while others are plunged in misery; production continues in its motion independently from any individual intervention of ours; and the possibilities of a better world spring to our imagination, or we deem they have been started elsewhere, even when we do not know where to begin to realize them in our own country. The argument of the free use of the language is either directly conservative, or it is at most a liberal argument. It sounds like the famous (and shameful) argument of the platonically unconstrained situation of workers faced with goods which for them are *in fact* unattainable. To give an Italian example: should the Sicilian miner want to abandon the sulphur-mine and go to Trieste to see the Science Fiction Film Festival, no external constraint would prevent him — he is thus "free to do so". Actually, he remains in the sulphur-mine, and can't avoid it. He is not even informed of the Science Fiction Film Festival, and perhaps doesn't know where Trieste is. Clearly, what is being confused here is the generic availability of men to use-values with their factual possession of some of them. A proposition like "everybody *is free* to eat a steak" is unduly derived from a proposition like "everybody *can* eat a steak". The social dimension is apparently added to the biological one through the same move by which, in fact, it is wiped off.

7.3.1.2 *Public nature of private property.* — The second point to be examined is the public nature of private property. What we call private is such only insofar as it is public. If it were not and did not continue to be something public, it would not be able to become, for an instant or for a thousand years, something private. As Marx says, «man is ... not only a social animal but an animal which can develop into an individual [*sich vereinzeln*] only in society» («Einleitung» of 1857: 2; McLellan's transl.: 17). 'Private' and 'public' are paired terms: they belong, even if in different manners, to the same totality, from which they derive all their meaning — just as do 'production' and 'consumption', 'thought' and 'language', and innumerable other pairs in which you can see instances of the one dialectically dividing into two.

Let us consider the case of private and public in the field in which it is most commonly discussed — economy proper, or, material exchange. Exchange itself, let us not forget it, is redistribution of what has already been distributed: the simultaneous passing over of two goods between two individuals according to their personal needs takes place insofar as the two goods have already been distributed according to supra-individual social laws (cf. 2.4.1). Capital and market certainly do not develop from the beginning by using private or individual items as their building stones. In order to isolate capital as private we must be able to have wealth available as a public thing — as are materials, instruments, and money, and as workers themselves are. One can act individually on a market, for instance by cornering it, precisely because the market is a social fact. The idea of an economic capital and market originally and constitutively private and individual not only would not explain anything: it would be inexplicable itself. Dialectically, material property itself is private *because it is* public. If it were not public, it would not be private either: the property of an isolated man would not be private because it would not be public either; indeed, it would not even be *property*. What is private is considered as such because it displaces something else which is private, breaking up internally a totality which is public but which even though broken up in this way continues to extend itself over the whole of its field. You are the private owner of *your* car insofar as the other members of the community you belong to are *not*. One certainly could not say that all the members of the community are private proprietors of the same car (whereas, it should be noted, one can indeed imagine a community in which each member enjoys the use of an object of public property). But this is not all. You are the private owner of *your* own car because your car is a public fact: it exists before the eyes of all, it is a collective product with the whole of history behind it, anyone who has learnt how to drive can use it, as indeed, in a different sense, can a non-driver. Without all these public dimensions, your car couldn't even be the object of a sale or a gift, that is, it couldn't become somebody else's private property.

There are two decisive passages in the *Grundrisse* on this dialectical inter-play, which are worth repeating not only because they reaffirm the "public" character of the "private", but because they also do this precisely with regard to language. Marx says:

The individual is related to a language as *his own* only as the natural member of a human community. Language as the product of an individual is nonsense. But so also is property.
Language itself is just as much the product of a community, as in another aspect it is the existence of the community – it is, as it were, the communal being speaking for itself (p. 390).

And again:

An isolated individual could no more possess property in land than he could speak. At the most he could live off it as a source of supply, as animals do (p. 385; Cohen's translation retouched, pp. 88 and 81 resp.).

Thus the building up of linguistic private property does not contradict the essentially public nature of the language, any more than the building up of private property in the economic sense, within material production, contradicts the public nature of wealth. Since a language as constant linguistic capital is something public and social, and since the linguistic market presupposes individuals united by the language, it is possible to isolate a linguistic private property and a personal or group linguistic use in it.

One may well ask what relationship there is between this notion of private property of the language and the notion of a *private language*, which has been so much debated in Wittgensteinian circles (cf., for instance, Ayer 1954b, Cook 1965, Cornman 1968, Funke 1968, Hintikka 1958, Hunter 1967, Morick ed. 1967, Thomson [Jarvis] 1964). Quite simply, one must be careful not to confuse the two notions. Linguistic private property is the successful seizure, by a privileged social group, of part of a public and social good. As we are going to say in 7.3.2, such a seizure takes place above all as control exercised on the formation, transmission, and reception of messages. The notion of a private language is counterposed instead to the notion of a public language, it wants to subtract something from the latter. To assert that there is something like a private language is one of the multifarious devices for evading reality or for asserting class privilege in a mystified manner. Individualism and personalism play here their reductionist role. Indeed, long before Wittgenstein, Marx and Engels had already brutally attacked the notion of a private language in the *German Ideology*, and Marx had come back to it in *Grundrisse*. To sum up: the language is public; the language *cannot be* private; but *precisely because* the language *is* public, there *can be* and usually is private property *of* the language.

7.3.2 *Communicative domination*

In 1.3 we dealt with the reasons why a priority is usually attributed to verbal sign systems, and in 1.4 with the tardy discovery of non-verbal sign systems. How is it that the programs of communication, especially of non-verbal communication, had hitherto escaped the attention of researchers, or had been gravely underestimated, or managed to emerge only in the sphere of declaredly non-scientific discussions? Western cultures within which intellectual techniques aimed at the conscious study of verbal, and later of non-verbal, messages and codes were formed — we said — are cultures which set great store on individuality and nonconformity. This happened precisely in the periods of the early formation and modern rebirth of those techniques. The doctrine of the independence, freedom, and responsibility (albeit relative) of the individual soul, which is at the basis of Christian civilization, and the bourgeois doctrine of the conscious psyche of the individual as an ideology of private property, could certainly not be conducive to a study of individual behavior as something programmed in advance. The fact that those two doctrines themselves were handed down through very careful programming made it more difficult, and not easier, to become aware of the models and programs involved (we shall take up again the general notion of "programming" in 7.5). This happens continually on the individual level too: the better engineered an unconsciously learnt program is, the less the subject is aware of executing it in his own behavior; indeed, he thinks he is acting independently from any program. Here too perfect socialization is presented as naturalness, the work done in the past is forgotten, previous products are assumed in their new immediacy; and it is only when hitches or defects emerge, that people begin to suspect something (cf. 6.5). But there is more to it than this. If a person knows that his own individual action is the execution of a program, this means that he sees it as a social fact, since a behavioral program *is* eminently social. On the other hand, if he ignores that his own individual action is performed according to programs, then he is cutting the action itself out of its background and makes it live as if it were exempt from social conditionings. In this latter case both his belief in individuality and his unawareness of models and programs are fortified.

It is certainly not fortuitous that the observation of non-verbal behavioral forms has for a long time been limited to societies other than our own. Here we are speaking of generalizing observation of a scientific kind; not of individualizing observation of a literary sort, typical of story-tellers and travellers. Bourgeois society allowed itself the exquisite torment of describing itself in bits in the form of individual stories of characters, who were certainly also investigated in their non-verbal behavior and in all their conditionings; but who, insofar as they were characters, remained bourgeois heroes, individuals not subject to generalizations of a scientific kind (Goldmann, especially 1963 and 1964). The generalizations were reserved for the others. We were informed with an ever greater wealth of detail about the traceable patterns in the behavior of so-called primitives long before attention was turned to the patterns which determine our own behavior. The techniques were too delicate for it to be possible to apply them to ourselves before having practiced them elsewhere; and "primitive" peoples were supposedly "less complex", therefore easier to study. And so, as a necessary premise to becoming aware of communicative programs, a typical dialectical procedure took place. As a result of previous codifying work, our society *in itself* enjoyed and suffered its lot without ever going back to that work. It ignored its existence and therefore couldn't certainly relativize its own codes. In a second moment, antithetically, we "came out" to see what the others were doing: in this way our society, *outside of itself*, learnt of the relativity of other people's codes. The very fact that there *is* a question of codes thus began to emerge. It was only in a third moment, however, that the new awareness of codes and programs returned to ourselves: this is the synthetic moment in which our society, now *in itself and for itself*, realizes both that it is living through the final moment of a dialectical procedure and that it is posing itself as a new thesis, that is, as the first moment of a new procedure. We have spoken of *moments* rather than of *phases* or *eras* in order to avoid the necessity of a reference to the temporal dimension; since, however, the process described is *also* historical, substitution of any of these words is feasible.

The discussion could be deepened if we were to study the way in which the change-over from capitalism to neo-capitalism has influenced the formation of a point of view capable of bringing out the structure of models and programs and of all sorts of behavioral programming. This however would go beyond the limits of the present research, and we have to content ourselves here with a few words. The organic structure of capital is the relationship between its constant and variable portions. With the progressive alteration of the organic structure in favor of the constant portion, the "value" of the workers has diminished. Any modification in the productive processes has become more and more expensive. It has been more and more the structure of non-human things which has emerged — which is just a way of hinting at one aspect of the technological development of the twentieth century. Due to the elephantiasis of the constant part of capital, neo-capitalistic man is completely instrumentalized in production. So one had to get to the point of seeing man himself in terms of the supra-personal structures of which he is a part in order to see him also in terms of his own internal programming. Just as the demystification of bourgeois economy was possible for Marx and Engels insofar as capitalism had been fully formed, so the study of the unconscious programs which determine non-verbal as well as verbal behavior would not have been possible before the consolidation of neo-capitalism. Previously also, the complex techniques of sound and vision recording which are necessary to bring out the programs were not available; and so the idea itself could not be formed. As Marx says, «the problem and the means of solution arise simultaneously» (*Kapital*, I, 1: 103; English transl.: 65). Man acts according to programs in any socio-economic situation, and certainly not only in the neo-capitalistic one. If the emergence of behavioral programming has been made possible or encouraged by the neo-capitalistic alteration of the organic structure of capital, the fact of becoming aware of it could contribute to the formulation of new and more human programmings. In order that the design for their use may have a liberating nature and not one of more refined forms of oppression, we must turn to a general theory of man and society; and for the design to be realized, to revolutionary praxis. The foundation of things is political.

All this brings us to face what is undoubtedly the most radical aspect of behavioral programming. No program exists in isolation — this would be meaningless. Each program, on the contrary, must be integrated with all the others within a society: all of the programs, together, must serve to preserve the cohesion of vaster social groups and the values of the culture. For this reason each program turns out to be controlled from a higher social level. Each totality in development is certainly not isolated; on the contrary, it develops together with other totalities of the same level. All these totalities are in their turn parts of vaster or more complex totalities. It follows that the development of a given totality is not determined only by the interplay of its parts, but also by the action of the totality itself as a part.

We must now ask ourselves who controls the programs from a higher level, and why he controls them. What are the vaster "social groups", what are the "values of the culture" which must be preserved? and why is this imperative posed? As Ivanov explains (from the Italian transl., 1969: 49, 53; see also the passage by him quoted in 1.4):

Sign systems serve the collectivity (just as they do the single individual) not only as means of communication, but also as means of control; this defines the role of semiotics in a cybernetic analysis of the collectivity. Given the presence, within a given collectivity C, of a sub-collectivity C_1, which constitutes the sub-whole C_1 and has the role of control-system over C, it is essential to clarify: what sign systems does C_1 make use of which C does not (problems of social cryptography)?; and what sign systems are common to C and C_1 (the problem, for example, of particular jargons used by the higher castes in India etc.)? what are the specific means available to C_1 for controlling C (mass communications)? . . . .

The model of the world which is constructed in a given sign system is generally common to the whole of a given collectivity and is introduced into each individual, who in this way becomes a member of the said collectivity.

At this point, however, semiotic discussion usually gets bogged down, not only when some social sign systems are investigated one by one, but also when the notion of all social sign systems is examined in general terms. Take the case of Émile Benveniste, who arrived at the following statement:

[There is] an appropriation by groups or classes of the apparatus of denotation which is common to all. Each social class appropriates general terms, attributes to these specific references and thus adopts them for its own sphere of interest and often constitutes them as a basis for new derivation. In their turn these terms, loaded with new values, come into the common language into which they introduce the lexical differentiations (1970: 26).[72]

What happens in reality is that there is a sole class which "appropriates general terms", and that is the ruling class. Benveniste seems almost to have arrived at the threshold of a theory of linguistic exploitation, linguistic private property, and linguistic alienation; a threshold which, however, he cannot cross because he lacks an appropriate political theory of society.

It is precisely when it gets to its own foundation that semiotics lends itself to being immediately wed to the doctrine of ideologies: more specifically, to the interpretation, in terms of communication, of the ideological role exercised by the ruling class. If one does not go back as far as this, and look for the foundation of semiotics outside of semiotics, or at least outside of what is usually called semiotics, then the very possibility of an all-embracing enquiry into social sign systems disappears.

The ruling class arrogates to itself the control of programs "from a higher social level". It becomes plausible to define 'ruling class' as *the class which possesses*

---

[72] «... une appropriation par des groupes ou des classes de l'appareil de dénotation qui est commun à tous. Chaque classe sociale s'approprie des termes généraux, leur attribue des références spécifiques et les adapte ainsi à sa propre sphère d'intérêt et souvent les constitue en base de dérivation nouvelle. A leur tour ces termes, chargés de valeurs nouvelles, entrent dans la langue commune dans laquelle ils introduisent les différenciations lexicales». Benveniste goes on to examine Saussure's comparison between economics and language and concludes in favor of studying «deep-seated analogies underneath superficial discrepancies» (28).

control over the emission and circulation of the verbal and non-verbal messages which are constitutive of a given community (Rossi-Landi 1967b). Ideology is a social design; the dominant design is precisely that of the class in power. All behavioral programs are submitted, on the part of those who hold power in a given historical moment, to a vaster and more fundamental programming which consists in preserving society just as it is, or in reducing change and absorbing it into the existing system as much as possible. *This is the foundation program beyond which one can go no further.* We call it a social design because it is the whole of society which is programmed in a unitary manner. To suppose an anterior or external program would only mean attributing an even deeper control to some other social group, that is, shifting the localization of the ruling class. The deepest control is by definition identified with ultimate possession of power. This is one of the senses in which the foundation of things is political. It thus happens that, in each sign- and communicative-market, the ruling class enjoys a private possession of the various sign systems in the following three dimensions: (i) control (or domination) of the code or codes and of the modalities of codification; (ii) control of the channels through which the transmitted messages run, *i.e.* of the modalities of the circulation of messages; (iii) control of the modalities of decodification and interpretation of the messages received. That here we are dealing with a form of "possession" phenomenologically different from material possession is only too obvious; but it doesn't follow at all that its substance is any different, or any less real.

Situations which merit the description of linguistic exploitation, linguistic private property, and so forth, are under the eyes of all. The press, radio and television belong to the dominant classes or groups. Whole cultural and artistic movements arise, develop, and die in function of the controls to which they are subjected. The "common people's" way of thinking is an aggregate of ever-repeated stereotypes. On a more radical level, ownership of communication begins with education and formation in all their gradations, right down to primary schools and above all to the determining, irreparable influence exercised on *speakers still being formed* long before they learn to read and write. As we have observed a number of times, right from birth the infant finds himself immersed in the sign systems governing the community to which he belongs. It is impossible not to notice in all this the dimensions of linguistic and communicative exploitation as an integral and indispensable part of exploitation in general.

The possession of modalities of codification is in the first place possession of codes. In this is reflected the fact that codes are products of previous codifications, which leads back to a previous possession of the pertinent modalities. In this early phase possession is furthermore exercised through explicit or implicit education: as control of the operations performed or undergone by the codifiers. Here the relationships between models and tokens, as well as between programs and executions, come out again quite clearly. We are always dealing with the possession of models and programs, concealed by the freedom, which is conceded, to produce tokens of those models and to execute those programs. Occasionally, however, even this freedom is denied. We then have cases of *direct* political repression: "You cannot even say such-and-such". Much more subtle precisely because it is concealed, much more serious because it refers to models and programs, and much more dangerous because it is imposed and accepted at a lower level of awareness, is the implicit order: "You may produce tokens only of these models (and you are inhibited from producing them of other models)", or, "you may execute only these programs (and you are inhibited from executing other programs)". Consider for example the social groups in which all sentences containing references to Communism *must* be used in determinate ways only, *e.g.* with horror, despisal, or detachment. Communism is then considered as a sort of social leprosy which must be immediately and energetically avoided. Furthermore other models of sentences have been linked to those centered on the idea of Communism as a social leprosy, and this is done in such a way as to arouse automatically negative reactions, or as a minimum, grave suspicion. Someone once asked a black American sailor in an Italian port if he felt *exploited*. The reaction was immediate: "You Communist?", asked the American, and hearing an affirmative reply, he immediately went away. The sole idea of exploitation, even if uttered on behalf of someone who was really exploited, and perhaps aware of the fact, immediately evoked the idea that the speaker was a Communist, *i.e.* someone to avoid.[73]

The system has taught or rather forced on the exploited class mental-verbal techniques whereby the modes of rebellion against exploitation are immediately rejected; indeed these techniques make even the first steps towards awareness impossible. We are clearly dealing with the *use* of the language: with the ways in which the language is used on a communitary level to produce and interpret messages. We are dealing in other words with the way in which linguistic constant capital is or is not used by linguistic workers, that is, by linguistic variable capital. The seriousness of this process is to be found in the fact that, as we know (5.2.2-3), the two portions of linguistic capital stand together, are not separable in reality. It is the *organic* structure of linguistic capital which changes over time. It is always total linguistic capital which moves; and it is its overall movement, therefore, which is dominated or conditioned by those who hold power.

The second phase, that is, the possession of the channels through which the messages run, is perhaps the most obvious aspect of communicative domination, at least in these days of mass media. But if this domination is so stridently obvious today, we must not forget that the channels have always been controlled by the

---

[73] Notice in the black American's question the absence of the verb; it is a traditional usage of the white North-American when addressing a red-skin. What we have here then, is a black North-American who derives from the white a linguistic usage felt to be appropriate when the addressee was a red-skin, and does so in addressing himself to a white whom he considers alien. The conditioning of thought-and-language is apparent down to the level of a precise stylistic device — a verbal omission.

ruling class. Today it is more conspicuous because its dimensions have grown so enormously. In the days of endemic illiteracy and before the invention of the printing-press, the control over the channels was perhaps less heavy-handed and pervasive; but it was more absolute and cruel than it is today. The same can be said of those regions which find themselves still in pre-industrial conditions (this usually means that they are the object of imperialistic exploitation). However, these are differences open to historical investigation —— an investigation for which we are here tentatively offering the subject.

Passing now to the third phase, that of the control of the modalities of decodification and interpretation of the messages received, one can say that, with due modifications, it is counterposed symmetrically to the first: once the first has been understood, the third also should become comprehensible. The point is that just as codification is conditioned, so is decodification: *only certain models* of messages are realized and transmitted, only certain communicative programs are executed. The linguistic workers who confection messages are the same as those who receive and interpret them. The planning consists not only in the imposition of certain models and programs, but also in the exclusion of others.

In terms of information theory, the control exercised by the ruling class over messages assumes fairly precise modalities. The ruling class increases the redundancy of messages which confirm its own position, and covers with noise or if necessary with real and proper disturbance or "jamming" the codification and circulation of messages which might instead weaken its position. The subordinate class is placed in the condition of being able to decodify with particular ease, and therefore of considering "real" or "natural", those messages which are sufficiently redundant to overcome the noise or disturbance which might distort their reception, or those messages which they receive with codifying modalities or through channels which are particularly free from noise or disturbance. For those messages, the operation of subtracting spurious from total information is either unnecessary or reduced to the minimum. It may be objected that redundancy is not due to the free choice of the transmitter, but rather to the statistical rules which govern the use of the signs in question, in our case, of words. But this does not change anything. The ruling class finds itself in the position of transmitter, and imposes on both its own members and on the members of the other classes the acceptance of certain sub-systems of signs rather than of others; alternatively, you have subaltern transmitters, who, overpowered by the ruling class, limit themselves to using its codes *or else keep quiet.*

What now happens in terms of linguistic production is that the single speaker comes to find himself in a position homologous to that of the single non-linguistic worker: the processes of linguistic production and circulation have become alien to him, are controlled from the outside, no longer serve to express his personality as a man insofar as they serve instead to reproduce the system. It is as if the speaker had been "hired by the society in which he is born". What is asked of him, is that he expend his linguistic labor-power according to obligatory modalities. We shall come back to this in 7.4.

In advanced capitalist societies, it is typical for the most dangerous messages to be absorbed with the aim of neutralizing them. This procedure comes into a widened notion of the *noise* with which the dominant class or group covers dangerous messages. Being left free to emit such messages means "being hired" in a yet more intimate and compromising manner. Thus, for example, the ruling class (the system, capital) may take pleasure in receiving even ferocious criticisms, which are directed against them "freely". The *noise* here consists in the cancellation of the fact that *even* such criticisms are programmed by those who hold power. This phenomenon of "absorption" would certainly merit a much deeper examination. Here we are referring to the simpler situation, which lies inside the more complex situation. The expenditure of linguistic labor-power according to obligatory modalities does not, however, undergo any substantial modifications. The fundamental fact remains always this: that if there were no speakers, there would be no ruling class either; indeed, every form of *human* deception and exploitation would cease. Those destined for exploitation must at least learn to speak. They are taught to speak so as to make them into machines which are more perfect and complex than any computer hitherto realized. The famous "machine of slavery" on which the charming Greek civilization stood was a *talking machine*. And so we have come back, in a circle, to face the problem of the programming which governs the whole of verbal as of non-verbal communication, *that is*, the whole of human behavior in all its aspects. We shall add to these some further remarks in conclusion (7.5), after briefly touching on linguistic alienation.

7.4 *A Hint at Linguistic Alienation*

In the dialectic between use-value and (exchange-)value of words, syntagms and messages, and between the two types of linguistic work corresponding to the two different basic forms of value (2.3.4; 6.1-4), is to be found the root of the type of alienation which can well be defined as linguistic. The root lies in the different types of work and in the values which derive from them. The developments concern language in its entirety — they concern it as an object of study, as an aggregate of linguistic materials, instruments, and money, which we use, and as a system which conditions the speakers. This conditioning reaches a point where it makes sense to say it is language that makes use of us.

The least one can say about linguistic alienation is that it is a particularly important sector of the general alienation of sign systems. Under various names, and in various of its aspects, it has been the object of study in many currents of contemporary thought. However, it does not appear to have ever been submitted to a frontal and unitary investigation on the basis of a theoretical system capable of comprehending it.[74]

Once the idea has been grasped that sign systems too are submitted to instrumentalization, distortion, mystification, estrangement, one can see no apparent reason why this alienation of theirs should not be taken into consideration alongside the various other kinds of alienation which have already been observed and

[74] The most telling insights into the nature of linguistic alienation are to be found *in nuce* in the founders of historical materialism. I am not referring only to the view that no criticism of alienation can make sense today without resorting to the Marxian demystification of bourgeois economy. I am referring also to something more specific. In *Die deutsche Ideologie* one can read incredibly modern pages on the ways in which a linguistic question can take the place of a real question, on the mystificatory linguistic techniques used by bourgeois ideologists, and on ways of combating such mystifications. That these analyses have been overlooked up to now by philosophers of language and by students of social communication is something either surprising or deeply significant. To the above *loci* one should add the references made to language and communication by Marx in his major work, particularly throughout the analysis of commodities, as well as the brilliant insights into the relationships between economic production and linguistic production which emerge here and there in *Grundrisse der Kritik der politischen Ökonomie* of 1857-1858.

After Marx, various branches of research have developed. We have in the first place the Lukács of *Geschichte und Klassenbewusstsein* and his direct or indirect followers — above all in Germany and in France, but also in Italy (and the vast production, part of which was antecedent to Lukács, of Karl Kraus, a mine of astute ideas: particularly *Die Sprache* and *Literatur und Lüge*). The Lukácsian concept of reification takes up and enlarges the Marxian concept of the fetish-character of commodities; the criticism that Lukács made of this concept offers a theoretical framework of which one might readily make use in the study of linguistic reification. The followers of Lukács have come still closer to such a study, but no one, as far as I know, has ever tried to construct a general theory of linguistic alienation. Let us give a few examples, choosing here and there from an already rather vast literature. The relationship between commodities, thought and language is doubtlessly present in *Dialektik der Aufklärung* by Horkheimer and Adorno, who see in language an extension of the division of labor, and whose treatment of the "cultural industry" necessarily involves the idea of an "industrialization" of language. Adorno's essay on «The fetish character of music and the regression of listening» (in *Dissonanzen*, 1963), can easily be transposed as a study of the fetish character of language and the regression of reading. Also to be kept in mind are the pages dedicated to the work of art as a commodity by Walter Benjamin and many clarifying points in his essay «On language in general and on the language of men» (in *Angelus Novus*, now 1955). One of the most convincing chapters of Marcuse's *One dimensional man* concerns the closing of the universe of discourse and studies such subjects as the "language of total administration", the anti-historical nature of "functional language", the "ritual-authoritarian language". Here we have problems which require *a theory* of linguistic alienation for their further clarification.

Many French Marxists are linked to these German scholars. Here too we will give a few scattered examples. Sartre touches on questions which can be referred to linguistic alienation in his monograph on literature, in *Critique de la raison dialectique* (1960) and elsewhere. The essay by Lucien Goldmann on reification (1958, in 1959) contains the beginning of a study of the "psychic mechanism" through which reification takes place. The distortion that makes man a spectator also expresses itself linguistically, says Goldmann; we can immediately add that the severing, due to reification, of the unity of subject and object and of producer and product cannot but directly regard language as well. If the ruling classes use the means of ideological influence in their possession to hinder the development of the consciousness of the working classes, the tendency of reification to take possession of the workers' minds is, *ipso facto*, a tendency to take possession of them *as speakers*. As we have seen in footnote 51, Henry Lefebvre (1966) has put forward, even if in an approximative and sometimes mis-

studied: religious, philosophical, political, social, economic alienation; and — as a specification of each of them referred to individuals — the alienation of the so-called alienated, who are the object of concern for psychopathologists.[75] The alienation of language cannot but penetrate right from the start all other kinds of alienation: for these in fact concern men, that is, definitionally talking beings. On the so-called "defects of language" various currents of contemporary research have done, separately, a large amount of analytical work; but they have not done so on the ground of, and fortified by, a theory of neo-capitalistic society and, through the study of this, of society in general. It can be maintained that linguistic alienation constitutes the common element at which, potentially, were aiming many attempts to discern in the malfunctioning of language one basic root of evil. However it is certainly not enough to state that language, as Wittgenstein said, «goes on holiday» and «is like an engine idling» (*leerfäuft*) rather than «working» (1953:

---

leading manner, some elements for a parallel between economics and communication, and has attempted an interpretation of language as subject to transformation-into-commodity. The importance of this approach did not escape George Steiner. Something similar, at least as far as "economic communication" is concerned, was indicated by George Herbert Mead (1934) whose work would be well worth returning to.

Among Italian authors, besides everything that is still to be learned from Vailati and Gramsci about the technical and social malfunctioning of language and, as direct examples of these malfunctions, from the philosophical mistiness of Croce and Gentile, let us recall some works of recent years. In his essay on the new avant-garde, Gianni Scalia (1966) deals with the "poverty of poetry" and the "transformation-into-commodity of words"; his argument is still confused but some of his intuitions are profound. Edoardo Sanguineti called a short book of his *Ideologia e linguaggio* (1965) in which he examines, though in passing, the plight of artistic products between the market and the museum. Lastly, it is remarkable that even a linguist of the classical school like Giacomo Devoto makes reference, in the preface to one of his collections of articles (1965) to «the alienation most characteristic of our time, linguistic alienation».

A second line of research is that of the analytic or linguistic philosophers, George E. Moore and Ludwig Wittgenstein and some of their followers, particularly in Great Britain. As I attempted to show in «Per un uso marxiano di Wittgenstein» (1966b, now in 1968c), there is a strong potential of linguistic demystification in the works of the Viennese philosopher as well as in those of Moore, John Wisdom, and Gilbert Ryle. This demystification, however, is rarely, if ever, presented as such; to the contrary, it is customary to limit whatever demystificatory analytical activity there may be to speech considered by itself, or worse, to some aspects of the "natural" language one happens to speak (cf. note 39). We must *bring to light* this potential demystification: then we see that it falls perfectly in line, and indeed, acquires force and meaning, within the framework of a general criticism of ideologies. This amounts to saying that what these philosophers actually concerned themselves with in the most worth-while part of their research was alienated language, linguistic ideology.

[75] Alienated language has been at the center of attention of psychologists and psychiatrists starting with Freud himself. One might rightly maintain that psychoanalysis grew up precisely as a research into alienated language. Lacan (1966) and Ricoeur (1965) are of course two scholars who must be mentioned at this point. Among the more recent contributions, we recall: *Insight and responsibility* (1964) by Erik H. Erikson; the trilogy dedicated by Jurgen Ruesch to communication as the social matrix of psychiatry (together with the anthropologist Gregory Bateson), to "disturbed" communication, and to therapeutic communication (1951, 1957, 1961); Julius Laffal's investigation of normal and pathological language (1965), and Sergio Piro's of schizophrenic language (1967).

38º and 132º); one has also to *ask oneself why this is so*. This apparently simple question opens up a boundless field of new research the existence of which the analysts of language have not even suspected. It is certainly not just a question of denouncing certain deviations from paradigms previously ascertained (or proposed) within the sphere of this or that language — a language, considered as a self-sufficient system independent of both other linguistic systems and non-verbal sign systems. Even less adequate would be any attempt to face linguistic alienation with the instrument of some presumptuous model of how language *ought to be*: by measuring reality with a subjective model only subjective changes can be proposed. Rather than combating ideology, these are themselves, in an unconscious way, loud ideological forms which withdraw from the task of becoming aware of socially real processes. In order to begin to reply to questions concerning the malfunctioning of language, one must consider verbal sign systems alongside non-verbal ones and social sign systems alongside natural ones. The first demand to be satisfied is an anti-separatistic demand. What is linguistic must be examined in its relationship with what is not linguistic. Language without society, in fact, does not exist, and vice-versa; and the first is a form and expression of the second; it is in language, or more broadly in sign systems, that society *manifests* itself. Perhaps these are commonplaces. It is not apparent, however, that students of language always extract the right consequences from them; while students of society do not always appear to take into account the fact that society, with the qualifications advanced in 1.3, *is* the functioning of sign systems. Precisely that upon which attention should be concentrated is often taken for granted, because it is too obvious, or too uncomfortable.

One of the hypotheses for research, to which I think we should turn for the study of linguistic alienation, is the hypothesis (already alluded to in 5.2.2, 5.2.3, and 7.3) that the individual speaker, who has no control over the codes and the channels, finds himself in a position analogous to that of the individual non-linguistic worker. As a worker, he no longer shares in the process of work and production to which he nevertheless belongs. The phases of a given working process, which once made up the personal task of the craftsman, are distributed in an equal number of phases external to the person: so that first the factory, and then the whole of capitalist production, become on an ever broader scale a sort of inhuman reproduction of man as a worker. Man with his productive processes has come badly out of himself, has objectivized himself in wrong ways; he now finds himself disarmed when faced with the organization of his very own products; his body is as it were distended outside himself, and the processes which govern it seem to proceed on their own like something alien. We can say similarly that the linguistic working process and, all the more, the entire process of linguistic production and circulation become external to the individual speaker precisely with the taking on of the institutionalized form of a linguistic capital and a linguistic market which no speaker can change at will. The speaker is, as we just said, "hired by the society in which he is born"; he is asked — or better compelled — to expend his linguistic labor-power in pre-established modalities which he is forced to accept and learn. The speaker works, but not for himself. We have seen in 6.5 and then again in 7.3.2 how a large part of linguistic behavior consists in using *already existing products*, in consuming them, unconsciously reproducing them according to models and programs which as a result are confirmed and perpetuated. The speaker must transmit certain messages and not others; he is able to understand only certain messages and not others. His freedom is limited to the use of everyday objects in both kinds of production, since in both kinds the behavioral programs woven into the social sign systems are immeasurably stronger than any single individual and thus also than any social group which has not yet been quickened by an appropriate revolutionary theory. Even if the individual speaker succeeds in refusing the models and programs imposed on him, by operating within himself a sort of linguistic-communicative inversion, the penalty he must pay is his expulsion or marginalization from the linguistic community, and thus, since society without language does not exist, from society itself. Anyone who does not learn to speak like the others or who starts out to speak a language personally deviated from the models, anyone who withdraws from the programs of communication which are considered normal by the society in which he lives, is no longer understood, and he is no longer capable of making himself understood even if he so wishes. Paraphrasing Shakespeare, he will lose his life for want of language. It is a situation which we can call *linguistic death*, or *communicative death*, and is just as serious as death from starvation or the civil death of forced labor. To such a death are condemned not only schizophrenics, chronic sufferers from aphasia, and all the so-called abnormal or demented: it manifests itself as at least a possibility to anyone who attempts radically new linguistic, or otherwise communicative, paths, just as it does to anyone who tries to recuperate the real social dimensions of language.

The linguistic worker, as an executor of programs and repeater of obligatory and suprapersonal models, comes to find himself in the situation of not knowing *what he is doing* when he speaks nor of *knowing why* he speaks as he does. He *belongs to* processes of linguistic production which condition him right from the start, which oblige him to see the world in determined ways and which make it difficult for him to perform any work which is original or just simply different.

Production as the mere use of products: this is what the system wants to have handed down. The materials upon which linguistic production is continuously renewed are linguistic materials handed down just as they are, without reverting again to the working processes, of which they were the products. In this way they are represented also as non-linguistic. The use of linguistic instruments is taught as if it were a set of equipment which anyone acquires once and for all, and this after having separated the instruments from the materials and the money (5.2.1.1). Linguistic money, which is continually made use of, is indeed ignored (apart from generic references to the "wealth of language": 5.2.1.2). The constant and variable portions of linguistic capital stand there face to face, without anyone's becoming aware of their dialectical opposition, and the problem of their reciprocal influence is grossly underrated. Above all, the programs which govern communication are ignored precisely in the act of their being most thoroughly exploited for the conditioning of individual behavior. Through all these omissions, distortions, reductions, and pseudo-naturalizations, the detachment of man from nature and of man from man fulfills and perfects itself, hands itself down, institutionalizes itself, and takes on a character of definitiveness and irreversibility.

What alienated society has programmed so successfully is precisely this: a way of barring the road along which one could try to go back to that very relationship for which a separation has been substituted. And it is a perfect road-block because it is itself dynamic. It is an expenditure of the type which seems to take place before the eyes of someone going along the aisles of a supermarket, even if it is obviously immensely more radical and vast. In fact precisely the products of the relationship between man and man and between man and nature have made themselves available — immediately and easily available; however, *no longer as products*, but instead as something natural upon which man no longer intervenes. It is the myth of the artificial pseudo-paradise immediately turning into its opposite, that is, the hell of consumer societies. That man *has* intervened in the production of himself — so that without such an intervention not one of those products would ever have emerged — is precisely what is ignored. The basic programming of alienated society consists in a de-totalized aggregate of piecemeal programs whose execution allows people to use all products as if they were not products; and this amounts to living in a fragmented way even on the level of fundamental relationships.

Now since the intervention we are discussing here is that of language, and of sign systems in general, in the division of labor — since it is, in other words, an intervention which presides over man's formation —, the overturning of the real situation causes man to deny himself as man. Within the pseudo-totality in which this negation takes place, this means that man establishes himself then as a mere cog-wheel: as a spokesman, repeater, and victim of the social process of linguistic reproduction. Since his own products have organized themselves in a system above and against him, his thrashing about under their weight pushes him further and further down, towards a situation which, no longer capable of being fully linguistic, necessarily becomes subhuman. In this way man is protagonist of a sort of grotesque "return to nature" in a completely false atmosphere. It is at this stage that exchange-values come back to the foreground as false use-values (cf. 5.2.2). We are doubly distant from a spontaneous relationship with nature.

The road for really going back to nature, for re-awakening it in ourselves, would be instead the diametrically opposite one of first giving man back to man. This can be done only through radically new social designs, that is — as we were saying — by consciously going through again some essential phases of homination. The basic choice, once again, is eminently political. Theories are not enough.

7.5   Conclusive Remarks on the Social Programming of All Behavior

We have maintained that everything that human individuals do and have done to them is programmed by the society to which they belong. The portions of behavior which can be considered casual, spontaneous, free, *purely* individual — that is, in one sense or another, *not* socially programmed — are much more limited than is commonly believed, at least in our Western societies. Even types of behavior which can be made to come under this heading are performed on the background or under the influence of existing social programmings[76] or may even use them: and in any case they themselves would not be comprehensible — indeed, not even identifiable as casual, spontaneous, free, or individual — if there did not exist other social programmings against which they can be measured.

The social programmings themselves can be conscious or unconscious, deliberate or simply assumed, long-term or transitional, unitary or differential. They can furthermore be more or less extended: they may concern all the members of a community or of various communities, or, alternatively, only one or more groups of members of one or more communities. The presence of similar programmings makes social groups homogeneous independently from their belonging to the same or to different communities. The most important instance of this supra-national homogeneity is obviously that of class division. The programmings vary continually according to the types of behavior being programmed, the structure of the society in which they are taking place, the historical moment, and so forth; they leave widely differing margins or illusions of fortuity, spontaneity, and freedom which in their turn are for the most part programmed; often they permit or rather foresee that the individual may *feel* himself to be an actor. The programmings hand themselves down from generation to generation with usually small changes, the amount of change depending upon the type of program involved. These changes create quantitative accumulations destined to give birth to qualitative leaps. A social action must be called revolutionary if it succeeds in changing in a more or less radical, but in any case general and long-term manner, a significant portion of the social programmings which were previously dominant.

Against the idea that *all* human behavior is *socially* programmed it is correct to raise the objection that men do, and have done to them, actions also on account of *natural* factors. This objection does not claim freedom or fortuity for certain types of behavior, but instead introduces conditioning factors of a different kind. All the same, in its obviousness, it proves much less than it may appear to prove. The dialectical criss-crossing of the two kinds of evolution — natural or biological,

---

[76]   Our main concern so far has been with models and programs with regard to sign systems. In this final sub-section communicative models and programs are related to wider forms of social programming (Mead 1968 may be consulted at this point as a partially similar outline of the subject). The word 'programming' has been introduced in a tentative manner as a comprehensive description not only of both models and programs, but also of all sorts of programming which may not be immediately reducible to the models and programs of sign systems.

and properly social evolution, which first began to overlap as soon as what could be called human aggregates emerged — makes it now almost impossible to isolate purely-natural factors within society. Even where it would seem most obvious to trace them, and that is in man's body itself, the natural factors always present themselves through social dimensions, by which they are in fact conditioned. A natural disaster like the Yellow River floods, or a disease like cancer, or a road accident, naturally, do *not present themselves* as being socially programmed. And this, not only in the sense that there are not individuals or groups who sit down round a table to study the actions necessary for the realization of a flood, a disease, or an accident (although, in determined circumstances, even this may happen); but also in the sense that it is not the custom even to suppose the existence of unconscious programmings on behalf of floods, diseases, and accidents. All the same, even the "natural" factors and events, which seem to condition human behavior independently from the social dimension, are, on the contrary, when examined more closely, inextricably entwined with the controllable consequences of social programmings. The Yellow River floods have been finally tamed; it was to the extent that Chinese society found itself in semi-feudal and semi-colonial conditions, that the human forces necessary for taming the floods could not be gathered together; this happened instead, after the revolutionary introduction of new social designs, *i.e.* of radically different programmings. Various diseases, including the scourge of cancer, are more widespread in certain societies and in certain historical epochs than in others; it will be possible to cure them much more completely and gradually to eliminate them when waste and exploitation have been abolished, and when the effort and expense today invested in armaments and in enterprises which are really mainly for prestige (like space exploration) are concentrated to that end. Road accidents also depend, more than on biological factors and on so-called "luck", on controllable factors such as the unrestrained planning of consumption for the benefit of the car-industry, the objective conditions of the traffic and of the road network, as well as on the courtesy, prudence, and psycho-physical conditions of the drivers. An "automobile civilization" without any accidents is perfectly conceivable.

The obviousness, and at the same time the inconclusive character of the appeal to natural factors, are further confirmed by the following fact. Not only social kinds of behavior, whether animal or human, nor only human kinds of behavior, whether social or individual, are programmed. Also programmed are kinds of behavior identifiable as biological. The programming of the living being begins with the genetic code and expresses itself in ecological programs which concern both men and non-human animals. It extends uninterruptedly from the most elementary levels of matter to the most complex — those which are called "social". There is therefore no sense in counterposing the realm of the biological to the realm of the social in function of programmings which are supposed to be present in the one but not in the other, or vice-versa: as if at a certain point there were an *onto-*

logical leap between the two realms. *All* behavior is programmed. The question is one of seeing how, why, and within what limits.

In order to clarify the general notion of the social programming of behavior with the aim of throwing the same amount of light on all its several areas, whether or not hitherto neglected, we must keep in mind the variety of the programmings and of the conditioning factors which they set in motion. In our opinion the following should be distinguished:

1) *modes of production* (the sum of productive forces and relations of production);
2) *ideologies* (social designs of a general type, over the long term);
3) *programs of communication* (both of non-verbal and of verbal communication).

Social programming takes place fundamentally according to the three dimensions indicated here. In reality the three dimensions are always present together and it can be difficult to disentangle them from each other. Each single instance of behavior is performed as a totality determined by multiple conditioning factors. From the point of view of the totality constituted by each given instance of behavior — if the purpose is that of understanding it in all its aspects — the various factors, and the programmings to which they belong, can be distinguished only in a provisional and artificial way. Even when it appears to be clear that an instance of behavior belongs to only one of the three programming dimensions, it can be grasped in its reality only on a background where the other two are also necessarily operating. Thus for example one's way of behaving at table, which in each community is programmed in the dimension of non-verbal communication, certainly does not take place *in the absence of* other communicative programs of the same community; and all the communicative programming certainly does not operate outside a situation which is also programmed by dominant modes of production and ruling ideologies. But, once this warning note has been struck and the anti-separatistic stance reaffirmed, the fact remains that the various programmings do lend themselves to being studied also on their own, and each one by itself, as matrices of conditioning factors and therefore as generators of behavior. The most important thing is to establish on each occasion the level of abstraction on which one is moving.

The study of the first dimension, that is of the modes of production, belongs to the demystification of bourgeois economy, and, after the proletariat's seizure of power, to the planning of socialist production; the study of the second belongs to the doctrine of ideologies understood as social designs which depend on the modes of production and vary accordingly, but at the same time get detached from them through numerous mediations, and furthermore retro-act on the modes of production themselves. With the arise of industrial capitalism in the late eighteenth and early nineteenth centuries, there emerged also the means for studying the capitalist mode of production and its relative ideologies, and lastly for projecting scientifically a better society, that is, new programmings destined to substitute the capitalistic ones. This also allowed for the emergence of a general doctrine of man in which the importance of modes of production and of ideologies was for the first time placed in a proper light. All the same, neither the first nor the second dimension, even if added together, gives us a *complete description* of the social programming of human behavior, if we do not add to them the dimension of those programmings which govern both verbal and non-verbal communication. This third dimension, which mediates between the first two, making possible, amongst other things, their reciprocal influence, had also been glimpsed by Marx's genius. It is, however, only with the arise of neo-capitalism that the means have emerged for a frontal study of the models and programs of communication. And since there is no communication without sign system, this study belongs to semiotics, the general doctrine and science of signs and of their systems. Semiotics finds its proper place, its significance, and its foundation alongside the study of modes of production and of ideologies, within the sphere of the social programming of all behavior.

(*Rome, July* 1971)

8. REFERENCES

While in the text and notes of this essay, references mainly follow the usual style adopted by *Current Trends* (e.g. Godelier 1969 : 101-110), in this Bibliography a more traditional style is adopted. This especially because a Bibliography like this one, which has historical, intercultural, and interdisciplinary dimensions, is necessarily different from one confined to publications belonging to a single field of enquiry and/or appearing in the last few years. Here entries are arranged alphabetically, and for each individual author chronologically; and the chronological order usually refers to the *date of publication*. Classics and many important contemporaries, however, are listed according to the *dates of writing*. This is for instance the case of Hegel and Husserl, where a chronological index of mere publication dates would have been unreasonable and misleading. In Husserl's case, however, the continuous realaboration of the various manuscripts and the fact that many of them were withheld from publication cause some overlapping of dates.

Translations are indicated under the text-heading, and are usually English translations, whenever these were available to the present writer. Some translations into other languages are given because of historical or technical importance.

ADORNO, THEODOR W. 1963. *Dissonanzen. Musik in der verwalteten Welt.* Göttingen, Vandenhoeck & Ruprecht, 160 pp.; Italian transl. and intr. by Giacomo Manzoni, Milano, Feltrinelli (1959), xxiii + 227 pp.

———. 1964. *Jargon der Eigentlichkeit. Zur deutschen Ideologie.* Frankfurt a. M., Suhrkamp Verlag, 139 pp.

———. 1966. *Philosophie der neuen Musik.* Frankfurt a. M., Europäische Verlagsanstalt, 201 pp.; *Filosofia della musica moderna*, with an introductory essay by Luigi Rognoni, Italian transl. by Giacomo Manzoni, Torino, Einaudi (1959), xxvi + 212 pp.

ADORNO, THEODOR W. and MAX HORKHEIMER, cf. HORKHEIMER.

ALBRIGHT, W. F., and T. O. LAMBDIN. 1970. The evidence of language. In *The Cambridge ancient history*, Vol. I, Part 1, Prolegomena and prehistory, ed. by I. E. S. Edwards, C. J. Gadd and N. G. L. Hammond, pp. 122–155, Cambridge, at the University Press.

ALTHUSSER, LOUIS. 1965–1966. *Pour Marx*. Paris, François Maspero, 261 pp. ("Théorie I").

ALTHUSSER, LOUIS, JAQUES RANCIÈRES, and PIERRE MACHEREY. 1965. *Lire le Capital*. Paris, François Maspero, Vol. I, 259 pp., Vol. II, 404 pp. ("Théorie II, III").

L'analogie, special number of *Revue internationale de philosophie*, 87° (XXIII, 1°), 1969, 150 pp. [Essays by various authors.]

Animal communication, ed. by Thomas A. Sebeok, 1968. Bloomington-London, Indiana University Press, xviii+686 pp.

Approaches to animal communication, ed. by Thomas A. Sebeok and Alexandra Ramsay. The Hague, Mouton & Co., 1969, 261 pp.

ARISTOTLE. 1935. *Metaphysics X–XIV, Oeconomica*, and *Magna Moralia*. Transl. by H. Tredennick and G. Cyril Armstrong. London, William Heinemann; revised and reprinted 1958, 688 pp.

——. 1926. *The Nicomachean Ethics*. Transl. by H. Rackham. London, William Heinemann; new and revised ed. 1947, xxix + 650 pp.

AUSTIN, J. L. 1955. *How to do things with words*. The William James Lectures delivered at Harvard University in 1955, ed. and with a preface by J. O. Urmson. Oxford, at the Clarendon Press, 1962, vii+166 pp.

——. 1961. *Philosophical papers*. Oxford, at the Clarendon Press, 242 pp.

——. 1962. *Sense and sensibilia*, reconstructed from the manuscript notes by G. J. Warnock. Oxford, at the Clarendon Press, ix + 144 pp.

Avanguardia e neo-avanguardia, by various authors, intr. by Giansiro Ferrata. Milan, Sugar, 1966, xviii + 263 pp.

AYER, A. J. 1953. The identity of indiscernibles. In Ayer 1954a, *q.v.*, pp. 26–35.

——. 1954a. *Philosophical essays*. London, MacMillan, xi+289 pp.

——. 1954b. *Can there be a private language?* Symposium, Aristotelian Society, Supplementary Volume 28, pp. 63–76; repr. in *The concept of a person and other essays*, London, MacMillan, 1964, vii+272 pp., at pages 36–51.

BACON, FRANCIS. 1622–1623. *De dignitate et augmentis scientiarum*. In Bacon 1858–1874, *q.v.*, Vol. I, pp. 415–837.

——. 1858–1874. *Works*, in fourteen volumes, collected and edited by James Spedding, Robert Leslie Ellis and Douglas Denon Heath. London.

BALES, ROBERT F., TALCOTT PARSONS, and EDWARD A. SHILS. 1953. *Working papers in the theory of action*. Toronto, Collier-MacMillan, 269 pp.

BALLY, CH., and A. SECHEHAYE, Eds. *Cours de linguistique générale*, by F. de Saussure, *q.v.*

BANFI, RODOLFO. 1965. Uno pseudo-problema: la teoria del valore-lavoro come base dei prezzi di equilibrio. *Critica marxista*, 3/3 (May-June 1965), 135–58.

———. 1966. Abbozzo di una ricerca attorno al valore d'uso nel pensiero di Marx. *Critica marxista*, 4/1 (January-February 1956), 137–75.

BARAN, PAUL A. 1957. *The political economy of growth.* New York, Monthly Review Press, 1967⁴, xliv+308 pp.

BARTHES, ROLAND. 1967. *Systhème de la mode.* Paris, Seuil, 326 pp.

BATESON, GREGORY. 1966. Information, codification, and metacommunication. In *Communication and Culture*, ed. by A. G. Smith, *q.v.*, pp. 412–26.

———. 1968. Redundancy and coding. In *Animal communication*, *q.v.*, pp. 614–26.

BATESON, GREGORY, and JURGEN RUESCH. 1951. *Communication: The social matrix of psychiatry.* New York, Norton & Co. [see Ruesch].

BEACH, FRANK A.: see FORD and BEACH, 1965.

BEAVIN, J. H.: cf. *Pragmatics of human communication.*

Behavior of nonhuman primates, modern research trends, ed. by Allan M. Schrier, Harry F. Harlow and Fred Stillnitz. New York, London, Academic Press, 1965, Vol. I, xvi + 286 + 33 pp., Vol. II, xvi + 287–595 + 33 pp.

BENJAMIN, WALTER. 1950. *Berliner Kindheit um Neunzehnhundert.* Frankfurt/Main, Suhrkamp, 171 pp.

———. 1955. *Schriften.* Frankfurt/Main, Suhrkamp Verlag; Italian transl. and intr. by Renato Solmi, *Angelus Novus: Saggi e frammenti.* Torino, Einaudi, 1962, xxxvii+289 pp.

———. 1961. *Illuminationen.* Selected Writings. Frankfurt/Main, Suhrkamp, 445 pp.

———. 1963. *Ursprung des deutschen Trauerspiels.* Frankfurt/Main, Suhrkamp, 272 pp.

———. 1966. *Versuche über Brecht.* Frankfurt/Main, Suhrkamp, 157 pp.

———. 1966. *Angelus Novus.* Selected Writings 2. Frankfurt/Main, Suhrkamp, 546 pp.

———. 1966. *Briefe 1.* Annotated edition by G. Scholem and Th. W. Adorno. Frankfurt/Main, Suhrkamp, 484 pp.

———. 1966. *Briefe 2.* Annotated edition by G. Scholem and Th. W. Adorno. Frankfurt/Main, Suhrkamp, iii+485–885 pp.

BENVENISTE, ÉMILE. 1954a. Tendences récentes en linguistique générale. *Journal de psychologie normale et pathologique*, 74/1,2 (January-June 1954), pp. 130–45; reprinted in Benveniste 1966, *q.v.*

———. 1954b. Catégories de pensée et catégories de langue. *Etudes philosophiques*, 419–429; reprinted in Benveniste 1966, *q.v.*

———. 1966. *Problèmes de linguistique générale.* Paris, Gallimard, iv+356 pp. (NRF, Bibliothèque des sciences humaines).

———. 1970. Structure de la langue et structure de la société. In *Linguaggi nella società e nella tecnica, q.v.*, pp. 17–28.

BERGOUNIOUX, F. M. 1961. Notes on the mentality of primitive man. In *Social life of early man*, q.v., pp. 106–18.

BERLIN, ISAIAH. 1960. The philosophical ideas of Giambattista Vico. In *Art and ideas in eighteenth-century Italy*. Roma, Edizioni di storia e letteratura, pp. 156–233.

——. 195. Sulla teoria del Vico circa la conoscenza storica. *Lettere italiane*, 17/4 (October-December 1965), 420–31.

BERNAL, JOHN D. 1969. *Science in history*. 4 Vols. London, C. A. Watts & Co. (1954[1]), Vol. I: pp. vii + 363 + xxv, Vol. II: pp. vii + 365–693 + xxv, Vol. III: pp. vii + 695–1008 + xxv, Vol. IV: pp. viii + 1009–1329 + xxv.

BIDNEY, DAVID. 1953. *Theoretical anthropology*. New York and London, Columbia University Press, 1964[4], xiii+500 pp.

BIRDWHISTELL, RAY L. 1966. Some relations between American kinesics and spoken American English. In *Communication and culture*, 1966, q.v., pp. 182–89.

——. 1968. L'Analyse kinésique. *Pratiques et langages gestuels*, special number of *Langages*, 10° (June 1968), 101–06.

BLACK, MAX. 1962. *Models and metaphors*, studies in language and philosophy. New York, Cornell University Press; repr. 1966, xi+267 pp.

BLOCH, BERNARD, and GEORGE L. TRAGER. 1942. *Outline of linguistic analysis*. Baltimore, Linguistic Society of America, ii+82 pp.

BLOOMFIELD, LEONARD. 1964. *Language*. New York, Holt, Rinehart and Winston (1933[1]), x+364 pp.

——. 1942. *Outline guide for the practical study of foreign languages*. Baltimore, Linguistic Society of America.

BOAS, FRANZ. 1911. Introduction to *Handbook of American Indian languages*, repr. together with *Indian linguistic families of America north of Mexico* (1891) by J. W. POWELL; ed. by Preston Holder. Lincoln, University of Nebraska Press, 1966, xii+221 pp.

——. 1966. *Race, language and culture* (1940). New York, Free Press, xx+647 pp.

BÖHM-BAWERK, EUGEN VON. 1959. *Capital and interest*. Transl. by Hans F. Sennholz. South Holland, Illinois, Libertarian Press. Vol. I: *History and critique of interest theories*, xxii + 490 pp.; Vol. II: *Positive theory of capital*, xi + 466 pp.; Vol. III: *Further essays on capital and interest*, viii + 246 pp.

——. 1966. *Karl Marx and the close of his system* (and RUDOLF HILFERDING: *Böhm-Bawerk's criticism of Marx*), ed. and intr. by Paul M. Sweezy. New York, August M. Kelley Publishers, xxx + 224 pp.

BOREK, ERNEST. 1965. *The code of life*. New York, Columbia University Press, xi + 226 pp.

BOUDIN, LOUIS B. 1907. *The theoretical system of Karl Marx*. Chicago, Charles

H. Kerr & Co.; repr. by the Monthly Review Press, New York and London, 1967, vii + 9–286 pp.

BRADFORD, JOHN. 1954. Building in wattle, wood, and turf. In *A history of technology*, Vol. I, *q.v.*, pp. 299–326.

BRADLEY, FRANCIS HERBERT. 1922². *Principles of logic* (1883). 2 Vols. London, Oxford University Press; repr. 1958, xxviii + 739 pp.

BRECHT, BERTOLD. 1968a. *Letters to a grown-up American*. In Brecht 1968b, pp. 293–302.

——. 1968b. *Schriften zur Politik und Gesellschaft*, ed. by Werner Hecht. Frankfurt/Main, Suhrkamp Verlag, 362 + 54 pp.

BRITTON, KARL. 1970. *Communication, a philosophical study of language*. College Park, Maryland, McGrath Publishing Company, xvi + 290 pp.

BRONFENBRENNER, MARTIN, and YUTAKA KOSAI. 1967. On the Marxian capital-consumption ratio. *Science & society*, 31/4 (Fall, 1967), 467–73.

BRONOWSKI, J. 1967. Human and animal languages. In *To honor Roman Jakobson*, *q.v.*, Vol. I, pp. 374–94.

BROWN, ROGER W.: see LENNEBERG, ERIC H.

BÜCHER, KARL. 1896¹. *Arbeit und Rhytmus*. 5th ed. Leipzig, 1919 (quoted by George Thomson).

BURGER, A. 1961. Significations et valeur du suffixe verbal français -e-. *CFS*, 18, 5–15.

CARPENTER, C. R. 1969. Approaches to studies of the naturalistic communicative behavior in nonhuman primates. In *Approaches to animal communication*, *q.v.*, pp. 40–70.

CATTANEO, CARLO. 1855–56. *Logica*. In Cattaneo 1960, Vol. III: Lezioni II, pp. 217–329.

——. 1960. *Scritti filosofici*, ed. by Norberto Bobbio. Firenze, Felice Le Monnier. Vol. I: Saggi lxix+493 pp.; Vol. II: Lezioni I, 382 pp.; Vol. III: Lezioni II, 444 pp.

CECCATO, SILVIO. 1952. Contra Dingler, pro Dingler. *Methodos*, 4, 223–65, with English transl. pp. 266–90 and reply by Dingler, pp. 291–96, transl. into English pp. 297–99.

——. 1940–1953. *Un tecnico fra i filosofi*. I: *Come filosofare* (1940–1947), 314 pp., II: *Come non filosofare* (1947–1953), 662 pp. Padova, Marsilio, 1964 and 1966.

A centenary of Marx's capital, special number of *Science & society*, 31/4 (Fall, 1967), 385–540.

CHANCE, M. R. A. 1961. The nature and special features of the instinctive social bond of primaes. In *Social life of early man*, *q.v.*, pp. 17–33.

CHENU, M. D. 1955. *Pour une théologie du travail*. Paris, Editions du Seuil, 123 pp.

CHERRY, COLIN. 1957. *On human communication: A review, a survey, and a criticism*. Cambridge, Mass., The M.I.T. Press, 1966², xiv+337 pp.

——. 1966. The communication of information. In *Communication and culture*, 1966, *q.v.*, pp. 35–40.

CHILDE, VERE GORDON. 1936. *Man makes himself*. New York, The New American Library, 1961 (1941²). [Especially Chap. II.]

——. 1942. *What happened in history*. Harmondsworth, Middlesex, Penguin Books (1954², 1964³), 300 pp.; *Il progresso nel mondo antico: L'evoluzione della società umana dalla preistoria agli inizi dell'età classica*. Transl. by A. Ruata. Torino, Einaudi, 1963, 312 pp.

——. 1954a. Early forms of society. In *A history of technology*, *q.v.*, Vol. I, pp. 38–57.

——. 1954b. Rotary motion. In *A history of technology*, *q.v.*, Vol. I, pp. 187–215.

——. 1956. *Piecing together the past, the interpretation of archeological data*. London, Routledge & Kegan Paul, 1969 (1964), vii+176 pp.

CHOMSKY, NOAM. 1957. *Syntactic structures*. JanL 4. 1965, 118 pp.

——. 1964. *Current issues in linguistic theory*. JanL 38. 1966, 119 pp.

——. 1965. *Aspects of the theory of syntax*. Cambridge, Mass., The M.I.T. Press, x + 251 pp.

——. 1966a. Three models for the description of language. In *Communication and culture*, 1966 (*q.v.*) pp. 140–52.

——. 1966b. *Topics in the theory of generative grammar*. The Hague-Paris, Mouton, 95 pp.

——. 1966c. *Cartesian linguistics: 17 chapters in the history of rationalistic thought*. New York, Harper & Row, xvi+199 pp.

——. 1968. *Language and mind*. USA, Harcourt, Brace & Co., 88 pp.

✗ ——. 1969. Linguistics and politics. *New left review* 57 (Sept.-Oct. 1969), 21–34 (Interviewers: R. B., G. S. S., L. R.).

Commodity fetishism and the value concept: Some Contrasting Points of View, 1966. By JACOB MORRIS, M. COLMAN, and DONALD CLARK HODGES. *Science & society*, 30/2 (Spring 1966), 206–27.

Communication and culture. Readings in the codes of human interaction. 1966. Ed. by Alfred G. Smith, New York, Holt, Rinehart and Winston, xiii+626 pp.

COOK, JOHN W. 1965. Wittgenstein on privacy. *The philosophical review*, 74/411 (3°, July 1965), 281–314.

CORNMAN, JAMES W. 1968. Private languages and private entities. *Australasian journal of philosophy*, 46/2 (August 1968), 117–26.

COSTA, FILIPPO. 1971. Prospettive sulla logica leibniziana. *Giornale critico della filosofia italiana*, 4th Series, Vol. II, 1st issue, 36–70.

CROCE, BENEDETTO. 1909. *Aesthetic*. Transl. by D. Ainslie. New York, The Noonday Press; revised ed. 1922, xxx + 503 pp.

DAVYDOV, JURIJ. 1962. *Il lavoro e la libertà*. Transl. and ed. by V. Strada. Torino, Einaudi, 1966, 143 pp.

DE MAURO, TULLIO. 1967. Eliminare il senso? *LeS*, 2/2, 131–51, with bibliography.

DERRY, THOMAS K., and TREVOR I. WILLIAMS. 1960. *A short history of technology*. Oxford, Clarendon Press, xviii+783 pp.

DEVOTO, GIACOMO. 1965. *Civiltà di parole*. Florence, Vallecchi, 234 pp.

Dictionnaire archéologique des techniques. Paris, Editions de l'Accueil, 1963–1964, vol. 2, 1122 pp.

A dictionary of the social sciences, ed. by Julius Gould and William L. Kolb. London, Tavistock Publications, 1964, xvi + 761 pp.

DINGLER, HUGO. 1913. *Die Grundlagen der Naturphilosophie*. Leipzig, Verlag Unesma, x+262 pp.

——. 1928. *Das Experiment: Sein Wesen und seine Geschichte*. München, E. Reinhardt, viii + 263 pp.

——. 1930. *Das System: Daes philosophisch-rationale Grundproblem und die exakte Methode der Philosophie*. München, E. Reinhardt, 133 pp.

——. 1931. *Philosophie der Logik und Arithmetik*. München, E. Reinhardt, 198 pp.

——. 1938. *Die Methode der Physik*. München, E. Reinhardt, 411 pp.

——. 1941. *Von der Tierseele zur Menschenseele. Die Geschichte der geistigen Menschenwerdung*. Leipzig, Helingsche Verlagsanstalt, 398 pp.

——. 1942. Das Unberührte. *Zeitschrift für die gesamte Naturwissenschaft;* now in *Grundriss der methodischen Philosophie* (ch. III, pp. 19–26). Füssen, C. F. Winter'sche Verlagshandlung, 1959, 143 pp.

——. 1955. *Die Ergreifung des Wirklichen*. Published posthumously by W. Krampf. München, Eidos, 239 pp.

DI SIENA, GIUSEPPE. 1969. Ideologie del biologismo. *Ideologie*, 9°-10°, 69–138.

DI SIENA, GIUSEPPE and FERRUCCIO ROSSI-LANDI. 1970. Corpo. *Ideologie*, 12°, 11–20. Article of *Dizionario teorico-ideologico*, ed. by the review.

DOBB, MAURICE. 1937. *Political economy and capitalism. Some essays in economic tradition*. London, Routledge & Kegan Paul. Rev. ed. 1940, repr. 1960, viii + 357 pp.

——. 1946. *Studies in the development of capitalism*. London, Routledge & Kegan Paul. Rev. ed. 1963, ix+402 pp.

——. 1948. *Soviet economic development since 1917*. London, Routledge & Kegan Paul. Sixth ed. 1966, viii+515 pp.

——. 1967a. Marx's capital and its place in economic thought. *Science & society*, 31/4 (Fall, 1967), 527–40.

——. 1967b. *Papers on capitalism, development and planning*. London, Routledge & Kegan Paul, vi+275 pp.

DUCHÁČEK, OTTO. 1968. Différents types de champs. *Zeitschrift für französische Sprache und Literatur*. Beiheft *Probleme der Semantik*. Wiesbaden, F. Steiner, pp. 25–36.

DUFFIELD, J. 1970. The value concept in capital, in light of recent criticism. *Science & society*, 34/3 (Fall, 1970), 293–302.

EBELING, C. L. 1960. *Linguistic units*. JanL 12. Repr. 1962, 143 pp.

ECO, UMBERTO. 1968. *La struttura assente: Introduzione alla ricerca semiologica*. Milano, Bompiani, 1968, 431 pp.

EMENEAU, MURRAY B. 1966. Franz Boas as a linguist. In *Portraits of linguists*, ed. by Th. A. Sebeok, *q.v.*, pp. 122–27.

Encyclopedia of philosophy. 1967. Ed. by P. Edwards. 8 vols. New York, The Macmillan Company and the Free Press.

Encyclopedia of the social sciences, ed. by E. R. A. Seligman and A. Johnson. 15 Vols. New York, Macmillan Company, 1963.

ENGELS, FRIEDRICH. 1935. *Socialism, utopian and scientific*, with an essay on "The Mark". Transl. by E. Aveling. New York, International Publishers, 1968, 93 pp.

——. 1940. *Dialectics of nature*. Transl. and ed. by C. Dutt, with a preface and notes by J. B. S. Haldane, New York, International Publishers, 1960, xvi + 383 pp.

——. 1941. *Ludwig Feuerbach and the outcome of classical German philosophy*, ed. by C. P. Dutt. New York, International Publishers, 95 pp.

——. 1948. *The origin of the family, private property and the state, in the light of the researches of Lewis Morgan*. Moscow, Progress Publishers, 1968[7], 181 + iii pp.

——.: see MARX, KARL. *The holy family or critique of critical critique*.

——. 1962. *Anti-Dühring. Herr Eugen Dühring's revolution in science*, third edition, Moscow, Foreign Languages Publishing House, 541 pp.

——.: see MARX, KARL. *The German ideology*.

ENGELS, FRIEDRICH, and KARL MARX. 1963, 1964–68. *Werke*. 39 Vols., 2 supplementary Vols. and 2 Index Vols. Berlin, Dietz Verlag.

ENGLER, RUDOLF, ed. of *Cours de linguistique générale*, by F. de Saussure, *q.v.*

ERIKSON, ERIK H. 1950. *Childhood and society*. New York, W. W. Norton & Co., 397 pp.

——. 1964. *Insight and responsibility: Lectures on the ethical implications of psychoanalytic insight*. London, Faber & Faber, 256 pp.

FANT, GUNNAR. 1967. The nature of distinctive features. In *To honor Roman Jakobson*, *q.v.*, Vol. I, pp. 645–42.

FANT, GUNNAR, MORRIS HALLE and ROMAN JAKOBSON. 1961. See *Preliminaries to speech analysis. The distinctive features and their correlates*.

FARRINGTON, BENJAMIN. 1947. *Head and hand in Ancient Greece: Four studies in the social relations of thought*. London, Watts & Co., 121 pp.

✕ FILLMORE, CHARLES J. 1970. Subjects, speakers and roles. *Synthese* 21/3, 4 (October 1970), 251–74.

FISCHER, GEERD. 1971. *Sprache und Klassenbildung: Die Bedeutung linguistischer Kode im Sozialisationsprozess.* Hamburg, Spartakus, iv + 97 + xxiv pp.

FISCHER-JØRGENSEN, ELI: cf. *Form and Substance*, phonetic and linguistic papers presented to Eli Fischer-Jørgensen.

FONER, PHILIP S. 1967. Marx's Capital in the United States. *Science & society*, 31/4 (Fall, 1967), 461–66.

FORBES, R. J. 1954. Chemical, culinary, and cosmetic arts. In *A history of technology, q.v.*, Vol. I, pp. 238–98.

——. 1956. Power. In *A history of technology, q.v.*, Vol. II, pp. 589–628.

——. 1958. *Man the maker, a history of technology and engineering.* New York, Abelard Schumann, 365 pp.

FORD, CLELLAN S., and FRANK A. BEACH. 1951. *Patterns of sexual behavior.* London, Methuen, University Paperbacks, repr. 1965, vi+330 pp.

FORDE, DARYLL. 1954. Foraging, hunting, and fishing. In *A history of technology, q.v.*, Vol. I, pp. 154–86.

Form & Substance. Phonetic and linguistic papers presented to Eli Fischer-Jørgensen, ed. by L. L. Hammerich, Roman Jakobson and Eberhard Zwirner. Copenhagen, Akademisk Forlag, 1971, x + 300 pp.

FORTI, UMBERTO. 1968–1969. *Storia della scienza nei suoi rapporti con la filosofia, le religioni, la società.* 6 Vol. Milano, dall'Oglio Editore.

FOUCAULT, MICHEL. 1966. *Les mots et les choses: Une archéologie des sciences humaines.* Paris, Gallimard, 400 pp.

FOX, ROBIN. 1967. *Kinship and marriage: An anthropological perspective.* Harmondsworth, Middlesex, Penguin Books, 271 pp.

✕ FRASER, LINDLEY M. 1937. *Economic thought and language: A critique of some fundamental economic concepts.* London, A. and C. Black.

FREUD, SIGMUND. *Gesammelte Werke*, chronologisch geordnet. 18 Vols. appeared from 1940 to 1968 in Frankfurt, Fischer Verlag.

——. 1953–1966. *The standard edition of the complete psychological works,* transl. from the German under the General Editorship of James Strachey, in collaboration with Anna Freud. 23 Vols. London, The Hogarth Press and the Institute of Psycho-Analysis.

From Max Weber. Essays in Sociology, transl., ed. and with an intr. by H. H. Gerth & C. Wright Mills: see WEBER.

FROMM, ERICH. 1963. *Marx's concept of man*, with a translation from Marx's *Economical and philosophical manuscripts* by T. B. Bottomore. New York, Frederick Ungar Publishing Co., xii + 260 pp.

FUNKE, GERHARD. 1968. Einheitssprache, Sprachspiel und Sprachauslegung bei Wittgenstein. *Zeitschrift für philosophische Forschung* 22/1 (January-March 1968), 3–30.

GEHLEN, ARNOLD. 1962[7]. *Der Mensch.* Frankfurt-Bonn, Athenäum, 410 pp.

——. 1963. *Studien zur Anthropologie und Soziologie,* ed. by H. Maus and F. Fürstenberg. Neuwied am Rhein-Berlin, Luchterhand, 355 pp. (Soziologische Texte, Vol. 17).

——. 1964. *Urmensch und Spätkultur: Philosophische Ergebnisse und Aussagen.* Second rev. ed., Frankfurt am Main-Bonn, Athenäum Verlag, 271 pp.

——. 1970. *Anthropologische Forschung. Zur Selbstbegegnung und Selbstentdeckung des Menschen.* Hamburg, Rowohlt, 150 pp. (Rowohlts deutsche Enzyklopädie, ed. by Ernesto Grassi).

GERBNER, GEORGE. 1967. Mass media and human communication theory. In *Human communication theory, q.v.,* pp. 40–56.

GEROW, BERT. 1964. Artifact. In *Dictionary of the social sciences, q.v.,* p. 37.

GILLE, BERTRAND. 1956. Machines. In *A history of technology,* Vol. II, pp. 629–62.

GODEL, ROBERT. 1957. *Les sources manuscrites du Cours de linguistique générale de F. de Saussure.* Genève-Paris, Droz-Minard, 283 pp.

GODELIER, MAURICE. 1969. La pensée de Marx et d'Engels aujourd'hui et les recherches de demain. *La pensée,* 143° (February 1969), 92–120; Italian transl. in Godelier 1970, pp. 80–119.

——. 1970. *Antropologia, storia, marxismo,* writings presented by M. de Stefanis and A. Casiccia. Parma, Guanda, 216 pp.

GOFFMAN, ERVING. 1959. *The presentation of self in everyday life.* New York, Anchor Books Edition, xvi + 259 pp.

——. 1966. Alienation from interaction. In *Communication and culture,* 1966, *q.v.,* pp. 103–18.

GOLDMANN, LUCIEN. 1959. *Recherches dialectiques.* Paris, Gallimard NRF, 357 pp. [the essay Sur la réification, of 1958, at pp. 64–106].

——. 1963, 1964. Introduction aux problèmes d'une sociologie du roman (1963) and La méthode structuraliste génétique en histoire de la littérature (1964), now in:

——. 1965. *Pour une sociologie du roman.* Paris, Gallimard NRF (1964[1]), 373 pp.

——. 1970a. *Structures mentales et création culturelle.* Paris, Éditions Anthropos, xxii + 493 pp.

——. 1970b. *Marxisme et sciences humaines.* Paris, Gallimard, 365 pp.

——. 1971. *La création culturelle dans la société moderne.* Paris, Éditions Denoël, 187 pp.

GOLDWAY, DAVID. 1967. Appearance and reality in Marx's Capital. *Science and society,* 31/4 (Fall, 1967), 428–47.

GRAMSCI, ANTONIO. 1952. *Passato e presente.* Torino, Einaudi, xviii + 274 pp.

——. 1954. *Letteratura e vita nazionale.* Torino, Einaudi, xx+400 pp.

——. 1955. *Il materialismo storico e la filosofia di Benedetto Croce.* Torino, Einaudi, xxiii + 299 pp.

——. 1966. *Gli intellettuali e l'organizzazione della cultura.* Torino, Einaudi, xv + 203 pp.

GREIMAS, ALGERIDAS JULIEN. 1966. *Sémantique structurale.* Paris, Larousse, 262 pp.

——. 1968. Conditions d'une sémiotique du monde naturel. *Pratiques et langages gestuels. Langages* 10 (June 1968), 3–35.

——. 1970. *Du sens: Essais sémiotiques.* Paris, Éditions Du Seuil, 317 pp.

GUDSCHINSKY, SARAH C. 1967. *How to learn an unwritten language.* New York, Holt, Rinehart and Winston, xviv + 64 pp.

HALL, A. R., E. J. HOLMYARD, and CHARLES SINGER, eds. 1956. *A history of technology,* Vol. I: *From early times to fall of ancient empires.* Oxford, at the Clarendon Press, lxiv+827 pp.

HALL, A. R., TREVOR I. WILLIAMS, CHARLES SINGER, and E. J. HOLMYARD. 1956–1958. *A history of technology,* Vols. II–V. Oxford, at the Clarendon Press.

HALL, EDWARD T. 1959. *The silent language.* New York, Doubleday; A Premier Book, Greenwich, Conn., Fawcett Publications, 1963, 192 pp.

——. 1966. *The hidden dimension.* New York, Doubleday & Co. Inc., repr. 1969, m xiv+217 pp.

HALLE, MORRIS, ROMAN JAKOBSON, and C. GUNNAR M. FANT: see *Preliminaries to speech analysis. The distinctive features and their correlates.*

HARRIS, ZELLIG S. 1951[1]. *Structural linguistics.* Chicago, The University of Chicago Press, 1963, xvi + 384 pp.

——. 1962[1]. *String analysis of sentence structure.* 3rd printing, The Hague, Mouton, 1965, 70 pp.

HARRISON, H. S. 1954a. Discovery, invention, and diffusion. In *A history of technology, q.v.,* Vol. I, pp. 58–84.

——. 1954b. Fire-making, fuel, and lighting. In *A history of technology, q.v.,* Vol. I, pp. 216–37.

HEGEL, G. W. F. *Hegels theologische Jugendschriften,* ed. by H. Nohl. Tübingen 1907.

——. 1803–1804. *Jenenser Realphilosophie,* I, ed. by J. Hoffmeister. Leipzig, Meiner, 1932, I, vii+392 pp. (Vorlesungen von 1803-1804; *Sämtliche Werke,* Band XIX).

——. 1805–1806. *Jenaer Realphilosophie,* II, ed. by J. Hoffmeister. Leipzig, Meiner, 1931, repr. 1967, viii + 290 pp. (Vorlesungen von 1805–1806; *Sämtliche Werke,* Band XX).

——. 1807. *Phänomenologie des Geistes,* ed. by J. Hoffmeister, according to the text of the original edition. Hamburg, Meiner, 1952, xlii+598 pp.; *The phenomenology of mind*, transl. with an introduction and notes by J. B. Baillie. London, Allen & Unwin, 1954 (1910[1]), 814 pp.

——. 1809–1811. *Philosophische Propädeutik, Jubiläumsausgabe*, ed. by H. Glockner. Stuttgart, Frommann, 1961, III, vi+335 pp.

——. *Sämtliche Werke*, Vol. VII: *Schriften zur Politik und Rechtsphilosophie*, ed. by G. Lasson. Leipzig, Meiner, 1932, 2nd. edition revised.

——. 1830. *Enzyklopädie der philosophischen Wissenschaften*. New edition by F. Nicolin and O. Pöggeler. Hamburg, Meiner, 1959, iii + 506 pp.

——. 1831. *Wissenschaft der Logik*. Hamburg, Meiner, 1963, repr. of the 1934 edition by G. Lasson, 2 Vols. of xii + 405 and viii + 512 pp.; *Science of logic*, transl. by W. H. Johnston and L. G. Struthers, with an introductory preface by Viscount Haldane of Cloan, Vol. I + II, London, Allen & Unwin, 1961 (1929[1]), Vol. I: 404 pp.; Vol. II: 486 pp.

Hegel and the philosophy of religion. The Wofford symposium, ed. by Darrel E. Christensen. The Hague, Martinus Nijhoff, 1970, xviii+300 pp.

HEIDEGGER, MARTIN. 1963. *Sein und Zeit*. Tübingen, Max Niemeyer Verlag, xii + 437 pp.; English translation: *Being and time*, transl. by J. Macquarrie and E. Robinson. London, SCM Press, 1962, 589 pp.

HILFERDING, RUDOLF. 1904. *Böhm-Bawerk's criticism of Marx* (and Eugen von Böhm-Bawerk: *Karl Marx and the close of his system*), ed. and with an introduction by Paul M. Sweezy. 1966. New York, August M. Kelley Publishers, xxx+224 pp.

HINTIKKA, JAAKKO. 1958. On Wittgenstein's 'solipsism'. *Mind*, 67/265 (Jan. 1958), 88–91.

Histoire générale des sciences. 1957–1964. Published under the direction of René Taton. 3 Tomes (Tome 3 in 2 Vols.). Paris, Presses Universitaires de France.

A history of technology. 1954–1958. Ed. by Ch. Singer, E. J. Holmyard, A. R. Hall and T. I. Williams. 5 Vols. Oxford, The Clarendon Press. Vol. I: *From early times to the fall of ancient empires*, 1965 (1954[1]), lxiv+827 pp., plus 36 plates.

HJELMSLEV, LOUIS. 1943. Langue et parole. *CFS*, 29–44; also in Hjelmslev 1959, *q.v.*, pp. 69–81.

——. 1947. Structural analysis of language. *Studia Linguistica*, 1/2, 69–78; also in Hjelmslev 1959, *q.v.*, pp. 27–35.

——. 1963. *Prolegomena to a theory of language*, transl. by F. J. Whitfield. Madison, The University of Wisconsin Press, vii + 144 pp. (revised English edition; Danish original).

——. 1954. La stratification du langage. *Word*, 10/2–3 (August-December 1954), 163–88; also in Hjelmslev 1959, *q.v.*, pp. 36–38.

——. 1959. Éssais linguistiques. *TCLC* 12, 275 pp.

——. 1958. Dans quelle mesure les significations des mots peuvent-elles être considérées comme formant une structure? *PICL*, 8 (Oslo, August 1957), 636–654; same as Hjelmslev 1959.

——. 1959. Pour une sémantique structurale. In *Essais linguistiques*, pp. 96–112. Copenhagen, Nordisk Sprog- og Kulturforlag, 275 pp.

HOBSBAWM, ERIC J. 1964. Introduction to Marx: *Pre-capitalistic economic formations* (1965), *q.v.* under Marx's *Grundrisse*.

HOCKETT, CHARLES F. 1954. The cultural content of language materials (discussion: pp. 148–68). In *Language in culture* (Conference on the interrelations of language and other aspects of culture), ed. by H. Hoijer. Chicago, The American Anthropological Association, xi + 286 pp.

HODGES, DONALD CLARK. 1965. The value judgment in Capital, *Science & society*, 29/3 (Summer 1965), 296–311.

——. 1967. The mothod of Capital. *Science & Society*, 31/4 (Fall, 1967), 505–14.

HOLMYARD, E. J., A. R. HALL, and CHARLES SINGER. Editors of *A history of technology*, Vol. I: *From early times to fall of ancient empires, q.v.*

HOLMYARD, E. J., A. R. HALL, T. I. WILLIAMS, and CHARLES SINGER. Editors of *A history of technology, q.v.*

HOOKE, S. H. 1956. Recording and writings. In *A history of technology, q.v.*, Vol. I, pp. 744–73.

HORKHEIMER, MAX. 1947. *Eclipse of reason*. London, Oxford University Press. Ital. transl., Milano, Sugar, 1962, 235 pp.

HORKHEIMER, MAX, and THEODOR W. ADORNO. 1942–1944. *Dialektik der Aufklärung, Philosophische Fragmente*. Amsterdam, Querido Verlag, 1947 (revised edition); Italian transl. by L. Vinci of the revised edition, *Dialettica dell'illuminismo*, Torino, Einaudi (1966), ix+279 pp.

HOWARD, DICK. 1969. On deforming Marx: the French translation of *Grundrisse*. *Science & society*, 33/3 (Summer-Fall 1969), 358–65.

Human communication theory, Original essays, ed. by Frank E. X. Dance. New York, Holt, Rinehart and Winston, Inc., 1967, vii+332 pp.

HUNTER, J. F. M. 1967. Wittgenstein's theory of linguistic self-sufficiency. *Dialogue*, 6/3 (December 1967), 367–78.

HUSSERL, EDMUND. 1913. *Logische Untersuchungen*. Tübingen, Max Niemeyer, 1968 (reprint of the 1913 edition), Vol. I, xxii + 257 pp.; Vol. II, Part I, xi+508 pp., Part II, xii+244 pp. — *Logical investigations*, transl. by J. N. Findlay from the Second German Edition (1913, 1921), London, Routledge & Kegan Paul, 1970; Vol. I, xvii+432 pp., Vol. II, xvii+433–877 pp.

——. 1893–1917. *Zur Phänomenologie des inneren Zeitbewusstseins*, ed. by Rudolf Boehm. Den Haag, Martinus Nijhoff, 1966, xliii+483 pp. (= *Husserliana*, Band 8). *The phenomenology of internal time-consciousness*, ed. by Martin Heidegger, transl. by J. S. Churchill, inr. by C. O. Schrag. Den Haag, Martinus Nijhoff, 1964. 188 pp.

——. 1918–1926. *Analysen zur passiven Synthesis, Aus Vorlesungs- und Forschungsmanuskripten*, ed. by Margot Fleischer. Den Haag, Martinus Nijhoff, 1966, xxiv + 531 pp. (= *Husserliana*, Band XI).

——. 1913–1930. *Ideen zu einer reinen Phänomenologie und phänomenologischen Philosophie*, Vol. I. Den Haag, Martinus Nijhoff, 1950, xvi+483 pp. (= *Husserliana*, Band III).

——. 1912–1917. Transcribed in 1924–25 by Landgrebe. *Ideen zu einer reinen Phänomenologie und phänomenologischen Philosophie*, Vol. II: *Phänomenologische Untersuchungen zur Konstitution*, ed. by Marly Biemel. Den Haag, Martinus Nijhoff, 1952, xx+426 pp. (= *Husserliana*, Band IV).

——. 1912–1915. *Ideen zu einer reinen Phänomenologie und phänomenologischen Philosophie*, Vol. III: *Die Phänomenologie und die Fundamente der Wissenschaft*, ed. by Marly Biemel. Den Haag, Martinus Nijhoff, 1952, vi+ 165 pp. (= *Husserliana*, Band V).

——. 1929–1931. *Cartesianische Meditationen und Pariser Vorträge* (= *Husserliana*, Band I). Den Haag, Martinus Nijhoff, 1949, 2. A. 1963, xxxiii+240 pp. – *Méditations Cartésiennes: Introduction à la phenomenologie*, transl by G. Peiffer and E. Levinas, Paris, Librairie Philosophique J. Vrin, 1931, 1966, vii+136 pp. – *Cartesian meditations, an introduction to phenomenology*, transl. by D. Cairns. Den Haag, Martinus Nijhoff, 1960, xii+157 pp.

——. 1935–1936. *Die Krisis der Europäischen Wissenschaften und die tranzendentale Phänomenologie*. Den Haag, Martinus Nijhoff, 1953, 2.A. 1962, xxiv +559 pp. (= *Husserliana*, Band VI).

International encyclopedia of the social sciences, ed. by David L. Sills. 17 Vols. New York, The MacMillan Company & The Free Press, 1968.

IVANOV, V. V. 1965. Ruolo della semiotica nell'indagine cibernetica dell'uomo e della collettività. In *I sistemi di segni e lo strutturalismo sovietico*, ed. by di Remo Faccani and Umberto Eco, pp. 41–54. Milano, Mompiani, 1969.

IVIĆ, MILKA. 1965. *Trends in linguistics*. JanL, series minor 42, 260 pp.

JACKSON, D. D.: cf. *Pragmatics of human communication*.

JAKOBSON, ROMAN. 1952. From the point of view of linguistics. Results of the conference of anthropologists and linguists (Indiana University, 1952) = *IJAL Memoir* 8, Supplement to *IJAL*, 19/2 (April 1953). French transl. in Jakobson, 1963a, p. 40.

——. 1961. Linguistics and communication theory. In *Structure of language and its mathematical aspects*, ed. by R. Jakobson, pp. 245–52. Vol. XII of *Proceedings of symposia in applied mathematics*. Providence, Rhode Island, American Mathematical Society, 1961.

——. 1963a. *Essais de linguistique générale*, transl. and preface by N. Ruwet. Paris, Les Éditions de Minuit, 260 pp.

——. 1963b. Parts and wholes in language. In *Parts and wholes*, ed. by Daniel Lerner, *q.v.*, pp. 157–62.

JAKOBSON, ROMAN, C. GUNNAR M. FANT, and MORRIS HALLE. 1961. *Preliminaries to speech analysis: The distinctive features and their correlates*. Cambridge, Mass., M.I.T. Press (orig. 1951).

JAKOBSON, ROMAN. 1966. Franz Boas' approach to language. In *Portraits of linguists*, ed. by Th. A. Sebeok, *q.v.*, pp. 127–39.

——. 1967. Linguistics in its relation to other sciences. *PICL*, 10/I, 75–122. Bucarest, Editions de l'Académie de la République Socialiste de Roumanie, 1969.

——. 1969. *Langage enfantin et aphasie*, transl. by J. P. Boons e R. Zygouris. Paris, Les Éditions de Minuit, 189 pp.

——. 1970a. Language in relation to other communication systems. In *Linguaggi nella società e nella tecnica*, *q.v.*, pp. 3–16.

——. 1970b. Linguistics. In *Main trends of research in the social and human sciences*, I, Chap. VI, pp. 419–63. The Hague-Paris, Mouton, Unesco.

——. 1971a. *Studies on child language and aphasia*. JanL, series minor 114, 132 pp.

——. 1971b. Introduction [without title] to *Form and substance*, phonetic and linguistic papers presented to Eli Fischer-Jørgensen. Odense, Akademisk Forlag, cf. pp. 9–10.

——. 1971c. *Selected writings*, Vol. II: *Word and language*. The Hague, Mouton, xii + 752 pp.

JOPE, E. M. 1956. Agricultural implement. In *A history of technology*, *q.v.*, Vol. II, pp. 81–102.

KEES, WELDON: see RUESCH and KEES, 1961.

KEY, MARY RITCHIE. 1970. Preliminary remarks on paralanguage and kinesics in human communication. *Linguistique*, 6/2, 17–36+figures.

KOECHLIN, B. 1968. Techniques corporelles et leur notation symbolique. *Pratiques et langages gestuels. Langages*, 10 (June 1968), 36–47.

KORSCH, KARL. 1923. *Marxismus und Philosophie*, ed. by E. Gerlach. Frankfurt, Europäische Verlagsanstalt, 1966, 181 pp.

——. 1938. *Karl Marx*. New York, Russell & Russell, 247 pp., reissued 1963.

——. 1934–1936. *Karl Marx*. Wien, Europa Verlag; Frankfurt, Europäische Verlagsanstalt, 1967, 280 pp.

KOSAI, YUTAKA: see BRONFENBRENNER, MARTIN.

KOTARBIŃSKI, TADEUSZ. 1948. *Principes du bon travail*. Seorsum impressum ex vol. III commentariorum societatis philosophicae polonorum studia philosophica. Cracoviae et Posnaniae, pp. 177–202.

——. 1966. *Gnosiology: The scientific approach to the theory of knowledge*, transl. from the Polish by Olgierd Wojtasiewicz, translation ed. by G. Bidwell and C. Pinder. Oxford, Pergamon Press, ix + 548 pp.

——. 1971. The methodology of practical skills: Concepts and issues. *Metaphilosophy* 2 (April 1971) 158–70.

KRAMPS, WILHELM. 1955. *Die Philosophie Hugo Dinglers*. München, Eidos Verlag, 71 pp.

——, ed., 1956. *Hugo Dingler Gedenkbuch zum 75. Geburtstag* [contains 14 essays by various authors and a bibliography]. München, Eidos Verlag, 222 pp.

KRÁMSKÝ, JIŘÍ. 1969. *The word as a linguistic unit*. The Hague, Mouton, 83 pp.

KRANZBERG, MELVIN, and CARROL W. PURSELL JR., eds. 1967. *Technology in western civilization*, I. New York, Oxford University Press, xii+802 pp.

KRAUS, KARL. 1905–1913. *Literatur und Lüge*. München, Kösel Verlag, 1958, 360 pp., being the sixth volume of the *Werke* edited by Heinrich Fischer.

——. 1915–1932. *Die Sprache*. München, Kösel Verlag, 1937, 1954, 1962⁴; being the second volume of the *Werke* edited by Heinrich Fischer.

KRISTEVA, JULIA. 1968. Le geste, pratique ou communication? *Pratique et langages gestuels. Langages*, 10 (June 1868), 48–64.

——. 1969. *Recherches pour une sémanalyse*. Paris, Éditions du Seuil, 381 pp.

KRISTEVA, JULIA, and M. LACOSTE. 1968. Bibliographie. *Pratique et langages gestuels. Langages*, 10 (June 1968), 132–49.

KRISTEVA, JULIA. 1969. Σημειωτικὴ. *Recherches pour une sémanalyse*. Paris, Seuil, 381 pp.

KRISTEVA, JULIA, JOSETTE REY-DEBOVE, and DONNA JEAN UMIKER, eds. 1971. *Essays in semiotics*. Paris, Mouton, x + 639 pp.

LACAN, JACQUES. 1966. *Écrits*. Paris, Seuil, 924 pp.

LAFFAL, JULIUS. 1965. *Pathological and normal language*. New York, Atherton Press, xx+249 pp.

LAMBDIN, T. O., and W. F. ALBRIGHT. 1970. See ALBRIGHT.

LANGE, OSKAR. 1959. *Ekonomia polityczna: Zagadnienia Ogólne*, Tom 1. Warszawa, Państwowe Wydawnictwo Naukowe, 302 pp.

LARSEN, EGON. 1961, 1969². *A history of invention*, London, Dent, 382 pp.

LAUER, H., R. N. LESNICK, and L. E. MATSON. 1960. *Servomechanism fundamentals*. New York.

LEACH, E. R. 1954. Primitive time-reckoning. In *A history of technology*, q.v., Vol. I, pp. 110–27.

LEAKEY, L. S. B. 1954. Graphic and plastic arts. In *A history of technology*, q.v., Vol. I, pp. 144–53.

LEFEBVRE, HENRI. 1966. *Le langage et la société*. Paris, Gallimard NRF, 377 pp.

LEISI, ERNST. 1952. *Der Wortinhalt: Seine Struktur im Deutschen und Englischen*. Heidelberg, Quelle & Meyer, 1961², 131 pp.

LENIN, V. I. 1955–1970. *Opere complete*. 45 Vols. Roma, Editori Riuniti.

——. 1914–15. *Filosofskie tetradi*, transl. into Italian, edited and introduced by Lucio Colletti: *Quaderni filosofici*. Milano, Feltrinelli, 1958, clxviii+517 pp.

LENNEBERG, ERIC H. 1953. Cognition in ethnolinguistics. *Lg*, 29, 463–71.

LENNEBERG, ERIC H., and ROGER W. BROWN. 1954. A study in language and cognition. *Journal of abnormal and social psychology*, 49/3 (July 1954), 454–462.

LENNEBERG, ERIC H., 1963. The relationship of language to the formation of concepts. Summary of oral presentation, November 1961, in *Boston studies in the phyilosophy of science*, Dordrecht, Reidel pp. 48–54.

——. 1966. A biological perspective of language. In *New directions in the study of language, q.v.*, pp. 65–68.

——. 1967. *Biological foundations of language*, with appendices by Noam Chomsky and Otto Marx. New York, London, and Sydney, John Wiley & Sons, xvii+489 pp.

——. 1968. Language in the light of evolution. In *Animal communication*, ed. by T. A. Sebeok, pp. 592–613. Bloomington and London, Indiana University Press.

——. 1969. Problems in the systematization of communicative behavior. In *Approaches to animal communication, q.v.*, pp. 131–37.

LEONI, BRUNO. 1962. «Obbligo e pretesa nella dogmatica, nella teoria generale e nella filosofia del diritto». *Studi in onore di Emilio Betti*, Vol. I: *Metodologia, ermeneutica, problemi generali*. Milano, Giuffrè, pp. 541–567; cf. pp. 547–548.

LEROI-GOURHAN, ANDRÉ. 1943. *L'homme et la matière: Évolution et techniques*. Paris, Albin Michel, 363 pp.

——. 1945. *Milieu et techniques: Évolution et technique*. Paris, Albin Michel, 512 pp.

——. 1964. *Le geste et la parole*, 1: *Technique et langage*. Paris, Albin Michel, 323 pp.

——. 1965. *Le geste et la parole*, 2: *La mémoire et les rythmes*. Paris, Albin Michel, 285 pp.

LERNER, DANIEL: ed. of *Parts and wholes, q.v.*

LÉVI-STRAUSS, CLAUDE. 1949. *Les structures élémentaires de la parenté*. Paris-The Hague, Mouton (1967²) xxx+591 pp. (= Collection de Rééditions II).

——. 1958. *Anthropologie structurale*. Paris, Plon, viii+454 pp.; English transl. by C. Jacobson and Brooke Grundfest Schoepf, New York, Basic Books, 1963, xxi+410 pp.

——. 1962. *La pensée sauvage*. Paris, Librairie Plon, viii+395 pp.

——. 1964. *Le cru et le cuit*. Paris, Librairie Plon, 402 pp.

——. 1966. *Du miel aux cendres*. Paris, Librairie Plon, 450 pp.

——. 1968. *L'origine des manières de table*. Paris, Librairie Plon, 478 pp.

LIBERMAN, A. M. 1957. Some results of research on speech perception; repr. in *Psycholinguistics*, ed. by S. Saporta, pp. 142–53. New York, Holt, Rinehart and Winston, 1961.

LILLEY, SAMUEL. 1966. *Men, machines and history: The story of tools and ma-*

chines in relation to social progress. New York, International Publishers, xiv+352 pp.

LINDSAY, A. D. 1925. *Karl Marx's Capital: An introductory essay.* London, Oxford University Press, Geoffrey Cumberlege (repr. 1947), 128 pp. ["OP" Xerographic Reprint by University Microfilms Ltd., London].

Linguaggi nella società e nella tecnica. 1970. Milano, Edizioni di Comunità, xxi+609 pp.

LOTMAN, JURIJ. 1967. Metodi esatti nella scienza letteraria sovietica. *Strumenti critici,* 1/2 (February 1967), 107–27.

———. Il problema di una tipologia della cultura (1967). In *I sistemi di segni e lo strutturalismo sovietico,* 1969, *q.v.,* pp. 309–18.

LUKÁCS, GYÖRGY. 1923. *Geschichte und Klassenbewusstsein: Studien über marxistische Dialektik* (1918–1922). Berlin, Malik-Verlag; French transl. by K. Axelos and J. Bois, preface by K. Axelos. Paris, Ed. de Minuit, 1960, iv+383 pp.; Italian transl. by G. Piana. Milano, Sugar, 1967, lii+419 pp.; *History and class consciousness: Studies in marxist dialectics,* transl. by R. Livingstone. London, Merlin Press, 1971, xlvii+356 pp.

———. 1948. *Der junge Hegel: Über die Beziehungen von Dialektik und Ökonomie.* Zürich-Wien, Europa Verlag, 720 pp. Third edition, Neuwied and Berlin, Luchterhand, 1967, 703 pp. (= Georg Lukács *Werke,* Band 8); Ital. transl.: *Il giovane Hegel e i problemi della società capitalistica,* transl. by R. Solmi. Torino, Einaudi, 1960, xii + 793 pp.

———. 1957. *Contributi alla storia dell'estetica.* Transl. by E. Picco. Milano, Feltrinelli, 490 pp.

———. 1963. *Die Eigenart des Aesthetischen.* Neuwied and Berlin, Luchterhand, pp. 851 and 857.

———. 1969. *Probleme der Aesthetik.* Neuwied and Berlin, Luchterhand Verlag, 811 pp. (= Georg Lukács *Werke,* Band 10).

LYONS, JOHN. 1968. *Introduction to theoretical linguistics.* Cambridge University Press, repr. 1969, x+519 pp.

MACHEREY, PIERRE. 1966. *Pour une théorie de la production littéraire.* Paris, Masp'ro, 1971, 3rd printing, 332 pp.

MALINOWSKI, BRONISLAW. 1966. *Argonauts of the Western Pacific: An account of native enterprise and adventure in the Archipelagoes of Melanesian New Guinea.* London, Routledge & Kegan Paul, xxxii + 527 pp.

———. 1929. *The sexual life of savages in North-Western Melanesia.* New York, Harcourt, Brace & World, Inc., xxx + 603 pp.

———. 1966a. *Soil-tilling and agricultural rites in the Trobriand Islands,* Vol. I of *Coral gardens and their magic.* London, George Allen & Unwin, xlvi + 500 pp.

———. 1966b. *The language of magic and gardening,* Vol. II of *Coral gardens and their magic.* London, George Allen & Unwin, xliv+350 pp.

——. 1963. *The family among the Australian aborigines: A sociological study.* Introduction by J. A. Barnes. New York, Schocken Books, xxx + 322 pp.

——. 1967. *A diary in the strict sense of the term,* transl. by N. Guterman. London, Routledge & Kegan Paul, xxii+315 pp.

MAO TSE-TUNG. 1937. On contradiction. Now in *Selected works,* Vol. I, 1967, pp. 311–47.

——. 1967–1969. *Selected works.* 4 Vols. Peking, Foreign Language Press; Vol. I (1967), 347 pp.

MARCUSE, HERBERT. 1955. *Eros and civilization: A philosophical inquiry into Freud.* New York, Vintage Edition, 1962, xviii+257 pp.

——. 1964. *One dimensional man: Studies in the ideology of advanced industrial society.* Boston, Beacon Press; Boston Paperback, 1966, xix + 260 pp.

——. 1970. *Five lectures: Psychoanalysis, Politics, and Utopia,* transl. by J. J. Shapiro and S. M. Weber. London, Allan Lane the Penguin Press, vi + 109 pp.

MAROUZEAU, JEAN. 1951. *Lexique de la terminologie linguistique.* Paris, Geuthner (1961³), xii + 267 pp.

MARSHALL, ALFRED. 1890. *Principles of economics,* an introductory volume. Eighth edition: London, MacMillan, 1966, xxxii+731 pp. (original eighth edition 1920).

MARTINET, ANDRÉ. 1949. La double articulation linguistique. *TCLC,* 5 (Recherches structurales), 30–37.

——. 1955. *Économie des changements phonétiques.* Berne, Francke, 1964², 396 pp.

——. 1957. Arbitraire linguistique et double articulation. *CFS,* 15, 105–16.

——. 1960. *Éléments de linguistique générale.* Paris, Armand Colin, 1966⁶, 224 pp.

——. 1962. *A functional view of language.* The Waynflete Lectures 1961. Oxford, Clarendon, ix + 165 pp.

——. 1965. *La linguistique synchronique: Études et recherches.* Paris, P.U.F., v+248 pp.

MARX, KARL, and FRIEDRICH ENGELS. *Werke.* 39 Vols. Berlin, Dietz Verlag, 2 supplementary Vols., 2 index Vols. 1963, 1964–1968.

MARX, KARL. *Frühe Schriften,* Vol. I, ed. by H.-J. Lieber and P. Furth. Stuttgart, Cotta-Verlag, 1962, x+998 pp.

——. 1844. *Economic and philosophic manuscripts of 1844,* ed. with an introduction by D. J. Struik, transl. by M. Milligan. New York, International Publishers, 1964, 255 pp.

MARX, KARL, and FRIEDRICH ENGELS. 1845. *The holy family or critique of critical critique,* transl. by R. Dixon. Moscow, Foreign Languages Publishing House, 1956, 299 pp.

——. 1845–1846. *The German ideology,* ed. by S. Rayzanskaya. Moscow, Progress Publishers, 1968 (1964¹), 751 pp. — Transl. of Part I and II by R. Rascal. New York, International Publishers, 1947, 1967⁶, xix+214 pp.

MARX, KARL. 1847. *The poverty of philosophy*, with an intr. by F. Engels. New York, International Publishers, 1963, 233 pp.

——. 1857–1858. *Grundrisse der Kritik der politischen Ökonomie* (Rohentwurf). Berlin, Dietz Verlag, 1953, xvi+1102 pp. – Transl. by E. Grillo: *Lineamenti fondamentali della critica dell'economia politica*. Firenze, La Nuova Italia, Vol. I. xv+424 pp., 1968, Vol. II, v+687 pp., 1970. — *Fondements de la critique de l'économie politique* (Ébauche de 1857–1858), transl. by R. Gangeville. Paris, Éditions Anthropos, 1967, Vol. I, xiv + 513 pp.; Vol. II, xi+762 pp. — *Pré-capitalist economic formations*, transl. by J. Cohen, ed. and with an introduction by E. J. Hobsbawm. New York, International Publishers, 1965, 153 pp. — *Marx's Grundrisse*, ed. and transl. by D. McLellan. London, MacMillan, 1971, 156 pp.

——. 1859. *A contribution to the critique of political economy*, transl. from the sec. German ed. by N. I. Stone. Chicago, Charles H. Kerr & Co., 314 pp.

——. 1861–1863. Resultate des unmittelbaren Produktionsprozesses [= *Das Kapital*, Vol. I: *Der Produktionsprozess des Kapitals*, VI Chap.]. Frankfurt, Verlag Neue Kritik, 1969, viii+314 pp. First published in *Arkhiv Marksa i Engel'sa*, 1933, II, VII).

——. 1867. *Capital*, Book One. 2 Vols., transl. from the fourth German ed. by E. and C. Paul, intr. by G. D. H. Cole. London, J. M. Dent & Sons, 1962 (1930¹), Vol. I: xxxv+548 pp.; Vol. II vii+549–929 + 16 pp.

——. 1867. *Capital, a critical analysis of capitalist production*, transl. from the third German ed. by S. Moore and E. Aveling and ed. by F. Engels, Vol. I. Moscow, Foreign Languages Publishing House, xii + 807 pp.

——. 1885 (posthumous). *Capital: A critique of political economy*, Vol. II, Book II: *The process of circulation of capital*, ed. by F. Engels. Moscow, Progress Publishers, 1967, xi+551 pp.

——. 1894 (posthumous). *Capital: A critique of political economy*, Vol. III (Book III: *The process of capitalist production as a whole*, ed. by F. Engels). Moscow, Foreign Languages Publishing House, (1962, 2nd Impression), xi +923 pp.

——. (written in 1862–1863). *Theories of surplus-value*, Vol. IV of *Capital*. Moscow, Progress Publishers, Vol. I: 1969 (1963¹), 506 pp., Vol. II: 1968, 661 pp.

MASTERS, ROGER D. 1970. Genes, language, and evolution. *Semiotica*, 2/4, 295–320.

MATES, BENSON. 1953. *Stoic logic*. University ofCalifornia Publications in Philosophy. Berkeley and Los Angeles, University of California Press, vii+ 148 pp.

MATORÉ, G. 1953. *La méthode en lexicologie: Domaine français.* Paris, Didier, 148 pp.

McLELLAN, DAVID. 1971. *Marx's Grundrisse.* London and Basingstoke, MacMillan, x+156 pp.

MEAD, MARGARET. 1968. *Continuities in cultural evolution.* New Haven-London, Yale University Press, xxi + 471 pp.

MEAD, GEORGE HERBERT. 1932. *The philosophy of the present,* ed. by A. E. Murphy, with prefatory remarks by J. Dewey. Chicago, The Open Court, repr. 1959, xl+199 pp.

———. 1934. *Mind, self and society from the standpoint of a social behaviorist.* University of Chicago Press, ed. and with an intr. by Ch. W. Morris, 13° pr. 1965, xxxviii + 401 pp.; Italian transl. by R. Tettucci: *Mente, sè e società.* Firenze, Universitaria G. Barbèra, 1966, 384 pp.

———. 1936. *Movements of thought in the nineteenth century,* ed. by M. H. Moore. Chicago, The University of Chicago Press, xxxix + 519 pp. (7th printing 1962).

———. 1938. *The philosophy of the act,* intr. by Ch. W. Morris in collaboration with J. M. Brewster, A. M. Dunnham, and D. L. Hiller. Chicago, The University of Chicago Press, lxxxiv+696 pp. (5th printing 1964).

MELANDRI, ENZO. 1968. *La linea e il circolo: Studio logico-filosofico sull'analogia.* Bologna, Il Mulino, 1096 pp.

MERLEAU-PONTY, MAURICE. 1942. *La structure du comportement,* précéde de «Une Philosophie de l'ambiguïté», by Alphonse de Waelhens. Paris, Presses Universitaires de France, 1963⁴, xvi+248 pp.

———. 1945. *Phénoménologie de la perception.* Paris, Librairie Gallimard, xvi + 531 pp.

———. 1948. *Sens et non sens.* Paris, Nagel, 1965⁵, 333 pp.

———. 1960. *Signes.* Paris, Gallimard, 438 pp.

———. 1961. *Les aventures de la dialectique.* Paris, Gallimard, 317 pp.

MISES, LUDWIG VON. 1949. *Human action, a treatise on economics.* London, William Hodge & Co., xv + 889 pp.

MOLES, ABRAHAM A. 1969. The concept of language from the point of view of animal communication. In *Approaches to animal communication, q.v.,* pp. 138–45.

MORRIS, CHARLES W. 1932. *Six theories of mind.* Chicago, The University of Chicago Press (repr. 1950), xii+337 pp.

———. 1938. *Lineamenti di una teoria dei segni,* intr., transl., and comment by F. Rossi-Landi [*Foundations of the theory of signs*]. Torino, Paravia, 1954, xxviii + 164 pp.

———. 1946. *Signs, language, and behavior.* New York, Prentice Hall, Inc., xiv + 365 pp.

——. 1964. *Signification and significance: A study of the relations of signs and values*. Cambridge, Mass., The M.I.T. Press, xii + 99 pp.

——. 1970. *The pragmatic movement in American philosophy*. New York, George Braziller, xii + 210 pp.

MOORE, GEORGE EDWARD. 1903. *Principia ethica*. Cambridge University Press, 1903, repr. 1960, xxvii + 232 pp.

——. 1912. *Ethics*. London, Williams and Norgate, Oxford University Press, repr. 1958, 160 pp.

——. 1903–1920. *Philosophical studies*. London, Routledge & Kegan Paul, 1922, 1965⁵, viii+342 pp.

——. 1953. *Some main problems of philosophy*. London, Allen and Unwin, xii + 380 pp. [a series of lectures delivered in 1910–1911].

——. 1954. Wittgenstein's lectures in 1930–33. *Mind*, 63/249 (January 1954), 1 + 5.

——. 1959. *Philosophical papers* (1923–1955). London, Allen and Unwin, 325 pp.

MORICK, HAROLD: editor of *Wittgenstein and the problem of other minds*, q.v.

MOWAT, FARLEY. 1963. *Never cry wolf*. Boston-Toronto, Little, Brown & Co., 247 pp.

NAPOLEONI, CLAUDIO. 1956. Economia (scienza). In *Dizionario di economia politica*, Milano, Comunità, pp. 565–78.

——. 1963. *Il pensiero economico del '900*. Torino, Einaudi, 204 pp.

New directions in the study of language, ed. by E. H. Lenneberg. 1966. Cambridge, Mass., The M.I.T. Press, ix+194 pp.

NICOLAUS, MARTIN. 1968. The unknown Marx. *New left review*, 48 (March-April 1968), 41–61.

NIDA, EUGENE A. 1946. *Morphology: The descriptive analysis of words*. Ann Arbor, The University of Michigan Press, 1949², repr. 1967, xvii+342 pp.

OAKLEY, KENNETH P. 1954. Skill as a human possession. In *A history of technology*, q.v., Vol. I, pp. 1–37.

——. 1959. *Man the tool-maker*. The University of Chicago Press: Phoenix Books, 1964⁴, vi+159 pp.

——. 1961. On man's use of fire, with comments on tool-making and hunting. In *Social life of early man*, q.v., pp. 176–93.

OLBRECHTS-TYTECA, LUCIE: see PERELMAN, CHAÏM, et OLBRECHTS-TYTECA, LUCIE: *Traité de l'argumentation. La nouvelle rhétorique*, Paris, P.U.F., 1958.

PAGET, SIR RICHARD. 1930. *Human speech: Some observations, experiments and conclusions as to the nature, origin, purpose and possible improvement of human speech*. London, Routledge & Kegan Paul, repr. 1963, xiv+360 pp.

PARKINSON, G. H. R. 1965. *Logic and reality in Leibniz's metaphysics*. Oxford University Press, 256 pp.

PARSONS, TALCOTT. 1937, 1949². *The structure of social action*. New York, The Free Press, xiii+817 pp.

——. 1954. *Essays in sociological theory*. Revised Edition, New York, The Free Press (1949¹), 459 pp.

——. 1966. *The social system*. New York, The Free Press (1951¹), xviii+575 pp.

——. 1967. *Sociological theory and modern society*. New York, The Free Press, xii+564 pp.

——. 1968. Systems analysis: Social systems. In *International encyclopedia of the social sciences*, vol. XV, pp. 458–73. New York, Macmillan Co. & Free Press.

PARSONS, TALCOTT, ROBERT F. BALES, and EDWARD A. SHILS. 1953. *Working papers in the theory of action*. Toronto, Collier-Macmillan, 269 pp.

PARSONS, TALCOTT, and EDWARD A. SHILS, with the assistance of James Olds. 1951. *Values, motives, and systems of action*. In *Toward a general theory of action*, pp. 47–243+figures. New York, Harper & Row, repr. 1965.

Parts and wholes, ed. by Daniel Lerner. 1963. New York, The Free Press, ix + 180 pp.

Pathologie du langage, by various authors. 1967. *Langages*, 5°, 126 pp.

PAUL, ANTHON M. 1970. Figurative Language. *Philosophy & rhetoric*, III, 4°, pp. 225–248.

PEI, MARIO. 1966. *Glossary of linguistic terminology*. New York and London, Columbia University Press, xviii+299 pp.

PEIRCE, CHARLES SANDERS. 1931–1935. *Collected papers*, Vol. I–VI, edited by Ch. Hartshorne and Paul Weiss. Cambridge, Mass., Harvard University Press.

PERELMAN, CHAÏM, and LUCIE OLBRECHTS-TYTECA. 1958. *Traité de l'argumentation. La nouvelle rhétorique*. Paris, P.U.F. 2 volumes of pp. iv+350+iii, iv+351–734; Italian transl. by various authors, preface by N. Bobbio, Torino, Einaudi, 1966, xix+593 pp.

PERLINI, TITO. 1968a. *Utopia e prospettiva in György Lukács*. Bari, Dedalo Libri, 470 pp.

——. 1968b. *Che cosa ha veramente detto Marcuse*. Roma, Ubaldini Editore, 211 pp.

——. 1969. Autocritica della ragione illuministica (Aspetti e momenti del pensiero negativo). *Ideologie*, 4°, 139–233.

PESENTI, ANTONIO. 1970. *Manuale di economia politica*, in 2 vols. Roma, Editori Riuniti. Vol. I: *Princìpi generali – Economia monetaria*, Two Appendixes by A. Pesenti and G. La Grassa, xxviii+928 pp.; Vol. II: *L'odierno capitalismo monopolistico o imperialismo*, appendixes by A. Lippi and C. Casarosa, xii+651 pp.

PIETRANERA, GIULIO. 1961. *Capitalismo ed economia. Idealismo e materialismo storico nell'economia politica*. Torino, Einaudi; new edition 1966, 245 pp.

PIKE, KENNETH L. 1947. *Phonemics: a technique for reducing languages to writing*. Ann Arbor, Michigan, The University of Michigan Press, xx+254 pp.

——. 1967. *Language in relation to a unified theory of the structure of human behavior*, Second, revised edition (1959[1]). The Hague-Paris, Mouton, 762 pp.

PIRO, SERGIO. 1967. *Il linguaggio schizofrenico*. Milano, Feltrinelli xii+590 pp.

PONZIO, AUGUSTO. 1967. *La relazione interpersonale*. Bari, Adriatica Editrice, 105 pp.

——. 1970. *Linguaggio e relazioni sociali*. Bari, Adriatica Editrice, 203 pp.

——. 1971a. Ideologia della anormalità linguistica. *Ideologie*, 15°, 50–73.

——. 1971b. Grammatica trasformazionale e ideologia politica. *Ideologie*, 16°–17°, 1971 [1972], 137–212.

POOLE, GORDON. 1971. Alle origini della concezione borghese della donna. *Ideologie*, 15°, 74–101.

Porraits of linguists, ed. by Th. A. Sebeok. 1966. Bloomington, Indiana University Press. Vol. I: xvii+580 pp., Vol. II: ix+605 pp.

Pragmatics of human communication: A study of interactional patterns, pathologies and paradoxes, by P. Watslawick, J. H. Beavin, and D. D. Jackson. 1967. New York, W. W. Norton, 296 pp.

Pratiques et langages gestuels. 1968. *Langages*, edited by A. J. Greimas, 10°, 149 pp.

Preliminaries to speech analysis: The distinctive features and their correlates, by Roman Jakobson, C. Gunnar M. Fant, and Morris Halle. 1965. Cambridge, Mass., The M.I.T. Press, viii + 64 pp.

PRICE, H. H. 1953. *Thinking and experience*. London, Hutchinson's University Library, 365 pp.

PRIMBS, EDWARD R. J. 1965. Contemporary American criticism of dialectical materialism. *Science & society*, XXIV, 2°, 129–172.

PURSELL, CARROL W., JR., and MELVIN KRANZBERG. Editors of *Technology in Western civilization*, Vol. I: see KRANZBERG.

RASTIER, FRANÇOIS. 1968. Comportement et signification. *Pratique et langages gestuels*. *Langages*, 10°, 76–86.

RICOEUR, PAUL. 1965. *De l'interprétation. Essai sur Freud*. Paris, Seuil, 534 pp.; Italian transl. by E. Renzi, Milano, Il Saggiatore, 1967, 599 pp.

RODOLSKY, ROMAN. 1971. *Genesi e struttura del "Capitale" di Marx*, transl. by B. Maffi. Bari, Laterza, 665 pp. (orig. 1955, 1967).

ROSENKRANZ, KARL. 1966. *Vita di Hegel*, transl. by R. Bodei. Firenze, Vallecchi Editore, 457 pp.

ROSSI-LANDI, FERRUCCIO. 1951. De la communication d'une langue au point de vue épistémologique et au point de vue opératif. *Congrès international de philosophie des sciences* (Paris: October 1949), *Actes*. Paris, Hermann, I: Colloque d'épistemologie, pp. 177–182.

——. 1953. *Charles Morris*. Milano, Bocca, 295 pp.

——. 1954. Del non-traducible. *Congresso di studi metodologici* (Torino, 1952), *Atti*, Torino, Ramella, pp. 112–117.

——. 1955. Della presente traduzione. Appendix to «Del tipo di lavoro svolto da Gilbert Ryle», pp. xlii–liv of the Introduction to Gilbert Ryle, *Lo spirito come comportamento, q.v.*

——. 1958a. Universo del discorso e lingua ideale in filosofia. In *Il pensiero americano contemporaneo*. Milano, Edizioni Communità. Vol. I: *Filosofia epistemologia logica*, pp. 133–182.

——. 1958b. Universi del discorso. *Rivista di filosofia*, XLIX, N° 3, 396–421.

——. 1961. *Significato, comunicazione e parlare comune*. Padova, Marsilio, 291 pp.

——. 1966a. Sul linguaggio verbale e non-verbale. *Nuova corrente*, 37°, 5–23 (now in 1968c, II, pp. 51–75).

——. 1966b. Per un uso marxiano di Wittgenstein. *Nuovi argomenti*, Nuova Serie, I°, 187–230 (now in 1968c, III, pp. 77–126).

——. 1967a. Note di semiotica: 1. Perché semiotica; 2. Su enunciato, proposizione e contesto; 3. Sul pregiudizio contrattualistico. *Nuova corrente*, 41°, 90–109 (now also in 1972).

——. 1967b. Significato, ideologia e realismo artistico. *Nuova corrente*, 44°, 300–342 (now also in 1972).

——. 1967c. Ideologia come progettazione sociale. *Ideologie*, 1°, 1–25 (now also in 1968c, VI, pp. 193–223).

——. 1967d. Lavorando all'omologia del produrre. *Nuovi argomenti*, N.S., 6°, 70–83 (now also in 1968c, IV, pp. 127–140).

——. 1968a. Per un rinnovamento dell'elaborazione ideologica. *Ideologie*, 3°, 3–8.

——. 1968b. Ideologie della relatività linguistica. *Ideologie*, 4°, 3–69 (now also in English transl.: The Hague, Mouton).

——. 1968c. *Il linguaggio come lavoro e come mercato*. Milano, Bompiani, 243 pp. (English transl. forthcoming; German transl.: München, Hanser; Spanish transl.: Caracas, Monte Ávila).

——. 1968d. Note di semiotica: 18. Sui segni del mare interpretati dai naviganti; 19. Sui programmi della comunicazione non-verbale. *Nuova corrente*, 46°–47°, 296–319 (now also in 1972).

——. 1969a. Extension de l'homologie entre énoncés et outils. *Xème Congrès international des linguistes* (Bucarest, 22.8–2.9.1967), *Actes*, I, 1969, pp. 503–508. Bucarest, Editions de l'Académie. (Italian transl. in 1972).

——. 1969b. *Dialettica e alienazione nel linguaggio*. [Conversation between E. Golino and the author]. *Paragone*, XX, n° 234, 78–160. Firenze, Sansoni (now also in 1972).

——. 1969c. Rivoluzione e studio. *Ideologie*, 9°–10°, 5–22.

——. 1970a. Calcolatori e cervelli. *Ideologie*, 12°, 3–10. Article of the *Dizionario teorico-ideologico*, ed. by the review (now also in 1972).

——. 1970b. Semiotica. *Ideologie*, 12°, 38–44. Article of the *Dizionario teorico-ideologico*, ed. by the review (now also in 1972).

——. 1971. Sul contributo di Mao alla dialettica. *Per lo studio della Rivoluzione cinese*, special issue of *Ideologie* (13°–14°), cf. pp. 519–540.

——. 1972. *Semiotica e ideologia*. Milano, Bompiani, 380 pp.

——. Forthcoming. *Lad and Lassie*.

ROUSE, IRVING. 1953. The strategy of culture history. In *Anthropology today, an encyclopedic inventory*, ed. by A. L. Kroeber, pp. 57–76. The University of Chicago Press, xv+958 pp.

RUESCH, JURGEN. 1957. *Disturbed communication: The clinical assessment of normal and pathological communicative behavior*. New York, W. W. Norton & Co. viii+337 pp.

——. 1961. *Therapeutic communication*. New York, W. W. Norton & Co., xvii+480 pp.

RUESCH, JURGEN, and GREGORY BATESON. 1951. *Communication: The social matrix of psychiatry*. New York, W. W. Norton & Co., vi+314 pp.

RUESCH, JURGEN, and WELDON KEES. 1961. *Nonverbal communication: Notes on the visual perception of human relations*. Berkeley and Los Angeles, University of California Press, ix+205 pp.

RYLE, GILBERT. 1931–32. Systematically misleading expressions. *Proceedings of the Aristotelian Society*, XXXII, pp. 139–164; repr. in *Logic and language: Essays* ed. by A. G. N. Flew, I, pp. 11–36. Oxford, Blackwell.

——. 1937–38. Categories. *Proceedings of the Aristotelian Society*, XXXVIII, pp. 189–206; repr. in *Logic and language*, II, 1953, *ib.*, pp. 65–81.

——. 1945. *Philosophical arguments: An inaugural lecture*. Oxford, Clarendon Press, 20 pp.

——. 1949. *The concept of mind*. London, Hutchinson's, 334 pp.; Italian edition by F. Rossi-Landi, *Lo spirito come comportamento*. Torino, Einaudi, 1955, lvii+372 pp.

——. 1953. Ordinary language. *The philosophical review*, LXII 167–186.

——. 1954. *Dilemmas*. Cambridge, University Press, vi+129 pp.

——. 1957. The theory of meaning. *British philosophy in the mid-century*, ed. C. A. Mace, London, Allen & Unwin, pp. 239–264.

——. 1961. Use, usage and meaning. *Proceedings of the Aristotelian Society*, Supplementary vol. XXV, pp. 223–230.

SABBATINI, MARIO. 1967a. Le formazione della società neocoloniale cubana. *Ideologie*, 1°, 52–80.

——. 1967b. La formazione delle ideologie neocapitalistiche, I: L'ideologia tradizionalista. *Ideologie*, 2°, pp. 1–35.

——. 1968a. La disgregazione politica della società neocoloniale cubana. *Ideologie*, 3°, 54–103.

——. 1968b. Il crollo dell'ordine neocoloniale a Cuba. *Ideologie*, 5°–6°, 7–95.

——. 1969. *Didattica della storia*. Treviso, Canova, 102 pp.

——. 1970. Formazione e ideologie della società industriale in Italia, I: L'impresa industriale e l'ideologia imprenditoriale di Alessandro Rossi. *Ideologie*, 12°, 160–171.

SAMARIN, WILLIAM J. 1967. *Field linguistics: A guide to linguistic field work.* New York, Holt, Rinehart and Winston, x + 246 pp.

SAMUELSON, PAUL A. 1949. *Economics*. Eighth edition, International Student Edition. New York, McGraw-Hill Book Company, 1970[8], xxvi+868 pp.

SANDBORN, HERBERT. 1952. Dingler's methodical philosophy. *Methodos*, IV, 15°–16°, 191–220.

SANGUINETI, EDOARDO. 1965. *Ideologia e linguaggio*. Milano, Feltrinelli, 105 pp.

——. 1966. Avanguardia, società, impegno. In *Avanguardia e neo-avanguardia.* q.v., pp. 85–100.

SAPIR, EDWARD. 1927. The unconscious patterning of behavior in society. In *The unconscious, A Symposium*, ed. by E. S. Dummer. New York, Knopf, pp. 114–142; repr. in *Selected writings of Edward Sapir*, ed. by D. G. Mandelbaum, pp. 544–559.

——. 1949. *Selected writings of Edward Sapir in language, culture and personality*, ed. by D. G. Mandelbaum. Berkeley and Los Angeles, University of California Press, xv+617 pp., 4th printing 1963.

——. 1952. *Culture, language and personality*. Berkeley and Los Angeles, University of California Press, x + 207 pp. (selected essays ed. by D. G. Mandelbaum).

SARTRE, JEAN-PAUL. 1948. *Qu'est-ce que la littérature?* Paris, Gallimard, 375 pp.

——. 1960. *Critique de la raison dialectique* (précédé de *Question de méthode*), I: *Théorie des ensembles pratiques*. Paris, Gallimard, 757 pp.

——. 1964. *Les mots*. Paris, Gallimard, 213 pp.

ŠAUMJAN, SEBASTIAN K. 1970. *Linguistica dinamica*, transl. and intr. by E. Rigotti. Bari, Laterza, xx+434 pp.

SAUSSURE, FERDINAND DE. 1957. Cours de linguistique générale (1908–1909), Introduction (d'après de notes d'étudiants). *Cahiers Ferdinand de Saussure*, xv, 3–103.

——. 1954. Notes inédites de Ferdinand de Saussure. *Cahiers Ferdinand de Saussure*, xii, 49–71.

——. 1915. *Cours de linguistique générale*, ed. by Charles Bally and Albert Sechehaye, and with the collaboration of Albert Riedlinger. Paris, Payot (1931[3], 1955[5], 1964, repr.), 331 pp.; Édition critique par Rudolf Engler, Wiesbaden. Otto Harrassowitz, 1967–68, issues 1, 2, 3, xii+515, double pages;

Corso di linguistica generale, intr., transl. and comment by T. De Mauro, Bari, Laterza, 1967, xxiii+487 pp.; *Course in general linguistics*, ed. by Ch. Bally and A. Sechehaye in collaboration with A. Riedlinger, transl. with an intr. and notes by W. Basin, New York-Toronto-London, McGraw-Hill Book Company, 1966, xvi+240 pp.

SCALIA, GIANNI. 1966. La nuova avanguardia (o della "miseria" della poesia). In *Avanguardia e neo-avanguardia, q.v.*, pp. 23–84.

———. 1967. Sulla società (e sulle ideologie) della reificazione (riflessioni marxiane). *Giovane critica*, 17, 34–43.

SCHAFF, ADAM. 1962. *Introduction to semantics*, transl. by O. Wojtasiewicz. Oxford, Pergamon Press, xii + 395 pp.

———. 1964. *Język a poznanie*. Warszawa, Państwowe Wydawnictwo Naukowe, 275 pp.

———. 1965. *Marxismus und das menschliche Individuum*. Wien, Europa-Verlag, 349 pp.

———. 1967. A propos de l'intégration des sciences de l'homme. *Actes du sixième congrès mondial de sociologie*, Evian, 4–11 Sept. 1966, II. Genève, Association Internationale de Sociologie, pp. 85–99.

SCHEFLEN, ALBERT E. 1968. Human communication: Behavioral programs and their integration in interaction. *Behavioral science*, XIII, 1°, 44–55 (with reference to previous writings of 1964, 1965, and 1966).

SCHLANGER, JUDITH E. 1967. Métaphore et invention. *Diogène*, 69°, 15–29.

———. 1971. *Les métaphores de l'organisme*. Paris, Librairie Philosophique J. Vrin, 269 pp.

SCHMIDT, ALFRED. 1962. *Der Begriff der Natur in der Lehre von Marx*. Frankfurt, Europäische Verlagsanstalt, 182 pp. (Frankfurter Beiträge zur Soziologie, Band II).

SCHUMPETER, JOSEPH A. 1950. *Capitalism, socialism and democracy*. New York and Evanston, Harper & Row (Harper Torchbooks), 3rd edition (1942[1], 1946[2]), xiv + 431 pp.

SEARLE, JOHN R. 1967. Human communication theory and the philosophy of language: Some remarks. In *Human communication theory, q.v.*, pp. 116–129.

SEBEOK, THOMAS A. 1962. Coding in the evolution of signalling behavior. *Behavioral science*, 7, 4°, 430–442.

———. 1963a. Lindauer: Communication among social bees; Kellogg: Porpoises and sonar; Lilly: Man and dolphin, Review article. *Language*, 39, 3°, part 1, 448–466.

———. 1963b. Aspects of animal communication: The bees and porpoises. *Language*, 39, 448–466.

———. 1965. Animal communication: A communication network model for language is applied to signalling behavior in animals. *Science*, 147, 3661°, 1006–1014.

———. 1967. On chemical signs. *Social Science Information*, 7 (1), 141–150; also in *To Honor Roman Jakobson: Essays on the occasion of his seventieth birthday*, q.v.

———. 1968. Goals and limitations of the study of animal communication. In *Animal communication*, q.v., chap. I, pp. 3–14.

———. 1969. Semiotics and ethology. In *Approaches to animal communication*, q.v., pp. 200–231.

———. 1970. Zoosemiotic structures and social organization. In *Linguaggi nella società e nella tecnica*, q.v., pp. 113–128.

———. Editor of *Portraits of linguists*, 1966, q.v.

———. Editor of *Animal communication*, 1968, q.v.

SEBEOK, THOMAS A., and ALEXANDRA RAMSAY: Editors of *Approaches to animal communication*, q.v.

SHANDS, HARLEY C. 1970. *Semiotic approaches to psychiatry*. The Hague, Mouton, 412 pp.

———. 1971. *The war with words: Structure and transcendence*. The Hague, Mouton, 128 pp.

SHERMAN, HOWARD J. 1970. The marxist theory of value revisited. *Science & society*, XXXIV, 3°, 257–292.

SHILS, EDWARD A., TALCOTT PARSONS, ROBERT F. BALES. 1953. *Working papers in the theory of action*. Toronto, Collier-Macmillan, 269 pp.

SHILS, EDWARD A., TALCOTT PARSONS, with the assistance of JAMES OLDS. 1965. Values, motives, and systems of action. *Toward a general theory of action*, New York, Harper & Row, pp. 47–243.

SHOUL, BERNICE. 1967. Karl Marx's solutions to some theoretical problems of classical economics. *Science & society*, XXXI, 4°, 448–460.

Simpozium po strukturnomu izučeniju znakovych Sistem: Tezisy dokladov, 1962, Moskwa. Cf. *I sistemi di segni e lo strutturalismo sovietico*.

SIMPSON, GEORGE GAYLORD. 1960. *The meaning of evolution: A study of the history of life and of its significance for man*. New Haven, Yale University Press, xvi + 364 pp.

SINGER, CHARLES, E. J. HOLMYARD, and A. R. HALL (editors). 1956. *A history of technology*, I: *From early times to fall of ancient empires*, q.v.

SINGER, CHARLES, E. J. HOLMYARD, A. R. HALL, and TREVOR I. WILLIAMS (editors). 1956–58. *A history of technology*, II–V, q.v.

I sistemi di segni e lo strutturalismo sovietico. 1969. By various authors, ed. by R. Faccani and U. Eco. Milano, Bompiani, 374 pp.

SLAMA-CAZACU, TATIANA. 1961. *Langage et contexte: Le problème du langage dans la conception de l'expression et de l'interprétation par des organisations contextuelles*. The Hague, Mouton, 251 pp.

———. 1964. *Comunicarea în procesul muncii* [Communication in the working process]. Bucarest, Editura Stiinţifică, 301 pp.

SMITH, ALFRED G., editor of *Communication and culture*, 1966, q.v.

SMITH, JOHN W. 1968. Message-meaning analyses. In *Animal communication*, q.v., pp. 44–60.

Social life of early man, ed. by Sherwood L. Washburn, 1961. Chicago, Aldine, ix+299 pp.

SOLÌMINI, MARIA. 1968. *Genealogia e scienza dei valori*. Manduria, Lacaita editore, 155 pp.

SOMMERFELT, ALF. 1938. *La langue et la société: Caractères sociaux d'une langue de type archaïque*. Oslo, H. Aschehoug & Co. (W. Nygaard), x + 233 pp.

——. 1954. Speech and language. In *A history of technology*, I, q.v., pp. 85–109.

SRAFFA, PIERO. 1960. *La produzione di merci a mezzo di merci: Premesse a una critica della teoria economica*. Torino, Einaudi, xiii + 129 pp.; English edition: *Production of commodities by means of commodities: Prelude to a critique of economic theory*. Cambridge, University Press, 1960.

STEINER, GEORGE. 1966. Babel and after, anonymous in the *Times Literary Supplement*, 10 November 1966; repr. in *T.L.S., Essays and Reviews from the Times Literary Supplement*, V, pp. 199–204.

——. 1967. *Language and silence*: Essays 1958–1966. London, Faber and Faber, 545 pp.

STÖRIG, HANS JOACHIM. 1965³. *Kleine Weltgeschichte der Wissenschaft*. Stuttgart, Kohlhammer, 1954¹, xix+686 pp.

SULLIVAN, NAVIN. 1968. *The message of the genes*. London, Routledge & Kegan Paul, vi + 198 pp.

SWADESH, MORRIS. 1959. Linguistics as an instrument of pre-history. In *Language in culture and society*, ed. by D. Hymes, New York, Evanston, and London, Harper & Row, 1960, pp. 575–584.

SWEEZY, PAUL M. 1942. *The theory of capitalist development. Principles of Marxian political economy*. New York, Monthly Review Press, repr. 1963, xv+398 pp.

TESNIÈRE, LUCIEN. 1966. *Eléments de syntaxe structurale*. Préface de Jean Fourquet. Paris, Librairie C. Klinksieck, xxvi + 670 pp.

TÉTRY, ANDRÉE. 1948. *Les outils chez les êtres vivants*. Préface de Lucien Génot. Paris, Gallimard, 345 pp.

THAO, TRÂN DUC. 1965. Le "noyau rationnel" dans la dialectique hegelienne. *La pensée*, N.S. 119°, 3–23 (original in Vienamese, 1956).

——. 1966. Le mouvement de l'indication comme forme originaire de la conscience. *La pensée*, 128°, 3–24.

——. 1969a. Du geste de l'index à l'image typique (I). *La pensée*, 147°, 3–46. 3–46.

——. 1969b. Du geste de l'index à l'image typique (II): La naissance du langage. *La pensée*, 148°, 71–111.

——. 1970a. *Fenomenologia e materialismo dialettico*, transl. from the French (1951) by R. Tomassini. Milano, Lampugnani Nigri, xix+282 pp.

——. 1970b. Du geste de l'index à l'image typique (III): L'alvéole de la dialectique de la connaissance. *La pensée*, 149°, 93–106.

——. 1973. *L'origine del linguaggio e della coscienza*, transl. from the French, forthcoming.

THOMSON, GEORGE. 1949–55. *Studies in Ancient Greek society*, I: *The prehistoric Aegean*, 1949, new edition 1954, repr. 1961, 626 pp.; II: *The first philosophers*, 1955, new edition 1961, 367 pp., London, Lawrence and Wishart.

THOMSON, JUDITH JARVIS. 1964. Private languages. *American philosophical quarterly*, I, 1°, 20–31.

TILGHER, ADRIANO. 1928. *Homo faber: Storia del concetto di lavoro nella civiltà occidentale: Analisi filosofica di concetti affini*. Roma, Dott. G. Bardi Editore, 1944³, 196 pp.

To honor Roman Jakobson: Essays on the occasion of his seventieth birthday [11.10.66]. 1967. The Hague, Mouton, 2464 pp.

TRAGER, GEORGE L., and BERNARD BLOCH. 1942. *Outline of linguistic analysis*. Baltimore, Linguistic Society of America, ii + 82 pp.

TRÂN DUC THAO: s. THAO, TRÂN DUC.

TRIER, JOST. 1931. *Der deutsche Wortschatz im Sinnbezirk des Verstandes: Die Geschichte eines sprachlichen Feldes*, I: *Von den Anfängen bis zum Beginn des 13. Jhr.* Heidelberg, Winter.

TUCKER, ROBERT. 1961. *Philosophy and myth in Karl Marx*. London, Cambridge University Press, 263 pp.

ULLMANN, STEPHEN. 1951. *The principles of semantics*. Oxford, Blackwell, 2ⁿᵈ ed., 1957, xii + 352 pp.

——. 1962. *Semantics, an introduction to the science of meaning*. Oxford, Blackwell, x + 278 pp.

VACHEK, JOZEF. 1966. *Dictionnaire de linguistique de l'école de Prague*, with the collaboration of J. Dubsky. Utrecht-Anvers, Spectrum, 104 pp.

VAILATI, GIOVANNI. 1911. *Scritti*. Ed. by M. Calderoni, U. Ricci and G. Vacca, with a biography by O. Premoli. Firenze-Leipzig, Seeber-Barth, xxxvi+ xxxii+976 pp.; a choice of 11 essays in *Il metodo della filosofia: Saggi di critica del linguaggio*, ed. by F. Rossi-Landi, Bari, Laterza, 1967² (1957), 223 pp.; «La grammatica dell'algebra» (in *Scritti*, 1911: 871–889), repr. in *Nuova corrente*, 38°, 1966, 131–157.

VERRI, PIETRO. 1771. *Della economia politica*. Livorno. Now in *Del piacere e del dolore ed altri scritti*, ed. by R. De Felice, Milano, Feltrinelli, 1964, xxxiii+422 pp.

VICO, GIAMBATTISTA. 1744. *La scienza nuova seconda*, ed. by F. Nicolini according to the 1744 edition. Bari Laterza, 1953, xl+575 pp.; *The new science,* transl. from the Third Edition and with a new introduction by T. G. Bergin and M. H. Fisch, New York, Anchor Books, Doubleday & Company Inc., 1961, liv+384 pp.

VITELLO, VINCENZO. 1963. *Il pensiero economico moderno*. Roma, Editori Riuniti, 130 pp.

WAGNER, ADOLPH. 1879. *Allgemeine oder theoretische Volkswirtschaftslehre*, I: *Grundlegung*. 2nd improved and augmented ed. Leipzig and Heidelberg (Vol. I of *Lehrbuch der politischen Ökonomie*), 1881–82.

WASHBURN, SHERWOOD L. (ed.). 1961. *Social life of early man, q.v.*

WATSON, O. MICHAEL. 1970. *Proxemic behavior*. The Hague, Mouton, 127 pp.

WATZLAWICK, P., J. H. BEAVIN and D. D. JACKSON. 1967. *Pragmatics of human communication: A study of interactional patterns, pathologies and paradoxes, q.v.*

WEBER, MAX. 1972. *Wirtschaft und Gesellschaft: Grundriss der verstehenden Soziologie*; with an appendix: Die rationalen and soziologischen Grundlagen der Musik. 5th newly published edition by J. Winckelman. Tübingen, J. C. B. Mohr (Paul Siebeck), (1925²), xviii+1033 pp.

——. 1964. *Essays in sociology*, transl., ed., and with an intr. by H. H. Gerth & C. Wright Mills. London, Routledge & Kegan Paul, (1948¹), xi+490 pp.

WELTY, EBERHARD. 1946. *Vom Sinn und Wert der menschlichen Arbeit: Aus der Gedankenwelt des hl. Thomas von Aquin*. Heidelberg, F. H. Kerke Verlag, 125 pp.

WENNER, ADRIAN M. The study of animal communication: An overview. In *Approaches to animal communication, q.v.*, pp. 232–243.

WHORF, BENJAMIN LEE. 1956. *Language, thought, and reality: Selected writings*, ed. and with an intr. by J. B. Carroll. Foreword by Stuart Chase. New York, John Wiley, and The Massachusetts Institute of Technology. 4th printing, 1959, xi + 278 pp.

WILLIAMS, TREVOR I., and T. K. DERRY. 1960. *A short history of technology*. Oxford, Oxford University Press, xviii + 783 pp.

WILLIAMS, TREVOR I., CHARLES SINGER, A. R. HALL, and E. J. HOLMYARD (editors). 1956–58. *A history of technology*, II–V, *q.v.*

WISDOM, JOHN. 1952. Ludwig Wittgenstein, 1934–1937. *Mind*, LXI, 242°, 258–260.

——. 1953. *Philosophy and psycho-analysis*. Oxford, Blackwell, vi + 282 pp.

——. 1965. *Paradox and discovery*. Oxford, Blackwell, ix+166 pp.

WITTGENSTEIN, LUDWIG. 1953. *Philosophische Untersuchungen* (1945). Text and English transl. by G. E. M. Anscombe. Oxford, Blackwell, x + 232 pp.; new ed. with a revised transl. and an analytical index, x+232 pp., 233–272 pp. (1958, repr. 1967).

——. 1956. *Bemerkungen über die Grundlagen der Mathematik* (1937–1944).

Text and English transl. by G. E. M. Anscombe. Oxford, Blackwell, xix + 196 pp.

——. 1960a. *Notes dictated to G. E. Moore in Norway, April 1914. Schriften,* pp. 227–253. Frankfurt/Main, Suhrkamp Verlag.

——. 1960b. *Schriften.* Frankfurt/Main, Suhrkamp Verlag, 545 pp. (contains the *Tractatus,* the *Philosophische Untersuchungen,* and minor writings).

——. 1961. *Tractatus logico-philosophicus.* The German text of Ludwig Wittgenstein's *Logisch-philosophische Abhandlung* (1920), with a new transl. by D. F. Pears and B. F. McGuinnes and the intr. by R. Russell, F.R.S. London, Routledge & Kegan Paul, xxii + 166 pp.

——. 1964. *Philosophische Bemerkungen* (1930). From his literary remains, ed. by R. Rhees. Oxford, Blackwell, 348 pp.

——. 1966. *Lectures and conversations on aesthetics, psychology and religious belief,* ed. by Cyrill Barrett. Oxford, Blackwell, pp. viii–72.

Wittgenstein and the problem of other minds. Ten essays by various authors, ed. by H. Morick. 1967. New York, McGraw Hill, xxiii + 231 pp.

PART NINE

LINGUISTICS AND EDUCATION

LINGUISTICS AND EDUCATION

AN OVERVIEW

I don't know anything about education.
                                    Anonymous psycholinguist.
The most pernicious thing linguists ever did was to sell the idea
of pattern practice drill to high school language teachers.
                                    Anonymous linguist.

It is often difficult to chart a way between the Scylla of indifference and the Charybdis of dogmatic misinformation. In this section, we have tried to point out the relevance of linguistics to education (and conversely of education to linguistics) while at the same time steering clear of the excessive claims that have caused so much damage to all concerned. It is tempting to suggest that linguists can be divided into three groups: the purists, to whom any application is anathema; the meddlers, who are convinced that they alone can solve the problems of language education; and the modest concerned minority, who understand what limited but vital contribution their field can make. Similarly, one would want to divide educators into three: the ignorant, a very large group, sadly, with the vaguest conception of the nature of language; the misinformed, who have picked up a phrase or two from a popular linguistics textbook or more likely at a two-day workshop; and the happy few who have had time to learn (and teachers to learn from) the relevance of current linguistic scholarship to their work.

For there can be no doubt that linguistics is relevant to education, that many aspects of the field have direct or indirect applications to, or implications for, much of the activity of schools. Children do a great deal of their language learning in school, and more important, do most of their school learning through language. Further, one cannot deny the importance of education to linguistics, as is shown by the fact that most linguists are employed by an educational system either to teach their field or a language. Educational linguistics then forms a vital area of inter-disciplinary activity.

This importance has been clearly recognized by the detailed attention given to the area throughout the twelve volumes of *Current Trends in Linguistics*. In all, over forty chapters treat of related topics.

In Volume 1, *Soviet and East European linguistics*, Jacob Ornstein describes foreign language teaching in the Soviet Union.

Six different chapters in Volume 2, *Linguistics in East Asia and South East Asia,* are on educational topics. Lukoff describes work in Korea, Cornyn reports the debate over the use of the vernacular in Burma, Uhlenbeck gives an account of the development of official languages in Indonesia and Malaysia, Akira describes English language teaching in Japan, and DeFrancis and Yamada Toshio write about the writing systems of China and Japan respectively.

Part III of Volume 4, *Ibero-American and Caribbean linguistics,* is titled 'Applied Linguistics'. It contains chapters on Spanish by Cisneros, on bilingualism by Di Pietro, on literacy by Lastra, on foreign language teaching by de Matos and Wigdorsky, on research by Contreras, and on the role of the language academies by Guitarte and Quintero.

In Volume 5, *Linguistics in South Asia,* there is a discussion of official language problems in India by Das Gupta.

Regional language issues are treated in Part IV of Volume 6, *Linguistics in South West Asia and North Africa.* Ferguson in his overview points out that many efforts have been made to deal with the problem of language in education. The situation in Iran and Afghanistan is described by Yar-Shater, in Israel by Landau, in Turkey by Hazai, and in the Arab countries by Altoma.

There is considerable discussion of language policy and language education in Volume 7, *Linguistics in Sub-Saharan Africa.* Spencer discusses colonial policies, Welmers the effect of Christian missions, and Whiteley the policies of independent African states. The complexities of multilingualism are further described by Alexandre. Dunstan writes a chapter on language teaching, and Foster and Tucker present two aspects of literacy.

Language policy, language engineering, and literacy are further treated in a number of chapters in Volume 8, *Linguistics in Oceania.* Wurm describes the situation in New Guinea and Australia, Lavondès in French Polynesia, Sibayan in the Philippines, Trifonovitch in the Trust Territory of the Pacific Islands, and Alisjahbana in Indonesia and Malaysia.

Volume 9, *Linguistics in Western Europe,* has a general review of work in the study of child language by Slama-Cazacu, and a chapter on language teaching by Strevens.

Volume 10, *Linguistics in North America,* includes chapters on the general educational aims of first language teaching (Marckwardt), the teaching of reading and spelling (Ives and Ives), and English as a second language (Allen).

When we came to plan this section, then, we could take into account the fact that the editors of *Current Trends in Linguistics* had already given very full recognition to the close interrelationship between linguistics and education. Additionally, there had just appeared the first yearbook in a projected annual review of foreign language teaching (Birkmaier 1969) and also a yearbook review of linguistics in school programs in the United States (Marckwardt 1970). While we hoped in this section to cover the main areas of educational linguistics, the contributors were invited to be as general and programmatic as they wished; they were assured that general theoretical statements would be in place rather than the detailed research reviews often written for such a volume as this.

In the first chapter of this section, I discuss the general relation of linguistics to education. I suggest the existence of a language barrier to education and the fact that linguistics makes possible an accurate description of the nature of this barrier. Sociolinguistics in particular provides the framework for a precise definition of the child's language situation, and psycholinguistics permits a more knowledgeable formulation of language education aims. There are important implications in linguistic theories and research for the implementation of these aims and for the evaluation of their achievement.

Much current work in linguistics is concerned with the acquisition of language by children; in the second chapter, Vera John and Marshall Peller consider the relevance of this work to the planning of education programs for young children. They set out some of the unsolved questions in the area, and then go on to assess the answers that are implied by a number of early childhood education programs in various parts of the world.

The general question of the relevance of linguistics to mother tongue teaching in the primary and secondary school is treated in a chapter by Rudolph Troike. He stresses the need to recognize a student's language ability and to build from that to the desired goal. Linguists are starting to show how this language ability can be characterized. Troike summarizes the contributions that linguists can make to bilingual education, to formal grammar instruction, and to the teaching of such subjects as reading, composition, and literature.

The field of reading instruction is the topic of a chapter by Richard Venezky. Some very strong claims have been made for the relevance of linguistics to the teaching of reading. In his wide-ranging and thorough review, Venezky puts these claims in perspective. He analyzes the nature of the reading process and of learning to read, emphasizing the linguistic aspects, but showing the importance of the full range of research in the field.

One special branch of reading instruction is literacy, treated in a chapter by Sarah Gudschinsky. Setting out the areas in which linguistic research is needed, she provides a model for analysis of orthography problems. Her chapter should be equally interesting to those who can have control of the choice of an orthography and to those who aim to teach literacy in an established orthography.

The many ways in which linguistics should influence second language pedagogy are analyzed by Glyn Lewis, who also stresses that other disciplines have contributions to make. He starts with an historical outline, considering the reasons that linguistics has generally had such a feeble effect on language teaching. After comparing the approaches in Western Europe and the United States, he gives a full account of Russian theory and practice. Overall, Lewis finds that the major linguistic influence on teachers has been in providing them with new concepts of language. He reviews the two alternative current models of language learning, the structuralist-associationist and the transformationalist-cognitive, and points how they are similar, where they differ, and what implications each has for language pedagogy. Finally, he discusses the organization of language courses and the question of language testing.

These chapters then are intended to add up to a general review of current trends in educational linguistics. A word about the title of the section. There was a brief temptation to call it 'Applied Linguistics'. The temptation was easily avoided, for the term is too wide in some of its uses (much of this volume could fit it in some definitions) and too narrow in others (as where it is used as a synonym for language teaching). It is also a potentially dangerous term in its central implication, that linguistics is to be applied to something. To anything available, often. In this mood, linguists are like little boys who rush out with their little hammers looking for something to bang. They are sometimes successful in beating the problem to death, but often they do no more than chip at its edges.

A more productive approach, it seems to me, is to recognize that one starts with a problem (here, for example, language education), and looks for the contributions that linguistics can make to its solution. With a problem-oriented approach, one is much more ready to remember that there are other disciplines with their own contributions to make, and that the application of linguistics will not be a panacea. The term 'applied linguistics' then is rather unsuitable. For the sense we are concerned with here, terms like 'language pedagogy' or William Mackey's 'language didactics' or perhaps 'educational linguistics' (on the model of 'educational psychology' and 'educational sociology') might give a clearer picture of the field, which is just as much a subfield of education as it must continue to be of linguistics. The title we have chosen, 'Linguistics and education', attempts to avoid too deep an involvement in these questions. There might be some argument with considering education an adjacent art or science, but the same objection might be made to medicine, which also draws on a number of basic sciences and technologies to handle its problems.

In this section, then, we have set out to show how linguistics and its various fields can help define and solve problems that reflect the centrality of language in the educational process.

BERNARD SPOLSKY

REFERENCES

AKIRA, ŌTA. 1967. The study of English in Japan. CTL 2.645–82.
ALEXANDRE, PIERRE. 1971. Multilingualism. CTL 7.654–63.
ALISJAHBANA, S. TAKDIR. 1971. Language policy, language engineering, and literacy: Indonesia and Malaysia. CTL 8.1087–1109.

ALLEN, HAROLD B. 1973. English as a second language. CTL 10.295–320.

ALTOMA, SALIH J. 1970. Language education in Arab countries and the role of the Academies. CTL 6.690–720.

BIRKMAIER, EMMA MARIE, ed. 1968. Britannica review of foreign language education, Vol. 1. Chicago, Encyclopaedia Britannica Press.

CISNEROS, LUIS JAIME. 1968. Spanish. CTL 4.379–98.

CONTRERAS, HELES. 1968. Applied linguistic research. CTL 4.534–42.

CORNYN, WILLIAM S. 1967. Burma. CTL 2.777–81.

DAS GUPTA, JYOTIRINDRA. 1969. Official language problems and policies in South Asia. CTL 5.578–96.

DEFRANCIS, JOHN. 1967. Language and script reform in China. CTL 2.130–50.

DE MATOS, FRANCISCO GOMES, and LEOPOLDO WIGDORSKY. 1968. Foreign language teaching in Latin America. CTL 4.464–533.

DI PIETRO, ROBERT J. 1968. Bilingualism. CTL 4.399–414.

DUNSTAN, ELIZABETH. 1971. Language teaching. CTL 7.570–86.

FERGUSON, CHARLES A. 1970. Regional language issues and studies: An overview. CTL 6.665–8.

FOSTER, PHILIP J. 1971. Problems of literacy in Sub-Saharan Africa. CTL 7.587–617.

GUITARTE, GUILLERMO L., and RAFAEL TORRES QUINTERO. 1968. Linguistic correctness and the role of the Academies. CTL 4.562–606.

HAZAI, G. 1970. Linguistics and language issues in Turkey. CTL 6.746–58.

IVES, SUMNER A., and JOSEPHINE PIEKARZ IVES. 1973. Linguistics and the teaching of reading and spelling. CTL 10.228–49.

LANDAU, JACOB M. 1970. Language study in Israel. CTL 6.721–45.

LASTRA, YOLANDA. 1968. Literacy. CTL 4.415–63.

LAVONDÈS, HENRI. 1971. Language policy, language engineering, and literacy: French Polynesia. CTL 8.1110–28.

LUKOFF, FRED. 1967. Linguistics in the Republic of Korea. CTL 2.735–57.

MACKEY, WILLIAM. 1965. Language didactics and applied linguistics. Vuosikirja 4. Suomen Uusien Kialtren, Opettajien Liitto.

MARCKWARDT, ALBERT A. 1973. General educational aims of native language teaching and learning. CTL 10.206–27.

——, ed. 1970. Linguistics in school programs. The Sixty-Ninth Yearbook of the National Society for the Study of Education.

ORNSTEIN, JACOB. 1963. Foreign language teaching. CTL 1.143–91.

SIBAYAN, BONIFACIO. 1971. Language policy, language engineering, and literacy: Philippines. CTL 8.1038–62.

SLAMA-CAZACU, TATIANA. 1972. The study of child language in Europe. CTL 9.512–90.

SPENCER, JOHN. 1971. Language policies of the colonial powers and their legacies. CTL 7.537–47.

STREVENS, PETER. 1972. Language teaching. CTL 9.702–33.

TOSHIO, YAMADA. 1967. The writing system: Historical research and modern development. CTL 2.693–731.

TRIFONOVITCH, GREGORY J. 1971. Language policy, language engineering, and literacy: Trust Territory of the Pacific Islands. CTL 8.1063–87.

TUCKER, ARCHIBALD. 1971. Orthographic systems and conventions in Sub-Saharan Africa. CTL 7.618–53.

UHLENBECK, E. M. 1967. Indonesia and Malaysia. CTL 2.55–111.

WELMERS, WILLIAM E. 1971. Christian missions and language policies. CTL 7.559–69.

WHITELEY, W. H. 1971. Language policies of independent African states. CTL 7.548–58.

WURM, STEPHEN A. 1971. Language policy, language engineering, and literacy: New Guinea and Australia. CTL 8.1025–38.

YAR-SHATER, EHSAN. 1970. Iran and Afghanistan. CTL 6.669–89.

LINGUISTICS AND THE
LANGUAGE BARRIER TO EDUCATION

BERNARD SPOLSKY

Just as language is central to human society, so the business of acquiring a language is a central part of socialization. The importance of this has recently been clearly recognized by linguistics with its emphasis on the explanation of the development of what Chomsky (1965) has called linguistic competence, and on the wider area of what the sociolinguists refer to as communicative competence (Slobin 1967). In order to become a full-fledged member of his society, a child must develop control not only of the rules of his language — its grammar and dictionary — but also of the rules of speaking, the 'situations and uses, the patterns and functions, of speaking as an activity in its own right' (Hymes 1962). The study of these systems and of their acquisition is a leading concern of linguistics, with general linguistic theory concerning itself mainly with the language rules, sociolinguistics with the rules of speaking, and psycholinguistics with the acquisition process.

We can usefully distinguish between the informal and formal acquisition of language and speech, using the term education to refer to the formal kind. Without at this time taking any position on the question of a theory of language acquisition, we may characterize as informal those activities that are left to normal, unstructured exposure, to the activities of such amateurs as siblings and parents, and to the free working of exposure or unorganized reinforcement. This informal learning, it has been argued by Chomsky and his followers, is possible because of an innate language learning propensity, species specific, as Lenneberg (1967) argues, that permits each normal human child to learn the language to which he is exposed.

There is reason to believe that this informal learning is not without its structure too. While the supporters of innate acquisition such as Menyuk (1969) and Carol Chomsky (1969) have argued for the fact that all children learn, in about the same order, the main rules of language, their arguments must not be allowed to obscure the fact that the quality and speed of such acquisition varies. And such variation may in fact turn out to be much more closely related to the kind of exposure than has been admitted. Thus Gordon (1969) has suggested the effect of the amount of mother-child verbal interaction on the quality of child language development.

There are many situations possible in which the whole of a child's language and speech acquisition is left to these informal activities, but it is more often the case that a society makes some efforts to formalize the education of its young, appointing certain times, places, and people to be responsible for passing on certain areas of traditional knowledge and values, among which language and speech play an important role. These formal educational systems may be described according to a number of linguistic dimensions. The first concerns the participants in the process: who is educated, by whom, and for what linguistic roles. The second is concerned with the choice of channel: pre-literate oral, written, or post-electronic oral. And the third is the choice of code or language: single or dual or multi-medium, and the types of languages — vernacular, standard, or classical.

Let us consider first the question of the participant in the educational process. We may distinguish here between universal and select education. In universal education, it is agreed that all children in the society should receive about the same amount of basic education. What this amount should be varies: in modern times, most societies accept universal primary education as a minimum ideal; more advanced technological societies aim at universal secondary education, with degrees of variation in kind of education at the secondary level; and some American educators speak of an ultimate right to universal tertiary education. When there is selection, one of the more common criteria is sex, with a distinction between the amount and kind of education provided for males and females. Equally common is the notion of elite education, with those chosen being selected on the basis of descent, wealth, race, religion, or intellectual qualification. The kinds and numbers of participants turn out to be very important in the linguistic quality of the education. There is good reason to feel that the failures of modern education — such as its inability to teach Johnny to read — can in large measure be attributed to the rapid increase in the numbers being taught and the subsequent linguistic heterogeneity introduced into the system.

The status and kind of teacher is also a variant. While teachers are often considered members of priesthoods, it is just as likely for them to be considered slaves (e.g. ancient Rome) or hard worked drudges (the East European Jewish *melamed*); the modern status of a teacher as a lower civil servant is an interesting compromise. In many societies, the teachers are elite guardians of an esoteric body of knowledge and a secret language; in modern society, however, with mass education, they tend rather to be members of the upwardly mobile lower middle class, one of whose self-appointed tasks is to teach the linguistic and other social mannerisms to be acquired by those who wish to move upward socially (Labov 1969). In linguistic terms, the teachers may be native speakers of the child's language or of the school language, with consequent effect on the methods they choose and their effectiveness.

In a pre-literate society, there is no problem about the choice of channel: it must be oral. As McLuhan (1962) argued, the development of writing, and perhaps more of printing, changed the emphasis from oral to visual learning. In the oral system, one goes to school to memorize the traditional lore, whether by learning it by heart, syllable by syllable, or by learning how to recreate its essential content in appropriate formulas. Given a writing system, however, the first task of the school is to teach reading and writing, and the written language becomes the special pre-serve of the school. An interesting example of two possible reactions to this situa-tion is given by orthodox Hinduism and Judaism; the former insists on memoriza-tion of the vedas, and their recitation from memory only. Judaism insists however that even if a reader is able to recite the Torah by heart, he must still follow the place in a written text. The third system is the post-electronic oral system, where it is possible to communicate over time and distance using speech; radio and tele-phones made recitation in class respectable again, and permitted the major swing back to oral second language instruction.

Finally, there is the choice of language or languages as medium of instruction or as languages to be taught. Mackey (1970) has proposed a useful typology of bilingual education, parts of which are relevant here. A school system may be single medium or dual medium. A single medium school becomes bilingual when the language used for instruction is not the same as that spoken by some of its students. A school may use two or more languages for instruction. It may intend to transfer its students from the use of one language to the use of another, or to maintain them in the use of their first language: it may aim that the students master two or more languages, choosing to establish them as equal for all purposes, or to make them different, so that one language would be used for certain domains, and the other for other domains. The classification of a bilingual (or any other) curriculum linguistically then involves first a statement of the child's situation, a statement of the linguistic objectives of the school in terms of the outside society, and a descrip-tion of the means it undertakes to effect these objectives.

A further dimension is the kind of language each is. For our purposes, I think useful three of the types set up by Stewart (1962): vernacular, standard, and clas-sical. For purposes of the educational system, we need simply to distinguish these three classes, which may be defined here as follows: a vernacular language is the language or dialect of the child; a standard language is the language or dialect associated with official, commercial, and cultural life of the community, and with a written form; and a classical language is one associated with national or religious history and traditions, but without living speakers.

This last classification permits us to consider what I will call the language barrier to education. The child acquires his vernacular in informal ways; the formal edu-cational system usually requires him to acquire either the standard language or a classical language. Interestingly enough, in the latter case, there isn't too much problem. Classical languages are either taught to select elites (as was Greek in ancient Rome, Latin in the Middle Ages and Renaissance, or Sanskrit to Hindus), or taught with the full force of a flourishing religious system (Hebrew in the East European ghetto, Arabic in the non-Arabic Moslem world; *The New York Times* reported recently the increasing enthusiasm with which the Malaysians greet the annual Koran-reading competitions for contestants from non-Arabic countries). And they are taught with the realization that learning a classical language is not simple, for it is a new language. But with standard languages, there has been an interesting unawareness of what is going on. Teachers and educational systems have often just assumed that everyone speaks the standard dialect or language, or that he will pick it up easily. Thus it has been and still is common for children to come to school and be classified as mentally retarded when they fail intelligence tests given in a language they don't know; to sit for years in a classroom where the teacher ignores that the whole of the class speaks a language he doesn't; to be treated as stupid because their dialect differs from the standard aimed at by the teacher. For it is not just that school is a place that teaches language: it is even more important that almost all of its teaching takes place through language. Unless the teachers and students can communicate, there is little possibility for effective education. A first task, then, in the understanding of language and education is an accurate picture of the language situation in which the educational system must function.

The description and analysis of these various language situations, as preliminary guidance on the need for language planning, is one of the areas in which socio-linguists are active. Particular emphasis has not unnaturally been given to the language problems of developing nations.

Sub-Saharan Africa, as described in more detail in *Current Trends in Linguistics,* Volume 7, exemplifies the nature of the problems and the various types of solutions. Pre-colonial Africa was to a certain extent multilingual, with multilingualism usually a result of tribal conquest or slavery. Some language education took place as initiation into secret groups with their own languages. The spread of Islam introduced a classical language taught in connection with religious observance. Colonization in the nineteenth century led to a new linguistic complexity. It set up new political units, the boundaries of which had little to do with the native ethnic or linguistic grouping, producing multilingual units, and introducing into them European languages. Part of the result of this was to encourage the spread of vehicular languages such as Hausa or Swahili, but the major effect was the new status of the European language. Generally, it was agreed that the European colonial administrators would continue to conduct the affairs of government in the European language: the first task of the education system was to produce a small group of native Africans able to work with them and as interpreters and lower civil servants. Thus, all colonial administrative systems assumed that such higher (secondary) education as there would be, would be in the European language; tertiary education for the tiny elite would be in metropolitan schools.

There were two distinct approaches to the early stages of primary education. The French and Portuguese, assuming that 'civilization' meant French (or Portuguese) language and culture, would have nothing to do with teaching in any other language. From his first day at school, the young African would be instructed in French (or Portuguese). The British, Belgians, and Germans, while still aiming at the use of their own languages in higher grades, accepted for a number of reasons the notion of initial instruction in the vernacular. For at least the first two years, instruction in the vernacular was provided, with a beginning of training in the European language. This policy led to the encouragement of literacy and literature in the various African languages, and is also associated with the Protestant missionaries who worked on translation of the Bible into as many African languages as possible.

The use of the vernacular first was the policy supported by international educators and UNESCO: once one accepts a universal right to education, it is a natural extension to postulate a right for everyone to be educated in his own language, at least until he has acquired sufficient knowledge of the standard language to work in it. One good example of a 'vernacular first' educational policy is the Soviet Union, where the various Republics provide education in the vernacular as far as it will go, at the same time teaching Russian and ultimately, in most cases, switching to Russian. How far the vernacular will go is a question of degree of standardization and modernization. A highly developed language like Georgian, with a well developed literature, makes possible tertiary education in the language; while a less standardized language, with little or no literature of its own, is likely to be found only for the first few years of elementary school.

The conflict between nationalistic and other values is particularly exemplified by countries of the Maghrib (see *Current Trends in Linguistics,* Volume 6). Morocco, Tunisia, and Algeria, originally basically Berber in language, were only slightly Arabized during the centuries of Arab dominion, but were intensively Europeanized in the hundred years or so of French rule. There was no place for Arabic education under French colonial status; all education was in French. Thus, the revolutionary leaders themselves were literate in French, and knew little of any Arabic at the time of independence. Independence was associated with pro-Arabic nationalism, and in the years since, the educational system has been working slowly to replace French with Arabic. The problems are immense, for Arabic itself is a language struggling to adapt itself to the modern world. The Arabic world is the classic original example of diglossia, a situation where two languages fill distinct roles in society. Classical Arabic is a written language with a long tradition, a tightly guarded notion of grammatical and rhetorical correctness, and a number of academies in various Middle Eastern countries. In each of these countries, the vernacular is quite different: different phonologically, grammatically, and lexically both from neighboring vernaculars and from the Classical language. The traditional view is that the vernaculars are corrupted versions of the classical language: that if vernacular speakers would only make the effort, they would use the correct classical forms. Attempts at modernization of Arabic follow two strategies: standardization of the vernacular, or modernization of the classical. There are signs of the emergence of a modern standard, with radio broadcasts playing a leading role in its spread.

Recent sociolinguistic work in the United States has made clear that here too there are many children for whom there is a language barrier to education.

Harold Allen's 1964 study was as important for the gaps it revealed as for its totals; it showed up the ignorance in many parts of the country of the fact that a large proportion of non-English speakers were coming to school. These children turned up in remedial reading classes, classes for retarded children, or most usually as early dropouts. The school, ignoring their knowledge of Spanish or French or Navajo, taught them as though they knew English; the few who succeeded would later be expected to study a foreign language with their monolingual peers. This squandering of linguistic resources, while NDEA money was still being used to reorganize the teaching of foreign language, was one of the ironies pointed out in the arguments that led to the 1969 Bilingual Education Act.

The new interest in bilingual education is a matter of the recognition of the coincidence of the linguistic barrier to education with other kinds of social disadvantage. The Coleman report (1966) showed clearly that Spanish, Indian, and Chinese students do poorer than average in the educational system, and as political pressures built up for minority groups, the linguistic minorities were recognized. That the motivation of Federal intervention is political rather than educational is clear, however, when one notes how the Office of Education tried in 1969–70 to cut out programs in TESOL and Bilingual Education at the same time it was planning campaigns for universal literacy in English.

Sociolinguistic studies in the last decade or so have drawn attention to a less obvious but probably equally effective language barrier to education, the use of the wrong variety. Teachers find it easier to consider the standard they teach, and teach in, as the correct and pure version of the language, and treat any variation as corrupt or debased, or careless. Thus, they see their role to persuade their students to take care to speak properly. Linguists in the 1930s and 40s moved to apply their doctrine that 'all languages are equally good' (sometimes paradoxically preceded by the claim that 'linguists do not make value judgments but simply describe what they find'), formerly used to attack references to 'primitive' languages, to varieties of languages classified previously as substandard. The war of the dictionaries, with *Webster's Third* dominated by the linguists, and the recent counterblast with the *American Heritage Dictionary*, was part of this struggle.

But more serious has been the question raised by Basil Bernstein (1964), who characterized lower-class English as a restricted code, with related limitations on cognition and perception. Here, a sociolinguist has set out not just to describe a variety of language that can be used to identify members of a particular group, but to propose that this variety is itself inherently limited and limiting. A user of the variety is at a disadvantage not just because the educational system is conducted in a different language, but because his language limits his ability to think in the way education demands.

Bernstein's claims raise questions of the sort that have continued to be discussed by anthropological linguists and tested by psycholinguists, the relations between language and thought. The linguistic relativity theory, associated especially with the names of Whorf and Sapir, has serious implications for education if its validity can be established. For, if it is true that language limits thought in any real sense, a linguistic disadvantage is a basic one. The child limited to using a language that is incapable of handling the thoughts called for in the modern world is condemned to second-class citizenship. His only hope is to be freed by massive programs to teach him the language of the school: some psycholinguists have even gone so far as to argue that lower-class children, having no real language, need to be taught language from scratch. But empirical studies have not in fact supported the strong form of the linguistic relativity theory. No experiments have been designed or conducted that show a clear advantage to speakers of one language over speakers of another in the performance of a specific language-aided task. Lenneberg's notion of codeability shows the greater ease of handling certain classifications when the language has a simple term for them, but there is no evidence of a real language barrier to thought.

But to education, there certainly is one, as other studies of lower-class varieties are showing. Studies of the speech of young black children point out the underlying regularities of the language system, its particular strengths, and the ways in which it varies from standard English. More importantly, work with social varieties suggests that the marks of social variation and of stylistic variation are similar, with a tendency to coincidence of informal higher socio-economic usage with formal lower socio-economic usage (Labov 1966). These and other studies are starting to make clear the nature of the language of the child, and of the society for which he is being prepared. Failure to control the standard language is a barrier to employment as well as to success in school. Much of the public activity of sociolinguists in the last few years appears to involve communicating to teachers the nature of the language of their students, and to explaining to them their own particular place in the sociolinguistic picture.

In these ways, linguistics has been contributing to the definition of language education aims. By the increasing light it has cast on the nature of the language barrier in education, it has permitted educators to understand the types of problems with which they are dealing. Given this understanding, and the decision on educational aims that follow, there comes the implementation of language education. Here again, various sectors of linguistics are offering assistance.

The establishment of curriculum models is a first area. The many complexities of bilingual educational models are starting to be unravelled, thanks largely to the typology prepared first by Willam Mackey, and elaborated by Theodore Andersson and Mildred Boyer (1970). Mackey's typology set out to classify any educational system according to the languages it used for instruction. It is a model strictly within the present sociolinguistic tradition, giving the language situation in each of the four domains of home, school, neighborhood, and State; it gives more detail then on the school domain, its language aims, and the techniques used to achieve them. Andersson and Boyer limit their coverage, setting out to describe types of curriculum supported by the Bilingual Education Act. They are able to go into greater depth in describing curriculum models.

It is general for linguists to be associated in one way or another with experimental bilingual programs, helping with the establishment of goals, the assessment of achievements, or the description of language of participants. Flanked on the one side by psychologists and on the other by child education experts, they attempt to delimit the central aspect of the bilingual program as linguistic.

The development of bilingual or vernacular education leads inevitably to problems with language standardization and modernization, the area somewhat inelegantly called language engineering. Indonesian schools, for instance, switched from Dutch to Indonesian during the Japanese occupation; in three years, 7000 new words, mostly for secondary school use, were decided on by the Language Office (Alisjahbana 1971). The curricular implications of language decisions like these are particularly interesting. The choice of a way to say 'triangle' has implications for later geometry teaching, for instance. At the same time that language academies tend to perpetuate the language barrier by their maintenance of the notion of correct language, they are most important in the development of new terms and expressions for vernacular education. Haugen (1966) has evaluated the linguist's role in language modernization, pointing out his special contributions and the limitations that arise from his lack of sensitivity.

The four main areas where linguistics has applications to and implications for education — mother tongue teaching, second language teaching, reading, and literacy — will be dealt with by others in this volume, but a few general remarks are perhaps in place.

Teaching the mother tongue is a central task of an educational system, although, as has already been suggested, this is often confused by an erroneous assumption that the 'mother tongue' is the standard language. The school very often ignores the child's own language or variety, and proceeds to instruct him in the grammar of the standard language. Recent years have seen a swing back from the grammarless teaching of the 30s and 40s to a newly-found faith in linguistics: very few American school textbooks offered today to teach language arts do not claim to have a linguistic approach or a linguistic adviser. The exact nature of the linguistic influence is interesting. Given the amount of time taken for ideas to filter down from scholarship to textbook writing, it is not surprising that 1970 textbooks find 1960 transformational grammar the main new thrust. Its similarities to the old diagramming, and its offer of a complete system, seems to be appealing. There are no signs yet of any real understanding in language arts books of the message of the sociolinguists.

Second language teaching has always been somewhat more susceptible to linguistic influence. The major force in American language teaching, with the NDEA supported thrust of the 50s, was the Audiolingual Method, a set of notions developed by linguists in the 40s. The failure of the panacea threatened relations between linguists and language teachers, but patient cooperation and a new acceptance of limitations, are once again leading to happier cooperation. As long as linguists argued that all one had to do to teach a language was to apply some bit of linguistic theory, conflicts were certain. Now that we admit that linguistics is only one of the fields whose findings have implications for the development of a theory, and subsequently, of methods, of second language pedagogy, there is a chance for a fruitful partnership.

Similarly with reading, where a few loud public claims to panacea led to 'linguistic' methods of teaching reading. The two main contributions linguists made were to point out the actual nature of the phoneme-grapheme correspondences, showing clearly the existence of underlying regularities, and to propose ways of obtaining a more perfect fit. The first activity is associated with the work of linguists like Bloomfield (1961) and Fries (1962). Having shown the nature of the regularities, they proposed to teach reading by presenting regular forms first. It has taken some time for others to point out that there is no logical connection between a linguist's description and a child's best order of acquisition: to show that the implications of the underlying facts are not the same as their direct application. Their activities were nonetheless sufficiently successful to set up a linguistic approach to reading teaching alongside the 'phonic' and the 'Look-say'. The work of Chomsky and Halle in *The sound patterns of English* (1968), by stressing the value of English spelling as the underlying pattern of English phonology, has added extra weight to the contribution to be made by linguists to the understanding of the nature of reading. The second thrust is the work of Pitman with his *Initial Teaching Alphabet*: a broad phonetic script chosen for its close phoneme-grapheme fit and for the ease of transition to standard English orthography. One of its key weaknesses is the same as any attempt at a phonological description of English in terms of phonemes: it has trouble with regional, stylistic, and social variations, particularly in vowels.

Linguists, especially those of the Summer Institute of Linguistics, have been very closely concerned with literacy work. In Africa, Central and South America, and Oceania, the establishment of orthographies by missionary-linguists, the translation of the Bible and hymnals, and the mass literacy campaigns, have brought literacy to speakers of hundreds of languages. Linguists have become involved in various ways in language reform and literacy campaigns in Africa and Turkey. But, as Foster (1971) points out, recent experience has raised questions on the economic justification for mass literacy. The lack of evidence of the long-term effects of literacy, the loss of impetus after the first stage, and the huge expense for a developing nation to establish a literate population add dimensions to the question beyond those normally considered by the linguist.

Indeed, if there is to be a single lesson to be drawn from the linguist's interventions in problems of language and education, it is the inadequacy of his preparation to solve the problems. Constantly, the linguist has offered his single-discipline-based panacea, ignoring the contribution of past practitioners or of other disciplines:

when his propaganda is successful, he quickly finds how inadequate his notions are in practice. At the same time, attempts to solve problems of language and education that ignore the implications of linguistics are equally unsatisfactory.

Perhaps some of the blame can be put on the notion of 'applied linguistics', the notion that there are problems waiting to be solved simply by the application of linguistic knowledge. That this is not so only becomes obvious when we look at a specific problem, its 'applied linguistic' solution, and the complexities this ignores. Let us take a case like setting up a bilingual kindergarten for an Indian tribe. The linguistic solution seems quite neat: have vernacular-speaking teachers carry on normal kindergarten activities, and establish appropriate language drills to teach English. The problems this does not touch are enormous in number and complexity: the question of community attitude to school language, the need to find and train vernacular teachers, the absence of vocabulary in the vernacular for normal kindergarten activities, the objections to language drills with five-year-old children, etc. This is not to deny the major implications of various parts of linguistics for the activity. Sociolinguists should offer guidance on community attitudes, and the type of bilingual teachers available; psycholinguists have much to say about the theoretical inadequacy of certain popular language drills; experts in semantics and language planning about problems of modernization and standardization. Implications, yes, but not direct applications.

Part of the problem must lie with the training of those concerned with language and education. In universities, the training of theoretical linguists tends to have a higher status than any of the related applied training. Very few educators are given enough exposure to linguistics to see its relevance to their activities. A few new programs are attempting to train graduates with a solid understanding of contemporary linguistics and a willingness to work out that understanding in the area of education.

Just as linguists can help choose appropriate language education aims and methods, they also have useful things to say about language testing. Examinations and tests have traditionally been used to control language education. Elite education systems tend to set formal barriers at various key stages of the process, and teaching tends to become preparation for these examinations. Emphasis on written examinations, essays, translations, and grammar questions all work against changes in language teaching methods.

New methods of teaching have called for the development of new methods of testing. In the United States, the new confidence in the objective, standardized test has set challenges for the development of item-types that have some relation to the various skills called for. The difficulty of finding a reliable test of more generalized ability has led to an emphasis on strict statistical control. Language tests such as those conducted by Educational Testing Service have extremely high statistical reliability. Such books as Lado (1961) present a method of writing such tests which shows very great similarity to structural linguistic description.

Each linguistic area is presumably to be described, sampled, and tested. But a number of scholars have recently questioned the theoretical base of tests of this sort, and their validity. Tests based on linguistic analysis assume the equal importance of each linguistic item (most psychometric techniques allot equal weight to all items), while in practice functional load certainly varies. Some have called for functional tests, the validity of which is more easily established. Such a testing system as the FSI language rating provides a reasonably reliable and definitely valid measuring stick against which to judge the item-type test. A second weakness of the test based on a linguistic description rather than a sociolinguistic function is its inability to measure the effectiveness of a particular language program. Language teaching materials usually follow a certain gradation in presenting the units of the language: it is theoretically possible to determine from examination of an item-type test and two sets of materials which set of materials will show up best in an experiment. Materials-independent functional tests are needed to evaluate effectiveness of different materials.

The full evaluation of language education will depend on a more effective method of assessing sociolinguistically and psycholinguistically, individual and group communicative competence. Often, the aims of language education go beyond language itself: the ability to function in certain domains with certain effects, is the important thing. The first of these aims must always be the same: the ability for all children to function effectively in the domain of school. Until the language barrier to education is overcome, a large proportion of the world's population is denied full access to education. Linguists have a great deal to offer to help reach this goal.

REFERENCES

ALISJAHBANA, S. T. 1971. Language policy, language engineering and literacy: Indonesia and Malaysia. CTL 8.1087–1109.

ALLEN, HAROLD. 1964. A survey of the teaching of English to non-English speakers. Champaign, Illinois, National Council of Teachers of English.

ANDERSSON, THEODORE, and MILDRED BOYER, eds. 1970. Bilingual schooling in the United States. 2 vols. Washington, D.C., USGPO.

BERNSTEIN, B. 1964. Elaborated and restricted codes: Their social origins and some consequences. AmA 66/2.55–69.

BLOOMFIELD, LEONARD, and CLARENCE L. BARNHARDT. 1961. Let's read, a linguistic approach. Detroit, Michigan, Wayne State University Press.

CHOMSKY, CAROL. 1969. The acquisition of syntax in children from five to ten. Cambridge, Massachusetts, MIT Press.

CHOMSKY, NOAM. 1965. Aspects of the theory of syntax. Cambridge, Massachusetts, MIT Press.

CHOMSKY, NOAM, and MORRIS HALLE. 1968. The sound pattern of English. New York, Harper and Row.

COLEMAN, JAMES S., *et al.* 1966. Equality educational opportunity. National Center for Educational Statistics.

FOSTER, PHILIP J. 1971. Problems of literacy in Sub-Saharan Africa. CTL 7.587–618.

FRIES, CHARLES C. 1962. Linguistics and reading. New York, Holt, Rinehart, and Winston, Inc.

GORDON, SUSAN. 1969. The relationship between the English language abilities and home language experiences of first-grade children from three ethnic groups, of varying socioeconomic status and varying degrees of bilingualism. The University of New Mexico. Unpub. Ph.D. dissertation.

HAUGEN, EINAR. 1966. Language conflict and language planning. Cambridge, Massachusetts, Harvard University Press.

HYMES, D. H. 1962. The ethnography of speaking. Anthropology and human behavior, ed. by T. Gladwin and W. Sturtevant. Washington, D.C., Anthropological Society of Washington.

LABOV, WILLIAM. 1966. The social stratification of English in New York City. Washington, D.C., Center for Applied Linguistics.

——. 1969. The study of non-standard English. ERIC Clearinghouse for Linguistics.

LADO, ROBERT. 1961. Language testing: The construction and use of foreign language tests. New York, McGraw Hill.

LENNEBERG, ERIC H. 1967. Biological foundations of language. New York, John Wiley and Sons, Inc.

McLUHAN, MARSHALL. 1962. The Gutenberg galaxy: The making of typographic man. Toronto, University of Toronto Press.

MACKEY, WILLIAM. 1970. A typology of bilingual education. Foreign Language Annals 3.596–608.

MENYUK, PAULA. 1969. Sentences children use. Cambridge, Massachusetts, MIT Press.

PITMAN, I. J. 1961. Learning to read: An experiment. Journal of the Royal Society of Arts 109.149–80.

SLOBIN, DAN I., ed. 1967. Field manual for the cross-cultural study of the acquisition of communicative competence. Berkeley, University of California.

STEWART, WILLIAM. 1962. An outline of linguistic typology for describing multilingualism. Study of the role of second languages in Asia, Africa, and Latin America, ed. by F. A. Rice, pp. 15–25. Washington, D.C., Center for Applied Linguistics.

LINGUISTICS AND LITERACY

SARAH C. GUDSCHINSKY

1. PRELIMINARIES

1.1 *The Scope of the Paper*

'Linguistics and Literacy' is a broad topic and my first problem is to limit the discussion to a manageable size. First of all, I choose to be programmatic rather than historical, pointing out the need for linguistic research rather than describing ways in which linguistics has been applied to problems of literacy. Most of what might be said about the history of the application of linguistics to problems of teaching reading and writing, with specific examples of such application, has already been detailed elsewhere in this series. (See, for example, chapters on literacy in the Americas, Asia, and Africa in *Current Trends* Vols. 4, 6, 7; and chapters on linguistics and reading in Vols. 10 and 12. For bibliographies of linguistics and reading in the United States, see Broz and Hays 1966, and Goodman and Goodman 1967.)

Secondly, I choose to be original rather than bibliographical. Throughout the paper there are references to literature which exemplifies or illustrates, but there is no attempt to be exhaustive.

Thirdly, I choose to discuss the teaching of reading, and to ignore writing, although both are necessary to complete literacy.

In general, I have ignored the differences between literacy for adults and for children. Most of the examples throughout the paper are taken from literacy programs for adults, but some are from bilingual primary education projects for children.

Although the choice of language and dialect as a medium for instruction is a linguistic problem that affects literacy, I will omit it from this discussion. I assume, however, what seems to me obvious, that the skills of reading and writing can only be taught in a language that the pupil already speaks. This means, of course, that either instruction must be in his mother tongue, or he must learn functional oral control of the language of instruction before he begins reading lessons (see Davis 1967; Gudschinsky 1967b; Hays 1965; Tucker 1952; UNESCO 1953; Wurm 1966).

Although much has been written about orthography, it has traditionally been far too narrowly conceived, and rather than excluding it, I have decided to use it as the core of the paper around which other observations can be organized. The body of the paper, therefore, consists of eight sections: introductory words on the linguist's role (2.1), and the nature of writing systems (2.2), five hierarchically ordered sections which deal with orthography in its widest sense, and its relationship to linguistic problems in literacy. Specifically, at the level of discourse and paragraph (2.3), sentence and phrase (2.4), word (2.5), syllable and morpheme (2.6) and phoneme (2.7). Then, a final word on lexicon (2.8).

I find that in developing this topic, I am torn between a desire to produce a typology of the linguistic and orthographic problems of the world as they relate to the teaching of reading, and a desire to discuss extensively the educational fallacies that might be cured by linguistic insights. I find that in practice I have done neither well. I can only hope that in this sketchy treatment that alternates between these two points of view, the reader will find some intriguing point that will lead him to further reading — or to carrying out some of the needed research.

1.2 *A Linguistic Model*

In the present state of turmoil and opposing models in linguistic theory, it is not easy to talk about the application of 'linguistics' to the problems of literacy, as though it were a monolithic discipline. Some of the earlier discussions of linguistics and reading used the structural model of Bloomfield and his followers (Bloomfield and Barnhart 1961; Fries 1952). More recently there has been considerable interest in psycholinguistics, orthography, and the application of linguistics to reading, on the part of the transformational-generative school. There are also useful insights from the stratificational model and from the scale-and-category model. I have chosen, however, to restrict myself mainly to the framework of tagmemics, the model in which I am most at home. I find particularly useful its emphasis on separate yet interlocking hierarchies of phonology, lexicon, and grammar; the notion of mutually substitutable items in a slot or position; and emphasis on levels of grammar above the sentence. (For discussions of tagmemic theory, see the bibliography in Pike 1966.)

1.3 *A Model of the Reading Process*

As background for further discussion, it will help to have a model of the reading process in mind. A number of such models have been proposed by various psychologists and psycholinguists (e.g. Venezky and Calfee 1970; Carroll 1970; Goodman 1968, 1970; and Rudell 1969. For the purposes of this paper I choose to follow Goodman's (1968) model of four stages of reading competence).

Goodman's model of Stage I competency views the VISUAL INPUT of the beginning reader as including Letters, Letter Patterns, and Whole Word Shapes which are *recoded* to the equivalent Phonemes, Phoneme Patterns, and Word Names, which are then mixed with the AURAL INPUT (which the reader brings to the process from his knowledge of the patterns of his language). This is then further *recoded* to ORAL LANGUAGE which is *decoded* for MEANING.

At Stage II, the reader is able to process larger chunks of the GRAPHIC INPUT, but the process is essentially the same.

At Stage III, however, the proficient reader *decodes* the GRAPHIC INPUT in large chunks direct to MEANING, and must *encode* the meaning to produce an ORAL OUTPUT. (This is why many proficient readers do not read aloud well.) Efficient oral reading is Stage IV, in which the reader simultaneously *decodes* the GRAPHIC INPUT for MEANING, and *recodes* it as ORAL OUTPUT.

1.4 *A Definition of Literacy*

Definitions of literacy have varied from the ability to sign one's name, to completion of a certain standard of elementary education. 'Functional literacy' has been defined as the ability to read and write sufficiently well to function in one's community. None of these definitions, however, provides a satisfying goal for literacy work.

Goodman's Stage III is a more adequate characterization of the reading processes of a fully literate person. My own definition adds reference to language, comprehension, and writing: 'That person is literate, who, in a language he speaks, can read and understand everything that he would have understood if it had been spoken to him; and can write, so that it can be read, everything that he can say' (Gudschinsky 1968b: 146). This degree of literacy implies full control of all the reading skills — control of the written signals for every level of all phases of the linguistic structure.

2. LINGUISTIC PROBLEMS IN LITERACY

2.1 *The Linguist's Role*

The linguist's primary contributions to the making of literacy materials, and decisions regarding teaching methods, include analyses of the linguistic — and psycholinguistic — structure of oral and written language, and the specification of the relationships of these structures to each other and to the writing system. It is of vital concern to the literacy worker to know how the writing system is related to oral language. He needs answers to questions like the following:

1) What units of the language are psycholinguistically real — at what depths of

focus or degree of sophistication (Gudschinsky 1958)? Which units, therefore, can the pupils focus on without special training, and which must they learn to focus on before they can relate them to written counterparts?

2) What chunks of the written language equate with minimum isolable units of the spoken language? Are those phonological units, grammatical units, or lexical units? If the isolable units in the three hierarchies are not isomorphic, how do they relate to each other?

3) Given the information in 1 and 2, what are the minimal pronounceable matrices within which the pupils may be taught to recognize letter-phoneme correspondences? What are the minimum meaningful matrices within which they can be taught to recognize specific morphemes and words? (e.g. a minimal matrix for English *and* is a phrase with two words: John ⸺ Bill. A minimal matrix for English *if* is two clauses: I'll go ⸺ it rains).

4) What elements of the writing system represent written styles that have no direct counterpart in naive speech, and so must be taught as new language rather than as mere recognition?

5) What are the inconsistencies of the orthography? Is there overdifferentiation of phonemes? Underdifferentiation? Other problems?

2.2. *The Nature of Writing Systems*

It is the thesis of this section, and the ones that follow, that to whatever extent writing systems symbolize spoken language, they represent in some measure all the levels of the three hierarchies: the lexical, the phonological, and the grammatical. This representation is usually incomplete, and the mixture of the hierarchies varies from one orthography to another, depending on the exigencies of the particular language, the bias of the orthography maker, or historical and sociological factors.

Orthographies have traditionally been viewed as devices for representing phonemes or morphophonemes by graphemes, with more or less accuracy depending on social pressures. Even linguists who share in devising orthographies have by and large taken this narrow view, so that the representation of higher levels of the phonology, and interlocking levels of the grammar and lexicon, is more by accident than design. Nor have any complete analyses of existing orthographies been made from a wider point of view. Even the recent investigation of English orthography by Venezky (1967), which relates graphemes to morphophonemes rather than to simple phonemes and so includes grammatical representation, fails to consider other aspects of the writing system.

It should be recognized at this point that an orthography represents more than the spoken language, even though that may have been the whole of its initial purpose. Inevitably when people write their language, they develop a written style that differs in some respects from their oral styles. (There are unpublished reports of the development of such written styles in the Aguaruna and Amhuesha languages of Peru.) These written styles, however, can be read aloud and some elements of them may find their way into the oral styles of the reader, so that our model of orthography is as follows:

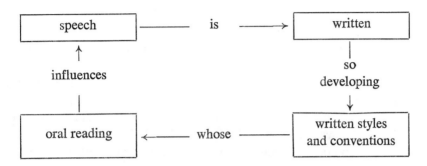

Thus one might hazard a guess that semicolon, some uses of parentheses, etc. arose in English orthography to meet needs in special written styles. These are matched, however, by certain elements of voice quality and intonation in the oral reading of such written material. The oral conventions in turn may be used in a formal speech, which in a measure mimics written style, but they are relatively rare in informal colloquial speech. (For example, the professor may say in a seminar or committee meeting: 'X is important because: a) ..., b) ..., and c) ...' but he does not converse with his small son in that style.)

2.3 Discourse and Paragraph

The largest linguistic levels relevant to the teaching of reading to beginners are discourse and paragraph — the 'stories' or 'connected material' of the beginning textbook — and their internal structure. In literacy materials for ethnic minorities, they tend to be the most neglected levels. In methods that begin with word or syllable, the use of connected material is sometimes delayed until late in the teaching sequence. Little attention is paid to naturalness of discourse genre and style, and even less to teaching the orthographic signals of discourse structure.

   There is a need for linguistic and cultural studies of discourse genre. Which are most appropriate for the beginning readers of various ages and backgrounds? Which of the written genres most closely approximate the oral language that the pupil already controls? It is traditional to use narrative for children's primers, and narrative or didactic how-to-do-it texts for adults. Are these the best choices? Would dialogue be closer to the spoken language? Or would well known poetry from the oral literature make a better starting point? There are scattered instances of imaginative choices that have been effective (e.g. an adult literacy text in one of the languages of Mozambique that begins with a song; and others described in section 2.8), but there has been no real study of the general principles involved.

An even greater problem is the production of the connected material for the literacy textbooks. In the writing of such material some restrictions are necessary if the pupil is to learn the elements of reading in a gradual and orderly way. Alternative kinds of restrictions are discussed in section 2.8, but we are concerned here with the effect of such restrictions on readability and style.

For many educators the notion of 'simplicity' in story writing requires restriction of the number of words used, and restriction of the variety of sentence patterns. The result is an unnatural 'primerese' in which, at its worst, the reader can neither find sufficient clues for guessing what the author has said, nor check on the correctness of what he has read. But the reader's ability to match a sampling of the text against his own knowledge of the language, and his ability to anticipate the author are essential to smooth reading (Carroll 1970; Goodman 1968 and 1970; and Venezky and Calfee 1970). This means that there is need for new, linguistically defined, criteria for simplicity and readability which take into account the degree to which the text matches the reader's expectations.

In linguistic theory there is a growing emphasis on the analysis of discourse and paragraph structure. See, for example, Fries (1952) on initiating and sequence sentences; Waterhouse (1963) on independent and dependent sentences; Bridgeman (1966) on paragraph structure; Wise (1968) on pronominal reference within discourse; and Longacre (1968) on paragraph and sentence within discourse, and many others. There is a lack of studies relating this level of linguistic analysis to readability, however. To what extent is readability impaired when the use of pronouns, functors, or sequence markers is limited in order to reduce the number of words used in a story? To what extent is it impaired by limitations on the choice of sentence types, or by unusual repetition of nouns or verbs? Are some styles more readable than others? Is readability of style a function of reading experience? Or are easy styles the same for beginners and for fluent readers?

There have been some tests of readability in use for some time. The interested reader will find a bibliography of readability and reading in Dale and Seele 1966; material on tests of naturalness and style in Grimes 1963, Gudschinsky 1967a, Larson 1967, and Moore 1964; and a first study of the relationship of sentence structure to readability in Schlesinger 1968.

It is not usually recognized that the devices that signal the boundaries of discourse and paragraph are part of the orthography. Discourse is usually set off by space, or sometimes by pictures or designs. It may have a title and/or a closure formula also set off by space and by capital letters or special type. Literacy teachers quite generally ignore the teaching of these devices. Apparently they expect the beginners to absorb an awareness of them incidentally. This does not always happen, however. There are reports of relatively fluent readers in some Amerindian groups who begin or end their reading where a page begins or ends — even in the middle of a hyphenated word — paying no attention to the beginning or ending of discourses.

The various kinds of discourse structure are also signaled in the orthography — and largely ignored in the teaching. Paragraphs are marked by indentation and/or wide vertical spacing at the beginning and end. Confusion for the pupil arises out of the fact that the units marked in this way are not always linguistically equivalent. The paragraphs of narrative or didactic text may be either lexical or grammatical divisions of the discourse, or both. Quotation paragraphs, on the other hand, usually signal change of speaker and cut directly across the lexical and grammatical units — e.g. in the following example, the quotation break occurs in the middle of a grammatical sentence:

'He is on his way —'
'Home?'

In poetry, wide spacing may signal stanzas which can be lexical or grammatical units, but which may well be primarily phonological units. (Note also the special use of capitals, line length, and diacritics such as apostrophe and accent to mark special phonological phenomena in poetry.)

For effective literacy teaching, the educator should know the linguistic correlates of orthographic signals at discourse and paragraph level. With this knowledge he can plan explicit lessons to help the beginner respond to these signals and make use of them in his comprehension of what he reads.

2.4 *Sentence and Phrase*

Sentence and clause levels are distinguished in tagmemic descriptions of language, but this distinction is somewhat less fruitful in the teaching of reading. It is relevant, however, to note that sentences are structural elements within paragraph and discourse. The notion that the sentence is the largest structural unit in language is responsible for many awkward pseudo-paragraphs in literacy materials.

Sentences are marked orthographically by a wider space than words, by terminal punctuation, and in many languages by capital letters. The sentence as such is usually a grammatical structure but the terminal punctuation may represent grammatical or lexical contrasts, or termination of a phonological structure, or various combinations of these. An analysis of English punctuation is beyond the scope of this paper, but the reader can easily find for himself instances of the use of the period and question mark to distinguish grammatical categories of affirmation and query even when the intonation is the same, and other instances that distinguish both the grammatical categories and contrastive intonation patterns. He can also find instances of exclamation points and italics signaling emphasis or focus which may belong high in the lexical hierarchy. Semicolon and period, both representing the end of grammatical sentences, may signal contrast between final and non-final intonation.

The exact role of punctuation and capital letters is not usually made explicit in the formulation of new orthographies or in the study of traditional ones (but see LeFevre 1964).

The deeper psycholinguistic problems with regard to how punctuation should be read by a beginner cannot be solved except on the basis of analyses of its linguistic meaning. Should the pupil be led to see the grammatical or lexical correlates of the punctuation in the expectation that correct intonation will follow? Or should he be taught the intonational equivalents in the expectation that this will lead to the understanding of the grammatical and lexical relationships? Answers to these questions will surely vary from language to language, as the precise interlocking of lexical, grammatical, and phonological criteria for punctuation vary.

There is clear evidence, however, that the reading of punctuation must be taught. Fox (1961) reports that in Quiché of Guatemala some rare but natural sentence orders are difficult to read. The readers ignore periods and attach subordinate elements from the beginning of such a sentence to the end of the preceding one — where subordinate elements are more likely to occur. From other sources there are reports of readers who treat each line of print as a sentence — with consequent loss of intelligibility.

Problems of phrases within the sentence are similar to the problem of sentences. Such phrases may be either grammatical or phonological or both. In many languages grammatical and phonological phrases are not coterminous. In Tzeltal of Mexico, for example, the pronominal verb prefix *s-* is attached phonologically to a preceding open syllable rather than to the following verb — even if the open syllable belongs to a subject noun phrase or a locational phrase, and not to the verb phrase at all. In such languages should space and comma be used to represent phonological phrase breaks, or to represent grammatical phrase breaks? And whichever choice is made in the orthography, how should the pupils be taught to read it?

Further problems of phrasing result from various kinds of sandhi within phrases. In Aymara of Bolivia, for example, many words have a final contrastive vowel that is lost within a phrase. Writing these vowels everywhere resulted in a tendency toward slow word-by-word reading, and hindered the development of fluency. Omitting the vowels from words within phrases forced the teaching of reading by phrases.

Fox (1961) also comments on problems of slow versus fast speech forms in the orthography of Quiché — essentially a choice between word and phrase as a spelling unit.

Other kinds of punctuation may be used primarily for the conventions of written style: e.g. colon, semicolon, parentheses, indentation of lists, footnote numbers, numbers or letters in parentheses, etc. What is the relationship of these conventions to oral language? At what point should they come into the teaching sequence, and how? To what extent do they pose a psycholinguistic problem to the naive reader? To what extent can they, or should they, be introduced into the orthographies of newly written languages?

2.5 *Word*

Words are usually considered to be the most basic units in the teaching of reading (Chall 1967; Fries 1962; Gray 1956). Educators talk of 'word attack skills', 'word analysis', 'word recognition' and sentences are conceived as built from words. Words are also the most prominent elements in the orthography — each separated from the others by word space. There are serious problems of orthography, psycholinguistic reality, and pedagogy at the word level, however.

Not all languages make the same use of the orthographic device of word space. In English the criteria are primarily grammatical with little reference to phonological isolability: e.g. *a* is written as a separate word although it is phonologically bound to the word which follows it, as is the infinitive marker *to* which is phonologically bound to a preceding main verb. In Mixtec and Mazatec of Mexico, on the other hand, hyphens are used to group clitics with grammatical words to form phonological words (Gudschinsky 1958; Hunter and E. V. Pike 1969; E. V. Pike 1956). There is need of more research to determine the best use of word space and hyphen in new orthographies, and to determine the psycholinguistic status of the units that are written as words.

Oddly enough, the educators and linguists-turned-educators who consider word to be the basic unit for the teaching of reading seem to have overlooked the fact that orthographic word does not necessarily represent intuitive units in the speech of the naive speakers of the language (but cf. Goodman 1969). Naive speakers differ in the ease with which they can use content words in isolation, but very few can isolate functors such as *the* or *at* without considerable teaching and sophistication.

In teaching reading I follow Fries (1952) in making a sharp distinction between content words and functors — often including function affixes as well as clitics and particles in the latter group. I advocate that pupils be taught strategies for equating symbol with phoneme (or morphophoneme) in the recognition of content words, but that they be taught to recognize entire functors at sight in context. Thus the functors provide the grammatical framework for the decoding of content words. This implies a literacy textbook in which lessons introducing new letters alternate with lessons introducing new functors, so that every lesson can be practiced by reading linguistically natural connected material (Gudschinsky 1968b, 1969b, 1970).

To produce such material, the literacy worker needs considerable information about the functors: Which are obligatory for the various discourse genre, paragraph types, and sentence and clause types? Which are rare (like *inasmuch* in English) and can be disregarded in the basic literacy lessons? Which are virtually automatic, needing little teaching (like the -*s* suffix on third person singular verbs)? Which are in contrastive sets that must be carefully taught (like English prepositions)? Which approach content words in their isolability (like *up* and *down* which are used by small American children as complete utterances)?

2.6 *Syllable and Morpheme*

Both syllable and morpheme may be important units in the teaching of reading, and both are relevant to at least some orthographies. Some languages — Amharic, for example — are written with syllabaries. Arabic and some of the Indian scripts use allographs to make syllable structure evident (see Butt 1967 on this phenomena in the Devanagari script used in writing Hindi). There are a few languages, such as Apinayé of Brazil, in which syllable boundary is contrastive, and has to be written in some words to prevent ambiguity (Burgess and Ham 1968). There are also languages like Mazatec of Mexico in which syllable boundary is marked as a by-product of the writing of tone (Gudschinsky 1959).

The primary usefulness of a syllable in the teaching of reading is as a pronounce-able matrix for the recognition of letters or digraphs (Gudschinsky 1968a). Non-linguists have supposed that the 'reality' of phonemes means that naive speakers could recognize and manipulate the phonemes of their language in isolation. This is not true, of course, except in situations where there are cultural pressures toward the abstraction of phonemes. In Huautla Mazatec, for example, the men communi-cate by whistling the tones alone, so they have no difficulty in abstracting tone phonemes. The use of tongue twisters and Pig Latin in word play helps some Americans to focus on initial consonants. In general, however, the naive speaker of a language tends to react to the phonemes as points in the contrast between lexical items rather than as abstract units and he must be taught to manipulate them. Attempts to pronounce phonemes in complete isolation produce distorted allophones unlike the actual pronunciation of the phoneme in any normal occur-rence. The use of a pronounceable matrix — such as a syllable — permits the perception of the phonemes and the letters that represent them as mutually sub-stitutable items in specific positions.

It should be noted, however, that in some languages a single syllable is not pro-nounceable, rather all isolated forms have a minimum of two syllables, and a couplet replaces syllable as the matrix for letter recognition. Couplets are also useful ma-trices for the recognition of letters with limited distribution: e.g. Spanish ñ which does not occur utterance initial, or the intervocalic single and double consonants of English which signal the quality of the preceding vowel (Glass 1969; Gudschinsky 1969a, 1970; Shand 1970).

The morpheme is important to the orthographies of languages in which some morphophonemic writing is needed. Venezky (1967) has described the English writing system in terms of morphophonemics. Gudschinsky (1958) describes the tone orthography of Soyaltepec Mazatec as partly phonemic and partly morphophonemic, giving the psycholinguistic evidence on which the choices were based. There are no broad-based criteria for deciding when to use phonemic writing and when to use morphophonemic, however. There are few studies of the psycholinguistic reality of morphophonemes, and even fewer of their relationship to phonemes (but see Newman 1968).

The morpheme may be a better teaching matrix than the syllable in the case of functors (see section 2.5), or in the case of morphophonemic writing. The effect of morphophonemic writing is to keep the spelling of all the allomorphs of a particular morpheme uniform, leaving it to the reader to make the phonemic changes required by various contexts. Eunice Pike (private communication) has suggested that phonologically conditioned allomorphs should be written morphophonemically, and that grammatically conditioned allomorphs should be written phonemically. This appears to be a reasonable solution in some cases (e.g. the English plurals -*s* vs. -*en*), but there are too few careful studies of the problem to assess its universality of application.

2.7 *Phoneme*

At phoneme level, we come finally to the elements that are often considered to 'be' the orthography — the letters and letter groups that represent the phonemes or morphophonemes of the language. These include the symbols used to represent lexical tone, nasalization, stress, or other suprasegmental phonemes, as well as the consonants and vowels. It is at this level that orthography is usually discussed (e.g. Berry 1958; Gudschinsky 1959; Ohannessian 1969; Sjoberg 1966; Smalley 1964).

In languages written with an alphabet, the letters, diagraphs, etc. represent phonemes more or less consistently. Traditional alphabets, of course, may continue to represent phonemic contrasts long since lost from the spoken language — e.g. the *c* and *s* which represent Mexican Spanish /s/, where Castillian had a contrast between /θ/ and /s/. Some new orthographies inherit inconsistencies from the prestige orthography they are modeled after — e.g. the use of *c* before back vowels and *qu* before front vowels to represent /k/ in Amerindian orthographies in Latin American countries where Spanish or Portuguese is the national language.

Many of the most severe problems of orthography making are a matter of phonemic interpretation, and sometimes these problems can be solved with psycholinguistic testing. Among the more dramatic examples of this are the Maxakalí of Brazil and the Brôu of Vietnam. Gudschinsky and the Popoviches (1970) present the evidence that in Maxakalí some sequences that are etically two syllables of the shape [CVCV] are emically single syllables of the shape /CVC/. Johnston (1968) presents evidence for 41 contrastive syllable nuclei in Brôu, along with the evidence for specific parameters of contrast including tense-lax, normal-short, and simple-glided.

The psycholinguistic data can be very complex, however, and the results of testing are not always the same for the bilingual as for the monolingual, nor for the educated person as for the naive illiterate. A Mazatec informant who is bilingual in Spanish may hear the allophones of his back vowel as /o/ and /u/ and be surprised if he discovers that he is not always consistent in making such a contrast. The educated Hindi speaker 'feels' the presence of a schwa vowel in words where the orthography implies it, even though he never actually pronounces a schwa in that position. The new literate in Hindi, however, who is led by the orthography to pronounce a schwa in that position, does not recognize the resulting word because it differs from the way he says it. Note also that a mature reader of English has difficulty in reading such sequences as: 'I went two see him', or 'I want to much' (see also Fries and Pike 1949).

Literacy programs can be built on even very inadequate orthographies, provided that the inadequacies are taken into account in the teaching process. Specifically, the person making literacy textbooks, and planning the course of instruction, should know exactly how the spelling differs from the phonemic analysis of the language. This includes overdifferentiation, in which a single phoneme is represented in more than one way; underdifferentiation in which some contrasts are not symbolized; irregularities of various kinds in which certain morphemes have unique spellings; ambiguities in which clusters and digraphs are not distinguishable, or in which syllable boundary is ambiguous, and the like.

The literacy worker also needs to know of the ambiguities which are a part of the language itself. Is there neutralization of contrast at some points? Are the phonemic elements written with the same letter in different positions psycholinguistically equivalent? (In some Vietnamese languages, for example, what is written as a normal vowel in open syllable equates with the short vowel rather than the normal one in checked syllables, so that the two occurrences of the same symbol cannot be equated as same in the teaching of reading.) Some inadequacies cannot be compensated for, however. If too many crucial contrasts are omitted from the orthography no amount of practice can eliminate the ambiguities (e.g. Longacre 1970).

2.8 *Lexicon*

One of the most important linguistic aspects of a literacy program is the choice of vocabulary for the basic textbook and for the follow-up literature. There have been two basic fallacies in the practice of educators. On the one hand, they have 'simplified' material by limiting the vocabulary used, and on the other hand they have chosen the vocabulary from lists of 'the most frequently used words'. Unfortunately, neither of these procedures is justified by the linguistic facts.

The formulas for limiting the vocabulary have included rules for the repetition of every word that is used. This leads to unnatural and boring style. It also prevents the use of vivid colorful words that are needed for specific stories, but cannot easily be repeated. In general, the rationale for such limitation is the notion that the pupil is learning to recognize words as such, and requires a certain number of repetitions for effective learning (see my earlier work, Gudschinsky 1951, for a statement of this point of view).

There are serious problems with this approach, however. There is psychological evidence that mature readers recognize words by internal detail rather than by 'whole word shape' (Carroll 1970). There is also ample pragmatic evidence that readers who depend on whole word recognition as their only strategy do not develop into good readers.

My present point of view is quite different. Functors and content words should be treated differently. The functors should be recognized as wholes on sight, but they are repeated often enough in normal text that artificial repetition is not necessary. The most frequent and familiar content words may also eventually be recognized at sight, but this is not the goal of beginning reading instruction. Rather the pupil should be taught to perfect his strategies for figuring out words that he does not recognize instantly. This means repetition of letters in certain positions in syllables or couplets, rather than repetition of content words as such. And this in turn leaves the way open for the use of a larger vocabulary, and the inclusion of some words that occur only a few times.

But how should the words be chosen? By frequency? But frequency in what? And by what kind of a count? The old method of choosing the most frequent words in running text meant, of course, that many functors were included (since the old counts did not distinguish between functors and content words). But it also often meant an artificial frequency depending on the particular type of text chosen for counting. Surely it is not important that a particular speaker may have used a particular word several times in a single text. Far more important is the percentage of the potential audience that uses that particular word. That is, 'frequency' of a word should not be counted in terms of its repetition in a particular body of text, but in terms of its use by a certain number of people. This kind of vocabulary count, obviously, is much more difficult and there is a need for experiment and research in techniques for making it.

Vocabulary is not a disembodied list of disconnected words. Vocabulary is embedded in a universe of discourse, limited by co-occurrence restrictions, used in a certain social register, by persons in certain sex, age, and occupational roles. Intuitive native speakers of a language may be able to choose appropriate vocabulary for a given audience without elaborate linguistic studies. Where materials are being prepared largely by non-participants in the culture, however (as is often the case in small minority languages in out-of-the-way places), there is serious need for better vocabulary studies.

The limitation of vocabulary in a beginning textbook to words made with certain letters does not necessarily mean dull or wooden content. This was illustrated at a workshop for the production of adult literacy primers at Literacy House, Lucknow,

India. All of the primers made at the workshop began with a very few letters, and added others one per lesson. In all of the primers, the introduction of letters alternated with the introduction of functors. The Oriya primer was written by a journalist. His primer contains a continued story of lurid melodrama. He introduces the town beggar, the loan shark, adultery, murder, suicide — and ends with the two main antagonists killing each other. The Telegu primer was written by a poet. Each word was chosen for its poetic quality, and the stories sing like Telegu poetry from the very beginning.

A further illustration comes from a primer production workshop in Vietnam. There the couple working on the Koho primer built into it their deep sense of the culture of the people. A highlander and a lowlander have a discussion. The highlander wonders how the lowlander can stand to eat rice grown in a wet paddy — or to work where the crocodiles eat the children. The lowlander in turn criticizes the sticky rice grown in a dry field, and wonders how the highlander can get along with the man-eating tigers in the hills. A reader from either dialect can identify with the speaker from his own area — and feel at home in a primer made with severe limitations on the use of letters.

REFERENCES

BERRY, J. 1958. The making of alphabets. PICL 8.752–64.

BLOOMFIELD, LEONARD, and CLARANCE L. BARNHART. 1961. Let's read, a linguistic approach. Detroit, Wayne State Univ. Press.

BRIDGEMAN, LORAINE IRENE. 1966. Oral paragraphs in Kaiwa (Guarani). Univ. of Indiana dissertation.

BROZ, JAMES, JR., and ALFRED S. HAYES. 1966. Linguistics and reading: A selective annotated bibliography for teachers of reading. Washington, D.C., Center for Applied Linguistics.

BURGESS, EUNICE, and PATRICIA HAM. 1968. Multilevel conditioning of phoneme variants in Apinayé. Linguistics 41.5–18.

BUTT, HELEN. 1967. Integrated literacy method. Haryana, India, Kurukshetra University Press.

CARROLL, JOHN B. 1970. The nature of the reading process. Theoretical models and processes of reading, ed. by Harry Singer and Robert B. Ruddell, pp. 292–303. Newark, Delaware, International Reading Association.

CHALL, JEANNE S. 1967. Learning to read: The great debate. New York, McGraw-Hill.

DALE, EDGAR, and BARBARA SEELE. 1966. Readability and reading. Annotated bibliography no. 10. Newark, Delaware, International Reading Association.

DAVIS, FREDERICK B. 1967. Philippine language-teaching experiments. Philippine Center for Language Study monograph series no. 5. Quezon City, Philippines, Phoenix Press.

Fox, David G. 1961. Some psycholinguistic considerations in Quiché literacy. A Cameron Townsend, ed. by Benjamin F. Elson and Juan Comas, pp. 265–72. Mexico D.F., Summer Institute of Linguistics.

Fries, Charles C. 1952. The structure of English: An introduction to the construction of English sentences. New York, Harcourt, Brace.

——. 1962. Linguistics and reading. New York, Holt, Rinehart, and Winston.

Fries, C. C. and Kenneth L. Pike. 1949. Coexistent phonemic systems. Lg Literacy 7.17–18.

Glass, Amee. 1969. A problem in Ngaanyatajara primer construction. Notes on

Goodman, Kenneth S. 1968. The psycholinguistic nature of the reading process. The psycholinguistic nature of the reading process, ed. by Kenneth S. Goodman, pp. 13–26. Detroit, Wayne State Univ. Press.

——. 1969. Words and morphemes in reading. Psycholinguistics and the teaching of reading, ed. by Kenneth S. Goodman and James T. Fleming, pp. 25–33. Newark, Delaware, International Reading Association.

——. 1970. Reading: A psycholinguistic guessing game. Theoretical models and processes of reading, ed. by Harry Singer and Robert B. Ruddell, pp. 259–71. Newark, Delaware, International Reading Association.

Goodman, Yetta M., and Kenneth S. Goodman. 1967. Linguistics and the teaching of reading. Annotated bibliography no. 13. Newark, Delaware, International Reading Association.

Gray, William S. 1956. The teaching of reading and writing. Paris, UNESCO.

Grimes, Joseph E. 1963. Measuring 'naturalness' in a translation. BT 14/2.49–62.

Gudschinsky, Sarah C. 1951. Handbook of literacy. Santa Ana, Calif., Summer Institute of Linguistics.

——. 1958. Native reaction to tones and words in Mazatec. Word 14.338–45.

——. 1959. Toneme representation in Mazatec orthography. Word 15.446–52.

——. 1967a. Frequency counts, naturalness, and style. Notes on Translation 28.12–14.

——. 1967b. Techniques for functional literacy in indigenous languages and the national language. El simposio de Bloomington, 1964, pp. 221–29. Bogotá, Instituto Caro y Cuervo.

——. 1968a. Highlights of the 1967 Vietnam workshop: Syllable teaching. Notes on Literacy 2.1–3.

——. 1968b. The relationship of language and linguistics to reading. Kivung 1/3.146–52.

——. 1969a. Matrix for letter recognition: Syllable or couplet. Notes on Literacy 4.4–7.

——. 1969b. The role of the linguist in the preparation of materials for the teaching or reading. To appear in Actas of the Fourth Symposium of the Inter American Program for Linguistics and Language Teaching at Sao Paulo, Brazil.

——. 1970. Psycholinguistics and reading: Diagnostic observation. Reading difficulties: Diagnosis, correction, and remediation, ed. by William K. Durr, pp. 154–63. Newark, Delaware, International Reading Association.

GUDSCHINSKY, S. C., and HAROLD and FRANCES POPOVICH. 1970. Native reaction and phonetic similarity in Maxakalí phonology. Lg 46.77–88.

HAYS, ALFRED S., ed. 1965. Recommendations of the work conference on literacy. Washington, D.C., Center for Applied Linguistics.

HUNTER, GEORGIA G., and EUNICE V. PIKE. 1969. The phonology and tone sandhi of Molinas Mixtec. Linguistics 47.24–40.

JOHNSTON, EUGENIA. 1968. Some psycholinguistic aspects of Brôu literacy problems. LL 18.15–27.

LARSON, MILDRED L. 1967. The relationship of frequency count and function. Notes on Translation 28.14–16.

LEFEVRE, CARL A. 1964. Linguistics and the teaching of reading. New York, McGraw-Hill.

LONGACRE, ROBERT E. 1968. Philippine languages: Discourse, paragraph and sentence structure. SIL Publications in Linguistics and Related Fields, 21. Santa Ana, Calif., Summer Institute of Linguistics.

——. 1970. An experiment in testing the reading of Trique without indication of tone. Notes on Literacy 8.1–3.

MOORE, BRUCE R. 1964. Second thoughts on measuring 'naturalness'. BT 15/2.83–87.

NEWMAN, PAUL. 1968. The reality of morphophonemes. Lg 44.507–15.

OHANNESSIAN, SIRARPI. 1969. Conference on Navajo orthography. Washington, D.C., Center for Applied Linguistics.

PIKE, EUNICE V. 1956. Tonally differentiated allomorphs in Soyaltepec Mazatec. IJAL 22.57–71.

PIKE, KENNETH L. 1966. A guide to publications related to tagmemic theory. CTL 3.365–94.

RUDDELL, ROBERT B. 1969. Psycholinguistic implications for a systems of communication model. Psycholinguistics and the teaching of reading, ed. by Kenneth S. Goodman and James T. Fleming, pp. 61–78. Newark, Delaware, International Reading Association.

SCHLESINGER, I. M. 1968. Sentence structure and the reading process. JanL series minor 69.

SHAND, JEAN. 1970. Couplets Manobo. Notes on Literacy 8.24–26.

SJOBERG, ANDRÉE F. 1966. Socio-cultural and linguistic factors in the development of writing systems for preliterate peoples. Sociolinguistics, ed. by William Bright, pp. 260–76. The Hague, Mouton.

SMALLEY, WILLIAM A., ed. 1964. Orthography studies, articles on new writing systems. Amsterdam, The United Bible Societies.

TUCKER, A. N. 1952. The linguistic aspect of mass literacy movements. Symposium on popular education, Leiden, pp. 1–18.

UNESCO. 1953. The use of vernacular languages in education. Monographs on Fundamental Education 8.

VENEZKY, RICHARD L. 1967. English orthography: Its graphical structure and its relation to sound. RRQ 2/3.75–105.

VENEZKY, R. L., and ROBERT C. CALFEE. 1970. The reading competence model. Theoretical models and processes of reading, ed. by Harry Singer and Robert B. Ruddell, pp. 273–91. Newark, Delaware, International Reading Association.

WATERHOUSE, VIOLA G. 1963. Independent and dependent sentences. IJAL 29.45–54.

WISE, MARY RUTH. 1968. Identification of participants in discourse: A study of aspects of form and meaning in Nomatsiguenga. Univ. of Michigan dissertation.

WURM, S. A. 1966. Language and literacy. New Guinea on the threshold, ed. by E. K. Fisk, pp. 135–48. Canberra, Australian National University.

THEORETICAL AND EXPERIMENTAL BASES FOR TEACHING READING

RICHARD L. VENEZKY

1. INTRODUCTION

1.1 *Purpose*

Reading is by any definition a complex process involving perceptual, linguistic and cognitive skills which themselves are not well understood. When confronted with something he recognizes as writing, the competent reader can locate an appropriate starting point for scanning, guide his eyes to fixation points, recognize words and some phrases as whole units, sense syntactic/semantic boundaries, generate expectations for words outside of his immediate vision, and 'understand' what the text says. He is also capable of translating written material into its oral form, both through sight recognition of familiar words (whose pronunciations he then retrieves as integrated units) and through application of letter-sound generalizations. Most of these skills are lacking in the child before he learns to read; in addition, the prereading child may not understand what reading is all about; that letters between spaces and other terminal markers can be translated into recognizable words and that the words together convey information, just as in oral communication.

The purpose of reading instruction is to aid children in the development of the skills possessed by a competent reader, which are, at a minimum:
1. An understanding of the reading process.
2. Appropriate scanning behavior.
3. Letter and word recognition.
4. Letter-sound generalizations.
5. Comprehension of written materials at least to the degree that the reader can comprehend the same message when received aurally.

This article is concerned with the nature of these skills and how they are acquired by healthy, normal children who learn to read their native language. It will not be concerned with either adult literacy or native literacy, or with reading disabilities that can be attributed to brain damage, emotional disturbances, or to the vagaries commonly lumped under the title of dyslexia.

It will first establish what the goals of reading instruction are by exploring further certain of the reading skills of literates; then, the development of reading skills will be described, and finally, the problems of teaching some of these skills to children will be discussed, with emphasis on the linguistic aspects of reading and in particular, the learning of letter-sound correspondences. The basis of this article is the experimental studies of reading and reading-related skills performed over the last 100 years by psychologists, linguists, and educators, among others. Special attention will be given to the present author's own work on orthography, started in collaboration with the late Ruth H. Weir at Stanford University, and on basic reading skills, done in collaboration with Robert C. Calfee at the University of Wisconsin.

This article will not be concerned with the merits of any particular reading programs, either existing or imagined, nor will it pick over the relative merits of phonics, whole-word, ita, or any of the other shibboleths of current reading practitioners. The major concern will be to understand what reading is and how it develops, so that a firm basis for teaching reading can be established.

1.2 On the Definition of Reading

The importance of literacy in modern society and the long and confusing history of reading instruction, spanning several millenia of comparing Method A to Method B, are adequately covered elsewhere, and will not be discussed here.[1] But the definition of reading, because of its importance in evaluating the outcome of reading instruction, requires clarification.

Reading is the translation from writing to a form of language from which the reader already is able to derive meaning. By this definition, reading is restricted to processes involving languages with which the reader can communicate by means other than reading (for all except the deaf and dumb, by speech). In addition, reading depends heavily upon the existing language habits of the reader, perhaps more so for the beginning reader than for the experienced one, but nevertheless, they form the basis upon which literacy is acquired. For the beginning reader the form of language mentioned in the definition above is usually overt speech, since this is, for practical reasons, the form of language which is easiest to manipulate in an instructional setting. As basic reading habits are established, the form of language gradually shifts to subvocalized speech, then to a more internal form that I will not attempt to define specifically.[2] The basic assumption here is that many of the same

[1] The most scholarly treatments of the history of reading methodology are Mathews (1966) and Chapter 1 of Fries (1963). On the history of reading research, there is no single, comprehensive source. Anderson and Dearborn (1952) discuss many of the early studies as does Gray (1925). The most concise summary of both methodology and research was made by Barton (1963:249): 'It does appear . . . from an analysis of manuals, texts on reading instruction, introductions to readers, and similar advice to teachers over the last 150 years, that almost all of the issues raised in the last ten years were being raised long before there was any such thing as educational research.'

[2] Subvocal speech in reading was studied experimentally for the first time at the end of the

language habits used in listening are available for reading; how they are utilized by the reader depends upon his reading ability and upon the particular reading task. Speed reading and rapid skimming, for example, utilize considerably different language habits than does more deliberate reading.

The emphasis in this definition for the teaching of reading is on the existing language and comprehension abilities of the reader. These, regardless of what they are, are what he must utilize in reading. Mismatches between the language and content of the reading material and the language and understanding of the reader are potential barriers for learning to read; or in different terms, if the learner can not understand the material when it is presented to him orally, he will have considerably more difficulty attempting to read it. Learning to read should not be confused with reading; in the latter situation, reading can be used to introduce new words, ideas, or language forms, but in the former task these are hindrances to achieving the intended goal.

Reading is not simply translation from writing to speech; that procedure, often called decoding, can be part of reading and appears to be a necessary ability for initial reading in normal children, but is not within itself reading. A person may learn to pronounce Hebrew or Russian from their respective orthographies, yet the acquisition of this skill does not result in an understanding of Hebrew or Russian texts. In the other extreme, reading is not translating from writing to meaning; that is reading plus some other abilities. A lawyer may have difficulty obtaining meaning from writings on microbiology and a microbiologist may have difficulty interpreting legal tracts, yet both might be competent readers within their own fields or within technically neutral fields. The writing-to-meaning definition would be acceptable if it could be shown that written language were so different from speech that the extraction of meaning required knowledge of numerous language structures and forms which did not occur in speaking. But this is simply not true for English or any other known language. There are, obviously, differences between writing and speech, and there are forms of writing, like legal tracts, that are difficult to understand orally, but the disjunction of writing and speech pales in comparison to the conjunction.

While this belaboring of definition may appear pedantic — and would be in many other disciplines – it is prompted by the identification of definition and teaching procedure which has pervaded the field of reading over the past 50 years. From the writing-to-speech definition comes a purblind concentration on oral reading, enunciation, and meaningless syllables; from the comprehension view, an

---

nineteenth century, and extensively in recent years by Edfeldt (1960) and Hardyck and Petrinovich (1969). But neither the role of subvocal speech nor the nature of the subvocalizations themselves has been clarified. Subvocalizing may be no more than a mechanism for decreasing silent reading speed when perception or comprehension becomes difficult. On the other hand, it might aid in the comprehension of difficult material by providing a phonological image for the reader to 'listen to'.

equally nihilistic devotion, but to meaningful units and comprehension rather than to sound units. The definition offered here is not a compromise of these extremes. It is an attempt to emphasize the distinctive processes that logically characterize the reading process, which by necessity requires attention both to sound and meaning, without assigning central roles to those that are common to other modes of communication.

1.3 *The Relationship Between Linguistics and Reading*

As a final introductory note, two important distinctions must be made. The first distinction is between the structure of a component of reading and the appropriate techniques for teaching skills based upon that structure. Or, stated differently, the first distinction is between a knowledge of the subject matter and a knowledge of the learner. There is a structure to both language and to English orthography, and it is to the credit of both Bloomfield and Fries that they labored long and hard to impress these facts upon those most responsible for the teaching of reading. But it was the failing of both to assume that knowledge of language and orthography was not only a necessary condition for deciding how reading was to be taught, but also a sufficient one. Reading involves language, but it also involves perception and cognition, no matter how they are defined, and no amount of ordering of phonemes, morphemes, letter-sound correspondences, or any of the other paraphernalia of modern linguistics can by itself produce an efficient pedagogy. Knowing the exact relationship between letters and sounds does not completely determine which orthographic patterns should be introduced in initial reading (if any), or their sequencing, or the teaching procedures to be employed.

Consider, as an example, the possible procedures for teaching the two pronunciations for the letter *a*, as they occur in the final *e* (e.g. *mate*) and final consonant (e.g. *mat*) patterns. Assuming that these patterns should be taught, should they be introduced sequentially as is done in most current reading programs, or should they be introduced simultaneously, as suggested by Levin and Watson (1963)? If sequentially, which correspondence should be introduced first, /æ/, which occurs in the simplest environments, or /e/, which is easier to manipulate as a separate sound and which has a wider distribution than /æ/? In sequential presentation, /æ/ is usually introduced first, yet there is neither experimental nor observational data to justify this choice. The data needed are primarily psychological and pedagogical, not linguistic: e.g., the time and effort required for teaching with each procedure and how each affects learning and transfer.

The role of the linguist, qua linguist, is to describe the structure of one of the components of reading. It is the task of others, however, to discover how such structures bear upon the learning process.

The second distinction is between the abilities of the competent reader and the development or acquisition of reading. Reading skills possessed by experienced readers represent goals for the teaching of reading, but they in no way tell us how reading should be taught. That adults may recognize whole words or be able to apply letter-sound relationships on request does not mean that beginning reading must be taught by means of whole words or by means of letter-sound correspondences.[3] How reading should be taught depends upon four factors: a) the skills which the child brings to the reading task, b) the learning abilities of the child, c) the teaching environment, which at a minimum includes teachers, resources, and the society in which the school is placed, and d) the relationship between writing and language.

If a child when he first begins to learn to read can not manipulate separate sounds, then it would be senseless to try to teach him individual letter-sound correspondences, regardless of how regular the letter-sound relations may be in the language he is to read. Similarly, if the child learns more efficiently from inductive than from deductive methods, we would tend less towards telling him the features he is to pay attention to in word recognition than we would towards attempting to have him induce these features through discrimination exercises.

And finally, even if all children could learn to read in a year or less through a program which required 18 hours per day of individual attention, we would reject this procedure because it exceeds the limits of time and resources that most modern societies are willing to devote to the teaching of reading.

2. ANALYSIS OF THE READING PROCESSES

2.1　*Goals of Reading Instruction*

In many countries, and especially those in the developing areas of the world, the primary goal of reading instruction is functional literacy: the ability to read at the level required for performing occupational, civic, and familial duties. But in other areas, including the United States, reading is taught for both functional and intellectual purposes; the good citizen reads not only to learn where he is to vote, how extensive his medical insurance is, and how many crankcases his assembly line is to produce each month, but he is also expected to use reading for entertainment and intellectual stimulation. A major segment of reading instruction in the higher primary grades, and of literature instruction in the secondary schools, is aimed towards these latter goals by devoting itself to the merits of the socially acceptable literary works of the western world. Every high school student learns

---

[3] Justification for teaching practices has often been drawn from misinterpretations of the extrinsic validity of experimental studies. Cattell's studies of word and letter recognition (Cattell 1885), in which perceiving was confounded with responding, were for many years the Sanctus for the whole-word approach, and the results of Erdmann and Dodge (1898), showing that word shape was a major cue for word recognition under an atypical reading were extended without question to typical reading situations, where they were no longer valid.

that the cultured reader is marked by a shelfful of expensively-bound Dickens, Shakespeare, and other well-established literati. A parallel goal of American reading instruction is that reading be a pleasurable activity — or, at least that gathering information through reading not be a tedious task.

Whether or not these goals are obtained is difficult to measure. The standardized reading tests given in the public schools are scaled for national norms, which can only roughly be correlated with levels of functional literacy.[4] To measure the level or amount of reading devoted to entertainment or intellectual drives is even more difficult. Sales tallies from publishing houses and circulation records from libraries might give an approximation to this quantity, although the effort required for collecting the data would far outweigh the value and reliability of the result. Furthermore, the amount of reading devoted to entertainment and intellectual curiosity is a function of available time and financial resources as much as it is of reading level. The desire and ability to appreciate modern American playwrights, for example, may not be reflected very accurately in the volumes of Edward Albee's plays which are purchased or borrowed.

What can be measured in the reader, however, are probably more important for the teaching of reading, and these are the more basic perceptual processes which the reader engages in, plus his ability to comprehend what he reads. These processes, as they are observed in the competent reader, are sketched below, followed by an outline of how certain reading abilities develop in children.

2.2 Basic Perceptual Processing

2.21 Eye movements

During reading the eyes move in *saccades* or jerks, in one direction while reading a line and in the opposite direction for the return sweep at the end of a line. This stop-and-go movement, first observed by the French ophthalmologist Javal (1879), consists of rapid movement during which no verbal material is recognized, followed by relatively long fixation periods during which as many as 30 letters may be perceived. For the average adult, reading (silently) nontechnical material, the fixations occupy approximately 94% of the reading time while the movements occupy the remaining time (Tinker 1965: 69).

In addition to the saccadic movements and return sweep, there are also regressive movements, composed of saccadic jumps in the opposite direction from the normal reading progression. These occur more frequently in the reading move-

---

[4] A recent full-page ad in a popular weekly news magazine, placed by a large American chemical firm, began 'Over 8,000,000 American workers have the reading, writing, and counting ability of a 4th grader, or less. In other words, 10% of our labor force is functionally illiterate'. Although one could quibble over the exactness of the figures, this description of functional illiteracy is probably as good as any that has been offered to date (*Time,* August 15, 1969, p. 51).

ments of poor than of good readers, and result from a variety of causes, the two most important being misreadings and beginning-of-the-line adjustment after a return sweep.

The number of fixations made per line varies according to reading ability, type of material being read, and to a lesser degree, the physical properties of the text: line width, type style, and type size. Buswell (1922) found that the average number of fixations per line for 13 college students reading easy material (3.5 inch line width) was about six, with each fixation lasting for an average of 225 ms. Comparable results have been found by Ballantine (1951) and Gilbert (1953).[5] (In Buswell's study, six fixations per line would yield seven letter-spaces per fixation.) There is a positive relationship between span of fixation and reading ability, but the size of the correlation has never been satisfactorily established.[6]

The factors which determine the distance that the eyes will move between the fixation points have not been thoroughly investigated. These distances vary widely for a reader, not only across different types of material, but also within a single line. For a given reader, the distance to be traversed is probably a function both of reading habit and of the immediate textual situation, that is, how much of the text lying immediately ahead he thinks he can recognize in one fixation, judging from the syntactic/semantic form of what he has read so far and the vague forms and spaces that he observes in his peripheral vision ahead of his fixation area. Published records of fixations during reading do not show a preference for either printing or blank spaces as fixation points; however, since an area is fixated rather than a point, almost all fixations during reading subtend printed matter.[7]

2.22 *Fixations*

Except for unimportant nystagmic movements, the eyes are locked on an area of text during the fixation period and intake of words, letters, punctuation, etc. must occur during this time. Whether anything more than dark and light is observed during the saccadic jumps is still a controversial issue, as is the claim that the backward masking of input during these jumps eliminates iconic storage of the last fixated material.[8] At a normal reading distance the most sensitive area of the retina, the fovea, subtends an angle of about 70 min. of an arc, which is

[5] The differences in results from Buswell (1922), Ballantine (1951), and Gilbert (1959) are discussed by Anderson and Dearborn (1952) and Tinker (1965). In general, both Ballantine and Gilbert found more improvement between Grades 4 and 8 in the basic perceptual skills than did Buswell, but the differences were not large.

[6] Buswell (1957) claims to have found in college students a high correlation (.63) between reading comprehension and span of attention as derived from eye movement records during silent reading. However, insufficient data are offered to allow a critical evaluation of this result. The data published in Buswell (1922) clearly do not show a high correlation for Grades 3-6.

[7] Except for the fixation following a return sweep, all fixations *may* be in areas observed during the previous fixation.

[8] Iconic storage is used here in the sense of Neisser (1967 : 15-35). The effects of backward masking in reading have been demonstrated by Gilbert (1959).

sufficient for about four letter-spaces of an average size. Visual reception declines gradually outside of the fovea, but recognition is still fairly accurate at a distance of 12-15 letter-spaces away for single letters (Ruediger 1907).[9] But letters within letter strings and words are considerably more difficult to recognize in indirect vision than are single letters surrounded by white spaces. Korte (1923) has shown that not only are single letters more legible than words, but also that capital letters are more legible in indirect vision than lower case ones and short words more legible than long words. Furthermore, images in the normal direction of scanning (to the right for English, to the left for Hebrew) are more likely to be perceived than those in the opposite direction.

According to Gilbert (1959:11) '... the fixation pause must be long enough in duration to allow time not only to see but also time to process the visual stimuli'. Gilbert tested college students on their ability to recognize tachistoscopically presented phrases. Immediately after each presentation, a 2/24-sec. mask of non-sense material was exposed. Without the mask, a 2/24-sec. exposure of a four-word string yielded a mean of 91.63% correct for 64 subjects, and with the mask, 56.14% correct.[10] The difference in mean percentage of words correctly identified between the best 25% of the readers and the poorest was significant at each exposure level in favor of the better readers.

Since tachistoscopic thresholds for word and phrase recognition are generally lower than those for actual reading, these data establish a lower bound on the fixation time for positive word identification. However, unclear images outside the foveal area play a large role in reading behavior. Their function is summarized succinctly by Tinker (1965:13):

These impressions, which vary greatly in clearness, provide preliminary partial perception of successive words. In addition they orient the reader for the perception of successive words in the sentence or phrases as well as provide essential stimuli for successive fixations of the eyes.

Support for this was found early in this century in an important experiment by Hamilton (1907). Sentences were exposed briefly on a screen and subjects were instructed to report everything they saw, including vague impressions. When subjects guessed at the identification of words which they could not positively identify, the responses they gave were similar enough to the stimuli in general form or in identical letters to indicate that recognition is not an all-or-none process, but that partial information is often obtained and stored. As would be expected, all of the reports of uncertain identification (marginal impressions) referred to materials to the right of the fixation area (English phrases, sentences, and nonsense words were used).

---

[9] Ruediger exposed single letters (u or n) to the left or right of the fixation point for 50ms. However, under normal reading conditions there is a considerably more dense perceptual field.
[10] The difference was significant at better than the .01 level (t test).

2.3 *Word Recognition*

2.31 *General processing*

Within a single fixation, words are usually recognized from left to right (or from right to left for Hebrew) as whole units, although the process of word recognition has not been settled beyond controversy. After nearly a century of experimentation, it is possible to hypothesize that two major sets of variables contribute to the word recognition process: stimulus variables and context variables. The stimulus variables include the shapes and positions of certain letters of a word, word length, and to a more limited degree, word shape. Context variables include expectancies of what words could occur at a given point in a sentence, based both upon the sentence context and upon the subject's prior experience with the material being read, and how familiar the subject is (visually) with the actual word. These two sets of factors most often work side-by-side, but also may be in conflict.[11]

Word recognition usually starts *de novo* at the beginning of a paragraph; in almost all other positions the reader brings to the recognition task expectancies derived from the preceding context and from his prior experiences, plus, for all except the first word of a line, partial identifying information from the TWILIGHT ZONE of the last fixation. Recognition in these circumstances can be viewed as hypothesis checking: further data are collected only to the point where a hypothesis is confirmed, then remaining data are ignored. The physical features which have been shown experimentally to be most important for recognition are the first and last letters of a word, and what Zeitler (1900) called DOMINANT LETTERS: the capitals, and the ascenders and descenders (b, d, f, h, k, l, t; g, j, p, q, y).[12] The greater legibility of initial and final letters over embedded letters has been demonstrated by Wagner (1918) and Woodworth (1938:720) for nonsense strings, but studies by Goldscheider and Muller (1893) and by Vernon (1931) indicate that the most important letters for recognition vary from word to word, and are not always the most discriminate ones.

Strong evidence against word shape as a consistent cue in perception has been provided by Smith, Lott, and Cronnell (1969), who tested visual search in passages of text printed in various combinations of letter case and letter size. Location speeds for words within normal text were no greater than those for the mixed case forms, created by alternating upper and lower case, letter-by-letter, throughout the text. In the latter situation, word shapes were altered significantly from those usually encountered in print, yet identification was not impaired. Word shape, nevertheless, may provide cues for recognition under special circumstances. Tinker (1956) hypothesized that general outline is important for recognizing sight-words (generally, function words) and McGinnies, Comer, and Lacey (1952), among others, have suggested that under some conditions word length is an important cue.

---

[11]   Proofreading is primarily a fight against this conflict.
[12]   Stimulus cues in word perception are reviewed by Tinker (1965), Anderson and Dearborn (1952), and Vernon (1931).

There is no evidence that letter-sound generalizations are consistently used in word recognition by adults, although they may be employed for recognition of unfamiliar or difficult to perceive words. Hardyck and Petrinovich (1969) have observed that even good readers begin to subvocalize when reading becomes difficult (either perceptually or cognitively) and most people are aware of attempting to sound out totally unfamiliar words in printed text. But the number of unfamiliar words encountered by the average reader is small compared to the familiar ones, and the average speed of silent reading is such that sounding of letter units could occur rarely. In oral reading, adults probably generate pronunciations not through letter-sound translation, but through retrieval of articulatory instructions after a word is recognized. The eye-movement patterns for oral reading reported by Buswell (1922) and others seem to preclude a letter-sound procedure.

2.32 *Context variables*

Whatever the exact stimulus cues are for word recognition, it is clear that they are highly influenced by context variables. Before the turn of the century Pillsbury (1897) demonstrated this through tachistoscopic presentation of familiar words into which typographic errors had been introduced. Subjects were asked to report everything they perceived — whole words, letters, etc. — and how certain they were of each item reported. 'In many cases it was noticed that the letters which were most certain and of whose presence the subject is most confident were not on the slide; but were added, subjectively' (Pillsbury 1897:362). Studies of experienced proofreaders (Crosland 1924) show similar results for words in context when meaning is observed.

Word familiarity has been repeatedly shown to have an influence on recognition. Vernon (1931) reported that unfamiliar words were misread more often in tachistoscopic presentations than familiar words.[13] More recently, the frequency effect has been demonstrated by Howes and Solomon (1951) and Solomon and Howes (1951).

The influence of context upon word recognition can be seen both in experimental data and in observations of reading errors. Tulving and Gold (1963) found that words which fit a previously exposed context were recognized significantly faster than words which did not, and both Swanson (1937:47) and Fairbanks (1937:93–94), in studies of oral reading errors made by adults, noted that the errors made by the better readers seldom changed the meaning of what was being read. The poor readers not only frequently changed the meaning of a passage through misreadings, but also recognized their errors less frequently than the better readers, as evidenced by self-correction (or lack thereof).[14]

---

[13]   Rebert (1932) reported a similar effect with numbers; familiar forms (e.g. 1776, 3.1416) were recognized in a single fixation, but unfamiliar ones required two or more fixations for recognition.
[14]   Weber (1968) reviews the literature on reading errors.

2.4 *Processing Model*

As a synthesis of the data just described, the following sketch for a processing model is offered.

A linear segment of text, stretching considerably farther to the right (for English) than to the left is placed in an input register which has a very rapid decay time. Scanning begins from the left and continues until either all words are identified or the image completely decays. Then, using partially identified segments in the right marginal field, plus data based upon the complexity of the material being read, a jump is made to another fixation point. During scanning, words are recognized as whole units and integrated as soon as possible into syntactic/semantic structures. Hypotheses are constantly being generated for what words should come next and constantly being tested.[15] For most words, recognition begins with partial knowledge gained from the previous fixation plus hypotheses formed from syntactic/semantic information. Recognition proceeds with identification of dominant or determining letter features, based upon the hypotheses generated, and stops when a hypothesis has been supported to the satisfaction of the reader. Through this process, details of function words are observed considerably less than those of less frequent and less predictable content words, and substitution errors tend both to fit the syntactic/ semantic context and to bear a physical similarity to the stimulus items they replace. Poor readers at the adult level tend to have shorter fixation spans than better readers and tend to make less use of the immediate syntactic/semantic context.

2.5 *Comprehension*

Although adequate comprehension is an important goal of reading instruction and most methods for teaching reading employ frequent tests of this ability, both the definition of comprehension and the acceptable means for gauging it are among the most controversial issues in modern pedagogy. The central problem is in separating reading comprehension from intelligence and experiential factors which might influence a person's ability to derive information from a text. A physician will probably derive more information from an article on advances in cardiology than will a literary critic, but from this difference it would not be advisable to conclude that the doctor reads better than the critic. Similarly, one child may bring to any given comprehension task specific knowledge which allows him to organize and retain the reading matter better than other children with the same basic reading skills.

---

[15] Neisser, Novick, and Lazar (1963) demonstrated that with extensive practice, scanning for multiple targets may not be any more difficult than scanning for a single target. The reader might attempt to test simultaneously several hypotheses about the identity of a single word, or, conceivably, several hypotheses about the identity of two adjacent words.

A similar problem occurs in comparing reading abilities across cultures. If different contents are used, then complexity of the passages will be difficult to compare, and if the same passages are used, one culture may be favored over another. The way around all of these difficulties is not to measure reading comprehension alone, but to measure both listening and reading comprehension for similar materials, using a variety of difficulty levels. The resulting measures, when appropriately combined, will not only give an assessment of individual reading comprehension relative to ability to comprehend orally, but will also give a measure for comparing reading abilities across cultures.

Several tests have been developed for comparing listening and reading comprehension, and at least one extensive study of the listening/reading comprehension ratio has been done. Goldstein (1940) tested both listening and reading comprehension in 280 adults (18 to 64 years of age), representing a wide range of intelligence, educational achievement, and cultural background. His results show:

1. For relatively easy materials, listening comprehension is significantly superior to reading comprehension, but this difference disappears progressively as the materials become increasingly more difficult. For difficult materials, neither mode is superior.

2. Intelligence is inversely related to superiority of listening comprehension on easy materials. The less intelligent subjects showed a greater superiority for listening comprehension than the more intelligent adults.

3. The greatest modality differences were obtained on medium-difficulty materials. Scores from both modalities were too high on extremely easy materials and too low on extremely difficult materials to allow adequate comparisons.

The reading-listening differential, as pointed out by Goldstein (1940:59), is an index of reading educability. A pupil who scores low on reading comprehension but high on listening comprehension has (assuming no physical defects) a high potential for improvement; a student who scores low on both probably does not.

3. DEVELOPMENT OF READING ABILITY

3.1 *Skills of the Prereader*

3.11 *Understanding the task*

Some children enter reading instruction with a well-formed concept of what reading is all about; they recognize many of the letters by name, know a few words by sight, and may attempt to sound out sentences. These children will learn to read under almost any teaching method, even one centered upon the local telephone directory. But most children in this world do not enter the reading situation so well prepared. More often than not they are unaware of either the purpose or the nature of reading; they do not know that letters represent sounds, and that these sounds can be blended into words and words into meaningful sentences. Reid (1960:60), who interviewed children during their first year of reading instruction in Scotland, writes: '... reading, prior to the experience, is a mysterious activity to which they (the children) come with only the vaguest of expectancies. In some cases the children ... were not even clear whether one "read" the pictures or the other "marks" on the paper.'[16]

In short, some children come to their first year of reading instruction ready to learn to read, but most do not. Those who do have been instructed already, either formally or informally, in identifying letters and in the process and value of reading. It should be no surprise, therefore, that the best single predictor at the end of kindergarten or at the beginning of first grade of later reading success is letter-name knowledge. The child who can name many of the letters has a high probability of succeeding, but the child who can name only a few may have difficulties.[17] Whether this is solely a function of the amount of instruction the child receives before he enters school, or is a complex of prior experience and mental development remains to be investigated.

3.12 *Language skills*

Although children come to the reading task with differing experiences and expectations, almost all can use language to communicate with adults and with peers. Articulation errors, though still occurring at the age of six, particularly for fricatives, result mostly from slow motor development and are not direct indicators of reading problems. Phonemic discrimination is also well-developed at the first grade level, as adequate testing will reveal, even for those children so cavalierly classed as 'verbally deprived'.[18] Morphology, syntax, and vocabulary continue to develop beyond this level, yet all three are sufficiently developed here to allow the child to express his immediate needs and impressions.[19] Reading problems related to morphology, syntax, and vocabulary often result, however, from the failure of instructors and textbook writers to estimate accurately the level of development of each of these skills at various ages.[20]

[16] Similar results are reported by Weintraub and Denny (1965).

[17] This result was reported in several independent studies: Wilson and Flemming (1938)–high IQ status; deHirsch, Jansky, and Langford, (1966)–average IQ children; and Durrell (1958)–high IQ children.

[18] Rudegeair and Kamil (1969), Berlin and Dill (1967) and Blank (1968) have all demonstrated that the standard phonemic discrimination test, upon which Deutsch (1964) and others have based their claims for inadequate phonemic discrimination in speakers of non-standard English, was invalid as was used for these subjects. When adequate testing procedures are used, the deficits tend to disappear.

[19] Reservations on this point have been expressed by Loban (1963) and Singer (1969).

[20] The mismatch between the syntax of commonly used reading series and that of the children who are taught with them has been explored by Hatch (1969). Studies of children's vocabularies have shown large individual differences, even within the same cultural setting, but the standard vocabulary tests now in use – in particular, the picture vocabulary tests – may not be measuring the vocabulary variables most important for reading. In reading,

The child's ability to use language for communication presents mostly tactical problems for the teaching of reading — selection of appropriate language forms and designation of what words must be taught orally before instruction begins. But the child's ability, or lack thereof, to treat language analytically is a far more serious concern and has been identified as a crucial reading variable in a number of different cultures. At some point in almost all reading programs sounds are treated as individual units which the child must manipulate, as in rhyming, matching of words by initial or final sounds, or by attaching sounds to letters and blending them into words. These tasks are, for reasons that are still not understood, difficult for many children at the kindergarten and first grade levels. Zhurova (1963) reports that Russian children still have trouble at the age of seven in isolating the initial sound of a word, especially if the sound is a stop. Bruce (1964) tested British children on their ability to remove a medial sound from a word to produce a second word (e.g. eliminating [t] from *stand* to give *sand*) and found that below the age of seven they could not learn the task. Schenk-Danzinger (1967) reports similar results in Austria as do Calfee, Chapman, and Venezky (1972) in the United States.[21] Once children learn to represent sounds with letters, these difficulties seem to disappear, but so far little success has been reported in teaching these skills to prereaders.[22]

3.13 *Perceptual and cognitive skills*

For the average child the perceptual and cognitive demands of initial reading instruction, aside from sound-abstraction, are not excessive. At the kindergarten level children can match letters of the alphabet, although left-right reversals (e.g. confusing lower case *b* and *d*) are common. Reversals may continue through first and even second grade, but are not considered to be a serious problem for reading. Most other skills required for learning initial reading — scanning left-to-right, following simple instructions, etc. — appear to be available by the end of kindergarten for children from middle-class environments. Some skills, however, such as those associated with sound manipulation and word identification appear to be

---

children are infrequently called upon to identify a picture. Rather, they must recognize words which they use orally but do not recognize visually. Furthermore, it may be more important to learn how rapidly a child can acquire new vocabulary than it is to sample what he has already learned. It is considerably easier to teach children a reading vocabulary than it is to develop a reading program using only those words that the majority of any large group of first grade children recognize.

[21] Schenk-Danzinger (1967 : 61) reports: 'Maturity for assigning sound-meanings to letter-signs ... does not develop before the age of 6-7. This faculty presupposes the first objectivity of language; the ability to analyze the written or spoken word ... Reading readiness for languages with correspondence of sound and sign can thus be defined as the stage when the child is able to isolate the sounds (phonemes) and identify them with their corresponding signs. About 20% of first graders do not reach reading readiness.'

[22] McNeil and Stone (1965) had limited success in training children to distinguish /s/ from /m/ in real and synthetic words.

lacking in many lower socio-economic children. (Cognitive functions like the use of context for generating word recognition hypotheses are important for the advanced stage of reading and are discussed under Perceptual Processing.)

3.14 *Patterns of skill deficits*

Since many children enter formal education with deficits in skills which relate to reading, it is important to know the distribution of these deficits. If children who are weak in any one skill tend to be weak in all other skills, a single prereading or remedial reading program might be appropriate. If, on the other hand, one skill deficit could not be predicted from another with a high degree of accuracy, then individual instruction would be required to meet the varying patterns of skill deficits present in any class. One insight into this problem can be gained from a study recently completed at the University of Wisconsin (Calfee, Chapman, Venezky 1972). The Basic Skills Test, composed of subtests for letter naming, single letter matching, letter group matching, rhyme production, and phonemic segmentation, was administered to 72 kindergarten children in the Fall of 1969. The intercorrelations for these subtests are shown in Table 1. For all of the tests except letter-naming, the distribution of failure and mastery scores is shown in Table 2, where mastery has been defined as better than

TABLE 1

Correlations Between the Basic Skills Subtests[a]

	2	3	4	5	6	7
1. Age in months	.107	.043	.165	−.281*	−.120	−.055
2. Matching — Letter Pairs + Groups, errors		−.309**	−.481**	−.236*	−.134	−.265*
3. Alphabet Production, correct			.599**	.204	.322**	.199
4. Alphabet Recognition, correct				.233*	.267*	.395**
5. Word Memory Span, correct					.157	.317**
6. Segmentation, List 1 Trials, correct						.457**
7. Rhyming, correct						

a Pearson Product-Moment Correlation Coefficients
 * $p < .05$, $r > .23$, df = 70, 2-tailed
** $p < .01$, $r > .30$, df = 70, 2-tailed

80% correct, and failure as chance performance or worse.[23] No child showed mastery of all four tests, yet only 15 of the 72 children failed all tests. The distribution of deficits is relatively even, indicating that the deficit patterns vary widely across children. There is no well-defined upper group which mastered all the tests and there is a relatively small group, composed of about 20% of the children, who failed all the tests. The implications of these results (assuming that the tests are valid) are that if prereading skill deficits are to be overcome through instructional

TABLE 2

Number of Children Mastering or Failing
BST Subtests, Fall, 1969

Totals	Number Mastering	Number Failing
Rhyming (R)	9	34
Segmentation (S)	4	49
Letter Groups (LG)	2	48
Single Letters (SL)	20	45
All Four Tests	0	15
Three of Four	2	22
R-S-LG	0	7
R-S-SL	0	5
R-LG-SL	2	2
S-LG-SL	0	8
Two of Four	5	20
R-S	1	3
R-LG	0	0
R-SL	3	1
S-LG	0	4
LG-SL	0	9
S-SL	1	3
One of Four	19	10
R	3	1
S	2	4
LG	0	3
SL	14	2

[23] Letter-naming has been omitted from this analysis because it bears no direct logical relationship to learning to read, and its correlation with reading success, when certain basic skills are partialed out, is not significant.

programs, then a high degree of individualization is required. Programs which treat an entire class as a unit, such as most of the so-called reading readiness programs now in use, may allow each child to make marginal, across-the-board gains, but fail to give the concentrated practice each child needs in his specific weaknesses. This may be an explanation for why reading ability at the end of first or second grade can be predicted so accurately from kindergarten tests — regardless of the intervening instruction.

3.2 *Stages of Reading*

The child's initial attempts at reading involve multiple fixations on each word, frequent regressive movements of the eyes, and a painfully slow response time for recognizing words or assigning sounds to letters. Oral reading errors are frequent, yet surprisingly, substitution errors by both good and poor readers most generally preserve meaningfulness although not always the meaning that would occur with the correct response (Weber 1970). According to Biemiller (1968), the error responses of beginning readers progress through three phases: an early phase, characterized by a predominance of context-errors (errors which fit the context, but show little graphic similarity to the stimulus word); a middle phase, characterized by a predominance of non-response errors, and a final phase, characterized by context errors on easy words and non-response or graphically similar substitutions on more difficult words.

By the end of first grade the average American child reads orally at a rate of about 45 words per minute (Durrell 1940:143) and makes somewhere between 15 and 16 fixations in silent reading for a 3.5 inch line (about one fixation for each pair of letters) with about four regressive movements per line (Buswell 1922).

By the end of second grade, the better readers know all of the invariant letter-sound correspondences and most of the major variant ones (e.g. long and short pronunciations of *a, e, i, o,* and *u*), although performance varies widely according to pattern (see section 5 below). In addition, most children by this level can sound out one and two syllable words that they have never seen before.

By fourth grade silent reading speed has overtaken oral reading speed (Durrell 1940:143), reading comprehension has overtaken listening comprehension for average difficulty material (Durrell 1969), the perceptual processes used in scanning and fixating have made their most important development (Buswell 1922), and some of the variable letter-sound patterns (for English) have been learned about as well as they ever will be (Calfee, Venezky, and Chapman 1969). While there is continual improvement, at least through the eighth grade, for all of these skills, this latter increase is nowhere as dramatic as the one between first and fourth grade.

4. LETTER-SOUND GENERALIZATIONS

4.1 *Importance*

Letter-sound generalizations are important for learning to read alphabetic or syllabic writing systems, although their use does not by itself guarantee competent reading behavior. Their primary function is to facilitate the development of word recognition ability, which they do by providing a means for a) checking the identification of a word previously encountered, but still not known well enough to be identified with high confidence from its visual features or from context, and b) generating the pronunciation of a word not encountered before in print, but which may be in the reader's listening vocabulary. For either of these aids, perfectly predictable correspondences are not necessary because in both situations the reader has other cues to work with; the pronunciation of the printed form must only approximate in most circumstances the actual pronunciation for the appropriate match to be made. For example, in the sentence 'The cowboy ran the horse into the street', the word *ran* may, if not recognized by sight or context, be pronounced [ren] initially, but if the reader is aware of the preceding context (and speaks a standard brand of English), he will probably recognize that this is not the correct form and try another pronunciation. Observations of children in oral reading show exactly this process at work.[24] Without the ability to approximate sound from spelling the child would be dependent upon other readers for substantiating his word identifications and consequently would develop this ability quite slowly.[25]

The reliance on letter-sound generalizations in word recognition slowly decreases as word identification ability increases, and the mature reader probably makes little use of them in normal reading. Nevertheless, the ability to apply letter-sound generalizations continues to develop at least through Grade 8. Whether this is due to a continual reliance upon sounding out words or is a result of increasingly more efficient memory organization is not known. But since the use of letter-sound generalizations appears to depend heavily upon examples stored in memory, organization probably accounts for a significant part of this development.

4.2 *The Notion of Regularity*

Regular spelling-to-sound relationships are assumed to be desirable features of an orthography and words with *regular spellings* are assumed to be healthy fodder for

---

[24] Studies of children's reading errors (Weber 1970) show that even the poorest readers at the first grade level make substitutions that are appropriate for the preceding context.
[25] The only record of a person learning to read (for his first reading task) an alphabetic language without letter-sound generalizations was Tarzan, who learned to read English by himself in the jungle at a time when his language repertoire was limited to Ape, Snake, and a little Alligator and Elephant. The feat was due, according to Tarzan's creator, to 'superior genetic endowment', a variable not since found to have such potency for reading (Edgar Rice Burroughs, *Tarzan of the Apes,* 1910).

the child learning to read, yet what *regularity* means in these contexts has never been properly defined. The problem with the term *regular* is that it implies a frequent recurrence of some entity, yet does not indicate either what entity is to be observed or what measure is to be used. The first of these problems is by far the most serious, since it requires an understanding of the orthography to resolve. Consider, for example, the correspondence of d-/d/ in *median*. While this is the most frequent correspondence for *d*, it is in some sense irregular in this environment since /d/ + /ɪ/ or /j/ should palatalize to /ǰ/ as in *cordial, deciduous,* and *gradual*.[26] On another level, *ou* in *thou* has its most frequently occurring pronunciation, yet is irregular in the sense that *u* is generally replaced by *w* in word-final digraphs.

A different problem is encountered in the correspondence of c-/k/ in *arcing*. We could say that /k/ is the most frequent pronunciation for *c*, therefore this correspondence is regular. Yet *c* is almost always /s/ before i (and e and y); therefore, c-/k/ in this word is irregular. But this doesn't complete the discussion, because the irregularity of c in *arcing* differs from that of c in *cello* or *facade*. In the latter two words unpredictable correspondences are clearly involved, but in *arcing*, something different has occurred. The base form *arc* has the predicted correspondence for *c*. In adding suffixes like *-ing* to words ending in *c*, a *k* is generally inserted after the *c* to preserve the /k/ pattern, e.g. *picnic:picnicking*. Thus the irregularity in *arcing* occurs in suffixation and not in the *c* correspondence per se.

To clarify the different classes of patterning in English orthography, the theoretical basis upon which spelling-sound relationships are built must be established. Then, the levels of patterning can be separated.

4.3 The Basis of Spelling-Sound Correspondences

4.31 Introduction

The theoretical basis for English spelling-sound relationship as developed by Venezky and Weir (Venezky 1970; Venezky and Weir 1966) is sketched below. Other treatments of English orthography can be found in Wijk (1966), Hall (1961), and Chomsky and Halle (1968). Some perceptive comments on the relationships of several of these analyses can be found in Wardhaugh (1968). The first task of this section is to establish the levels of units which are required for discussing the orthography, beginning with the grapheme. For reasons which are discussed in detail elsewhere, the theoretical mapping from spelling to sound is achieved in three steps.[27] First, graphemes are mapped into morphophonemes. Then, rules which

---

[26] The general pattern involves the palatalization of the post-alveolars /t/, /d/, /s/, and /z/ to /č/, /ǰ/, /š/, and /ž/ respectively, before a high front vowel or high front glide. This process does not occur, however, when the high front vowel is stressed. In several words containing *-di* + Vowel, including *Indian,* an earlier /ǰ/ pronunciation was depalatalized under the influence of the eighteenth century hypercorrectionists.

[27] The rationale for the morphophonemic approach is discussed in Venezky (1970).

map one set of morphophonemes onto another are applied, and finally morphophonemes are mapped into phonemes. Although this tripartite classification is not
directly applicable to reading instruction, it is important for distinguishing relationships which are totally new to the non-reader (grapheme to morphophoneme) from
those which may already be components of his language habits. For example, the
various correspondences for *g* depend upon peculiarities of the writing system and
must be learned as such,[28] but the /n/ and /ŋ/ pronunciations of *n* are conditioned
by phonological environment and undoubtably do not need to be taught (excluding *ng*).

4.32 *Basic units*[29]

The basic unit in the orthography is the *grapheme*, which is a letter class; in this
paper the alphabetic characters *a* through *z* are classed as *graphemes* and the term
GRAPHEMIC LEVEL will refer to the spelling level. The language-dependent units
on the graphemic level which are significant for the prediction of sound are called
FUNCTIONAL UNITS and are divided into RELATIONAL UNITS and MARKERS.

A RELATION UNIT is a string of one or more graphemes which has a MORPHO-
PHONEMIC CORRESPONDENT which cannot be predicted from the behavior of the
unit's smaller graphemic components.

A MARKER is a string of one or more graphemes whose primary function is to
indicate the correspondences of relational units or to preserve a graphotactical or
morphological pattern. It is mapped into a zero morphophoneme.

4.4 *Relational Units*

The same grapheme string can be part of more than one relational unit. Thus, *gn*
in *cognac* and *poignant* is a single relational unit which corresponds to the morphophonemic cluster {nj}, but *gn* in *sign* and *malign* is not a relational unit, but a
sequence of two relational units which correspond to the morphophonemes {g}
and {n}. Morphophonemic rules map {g} into either {ø} or into {g}, depending
upon allomorphic considerations (cf. *signal* and *malignant*). The selection of relational units is based upon function and composition. Any string of graphemes that
corresponds to a non-zero morphophoneme is a potential relational unit. However,
only those strings whose morphophonemic correspondences cannot be predicted by

[28] That the conditioning for *g* can be stated in phonological terms (e.g. *g* followed by front
vowels or front glides is mapped into /ǰ/) does not make the correspondences morphophonemic,
because no phonological conditioning is involved. Both /g/ and /ǰ/ can appear before front
vowels and glides.

[29] The discussion which follows is adapted from Venezky (1970 : 39-46). Morphophonemic
units will be enclosed in brackets – {x}. However, in discussing letter-sound relationships in
the sections after this one, the morphophonemic designation will be dispensed with except
when theoretical issues are involved.

general rules based upon smaller units contained in the string are classed as relational units. *ch* in *chair*, for example, is a relational unit since the morphophoneme {č} cannot be predicted from rules based upon *c* and *h* separately. Geminate consonant clusters, on the other hand, are not single relational units since their morphophonemic forms can be obtained from rules based upon their separate constituents. (The leveling of clusters like {ff} to {f} can be accounted for by a general phonotactical rule.)

Consonant relational units are classed as functionally simple or functionally compound. This distinction is needed for an accurate statement of a number of rules. In the sequence VOWEL + CONSONANT + final *e*, for example, VOWEL is generally mapped into its free alternate if CONSONANT is a functionally simple unit (or this type of unit plus *l* or *r*), and into its checked alternate if CONSONANT is a functionally compound unit, or a cluster. Thus,

Free alternate	*Checked alternate*
b*a*ke	*a*xe
*a*che	b*a*dge
conc*e*de	*e*dge
cl*o*the	h*o*dge

Vowel units are classed as primary (*a,e,i,y,o,u*), or secondary (all others).

Examples of markers are the final *e* in *mate* and *peace*, the *u* in *guest* and the *k* in *trafficking*, all of which indicate the pronunciation of a preceding grapheme. *ue* in *plague, catalogue*, etc. is a sequence of two markers. The *u* after *g* marks the correspondence *g* -{g} rather than *g* -{ǰ}. Since *u* generally does not appear in final position in English words, a final *e* is added, as in *continue* and *blue*. Only graphemes mapped into zero (i.e. silent graphemes) can be classed as markers (this is a necessary, but not sufficient condition). Graphemes with non-zero morphophonemic correspondences, however, though properly classed as relational units, can also perform marking functions. The *i* in *city*, for example, besides corresponding to {ɪ}, marks the correspondence *c* -{s}. A geminate consonant cluster also performs a marking function since it regularly indicates the checked correspondence of the preceding vowel.

The strongest evidence for a separate class of markers in English orthography is found in orthographic alternation patterns.[30] For example, final *e* as a marker for

---

[30] Markers are not unique to English. Spanish, for example, uses a *u* to mark a stop pronunciation of *g* in environments where the fricative pronunciation would occur, e.g. *guiar* 'to guide' /gjar/. An additional marker, a diaresis, is placed over a *u* to indicate a shift in pronunciation towards a full vowel, that is, to /w/ in environments where it would otherwise be a silent marker (e.g. *güipil* 'sack' /gwipil/), and to /u/ in environments in which it would otherwise be a glide, /w/) (e.g. *püado* 'teeth of a comb' /puedo/). In Hebrew, a final, silent *he* marks feminine gender (generally, the vowel under the preceding consonant is a *kamatz*), and the mid-line point (*dagesh*) can be viewed as a marker for the stop pronunciations of *beth* (/b/), *kaph* (/k/) and *pe* (/p/). Without the dagesh, these letters are pronounced /v/, /x/, and /f/, respectively.

the pronunciation of a preceding *c* or *g* is dropped before a suffix which begins with a letter that will perform the same function as the *e*. Therefore, *notice* drops the final *e* before *ing* (*noticing*) since *i* also marks the correspondence *c* -{s}, but retains the *e* before *able* since *noticable* would have *c* -{k}. Similarly, the *e* added to an otherwise terminal *u* is dropped before any suffix since the only function of the *e* is to avoid having word-final *u*, e.g. *argue*, *arguing*.

Relational units are classed as consonants or vowels depending upon the class of the morphophonemes into which they are mapped (glides are classed as consonants). Some RELATIONAL UNITS are classed as both consonants and vowels, e.g. *u* in *language* (consonant) and *during* (vowel). Within these classes major and minor patterns are distinguished on the basis of frequency of occurrence. Thus, *ch* is classed as a major consonant unit, but *kh* (*khaki*) is classed as a minor unit. While the major-minor classification is arbitrary, it distinguishes frequently occurring, productive patterns from infrequent patterns which would seldom be introduced in teaching reading.

The consonant and vowel relational units are shown in Table 3. Units followed by an asterisk are discussed in the following paragraphs.

TABLE 3

List of Relational Units

MAJOR RELATIONAL UNITS

Consonants						Vowels		
simple				*compound*	*primary*	*secondary*		
b	gh	n	s	w*	ck*	a	ai/ay	ie	ue
c	h	p	sh	y*	dg	e	au/aw	oa	ui
ch	j	ph	t	z	tch	i	ea	oe	
d	k	q	th		wh	o	ee	oi/oy	
f	l	r	u*		x	u	ei/ey	oo	
g	m	rh	v			y	eu/ew	ou/ow	

MINOR RELATIONAL UNITS

Consonants		Vowels
simple	*compound*	*secondary*
kh	gn	ae
sch		eau
		eo
		uy

u is a consonant unit when it corresponds to {w} as in *quack*, *language*, and *assuage*. It may also be a vowel unit, or part of a vowel unit (*ou*), or a marker (*guest*, *plague*).

w is a consonant unit when it corresponds to {w}, e.g., *warm, beware*. It also appears as part of a vowel unit (*ow, aw*) but never as a vowel by itself.

y is a consonant unit when it corresponds to {j}, e.g., *yes, beyond*. It also appears as a vowel unit, and as part of a vowel unit, e.g., *cycle, boy*.

ck is a consonant unit in words like *rack* and *tack*. In instances like *picnicking*, however, the *k* is a marker. That *ck* in *picnicking* is identical to the relational unit *ck* is immaterial, since the base form *picnic* ends in *c*, not *ck*.

4.5 *Markers* [31]

Markers of vowel correspondences:

   e to mark a free vowel: *cute* (cf. *cut*).

Markers of consonant correspondences:

   e marking 1.   *c.* -{s}: *farce* (cf. *arc*).

            2. syllabic *l* or *r*: *table, acre*.

            3. *g* -{ǰ}: *change* (cf. *rag*).

            4. *th* -{đ}: *bathe* (cf. *bath*).

   u marking *g* -{g}: *guess*.

   k marking *c* -{k}: *picnicking*.

   gemination marking a checked vowel: *annals* (cf. *anal*).

Markers of graphotactical patterns:

   e 1. to remove *u* or *v* from the end of a word: *love, glue*.

      2. to prevent two-letter words: *doe, toe*.

   e to mark non-morphemic *s*: *moose*.

4.6 *Levels of Patterning*

4.61 *Introduction*

With the classifications established in the preceding section, it is now possible to refine the quest for regularity to distinct levels of patterning. These are:

Graphotactic   The allowable distributions of relations units and markers. E.g. *q* must be followed by *u*; *k, j, x, w, y, h, q*, and *v* rarely if ever double.

Spelling-to-morphophoneme   The arbitrary correspondences of relational units to morphophonemes, that is, those relationships which are not conditioned by morphophonemic alternates. For example, V in the pattern VCe corresponds to its free form.

Morphophonemic   Alternations which result from phonological/morphological patterning, as opposed to graphemic patterning; for example, palatalization of {sj} to {š} as in *issue*.

---

[31] These are discussed more fully in Venezky (1970 : 55ff). Some examples given there are not included here.

By this classification, *c* in *arcing* involves an irregularity on the graphotactic level; *c* in *facade* involves an irregularity on the grapheme-to-morphophoneme level, and *d* in *median*, an irregularity on the morphophonemic level. But this leaves unanswered the question of how we decide for any pattern (on any level) what is regular and what is irregular. The real problem is in deciding which features to admit for determining regularity and which ones not to.

A feature that is clearly not admissible is etymology. Native speakers are generally not aware of the origins of most words in their vocabularies, and the graphemic shape of a word seldom provides adequate clues for such decisions. If etymology were to be accepted, considerably more than 'LANGUAGE OF ORIGIN' would need to be specified. Consider, as an example, the correspondences of *ch*. At first glance it appears that the {č} forms are derived from Old English, the {š} forms from French, and {k} from Greek. But this is hardly adequate, for although the {š} forms (e.g. *chaise, chalet, champagne*) are borrowed from French, so are most of the {č} forms, e.g., *chafe, chain, challenge, chamber, chance* and *change*. The latter words were borrowed before French {č} shifted to {š}, the former group, after this change took place. For Greek words, a further complexity arises, in that many Greek forms were borrowed through Latin and French and consequently lost their {k} pronunciations. In this class are such forms as *chair*, *archbishop*, and *machine*. And finally, from Latin come both {č} and {k} forms, depending generally upon the date of borrowing; thus, *cheese* and *chalk* alongside *chord* and *choral*.

Another feature which cannot be used is syllable boundary, because such entities are often not determinable either from writing or speech.[32] The features which could be used for predicting sound from spelling are discussed below under the headings graphemic, morphemic, and phonotactical.

4.62 *Graphemic features*

Both position within the printed word and graphemic environment can determine correspondences for a relational unit. Initial *gh*, for example, is always mapped into {g}, as in *ghost, ghetto*, and *gherkin*, but medial and final *gh* have a variety of correspondences, most of which can not be predicted.

4.63 *Morphemic features*

The spelling *ph* regularly corresponds to {f} as in *phase, sphere*, and *morpheme*. In *shepherd*, however, *ph* clearly does not correspond to {f} but to {p}. One way to explain this is to say that *shepherd* is an exception to the more general rule of *ph* -{f}. But if this is done, then the same process must be repeated when faced with *uphill, topheavy* and every other form in which *ph* occurs across a morpheme boundary. The most satisfactory procedure is to say that *ph* corresponds to {f}

---

[32] Syllable boundaries in spoken words should not be confused with hyphenation divisions in printed words. The latter are, in part, arbitrary. On the pedagogical utility of syllabification rules, see Wardhaugh (1966).

when it lies within a single graphemic allomorph and that across morpheme boundaries *ph i*s treated as the separate letters *p* and *h*.

Other situations in which morpheme boundary is important are:

(1) Within graphemic allomorphs geminate consonant clusters as in *letter, add,* and *canned* are pronounced as single consonants. Across morpheme boundaries, however, both graphemic consonants may correspond to separate phonemes, as in *midday* and *finally*.

(2) All of the digraph and trigraph spellings are subject to the same morpheme boundary problem as *ph*, e.g. *hothead, changeable*.

(3) The spelling *n*, before spellings in the same morpheme which correspond to {g} or {k} corresponds to {ŋ}, as in *congress, finger, anchor*. Across morpheme boundaries this may not hold, e.g., *ingrain, ingratiate*.

(4) Many word-final clusters contain silent letters, e.g. *gm, gn, mb* (*paradigm, sign* and *bomb*). Across certain morpheme boundaries, the silent letter remains silent, as in *paradigms, signer*, and *bombing*. As long as the morpheme boundary is recognized, the correct pronunciation can be predicted. If the morpheme boundary is not recognized, then the three forms above would be thrown together with *stigma, ignite*, and *bamboo*.

The discrimination of a morphemic spelling from an identical, non-morphemic spelling is necessary for the prediction of the pronunciations of final *s* and *d*. For example, the pronunciations of *s* in *boys, judges* and *cats* are governed by different ᵔules from those for *s* in *stylus, apropos* and *summons*.

The correspondence of any form ending in *nger* or *ngest* cannot be predicted unless the morphemic identities of *er* and *est* are known. If these are the comparative and superlative markers, then ng is {ŋg} as in *stronger*; in most other cases the {ŋg} cluster is leveled to {ŋ}, just as it is in word final position. Morphemic identity is also important for predicting the pronunciation of word final *ate*. In adjectives and nouns, the ending is generally {-it}, e.g. *duplicate, frigate, syndicate*, while in verbs, {-et}, e.g. *deflate, duplicate, integrate*.

Finally, morpheme identity is necessary for the correct pronunciation of initial *th*. Functors beginning with this cluster have the voiced inter-dental spirant {ð}: *the, then, this, those*, while contentives have the voiceless spirant {θ}: *these, thin, thumb*. (But *th* before *r* is an exception: *through*.)

4.64 *Phonotactical features*

4.641 *Consonant clusters*. A knowledge of phoneme arrangements which are not allowed in English words is a necessary prerequisite for analyzing many spelling-to-sound correspondences. Sequences like /bp/ and /pb/ do not occur within English words except when separated by juncture. Where they would occur, as in *subpoena* and *clapboard*, the speaker drops one sound or the other (with /pb/ and /bp/, the first sound is always omitted). The elision of sounds in consonant clusters can also be predicted in initial and final positions, as in *knee, grant, bomb,* and *sing*. (In all of these cases, the correct pronunciations can be derived by first mapping all spelling units onto a morphophonemic level and then applying the rules for leveling non-English clusters to obtain the phonemic forms. Thus, *knee, gnat, bomb, sing*, become first {kni}, {gnæt}, {bamb}, {sɪng}, and then the non-allowed clusters are leveled, giving /ni/, /næt/, /bam/, /sɪŋ/.)

4.642 *Stress*. Stress is a conditioning factor on the pronunciation of unstressed vowels. While the reduction of unstressed vowels to schwa is not entirely regular, it can still be predicted in many cases. The patterns, however, are highly complex and are beyond the scope of this paper. A less complex example of stress conditioning occurs in the correspondences for intervocalic *x*, which corresponds either to {ks} or {gz}, depending upon the position of the main word stress. If the main stress is on the vowel preceding *x*, the correspondence generally is {ks} as in *exit, exercise*. Otherwise, it is {gz} (cf. *examine, exist*). While this rule is similar to Verner's Law for the voicing of the Germanic voiceless spirants, it is not a case of pure phonological conditioning. Words like *accede* and *accept* have the identical phonetic environments for {gz}, yet have {ks}.

The retention or deletion of medial {h} in most cases also depends upon the position of the main word stress. Compare *prohibit: prohibition; vehicular: vehicle*. In each pair, the first member, which has the stress on the vowel following *h*, has a fully pronounced {h}, while the second member, with an unstressed vowel after *h*, has no {h}. This rule also holds for *vehement, shepherd, philharmonic, annihilate, rehabilitate* and *nihilism*.

4.643 *Palatalization*. Another type of correspondence in which stress is important is the palatalization of {sj, zj, tj, dj} to {š, ž, č, ǰ}. This form of palatalization occurs when {sj, zj, tj, dj} are followed by an unstressed vowel, as in *social, treasure, bastion,* and *cordial*.

4.7 *Pattern Classes*

It should be apparent at this point that when proper consideration is given to the basic units of the orthography, the different levels of patterning, and the features which determine pronunciation from spelling, the terms *regular* and *irregular* are neither theoretically nor pedagogically adequate. Once the notion that every deviation from a one-letter, one-sound system is an irregularity is discarded, then the complexities just described must be considered and the notion of regularity replaced by something more adequate. What can be offered in its place is a classification based upon PREDICTABILITY, as sketched below.

I. Predictable: patterns that can be predicted upon the basis of features of the words or sentences in which they occur.

   A. Invariant: spellings which have a single correspondent and which admit no (or very few) variations or exceptions (e.g. *f* - {f}).

B. Variant: spellings which relate to two or more correspondences, all of which are predictable (e.g. *n* - {n} or {ŋ}).
II. Unpredictable: patterns which cannot be predicted.
A. High-frequency: (e.g., *ea* - {ɛ}, {i}).
B. Rare: (e.g., *c* - {ø} as in *indict*; *o* - {ɪ} as in *women*).

Invariant, predictable correspondences, although confined to a group of consonants, form the backbone of most introductory reading programs. Variant, predictable correspondences must be further classed according to the features upon which the predictability is based, because graphemic features require a different teaching approach from any other class of features. Among the unpredictable correspondences, the high frequency ones deserve special attention because (by definition) of their functional value. However, it is not yet certain whether the definition of frequency in this class should be based upon word types alone, or upon both types and tokens.

5. LEARNING LETTER-SOUND CORRESPONDENCES

5.1 *Introduction*

The patterning just discussed was derived through analysis of the writing and the sound system, without regard for the psychological reality of each of its components. It is, therefore, not by itself a model of how readers generate sound from spelling, but a basis for testing whether or not particular types of spelling-sound generalizations are actually acquired. In this section some experimental results on the acquisition of selected generalizations are discussed.

5.2 *C Patterns*

The different pronunciations for the letter *c* are among the most predictable in English orthography. The pronunciation of *c* in initial position before *i*, *e*, or *y* is /s/ as in *city*, *cent*, and *cycle*; otherwise it is /k/, e.g. *clap*, *cross*, *carrot*, *come*, *cut*. (The one exception to this distribution is *cello*.) In final position it is invariantly /k/, although there are few examples of final *c* among the more common English words, except in the ending *-ic* (e.g. *traffic*, *picnic*, *panic*). The non *-ic* forms are borrowings, primarily from French: *arc*, *havoc*, *sac*, *shellac*, *sumac*, *talc*, and *zodiac*. Medial *c* before a consonant or juncture, is identical to initial *c*. Before *i* and occasionally *e*, plus another vowel, and with the primary word stress on the syllable before *c*, *c* plus the following vowel tend to palatalize to /š/: e.g. *conscious*, *social*, *ocean*. The exceptions to these patterns are three words in which *c* is silent: *victual, czar,* and *indict,* plus *facade* and *sceptic* (a variant spelling for *skeptic*).

In spite of the predictability of the *c* pronunciations, appropriate transfer of the *c* pattern to new words develops slowly through the elementary grades and seldom approaches the theoretical level of predictability. Students (2nd, 4th, 6th, and 8th graders, plus college undergraduates) were shown, one at a time, the spellings displayed in Table 4, which they were told were either English or English-like words, and asked to pronounce them.[33] Results were tape-recorded, and later transcribed and analyzed.

TABLE 4

Synthetic Words for Testing c *Pronunciations*

Initial		Medial		Final
cade	cefe	mecal	roce	dac
carg	comp	nacom	hacen	mec
cobe	cipe	licul	recilt	jic
corb	cilf		necy	woc
cuse	cyfe			huc
cung	cylm			zyc

Subjects for the 2nd, 4th, and 6th grades were drawn from the same three schools, representing middle-class urban, lower-middle class urban, and rural school districts. The eighth grade sample was drawn from the rural school above and the college subjects were selected from freshmen and sophomores attending an introductory psychology class at the University of Wisconsin. A total of 561 subjects were tested. (Since no important differences were found between male or female subjects or among the various schools used for the 2nd, 4th, and 6th grades, results will be given for grades only.)[34]

The results shown in Table 5 show that while correct responses for *c* in initial and medial positions before *a, o, u* and in final position are well learned by 6th grade (91.6%, 85.6%, and 82.1% respectively), the responses to initial and medial *c* before *e, i,* and *y* at this grade level are correct in only 58.9% and 63.7%

[33] The material reported here is based upon a recent study done at the Wisconsin Research and Development Center for Cognitive Learning. It will be reported in a forthcoming technical report from the Center. An earlier study of some of the patterns described here is presented in Calfee, Venezky, and Chapman (1969). The schools tested for grades 2, 4, 6, and 8 used a three-track reading program in the lower primary grades, with formal instruction in reading ending after third grade, except for the poorer readers. Except for one variation in the middle track, the three schools used identical reading series. There were no significant differences (.01 level or better) between schools at any grade.
[34] While this study is not longitudinal, the sampling of grades 2, 4, and 6 from the same schools allows a fairly reliable comparison across these grades. Therefore, the major emphasis in the discussion which follows will be upon these grades.

of their occurrences. Initial *c* before *a*, *o*, and *u* shows the highest percentage of correct responses, progressing from about 82% in 2nd grade to almost 92% by 6th grade. Initial *c* before *i*, *e*, and *y* on the other hand shows the lowest percentage of correct responses, advancing from about 22% in 2nd grade to 59% in 6th grade, and never quite reaching 70%, even with college students.

Additional information on response strategies is revealed by the figures for correct plus plausible responses for the two categories of initial *c* (Table 6). That these percentages are quite high, and are nearly identical for *a, o, u* and *e, i, y* even in 2nd grade where there is a highly significant difference between correct responses for the two patterns, indicates that the range of plausible responses for *c* is learned early, but that the /k/ pronunciation is so dominant that it persists for *c* before *e, i,* and *y* past the 4th grade. If the subjects were attempting to apply the appropriate rule, we would expect a greater similarity between the correct response totals for the two patterns. Instead, it appears that a single response, /k/, is available for all occurrences of initial *c*, and only slowly does it give way to /s/ for *c* before *e, i ,y,* but surprisingly still occurs in about 30% of the *e, i, y* responses at the college level. A possible reason for this responses bias is that words with *c* before *e, i,* and *y* are rarely introduced in reading lessons until after the time when emphasis is given to letters and sounds. In part this results from the distribution of *c* pronunciations in the English vocabulary; among the more common words, only the following have initial *c* before *e, i,* or *y* and most of these, by tradition, are proscribed from readers before the fourth grade: *ci*der, *ci*nder, *ci*rcle, *ci*tizen, *ci*ty, *ci*vil, *ce*ase, *ce*iling, *ce*lery, *ce*ll, *ce*llar, *ce*nt, *ce*nter, *ce*rtain, *cy*cle.

TABLE 5[a]

Percentage of Correct Responses to
c Patterns

POSITION	2	4	6	8	Coll.
Initial					
before a,o,u	82.4	88.5	91.5	91.9	88.1
before i,e,y	22.4	41.4	58.9	69.9	69.8
Medial					
before a,o,u	63.6	81.0	85.6	83.3	87.3
before i,e,y	39.3	53.7	63.7	73.9	73.8
Final	65.1	77.5	82.1	81.2	97.6

[a] Differences between means within a grade which exceed 1.1 are statistically significant (t test, p<.005), differences between means across grades which exceed 7.3 are statistically significant (t test, p<.005).

TABLE 6[a]

Percentage of Correct and Plausible
Responses to c Patterns

POSITION	2	4	6	8	Coll.
Initial					
before a,o,u	89.9	90.9	95.3	88.6	95.2
before i,e,y	87.9	92.0	95.8	93.0	100.0
Medial					
before a,o,u	76.5	89.1	95.9	96.8	100.0
before i,e,y	77.6	90.9	95.8	95.7	94.0
Final	82.1	87.8	92.8	94.5	98.4

[a] Differences between means within a grade which exceed 1.1 are statistically significant (t test, $p < .005$), differences between means across grades which exceed 7.3 are statistically significant (t test, $p < .005$).

The data for medial and final *c* are similar to those for initial *c*. Percentages of /k/ responses to medial *c* before *a*, *o*, and *u* and to final *c* are almost identical, except for the college level, where the final *c* responses rise to almost 100% correct. And similar to the initial position responses, correct-plus-plausible percentages for the two different medial patterns are both close to 100% and nearly identical. Responses for medial and final position also show the gradual influence of an increasing reading vocabulary as opposed to the acquisition of overtly stated rules.

Equal in significance to the overall responses are the individual responses to *c* before *e*, *i*, and *y* for each class quartile, shown in Figure 1.[35] What is most important is that while the top quartile continues to give more correct responses than the other quartiles, all four curves show the same general upward trend, indicating that the differences between the upper and lower quartiles (that is, between the best and poorest readers) is quantitative rather than qualitative; the poorer readers are continuing to acquire the correct responses. (This same pattern is observed in almost all letter-sound tests we have performed so far.)

5.3   G Patterns

The *g* patterns are theoretically quite close to the *c* patterns, both behaving differently before high front vowels than they do in any other environment. However, *g* has no parallel to the palatalized *c* as in *social* or *ocean*. Before *e*, *i*, or *y*, *g* (theoreti-

[35] Quartile breaks were based upon scores received on standard reading and intelligence tests administered by the different schools. In all instances, the closest approximation possible to a reading score was used.

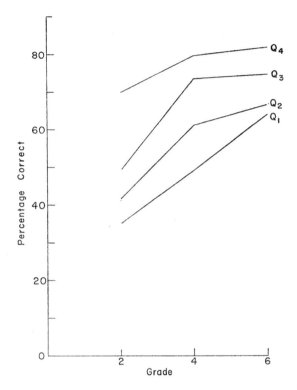

Fig. 1. Responses by Quartiles* to Initial and Medial c before e, i, and y.
*   Q₁ is the lowest quartile; Q₄ the highest.

cally) is pronounced /ĵ/ as in *gem, giant, gym, orgy* and *origin*; elsewhere, it is /g/: *game, goat, gum, rag, grow, glow*. But there are many exceptions to the first generalization, and these exceptions tend to occur in the more common English words. In initial position the exceptions among common words outnumber the examples and include such forms as *get, gift, girl,* and *give*. For medial position, the exceptions are restricted to *-ger* forms (*anger, finger, tiger,* etc.) plus a few miscellaneous items (e.g. *begin, target, bogey*).

Tests for *g* pronunciations were run on the same subjects described above, using the test items shown in Table 7. The results, shown in Table 8 show that /ĵ/ pronunciations before *i* and *e*, even at a college level are relatively infrequent in initial position and exceed 50% for medial position only at the college level. The percentages correct when /g/ is the correct response are nearly identical to the corresponding *c* responses when /k/ is correct, all showing a high percentage of correct responses by the end of 6th grade.

The low number of correct responses through college for *g* before *e* and *i*, particularly in initial position, suggests that examples are more influential than verbali-

TABLE 7

Stimulus Words for g Patterns

Initial[36]		Medial		Final
gade	geme	hugan	noge	dag
gand	geft	nigom	ponge	feg
gope	gite	legute	agime	lig
golb	gink			pog
gube				sug
gurk				

TABLE 8[a]

Percentage of Correct Responses to g Patterns

POSITION	2	4	6	8	Coll.
Initial					
before a,o,u	85.6	90.0	95.8	95.3	91.2
before i,e	12.6	21.8	23.6	23.4	25.0
Medial					
before a,o,u	63.5	78.8	86.1	82.3	95.2
before i,e	26.1	42.2	44.7	50.0	57.2
Final	76.5	88.7	91.4	88.0	97.00

[a] Differences between means within a grade which exceed 1.1 are statistically significant (t-test, $p < .005$), differences between means across grades which exceed 7.3 are statistically significant (t-test, $p < .005$).

zation of rules for *g* pronunciations. For initial position, the only common words with *g* pronounced /ǰ/ are *gem, general, germ, giant,* and *ginger.* Less common are *generate, genius, genuine, geography, geometry, gin, giraffe,* and *gist.*[37] The exceptions, as mentioned above, make a formidable list: *gear, geese, geld, get, geyser, giddy, gift, gig, giggle, gild, gilt, gill, gimlet, gird, girdle, girl, girth, give, gizzard.* If a generalization for *g* before *e* or *i* is to be taught, then a suitable pool of examples will be required, but these can not be introduced under present attitudes towards grade-level vocabulary until the higher primary grades, and at these levels letter sound-generalizations are rarely stressed. Even under ideal circumstances, it is not clear that this generalization merits any attention. From the child's

[36] Since the sequence *gy-* is rare in English words, occurring commonly only in *gym, gyp,* and *gypsy,* it was not tested.

[37] The generalization that *g* before *e* and *i* is often pronounced /ǰ/ frequently occurs in phonics texts. Clymer (1963) gives it a utility value of 64 %, based upon an analysis of 2600 words found in four primary grade readers (Grades 1-3). Emons (1966) extended Clymer's tabulations to the fourth grade using the Thorndike and Lorge wordlist (Thorndike and Lorge 1944) and gave the *g* before the *e/i* rule an 80 % utility rating. In neither of these studies, however, was initial position differentiated from medial position.

standpoint, it may be easier to handle a list of exceptions to *g* -/g/ than to have a fairly complex with an equally long list of exceptions.

5.4 *Checked and Free Vowel Patterns*

In the pattern -VCe where C is any single consonant letter except *x*, or any digraph except *ch, dg,* or *wh,* and V is a simple vowel spelling (a, e, i/y, o, u) V receives its free pronuciation, e.g. *mate, ache, mete, site, writhe, robe, cute.* Otherwise, V receives its checked pronunciation; e.g. *mat, met, sit, rob, cut.* Several distinct subpatterns exist, the most important being the $V + r$ patterns, which will not be discussed here.[38] Other patterns and exceptions which are important for the tests reported here are:

1. The letter *o* in both the checked and the free pattern is often unpredictable before *m, n,* and *v*;

2. After *w* in the checked pattern, *a* becomes /a/ except when followed by a velar consonant spelling (spellings for /k, g, ŋ/) e.g. *wad* vs. *wag, wax.*

3. -eCe is rare in monosyllables, occurring only in *mete* and *plebe* (aside from *-ere* words).

4. Whether *u* is pronounced /u/ or /ju/ in the -uCe pattern is conditioned by the consonant preceding *u.*

To test for the pronunciations of simple vowel spellings, matched pairs for each vowel were constructed as shown in Table 9.

The percentages of correct and correct plus plausible responses for the free and check vowel patterns are shown in Table 10. Correct responses for free and checked pronunciations (collapsed across vowels) are plotted in Figure 2.

TABLE 9

Test Words for Free and Checked Patterns

letter	test words		correct responses	plausible responses
a	dape	nade	e	æ
	dap	nad	æ	e
e	kete	lebe	i	ɛ
	ket	(leb)*	ɛ	i
i	bime	kipe	aɪ	ɪ
	bim	kip	ɪ	aɪ
o	jode	wome	o	a
	jod	wom	a	o
u	fube	vune	ju	ʌ
	fub	vun	ʌ	**ju**

* Omitted by mistake from the stimulus list.

[38] For a full treatment of these patterns see Venezky (1970 : 109-114).

TABLE 10[a]

Percentage of Correct Responses
to Free and Checked Vowel Patterns

PATTERNS	2	4	6	8	Coll.
VCe-					
Correct	49.2	67.5	74.2	66.0	67.8
Correct +					
Plausible	75.5	86.2	89.9	90.7	81.1
-VC#					
Correct	62.0	75.0	78.0	75.5	80.0
Correct +					
Plausible	75.0	86.0	89.3	89.0	89.5

[a] Differences between means within a grade which exceed 1.1 are statistically significant (t test, $p < .005$), differences between means across grades which exceed 7.3 are statistically significant (t test, $p < .005$).

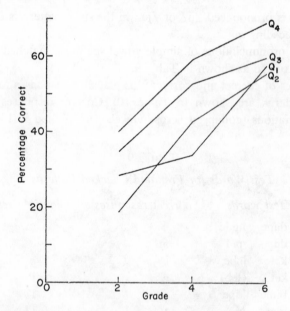

Fig. 2. Responses by Quartiles[a] to Free and Checked Vowel Pattern.

[a] Q_1 is the lowest quartile; Q_4 is the highest.

The free-checked patterns show their steepest improvement between 2nd and 4th grades; the college averages are not significantly higher than those reached by the 6th grade. The improvement from grade to grade by quartiles is similar to that shown for *c* before *e, i,* and *y,* with the lower quartiles continuing to improve through 6th grade. The lack of an appreciable difference between correct responses for free and checked vowels is surprising, in that the checked vowel patterns are usually introduced first in the reading program. Of special interest is the contrast between the development of these patterns and the *c* ones. In both instances there are two major pronunciations which can be predicted on the basis of following graphemes. Furthermore, in both instances one pronunciation is usually introduced first in the teaching of reading and learned to some criterion before the second pronunciation is exposed. Yet there are major differences in the developments of the correct pronunciations. For *c*, there is a strong bias towards the pronunciation introduced first (/k/), yielding a high percentage of correct responses in 2nd grade for *c* before *a, o,* and *u,* but a low percentage of correct responses at the same level when *e, i,* or *y* follows. The most significant improvement in the *c* pronunciations involves a gain in /s/ at the expense of /k/; the percentage of correct plus plausible showing little gain.

For the checked and free vowels, on the other hand, there are gains in both correct responses and in combined correct plus plausible responses for the two different categories. What is learned over this period is not just the appropriate responses for each pattern, but also the range of plausible responses. There is no tendency at the 2nd grade level to assign one pronunciation to both the checked and free environments of each letter. Furthermore, at all levels except 8th grade, there are more correct responses to the free/checked patterns than there are to *c* before *e, i* and *y*.

The differences between these patterns is probably due to the relatively early introduction of the free pronunciations of the vowels as opposed to the /s/ pronunciation of *c*, plus the relatively large number of words available for demonstrating both checked and free pronunciations. It appears from these data that if predictable, variant pronunciations exist for a spelling unit, they must be introduced early in the reading instruction and illustrated with numerous examples. Exactly what 'early' means can not be determined precisely from these data; certainly before 4th grade, and probably before 3rd grade. Whether or not the variant pronunciations should be introduced simultaneously as suggested by Levin and Watson (1963) and others needs to be determined experimentally.

5.5 *Invariant Consonants*

One of the most important distinctions between good and poor readers at the 2nd and 4th grade levels is their responses to invariant consonant spellings. Shown in Figure 3 are percentage correct responses for the lowest (Q1) and highest (Q4) quartiles to the spellings *b, d, l,* and *m*.

For initial position the lowest quartile is only slightly lower than the highest quartile in percentage of correct responses, but for medial and final positions the

2092   RICHARD L. VENEZKY

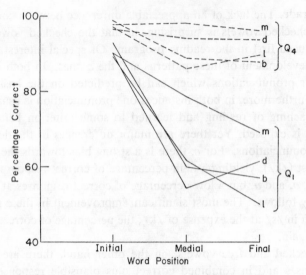

Fig. 3. Responses by Quartiles to Invariant Consonants: Grade 2[a].

[a] Q_1 is the lowest quartile; Q_4 is the highest.

differences in performance are large, with the lowest group showing a marked
degeneration. That the responses for the lowest quartile for initial position are
consistently in the 90% range shows that the letter-sound correspondences
have been learned. What appears to be lacking is a concern for word details beyond the beginning of the word, a phenomenon also reported by Marchbanks and
Levin (1956) for word recognition by kindergarten and first grade children and by
Bennett (1942) for oral reading errors of poor readers in the 3rd, 4th, and 5th
grades. Although this is not the only problem that poor readers exhibit, it is
frequently reported not only for learning to read English, but also for Hebrew,
where inflectional suffixes are extremely important. Whatever the source of the
problem — lack of appreciation of detail, low criterion level for identification,
impulsivity, etc. — training procedures for overcoming it are needed before certain
letter-sound relationships can be used.

6. TEACHING LETTER-SOUND PATTERNS

6.1 *Introduction*

For a child to give the appropriate responses to any of the patterns just described,
he must at a minimum have learned to recognize letters, remember sounds, and
associate the appropriate sound with each letter. The first task has been shown
by Olson (1958) and Calfee, Chapman and Venezky (1972) to be easily accomplished by kindergarten children. The remaining two tasks, however, have not been

adequately examined. In general, it has been observed that when kindergarten children are required to learn oral responses for visual stimuli, no difficulty is encountered for small stimulus sets as long as the responses are familiar to the child (Muehl 1962). That is, a kindergarten child can learn to respond 'dog, tree, house', etc. to geometric forms or to letter strings, indicating that the task of associating a familiar response with either a familiar or unfamiliar stimulus is not the central problem in learning letter-sound correspondences. But the same task with meaningless individual sounds or with meaningless syllables is quite difficult for most kindergarten children (Calfee, Chapman, and Venezky 1972). That the difficulty is not in the child's ability to produce the required responses can be seen from tasks which require children to imitate pronunciations of meaningless sounds (Zhurova 1963; McNeill and Stone 1965; Marsh and Sherman 1970). The difficulty, therefore, appears to be in the storage and retrieval of the sound.

It is speculated further that the core of the problem is in memory organization — the ability to arrange the sounds by themselves in memory and to retrieve them at the proper time. This speculation is based upon two observations: first, that young children seem to learn fairly easily to recall certain meaningless sounds, in particular, those that represent noises made by animals or objects (e.g. the hoot of an owl, the hiss of a radiator); and second, in the teaching of sounds for letters, considerable success is reported when proper mediation is provided.[39]

But even if it can be shown that certain forms of mediation lead to rapid acquisition of letter-sound associations, this can not be accepted as proof that such associations should be the basis of early reading instruction. Aside from examining sound-blending,[40] which is required for pronouncing all words of more than one letter, it would remain to be shown that this teaching procedure was more efficient for letter-sound learning and later word recognition than various other commonly employed procedures, especially those that begin with whole word identification and then proceed to letter-sound generalizations. Attempts to compare training methods on adults (Bishop 1964) and on children (Jeffrey and Samuels

[39] Letter names, upon which the initial teaching of reading was based for almost 2000 years, are poor mediators for English letter sounds. The name for *h* does not contain the sound it represents; that of *w* retains its descent from two *u's*, and that of *y*, neither its sound nor its origin. (According to the *OED*, the English name for *y* is ' . . . of obscure origins'). The names for *f*, *s*, and *x*, and for the sonant symbols *l*, *m*, *n*, and *r* are composed of a checked vowel, followed by a consonant sound (or sounds). The remaining consonant names in English are open syllable names based upon the acrophonic principle.

[40] The most important studies on sound-blending are Laumbach (1968) (reported in Coleman 1970) and Desberg (1969). Laumbach tested seven preschool children between the ages of 66 and 75 months on blending 293 two-sound words. Her major finding was that blendability was primarily a phonological function, and not related to frequency of word usage. However, the small subject population size and the high probability of practice effects on the 293 item list reduce the reliability of this result. Desberg tested the effects of frequency of occurrence of different sounds and of inter-sound interval on the blending abilities of 60 beginning readers. Neither variable was found to be significant.

1967) have been limited, so far, to short training sessions, with limited and highly artificial reading situations.

6.2 *Correspondences vs. Whole Words*

Almost all modern methods for teaching reading include letter-sound learning somewhere in the teaching sequence, although the amount and exact placement of this training accounts for the central disagreement between methods. PHONICS or LINGUISTICS programs tend to initiate the teaching procedure with emphasis on letters and sounds, while GLOBAL or SYNTHETIC-ANALYTIC methods tend to begin with whole words or phrases, which only at a later stage are analyzed into syllables and unit sounds. Non-systematic procedures, such as those that Bloomfield inveighed against in the 1940s are no longer in the majority. Hence the differences between methods have become more and more reduced to differences in the sequencing of learning as opposed to differences in goals, or basic philosophy. On one hand, this allows more rigorous comparisons of methods, since the desired outcomes of training are nearly identical, but on the other hand a more exacting criterion has emerged, in that the comparison of any *letter-sound method* with any *whole-word method* is no longer valid (if it ever was). One must find the optimal teaching sequence based upon letters and sounds, and compare this in terms of desired outcomes with the optimal teaching sequence based upon whole-words. From a practical standpoint, this requires that comparisons be made within common approaches before comparisons can be made across methods. Otherwise, one may compare the worst of Procedure A with the best of Procedure B. This may have some interest within itself, but its application to the teaching of reading is questionable.

The basic tenet of the phonics school is that since letter-sound relationships are needed in reading, they should be taught from the beginning of reading instruction. The counter-argument is not that letter-sound correspondences are unnecessary, but that the beginning reader has difficulty in dealing with such abstractions, and that *more efficient* learning is achieved by beginning with whole words.

6.3 *Methodology*

The experimental approach to questions of reading methodology has generally involved experiments with small numbers of children (20 to 60 or so) who are paced individually through a few training and testing sessions, with small lists of letters, words, syllables, or correspondences. Yet the results of these studies are offered, albeit with *caveat emptor* inoculations, as evidence for how children in groups should engage in sustained learning over a school year or more, absorbing not four or eight items, but many hundreds or thousands. Success and failure in a half-hour laboratory session may not be isomorphic to success and failure in the on-going classroom.

On the other hand, experiments done over long periods in the classroom are difficult to control to the same degree assumed necessary for the laboratory, are expensive, and require continual preparation and monitoring — tasks which few experimenters who are not working full time on research are willing to undertake. What appears to be needed is a re-evaluation of the methodology of reading investigation. The relative values of the experimental procedures now in vogue may need recalculating, and different forms of classroom experimentation may need to be introduced. There does not appear to be any escape from using the classroom to test many of the important phases of reading methodology, but this should not imply that the only legitimate classroom procedure is to dump different reading programs into similar classrooms and compare the final products. Over 70 years of such tests have contributed little to anything except the national debt.

A more valid procedure might be to work with existing (or new) programs, altering small, discrete segments of the materials and methods and measuring marginal gains. In this way critical components — that is, components that show the greatest sensitivity to differing procedures — could be isolated and methods perfected to the point that over-all comparisons could be made if any need exists for them. This will be a lengthy procedure, devoid of the instant solutions offered by the neatly controlled laboratory study, but the relevance of significant results will have been established *in situ* rather than by post-experimental speculation.

7. CONCLUSIONS

From a logical standpoint, both reading and learning to read are complex processes, each composed of a multiplicity of poorly understood subprocesses. Memory, language processing, word and letter recognition, letter-sound translation, sound-blending, visual scanning and a variety of other tasks are all involved, yet none of these is well-enough understood that its role in reading and reading acquisition can be assayed with certainty. The procedures employed by the competent reader, whatever they are, represent endpoints or objectives for the teaching of reading, but they translate no more readily into pedagogical procedures than do the pyramids into the techniques used to construct them. For both of these developments, the scaffolding that was so essential for construction is no longer visible in the final product. Utilization of letter-sound generalizations, for example, appears to be essential for acquiring word recognition abilities, yet in the competent reader such generalizations are infrequently observed in application.

The initial barriers to learning to read center primarily upon functions in the auditory domain, viz. recall, blending, and replacement of speech sounds; for more advanced reading, the vagaries that enter into comprehension become the limiting factors.

From all of these uncertainties, there is some comfort to be derived for our humanistic souls from the observation that the average child has considerably less trouble in learning to read than psychologists and linguists do in defining reading.

REFERENCES

ANDERSON, IRVING R., and WALTER F. DEARBORN. 1952. The psychology of teaching reading. New York, The Ronald Press.

BALLANTINE, FRANCIS R. 1951. Age changes in measures of eye-movements in silent reading. Studies in the psychology of reading, pp. 65–111. Monographs in Education 4. Ann Arbor, University of Michigan Press.

BARTON, ALLEN N. 1963. Reading research and its communication: The Columbia-Carnegie project. Reading as an intellectual activity, ed. by J. Allen Figurel. Newark, Delaware, International Reading Association.

BENNETT, ANNETTE. 1942. An analysis of errors in word recognition made by retarded readers. JEdPsych 33.25–38.

BERLIN, C. I., and A. C. DILL. 1967. The effects of feedback and positive reinforcement on the Wepman Auditory Discrimination Test Scores of lower-class Negro and white children. JSHR 10.384–89.

BIEMILLER, ANDREW. 1968. A guide to oral reading errors. Mimeographed manuscript, University of Toronto, Institute of Child Study, March 1968.

BISHOP, CAROL H. 1964. Transfer effects of word and letter training in reading. JVLVB 3.215–21.

BLANK, MARION. 1968. Cognitive processes in auditory discrimination in normal and retarded readers. CDev 39.1091–1101.

BLOOMFIELD, LEONARD. 1942. Linguistics and reading. EERev 19.125–30, 183–86.

BRUCE, D. J. 1964. The analysis of word sounds by young children. BrJEdPsych 31.158–69.

BUSWELL, GUY THOMAS. 1922. Fundamental reading habits: A study of their development. Supplementary Educational Monographs, No. 21. Chicago, University of Chicago Press.

——. 1957. The relationship between perceptual and intellectual processes in reading. California Journal of Educational Research 8.99–103.

CALFEE, ROBERT, ROBIN CHAPMAN, and RICHARD VENEZKY. 1972. How a child needs to think to learn to read. Cognition in learning and memory, ed. by Lee Gregg. New York, John Wiley.

CALFEE, ROBERT, RICHARD VENEZKY, and ROBIN CHAPMAN. 1969. Pronunciation of synthetic words with predictable and unpredictable letter-sound correspondences. Technical Report No. 71. Madison, Wisconsin Research and Development Center for Cognitive Learning.

CATTELL, JAMES MCKEEN. 1885. Über die Zeit der Erkennung und Benennung von Schriftzeichen, Bildern und Farben. Philosophische Studien 2.635–50.

CHOMSKY, NOAM, and MORRIS HALLE. 1968. The sound pattern of English. New York, Harper and Row.

CLYMER, THEODORE. 1963. The utility of phonic generalizations in the primary grades. RT 16.252–8.

COLEMAN, E. B. 1970. Collecting a data base for a reading technology. JEdPsych, Monograph 61, No. 4, Part 2.

CROSLAND, H. R. 1924. An investigation of proofreaders' illusions. University of Oregon Publication, Vol. 2, No. 6. Eugene, Oregon, University Press.

DE HIRSCH, KATRINA, JEANETTE J. JANSKY, and WILLIAM S. LANGFORD. 1966. Predicting reading failure. New York, Harper and Row.

DESBERG, PETER. 1969. Blending: Preliminary analysis and literature review. Southwest Regional Laboratory Research Memorandum, Inglewood, California.

DEUTSCH, C. P. 1964. Auditory discrimination and learning: Social factors. Merrill-Palmer Quarterly 10.277–96.

DURRELL, DONALD D. 1940. Improvement of basic reading abilities. New York, World Book Co.

——. 1958. First-grade reading success study: A summary. Journal of Education (Boston University) 140.2–6.

——. 1969. Listening comprehension versus reading comprehension. JR 12.-455–60.

EDFELDT, AKE W. 1960. Silent speech and silent reading. Chicago, University of Chicago Press.

EMONS, ROBERT. 1966. The usefulness of word pronunciation rules. Paper read at the Annual Meeting of the American Educational Research Association. Chicago.

ERDMANN, B., and R. DODGE. 1898. Psychologische Untersuchungen über das Lesen auf experimenteller Grundlage. Halle, Niemeyer.

FAIRBANKS, GRANT. 1937. The relation between eye movements and voice in the oral reading of good and poor silent readers. PsychM 48.78–107.

FRIES, CHARLES C. 1963. Linguistics and reading. New York, Holt, Rinehart and Winston.

GILBERT, LUTHER C. 1953. Functional motor efficiency of the eyes and its relation to reading. UCPE 2.159–232.

——. 1959. Speed of processing visual stimuli and its relation to reading. JEdPsych 50.8–14.

GOLDSCHEIDER, ALFRED, and ROBERT F. MULLER. 1893. Zur Physiologie und Pathologie des Lesens. Zeitschrift für Klinische Medicin 23.131–67.

GOLDSTEIN, HARRY. 1940. Reading and listening comprehension at various controlled rates. Teachers College Contributions to Education No. 821. New York, Bureau of Publications, Teachers College, Columbia University.

GRAY, WALTER S. 1925. Summary of investigations relating to reading. Supplementary Educational Monographs 28. Chicago, University of Chicago Press.

HALL, ROBERT A., JR. 1961. Sound and spelling in English. Philadelphia, Chilton Book Co.

HAMILTON, FRANCIS M. 1907. The perceptual factors in reading. Archives of Psychology 1/9.1–56.

HARDYCK, CURTIS D., and LEWIS F. PETRINOVICH. 1969. Treatment of subvocal speech during reading. JR 12.361–68, 419–22.

HATCH, EVELYN. 1969. Four experimental studies in syntax of young children. Report TR 11. Southwest Regional Laboratory for Educational Research and Development. Inglewood, California.

HOWES, D. H., and R. L. SOLOMON. 1951. Visual duration threshold as a function of word-probability. JExPsych 41.401–10.

JAVAL, ÉMILE. 1879. Essai sur la physiologie de lecture. Annales d'Oculistique 82.242–53.

JEFFREY, W. E., and S. J. SAMUELS. 1967. Effect of method of reading training on initial learning and transfer. JVLVB 6.354–8.

KORTE, WILHELM. 1923. Über die Gestaltauffassung im indirekten Sehen. ZPsych 92.17–82.

LAUMBACH, J. D. 1968. Rank-ordering two-sound words as to phonic blendability. Unpublished Master's Thesis, University of Texas at El Paso.

LEVIN, HARRY, and JOHN WATSON. 1963. The learning of variable grapheme-phoneme correspondences. A basic research program on reading, ed. by Harry Levin. Ithaca, New York, Cornell University.

LOBAN, WALTER. 1963. The language of elementary school children. NCTE Research report No. 1. Champaign, Illinois, NCTE.

McGINNIES, E., P. B. COMER, and O. L. LACEY. 1952. Visual recognition thresholds as a function of word length and word frequency. JExPsych 44.65–69.

McNEILL, J. D., and J. STONE. 1965. Note on teaching children to hear separate sounds in spoken words. JEdPsych 56.13–15.

MARCHBANKS, G., and HARRY LEVIN. 1956. Cues by which children recognize words. JEdPsych 56.56–61.

MARSH, GEORGE, and MARJORIE SHERMAN. 1970. Children's discrimination and production of phonemes in isolation and in words. Southwest Regional Laboratory Technical Note, TN–2–70–43. Inglewood, California.

MATHEWS, MITFORD M. 1966. Teaching to read, historically considered. Chicago, The University of Chicago Press.

MUEHL, SIEGMAR. 1962. Effects of letter-name knowledge on learning to read a word list in kindergarten children. JEdPsych 53.181–6.

NEISSER, ULRIC. 1967. Cognitive psychology. New York, Appleton Century Crofts.

NEISSER, ULRIC, R. NOVICK, and R. LAZAR. 1963. Searching for ten targets simultaneously. PMS 17.955–61.

OLSON, ARTHUR. 1958. Growth in word perception abilities as it relates to success in beginning reading. Journal of Education (Boston University) 140.25–36.

PILLSBURY, WALTER B. 1897. The reading of words: A study in apperception. AJPsych 8.315–93.

REBERT, NEVIN G. 1932. A laboratory study of the reading of familiar numerals. JEdPsych 23.35–45.

REID, J. F. 1966. Learning to think about reading. EdR 9.56–62.

RUDEGEAIR, ROBERT, and MICHAEL KAMIL. 1969. Assessment of phonological discrimination in children. Technical Report No. 75. Madison, Wisconsin Research and Development Center for Cognitive Learning.

RUEDIGER, W. C. 1907. The field of distance vision. ArchPsych 1/5.

SCHENK-DANZIGER, LOTTE. 1967. The concept of reading readiness in Austria. Reading instruction: An international forum, ed. by Marion D. Jenkinson, 61–69. Newark, Delaware, International Reading Association.

SINGER, HARRY. 1969. Theoretical models of reading. JC 19.134–56.

SMITH, F., DEBORAH LOTT, and B. CRONNELL. 1969. The effect of type size and case alternation on word identification. AJPsych 82.248–53.

SOLOMON, R. L., and D. H. HOWES. 1951. Word-probability, personal values, and visual duration thresholds. PsychRev 58.256–70.

SWANSON, DONALD E. 1937. Common elements in silent and oral reading. Psychological Monographs 48.36–60.

THORNDIKE, E. L., and I. LORGE. 1944. The teacher's word book of 30,000 words. New York, Bureau of Publications, Teachers College, Columbia University.

TINKER, MILES A. 1965. Bases for effective reading. Minneapolis, University of Minnesota Press.

TULVING, E., and C. GOLD. 1963. Stimulus information and contextual informaton as determinants of tachistoscopic recognition of words. JExPsych 66.-319–27.

VENEZKY, RICHARD. 1970. The structure of English orthography. The Hague, Mouton.

VENEZKY, RICHARD, and RUTH W. WEIR. 1966. A study of spelling-to-sound correspondence patterns. Final report, Cooperative Research Project No. 3090 (U.S. Office of Education). Stanford University.

VERNON, M. D. 1931. The experimental study of reading. Cambridge, University Press.

WAGNER, JULIUS. 1918. Experimentelle Beiträge zur Psychologie des Lesens. ZPsych 80.1–75.

WARDHAUGH, R. 1966. Syl-lab-i-ca-tion. EE 43.785–8.

——. 1968. Linguistic insights into the reading process. LL 18.235–52.

WEBER, ROSE-MARIE. 1968. The study of oral reading errors: A survey of the literature. RRQ 4.96–119.

——. 1970. First graders' use of grammatical context in reading. Basic studies in reading, ed. by Harry Levin and Joanna Williams. New York, Harper and Row.

WEINTRAUB, SAMUEL, and TERRY P. DENNY. 1965. What do beginning first-graders say about reading? CEd 41.326–7.

WIJK, AXEL. 1966. Rules of pronunciation for the English language. An account of the relationship between English spelling and pronunciation. London, Oxford University Press.

WILLIAMS, JOANNA. 1968. Successive versus concurrent presentation of multiple grapheme-phoneme correspondences. JEdPsych 59.309–14.

WILSON, FRANK T., and C. W. FLEMMING. 1938. Correlations of reading progress with other abilities and traits in grade 1. JGenPsych 53.33–52.

WOODWORTH, ROBERT S. 1938. Experimental psychology. New York, Henry Holt.

ZEITLER, JULIUS. 1900. Tachistoskopische Untersuchungen über das Lesen. Philosophische Studien 16.380–463.

ZHUROVA, L. E. 1963. The development of analysis of words into sounds by preschool children. Soviet Psychology and Psychiatry 2.17–27 (published originally in Russian in Voprosy psikhologii, No. 3. 1963).

LANGUAGE IN EARLY CHILDHOOD EDUCATION

VERA P. JOHN and MARSHALL I. PELLER

INTRODUCTION

The acquisition of language in the young child has frequently been compared to his mastery of walking. While few educators have as yet concerned themselves with teaching children in a school setting to walk better, they do recognize that the development of language skills is an important aspect of educational programs for young children.

Why suddenly is there so much interest in the skill of words among the very young? The reasons are varied. One of them is the challenge to the long-held assumption that the six-year old child has achieved a fundamental competency in language and is ready to learn the written forms of his native tongue. The critics of this favored generalization include the transformational grammarians who ascribe the process of mastery to a biologically determined 'language-acquisition device'. Carol Chomsky (1969) articulates this criticism in the beginning of her study of school-age children: 'the child of five or six may still not have mastered certain — perhaps surprisingly many — aspects of the structure of his language that the mature speaker takes for granted and commands quite naturally.' Students of social class differences also question the accuracy of this long-held tenet about language and the young child. They have asserted that the lower academic achievement of the child of poverty is due, to a large extent, to the limitations of his language skills at the time he starts school. While some linguists, for example Labov (1970), have challenged these conclusions, the very controversy concerning class-linked differences in language performance has kindled interest in these issues.

Of greatest significance, we think, is an emerging concern, on the part of some students of behavior, about uniquely human skills and their importance to educability. In the wake of a primarily reductionist psychology, young scholars are searching for relevance in their scientific endeavors. Members of the middle class are no longer isolated from the experiences of their non-white and poor neighbors. Concern for the millions who have been uprooted from their homes and alienated from their traditional ways of life, as a result of wars, forced migrations, economic and technological changes, characterizes the outlook of some professionals. The fate of these individuals, particularly the young among them, has been the subject of considerable rhetoric and many short-term projects. Among these is the interest in, and stress upon, early intervention programs with a language focus in ghetto and reservation communities.

Language, it is argued, is basic to the ways in which we learn to deal with changing social realities. The representational function of words serves to internalize and stabilize the fleeting and conflicting aspects of the world experienced by the child. But the attitudes of the non-English speaking child toward those who natively speak the language he is expected to acquire as a second language plays a significant role in the speed and breadth of his acquisition. Similarly, an uprooted child even in a monolingual environment is confronted with many new and baffling experiences. How, and by whom, should these children be taught to speak? Is there a need to modify or develop their skills of speech acquired from parents whose use of language may differ profoundly from their new city neighbors?

Answers to these questions are advanced based on pragmatic considerations. In spite of the need articulated by younger scholars for socially relevant knowledge in these realms, we are sorely lacking theoretical work connected to these problems. A well-developed field of language pedagogy, complex and interdisciplinary, proposed by Spolsky (1970) is not yet in existence; in its absence, contemporary programmatic efforts aimed at young children are flawed. (In this context, the attitude of many established psychologists and linguists is disturbing. The comments of one outstanding psycholinguist of the tarnsformational bent may be typical. When queried about the educational implications of his research in language acquisition, he was shocked by the question. He protested, 'I know nothing of education'.)

It may be redundant to argue, in a volume such as this, for greater cooperative efforts on the part of theoreticians and scientists in the field. It is obvious to most individuals that educative efforts have suffered greatly because of the lack of concerted efforts by all those who are gathering knowledge related to language; thus, we are deprived of a worthy theory and practice of language pedagogy.

In light of these concerns, we have chosen to present descriptions of early childhood programs as they relate to some as yet unresolved, but crucial, issues in the disciplines of language. An additional reason for such a strategy is the writers' need to avoid repeating themselves. The interested reader is referred to a recent review of language programs by John and Moskovitz (1970). A comprehensive evaluation of these programs (forthcoming), currently directed by Courtney Cazden, will offer the needed detail to complement this and other reviews.

1. IS THERE A DISTINCTION BETWEEN RECEPTIVE AND PRODUCTIVE COMPETENCE?

Frequently, deviations from experiences that most humans take for granted offer the scientist an approach to a thorny problem. The closely entwined cycle of hearing and speaking makes it difficult to separate the contributions of each in the process of language acquisition. The training program devised by the French physician Itard for Victor, *The wild boy of Aveyron* (1932), was an interesting method of dealing with the complexities of comprehension.

Itard had worked intensively for five years with this feral child, but little progress in production was made by the tutored. Victor could say but two exclamations, although his comprehension of words and phrases, both oral and written, was considerable. Recognizing some lack in Victor's auditory channel, Itard trained his pupil by associating written names with objects and eventually classes of objects.

The method Itard developed is not too different from that which is used at present by the tutors of the deaf. They, too, rely upon a visual channel for the training of comprehension. The painstaking and imaginative work in lip-reading, conducted in institutions such as the John Tracey Clinic for the preschool deaf child, is based upon associations between names and referents, eventually including classes of referents. The names are mouthed by the tutor in the presence of the referent. Just as Itard was not satisfied with linking the word 'book' to a single object, similarly, in the course of work with active three-year-old toddlers, the tutors of the deaf choose multiple instances of 'airplanes' to associate with the lip-read label.

The recognition that training in comprehension can take place in the absence of much progress in production skills is understood by individuals who work with biologically damaged children. However, in the many programs aimed at ghetto and reservation children this understanding is not incorporated. Their emphasis is overwhelmingly upon increasing spoken vocabulary and developing sentence complexity in young children's speech without realizing that the antecedents to the production of oral speech are in comprehension. We shall return in greater detail to a discussion of this issue, particularly in its relevance to the bidialectal speaker and the formal proposal made by R. Troike (1970) which has grown out of his research with speakers of non-standard dialects of English, concerning receptive and productive competence.

The frequent, and nearly unconscious, identification of growth in language with overt speech needs to be challenged from another point of view as well. Neurophysiological evidence seems to substantiate the existence of some independence between comprehension and production. Geschwind (1967) presents a simple two-step model in which the linkage between the visual and auditory cortex, necessary for much of language comprehension, represents a different system from that linking the auditory association area with the motor cortex, the latter being primarily involved in production. The evidence he cites is based upon his work with brain lesions.

These various strains of language-related research and experience suggest quite strongly that the neglect of the importance and the development of receptive competence in most language programs may be a serious oversight. Susan Ervin-Tripp (1970) argues that in bilingual programs there is a need for an intense period of training in comprehension preceding speaking. This approach replicates the sequence of language development in infancy.

2. FROM WORDS TO PHRASES:
CREATIVE ASPECTS OF LANGUAGE OR HABIT?

Parents celebrate the first words of their infants as the dividing line between infancy and childhood. But the linguist considers a slightly later achievement as crucial, that of combining words into utterances: it is patterned speech that forms the basis of the study of grammar.

Psychologists, like parents, have been particularly interested in the first words of children. Many studies of the last half-century have been devoted to an assessment of vocabulary growth of children from various backgrounds. The close correspondence between performance on vocabulary tests and other measures of achievement and intelligence has led to the belief that semantic growth is fundamental to academic achievement. Thus, there has been the creation of many preschool programs which have an ambitious curriculum aimed at vocabulary growth. (In Vineland, New Jersey, migrant children are expected to have mastered a vocabulary of 2,000 words at the end of a preschool program, including 170 terms devoted to body parts.) This simple-minded approach to language development, illustrated by such programmatic endeavors, is a further example of the need for a theory of language pedagogy as the basis of intervention methods.

While research on patterned speech has been flourishing during the last decade (see the chapter by Ursula Bellugi in this volume), the impact of this work on educational intervention is debatable. Bereiter and Engelmann (1966) describe their approach to intervention in *Teaching disadvantaged children in the preschool*. In order to improve the use of grammatical structures among their students — ghetto children drawn from predominantly black, inner city neighborhoods — they have adopted the model of pattern drills, borrowed from the foreign language teacher. Some of their objectives are: the production of 'complete sentences', plural forms and negatives in the speech of these children.

This approach has been criticized by linguists, both directly and indirectly. The alternative concept of language development from that which governs the work of Bereiter and Engelmann is expressed by Spolsky (1970: 150) in a series of assumptions:

(1) Language use is essentially creative; thus the notion of language as habit is not possible.
(2) The best explanation of this aspect of language is to say that the speaker of a language has available a system of rules to be used to produce and understand new sentences.

In criticizing the concept of habit as relevant to language use, Spolsky attacks the very foundations of the Bereiter-Engelmann program. Labov as well has attacked the basic assumptions upon which their intervention program is based: he questions the accuracy and the interpretation of their observations of the language of Black children. For example, in these programs much effort is devoted to the copula in the language drills in which the four-year old students partake. Labov argues, based on his own comprehensive research efforts among children of all ages in Harlem, that the copula is not absent from their speech. Depending upon the social context and/or communicative intent, it may or may not be included in the speech of black ghetto children. Interestingly, the frequency of copula inclusion is greater among the younger children whose age corresponds to those enrolled in these educational preschool programs.

In spite of these severe criticisms by linguists, the Bereiter-Engelmann program is exceedingly popular among educators. Their faith in the approach is based upon changes in test performance on the part of children who have participated in the academically-oriented preschool designed by Bereiter and Engelmann. In a published report, the research director of the New York State Department of Education, Louis DiLorenzo, urges the wide-scale adoption of this model (1969). This recommendation is based upon a three-year study in which a number of preschool programs were compared. While the greatest gains in intelligence test scores and in performance on some parts of the Illinois Test of Psycholinguistic Abilities were shown by those in the academically-oriented preschool, children gained in vocabulary scores in less structured programs as well.

There are some important questions this kind of report raises. White children from economically disadvantaged homes profited most from the intervention efforts, according to this report, while middle class children failed to gain in tested scores. These findings can be interpreted as follows: speakers of non-standard Negro English (NNE) when exposed to training in test-English (which is what this program specifically aimed at) have to learn a new dialect as well as a new style. White, low-income children face a more limited task: they are receiving training in a style more formal than that which they speak. Middle-class children, on the other hand, already have some skill in the style required for effective performance on the Bereiter-Engelmann program, and thus, they are least likely to gain from it.

In contrast with the claims of Bereiter and Engelmann that their program helps to overcome the deficiencies of thought associated with deviations in grammar, Labov (1970) interprets the effects of this intervention as teaching ghetto children to produce slightly different forms of language than those they already speak. While such changes may ease the task of the teacher unfamiliar with non-standard English, Labov claims that the eventual outcome of programs, such as the academically-oriented preschool, may be disastrous: 'Those who know the sociolinguistic situation cannot doubt that reaction against the Bereiter-Engelmann approach in later years will be even more violent on the part of students involved, and their rejection of the school system will be even more categorical' (Labov 1970: 28).

If instructional programs characterized by drill are open to severe linguistic and sociological criticism, what alternatives are there to the educator concerned with improving the language skills of poor children? One approach, suggested by Spolsky, is that 'language can be acquired by active listening (listening and doing) even better than by listening and repeating' (Spolsky 1970: 150). Support for this statement comes from Courtney Cazden's work with young ghetto children: she found gains in syntactical growth on the part of those children who participated in individual learning sessions. The most beneficial treatment consisted of exposure to well-formed sentences (Cazden 1965). She interprets these findings to mean that a child's exposure to variations in the patterns and content of language contributes to his forming and testing grammatical hypotheses; those variations may enhance his attentional processes as well.

These results have been discussed by a number of linguists, but less attention has been paid to them by psychologists interested in the interpersonal context of language acquisition. Of significance is the individualized nature of instruction in the case of children who spend most of their waking hours in the company of many age-mates and only one adult.

3. THE WISH TO SPEAK

Many scholars devoted to language have emphasized the universality of speech acquisition, while others are primarily concerned with the large number of children whose language deviates from the normal. Menyuk analyzes the syntactic features characterizing the production of language by children labeled as 'immature' speakers; they formulate their sentences by using only the most general rules. While criticizing the simplistic notion that this type of speech resembles that of the chronologically younger child, she does not offer any explanations for the etiology of these deviations (Menyuk 1967).

Psychologists and clinicians of speech have put forth theories of language acquisition to account for normal as well as deviant development. In the recently published, *Language learning and communication disorders in children,* Gertrude Wyatt presents the following assumption:

The optimum condition for successful language learning in early childhood is a continuous, undisrupted, and affectionate relationship between mother and child, manifested in frequent and appropriate communication, both verbal and non-verbal. (Wyatt 1969:19)

In stressing the mother-child relationship, Wyatt articulates the Freudian view that the learning of the 'mother-tongue' is an intensely emotional process. Of particular significance to the psychoanalysts is the child's identification with a loved adult and his wish to imitate him or her. The evidence often cited in favor of this position is studies of institutionalized children. 'All observers agreed that the majority of children in this category (institutional and hospitalized children) were retarded in their development and that language was the area most affected' (Wyatt 1969:22).

Linguists have questioned the naïveté of some of the measures used to arrive at such conclusions: to them, the speed and universality with which children learn to internalize syntactical structures is ample evidence of the biological instead of the social-emotional roots of learning. However, these two groups concern themselves with different aspects of the verbal process. The clinician studies articulation and the rate of language acquisition; he lacks sophistication about grammar. He/she is also interested in the functional use of words, in communication and cognition. His therapeutic endeavors are aimed at children with halting or indistinct speech, or, as in the case of the autistic child, with one who fails to communicate altogether.

The failure to talk on the part of some children raises the question: why do children have the urge to speak? The contemporary language scholar is reluctant to speculate about the historical and individual origins of language beyond the statement made by Chomsky and his students that language is a uniquely human accomplishment. Lenneberg (1966) criticizes the concept of 'need' in the analysis of language acquisition: he argues that biology accounts for the nature of language universals and for the inevitability of language acquisition as well.

But the observations on the functional diversity of language use in distinct cultural and familial environments forced us to question a purely biological position. In this chapter we will explore only a few psychological considerations, recognizing the vastness and difficulty of the subject.

The very young child resists the physical separation between himself and his caretakers which so inevitably takes place in the course of growth. He cries; he extends his arms, asking to be picked up; he throws tantrums; and some children, who fail in their efforts to reach a desired end, turn to animals and toys as substitutes. Smiles, cooing and the slow growth of intelligible speech bridges the physical distance between mother and child. Communication takes the place of direct manipulation: the child asks for what he wants instead of tugging and pointing; the parent offers, directs, protects and instructs by words as well as deeds. While much early verbal play is not goal-directed, it is possible to recognize several needs that language serves in the life of the very young child. Wyatt delineates some of these:

Thus language, even at this early stage, already has a variety of functions: to structure reality selectively and thus protect the child against overwhelming sensory-motor stimulation; to express wishes and desires; to make people do things for the child; to communicate with others; and finally, to help the child to cope with anxiety-provoking experiences. (Wyatt 1969: 60-61)

We are not suggesting that children learn to speak because of these needs, but that the capacity for speech, the playful exploration of speech and the functional usefulness of speech *together* form the basis of language acquisition.

The social context in which language acquisition takes place is of great interest to the sociolinguist. While comparative studies have just been started (Slobin 1967) their promise is a substantial one. Kernan (1969) found that Samoan children who spent most of their day with peers do not combine words into pivot structures until their third year of life, while most Western children studied accomplish this significant step during their second year. (It is interesting that Samoan as well as American children often produce two-word sentences denoting possession and territoriality — Brown 1970.)

The rate of language acquisition is affected by familial as well as cultural factors. In technologically developed societies, alienation from nature and the security of the kinship society forces parents and children alike to rely heavily upon verbal communication as a respite from such alienation. In tribal and agricultural societies, on the other hand, the conveying of skills as well as emotional closeness is achieved by shared activities as well as verbal communication. Because of the inordinate reliance upon language in the world of professional fathers and college-educated mothers, any break in the communicative network presents a particularly severe threat to the growing child. The high percentage of kindergarten and 1st grade children, identified by the predominantly middle-class Wellesley, Massachusetts school system as being in need of speech therapy, may be explained by the vulnerability of these children to communication breakdowns (Wyatt 1969).

In short, the wish to speak, though present in all children, may be differently patterned according to the social and emotional environment of the growing child. In neglecting some of the suggestions of the clinically oriented student of speech we may underestimate the impact of these variables in the acquisition and educationally-facilitated development of language.

4. THE ROLE OF MEANING IN LEARNING

We mentioned earlier in this chapter that some preschool educators have a rather naïve notion of language objectives for their programs: they wish to teach a certain number of words to their pupils. While the notion that mastery of words is all there is to language is rightly challenged by linguists, the contemporary neglect of semantics in the study of language acquisition is a distressing phenomenon. One is reminded of the structure-function debates in biology. The study of the acquisition of syntax is reminiscent of growth studies of the anatomy which neglected the functional aspects of body use.

There is an elegance to studying a system which has internal rules and in which the difference between children and adults can be represented by a logical progression of differentiations. Such is the study of syntax. The role of word meaning, however, is a messy affair. The way young children assign meaning to their sounds is often arbitrary — witness the example of Lewis of 'fafa' which refers to flowers as well as a design on a biscuit (Lewis 1959); or the delightful description by Gertrude Wyatt of her child's use of 'foffa' originally the name of a favorite baby-sitter (Sophie), who came home once with a colorful umbrella. Later, 'foffa' is used as an adjective in many of the child's utterances describing colorfulness (Wyatt 1969).

The development of meaning is closely tied to the non-verbal experiences of the child as defined by the specific aspects of his social environment. We know little about the earliest attempts at the acquisition of meaning beside the stimulating accounts of it presented in diary studies. It seems clear, however, that the role of tuition is of greater significance in semantic learning than in the acquisition of grammar (Cazden 1965). The issues of meaning are closely tied with the role of language in thought, a topic of engaging controversy at present.

5. THE LANGUAGE OF THOUGHT, OR THOUGHT BEFORE LANGUAGE

Most students of development acknowledge the importance of the earliest, non-verbal stages of thought, best described by Piaget in his work on sensory-motor intelligence. But theoretical differences emerge among child psychologists regarding the importance ascribed to language for thought once the child has reached the age of a speaker. Piaget and his students do not view language in a causal role; its purpose is communication rather than knowing. Speech, conceived as the vehicle of communication rather than as a reflection of logical thinking, is analyzed in its use socially.

An argument presented in favor of this position is as follows: there does not necessarily have to be any linguistic difference between a logically correct and incorrect answer. Furth (1969) presents an example illustrating this point. When asked why the sun is called the sun a child may reply 'because it is yellow' or 'because the sun gives more light than the moon and people thought it was the best name' before he realizes that a name is distinct from the objective reality of the referent, and says something like 'for no reason, it is just a name'. Both types of reply demonstrate a similar level of language ability, but at the same time they indicate that progress in logical thinking may not be linked with progress in linguistic skills.

Piaget is not claiming that language and thought are unrelated. He definitely acknowledges a relation between the development of these two processes, but states that thought can be neither reduced to nor explained by language. Ordering objects, grouping them and other such motor abilities are the foundations upon which mental operations and abstractions are conducted, while language (according to the psychologists of Geneva) is built from imitations of patterns provided by experiences with adults. Once acquired in this manner, language facilitates the expansion and mobility of thought.

The great emphasis upon language by those working with young disadvantaged children is criticized by Kohlberg from a Piagetian framework:

The stimulation of cognitive development involves something much more refined than the focus upon verbal labeling and grammar characterizing current pre-school programs. (Kohlberg 1968: 1043)

Though the pedagogical implications of his theory have been of limited interest to Piaget, there have been a number of attempts to implement his notions in educational settings. Stendler-Lavatelli (1968) described a program in the Oakland Children's Center in which operations such as one-to-one correspondence, classification and seriation were taught to the preschoolers. Facilitation of cognitive reorganization requires a carefully planned, long-term program in which the children participate actively, manipulating a wide variety of materials. Even under these conditions, modifications of cognitive structures are likely to occur within a stage (as defined by Piaget). The aim of the Oakland program was to offer 'environmental facilitation to logical thinking'; the lesson plans were designed in accordance with Piaget's research on the order of development of the concepts.

The tutorial approach of Marion Blank (1968) is based on a set of assumptions about language and thought different from those of Piaget. While the latter emphasizes the role of manipulation, Blank stresses the importance of the verbal dialogue in the formation of an 'abstract attitude'. She has described her approach as a combination of 'Socratic dialogue' and discovery learning. The one-to-one tutorial interaction she recommends is modeled after the verbal exchanges characteristic of some middle-class homes. The child is taught to question, probe and investigate in order to build upon previous experience. Young, disadvantaged children are seen as suffering from a lack of an adequate symbolic system for organizing all the stimulation surrounding them rather than from experiential deficits. In criticizing other approaches to preschool education, Blank argues that disadvantaged children are not devoid of experience and that merely presenting them with a wide array of 'enriched' stimuli may not be synonymous with its being incorporated into their cognitive repertoire. The tutorial sessions described by Blank and Solomon (1968) are taught by specially trained nursery school teachers. The sessions are short, individualized and take place in nursery school settings.

The focus upon language as basic to the development of cognition characterizes other preschool programs as well. The work of Martin Deutsch and his collaborators at the Institute for Developmental Studies illustrates this kind of an orientation (1967). The preschool teachers trained by Susan Gray in Nashville also stress language skills and cognition. The most pervasive approach to thinking via language is evident in the writing of Soviet educators. Their concern for the development of speech in all Soviet children educated in nurseries and kindergartens is reflected in the recently translated manual, *Soviet preschool education* (Chauncey 1969). In the section devoted to the first infant group, childcare workers are urged to

encourage humming and babbling, since at this time the organs involved in articulation and aural attention are developing, and these activities will establish the necessary foundation for the development of speech. (Chauncey 1969: 14)

Further in the manual, age-specific recommendations are made for the development of speech, stressing its role in communication and cognition. For instance, in discussing two- to three-year old children, the authors stress 'primitive comparisons, deductions and generalizations' as examples of language activities characteristic of that age. In reading this volume, one is struck by the influence of Soviet psychologists such as Luria and Vygotsky, recognizing, of course, that the full complexity of their thinking is not used in the development of the educational recommendations. (A similar difficulty in relating articulated theory to educational practice has plagued the followers of Jean Piaget.)

Thought and language, which reflect reality in a way different from that of perception, are the key to the nature of human consciousness. Words play a central part not only in the development of thought but in the historical growth of consciousness as a whole. A word is a microcosm of human consciousness. (Vygotsky 1962: 153)

Throughout *Thought and language,* Vygotsky emphasizes the changing connections between words and thought. Developmentally, the links are constantly modified. Historically, our need for verbal thought has been dependent upon the way in which we insure our survival and relate to our fellows. Views of language and thought by students of human behavior also reveal a history of change. At a time when studies of speech and cognition were limited, the simplistic views of J. B. Watson (1930), postulating the identity of the two, were accepted by many of his colleagues. Today, with the great increase in research in these two fields, theories of greater differentiation are proposed. However, our present approaches still lack the definitiveness needed by practitioners in the field. They are forced to make their own pedagogical decisions about fostering the language of thought and thought before language.

6. TEACHING AND TESTING

The impact of instruction is traditionally assessed by changes in tested achievement. Standardized tests are constructed to measure most aspects of human performance from birth to death. Tests of verbal proficiency are available in great number and are frequently used as indicators of program effectiveness. It is questionable whether instruments such as the Wechsler Preschool and Primary Scale of Intelligence (WPPSI) in its verbal scales or the Illinois Test of Psycholinguistic Abilities (ITPA) do indeed measure changes in language.

Tests of vocabulary appear to be synonymous with language in the work of the psychologist of measurement; and Standard English is assumed to be the universal medium of communicative exchanges for the children of the United States. Though linguists would question whether information, comprehension and vocabulary items are effective indicators of language growth, these are the types of items which saturate most tests used in evaluating the results of first language pedagogy.

A test is a sample of behavior elicited under standardized conditions. It is possible that in sampling over-learned, quasi-automatic behavior (for example, the speed of typing) reliable estimates of behavior can be obtained. But, when measuring complex behavior such as language or cognitive performance, the assumptions governing most tests need to be challenged.

The first issue of concern is the choice of *test content*. Are the aspects of language measured of true significance, and what are some of the hidden task requirements which really determine performance? Elsa Roberts (1970) argues quite convincingly that psychologists are not aware of the grammatical features of test items aimed at assessing information or analogies. Though syntactical cues are essential for correctly answering certain items, these are rather haphazardly included in tests of comprehension. The children who are speakers of non-standard dialects are particularly penalized on tests such as the ITPA with its grammatical closure sub-test which requires them to produce plural forms which are often absent or infrequently used in their dialect.

Many children, however, improve their performance on standardized tests after participating in an instructional program. The graduates of the Bereiter-Engelmann preschools have scored higher on the ITPA than control subjects (DiLorenzo 1969). But has their language truly improved? Are they more competent speakers? We mentioned earlier Labov's position, that the effects of such a program are to teach children slightly different forms of speech, but at a great price. The children become familiar with the communicative styles of the school. These objectives are the result of programs which are tailored to improve test performance, in the absence of either a true knowledge about language or a precise understanding of the role of tuition in the development of verbal proficiencies.

Even those devoted to the study of language acquisition occasionally use standard measures. However, their purpose, as phrased by Roberts, 'is to use tests to learn about the language of children rather than to fit children into pre-determined categories' (1970:9). It is recognized that performance in a standardized situation can give a false impression of the level of language development, even in the case of middle-class children. Braine (1967) quotes one example: according to his own studies and those of other workers, three-year-olds show a nearly universal control of the subject-object distinction when analysis is based upon free-speech samples. But children assessed by a standardized measure, as were the subjects in Fraser, Bellugi and Brown's study (1963), produced these distinctions accurately only fifty percent of the time. Young children are particularly affected by the artificiality of the testing situation; they display what they know when they are secure, motivated, and understand what is expected of them. Only under the most unusual conditions can tests approach an accurate reflection of knowledge; and in measuring verbal proficiency, the child is tested under circumstances in which even the process is as yet poorly understood. The detailed study of language acquisition is still in its infancy. Though some findings have been substantiated by a number of workers, these do not constitute a pool of items for those who construct tests of 'language'.

The emergent findings from language acquisition studies continue to be ignored by test constructors. Their efforts maintain a circularity of reasoning reminiscent of the oft-heard comment, 'intelligence is that which intelligence tests measure'.

We would like to urge the adoption of a different point of view. If a human process cannot be adequately described, and/or knowledge is insufficient for effectively teaching it, let us then refrain from testing such a process.

A precise definition of a 'behavioral objective' can be given in certain spheres of language such as the appropriate uses of negation in the speech of the child. Nevertheless, the acquisition of such a marker still may not fit the form of linear increment learning. The acquisition of grammar offers many examples of the circuitous road by which new forms are acquired. Children tend to overgeneralize in their testing of grammatical and semantic hypotheses. They reveal significant increases of error, as well, followed by a sudden drop of incorrect forms preceding usage akin to that of adults. To scale such a process of acquisition in the traditional manner of linear increases is highly questionable. The popularity of vocabulary tests derives to a large extent from the apparent simple additive nature of word acquisition. However, this, too, is an untested assumption, since the relationship among words is frequently more crucial than the number of items in the child's repertoire.

In short, the current emphasis on testing may be questioned on many grounds, including the content of the tests, the conditions under which children are tested (particularly with its impact on the minority child) and the danger of instruction being tailored to fit tests in order to heighten gain scores. Also, specifically in the area of language, it is necessary to question the assumption that learning is simply incremental since that notion seems to be contradicted by findings in different areas of language acquisition.

In appearance, the aims of early intervention programs may seem deceptively simple: to increase the child's vocabulary, to encourage him/her to speak in full sentences, and to make him verbal and articulate in the manner of his middle-class peers. The methods chosen to achieve these ends are varied: pattern drills, tutorial instruction, and the catch-all category of verbal enrichment. Prevalent in all these attempts is the notion that children can be shaped through education into young learners who are acceptable to their teachers.

Our view is that language is not an isolated skill, an occasional performance to be rewarded by a smile or a cookie; language is a most pervasive force in the life of the growing child. The development of communicative competence depends first of all upon the intactness of the human body and human spirit. Most educators ignore the extent to which ghetto children are handicapped in the development of their full learning capacities by poor nutrition, frequent illnesses and the sequelae of reproductive injuries. It is our conviction that the improvement of the quality of life in the ghettos and reservations is more crucial to the development of language and cognitive capacities in young children than programs aimed at eradicating their dialects.

Children need many opportunities for exploring their language, for building and testing hypotheses, for hearing the speech of others while playfully improving their own. The preschool environments that offer such opportunities together with medical, nutritional and social facilities can contribute to the development of communicative competence in young children. Although specific instructional goals are hard to formulate at this stage of our knowledge, linguists familiar with the range of competencies of ghetto children are beginning to address themselves to this task (Labov, personal communication).

These criticisms of most extant programs of first-language pedagogy are based upon a disagreement with the oft-stated view that a child can, and should be, molded and shaped by the teacher, as though the child were an object. Piaget has stressed that 'knowing' is the result of active exploration; Chomsky has spoken of the creative aspects of language development; Vygotsky has written of the importance of a child engaging in meaningful dialogue with those around him. It is our belief that a child should not be an object of education, but rather that education should be an integral force in the growth of the child.

Language development is not separate from human development. In both words and life, the active role of the growing child is essential.

REFERENCES

BEREITER, C., and S. ENGELMANN. 1966. Teaching disadvantaged children in the preschool. Engelwood Cliffs, New Jersey, Prentice-Hall, Inc.

BLANK, MARION, and FRANCES SOLOMON. 1968. A tutorial language program to develop abstract thinking in socially disadvantaged children. CDev 39.379–90.

BRAINE, M. D. S. 1967. The acquisition of language in infant and child. Washington, D.C., Walter Reed Army Institute of Research. MS.

BROWN, R. 1970. First sentences in child and chimpanzee. Harvard University, mimeo.

CAZDEN, C. 1965. Environmental assistance to the child's acquisition of grammar. Ph.D. Dissertation, Harvard University.

——. 1968. Some implications of research on language development for preschool education. Early education, ed. by Robert D. Hess and Roberta M. Baer, ch. 11. Chicago, Aldine Publishing Company.

——. 1970. Transplanting English Infant School ideas to American classrooms and some effects of language use. Paper read at AERA Symposium on Anthropological Approaches in Educational Research, March 1970.

CHAUNCEY, HENRY, ed. 1969. Soviet preschool education, vol. 1. New York, Holt, Rinehart & Winston for Educational Testing Service.

CHOMSKY, CAROL. 1969. The acquisition of syntax in children from 5 to 10. Research Monograph 57. Cambridge, Mass., The M.I.T. Press.

DEUTSCH, MARTIN. 1967. The disadvantaged child, selected papers of Martin Deutsch and associates. New York, Basic Books, Inc.

DiLORENZO, L. T. 1969. Prekindergarten programs for educationally disadvantaged children. Washington, D.C., Office of Education, Bureau of Research.

ERVIN-TRIPP, S. 1970. Structure and process in language acquisition. Report of the 21st Annual Roundtable Meeting on Linguistics and Language Studies. MSLL 23.313–54.

FRASER, C., U. BELLUGI, and R. W. BROWN. 1963. Control of grammar in imitation, comprehension, and production. JVLVB 2.121–35.

FURTH, H. G. 1969. Piaget and knowledge: Theoretical foundations. Engelwood Cliffs, New Jersey, Prentice-Hall, Inc.

GESCHWIND, N. 1967. The neural basis of language. Research in verbal behavior and some neurophysiological implications, ed. by K. and S. Salzinger, pp. 423–27. New York, Academic Press.

ITARD, J. M. G. 1932. The wild boy of Aveyron. New York, Century.

JOHN, V., and S. MOSKOVITZ. 1970. Language acquisition and development in early childhood. Linguistics in school programs, 69th yearbook of The National Society for the Study of Education, ch. 4. Chicago, University of Chicago Press.

KERNAN, K. T. 1969. The acquisition of language by Samoan children. Language Behavior Research Laboratory, Working Paper 21.

KOHLBERG, LAWRENCE. 1968. Early education: A cognitive developmental view. CDev 39.1013–62.

LABOV, W. 1970. The logic of nonstandard English. Language and poverty: Perspectives on a theme, ed. by F. Williams, pp. 153–89. Chicago, Markham.

LENNEBERG, E. H. 1966. The natural history of language. The genesis of language, ed. by F. Smith and G. A. Miller, pp. 219–52. Cambridge, Mass., M.I.T. Press.

LEWIS, M. M. 1959. How children learn to speak. New York, Basic Books, Inc.

MENYU, P. 1967. Acquisition of grammar by children. Research in verbal behavior and some neurophysiological implications, ed. by K. and S. Salzinger, pp. 101–10. New York, Academic Press.

PIAGET, J. 1967. Six psychological studies. New York, Random House.

ROBERTS, ELSA. 1970. An evaluation of standardized tests as tools for the measurement of language and development. Cambridge, Mass., Language Research Foundation, mimeo.

SLOBIN, DAN I. 1967. A field manual for cross-cultural study of the acquisition of communicative competence. University of California at Berkeley, mimeo.

SPOLSKY, B. 1970. Linguistics and language pedagogy — applications or implications. MSLL 22.143–57.

STENDLER-LAVATELLI, CELIA. 1968. Environmental intervention in infancy and early childhood. Social class, race, and psychological development, ed. by M.

Deutsch, I. Katz, and A. R. Jensen, pp. 347–80. New York, Holt, Rinehart & Winston, Inc.

TROIKE, R. 1970. Productive competence and performance. MSLL 22.

VYGOTSKY, L. S. 1962. Thought and language. Edited and translated by Eugenia Hanfmann and Gertrude Vakar. Cambridge, Mass., M.I.T. Press.

WATSON, J. B. 1930. Behaviorism. New York, Norton.

WYATT, GERTRUDE L. 1969. Language learning and communication disorders in children. New York, The Free Press.

LINGUISTICS AND THE LANGUAGE ARTS IN ELEMENTARY AND SECONDARY EDUCATION

RUDOLPH C. TROIKE

Although the science of linguistics is now over a century and a half old, its impact on education in the United States has come only in the last two decades, and only as a result of the dedicated efforts of a small number of leaders in the profession. The rapid progress of this development has been adequately documented elsewhere in this *Current Trends in Linguistics* series (Volume 10) in papers by Ives and Ives and Albert H. Marckwardt, and so will not be dealt with here. The present paper will attempt to define the relevance of linguistics to the content and teaching of English and the language arts, and will try to identify certain needs in the areas of application and research.

1. LANGUAGE LEARNING, GRAMMAR, AND LANGUAGE VARIETY

From the linguist's point of view, probably the single most important thing the language arts teacher — and curriculum designer — can do is to implement to the fullest possible extent the first precept of all education: to accept the pupil where he is. The principal difficulty in the way of acting on this precept — which has been more honored in the breach than in the observance — is that teachers are poorly informed about the facts of language development, and often have a false set of expectations regarding the competence of their students. At the same time, they lack the necessary training which would enable them to discover where their students actually are. Unfortunately, test-developers are little better informed, so that most evaluational devices are woefully inadequate, and not infrequently are strongly biased, both in language and culture.

The first step, then, in putting this precept into practice is learning something about how children acquire language, and about what it is that they acquire. Research in child language acquisition is only just beginning, and there are at present more questions than answers, but enough information is available to provide some guidelines for educational policy.[1]

It appears that all normal children are born with a built-in ability to acquire

---

[1] Some of the most important and accessible references are as follows (see also the papers by Bellugi, Fishman, and Bernstein in the present volume): Lenneberg (1964), Smith and Miller (1966), Menyuk (1969), and Chomsky (1969).

language. This ability is identical in children of all races, and is unique to the human species ('species-specific'). How the child acquires his language is largely unknown, but the brain is evidently 'pre-programmed' to carry out an analysis of the linguistic data to which the child is exposed, and to extract from that data his own internal grammar. By the time the child is six years old, he knows, i.e. has internalized, roughly 80 percent of the grammar of his language. In order for one to appreciate the extraordinary nature of this fact, it should be recognized that the average six-year-old knows more of the grammar of his language than any grammarian has ever been able to collect in a book, even after a lifetime of work.

Of course there remain aspects of the grammar of the language which the child will not ordinarily acquire until later, in particular certain complex syntactic structures, but by the time the child comes to the first grade, or even kindergarten, he has mastered most of the basic grammatical structures and has been practicing them intensively for several years. By this time also most children have mastered the pronunciation (the PHONOLOGY) of their language, and have control of a functional vocabulary adequate to their nonscholastic needs (because there is no basic agreement on how to count 'words', estimates on the number vary widely and are quite unreliable).

A crucial concept for the educator, though a very unfamiliar one, is that of GRAMMAR, and what it means to 'know', or to have 'internalized', the grammar of a language. In the view of most linguists, grammar is not a descriptive account in a book, and especially not a set of prescribed 'do's' and 'dont's' (e.g. say 'It is I', not 'It is me'; don't use double negatives; etc.). Rather, grammar is the knowledge in the head of the speaker which enables him to construct and comprehend sentences in his language. One cannot speak and understand a language without knowing its grammar. A FUNDAMENTAL ASSUMPTION, THEN, WHICH MUST GUIDE ALL LANGUAGE ARTS INSTRUCTION, IS THAT THE STUDENT ALREADY KNOWS THE GRAMMAR OF HIS LANGUAGE BEFORE HE ENTERS SCHOOL.

This idea is often very hard to accept at first, and frequently evokes the reaction, 'But what about students who say "I ain't got no money", instead of "I don't have any money", or "I seen him" instead of "I saw him", or "Her pretty" instead of "She is pretty"? Surely they don't know the grammar?' The answer is that they do indeed know the grammar, but in order to grasp this fact it is necessary to understand something about the nature of linguistic variation, and the character of 'standard' languages.

When two groups of speakers using the same language become separated for any length of time, changes — in pronunciation, grammar, and vocabulary — will gradually develop in the usage of each group, particularly as new generations grow up, until in time it becomes readily apparent from the speech of an individual which group he belongs to. If the groups are separated geographically, their speech-forms are termed REGIONAL VARIETIES (dialects); if the groups are separated socially, in a class-stratified society, the distinctions in speech are termed SOCIAL VARIETIES (dialects). Linguists have long recognized that change in language is a natural and inevitable phenomenon, and does not lead to deterioration of a language. If it did, we could not explain the fact that French, Spanish, and Italian, which all derive from Latin, still function just as well as Latin as mediums of communication.

Most change in language results from shifts in fashion, and goes on nowhere more rapidly than among the educated upper classes in major urban centers. Conversely, the speech of the lower classes, and the most isolated rural inhabitants, tends to remain relatively conservative. Many of the features of such dialects, such as the double negative, or the use of *holp* as the past tense of *help*, were once in use by all classes of speakers, but have fallen out of fashion among the upper classes and today survive primarily among the poor and the rural population.

Because of the social and economic prestige of the middle and upper classes, and ONLY because of that, their variety (dialect) of the language comes to be considered the 'standard' form of the language, and is used as the basis of literature, education, and formal communication. The so-called 'standard language', therefore, is itself nothing more than a class dialect, and has no more claim to purity or grammaticality than any form of the language — in fact, from a historical viewpoint, often less. The dialects of the poor and the country dweller become, by definition, stigmatized as nonstandard, even though they may represent the majority of speakers and be historically 'purer'. In some countries, such as France or England, only one dialect, usually that of the capital, becomes the standard, but in the United States there are a number of equally-accepted regional standard dialects, with no single dialect dominant over any of the others.[2]

Our schools have since the eighteenth century inculcated a belief in the sanctity of the standard dialect by applying such morally-tinged epithets as 'good' and 'bad', 'right' and 'wrong', 'correct' and 'incorrect' respectively to the standard and deviations from it. Generations of children not born into privileged environments where they might have internalized the standard dialect from the beginning have been taught to feel linguistically insecure and ashamed of their speech, while their more fortunate classmates have been taught the shibboleths of linguistic intolerance and social snobbery. They have, in short, been taught to judge a person by how he speaks, rather than for what he is.

It does not at all follow that a person who speaks a nonstandard dialect should have any reason to be ashamed of it. Language is often an affectively powerful badge of group membership and identification. A child learns his language from his family and close friends, and uses it as a basis for identifying with them and for mediating his relations with them. Criticism of an individual's speech carries with

---

[2] Linguists working since the 1930s have defined four major dialect areas in the United States: the Northern, North Midland, South Midland, and Southern. The pre-scientific designation 'General American' found in many older works (and some less well-informed current writers) is roughly to be identified with North Midland. For further information on American dialects, see Chapter 9, "The dialects of American English", by Raven I. McDavid, Jr., in Francis (1958); Reed (1967), and Chapter 4 in Troike (forthcoming).

it the implication of a rejection of him as a person, and of those whom he likes and admires. There is perhaps no more effective way to injure a student's self-image, or to depreciate his personal allegiances, than to criticize the way he talks. A child who moves from one dialect area to another may, if he wishes to identify with his new peers, learn their dialect; if, on the other hand, he rejects them (or vice versa), he may continue to cultivate his native dialect as a symbol of that rejection.

A third type of language variation which needs to be touched on before the role of the teacher and the school can be viewed in its proper perspective, is what has been called 'functional variety', 'style', or 'register'. These have been discussed at greatest length by Martin Joos in his provocative little book *The five clocks* (1967). Joos defines four 'styles', or 'registers', in English,[3] which he labels intimate, informal, consultative, and formal, the last two of which we may re-label for clarity as 'business' and 'platform' or 'essay' styles. These styles correspond to different stages in the socialization cycle of the individual. The first two, the INTIMATE and INFORMAL, are used with close friends or family, and with casual acquaintances, respectively; they may be grouped together as primarily PRIVATE styles. The BUSINESS style is typically used in semi-formal situations, as between strangers, or between teacher and student, or employer and employee, while the PLATFORM or ESSAY style is used for formal speaking or writing; these last two styles may be considered primarily PUBLIC styles. Styles and dialects cross-cut one another, so that within each regional variety there will be standard and nonstandard class dialects, and within each class dialect there will be private and public styles or registers.

The average child, when he comes to school, will have four years of language learning behind him (three, if he is entering kindergarten), during which time he has internalized the grammar governing the private styles of his regional class dialect. While he has developed PRODUCTIVE COMPETENCE in these styles within his particular dialect, he may or may not have developed RECEPTIVE COMPETENCE in other styles and dialects. A common problem for white teachers in newly-integrated schools in the southern United States is that they find themselves unable to understand the dialect of their Black students; in many cases, however, the Black students are readily able to understand their white teachers. Thus the students are often RECEPTIVELY BI-DIALECTICAL, whereas their teachers are not (at least with regard to their students' dialect).

Within this context, the role of the school may be seen as HELPING THE STUDENT TO DEVELOP AND EXPAND HIS LINGUISTIC COMPETENCE. For all students, this will involve helping them gradually to develop productive control over the public styles of the language; it is an enterprise which will continue throughout the school years and even into college, and involves training not only in the use of the appropriate linguistic forms, but also in the recognition of social contexts in which the 'business' style, as opposed to the informal style, would be appropriate. Teachers in the past

---

[3] Joos adds a fifth style (hence the title of the book) which he terms the 'frozen', or artistic-literary style.

have often made the mistaken assumption that because the consultative or business style (sometimes called 'school language') was appropriate in the classroom, it should also be required on the playground, but students, often more aware of the social functions of language than their teachers, have usually rejected such absurdities.

For the student who comes to school having mastered a nonstandard dialect, the role of the school is to provide him with the opportunity to ADD a standard dialect to his repertoire. This can probably best be facilitated by oral language games, pattern practice, and language laboratory work, using many of the techniques employed in second language teaching.[4] In this way the teacher will be recognizing the student's existing competence, and will simply be BUILDING UPON his already developed strengths. Every effort should be made to avoid changing or stigmatizing the student's native dialect, much less 'eradicating' it — a task which would be impossible in any event, short of brain surgery. Emphasis should be on the POSITIVE aspects of acquiring productive control over a second dialect. Acquisition of the standard regional dialect will help make available to the student more of the benefits of education, and provide him with a broader range of options for achieving a full and satisfactory life.

Accepting the student where he is, then, requires the teacher's being aware of the nature and sources of language variation, and being willing to accept the student, and his language, as worthy of respect. If the teacher is to determine where the student is, she must be willing first of all to put aside any prejudices and stereotypes which interfere with objective assessment, and, recognizing the inadequacy of existing instruments, learn to observe the speech of her students closely in order to develop a more valid basis for judging the state of their linguistic development.

One of the most serious, and as yet unanswered, questions regarding the development of language in the child is whether economic deprivation has a retarding or limiting influence on language acquisition (other than on vocabulary size, which is not relevant). Many studies by psychologists would appear to indicate such an effect on cognitive development, but it is not certain that such studies were adequately culture-fair, i.e. that they did not just test for competencies found in middle-class children, and overlook the presence of different competencies among lower-class subjects. In a similar way, the conclusions by Loban (1966) in his large-scale longitudinal study, that lower-class children lagged behind middle-class children in acquiring 'standard' grammar, at least in part reflected a difference in class-dialect between the two groups. Nevertheless, if it should be shown that economic (and by consequence, nutritional) deprivation does exert a retarding effect on language development, this will have major significance for educational policy.

To the charge by certain psychologists that ghetto Black children were non-verbal and had no grammar, Labov (1970) has produced a vigorous answer demonstrating that, given a non-threatening situation, such children are highly verbal,

---

[4] See some of the papers in Alatis (1970), which was devoted largely to teaching standard English as a second dialect.

and that far from having no grammar, their grammar is quite consistent and systematic. Labov showed that the children's dialect was merely different from that of the white investigators (e.g. in the regular omission of *is*, as in *He working*), who ethnocentrically assumed that any departure from their own grammars meant a lack of grammar.

2. BILINGUAL EDUCATION

The passage of the Bilingual Education Act of 1967 for the first time gave official recognition to the use of native languages other than English as mediums of instruction in United States schools, although bilingual schools have existed in other countries for some time. Sizeable funds have been appropriated by the U. S. Congress for bilingual programs, without consideration for the training of teachers in these programs or for the conduct of research needed to support materials development and program evaluation. The result has been a rash of programs covering a number of language groups, including certain American Indian groups, but concentrated in the Spanish-speaking areas of the Southwest.[5] Most of the programs exhibit a great amount of zeal and goodwill, but many lack any knowledge or realization of the relevance of linguistics to their instructional needs and problems.

This is not the place to give a detailed discussion of the significance of linguistics in bilingual education,[6] but some of the major considerations may be briefly mentioned. A bilingual program typically involves content instruction in the native language, often leading to literacy, while the official language (e.g. Spanish in Peru, English in the U.S.) is taught as a second language until students have learned it well enough that it can be used as a medium of content instruction. In the native-language instruction component of a bilingual program, many of the same considerations discussed in the preceding section must be recognized and dealt with. For example, Spanish-speaking students from a lower socio-economic background usually bring a nonstandard regional dialect to school. In order for teaching to be effective and not frustrating, it is important for the teacher to know just what the features of the dialect are and how they differ from whatever regional standard is to be taught. However, there is as yet very little information available on such dialect variations, and research is badly needed. For the present, teachers must be trained to rely on their own observations.

In addition, students from different areas may have different pronunciations, vocabulary, or grammatical forms. Teaching materials or tests formulated for use in one area often cannot be used in another until they have been modified. This has proven to be true even for Navajo speakers on different parts of the reservation.

However, the most direct application of linguistics is in teaching English (or Spanish, etc.) as a second language to nonnative speakers, which may be carried

---

[5] The best available source of information is Andersson and Boyer (1970).
[6] For this, see Saville and Troike (1970).

out separately from, or as part of, a bilingual program. Here, an effective teaching program should be based on a CONTRASTIVE ANALYSIS of the native and the second (target) language.[7] Such an analysis will show the differences in the sounds (phonemes) of the two languages and their distribution, in the respective grammatical patterns, and in the semantic system, and will make it possible for the teacher to PREDICT and DIAGNOSE learning problems and to adopt appropriate teaching strategies to help students overcome them. For example, such an analysis will show that Spanish speakers have difficulty hearing, or producing, the differences in such pairs of words as *beet-bit, bet-bat, boat-bought, sing-sin, watch-wash,* or *ladder-lather,* because the relevant sounds are not distinguished in Spanish. Drills are needed to provide ear-training in hearing such differences before students can be expected to produce the differences with any degree of consistency.

It is also important to note that the teacher should be aware of her own dialect, especially in attempting to use previously-prepared material. Whereas a teacher from the southern U.S. will not ordinarily distinguish such words as *pin* and *pen,* a teacher from parts of the North or the West Coast will not differentiate *stock* and *stalk.* Still others will not differentiate *feel* and *fill,* or *which* and *witch.* A teacher should be careful never to attempt to teach sound-distinctions which she does not normally make herself.

Although it is sometimes erroneously thought that drill-type activities for language teaching are not suitable for young children, experience has shown that in fact children actually like such drills, since they enjoy engaging in disciplined activity. For drills to be effective, however, they need to be made meaningful; frequently drills can be structured in the form of games to provide additional motivation (the same is true in second-dialect teaching). In general, it is not enough for children simply to be exposed to the second language, even in meaningful contexts. An organized program is required, with an orderly sequenced presentation of structures, giving special attention to points of difference in the two languages, and regular patterned drill activities which will insure adequate individual practice in mastering the structures, sounds, and vocabulary of the new language.

3. FORMAL GRAMMAR INSTRUCTION

Although the most significant contribution of linguistics to the teaching of English and the language arts is in helping the teacher develop a greater understanding of the nature of language, language variation, and language learning, probably the most conspicuous impact of linguistics on the curriculum has been in the teaching

---

[7] The best available discussions of contrastive analysis are Lado (1957) and Alatis (1968). The most detailed comparison of English and Spanish available is Stockwell and Bowen (1965), and Stockwell, Bowen, and Martin (1965). See also Ohannessian and Gage (1969), and Saville and Troike (1970).

of formal grammar. The growing displacement of traditional grammar in the schools by grammatical descriptions based on the structural and generative-transformational linguistic models reflects a dissatisfaction with the sterility of traditional grammar instruction and its demonstrated non-utility. To some extent, the success of linguistically-based models in the schools can be attributed to the intellectually moribund state of traditional grammar, which was unable to answer the criticisms brought against it by linguists. But probably most decisive was the evidence that the new approaches, though they described the same phenomena, engaged the interest and intuition of students in a way which led to much more successful learning.

All of the linguistically-based approaches to grammar instruction begin with the common assumption that the student, as a speaker of the language, ALREADY KNOWS THE GRAMMAR OF THE LANGUAGE, though only unconsciously. From this assumption it follows that the teaching of 'formal' grammar primarily involves MAKING THE STUDENT CONSCIOUSLY AWARE OF WHAT HE ALREADY KNOWS. It also follows that to make the student consciously aware of his existing knowledge, an inductive approach is the best method for teaching grammar. Rather than having students memorize unanalyzable rules and pseudo-definitions as in the past, students can be invited to develop their analytical faculties by examining selected samples of language data and consulting their own linguistic knowledge in order to come up with scientifically defensible statements and generalizations. In such an approach, students are challenged to formulate descriptive rules and frame valid definitions, and grammar study can become an exciting process of self-discovery rather than an irrelevant and often frustrating pursuit of a rigid and meaningless catechism.

After a period of transition in the textbook market, most publishers have now fully committed themselves to the development of linguistically-oriented texts for the public schools. The pattern which has emerged as most pedagogically effective is one which begins with structural grammar, using characteristic positional slots in sentences and typical function-words and morphological markers as identifying features for the major parts of speech. Certain morphological and syntactic patterns are then examined in order to define various subclasses, particularly of verbs. Instruction moves from the observable surface features of the language to an examination of the underlying structure of sentences, using transformations as a tool to analyze and discover this deeper structure. Grammar study, rather than being a fixed body of facts to be reviewed every year from the eighth grade onward, is seen as an open-ended, continually growing understanding of the operation of the language, and by implication, of the operation of the human brain in producing and understanding sentences.

Although as will be mentioned below, a structural-transformational approach to the study of grammar does have utilitarian benefits which traditional grammar did not (despite a naive faith to the contrary), its primary justification may be seen as a humanistic one — that by better understanding how our grammar works, we can come to a better understanding of ourselves, and of what it means to be human.

4. READING

The study of reading has been pursued for a number of years in almost complete isolation from the field of linguistics. Only recently have specialists in reading begun to recognize that reading is primarily a linguistic process — a surrogate for hearing — which, in addition to involving the association of marks on paper with stored phonological sequences, involves even more crucially the recognition and analysis of grammatical structures in sentences. Nevertheless, with the major thrust from the U. S. Office of Education in the decade of the 1970s being directed at problems of reading, little attention is being given to the potential contribution of linguistics to the solution of these problems. Regrettably, many millions of dollars will undoubtedly be wasted because the relevance of linguistics to reading is not being taken into account.

After a long and unfortunate enchantment with a 'whole-word' approach to the teaching of reading (which treated English as though it were written with Chinese characters instead of alphabetic symbols), schools have now begun a swing back to 'phonics'-based instruction, which recognizes the relationship between the graphic symbols of writing and the spoken sounds (phonemes) of the language. Earlier 'phonics' approaches were very naive regarding the relation of writing to speech, often assuming that writing was more basic than speech and treating children as though they had no language until they learned to read. The better modern phonics materials, however, deal more sophisticatedly with phoneme-grapheme correspondences, and otherwise show definite influence from the field of linguistics.

In addition, many reading and spelling texts have begun to show an awareness of regional dialect variation. In the past, textbook writers from one part of the country naively assumed either that everyone spoke as they did, or that theirs was the only acceptable form of the language. As a result, students and teachers in other parts of the country found words listed as homonyms which they knew were not, such as *hoarse* and *horse*, or found themselves enjoined to make a distinction between words which they knew to be homonyms, as *pin* and *pen*, or *which* and *witch*. However, as teachers become more knowledgeable about dialect differences and realize that there is more than one standard regional dialect, they are becoming less willing to accept textbooks and textbook writers as infallible, and are beginning to be more critical of the texts offered by publishers for adoption.

The same problem of dialect variation is relevant for beginning reading materials which use a phonics approach, since words which rhyme in one dialect may not do so in another. Thus in some dialects *hog, log,* and *dog* may rhyme, while in others they may not. The teacher — and preferably, the textbook writer — needs to be aware of POSSIBLE differences, and should check these with her class before beginning instruction. In any cosmopolitan classroom with students from various parts of the country, there may be a number of quite different dialect patterns to deal with in teaching sound-symbol relationships.

Although the application of linguistics to the problem of initial reading instruction has begun to make some progress, the relevance of linguistics to the problems of advanced reading instruction has received almost no attention. The focus of most reading work in the early years is on the development of word-recognition ability, after which the focus shifts to a generalized concern with content, or with such external matters as motivation or reading speed. Missing is any methodology for carrying students beyond the word level to the level of the grammatical construction and the sentence. Yet the crucial need for such a step in reading instruction has been almost totally missed. The importance of this step may be easily grasped if one attempts to read any fairly long and complex sentence three words at a time (as did one college senior who reported that she had difficulty understanding her reading assignments). When sentences are broken up into such mechanical spans, it becomes almost impossible for the brain to process them in any intelligible fashion. Nevertheless, reading instruction abandons the student, once he has been helped through the word-recognition level, to devise his own means for working his way through the structure of the sentence.

A generally unrecognized linguistic problem in advanced reading is that the student may be unfamiliar with some of the complex grammatical structures he encounters in mature writing, and may therefore experience difficulty in comprehending their contents. That is, he may encounter structures which he has not previously internalized, so that his brain is unable to decode them. This is a situation in which a program of linguistically-based grammar study, containing work in transformations and complex sentence formation, can be potentially very helpful in improving students' reading ability. To be maximally effective, such a combined program should be accompanied by work on oral language development, once a central part of the curriculum but now largely overlooked.

Another source of difficulty in reading may result from disparities between the student's dialect and that of the textbook. This seems to be a particularly marked problem for Black children with a nonstandard dialect which is one of the most divergent of any in the United States. Using material rewritten into the grammatical forms of the students' dialect (keeping standard spelling), or employing direct experience accounts dictated by the students themselves, may help provide a bridge into their reading of standard English.

A related, and very serious problem in many areas, is that of the 'slow reader' whose difficulties stem from the fact that he is not a native speaker of English. The real tragedy for such students is that the source of their difficulties is usually not recognized, and they are mistakenly regarded by teachers as 'stupid' — the pejorative epithet most often encountered. The problem is being attacked in bilingual programs by the procedure of teaching the basic reading skills to these students first in their native language, and later having them apply these skills to English, once their command of English is adequate. But unfortunately, most ordinary school programs totally fail to recognize the special problems of non-English speakers, and attempt to deal with their difficulties by placing them in remedial reading classes, where teachers are not trained to diagnose and treat the real cause of their reading problem. When traditional remedial techniques prove ineffective with such students, this is taken to confirm their supposed lack of intelligence. Only rarely is it suspected that the inappropriateness of the techniques may be at fault.

Ironically, the very teachers most responsible for teaching reading — at whatever level — are also most likely to be those who have had the least training in English phonology and grammar. The obvious conclusion is that certification requirements for elementary teachers and others concerned with reading should be changed to include at least one general course on English linguistics. If reading instruction is to be more effective than it now is, it must be recognized that the reading teacher is as much a teacher of language as is the English teacher, and that a knowledge of the English language is essential to them both.

5. COMPOSITION

Composition is a complex skill involving the integration of structures on at least three levels: conceptual, rhetorical, and linguistic. Of the three, the linguistic is the most tangible, and at the same time the most pervasive, since it is through language that the other two levels are expressed.

Until recently, traditional grammar provided the only framework for talking about syntactic problems, where these impinged on matters of style or rhetorical organization. Nevertheless, research has repeatedly shown that a knowledge of traditional grammar bears no relation to writing ability. Recently, however, it has been found by such researchers as Kellogg Hunt (1965) and John Mellon (1969) that work with transformational grammar can accelerate the growth of students' linguistic maturity (as measured by the complexity of their written sentences) by several years. This finding, which linguists have predicted for some time, is perhaps one of the most significant applications of linguistics to language arts instruction in many years.

When composition and reading are both seen as containing a fundamental linguistic component, their complementary nature as productive and receptive aspects of language use becomes immediately apparent. Ideally, the two should be reciprocally reinforcing, since reading can lead a person to internalize grammatical patterns not part of his previous competence, and composition can give him practice in the use of these structures, which will in turn help strengthen his ability to recognize and decode them in reading. However, the poor reader who is unable to analyze the complex structures in his reading to start with, certainly cannot be expected to use them fluently in his writing. It is here that the formal study of how these structures are produced can be mutually beneficial to both the student's reading and writing, for it can help him to incorporate these structures into his own internal grammar.

6. LITERATURE

Linguistics is pertinent to the study and teaching of literature in at least two important ways. The first, which should be self-evident but often is not, is that students cannot be expected to enjoy literature, much less appreciate it, if they cannot read it. The second arises from the fact that language is the medium of literature. Since linguistics provides the best available tools for the analysis of language, it follows that it has a great deal to contribute to our understanding and appreciation of literature as the art of language.

It is not possible here to do more than merely mention some of the ways linguistics can aid in the study of literature. In dealing with prose, a knowledge of dialect variation can lead to an awareness of how successfully an author has used features of regional, social, or functional varieties to characterize individuals in a story, or to indicate the nature of their social relationships. An examination of the types of sentence structures and transformations an author uses, and how he uses them, can help in defining certain elements of his style, as well as in making students consciously aware of how stylistic effects are achieved.

A linguistically-based approach to the study of literature views the writer as the artist of language, and seeks to examine the ways in which a writer has used his medium to achieve particular effects. Perhaps the interplay of language and artistic form is most observable in poetry, where the writer must fit his linguistic material into a poetic structure of stress and rhyme. Rewriting a poem into its normal prose form is a useful means of revealing what changes the poet had to make in the normal syntactic order of the constituent sentences so as to fit the right syllables of the right words into the stress-patterns of the lines, or to bring parallel ideas into parallel grammatical sequences.[8] At the same time, such matters as alliteration or rhyme can be examined for their effect on word choice and placement in the line. Students with a knowledge of the structure of the language will be better equipped to understand the challenge the poet faces in molding linguistic structure into poetic structure, and thus will be better able to appreciate the craftmanship involved in the creation of a good poem.

7. LINGUISTICS IN THE CURRICULUM

To this point we have dealt with the relevance of linguistics for the language arts-English curriculum, but we have not considered the possibility of a separate course in linguistics per se. There have been several successful summer institutes in lin-

---

[8] This practice of rewriting a poem into normal sentences, keeping the same words, is a valuable means of testing student comprehension of a poem (such a procedure can even catch critics in errors of misreading). Because of its distorted syntax, students often need special training in reading poetry. Oral reading, in particular, can be both a good training and a good testing device.

guistics for bright high-school juniors, and a few schools are already beginning to offer an elective course entitled 'Linguistics' at the high school level. The concepts and techniques of linguistic analysis are not too difficult for high school students to learn, and a linguistically-based language arts-English curriculum would provide a good foundation for such a course. In addition, the course itself would be valuable as background for college study in any of a number of fields, including, of course, linguistics itself. In time, we may be able to see the fulfillment of William Dwight Whitney's declaration of a century ago (1875:5) that

No educated person can afford to lack a clear conception of at least a brief connected outline of a science possessing such claims to attention.

REFERENCES

ALATIS, JAMES E., ed. 1968. Report of the Nineteenth Annual Round Table Meeting on Linguistics and Language Studies. MSLL 21.

——, ed. 1970. Report of the Twentieth Annual Round Table Meeting on Linguistics and Language Studies. MSLL 22.

ANDERSSON, THEODORE, and MILDRED BOYER. 1970. Bilingual schooling in the United States. Washington, D.C., U.S. Government Printing Office.

CHOMSKY, CAROL. 1969. The acquisition of syntax in children from 5 to 10. Cambridge, Mass., The M.I.T. Press.

FRANCIS, W. NELSON. 1958. The structure of American English. New York, The Ronald Press Company.

HUNT, KELLOGG W. 1965. Grammatical structures written at three grade levels. Champaign, Ill., National Council of Teachers of English.

JOOS, MARTIN. 1967. The five clocks. New York, Harcourt, Brace & World, Inc.

LABOV, WILLIAM. 1970. The study of nonstandard English. Champaign, Ill., National Council of Teachers of English.

LADO, ROBERT. 1957. Linguistics across cultures. Ann Arbor, The University of Michigan Press.

LENNEBERG, ERIC H. 1964. New directions in the study of language. Cambridge, Mass., The M.I.T. Press.

LOBAN, WALTER. 1966. Problems in oral English. Champaign, Ill., National Council of Teachers of English.

MELLON, JOHN C. 1969. Transformational sentence-combining: A method for enhancing the development of syntactic fluency in English composition. Champaign, Ill., National Council of Teachers of English.

MENYUK, PAULA. 1969. Sentences children use. Cambridge, Mass., The M.I.T. Press.

OHANNESSIAN, SIRARPI, and WILLIAM W. GAGE. 1969. Teaching English to speakers of Choctaw, Navajo, and Papago. Washington, D.C., Bureau of Indian Affairs.

REED, CARROLL E. 1967. Dialects of American English. Cleveland, World Publishing Company.

SAVILLE, MURIEL R., and RUDOLPH C. TROIKE. 1970. A handbook of bilingual education. Washington, D.C., ERIC Clearinghouse for Linguistics. (2nd ed., 1971. Washington, D.C., Teachers of English to Speakers of Other Languages (TESOL).)

SMITH, FRANK, and GEORGE A. MILLER, eds. 1966. The genesis of language. Cambridge, Mass., The M.I.T. Press.

STOCKWELL, ROBERT P., and J. DONALD BOWEN. 1965. The sounds of English and Spanish. Chicago, University of Chicago Press.

STOCKWELL, ROBERT P., J. DONALD BOWEN, and JOHN W. MARTIN. 1965. The grammatical structures of English and Spanish. Chicago, University of Chicago Press.

TROIKE, RUDOLPH C. Forthcoming. An introduction to English linguistics for the teacher of English. New York, McGraw-Hill, Inc.

WHITNEY, WILLIAM DWIGHT. 1875. The life and growth of language. New York, D. Appleton and Company.

LINGUISTICS AND SECOND LANGUAGE PEDAGOGY[1]

E. GLYN LEWIS

1. INTRODUCTION

Linguistics is an autonomous discipline, but with close links with other studies such as mathematics, sociology and especially philosophy and psychology: Bloomfield's rejection of mentalism was only the negative aspect of his commitment to an equally influential empiricist epistemology. The association of linguistics with other disciplines is due to the fact that language is only one element in a unified system of behaviour, and though its study has to be pursued as far as possible as an independent discipline the extent of that independence is limited. Whatever justification there may have been for the traditional isolationism of linguistics it is now being abandoned in favour of a 'willingness to explore connections in other directions' (Greenberg 1957 : v).

One of these connections is psychology, and because the teaching of languages necessitates a contribution from both disciplines, the connection of linguistics with teaching has to be reviewed in the light of the kind of contribution made by psychology as well. The connection of structuralist linguistics with a particular school of psychology is well recognised. The same thing is true of other linguistic theories: for 'since the psychologist and the mentalistic linguist are constructing theories of the same kind . . . it follows that the linguist's theory is subject to the requirement

---

[1] In spite of Lionel Trilling's confession that pedagogy is a depressing subject to all persons of sensibility, this review is written strictly from the standpoint of a pedagogue rather than a linguist. Consequently it interprets 'Linguistics' fairly liberally and for that reason it may offend the strict austerity of academic linguistic puritanism. Pedagogy is a useful term, though in little favour in Britain; and so far as this review is concerned it, too, is conceived liberally to include not only actual class teaching, teacher training and the preparation of materials but the preparation of courses and curricula. Of the many defects of this study the most important is the failure first to take into account the differences in linguistic impact arising from the very many pedagogic variables such as age of student and of introduction to the language, learning the language in the national's own country or in the native country of the second language, differences between second and foreign language acquisition, and perhaps most important of all, differences of impact according to the aims proposed for the second language course. The nature and extent of a specifically 'linguistics' influence will alter considerably with each of these pedagogic variables. To emphasise the strictly pedagogic standpoint I have to acknowledge that the study was undertaken to some extent as part of a languages research project financed at the University of Wales, Swansea, by the Schools Council of England and Wales.

that it harmonize with the psychologist's theories dealing with other human abilities ...' (Katz 1964: 127). Others go beyond the need to harmonize concepts and insist on the proposition that 'Linguistic theory *is* psychological theory' (Bever 1968: 478). One could, of course, regard the contribution of linguistics to pedagogy as simply the provision of a description of the language being taught, its regular system and underlying rules (Gefen 1966). Such a restricted approach would result in the need to inject linguistic considerations into such other explanatory models of language pedagogy as are proposed by psychology and sociology. In fact, alternative linguistic theories are necessarily embedded in psychological and epistemological considerations.

The teaching of languages also has its own equally independent set of theoretical and practical principles and postulates, but as is the case with linguistics, it becomes unprofitable to pursue a consideration of these principles independently of a consideration of the principles governing the teaching of other subjects. It would be inconsistent with contemporary educational theory to limit the boundaries of the several subjects of the curriculum unduly, or to attempt to ensure that the contribution of a particular discipline to the teaching of one of those subjects should be considered in total isolation from any other. So far as the teaching of languages is concerned, one result of a restricted interpretation of the nature of the contribution of linguistics would be to encourage the return of formalism in the classroom. While linguistics itself has refined the content of the language course it is the interplay between linguistics and the related disciplines which has broadened and deepened our understanding of the teaching of languages. This is what has led to the concept of a second language not only as an additional number of skills or an extension of the means of communication at the disposal of the student, but as part of the process of individual development similar to, though not identical with, the process of development we call acquiring the mother tongue. This broadening of our concept of second language learning has led to a more humane, less formal approach to actual practice in class.

One can favour a broad view of the relations of linguistics to philosophy, psychology and sociology as they affect language pedagogy, and yet be able to restrict our interpretation of linguistics itself, by excluding phonetics, for instance, as Trager does (1949), or semantics following the example of Bloomfield (1933). But this would hardly be a realistic procedure. The only acceptable standpoint the teacher can take is to regard linguistics as the study of a particular aspect of intelligent behaviour in general, and the linguist as one who is 'above all concerned with what people *do* when they interact by means of language' (N. E. Conference 1962). Language is but one structured phase of all human overt and covert activity (Pike 1967: 32).

All this implies our believing that linguistics can and must contribute to language teaching not only a model of linguistic competence, a theory of the language, but help in formulating possible models of acquisition and of presentation as well. The attitude of the teacher is that there can be little advantage in insisting on a sharp separation of theoretical and applied linguistics; and that there is no point, for example, in looking for essential differences between a scientific and a school grammar It is probably also true that however closely related a theory of language may be to the model of presentation which the teacher chooses, it is unlikely that he will be determined in his choice of presentation model by the appropriateness of a theory of language — a good deal of electicism is inherent to the professional approach of the teacher. Consequently the contribution of linguistics can be understood and measured only if linguistic theory, so far as it concerns pedagogy, is conceived within a broad system of references.

Such a frame of reference must reflect the fact that linguistics influences teaching a second language on at least four levels. First, there is the highest level of abstract theory concerning the nature of language. Even at this level non-linguistic considerations operate; for instance, distinctive epistemological concepts enter into the differences between empiricist and cognitive models of language and of its acquisition. On the second level, that of sophisticated description and analysis of particular languages also, more than the objective layout of the linguistic map is involved. Such sociological considerations as 'the *acceptance* of the norm even by a small but influential group is the life blood of the language' (Haugen 1966:933). Third is the level of the teacher-theoretician, concerned to exploit the contribution made at the two highest levels, in preparing courses, training teachers, and initiating discussions of language teaching in periodicals and textbooks. At this level the contribution of linguistics has to be firmly integrated with, and in fact is determined to a considerable extent by the contributions of other disciplines such as psychology and sociology, and by mundane but important practical considerations. Finally, there is the level of the classroom practice, where even more than on the level of teacher-theoretician the integration of the disciplines referred to, and the practical considerations have to be ensured. Whatever light linguistics sheds on language pedagogy is inevitably coloured by the contributions of other disciplines.

2. WHAT IS THE SECOND LANGUAGE?

In defining what we mean by 'a second language' a distinction has to be drawn between a historical, naturally developed language such as English, Russian or Welsh and an artificial language, like Esperanto — to say nothing of 'minimal languages' used for experimental purposes. A distinction among natural second languages needs to be made between a *langue vivante* and the classical languages, like Latin and Greek. Reforms in the teaching of 'dead' languages take into account recent developments in linguistics.[2] The impact of linguistics on the teaching of

---

[2] The fairly informal but nevertheless interesting and potentially valuable study of the relationship of transformational theories and the teaching of the Classics at the Universities of Birmingham and Oxford are to be noted as significant in this respect.

second languages inevitably varies according to the category of second language with which we are concerned, but this review will deal almost exclusively with the teaching of *langues vivantes,* as the most relevant pedagogical problem, and the one where central issues of the contribution of linguistics are revealed most clearly.

Even among modern languages it is difficult to know, from the standpoint of pedagogy, where the limits of the second language category begin and end. For instance the characteristics of an extreme regional dialect such as that of Pitea in Sweden (Österberg 1961), or of major dialects such as the six of modern China, are known to necessitate the teaching of the standard language, or any of the dialects, as a second language. Equally important, diglossic differences between High and Low forms of a language as in the case of Swiss German involve similar pedagogical considerations (Ferguson 1959): while the characteristics of social dialects, of Creoles and Pidgins have been taken to justify the teaching of the standard language as a quasi-foreign language (Stewart 1964). It is questionable, however, whether the differences between variants of the same language, particularly variants arising from social stratification in a fairly mobile society, justify teachers in treating the standard form as a second language in the way they must in teaching a different language. No matter how many the variant characteristics of the dialect may be, the opportunity for transfer of learning between the dialect and the standard language are usually greater than between two different languages.

So far we have assumed that all separate languages acquired subsequent to the mother tongue can be regarded as a uniform set of second languages. It is doubtful, to say the least, whether we should do so. Marckwardt favoured the careful distinction which British linguists and teachers draw between a second and a foreign language (Marckwardt 1962). The distinction has not found acceptance in the U.S. nor, for that matter, in many European countries, except the U.S.S.R. Nevertheless the distinction is convenient. To speak of the 'two first languages' of Mexican-American bilingual children is to cloud the teacher's judgement (Rafferty 1963:21). Among bilinguals in Wales, for instance, it is necessary to be able to distinguish between the learning of a second language — Welsh or English, and a foreign language, usually French or German. The introduction of the foreign language to a Welsh-speaking child involves very different approaches from those used to teach him English. For a large number of such children the gap between their acquisition of the mother tongue and their introduction to English may be five years, so that the latter can in no sense be regarded as the second of two first languages. Nor is English a foreign language in their case; since there is a strong supporting background to English in the Welsh-speaking community, the use of foreign language strategies of teaching is both uneconomical and frustrating (Lewis 1952, 1962).

There are other differences which necessitate drawing the distinction we are discussing, and which govern the kind of contribution linguistics can make in either case. Facts account for a large part of the acquisition of second language vocabulary, though not to the same extent as in the first language. In the foreign language, though it may be more advantageous to associate new words, where it is appropriate, with the concrete referents, it is difficult, and in the majority of cases impossible, to rely on such associations. Secondly, there is usually no need to emphasize the primacy of speech since the second language is acquired very largely in the normal speech situation. Third, the model of the second language is less strictly formulated and the adult criteria and norms less consistently stressed than in foreign language teaching. Consequently even where a second language is taught formally in school the teacher may permit semi-sentences, which, compared with the model normally referred to in the foreign language, must be regarded as grammatically incomplete (Jakobovits 1968). Finally the same psychological factors operate differently in the learning of the second and the foreign languages. Both attitude and motivation play their part in each case but the former is more important in learning a second language since the second language involves active and immediate participation in the life of the ethnic group speaking the second language (Spolsky 1969a). In learning the foreign language, because such group considerations are usually remote, attitude is less powerful in influencing learning compared with motivation (Pimsleur 1962, 1964). For these reasons it would be interesting to deal with second and foreign language acquisition separately. All that it is convenient to do at the moment is to encourage the use of the distinction.

3. HISTORICAL CONSIDERATIONS

3.1 *Early Debates*

The fact that students received a very efficient linguistic education in the Royal Colleges of ancient Babylonia and Assyria is an indication of the length of the tradition of second language teaching, and we need refer only to Panini to establish an equally respectable tradition of linguistic scholarship. Moreover it is on record that many of the most interesting pedagogic issues, to the discussion of which contemporary linguistics has contributed, have always been the concern of linguists. For instance, the primacy of speech is not a new discovery: during the 17th century and especially in the 18th and 19th centuries missionaries, like Lorenzo Hervas (1800), scholars like Ellis (1845) to say nothing of more recent linguists like Sweet (1899), Vietor (1902) and Palmer (1917) or Jespersen (1904) contributed to the discussions. Even early in the 17th century the Welsh scholar Sir John Price (*Camden Remaines*) basing his argument on the advances which the phonetic spelling of Welsh offered those who learned it as a second language, urged the usefulness of a phonetic alphabet. The importance of linguistic context in the acquisition of new material was stressed by Sweet, and the possible advantage and disadvantages of the explicit introduction of grammatical rules were canvassed not only by Sayce (1880) at the end of the last century, but at the beginning of the 17th century as well by Libinius of Amerang (Lubinus) and John Amos Comenius in his *The Great Didactic* (1628-32). The problem of linguistic interference between Latin and Greek was much in the mind of Quintilian (*Institutio*) and the same phenomenon led Comenius to suggest contrastive analysis since it was important that 'stress be laid on the points in which the languages differ' (Comenius).

What is of even greater interest is that discussions concerning the comparative validity of cognitive and associationist models of acquisition date back to the Middle Ages and were pursued in the 17th century. The empiricist theory was set out by Joseph Webbe in the 30s of that century — 'Looke upon children in their learninge languages, nature teacheth them to use the sence before the judgement . . . wherein I see an action of memory taken from the outward sense than of judgement or understanding. As in dogges, that once hearinge the bell and presently feeling the lash, will never after heare the bell, but will runne away barking or crying' (Webbe). His argument was controverted shortly afterwards by William Brooke, who advanced the mentalist argument that it is through the operation of central processes that languages are acquired. Language which relies on habit and association being 'contrary to the course of nature will be long adoeing' (Brooke). Arising from the argument whether to teach Latin by drills or by concentrating on the acquisition of grammatical rules, this discussion went to the heart of the major issue in contemporary linguistics and language pedagogy.

3.2 *Criticism of the Slender Contribution of Linguistics*

In spite of these adumbrations of vital issues in language teaching and the advances which were made in linguistic science, little evidence, it has been alleged, exists for any significant contribution by linguistics to language teaching, until new objectives consequent on the democratic expansion of educational opportunity made it necessary to organise instruction economically and effectively. It is this social advance rather than any deliberate or pronounced interest on the part of linguists in language teaching that ensured that teaching languages should be based on more solid or broader foundations than the teacher's command of the language alone. Whatever contribution linguistics has made is due to the fact that mass education necessitated a more scientific and rational set of principles than individual competence alone could command.

However, even within the limits of very recent changes in linguistic and pedagogic theory, it is hard not to agree with those who have claimed that the response of linguists to the demands of the schools, and the awareness among teachers of the importance of linguistic theory have been slow to mature, so that the actual impact of linguistics has been weak and dull. The disenchantment of European teachers with the kind of contribution made by linguistics is pronounced (W. Haas 1960). They maintain that linguistics has not, for instance, led to any improvement in the preparation of textbooks. There are also doubts about the very possibility of a linguistics contribution. Whatmough, who maintained that even a linguistic description of the language is of little help in learning it, recently published structural accounts notwithstanding (Whatmough 1956 : 213). Bloomfield argued that language learning depended less on theoretical formulations than on 'the conditions of teaching and the competence of the teacher' (Bloomfield 1933 : 503). Chomsky, if in little else, agrees with Bloomfield in this matter — since he is 'rather sceptical about the significance for the teacher of languages of such insights and understandings as have been attained in linguistics and psychology' (Chomsky 1968b : 43). Some go beyond mere doubt and argue as Vogt does 'that there is not necessarily any point of contact between linguistics and language teaching' (quoted in Christophersen 1964 : 17). This apparent fear of contamination inspired Mackey to insist that language learning cannot be the purpose of linguistics (Mackey 1966 : 199), though to my knowledge there are few if any teachers or linguists who have made the claim.

The feebleness of the impact on any reckoning is inevitable. In the first place contemporary linguistics, with justifiable pretensions to scientific status, has rightly been concerned principally to discover and explain the facts, the internal relations of particular languages, their inherent structure, and to throw light with these descriptions on general linguistic theories. In this sense linguistics is closer to logic and mathematics than to the humanities — the traditional associates of philology (Jakobson 1958 : 87). Contrary to contemporary linguistics the traditionalists sought the objectivity of their discipline by adopting an external criterion of significance (Haugen 1951 : 360). To the extent that contemporary linguists have sought to insulate their discipline from criteria which give 'linguistic data concrete validity in the real world' they have been incapacitated from seeing any striking relevance for their discipline in language teaching.

Furthermore, contemporary linguists highly favour abstract metalanguages necessitated by their conception of the science they are pursuing and by the abstract nature of their hypotheses. These abstractions are difficult to interpret or to adapt to practical studies except by those who formulate them. In addition the conflict between theories results in bewildering inconclusiveness so far as concerns language pedagogy. However persuasive the linguists may be, the attempts to validate their theories in terms of improved performance are not infrequently contradictory (Chastain and Woerdehoff 1969 : 224).

Second, some well cultivated areas of investigation are unproductive, and it is not unlikely that this is so because they are peculiarly unsuited to second language teaching research. The psycholinguist, in order to ensure control of a large number of variables in the learning situation, has to break up a complex process into isolated elements. Simple processes are chosen before complex problems for investigation and this leads to the use of pedagogically insignificant and artificially limited language situations to validate the learning theories. Verbal paired associate learning tests are a case in point (Sapon). Nonsense stimuli and exaggeratedly specific language materials have also been referred to as unfruitful, if not irrelevant, areas of investigation so far as second language learning is concerned (Crothers and Suppes 1967:4; Cofer 1968:535). In the Soviet Union the investigation of second language problems is pursued in normal complex classroom situations. It is axiomatic for Soviet teachers that educational developments 'like other forms of living activity are determined by the conditions of the organism's existence' (Teplov) and the development of the intellectual aspects of this development 'cannot be adequately discussed in isolation from the development of other qualities' (Kostiuk). Consequently, to carry out research into second language learning in an unduly restricted and artificially limited framework is unacceptable. It is for this reason that a considerable amount of the most seminal investigation of second language problems is pursued in the experimental classes attached to teaching training colleges and institutes, like the Herzen Institute.

Third, because it is easier to change a theory than to abandon a practice, there will always be a gap between linguistic and pedagogic advance. Furthermore, the traditional practice of language teaching, because of its association with humanist classical scholarship, has identified itself with an emotionally charged philosophy of education. Teachers have been inhibited from adapting linguistic advances to their requirements as teachers, and from adopting a critical attitude to traditional language practices simply because it appeared to involve questioning a whole educational ethos, a *paideia*, a method of shaping the whole character. This reluctance has been accentuated by the fact that the sources of innovation in language pedagogy are the results of scientific enquiry, the basic postulate of which is the existence of one and only one true solution of any problem. This necessarily imposes unaccustomed constraints on the teacher. 'The influence stemming from his own personality as moulded not only by tradition and environment but also by his individual history, constitution and inclination' (Myrdal) have to be abandoned. The more scientifically oriented linguistics becomes, and the more the teaching of languages places itself under the influence of linguistics, the more technical and objective the teacher's approach will be. Occasional brilliant virtuosity is replaced by higher average but impersonal competence; and an intuitive approach to teaching is replaced by standardized, objective and often mechanized techniques. The teacher's traditional prerogative to organise a sometimes idiosyncratic program has to be abrogated in favour of universally valid materials and techniques.[3] All school disciplines are influenced at present by scientifically based innovations; but the

---

[3] The influence of the scientific or technological approach has been long maturing – it certainly owes its theoretical origin to the empiricist philosophy of Francis Bacon – 'My way of discovering sciences goes far to level men's wits; and leaves but little to individual excellence, because it performs everything by the surest rules and demonstrations.' (*Works* III 221).

consequences for second language teaching are exacerbated by the long humanist tradition which, in Europe certainly, still prevails, and delays the acceptance of advantages offered by advances in linguistic science.

Finally, it is possible that some unfortunate characteristics of the methodology of linguistics with respect to second language learning have contributed to the teacher's hesitance. It has been suggested that because 'a theory of grammar is not itself a theory of performance', linguists, whose main concern is with the former, are indifferent 'to presentation or analysis of any systematic empirical data' about language learning. Related to this is the alleged 'contentious philosophical tone' of the linguists' discussion of the problem of language learning (Crothers and Suppes 1967 : 2).

4. NATIONAL DIFFERENCES

4.1 *Western Europe and the United States*

Historical factors have produced marked differences between various countries. Even within such closely related communities and educational systems as those of Western Europe there are characteristic disparities of linguistic and pedagogic outlook, though these are fewer and less important than the differences between Western Europe and America. In Europe changes in linguistic theory or outlook have been assimilated gradually and almost imperceptibly by language pedagogy. Therefore there are fewer of those marked cleavages between linguistic theory and practice in the schools, which have been noted in the U.S. For instance, during the last decade of the 19th century, linguistic science in Europe produced the gradual reform of language teaching through the introduction of phonetics, and this was never felt as a change of direction. In Europe the distance between theory and practice has been shorter partly because the theory has tended to be less abstruse, or less abstractly formulated, partly because the contact between schools and universities is usually close, and partly because in most European countries, and particularly Britain, teaching is less theoretically biased — the attractiveness of an approach is often inversely proportionate to its theoretical cogency. Such an approach has considerable disadvantages, but it has resulted in greater realism with regard to language teaching — a characteristic of H. E. Palmer's work, and a greater insistence on the relevance of pragmatic criteria of success as distinct from theoretical consistency.

The Western European tradition is classical and humanist both in origin and orientation. While in the U.S. linguistics has tended to find its social, external reference in anthropology and sociology, in Europe it has been sought, through philology, in literature and the humanities (Hall 1950 : 124). Because it has been so clearly related to classical and humanist studies, an emphasis on semantics has always characterised linguistic science in Europe. In Britain certainly, the aim is to elucidate meaning at its various levels as distinct from exhibiting the internal structure by means of which meaning is conveyed (McIntosh and Halliday 1966:4). It is one of the central features of Firth's theories (1937, 1957), which in turn have had considerable influence in maintaining what was best in traditional pedagogy. In Germany, too, a similar emphasis on meaning-orientated grammar, *inhaltsbezogene Grammatik,* is evident in the work of the Bonn school of Weisgerber (1929, 1949). This humanist tradition and the consequent insistence on the semantic component helped to justify an approach to language teaching through reading, exemplified in the work of West, who, before the structuralist revolution, had considerable influence in the U.S. (West 1926). In France, Belgium, and Holland the humanist and reading approach provided the rationale for *explication de texte.* The same emphasis on semantics is undoubtedly part of the explanation of the attractiveness of the contextual theories which are basic to British language teaching, and are an essential and remarkably well refined element in the work produced in France under the direction of Gougenheim, Rivenc and Guberina (CREDIF 1963; Girard 1964: 22).

In the U.S. on the other hand, linguistics developed in conjunction with social anthropological investigations initiated by scholars such as Powell, Brinton, and Gatschet, but principally Franz Boas, whose attitude to linguistic analysis as the elucidation of purely internal relationships attracted Bloomfield. A structural approach, independent of external semantic references was advisable and possibly necessary in the early work with little known indigenous American languages; and the undoubted success of such work, and the academic orientation of linguists brought up in that school, inspired teachers of languages where an exclusively internal analysis might be less easy to justify. It began mainly through the efforts of Fries (1945, 1952) with the teaching of English as a second language, and extended as an almost established orthodoxy to other foreign languages.[4] It should

---

[4] While in the U.S. it is usually accepted that the linguistics breakthrough into foreign language teaching came via the teaching of English as a second language, the reverse is the case in Britain. The teaching of English as a second language until comparatively recently was (apart from the University of Wales) based almost exclusively on the University of London Institute of Education, and maintained a predominantly humanist, not to say literary approach. Under the influence of Firth, first in London and later at Edinburgh, a school of young and lively linguists whose basic languages of study ranged from Chinese, Arabic and African languages to Greek, were trained. And when, with the encouragement of the Ministry of Education and the British Council, the training of teachers of English as a second language for work abroad considerably expanded the Firthian linguists, as occupiers of new Chairs of Linguistics, were able to exercise a very different kind of influence on the study of English. The focal point of these early activities, apart from Edinburgh and London was the University of Leeds under Peter Strevens, later at Essex. In France, as I understand it, the situation is nearer to that of the U.S. for it is the development of work in French that has influenced other second language work. The most influential organisation is B.E.L. under G. Capelle. Mention should also be made of the importance of the work of the Center for Applied Linguistics in Washington, D.C. under Ferguson, and later J. Lotz and the International Committee on Second Language Problems which Ferguson organised and the Ford Foundation financed, to coordinate second language studies internationally.

be noted too that the requirements of the armed services during the early 40s necessitated an intensive programme of language teaching which precluded the use of more humanistically directed teaching, and put a premium on highly structured teaching programmes (Graves and Cowan 1942:100). The success of such programmes, albeit within severely restricted terms of reference, encouraged their adaptation to courses and materials to be used with children in schools. From the European standpoint, it must be confessed that the highly structured programmes typical of U.S. linguistics, however they might be justified originally and with adults, are somewhat suspect. Reliance on highly sophisticated mechanical devices is acceptable to 'Americans who by cultural conditioning are so impatient with the hard labor of acquiring linguistic skill' (Ornstein and Lado 1967:17) and their general outlook appears to demand a fairly immediate return for extremely intensive study. These features point to a basic difference from the general tenour of European teaching.

4.2 *USSR*

4.21 *Russian as a second language*

The USSR presents one of the most convenient units for studying national characteristics in language pedagogy at present. For a long time it sought comparative isolation academically, and developed its own theories and practices with little influence from abroad. Its system of educational administration ensures that both practice and theory are fairly uniform throughout the school system. Structuralism played rather an unimportant part in Soviet linguistics for some time, and only gradually came to be regarded with favour (Haustrate 1968:137). Transformational theories, when they appeared, received more sympathy. The fundamental postulates of contemporary linguistics, for instance an emphasis on a synchronic approach, do not always inform the work of even major figures like Vinogradov (Van Schooneveld 1963:24), in consequence it is not unusual to find courses drawing their illustrative instances from different periods of linguistic development. The intervention of the Marrist school also affected not only the theories upon which courses were framed but the practical importance with which the basic skills were regarded — 'orthographic skills were relegated to the background and semantics replaced the study of concrete language phenomena' (Tekuchev 1967:23). In line with this self-imposed isolation the textbook writers tended and still tend to disregard material prepared in the country of origin of the language which may be under consideration.

At present foreign languages are next in importance only to the sciences in the school curriculum: they are taught in all schools, and in many of them with remarkable intensity. They are introduced from a very early age — in some kindergartens at ages 3 and 4 — and they are used in the senior grades of the high schools to

teach at least one non-linguistic subject (Lewis 1962). In addition to all this
foreign language activity there is the problem of presenting a native second language, partly because of the enormous number of different nationalities in contact,
and partly because the phenomenal mobility of masses of the population makes the
teaching of a lingua franca, Russian, obligatory. Even without such mobility administrative requirements and opportunities for higher education promote the learning
of Russian as a second language. Not only are all national groups taught Russian
as a second language but, in spite of the statutory right of parents to have their
children taught in their mother tongue if they wish, many receive all their education from the beginning in their second language. Therefore, the need for a methodology for non-Russian speaking students is pressing. Some work has been done
but the attitude adopted up until recently has not been unlike that of the British
in India and Africa during the last century, and of the French even now in large
areas of Africa, resulting in linguistic assimilation and a refusal to regard the
lingua franca as a second language. In fact, looking at the teaching of Russian as
a second language what strikes the observer is its remarkable formalism because
of the transfer of the characteristics of the teaching of Russian as the mother tongue.

Since the revolution and particularly since the war many factors have served to
promote the closer relationship of linguistics and the teaching of languages, especially the teaching of Russian to speakers of other Soviet languages. In the first
place steps were taken by linguists and teachers jointly to reconcile school and
academic grammars of the Russian language (Tekuchev 1967:32). The need for
such improvements in the school grammars is apparent from the fact that it was
thought 'the school programmes cannot include the teaching of voices because there
is not an established classification of voices in the science as yet' (Rozhdestvenskii
1966 : 39). The same is true, it is claimed, of punctuation where 'even an individual
with an excellent linguistic background would have to find his way alone' (Tekuchev 1967 : 7). Much of the scientific work was inspired by Shcherba (Friedl 1944)
who as one of the leaders of the Leningrad school attempted among other things
to ensure that there should not be the kind of separation of levels of language, in
description and teaching (especially the separation of phonetics from other levels),
that had been customary (Halle 1963:48). He had little success in this matter,
for the tendency of Soviet teachers and especially teacher-trainers is to teach the
linguistic levels separately, and to allocate separate parts of the language curriculum
to the task. Shcherba's discussions of syntax and parts of speech, and of lexicology
(Worth 1963:35; Weinreich 1963:65) together with the work of other linguists
influenced teachers to adopt an emphatically grammatical approach to language
teaching. Shcherba entered vigorously into discussions with teachers and published studies on detailed aspects of teaching, for instance *Bad spelling and its
causes* (Shcherba 1927).

The scientific work of the 30s and earlier which was pursued even more vigorously after the war, together with advances in mathematical linguistics, have led

to intensified efforts in foreign language pedagogical research to use highly formalised algorithmic concepts, characterised by logical analysis of linguistic processes
(Malash'chenko 1966; Artemov 1967). This form of linguistic academicism is
still active in the minds of some Soviet teachers and researchers, for whom grammar
is 'not only an aggregate of theoretical information . . . but one of the most important foundations for the development of their cognitive capabilities'; and on these
grounds they argue its separate teaching is to be encouraged (Rozhdestvenskii
1966 : 45).

The teaching of Russian as a second language suffers from the transference of the
formality of the teaching of Russian as the first language. As far back as 1928 the
'prominence given to theoretical linguistic information' was noted and even in the
standard curriculum of 1931 systematic grammar instruction was given, and very
general Russian language concepts were introduced (Tekuchev 1967:20). The
general direction of the thinking of psychologists like Vygotsky, and later Luria
and Leontev, and of educational psychologists such as Belayev (1963) has been
to encourage teachers to introduce formal grammar at an early age. In 1967 the
justification of grammar teaching was that 'theory produced mastery of material'
(Rozhdestvenskii 1967), and the influence of transformationalist thinking also is
apparent here. The relationship between theory and practice formulated so explicitly is the basis on which the content and amount of the primary school second
language course is organised. Consequently, even the primary school Russian
course introduces information about 'relationships between sounds and letters,
vowels and consonants . . . stress, stressed and unstressed vowels, voiced and un-
voiced (paired) consonants, and silent and double consonants . . . The pupils
acquire an elementary concept of the composition of the word (root, prefix, suffix)
etc.' (Rozhdestvenskii 1966: 31). This heavy injection of linguistic information at an
early age is one of the main characteristics of the teaching of Russian as a second
language to other nationalities in the Soviet Union, although in 1965 the amount
was reduced (Rozhdestvenskii 1967: 4).

4.22 *Work on Soviet national languages and foreign languages*

In spite of the overwhelming emphasis placed on the scientific description and
analysis of Russian and on its teaching to speakers of other Soviet languages little
has been done to adapt the researches to second language requirements.[5] This is

---

[5] Some work has been done especially in the Universities of some of the larger Union
Republics such as Ukraine (Cherednichenko 1957), Georgia (Purtseladze 1960-66), Uzbekistan
(Mirtov 1962), and some little work among the smaller nationalities, for instance Buriats
(Kudriavtsev 1965). To my knowledge there is one work which is concerned with the general
principles governing Russian second language teaching (Chistiakov 1969). In addition there
are two periodicals concerned with Russian as a second/foreign language – *Russkii jazyk v
national'noi shkole* (The Russian Language in the National School), and *Russkii jazyk
zarubezhom* (The Russian Language Abroad). Azerbaydzhan teachers of Russian have a
periodical, *Russkii jazyk v azerbaydzhanskoi shkole* (The Russian Languages in the Azerbaydzhan school), and this practice seems to be growing.

less true of the treatment of the other national languages, not because of any par-
tiality for them, but because of the force of circumstances. Because of the immense
literacy campaign after the revolution, considerable stress was laid on the accumulation of linguistic data, the description of the little known languages, the practical
task of creating for them alphabets, school grammars and dictionaries. While
this work was in progress, in order to facilitate social and political aims, attempts
were made to bring the various languages together, to plan them linguistically in
such a way that those who spoke them could transfer more easily to the official
second language, Russian. This was attempted partly by changes in the alphabets
of the non-Russian languages. The diverse Republics were encouraged and later
obliged to change to a uniform Latin script, but even before the change to Latin
had been completed a movement to introduce Cyrillic uniformly was inaugurated
(Winner 1952). The reason given for these changes was that 'the mass popular
movement for mastering the Russian language has led to the necessity for reforming the archaic alphabets, which have impeded the study of Russian' (Mordvinov
1950). In fact Baskakov, in setting out the criteria to be employed in modifying a
national script argued that 'further modification should be directed towards the
object of facilitating the learning of both the national and Russian languages . . .
and towards reconciling and co-ordinating the values of each symbol in the alphabet
of the language with the Russian alphabet' (Baskakov 1952 : 20). Every encouragement has also been given to the transfer of Russian loanwords and as a rule
'Russian and international terms were taken over in their Russian orthography and
this simplified the teaching of Russian' (Boskakov 1952 : 22). The Russian borrowings have also brought the phonetic systems of the national languages nearer to
Russian and linguists have formalised these changes to ensure the easier learning of
Russian as a second language (Baskakov 1952 : 28). It is no exaggeration to say
that the second most powerful motive (some would say the first) for language
planning in the Soviet Union has been to promote the learning of Russian by
speakers of other Union languages.

An area of second language teaching which has received some attention in the
USSR is the problem of interference. Serdyuchenko (1955), Rastorgueva (1952),
Grunberg (1960), and Ubryatova (1956) have drawn attention to this aspect of bilingualism, and school practice based on admittedly rudimentary contrastive of analysis is fairly commonplace (Galazov 1965). Stress is laid on the advisability of studying Russian with texts prepared locally 'because they take into account the specific
features of the national language and are a greater help in mastering those aspects
which are difficult for the Ossetian student' (Galazov 1965 : 54). Linguistic investigations relating to the Uzbek language were used in identifying phonetic difficulties
and 'these showed that Russian auditors heard the length and volume of the
stressed vowels as the basic component of stress, while the Uzbeks heard the volume and pitch of the fundamental tone' (Artemov 1960: 13). Similar work has been
done for Armenian and Russian. Lithuanian linguists have made a study of British

English and the native language, which can be used by English or Lithuanian students (Schalmstieg 1963:297). This work has been extended to foreign languages such as English, French and German. However, Soviet teachers are reluctant to rely on a theoretical contrastive analysis exclusively and they supplement theoretical analysis with observation of actual difficulties and error analysis (Menchinskaia 1967:12).

One marked difference, as one might expect, between teaching Russian as a second language and the teaching of a foreign language in the Soviet Union is the orientation of the former towards the assimilation of the Russian culture (or alternative concept of Russian as the medium of a new Soviet culture); while the approach to the teaching of foreign languages is minimally cultural and mainly instrumental. In this respect, so far as foreign languages are concerned, very interesting work has been done in the linguistic analysis of special or restricted registers of foreign languages. If, as the argument goes, 'life requires the use of only part of a foreign language and the time allotted for its study is extremely limited . . . it is better to study not the language in general but a specialised micro-language' (Artemov 1967:13). Mathematic and probability analysis help the Soviet linguists to restrict the English verb forms taught to the medical student to the present indefinite, present perfect, and past perfect; and only the indicative mood is taught' (Artemov 1967:13).

The pioneering work of Soviet psychologists and neurologists has changed our understanding of the function of the mother tongue, and this has tended to justify a place for the first language in the teaching of the second. Class teachers of Ossetian children, for instance, are praised for the 'skillful use of the children's native language in the process of Russian instruction' (Galazov 1965:47). They are confirmed in this approach by the argument that 'comprehension of the meaning of words in the foreign native language proceeds on the basis of knowledge of the meaning of corresponding words in the native language' (Artemov 1960:44).

Then again, in spite of the tradition of behaviourism in the USSR, Soviet linguists are disinclined, like Chomsky, to 'reduce speech mastery to habits, and habits to systems of . . . associations'. Language learning is 'a particular case of the learning process which requires an integral dynamic comprehension of the whole process' (Artemov 1967:15). At the same time, there is complete rejection of the metaphysical components of the transformationalist theories, more especially the hypothesis of innate linguistic features or a special capacity for language. Vygotsky, as early as 1926, criticised such theories, and among Soviet psycholinguists there is no sympathy for the rationalist tradition in linguistics — 'What are inborn are not capabilities but those anatomical and physiological characteristics . . . upon which capabilities are built' (Menchinskaia 1967:12). Soviet teachers, in consequence, are led to place less importance on the process of maturation and simple exposure to a language and to rely much more than British teachers are inclined to do, upon very carefully controlled instruction. The Soviet psycholinguist places the teacher at the very heart of second language pedagogy. In this adherence to a strictly controlled programme they are nearer to the U.S. than to the main tradition of European teaching.

The Soviet attitude also places a premium on and provides a rationale for *conscious automation,* which Shcherba puts at the centre of linguistic pedagogy — a progression to unconscious control through the explicit awareness on the part of the student of the features of language he is learning and their relation to each other. Leontev is unwilling to accept that language learning proceeds from maturation, 'spontaneously or a matter of passive imprinting' (Leontev 1963:217). Consequently the teacher is told that conditions must be created that will maximize the child's conscious activity as he learns the rules of a foreign language (Artemov 1960 : 65). Such a theory of language learning differs from the mainstream American attitude where the existence of conscious awareness of the learning task, to say nothing of structuring the teaching to promote such awareness, are thought to handicap language learning (Creelman 1966:18). Furthermore such an approach provides further justification for the Soviet grammatical approach to teaching the second language.

Finally, the Soviet psycholinguist contribution insofar as it emphasises instruction as distinct from encouraging maturation, favours programmes of accelerated learning, partly by intensive teaching in special foreign language schools with classes of 12-15 students, and partly by early introduction. 'It is possible for school children of the younger and intermediate age groups to attain higher levels of . . . language acquisition' (Menchenskaia and Saburova 1967:7) than is normally accepted, and they cite with approval work which demonstrates that under appropriate conditions it is possible to teach children a great deal more language than is possible by relying on the normal developmental processes merely. It would of course be absurd to insist unduly on the dichotomy between maturational learning and instruction, but there is no doubt that the emphasis is very differently placed in the Soviet Union from most countries in Europe and possibly, but less emphatically, in the United States.

5. LINGUISTICS AND THE TEACHER'S CONCEPT OF LANGUAGE

5.1 *Introduction*

A new orientation towards the idea of what language is and does, a redefinition of the concept of language, is possibly the most important contribution contemporary linguistics has offered language pedagogy. A definition controls the area within which the purpose of teaching a subject should be discussed. The teaching of a language as a corpus of etymological or historical information, as a set of mechanical skills, or of grammar as a mental discipline and a form of logic, is justified or not according to the concept of language which informs the course. It is true that linguistics contributes more than this — it offers better descriptions or models of particular languages, helps to determine the design of alternative models of language acquisition, and, according to the alternative the teacher or course designer chooses, linguistics helps to justify certain techniques of language teaching. Nevertheless, logically prior to these contributions, linguistics, by precisely circumscribing theoretically the area within which the teacher of languages operates, helps him to decide his aims and his general mode of approach. The changes which have occurred in the way we look at language characterise in precise terms the difference between the teacher of languages now and at the beginning of this century.

Not all the characteristics which are used to define language are equally important in forming the teacher's concept and in directing his approach to his practical tasks, and we shall be concerned only with those which appear most relevant. Furthermore, though it is probably the case that most of the defining characteristics have been recognised by linguists and teachers for as long as languages have been studied, the relative weight of importance attached to various characteristics has changed, and it is this new pattern of emphasis which constitutes the new orientation.

5.2 *Language a Part of a More General System of Symbolic Behaviour*

Increasingly significant in second language teaching is the realization that language is only one aspect of, and in point of time succeeds other forms of, intelligent behaviour. The recent stress on this fact, consequent on the work of C. S. Morris (1946), Osgood (1953), and Bruner (1966) supported by the work of Pike (1967) for instance in the U.S., and Vygotsky and Piaget in Europe, gives importance to the realization that 'the phenomena of language are perfectly and completely co-existent with the phenomena of behavior in general and any adequate theory of one is at once an adequate theory of the other' (Osgood 1963:240). The almost exclusive concern of traditional linguists and teachers with the written language, and even when their interest did extend to speech, a limitation to connected, formal discourse, meant that the argument for language as behaviour was not pursued vigorously. Now teachers are attending to aspects of behaviour which complement speech. Cassirer (1923, 1945) and following him Susanne Langer (1942) have encouraged teachers of languages to see other symbolic systems, like music, dance and art, not only as resources for illuminating the cultural background of the language but as essential components of a linguistic education. For instance experience of traits of the traditional culture of Wales may not help the English child to master the complicated system of initial consonant mutation, but he is unlikely to want to do so unless he has some awareness of the culture and life to which the language belongs. It is not simply the concept of language as speech, but of speech as intelligent behaviour linked to other aspects of culture, which has liberated the teacher of languages from the academicism of the past. Even at the more immediately practical level of classroom practice the behavioural approach to language has directed attention to a variety of paralinguistic features, the varying pattern of gestures for instance among different language groups, and the need to ensure that students are able to interpret these with verbal associates (Brault 1963:436).

The emphasis on the relation of language learning to general symbolic behaviour has broadened and deepened the teacher's interpretation of his discipline.[6] If there is one promising element in the present approach to language teaching, it is the realization in several countries that language learning cannot consist entirely of shaping language repertoires by mainly external means. However feasible that might be in respect to some aspects, language learning as a form of intelligent behaviour is succoured as well as shaped. Furthermore, not only does the learning of a foreign language manifest intelligence, it helps to influence mental development. Consequently, aspects of development like the stability of emotional behaviour, which may be termed problems of psychological interference and conflict and until recently were regarded as affecting only the traditionally bilingual child, are now seen, especially with the tendency to bring forward the age of introduction of a second language, to be important considerations for the teaching of foreign languages as well (Luria 1932). The linguistic contribution to language learning can be exploited satisfactorily only if the psycho-social setting is harmonious (Lewis 1970a).

The idea of language as part of a more general symbolic universe gives added weight to the teacher's understanding of the culture related to the language he is teaching. The linguist has little contribution to make regarding a decision about the depth at which it is intended a student should participate in the related culture. Nostrand (1966: 15–9) has identified at least six levels of possible participation, and the teacher in selecting a language course will take the proposed degree of cultural

---

[6] The teacher does not usually consciously concern himself with the philosophical bases of language and language pedagogy. But there are very important reasons why these bases should be taken into account in any study, since they help to determine the aims of language teaching and therefore the choice of method. The teacher cannot teach a language without being influenced, consciously or unconsciously by his idea of the importance of his task, its value: and while he might not go so far as G. K. Chesterton in arguing that the question is not in the long run whether anything else but these 'considerations of value' affects them, it is certainly the case that omissions from the study of the relationship of linguistics and pedagogy of any consideration of the philosophical climate in which teaching languages occurs is a defect. At the present time teachers and linguists are influenced directly and indirectly by the intellectual consequences of a considerable philosophical interest in language on the part of symbolic logicians and philosophers. The influence of their work on the teaching of language through their views on the value of language and its place in intellectual behaviour generally cannot be ignored any more than could the work of Haman, Herder and Humboldt. Language teaching is what philosophy and the philosophy of language proclaim its purpose to be.

immersion into account. The linguist has little to offer in determining this choice, but the interpretation of the sensitive interplay of language and social patterns is part of his contribution. The part linguistics plays in language teaching is in some ways proportionate to the account taken of cultural considerations. Such considerations determine choices of linguistic alternatives, like *tu* or *vous* in French, *ti* and *chwi* in Welsh. The teacher of Japanese has to teach not only the acquisition of alternative linguistic forms but their relationship to the sex of the speaker. In teaching Thai, regard has to be paid to the social status of the interlocutors, degree of familiarity, family relationship and age. At the beginning of a language course such cultural factors do not weigh unduly, but as the student reaches the higher levels of linguistic competence and of conceptual sophistication the cultural considerations become very relevant. The difference between languages in the way they reflect patterns of cultural organisation and behaviour necessitate a full understanding of the relationship of language to culture in general, and of the precise ways in which particular languages differ in this respect. There is no doubt that the main contribution in this field has been made by the anthropologically oriented linguists of the U.S. (Hymes 1964; Lado 1957).

5.3 *Language as Speech*

Speech, another of the defining characteristics which have appeared in a new light, is at the heart of modern language teaching. Linguists have revived interest in the observation, description and measurement of the sounds of speech for the purposes of teaching. This has encouraged the development of pre-linguistic phonetic components of foreign language courses, consisting in the main of discrimination training leading to articulation practice. Sometimes the introduction of such phonetic components is explicit but occasionally some A/V courses disguise the phonetic instruction, as in the Cours Audio-Visuel entitled Voix et Images de France. The interest in the phonetics of particular languages, and so far as the teacher-trainer is concerned in the study of the general science of phonetics, has meant the encouragement of specialised departments of the science, like acoustic phonetics, as well as new techniques within the specialised department like the use of the spectogram. At the classroom level it has meant among other things, the development and use of transcription techniques which most language teachers find useful at some point or another (Halliday et al. 1964).

Since writing and reading are also important parts of even the elementary language course, the relation of speech to its written representation must always concern the teacher. In the case of some languages, such as Spanish, Italian or Welsh, the spelling of which is more or less phonemic, the need for a systematic transcription to bridge the two modes of speech and writing is not urgent. For teachers of other languages this is not the case, and it sometimes happens that

rationalization of the spelling system is desirable, in order to facilitate its acquisition by foreigners. This has been one of the arguments used to support the teaching of Initial Teaching Alphabet, though its indebtedness to the linguistic sciences
is slight. Apart from the need to rationalize an idiosyncratic spelling system is the
problem of ensuring as little interference as possible between different types of
alphabet — Chinese ideographs, the Japanese supplementary Kana or syllabary,
and the alphabetic scripts of most countries. The differences among languages
using the same kind of script may also be important as we have seen in the changes
inaugurated in the USSR involving Cyrillic, Central Asian scripts and Latin.

Finally a descriptive, as opposed to prescriptive, approach to speech is less relevant to the teaching of a foreign language than linguists normally assume to be the
case. This fact helps to reinforce the distinction which has to be made between
second and foreign language instruction. The teacher of a foreign language has
to ensure that the linguistic norm at each intermediate stage of learning conforms
to the ideal, final stage or competence model of the language; whereas the teacher
of the second language is much more permissive. At any one stage of learning
he accepts speech or grammatical approximations, the appropriateness of which is
determined as much by the child's age and level of general development as by
linguistic criteria. The foreign language teacher in the framing of the programme
for the whole course takes these non-linguistic criteria into account also, but once
the course has been framed he tends firmly to retain his prescribed norms. Problems of correctness, which do not have the same relevance in the learning of a
second language in close contact situations are pervasive in the handling of speech
and grammar in the foreign language. Furthermore, the relative importance of
linguistic prescriptiveness and psychological considerations will tend to shift and
approach more nearly to second language practice as the foreign language is
introduced at progressively earlier ages.

5.4 *Language as System*

Regard for language as a system is not an innovation in language teaching, but
changes in the manner in which teachers conduct the discussion of the question
have affected present day teaching. System is no longer one feature among many —
it is considered to be the essence of language and of its teaching. 'To those who
have felt something of the spirit of a foreign language it is certain that there is
such a thing as a basic plan, a certain cut to each language' (Sapir 1921: 120).
Structuralism, according to this view, is not only a possible, or alternative way of
teaching, it is the only way. Of course the systemic nature of language is important
in teaching the mother tongue but in second language teaching it has a new
dimension of importance. In noisy channels more words are recognised when they
are included in a structured context than when produced alone (O'Neill 1957 : 220).
It is undoubtedly the case that distortion, imprecision and mere approximation are

more confusing in learning the second language than in acquiring the mother tongue, where the context of the situation provides a surrogate for linguistic redundancy in structure.

Second, the extension of the idea of system beyond grammar, to include the sound system, made possible the structural approach to teaching speech. The present day teacher of French prefers to practice significant oral contrasts like *il/elle* or *le/les* than to drill the precise articulation of single discrete sounds. The idea of distinctive features as the basis of the system is among the most fruitful principles in teaching foreign languages since it economises effort in course design and teaching, by identifying a selection of features which must have priority. The same is true of the concept of a hierarchy of units, among which priority has to be given to those which are important not only in themselves but also because they enable the learner to make judgements about subsequent data presented to him. In learning Russian as a second language for instance 'the students made judgements according to syntactic constructs . . . to a lesser degree by perception of individual words, and even less by particles' (Crothers and Suppes 1967: 288).

Differences among linguists about the degree of openness of the linguistic system influence teachers of languages. Not only do the present advocates of transformational grammar tend to regard language as a *well defined system,* but the trend of linguistics in the U.S. for a long time incorporated 'without question the Saussurean-Bloomfieldian characterisation of language as a rigid system'; and among some of the more influential British linguists, the closedness of grammar is its main characteristic (McIntosh and Halliday 1966:5). On the other hand, some linguists are reluctant to continue in this tradition or to accept a linguistic model based on exclusively and/or alternatives (Nida 1969:48). This argument is important because it brings into focus once again the status of linguistic ontogeny in the teaching of foreign languages. The teacher of the mother tongue, or of the second language in situations of close contact must allow for the operation of linguistic change, and consequently for a relatively open system. No teacher of the mother tongue or of the second language to a bilingual child ever pretends that he is regulated by a precise and well formed model. So far as the teaching of a foreign language is concerned however, the instruction is programmed according to a previously defined model and to that extent the system taught has been closed and at each stage of the course the aim is to conform as closely as possible to that model.

5.5 *Semanticity*

Language taught without regard for its semanticity, as very often happened with the traditional grammar approach, is simply an elaborate game or at best an exercise in logical analysis. The establishment of meaning is the life blood of successful language teaching and the extension of communication is its only justification. The conviction of many linguists that it is possible to describe a language without recourse to meaning (Hockett 1968:24) and the equally strongly held conviction of other linguists (Trager 1949; Harris 1951) that rejection of meaning as a criterion is not only possible but necessary, have encouraged a similar disinclination to introduce meaning into teaching a language among some teachers. For instance Mueller (1961) and Morton (1960) maintain that directing the student's attention to the meaning of the sound patterns he is being taught interferes with the development of automatic response and control of the patterns. This view carries weight with many teachers and course designers, especially those involved in programmed instruction. However the rejection of meaning, where it does occur, is usually a feature of the prelinguistic stages of oral instruction. When it comes to thematic stages, the consideration of meaning is unavoidable. However justifiable the descriptive linguist himself may be in employing exclusively formal criteria, the classroom teacher usually approaches language through meaning. Furthermore, apart from the technical necessity, the need for motivation suggests the advisability of including meaning in teaching: repeated drills without interest offer ever diminishing returns to the learner and teacher. It is at least arguable that projecting into the teaching of languages at even the earliest stages, the descriptive linguist's formal criteria has been disadvantageous.

To the extent that linguistics has focussed the problem of meaning and made clear the implications, it has made a contribution to teaching. Insofar as linguists have helped the teacher to recognise the differences between levels of meaning — lexical, syntactic, morphemic, tonal, etc., and between kinds of meaning — linguistic, immediately situational and broadly cultural, it has sharpened the teacher's awareness of the pervasiveness of meaning and governed the relative emphasis he places on each kind. It accounts very largely for the contextually determined approach in Britain. Whatever the differences in levels and kinds of meaning may be, the teacher finds it more in keeping with the realities of language to regard meaning as something which is 'relevant from the discourse of the sounds . . . One must recognize that creativity in the communication process begins with discourse, where the semantic component is most involved' (Nida 1969:488). Consequently the importance of the use of dialogues which, though structured to bring out the features to be taught, convey meaning creatively.

5.6 *Linguistic Diversity*

5.61 *Differences within languages*

The linguistic behaviour of even a monoglot is not uniform, and a modern language reveals, if it does not consist of, a reticulation of varieties. Linguists have contributed to the teaching of languages by drawing attention to this fact as well as by identifying and describing the varieties to which the student of a foreign language has to adapt. The long tradition of teaching classical languages, which have all the appearance of uniformity because the literary corpus has been so severely selected, seriously delayed the realisation of the importance of diversity in second language pedagogy. Differences between the grammar of speech and writing, identified and emphasised by linguists as we have seen already, have become important because of the oral direction of instruction (Rojas 1969: 56–7). Differences within the language, whether spoken or written, arising from the social situation are equally important to the learner. Though his mind is directed, in the main, to the ability to use the standard forms of the language he has to recognise the meaning of a discourse appearing in a variety of other forms. The variants of *il ne veut pas* /ildvøpa/invøpa/inøpa/ have all to be understood. Again the teacher of French as a foreign language has to help his students to appreciate the differences, for instance, between *langue contemporaine*, and *langage classique*; within the former, distinction between *langue populaire*, *bon usage* and *langue literaire* have to be established. Even within the subcategory of *bon usage* differences between *langue familière*, *langue courante* and *langue soignée* need to be recognised. And within *langue courante* differences between the spoken and written languages occur. These different *niveaux de langue* have characteristic formal features some of which insofar as they affect the English language, for instance, Martin Joos (1961) and others have described and are incorporated in teaching programmes. Some of the varieties constitute special or restricted languages and we have seen how the linguistic analysis of the kind of English to which a medical student is exposed is made the basis for a language course in the USSR. In Britain and elsewhere colleges provide courses which combine technological training like engineering with instruction in an appropriate restricted language on the basis of linguistic analysis (Koutaisoff 1965).

Sometimes two or more varieties of the same language have been stabilized and institutionalized. Socially and traditionally determined High and Low varieties, diglossia, have received the attention of teachers (Ferguson 1959). While the teaching of Arabic as a second language must be directed for the most part to the acquisition of the classical or High form, a student needs to have an acquaintance with the Low form if he is to communicate with servants and workmen, carry on a conversation with friends or enjoy popular entertainment in Arabic countries. A range of vocabulary and a set of grammatical features not normally included in the standard course have to be taught. In the same way a student has to learn more than one regional dialect if divergencies such as those of modern China exist. Marked regional dialects are also important if they occur in the mother tongue of the student. For instance in Italy, where more than half the population make use of one dialect or another in most of their private and public activities it is inadvisable to use a uniform Italian/English contrastive analysis for all students learning English, since certain consonants and vowels in some dialects do not contrast with English in the same way as they do in other dialects. The same thing occurs in respect to Italian/French contrast, some French vowels, for instance /y/, /ø/, /æ/, presenting particular difficulty for speakers of Southern dialects but not speakers of Lombard dialects and Piedmontese (Titone 1965:159). Similarly, speakers of German dialects, for instance Swabian, make distinctions which differ from speakers of High German. 'Swabians do not distinguish between *fortes* and *lenes,* consequently they do not notice differences between big and pig', which Germans normally do (Ludwig 1965:230).

5.62 *Differences between languages*

Comparative linguistics has played a useful role in enabling teachers of a second language first to exploit, scientifically, the similarities between languages, and second to minimize the inevitable confusions which differences between languages create in the mind of the student. One category of similarities includes the hypothesised universals of language (Greenberg 1963). This field of enquiry has not offered any significant contribution to the teaching of languages up to the present. Linguists have identified to their own satisfaction some of these universals — for instance the phonemic character of all languages and their hierarchical organization, the existence of units, structures, systems, classes in all languages (Halliday et al. 1964). If it were agreed that such categories constitute universals of language they would have little relevance to the teaching of any second language, since all their existence would imply is the precondition of, or possibility of, learning a second language; universals are the presupposition of moving on from one language to the next, their existence cannot be said to facilitate the learning of any particular language.

There are less abstract or hypothetical points of comparison between languages, and it is the existence of these and especially if they are favourable to the learning of a second language, which the practical teacher has to take into account. The importance of these similarities has been discounted during the last half century and more, partly because linguists and anthropologists brought up in the Humboldtian Romantic philosophical tradition have tended to stress the uniqueness of languages and the multiplicity of differences which uniqueness implies.[7] With the revival of the interest in universals, and of the nationalist tradition in linguistics the feasibility of exploiting the similarities among languages is bound to become increasingly evident. Recent studies by Lane (1964), Pimsleur (1963), Galanter (1962) and others suggest that students transfer from first language discrimination of sounds to the discrimination of sounds in the second language, and that learning proceeds more rapidly for that reason. Such transfer is more likely to occur between languages which have a genetic or contact relationship (Lane 1964).

[7] One is apt to ignore the fact that but for the combination of the influence of Romantic (folk) linguistics, democratic (folk) stress on the necessity of using the vernacular in education, and Romantic (folk) nationalism insistence on the need to preserve and possibly revive minority languages, there would be little call to consider tne teaching of a second as distinct from a foreign language in some countries. Cf. Welsh, Irish, Breton, Fries, etc.

However it is the study of differences which is most characteristic of the linguists' contribution to teaching. There are two chief sources of error in learning a second language — rivalry and resulting confusion between the new and the native language patterns, and rivalry and resulting confusion among the new language patterns which are being acquired. This second source of confusion is almost as important as the first. Wolfe (1932) suggests that consistency in the structure of a language is favourable to its acquisition; and the inconsistencies in a language can be most frustrating to a student. Anyone learning Japanese is introduced to the Kanji (Chinese characters) as ideograph, as well as to the Kana or phonetic symbols, the Roman letters and the Arabic numerals. In addition to their enormous number, Kanjis have more than one pronunciation, and the 74 Kanas have two written forms. The inconsistencies of the English language are a by-word. Consequently an approach which has appealed to some teachers is the rationalization of the target language and this has been the motive for the foundation of Basic courses in several languages (Richards 1930:48).

Such limited languages are possible and useful (Richards 1939) but rationalizing the language is not the only way to minimize inconsistency. Confusion can be kept within bounds by judicious selection and grading. Although these aspects of a language course are mainly aspects of the presentation of the language, and, it has been argued, are not linguistic issues, it is a fact that linguistic considerations and not simply pedagogic convenience enter into the selection and grading of units of the course. Among the two most important criteria specified by Fries in selecting language patterns, regularity of form is one (Fries 1952 : 32). And of the seven criteria of vocabulary selection listed in the *Interim report on vocabulary selection* two linguistic criteria are given — structural value and value for word building (Faucett et al. 1936).

The second approach to rationalising the presentation of the second language is to reduce possible interference between the two languages and so eliminate confusion in the process of learning. There are two theoretical foundations to this approach, one psychological and the other linguistic.

A basic assumption of interference theory is that when incompatible responses are stimulated and the incompatibility is between old and newly acquired responses 'there is competition between the old and new habits at the time of recall, with the stronger of the competing responses achieving dominance; an important application of this analysis is to the transfer effects of pre-experimental language habits on the acquisition of new verbal sequences' (Postman 1963 : 40). To the extent that the new associations are compatible with the old, the learning of the new is facilitated, but any incompatability of old and new language habits results in interference and negative transfer.

The second basis of the theory is provided by Bloomfield's discussion of the problems which occur when sounds that are phonemic in one language are not phonemic in another. Such a lead was followed by Haugen (1956) and Weinreich

(1953) in their studies of bilingualism. While the psychological theory explains how interference occurs, it requires the structural linguist to predict the areas where it is likely to occur and in what form. In fact, linguists maintain that they are able to supply teachers with very precise predictions, and in this they are supported by mathematical learning theorists (Jakobovits 1968). Precise prediction extends to all levels of language, though because of the emphasis on speech in contemporary linguistics it is the prediction of sound-interference that has been in the forefront of teacher's minds. Teachers have taken advantage of contrastive analysis to provide such things as bilingual contrastive vowel charts, for instance between Romanian and English (Vasu 1961); or lists of contrast pairs directed to a particularly troublesome combination of sounds characterising the language (Wolf 1962). Similar contrastive analyses have been offered for structures and for the orthography of different languages. The system has been extended to punctuation problems such as those which English students meet in learning to read and write Scandinavian languages (Nichols 1962).

One area of contrastive analysis has not received the attention it requires in pedagogy. Hardly anything of significance has been attempted in the differential comparison of vocabulary. At first sight, it might be expected, because of the work of Whorf in showing how various languages reflect the common experience of mankind differently, that as much would have been attempted in this area as in speech. The need is certainly as great, for even in languages as nearly related as Danish and English, words like *morning,* Danish *morgen* and *foremiddag;* or *family,* Danish *familie* and *born,* and the Danish *hund,* English *dog* and *hound* cause confusion. Some systematic work has been attempted by Prator (1965) in his discussion of the adjectives of temperature in English, Chinese, French, Spanish and Tagalog. His purpose is specifically to identify and predict the difficulties which a native speaker of any one of the five languages will have in learning to use the temperature terms of any of the other four. Colour terms have been used by research workers to test Whorf's ideas but in spite of the availability of the results and the importance of colour terms, such research has had little impact on teaching or course designing (Lenneberg 1953, 1961, 1967). Contrastive analysis of meaning must surely make increasing demands upon the attention of linguists, especially as interest in semantic studies intensifies. When such an interest does develop it is more than probable that Prator's view that vocabulary and grammar will have to be treated together will be substantiated. That being the case there is everything to be said for on-going contrastive analysis of grammatical structures taking greater account of semantics.

Reference has already been made to the Soviet interest in contrastive analysis in teaching second and foreign languages. Contrastive studies have been produced in France as bases for French courses for Laotian and Cambodian students, and similar work is being produced for teaching French to speakers of African languages (Girard 1964:23). Vinay and Darbelnet have produced a good comparison of French/English (1958). In Britain there is no great enthusiasm for the approach. The main impetus, theoretically and practically, has occurred in the U.S. Lado's exposition of the problem (Lado 1957) and the fact that the Michigan materials for English were built around English/Spanish contrasts, have been important factors. The same principles were applied in the ACLS series for speakers of such languages as Serbo-Croat, Thai, Turkish, Greek, Mandarin Chinese, etc. From these beginnings progress was made with the C.A.L. contributions to English/German studies in the first place and later to Russian and French, etc. (Hammer and Rice 1965).

The approach has not been without its critics among teachers. It has been suggested that the method is difficult to control because of the complexity of its operation — its effect on performance and competence may not be similar; understanding, speaking, reading and writing the language may be differentially affected by interference, and there are possible differences in interference with respect to phonology, syntax and lexis (Jakobovits 1968). Then again, apart from the complexity of interference it has been denied that contrastive analysis is needed at all, since the errors which are predicted are already known to the teacher (Mackey 1966:200). In such cases the use of contrastive techniques may do positive harm (Pilch 1964). Some critics have argued that the predictions have seldom been attested, though work undertaken by Suppes suggests that prior contrastive analysis was a good predictor of the relative difficulty which students encountered in learning some Russian sounds (Lane 1964a: 260). Titone's investigations (1965: 150) of the ability of Italian secondary school students to discriminate four constituents of the sounds of English and French found a high correlation between actual and predicted performance. These investigations into the relationship between predicted and actual performance are helpful to the teacher, who is concerned not only with identifying the difficulties but with measuring their extent or intensity. Some difficulties exist but are insignificant — thers are crucial. Only error analysis can provide a check on their relative significance and discover the intensity of the difficulty of a particular case (Titone 1965:153; Lane 1964a:269; Lewis 1969b).

Other observations have been offered by teachers — for instance that in teaching young children the value of contrastive analysis is questionable (Titone 1965 : 151). It is my experience that it has less to offer the teacher of a second as distinct from a foreign language. There is some support for this view in psychological interference theory. Contextual constructs derived from the circumstances in which a language is learned and serving, so far as the second language is concerned, to provide redundancy within the learning task, radically influence the amount of possible interference (Postman 1963:45). It is also the case that the use of contrastive analysis must vary with the model of acquisition favoured by the teacher. Contrasts may be used explicitly and the attention of the student may be directed consciously to them, in which case it adapts easily to the cognitive, code-learning model. On the other hand the contrasts may be built into drills which the student is required to practice without necessarily being aware of the principle on which the drill is based. In general, this adapts very well to the Audio-Lingual approach. In the main those who favour contrastive analysis also favour the explicit approach since 'resistance to interference increases with the amount of explicit information given to the subjects about the rules involved' (Postman 1963 : 46).

Finally, the comparison of languages affects teaching through the importance which may be attached to translation, both as an objective to be pursued and as a component of the method of achieving other aims. The consideration affecting translation as a main aim of learning a second language cannot conveniently be included in this discussion for the reason that, unlike other elements within method, translation poses a large number of questions which are outside the province of teaching, and because there are criteria of success in translation which go well beyond the needs of teaching. Nevertheless, it is difficult to deny an element of translation in most forms of second language learning. Lambert (Segalowitz and Lambert 1969 : 564) suggests that 'the first language used by the bilingual may develop as the pivot language'; and it is consistent with the experience of most teachers in spite of the views of language programmers (Lane 1968 : 109) that the vernacular meaning helps to determine, for the beginner at least, the point of reference for comprehension. Even those who are most committed to the elimination of meaning in language programmes are prepared to compromise to some degree (Morton 1960). Crothers and Suppes (1967) argue that the acquisition of a language is facilitated if translation techniques are introduced intentionally and deliberately, and that these are more successful if instead of using complete sentences they are limited to isolated words. A similar conclusion has led to the development of bilingual method courses (Dodson and Price 1969) which adopt the prompting techniques employed by Israel (1960).

6. MODELS AND THEORIES

6.1 *Introduction*

So far we have been considering the influence exerted on teachers by new ideas about language and by the changes in our attitude to various characteristics of language which linguists have brought about. In consequence of these changes teachers tend to link language more closely to other non-verbal forms of intelligent behaviour constituting our culture, to regard speech as our primary concern, to teach language as a system rather than an aggregate of discrete units, to have a new regard for semantics and to put 'meaning back in the driver's seat' (Osgood 1968 : 503); to recognise the diversity within language as well as the systematic comparison of differences between languages as a technique of teaching. The acceptance of any particular theory of language is unnecessary to justify these changes in emphasis: it is mainly a matter of attitude to certain characteristics of language, the existence of which all theories are prepared to postulate. The influence of linguistics at this level has been pervasive and together with the contribution it has made by refining the descriptions of particular languages it may be the most important, as it is certainly the most evident support linguistics has given to language teaching.

Nevertheless, theories are necessary to a science, whether of language or teaching language, and pedagogy reflects the interplay of several explanatory models or theories which have many linguistic elements. The linguist has to be concerned with three questions — first, what knowing a particular language involves, that is, what it is that the student is learning; second, he is concerned not only with the description of the language but with how the language is used, how communication is being promoted by means of what is being acquired; and third, between the first and second issues, that is, what is available to the student and the use to which he puts it, there is the question of how the student took possession of what he is using (Katz 1964:78). It is perfectly proper for a linguist to restrict the area of his interest to any aspect of any one of these questions, and it is probably necessary that many should do so. But the science itself ranges over the three issues and is concerned with the theoretical constructs and hypotheses which are devised to elicit the answers.

Before we discuss the influence of linguistic theories within any one of the three fields we have referred to, some reservations need to be expressed. In the first place the amount and kind of theorizing varies according to the area of investigation. For instance, there is no doubting the value of such studies as Leopold's meticulous description of the bilingual development of his daughter, Hildegard; but though theories may be proposed to explain his data, Leopold himself does not attempt to articulate or employ a theory (Leopold 1939-49). Then again, no theory is watertight, like grammars every one leaks, and any model whether of the language itself, or of acquisition or presentation will necessarily be partial and to that extent inadequate (Leontev 1963:215). The linguist is justified in elaborating his theories so far as the criteria of his discipline permit but he has to allow for a degree of *play* or looseness in any formulation.[8] Thus though it may not be true that in 'some instances it matters very little whether a foreigner distinguishes between two phonemes' (Christophersen 1964:30), it is a fact that within phonemic theory a good bit of latitude is allowed — a wide variation in the production of a phoneme does not necessarily prohibit its identification (Lane 1965:288). The teacher for his part handles a model arbitrarily; he makes a useful distinction between what is *acceptable* and what is *good*. Because of the difficulty even a native speaker has in conforming to any norm, the teacher of a second language settles for optimum rather than maximum control (Nostrand 1966:4; Chao 1968:

---

[8] 'Scientists do tolerate uncertainty and frustration, because they must. The one thing that they do not tolerate is disorder' (quoted in Lévi-Strauss 1966:9).

140). He need not accept the precision or the elaborateness proposed by the linguists' model of the language. A strong French accent is not a barrier to communication in another language and very often an attempt religiously to overcome such an accent sets up resistance to reciprocal social contact. Some teachers believe that the pursuit and presentation of theoretically more convincing descriptions of English intonation for the use of African students may be unjustified (King 1967). In the same way the teacher's traditional operation with at least 6 English tenses, modelled on Latin, though less elegant, may be more useful than the linguist's more austere categorization (Christophersen 1964:27). The single-mindedness of linguists in the pursuit of exactitude results in their descriptions and theories becoming as unintelligible to other linguists as they are unhelpful to teachers (Haugen 1951:363).

Models are built for specific purposes: there is no one absolute model of language or acquisition or presentation. The kind of analysis that is best is determined by extra-linguistic goals (Haugen 1951:363), though any model to be at all helpful must meet certain requirements (Postal 1964 : 197). It follows that a teacher or course designer is entitled to choose from among the models available the one which best suits his own purpose and predilections (Gefen 1966 : 230). Nevertheless, the acceptance of a particular model at one level, for instance a theory of language, though it does not absolutely determine his choice of a model of acquisition and a model of presentation, helps him to evaluate the suitability of such theories. Similarly if he prefers to organise a course in a particular way and to use certain kinds of materials he tends to look to a particular theory of language or a particular model of acquisition to justify or explain his choice and to provide the rationale which every good teacher seeks. In this sense, though a theory of language may imply a particular theory of acquisition so far as teaching is concerned, the relationship between the different levels of theory is tenuous to say the least, though insofar as language pedagogy seeks to achieve the status of a science it should perhaps seek to remedy the defect.

The fact that relationships of implication exist between the levels of theory does not mean that there are no differences in their formulation — in fact there are essential disparities. For instance, it has been suggested that between possible models of language and of language acquisition there are at least the following differences. First, the model of language, though it reflects a relatively finite system, should provide for the possibility of infinitely varied production; whereas the model of acquisition is limited by the given capacities and inherent endowment of the learner. Second, the model of the language reflects an abstract system, a blueprint or map, whereas the model of acquisition needs to take account of the speaker's use of the language along a dimension of time. Third, the model of the language does not need to take into account any non-linguistic context — it is not only abstract but autonomous: whereas the model of acquisition is hardly adequate if it omits contingent factors like motivation. Fourthly, the language model can theoretically be described without reference to meaning while in the acquisition model meaning is central (Osgood 1968:494).

There is one final reservation about the relationship of the theories we are discussing: it does not follow of necessity that because we have a model of language as well as an account of the principles of language acquisition, that a student actually operates the models or adheres to those principles in his learning of a second language. On the other hand there is nothing to suggest that he might not do better and learn more easily if in fact his course recognised and adhered to the model. A reasonable consistency not only within a theory but between levels of theory is what the science of language pedagogy should seek to achieve. A mass system of education (unfortunately perhaps) cannot afford the luxury of idiosyncracy. The learning of a foreign language proceeds without the supports of a strong social reinforcement of the language — the student's success depends very much on how the new material is presented formally and on the consistent application of the principles which govern instruction. We need in second language pedagogy a theory of instruction that at least reflects if it does not conform to a theory of acquisition, itself a reflection of a theory of language. Linguistics has contributed something to the tentative design of a theory of instruction mainly through its contributions at the other theoretic levels, and it is in this direction that its influence will be exerted in the future.

6.2 *Two Alternatives*[9]

The teacher and course designer are offered two alternative approaches and theories by means of which they may evaluate the linguistic adequacy, as distinct from the pedagogic convenience of using types of teaching materials and exercises: the alternatives are a structural linguistic theory related to an associationist and empiricist theory of acquisition, or a transformationist theory of language with a cognitive model of acquisition. This dichotomy, it will be immediately apparent though basically valid and useful, is a rash over-simplification because there are variations within the structural approach, and at least some differences in emphasis among the transformational theorists. Moreover, though some psycholinguists state the alternatives in stark opposition (Katz 1964:75), one suspects that the differences between the two schools are not as wide as the vehemence of their discussions suggest. More and more ground which is common to both sides is being identified:

---

[9] Pribram's account (1965) of two possible models of behaviour analysis is highly relevant to the articulation of language and language models, in general respects: One alternative model is constructed as a result of the analysis of systems of input variables, and the other is based on the consideration of the effect of action on the system. Second, one alternative is a structured model while the other is a topographical model. These correspond, to my way of thinking, to the two models we are discussing, the empiricist and the cognitive models of acquisition. The third point Pribram makes is that because of these differences the two models complement each other, and for that reason, I suggest teachers must take both into account.

neo-behaviourists recognise that command of language depends on the student's internal condition as well as on external stimuli; and among those who are identified with the associationist school like Postman, Keppel, and Osgood there has long been a recognition of the existence of the *principles* underlying the organisation of verbal learning, of the function of coding rules (Cofer 1968:529) and of the need to postulate central integration as a factor in learning (Osgood 1956:55). It has been pointed out that tagmemic-substitution grammarians recognise the place of transformations as in Longacre's work (1958) and 'transformationalists propound syntactic features . . . which select a certain sub-category (e.g. an abstract noun) to fill a place . . . as subject or object of a verb (the function of tagmemics) in a sentence' (Gefen 1966:232). In any case, whatever the system for differentiating the various schools of linguistic description and theory we have to agree that 'we do not have a satisfactory theory of language learning, nor do we know what form a theory will take' (Crothers and Suppes 1967:75), so our habits of mind may incline us one way or another. This tendency towards reciprocity between schools of thought, the large measure of uncertainty and, much more serious, the abstractness of the discussions of the proposed theories impel teachers to adopt a pragmatic and eclectic rather than consistent attitude, and delay the development of language pedagogy as a science with a coherently expressed set of principles.

From the structuralist, the teacher learns that a language consists of a finite, unordered list of ordered pairs of elements, to which he may attach one of several labels — constituent, phrase construction, or tagmeme, etc. His concern is with presenting the systematic analysis of these structures. The teacher depends on the linguist's description of the linguistic units, their distribution and combinational possibilities in the chain of speech. The distribution of these units is tested by the linguist according to a method of substitution, the replacement of the unit under consideration by another unit in the same context, the interavailability of units constituting a grammatical class. The approach is taxonomic and the teacher is interested not only in the units but in the classes to which they belong. From the linguist of this school, the teacher learns to adopt an analytical, step-by-step procedure for presenting the features of the language, conforming to the procedure adopted in arriving at the description.

Bloomfield's original development of structural analysis reflects a behaviourist theory of language acquisition and the empiricist features are still associated with structuralism in language teaching. So far as the teacher of a second language is concerned, the most important of these characteristics is the insistence, in the first place, that language is learned by the strength of habitual associations and by context generalization. Second, reinforcement which may be interpreted or conceptualized as the information conveyed or fed back to the student, and the support given him by confirmation or correction of his response plays an important part in this learning. The stress on habit formation leads to the belief in the value of overlearning. At one time it might have been true to say that in the empiricist approach the burden of ensuring language learning was placed on the environment, that the role of the student was relatively passive and that the account of the learning process itself, the ordering of words according to the probability of their association, underestimated the complexity of the process. This is hardly the case at present, and the two stage mediation theories of Jenkins, Braine, Mowrer, Osgood and others, and especially Osgood's three stage hypothesis have gone a long way to meeting the former objections. However, it is still the case, in spite of the claims of psycholinguists like Staats (1968) that, for the empiricist, using a language is very much a reproductive event, manipulating a finite repertoire of responses. To this extent the teacher may very well claim that the approach fails to take 'adequate account of intelligence ... the power to make a new departure instead of repeating the old habit' (Whatmough 1965: 75).

A feature of the empiricist approach which is important to the language teacher is its ability to account for language as part of a general theory of behaviour, and consequently to justify the placing of language teaching very firmly within the framework of the child's behavioural development. The empiricist psycholinguist, while prepared to accept the fact that language, the second signal system, plays a unique role in the development of intelligent behaviour, does not accept that the linguistic process itself either in acquisition or use is unique, or essentially different from other forms of behaviour. Consequently, the teacher of a second language is encouraged by empiricist theory to link language development, including the acquisition of the second language, to the general psychological development of the child. Moreover, there is another distinction which the empiricist refuses to make, at least in the form in which it is gaining popularity, namely the distinction between competence and performance (Chomsky 1965a: 15). For the teacher and course designer the empirical attitude has considerable attractiveness. Contemporary teaching theory attempts to work to an integrative model making little distinction between the process and the substance of learning. To the extent that he adheres to this principle the teacher judges linguistic competence in operational terms only. Not only is there no way of knowing the student's competence except in terms of performance but the distinction itself is meaningless. It is true, as Spolsky argues, that one knows a language even though one speaks it confusedly and somewhat incoherently (Spolsky 1966a: 124). This is something all teachers accept; but knowing a language in this sense is not to be identified with linguistic competence in the sense that it is used by contemporary linguists. One speaks it incoherently because one's knowledge is limited. There are at least three levels on which the teacher has to operate — the level of *available* knowledge — what it is possible to know and use, an ideal linguistic concept. As I understand it, this is what is generally meant by *competence*. Second, the level of *acquired* knowledge, a psychological concept which is variable; and the level of *operative* knowledge, performance, which is a pedagogic concept. The empiricist and the teacher make no distinction between the second and third levels — 'how do I know what I mean until I say it'.

From the point of view of the teacher of a second language, the salient feature of transformation theory is the attempt to explain the production of utterances to which a student has not been exposed, and the theory of grammar which is used to give an account of this fact offers him considerable advantages. The grammar of a language in this theory contains syntactic, semantic and phonological components the first of which is characterised by a base consisting of a categorical element and a lexicon, and which generates deep structures. These in turn receive a semantic interpretation. The second component of the base is the transformation system or rules which operate on the deep structures to produce a variety of surface structures which are realized phonologically. The rules of the base produce, or are identical with, deep seated regularities of language, some of which have been identified as the subject and predicate group, main verb and object of a phrase, etc. These may be omitted from the grammar of particular languages but they have to be included in any account of the student's competence. This characterises the grammar of the language — what it is ideally possible for the student to acquire. The use of the language is reflected in performance. It is part of the theory of transformational grammar that competence is largely a matter of the rules and of being in a position to operate them at various levels.

Language is therefore a manifestation of an extremely complex central integration of intellectual processes. This position is essentially a version of cognitive psychology according to which the learner brings to any task schemes, strategies, plans or hypotheses that influence the entire process of learning (Miller, Galanter and Pribram 1960). In the process of language teaching the emphasis is placed on the intricate system of rules by which the patterns of the language are formed, modified and elaborated rather than on the patterns or structures themselves (Chomsky 1968a). This conforms to the main stream of contemporary educational thinking, with its emphasis on learning to learn rather than on accumulation of knowledge or ideas. Insofar as the teaching of languages reflects the prevailing mode of general educational thought it will almost inevitably lay stress on the learning of language through the development of the rules rather than through the accumulation of linguistic forms.

Another feature of transformational grammar which is of interest to language teachers is the nature of the 'deep seated regularities' of grammar which the transformationist tends to speak of as 'universals of language', and 'innate properties of mind' (Chomsky 1965a: 53, 1968b: 59). Before a child can begin to learn a language, it is alleged, 'he must possess the form of grammar of a possible human language' (Chomsky 1965a: 26). 'Language is not acquired through training, but is a matter of growth and maturation of relatively fixed capacities . . . the form of the language that is acquired is largely determined by internal factors' (Chomsky 1968b: 64). The innate universals provide the child with a set of templates and it is only so far as the language he hears conforms to this innate pattern that it is helpful to him in his learning of it (McNeill 1966). In fact the transformational theory postulates a *faculté de langage,* a unique cognitive capacity, though Chomsky himself disavows the uniqueness (Chomsky 1965b: 56). Furthermore, the acquisition of language is independent not only of the experience available in society but of other aspects of the child's intelligence, there being 'little useful analogy between linguistic structure and other systems of mental organisation, nor much promise in extending the concepts of linguistic structures to other cognitive structures' (Chomsky 1968b: 53, 56, 77).

Language acquisition according to this hypothesis is autogenic and we 'do not know that a child needs tuition nor is it even certain that he profits from the tuition when it is given to him' (Jenkins 1966:351). The influence of the environment is largely restricted to triggering off the process of maturation and does not affect acquisition in a formative fashion: 'patterns of development emerge according to a maturational schedule in every child raised in an adequate environment. The emergence of such patterns is independent of training procedures and extrinsic response shaping' (Lenneberg 1967:127). Chomsky's review of Skinner's researches has set the tone of the criticism of reinforcement techniques, and Lenneberg generalises such criticism to embrace instruction models of all kinds since 'we have neither a good theoretical model nor any practical insight into how we could teach an organism to respond for instance to plurality, third personness, let alone how we could train him to use these responses' etc. (Lenneberg 1964: 599).

From this it will be clear that a crucial difference between the two alternatives is the function attributed to instruction. So far as the associationist is concerned, whatever minor instances of transfer may exist between the learning of the first and second languages, the process of learning the latter is repetition of the whole process of learning the former: the habits, associations and generalizations which governed the acquisition of the first language have to be repeated with different data in the acquisition of the second. There is relatively little place for 'learning to learn'. On the other hand, the cognitive theorist is concerned with discovering how linguistic competence, linguistic potential is acquired, and it needs to be acquired only once: learning the second language depends on the processes which have led to the acquisition of the first, but the two are not identical. This disposes of a point which is sometimes made, that since the deep-set regularities are innate they operate more effectively when the child is very young than when he is older: that, it is claimed, is an argument for the early introduction of a second language (Saporta 1966:85). This is not the case. Transformational grammar can say nothing about this question: its concern is with the establishment of a universal mechanism, the development of a code-operated behaviour which is thereafter available for the learning of any language. Indeed it is equally possible to argue that transformational theories, since they tend to suggest the value of the understanding of the code, and therefore of consciously controlled learning, may favour later rather than earlier learning of a second language. But the fact is that the cognitive, transformationist theory does not support one view or the other.

Insofar as the transformationist model of first language acquisition is applied to the second language the teacher is faced with some difficulties, for it does not take into account the contingencies which differentiate the acquisition of the two languages. In the first place the theory is heavily weighted, as we have seen, in favour of maturational explanations of development. Assuming this to be acceptable so far as the mother tongue is concerned, and there is no agreement even here, it will not do for the learning of the second language. When the child comes to learn a second language other than in situations of close contact, or where the two languages are learned simultaneously from birth, it can be assumed that the child's linguistic competence has already matured, so that the innate factors of linguistic learning become progressively and relatively less important compared with social factors. Tutoring and the reinforcement available from speakers of the foreign language are then not only the necessary but the sufficient cause of learning.

All this is acknowledged by the transformation theorist. A theory of actually learning a language as distinct from developing the rules or the code which makes possible the learning of any language involves questions the transformationist does not investigate such as 'the continual accretion of linguistic skill and knowledge' (Chomsky 1965a: 202), the additions to the linguistic repertoire as well as the enrichment of any command of languages. In terms of this approach the learning of a second language belongs to the level of performance, the realization or actualisation of the deep set rules or universals which have been acquired in learning the mother tongue, and it is a mistake to believe 'that a generative grammar in itself provides or is related in some obvious way to a model for the speaker' (Chomsky 1957: 144). Osgood has seized upon this point — 'transformational grammars *per se* have nothing to say about learning' (Osgood 1968: 503); and since the principles on which learning depends have to be acquired before the second language is introduced, what is peculiar to the second language belongs to the learner, speaker and teacher phase.

In spite of this disavowal by the generative theorist, teachers of second languages have been at pains to draw out possible implications of the transformational approach. It has been suggested for instance that the identification of, and limitation of early instruction to kernel sentences would be economical in any course (Politzer 1967: 212). Furthermore, if translation is involved in teaching a second language, either implicitly or explicitly, the argument goes that it should be based on the kernel sentences because 'the kernel sentences of different languages are remarkably similar, so that transfer might be affected with the least skewing of the content' (Nida 1969: 489). It is the case also that because the interpretation of grammaticality may be more liberal in the learning of the first language than it can afford to be in teaching the second, and because it requires a sharp distinction between grammatical and ungrammatical sentences, generative grammar is more in keeping with theories of second language acquisition. This has a bearing on the possibility that the understanding for instance of the grammatical structure of a number of discontinuous and elliptical verb constructions is best attempted in terms of the deletion transformation of generative grammar.

An important aspect of any model of second language instruction is the order of presentation both of the various linguistic levels and of the elements within any one level. Here the two approaches we are considering differ markedly. The well established audio-lingual approach based as it is on habit formation and drilled assimilation of an inventory of linguistic units such as phrases, morphemes and grammatical structures is closely related to a taxonomic theory of language and an empiricist theory of acquisition. It has adopted the order of presentation characteristic of phoneme-morpheme theory and moves from intensive sound discrimination, articulation training, through small grammatical units to sentences. The transformational grammarian has taken over the specification of linguistic units but has reversed the order in which we are accustomed to meet them in courses, so that the progression is from grammar to phonology. Any related teaching model therefore is very different in the place and emphasis it gives to discrimination and articulation of sounds, and the recognition it affords to phonemic analysis. Movement from grammar to phonology is the obligatory direction. The same kind of obligation is laid on movement from base structures 'which must be presented before a child can formulate transformations' (McNeill 1968:414). Each rule of transformation has a more or less fixed place. The taxonomic model however makes no such imposition on the teacher and the primacy of speech, characteristic of the audio-lingual approach, is not a necessary derivation from the empiricist model. If, therefore, transformational grammars do more than is claimed for them by their promoters, and if they have more than a fortuitous connection with any second language teaching model, they will reverse the customary order of presenting linguistic levels, and at the same time set a fixed schedule for presenting transformational rules. Another possible consequence of the transformational model, which may lead to a relaxation of the convention of speech primacy in language teaching, is the integration of all the language skills and their simultaneous presentation as early as possible. This possible consequence does not make it any less acceptable to teachers brought up in a European classically oriented tradition (Robins 1967:231).

The main contribution of the transformational approach is to emphasise the need for rule oriented teaching, and this again is what has made it more acceptable than structuralist teaching in the USSR, and has helped also to ensure for it a fairly favourable reception in the rest of Europe. The associationist theory of language tends to provide a rationale for the audio-lingual approach, and the inductive presentation of the grammar of a language; whereas the transformational grammarians regard the acquisition of the set of base regularities of language and the rules which govern the generation of new sentences, as requiring some degree of conscious awareness of the grammar. The exercises which the approach favours are designed to teach grammatical understanding of the concepts being introduced. Because of the general acceptance of the structuralist/behaviourist models, researches into second language acquisition until recently have been largely coloured by inductive presuppositions, so that the relative merits of the two alternative models in respect to inductive-deductive approaches have not been assessed. Crothers and Suppes (1967) in their study of the learning of Russian as a second language were concerned to identify and measure the possible differences that might arise from using the two approaches in a given instance. Swedish scholars (Carlsson et al. 1969) have also investigated the effects of theoretical explanations in juxtaposition with drills, and the comparative advantages of using the mother tongue or the second language for this purpose. Scherer and Wertheimer's (1964) recent study of this problem does not draw the distinction between the two possible approaches with sufficient sharpness to permit a valid conclusion to their research. In other areas of language learning there is evidence for the claim that implicit discovery methods tend to favour retention (Haselrud and Meyers 1958). However the results of most, if not all, the researches into this aspect of second language learning, an aspect which is inextricably bound up with a choice of alternative linguistic theories, is inconclusive.

The type of exercise included in any teaching model will be influenced, if not determined, by the differences between the language and language-acquisition theories we have discussed. It is still the case that a considerable amount of foreign language teaching, to say nothing of the teaching of a classical language, depends upon the analysis of sentences and parsing, and these exercises conform to the traditional theories of linguistic description, and the mechanistic, constructionist concept of acquisition — a process of building unit upon unit. The immediate constituent version of the structuralist account of language favours the use of expansion and substitution exercises, while the tagmemic version, because of its postulation of slots and fillers, also favours substitution drills but cannot justify the use of completion exercises. The transformationist-cognitive theory can justify reduction or expansion exercises but it relies mainly on conversion drills involving tense, voice and mood changes, etc.

It would be idle to deny the deep theoretical differences between the two alternative approaches of language and language acquisition, and the practical implications of these differences persist to confuse teachers and beguile the course designers. Nevertheless the amount of common ground between them is increasing.[10] Cognitive psycholinguists are willing to accept that conditioning governs the learning of referential meaning though such a contribution amounts, in their view, to no more than 1% of the solution of the learning problem (Miller 1962). Most teachers agree, too, that there are some things an associationist technique does better than the transformational model, for instance the acquisition of the formal repertoire,

[10] An interesting account of the historical roots of some of the similar positions taken up by the two schools of thought is given in Teeter (1969: 1-6).

while the cognitive approach is better able to handle the thematic learning stages —
a stubborn obstacle to the empiricist. It is probably true that transformational
grammar handles the delicate issues of language learning at the advanced stage
better than the associationist. There is no reason to doubt that from the teacher's
point of view a 'two factor' model incorporating some empiricist and some cognitive
elements has considerable attractions. If such a theory can be validated it would
undoubtedly provide them with a rationale for what is undoubtedly their current
highly pragmatic practice (Peizer and Olmsted 1969).

7. ORGANISATION OF THE LANGUAGE COURSE, AND TESTING

7.1 *Courses*

The actual organisation and planning of a second language course has to take into
account considerations which are only remotely connected with any discipline,
linguistic or otherwise, which contributes to language learning — size of class,
amount of time available and its distribution, experience of teachers, etc. Some
considerations have to do mainly with the differences between individuals — attitude and motivation and preference for learning visually or aurally, for instance.
Some independent factors, however, have a bearing on the nature and extent of
any contribution which linguistics can make to the school programme.

Age is one such factor. A course for young learners may have to be created
around a number of situations rather than according to strictly linguistic criteria,
though the linguistic criteria will not be ignored. The justification of such an
approach is that 'a pupil tends to remember only that which he has actually experienced . . . and the best possible materials according to the best possible procedures' (Stevick 1969:10). Among courses which are designed, in the first place,
to create interest are the St. Cloud audio-visual courses for French, English, and
other foreign languages, and some Australian programmes for non-English speaking immigrants. The same criteria have been used in devising courses for young
non-English speaking immigrants to Britain. The need to take interest into account
is greater with younger pupils than with older school children or adults.

Similarly, the need to take psychological, developmental processes or stages into
account decreases with age of student and to that extent strictly linguistic criteria
take progressively a more prominent place in the design of a course. The younger
the student, the closer the models of acquisition of the first and second languages
have to be. And this is vital in the programming of the second language course.
For instance age and stage of development impose limitations on the possibility of
acquiring certain aspects of the mother tongue — in the early stages competence
does not include the ability to perform certain transformations (McNeill 1966:
53–65) and similar limitations are imposed on second language learning by the im-

maturity of cognitive development. In such cases adherence to strictly linguistic criteria in preparing a course is likely to be frustrated, and in any case extremely uneconomical.

On the other hand, beyond the cognitive stage of the development of Piaget's 'formal operations' for instance, and certainly with adults, it becomes possible and perhaps desirable to take account almost exclusively of strictly linguistic criteria, as was done with the U.S. Foreign Service Instruction courses. In such cases the structure of the target language is the determining factor in sequencing the course. Whether a particular linguistic feature, for instance the genitive, is introduced at a certain point depends entirely on whether it is necessary for the understanding of the next step. Other non-linguistic factors are largely ignored (Hodge 1968:18). The same considerations make the strict 'programming' of a language course more suitable for older school children or adults.

Sequencing and grading of the language material within a course are often stated to be aspects of course design which are outside the competence of linguists to discuss. But there is little doubt that purely linguistic characteristics influence optimal sequencing. The regularity or irregularity of linguistic units or patterns must influence the point at which they may be introduced most appropriately. In the same way, within an agreed sequence of items, step size, the gradation of the course is influenced, though not governed, by purely linguistic considerations. Though the difficulty of a particular item in the course is a function of the subjective behaviour of the student (Lane 1968:87) the purely objective linguistic character of the item, such as, for instance, the 'pronounceability value' or the 'stimulus word length', in the learning of Russian are factors to take into account. For such factors it is possible, it has been suggested, to prepare a difficulty rating in absolutely linguistic terms (Crothers and Suppes 1967). The order in which the teacher presents the modalities of languages — whether of speech or writing — being largely dependent on individual student preference for their success, is less under the control of purely linguistic factors, though here again it has been suggested that the amount of transfer from learning in one to learning in the other modality is influenced by the characteristics of the language being learned (Chastain and Woerdehoff 1969).

7.2 *Testing*

Language testing, whether it is to assess individual or group achievement, to evaluate the impact of instructional techniques, or to diagnose individual difficulties, is part of language pedagogy. But the contribution of linguistics to this aspect of our subject, especially to the growing sophistication and refinement of language tests, is not different from its contribution to actual teaching. It is what has been taught that should be tested and for that reason the contribution of linguistics to the refinement of testing procedures is indirect. Nevertheless, there are some additional issues which should be referred to. The evaluation of instruction must take into account first the environment of learning, and this, as we have suggested, can differentiate second from foreign language learning. Since linguistic problems are likely to be more acute in the former situation, for instance problems of uncontrolled interference, the testing of these difficulties has to be regarded differently. The comparison of the linguistic issues involved in testing bilingual and foreign language students has hardly begun (Lewis 1969b).

A second aspect of instruction which testing has to take into account is the intellectual processes of the learners. As we have remarked these will vary with age and stage of cognitive development. This means that tests which are satisfactory for one set of students may be entirely unsuitable to others though the number of years they may have been taught the language may be the same. Tests which can be directed at children and adults of assumed equal linguistic proficiency may not be equally appropriate. Consequently, granting hypothetically similar levels of achievement in the language for both groups, the individual linguistic items used to test for that achievement and their distributional pattern need to be different.

The third element in testing is the learning itself — the content of the course. Here, to be acceptable, a test has to take into account the models of the language and language acquisition which have influenced the design of the course the student has followed. The linguist can help the teacher in identifying those aspects of language acquisition which a particular model promotes most successfully and which therefore should be tested for.

Another area where the linguist will be required to assist is cross-national evaluation of language achievement. Certain forms of educational research entail more detailed comparison of achievement in different countries. Language learning because of its importance and its universality within school curricula is an area of school instruction which invites comparison. There are some aspects of the curriculum like mathematics where it is fairly easy to agree upon uniform tests since the symbolization is uniform and the mathematical processes are possibly the least culturally skewed. In testing second language achievement across cultures, account has to be taken of the influence of the mother tongue, and problems or interference and negative transfer. At the same time, such tests have to be uniform if a basis of valid comparison is to be ensured. In the interpretation of the results of such uniform tests it is necessary to have a differential weighting corresponding to the distances of the various mother tongues from the second language. A model which provides a measure of distance for each important linguistic level, phonology, grammar and semantics is needed. The linguist has been interested in measures of linguistic distance, and though the measures will be difficult to devise and complex in their operation they are vital to the prosecution of certain aspects of research into second language pedagogy (Lewis 1968a).

It must be confessed that the linguists' interest in the test design has lagged behind the interest of the psychologist and the statistician. All that can be done at the moment is to suggest areas where the linguist should intervene.

8. CONCLUSION

In the course of this review it has been difficult to determine at various specific points the relative importance of linguistics to pedagogy and of pedagogy to linguistics — for instance Braine, and Bever and his associates. Fodor and W. Weskel have argued about the possibility of using studies of child language to decide questions in linguistics and there is no reason to confine such a possibility to the first language. Then again the adoption of a particular model of language because of its pedagogic convenience has been proposed (McNeill 1968:406). Sometimes the contribution of pedagogy is more direct and precise: for instance Daniel Jones placed at the head of his motives for prosecuting his phonetic studies 'to help learners of the foreign language to acquire a good pronunciation', and phonetic analysis was included by him in the pedagogically oriented parts of his discipline. We have referred to the impact of the American Intensive Language Program, and it is notable that though the normal development of linguistic scholarship would have meant that the structuralist system would probably have taken the form it did, it was the need of the armed forces for complete analysis of languages and their adaptation to practical teaching that was the main cause for the rapid development of structuralism (Hall 1950). It was also undoubtedly the case that the rapid expansion of the programme and the need for a single minded commitment in one theoretical direction ensured the almost universal acceptance of the approach, not only in teaching adults but in schools as well.

There is no doubt that as the teaching of a second language becomes more scientific, more under the control of identifiable and measurable factors, the impact of pedagogy on linguistics will be intensified. For instance, it ought to be possible to judge the efficacy of reinforcement theory and so evaluate the validity of one element in the associationist theory of language. Similarly, the relative value of implicit and explicit acquisition of the rules of language should throw some light on the importance of the transformationist insistence on the code oriented theory of acquisition. Third, the investigation of the use of translation, explicit or implicit, in the learning of a second language should cast some light on the level on which languages tend to coincide, whether at the level of linguistic universals, or the basic structures, the kernel sentences or the surface levels (Nida 1969). The investigation of the teaching of extreme social and regional dialects should illuminate the discussion of the linguistic nature of such dialects and their relation to standard forms. Finally there is a whole range of problems in semantics, the solution of which can be assisted by the investigation of how and under what circumstances students of a second language confuse meanings in the two languages, to say nothing of the way in which the development of error analysis techniques can help validate and support theoretic contrastive analysis of languages. Linguists and language teachers are engaged on a cooperative enterprise and there is no area of the activities of either partner in the common enterprise which can fail to be of interest to the other. The measure of the contribution to date is no indication of future possibilities.

REFERENCES

ABERCROMBIE, D. 1964. English phonetic texts. London, Faber.

AGARD, F. B., and H. B. DUNKEL. 1948. An investigation of second language learning. Boston, Ginn.

AGUROVA, N. V. 1959. An experiment in teaching English to first and second graders. IJaS 1959/4. Translated in SovED 2/2.

ARTEMOV, V. A. 1960. Some problems of speech psychology in teaching students to speak a foreign language. Translated in SovED 4/1.

——. 1967. Basic problems in the modern psychology of foreign language study: Conditions for the effectiveness of teaching methods. IJaS 1967/1.

ARTEMOV, V. A., et al. 1947. Voprosy psixologii i metodiki innostrannim jazykam. Moscow.

BASKAKOV, N. A. 1952. The Turkic people of the USSR: The development of their languages and writing. VJa, June 1952. Translated 1960 by C.A.R.C. at St. Anthony's College, Oxford.

BELAYEV, B. V. 1963. The psychology of teaching foreign languages. London, Pergamon.

BENEDIKTOV, B. A., and V. E. IARNATOVSKAIA. 1960. Method of teaching foreign languages. Translated in SovED 3/2.

BEVER, T. G. 1968. Associations to stimulus response: Theories of language. Verbal behavior and general behavior theory, ed. by T. R. Dixon and D. L. Hortin, pp. 88–102. Englewood Cliffs, N.J., Prentice Hall.

BLOOMFIELD, L. 1933. Language. New York, H. Holt and Co.

——. 1942. Outline guide for the practical study of foreign languages. Baltimore, Linguistic Society of America.

BOAS, F. 1940. Race, language and culture. New York, Macmillan.

BRAULT, G. J. 1963. Kinesis and the classroom: Some typical French gestures. FR 1963.374–82.

BROOKE, W. British Museum Mss. (Sloane Collection 1466) Folio 290.

BROOKS, N. 1964. Language and language learning. New York, Harcourt Brace.

BRUNER, J. S. 1966. Studies in cognitive growth. London, and New York, John Wiley.

Camden Remaines. Quoted in English examined, ed. by S. Tucker. London, Cambridge University Press. 1967.

CARLSSON, I., et al. 1969. GUME-projektet 1–4. Goteborg, Pedagogiska Institutionen Lararhogskolan i Goteborg.

CARROLL, J. B. 1963. Research on teaching foreign languages. Handbook for research on teaching, ed. by N. L. Gage. Chicago, Rand McNally.

——. 1966. Research in foreign language teaching. Language teaching: Border contexts, ed. by R. Mead. New York, Modern Language Association.

CASSIRER, E. 1923. The philosophy of symbolic forms. Translated 1953. London.

——. 1945. Structuralism in modern linguistics. Word 1.99–120.

CATFORD, J. C. 1962. A linguistic theory of translation. London, Oxford University Press.

CHAO, YUEN REN. 1968. Language and symbolic systems. London, Cambridge University Press.

CHASTAIN, K. D., and F. WOERDEHOFF. 1969. A methodological study comparing the A/L habit theory and the cognitive code theory. MLJ 1969.268–79.

CHEREDNICHENKO, I. G. 1957. Metodika prepodovanniia russkogo iazyka v shkolakh s ukrainskim iuzykom obuchencia. [Russian in Ukrainian middle schools.] Kiev.

CHISTIAKOV, V. M. 1960. Osnovy metodika russkogo iazyka v nerusskikh shkolakh. [Russian in non-Russian schools.] Moscow.

CHOMSKY, N. 1957. Syntactic structures. The Hague, Mouton.

——. 1959 Review of B. F. Skinner, Verbal Behavior. Lg 35/1.26–58.

——. 1961a. On the notion 'rule of grammar'. Structure of language and its mathematical aspects. Proceedings of the 12th Symposium in Applied Mathematics, pp. 6–24. Providence, R. I., American Mathematical Society.

——. 1961b. Some methodological remarks on generative grammar. Word 17.219–39.

——. 1962. A transformational approach to syntax. Proceedings of the Third Texas Conference of Linguistic Analysis, ed. by A. A. Hill, pp. 65–73. Austin, University of Texas.

——. 1964a. The logical basis of linguistic theory. PICL 9.914–77.

——. 1964b. Current issues in linguistic theory. CTL 3. *Also* JanL series minor 38.

——. 1965a. Aspects of the theory of syntax. Cambridge, Mass., M.I.T. Press.

——. 1965b. Cartesian linguistics. New York, Harper & Row.

——. 1968a. The formal nature of language. *In* Lenneberg 1967, Appendix A, pp. 397–442.

——. 1968b. Language and mind. New York, Harcourt Brace.

CHRISTOPHERSEN, P. 1964. The application of linguistics to the teaching of foreign languages. Oslo, Sprockforskning og Sprakopplaering.

COFER, C. N. 1968. Problems and issues and implications. Verbal behavior and general behavior theory, ed. by T. R. Dixon and D. L. Horton, pp. 45–70. Englewood Cliffs, N.J., Prentice Hall.

COMENIUS, J. 1628–32. The great didactic. London. [*See* The analytical didactic of Comenius by V. Jelinek. Chicago, University of Chicago Press. 1953.]

COOK, V. J. 1969. The analogy between first and second language learning. IRAL 7/3.207–16.

CROTHERS, E., and P. SUPPES. 1967. Experiments in second language learning. London, Academic Press.

CREDIF. 1963. Bonjour Line. Paris.

CREELMAN, M. B. 1966. The experimental investigation of meaning. New York, Springer.

DMITRIEV, N. K., et al. 1952. Ocherki po metodiki prepodavanija russkogo i rodnogo jazykov v tatarskoj skole. Moscow.

DODSON, C. J., and E. PRICE. 1969. Towards bilingualism: Studies in language teaching method. Cardiff, University of Wales Press.

ELLIS, A. J. 1845. The alphabet of nature. London.

FAUCETT, L., et al. 1936. Interim report on vocabulary selection. London, King.

FERGUSON, C. A. 1959. Diglossia. Word 15.325–40.

FILIPOVIC, R. 1970. Contrastive trends in applied linguistics. Contact 14 (Jan.).

FIRTH, J. R. 1937. The tongues of men. London, Watts.

——. 1957. Papers in linguistics, 1934–51. London, Oxford University Press.

FISHMAN, J. A. 1966. The implications of bilingualism for language teaching and language learning. Trends in language teaching, ed. by A. Valdman, pp. 121–32. New York-London, McGraw Hill.

FRIEDL, B. C. 1944. Techniques in spoken language: Specific procedures in the Army Specialized Training Program. MLJ 28/6.

FRIES, C. 1945. Teaching and learning English as a foreign language. Ann Arbor, University of Michigan Press.

——. 1952. The structure of English. New York, Harcourt Brace.

GALANTER, E. 1962. Contemporary psycholinguistics. New directions in psychology, ed. by T. Newcomb. New York, Holt, Rinehart and Winston.

GALAZOV, V. 1965. The native and Russian languages in our schools. Narodnoe obrazovanie. Translated in SovED 7/12.

GEFEN, R. 1966. Theoretical prerequisites for second language teaching. IRAL 4/4.227–33.

GEZ, N. I. 1966. Inter-relationships between oral and written forms of communication. IJaS 1966/2. Translated in SovED 8/8.

GINSBERG, V. S. 1960. An experiment in teaching pre-school children a foreign language. Sovetskaia Pedagogika. Translated in SovED 5.

GIRARD, D. 1964. New trends in language teaching in France. NAFSA Studies and Papers 9, ed. by D. P. Harris. New York, NAFSA.

GOUGENHEIM, G., et al. 1956. L'élaboration du français élémentaire. Paris, Didier.

GRAVES, M., and M. COWAN. 1942. Report of the first year's operation of the Intensive Language Program. New York, American Council of Learned Societies.

GRAVIT, F. V., and A. VALDMAN. 1963. Structural drills and the language laboratory. IJAL 29/2.

GREENBERG, J. H. 1957. The nature and use of language typologies. IJAL 23.68–77.

——. 1963. Essays in linguistics. Chicago, Phoenix Books.

GRUNBERG, A. L. 1960. On the question of language influence — the materials of the language of the Northern Azerbaydzhan Tats. Brief Reports of the Central Institute, Moscow.

HAAS, M. R. 1953. The application of linguistics to language teaching. Anthropology today, ed. by A. L. Kroeber. Chicago, University of Chicago Press.

HAAS, W. 1960. Linguistic structures. Word 16.251–76.

HALL, ROBERT A., JR. 1950. American linguistics 1925–50. AL 3/2.101–25.

HALLE, M. 1963. Phonemics. CTL 1.5–21.

HALLIDAY, M. A. K. 1962. Linguistique générale et linguistique appliquée. ELA 1.

HALLIDAY, M. A. K., et al. 1964. The linguistic sciences and language teaching. London, Longmans.

HAMMER, J. M., and F. A. RICE. 1965. A bibliography of contrastive linguistics. Washington, D.C., Center for Applied Linguistics.

HARRIS, Z. S. 1951. Methods in structural linguistics. Chicago, University of Chicago Press.

HASELRUD, G. M., and S. MEYERS. 1958. The transfer value of given and individually derived principles. JEdPsych 49.

HAUGEN, E. 1951. Directions in modern linguistics. Lg 27.211–22.

——. 1956. Bilingualism in the Americas: A bibliography and research guide. PADS 26. [Reprinted 1964 and 1968].

——. 1966. Dialect, language and nation. AmA 68.922–35.

HAUSTRATE, M. 1968. Quelques tendences nouvelles de la linguistique soviétique. Babel 14/4.222–24. Avignon.

HERVAS, PANDERO LORENZO. 1880. Catalogo de las lenguas de las naciones conocidas. Madrid.

HOCKETT, C. F. 1954. Two models of grammatical description. Word 10.218–34.

——. 1968. The state of the art. The Hague, Mouton.

HODGE, C. 1968. In Language Sciences, December, pp. 17–20. Bloomington, Ind.

——. 1963. The influence of linguistics on language teaching. AnL 5/1.50–59.

HOLMER, N. M. 1949–1950. Comparative semantics: A new aspect of linguistics. Yearbook of the New Society of Letters at Lund. Lund.

HYMES, D. H., ed. 1964. Language, culture and society. New York and London, Harper & Row.

ISRAEL, M. L. 1960. Variably blurred prompting: Methodology and application and analysis of paired association learning. JPsych 50.43–52.

JAKOBOVITS, L. A. 1968. Implications of recent psycholinguistic developments for the teaching of a second language. Urbana, University of Illinois [mimeo.].

JAKOBSON, R. 1958. Typological studies and their contribution to historical comparative linguistics. PICL 8.17–25.

JAMES, C. 1969. Deeper contrastive study. IRAL 7/2.83–95.

JENKINS, JAMES J. 1966. Reflections on the conference. The genesis of language: A psycholinguistic approach, ed. by F. Smith and G. A. Miller, pp. 347–60. Cambridge, Mass., M.I.T. Press.

JESPERSEN, OTTO. 1904. How to teach a foreign language. London, Allen and Unwin.

JONES, D. 1948. Differences between spoken and written language. London, International Phonetic Association.

——. 1950. The pronunciation of English, 3rd ed. Cambridge, Cambridge University Press.

——. 1960. An outline of English phonetics, 9th ed. Cambridge, Heffer.

JOOS, M. 1961. The five clocks. New York, Harcourt Brace.

KARPOV, I. V., and V. RAXMANOV. 1958. Metodika nacal'nogo obucenja inostranym jazykam. Academy of Pedagogic Science, Moscow.

KATZ, J. J. 1964. Mentalism in linguistics. Lg 2.124–37.

KING, A. H. 1967. Intercomprehensibility. London, British Council [Mimeo.].

KOLJADENKOV, M. N. 1960. Russkij jazyk v mordowskoj skole. Saranask, U.S.S.R.

KOSTIUK, G. S. 1956. Some aspects of the inter-relation between education and the development of personality. Education psychology in the U.S.S.R., ed. by B. Simon. London, Routledge.

KOUTAISOFF, E. 1965. New trends in modern language studies. MLJ 46/3.112–15.

KREUSLER, A. 1963. The teaching of modern foreign languages in the U.S.S.R. Leiden.

KUDRIAVTSEV, V. D. 1965. Prepodovanie russkogo iazyka v buriatskoi shkoly. [Russian in Buriat schools.] Moscow.

LADO, R. 1957. Linguistics across cultures. Ann Arbor, University of Michigan Press.

——. 1964. Language teaching: A scientific approach. Boston, McGraw-Hill.

——. 1967. Language testing: The construction and use of foreign language tests. London, Longmans.

LAMBERT, W. E. 1956. Developmental aspects of second language acquisition. JSocPsych 43.83–104.

LANE, H. 1964a. Programmed learning of a second language. IRAL 2/4.249–301.

——. 1964b. Transfer in auditory discrimination. AmJPsych 27.230–48.

——. 1965. The motor theory of speech perception. PsychRev 72–4.

——. 1968. Research on second language learning. Developments in applied psychology, ed. by S. Rosenberg and J. H. Koplin, Ch. 3. London.

LANGER, S. 1942. Philosophy in a new key. Cambridge, Mass., Harvard University Press.

LENNEBERG, E. H. 1953. Cognition in ethnic linguistics. Lg 29.463–71.

——. 1961. Color naming, color recognition and color discrimination. Perception and Motor Skills 12.375–82.

——. 1964. The capacity for language acquisition. Structure of language, ed. by J. Fodor and J. J. Katz. Englewood Cliffs, N.J., Prentice Hall.

——. 1967. Biological foundations of language. New York and London, John Wiley.

LEONTEV, A. A. 1963. The plurality of language models and the problem of teaching languages and grammar. IRAL I.211–22.

LEOPOLD, W. F. 1939–49. Speech development of a bilingual child, 4 Vols. Evanston, Ill., Northwestern University Press.

LÉVI-STRAUSS, C. 1966. The savage mind. London, Weidenfeld and Nicolson.

LEWIS, E. GLYN. 1952. The place of Welsh and English in the schools of Wales. London, H.M.S.O.

——. 1960. Bilingualism in education. London, United Kingdom Commission for UNESCO.

——. 1962. Foreign and second language teaching in the USSR. London, British Council.

——. 1964. English as a second language in Britain. Studies and papers, ed. by D. P. Harris. New York, NAFSA.

——. 1968a. International educational assessment: English as a foreign language. LL Special No. 3.

——. 1968b. Hwanner en hoe in twadde tael yn to fieren. [When to introduce a second language.] It plak fan it Frysk yn it underwiis. [The place of Frisian in the schools.] Leeuwarden, Fryske Academy.

——. 1969a. Language and the intellectual development of children. (Address to Education Section of the British Association, Exeter.)

——. 1969b. Taxonomy of language testing objectives. Statens Erhvervs pedogigiscke Laereruddanelse, Copenhagen.

——. 1970a. Migration and language in the USSR. International Migration Review 5.

——. 1970b. Immigrants and their languages in Trends. London, H.M.S.O.

LIAKHOVILSKII, M. V. 1960. An urgent demand of life. Vestnik Vysshei Shkoly 3. Translated in SovED 2/2.

LONGACRE, R. E. 1958. Items in context: Their bearing on translation theory. Lg 34.482–91.

LUBINUS. 1617. Didactic. Amsterdam.

LUDWIG, E. 1965. Practical exercises in English phonetics. International Conference of Modern Foreign Language Teaching. Berlin, Paedogogische Arbeitstelle.

LURIA, A. R. 1932. The nature of human conflicts. American edition, 1967.

——. 1959. An objective investigation of the dynamics of semantic systems. BrJGPsych 50/2.

——. 1966. Human brain and psychological processes. London.

——. 1967. Problems and facts in neurolinguistics. IntSocSciJ 19/1.

MCINTOSH, A., and M. J. K. HALLIDAY. 1966. Patterns of language: Papers in general, descriptive and applied linguistics. London, Longmans.

McNeill, D. 1966. Developmental linguistics. The genesis of language, ed. by F. Smith and G. A. Miller. Cambridge, Mass., M.I.T. Press.

——. 1968. On theories of language acquisition. Verbal behavior and general behavior theory, ed. by T. R. Dixon and D. L. Horton, pp. 124–32. Englewood Cliffs, N.J., Prentice Hall.

Mackey, W. F. 1966. Applied linguistics: Its meaning and use. ELT 20/3.197–206.

——. 1967. Language teaching analysis. London, Longmans.

Malash'chenko, V. P. 1966. Ispol'zovanie algoritmov pri obuchenii russkomy jazyku. Rostov-on-Don.

Marckwardt, A. H. 1962. English as a second and English as a foreign language. PMLA. 25–28.

——. 1967. Teaching English as a foreign language: A survey of the past decade. The Linguistic Reporter, Oct. Washington, D.C., C.A.L.

Mathews, W. K. 1951. Languages of the USSR. London, University of London Press.

——. 1947. The language pattern of the USSR. SIR 25.427–54.

Menchenskaia, N. A. 1967. Fifty years of Soviet psychology of learning. Translated in SovED 10/6.

Menchenskaia, N. A., and G. C. Saburova. 1967. The problem of instruction and development. Translated in SovED 10/July.

Mescaninov, L. L. 1948. Sovetskoe jazykozanie. Moscow.

Miller, G. A. 1962. Some psychological studies of grammar. Am. Psych. 17.-748–62.

Miller, G. A., E. Galanter, and K. H. Pribram. 1960. Plans and the structure of behavior. New York, Holt.

Miroljubov, A. A. 1960. O prepodvanaii innstrannie jazykov v vos'miletnei skole. Moscow.

Ministère de l'Education Nationale. 1960a. Vocabulaire d'initiation à la critique et à l'explication littéraire. Paris, Didier.

——. 1960b. Le français fondemental (2e degré). Paris, Didier.

Mirtov, A. V. 1956. Ocherki po metodike prepodavaniia russkogo jazyka azerbaydzhanskoi shkole. [Russian in Azerbaydzhan schools].

——. 1962. Ocherki po metodike prepodavaniia russkogo jazyka uzbeksoi shkole. [Russian in Uzbek schools].

Mlikotin, A. M. 1967. Soviet methods of teaching foreign languages. MLJ, Oct. 337–43.

Mordvinov, A. E. 1950. The development of the languages of the socialist nations of the USSR. Problems of Philosophy 3.

Morris, C. S. 1946. Signs, language and behavior. New York.

Morton, F. R. 1960. The language laboratory as a teaching machine. Ann Arbor, University of Michigan Press.

MOSKOLSKAIA, O. I. 1962. The development of foreign language study in the USSR. Innostrannye Jazyki v Skole.

MOULTON, W. G. 1961. Linguistics and language teaching in the U.S. 1940–60. Trends in European and American linguistics 1930–60, ed. by C. Mohrmann et al. Utrecht.

——. 1966. A linguistic guide to language learning. New York, Modern Language Association.

MUELLER, T. 1961. Programming morphemic structures. Programming A/L skills. Ann Arbor, University of Michigan Press.

MYRDAL, GUNNAR. 1969. Objectivity in social research. London. (Quoted in T.L.S. 19.2.70.203.)

NEWMARK, L. 1964. Grammar theory and the teaching of English as a foreign language. Studies and papers, ed. by D. P. Harris. New York, NAFSA.

NICHOLS, A. E. 1962. Punctuation problems for speakers of Germanic languages. LL 195–204.

NIDA, E. A. 1969. Science of translation. Lg 45/3.483–97.

NORTH EAST CONFERENCE ON THE TEACHING OF FOREIGN LANGUAGES. 1962. IRAL 2.37–52.

NOSTRAND, H. L. 1966. Describing and teaching the sociocultural context of a foreign language and literature. Trends in language teaching, ed. by A. Valdman, pp. 1–26. New York-London, McGraw-Hill.

NOSTRAND, H. L., et al. 1962. Research on language teaching: An annotated bibliography for 1945–61. Seattle, Washington University Press.

O'NEILL, J. J. 1957. Recognition of intelligibility of listening materials in context and in isolation. JSHD 22.87–90.

ORNSTEIN, J. 1963. Foreign language teaching [in the USSR]. CTL 1.143–91.

ORNSTEIN, J., and R. LADO. 1967. Research in foreign language teaching methodology. IRAL 5/1.11–25.

OSGOOD, C. E. 1953. Method and theory in experimental psychology. London, Oxford University Press.

——. 1956. Behavior theory and the social sciences. BS 1/3.167–85.

——. 1963. Psycholinguistics. Psychology: A study of a science, ed. by Koch. New York, McGraw-Hill.

——. 1968. Towards a wedding of insufficiences. Verbal behavior and general behavior theory, ed. by T. R. Dixon and D. L. Horton. Englewood Cliffs, New Jersey, Prentice Hall.

OSGOOD, C. E., and T. A. SEBEOK, eds. 1965. Psycholinguistics. Bloomington, Indiana University Press.

ÖSTERBERG, TORE. 1961. Bilingualism — illustrated by results from a Swedish dialect area. Umea Vasterbottens Tryckeri.

PALMER, H. E. 1917. The scientific study and teaching of languages. London, Harrap.

——. 1922. The principles of language study. Republished, London, Oxford University Press. (1962)

PASSY, P. 1899. De la methode directe dans l'enseignement des langues vivantes. Cambridge, International Phonetic Association.

——. 1929. La phonetique et ses applications. London, International Phonetic Association.

PEIZER, D. B., and D. L. OLMSTED. 1969. Modules of grammar acquisition. Lg 45/7.60–96.

PIKE, K. L. 1967. Language in relation to a unified theory of the structure of human behaviour, 2nd ed. The Hague, Mouton.

PILCH, H. 1964. Phonemtheorie. I Teil. Basel/N.Y.

PIMSLEUR, P. 1962. Foreign language learning ability. JEdPsych 53/1.15–26.

——. 1964. Under-achievement in foreign languages. IRAL 2/2.113–15.

POLITZER, R. L. 1965. Foreign language learning, preliminary ed. Englewood Cliffs, New Jersey, Prentice Hall.

——. 1967. Two schools of language and foreign language teaching. Proceedings of the 1967 MLA Conference. MLJ 53.

POSTAL, P. 1964. Underlying and superficial linguistic structures. Harvard Ed. Rev. 34.

POSTMAN, L. 1963. Does interference theory predict too much forgetting? JVLVB 2.40–48.

POTTIER, B. 1962. Introduction à l'étude des structures grammaticale fondementale. Paris.

PRATOR, C. H. 1950. Language teaching in the Philippines. Manila.

——. 1964. Development of manipulative-communication scale. Studies and Papers 9. New York, NAFSA.

——. 1965. English as a second language. Teaching English as a second language: A book of readings, ed. by H. B. Allen, pp. 87–92. New York-London, McGraw-Hill.

PRIBRAM, K. H., ed. 1965. Proposal for a structural pragmatism. Brain and Behaviour, ed. by K. H. Pribram, Vol. 4.

PURTSELADZE, S. D. 1960–66. Osnovy metodiki prepodavaniia russkogo jazyka v gruzinskoi vos'miletnei shkole. [Teaching Russian in Georgian schools] 3 vols. Tbilisi.

QUINTILIAN. Institutio Oratio 1/1.12–14.

RAFFERTY, M., ed. 1963. Language instruction. California State Dept. of Education, Sacramento.

RASTORGUEVA, V. S. 1952. On the stability of the morphological system of the language. Questions of theory and history of language. Moscow.

REAL, W. 1939. Linguistique et pédagogie. Mélanges Bally, pp. 63–71. Geneva, Georg.

REVZIN, I. I. 1966. Models of language. Translated from Russian by N. F. C. Owen and A. S. C. Ross. London, Methuen.

RICHARDS, I. A. 1930. Basic English. London, Psyche Miniatures.

——. 1935. Basic in teaching: East and West. London.

——. 1939. Basic English and its application. J. of the R. Soc. of Arts. June.

——. 1948. The pocket book of basic English. New York, Pocket Books, Inc.

RIVERS, W. M. 1964. The psychologist and the foreign language teacher. Chicago, University of Chicago Press.

ROBINS, R. H. 1964. General linguistics: An introductory survey. London, Longmans.

——. 1967. A short history of linguistics. London, Longmans.

ROJAS, C. 1969. L'enseignement de la grammaire. Le Français dans le Monde, Juin. 51–7.

ROZHDESTVENSKII, N. S. 1966. The grammar course in the primary school. Translated in SovED 7/5.

——. 1967. Composition and structure of the Russian language syllabus. Translated in SovED 10/2.

SACKS, N. P. 1964. Some aspects of the application of linguistics to the teaching of modern foreign languages. MLJ 48/1.7–17.

SAPIR, E. 1921. Language. New York, Harvest Books.

SAPON, S. M. 1964. Micro-analysis of a second language learning behaviour. In International Conference on Modern Language Teaching. Paedogogische Arbeitstelle, Berlin.

SAPORTA, S. 1966. Applied linguistics and generative grammar. Trends in language teaching, ed. by A. Valdman. London, McGraw-Hill.

SAYCE, A. H. 1880. Introduction to the science of language. London, Kegan Paul.

SCHERER, G., and M. WERTHEIMER. 1964. A psycholinguistic experiment in foreign language teaching. London, McGraw-Hill.

SCHMALSTIEG, W. R. 1963. Lithuanian. CTL 1.287–300.

SEGALOWITZ, N., and W. E. LAMBERT. 1969. Semantic generalization in bilinguals. JVLVB 8.559–66.

SERDYUCHENKO, G. P. 1955. The language of the Abazins. Information Bulletin 5. Academy of Pedagogic Sciences, Moscow.

——. 1962. The eradication of illiteracy and the creation of new written languages in the USSR. Int. J. of Youth Ed. 14.

——. 1965. Elimination of illiteracy. Unesco, Moscow.

——. 1962. The linguistic aspects of bilingualism. Bilingualism in education, ed. by E. G. Lewis. London, H.M.S.O.

SHCHERBA, L. V. 1927. Bezgramotnost i ee preckiny. Voprosy Pedagogiki 2. Leningrad.

——. 1947. Prepodavanie inostrannie yazyki v srednet shkole obschie voporsy metodiki. Moscow.

SOBOLEVA, P. A. 1956. Primenenie sopastavitel'nogo metoda pri obicenii lekiske inostranogo jazyka. Moscow.

SOVETKIN, S. S., and V. CISTJAKOV. 1960. Metodika obucenija russkomu jazyka v nacal'noj neerusskoj skole. Moscow.

SPOLSKY, B. 1966a. A psycho-linguistic critique of programmed foreign language instruction. IRAL 4/2.

——. 1966b. Man-machine communication in programmed instruction. Computation in linguistics, ed. by P. L. Garvin and B. Spolsky. Bloomington, Indiana University Press.

——. 1969a. Attitudinal aspects of second language learning. LL 19.271–85.

——. 1969b. Reduced redundancy as a language-testing tool. Applications of linguistics, ed. by G. E. Perren and J. L. M. Trimm, pp. 383–90. Cambridge University Press.

STAATS, A. W. 1968. Learning, language and cognition. London, Holt, Rinehart and Winston.

STERN, H. H., ed. 1962. Foreign languages in primary education. Hamburg, Unesco Institute.

——. 1969. Languages and the young school child. London, Oxford University Press.

STEVICK, E. W. 1969. *In* Language Sciences, August. Indiana University.

STEWART, W. A. 1964. Non standard speech and the teaching of language. Information Series 2. Washington, D.C., Center for Applied Linguistics.

STRANG, B. M. H. 1964. Metaphors and models. Inaugural Lecture, University of Newcastle-upon-Tyne.

STREVENS, PETER. 1965. Papers in language and language teaching. London, Oxford University Press.

SWEET, H. 1899. The practical study of languages. London, Dent.

TEETER, K. V. 1969. Leonard Bloomfield's linguistics. Language Sciences 7. Indiana University.

TEKUCHEV, A. V. 1967. Major landmarks in the history of the development of Soviet methodology in the teaching of the Russian language in the secondary schools (1917–67). Translated in SovED 7/10.

TEPLOV, B. M. 1952. Objective method in psychology. Psychology in the USSR, ed. by B. Simon. London, Routledge.

TITONE, R. 1965. A plea for experimental studies in Applied Contrastive Phonology. ELA.

TRAGER, G. L. 1949. The field of linguistics 4. Norman, Oklahoma.

TWADDEL, W. F. 1966. Linguistics and language teachers. On teaching English to speakers of other languages, ed. by C. Kreidler. Champaign, Ill., NCTE.

UBRYATOVA, E. I. 1956. Notes. Report and notes of the Linguistic Institute of the ASUSSR, pp. 86–92. Moscow.

ULLMANN, S. 1962. Semantics: An introduction to the science of meaning. Oxford, Blackwell.

——. 1963. Language and style. Oxford, Blackwell.

U.S.S.R. COUNCIL OF MINISTERS. 1961. Decision on improving foreign language instruction. Pravda, June 4. Translated in SovED 3.

VALDMAN, A. 1964. Towards a redefinition of teacher role and teaching context in foreign language instruction. MLJ 48.177.

VAN SCHOONEVELD, C. H. 1963. Morphemics. CTL 1.22–34.

VASU, L. V. 1961. Bilingual vowel charts. Rev. U.S. Army Language School, Summer 1961, pp. 12–23. Monterey, Calif.

VIETOR, W. 1902. Die Methodik des Neusprachen-Unterrichts. Leipzig.

VINAY, J.-P., and J. DARBELNET. 1958. Stylistique comparée du français et de l'anglais. Paris, Didier.

WEBBE, J. British Museum mss. Sloane Collection 1466, fol. 267.

WEINREICH, URIEL. 1953. Languages in contact. New York, Linguistic Circle of New York.

——. 1963. Lexicology. CTL 1.60–93.

WEISGERBER, L. 1929. Muttersprache und Geistesbildung. Göttingen.

——. 1949–50. Von den Kraften der deutschen Sprache. Düsseldorf, Schwann.

WEST, M. P. 1926. Learning to read a foreign language. London, Longmans.

WHATMOUGH, J. 1956. Language: A modern synthesis. London, Secker.

WINNER, T. G. 1952. Problems of alphabetic reform among the Turkic peoples of Soviet Central Asia. S1 Rev. 1952.132–47.

WOLF, E. M. 1962. Contrastive pronunciation practice in German. San Diego.

WOLFE, J. 1932. The relationship between language structure and associative interference in artificial language material. Lang. Monograph 2.

WORTH, D. S. 1963. Syntax. CTL 1.35–59.